SACRED V

African Christians and Sectarian Hatred in the Age of Augustine

BRENT D. SHAW

CAMBRIDGE
UNIVERSITY PRESS

CAMBRIDGE
UNIVERSITY PRESS

University Printing House, Cambridge CB2 8BS, United Kingdom

One Liberty Plaza, 20th Floor, New York, NY 10006, USA

477 Williamstown Road, Port Melbourne, VIC 3207, Australia

314-321, 3rd Floor, Plot 3, Splendor Forum, Jasola District Centre, New Delhi - 110025, India

79 Anson Road, #06-04/06, Singapore 079906

Cambridge University Press is part of the University of Cambridge.

It furthers the University's mission by disseminating knowledge in the pursuit of education, learning and research at the highest international levels of excellence.

www.cambridge.org
Information on this title: www.cambridge.org/9780521127257

First published 2011

A catalogue record for this publication is available from the British Library

Library of Congress Cataloging in Publication data
Shaw, Brent D.
Sacred violence : African Christians and sectarian hatred in the age of Augustine / Brent D. Shaw.
p. cm.
Includes bibliographical references and index.
ISBN 978-0-521-19605-5 (hardback)
1. Christianity – Africa – History.   2. Africa, North – Church history.
3. Violence – Religious aspects – Christianity.   4. Church history – Primitive and early church, ca. 30–600.   5. Donatists.   6. Augustine, Saint, Bishop of Hippo.   I. Title.
BR1369.S53   2011
273′.4 – dc22   2010054601

ISBN 978-0-521-19605-5 Hardback
ISBN 978-0-521-12725-7 Paperback

SACRED VIOLENCE

One route to understanding the nature of specifically religious violence is the study of past conflicts. Distinguished ancient historian Brent D. Shaw provides a new analysis of the intense sectarian battles between the Catholic and Donatist churches of North Africa in Late Antiquity, in which Augustine played a central role as Bishop of Hippo. The development and deployment of images of hatred, including those of the heretic, the pagan, and the Jew, and the modes by which these were most effectively employed, including the oral world of the sermon, were critical to promoting acts of violence. Shaw explores how the emerging ecclesiastical structures of the Christian Church, on one side, and those of the Roman imperial state, on the other, interacted to repress or excite violent action. Finally, the meaning and construction of the acts themselves, including the Western idea of suicide, are shown to emerge from the conflict itself.

BRENT D. SHAW is the Andrew Fleming West Professor of Classics at Princeton University. He has published widely on the regional history of the Roman empire, with particular emphasis on the North African provinces and the problem of violence in its historical contexts, in major journals including the *Journal of Roman Studies*, *Past & Present*, and the *American Historical Review*. He has also co-authored a new world history text entitled *Worlds Together, Worlds Apart* (2010).

Shauna
devotissimo animo

Vengeance is mine – I shall repay (Romans 12: 19)

Contents

Abbreviations

All periodical, serial, and collection abbreviations, other than those noted below, are taken from the standard list in *L'Année philologique*.

AASS   *Acta Sanctorum*, Antwerp, Société des Bollandistes, 1643–

AfrRom   *L'Africa romana*, Atti del Convegni di Studio, Sassari, 1984–

AtlArch   S. Gsell, *Atlas archéologique de l'Algérie*, Paris, Gouverne-ment générale de l'Algérie, 1911 (reprint: Osnabrück, O. Zeller, 1973)

AugLex   *Augustinus-Lexikon*, ed. C. Mayer, Basel, Schwabe, 1986–

BA   *Bibliothèque Augustinienne: Oeuvres de saint Augustin*, Paris, Desclée de Brouwer, 1948–

CCL   *Corpus christianorum, series Latina*, Turnhout, Brepols, 1954–

CIL   *Corpus Inscriptionum Latinarum*, Berlin, 1863–

CLE   *Carmina Latina Epigraphica*, 2 vols., Leipzig, 1895–97 ed. F. Buecheler; E. Lommatzsch, *Supplementum*, Leipzig, 1926

CSEL   *Corpus Scriptorum Ecclesiasticorum Latinorum*, Vienna, Tempsky, 1866–

CTh   T. Mommsen and P. M. Meyer eds., *Theodosiani libri XVI cum Constitutionibus Sirmondianis et Leges Novellae ad Theodosianum pertinentes*, 2 vols., Berlin, Weidmann, 1905

DACL   *Dictionnaire d'archéologie chrétienne et de liturgie*, ed. F. Cabrol and H. Leclercq, Paris, Letouzey et Ané, 1907–53

DHGE   *Dictionnaire d'histoire et de géographie ecclésiastiques*, ed. A. Baudrillart, Paris, Letouzey et Ané, 1912–

GCC   *Gesta conlationis Carthaginiensis anno 411*, ed. S. Lancel (see texts s.v. Church Councils)

GCS   *Die griechischen christlichen Schriftsteller der ersten drei Jahrhunderte*, Leipzig and Berlin, Akademie-Verlag, 1897–

ICUR	A. Silvagni & A. Ferrua eds., *Inscriptiones Christianae Urbis Romae*, nova series, Rome, 1922–
ILAlg	*Inscriptions latines de l'Algérie*, Paris, 1922–
ILCV	*Inscriptiones Latinae Christianae Veteres*, ed. E. Diehl, Berlin, Weidmann, 1925–31 (reprint: 1961–67)
ILS	*Inscriptiones Latinae Selectae*, ed. H. Dessau, Berlin, Weidmann, 1892–1916 (reprint: 1954–62)
ILTun	*Inscriptions latines de la Tunisie*, ed. A. Merlin, Paris, Presses Universitaires de France, 1944
IRT	J. M. Reynolds and J. B. Ward Perkins, *The Inscriptions of Roman Tripolitania*, Rome, British School at Rome, 1952 [and supplements: *PBSR* 23 (1955), 124-47; *LibStud* 20 (1989), 117–26]
MGH AA	*Monumenta Germaniae Historica, auctores antiquissimi*, Berlin, 1826–
MiAg	*Miscellanea Agostiniana: testi e studi pubblicati a cura dell'ordine Eremitano di S. Agostino nel XV centenario dalla morte del santo dottore*, 2 vols., Rome, Tipografia Poliglotta Vaticana, 1930–31
PAC	A. Mandouze ed., *Prosopographie chrétienne du Bas-Empire*, vol. 1: *Prosopographie de l'Afrique chrétienne (303–533)*, Paris, CNRS, 1982
PG	*Patrologiae cursus completus, series graeca*, ed. J.-P. Migne, 161 vols. in 166, Paris, Editions Garnier Frères, 1857–66
PL	*Patrologiae cursus completus, series latina*, ed. J.-P. Migne, 222 vols., Paris, Editions Garnier Frères, 1844–66; second edition, 1878–90
PLRE	A. H. M. Jones, J. R. Martindale, J. Morris *et al.*, eds., *The Prosopography of the Later Roman Empire*, 3 vols. in 4, Cambridge University Press, 1971–92
PLS	*Patrologiae Latinae Supplementum*, ed. A.-G. Hamman *et al.*, 4 vols., Paris, Editions Garnier Frères, 1958–74
RAC	*Reallexikon für Antike und Christentum*, Stuttgart, A. Hiersemann, 1941–
SC	*Sources chrétiennes*. Paris, Editions du Cerf, 1942–

Maps

Acknowledgments

I would like to record some personal marks of gratitude. I must thank all the persons at Cambridge University Press who were involved in the publication of this book, beginning with Michael Sharp for his willingness to consider a large and daunting manuscript. My production editor, Thomas O'Reilly, remained throughout a modulated source of discipline and encouragement. I am also in debt to the anonymous readers of the Press for their perspicacity, their necessary cautions, and their constructive recommendations. Finally, Mr. Adam Gitner, a talented graduate student in the Classics at Princeton, brought his eagle eye to the checking of the primary texts cited in the annotation. The lapses of interpretation and fact that remain, as they say, are my responsibility. In the struggle of the writing, I was assisted by able and generous helpers. At the onset, at my request, Ineke Sluiter, at Leiden, photocopied a whole book and sent it to me, gratuitously—what else are good friends for? In the interim, to those who generously answered pestering questions on points of detail, and who offered other much needed help: Denis Feeney, Joseph Farrell, Bob Kaster, AnneMarie Luijendijk, Ann Matter, Aislinn Melchior, and Eric Rebillard. In the end, there were two wonderful colleagues and fellow historians, Peter Brown and Johannes Hahn, who took from their own valuable time and gave it to a reading of the final draft. I must thank the latter for his series of acute challenges and observations, as well as for his critical corrections. Quite apart from his creative insights and provocative suggestions on a draft of the book, my debt to Peter Brown is exceedingly great. Without him, as I am sure many other historians would happily confess, this work of mine would never have existed.

The dedication marks another ineffable debt. Shauna Shaw read several drafts of most of the chapters, a near endless rota of drudgery and thankless hard work. She made numerous helpful suggestions in aid of enhancing the readability of the text. I owe her for this, and for more of which she alone knows. And then there is the music, reminding one of true value. My thanks to E.C. and Derek Trucks at Philadelphia in November 2006, and to D.T. and his talented fellow players at the McCarter, Princeton, in May 2007. Life came back.

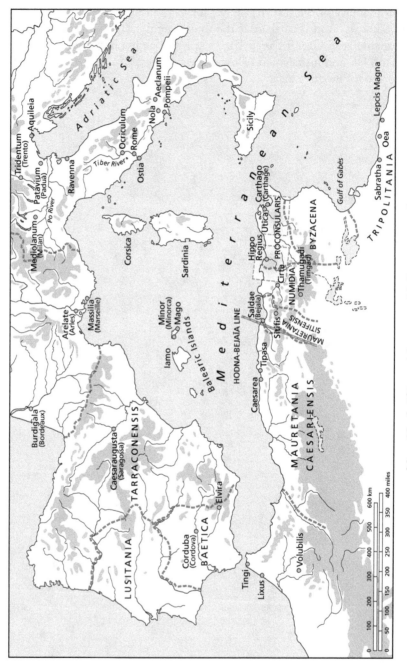

Map 1 North Africa and the western Mediterranean empire

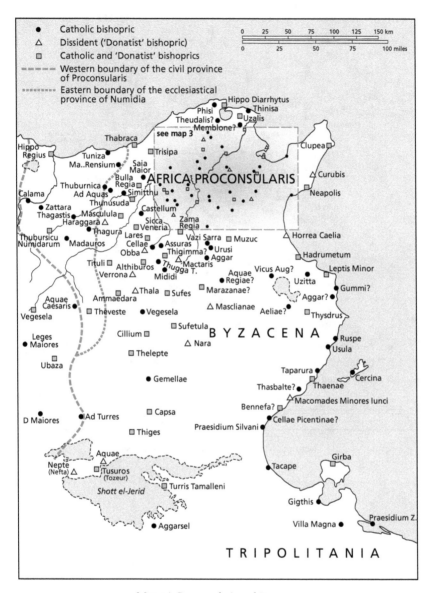

Map 2A Proconsularis and Byzacena
(The area in the dotted-line square is shown in Map 3.)

Map 2B Numidia and Mauretania Sitifensis

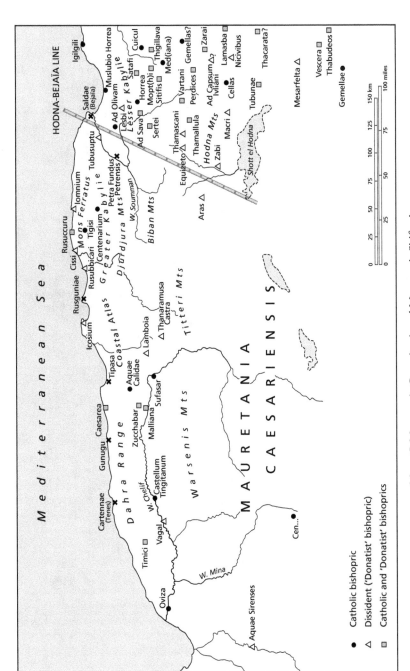

Map 2C Mauretania Caesariensis and Mauretania Sitifensis

Legend:
● Catholic bishopric
△ Dissident ('Donatist' bishopric)
▣ Catholic and 'Donatist' bishoprics

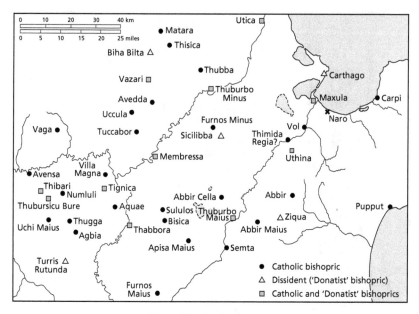

Map 3 The Carthage region

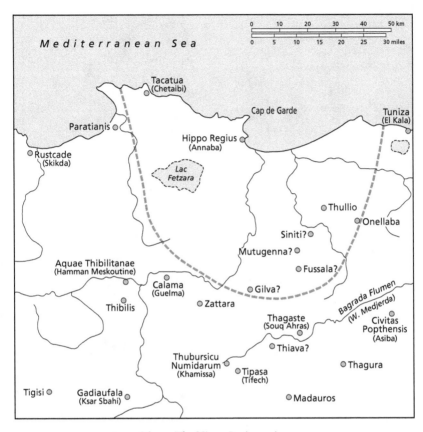

Map 4 The Hippo Regius region
(The area within the dotted line approximates the boundaries of Augustine's diocese of Hippo Regius.)

Introduction

This is not a nice book. It begins with betrayal and ends with suicide. Set on this sad trajectory, the narrative suggests a mundane parallel to the city of God, a fallible human city. If the ideas created by its actors were transcendent, the story itself was enacted in an imperfect human way. The problem confronted in the following investigation is the meaning of religious violence. This story of violence happened in the age of Augustine in his native Africa, when its lands were provinces of the Roman empire. The events begin in the last decade of the fourth century and they end with the armed incursions of foreign Vandal invaders into Africa about the year 429. The spate of killing and destruction that accompanied the arrival of these "barbarian" outsiders put an end to the small story of sectarian violence that is our focus. The new Vandal lords of Africa swept away the cultural underpinnings of institutions and thought that had sustained the special hatreds of the generations that concern us here. There were now to be new dislikes, as one kind of violence decisively trumped another.

The diminutive tradition of sacred violence that I am considering served to create and to confirm intimate values and personal relationships in Africa. The war brought by the Vandals erased these rich meanings that had been created by sectarian conflict. Our attention is focussed on the earlier church struggles that were an integrating force of a social and religious world that disappeared in 430. Our interest is directed as much to the question of how acts of sectarian violence were thought about and represented in words as it is to the actual threats, beatings, burnings, and killings. In this light, it is perhaps disappointing that our narrative diminishes rather than exalts. Events claimed as peasant rebellions and revolutionary social struggles turn out, on closer inspection, to be smaller and meaner things. The principal actors were moved by the logical, if fulfilling, credulities of religious faith and by not much more. What I have encountered is a history of hate – a story of intimate dislike that was motivated by the profound love for one's own people, beliefs, communities, and traditions.

I

The age concerned is the lifetime of Augustine of Hippo, the greatest churchman of western Christendom. So it is perhaps best to begin with a warning. There can be no concealing the plain fact that the great body of writings of the bishop of Hippo make this work possible. But this is *not* a book about Augustine. It is an investigation of what he, along with many others, persuaded, explained, demanded and cajoled, and concealed, and sometimes just reported. Of the mountain of these words, it is the sermons that were preached to the parishioners who crowded basilicas at Hippo Regius, to congregations in the great basilicas at Carthage, and to audiences gathered in the humble churches in smaller provincial towns that are especially significant. Improvised to connect with a wide range of persons who listened to the preacher, they were meant to persuade on that occasion. We should listen to them with care. The written letters that were communications with peers, with the literate elites of Augustine's world, provide information bound by time and place, and by person. And there are the acerbic and polemical writings composed by bishops and laymen on the opposing sides – bitter attacks on their enemies. It is these real-time writings, much more than the elevated, consciously and elaborately wrought world of the theological treatise, that are of special significance to our inquiry.

To repeat: this is not a study of an individual man and his ideas, whether that individual was an Augustine or a Petilian, an Optatus or a Tyconius. Augustine, it is true, was a marvelous creator and marshaler of ideas, and of men. The mountainous weight of his writings and, even more, the ways in which they have profoundly shaped basic ideas of ours, dominate our understanding of the time. Insofar as they pertain to the problems that confront us, however, matters such as the essence of a Trinitarian god, the nature of the mystical or real body of Christ, fine distinctions in the dispensation of grace, the idea of predestination, or the doctrine of original sin are *not* our direct concern here. The long-term impact of Augustine's ideas – not in north Africa where they have all but vanished, but in western Europe and its cultural heirs and legatees – is no concern of mine here. In this investigation, my interest in Augustine is limited to his participation in events in Africa in his own lifetime and not in the later history of his magnificently successful project of self-promotion.[1]

As a history, the analysis here is drawn in a direction contrary to the natural course of the progressive unraveling of events. It is attracted, instead,

---

[1] There are already a number of outstanding biographies, including Brown, *Augustine of Hippo*, still the classic; Lancel, *Saint Augustin*, all the facts, and in order; and O'Donnell, *Augustine*, for the age.

to the backwards rerunning of memory. My purpose is not to reconstruct events serially as they occurred from some point in time, beginning, say, with the first steps of the Great Persecution under the emperor Diocletian in the year 303 and working forward step-by-step to Augustine's death in his bed at Hippo Regius on 28 August 430. Our path will be the reverse of this. Attention will be focussed on the specific hatreds of Augustine's own generation. The majority of incidents of sectarian violence in Africa that can be studied in any coherent fashion occurred in his own lifetime, for the most part during his tenure as bishop of Hippo Regius from 395 to 430. The first problem is to understand the function of earlier quarrels and battles as part of the collected memories of the generation who lived in this later age. I am not especially interested in a blow-by-blow reconstruction of a grand narrative of the dissident Christian community in Africa, the so-called Donatist Church, from its inception to the final dissipation of Christian communities in the Maghrib. There already exist narratives, however imperfect, of this story.[2]

I am also less entangled in the struggle to determine precisely what happened during the state-directed persecution of Christians in Africa in 303–05, or the struggle to determine the facts of what happened in the bitter internecine struggles that emerged in its aftermath. I am more attracted to what each side remembered of this past. What men like Tyconius, Optatus, Augustine, Possidius, Petilian, Emeritus, Cresconius, and their peers and followers, could know is of direct relevance to why they were willing to encourage and engage in coercive and violent action. How the bishops and learned laymen construed the little that they knew of their past is one part of my problem. No matter how public or common this knowledge might seem, it was anything but given or natural. It was a matter of bishops, literary elites, imperial administrators, and teachers and pedagogues constructing this knowledge, and then educating and persuading the ignorant, as they called them. It is this constant rebuilding and replaying of the past by Augustine's peers that formed the context in which the violence was enacted in their present. The script was managed and manipulated. When the writers changed their minds, or disappeared, so did the peculiar acts of hate and harm that were tied to the script that they had made.

In this investigation, violence is understood not just as the specific acts of physical hostility – the threats, the beatings, the blindings, the cuttings,

---

[2] Frend, *Donatist Church*, the standard treatment in English, innovative and influential in its time; and Brisson, *Autonomisme et christianisme*, more perspicacious on the motivating issues (and more accurate on the facts), are exemplary.

the mutilations, and the murders – but also the surrounding world of speech and writing of which these acts were a living part. The violent deeds were living extensions of the rhetoric in which their values and causes were formed. The acts of physical harm and material damage served specific tactical ends that must be understood. The investigation is difficult if only because, as many have already noted, violence is rarely seen as a thing in its own right and is radically under-theorized.[3] The interpretations and representations of violence fed on themselves and were seedbeds for novel and innovative acts of physical harm. But they were all part of a peculiar order of talking, thinking, and writing, at the center of which were new Christian narratives and discourses. The extent to which this new Christian story both displaced and substituted for all others is breathtaking. The power of this Christian talk was produced by many things, among them a remorseless hortatory pedagogy, a hectoring moralizing of the individual, and a ceaseless management of the minutiae of everyday life. Above all, it was a form of speech marked by an absence of humor. It was a morose and a deadly serious world. The joke, the humorous kick, the hilarious satire, the funny cut-them-down-to-size jibe, have vanished. What passes for a laugh is a ghastly gloss on your enemy's spiritual death, on your own coming demise, or on the misfortunes of the sinful and the stupid. Whatever it was, this violence was not funny.

This is also an experiment in time with its own bounds and closures. The contests and values, the affairs and the debates that mattered so intensely to the people that I describe were to become dead matters, things done and past in the generation after Augustine's death. In these later years, different and more pressing concerns were to consume public and personal agendas. In witnessing these ideas and actions at their most intense and meaningful, we are always close to an end when they were to become irrelevant. In the great age of transformation that engulfed the Maghrib at the end of the seventh century and through the remainder of the eighth, all these vitally significant beliefs and actions, the people involved in them, their writings and sermons, their emotional commitments and memories were to disappear forever from the valleys and fields, towns and villages in which they had been lived with such passion. Their only life now was in the memories and ideas borne on a refugee flotsam of Christian writings drifting to European shores. Although it is true that the people and their communities were not suddenly buried under layers of volcanic ash, what

---

[3] See Pandey (1992), esp. pp. 27, 41–42; Brubaker (2004), pp. 90–92; and Zizek, *Violence*, *passim*, for some of the cris-de-coeur, emphasizing the radical "under-theorizing" of violence, and its status as a phenomenon that has to be taken more seriously and understood as a thing in its own right.

they valued was subverted and replaced by different languages and narratives. One might like to imagine a transhistorical world of behaviors and purposes that informed so much of Western history, to imagine that they were part of continuous connections of a grand metahistorical narrative. This is not so. In the end, everything these people did, every communal conflict and personal battle to which they committed themselves out of a belief in transcendent values, became meaningless and worthless. It is enough to give history a bad name.

But bad names are at the very heart of my problem, and from this fact stem even more problems for the historian. In those days, there were good social and political reasons for calling someone a Maximianist, a Donatist, a Rogatist, or a Caecilianist. Sometimes these labels cohered with an accepted reality, but in others they did not. My approach will be to avoid the name-calling as much as possible. More neutral terms can be found to designate each side, words that the participants themselves would have found more or less acceptable as names of their own communities. The more powerful Christian community – in the sense that it was approved by the church in Rome and also recognized by the imperial state – was the one headed by Aurelius, bishop of Carthage and Primate of Africa, but which is most identified in our own age with the dominant literary personality of Augustine. This religious community did succeed, at some level, in asserting a claim to an identity as Catholic. But their opponents, persons whom they labeled "Donatists," consistently, and insistently, claimed to be just as Catholic as the party of Aurelius and Augustine. They insisted with some reason, since even their Catholic opponents admitted that, apart from the division between them, both sides shared the same trinitarian god, the same churches, the same baptism, the same approved canon of sacred scriptures, the same rituals, and the same sacraments. What divided them so bitterly was something else that was rather difficult for them to name and to describe.

Although both parties were Catholic, I have called the Aurelian–Augustinian church "Catholic" because this was their success-in-power identification of themselves. Their opponents are more difficult to designate with any neutral term. The word "Donatist" should be avoided since it was nothing more than a pejorative label foisted on them by the Catholics. In their own self-identity these others thought of themselves as both Christian and Catholic, and that was that. I had once thought that the term "African" Christians would be good since this caught the sense of regionalism that defined a critical part of their identity. I now think that this name must be avoided. They themselves would have found it an odd distinction. More important, the label creates a fundamentally misleading impression that the Catholics in Africa did not share just as many African characteristics as did their opponents. I have therefore lapsed onto a general description of them as a dissident or dissenting party in a descriptive sense, since, even in their own terms, they saw themselves as a persecuted minority who fundamentally disagreed with the majoritarian party.[4] This means that I have committed myself to an imperial view of the situation since "the Donatists," although a minority in the empire, were a majority in their homeland. The imperial perspective is, I think, justified in part by the imperial stage on which Christians acted, and the critical role of the imperial state as a player in this drama. The signal warning, however, is that on their own home ground, in Africa, "the Donatists" were in the majority in numbers and could easily and quite legitimately see their own way as the right one.

As for those objects of our inquiry – the styles and modes of hatred – these are nothing new or unusual. Consider the following story of two chess venues in New York City at the end of the 1990s.[5]

In the Far East, where the game of chess was invented around 600 A.D., stones were supposed to be placed on each corner of the board to keep the evil of the match from spilling over into the world. But there are no stones on the boards in the rival chess shops on Thompson Street in Greenwich Village. And people here see evil all over the place.

The owners of the Chess Shop, at 230 Thompson Street, and the Chess Forum, at 219 Thompson Street, along with the patrons who will go to one shop and not the other, are bitter rivals. The two owners, former partners, have filed lawsuits, had their customers take loyalty oaths and accused each other of spying and theft. They have engaged in name-calling and what each side considers character assassination. One shop briefly debarred disloyal patrons. The shops unleashed price wars where each lost money. And all those involved, cursed with minds that often see life as an intricate battle between pieces on a board, have created whirlpools of intrigue.

The battle will probably not end until one of the shops goes into foreclosure.

"It does not make very good business sense," said Imad Khachan, 37, who owns the Chess Forum. "We would both make more money if we worked together . . . If I had to give him one book it would be King Lear," said Mr. Khachan of his former partner, George Frohlinde, at the Chess Shop. "He is the man who divided his kingdom. This did not need to happen."

---

[4] Georg Michels, facing an analogous problem with the labeling of the "Old Believers" in seventeenth-century Muscovy, has been compelled to this same solution: *At War with the Church*, pp. 16–18.
[5] Chris Hedges, "A Perpetual War Consumes Competing Chess Shop Owners," *The New York Times* (Monday, 23 December 2002), B 1 and 6.

The two shops are similar. They are dominated by tables where players sit, their heads bent over chess boards, for a dollar an hour. There is soft background music, with the Chess Shop preferring classical and the Chess Forum light pop. The players rarely speak . . . The walls in each shop could use a coat of paint, the bathrooms are a bit grimy . . .

The [biblical] commandment against bearing false witness calls on people not to defame and slander their neighbors. On Thompson Street, though, defamation and slander have divided the rival shops as neatly as two lines of pawns.

The dispute began with an exiled Russian grandmaster, Nicholas Rossolimo, a cabdriver who ran a small chess shop on Sullivan Street in the 1950's. He hired Mr. Frohlinde to run it for him in 1963, and eventually left to live in Paris.

The two eventually had a falling out and Mr. Frohlinde opened the Chess Shop in 1972. Mr. Rossolimo, an aristocratic exile from communist Russia, came back to try to save his shop but fell down a flight of stairs in 1975 and died; his shop perished not long after he did.

Those who are set against Mr. Frohlinde seize on the story of how he began his life in America by betraying Mr. Rossolimo. The Russian grandmaster has assumed the role of the martyr in the narrative spun out by those who seek to demonize Mr. Frohlinde.

Mr. Frohlinde, however, said it was he who was betrayed . . . and once he opened his own shop, he said he never spoke to his former employer again.

Enter Mr. Khachan, a graduate student at New York University who was also fleeing war, in this case from Lebanon. He soon became the manager of the Chess Shop. He dropped out of graduate school because he was promised a partnership which, he says, was never delivered . . . Mr. Khachan walked out in 1995 and opened the Chess Forum.

Some of the patrons walked out with him. The newest game began. When asked what happens when he bumps into his former manager on the street, Mr. Frohlinde answered, "You don't see people you don't like."

He paused, seated under a fly strip with numerous dead bugs stuck to it and a bare neon light, and grimaced at the thought of his rival across the street.

"I have not seen him since," he said.

Those who defected to the Chess Forum began to refer to Mr. Frohlinde as "the Nazi." Those in the Chess Shop began to call Mr. Khachan, a Muslim, "Yasir Arafat" . . .

The vitriol does not at all surprise Mr. Khachan, who said that during the war in Beirut he noticed that the worst savagery was always between those of the same religious or ethnic group.

"Former partners always tend to be worse than others when they go to war," he said. "People are meaner to their own people. Maybe this is human nature. You become more self-righteous with your own family. You feel the violence is more justified. You are the big brother who will whip everyone into shape, even if you have to kill them all."

Ernie Rosenberg said that he and his son were barred from entering the Chess Shop after they defected to the Chess Forum. "I printed up leaflets and told the owners of the Chess Shop I would distribute them on the sidewalk during the Christmas season unless they lifted the ban on my son," he said. "Why did they ban my son? Because he was my son. My son did not really want to go in there . . . I used to go in the shop just to annoy them. They would try and throw me out."

Mr. Khachan threw in that when he worked at the Chess Shop . . . "the place was crawling with cockroaches." "With all the fear and prosecution [sic] in the Chess Shop, it saves you from having to read Kafka," he said . . .

Mr. Khachan stood one evening in front of the plate glass window that displayed his chess sets. He watched a young man in a black fatigue jacket and a black wool hat pulled down to his ears linger at the door. The man carried a folded chess board under his arm.

"He's a spy," Mr. Khachan said in a whisper . . . Mr. Nash scoffed at the charge, calling Mr. Khachan paranoid . . .

"He's been doing this for years. He doesn't let some customers into his shop because he says they are spies, but they are just players who like to play in both shops. It is all very weird."

It *is* all very weird. A foundation, a betrayal, a split, a separation, martyrdom, bad names, traitors, libelous leaflets and pamphlets, banned sons who have inherited the stain of betrayal, claims to the truth, and sheer paranoia. It is all here in a smaller and neater scale. So mine is just another history, an attempt at understanding another specific instance.

In the late summer of 2005, a colleague at Princeton noted that I was busy re-reading Truman Capote's *In Cold Blood*; with her usual acumen, she also noted that the reading was incited because "your heart is set on murder." It was. This is not a good mood in which to write history. But as my focus slowly but surely mutated from violence to lying, so did the avenues of approaching my problem. I now understood that it was no accident that Augustine had come to be so concerned with mendacity. His worry was not just the spinoff of a theological tiff with Jerome. It intimately involved himself and his own history. The special qualities of mendacity encompass another species of story telling, one that Professor Frankfurt at Princeton has formally labeled "bullshit," that is at the heart of my problem.[6] I would have preferred to title the book "All Men are Liars." The biblical verse – much quoted by the Christian protagonists in the course of their murderous conflicts in Augustine's Africa – would have raised dangerous questions about historians and the making of fictions. As Verkhovensky once remarked to his sly little friend, "She lied to me so very well – it was almost as good as the truth." My memory of *The Demons* is so thin that I have perhaps mistaken the gender. But the words speak just as well to the history of anything.

---

[6] See Frankfurt, *On Bullshit* – an analysis to which I shall have occasion to return.

CHAPTER I

This terrible custom

Under the burning midsummer sun of the year 418, Augustine, the Catholic bishop of Hippo Regius, already in his mid-sixties and increasingly burdened with the ailments of old age, undertook a journey of unusual length and direction. The long trek took him well outside the heartlands of Africa with which he was familiar. He travelled the roads to Caesarea, the capital of the imperial province of Mauretania Caesariensis, well over 350 miles to the west.[1] Given the deliberate pace of an average day's travel on mule or horseback, the journey would have taken him and his companions about two weeks to complete. What is more, Augustine suffered badly from hemorrhoids and anal fistulae, afflictions that would have made the ride all the more painful.[2] Quite apart from the arduous nature of the trek, the people who lived in Augustine's part of Africa thought of Caesariensis, the far western province of Rome's African empire, as a barbaric and dangerous frontier land.[3] To them, its hinterland did not really belong to the civilized regions of the east. The people of Mauretania knew that they were

[1] Augustine himself regarded the place as remote and far off the beaten paths of the Africa that he knew: see Aug. *Ep.* 190.1 (CSEL 57: 137–38); dating to later in 418, this must reflect his opinion after his visit to Caesarea. For his journeys, see Perler, *Voyages de saint Augustin*, pp. 17, 25–26, 41. In fact, Augustine hardly traveled at all outside the core area of "Africa" well known to him. He had a brief three-year stint in Italy in 384–87. Following his return to Africa in 387, and his ordination as priest and then bishop, Augustine's travels were almost all by land and made in connection with business that directly occupied him in the strategic area west of Carthage, north of Numidia, and east of Mauretania.

[2] For Augustine's sicknesses in old age, see Legewie (1931), 10–14; Lancel, *Saint Augustine*, 193–94; for the hemorrhoidal problems, see Aug. *Ep.* 38.1 (CCL 31: 156): "corpore autem ego in lectum sum, nec ambulare enim nec stare nec sedere possum rhagadis vel exochadis dolore et tumore." *Rhagades* were internal fistulae or haemorrhoids; *exochades* were external piles. His personal difficulties with these afflictions probably provoked his interest in recording the miraculous healing of the anal fistulae of one Innocentius, a former advocate in the office of the Vicar of Africa at Carthage – an event that he himself witnessed: Aug. *Civ. Dei*, 22.8 (CCL 48: 816).

[3] Perler (1958), p. 25, presumes that the journey was made by land, citing Aug. *Ep.* 122.1 (CSEL 34.2: 742) and *Ep.* 193.1 (CSEL 57: 167) in support. But the earlier letter, dating to 410, only speaks of long journeys made by sea *and* land from which Augustine had been exempted at that time for reasons of ill health. The latter letter does not give any indication of the mode of travel to Caesarea. Nor is it clear why the journey would have had have been made all the way directly from Carthage, as Perler

different; some of them did not even wish to be called "Africans."[4] As he made his way through Mauretania Sitifensis, the province just to the east of Caesariensis, Augustine already felt that he was on the frontier next to "the land of the barbarians."[5] The forbidding mountains of Caesariensis, immediately to the west, harboured "innumerable barbarian peoples" to whom the Christian message had not yet been preached. Anyone could see as much by observing its "barbaric" inhabitants who were hunted down, men and women who were transported to the cities of the coast to feed the imperial slave trade.[6]

The reasons why Augustine made this arduous journey have been much debated, but the mission was sufficiently urgent to require the presence of the most prestigious bishop of the Catholic Church in Africa, and it was undertaken at the request of Zosimus, the bishop of Rome.[7] Augustine took with him two of his most-trusted fellow-bishops, Alypius of Thagaste and Possidius of Calama. All three were acting as legates sent on a mission by the Church of Rome. But they also had an agenda of their own. As one of the most talented, energetic, and committed leaders of the Catholic Church in Africa, Augustine decided to take advantage of his presence in Caesarea – which he reached by mid-September – to confront Emeritus, bishop of the dissident or "Donatist" Christian community in the city, and to do this in the basilica that had once been Emeritus' own church. Only a few years earlier, the basilica had been seized by the Catholics under the authority of decrees issued by the emperor that had ordered dissident bishops, like Emeritus, to hand over their places of worship to the

presumes. If Augustine took the usual inland routes and all the way from Carthage, the journey would have been 720–40 Roman miles (about 1,000 km); if made from Hippo, however, as seems more likely, the journey would have been about 530 Roman miles (about 785 km). If Augustine did brave the sea voyage, it would have been much shorter and conceivably quicker (*Itin. Anton.* 15.2–20.3 = O. Cuntz, ed. *Itineraria Romana* (Leipzig, 1929), pp. 2–3), only 378 Roman miles or about 560 kilometres. It would have been the *only* sea voyage other than the two that he made in the 380s, to Italy and back.

[4] Aug. *Ep.* 93.8.24 (CCL 31A: 185): "Mauretania tamen Caesariensis, occidentali quam meridianae parti vicinior, quando nec Africam se vult dici"; cf. Lepelley, *Cités d'Afrique romaine*, 1, p. 50 and 50 n. 95.

[5] Concil. Carth. 28 Aug. 397, canon 4 = *Reg. Eccl. Afr. Excerpt.* canon 52 (CCL 149: 189): "Tunc de provincia Mauritania, propterea quod in finibus Africae posita sit . . . siquidem vicinae barbarico," where it is also compared to the land of the Arguzes in Tripolitania; the people of the ecclesiastical province often redeemed prisoners taken by "barbarian" raiders: Concil. Carth. 13 Sept. 401, canon 7 = *Reg. Eccl. Afr. Excerpt.* canon 72 (CCL 149: 202): "Hinc etiam legati Maurorum, fratres nostri, consuluerunt, quia multos tales a barbaris redimunt."

[6] Aug. *Ep.* 199.12.46 (CSEL 57: 284): "Sunt enim apud nos, hoc est in Africa barbarae innumerabiles gentes, in quibus nondum esse praedicatum evangelium ex his, qui ducuntur inde captivi et Romanorum servitiis iam miscentur, cotidie nobis addiscere in promptu est."

[7] See Bonner (1964) with Lancel (1984a and 1984b) and his "Le long voyage vers Caesarea (Cherchell), en l'été de 418," in *Saint Augustin*, pp. 489–92, for some of the debates.

state-approved Catholic Church. State coercion had transformed Emeritus'
basilica into a Catholic place of worship. To drive home who was now in
power, Augustine delivered a long sermon to the local congregation on the
evils of his sectarian enemies in the very basilica that had once belonged to
them. He expatiated on the good of the unity imposed on all Christians
by imperial laws that had made "the Donatists" an illegal heretical sect and
had forced them to return to the Catholic fold.

In what might be considered a calculated insult, Augustine invited Emeritus to come back to his former church to engage in a face-to-face public
debate over the main points of contention between "the Donatists" and
"the Catholics." The expected verbal fireworks turned into a strange and
abortive confrontation between the two old enemies. Emeritus did turn
up for the occasion. To enter as a legal outcast into what had once been
his own church must have evoked feelings of bitterness and resentment.
In the end, he did no more than utter one word – *fac* – "do what you
want" – and then kept his silence for the remainder of the meeting.[8]
The deliberate stonewalling left Augustine, suddenly, out on a limb. With
the expected show aborted, he had to improvise a make-shift debate on the
spot, a challenge that he met with his usual verve and skill: "I say this . . . " –
"In reply, you would have said this . . . " – and so he went on for an hour
or more.[9] One wonders. Was it in the same voice? Or did Augustine shift
force and timbre to imitate his old enemy's tone? For the entertainment
and the edification of the crowd, he acted out a lengthy virtual dialogue
with his detested enemy.

It is not these sectarian hatreds, however, or any matters of the church
that concern us about what happened in Caesarea in that year. What
will claim our attention has no special connection with the Christian
inhabitants of the city or their quarrels. It is, rather, a strange and violent
episode that was revealed by Augustine, incidentally, in a work that was
not even concerned with the city. In the year 426, eight years after his
mission to Caesarea, while writing the closing chapters of his treatise on

---

[8] Aug. *Gesta cum Emerit.* 3 (CSEL 53: 184), the words come at the end of the five lines of dialogue
that Emeritus did deign to exchange with Augustine; they were cued by a knowledge of the martyrs'
responses to their persecutors, such as Polycarp, *Mart. Poly.* 11 (SC 10: 258): φέρε ὃ βούλει. In this
case, however, it is more probable that Emeritus was intentionally echoing the final words of the great
African bishop martyr Cyprian to the governor Galerius Maximus: *Acta Proconsularia*, 3.4: 'Fac quod
tibi praeceptum est . . . ' (A. A. R. Bastiaensen, ed., *Atti e passioni dei martiri*, Milan, Mondadori,
1987, p. 224).

[9] Augustine was able to do this, in part, because he was so well practiced in these "virtual debates"
from days as early as his confrontations with the Manichees in Africa: see, for example, his *Contra
Faust.* praef. (CSEL 25.1: 251): "Commodum autem arbitror sub eius nomine verba eius ponere et
sub meo responsionem meam" – followed by no less than twenty-three books of dialogic refutation.

Christian education, the *De Doctrina Christiana*, Augustine recounted an unusual event. It was so unusual that he remembered it many years later when completing his work on Christian rhetoric. However odd it might have been, the shocking behavior was something that happened regularly and ordinarily in the Roman city of Caesarea.

A LATE ROMAN CITY

First, a little background. Caesarea's history went back to its foundation as a colony by the Phoenicians in the sixth century BCE. Then it was known by its Punic name of Iol, meaning "the island" immediately offshore where the Phoenicians first landed. From its origins, Caesarea had always been connected with the metropolis of Carthage far to the east. The African king Juba II, put in place as ruler over the region of Mauretania in 25 BCE by the emperor Augustus, renamed Iol "Caesarea" in honor of his imperial patron. Furnished with Hellenistic-style architectural embellishments that marked it as a magnificent Roman-style *urbs*, it became an instant if somewhat artificial city – a symbol of the Roman imperial presence along the coastline of Mauretania. With the end of the African kingdom in 40 CE and the annexation of the region as a province of the empire by the emperor Claudius, this part of the former kingdom of Mauretania was named *Caesariensis*. The city of Caesarea became the capital city of the new province.[10]

Caesarea long retained its character as a government town. It has aptly been called a *ville vitrine*, an urban showcase of Roman power in this part of Africa. A core of bureaucrats, soldiers, imperial slaves, and the other agents of the provincial administration, including the governor and his entourage, anchored the most visible elements of its population.[11] The Italian soldiers, administrators, artisans, traders, and others, who came as emigrants to populate Caesarea would have found themselves in a familiar landscape. It has been remarked, rather poetically, that the countryside has a beauty and charm that is "entirely Campanian."[12] First as a royal center of local

[10] Coltelloni-Trannoy, *Royaume de Maurétanie*; Gsell, (1948) and *Cherchel*; Lepelley, "Caesarea," in *Cités de l'Afrique romaine*, 2, pp. 513–20, 547–48.

[11] Leveau, *Caesarea de Maurétanie*, chs. 1–6 on the development of the city and its history to Late Antiquity. On its type as an urban settlement, see p. 79: "Caesarea m'apparaît comme une ville résidentielle, capitale d'une province et lieu de résidence d'une aristocratie urbaine vivant de l'exploitation de la terre, et non comme un grand centre commercial ou industriel attirant des populations pauvres acceptant de vivre dans un habitat à forte densité" (an interpretation which I take to be essentially correct).

[12] Gsell, "Cherchel," in *Promenades archéologiques*, pp. 7–83, at p. 7: "Le paysage, dit M. Louis Bertrand, est 'd'une noblesse et d'une grâce toutes campaniennes'."

kings and then as a capital of a Roman province, African monarchs and then Roman emperors furnished the city with a full range of palatial and monumental edifices of power. Their benefactions encouraged imitation by the local wealthy who generously constructed facilities for the staging of spectacles: an impressive theater in the center of the city, an amphitheater for gladiatorial contests on a height to the east, and a circus for chariot racing to the west.[13] Its citizens enjoyed the amenities offered by three massive bath complexes. Like the rest of the city, the baths were supplied with water by means of an elaborate system of monumental aqueducts that transported water from a source some twenty miles away to the south.[14]

In the year that Augustine came to the city, in 418, Caesarea was as thriving a city as it had ever been in the halcyon days of the high empire. Its hinterland was densely exploited by agricultural establishments of every size and type. In the late fourth and early fifth centuries, its farms and villas were flourishing on an unprecedented scale. An impressive three-mile-long perimeter wall framed a great quadrant around its core, a large well-defended living space.[15] Within the walls, an urban populace, numbering perhaps 20,000 souls, formed a vibrant face-to-face community.[16] The sense of closeness was tightened by the cocoon-like environment of the city. If one thing was true of Caesarea and of the other Roman cities that dotted the Mediterranean shore of Mauretania, it was their relative isolation from each other and from the lands immediately inland. Like them, Caesarea was ensconced in a small niche of coastal territory, encircled on all sides by high hills and rugged, jumbled mountains. As island-like settlements along the coast, each of these towns was simultaneously a Mediterranean port-of-call and a settlement anchored precariously against a mountainous hinterland.

---

[13] Leveau, *Caesarea de Maurétanie*, pp. 33–36 (theater), 36–39 (amphitheater), and 39–40 (circus).

[14] On the baths, see Leveau, *Caesarea de Maurétanie*, pp. 51–57; on aqueducts, ibid., pp. 57–63; cf. P. Leveau and J. Paillet, *L'alimentation en eau de Caesarea de Maurétanie et l'aqueduc de Cherchel*, Paris, Editions l'Harmattan, 1976; and P. Leveau and J. Paillet, "Alimentation en eau de Caesarea de Maurétanie et l'aqueduc de Cherchell," in J. P. Boucher ed., *Journées sur les Aqueducs*, Paris, 1977, pp. 231–34, on the aqueduct and water supply.

[15] Leveau, *Caesarea de Maurétanie*, pp. 26–28, recapitulating the basic work by P.-M. Duval, *Cherchel et Tipasa. Recherches sur deux villes fortes de l'Afrique romaine*, Paris, 1946.

[16] Gsell, "Cherchel," guessed, certainly much too high, at 100,000; Courtois, *Les Vandales*, p. 108, placed his estimate at 37,000 based on an area coefficient of 140–150 persons per hectare, which Lezine argued, correctly I think, to be much too high since it did not take into the consideration the 20–30% of city space that was open and not inhabited in the city. See Leveau, *Caesarea de Maurétanie*, p. 79. The modern town of Sharshall, which occupied about a fourth of the site of the original Roman city, numbered about 2,500 inhabitants in 1830, about 5,300 in 1921 (Gsell, *Promenades archéologiques*, p. 26); and about 5800 inhabitants in 1951 (Gsell, *Cherchel*, p. 36). It is therefore to be doubted that the *intra muros* population of the Roman city greatly exceeded a figure on the order of 20,000 or so.

African outsiders who came to live at Caesarea whose origins are known without exception came from the other harbor towns that were strung out, archipelago-like, along the northern coast: Tingi, Gunugu, Icosium, Saldae, Tipasa, Rusguniae, Hippo Regius, and Carthage.[17]

The proximity of Caesarea's inhabitants by kinship, neighborhood, and occupation is something to remember. This sense of closeness must have been typical of many other African cities. Almost all of these towns, apart from the great metropolis of Carthage, were of rather modest to middling size. The cities were urban, but with a peculiar compactness that highlighted their urban skyscapes against the agrarian worlds pressing in immediately around them. Starkly distinguished from the countryside round about, the towns deep in the agrarian hinterland were intense islands of urbanity in vast oceans of rural space. To come upon them from the outside was to be introduced suddenly and abruptly to a world of walls, gates, paved streets, imposing fora, fountains, libraries, and monumental buildings. So it was at Caesarea. But with the recurrent advent of a new governor and his staff every few years, the rotation of military personnel, and the shipping of produce and tribute, the arrival and departure of vessels bearing travelers and traders, the city was more continuously connected with other big urban centers of the Mediterranean, including the imperial metropolis of Rome, than were most of the inland towns of Africa.

Seaborne connections enabled the inhabitants of the small coastal cities to move onto the larger imperial stage. Most spectacularly in the case of Caesarea, one of its native sons, Marcus Opellius Macrinus, became emperor of Rome in 217. His rise to power illustrates the close, if strange and unexpected, interpellation of high and low in the city. An African or *Maurus* who was born in Caesarea, Macrinus was the offspring of "most unillustrious parents." In appearance he had followed the customs of the Mauri by piercing one of his earlobes to take prominent earrings."[18] It was an African custom, one connected with magic and occult power.[19] But outsiders, like the Roman historian who reports this fact, no doubt tended to exaggerate the perceived "Africanness" of the locals. However much it was an isolated insular world on the African coast, Caesarea was well enough connected with the outside to provide ways by which men of refinement and connection might rise. The presence of all of the apparatus of imperial administration – most importantly, the governor's courts – meant that the city was also a center of rhetoric and education. The dissident Christian

---

[17] Leveau, *Caesarea de Maurétanie*, p. 96.   [18] Dio 79.11.1–2.
[19] And therefore condemned by some Christians, including Augustine: see *De Doct. Christ.* 2.20.30 (CCL 32: 554) and *Ep.* 245.2 (PL 33: 1060–61).

bishop of Caesarea, Emeritus, a man of considerable talent with whom Augustine dueled throughout his life, was one of these professional men of law and speech. The rhetors were skilled politicians and leaders in a general sense, and the teachers who trained them were among the best. The last of the renowned Latin grammarians, the great Priscian, who flourished as the leading teacher of Latin letters and grammar at the eastern imperial capital of Constantinople in the first decades of the sixth century, was a native of Caesarea. And like Emeritus, he was also a Christian.[20]

In the age of Augustine, Caesarea played the role, as it had in the past, of a major staging port when the imperial government brought in expeditionary forces from abroad to repress outbreaks of violence of a kind that were deemed sufficiently large-scale and threatening to the empire to be recognized as wars. One of these incidents is retold in some detail by the historian Ammianus Marcellinus. It was an armed insurrection in the early 370s led by an African rebel named Firmus. The outbreaks of violence of the Firmus war included assaults on the isolated coastal cities of Mauretania in 372, attacks in which some of them, like Icosium (modern Algiers) and Caesarea, were pillaged and burnt. Tipasa, only seventeen miles to the east of Caesarea, managed successfully to repel the armed marauders.[21] Ammianus describes the consequences for Caesarea:[22]

Then he [sc. the general Theodosius] turned to go to Caesarea, once a wealthy and noble city . . . and having entered it, he found the city almost entirely burned from widespread fires, with even the paving stones turned white from the scorching heat. He commanded the first and second legions to be quartered there for a time, with orders to clear away the heaps of ashes and to stay on guard, so that the city would not be devastated by a renewed attack made by the barbarians.

To exalt the image of the Roman commander Theodosius and to disparage "the barbarians," Ammianus might well have exaggerated the effects of the assault on the city. Even so, some seven or eight years later the local dignitaries of Caesarea were still expending their wealth to recover from the damage. But recover they did. By the early decades of the fifth century, the ornate houses of the wealthy were once again resplendent, dominating the heights just inside the city walls to the south, overlooking its

---

[20] Because of his consistent identification of himself with speakers of Latin, Niebuhr held that he probably came from Caesarea in Mauretania: R. Kaster, *Guardians of Language: The Grammarian and Society in Late Antiquity*, Berkeley and Los Angeles, University of California Press, 1988, no. 126, pp. 346–48; arguments have been made that his home city was Caesarea Maritima in the East – see Geiger (1999). I am not persuaded.

[21] On Tipasa and Iconium, see Amm. Marc. 29.5.16–17; Orosius 7.33.5 on the fate of Caesarea.

[22] Amm. Marc. 29.5.18; cf. 29.5.42, where he adds: "Qui [sc. Theodosius] Caesaream mitti dispositus, ubi saeva iniusserat monumenta facinorum pessimorum, dilatato vulneris hiatu discessit."

monumental center. Decorated with brilliant frescoes and mosaics, and statuary that replicated the prevailing modes of high-style Mediterranean fashion, the homes of the elite exuded a new confidence. The people of the late antique city of Caesarea, nested in their protective urban environment, were exemplary Romans. A wealthy curial class controlled the city's public affairs. A varied artisanal class provided for the material demands of everyday living. And there was the ever-present urban proletariat, large numbers of the not-so-well off whose names are not seen even in the simplest of funeral epitaphs that marked the gravestones in the city's cemeteries.

There was also a Jewish community of some importance. It boasted a chief rabbi, a synagogue, and an *archisynagogus*. And a separate Christian community had grown, developing its own sense of identity. A Christian basilica was located in the center of the town on the edge of the forum, probably the main church of the city.[23] In the generations after Constantine, this new community of believers had flourished. A local Christian, a self-styled Worshiper of the Word, a *cultor verbi*, had bestowed on the church a large piece of property just to the west of the city to serve as the burial ground for his fellow believers. In the late fourth century, the area had been repaired by Severianus, a Christian of senatorial rank. His act of benevolence was later remembered in a verse inscription restored by Asterius, acting in concert with his Christian "brothers."[24]

This same Christian community had an important role in the restoration of the city following the damage caused by the Firmus revolt. Clemens, the bishop, is mentioned in a letter written by the grandiose Roman senator Symmachus to his brother Celsinus Titianus in 380–81. In the letter, Symmachus solicited whatever interventions Titianus might be able to make in his capacity as Vicar of Africa to assist the hard-pressed magistrates of Caesarea.[25] They were being held responsible for replacing the monies robbed from the provincial treasury in the city during the violent raid staged by Firmus' partisans. Symmachus was able to help them because he was a powerful man in the imperial elite and he was someone with whom the men of the city had connections: he possessed estates in the province of which Caesarea was capital. The Firmus raid is worthy of consideration because it was one of the rare instances of hard war, of big violence, that marked the history of Africa in the fourth century. The ways in which it

---

[23] Potter, *Iol Caesarea*, p. 33, fig. 14, 42–44 and fig. 43; Potter (1996); and Potter and Benseddik (1993).

[24] CIL 8.9585 = ILCV, 1583 (Caesarea); see Duval, *Loca sanctorum*, I, no. 179; "Severianus (2)," PAC, p. 1068; Gsell, *Promenades archéologiques*, p. 19.

[25] Symm. *Ep.* 1.64 (MGH AA 6.1: 29); see "Clemens (1)," PAC, pp. 212–13; for Titianus, see "Titianus (1)," PAC, p. 1115 and "Celsinus Titianus (5)," PLRE, I, pp. 917–18.

affected the city of Caesarea suggest the significance that the violence of war had for African affairs of the time. But first, we must turn to the unusual event that happened in the city and to Augustine's connection with it.

THE GANGS OF CAESAREA

It was neither violence between the bitterly divided Christians inside Caesarea during these years – although such divisions marked by deep hatreds certainly existed – nor the damage caused in the war with Firmus that Augustine remembered from his visit to the city in 418. It was something different from full-blown war on the one hand and from sectarian violence on the other. The Caesarea that recovered and rebuilt after the Firmus war was a confident and burgeoning late Roman city. Embedded in the normality and order of its renewed urban life, however, were things that were not so ordinary. These events bring us back to Augustine, the *De Doctrina Christiana*, and to his memories of Caesarea.

In the year 426, in composing the final book of his treatise on Christian education and communication, Augustine described the different styles of speaking to an audience in ways designed to influence its behavior: the temperate, the subdued, and the grand styles of formal speaking. In writing these words, he recalled the visit that he had made to Caesarea some eight years earlier.[26] What provoked his memory was the reason that had driven him to deliver a speech in the grand style to the people of the city.[27]

By its very weight, the grand style of speaking often crushes opposing voices, but it also elicits responses of tears. This was the case when I was persuading the people of Caesarea in Mauretania to desist from their civil battles, or rather something much worse than a civil conflict – something which they called "the *caterva*." At the same time every year, not just the citizens as such, but rather close relatives, brothers, and even parents and children ceremonially divided themselves into two parts and for several successive days they fought each other with stones, each one of them attempting to kill whomever they could.

---

[26] The reasons that prompted Augustine's visit to Caesarea in 418 are a matter of debate; suffice it to say that they had nothing to do with the *caterva*. See Lancel (1984a and 1984b) for a comprehensive discussion of the evidence. He estimates, rightly I think, that the affair had something to do with the need to confirm the position of a "primate" for the new ecclesiastical province of Caesariensis.

[27] Aug. *De Doct. Christ.* 4.24.53 (CCL 32: 159): "Grande autem genus plerumque pondere suo voces premit, sed lacrimas exprimit. Denique cum apud Caesaream Mauritaniae populo dissuaderem pugnam civilem vel potius plus quam civilem, quam *catervam* vocabant – neque enim cives tantummodo, verum etiam propinqui, fratres, postremo parentes ac filii lapidibus inter se in duas partes divisi, per aliquot dies continuos, certo tempore anni solemniter dimicabant et quisque, ut quemque poterat, occidebat."

In this unexpected way, Augustine unveils for us a violent, indeed lethal custom that annually divided the inhabitants of this coastal city, the capital city of a Roman province, into two warring factions who viciously set at each other purposefully to inflict physical harm. He continues:[28]

> I pleaded with them, in the grand style, as far as I was able, to convince them to drive from their hearts and from their behavior such a cruel and chronic evil. It was not as much when I heard them shouting and chanting their approval that I thought that I had achieved anything as when I saw them weeping. Their shouts of approval indicated that they had been taught and that they had understood, but their tears showed that they had actually been changed. When I saw those tears, I believed that this terrible custom handed down by their fathers and grandfathers, and by even more remote ancestors, which had besieged their hearts like an enemy, or rather had occupied their hearts, had been overcome even before the victory had been proclaimed. As soon as my speech was finished, I directed their hearts and lips to give thanks to God. By the grace of Christ, nothing similar has been attempted there for eight years or more by now.

The strange violence that divided the community internally against itself was so thoroughly entrenched that only the grace of the supreme deity could eradicate it. The custom was so deeply ingrained because it defined the people who participated in it. Every year they willfully engaged in a murderous ceremony that demonstrated to themselves, even to the point of death, who they were. Its primal causes were almost irrelevant. More significant was the long-lived history and tradition. Handed down from distant ancestors, and more immediately from fathers and grandfathers, this violent custom – a *consuetudo* as they called it – was re-enacted ceremoniously year after year because, quite simply, it was what the people of Caesarea had always done. It was irrelevant that it involved real violence, injury and suffering, and even the occasional death; or that it pitted brother against brother. Splitting the community into two contending parts, the violent celebration took place every year under the eyes of the Roman governor and the units of guards and the army that were stationed in the city. They did nothing to to prevent it. They, too, must have accepted that this was something that everyone did because it had always been done.

---

[28] Aug. *De Doct. Christ.* 4.24.53 (CCL 32: 159–60): "egi quidem granditer, quantum valui, ut tam crudele atque inveteratum malum de cordibus et moribus eorum avellerem pelleremque dicendo, non tamen egisse aliquid me putavi, cum eos audirem acclamantes, sed cum flentes viderem. Acclamationibus quippe se doceri et delectari, flecti autem lacrimis indicabant. Quas ubi aspexi, immanem illam consuetudinem a patribus et avis longeque a maioribus traditam, quae pectora eorum hostiliter obsidebat, vel potius possidebat, victam, antequam re ipsa id ostenderent, credidi. Moxque sermone finito ad agendas deo gratias corda atque ora converti. Et ecce, iam ferme octo vel amplius anni sunt, propitio Christo, ex quo illic nihil tale temptatum est."

The *caterva*, as it was called, is a difficult thing to explain.[29] Examples from other cities in Africa are hard to find, and the fact that Augustine designates the practice by a local term – "*they* call it the *caterva*" – almost guarantees that even he found it a strange and unusual custom. But the word by which the local inhabitants designated this form of civic violence was appropriate, since it usually designated violently opposed groups of men, sometimes chaotic and violent, sometimes "barbaric" in nature, and sometimes informally organized and undisciplined.[30] As we shall see, it was conventionally used to describe the armed and violent bands of circumcellions who were some of the main propagators of sectarian violence in Augustine's Africa.[31] But any loose collection of things, from a farrago of words to a herd of wild animals, could be designated a *caterva*, but it could also be used to designate a group of men as organized, violent, and dangerous as a band of trained gladiators.[32] All of these uses are reflected in Augustine's prose, and *caterva* continued to have a negative connotation associated with violence in late Latin long after his time.[33] But it had an early history too. In Roman Pompeii of the mid-first century CE, the people celebrated the benefactions of Aulus Clodius Flaccus, one of the mayors or *duumviri* of the city. As part of the Apollonian Games that he staged in gratitude for being elected, Flaccus presented a parade, bulls, bullfighters, three pairs of *pontiarii*, and gangs of fist-fighters or *pugiles catervarii* – all followed by plays and pantomimic performances, one of them featuring the famous dancer Pylades. To celebrate his second duumvirate in which he was *quinquennalis* or town censor, Flaccus provided much the same range of entertainments displayed in the town forum which, in additional to gladiatorial contests, again included gangs of fist-fighters or *catervarii*.[34]

---

[29] For some recent attempts, see Rohozinski (2002) and Cecconi (2007), whose proffered explanations seem far-fetched, even if they do offer some interesting "anthropological parallels."

[30] Equivalent, therefore, to *manus* and *turba*, both of which were frequently used to designate informal collections of persons gathered in episodes of civil violence: Cic. *Verr.* 2.5.43.184; *Mur.* 33.69; Sall. *Bell. Cat.* 14.1; of animals (but usually a poetic usage): Lucr. *De rer. nat.* 6.1092; Verg. *Aen.* 11.456.

[31] See ch. 14, p. 657.   [32] Suet. *Calig.* 18.

[33] Aug. *Ep.* 10.5.1* (CSEL 88: 49): Africa is losing its indigenous inhabitants to slavers not in "herds" (*gregatim*) or by groups (*catervatim*), but in a continuous stream; *Confess.* 6.3.3 (CCL 27: 75): importunate clutches of busybodies (*catervae negotiorum hominum*) pester Ambrose. More colorfully, the term is used of disorganized groups of ideas and images that "crowd" our minds: *Confess.* 10.8.12, 10.35.57 (CCL 27: 161 and 186); *De quant. anim.* 33.71 (CSEL 89: 219); or of batches of sins and evil desires: *En. In Psalm.* 57.19 (CCL 39: 725), 129.2 (CCL 40: 1891), 140.18 (CCL 40: 2039): all with generally negative connotations, as of bands of "nay-sayers" and sinners: *Sermo*, 216 (PL 38: 1082), 313 (PL 38: 1424), 363 (PL 39: 1635); for its continued negative associations with bad and violent behavior see Halsall, *Violence and Society*, pp. 8–9 and 9 n. 8.

[34] CIL 10.1074d = ILS 5053; for more comment, see J. L. Franklin, *Pompeis Difficile Est: Studies in the Political Life of Imperial Pompeii*, Ann Arbor, University of Michigan Press, 2001, pp. 23–25 (no. 9). To celebrate his third duumvirate, Aulus records "games of the first faction": *ludos prima factione*.

Two such men of violence, each of whom called himself a *catervarius* or gangster, are actually recorded. Perhaps equally significant is the fact that they both come from Africa, from the city of Cirta.[35] What were these *catervarii* or gang men – for that is what the word literally means – doing? The primal elements of fist-fights and the importance of neighborhoods takes us back to a passion of the first emperor, Augustus. In noting the emperor's attraction to the world of games and contests, his biographer reports:

He was an avid and very knowledgeable spectator of boxers, and especially of the Latins, and not only of the professional and trained ones whom he was accustomed to pit against Greeks, but also of local town toughs, *catervarii oppidani*, who, at the drop of a hat, engaged in fist-fights in the narrow alleyways in the city's neighborhoods, but who were lacking in skill.[36]

By this chance notice, we happen to learn that there existed in the *vici* or neighborhoods of the city of Rome gangs of roughs, members of fight clubs who were accustomed to participation in neighborhood battles. They were the informal side of a sport that had an element of ethnic labeling to it, in which the locals, that is to say "the Latins," could be pitted against outsiders, called "the Greeks."

Ritualistic or entertainment-based fist-fighting in cities like Rome and Cirta, and their neighborhoods, could have been influenced in some fashion by the circus and theatrical violence known from other urban environments in the empire.[37] In condemning an immensely popular festival, the great "Day of the Torches," that took place in his own city of Hippo Regius on 24 June of every year, Augustine noted that the uproar could get out of hand. What else could one expect when many demons and much devilry was abroad? "Now the demons take pleasure," he says,

don't they, in these pop songs, they take pleasure in vapid spectacles, in the manifold indecencies of the theaters, in the mad frenzies of the chariot races, in the cruelties of the amphitheater, in the unrelenting rivalries of those who take up quarrels and disputes to the point of open hostilities – all this on behalf of some comedian, actor, jester, charioteer, or wild-beast hunter.[38]

---

[35] CIL 8, 7413 = ILS 5176 (Cirta): d. m. / T. Iotelus / citirva/rius [sic], v. / a. LXXXI / h. s. e. / o. t. b. q. f.; and CIL 8, 7414 = ILS 5176A (Cirta): Cirius ca/thruarius / v. a. XXII. But one should perhaps not make too much of any negative element in the word, since a *Comes sacrarum largitionum* could bear the name Catervius (CTh 6.30.3).

[36] Suet. *Aug.* 45.2: "Spectavit autem studiosissime pugiles et maxime Latinos, non legitimos atque ordinarios modo, quos etiam committere cum Graecis solebat, sed et catervarios oppidanos inter angustias vicorum pugnantis temere ac sine arte."

[37] Cameron, *Circus Factions*, esp. ch. 10, "Riots and Politics," pp. 271–96.

[38] Aug. *Sermo* 198.3 (PL 38: 1026).

/

These theatrical venues of factional fan-driven rivalries and violence, all of them involving young men, also existed in Caesarea. But it is almost certain that the *caterva* was different from entertainment violence and rioting. Its purpose was simply the violence itself, not the support of some actor or gladiator, or a battle over a contested referee's call. And it involved everyone, the old and the young, women and men. It was a form of communal violence.

The city of Rome and, for that matter, Caesarea were not alone in exhibiting this behavior. Take the northern Italian city of Patavium, modern Padua, the home town of the historian Livy. He reports that in the year 174 BCE one of the two consuls, M. Aemilius Lepidus, had been assigned as his special task or "province," the repression of an inside war, a *bellum intestinum*, in the city that was caused by the struggle of gangs or *factiones* in the town.[39] We learn about this, surely, because it was a fragment of local knowledge that the historian knew because it came from the annals or the verbal lore of his home town. So the story, a little bit of Padua, was artificially inserted into his history of the city of Rome.[40] Another accident of recounting, like that of Augustine on Caesarea, it discloses to us the inner workings of community life. Was the split a *stasis* cutting vertically across the layers of the more and less well-off in the city, with battles that pitted the poor against the rich? It does not seem to have these characteristics.[41] Or was the community divided horizontally: neighborhoods turning violently against each other? The latter seems more likely. Brothers against brothers – rough contact in which young men clustered according to neighborhood sections, fighting each other. Violent ceremonials of this kind were part of life in the Renaissance city-states of Italy, perhaps best attested in the case of Siena.[42] But not there alone. There is the wonderfully well-documented history of the *pugni* of Venice, battles fought with fists and staves that involved divisions within the city that can be traced to post-Roman times when the town was still a series of settlements on the islands off the

---

[39] Livy 41.27.3: "Ex iis [sc. consulibus] M. Aemilio senatus negotium dedit ut Patavinorum in Venetia seditionem comprimeret, quos certamine factionum ad intestinum bellum exarsisse et ipsorum legati attulerant."

[40] Marcus Aemilius Lepidus was consul in 175 BCE (MRR, I, p. 401) when he commanded military forces in Liguria; it would be logical that this particular bit of "business" or *negotium* was appended to his duties in his northern Italian *provincia*.

[41] A. Lintott, *Violence, Civil Strife and Revolution in the Classical City, 750–330 B.C.*, London, Croom Helm, 1982, offers a convenient survey. The "classical city" is the Greek polis, and none of the cases of violence studied by Lintott is like the type documented for Caesarea.

[42] L. Martines, *Power and Imagination: City-States in Renaissance Italy*, New York, A. Knopf, 1979, pp. 34–41.

mainland.[43] Initially, the mini-combats were mêlées that involved districts or neighborhoods set against each other. As the city grew and unified, however, so did the opposing districts. In the end, they coalesced into two opposing sides and became an annual dyadic struggle.

As for Africa, the people of Caesarea had good reason to appeal to distant ancestors. The dyadic civic battle attested for Caesarea was not an isolated occurrence in Africa. In the earliest external ethnography that we have of Africa, Herodotus, in the fourth book of his *Histories*, reports a ritual that took place at a site inland of the Gulf of Gabès where two ethnic groups, the Machlyes and the Ausees, lived.[44]

During a festival dedicated to the goddess Athena, their young women divided into two camps and then set to fighting each other with blows from stones and wooden clubs, thereby enacting, as they say, a ceremonial that was instituted by their ancestors in honor of the indigenous deity whom we call Athena. Some of them who die from the wounds are called false virgins.

It has been noted that in modern times in this same region near the Shatt al-Jerid, in the springtime, there have been festive chanting, dancing, and violent confrontations in which the young men of Tozûr and of Nefta divided into two camps and attacked each other, using stones and wooden clubs. The confrontation is violent and the participants risk serious injury. The ritual is an annual one for which those involved plan in detail, assembling in advance stores of the necessary ammunition, mainly staves and stones.[45] Detailed ethnographic reports of this festive moietic battle have occasioned much comment about "religious survivals" in this part of the Maghrib.

The custom of the *caterva* at Caesarea, as well as the violent annual rituals found inland of the Gulf of Gabès from Herodotus to our own day, points to another deep structure that is important to sustaining ongoing violence: the power of tradition. In the division that split the community of Caesarea into two sides, pitted against each other, most of the participants defended their actions on the basis of the past: the practice had been handed down to them by their fathers and their fathers' fathers. What one's ancestors or *maiores* had done was what you did because it was, by that very fact, justified. In any premodern society this is usually true to

---

[43] Davis, *War of the Fists*, with the earliest surviving references going back to the ninth century; see pp. 19–20; 32–46 on connections with urban factionalism; and 117–28 on the role of neighborhoods.

[44] Hdt. 4.180; he goes on to offer some interpretation of the behavior and the antecedent ritual in which one of the girls was dressed up in armor and paraded around.

[45] Payre (1942), pp. 171 f., with the oral reports confirmed by Decret and Fantar, *L'Afrique du Nord*, pp. 248–50.

some extent. It was particularly true of the societies of the ancient western Mediterranean. But even among these, it was especially true of ancient north Africa. Everywhere where we can measure degrees of affection, duty, and other sentiments, Africans showed an unusual respect for age and seniority.[46] As at Caesarea, this devotion to old age had nothing to do with Christian influences; rather it had a profound impact on the structure of Christian practices and institutions in their local African form.

How many other urban communities in Africa had factions that engaged in *catervae*? And did these traditional violent rituals, where they existed, spill into the new religious factionalism of the fourth and fifth centuries? We do not know. What can be noted are a few circumstantial details. Few cities of the late empire of any size escaped violent factionalism of some kind. In larger towns it was often associated with the *factiones* or fans of the circus. Carthage was no exception. Augustine's testimony regarding his life as a young man in the city confirms the presence of this violence. He reports how he encountered "The Destroyers," groups of young men called *Eversores* that were prevalent when he came to the city as a young man in 371.[47] Although it is possible that such hell-raising was no more than a violent style engaged in by young men as individuals, it is more likely that they were groups, however passing and informal, tied to neighborhoods, work associations, or entertainment venues. They were engaged in violent gang-like acts. In other words, they too were *catervae*.[48]

How very calmly I behaved, my Lord, you know – I was completely removed from the acts of violence that the Destroyers, the *Eversores*, committed – an insidious and diabolical name which was adopted as a mark of stylish urbanity. I lived with them, but with a sense of shame because I was really like them. When I was with them and when I delighted in their friendships, I was still always horrified by the acts which they committed, by their violent deeds. In these, they would brashly harass some unsuspecting victim, gratuitously affronting his sense of decency, all for their own amusement and as a way to get their kicks. Nothing in their acts was more similar to those of demons. There could be no truer name for them than

[46] See Shaw (1984), pp. 479–81, on seniority, with the studies (1982) and (1991) documenting its social effects.

[47] Brown, *Augustine of Hippo*, pp. 26–27; Augustine was seventeen at the time.

[48] Aug. *Confess.* 3.3.6 (CCL 27: 29): "quamquam longe sedatior, domine, tu scis, et remotus omnino ab eversionibus, quas faciebant eversores – hoc enim nomen scaevum et diabolicum velut insigne urbanitatis est – inter quos vivebam pudore impudenti, quia talis non eram: et cum eis eram et amicitiis eorum delectabar aliquando, a quorum semper factis abhorrebam, hoc est ab eversionibus, quibus proterve insectabantur ignotorum verecundiam, quam proturbarent gratis inludendo atque inde pascendo malivolas laetitias suas. Nihil est illo actu similius actibus daemoniorum. Quid itaque verius quam eversores vocarentur, eversi plane prius ipsi atque perversi deridentibus eos et seducentibus fallacibus occulte spiritibus in eo ipso, quod alios inridere amant et fallere?"

Destroyers, since they were already themselves destroyed and thoroughly perverse in nature. The mockery and deceit which they loved to vent on others were the seductive hidden traps of the One [i.e. the Devil] by which they themselves were mocked and deceived.

This African youth violence is no imaginary thing of Augustine's, exaggerated for personal purpose. In the year immediately preceding the year of this incident in the *Confessions*, the emperors had issued an edict against the violent acts of student gangs in Africa, principally, one assumes, the youth gangs in Carthage.[49] When Augustine speaks from his own experience of "stylish urbanity" he cues another significant element of violence: style. It reminds us of the town of Hypata as imagined by the African writer Apuleius in the 180s, in which young men from the local town elite congregated in gangs to pulverize unsuspecting wayfarers who happened to stray though their part of town or who happened to run into them by accident. Their presence was well known, their activities mostly uncontrolled, and their violence part of a young man's style.[50]

In the imperial capital of Constantinople in the later empire, we have a good description that combines the elements of stylishness and violence among the members of such gangs of young men. Their hair was cut in the radical mullet skater style, the rough ponytail of the biker, the exaggerated ballooning clothes of the forties zoot-suiter or the seventies rapper, all purposefully meant to imitate a stylish civilized-barbarian mode. Here, again, we see Augustine's "stylish urbanity."[51]

First among the factions, they [i.e. the Blues] changed their hair to a completely new style. They had it cut and shaped very differently from all the other Romans. They did not alter the beard or moustache in any way, but took care to grow them as long as possible, like the Persians. But the hair on the head they cut right back to the temples, allowing the long growth to fall down behind to its full length in a mangled mess, like the Massagetai. That is why they call this fashion the "Hun style." Then, for their mode of dress, they all think it right to be wear rich clothing, putting on styles too ostentatious for their proper status – it is just that they were in a position to obtain such clothes at other people's expense. The part of the top covering their arms is drawn in very tight at the wrists, while from there

---

[49] CTh 14.9.1 (Valentinian, Valens, and Gratian, from Trier, to Olybrius, Praefectus Urbi; 12 March 370): in an attempt to control student violence in Rome, various controls were to be instituted, including the requirement of letters of reference and birth registrations; the students who were so violent that they had to be returned to Africa ("and other provinces" added for good measure, but indicating the main source of the problem) were to be registered by the authorities.

[50] Apul. *Met.* 2.18, cf. 2.31–32. Photis warns Lucius against the violent youths; Apuleius is probably reflecting African town life of his own time; a long-standing "fear" in the larger cities of the empire: see Juv. *Sat.* 3.268–301 on the streets of Rome.

[51] Procop. *Historia arcana*, 7.8–14 (ed. J. Haury).

to the shoulder it is spread out to an enormous width. Whenever they waved their arms as they chanted slogans in the theaters or the circuses, and urging on their favorites in their usual way, up in the air went this part of their clothing . . . Their capes and pants were also in the "Hun style" in both name and fashion.

Such violent youths in the towns and cities of the empire were very much part of Carthage in the later empire. They were still there ten years after Augustine's first encounter with the Destroyers, when, in 382, at age twenty-eight, he offered the continued violence of young men as his main reason for leaving the metropolis of Africa for Rome, where (as he heard) things were more peaceful.[52] Augustine was not thinking of the gangs of *Eversores*, as much as he was of the violent behavior of young students: "Their recklessness is unbelievable. They often commit outrages which ought to be punished by law, were it not for custom that protects them."[53] Like the Mohocks of early eighteenth-century London, the rowdy and violent gangs of the elite had protection to engage in the little acts of violence for their own enjoyment.[54] Custom was also central to this violence – *consuetudo* as Augustine puts it. Important persons had always offered a sort of patronal protection to the students: their violence was a place where custom and style converged. In other sources of the period, the sense of *caterva* is that of a gang, a group of persons gathered for violent purposes. It could be legal, as in a gang of torturers who vented violence on the bodies of others under the approval of the government.[55] More to the point, however, it could be a voluntary assemblage of private persons gathered to exert violent force as, for example, the "hired gangs" employed to provide "muscle" in the enforced repossession of a property from the current possessor – only after, of course, a court had given a judgment that legitimized the use of private force in effecting the dispossession of the current illicit owner.[56] It was the congregated force of young men.

[52] Aug. *Confess.* 5.8.14 (CCL 27: 64): "the greatest and indeed almost my sole reason [sc. for going to Rome] was that I heard that the youth at Rome were quieter in their studies and that, under a more regular compulsion, they were more attentive to their studies" ("sed illa erat causa maxima et paene sola, quod audiebam quietius ibi studere adulescentes et ordinatiore disciplinae coercitione sedari").

[53] Aug. *Confess.*, 5.8.14 (CCL 27: 64): "Multa iniuriosa faciunt mira hebetudine et punienda legibus, nisi consuetudo patrona sit, hoc miseriores eos ostendens . . . et impune se facere arbitrantur."

[54] Statt (1995) who points out, however, how exaggerated the short-lived phenomenon was.

[55] For example, in the *Passio Isaac et Maximiani*, 5.27 (Mastandrea, 1995: 79): the "savage gang of torturers" who punish Maximian after his arrest: "sine ulla dilatione proconsulis iussu vallatus est effera caterva tortorum."

[56] For example, in the *Passio sancti Donati*, 3 (Dolbeau, 1992: 259): speaking about the enforcement of the decree of *c.* 317, and the seizure of basilicas, the preacher speaks of a "superinducta gentilitatis caterva": the use of "a hired gang of pagans," revealing the use of such gangs for purposes of enforcement.

The good people of Caesarea were not the only ones to engage in catervic behavior. In the sectarian violence that rent the Christian communities of Africa in the fourth and fifth centuries, gangs of young men and women called circumcellions gathered in loose bands of violent proclivity. They were also called *catervae* by those who sought to label their behavior as chaos-ridden and subversively violent, including the same Augustine who preached to the people of Caesarea in 418.[57] More important is the ritual-like nature of low-level violence in forging local identities in every city, town, and village. So the people of Caesarea divided into two mortally hostile sides and the two opposing camps maintaining a brutal and vicious combat from one generation to the next, having been taught to do so by their ancestors for some primeval cause that was now dim in memory. Something like this was nothing novel for the inhabitants of Caesarea. Or in the dozens and dozens of other towns and cities like Caesarea. It was deeply bred in them. It was part of them. It defined who they were, and they loved doing it. Could these same sentiments and impulses be mobilized for sectarian violence? Perhaps. But the fact would have to be demonstrated.

After all, Caesarea was an enclosed town in which many if not most of the people who were Christians would also have participated in the annual rite of violence of the *caterva*. Popular behavior already had existing templates and modes of organization. In this light, events in Caesarea in 419, the year immediately following Augustine's visit, are of some importance. This time, the story concerns a bitter dispute within the Catholic Church in Caesarea in which the Christians were creating "a huge scandal." After the death of Deuterius, the "metropolitan" or senior bishop of the province, Honorius, another bishop in Mauretania, wished to be seated as Deuterius' successor in the provincial capital.[58] Some churchmen had written to Augustine to inform him about the resulting troubles in the city.[59] The bishops of the

---

[57] Aug. *Contra ep. Parm.* 2.3.6 (CSEL 51: 50): "quorum et catervae gregum furiosorum huc atque illuc armatae ferro ac fustibus volitant" of circumcellions; *Contra litt. Petil.* 2.14.33 (CSEL 52: 37): "quas furiosi vestri principes circumcellionum et ipsae catervae vinulentorum atque insanorum . . ."; 2.47.110 (CSEL 52: 84): "certe fatereis istum psalmum non ibi pertinere ad furiosas catervas circumcellionum"; and 2.96.222 (CSEL 52: 140): "Respicite paululum catervas vestras, quae non antiquo more parentum suorum solis fustibus armantur" (of the circumcellions).

[58] See "Deuterius (4)," PAC, p. 275–76; that he was already "metropolitan" bishop of the province is stated in *Gesta cum Emerit.* 1 (CSEL 53: 181); see S. Lancel, "Episcopus metropolitanus," *BA* 46B (Paris, 1987), pp. 527–30. As Lancel cautions, this man is not necessarily the one who held the *prima sedes*, the man who would have been the most senior in the line of succession.

[59] Aug. *Ep.* 22.5* (CSEL 88: 115); Lancel (BA 46B, p. 353 n. 9) thinks that these are local monks or monastics (seeing that in *Ep.* 23* the monk Renatus is one of his informants; were they part of an information network built up by Augustine?).

province had assembled in Caesarea to supervise the election of a bishop whom *they* wished to ordain.[60] They had been frightened by the harassment and the serious injuries inflicted on them by the turbulent crowd that supported Deuterius. A large faction of people in the city wished to have the man whom *they* wanted transferred to the city. Following more threats and violence, they insisted that the bishops send a delegation to the First Seat at Carthage to see if their wish could be allowed. Augustine says that the reply came to him that no "metropolitan" was yet properly seated for Caesariensis. Therefore the local bishops were not to cede to what the "seditious mob" was demanding, namely the seating of Honorius.

The finale of this incident is not known, but what the rough actions of 419 reveal are the discordant overlappings of violence in a late antique town. The Christians who were organizing in "turbulent crowds" in this year probably included many of the same persons who had annually participated in the *caterva* in these same years. The coexistence of different types of civic violence in the cities is therefore a problem that must be faced. How might one kind of violence feed into or affect another? What were the mechanisms?

A POPULAR LYNCHING

However it is construed, the year-in and year-out celebration of violence at Caesarea was not a conflict that mobilized the community against some hated alien presence. It was, rather, a violent ritual in which the community turned inwards on itself. Sudden outbursts of violence that were not so ritualized or regular as the *caterva* were also common, but they were mobilized in a rather different fashion.[61] An outburst of this type occurred at Hippo in the year 412 in conditions that were close to those of a general riot: an incident in which a crowd – or rather a collection of men drafted out of family, workplace, and other connections – was mobilized to hyperviolence, although only for a brief instant and for a specific purpose.[62] It

---

[60] Aug. *Ep.* 22.5* (CSEL 88: 115): "Interim episcopi cum ad ipsam civitatem necessitatis ipsius gratia convenissent, ut eligeret populus quem sibi cuperent ordinari."

[61] The extent of ritualization in such cases is, of course, debatable: Tilly, *Collective Violence*, pp. 81–98; cf. S. Silverman, "The Palio of Siena: Game, Ritual, or Politics?," in S. Zimmerman and R. Weissman, eds., *Urban Life in the Renaissance* (Newark DE, 1984), pp. 224–34; and Davis, *War of the Fists*, pp. 32–44, for some comparative cases.

[62] For what follows, see Aug. *Sermo* 302 = Guelferbytanus 25 + Mainz 37 (MiAg 1: 527–28; Lambot, *Sermones selecti duodeviginti* = SPM 1 [1950], pp. 100–11) and the edition and commentary by Pieri (1998). The date is that urged by Hombert, *Chronologie Augustinienne*, pp. 495–506. Not much can be added to the analysis of Magalhães de Oliveira (2004).

also happened in the heat of midsummer. Perhaps tempers had flared over an igniting issue. What happened next can only be gleaned with some difficulty from a sermon delivered by Augustine to his parishioners on 10 August, the festival day of the Roman martyr Lawrence, a day not long after the frightening event itself.

An imperial official who had a supervisory function connected with the collection of transit dues had been colluding with other officials and private persons in the systematic extortion of kick-backs, rake-offs, and other such extra payments out of merchants, transshippers and buyers: *concussiones* or "shake-downs" as they were popularly called.[63] Naturally, the businessmen and craftsmen, especially, became increasingly resentful. Matters reached a breaking point. The angry middling ranks of the town mobilized their familial and other dependents, including their slaves, all of them rough young men. According to one's point of view, these men either constituted themselves as "the people" who were enforcing popular justice or they were a crazed lynch mob. The "bad man" was not just killed by popular action. His body was badly mutilated.[64] Whatever he had done had roused the ire and the frustrated hatred of a community.

The crowd thought their actions to be a kind of popular justice, however rough, and the death of the official to be a well-deserved punishment. In what appears to be an angry disciplinary sermon, Augustine reprimanded his Christian parishioners who had participated in the riot. He denounced their violent actions as not constituting any kind of legal punishment, but rather as the brazen and lawless acts of bandits.[65] He denounced the murder not as a proper form of lawful retribution, but as an act of madness and insanity, denying that such legal powers had ever been placed in the hands of "the people." The bishop's concern was not just with the legality of the crowd's behavior and its relationship to duly constituted legal powers of the state) on which matters he did indeed have much to say (but also with the fact that the man, the object of their violence, had sought refuge in the church at Hippo. The mob had dragged the terrified miscreant out of the holy place and had proceeded to murder him. It may well be that the Christians had hesitated to violate the sacrosanctity of their church. The non-Christians probably had no such qualms. They dragged the man

---

[63] See Aug. *Sermo* 302.15–16 (Lambot, *Sermones selecti deodeviginti* = SPM 1 [1950], pp. 107–08).

[64] At least this seems to be what Augustine is alluding to *Sermo* 302.10 (Lambot: 105): "Quid saevis in malos? Quia mali sunt, inquis . . . Postremo saevit usque ad mortem. Quid et post mortem, ubi ad illum malum iam non pervenit poena, et alterius mali sola exercetur malitia? Hoc insanire est, non vindicare."

[65] Aug. *Sermo* 302.10 and 13 (Lambot: 105 and 106): "Tu quare saevis? Quam potestatem accepisti, nisi quia sunt ista non publica supplicia, sed aperta latrocinia?"

out. At last, the Christians themselves felt free to join in the killing of the man and the mutilation of his body.[66] Or so it seems. All of it done by religious and self-respecting citizens of the municipality.

Here we see more of the same convergences. Christians, who were used to violence in their own sectarian struggles, were now participating in a popular form of public retribution. Or perhaps, it was the other way around. Brief, violent, and final, it enforced community standards against a tyrannical outsider. Both in the arming and marshaling of dependants, and in the lynching of a hated imperial official, this incident was a miniature version of the violent *coup d'état* of 238 (which we shall consider presently). Instead of well-connected and powerful imperial aristocrats with high social connections, its leaders were less powerful municipal men and so the violence did not have the empire-wide implications of the assassination of the imperial procurator at Carthage. Both in the nature of the mobilization and in the manner of the killing, in the systemic mutilation of the body, it shared more with small-town ritual behaviors like the *caterva*. Here, then, was another form of collective violence, one that was not defined and periodic, but was rather provoked by specific kinds of hostilities tied to the "unjust actions" of one person. So how did the *caterva* or the lynching relate to the standard acts of sectarian violence of the time? This question prompts a prior one concerning the range, quality, and quantity of violence in late antique Africa.

WHAT WAS VIOLENCE?

The ritual internecine rioting that happened annually in the city of Caesarea was one kind of violence. It was a local affair that involved clubbings, beatings, stonings, and a lot of civic joy and festivity. Lower-level violence, like individual homicides, beatings, or robberies, happened everywhere and all the time. But Africans could and did face more serious, bigger, and more destructive kinds of disorder. At the other end of the spectrum of violent acts from the individual fist-fight, tavern brawl, or street mugging was the larger-scale violence of war. Everyone accepted the common presence and reality of war. On the possibility of "banishing wars to the ends of the earth," Augustine ruefully commented that it was not likely in the present time. In his eyes, these wars included the religious conflicts of the age.[67]

---

[66] I follow the reconstruction by A. Ducloux, *Ad ecclesiam confugere. Naissance du droit d'asile dans les églises (IVe-Ve s.)*, Paris, 1994, pp. 176–80, which is also accepted by Magalhães de Oliveira (2004), pp. 317–18.

[67] Aug. *En. in Ps.* 45.13 (CCL 38: 527): commenting on Psalm 45: 10: *Auferens bella usque ad fines terrae*; he ends by noting, plaintively, that "someday this might happen."

We do not yet see this fulfilled. There are still wars. Wars are fought between peoples to establish rule. They are fought between sects, between Jews, pagans, Christians, and heretics. Wars are fought, and with increasing frequency – some fighting for truth and others for untruth.

In the instances that he notes, the actors were not individuals or smaller ad hoc groups, but larger social entities like ethnic societies, cities, and states that created greater concentrations of violent force. As we have already seen, in the early 370s the city of Caesarea itself was implicated in the larger type of violence, the scourge of war, in which the city had suffered considerable destruction from which it was recovering only some decades later. This one place, we might note, like many in Africa, witnessed ordinary violent crimes, an annual ritual of civic mayhem, sectarian battles, and the frontal assaults of full-scale warfare.

But how are individual assaults that aimed at bodily injury or homicide, the group violence of sectarian religious battles, and the huge collective violence of war – all of which Africans experienced in various places and times – to be plotted? At one end of a simple linear spectrum of types of violence is the full-blown war: a conflict conducted with the full resources of a state that opposes enemy forces whose defeat will either conserve the existence of the state or might even extend its existing territorial and demographic resources. At the other end are highly localized and episodic fits or mini-events of violence in which the participants have as their targets individuals or tiny bits of property whose harm or elimination will serve not only to achieve their personal aims but also to confirm the norms of their society.[68] The one kind of violence is an immediate threat to the state, the other is not. The one kind upsets the locals on a Saturday night, tears families apart, and destroys individual lives, while the other transforms the status of regions and threatens to sweep social and political orders from existence. The levels of organization, of supply, of maintenance and continuity, the aims and purposes of the violence in each case are so different that in many ways they only share the instrumentalities of force and harm. Everything else in which the violence is embedded is so different that the languages in which the violence speaks are not the same.

Acts of violence are not uniform and transcendental universals, but rather variable elements of normal human behavior that are informed by culture and conditioned by human ecology. To begin to answer questions about violence demands a prior answer to the social and geographic contexts of

---

[68] Tilly, *Collective Violence*, pp. 12–21, argues for links between these apparently different kinds of violence.

the individual episodes of violence themselves. We might begin with the general place of Africa within the wider context of the Roman empire in the West. Despite several strands in historical argument that have suggested that Africa was a foyer of armed resistance, a hotbed of violent opposition to Roman rule, it must be firmly stated – in comparative terms at least – that such claims are far from the truth. Only by focussing narrowly on episodes within Africa itself and by carefully culling selected literary sources in ways that deliberately exclude the wider context of empire can this "armed resistance" hypothesis be sustained. This is not to say that Africa cannot provide its list of so-called provincial rebellions, as they have been mistakenly labeled, or "ethnic revolts" or "nativist insurrections." They have been duly catalogued.[69] Given the long six or seven centuries of Roman imperial rule in Africa, and the potential extent of problems caused by violent resistance, the one thing that is strikingly apparent about these incidents in context is that they are thin in social depth and sparse in number.[70] At no point until the early 430s of the fifth century did Africans face large-scale violence as it was experienced on the war frontiers of the empire, to the north along the Rhine and Danube and to the east along the frontiers with Sassanid Persia.

By contrast, violence in Africa tended to assume a number of rather limited kinds and types, none of which threatened the Roman imperial order. Even knowing about specific incidents is, of course, a big problem. A lot of violence that happened was never reported because it was a kind of harm that was not of interest to those who kept records. Like the *caterva* at Caesarea, we happen to learn about these cases because of accidental connections with concerns of greater relevance to the writer. A good example is provided by the Catholic Council of Carthage held in the year 403. Of all the considerable number of Catholic bishops from the province of Numidia, only three of them – Augustine, Alypius, and Possidius – made it to Carthage. The others could not, we are told, because of incidents of violence caused by army recruiting.[71] To prevent the numerous Catholic bishops from all of Numidia traveling to Carthage, the violence must have been very serious and widespread. But we only hear about it quite by chance. And we have no knowledge of the details of its events, structure,

---

[69] See Bénabou, *Résistance africaine*, pp. 67 ff., and Rachet, *Rome et les Berbères*, pp. 82 ff.

[70] For what follows, the standard references are the works of Rachet and Bénabou (above); and reviews and discussion of these, especially of Bénabou's work through the 1980s.

[71] *Reg. Eccl. Carth. Excerpt.* canon 90 (CCL 149: 209): "sed de Numidia legatio mitti non potuit, quod adhuc tumultu tironum episcopi propriis necessitatibus in civitatibus suis aut impediti aut occupati sunt."

or extent. Instances like this can be multiplied many times over. In the history that does survive, however, the big violence typical of Africa divides into two broader types connected with large organizing entities like ethnic groups or states.

The first was a regional response where local men who were mostly independent of direct Roman control, or who had been integrated with the Roman order and then withdrew from it, engaged in various kinds of entrepreuneurial or autonomist violence. The best-known of these episodes, because it was written up by the Roman historian Tacitus to promote his personal agenda in interpreting the Principate, was a series of incidents involving an African named Tacfarinas. In the late teens and early 20s of the first century, this former auxiliary in the Roman army in Africa spearheaded a spasmodic series of bandit raids along the southern frontiers from Gigthis in the southeast to Auzia in the west.[72] No subsequent incidents of a similar kind and scale are known to have happened in the whole of the eastern Maghrib down to and including the age of Augustine.

The normal location of the most serious threats of autonomist violence was, rather, in the mountain highlands west of the Hodna-Bejaïa longitudinal line (see map 2c). The rugged highlands and arid plateaux of the Mauretanias in the western half of the Maghrib formed the real cultural and military frontier of late Roman Africa. Its landscapes, especially the lowland valleys, were studded with chain-like links of army camps, forts, observations towers, and supply roads. The forts were manned by infantry units and fast cavalry detachments. Zones of detention marked out the lowlands, and the highlands were cordoned off by lines of forts, ditches, and roads. The roads and fortifications were not outer defensive lines, but rather a complex web-like network that covered the whole region in which raiders could be caught and trapped. It was this mountainous zone of the Mauretanias and not the periphery of the Sahara to the south, the romantic source of desert raiders, that was the real Wild West of Rome's hegemony in Africa. The mountain highlands immediately west of Sitifis were known to be populated with dangerous "barbarians." Occasionally, they descended into the plains to plunder, to rape, and to take captives.[73]

---

[72] The bibliography is immense. See Bénabou, *Résistance africaine*, pp. 75–84, and Rachet, *Rome et les Berbères*, pp. 84–126, for summaries to the mid 1970s; of the many items since, Bénabou (1978), Lassère (1992), and Gonzales (1998) are worthy of consideration.

[73] Aug. *Ep.* III.7 (CSEL 34.2: 653–54): discusses a recent case ("a few years ago": i.e. before November of 409) of women who had been raped and captured by "barbarians," one of them a niece of Severus, the bishop of Sitifis.

COUP D'ÉTAT

Over the whole age between Tacfarinas in the 20s and a rebel named Firmus in 370s, the single most destructive episode that the provinces of Africa experienced was not any conflict with indigenous rebels, but rather a different kind of violence marked by the upheavals of the 230s. This short burst of killing and destruction was not caused as much by forces within Africa itself, as in the Tacfarinas case, as by external structural changes in the imperial state. The episode points to a second type of big violence: local repercussions caused by strategic shifts in the structure of the empire as a whole. With increasing military pressures along the Rhine and Danube frontiers in the 220s and 230s, a fundamental shift in the traditional civil mode of governing the empire took place, marked by the rise of a new breed of emperors rising from the ranks of the Rhine and Danube armies. The first of these new emperors was Maximinus "the Thracian." With his ascent to the throne in 235, the agenda of the northern military establishment became the driving force of imperial policy. The army needed more resources: more men, more pay, more equipment, more "subventions" for allies, and more and better fortifications. All of this would cost a lot more.

The military needs drove the new regime's concern with higher and more efficient levels of tribute collection.[74] These drives ran directly counter to the interests of the wealthy landowners and their peers. The landholders in Africa who were responsible for the bulk of the tax felt the new impositions most keenly. Africa was furthest removed from the military threats of the northern frontiers. Living in an isolated and protected land of peace and prosperity, there arose in the minds of its upper-class tribute payers resentments over the hugely increased tax burdens for problems that they did not see as particularly theirs. Three years into Maximinus' new regime, in March 238, the landowning elites rebelled. Faced with ever more severe tribute exactions and harsh treatment from the provincial procurators, aggressive young aristocrats, sons of the powerful, who were resident in Carthage, armed themselves with knives and their peasant dependants with wooden clubs and axes.[75] Seeking the provincial procurator at his

---

[74] These structural elements are difficult to apprehend because the literary sources, written by the usual civil upper-class authors, interpret them in such negative, hostile, and moralizing terms. So the new emperor Maximinus is portrayed as a brutish and violent barbarian, and his need for more funds is pictured as nothing more than an extreme personal avarice.

[75] The primary sources, the historian Herodian and the biographer of the *Scriptores Historiae Augustae*, are confused and misleading. This is my construal of the general course of events and the main

headquarters, they assassinated him, stabbing him to death in his office. Other landowners in the southern parts of the province stormed the official residence of the proconsul of Africa, M. Antonius Gordianus, who was then on assizes at Thysdrus in the region of Byzacena, and hailed him as their emperor.[76] From the arming of peasants with wooden clubs, to the lynching of a hated imperial official, this violence, as we shall see, had smaller-scale analogues in the age of Augustine.

The *coup d'état* was quickly countered by Maximinus who ordered the army in Africa, commanded by one Capellianus, the legate of the Third Augustan Legion, to take immediate action.[77] The result was not just the defeat of Gordianus' ramshackle civilian forces under the command of his son just outside the suburbs of Carthage, and his own death by suicide, but a murderous rampage of the soldiery that was vented on the municipal elites that had supported the tax revolt, men whose actions and attitudes threatened the legionaries' wages. Since Africa was not normally a war frontier of the Roman state, the function of the army was more like that of a national police force or a regional militia. Africa, indeed, was one of the most peaceful areas of the empire. The majority of its inhabitants were unarmed, and most of its cities east of the frontier zone of the Mauretanias were unwalled. This was Gordian's main problem. He had no ready access to a trained force of violent men, and not many of the ordinary inhabitants of the towns and cities of Africa had the requisite experience or skill with arms. They were too used to peace.[78] The result was a murderous disaster for himself, his family, and large numbers of the civilian elites who had supported him. Although it was an unusual and rare event, the regional *coup* of Gordian foreshadowed a type of violence that was to recur with greater frequency in the Africa of the later empire. Shifts in the attitudes of emperors and politicking at their courts produced these strange and violent local repercussions.

parties to it. The month of March is a best guess at a date. For a critique of the sources and a rather different reconstruction of the events, see Kolb (1977). The fact that peasant farmers were normally armed with wooden clubs, and such instruments, for acts of enforcement is an important fact to which we shall return.

[76] For the events, see Romanelli, *Storia*, pp. 447 f.; the principal literary source is the historian Herodian, 7.4.1 f. (on which see the valuable comments in C. R. Whittaker's Loeb edition). For Gordian as governor, see Thomasson, *Fasti Africani*, "Africa Proconsularis – Proconsules," no. 121, pp. 89–90.

[77] The figure of "Capellianus" is as obscure as most of the others in this drama; see Thomasson, *Fasti Africani*, "Legio III Augusta – Numidia," no. 63, pp. 184–85; the main references are SHA, *Gord. tres*, 15.1–16.2; Herodian, 7.9.

[78] Herodian, 7.9.4; rhetorically formed, of course, but nonetheless credible.

STRANGE WARS: FIRMUS TO HERACLIAN

By the fourth and fifth centuries, the structure of the Roman army in Africa had been fundamentally transformed. Military commands were systematically separated from the civil administrators of the provinces, and army commanders were more than ever directly responsible to the imperial court. The emperor himself appointed the generals or *duces* who commanded the different sectors of the African frontier. Over all of these forces, he placed a supreme commander, the Count of Africa, the *comes Africae*, who was the local commander-in-chief of the Roman army in Africa. To ensure a dependable control over the empire's armed forces in Africa, emperors were willing to concede an unusual term of office to the Count of Africa. On this frontier – the most peaceful and the least threatened by large numbers of external enemies – the long-term tenure of the commander-in-chief was not a bad idea. For one thing, measured in strategic terms against the entire military force of the empire, Africa was just not that important. The installing of the *comes Africae* was comparable to appointing the head of a home guard. While successive emperors and ever-rotating field commanders attended to unending warfare on the northern frontiers of the empire, its relatively quiet southern front could be held by a dependable man whom the emperors trusted. If a good man could be kept in place in Africa for a longer time, this would be one large sector of the frontier about which the emperors would not have to concern themselves on an ongoing basis. Trust was the key. The evidence that survives (admittedly thin) indicates that the Counts of Africa were kept in place for long periods of time when compared to the annual rotation of offices typical of other higher-level officials of the state, including provincial governors.[79] Being in power for so long, they were able to develop a wide range of social dependants and to acquire landed wealth. A man like Romanus, who was Count of Africa for about a decade, from *c.* 365 to 375, accumulated considerable personal wealth and power.

The position of the Count of Africa was therefore something of a paradox. The Counts held the power of violent force that permitted the usual

---

[79] The Counts of Africa relevant to our story include Gratian, the father of the emperor Valentinian, who seems to have held this position over a period as long as two decades, between the 320s and 340s (see "Gratianus (1)," PLRE, 1, pp. 400–01); Amm. Marc. 30.7.3; Symm. *Or.* 1.1 (MGH AA 6.1: 318); Cretio – his name is probably a misunderstanding of an African name – who had a son named "Masaucio" that is related to the African name Mausakes, who was raised in Africa when "Cretio" was there, was probably *comes Africae* from the late 340s until the early 360s (see "Cretio," PLRE, 1, p. 231; Amm. Marc. 21.7.4; 26.5.14; CTh 7.1.4, dated to 349–50); and Romanus, who was *comes Africae* from the early 360s until 372–73.

civil business of empire to continue behind the defensive perimeters of the frontier. The normal collection of tribute and the administration of justice, the principal concerns of the imperial court, were enabled by the Count's successful tenure of office. The paradox is that the better he performed this task, the more he might come under deep suspicion as a potential threat to central power. As the latter decades of the fourth century wore on and the first decades of the fifth ensued, this problem emerged with force and was exacerbated as the standing of the Count of Africa was increasingly enhanced, almost by default, by the concurrent decline in the power of the central court, first at Milan and then at Ravenna. As trust mutated into apprehension, a considerable part of the structural problem was one of perception. As the position of the central court progressively deteriorated, the more its leaders, fearful of possible threats to their position, were subject to a kind of paranoia. While the court lost one provincial region after another in the west, the man who controlled the flow of tribute and other resources from Africa – whether he liked it or not – found himself in an increasingly important and sensitive position.

Because of this emerging nexus of forces, the episodes of big violence in which Africa was involved in our period were far less ones of repelling "barbarian" incursions than they were conflicts between the commander of the state's armed forces in Africa and the imperial court. The problem is that the Counts of Africa, and men like them who were serving the Roman state in Africa, could easily be accused of holding power for their own purposes and of plotting to establish their own autonomous domain against the crown. Once accused of "rebellion" and "acts of treason" by their enemies in a distant and suspicious court, it was almost impossible for these men to correct the maliciously biased pictures of themselves and their actions. Any serious moves taken to defend themselves only "proved" to the court that they were dangerous men who had to be eliminated. The result was a self-reinforcing spiral of violence in which the court, increasingly protective of its one safe and sure source of supplies, the wealth of Africa, was willing to strike first against a perceived threat to its resources rather than to risk losing them.

This brings us to the strange episodes that are the closest to large-scale violence or war found in Africa before the Vandal incursions of the late 420s. These are the so-called rebellions of Firmus, Gildo, and Heraclian at the end of the fourth century and at the beginning of the fifth. Firmus and Gildo were supposedly "brothers" who were local leaders of the powerful and influential ethnic groups in the rugged mountain region of the Grande Kabylie in what is today north-central Algeria.[80] Although they were men of regional power, their fates were inextricably bound up with the changing configurations of power in the late Roman state in the west. Both men came to be portrayed as rebels by the imperial court – men who set out with deliberate plans to attack the Roman state and its interests and who premeditated secessions from its imperium. These ancient prejudices, recycled in modern histories, do little more than parrot willfully contorted views created for and repeated by supporters of the court. In usual circumstances – almost all of the time – these Africans were loyal subjects of the state. Their dissent was provoked not by any conscious drive to independence in Africa, but rather by the changing configuration of the imperial state of which they were part. To apply to them the modern idea that they were guerrilla fighters for some notional regional autonomy is to overstate who they were and what they did to the point of falsehood. They were men who were caught in a power trap, forced into corners in which they had few alternatives left except to defend themselves. When they did so, they were labeled "rebels." This only incited more defensive behavior on their part. A frightened and factionalized court finally declared them to be enemies of the state. In the case of Firmus, the first of these "rebels," an analysis of the events helps in understanding this peculiar type of violence.

AN AFRICAN REBEL?

The best-documented episode of big violence that struck Africa in the later fourth century is the so-called "Firmus war."[81] The course of this conflict reveals not only its limited and marginal nature as large-scale violence, but also its pathology as a typical kind of conflict generated by the restructuring of the western empire. The regime of Romanus, who had been Count of Africa from the early 360s, involved disputes not just with local urban elites, such as those of the city of Lepcis Magna, but also with the quasi-autonomous big men who controlled large ethnic areas

---

[80] I say supposedly because, although they might have been biological siblings, I think it more probable that the word indicates a fictive kinship relationship between them: see Shaw (1997) for a discussion of these artificially "made" relationships between powerful men.

[81] Ammianus Marcellinus 29.5 is the principal, indeed the sole continuous prose narrative of any distinction. The other sources are minor and contribute only occasional detail: Augustine, *Contra ep. Parm.* 1.10.16; 1.11.17 (CSEL 51: 36–39); Aurel. Vict. *Epit. de Caes.* 45.7; Claudian, *De bell. Gild.* 330 f.; Orosius 7.33.5; Symmachus, *Ep.* 1.64 (MGH AA 6.1: 29), *Relat.* 10.1 (MGH AA 6.1: 279); Zosimus, *Hist. nov.* 4.16.3; *Passio Sanctae Salsae*, 13 (Piredda: 100–06). Among the modern treatments, see Seeck (1909), Kotula (1970), and Moreau (1973b).

for the Roman state, especially in the mountains of the Mauretanias. The highland lords had a double identity. They served both as local leaders of their own ethnic groups and as military commanders for the Roman state. In artistic representation, they portrayed themselves in mixed Romano-African mode as addicted to banqueting and armed for the hunt.[82] One of these powerful men was Nubel (or, Nuvel), the father of Firmus. His African side was highlighted by the Roman historian Ammianus – practically the sole contemporary source for the war – who labels him "a most powerful minor king among the Maurian peoples."[83] What Ammianus does not say is just as significant. This same African, Nubel, had a Roman name, Flavius Nubel. He was a Roman citizen, and he was the commander of Roman army units in northern montane regions of the Mauretanias: he was *praepositus* or head of the *equites armigerorum iuniorum*, a regional cavalry unit of the army. It is also known that Nubel was the son of an African named Saturninus, and that he was married to a local woman named Nonnica (that is, Monnica, the same name borne by Augustine's mother). Together with her, he constructed a Christian basilica in the coastal city of Rusguniae (modern Borj el-Bahri) and placed in it a piece of the true cross.[84] Nubel therefore belonged to an African family that had served the Roman state at least from the generation of his father, who himself ranked among the elite "companions" or *comites* of the emperor.[85]

Nubel's son, Firmus, was just one of several ethnic heads in the mountainous redoubt of the Kabylie. Another player in this little drama was a man named Sammac, supposedly one of Firmus' "brothers." Like Firmus, Sammac was local man of power in the mountain highlands. He had constructed a mountain stronghold at a place named the *fundus Petrensis*. He had built this place up, Ammianus says, in the manner of a town or city.[86] In one of those wonderful accidents of discovery, we know precisely where Sammac's domain of Petra was located, and we know more about the owner himself. An eight-line Latin poem in hexameters was set up at the fortified

---

[82] Février (1973).

[83] Amm. Marc. 29.5.2: "Nubel velut regulus per nationes Mauricas potentissimus."

[84] CIL 8.9255 = ILCV 1822 (Rusguniae, Bordj el-Bahri): "D(e) sancto ligno crucis Christi salvatoris adlato / adq(ue) hic sito Flavius Nuvel ex praepositis eq(u)itu/m armicerorum <i>unior(um), filius Saturnini viri / perfectissimi ex comitibus, et Col<e>cia<e>[?] honestissima/e feminae, primepos [sic] Eluri Laconiq [sic], basilicam voto / promissam adq(ue) oblatam cum coniuge Nonni/ca ac suis omnibus dedicavit"; cf. PAC, p. 790 and Duval, *Loca Sanctorum*, 1, p. 352, no. 167.

[85] If the fourth line is read properly, it seems to indicate that he is the grandson of one Elurus Laconiq(us) [?].

[86] Amm. Marc. 29.5.13: "Inter quos clades eminuere fundi Petrensis, excisi radicitus, quem Salmaces (Firmi frater) in modum urbis exstruxit."

site, boasting of Sammac's power.[87] In hiring a poet to create this little
Latin display piece, Sammac was not so much vaunting his own status as
he was advertising his loyalty to the state and his connections to certain
powerful persons. Yet another one of the fanciful literary tours-de-force
typical of the more spectacular gymnastic poetics of the age, the poem is a
double acrostic. The first letters and the last letters of each line, when read
vertically, spelled out the name of the place: **P R A E D I U M S A M M-
A C I S**, The Great Domain of Sammac.

> **P** raesidium aeternae firmat prudentia paci **S**
> **R** em quoque Romanam fida tuta undique dextr **A**,
> **A** mni praepositum firmans munime monte **M**
> **E** cuius nomen vocitavit nomine Petra **M**
> **D** enique finitimae gentes deponere bell **A**
> **I** n tua concurrunt cupientes foedera, Samma **C**
> **U** t virtus comitata fidem concordet in omn **I**
> **M** unere, Romuleis semper sociata triumfi **S**

> The wisdom of eternal peace makes strong this fort.
> With sure loyalty it guards Rome's power on all sides;
> set high above the river, it guards the mountains with its walls
> by which it continually proclaims its name of Petra: "The Rock."
> All the neighboring peoples, ceasing from their wars,
> wish to rush into alliance with you, Sammac,
> so that your virtue, adorned with loyalty, is strong in its
> every duty, always allied with the victories of Rome's sons.

The inscription boasts of the great strength of the fortified place and of
the loyalty of Sammac to the Roman state: his trust, his *fides*, in protecting
Roman power, and his connections with the "sons of Romulus." The
reference to the *Romuli* was perhaps intended to draw attention to his
powerful patron, the Count Romanus. The historian Ammianus confirms
the connection, speaking of the fact that Sammac had been received into
the *fides*, that is, into the personal protection of the Count of Africa. These
personal connections were part of the difficulties in which Firmus was to
become implicated.

What happened next? No one knows for sure. For reasons beyond
recovery, in the early 370s Firmus was drawn into an armed conflict with the
Roman state. The war's only historian, Ammianus Marcellinus, certainly
did not know why. Having no information other than the bare record of
a few events, he composed his narrative as a replay of the *Jugurthine War*

---

[87] ILS 9351 = CLE 1916 (Ighzer Amokrane); see. S. Gsell, "Une inscription d'Ighzer-Amokrane," *CRAI*
(1901), p. 176; Gsell (1902), p. 22 = *Scripta Varia* (1981), p. 114, no. 1; Lengrand (1994), pp. 159–61.

by the historian Sallust – the only model of an African war that he had at his disposal. As with King Micipsa and his sons in Sallust's account of the 120s BCE, all the major players in the Firmus episode are turned into sons of "King" Nubel. They are said to be born from legitimate wives or from concubines – Sammac being one of the latter – a fact that leads to inevitable conflicts between them. Ammianus also sets up his account as an extension of the Romanus affair, with which, in reality, it seems to have had only a tenuous connection, if any. Chronology is another problem since at this point in his history, Ammianus decided, in Sallustian fashion, to switch from an annalistic year-by-year framework into a continuous unbroken narrative of this one story. Some of the earliest events might well have happened as early as 370 or 371.[88] But even this much is uncertain.

The problems began with Firmus' murder of his "brother" Sammac, a killing that precipitated a breakdown of order in the mountain highlands of the Mauretanias. The collapse pitted powerful mountain barons, like Firmus and Sammac, against each other. The violence was especially dangerous since some of them, like Firmus, commanded units of the Roman army and state resources, they knew the terrain and people, and they knew the richest targets, including isolated coastal cities like Caesarea. The petitioning of the emperor Valentinian and the court at Trier by Firmus on the one side (pleading his innocence) and by Romanus on the other (condemning the African as culpable) only further complicated matters. Embassies went back and forth, each attempting to sway the sentiments of the emperor. According to Ammianus, Romanus, having greater clout at court with the support of his kinsman and ally, Remigius, the *magister offi-ciorum*, won the first round.[89] Firmus is represented as not having intended any rebellion, but as having been driven into a corner by false accusations. Reasonably fearful of the unmerited consequences of arrest and execution, he chose the practical course of self-defense.[90]

The nature of the violence belies this easy personal story. The main assaults on Roman interests by Firmus' partisans in 372 were attacks on the vulnerable coastal cities. Icosium was attacked and occupied. Just to its west, Tipasa was also attacked but, relying on the strength of its fortifications, or so later memory held, the city successfully repelled the raiders

---

[88] Demandt (1968), p. 283 and (1972) favors dating the first events as early as *c.* 370, based on the fact that Remigius was no longer Magister Officiorum after 371; the latter's dates, however, are not as fixed as one might wish.

[89] Amm. Marc. 29.5.2: "Remigio tunc officiorum magistro, affine amicoque Romani, inter potiores imperatoris necessitates..."

[90] Amm. Marc. 29.5.3.

sent against it by the "tyrant" Firmus.[91] Finally, even further to the west, Caesarea, the capital of Mauretania Caesariensis, was burned and looted.[92] Pleas for help from these cities, and from the governor of Mauretania Caesariensis, elicited a heavy response from the imperial court. In the summer of 373, the situation in Africa was deemed sufficiently threatening for the emperor Valentinian to dispatch one of his more able, experienced, and successful commanders, Theodosius, the *magister militum*, a man who might well have had earlier field experience in Africa, to deal with the problem. Theodosius sailed from Arelate with a small force and landed at the port of Igilgili, well to the east of the main troubled region.[93] He moved quickly inland to the city of Sitifis (modern Sétif) to establish his main base in the heart of the great plains region immediately to the east of the mountain highlands.

Far from supporting Romanus' complaints about Firmus, Theodosius' brief was to bring the Count of Africa under control. To this end, he employed a local chief in Roman service, one of Firmus' "brothers," named Gildo, to arrest Romanus and to detain several of the Count's officials.[94] On the other front, what followed next was a rather strange on-again-off-again conflict in which Firmus repeatedly tried to meet with Theodosius to prove his innocence and to rehabilitate himself as part of the Roman administration in Africa. The first of these attempts was made soon after Theodosius arrived in Africa. It was a gesture to which Theodosius responded positively, saying that a peace agreement was possible if Firmus provided the required hostages to guarantee his words and behavior.[95] Theodosius had moved his main military forces to the city of Tubusuptu, just inland from Saldae on the coast. The shift enabled him to run his army units more easily into the interior, up the valley of the Wadi Soummam, the major riverine system that drained the most rugged of the coastal mountain ranges in north Africa: the Lesser Kabylie to the east of the river centered on the Babors Range, and the Greater Kabylie to the west of it, centered on the Djurdjura Range.[96] It was a forbidding region, heavily populated in antiquity, and difficult for any power anchored in the plains to control.

[91] *Passio S. Salsae*, 13 (Piredda: 104): "Illis enim temporibus quibus provinciam totam Firmianae labes tyrannidis devastaverat, incensis finitimis civitatibus, quarum aggeres ruinarum dabatur aestimare cineribus." The passage advances to speak of Firmus' ambition for imperial rule and the eight-day battle against the *catervae praedonum* of the the cruel and savage tribesmen.

[92] Amm. Marc. 29.5.16.

[93] Amm. Marc. 29.5.4–5: "abolendum cum Comitatensi auxilio militis pauci Theodosius magister equitum mittitur . . . Proinde ab Arelate secundis egressus auspiciis, emeatoque mari cum classe, quam ductabat . . . defertur ad Sitifensis Mauretaniae litus, quod appellant accolae Igilgilitanum."

[94] Amm. Marc. 29.5.6–7; see Oost (1962).   [95] Amm. Marc. 29.5.8.

[96] Despois and Raynal, *Géographie*, pp. 156–65; Admiralty, *Algeria*, vol. 2, pp. 53–55.

These particular mountain ranges – the *qabiliyya* or "tribal lands" as they have been called in Arabic – have been reservoirs of local autonomy over the ages of Maghribi history. It was not without significance that, in antiquity, the highland was called the Iron Mountain, the *Mons Ferratus*. As Theodosius moved his forces into this montain zone, a second peace feeler was sent out by Firmus. It was rejected by Theodosius, apparently because the required hostages had not been provided.[97] Leading his forces up the Wadi Soummam, Theodosius founded a supply base at Lamfoctense at a place that would allow him to divide the ethnic groups of the Tyndenses and the Masinissenses, headed, respectively, by Mascizel and Dius, two other "brothers" of Firmus. On the way upriver he attacked and seized the Fundus Petrensis, the fortified place once held by Sammac and now defended by Firmus' supporters.[98] Under this unrelenting pressure, Firmus again attempted to contact Theodosius, sending two Christian bishops as intermediaries to ask for a peace agreement. This time, they brought the required hostages. A meeting was arranged between the two men and their forces, a colloquy marked by much pageantry and display on both sides. Terms were agreed. Theodosius kissed Firmus. Firmus promised to return prisoners he had taken and, two days later, also as promised, his followers handed over the city of Icosium to the Roman authorities.[99]

No doubt considering the matter on the way to resolution, Theodosius moved quickly around the mountain mass of the Great Kabylie to the coastal city of Tipasa, to the west of Icosium, to receive reassurances from the local Africans, collectively called "the Mazices," who had originally sided with Firmus. He then moved further westwards to the provincial capital of Caesarea. Here he stationed two legions to prevent the return of "raiding barbarians."[100] It is at this point that the events became murky. Certain men, it is said, intimated to Theodosius that Firmus might be breaking his word. Theodosius immediately headed inland from Caesarea to Zucchabar to deal with military units that had been under the command of Firmus, including the *equites cohortis quartae sagittariorum* (Fourth Cohort of Mounted Archers) and the *pedites Constantiniani* (Constantinian Infantry Regiment). He ordered both units to go to Tigava Castra, to the west, where they were severely punished with demotion to the ranks, with decimation, and with the ritualistic amputation of right hands.

Theodosius' subsequent armed forays were concentrated in this same far western sector until he returned to the coastal base at Tipasa in

---

[97] Amm. Marc. 29.5.11. [98] Amm. Marc. 29.5.11–13.
[99] Amm. Marc. 29.5.15–16. [100] Amm. Marc. 29.5.17–18.

February 374.[101] It is manifest that his military operations had not resulted in the hoped-for success, so he decided to change his tactics, shifting to a more diplomatic approach to the problem in which he tried to gain the cooperation of the local tribes. This negotiating phase in which Theodosius no longer depended mainly on military force is glossed by Ammianus as a wonderful imitation of the tactics of Quintus Fabius Maximus "the Delayer" in the war between Rome and Carthage in the third century BCE.[102] Focussed less on the deployment of violent force, Theodosius' new strategy was more successful. Firmus was gradually hemmed into a region inhabited by the Isaflenses, and the Jubaleni, the "royal tribe," who were the original ethnic group from which his father Nubel came. Going to ground in his home turf, however, was not sufficient to protect him.

One of Firmus' main supporters at this time, another of his "brothers," named Mazuca, who was head of the Isaflenses, had been severely wounded in a clash with Roman forces; he died on the road and his corpse was dispatched to Theodosius. Mazuca's head was hacked off his body and was paraded around the streets of Caesarea, to the great joy of its inhabitants.[103] Increased pressure on the new chief of the Isaflenses, one Igmazen, finally worked. He betrayed Firmus to the Romans, so neatly completing the replay of the Jugurthine War in Ammianus' narrative. The parallel was not quite so neat, however. Realizing that he was to be handed over to Theodosius, Firmus managed to escape. He took his own life by hanging himself. A much-disappointed Igmazen had the body taken on camel-back to Theodosius. After a positive identification of Firmus' face by locals, Theodosius made his triumphant return to Sitifis.[104] The end came either late in 374 or early in the next year. A final footnote: if Firmus had been deemed a very dangerous man by the court, then, by definition, so was the man who finished him off in such an expeditious manner. In suitably mysterious circumstances, Theodosius was murdered, a demise no doubt engineered by other fearful and suspicious elements at the court.

Some characteristics of state-based violence in late fourth-century Africa should now be manifest. First of all, it was not all that violent. The largest field force that Theodosius mounted is said to have been about 3,500 men strong. The entire war from Theodosius' arrival to the death of Firmus

[101] Amm. Marc. 29.5.25–31.
[102] Amm. Marc. 29.5.32–33, where the ethnic groups involved are named.
[103] Amm. Marc. 29.5.40–42.
[104] Amm. Marc. 29.5.45–54. Note that Firmus hanged himself. This was not a mode of self-killing chosen by Christians of the time. The display of the corpse of a dead enemy on camel back was a typical mode of humiliation used in the display of a defeated enemy.

lasted two years at most. And all of it was restricted to the mountain zone well to the west of the "civilized Africa" where Augustine lived, a region that was admitted by all concerned to be a region of "barbaric" peoples. It was a zone of permanent dissidence where isolated towns – indeed, unusually isolated by the standards of the rest of Africa – were heavily walled and defended. The reality of the threat that Firmus posed was supposedly proved by his acclamation as emperor by some of his men. But the whole episode as told by Ammianus is a doublet of his description of the hailing of Julian as emperor by his Gallic troops in 363. It is not sustained by any other evidence. And the claim flies in the face of the repeated attempts by Firmus to reach a normalization of his status through Theodosius.[105] It is of a piece with the parallel claim that Roman military units were "deserting" to Firmus when in fact they were units of the army that had always been under his command. What was normal was being deliberately re-read as something strange and aberrant. When the senator Symmachus travelled westwards, following the end of his governorship of Africa in 373, to inspect domain lands of his in Mauretania, he dismissed the uproar as nothing more than another *rebellio barbarica* typical of the region.[106]

Nor is there any sign of systemic linkages between this kind of political violence and the sectarian religious violence of the time. What little evidence has been scraped together to support this hypothesis is utterly unconvincing. The fact, for example, that Firmus sent two Christian bishops to act as intercessors in making his appeal to Theodosius is not evidence of any special cooperation between Firmus and the dissident "Donatist" Christians.[107] In attempting to seek peace with Theodosius, it is most unlikely that Firmus would have deliberately chosen to insult a most orthodox Catholic Christian by purposefully sending to him bishops of a dissident church that had been repeatedly condemned by the imperial government. Nor is there anything to indicate that Firmus himself was especially inclined to favor the dissident church. His father Nubel had built a church containing a piece of the cross of Jesus, almost certainly an indication that he was an orthodox Catholic. Mascizel, another of the "brothers" of Firmus, is described by both Orosius and Paulinus of Milan as a fervent Christian.[108] Given the religious predilections of these men, they

---

[105] Amm. Marc. 29.5.20; refuted, rightly, by Kotula (1970), p. 141.
[106] Symm. *Ep.* 1.64 (MGH AA 6.1: 29).
[107] Argued by Frend, *Donatist Church*, p. 73, but rejected, for example, by Matthews (1976), pp. 178 and 186 n. 93.
[108] Oros. *Adv. pagan.* 7.36.5–7; Paulinus, *Vita Ambros.* 51.1–2 (Bastiaensen: 118).

must have believed that Mascizel was an orthodox Catholic. All the evidence connecting Firmus and "Donatist" violence comes from one source: from Augustine's polemical assertions made three decades or more after the events to defend the Catholic Church's use of the violent force of the Roman state to repress its sectarian enemies in Africa.

ALL AFRICA GROANS

Two decades and more passed with no hint of comparable violence in Africa. Then one of Firmus' so-called brothers – the same Gildo who had helped Theodosius to contain Romanus and to rally the mountain tribes of the west to his side – became implicated in a carbon-copy "rebellion." The violence surrounding Gildo in the late 390s is significant not just because he was a "brother" of Firmus, but also because his rebellion was later presented as a dire threat to the court at Ravenna.[109] In these hostile accounts, the dissident church is presented as being in league with this dangerous enemy of the state. Gildo himself is said to have been involved with circumcellion gangs who were serving as violent sectarian enforcers for the "Donatists."[110] As just noted, Gildo had been closely involved with the *magister militum* Theodosius in the repression of Firmus in the mid-370s. Given this fact, it is notable that he was rewarded for his loyalty by Theodosius' son, also called Theodosius, when the latter became emperor of Rome. It was probably in the mid-380s that the junior Theodosius appointed Gildo the commander of all Roman forces in Africa.[111] He was grandly styled *comes et magister utriusque militiae per Africam*: Count and Master of Both Armies in Africa.[112] From the time he was appointed to high office until his demise in 398, Gildo wielded considerable power for

---

[109] The main literary sources on Gildo are Claudian, *De Bello Gildonico, Libri in Eutropium*, and the *De consulatu Stilichonis* (MGH AA, 10: 189–233); Orosius, 7.36.2–13 and Zosimus, 5.11 (the main historical accounts); the main legal sources are: CTh 9.7.9 (Dec. 393), 9.39.3 (March 398), 9.42.16 (December 399), 7.8.7 (June of 400), 9.42.19 (April 405), 9.40.19 (November 408), and 7.8.9 (August 409). Ancillary are Symmachus, *Ep.* 4.5 (MGH AA 6.1: 99); Augustine, *Contra ep. Parm.* 2.4.8 (CSEL 51: 47); *Contra litt. Petil.* 1.24.26 (CSEL 52: 20–22) and Jordanes, *Rom.* 320 (MGH AA, 5.1: 41). See also Seeck (1910).

[110] The connection has been accepted as standard in most histories; see, e.g., Monceaux, *Hist. litt.* 4, pp. 188–90; Baldwin (1961), p. 8; Frend, *Donatist Church*, pp. 213, 220–23; and Congar (1963c), pp. 729–30; at length, more recently, in Rubin (1995), pp. 168–72; Atkinson (1992), p. 490, almost alone of all the more recent studies, candidly admits that the evidence is "circumstantial."

[111] For the sources, see "Gildo," PLRE, 1, pp. 395–96: he seems to have become *Comes Africae* in 385, a date deduced from Claudian, *Bell. Gild.* 154; cf. Olechowska, *De Bello Gildonico*, 161–62.

[112] CTh 9.7.9 (30 December 393), given at Constantinople by Theodosius, Arcadius, and Honorius: "Gildoni com(iti) et mag(is)tro utriusque mil(itiae) per Africa(m)."

much longer than any other imperial official sent to Africa – for longer, in fact, than most emperors held power at Milan and Ravenna.[113]

During all of the long tenure that Gildo held his office, there is no good contemporary evidence that he failed to show due loyalty to the central government or that he had any pretensions to local autonomy. Gildo's high status had been created by the court. And his demise was determined not by events in Africa, but by happenings at the imperial court in the aftermath of the death of Theodosius on 17 January 395. The instability of central power threw the status of regional power-holders like Gildo into doubt. Theodosius' sons, Honorius and Arcadius, became nominal emperors, respectively, of the western and eastern halves of the empire – but in tenuous circumstances. At the time, Honorius was an eight-year-old child surrounded by influential courtiers and by a guardian regent general, Stilicho. Radical uncertainty about the court encouraged the emergence of regional contenders to imperial power, like Maximus and Eutropius. In the confusion, the position of Gildo – a critical one since he controlled security in one of the richest resource bases for the western court – came under nervous scrutiny. A combination of fear, mistrust, and misunderstood intentions led the court in Ravenna to label Gildo as an enemy of the state. In this situation, Gildo's options were few. He could stand fast and hope for the best, or he could do what his enemies at court were accusing him of doing: he could form an alliance with the eastern court at Constantinople.

Up to the year 397, there is no evidence to sustain a picture of Gildo busily preparing a local power base independent of the court or of showing any signs of disloyalty to the central government. It was the situation of extreme fluidity in 396–97 that compelled Gildo to reconsider his position. Even so, there is no evidence to support the assertion that in the autumn of 397 he decided to suspend the normal grain shipments to Rome.[114] But it was on the basis of such *fears* that Stilicho had him declared a public enemy. Once this step was taken, Gildo had no practical alternative except to confirm his own position in Africa. Even in this final extremity, there is

---

[113] Between Julian in 360 and Gratian in 383, no emperor in the West had held power for more than eleven years, many for less than this; Theodosius himself, exceptionally, was to hold imperial power for about a decade and a half.

[114] *Chron. Gall.* a. CCCCLII.36 (MGH AA 9:650). Gebbia (1988), p. 125, based on Courtois, *Les Vandales*, p. 145n. asserts the standard view of a stoppage of grain supplies to Rome, but neither cites any evidence in support of the claim. As Modéran (1989), pp. 863–65, points out, however, neither CTh 14.15.3 (15 April 397) nor CTh 14.15.6 (28 September 399) are relevant; both speak of the illegal manipulation of grain supplies by certain powerful persons and nothing more. So, rightly, Romanelli, *Storia*, p. 609.

no evidence to show that Gildo was doing much to prepare a military strike against the hostile court. On its side, Ravenna used the same device against him that had succeeded against Firmus in the 370s. It found a Gildo to fight a Gildo. A "brother" of Gildo's, named Mascezel, was dispatched to Africa with a modest military force.[115] Whatever support Gildo had seems to have had melted away. He died in a minor skirmish in the spring of 398. The whole of his "great armed threat" to the Roman state had not lasted even a year.

In the morass of the surviving evidence, all of it biased beyond redemption, it is almost impossible to say where the truth lies. One hostile series of sources, those close to the court at Ravenna, including the poet Claudian, tried to portray Gildo as someone who was planning to betray Africa to forces in the eastern court.[116] Another hostile line promoted Gildo as someone who intended to go his own way to form an autonomous state in Africa.[117] Both claims were equally distorted and both threw up a barrage of fictions about Gildo.[118] Most of the rabid assertions about him as a threatening barbaric African were nothing more than derivative literary types plundered from images of "bad Africans" found in Livy and Vergil. The stereotypes of bad Africans were then placed in an ethnographic background copied from Sallust. These were book-learned prejudices about literary Africans that had little or nothing to do with living contemporary Africans of the late fourth century.[119] They tell us nothing about Gildo's motives, which surely shifted and changed during this period as he found some options opening to him while others were closing.

Relying on these distorted fictions, modern historians have portrayed Gildo as an African rebel who allied himself with the dissident church in Africa and with its "armed wing," the violent circumcellions. If true, these claims would establish a basis for a connection between the secular armed force of the state and the armed gangs fronting the sectarian violence of

---

[115] This Mascezel is very probably the same Mascizel who was involved in the Firmus revolt in the 370s, see "Mascezel," PLRE, 1, p. 566; cf. Melani (1998).

[116] Claudian, *De Bello Gildonico*, esp. ll. 4–6, 235–40, 277–78, 283–87, and 324; see Gebbia (1988), p. 125.

[117] Orosius, 7.36; Zosimus, 5.11.1–2. Jordanes' statement, *Rom.* 320 (MGH AA 5.1: 41): "sibi velle coepit Africam optinere" is simply derivative of the earlier traditions; see Gebbia (1988), p. 125.

[118] Modern interpretations, like those of Gebbia (1988), Olechowska, *De Bello Gildonico*; Courtois, *Les Vandales*, pp. 145–46, and Frend, *Donatist Church*, pp. 208–10, 225–26, are fantasies, based on the outsiders' fiction of the "African rebel"; they have no independent evidence to support their main hypotheses (the supposed collapse of African grain prices and his alliance with circumcellions are just a few of the modern inventions).

[119] Modéran (1989), pp. 825–38, based, in part, on the literary analyses of Cameron (1970) and Olechowska, *De Bello Gildonico*.

the time. That is to say, an historical case of salience in violence. But the hypothesis raises a simple and basic question. Did the man who held the power of state violence in his hands in Africa up to the year 398 involve himself and the military forces at his command in the sectarian battles of the age? Despite a long historical tradition that has held this to be so, the evidence in support of the assertion is wholly without merit.[120] In its various forms, the argument is that Gildo was an African nationalist rebel who gave special support to the dissident church since it was "more African" than the Catholic church.[121] The only data arraigned in support of the claim are a series of tendentious statements made by Augustine in his polemical writings in which he refers to Optatus, the dissident bishop of Thamugadi (modern Timgad), as a "Gildonian," that is to say, a supporter and adherent of Gildo.[122]

Following his condemnation as an "enemy of the state" by the western court in 397, and his murder in 398, Gildo became a loser who had successfully been labeled as a traitor by the central government. If an important dissident bishop and his supporters could be closely identified with Gildo, this bad connection would add to the negative picture that was being constructed of them and their faction as a real danger to the state. It would condemn "the Donatists" as hypocrites. Rather than being just critics of the state's intervention in church affairs, the historical record would show that the dissidents were just as willing as the Catholics to join hands with a secular power when it suited their interests. But other than the device of name-calling – labeling Optatus as a "Gildonian" – Augustine offers no evidence in support of any effective or special alliance between the bishop of Thamugadi and the Count of Africa. Since Optatus was bishop of Thamugadi in the same years that Gildo was *comes Africae* and since Thamugadi was a major army settlement close to the southern frontiers of Numidia, there must have been some normal dealings between them, as was generally true of Christian bishops and officials of the Roman

---

[120] Tengström, "Die Donatisten und Gildo," in *Donatisten und Katholiken*, pp. 84–90, was the first seriously to question the connection.

[121] The idea is basic to Frend, *Donatist Church*, pp. 220–26; Romanelli, *Storia*, pp. 606–09, 617–18, thinks of him as an autonomist rebel, with interests parallel to those of "the Donatists"; Kotula (1972) and Diesner (1962b) see him as a populist leader forging links with "the masses."

[122] On Optatus, see Quinot (1967a) and De Veer (1968b); Aug. *Contra ep. Parm.* 2.2.4 (CSEL 51: 47) of "the Donatists . . . who, surrounding with honors as a bishop and a colleague Optatus the Gildonian, that man who made all Africa groan for ten years, whom they kept in their communion." *Contra litt. Petil.* 1.24.26 (CSEL 52: 20) just repeats the same phrase: "et sub uno Optato Gildoniano decennalem totius Africae gemitum"; *Contra litt. Petil.* 2.83.184 (CSEL 52: 112–14) where he refers to "the time of Gildo" and the fact that "one of your colleagues (sc. Optatus) was his very close friend."

state in general. But there is no hard evidence supporting anything more sinister.

HERACLIAN

The same violent cycle was repeated again in the crisis of 413 in which Honorius and the court at Ravenna turned on Heraclian, the *comes Africae*, who found himself similarly driven to rebellion, again facing few other good alternatives.[123] The incident was similarly court-driven, but it shows how one of these typical "revolts" might involve very little violence for Africa itself. Heraclian had been appointed to the position of Count of Africa for his proven trust and loyalty. When the emperor Honorius turned on his regent, Stilicho, in 408, Heraclian acquired great kudos by personally murdering the German on 22 August. The court also ordered the assassination of the sitting Count of Africa, Stilicho's brother-in-law Bathanarius. With no clear line of succession evident to the people in Africa, a man already on the ground named Johannes took over following Bathanarius' death. Knowing that he was unacceptable to the court, popular mobs in Carthage were encouraged to lynch the poor man.[124] These murders opened the way for the appointment of Heraclian as the emperor's trusted man in Africa. He probably assumed the position of *comes Africae* in early 409. Throughout the events that transpired over the years immediately following, the court at Ravenna found itself almost without an empire. When Alaric laid siege to Rome and pillaged the city in the summer of 410, Heraclian not only remained loyal, but sent additional funds and resources to Honorius that enabled him to survive. The Africans were rewarded for their loyalty by the court with imperial benefactions, as was Heraclian when he was appointed consul for 413. To the last months of 412, therefore, there were no apparent signs of trouble.

The best guess for the immediate cause of what transpired next is that an old friend of Stilicho's, the new *magister equitum* or Commander of the Cavalry army, Flavius Constantius, began making trouble for Heraclian. Given Heraclian's manifest power, it would not have been difficult to

---

[123] The principal sources for the Heraclian episode are Zosimus, 5.37.6, 6.7–12; Orosius, 7.42.10–14; Sozomen, 9.8; Philostorgius, 12.3; Procop. *Bell. Vand.* 1.2; among the analyses, see Oost (1966), Kotula (1977), and Gaggero (1991).

[124] See "Ioannes (5)," PLRE, 2, p. 594; the dating of this incident depends on the credibility of the Gallic chronicler who places it in this year: "Iohannes comes Africae occisus a populo est" (Chron. Gall. 452, no. 59, s.a. 408–09). But there are arguments that the chronicler might be in error and that the incident is to be connected with one mentioned in Aug. *Ep.* 15*–16* and 23* and therefore to be dated to the year 419: see Delmaire and Lepelley (1983b). I am not convinced.

suggest to the emperor and his circle that Heraclian might be planning "something." It is said that Heraclian feared certain dangers and suspicions being mooted about his power. Finding himself cornered, Heraclian had no other pragmatic alternative except to assert his own defense. He apparently stopped critical grain shipments to Rome in April 413. The court reacted by declaring him a public enemy. Heraclian responded by mobilizing the grain fleet and transporting part of the army in Africa to Italy. The only fighting took place in Italy not in Africa (Heraclian's force was quickly defeated at Ocriculum on the Via Flaminia, to the north of Rome). Heraclian fled back to Africa. He was hunted down by agents of the emperor who, in July, found him hiding in the Temple of Memory at Carthage. They had him put to death. In Heraclian, the same cycle of causes involving the court at Ravenna repeated itself, but with different results for the problem of violence.

All these violent episodes in Africa, from Firmus to Heraclian, were insignificant when compared with the wars along the northern frontiers of the empire. The African incidents were fundamentally different in cause in that they were primarily driven by the suspicion, even paranoia, in which the central court increasingly operated. They bear striking structural similarities to each other and they occurred more frequently as the central state in the West entered the recurrent crises that marked its end. The focussing of the court's apprehensive perceptions, and frights, on the figure of the supreme military commander in Africa provoked the very instability that it feared. These occurred in 308–11 with Domitius Alexander, the Vicar of Africa; in 370–73 with Romanus, the *comes Africae*, and in 396–98 with Gildo, also as Count of Africa. The last of these frights, these self-inflicted crises, involving the *comes Africae* Bonifatius in 427–28, indeed, was to signal the final end of the Roman hegemony in Africa.

The type of violence produced by the fissioning of the late Roman state, as with the state-induced violence of the Mauretanian highlands, was, in most of its most important aspects, markedly different from the modalities of the sectarian violence of the time. Rhetorical assertions constantly tried to identify one's sectarian enemies with the hated enemies of the state. Within this tactic, it was always the "barbarian" African rebels, Firmus and Gildo, who were the favorite *bêtes noires* that were identified with the dissident Christians. The other option was just too dangerous. In the cycle of causes peculiar to it, each kind of violence had its own history. To connect the sectarian gangs and the religious violence with the political meltdowns and the regional *coups d'état*, quite artificial and fictitious links had to be suggested by lobbyists, that is the ecclesiastical parties who were seeking the state's approval. But their biases do not count as evidence.

HOW VIOLENT WAS VIOLENT?

In terms of large-scale killing and damage, these preliminary stories serve to show how relatively non-violent Africa was in late antiquity. Indeed, in comparative terms, it was actually becoming *less* violent than many other regions of the empire. Apart from strange episodes of political-military breakdowns that were much smaller and short-lived versions of the great military fissionings that were afflicting the rest of the empire, there is little else to note. But to say that Africa in late antiquity was, relatively speaking, a rather civil and peaceful society is to suggest *what*? In the face of an absolute deficit of the relevant evidence, one can only speculate. Not including all sorts of other attacks on persons and property that do harm and surely count as violence, homicide rates alone in hyper-peaceful post-industrial countries in our own time usually range between 1 and 2 persons per 100,000. The United States is an exception, where, over recent decades, homicide rates have ranged between 7 and 10 per 100,000. These higher rates are still rather low when compared with the rates of less stable communities that are several orders of scale higher.[125] The low rates are created by a combination of modern manners of civility, a generally disarmed population (the United States is a modest exception), and the pervasive effect of civil policing.

Africans in the age of Augustine shared few of these civilizing virtues, and the institutions in the measure needed effectively to repress civil violence to low modern levels were generally absent. So let us hypothesize that Africa of the time managed to be as civil and peaceful, say, as England in the sixteenth or seventeenth centuries. What would that mean? In Elizabethan England homicide rates perhaps ran at about 7–9 per 100,000; in the following century at about 5–7 per 100,000 population.[126] If Africa was no more violent than this – a stretch, but useful for the purpose of argument – then there were would have been over a thousand murders every year – a total of about 35,000 homicides over the years that Augustine was bishop. Even if one settles on a number as very low as this, there is no sign of a special awareness of these deaths, records of them, or any particular significance attached to them in the writings of Augustine or his peers. But

---

[125] A. Underwood and M. Carmichael, "Guns: The Global Death Toll," *Newsweek* (30 April 2007), pp. 44–46.
[126] Stone (1983), but see the serious reservations offered by Sharpe (1985) and by Cockburn (1991).

homicide rates in premodern western Europe often ran to figures much higher than 7–9 per 100,000; rates at three times this level were not at all uncommon, especially in particular social or regional contexts.[127] At these not at all unbelievable levels, Africa in the age of Augustine would have witnessed something on the order of 100,000, or more, violent murders. Compared to these numbers, the total number of all known and imputed deaths caused by sectarian attacks in the period is a slight thing.

This is hardly surprising. Public sensibilities of violence are matters of perception and commitment. In the years around 2000 CE, about a third of a million people in the global population suffered violent deaths caused by the armed conflicts that dominated the big news of the age. About four times that number died equally violent deaths in automobile crashes.[128] The first kind of death is highly public and very politicized, the second more private and personal. The one kind of death causes collective fear and public lament, the other, generally speaking, does not. Consider another example. Between 1950 and 1975, the United States was engaged in an armed conflict in Vietnam in which its military forces suffered about 52,000 combat deaths. Over these same years, about 225,000 Americans were murdered by their fellow Americans in homicides, a substantial portion of them inflicted by hand guns and other firearms.[129] This internal war, broken down and isolated into small one-by-one killings, never had the same impact on the "national psyche" or public action as did deaths in the foreign war. During this same period, for the sake of comparison, more than 600,000 Americans were violently killed in motor vehicle accidents. The slaughter on the highway greatly surpassed that on the battlefield but, once again, these violent deaths produced none of the same public emotional response in writing or oral debate. The latter two, but especially the second, are rarely, if ever, featured in general histories of the 1960s and 1970s.

This brief foray into numbers is only intended as a small caution. It indicates that there is a romanticizing of violence that leads one to assume that violent causes and effects are connected in a certain fashion. It might come as a surprise to find that the horse – a normal mode of transport in Roman Africa – was one of the most dangerous of tools commonly employed by humans. In the prime of their use, horses were generally responsible for as large a proportion of violent deaths as caused by motor

[127] Ruff, *Violence in Early Modern Europe*, pp. 120–22, 130–31.
[128] *Time Magazine*: Global estimates for 2000/2003 (26 May 2003), p. 24.
[129] Sourcebook of Criminal Justice Statistics Online (http://www.albany.edu/sourcebook/pdf/t31062004.pdf), Table 3.106.2004.

vehicles in our own age.[130] Sensitivity to values and perspective is required. The actions that the selective and biased literary sources of late Roman Africa portray as violent and harmful are ones of which the writers of the time chose to be aware. They had an interest in highlighting particular kinds of violent acts while ignoring most others. They made heartfelt assertions about violent threats to the general social order: that dangerous movements involving peasant uprisings of rural workers were taking place, and that a general and widespread insurrection was being abetted by their hated sectarian enemies and their violent supporters. Why? Almost all the claims have to do with the writers' interests in forming certain kinds of knowledge. The result is that the reader is not presented with an even-handed or balanced reportage of violence, but rather with an aesthetic and moral ordering of it mainly for the purpose of persuasion. This is not to say that the violent acts that I am about to describe did not happen, but rather that, between individual murders on the one side and wars and rural rebellions on the other, there was a large and sometimes amorphous middle ground of violent acts that were interpreted as bearing a terrible meaning or which, in these terms, were simply ignored: the meanings were susceptible of being pushed to amnesia on the one side or to repeated celebration on the other.

INVENTED CONNECTIONS

To begin with interpretation, it is misleading to understand the violence involving the African military man Firmus as the core of a proto-nationalist or autonomist movement. The false assumption on which this argument rests is the assertion that his actions were part of the rebellion of an indigenous African who had the conscious aim of establishing a local power base independent of the Roman state. This is a misunderstanding of the context of the Firmus incident, which was typical, even if it was regionally specific. His violent actions fit into a frame produced by the shifting configurations of power implicating the western court. The ancillary claim that violent sectarian gangsters known as circumcellions formed a working alliance with Firmus and his forces is equally implausible.[131] This alliance, if it had existed, would be important since it would confirm links between different kinds of violence, with the one reinforcing the other. Gangs

---

[130] Hair (1971), pp. 7–12.

[131] It is in this context that the circumcellions are most frequently compared to the Bagaudae of late Roman Gaul: Monceaux, *Hist. litt.* 4, pp. 181–82; Frend, *Donatist Church*, p. 73; Rubin (1995), pp. 137–56, implicitly, specifically with p. 166.

purveying a localized and low-level sectarian violence could join a regional warlord seeking to assert his independence of the central government. But the claim is baseless. It is pure fantasy and invention, and not underwritten by any evidence. Only on two occasions does our best source on these events speak of any relationship between the dissident Christians and Firmus. It is in the context of the argument that Augustine makes that "the Donatists" were willing to use the violence offered by secular power to repress dissidents within their own church. It is in this context that he claims that they persecuted Rogatus "the Moor," who was the dissident bishop of Cartenna, through the agency of Firmus "the barbarian." But Augustine then goes on specifically to separate this violence in Mauretania against the so-called Rogatists from that of the circumcellions, which he sees as quite different in kind.[132] So not only does Augustine, our *only* witness to these events, *not* connect the circumcellions with Firmus, he explicitly *denies* the connection.

In the face of this denial, Augustine still uses Firmus to reprimand "the Donatists" for their hypocrisy. They had acted no differently than the Catholics. They too had used the secular force offered by Firmus to discipline one of *their* dissidents, Rogatus the bishop of Cartenna. This was the reason why his followers, the Rogatists, had called the mainstream dissidents *Firmiani*, the "adopted sons" or followers of Firmus.[133] It was a rhetorical term of condemnation that Augustine himself adopted: "the Donatists" in general were *Firmiani*, known supporters of the rebel Firmus.[134] Augustine suggests that there was a reported case where a "Donatist" bishop had allowed the partisans of Firmus to enter the coastal city of Rusubicari (modern Mers el-Hadjedj).[135] Not one of these assertions is persuasive.[136] Not one of them is supported by any credible independent evidence. Let us consider some of Augustine's rhetorical assertions more closely. In an initial foray, he rebuts the dissident bishop Petilian's claims about the Catholic use of compulsion to force people to adhere to the Catholic view of the Christian faith. Augustine defends the use of compulsion. After all, it is in the nature of God Himself who uses force to punish wrongdoers. He

---

[132] Aug. *Contra ep. Parm.* 1.11.17 (CSEL 51: 39): "quae etiam ad persequendum Rogatum Maurum ab eis per Firmum barbarum gesta sunt"; *Contra litt. Petil.* 2.73.184 (CSEL 52: 113): "Bello Firmiano quae a vobis Rogatus Maurus pertulerit."

[133] Aug. *Contra ep. Parm.* 1.11.17 (CSEL 51: 39).   [134] Aug. *Contra litt. Petil.* 2.83.184 (CSEL 52: 114).

[135] Aug. *Ep.* 87.10 (CCL 31A: 138): "Memento quod de Rogatensibus non dixerim, qui vos Firmianos appellare dicuntur, sicut nos Macarianos appellatis. Neque de Rusicazensi episcopo vestro, qui cum Firmo pactus perhibetur incolumitatem suorum"; "it is said," says Augustine, further adding that the anonymous bishop handed Catholics over to Firmus to be slaughtered.

[136] As Tengström, "Die Donatisten und Firmus," in *Donatisten und Katholiken*, pp. 79–83, clearly saw.

then proceeds to use the "what about you" ploy, a defense based on the other's hypocrisy. Augustine selects examples where his sectarian enemies had themselves been content to use compulsion.[137]

When Julian, in his invidious dislike of the Peace of Christ, returned to you the basilicas of the Unity [i.e. the churches that had been handed over to the Catholics by imperial decree in 347], what slaughters were committed by you at that time. It was a time when even the demons themselves were rejoicing with you when their temples were opened. Who has enough energy to retell the whole story? During the war with Firmus, what did Rogatus the Moor not suffer at your hands? The province of Mauretania Caesariensis itself should be asked.

Augustine's second statement is a little more explicit on the relationship. In it, he is once again attempting to refute the dissidents' charge that the Catholics were unjustly using secular force to compel adherence to their side.[138]

Perhaps they [i.e. "the Donatists"] say that have suffered more serious things at the hands of Catholic emperors than they themselves inflicted on the followers of Rogatus through the agency of the kings of barbarians, or by means of the civil judges [i.e. provincial governors] of Catholic emperors against the Maximianists, or which they committed against whomever they could by the mad actions of the circumcellions. As if indeed the question is simply whether they suffered *more* serious harm than they themselves inflicted on others – which, even if it is what you mean, I would never concede it. The most savage and violent acts are so numerous that they cannot be counted. And even if they were fewer in number or if those against whom these acts were committed were somehow harmed less, then on the following grounds alone they would be very serious: the fact that such acts were not ordered by established legitimate powers but were left to the extralegal

---

[137] Aug. *Contra litt. Petil.* 2.83.184 (CSEL 52: 113): "Quando Iulianus vobis Christi invidens paci basilicas reddidit unitatis, quae strages a vobis factae sint, quando vobiscum apertis templis suis etiam daemones exultabant, quis commemorare sufficiat? Bello Firmiano quae a vobis Rogatus Maurus pertulerit, ipsa Mauritania Caesariensis interrogetur."

[138] Aug. *Contra ep. Parm.* 1.11.17 (CSEL 51: 38–39): "Fortassis enim dicunt graviora se perpessos a catholicis imperatoribus quam isti fecerunt vel per reges barbarorum Rogatistis vel per iudices catholicorum imperatorum Maximianistis vel etiam faciunt per furorem circumcellionum quibuscumque potuerint. Quasi vero inde quaestio est, utrum graviora patiantur quam faciunt, quod quidem nullo modo concesserim. Multa enim eorum saevissima et acerbissima numerantur, immo numerari non possunt, quae si pauciora essent vel eos in quos admittuntur minus affligerent, eo ipso essent certe graviora, quod non ab ordinatis potestatibus iubentur, sed extraordinariis furoribus admittuntur. Non enim tam multa sunt quae adversus Maximianistas per iudices humanae constitutionis egerunt. In eo genere actionum ponant, si volunt, quae etiam ad persequendum Rogatum Maurum ab eis per Firmum barbarum gesta sunt, et illum licet hostem immanissimum Romanorum in legitimis potestatibus numerent. Sed haec non tam multa sunt, quam multa cotidie per furiosos ebriosorum iuvenum greges quibus principes constituunt, qui primum tantummodo fustibus, nunc etiam ferro se armare coeperunt, qui circumcellionum notissimo nomine per totam Africam vagantur et saeviunt, contra omnem ordinem legum potestatumque committunt."

acts of madmen. But, in fact, they [i.e. "the Donatists"] never experienced as many cruelties as they themselves committed against the Maximianists through judges established by earthly powers. They can also place in this same category of actions, if they so wish, those which were accomplished through the agency of Firmus the barbarian in their persecution of Rogatus "the Moor," and so to count amongst their duly recognized "legitimate authorities" an enemy who was so dangerous to the Romans. But none of these things is as serious as the multiple acts of cruelty that are committed every day – against the general order of laws and legal powers – by means of the mad herds of drunken young men whose leaders they appoint – men who at first were armed only with wooden clubs, but who are now beginning to use swords, and who wander and rage throughout all of Africa under the most infamous name of circumcellions.

This is a list of sectarian atrocities that catalogues the relationships that Augustine claims to have linked. First of all, he refers to court actions by which the dissidents used the civil authorities of the Roman state to reclaim basilicas and properties that were held by a renegade faction of their own party, the so-called Maximianists. He then castigates the use of Firmus – how is not specified – to direct similar punitive measures against another internal renegade within the dissident church, Rogatus, the dissident bishop of Cartenna and his followers. Finally, he refers to the quotidian acts of violence committed by the circumcellions, men whom he regards as more harmful by far.

A number of conclusions can be drawn. Augustine does make the explicit statement that Firmus or forces identified with him were somehow engaged in the "persecution" or "harassment" of bishop Rogatus and his followers. But this seems to be the full extent of any alliance with the dissidents. If there were any other facts concerning the serious consequences of this collusion, then Augustine would surely have offered them. Another important point emerges. It is that Augustine separates circumcellion violence from these other episodes of violence. In his eyes, the violent acts of the circumcellions are worse in kind and *different from* either the court actions against the Maximianists or the vicarious acts committed by the followers of Firmus against the bishop Rogatus. There is no evidence that there was any collaboration between the circumcellions and the forces of the rebel Firmus. The incidents are listed in serial order, and they are not linked in any fashion.

Since this is the sum total of the evidence bearing on an alliance between "the Donatists" and Firmus, it bears repeating how allusive and slippery it is. All that Augustine says is that during the war with Firmus, at that time and in those circumstances, the mainstream "Donatists" of his region of Africa had reaped a vicarious advantage of the forces that Firmus' supporters used against the coastal city of Cartenna. At most, Augustine *suggests* that there might have been a link with Firmus, but the impression that one gets from a close reading of the evidence is that it is nothing more than a rhetorical incrimination by association. If Augustine had hard facts to sustain an active alliance between the two, he surely would have given explicit details of the collaboration. Even so, such acts did *not* include the circumcellions, whom Augustine sees as representing a different kind of violence that he locates precisely in the non-barbarian, non-frontier civilized core of lands in Africa between Sitifensis in the west and the heartlands of the old proconsular province in the east.

So much for Firmus. What then is the explicit testimony of the involvement of dissident church leaders with the "rebel" Gildo? Once again, the data are limited to an exiguous and finite number of polemical assertions made by Augustine. In his reply to the dissident bishop Parmenian, Augustine begins with the summary of a dissident complaint in which they used a biblical text – "The one who judges the just unjustly and the one who unjustly judges the just is an abomination before God" (Proverbs 17: 15) – to condemn the Catholics.[139] But, Augustine retorts, the execration is more appropriately directed against "the Donatists" themselves.

In this way they have judged unjustly that which is just. On the other hand, they have judged just that which is not just, as when they held in high honor both as a bishop and as a colleague Optatus "the Gildonian" – that man who made all Africa groan for a decade – a man whom they kept in their communion.

Later, in his reply to the dissident bishop Petilian of Cirta, he elaborates:[140]

Let's consider your achievements. I'll omit consideration of the tyrannical regimes that you run in the towns and cities, and especially on the rural domains that belong to others. I shall pass over the madness of the circumcellions and the sacrilegious and profane worship of the bodies of those who willingly hurl themselves off great heights, the bacchic orgies of drunken men, and the decade-long groan of all Africa under Optatus "the Gildonian" . . .

---

[139] Aug. *Contra ep. Parm.* 2.2.4 (CSEL 51: 47): "Hoc ergo modo quod iustum est iudicarunt iniustum, quod autem iniustum est iudicarunt iustum, cum Optatum Gildonianum, decennalem totius Africae gemitum, tamquam sacerdotem atque collegam honorantes in communione tenuerunt."

[140] Aug. *Contra litt. Petil.* 1.24.26 (CSEL 52: 20): "Vestros autem fructus si consideremus, omitto tyrannicas in civitatibus et maxime in fundis alienis dominationes, omitto furorem circumcellionum et praecipitatorum ultro cadaverum cultus sacrilegos et profanos, bacchationes ebrietatum et sub uno Optato Gildoniano decennalem totius Africae gemitum."

At the end of this same passage, he points to the dissidents' willingness to use official force under the brief reign of the emperor Julian, their treatment of Rogatus "the Moor" during the war of Firmus and, he continues, "In the time of Gildo, because one colleague of yours was his [i.e. Gildo's] very close friend, the Maximianists understood what they would have to suffer."[141] When challenged, however, Augustine had to admit that he had no hard written evidence or documentation to support his claims about Optatus. They were all matters of oral hearsay.[142] In the barrage of vituperation, a single theme stands out: that Optatus, the dissident bishop of Thamugadi, did indeed have some sort of relationship to Gildo. At various times, Optatus is labeled as a "Gildonian," as a friend or *amicus* of Gildo, and an accomplice or henchman, a *satelles*, of the Count of Africa.[143] And, further, that Optatus regarded Gildo as being something of a "god" to him.[144] Although he rhetorically denies the fact, all that Augustine can claim was a general hearsay knowledge that Optatus was someone who regarded Gildo as one of his patrons.[145] This is all that being a *Gildonianus* would technically mean.[146] This is hardly surprising and it does not add up to much. One would expect a very powerful Christian bishop, seated in the major city and army base in southern Numidia – it was also the seat of the *comes Africae* – to have had some such relationship with the Count of Africa. The latter needed to ensure conditions of peace and stability, and he had personal interests such as the need for a labor supply for his huge domain lands throughout Africa. Friendship of this sort with a powerful Christian bishop would be normal. It does not mean, as Augustine repeatedly insinuates, that as a high-ranking official of the empire Gildo was ready to put the armed forces of the state at the disposal of a Christian bishop, for which there is no evidence whatsoever.

---

[141] Aug. *Contra litt. Petil.* 2.83.184 (CSEL 52: 112–14): "Tempore Gildoniano, quia unus collega vester familiarissimus amicus eius fuit, viderint Maximianistae quae senserint."

[142] Aug. *Contra Cresc.* 3.12.15–16 (CSEL 52: 422–23).

[143] Optatus as a "Gildonian": Aug. *Contra ep. Parm.* 2.2.4 (CSEL 51: 46–47); *Contra litt. Petil.* 1.9.10; 1.14.14; 1.24.26; as a *satelles*: Aug. *Contra ep. Parm.* 2.4.8; 2.15.34; 2.29.209; *Contra Cresc.* 2.12.16; as an *amicus*: Aug. *Contra litt. Petil.* 2.27.88; 2.84.184.

[144] Aug. *Contra litt. Petil.* 2.33.78; 2.37.88; 2.100.230; to call someone *dominus* or *deus* in a context like this was just to indulge in the exaggerated language of clientage.

[145] Aug. *Contra litt. Petil.* 2.103.237 (CSEL 52: 151): "Itane vero Optatus, quem pagani Iudaei christiani nostri vestri per Africam totam furem raptorem proditorem oppressorem separatorem et illius, quem quidam vestrum eius dixit comitem deum, non amicum, non clientem, sed satellitem clamant, non fuit vel qualiscumque peccator?"

[146] The "-ianus" suffix in Latin words usually indicates an artificial kin-like identity such as this: adoption, clientage, or otherwise being the self-adopted member of a family or community – like "Christ-ianus," for example.

Given that this is the sum total of evidence linking one of the dissidents' bishops, Optatus of Thamugadi, to Gildo, the "brother" of Firmus, a few basic conclusion can be drawn. At no point are circumcellion gangs identified as part of this larger violence, much less as allies of Gildo's. The evidence connecting Optatus with Gildo is flimsy, but perhaps sufficient. It consists of nothing more than an epithet: Optatus was a "Gildonian," which has all the hallmarks of being not much more than standard polemical rhetoric: "such-and-such" is a "so-and-so," indeed a "bad so-and-so." A standard way of demonizing a hated opponent was to claim that his followers were nothing but the acolytes of a bad man. In calling Optatus a *satelles* of Gildo, Augustine was deliberately echoing the official pronouncement of the state which had used this precise word to condemn adherents of Gildo and to impose harsh penalties on them.[147] By saying that Optatus was one of them, Augustine was attempting to create dangerous links connecting political and military treason, a specific type of threat to the state, and the dissident bishop. The modern historian must make a better attempt to understand the causes of the Firmus and Gildo insurrections and their relationship to the Christian communities of the time. As the parallel incident of Heraclian shows, both sides played the game of appealing to local holders of secular power. It was not without reason that Augustine suspected that his man, Flavius Marcellinus, and his brother, Apringius, had been executed because "the Donatists" had successfully suggested that *these men* had been implicated in the "revolt" of Heraclian. The rhetorical fictions could cut both ways.

THE GOOD USE OF TREASON

Analysis of the incidents of large-scale violence in Africa of the fourth and fifth centuries that are the closest to war in type cautions against the exaggerated impression of the high levels of violence that are suggested and encouraged by tendentious literary sources. The violent episodes that involved Firmus, Gildo, and Heraclian are typical political crises in which local men who were high-ranking servitors of the Roman state found themselves cornered and could not convince the court of their loyalty. A huge official and quasi-official polemical literature of hatred directed

---

[147] See CTh 9.40.19 (11 November 408) on the *satellites Gildonis* and the penalties imposed on them (one must have suspicions about the date, but the governor, Donatus, to whom it was addressed and the consuls date to 408); in its legal condemnation of the supporters of Heraclian, the central court similarly labeled them as his "henchmen" or *satellites* (CTh 9.40.21; 5 July 413) – it was officialspeak for the supporters of a political enemy of the state.

against them sustained their labeling as enemies of the state, tyrants, and rebellious barbarians. It was then easy for others to exploit these hostile official lines for their own purposes. In doing so, they were all too willing to embrace and to expand the exaggerated picture of these men as native African enemies of the Roman state and their strange insurrections as genuinely threatening wars. To the extent that the big violence of war could be attached to the little violence of sectarian conflict, the connection could be used to convince the court of a serious link between the two: between religious dissidence and political conspiracy and rebellion.

The ordinary day-to-day reality was different. Rather than a war involving direct confrontation between the Roman state and perceived usurpers of power, it was the bloody little battle that was ritually repeated in the streets of Caesarea every year that better mirrored what African Christians were doing to each other in these same decades. They, too, had split into two opposing sides within their own community. They had also appealed for generations to what their ancestors or *maiores* had decided as the basis for their daily treatment of each other. And they kept nourishing their conflict with the food of tradition. The two sides had identified with themselves and had attacked each other over a number of generations because that is what their ancestors did. In their own peculiar way, the Gildo and Firmus episodes might reflect other cultural aspects of violence. Brothers fought and betrayed each other and, in the end, the violence was a manic and demented rage caused by the unfounded fears, illogical responses, and the bumbling and ignorant intrusion of a heavy-handed and suspicious imperial court armed with the resources of a great state. These aspects of violence were indeed shared.

In the age of Augustine, the two Christian communities behaved in a similarly divisive way and gave much the same reasons for their adhesions and actions. The causes proffered were so pragmatic and profound that even Augustine had to admit that they would be very difficult to eradicate and to overcome. Why were the two hostile Christian communities doing what they did? What was it that their ancestors had done to set them on this remorseless and repetitious course? The embittered hostilities were less the result of a neatly delineated series of causes and effects that produced the present hatreds. They were more a matter of contemporary memory and action. And if anything can be said about this memory where it concerned the contentious matter of faith, it is that the remembrance was very selective and that it depended on a few narrative lines that were firmly believed and acted upon by each side.

Other than oral tradition and a scattering of written documents contained in dossiers, the big single account for the Catholics in the last decades of the fourth century was a five-book treatise composed in the mid-360s by Optatus, the Catholic bishop from the city of Milevis in the province of Numidia. In his polemical treatise, he described the origins of the great division that had occurred within the Christian church in Africa. For African Catholics in the age of Augustine this account was both the history and the memory that justified and explained "who we are." The primal events that he retailed had occurred during and immediately after the trauma of the great persecution of Christians that had been initiated by a decree issued by the emperor Diocletian at Nicomedia in February 303. The heavily freighted act that subsequently came to be the litmus test for who was to be identified as on what side was that of collaboration with the authorities during the persecution. To be precise, who among the priesthood, the bishops, had collaborated in betraying or handing over the Word of God, the books or *codices* of Holy Scripture to the authorities when they demanded them? The identification of these traitors or *traditores* became central to separating the supporters of Caecilianus in his ordination as bishop of Carthage from those who supported his rival Maiorinus.

The contributing factors to the conflict quickly crystallized in the years immediately after the Great Persecution, in late 305 and in 306.[148] The division produced an odd sense of minority and majority parties, but the unusual nature of the conflict was provoked by the involvement of the imperial state in the conflict which, oddly enough, did not happen for a significant number of years. Seven or eight years passed until, following the involvement of the new Christian emperor Constantine and his entourage in the disputes, beginning in the year 313, the one side was declared, at the prompting of the emperor and his advisors, to be right and the other to be wrong. And yet, the "wrong" side, from the perspective of the central government, the "Rebaptizers" as they were called, were clearly the majority party on the ground in Africa in terms of numbers, and they appear to have remained so throughout the rest of the fourth century.[149]

In all of this, the hostility and hatred between the two sides increased and the gap between them grew. They viewed each other through the

---

[148] See Appendix B on the chronology of the events.

[149] Possidius, the biographer of Augustine, admits as much in his synopsis of the situation in Africa at the time that Augustine became bishop in the mid-390s: "rebaptizante Donati parte, maiore multitudine Afrorum" (*Vita Aug.* 7.2: Bastiaensen: 146), unless one wishes to dismiss it as a rhetorical ploy.

screen of labels that each imposed on their enemies. Some of these grew out of the incessant court battles that each side undertook with the civil authorities in order to enforce possession orders or to recover property, mainly the churches currently possessed by their enemies. In Carthage, the main venue for such actions, the representatives of the dissidents were therefore called the "party of Majorinus" or the *pars Maiorini* and the "party of Donatus" or *pars Donati*, as they would be identified in order to provide the court with a legal person or *persona* on whose behalf legal actions could proceed. This labeling of one side or the other was a function of the Roman civil court system which, from the beginning of the dispute – quite unlike the *caterva* in Caesarea – was a critical referee in the process. The courts were an ever-present third-party representing the arbitrating power of the state that continually affected the ways in which the two sides were represented: not as catervic gangs but rather as parties to a legal dispute.

Yet how each side construed the other in these battles was not constant, but varied, sometimes considerably, as the surrounding circumstances of the time changed. If the immediate circumstance favored a conciliatory approach, the one side could present the other charitably as fallen "brothers" who could be reconciled with "the truth." In harsher and harder moments, they could just as easily construe their opponents as mortal enemies aligned with Satan or the Antichrist. Since the surviving literary evidence is very unevenly distributed chronologically, it is difficult to be certain about which perspective was dominant in any year or decade. But situational changes certainly defined the conflict. For example, in his long reply to the "Donatist" bishop Parmenian of Carthage – the man who commanded the dissident church in the decades after the death of the emperor Julian – the Catholic bishop Optatus consistently hewed a line that was conciliatory in tone. In his rhetoric, Optatus deliberately tried to minimize the differences between the two communities. He referred to the two sides as children of the same mother, Mother Church, and as the adopted children of the same God the Father. The dissidents and the Catholics are portrayed as brothers or *fratres* who share a common brotherhood or *fraternitas*. Throughout his treatise, Optatus directly addresses Parmenian as "brother Parmenian" or "my brother, Parmenian."

If he so chose, Optatus *could* portray the split as a family squabble, an unfortunate division between siblings of the same household – between brothers who ought to resolve their familial differences. In this mode, any bishop like Optatus (and, later, Augustine) *could* consciously draw attention to the plain fact that there were really no differences of doctrine, belief, scripture, or ritual that separated the two sides. As Optatus said, the two sides shared all the same fundamentals of Christian belief and practice.[150]

> Between you and us there is one and the same manner of church life, the same shared scriptural readings, the same faith, the same sacraments of the faith, the same mysteries.

So Augustine himself would later ply this same line.[151]

> "Are you a Christian?" And the other replies, "Yes, I am" . . . and in many respects they have in fact been with me. We have the same baptism. In that they were with me. We have both customarily read the gospels. They were with me in that. We have both customarily celebrated the holidays of the martyrs. In this too they were with me. We both always observed the festival of Easter. And in this they were with me too.

On the other hand, not far removed from this position, and implicit in it, there always lurked a more sinister construction of one's opponents. Given different conditions, it came to the fore just as easily. In this perspective, the struggle was over real and finally irreconcilable basic differences, less a family squabble than a deeply embittered civil war scarred by the special hatreds of fratricidal killing. The fight was against evil and the final destruction of humans, over the damnation or salvation of a host of human souls. In the eyes of each party to the dispute, the loss of those souls was an unacceptable cost of acceding to the demands of the other. Reconciliation would require the surrender of bedrock values by one of the two sides. In the later 380s, when Optatus added a seventh book to his refutation of Parmenian, the dissident bishop of Carthage, he ended it on a rather darker note. Now the biblical model for the struggle was the fratricidal one modeled on the primal murder of Abel by Cain. The shift to a harsher way of seeing things should not be taken to mean that there was some predictable gradual narrative of these hatreds that worked its way, evenly, from beginning to end. Optatus' different attitude of the 380s was part of a

---

[150] Optatus, *Contra Parm.* 5.1.11 (SC 413: 116): "Denique et apud vos et apud nos una est ecclesiastica conversatio, communes lectiones, eadem fides, ipsa fidei sacramenta, eadem mysteria." This brief statement sums up the whole argument in book four on the substantial "brotherhood" between the two sides.

[151] Aug. *En. in Ps.* 54.19 (CCL 39: 670–71), leading, however, to an emphasis on difference: "but they are not with me in all respects." Similarly, Augustine, in a letter addressed to Macrobius, the dissident bishop of Hippo in 409 (*Ep.* 108.1.3–2.5 = CCL 31B: 65–68), goes out of his way to emphasize how much the two communions had in common.

changed set of circumstances that encouraged the use of a different part of an existing repertoire of hatred. What people selected from memory was a dynamic process. But everyone implicated in the struggle had learned from their ancestors that one hard fact was certain: a damnable act of betrayal lay at its origins.

CHAPTER 2

Church of the traitors

When evening came, he reclined to dine with the twelve.
When they were eating, he said:
I tell you that one of you is going to betray me...
and that man by whom the Son of Man is betrayed will be cursed.
It would be better for him that he had never been born.[1]

(Jesus)

It would take too long to explain the intimate alliance of
contradictions in human nature which make love itself
wear at times the desperate shape of betrayal.

(Joseph Conrad)[2]

A primordial evil lay at the base of the conflict: an act of betrayal. And
no one doubts that deep perfidy generates irreconcilable hatred. Betrayal
moves and it paralyzes.[3] It was not for any trivial offense that Dante
placed Brutus and Cassius, along with Judas Iscariot, in the ninth circle
of Hell, freezing on eternal ice, being ripped apart by the maws of Satan
himself. It was for the sin of betrayal.[4] And the betrayal at the heart of the
sectarian conflict in Africa was not a personal betrayal of the usual kind.
The betrayal was permanently branded by the handing over or *traditio*
of the Holy Scriptures, the Words of God Himself, to secular authorities
by Christian collaborators during the Great Persecution of 303–05. The
history of this betrayal was incessantly asserted and denied, extended and
elaborated by both dissidents and Catholics. It called out for explanatory

---

[1] Matt. 26: 20–24.   [2] J. Conrad, *A Personal Record*, London, Dent, 1946, p. 36.
[3] The modern analytical literature on the phenomenon is strangely thin. A good beginning is found in
Akerström, *Betrayal and Betrayers*, but even he remarks that as of the date of his foray into the subject
(1991), his was a solitary and lonely piece of research. G. Simmel, "The Fascination of Betrayal," in
K. H. Wolff, transl. and ed., *The Sociology of Georg Simmel*, New York, 1950, pp. 333–34, provided
some early insights; on the strong emotions, see Akerström, pp. 1–2, 18–21, based in part on the work
of Gregory Bateson on the behavior of higher primates.
[4] On this betrayal as a form of inherited sin, see De Veer (1968m).

storytelling, and a lot of it.[5] The traitors, the *traditores*, were at the heart of their mutual hatreds and fears. The universal conviction was that certain detestable men had betrayed God Himself. In handing over His holy words to earthly officials to be destroyed, they deserved their notorious status as agents of the Devil and of the Antichrist. But real ambiguities about who precisely had done what meant that no one could let the question fade or slip from knowledge or from endless debate.

The act of faithlessness was meditated upon and condemned by the dissident Christians. They felt that their enemies were not just personal sectarian foes: they were the betrayers of God's words, traitors to his divine laws. The acts of betrayal were a common currency. They became a creative seedbed, causing a new community to come into existence whose members identified themselves as "not them," not the traitors.[6] In the eyes of dissident Christians in the age of Augustine, their Catholic enemies were genetically descended from the original collaborators. They had inherited the primal sin. And no one, not even the sometimes innovative Augustine, doubted the African conviction that primal sin was inherited – passed down from one generation of sinners to the next.[7] He himself was made to face his inheritance. At the great conference at Carthage in 411, the dissident bishop Petilian from Constantina verbally challenged him: "Who are you? Are you a son [sc. of that traitor] Caecilian or aren't you?"[8] "Was Caecilian your daddy, or your mommy?" Petilian then goaded, to which Augustine replied "He's my brother." Which only provoked the acidic counter from Petilian: "The person who procreates children is not a brother."[9] The answer, to Petilian, was manifest. All the talk about kinship was because the great sin was inherited, and to show who had acquired it. On these grounds, the Catholics were not just any congregation of bad Christians. They were a

---

[5] In the terms outlined by Tilly, *Why?*, pp. 14–17, there is some recourse in the stories, in his terms, to codification, that is, to a theodicy within which betrayal and martyrdom were embedded and in which everyone accepted the shorthand of why the events had to happen and made sense. In this way the combined discourse united his "popular" and "specialized" modes of explanation, see Tilly, *Why?*, pp. 18–20.

[6] Akerström, *Betrayal and Betrayers*, pp. 21–23; cf. Simmel, "The Fascination of Betrayal," p. 334.

[7] See Lamirande (1965a and 1965g); Augustine's final position was staked out in his little handbook on Christian doctrine: *Enchirid.* 13.46 (CCL 46: 74); for its relevance to the status of the Church, see Adam, *Kirchliche Sündenvergebung*, pp. 75–87; his views were nuanced, of course, and pushed first one way in his disputes with the dissidents in Africa and then the other in the disputes with Pelagius; see Dubarle (1957), pp. 113–20.

[8] GCC 3.221 and 227 (SC 224: 1162, 1168): Petilian challenges Augustine: "Tu, quid es? Filius es Caeciliani, an non?" and "Tu quis es? Filius es Caeciliani, an non? Tenet te crimen Caeciliani, an non?"

[9] GCC 3.231–32 (SC 224: 1170–72): Petilian: "Caecilianus tibi pater aut mater est, ut dixisti?"; Augustine: "Iam audisti quia frater erat." Petilian: "Frater non est qui generat filios."

segregated and polluted church of traitors.[10] This much was stated frankly
in the programmatic statement about "who we are" enunciated before the
conference of Carthage by the belligerent dissident bishop of Arusuliana
who bore the wonderful name Habetdeum ("He-Hath-God"). Habetdeum
read aloud a statement on behalf of "the bishops of Catholic Truth: the
church which is suffering persecution – *not* the one that is conducting it."
In it, the collected dissident bishops stated bluntly: "Our adversaries are
traitors and they are our persecutors."[11] Habetdeum's statement advanced
to link the Catholics closely with the arch-traitor Judas, going so far as to say
that Judas was their patron, the one whose example they were following.[12]

   Once the fact of betrayal was established, it had a long life. Few other
human emotions and commitments possess such a natural longevity. To be
caught up in collaboration is to invite a deep and powerful memory fixed
on retribution. In this way Pierre Taittinger, founder of the house built on
champagne, later remembered his arrest and transport to the Vélodrome
d'Hiver in Paris that was serving as a prison in the fetid heat of August
1944 – just as it had not long before for Jews who were being transported
to Auschwitz. As they were about to unload the prisoners, the guards
incited the awaiting crowd, intent on vengeance: "You're about to see a
gang of collaborators, agents of the Boches, traitors!" And so, "the dirty
collaborator" Sacha Guitry, actor, writer, and director, was severely beaten
as he fell from the prison van. As he lay on the ground, Guitry witnessed
the beating of another prisoner, a distinguished scholar. His face covered
with blood from the attack, the man collapsed and fell into Guitry's arms.
This man, the eminent historian of imperial Rome, Jérôme Carcopino, was
the target of a savage rage fueled by those who hated the government with
which he had collaborated – in his case, as the Vichy regime's Secretary of
State for National Education, no less.[13] The sentiments excited by betrayal
are not far from our modern understanding or from the doing of ancient

[10] For a summation of the problem, with attendant literature, see B. Kriegbaum, "Die afrikanische
    Sicht der *traditio* und ihre Bedeutung für die innerkirchliche Kommunikation," ch. 6 in *Kirche der
    Traditoren*, pp. 150–72.
[11] GCC 3.258 (SC 224: 1194): "et ceteri episcopi veritatis catholicae, quae persecutionem patitur, non
    quae facit . . . Adversarii igitur traditores persecutoresque nostri," this coming at the beginning of
    a long statement (SC 224: 1194–1218) in which Habetdeum outlines the basics of the dissidents'
    self-definition.
[12] GCC 3.258 (SC 224: 1208): "In defensionem deinde sceleris sui auctoritatem sibi exemplo Iudae
    traditoris adsumunt" (SC 224: 1210): "sed cum ipsa postmodum turba ad tradendum Dominum
    venit. Vadant ergo cum suo Iuda patrono inimici dominicae veritatis, qui suo more defendere reos
    manifestissimos elaborant."
[13] P. Taittinger, . . . *Et Paris ne fut détruit*, Paris, 1948, p. 239; as reported by H. Lottman, *The Purge*, p. 80;
    and Corcy-Debray, *Jérôme Carcopino*, pp. 270–85 (on the Vélodrome d'Hiver incident); pp. 276–82;
    on "Carcopino, traître à la patrie"; and pp. 295–97, on his difficult post-war "rehabilitation."

history. This same rage, we must imagine, was implanted deep in the Christian community in Africa, defining it for a century, and more, of inside war.

In a circular letter composed by a dissident writer in the conflicts of the late fourth and early fifth century – but paraded as a composition written a century and a half earlier by the great bishop Cyprian – the entire range of traitors is broken down into various subcategories of betrayers who merited different kinds of responses.[14] The writer mimics the legal language of the courts, and of imperial government decrees, to issue his own edict, in his guise as Cyprian, the founding father of the African Church, on how true Christians should abjure polluting contact with condemned persons.[15] His instruction taught men how to think in categories of traitors. Another more powerful reminder of the primal crime of betrayal was the rewriting and dramatic re-enacting of the stories of persons who had bravely stood their ground and who had perished in the Great Persecution. The sacred narratives, or selections from them, were replayed every year on the "birthdays" of the martyrs, the anniversaries of their deaths. In these mini-dramas, the holy martyrs addressed the parishioners directly. Because they had voluntarily sacrificed their own lives in order *not* to give in to the demands of the authorities to surrender the scriptures, they spoke with a singular, imperishable authority. Their response to Diocletian's edict requiring them to hand over the words of their God was refusal and the acceptance of torture and death. The judgments of these loyal persons on those who had betrayed the word of God echoed with a particular force in a host of churches throughout Africa every year.

One of these death narratives retells the story of the Christians from the small town of Abitina (Avitina), about fifty miles to the southwest of Carthage. Their case was heard by the Roman governor Anullinus at Carthage on 12 February 304. The story of their deaths as we now have it is a confection of a much later time, perhaps reaching its final form in the early decades of the fifth century. It therefore offers a window into

---

[14] It is normally included in the numerous pseudo-Cyprianic writings that form part of the larger "Cyprianic corpus" (CSEL 3.3: 273–74). See Mercati (1899/1937) for some analysis; of its author, he says, rather humorously: "il nostro deve essere un ignorante fanatico, forse vissuto in alcune delle provincie meno romanizzate dell'Africa Romana" (p. 277 n. 2), further pegging him as "un vero circoncellione letterario" (p. 270). The composition is most probably of late fourth- or early fifth-century date. The attribution to Cyprian was made, obviously, in order vicariously to claim the authority of the founding father of African Christianity.

[15] Ps.-Cypr., *Ep.* 3 (CSEL 3.3: 273–74); compare the frequent use of such officialese in the passion of the Abitinian martyrs: *Passio sanctorum Dativi, Saturnini presbyteri et aliorum*, 19 (Maier, *Dossier*, 1, no. 4, p. 84): "decreta coniungere constitutionesque sanctissimas . . . ex auctoritate legis divinae sanxerunt servandaque posteris reliquerunt . . . etc."

the ways in which the history of the Great Persecution was manipulated to produce current values in the age of Augustine.[16] In the narrative, a forceful point is made of the continued refusal to obey demands made by state officials.[17] Of all later African martyr stories, this one contains a vivid and almost complete replay of the blood sacrifices made by the Christians who courageously refused an imperial command. In obedience to the edict issued by the emperors, they were to hand over the Holy Scriptures to be burned.[18] Loyalties in the small town of Abitina at the time of the posting and enforcement of the so-called first edict of Diocletian polarized along the fault line dividing collaboration from resistance. The municipal authorities, aided by a local police detachment of the Roman army, arrested forty-six Christians, including seventeen women, and hauled them from their homes to a place of assembly in the town forum. Once registered and accounted for, they were marched from Abitina to Carthage, the capital of the proconsular province. Here they were put in holding cells to await the hearing before the governor.

The Christians of Abitina had been arrested and detained because they had refused to cooperate in the betrayal of their places of assembly and the Holy Scriptures. In the extreme emotions of the event, they faced a crisis that forced on them a decision about their identity. Their bishop, named Fundanus, faced with the same demands made by local municipal

---

[16] Monceaux, *Hist.litt.* 5, p. 53, who outlines the stages in the production of the document as we have it, including an original transcript-type, and then two later dissident recensions; cf. Dearn (2004), p. 16: "The text is not a reliable source for nascent Catholic or Donatist attitudes at the time of Caecilian's consecration or before, but for the way in which later attitudes were projected into the past for polemical purposes."

[17] On Abitina, actually formally called Avitina, see Lepelley, *Cités de l'Afrique romaine*, 2, pp. 56–62; on its identification with Chouhoud al-Batel, now confirmed, see Beschaouch (1976).

[18] *Passio sanctorum Dativi, Saturnini presbyteri et aliorum*, sometimes also known more generally as the "Acts of the Abitinian Martyrs." The standard text is printed in Maier, *Dossier*, 1, no. 4, pp. 59–92, who reprints (with only some minor changes) the edition by Pio Franchi de' Cavalieri (1935a), and takes into consideration the important review by Delehaye (1936). In their current state, the *acta* appear to go back to a series of documents written and assembled in the aftermath of the persecution of 303–05, but in the years after Caecilian was raised to the position of bishop (probably in 307–08). There is no date on the *acta* as they survive, but when *acta* like them were introduced at the third day of the proceedings of the conference at Carthage in 411, there was a specific consular year as well as day (GCC 3.432–433–35; SC 195: 528; cf. Aug. *Ad Donatist. post Coll.* 14.18 = CSEL 53: 115–16). In his later report on the third day of the council, Augustine specifically states what this date was: "Nam gesta martyrum quibus ostendebatur tempus persecutionis consulibus facta sunt Diocletiano novies et Maximiano octies pridie idus februarias" (*Brev. Coll.* 3.17.32; CCL 149A: 297), which is to say 12 February 304. I accept this as valid. I can only presume that the consular year-date was deliberately "obscured" in the new preface to the document written by a later dissident editor of the documents, precisely because the date of 304 was not supportive of their interpretation of the "council" of Cirta. The full document as we now have it, I presume, is the "edited" one produced in the aftermath of the Conference of 411, obviously as a confection of the dissidents: see also Dearn (2004) for detailed argument.

authorities, had surrendered to pressure and had handed over the Holy Scriptures to be burnt in public.[19] He had committed this act of betrayal at some point before the arrests of the Christians began in earnest. The books of scriptures were brought into the forum of Abitina to be fired in a conflagration that was witnessed by the Christians of the town. A sudden rainfall and hailstorm miraculously prevented the destruction of the holy books, or so the writer of the martyr narrative asserts. The justification of the terrible sufferings, the incarcerations, the judicial tortures, and the executions inflicted on the Christians of Abitina was that they had refused to surrender God's laws. Unlike the traitors, including, most shamefully, their own bishop, they defended the integrity of the scriptures and refused to hand them over to the authorities. The whole point of the story that retold the anguish of the martyrs from Abitina – a record that was read aloud every year in dissident churches throughout Africa – imprinted this historical fact on the minds of subsequent generations.

A dissident sectarian who later added to the narrative of the Abitinian martyrs made the issue of betrayal manifest in his vivid introduction to the story of their execution.[20]

The person who is enriched by the belief of our most holy faith is happy and is glorified in Christ. He rejoices in our Lord's Truth. He condemns error so that he might hold fast to the Catholic Church and so that he can distinguish the holy communion from the profane. Let him read the acts of the martyrs which have been inscribed in the indispensable archive of memory so that, with the passage of the ages, the glory of the martyrs and the damnation of the traitors will never be forgotten.

The serial redactions of this story by the hands of later dissident writers allows us to see some of their perspective, including their claim, as this writer states, that *they*, the dissidents, were "the Catholic Church." Although the martyrs and the traitors are vitally connected with each other – both are shown to be part of the same living Christian community – they are presented as completely opposite types. There is no grey area between them. The aim of the story, as the writer states, was to provoke imitation

---

[19] *Passio sanctorum Dativi, Saturnini presbyteri et aliorum*, 3 (Maier, *Dossier*, I, no. 4, p. 64): "In isto namque foro iam pro dominicis scripturis dimicaverat caelum, cum Fundanus ipsius civitatis quondam episcopus scripturas dominicas traderet exurendas." For context, see Monceaux, *Hist. litt.* 5, pp. 53–59.

[20] *Passio sanctorum Dativi, Saturnini presbyteri et aliorum*, 1 (Maier, *Dossier*, I, no. 4, pp. 59–60): "Qui religionis sanctissimae fide praeditus exsultat et gloriatur in Christo quique dominica veritate gaudet, errore damnato, ut ecclesiam catholicam teneat, sanctam quoque communionem a profana discernat, acta martyrum legat quae necessario in archivo memoriae conscripta sunt ne, saeculis transeuntibus, obsolesceret et gloria martyrum et damnatio traditorum!"

of correct behavior: the reader was to be ready to die in defense of the scriptures and to avoid the fate of becoming a traitor.[21] The aim of the author in manipulating the narrative was that the listener would learn "the rewards of the martyrs and the punishments of the traitors."[22] The story therefore embodies a series of responses – in this case by at least two sectarians, one writing soon after the division between the two churches and one rather later.[23] Both dissident writers were using the powerful emotions surrounding the story of the martyrs to mobilize sentiment and action by highlighting the inflammatory issue of betrayal.

The basic lesson imparted by these later fabrications about the Christians of Abitina is that some persons in 304 had kept the faith in the war against the Devil, whereas others, faced by this same critical test, "fell away from the main path of the faith." These other despicable persons had betrayed God's words to non-Christians so that they could be burned in fire. The optimistic finale of the narrative, however, was that the bad were outnumbered by the good.[24]

To save these same writings, what great numbers of people freely poured out their blood for them. Filled with God, and having defeated the Devil and having laid him low, in their suffering they waved the palm branch of victory. With their own blood, they sealed the final sentence against the traitors and their supporters. *This* was the judgment by which they cast them out from communion with the Church. For it is not right that there should be both martyrs and traitors together in the Church of God.

In the sequence of tortures that the loyal endured, the attacks were inflicted first on the body of the priest Saturninus. The priest is shown to be more faithful to preaching the word of God than was his own

---

[21] *Passio sanctorum Dativi, Saturnini presbyteri et aliorum*, 1 (Maier, *Dossier*, 1, no. 4, p. 60): "consulto quidem hoc faciens duplici scilicet modo, ut et imitatoribus eorum ad martyrium animos praeparemus" [the other aim being to preserve memory of the persons themselves].

[22] *Passio sanctorum Dativi, Saturnini presbyteri et aliorum*, 1 (Maier, *Dossier*, 1, no. 4, p. 61): "et praemia martyrum et poenas quis noverit traditorum."

[23] Monceaux, *Hist.litt.* 5, p. 56, draws a rather severe, but useful, distinction between the two subsequent redactors: the first "intelligent" and "moderate," the second "a hate-filled and brutal pamphleteer, only half literate." It would seem that the first writer actually knew the circumstances of 304; he might have been writing in the aftermath of the crisis of 317; the second was writing much later and was, indeed, a pamphleteer, indicating the crisis of 347 or a later one.

[24] *Passio sanctorum Dativi, Saturnini presbyteri et aliorum*, 2 (Maier, *Dossier*, 1, no. 4, pp. 61–62): "Et quamvis tradendo gentilibus scripturas dominicas atque testamenta divina profanis ignibus comburenda a fidei cardine cecidere nonnulli, conservando tamen ea et pro ipsis libenter suum sanguinem effundendo fortiter fecere quam plurimi. Quique pleni Deo, devicto ac prostrato Diabolo, victoriae palmam in passione gestantes, sententiam in traditores atque in eorum consortes qua illos ab ecclesiae communione reiecerant cuncti martyres proprio sanguine consignabant; fas enim non fuerat ut in ecclesia Dei simul essent martyres et traditores."

bishop.[25] The sequence of tortures finally ends with the reader, Emeritus, in whose house the meetings of the faithful were held. Readers held a special position in the Great Persecution precisely because they possessed copies of the scriptures that the authorities were seeking. The questions put to him by the governor Anullinus therefore repeatedly focussed on the question of whether or not Emeritus had any scriptures in his house at Abitina.[26] In response to the governor's demands, Emeritus replies, again and again, that he knows the scriptures since they are "written down in my heart." His words provoke the comment by the author of the narrative: "O martyr, best and most diligent guardian of the sacred law! Struck with horror at the crime of the traitors, he had placed the scriptures of the Lord in the innermost recesses of his heart, so that he would not lose them."[27]

This second narrator of the deaths of the Abitinian martyrs, who added his own views in a piece appended to the end of the narrative – a little pamphlet of violent disposition – is more passionate and forceful in his words. In a fervid and fiery rhetoric he denounces the "shamelessness of the traitors."[28] With the rhythmic attacking style of a preacher, he emphasizes, again and again, that their fatal flaw was that of betrayal:

The Holy Church follows the example of the martyrs and curses the treachery of the traitor Mensurius... What person... could think that the church of the martyrs and the conventicles of the traitors are one and the same thing? No one! No one! The two are *absolutely* hostile to each other! They are as opposite to each other as light is to darkness, life to death, a holy angel to the Devil, Christ to the Antichrist... The good and faithful must carefully avoid the conspiracy of the traitors, the houses [i.e. churches] of the hypocrites, and the opinions of the Pharisees.

They had better, for not to do so was to associate oneself "with the polluted traitors."[29]

---

[25] Insofar as it might have had a name in antiquity, the story probably bore the title *Acta Saturnini*, since it was Saturninus' martyrdom that was the model of behavior that was being exalted, while the response of Fundanus, by comparison, was being condemned.

[26] For the *lectores*, see the parallel search conducted by municipal magistrates at Cirta in May of 303: *Gesta apud Zenophilum* (CSEL 26: 187–88). In this case: *Passio sanctorum Dativi, Saturnini presbyteri et aliorum*, 12 (Maier, *Dossier*, I, no. 4: 75): "Cui tali precanti haec proconsul iniecit, 'Habes ergo scripturas aliquas in domo tua?'"

[27] *Passio sanctorum Dativi, Saturnini presbyteri et aliorum*, 12 (Maier, *Dossier*, I, no. 4, p. 76): "O martyrem legis sacrae idoneum diligentissimumque custodem. Qui traditorum facinus perhorrescens scripturas dominicas ne perderet intra secreta sui pectoris collocavit."

[28] It is difficult to desist from quoting Monceaux's vivid denunciation of the author: "Tel est cet étrange pamphlet, tout vibrant du haine, où la dévotion se mêle à la violence... L'oeuvre est médiocre, assurément: lourde et brutale, confuse, incohérente" (*Hist. litt.* 5, p. 59).

[29] *Passio sanctorum Dativi, Saturnini presbyteri et aliorum*, 21–22 (Maier, *Dossier*, I, no. 4, pp. 89–90): "Exinde ecclesia sancta sequitur martyres et detestatur Mensurii perfidiam traditoris... quinam..."

Because of the myriad consequences that were seen to flow from the primal act of betrayal, it was constructed as the defining moment that divided the two communities. Not long after assuming office as the bishop of Carthage in the mid-360s, Parmenian, the dissident Primate of Africa, composed a five-volume work against his sectarian enemies entitled *On the Church of the Traitors*, the *De ecclesia traditorum*, a work of attacking polemic aimed at the Catholics. Not surprisingly, it provoked a longer six-book reply by Optatus, the Catholic bishop of Milevis – and later, an even longer seven-book version from the same hand.[30] One side conceived the other as a nest of traitors, and so a visceral animus and unshakable convictions about rights and wrongs entered the conflict. And, after all, the effects of hatreds engendered by betrayal were well known from the ordinary experiences of daily life.[31]

> There are many examples in everyday life of what we're saying here. Sometimes your dearest friend has a personal enemy who is a friend to both of you. What is the person left in the middle to do? Your friend wants, insists, begs you to hate with him the one whom he has begun to hate, and speaks to you with these words: "You are not my friend since you are my enemy's friend" . . . If you hear terrible things about each of them from the other, you should not betray them to the other, or else, although enemies now they might become friends later and betray to each other their own betrayers.

The emotions of anger and hatred that naturally occurred in mundane daily personal acts of deceit could easily be understood by everyone. Each parishioner had events in his or her own life from which they could readily sense the same violent feelings generated by the past events of their own community.

In the year 307, the Christians who rejected the election of Caecilian as bishop of Carthage elected their own man, Maiorinus, as bishop of the metropolis. Whether he deserved it or not, Caecilian had come to be stained with the name of traitor, as had the men who had ordained him as bishop. Here, too, distaste ran so deep that the very name was both fixed in memory and avoided like the plague in the aftermath. No dissident is found bearing the name Caecilianus in the aftermath of his ordination as bishop. Other Catholic bishops and high-ranking "pagan" officials of the

---

unum atque idem esse existimet et ecclesiam martyrum et conventicula traditorem? Nemo, scilicet, quoniam haec inter se ita repugnant contrariaque sunt sibi ut lux tenebris, vita morti, sanctus angelus diabolo, Christus Antichristo . . . Quam ob rem fugienda bonis et vitanda semper est religiosis conspiratio traditorum, hypocritarum domus pharisaeorumque sententia." " . . . eos pollutis traditoribus iungens sub praetextu sanctissimae religionis exstinguat."

[30] Monceaux, *Hist. litt.*, 5, pp. 227–30.   [31] Aug. *Sermo* 49.6 (CCL 41: 618).

age bear the name, but no dissident ever perpetuated it.[32] The intensity of feelings that provoked this kind of memory and will to forget can be sensed from the hearings before the governor of Numidia, Zenophilus, in the year 320.[33] It was one of those typical outings of internal quarrels in which much dirty laundry is ventilated in a public venue. In this hearing, all of it was dirt from within the ranks of the dissident church, a church that portrayed itself as the assembly of the white, the spotless, and the pure.

For some unknown reason, a deacon named Nundinarius in the church at Cirta had entered into a quarrel with his bishop Silvanus.[34] The hostility between the two men became bitter. But it was Nundinarius' circulation of a written statement containing a record of the misdeeds of Silvanus that forced the bishop's hand: he had Nundinarius stoned.[35] Frustrated by the throttlehold that Silvanus had over the church and his own inability to make any headway, Nundinarius took his campaign against his own bishop to the bishops of the neighboring communities. In the manner typical of an aggrieved person who harps away at a litany of personal injustices, Nundinarius visited fellow clerics, collated damning documents, and repeatedly circulated letters and written petitions in support of his case. Meeting with no favorable response and perhaps even disinterest on this front, Nundinarius threatened to go public with the whole matter – an alarming prospect for the clergy in the local hierarchy. They knew that there was good evidence that they were guilty of the most heinous crime of all: the betrayal of God's words and properties to state authorities. Although these acts had been committed some seventeen years earlier in the throes of the Great Persecution, memories and feelings about them in the local Christian community were still alive and intense, and therefore dangerous.

---

[32] See the entries on Caecilian in PAC, pp. 165–79; on the parallel fate of the name Quisling, see Akerström, *Betrayal and Betrayers*, p. 28.

[33] For the text of the *Gesta apud Zenophilum*, see C. Ziwsa's "Appendix: Decem monumentorum veterum ad Donatistarum historiam pertinentium," in his edition of Optatus' works: CSEL 26: 185–97; and Maier, *Dossier*, 1, no. 29: 211–39, who reprints the text of von Soden–von Campenhausen, *Urkunden des Donatismus*, pp. 37–50. The whole of it depends on one manuscript, the Colbertinus no. 1951 = BN, Parisinus, no. 1711, from which the last pages of the proceedings before the governor have been lost. Duval, *Chrétiens d'Afrique*, pp. 70–85, provides a photocopy of the original manuscript. On background, see De Veer (1968f).

[34] On the man, see De Veer (1968g); since Nundinarius was not in the clergy of the church in 303, but was later ordained in his position as deacon by the bishop Silvanus, the very man with whom he quarreled, the incident must have taken place some time after 305: *Gesta apud Zenophilum*, 11; in the letter of Sabinus (?) to Silvanus (CSEL 26: 191): "quem (sc. Nundinarium) tu nutristi et ordinasti."

[35] *Gesta apud Zenophilum*, 7; in the letter of the bishop Purpurius to Silvanus (CSEL 26: 189): "Manu sua enim mihi tradidit libellum rei gestae, pro qua causa tuo praecepto fuerit lapidatus"; 10: in the letter of the bishop Fortis, to the clergy and Elders (CSEL 26: 191): "ut talem insaniam passi a quibus lapidarentur pro veritate."

The fear provoked repeated pleas on the part of several of the bishops, citing biblical verses in support, not to take matters between "Christian brothers" to the civil courts. They expressed fears about the dangers
involved should these inside matters become public. Their letters are filled
with pleas for reconciliation and the need to hush up the entire matter.
Almost every one of their missives ends with the mantra: "Let no one
know."[36] Their implorings did not move either side. Nundinarius went off
to the civil courts with his dossier of documents. The case was heard at
Cirta on 13 December 320 by the governor Zenophilus who was, indeed,
not a Christian.[37] Prize among the documents that Nundinarius submitted
to the court was a copy of a record from the municipal archives of Cirta,
a schedule that carefully recorded the search made by municipal officials
in May 303 in accordance with the emperor Diocletian's decree.[38] Among
other things, it revealed the collaboration of the bishop Paul, as well as of
several of his clergy, including the (then) subdeacon Silvanus. Despite the
fact that this official municipal record clearly indicated who had handed
over the codices of the sacred scriptures to the authorities in 303, in the
trial in 320 the guilty went to great lengths to deny that they had ever done
such a thing. In the hearing before Zenophilus, Victor the grammarian,
who held the position of Reader in the events of 303, tried to claim that he
was not even in Cirta at the time. "If I'm lying, may I perish," he added
for good effect. But the official proceedings showed that he *was* at Cirta
in 303, that he *did* hand over the scriptures – in short, that he was lying.
His behavior was normal. The greater fault of betrayal was covered by the
lesser sin of mendacity.

To avoid the label of traitor, every kind of evasive action was taken.
The governor Zenophilus asked one witness, Saturninus, if he knew that
Silvanus, his bishop, was a traitor. Saturninus knew full well, but the most

---

[36] Every one of the bishops' letters, directed to Silvanus himself and, separately, to the clergy and Elders
of the church at Cirta, begged for a reconciliation between the two men; all emphasize the urgent
need to hush up the whole matter: *Gesta apud Zenophilum*, 7: Purpurius to Silvanus (CSEL 26: 189):
"Omnes nos occiditis"; 8: Purpurius to clergy and Elders (CSEL 26: 190): "Elaborate, nemo sciat,
quae sit coniuratio haec"; 9: letter of Fortis to Silvanus (CSEL 26: 190): "Nemo sciat"; 11: letter of
Sabinus (?) to Silvanus (CSEL 26: 192): "Nemo sciat." 12: letter of Sabinus to Fortis (CSEL 26: 192):
"Nemo sciat."

[37] It is difficult to understand what the formal charge was. The incipit to the proceedings says that the
main finding was to have shown that Silvanus was a collaborator (*traditor*), but it is almost certain
that civil court headed by a Roman governor under Constantine would not have agreed to hear such
a charge. The introduction is therefore a later "Donatist" addition. Under what heading, therefore,
did Nundinarius petition the court to hear his case?

[38] Nundinarius had this document, recording the search made by municipal officials at Cirta on
19 May 303, read into the record of the proceedings: *Gesta apud Zenophilum*, 3–5 (CSEL 26: 186–88;
Maier, *Dossier*, 1, no. 29, pp. 217–22).

that he could bring himself to admit was that Silvanus had "handed over a silver lamp."[39] Silvanus himself behaved no differently. In his campaigning to be elected bishop at Cirta, Silvanus had made a speech to the assembled Christians in which he downplayed the extent of his betrayal. Perhaps he had not really betrayed anything at all? "For what do they call me a traitor? For a mere lamp and a casket?"[40] He, too, was not averse to outright lying.[41] A direct confrontation with betrayal was made, however, when the primate of Numidia, Secundus of Tigisis, held a mini-conference at Cirta on 13 May 306, in which he directly confronted the bishops who were about to ordain Silvanus as the newly elected bishop of the city.[42] Asking each bishop if he himself was involved in handing over the scriptures to the authorities, Secundus met with obfuscation, excuses, and lies. They had turificated, but not much else; they had handed over medical books instead of real scriptures; they had handed over scriptures that were in such bad condition that they really didn't count as scriptures. The excuses worked, in part, because a sufficient number accepted them. After all, whatever his terrible deeds, the people had still elected Silvanus as their bishop and he had been ordained by fellow bishops, whose numbers included admitted "traitors" and a self-confessed murderer.

The powerful place of betrayal within the dissident church at Cirta in the first generations of the conflict is a small sign of how it was to configure sentiments on both sides in almost every local church in Africa. The dislikes on either side came to be set in fixed patterns not only because of the deep-seated emotions fired by betrayal, but also because no one could deny that such an act was in itself a very bad if not an evil thing. There was little room for maneuver. On the one side, the dissidents were able to launch a devastating *j'accuse* at the Catholics, who had little room to maneuver by which to extract themselves from the indelible polluting stain of the charge. One good defense was to say "well, you did it too." Documents, such as those relating to the behavior of the dissident bishop Silvanus at Cirta, were carefully preserved to demonstrate that there was good evidence to prove that clergy on the dissident side had behaved in

---

[39] *Gesta apud Zenophilum*, 14 (CSEL 26: 193): "Zenophilus v. c. consularis dixit: 'Silvanum scis esse traditorem?' Saturninus dixit: 'Scio lucernam tradidisse argenteam.'"

[40] *Gesta apud Zenophilum*, 15 (CSEL 26: 193)): "Ibi coepit alloqui populum dicens: 'De quo dicunt me traditorem esse, de lucerna et capitulata?'"

[41] Duval, *Chrétiens d'Afrique*, p. 73.

[42] The transcript of the proceedings was quoted by Augustine, *Contra Cresc.* 3.27.30 (CSEL 52: 435–37 = Maier, *Dossier*, 1, no. 7, pp. 115–18); on the date, see Appendix B.

no less traitorous a fashion.[43] There was a bolder defense: "There's been a mistake here. Actually, we can show that it was *you* and not we who did it." But such counter-strategies only tended to reinforce the feeling that whatever it was that had been done was an indelible and ineradicable wrong. In the legislation passed by their church council in 348 at Carthage, even the Catholics publicly excoriated the crime of betrayal or *traditio*, stating that it had already been condemned by councils of their forefathers.[44] It was a grave error. It is just that *we* did not do it. In his popular *Song against the Donatists*, Augustine preferred this harder line: "It was *you* who actually did it."[45]

> *They* betrayed themselves to the Devil
> while they fight about the issue of betrayal,
> and the crime which *they* committed
> they wish to charge against others.
> *They* themselves handed over the [sacred] books
> and yet *they* dare to accuse us,
> so that they commit a crime that is worse
> than the one they committed before.

The counter-move was already a long-standing tactic by the time Augustine composed his song in the early 390s.

In the mid-360s, Optatus, the Catholic bishop of Milevis, counted betrayal as among the three or four basic issues that divided the two churches. It is not accidental that this was what he tackled first – the problem to which he devoted the whole of the first book of his reply to Parmenian's attack on the Catholics. The emphasis was appropriate and logical, since Optatus' riposte was directed against Parmenian's work that bore the title *The Church of the Traitors*.[46] The damnation of betrayal and the traitors was something that Optatus shared with his opponents: "Along with you, we too condemn traitors."[47] The first book of his massive

---

[43] *Gesta apud Zenophilum* (CSEL 26: 185–97), see Duval, *Chrétiens d'Afrique*, esp. pp. 65–73; see "Silvanus (1)," PAC, pp. 1078–80.

[44] Concil. Carth. 348, canon 14 (CCL 149: 10): "Sane credo vos tenere multis conciliis a patribus nostris et traditionem esse damnatam et rebaptizationis impietatem esse puniendam; quas res etiam nostro concilio credo iam terminum accepisse."

[45] Aug. *Psalmus contra partem Donat.* 24–27 (BA 28: 152–54): "Diabolo se tradiderunt cum pugnant de traditione / et crimen quod commiserunt, in alios volunt transferre. / Ipsi tradiderunt libros et nos audent accusare, / ut peius committant scelus quam quod commiserunt ante."

[46] Optatus, *Contra Parm.* 1.5.4–7 (SC 412: 182); 1.6.2 (SC 412: 184): "Tertio loco traditores nullis certis personis aut nominibus accusasti" (i.e., as third in sequence among the five issues to which Optatus will have to reply); 1.7.1 (SC 412: 184): "Sed mihi videtur primo loco traditorum et schismaticorum indicandas esse civitates, personas et nomina."

[47] Optatus, *Contra Parm.* 2.13.2 (SC 412: 266): "Traditores vobiscum et ipsi damnamus" ("as you remember that I have demonstrated in the first book of my work," he adds).

broadside against Parmenian was composed to prove that it was in fact "the others" who had committed the despicable act of betrayal. Once this fact was established, Optatus was not far from making a genetic argument: since these people were your "parents" and you are their "heirs," it is *you* who *inherited* the primal stigma of betrayal. "Since we have shown when and who were the traitors and what the real origin of the division was," is the statement with which Optatus began the second book of his counterattack, referring back to the argument that he had just finished in the first book of his treatise.[48] That is the position that he had reached in the summary at the end of his treatment of the origins of the conflict between the two communities.[49]

A little earlier, we showed that *your parents* were the ones who were the schismatics and traitors. And *you* who are the heir of these very same persons did not wish to spare either the traitors or the schismatics . . . all the spears that you wished falsely to hurl against others, repelled by the shield of the Truth, have been deflected back with a return blow against your parents. Therefore everything which you were able to claim against traitors and schismatics in fact concerns *you*.

Optatus never once denies the terrible stigma of betrayal. His interest was to show *who* it was that had received this *damnosa hereditas* from their ancestors. Although cast in formal legal language, the idea of a primal sin that had been inherited in an almost congenital fashion was never far away.

In his counterattacking books against Parmenian, Optatus returned again and again to this primal act, beginning each book with a phrase like "having shown in my first book who the traitors really were."[50] Although there are other issues to which he attends – both theological ones like the status of baptism and more secular ones like "who" was responsible for the use of secular force – the hue of this base tint colours all of the rest. The stories of the original acts of betrayal, and Optatus' construal of them, anchors his entire work. The same issue, surely, must have constituted the substance of Parmenian's attack on the Catholics. But there is more. The first six-book version of Optatus' reply to Parmenian was published in the mid-360s. About two decades later, he felt compelled to return to

---

[48] Optatus, *Contra Parm.* 2.1.1 (SC 412: 236): "Quoniam et qui fuerint traditores ostensum est et schismatis origo ita monstrata est."

[49] Optatus, *Contra Parm.* 1.28.2–3 (SC 412: 234): "Paulo ante docuimus vestros parentes fuisse schismaticos et traditores. Et tu ipsorum heres nec schismaticis nec traditoribus parcere voluisti . . . omnia tela quae falso in alieno iactare voluisti veritatis clipeo repulsa in tuos parentes reciproco ictu vertuntur. Omnia igitur quae a te in traditores et schismaticos dici potuerunt vestra sunt."

[50] Optatus, *Contra Parm.* 2.1.1 (SC 412: 236): "Quoniam et qui fuerint traditores ostensum est"; 5.1.1 (SC 413: 110): "Traditores legis qui fuerint . . . in primo libro manifestissimis documentis ostendimus".

the line of battle with a new edition of his work, this time adding a supplemental seventh book. Returning to the core problem of the cause of the division between the two Christian communities in Africa, he began the new book with the telling phrase, "having shown who were the traitors." What had remained such a pressing issue in the intervening two decades in Christian communities that Optatus felt that he had to add a seventh book to his original attack? The answer is betrayal, and the question of how the traitors and their descendants were to be treated.

The issue had continued to smolder, not only because of its fixed place in the whole debate, but also because in the interim an interesting dissident riposte to the Catholics had developed: If *we* are the traitors, as *you* say, then why are there all these hard demands and coercive measures to compel us to enter your church? If we're that bad, why even bother? This is the question that Optatus attempted to answer in the new seventh book that he appended to the first edition of his *Against Parmenian*. It was a difficult and complex matter. The subversive counter-question that Optatus had to create was: What grounds existed on which the Catholics could be forgiven for the primal act of betrayal? The rhetorical subterfuge that allowed him to avoid answering the dangerous question was simply to reverse the equation. By founding his answer on his earlier "proven" position that it was the dissidents whom he had demonstrated to have been the traitors, he could answer the same question by wittily giving a whole string of reasons about why *your* ancestors might have been exonerated of the stigma of betrayal. In this way, Optatus could suggest to the dissidents, without having to say so in actual words: Here are a series of just defenses that *we* could offer against the charge of betrayal. The whole of the additional book was made up of a series of arguments about grounds on which collaboration with the authorities might be excused.[51]

The problem is that the crime or, worse, the sin of betrayal had become so heavily valued by the process of accusation and counter-accusation that the attacks and counterattacks – of which Parmenian and Optatus' works were part – only served to make it more important. It was a terrible crime. It is *you* who did it rather than us. *You* committed an even worse crime by having the audacity falsely to accuse *us* of it. There can be no denial that sacred books were handed over. But the welter of criss-crossing accusations about who actually did it only succeeded in fixing the conviction in both sides that the act was never in issue as an immoral and criminal thing of such momentous consequence that it damned the perpetrators to perdition.

---

[51] These closely match the list in Akerström: *Betrayal and Betrayers*, pp. 11 f.

Talk of this kind, rife in the polemical writings of both sides, only served further to entrench a conviction about the transcendent evil of betrayal. So Augustine spun it, yet again, in the lines of his popular song:[52]

> Because rumour was already spreading the news
> concerning the betrayal of the [sacred] books,
> those who committed the act were concealing
> themselves in the confusion and uproar.
> Behind this cover, they began falsely to accuse others
> so that they would be able to hide themselves.

The insidious nature of the struggle was such that the hypocrisy of these words was perhaps not manifest even to an Augustine. After all, he could just as easily have been writing them of Optatus and others among his fellow bishops.

Any aspect of crossing over to the other side, of betraying one's own community of belief, came to be measured with a heightened sensitivity. To do anything that associated oneself with *traditio* was something that connected the culprit with the original indelible polluting stain.[53] The long history of the competing arguments over the acts of betrayal in the persecution of 303–05 influenced almost all aspects of other ecclesiastical debates. But in a paradoxical, one might say hypocritical sense, betrayal was precisely what each side was hoping for in the members of the other. For the reasons just adduced, they could not openly say that it was so. And so, more hypocrisy. For Catholics to ask the members of the dissident Christian community to leave the church of their birth, the church of their ancestors, and their own communion, to go over to the right side – to the side of peace, unity and the truth – was to ask them to turn on their basic loyalties. "Donatists" were encouraged to give up everything that was important to them – in short, to betray themselves and their core values. To ask persons who defined their very existence in terms of the transcendentally negative value of a primal act of betrayal to engage in such a traitorous act themselves was to ask too much.

The issue of betrayal was so incendiary that everyone who wished to count was compelled to take his or her own position on it. Its centrality continued to provoke the production of whole literary works that were

---

[52] Aug. *Psalmus contra partem Donat.* vv. 66–68 (BA 28: 158–60): "Quia fama iam loquebatur / de librorum traditione. / Sed qui fecerant latebant / in illa perturbatione. / Inde alios infamarunt / ut se ipsos possent celare."

[53] Lamirande (1965c).

devoted to the problem.[54] The fascination with traitors riveted the thinking and emotions of all who shared in the struggle.[55] They returned to the subject of infidelity time and again, as it was colorfully put in one of the favorite Proverbs frequently quoted in the age, like dogs to their own vomit. The conviction that the Catholic bishops were the congenital heirs of the original traitors in the Great Persecution and that they suffered from an indelible and polluting stain of betrayal served to construct a permanent no-go zone between the two sides. Primian, the dissident bishop of Carthage, was compelled to reply to a Catholic request, supported by the Roman governor of Africa in mid-September of 403, that the two sides meet in a conference to discuss their differences. In the letter of reply delivered by one of his deacons to the proconsul, he angrily noted that "it is not right for the sons of martyrs and the offspring of traitors to meet together."[56]

A PERFECT HATRED

Despite its brevity, the Diocletianic persecution in Africa had such an intense impact that betrayal or *traditio* had become central to all subsequent Christian identity in Africa. It engendered the perfect hatred.[57] No one, on either side, had enough latitude to reconfigure the essentially evil nature of such an act. If implicated, other avenues of apology had to be taken. Optatus offers what must early on have become a common set of defenses. First, the documentary record proved that some of the most important luminaries of the dissidents' own church had betrayed the scriptures to the authorities. If there were incurable faults incurred by the act of betrayal, then "they were just as blameworthy in your people whom we have shown to have been traitors."[58] It is a line that he returns to again and again: If something is not permitted to certain men because they were traitors, then it ought not to be allowed to your people, whose leaders we have proven to have been traitors."[59] Another defense was that the specific men who had

---

[54] Gennadius, *De scriptoribus ecclesiasticis*, 4 (PL 58: 1063) mentions a Vitellius Afer "the African" who had written a work on the subject in the reign of Constans: "Vitellius Afer Donatianorum schisma defendens scripsit *De eo quod odio sint mundi servi Dei*... Scripsit et adversum gentes et adversum nos velut traditores in persecutione divinarum scripturarum... Claruit sub Constante, filio Constantini principis."

[55] So in the classic work of Georg Simmel, "The Fascination of Betrayal," ch. 4.3.2 in K. H. Wolff, ed., *The Sociology of Georg Simmel*, New York, 1950/1964, pp. 333–34.

[56] Aug. *Ad Donatist. post Collat.* 1.1 (CSEL 53: 98), quoted by Augustine at the Conference of 411: GCC 3.116 (SC 224: 1074): "Indignum est ut in unum conveniant filii martyrum et progenies traditorum."

[57] Aug. *En. in Ps.* 138.27 (CCL 40: 2009–10), discourses on this kind of hatred at some length.

[58] Optatus, *Contra Parm.* 1.5.4 (SC 412: 182).

[59] Optatus, *Contra Parm.* 1.5.6 (SC 412: 182): "Si traditoribus non licet, vobis licere non debuit, quorum principes probamus fuisse traditores."

been accused of betrayal were innocent. Using documents that an earlier Catholic source had carefully assembled, Optatus could demonstrate that neither Caecilian nor the men who had ordained him as bishop had been convicted of handing over sacred scriptures or vessels or of surrendering churches to the persecuting authorities.[60]

The problem was that the collected documents were less than manifest in their exculpation or condemnation of anyone. They were difficult to decipher, obscure, and hard to understand, and so probably did not have the desired impact on those who firmly believed that the acts of betrayal had been committed by the other side. The written word, even authoritative Roman court records, would have to prevail against a long and deeply entrenched oral tradition – rumor as it was called in Augustine's pop song – that sustained a simpler and more powerful narrative. Against the written records, it was known that official documents could be faked. Their effect was limited. They would have to countervail a huge world of verbal talk. This is where the power of common discourse was finally rooted: in every field and at every street corner. As much had to be admitted in sermons delivered to attentive congregations, since parishioners encountered this sort of behavior in their daily life. "Brothers, at every street corner you hear their strident accusations: 'That man was a traitor... and that man over there, he was a traitor too.'"[61] Such identifications affected judgments of actions, the most significant of these being baptism. Which also led to verbal confrontations: "Who gave that baptism to you?" a dissident asks, and then he tells you: "A wicked person gave it to you." "Didn't *someone* give it to me?" the Catholic asks. "Sure *someone* gave it to you, but he was a traitor," is the reply.[62] Or again, a dissident might walk up to a Catholic and say: "That man betrayed the sacred books." No, he didn't. "But, I tell you, that man certainly *did* betray the sacred books," is the persistent and confident retort.[63]

The emotional experience of betrayal was recursively replayed for Christians, whether dissident or Catholic, as part of their normal church-going. For just as their different churches had been born out of a primal act of

---

[60] Optatus, *Contra Parm.* 1.6.2 (SC 412: 184): "Tertio loco traditores nullis certis personis aut nominibus accusasti"; and 1.7.1 (SC 412: 184): "Sed mihi videtur primo loco traditorum et schismaticorum indicandas esse civitates, personas et nomina, ut quae a te de his dicta sunt, veros auctores et certos reos suos agnoscant."

[61] Aug. *En. in Ps.* 95.11 (CCL 39: 1350): "Ille tradidit, et ille tradidit."

[62] Aug. *Tract. in Ioh.* 5.13.2 (CCL 36: 48); to which the supplementary conversation is added: even if he was a bishop, he was a bishop in communion with them, and the "them" are traitors: 5.13.4 (CCL 36: 48).

[63] Aug. *Sermo* 88.19.21 (PL 38: 550).

betrayal, so had the very Christian Church itself. The most fundamental materials of the faith were readily to hand to be explicated in the elaboration of a more contemporary story of betrayal. Every year, as the Easter season approached, there was a heightened sense of the impending tragedy, the trial and execution of Jesus by Roman authorities, to be commemorated by believers over a prolonged and intense period of ritual action in ceremonials, readings, songs, and sermons. This foundational story of Christian faith hinged on the act of betrayal of Judas Iscariot. In the annual emphasis on betrayal, the surviving Easter sermons leave no doubt about how often Judas and his act of betrayal were brought up and intensely contemplated. The same story was also replayed in minor ways throughout the rest of the year. In every church service, as the mass drew to its conclusion, and the offertory prayers had been said, for example, there followed the Lord's Prayer, and the ritualistic "kiss of peace" exchanged by the worshipers. How were they to kiss each other?[64] "After this comes 'Peace be with you' – a great sacrament, the kiss of peace. So kiss in such a way as is really meaningful for Christian love. Don't be a Judas. Judas the traitor kissed Christ with his mouth, while setting a trap for him in his heart."[65] Both sides had the perfect model of betrayal and cosmic condemnation buried right in the heart of their sacred texts.

HE WHO IS NOT WITH ME IS AGAINST ME

One of the main tactical aims of both the Catholics and the dissidents was to encourage others to cross over to their own side. A dissident Christian would repent of his or her past error and become a true Catholic. Or the reverse. The most prestigious and spectacular transition was one that involved a ranking member of the ecclesiastical hierarchy in either church: a deacon, a priest or best of all, a bishop. It was hoped that the head of a congregation would be able to bring with him some or all of his flock. Both sides engaged in tactics of enticement. In the great reformation of their church that began in the early 390s, the Catholics made it a specific part of their church policy to encourage crossovers and to offer inducements that would help them to make the transition. Among the sweeteners was the preservation of rank and status. For one side, such a crossing over was happily construed as seeing the light, recognizing what was right, admitting the truth, entering into blessed unity, or embracing the general peace. The other saw it as an individual act of treachery, vitally connected with the

---

[64] Aug. *Sermo* 229.3 (PL 38: 1103).   [65] Aug. *Sermo* 229.3 = Denis 6 (MiAg 1: 33–34).

whole history of betrayal. Yet if one side or the other was to win, then there would have to be many betrayals and many real traitors.

Nothing could disguise the fact that conversion was a species of betrayal. It was therefore advantageous to emphasize, where possible, that the numbers of such converts were substantial. Numbers imparted a sense of truth to claims of success, and bestowed legitimacy on the process.[66] "*Many* of them [i.e., the dissidents] recognize the truth because they have come to life again and at their arrival we rejoice daily in the name of Christ."[67] For the one side, these persons were traitors, while for the other they were thoughtful people who had reasonably come over – the neutral verb *transire* ("to cross over") was used – to the right side. What was involved was both a matter of construing what had happened and a numbers game.[68] If someone had not actually crossed over, a hostile critic could still achieve the same effect by claiming that they had, by planting rumours which, given time and distance, might be difficult to disprove. This is precisely what the dissident bishop Gaudentius of Thamugadi accused Augustine of doing in the decade after the Conference of 411: spreading rumours that men like dissident Bishop Emeritus, in distant Caesarea, had "gone over." It was a rumor that Augustine finally had to admit was false. Not only could actions be imputed; motives could be too. In conversion or betrayal – flip sides of the same coin – there were options. In the case of Emeritus, Augustine states that he *could* have crossed over, indeed *should* have, had he "yielded to the truth." But if Emeritus had embraced Catholic unity, then the dissidents in his own church would have said that he had done it out of fear, bowing to the forces of persecution.[69] It was not an unbelievable explanation. Obviously there were such traitors or converts and so each side needed a way to explain them away. The dissidents quoted Romans 3.3–4 to dilute the effect of the acts committed by their own traitors: just because a few have deserted does not destroy the faith of God. "Far from it!," they exclaimed.[70]

In his cutting response made in 405 to the grammarian and dissident lay exegete Cresconius, Augustine mentions that Cresconius had made a great to-do about the bishops Candidus and Donatus who had

---

[66] That numbers really counted: see MacMullen, *Voting About God*, pp. 12 f.
[67] Aug. *Tract. in Ioh.* 6.4.3 (CCL 36: 55).
[68] Crespin, "L'accueil des clercs convertis," 2.1.4 in *Ministère et sainteté*, pp. 170–74.
[69] Aug. *Contra Gaud.* 1.14.15 (CSEL 53: 209–10): "sed ponderi persecutionis humana infirmitate cessisse . . . suspicarentur hominem formidantem."
[70] Aug. *Contra Gaud.* 1.15.16 (CSEL 53: 210).

crossed over and had been accepted by the Catholics as bishops.[71] We know nothing about their motives or anything about the men themselves other than their names. Situations that called for internal discipline within one of the two churches – as probably the case of these two crossovers – might only succeed in driving the miscreants into the opposing camp. All kinds of misdeeds might call for discipline, but because of the public shame and dishonor incurred by them, matters of gross moral malfeasance were high on the list. In his debates with Petilian, Augustine noted a case that had been mentioned in the original letter circulated by the dissident. In it, Petilian had excoriated a crossover from "the Donatists" to the Catholics, presumably to castigate the impure motives that had provoked the opportune conversion. It was the case of one Quodvultdeus, a bishop who had been twice convicted by the dissident church of adulterous affairs and had been thrown out of their church. His logical response was to cross over to the Catholic side, where he was received, happily, into his new church.[72] He was not alone. Similar motives for betrayal are documented in the Conference of 411. There is the case of Vitalis, the dissident bishop of Mascula. Once he had declared his presence at the conference, Aurelius, the Catholic bishop of Macomades, leapt up and declared: "This Vitalis here was once a Catholic deacon in the city of Sitifis. Rebaptized by *them*, he was turned into a priest. Thrown out on a charge of adultery, he was then turned into a bishop."[73] External blandishments and opportunities on the one side, and internal hostilities and pressures on the other: the dual dynamic certainly provoked some of the conversions.

Harsh sectarian battles within the dissident church itself not unnaturally produced situations where alienated bishops would see the option of passing over to the other side as preferable to accepting punishment or a continued inferior status within their own communion. The conflict within the dissident church between Maximian and Primian, the mutually hostile bishops of Carthage in the early 390s, produced more than a few such traitors. By chance, we know of one of them. Two supporters of

---

[71] Aug. *Contra Cresc.* 2.10.12 (CSEL 52: 370): "nominando Candidum Villaregensium et Donatum Macomadiensem, qui ex vestris episcopis etiam apud nos episcopi fuerunt." As De Veer (1968b) points out, nothing is known about these men as bishops. A certain Cresconius was bishop of Villaregia around 400, and an Aurelius bishop of Macomades in 411 (GCC, 1.116 = SC 195: 706).

[72] Aug. *Contra litt. Petil.* 3.32.37 (CSEL 52: 192): "Quid quod etiam ipse posuit in epistula sua Quodvultdeum de duobus adulteriis apud vos convictum et abiectum a nostris esse susceptum?" For his identity, see PAC, "Quodvultdeus (4)," p. 946, whose compilers reject the identification of this man with Quodvultdeus (2), bishop of Centuriensis in Numidia, whose case was being heard at the Council of Milevis in August of 402 (CCL 149, p. 207).

[73] GCC 1.201 (SC 195: 866): "Iste Vitalis diaconus fuit Catholicus in civitate Sitifensi. Rebaptizatus, factus est presbyter. Proiectus est causa adulterii, et factus est postea episcopus."

Maximian were Felicianus, bishop of Musti, and Praetextatus, bishop of Assuras. The congregation of Assuras, staying loyal to the main dissident church, had taken matters into their own hands. Either before or shortly after the condemnation of Praetextatus, a replacement for him named Rogatus had been ordained. When the conflict between the two bishops of Carthage had finally been settled in favor of Primian, Rogatus must have had every expectation that he would remain the dissident bishop of Assuras – after all, he had been on the right side.[74] After the condemnation of Maximian, Rogatus, a "Primianist," must have had every reason to believe that he would be rewarded by having his seat confirmed. The result of a deal brokered by Optatus, the dissident bishop of Thamugadi, however, was that Felicianus and, more important to this case, Praetextatus of Assuras, the bishops who had supported the loser Maximian, were to be received back into the church and confirmed in their original positions. Rogatus' disappointment must have been profound, bordering, certainly, on a sense of betrayal by his own church. He had been stabbed in the back by his own people. What could he do? He could accept the humiliation or he could defect. Which is precisely what he did. He went over to the Catholics.

Within each church, attitudes towards these crossovers were especially bitter. They embodied a "stab in the back" that was unlikely to be forgotten for a long time. It is not surprising that so few of these converts advertised themselves. A certain Euticius attested in the hinterland of Hippo Regius – who was "dragged out of errror and reborn, and restored to the bosom of the Catholic faith" – is one of the few.[75] Although the existence of sectarian traitors and the labeling was not peculiar to African Christianity it had a special centrality in it.[76] If such detested persons became involved with their former colleagues and believers – which was likely to happen if they continued to serve in the same small town or village – the bitterness was compounded. In his second letter of reply to the imperial tribune Dulcitius in the year 419, Gaudentius, the dissident bishop of Thamugadi, gave voice to acrid complaints about a certain Gabinius. Gaudentius states that he could not agree that Gabinius was an innocent party to actions involving

---

[74] Aug. *Gesta cum Emerito*, 9 (CSEL 53: 192).

[75] Gagé, "Un donatiste rallié à l'église catholique," pt. 2 in (1935), 45–53; cf. Albertini in *BCTH* (1924), p. lxxvii and (1928), 90 n. 1: "Euticius quem genu[it . . . is]to in loco quies[cit]. / Errori subtractus [. . . postquam?] fuerat renat[us, / Cat[olicae fidei . . .] / est gremio reservat[us. / . . .] s(an)c(t)a progenies, quem [probavit ?] fides, / confessio[ne memo]riam, decoravi[sti aeter]nam ." Alas, the nature of the "error" from which he was saved is not certain, but Gagé's arguments for it being membership of the dissident church are appealing.

[76] For the parallel labeling of traitors and betrayers in the East see, e.g., Sizgorich, *Violence and Belief*, pp. 66 f., 75 f., 109 f. – all in the context of what he calls the "boundary defense" or policing of the community.

Gaudentius himself. The poison dripping from the word "innocent" is easier to understand, as is Gaudentius' bitterness, when we are told that Gabinius had been used in efforts "to discipline" Gaudentius. The hatred was fueled by a double hostility: not only was Gabinius working for the other side, he was also a traitor. Once a bishop in the dissident church, he had crossed over to the other side, to the Catholics, apparently some time in the aftermath of the measures of 412–14. Catholic bishops like Augustine naturally glossed this betrayal as a good thing: "Gabinius is now one of ours, who was once one of yours, just like very many others who crossed over from your side to ours once they had given due consideration to Catholic truth, men who do not seem to you to have been purged of your contagion."[77]

The common use of coercion in forcing people to convert, however, did offer a cover that effaced the impression of a nakedly voluntary and self-interested betrayal. If one was compelled by superior force and could not be expected to endure martyrdom, then one had been forced against one's will. It worked for each side. Both parents of Petilian, the renowned dissident bishop of Constantina, were Catholics. He himself had been a Catholic catechumen in the local church. He was a talented young man, a brilliant orator, and the dissidents were not about to let a good thing go to waste. They suddenly pounced on him one day, kidnapped him, rebaptized him, and ordained him as bishop of their city. All against his will, says Augustine. "What violence was done against one of ours. They dragged him to his death!" he exclaims.[78] But for Petilian, the compulsion was something that could be accepted, embraced, and presented as the heavy hand of the Almighty. He had been struck down, as it were, on his own little road to Damascus. Finding his way upwards blocked by the sitting Catholic bishop at Constantina, the ambitious Petilian might have wanted to "cross over" to a more powerful and available local community. If a voluntary move would have been construed as a terrible betrayal, then being kidnapped and forced to act against one's will neatly covered and defused that potential vice.

---

[77] Aug. *Contra Gaud.* 1.11.12 (CSEL 53: 206); Monceaux, perhaps correctly, identifies this Gabinius as the man who came to the Conference of Carthage in 411 as the Catholic bishop of Vegesala; followed by the editors of PAC, see "Gabinius," PAC, p. 515.

[78] See "Petilianus," PAC, pp. 855–68, at p. 856; Monceaux, "Petilianus de Constantine," *Hist. litt.* 6, pp. 3–5, at p. 5; Aug. *Contra litt. Petil.* 2.104.239 (CSEL 52: 155); *Sermo ad Caes. Pleb.* 8 (CSEL 53: 177): "Pars Donati quando praevalebat Constantinae, laicum nostrum catechumenum natum de parentibus catholicis Petilianum [mss: Petialius] tenuit, vim fecit nolenti, scrutatus est fugientem, invenit latentem, extraxit paventem, baptizavit trementem, ordinavit nolentem. Ecce qualem violentiam in nostro! Rapuit illa ad mortem." A fine rhetorical rampage. How much of it was actually so?

The reality of betrayal provoked two responses that can be seen in detail for only one side in this struggle. We can presume that both sides engaged in the same tactics. The first response was embedded in the oral and written communications in which betrayal and conversion were repeatedly glossed and explained in letters, pamphlets, and sermons. The other response was focussed on the institutional efforts that were made to reduce the incidence of crossing over. Both sides struggled to create a disciplinary structure that would impede betrayals and, if necessary, punish them severely. But such efforts were undercut by inducements to betrayal – glossed as conversions or returns to the truth – that both churches proffered. When Augustine addressed the Christians of Caesarea in 418, he began by drawing a distinction between those who were "original Catholics" and those who had "come over" from "the Donatist side." Although the latter had recognized their error and now saw the light and the truth, Augustine knew of and publicly acknowledged the distinction between long-standing Catholics – those who had been born into the community – and those who had recently entered it after abandoning their community of origin.

It is possible that the years after 412 witnessed many such converts for the Catholics.[79] This is usually asserted as fact, although there is nothing save the rhetorical claims of one side to support it. Even if the numbers were substantial, the problem was that the stigma of betrayal was fixed on these crossovers, even by the Catholic parishioners who were being asked to accept them into their community. The powerful effect of generations of hatred meant that the newcomers could not easily be received on equal terms. The problem excited much preaching on the theme of the prodigal son. Not a few of those who had remained steadfastly loyal to the Catholic Church through the previous generations felt that the new converts were second-class Christians. The normal stigma that attached to traitors or betrayers also attached to them, however well-meaning or exalted the grounds for their behavior.[80] The betrayals, although eagerly sought and encouraged by both sides, were potentially difficult in real life.

Not all persons who betrayed their own communities to go over to the other side, for whatever reason, made successful transitions. When a preacher cautioned his parishioners about these problems, he illustrated his warnings with examples of good and bad converts. He hints at the personal motives of some of the crossovers.[81]

---

[79] Aug. *Gesta cum Emerito,* 9 (CSEL 53: 192).
[80] Akerström, *Betrayal and Betrayers,* pp. 27 f., discusses the permanent contempt that attaches to crossovers.
[81] Aug. *En 2 in Ps.* 36.11 (CCL 38: 353–54).

It was the same when a certain man, having been accused and excommunicated by his own people, came over to us from the Donatist side, seeking what he had lost among them. There was no way that I could receive him, except in a way that was his due. For he had not abandoned their party as someone who was a good man, so that he would seem to have come over to our side not by compulsion but by free choice. Rather, because he could not have what he wanted among them – he was seeking empty rank and false honours – he came to us to find what he had lost there. But he did not find it, and so lost himself. . . . Firebrands of humiliation and injury burned in him. His mind was in violent upheaval . . . so that he had finally to be thrown out of our communion. . . . You should not despair, however, about any person so long as he lives. Lest anyone perhaps suggest differently to you, you ought to know this, my brothers, from the following case. A subdeacon of theirs, with no investigation being made against him, chose Catholic peace and unity and, having abandoned them, he came over to our side. He came as one returning to the truth and not as one rejected by evil men. So he was accepted by us and we rejoiced in his conversion.

There was an awareness on all sides that the presence of the two religious communities offered choices to men and women who might be having troubles inside their own communions. But the dynamic of attraction and repulsion was surely a modulated one, varying in each individual case. Even for the hard-pressed, there were other alternatives within each community and the choice to become a convert or a traitor – depending on how one saw it – must have been a difficult one, provoked by what the person felt was an unbearable slight or an excessive penalty imposed for a minor delict. On the other hand, the very existence of the alternatives made imposing too stringent an internal discipline a big problem for the leadership in each church. If a bishop came down too hard on an ordinary parishioner or, more dangerously, a junior member of his clergy, he might propel the disaffected into open dissidence. There might also be more mundane motives of secular advantage. These baser motives, too, had to be admitted.[82]

Sometimes the winds that blow the chaff off the threshing floor blow the chaff again from the direction of the hedgerow where it has stuck, blowing it back onto the threshing floor. Just as, for the sake of an example, we see in a certain man who was well established in the Catholic Church and who had suffered some blow of misfortune. He sees that he can be assisted materially in his worldly business affairs by the Donatists. He's told: "You won't be given any assistance unless you join our communion over here." So the wind blows him and drives him into the spines of the hedgerow. If it happens that he has some other worldly business that can only be successfully completed in the Catholic Church – and he does not

---

[82] Aug. *Sermo* 252.5.5 (PL 38: 1175).

concern himself too much with where he is located, but only with where he can more conveniently do his business – then he's blown back onto the threshing floor of the Lord.

Were such marriages of convenience interpreted as betrayals? Probably, but in a minor key. Everyone seemed to recognize the secular motives that drove some persons back and forth, seeking advantage first in one religious community and then in the other. Christian truth, although averred, was not the only, even the biggest, thing at stake.

Despite all of the incitements, inducements, pressures, and dangers, the self-policing of both communities against betrayal seems to have been rather successful. Certainly at higher leadership levels, the numbers of crossovers that can be confirmed are rather small. Despite suffering fearful threats and humiliations, disappointments, and developing a seething anger over their maltreatment, most aggrieved clergy, it seems, decided to remain within their own religious communities. The risks and costs of going over were just too high. The deacon Nundinarius in the dissident church at Cirta suffered hurtful slights and insults at the hands of Silvanus, his bishop. He was stoned. He was denied normal participation in the liturgy. Naturally, he nursed a festering anger over the injustices committed against him, lobbying bishops in towns around Cirta to seek fairer treatment from Silvanus. But in the end, he did not go over to the other church or form his own breakaway church at Cirta, as he surely could have done. Rather, he took the whole dispute to the civil courts. Although all the aggrieved participants in this quarrel held the trump card of "crossing over" in their hands, and even threatened to play it, none of them actually took the final step.[83]

But the threat was real enough. As part of earlier events in the same scandal at Cirta, the primate of the dissident church, Secundus of Tigisis, held a meeting in the city in May 306 in which he scrutinized the credentials of the bishops who had assembled to ordain the newly elected Silvanus. He put hard questions to the bishops about their part in the betrayal of Holy Scriptures to the authorities. The first three bishops who were cowed and frightened when they were interviewed, attempted evasive strategies that mitigated or explained away their actions as traitors. When Secundus confronted Purpurius, the bishop of Liniata, with his misdeeds, however, the man counterattacked, declaring that, more than being a mere traitor, he was a self-confessed killer who was prepared to murder anyone who

---

[83] There is no sign that Nundinarius ever crossed over, whatever the result of the trial in 320 (which we do not know); had he done so, the Catholics would surely have signaled it.

threatened him or his interests. Now it was Secundus' turn to be afraid. It was more than the fear of his death at Purpurius' hands, however, that moved Secundus' nephew to proffer some good advice to his uncle.[84]

Do you get what he's saying to you? He's ready to leave [us] and to create his own church. And not only him, but also all those to whom you've put to the question. I know that they'll leave you. Then they'll bring an accusation against you and you'll end up stranded, all on your own, as a heretic. So, let's face it . . . of what real importance is whatever was done by this person or by that one? Let each one render his own account to God.

Secundus saw the light and let the issue die. The remaining three bishops were not questioned, but simply allowed to seat themselves in the session without facing more questions. The threat that these men might have "gone over" was real enough. Although teetering on the brink of provoking them, Secundus stopped short of doing something that would have forced real betrayal – and so it must have been in most cases. Apart from the striking effect of these individual betrayals, one must wonder if the total numbers were very great. In all of the years of the threats and enticements directed at his opposite numbers in the very large diocese of Hippo Regius, Augustine only mentions one single high-ranking crossover, the bishop Maximinus from the hamlet of Siniti.[85] Siniti was just not a very significant place within the diocese. Had others existed, Augustine would certainly have mentioned them.

The impression given by this single instance is confirmed by another body of data. Since it lists all the bishops in either church who were present, the documentary record of the conference at Carthage in 411 is the most detailed and coherent picture that exists of the leadership of both churches. Because of the acerbic formal face-to-face confrontations that took place at the conference for the purposes of identifying the bishops, if there was any opportunity to identify one's opposite number with the horrible epithet of *traditor*, it was taken. Such men were traitors and their presence provoked a visceral response in those whom they had betrayed. Something had to be put on the record publicly to mark these detestable men. For example, when the name of Maximinus, the Catholic bishop of Turres, was called out by the court secretary, he made the formulaic reply: "Present. I have no bishop in my diocese against me." This apparently bland statement provoked an acidic aside, shouted out by the dissident bishop Adeodatus: "He was once

---

[84] Apud Aug. *Contra Cresc.* 3.27.30 (CSEL 52: 437 = Maier, *Dossier*, I, no. 7, p. 117).
[85] Aug. *Ep.* 23.2 (CSEL 34.1: 65); 105.2.4 (CSEL 34.2: 597); *Civ. Dei*, 22.8.6 (CCL 48: 820); for Maximinus of Siniti, see "Maximinus (2)," PAC, p. 728.

one of ours."[86] Of the nearly six hundred diocesan heads attested at the meeting, however, only eighteen are specified as clergy who had crossed over from one side to the other. Twelve were former dissident clergy who had defected to the Catholic side. Only six Catholics had betrayed their own and gone over to the dissidents.

A consideration of the traitors who were singled out at the conference of 411 might reveal who was betraying and why. Of the Catholics who abandoned their community, three were deacons and two were bishops. Of one of the deacons, Felix of Boseth, we know nothing more than that he crossed over and was rebaptized by the dissidents.[87] The same is true of Rogatus of Zaraï.[88] Some of the other cases for which there is more information are more revealing. Of the bishops, Leontius of Rusticiana left the Catholic Church and went over to the dissidents, leaving no opposing orthodox bishop in his diocese. The reasons seem to have been liturgical and ecclesiastical practices that put him at odds with his own church. He was insisting on the rebaptism of converts. Since the practice had been condemned by the Catholic Church, Leontius probably felt that he had no alternative except to enter the communion of his erstwhile enemies.[89] The case of Simplicius of Thibilis seems to be a similar, although the circumstances are not certain: "He recognized the truth," is all that the dissident bishop Adeodatus says.[90] At the lower level of the deaconate, however, matters were different. Vitalis of Mascula had once been a Catholic, but was now a bishop of the dissident church. Why had this happened? Aurelius, the Catholic bishop of Macomades tells us: "This Vitalis was once one of our deacons in the city of Sitifis. Rebaptized, he was made a priest by them. He had been thrown out of our church for reasons of adultery. He has subsequently been made a bishop."[91] In terms of geographic origins, it might be noted that four of the five cases of Catholic crossovers came from towns in Numidia where the surrounding pressures of the dissidents were greater and support from their own weaker.

---

86 GCC 1.121 (SC 195: 712): "Item recitavit: 'Maximinus episcopus plebis Turrensis.' Idem dixit: 'Praesto sum. Sed non contra me habeo episcopum.' Adeodatus episcopus dixit: 'Noster fuit.'"
87 GCC 1.126; 1.202 (SC 195: 726, 872).   88 GCC 1.128; 1.203 (SC 195: 736, 873).
89 GCC 1.198 (SC 195: 858): "Adversarium non habeo," Leontius is able to state. But this provokes a gloss by the Catholic bishop Terentius: "Iste rebaptizabat post partem Donati. Rebaptizatus est postea, et sic est ordinatus."
90 GCC 1.197–98 (SC 195: 848): He too "had no adversary" in his diocese, which prompts the remark by Aurelius, the Catholic primate of Africa: "Iste est episcopus qui rebaptizatus est et factus est audiens." And the countershot by Adeodatus: "Hoc cognitioni servandum est. Agnovit veritatem."
91 GCC 1.128; 1.201 (SC 195: 734, 866).

Of course, other cases were known, but they reveal the same circumstantial factors: a combination of pull and push, but mainly the latter. Take two examples from the diocese of Hippo in 409 or in the years just before.[92] One involved a subdeacon named Rusticianus. Another was a Catholic deacon who moved to the dissident church where he was welcomed in his same rank, and rebaptized. He became the head of a circumcellion gang, leading attacks on his former Catholic brothers. He was killed in one of the raids. The reason for his betrayal? He had been excommunicated by his priest for an unspecified delict. In the instances of dissident crossovers to the Catholics, greater in absolute numbers, the same basic patterns recur, the same signs of disaffection among the lower-ranking clergy. Cassianus was once a priest of the dissident bishop of Vamaccura.[93] Concerning one Sabinus from Tucca, the dissident bishop, Adeodatus remarked: "he was ordained in my diocese. He came from the ranks of my priests."[94] Sabinus' response reveals a complex set of factors leading to his act of betrayal. On the one hand, he claims that the parishioners in his diocese petitioned him to take them over into the Catholic communion; but he also had to admit that there was a personal rise in rank involved. Only a priest in the dissident community, he was now ordained as a bishop in the Catholic Church.[95] Again, on seeing Felix, Saturus the dissident bishop of Iziriana remarked, "He was once one of my priests," signaling yet another case of a man driven by some combination of causes to seek refuge in the enemy camp.[96]

Difficulties therefore arose with policing obstreperous clergy who held in their hands a trump card: the threat of going over to the other church. There is the case of Felicianus of Cufruta. Primian remarks of him that he was a man who had been condemned by both sides for his bad deeds. While still a defendant on charges within the dissident church, he had crossed over and "they" (i.e. the Catholics) knowing that he was an accused still ordained him as bishop.[97] A similar moral failing accounted for the actions of Niventius, the bishop of Thunigaba. He had no bishop opposing him because he had deserted his post as the dissident bishop of the town and had crossed over to the Catholics. Primian, the bishop who was called upon

---

[92] Reported by Aug. *Ep.* 108.19 (CCL 31B: 82–83); cf. "Rusticianus (2)," PAC, p. 1011.
[93] GCC 1.128 (SC 195: 736).   [94] GCC 1.130 (SC 195: 742).
[95] GCC 1.130 (SC 195: 742): This seems to be the meaning of his words: "Cum saepe a civibus meis peterer ut eos in communionem ecclesiae Catholicae suscepissem, rogaverunt eam ut eis episcopus daretur. Petiverunt me, et ordinatus sum."
[96] GCC 1.133 (SC 195: 764).
[97] GCC 1.128–29 (SC 195: 740): "Primianus episcopus dixit: 'Ille qui fuit damnatus est a nobis et ab illis; cum scirent illum reum, et ipsi confirmaverunt.'"

to comment on these cases by the dissidents, noted that Niventius "had been condemned on the charge of adultery. He had been our bishop in that place right up to the present year."[98] In cases where men like Niventius were designated as crossovers and had no bishop from the dissident side yet opposing them in their diocese, one must suspect that it was a bishop who had gone over and who tried to take the whole of his congregation with him: men like Hilarus of Boseth, Maximinus of Turres, and Rogatus of Gaguar.[99] A few examples of these group crossovers, like that of Primulus of Vaga, are confirmed.

Mass betrayals would be easier for all concerned. The bishop would take all of his potential accusers along with him to the other side. Everyone could agree they had done a good thing. Against accusations of betrayal, Ampelius, the Catholic bishop of Vaga, explained in defense of his new colleague:

Recognizing perfect unity by his conversion, my brother bishop Primulus declares the most correct faith along with me. Earlier he was a bishop on the Donatist side. Now, having converted, along with his congregation he professes the true faith as a result of his conversion. Unity is perfect there, not only in the city itself, but also in all of the dioceses.[100]

A bishop who crossed over, and who took all of his flock with him, had much self-justification to offer. And it could be offered in various ways. There is the chutzpah of Rufinianus of Bonusta, who crossed over to the Catholics with his whole flock – logically leaving himself with "no opponent" and who explained himself, perhaps somewhat illogically, before the conference as follows: "There never were any Donatists in that place." Primian, the dissident Primate, replied to his claim: "He was once one of ours. But we still have congregations there with whom to ordain someone." Rufinianus retorted to the judge: "He never had any people there."[101] Even on his own accounting, the statement makes his earlier position as the dissident bishop of Bonusta a bit of an existential puzzle.

At the higher leadership level, however, the total number of traitors was not great, and the proportions even less so. A 2–3 percent betrayal rate

---

[98] GCC 1.129–30 (SC 195: 740).

[99] GCC 1.120 (SC 195: 710), 1.121 (SC 195: 712) and 1.128 (SC 195: 738): "noster fuit, a nobis illo transiit."

[100] GCC 1.176 (SC 195: 818–19): "Perfectam unitatem ex conversione sua cognoscens, rectissimam fidem mecum frater meus Primulus loquitur episcopus. Episcopus enim tunc fuit partis Donati. Nunc conversus demonstrat cum plebe integram fidem ex conversione sua. Unitas illic perfecta est, non solum in ipsa civitate, verum etiam in omnibus diocesibus."

[101] GCC 1.133 (SC 195: 746); Augendus of Villa Magna seems to be a similar case; see 1.133 (SC 195: 748): "Ille est qui iamdudum ad illam partem transiit."

is open to different interpretations. On the one hand, it indicates that of the total cohort of bishops known for 411, about 97 or 98 out of every 100, were firm in their loyalty to their positions and to their communities. On the other hand, the low incidence of such occurrences only served to highlight and make more significant the two or three who did betray their church of origin. It might be argued that greater numbers among the common parishioners would tend to go over to the other side, since they had less to lose by their transition. But evidence for such a claim is thin. The impression – and it is that – is that most ordinary persons hewed rather closely to the traditions of their ancestors, to the values of the community into which they had been born and raised, and that they were unlikely to move in large numbers unless led by an ecclesiastical figure of authority or by the compulsion of a secular lord. In other words, they followed their leaders.

THE CRIME OF JUDAS

The troubling problem was how to construe betrayal in Christian terms. The subject recurs repeatedly in the tracts, theological treatises, letters, and sermons of the period. The imagery was commensurately powerful not only because of the emotional commitment to the importance of the act within African Christianity, but also because of the profound parallel between the birth of the division in the African church and the birth of Christianity. Both had been signaled by an act of betrayal. Christian sacred texts contained many figures that could be used as tropes for the traitor. So the dissident bishop, Cassianus of Vamaccura, who crossed over to the Catholics in the aftermath of repressive imperial legislation in 405, was branded as an "Absalom" by his own people, recalling the son of David who rebelled against his own father (and suggesting the fate that was in store for such a betrayer).[102] But from the number of times that he is mentioned, and the strident language used in the references, it is the figure of Judas that was deployed by both sides as the most powerful archetype. Neither party denied the terrible and unspeakable awfulness of Judas' crime. The dissidents emphasized the terrible nature of the crime – the original sin at the birth of Christianity. The Catholics agreed with the extreme gravity of Judas' act. Augustine can expatiate on "the unspeakably awful crime of that traitor Judas" in terms no less harsh than those used by

---

[102] An action remembered later at the conference of Cathage in 411: GCC 1.187 (SC 195: 836); cf. 1.128, ll. 744–47 (SC 195: 736).

the dissidents.[103] Although a great good had been achieved by the agency of this betrayal, nevertheless the act and the man himself were utterly wicked and damned.[104]

In addition to the ever-present image of Judas, there was a rich conciliar tradition to which the bishops and parishioners of both sides had access. The primal font of such opinions were the judgments enunciated by eighty-seven bishops at a conference held at Carthage in September 256 where they had debated the need to rebaptize Christians who had lapsed during the Decian persecution, and who were regarded as heretics.[105] Caecilius of Bahia Bilta, who was the first bishop to give his opinion on the matter, stated that the voices of the traitors actually emitted a kind of cancerous infection. They were stained like the Antichrist and had become "bishops of the Devil" who polluted the priesthood.[106] All the bishops emphasized that there was only one church, one faith, and one baptism, and that those who had been baptized "among the heretics" (i.e. by lapsed or traitorous clergy) had to be rebaptized in the only true church. The beliefs of the heretics were repeatedly excoriated by the bishops as cancerous diseases and the persons themselves were condemned as enemies of Christ and of the truth. The effects of actions taken by them were permanently polluting, performed by men who were "worse than the pagans." Such men could not baptize others. As seducers, adulterers, and sexual predators, they could only corrupt.[107] Faced with such a threat, they felt that it was best to quote the words of Jesus: "He who is not with me is against me" (Mt. 12: 30).[108] And so came the almost inevitable identification of such bad persons with "the Jews" and with Judas.[109] Although this official tradition offered other possible images for the effects of betrayal, from the physical distortion of cancer to the contamination of disease, it was the figure of Judas and his betrayal that overshadowed the rest.

---

[103] Aug. *En. in Ps.* 93.28 (CCL 39: 1328): "de ipso immanissimo scelere Iudae traditoris."
[104] Aug. *Tract. in Ioh.* 113.1.1 (CCL 36: 636): Judas is "useful" for his betrayal, but damned for the willfulness of his wicked act.
[105] For the text, see Cyprian, *Sententiae episcoporum numero LXXXVII "De haereticis baptizandis"*, ed. G. F. Diercks (CCL 3E).
[106] *Sententiae episcoporum LXVIII*, 1 (CCL 3E: 9).
[107] As Antichrists: 11, 64 (CCL 3E: 31, 87: the last is Cyprian's own view); cancerous beliefs: 10, 18 (CCL 3E: 31, 37); enemies of Christ: 7, 87 (CCL 3E: 25, 107: the last the view of Cyprian himself); enemies of truth: 38 (CCL 3E: 65); polluting: 18, 26, 40, 41 (CCL 3E: 39, 47, 67); they import filth into the church: 42 (CCL 3E: 69); worse than pagans: 37 (CCL 3E: 63); adulterers and seducers: 22, 31, 49 (CCL 3E: 43, 55, 75).
[108] Quoted by Secundus, bishop of Cedias (CCL 3E: 31); and Secundinus of Carpi (CCL 3E: 45).
[109] For these people as "the synagogue of Satan": 60 (CCL 3E: 85); as being like Judas: 61 (CCL 3E: 85).

A general picture of the hatefulness of the act of betrayal can be fleshed
out from Augustine's picture of the sin. First of all, the betrayal was literally
satanic. It was because the Devil himself had entered into Judas' heart that
he was led to carry out the betrayal.[110] By his acts, the traitor became a
damned man.[111] Judas himself is defined as a Jew, and so he was connected
with the evil designs that the Jews had in plotting and carrying out the
murder of God, to which plans Judas was central.[112] The traitor reduces
Christ to the level of a slave, the object of his betrayal. He sells, and the
Jews buy. The image of Judas the vendor of God recurs time and again in
sermons and treatises.[113] All of these elements could be, and were, drawn
together as the main themes of whole sermons in which the nature of the
betrayal, the character and type of the traitor himself, and the meaning of
this ultimate sin was drawn out at length for parishioners.[114] The kindest
interpretation that could be placed on Judas and his act was that his betrayal
was one of the best examples of how good could be achieved through evil
(although such, to be sure, was not Judas' intent). On the other hand,
the betrayal was itself a quintessentially evil act, and the traitor damned
forever by it. More directly relevant to African Christians was the fact that
Judas' betrayal became a template of what had happened in Carthage at
the inception of the division between the two churches, although who was
to be identified with Judas depended on which side one was on. Judas
deliberated a conscious separation from the Lord; his decision to betray
Jesus was therefore *the* primal act of separation, of schism.[115] The consistent
image of the *traditor* always evoked the image of the arch-traitor himself:
a diabolical man of satanic evil, rightly damned by everyone as someone
who embodied the absolute worst of human misbehavior.

---

[110] Aug. *En. in Ps.* 136.9 (CCL 40: 1969): "Quomodo autem diabolus intravit in cor Iudae, ut traderet
Dominum"; cf. *Sermo* 284.5 (PL 38: 1292).

[111] Aug. *Sermo* 56.2 (*RBén* 68: 27): "in quo praedictus est damnabilis traditor Iudas"; *En. in Ps.* 61.22
(CCL 39: 791): "Judas, the malevolent betrayer of Christ, and all persecutors of Christ, all evil
people, all the impious, all the unjust – all of them deserve condemnation."

[112] Aug. *Sermo* 214.3 (*RBén* 72: 16): "per malitiam Iudaeorum, per malitiam Iudae traditoris impletum
est . . . quemadmodum Deus etiam malis operibus diaboli, Iudaeorum et Iudae traditoris bene usus
est ad nostram redemptionem ac salutem."

[113] Aug. *Sermo* 46.23 (CCL 41: 551): a *venditor* of Christ; *Sermo* 262.4.4 (PL 38: 1208): Judas sells and
the Jews buy; *Sermo* 336.4.4 (PL 38: 1473–74) dilates on the theme of Judas the *emptor* and *venditor*
at length, along with a consideration of his motives.

[114] Aug. *Sermo* 313E.3–5 = Guelferb. 28 (MiAg 1: 537–39) provides one example at length on Judas
the traitor, how he separated himself from the Lord, how the Devil entered him, he sold, the Jews
bought, etc.; § 5, significantly, leads directly to "the Donatists."

[115] Aug. *Sermo* 313E.3 (MiAg 1: 537): Judas the *traditor* separated himself from the Lord: it was the
origin of a schism; it is paralleled to the schism of "the Donatists."

To catch some of the dissidents' play on Judas one has only to listen to the debate between Augustine and Petilian, the dissident bishop of Constantina, whose words Augustine has quoted verbatim. For Petilian the act of betrayal is absolutely essential and primal. The original act of betrayal was so powerful in its effects that it permanently polluted and disabled the priests and bishops who were descended from the first traitors in the Great Persecution of 303–05. Any discussion of this kind evoked the image of Judas. The case of Judas, it was argued by Catholics, simply did not apply to their communion, since "those men" who might have committed "that act" were dead men who had done that "long ago." Their acts, however despicable and wrong, could not stain or pollute those in the present. For Petilian, the dissident, the matter was quite different. The primal act of betrayal had precisely this permanent polluting effect. The clergy of the Catholic Church in the 390s and early 400s were the heirs of the original traitors. For him, the figure of Judas was commensurately more immediately powerful and more relevant; Petilian drew a strong parallel between Judas the traitor and the traitors in the African church.[116] He went on to point out that the men who did what they did at Carthage and elsewhere in Africa during the Great Persecution were *worse* than Judas himself. Judas betrayed Christ in the flesh, but these false Africans had betrayed the word of God for which the Maccabees had been willing to die. Augustine took the trouble to reply at great length to Petilian's views. The obvious reason for the amount of time, paper, and ink deployed was the effect that these charges had on many people and the manifest difficulties of overcoming the powerful effect of the comparison.

The dissidents placed as great an emphasis as did their opposite numbers on the record by the evangelist John on the betrayal of Jesus (John 6: 66–71). To them it made certain fundamental points. One was that Jesus had had many more than the twelve disciples. They noted that it was the many – most often identified as sixty in number – who abandoned Jesus when the going got rough and dangerous. There was one man who was like the sixty in that he too abandoned Jesus: Judas son of Simon the Iscariot. It was just

---

[116] Aug. *Contra litt. Petil.* 2.8.17 (CSEL 52: 29–30): "Petilianus dixit: 'Agendum, inquam, nobis dicendumque est, quatenus perfidus traditor vita mortuus habeatur. Iudas apostolus fuit, cum traderet Christum, idemque honore apostoli perdito spiritaliter mortuus est, suo postea laqueo moriturus, sicut scriptum est . . . ecce quantus est spiritus prophetarum, ut cuncta futura pro praesentibus viderit, ut ante plurima saecula nasciturus traditor damnaretur . . . hoc igitur facto episcopatum tibi quid vindicas, heres nequioris traditoris? Iudas Christum carnaliter tradidit, tu spiritaliter furens evangelium sanctum flammis sacrilegis tradidisti. Iudas legislatorem tradidit perfidis, tu quasi eius reliquias legem dei perdendam hominibus tradidisti. Qui si legem diligeres, ut iuvenes Machabaei, pro dei legibus necareris . . .'"

that his betrayal was more blatant, and more aggressive, than the rest. Jesus referred to this one man as a devil incarnate. In the debate between Petilian and Augustine, the figure of Judas the traitor is brought up repeatedly, and Petilian finally clinches the identity between the Catholics and the permanent stigma of betrayal.[117]

Was it for you that the traitor Judas died with his hanging rope?

... After all, *you* imitate *his* acts, you pillage the goods of the Church and you sell [i.e. into slavery] the heirs of Christ, whom *we* are, to the powerful of this world.

By any measure, it is a powerful statement. Continued protests by Augustine that it was "the Donatists" who were "like the Jews" were a rather weak response to Petilian's strident assertion that the Catholics were the real descendants of Judas. He was their ancestor. Through baptism, true members of the church clothed themselves in Christ; because of the contagion with which the Catholic bishops were infected, they clothed themselves in the person of Judas the traitor.[118] And so Petilian identifies the Catholic clergy as destroyers of good humans. They are like ravenous wolves ravaging innocent sheep. "You wretched traitors!" he explodes. It was an emotional charge that provoked the bitter response, "*You* wretched heretics," from Augustine.[119] But it was Augustine himself who had brought into the argument the images of betrayal that nourished the picture of traitors. In this discourse, Judas is constantly referred to as an archetype and as one into whom Satan himself had entered. The saying from the evangelist John (Jn 6: 71) that Christ identified Judas by saying "One of you is a devil" is repeated again and again, especially during the sermons that recurred every year with the coming of the Easter season.[120]

The Catholic response was that the true traitors were those who had betrayed the church. Those who truly deserved the label of being Judases were those who were "false brothers," persons who formed a fifth-column that had infiltrated the true church and were spreading false charges against it. For Augustine, and the standard ideas upon which he drew in composing his *Song Against the Donatists* in the early 390s, there was no better exemplary role for Judas. No one could deny his betrayal or the parallel

---

[117] Aug. *Contra litt. Petil.* 2.43.101 (CSEL 52: 79): "Petilianus dixit: 'Numquid pro vobis laqueo suo Iudas traditor mortuus est... cuius facta sectantes raptis thesauris ecclesiae nos Christi heredes potestatibus saeculi venumdatis?'"

[118] Aug. *Contra litt. Petil.* 2.44.103 (CSEL 52: 81): "Petilianus dixit: 'Nos enim, ut scriptum est, baptismo nostro Christum induimus traditum, vos vestro contagio Iudam induitis traditorem.'"

[119] Aug. *Contra litt. Petil.* 2.74.165–66 (CSEL 52: 105).

[120] For example, Aug. *Tract. in Ioh.* 55.3.1 (CCL 36: 465); 60.1.1 (CCL 36: 478): where the verse is quoted; 62.1.1 (CCL 36: 483).

betrayal of the word of God during the persecutions that struck Africa under Diocletian. The question could then be construed as one about the effects of the betrayal and about what "we" are to do about it. In his popular song, Augustine already hinted at the possibilities.[121]

> There is the example of the Lord
> and [his actions] towards that traitor Judas...
> For they [i.e. "the Donatists"] were worse than that traitor Judas,
> with whom the apostles took the first sacrament of the dinner,
> although they knew that the man
> guilty of such a terrible crime was among them...

In other words, even if Judas was a traitor, the Lord and the disciples showed an infinite patience with him. They did not condemn him. Rather, he will be condemned by God at the end of time. If Judas is anything, and if any parallel is to be drawn with the guilty men who betrayed the word of God in the time of Diocletian, it is that we should not judge such men. Jesus himself presented us with a paradigm of patience. A tactic of almost infinite delay was therefore a useful and workable response to dealing with an intractable problem.

THERE ARE GOOD REASONS

Any betrayal can be interpreted, made stronger, or have its effect diluted or wholly exculpated, based on a spectrum of possible responses and circumstances.[122] Those who handed over the scriptures did so out of an understandable and forgivable motive. But along a spectrum between Judas' unforgivable act and Peter's allowable thrice denial of Christ before the cock crew, where did true betrayal and treason lie? The question arose even in the case of Judas, for if he had betrayed Christ had he not done so with the connivance of God? Had not God himself "handed over" his own son? After all, the acts were structurally similar. And so debates arose about betrayal. Why is one kind good and another bad?[123] The Father handed over Christ. Judas handed him over. Does not each action seem

---

[121] Aug. *Psalmus contra partem Donati*, vv. 205, 262–64 (BA 28: 178; 186): "Habet iam Domini exemplum / et in Iuda traditore... Non enim peiores erant / illo Iuda traditore, / cum quo apostoli acceperunt / primum sacramentum cenae. / cum tanti sceleris reum / inter se iam scirent esse."

[122] Akerström, *Betrayal and Betrayers*, pp. 18 f., is good on these "mitigating circumstances."

[123] A paraphrase of Aug. *Tract. in 1 Ep. Ioh.* 7.7 (SC 75: 326). Hewing this even more extreme line of defense: did not God himself betray his own son? Quoting Galatians 2: 20: "Qui me dilexit, et tradidit seipsum pro me." This was the logical consequence of the act of betrayal made by God himself: "Qui filio proprio non pepercit, sed pro nobis omnibus tradidit eum, quomodo non et cum illo omnia nobis donavit." (quoting Romans 8: 32).

similar? Far from it. Judas is a traitor. Is God the Father also a traitor? Far from it. The same thing, handing over, was done by them all. But what distinguishes them?. The Father and the Son did it in love, but Judas did it as an act of betrayal. We bless the Father, we detest Judas. Why do we bless the Father and detest Judas? We bless love, we detest evil. Fear was proffered as a reasonable mitigating circumstance. If one acted abnormally under extreme compulsion, then it was understandable. Bad, but not in the same category as Judas' action. So Peter was "frozen by fear" when he denied Christ.[124]

These debates did not take place in a vacuum. They were integrally connected with the single ritual that marked the passage from death to life for every Christian, the living waters of baptism. That baptism and debates over it became central to this dispute is not accidental. It was not just a theological debate about the efficacy or not of baptism, depending on who gave it or how it was given.[125] It was a powerful struggle over claiming the past and, especially, over claiming authority. Just as true martyrs had stood up and been counted, refusing to betray the word of God to secular authority, that much was expected of any person who could claim to be a true leader in the church. Such persons were to be like the priest Saturninus at Abitina and not like his weak and traitorous bishop Fundanus. The issue was unavoidable because that vital connection had been permanently implanted in African tradition with the death of Cyprian. As bishop of Carthage, he was the first man of such high rank who was known to have stood up and accepted death as the price of his office. With this decision, Cyprian powerfully merged the status of the martyr with the high rank of a bishop. When he was further elevated by the aura of his unique position as a high-status expositor of Christian ideology, his position as the founding father of African Christianity was placed beyond challenge. There had been no one even remotely like him. Cyprian was the one who placed the stamp of an aristocratic legitimacy, and the required high ideals of behavior, on the position of the Christian bishop in Africa. There was no way in which any subsequent Christian authority in Africa could dispute his status. His writings had near-canonical authority. Not a word of them was to be tampered with; not a sentence was to be altered

---

[124] Aug. *Sermo* 135.7.8 (PL 38: 750).

[125] The bibliography is simply immense. For a few guides, see Dattrino (1990) for Optatus, whose views recapitulate the substance of the debates in the African church; Finn, *Early Christian Baptism*, pp. 129–71, collates the important historical documents for Africa in context. Frend, *Donatist Church*, pp. 135–39; Brisson, *Autonomisme et christianisme*, pp. 78–86, 164–78.

or added to what he had said and written. His words were that carefully guarded and venerated.[126]

The ways in which Cyprian linked the problem of betrayal and baptism could not be evaded or traduced. Those who had betrayed the true church were like heretics and had to be rebaptized to re-enter it. When Augustine wrote his seven-book treatise "On Baptism," around the year 400, he had to work within these given parameters. It is interesting to consider the division of labor in this, the largest single work in his polemical attacks on the dissidents – written, in his own words, "to shut up the Donatists." One book was devoted to the theological implications of baptism, six to the status of Cyprian. There were good reasons. Cyprian's words manifestly underwrote the position held by the dissidents. They could claim the high ground of hallowed tradition. It was his views on betrayal that mattered: the implicit linking of those who had lapsed in the Great Persecution with those who had lapsed in the persecutions of the 250s. Cyprian's perspectives on the status of baptism were closely connected with his views on the status of betrayers. For the dissidents, and as much for those who opposed them, baptism had become a pivotal question because it had been the means by which a primal sin was passed from one generation to the next. It mattered so much because this means and this stigma were said wholly to disable the authority of the bishops of the Catholic Church. But there is something more. In competing for the same place, the two sides were moved by heavy emotions, the one side by the sense of betrayal and the other by the need for autonomy. As has been acutely noted, such competitiveness is manifested at the micro-level in quarrels, but most such disputes remain merely verbal, and that they only occasionally escalate into violence.[127] So it was to be here as well that baptism mattered a lot.

WHO CARES?

But there was a final, somewhat paradoxical riposte to the charges of betrayal: "It really doesn't matter." Catholics could admit that some of our people *might* have betrayed the scriptures to Roman authorities during the persecution, but even if they did – which the Catholics were not

---

[126] Rouse and McNelis (2000) on the discovery of the reference work of a dissident preacher that makes manifest how important the works of Cyprian were and that one did not mess around with him or his writings.

[127] Collins, *Violence*, pp. 365–66: note that the words "sense of betrayal," "need for autonomy," "micro-level," and "merely verbal" are quoted from the author in his analysis of the Sinclair Lewis–Theodore Dreiser conflict – in a case where a lot of public status, and literary production, was at stake.

admitting, of course – it would not matter anyway since there was no connection between those earlier people and "we today, many generations later" in terms of the responsibility that "we have for our own age." In this case, there were mitigating grounds of betrayal. The men who actually handed over the scriptures were liable, and should be held liable, for their bad act, but the stain of their fault, their sin, did not pass down to *us* – to the Catholic bishops of Augustine's own day. In an extensive anti-Donatist sermon preached in 403 in the Restoration Basilica at Carthage, Augustine made the point.[128]

> They speak their own words. They speak vain and hollow words: "That fellow there handed over the books," they say, "and that one over there too." Yes – OK – I'll say the same: "That guy over there handed over the scriptures and so did that other one over there." And I'd be speaking the truth. But what does all of this have to do with *me*?

The implication is that it had nothing to do with his contemporaries in the early fifth century; it was an interpretive point of exculpation that he therefore repeated. In one of his longest sermons, the magnificent *On the Shepherds*, a prolonged castigation of "the Donatists" as enemies, he reran the whole history of the conflict. He placed the act of betrayal at its center, but only to turn the tables on the dissidents: it was *they* who had betrayed themselves and the church by their dogged and prolonged litigating of the case. He put the typical dissident charge into the mouths of one of his sectarian enemies.[129]

> "But *those men* betrayed the sacred books and *those men* offered incense to idols, this man here and that man over there." Well, what do "this man" and "that man" mean to me? If they actually did these things, then they're not shepherds... you bring out your court records to prove your case and I bring out my court records to prove mine. Let's believe yours. Then *you* must believe mine. I don't believe yours and you don't believe mine. Let's take away these human documents and let divine words resound instead.

That is to say, no one can really be certain what the written records really said, so any condemnation of some men as traitors based on some carefully hoarded human documents was uncertain at best. Persons in the present cannot be held liable for the actions of men in the long-distant past, even

---

[128] Aug. *En. in Psalm.* 57.6 (CCL 39: 714):. "loquuntur sua, loquuntur inania: 'Ille tradidit, et ille tradidit.' Immo et ego dico, 'Et ille tradidit, et ille tradidit.' Et verum dico. Sed quid ad me?... Auferantur de medio chartae nostrae, procedat in medium codex Dei."

[129] Aug. *Sermo* 46.33 (CCL 41: 558–59): delivered in 414.

if they did do what they are averred to have done. The other side of this coin was the Catholic claim that many of the dissidents were themselves polluted with the stain of betrayal, a point that Augustine made in his epic sermon twinned with *On the Shepherds*, the monumental *On the Sheep*.[130]

> You shout out about traitors, but you can't *prove* it . . . I'm not saying to you, as I could, "It's rather you who are the traitor." If I did say this, however, I could easily prove it. But the reason I don't want to say this is that it was *your people* who did it, not you yourself.

In saying this, Augustine was not denying either the reality or the power of betrayal, but rather trying to fix its precise place. In preaching to his own congregation, he was saying that the shepherds and their sheep had their own roles to play. And part of this role was to make sure who, precisely, would be branded with the label of traitor.

To maintain its integrity in this long cold war, each community had to be constantly vigilant for signs that any of its own might defect to the other side. Such vigilance could be systematically inculcated into the members of the congregation by images of predators, mainly wolves, against whom they had to be on guard. Of course, the bishop as the shepherd of his flock had to be especially vigilant, to care for the sheep that were his. But there were bad shepherds and, even worse, people who did not act according to the model of the good shepherd, but rather assumed the lackadaisical attitude of hired hands who had no vested interest in their sheep, and who did not adequately police the frontiers of their community.[131]

> When a salaried worker, a man who is not a shepherd who owns his own sheep, sees the wolf coming, he abandons the sheep and runs away. Then the wolf snatches and scatters the sheep . . . Such a person would not be called a hired man unless he received pay from his employer. So who is this employee and who is his employer? . . . And who is the wolf if not the Devil? And what was said about the hired man? "When he sees the wolf coming, he flees because the sheep are not his and he has no special care for them."

Neither side wanted such disinterested hired hands. They wanted and needed committed shepherds. The sheep, the parishioners, for their part, had to be encouraged to be watchful. To be on guard, they had to be

---

[130] Aug. *Sermo* 47.17 (CCL 41: 587–88).

[131] Aug. *Tract. in Ioh.* 46.7–8 (CCL 36: 401–03): where the Devil is also someone who persuades the faithful to adultery and is identified with the wolf; cf. *Sermo* 137 (PL 38: 761) and 77C (*RBén* 84: 253, cf. PL 39: 1732–33).

knowledgeable: they had to be educated. Even the dense, the obdurate, and the stupid, the *stulti*, had to be taught and they had to learn. What they had to learn was not only "why we are right and why they are wrong," but also "how it is that we came to be who we are." The one suggested a lifelong program of moral training and discipline, the other a sense of one's own history.

CHAPTER 3

A poisonous brood of vipers

If the religious conflict in Africa had been ignited by betrayal in the reign of Diocletian, it developed in complex and unforeseen ways during the last decades of Constantine's reign and over the remainder of the fourth century. This erratic history was marked by fluctuations between spates of violence and long periods of relatively peaceful coexistence. The back-and-forth shifts were provoked mainly by the changing agenda of emperors, although to a considerable degree the attitudes of the imperial court were deeply implicated in the provocations of the religious parties themselves. In these shifts, the Catholics and the dissidents found themselves variously advantaged or disadvantaged. In the decades after the mid-360s, following the watershed of Julian's reign, the hostile churches settled into a prolonged trench warfare in which each side carefully guarded its own flocks and made few inroads into the membership of the other. Because the written sources covering the period are so sparse, it is possible that this conclusion is too starkly drawn. Through the 370s and the 380s, however, the distinct impression is that each community strengthened its base and that a general balance between the two sides had settled in.

Little is known about the leadership ranks of the Catholics in these years. On the side of the dissidents, there was long-term stability under Parmenian, the bishop of Carthage and Primate of Africa. He had succeeded the great Donatus in the leadership of the dissident church around the year 360, and he remained in this commanding position until the early 390s.[1] The successive long reigns of Donatus and Parmenian provided the

---

[1] For the basic facts, see "Donatus (5)," PAC, pp. 292–303, whose editors opt for a death date around 355, and "Parmenianus," PAC, pp. 816–21, where they are only willing to concede evidence for Parmenian's presence from a date "after 362." Our documentation for the two churches over the mid-fourth century is so spotty that it is not possible to say precisely when Donatus died and when Parmenian succeeded him. We can only say that Parmenian died sometime *before* 24 June 393, when his successor Primian was condemned by the Council of Cabarsussi; how long before depends on how long one judges it necessary for the intervening events to unfold.

dissident church with an enviable firmness at the helm. But Parmenian's three-decade-long tenure as Primate of Africa also had a hidden danger, since episcopal succession always had the potential for dissension and dispute. If there were serious competitors who brought political baggage with them into the struggle for power, the problem was only exacerbated. More tension was likely where the diocese was larger, boasted greater prestige, and had more resources at its command. The contentious election of Augustine as bishop of the diocese of Hippo Regius in 395 is one such reasonably well-documented case. Hippo was an unusually large, wealthy, and important diocese. Augustine's much-disputed choice as co-bishop to the aging and unimpressive Valerius was met with hostility that was only gradually overcome by hard lobbying and persuasion. If such potential for conflict existed at Hippo, it was much greater at Carthage, the pre-eminent see of all Africa. Here the ultimate in the way of material resources and rewards of authority and prestige were at stake with the selection of each new bishop, for the successor was not only chosen from a competitive field of candidates and became bishop of Carthage, he also became Primate of all Africa.

Adding to these difficulties was the fact that the metropolitan diocese was one where the seated bishop of the dissident church, the great Donatus, had been in place for a long time. His long tenure must have created a considerable backlog of competing candidates, all of whose ambitions had to be held in check in a long, sometimes exasperating wait. These same problems were found in abundance in Carthage at the time of Parmenian's accession to the seat of the dissident bishop and Primate of Africa in a year close to 360, and they remained structurally part of succession to the top position in the city. There is no doubt that it was these same factors that contributed substantially to the infighting at Carthage that produced the original division inside the church in 305–07. In the case of Parmenian's election around 360, the internal tensions probably go some way to explain why the electors chose a foreigner – a very unusual thing in the election of African bishops – to hold the seat at Carthage and to become Primate of Africa.[2] As an outsider, Parmenian was probably a compromise or a neutral

---

[2] That Parmenian was "not African" is often asserted (for example, by Frend) on the basis of the polemical statement of Optatus (*Contra Parm.* 1.5.4; SC 412: 182): "quaedam contra vos per ignorantiam, quia peregrinus es," and so must be accepted only with due caution. But the precise sense of "peregrinus" here is unclear. In the Christian *Sondersprache* it seems to have meant someone not in the fold of the Church, and in Africa someone of the "other Church" – see *Passio Isaac et Maximiani*, 18 (Mastandrea 1995: 78) – but it is unclear how this would apply to Parmenian.

candidate upon whom the competing parties could agree to ground their differences.[3] Whatever the reasons, the choice was a good one. Parmenian proved to be a capable leader.

The history of primatial elections at Carthage set up expectations and portended dangerous trouble. It was hardly surprising that Parmenian's death, *c.* 390, produced a dramatic upheaval within the ranks of the dissident church. The internal breakdown revealed to its enemies that there might be fresh opportunities to orchestrate a new campaign against their internally divided and weakened opponents. If matters had been relatively quiescent between the two churches up to 392, then they were to be quite different in the aftermath of the internal conflict that broke out in this year.[4] If Parmenian's accession in the mid-360s had been marked by concession and compromise, his death in early 392 set off a detonation inside the dissident community. Parmenian's long tenure as the dissenting primate of Africa had left a powerful imprint on his church, its organization, and its power.[5] But after three decades of his firm hand, insufficient precautions had been taken to dampen the long rivalries that were simmering just beneath the surface of the hierarchy of the church at Carthage. The pent-up reservoirs of resentment that normally threatened the selection of a new bishop were unleashed in full and superabundant fury.

The resulting infighting at Carthage, which spread from the metropolis to the rest of Africa, split and shattered the dissident church. It was these internal wars within the dissident church in the early 390s that set the stage for what was to be the final phase of the larger struggle between the Catholics and the dissidents in Africa. Parmenian's death had disclosed an unseemly underside of ecclesiastical politics that not infrequently marred the elections of bishops at Carthage. On the one side was a duly constituted successor named Primian, who probably held one of the senior priesthoods in Carthage before his elevation to the rank of bishop.[6] His elevation to

---

[3] Despite claims made about him being from Gaul or Spain, there is no independent evidence in support of either.

[4] For example, as late as the summer of 392, both the dissident and the Catholic Christian communities at Hippo Regius could combine their interests in soliciting the action of the local Catholic priest, Augustine, against the Manichees in their city: Possid. *Vita Aug.* 6 (Bastiaensen: 142–46), cf. Lim, *Public Disputation*, pp. 93–94.

[5] Frend, "The Age of Parmenian, A.D. 363–91," ch. 13 in *Donatist Church*, pp. 193–207, offers a narrative of the events of the period.

[6] See "Primianus (1)," PAC, pp. 905–13; Monceaux, *Hist. litt.* 6, pp. 57 f.; Frend, *Donatist Church*, p. 213, characterizes Primian as "a man of extreme views and ruthless violence," and (p. 213n4) as "a violent individual and clearly from the first the nominee of an extremist group." I disagree. The

the primatial seat, however, was virulently opposed by a deacon named Maximian. Maximian's special strength was a close relationship, a *propinquitas*, that he had had with the great bishop Donatus – the bishop who had headed the dissident church over the first four and a half decades of its existence, and who was its founding father.[7] In a belief system that placed a high premium on the power of inherited blessing, this was not a slight claim. Details about other causes of the hostility between the two men are lost, but the ugly consequences of their conflict are not: they have been preserved in lurid and unseemly detail.

For whatever reason – probably not because of the egregious merits of his purity that apparently set him so much apart from Primian (as his own partisans claimed) and not, as Augustine later asserted, because of his overbearing pride – Maximian entered into a direct confrontation with Primian. The matter came to a head first in the form of a hearing before an ecclesiastical tribunal held at Carthage that was meant to discipline Maximian. The internal hearing was chaired by Primian. The advisors of his court were recruited out of his priests who functioned much like *adsessores* or the advisors who sat in session with the judge of a Roman court of the time. Maximian was supported by four of his fellow deacons; it was this group of five men who were hailed before Primian's tribunal. Either nothing of any significance was found by the hearing or the defendants were exonerated of any misdeeds. In either case, Primian overrode the decision of his own tribunal. Using his powers as bishop, he moved to excommunicate Maximian, apparently without any formal hearing. It was later claimed that Primian had not accepted any witnesses and that he had issued his judgment when Maximian himself was not able to be present because he was sick in bed.

The subsequent conflict between the two men and their followers split the dissident church at Carthage into two hostile camps. With the bishop and the anti-bishop at loggerheads, in the resulting vacuum of a single accepted center of authority in the city, a third party inside the church, the Elders (or *seniores* as they were called), entered the scene. Although they were not a formal part of the ecclesiastical hierarchy in African churches, the Elders formed a quasi-formal body whose position and authority was derived, as their name indicates, from the aura of respectability that

---

imputations of violence are difficult to trust, derived, as they are, from a purposefully constructed dossier that is patently so hostile to Primian.
[7] See "Maximianus (3)," PAC, pp. 719–22; for his status as a deacon at the time of the outbreak of hostilities, see Aug. *Ep.* 185.4.17 (CSEL 57: 15); *Contra Cresc.* 4.4.4 (CSEL 52: 501); *Gesta cum Emerit.* 9 (CSEL 53: 190); *En. 2 in Ps.* 36.2.19 (CCL 38: 359).

attended older age. In normal circumstances, they acted in an advisory capacity to the bishop.[8] They embodied the special respect, and therefore power, that was attributed to older males in African society. This unusual authority of elder men was reflected in the formal ecclesiastical organization of both churches in Africa – as, for example, in the ranking of bishops or in the appointment of provincial primates where length of time served in the position determined status and rank. The power derived from a special respect for old age that characterized African social relations, a peculiarity that is seen in the function that older males had in pre-Roman towns and villages in Africa. Even after many generations of Roman occupation, the Elders in these towns retained real elements of judicial and arbitrative authority in their hands, and they did so despite the presence of new formal institutions of authority in their communities – whether the offices of a Roman municipality or the formal hierarchy of the Christian church. At most times – which is to say in ordinary peaceful conditions in the day-to-day running of the churches – not much is heard of these men. They usually functioned in a quieter, more responsive role, in the background of their affairs.

Occasionally, however, the Elders surfaced in a more dramatic fashion in the politicking within each church. As, for example, when a bishop suffered a loss of authority or where there was a sudden breakdown of local hierarchy, as happened at Carthage in the aftermath of Parmenian's death. In the widening power vacuum, the Elders suddenly found their power and authority considerably enhanced. Should other centers of power fail, by default they became a major locus of authority. In the year 390, the Elders of the dissident church at Carthage found themselves in just such a situation. With the newly elected bishop Primian acting in ways that alienated significant numbers in the ranks of the priests, as well as a powerful group of deacons, the Elders were the only recognized figures of authority who could arbitrate the dispute. They suddenly found themselves invested with significant decision-making power.

In the flurry of partisan claims and counterclaims that proliferated in the uncertainty – accusations circulated by word of mouth and by written posters and pamphlets – everything that Primian did was given a negative "spin" by his opponents. A group of coreligionists led by Claudian, the dissident bishop of Rome, had become divided from the main dissenting church. When Primian decided to let them re-enter the communion of

---

[8] Shaw (1982), with additions in the reprint version, where the relevant earlier scholarly literature can be found.

the dissident church in Africa, his conciliatory offer was interpreted as a vile error. One can easily imagine that such a forgiving move affronted sensibilities of purity shared by some and raised the old problem of the status of rebaptism. If Primian tried to broaden the range of persons who could be formally received as members of the church, then he was inviting "the impure" to pollute its pure body. The subversive concern was that he was deliberately lowering standards for church membership in order to increase the number of his partisans.

It is in this context that the accusations made against Primian for his illicit use of violence first surfaced. Whatever the animus behind them, the incidents were very limited in number. A few situations are typical. For example, when the Elders objected to some of Primian's actions, like those noted above, they claimed that he had used threats and force to intimidate them. There were apparently other isolated individual acts of violence that were part of the same campaign of coercion, as when Primian had a priest named Fortunatus thrown into one of the city sewers, ostensibly for doing nothing other than offering baptism to the sick. Given the continual flow of partisan rhetoric generated by each side, the actual number of violent acts on record is small. It is therefore difficult to assess the true extent of the use of physical force to coerce.

The collected body of accusations generated during the struggle in the early 390s bear all the hallmarks of an information dossier that was being assembled for the purpose of lobbying against Primian. The persons who oversaw the collection are manifest: they were the Elders who were taking control of the situation in the city. They met in council at Carthage and decided to take a stand in favor of Maximian. In pursuit of their program, they sent a circular letter to the bishops of the dissident church that contained an enumeration of Primian's faults. They assembled a dossier of documents in support of their case and then demanded that a council of bishops meet to resolve the crisis. At some time in late 392, a large number of dissident bishops made their way to Carthage to attempt to deal with the disputes that had arisen within their church. More problems arose, however, when Primian refused to recognize their assembly. No less than three times he rejected a summons to appear before the bishops. He had good grounds for his refusal. It must have been irregular, in terms of traditional practice, for an informal body of Elders to be have the right to summon a full council of the church.

Two new developments then served to excite more conflict. The first was the mobilization of large numbers of ordinary parishioners by the bishop Primian. The second was the increasing involvement of the Roman civil authorities in the sectarian struggle. The gradual intrusion of state officials into conflicts within the dissident church was caused primarily by disputes over who had property rights to what church buildings and, more precisely, to the basilicas at Carthage in which the supporters of Maximian were meeting. The hostile rhetoric of his enemies pictured the attempts by Primian to assert rights of ownership over these churches as freewheeling violent attacks on the basilicas and their occupants. What was actually happening was more mundane. Imperial officials were present at these actions because a formal petition or request for legal action had been put to them by Primian. The nature of the petition is not specified, but the range of matters on which he could have requested action from the state was rather limited. The obvious one was that the churches in question were the property of the church at Carthage and that the persons using them (that is, Primian's enemies) had no right to their possession. If he succeeded in his claims, then he had a right to repossess the basilicas concerned and, in the repossession, to use reasonable force. He surely would have organized whatever number of "good men" he needed to enforce the court order. His enemies later represented this private enforcement force as a mob of desperadoes, a *multitudo perditorum*. Even from this hostile description of them, however, the point of Primian's actions was to bar the doors of the basilicas to prevent access to them by the supporters of Maximian and to prevent the use of these churches for liturgical purposes by his sectarian opponents.

DOWN THE SEWER

Deprived of their own basilicas, the supporters of Maximian – in particular the investigating bishops – had to retreat to the suburban churches in the outlying districts of Carthage. In these more remote venues, they constituted themselves as a tribunal hearing the dossier of charges against Primian. Before returning to their homes, they issued a preliminary judgment against him that they circulated to the other bishops in Africa. These hostile moves transpired during the winter of 392–93. Early in 393, the forces that opposed Primian insisted on the holding of a larger church council at a place well outside of Carthage where the case against him could be judged free of the bishop's interference. The council finally assembled on 24 June at the town of Cebarsussi in the southern province of Byzacena. It was chaired by Victorinus of Munatiana, the Old Man, or *Senex*, the senior-ranking bishop or Primate of the ecclesiastical province of

Byzacena.[9] The large numbers of bishops who met in council at Cebarsussi were, by and large, favorably disposed to Maximian.[10] This bias was
also apparent to the Catholics who were observing the struggle within the
dissident church from the outside.[11] The fifty-six bishops whose names
still survive on the decision issued by the council came almost solely from
the ecclesiastical provinces of Byzacena and Tripolitania.[12] The words of
the *tractatoria*, the final decree issued by the council, are worth quoting
because they suggest the sentiments of the participants, as well as the terms
in which the violence at Carthage was interpreted by one of the two sides
to the conflict.[13]

---

[9] See "Victorinus (6)," PAC, p. 1196; episcopus Munatianensis (a seat not otherwise known); Aug.
   En. 2 in Ps. 36.2.20 (CCL 38: 361, 365).

[10] The actual numbers are much disputed. Frend, *Donatist Church*, p. 216 n. 1 (with others) accepts
   that there were only 53 bishops in total, but Augustine's repeated claim that there were about 100,
   or more, bishops present – as Maier, *Dossier*, 2, p. 82 n. 45 argues (with full references) – was
   never contested by the dissidents. On the evidence of the known names of bishops at the council,
   there were clearly more than fifty-three in attendance, since fifty-six names, at a bare minimum,
   can be reconstructed: see Wiedmann, *Maximianistenkonzil von Cebarsussi*, pp. 40–42 and Table 4,
   pp. 54–56, even after discounting several possible "duplicates." A possible explanation for the "omnes
   numero quinquagenta tres" at the end of the list is that this was the total number of names preserved
   in the defective manuscript that a copyist had before him, and that this is the copyist's addition of
   the names at the end of the document. The remainder of the names, constituting the last half of
   the list, had been lost in the process of manuscript transmission.

[11] Aug. *Ep.* 93.8.24 (CCL 31A: 185): "omnes vos Maximianistae superabunt, quorum schisma in
   Byzantio et in Tripoli exarsit"; cf. *Ep ad Cath. de secta Donat.* 3.6 (CSEL 52: 237): "Si in paucis
   Tripolitanis et Byzacenis et provincialibus, Maximianistae ad eam [sc. ecclesiam] pervenerunt."

[12] Weidmann, *Maximianistenkonzil von Cebarsussi*, Table 4, pp. 54–56, has produced the following
   figures for the bishops whose locations can be determined with reasonable certainty: Tripolitania: 2;
   Byzacena: 27; Proconsularis: 8; Numidia: 2; Mauretanias: 0 (but note that there is some guesswork
   with these "known" assignations).

[13] The *tractatoria* or the text of the decision is quoted by Aug. *En. in Ps.* 36.2.20 (CCL 38: 361–
   66), whence the edition in Maier, *Dossier*, 2, no. 54, pp. 73–82. All the versions on which he
   depended, however, are somewhat defective and will be superseded by the new edition in CSEL:
   see Weidmann, *Maximianistenkonzil von Cebarsussi* for background and comment on the earlier
   editions. It is important to point out that we might not have the whole original, but rather only
   the parts of it as quoted by Augustine. The Catholics had obtained the document out of the
   files of the proconsular governor in 403. A copy of the decree had been filed as one of the legal
   documents submitted to the court in connection with proceedings before proconsular governors
   involving the two factions of the dissident church at Carthage: Aug. *En. in Ps.* 36.2.19 (CCL 38:
   359): "Venerunt ad Carthaginem, sicut se habet tractatoria, quam etiam gestis allegaverunt, cum
   litigarent de domo cum procuratore illius, qui praetermittit ablata." An important corrected reading
   of the text by Weidmann, "allegaverunt," shows that the copy of the decree was *attached* to the
   dossier of documents involved in the dispute over a house at Carthage that belonged to the Exorcists
   (see p. 120 below). Importantly, this additionally shows, contrary to claims by Frend and Maier,
   that the dispute over the house dates to some time *after* the council at Cebarsussi: Weidmann,
   Maximianistenkonzil von Cebarsussi, pp. 13–15. On the language of this decree and the one from the
   Council of Bagaï below, see Hoogterp (1940).

Decree of the Council of Cebarsussi

To our most holy brothers and colleagues [i.e. bishops] throughout the whole of Africa – that is, in the Proconsular Province, Numidia, Mauretania, Byzacena, and in Tripolitania – and also to the priests and deacons, and to all congregations who are fighting with us for the Truth of the Gospel.

Those who attended the Council at Cebarsussi – Victorinus, Fortunatus, Victorianus, Miggin, Saturninus, Constantius, Candorius, Innocentius, Cresconius, Florentius, Salvius, another Salvius, Donatus, Geminius, Praetextatus, Maximianus, Theodore, Anastasius, Donatianus, Donatus, another Donatus, Pomponius, Pancratius, Januarius, Secundinus, Pascasius, Cresconius, Rogatianus, another Maximianus, Benenatus, Gaianus, Victorinus, Guntasius, Quintasius, Felicianus, Salvius, Miggin, Proculus, Latinus – and the others who were present in the council at Cebarsussi – eternal salvation in the Lord!

There is no one who does not know, most beloved brothers, that God's priests [i.e. bishops], compelled not by their own will, but by Divine Law, pronounce sentence against the guilty and – as is also legal and right for them to do – remove any sentence that has been decreed against the innocent. For anyone who either pardons a guilty person or attempts to ruin an innocent one is exposed to no small danger, especially since it is written: *You shall not put an innocent and just person to death, nor acquit the guilty man with an excuse* [Ex 23: 7].

Warned by this decree of the Divine Law, we were obliged to hear and to debate the case concerning Primian – whom the Holy People of the Church at Carthage had chosen as their bishop over God's sheepfold – and to make a decision on the matter, because the Elders of the same church filed the formal written petition with us. Then, once everything had been properly investigated, we might either acquit him – which would have been the most desirable outcome – or, having found him guilty, demonstrate beyond doubt that he had been condemned deservedly because of his own acts. Our fondest wish was that the Holy People of the church at Carthage might joyfully recognize the honor that had been conferred on their church by a bishop who would be found to be holy in all respects and blameworthy in none. A priest [i.e. bishop] of the Lord ought most certainly to be of such character that when the people's prayers are of no avail, the priest [i.e. bishop] deserves to obtain from God what he asks for on behalf of the people, since it is written: *If the people sin, the priest will pray for them. But if the priest sins, who will pray for him?* [cf. 1 Sam. 2: 25]

The scandalous acts of Primian and his unique wickedness have called down upon him the judgment of Heaven, making it inevitable that the one who committed such crimes should be entirely amputated from our body. Having only recently been ordained as bishop, he forced the priests of the aforesaid congregation to swear an oath to join an unholy conspiracy. As a further favor, he requested that they promise him on the spot to give their agreement to the condemnation of four deacons, outstanding men of good reputation for their excellent qualities, namely Maximianus, Rogatianus, Donatus, and Salgamius. Although these men were shocked by his unprincipled audacity, and implicitly rejected his plan with their silence, Primian still did not hesitate to implement this crime of his own devising – to the extent that he believed himself competent to pass sentence on the deacon Maximianus, who, as everyone knew, was an innocent man. He did this without a formal trial, without the presence of any accuser, without any witnesses, and in the absence of Maximianus himself, who was ill in bed at the time. Indeed, for some time prior to this event, he [i.e. Primian] had already been punishing clerics with similar savagery.

In contravention of the law and decrees of all bishops, he [i.e. Primian] was in the habit of admitting to the holy community men who were impure. Although the majority of the people were opposed to this practice, and furthermore a letter from the most distinguished Elders agreed that Primian himself should correct what he had done, possessed by his own audacity, he disdained to correct his error. Deeply distressed by these events, the Elders of the aforesaid church dispatched a circular letter and legates to the whole family of bishops, begging us with tears to come to them in the greatest haste so that their charges could be investigated in a fair and balanced way – in order that the reputation of the Church could be cleansed. We came [to Carthage] in response to the letter of the aforementioned persons. When this accounting became known, Primian, seething with rage, absolutely refused to meet with us. In every possible way, he displayed his defiance and persisted in his evil actions, hiring a mob of desperate men who, after petitions had been filed with the authorities, blocked the doors of the basilicas in order to deny us the possibility of entering them and celebrating the liturgy. Let anyone who is a lover and a champion of the Truth consider these actions and judge whether such behavior befits a bishop – indeed, consider if it is even permissible for a Christian or if the Gospels proclaim it. Yet it was a man who had been our own brother who treated us in a manner such as a stranger would never have done.

All of us, as God's priests [i.e. bishops], in the presence of the Holy Spirit, have issued a decree against this same Primian because:

- he substituted new bishops for bishops who were still living
- he introduced impure persons into the communion of the saints
- he attempted to force priests to involve themselves in a conspiracy
- he had the priest Fortunatus thrown into a sewer because he had offered baptism to those who were sick
- he denied communion to the priest Demetrius so that he [i.e. Demetrius] would disinherit his own son
- he severely reprimanded this same priest because he had received bishops with hospitality
- the above-mentioned Primian sent a mob that pillaged the "houses" of Christians
- the bishops were besieged along with other clergy and they were then stoned by his henchmen
- the Elders were beaten in the basilica
- he unworthily permitted Claudianists to be admitted to our communion
- he thought it necessary to condemn innocent clergy
- he refused to present himself before us for a formal hearing while he barred the doors of the basilicas with his mob and with state officials so that we could not enter them
- he insolently rejected the emissaries sent to him by us, and
- he seized many places, initially by force and then by the authority of the courts

. . . not to mention the many other unlawful things which we pass over in silence so as not to dishonor our quill.

We have therefore decreed that he be condemned in perpetuity by our priestly family. We do this fearfully, lest through contact with him the Church of God be polluted by any contagion or crime of his. It is to this very course that the apostle Paul exhorts us when he warns: *In the name of our Lord Jesus Christ we command you, brothers, to separate yourselves from any brother who is walking in a disorderly way* [cf. 2 Th 3: 6]. Not unmindful of the purity of the Church, we have therefore judged it useful that, since he has been condemned, all our fellow holy priests [i.e. bishops] and all clerics and all congregations who call themselves Christian should be warned by this circular letter of ours that they should take great care to shrink in horror from any communion with this man. That person will render an account concerning his own death who attempts to violate our decree by not listening to it.

It is manifestly pleasing both to us and to the Holy Spirit that a period of time should be set aside for those who are slow to change sides. This period [of grace] is to extend from the eighth day before the Kalends of July [24 June] to the eighth day before the Kalends of January [25 December].[14] Whoever among his [i.e. Primian's] fellow priests [i.e. bishops] or clerics are not mindful of their own salvation, as of the day of the condemnation of the above-named Primian, if they have not removed themselves from partnership with this man, let them be held to the prescribed penalty. And unless they will have separated themselves from the communion of the above-named man between the day of his [i.e. Primian's] condemnation and the day of the forthcoming Easter, laypersons shall not be able to be restored to the Church, unless they will have remembered [their true allegiance], and then only by means of penitence.

The words of the decree, a mélange of emotional churchspeak and government-like officialese, show that the context in which the assembled bishops framed Primian's violence was a judicial one. His supposed acts of violence are enumerated as part of a large legal-like dossier of evidence that had been assembled to convict him before the Christian counterpart of a Roman court of law. The number of illicit acts allegedly committed by Primian was not very great, nor were they particularly violent. No physical deaths actually occurred: the only deaths, including the "death sentences," referred to in the decree of the council, are spiritual ones. There is no doubt that Primian had employed force to impose his will on the dissident community at Carthage. Even here, however, some caution is required. There are some incidents, such as the dumping of the priest Fortunatus into the sewers of Carthage, that should be interpreted as symbolic ways of marking a bad person (in this case, the heretic as excrement). But the more serious collective violence that involved larger numbers of enforcers – Primian's "hired mob" – must be seen in a different context. The focal points of anger at Carthage were disputes over church property including questions of who controlled church buildings. Whereas Roman courts and

---

[14] The dates are not random: 24 June was the summer solstice, originally the pre-Christian "Day of the Torches" (see ch. 5, p. 221 below), but in Christian terms the Feast of St. John the Baptist; and it was in this period that 25 December was coming to be recognized as Christ's birthday. So the time of grace was bounded by sacral time. So, too, the mention of Easter later in the *sanctio* of the edict.

civil judges might have been adverse to having their courts used to resolve theological or ecclesiastical issues, disputes over property ownership were something that they were well equipped to handle and which they were probably willing to entertain as valid legal actions. Who did own the churches and who had the right to possess and to use them? This was an issue that *could* be resolved by the civil courts and by normal judicial procedure.

The one serious act of violence of which Primian stood accused was the use of private force – rhetorically described in hostile terms as his hired mob – to enforce his claim to certain basilicas in Carthage. He did this by barring entry to outside persons. No other specific violence is connected with the episode. Furthermore, even his enemies conceded that Primian had first filed petitions with the courts and that he had *officiales* with him during the process of enforcing his claim. What Primian had done was legal: he had followed normal practice in enforcing claims to property. He first went to the civil courts and received a decision that the basilicas were owned by the church of which he was the legally established head. He then had recourse to private force (although in the presence of state officials) to enforce a legally settled claim. The dossier of charges against Primian suggests that this is what had happened, although it inverts the order "force" and "by legal authority." It is just possible that this sequence *was* the order in which events transpired. Primian might have tried first to enforce his property claims by attempting to take possession of them. Only when this approach failed did he then go to the civil courts to seek a decision that would allow him legally to use force to repossess them. Either way, the incident shows how much of the violence in these intra-Christian conflicts revolved around claims to property: the ownership of basilicas, church buildings, and other valuables. It is in this specific context that the leaders of Christian communities had good reason to bring in secular civil authorities who might otherwise have been reluctant to enter ecclesiastical quarrels.

Primian was also accused of pillaging houses belonging to Christians. This might refer to actual vendettas or to the use of violence as a form of threat or enforcement against persons in their own homes. But it might not. What a house was and who owned it would also be in dispute whenever a serious division occurred within a Christian community. Churches were often referred to as "houses," but the church at Carthage owned ordinary houses that were part of its property. Whoever was considered to be the legally constituted head of the church had a right to assert ownership and use of these houses. And disputes over properties other than basilicas were another aspect of the conflict between Primian and Maximian.[15] Perhaps after an initial attempt to assert ownership over such houses, Primian resorted to the civil courts on this matter as well. Maximian saw the houses as his, whereas Primian claimed that they were his insofar as they were property belonging to the church of which he was the legally constituted head. Just as probably, however, the term might have been used here in the precise Christian sense of a "house" of God, meaning a church or a basilica. Again, Primian would have been doing nothing other than sending enforcers to claim what he saw as being property belonging to his own church. So when he "besieged" the Elders in the houses in which they were meeting, he was probably doing nothing more than enforcing the same claim.

The case against Primian was heard before no less a figure than the son of the proconsular governor of Africa, Tiberius Flavius Sacerdos, who held the position of his father's judicial legate.[16] It was from the minutes of the court proceedings that later commentators were able to report on what had happened:

I am reading the *acta*, in which it is shown that the house that Maximian had defended as belonging to himself, Primian had seized back in the name of the Exorcists of the church through an agent to whom he had given this task. This was when the judicial legate Sacerdos gave him a favorable decision, as the court records themselves show.[17]

The fact that Primian filed his petition through a legal agent "in the name of the Exorcists," shows that the house in question was probably one of theirs, a residence where they lived. In this case, it was thought that the judge had ruled justly, and not out of a sense of personal favoritism. It is alleged that there had been several legal actions taken before more than one proconsular governor of Africa during this period asserting the ownership of such buildings.[18]

---

[15] Quinot (1967b).

[16] On Sacerdos, see de Veer (1961), although he seems unaware of the fundamental article by Pallu de Lessert (1917) who first presented the elegant and simple explanation for the word. As *legatus*, Sacerdos was stationed in Carthage to act as his father's representative, especially when the latter had to be absent from the city on his conventus circuit. As such, Sacerdos held the position of *legatus almae Karthaginis*. As we know, it was not unusual for sons of governors in the Principate to hold the position; presumably, the same practice was followed in the fourth century: Thomasson, *Statthalter*, I, pp. 60–61.

[17] Aug. *Contra Cresc.* 4.47.57 (CSEL 52: 554): "et recito gesta, quibus ostendam domum, quam Maximianus propriam defendebat, Primianum procuratione mandata exorcisterii ecclesiastici nomine, favente sibi Sacerdote legato, quod ipsa gesta indicant, abstulisse."

[18] Aug. *Contra Cresc.* 4.47.57 (CSEL 52: 554): "dico episcopos vestros et clericos vestros Maximianensibus in eis sedibus manentibus, in quibus antiquitus fuerant ordinati, fecisse persecutiones,

The petitions for legal actions filed with the civil court of the governor resulted in judicial orders which were then executed with the assistance of officials of the state. This is a pattern consistent with the events referred to in the decision of the Council of Cebarsussi. Disputes over properties other than basilicas may well have erupted early on in the disagreement between the two men, and might have been one of the main causes of their division. As much seems to be suggested by Augustine (who had access to the court *acta*) when he states:

in earlier days . . . when Maximian was still a deacon under Primian, some bishops who supported Maximian came to Carthage, as we find in the circular letter which they included in the *acta*. These Maximianists were in a legal dispute over a house with the agent of this same Primian who declared that he would "release" any property taken from him.[19]

The events at Carthage in the early 390s involving these two men with the state were civil matters that provoked the use of force, although they involved not much more than the normal and legal means of enforcing court decisions in one's favor.

The involvement of the state gave one side the legal right or cover under which it could legitimately use force to assert its property claims. The other side, naturally, did not see things so innocently, and with some justice. It was commonly known that judges were open to being influenced by bribes and other inducements (*gratia*, as it was known) to issue biased decisions. The not unexpected result was that more violence would occur as the one side brought "hired private thugs" (as they were seen to be) to use force to execute what the other side perceived to be an unfair judicial order. In consequence, it was considered just to resist these judicial enforcements with violence in kind. So it was that the battles between the two factions within the dissident church at Carthage were to consume the time of one proconsular judicial legate, Sacerdos, and at least three more Roman proconsular governors: Herodes, Theodorus, and Serenus.[20] It is in the context of judicial decisions that the incidents of violence must

apud proconsules accusasse, impetrasse iussiones eisdemque iussionibus exsequendis officiorum instantiam et civitatum auxilia meruisse."

19 Aug. *En. 2 in Ps.* 36.2.19 (CCL 38: 359–61). In this version, all of this takes place before the visiting bishops sent around their circular letter complaining that Primian had refused to come to meet with them.

20 Aug. *Contra Cresc.* 4.3.3 (CSEL 52: 500): "apud legatum Carthaginis et apud quattuor vel amplius proconsules factum est"; cf. *Ep.* 108.2.5 (CSEL 34.2: 615–16): where he mentions only three or more proconsuls; and *Brev. Collat.* 3.11.22 (CCL: 149A: 287–88); he mentions Sacerdos the legatus (above), Herodes and Theodorus (*Contra Cresc.* 3.56.62 [CSEL 52: 467]) and Seranus (*Contra Cresc.* 4.48.58 [CSEL 52: 555]) the proconsuls.

be interpreted. Quarrels that could be adjudicated by the law and civil authorities were taken to them and state officials were willing to accept these legal petitions because property actions, unlike disputes over the essential nature of the Trinity or about the efficacy of rebaptism, fell within their authority and expertise. But the court decisions implicated the government not just in property disputes, but also in ecclesiastical quarrels and, even if inadvertently, provided a legal basis for more violent provocations.

The first result caused by the decision of the council of Cebarsussi was to unseat Primian and to replace him with Maximian as the dissident bishop of Carthage. The excommunication of Primian from the church technically left the seat open, clearing the way for Maximian legally to take his place. At some time after the conference at Cebarsussi, almost certainly by August or September of 393, a large number of bishops assembled in the metropolis, out of whom twelve, the number formally required for a fully legitimate consecration of a bishop of a large and important province, moved to ordain Maximian as the dissident bishop of Carthage. The response by Primian was to fight back and to assert the original legitimacy of his position. For this, he required a larger, more numerously attended church council which, for that reason, would issue a more powerful and compelling declaration in his favor.

The words in the decree issued by this second council were inflected in a polemical rhetoric that is difficult to interpret. When reading its words, we must ask "just how violent was violent?" especially given the religious rhetoric of the period. Frequently, when Christian writers speak of death or murder or killing, as is clear from the words of the council of Bagaï already quoted, they were not speaking of secular homicides that were part of hard physical violence, but rather of spiritual deaths. For the bishops, "murder" was the driving of a soul out of the life of the church: this death was the death of the soul suffered by the pagan, the heretic, or the Christian who had gone bad. There is always an interpretive problem of where the line of interpretation is to be drawn between the two kinds of "killing." Let us consider one example. We have already encountered the frank-speaking and brutish Purpurius, the dissident bishop of Liniata, as a self-confessed murderer. But was he?

Quite apart from suspicions about the potentially fraudulent nature of the documents that attest to his badness, there is the additional problem of Christian rhetoric. It was normal to speak of converting or subverting the minds of the simple to a new belief or heresy as tantamount to murder: the seduction or traducing of someone's soul was committing homicide of the soul – it was much worse than physical murder.[21] The confirming evidence is found in the transcript of the meeting held by Secundus the bishop of Tigisis at Cirta in 305. If this document is genuine (a big "if"), Purpurius appears to assert that he had two of his sister's sons, his nephews, killed and that he would kill anyone who got in his way.[22] But is it possible that the uncritical have fallen into a trap and have created the murderous monster of a bishop that the Catholic preservers of these documents wished others to see? This is, for example, how Optatus glosses Purpurius: as a common murderer.[23] But it is interesting to note that Purpurius had a penchant for using caustic and cutting language, and it is conceivable that he was speaking, well, metaphorically. For example, at the end of his letter to the bishop Silvanus in which he was attempting to get him to make-up with his accuser Nundinarius, Purpurius says of Silvanus: "You're killing all of us."[24] The same verb "to kill" – *occidere* – is used. But did Purpurius literally mean that Silvanus was committing multiple acts of homicide? Surely not. He only meant that Silvanus, by his oburate and harsh actions towards Nundinarius, and his refusal to compromise, was threatening the privileged cabal of which he and Purpurius were part. Nothing more.

That this was the kind of homicide involved in a lot of the churchspeak of the time is almost certain. Both sides shared a soul-based definition of murder. Consider the following long sermon by a dissident preacher in Africa to his flock.[25]

This is the voice of the apostle John: "He who hates his brother is a murderer." Homicide is the worst evil and the greatest of harms, the first of all wrongs, the most savage of all crimes, the most horrifying of all sins. This is what destroys a man, takes away life, condemns to death. This, I say, is what is forbidden by the law, commanded to be feared, ordered to be avoided by Divine Law . . . The evil of hatred kills without a weapon, murders without a sword. The evil of hatred found at the beginning of the world made Cain kill his brother and crowned the

---

[21] For example, Optatus, *Contra Parm.* 1.2.2 (SC 412: 174–76): "nec nos eversas aut occisas innocentium animas doleremus," citing Ezechiel (13: 18) to the effect that it was a kind of murder: "Animae eversae sunt populi mei et maledicebant mihi in populo meo, ut occiderent animas quas non oportuit mori, dum adnuntiant populo meo vanas seductiones."

[22] See ch. 2, pp. 91–92 above.

[23] Optatus, *Contra Parm.* 1.13.3–4 (SC 412: 200): "et homicida Purpurius Liniatensis, qui interrogatus de filiis sororis suae quod eos in carcere Milevi necasse diceretur confessus est dicens: 'Et occidi et occido non eos solos sed et quicumque contra me fecerit.'" It should be noted that Optatus is not quoting the text verbatim as we have it.

[24] The letter was part of the dossier submitted by Nundinarius to the trial before the governor Zenophilus in 320; *Gesta apud Zenophilum*, 7 (Maier, *Dossier*, I, no. 29, p. 224): "Omnes nos occiditis . . ."

[25] Anon. *Sermo Escorial.* 55 (Leroy 1999: 215–17).

innocent Abel with martyrdom... The evil of hatred among brothers is absent within the Church, if it is even possible for one who hates a brother to be in the Church.

In this way, the preacher weaves a complex story, appealing to biblical parallels of fratricidal hatred, and actual murder, to caution against a more subtle wrong that counts in his eyes as homicide and makes the killer just as surely a murderer. He is suggesting that the Catholics, like the Jews whose evil hatred against good men the preacher details with relish, have been consumed by a hatred that has turned them into persecutors. Just as they destroy souls, so they murder them. Such talk of murder, when used freely in speaking about killing Jews, for example, and the logical fears of "death" were perhaps meant to be read in an allegorical fashion to refer to the "death" of one's culture, beliefs, or soul, but the general impact of such talk amongst the *imperiti* was bound to be more literal.[26]

The problem highlights a parallel one in the rhetoric of violence. In a civil society that already harbored every kind of low-level violence from the severe corporal punishment of schoolboys and slaves to the harsh physical disciplining of wives, the ability to talk a violent talk was perhaps less inhibited, especially so in the new allegorical talk of the Christian preacher.[27]

"He slaughtered many peoples, he killed mighty kings..." Obviously, he killed them. And so may he exterminate them now from the hearts of his slaves. Kill them, so that the church might no longer be tested by them. May his hand not cease from the slaughter of such kings and such peoples.

Just so, the loss of a soul by one church to the other through rebaptism, excommunication, or conversion (sc. betrayal) was commonly described as a tragic death, a homicide, or a murder, depending on one's point of view.[28] Indeed, intense dislike of one's Christian brother was itself construed as murder.[29] The step from this kind of rhetoric to positive injunctions that "the saints" should be armed for killing was not a big one.[30]

---

[26] See Fredriksen, *Augustine and the Jews*, pp. 270–74, on the metaphoric meaning.

[27] Aug. *En. in Ps.* 134.20 (CCL 40: 1951).

[28] Aug. *Ep.* 23.8 (CCL 31: 67): Augustine of the rebaptism of one of his own deacons at Hippo, refers to the matter politely – he is writing to a dissident bishop – as "death," but doubtless "murder" or "killing" in other terms.

[29] Aug. *En. in Ps.* 138.26 (CCL 40: 2008), where Augustine asks "Who are the men of blood? John says 'Everyone who hates his brother is a murderer.'" (referring to 1 Jn 3: 15): "Qui odit fratrem suum, homicida est."

[30] Aug. *En. in Ps.* 149.13 (CCL 40: 2186–87).

Now, brothers, you see that the holy men of god are armed. Expect slaughter, expect glorious combat. If there is a commander, then there is a soldier; if there is a soldier, then there is an enemy; if there is war, then there will be a victory . . . How will there be a double payback? The holy men now wage war, drawing their double-edged swords: there will be slaughters, killings, and deaths . . . soon there will be a double payback. The pagans will be exterminated and their idols smashed.

And so the preacher goes on, this time at great length, ramping up the violent language of killing and bodily harm, all of it aimed directly at the enemies of his church. Now they will pay, twice over. In this fashion, one walked the easy walk from metaphor to what would readily be perceived by most parishioners, surely, as an incitement to do the right thing.

THEIR COLLECTED EXCREMENT

The legal actions that Primian and his supporters had undertaken to enforce their ownership of church properties in Carthage and elsewhere were a core element of the charges filed against him at the council at Cebarsussi. On the other hand, the formal condemnation of this same council created the legal grounds for a return to the civil courts by his enemy Maximian. His supporters could now demonstrate that it was *they* who deserved legal enforcement of ownership of the basilicas and other church properties. For Primian and his side this was a dangerous development. As far as the records of the council allow us to see, there appears to have been a regional division in support for the two contending parties at Carthage. Almost all of the bishops whose bishoprics can be identified who signed the condemnation of Cebarsussi came from the proconsular province and the region of the Tunisian Sahel – the ecclesiastical province of Byzacena – and Tripolitania. They represented a more open-to-the-outside and cosmopolitan Mediter-ranean face of Africa.[31] A different group of bishops, part of a socially and regionally distinct group within the dissident church that was centered in the High Plains regions of Numidia far to the southwest of Carthage, rejected the findings of the council of Cebarsussi and called for a more universal council to be held that would finally decide the whole dispute. The latter men succeeded in their demand. The larger council was to be

---

[31] A point made by Frend, *Donatist Church*, pp. 215 f., who should not, however, have conceded the bishop of Theveste as a "Numidian" signatory; Theveste was always part of the proconsular province; nor does his other "Numidian," Pomponius of Macri, count: the Macri concerned is probably in Byzacena, not Sitifensis (so, correctly, see "Pomponius (2)," PAC, p. 882). The not inconsiderable cautions are two. First, many of the dioceses that are specified in the list still cannot be identified; second, the fifty-three names that survive are only half the original number. Still, the pattern seems to be there in the surviving evidence.

held at Bagaï. The choice of place was significant. Bagaï was the basilica center which, ever since the traumatic events of 347, had been one of the most highly charged holy sites of the dissident church; it was a special place that was a focus of pilgrimage to the monuments of the holy martyrs of that awful year. The new council convened in the spring of the following year, on 14 April 394. It was a much larger meeting of 310 bishops of the dissident church. Unfortunately, the list of signatories does not survive, so we are dependent on a later, perhaps biased claim that the great majority of these bishops came from the Mauretanias and Numidia, and only a few of them from Byzacena and the proconsular province.[32]

The bishops who assembled at Bagaï re-debated the entire problem of the quarrel between Primian and Maximian. They issued a decree of their own which was then sent around to all of the dissident churches in the form of a circular letter. Although this decree has survived only in the selected bits of it that were quoted by later writers, the words of the fragments that have survived are worth repeating verbatim to convey a sense of the increasingly violent language that was emanating from the quarrels within the dissident church.[33] The council's formal sentence was pronounced by our old friend, Emeritus, the dissident bishop of Caesarea in Mauretania.[34]

Decree of the Council of Bagaï

Since it is by the will of Almighty God and his Christ, our Saviour, that we have come from all the provinces of Africa to the Holy Church of Bagaï and have here held a council – Gamalius, Primian, Pontius, Secundianus, Ianuarianus, Saturninus, Felix, Pegasius, Rufinus, Fortunius, Crispinus, Florentius, Optatus, Donatus, Donatianus, and all others to the number of three hundred and ten – and since it pleases the Holy Spirit, who is in us, to confirm the perpetual peace and to cut away sacrilegious schisms . . .

. . . indeed, the conjoined brotherhood of peace and concord is very much hoped for, as it is written: *Justice and Peace kiss each other in turns*

---

[32] This *seems* to be the import of Augustine's words, however biased and rhetorically skewed they might be: Aug. *Contra Cresc.* 4.58.69 (CSEL 52: 568): "Si hoc iustissime dicturae sunt plebes et clerici eorum locorum, ex quibus erant trecenti et decem, qui contra Maximianenses Bagaiense concilium condiderunt, si hoc, inquam, recte dicturi sunt Afri Afris, Numidae et Mauri quam plurimi paucis Byzacenis et provincialibus."

[33] Maier, *Dossier*, 2, no. 56, pp. 84–91 (cf. CSEL 53: 276–78), who lists the original sources behind the five fragments of the decision that survive. As he rightly points out, it is not always clear what part of which fragments are from the decree proper, as opposed to embodying some of the discussion and debate in the council.

[34] Aug. *Gesta cum Emerit.* 10 (CSEL 53: 192): "ab isto Emerito est dicta sententia ubi illi damnati sunt."

[Ps. 85 (84): 11]. But the waves of the Truth have driven onto jagged rocks the shipwrecks of some men – following the example of the Egyptians – and the shores are littered with the funereal remains of those who have perished. The penalty that they will suffer is worse than death itself, since after life has been driven out of them by the avenging waters they shall find no burial . . .

The belly of a poisonous uterus can hide the deadly offspring of a viper's seed for a long time and the concealed dampness of the evil which has been conceived in this way will later, when slowly warmed, burst forth in the form of the bodies of vipers – and the poison thus created, once the dark and covering shadows disappear, can no longer be hidden. For sooner rather than later, the fetid lusts of their sins will give birth to parricide and brazen criminal acts – as has been foretold: *He is pregnant with unfairness; he shall conceive suffering and give birth to injustice* [cf. Ps. 7: 15]. A serenity already shines from amidst the dark clouds, however, and the dark forests are not completely convulsed with crimes, since there are specific names designated for punishment – although up to now a certain indulgence has been granted to the guilty – and since we now find ourselves beyond the limits of clemency, the facts plainly reveal to us those who must now be punished . . .

. . . we are speaking, dearest brothers, about the causes of schism, since we are no longer able to remain silent about the persons who are legally responsible. The lightning bolt of our judgment has struck Maximianus from the lap of peace – that very man: the adversary of the Faith, the adulterer of the Truth, the enemy of Mother Church, the helper of Dathan, Cora, and Abiron [cf. Num. 16: 32]. Since the earth has not yet swallowed him up, he is reserved for a greater punishment in what is to come. For having been thus torn from his position, although he might have saved himself the expense of a funeral, he will now pay the usurious interest of a much heavier loan, since he is now no more than a dead man among the living [cf. 1 Tim. 5: 6] . . . He is not the only man whom a just death condemns for his crimes. He has enticed very many men into a common share of his crimes, shackled them to his sacrilegious acts – those men of whom it is written: *The poison of vipers is on the lips of those whose mouths are filled with hatred and bitterness. Their feet rush to shed blood. Sadness and unhappiness mark their paths, and they do not recognize the way of peace. There is no fear of God before their eyes* [cf. Rom. 3.13–17]. We do not actually want these limbs to be amputated from our own body. But since the putrefying disease of a chronically debilitating wound benefits more from amputation than it does from the help of medicine, the healthier course of action is manifest. Care must be taken that this deadly poisonous infection does not spread through all of the limbs of our body – and so, even if at the price of some pain, we must cut out this lesion at its birth.

Therefore, the following defendants who are guilty of this infamous crime – Victorianus from Carcabia, Marcianus from Sullecthum, Beianus from Beiana, Salvius from Ausafa, Theodore from Usula, Donatus from Sabratha, Miggin from Elephantaria, Praetextatus from Assuras, Salvius from Membressa, Valerius from Melzi, Felicianus from Musti, and Martialis from Ad Pertusa – men who in their deadly work of damnation gulped down a filthy bowl filled with their own collected excrement – and also those members of the clergy of the church at Carthage, who, as they aided and abetted this crime, showed themselves to be the pimps and whoremongers of a criminal act of incest – let all these men know that they have been condemned by the True Voice of a universal council and by the decision of God who presided over it.

We do permit those men, whom the sucker shoots from that sacrilegious tree have not yet polluted, to return to Mother Church – that is, those men who, out of true shame for the faith, removed their hands from the head of Maximianus. For as much as we are purged by the deaths of the guilty, to that same degree we rejoice in the return of the innocent. And out of fear that too narrow a span of time allowed for those who wish to return will not sap the hope of safety because of the pressures of the day, we shall keep open the door for all those who recognize the Truth until the eighth day before the Kalends of January [25 December]. We also preserve the force of all earlier decisions, such that those who do return will have the basic parts of their status and of their faith kept intact. But to the extent that anyone does not come back because of an excessive sloth, let that person know that he himself, of his own volition, is shutting off all the roads to his re-entry. Against such persons, the sentence that has been decreed shall remain in force. And for those who return after the day indicated above, a set penitence shall be fixed.

The writers of the decree deliberately cast their condemnation in an aggressively harsh language. The hard-edged words forged a judgment that left no doubt in the minds of listeners where matters now stood. The damnation of Maximian and his supporters was of an absolute kind that made manifest not only their excommunication, but also their share in a quality of guilt that transformed them into poisonous vipers. In the animal language of Christians, the viper was usually the source of a repulsive and

Satanic evil, so the words could be counted on to evoke the appropriate hostile emotions from Christian believers. What else would be the response in the congregations of dissident churches throughout Africa as they heard the words of the decree read aloud to them? They heard vivid animal imagery in which the enemy within was compared to "the offspring of vipers." If they did not already know, the preacher would remind them of the judgment of the apostle John on the Jews – these people were poisonous, just like the rebels in their own church.[35] The judgment drew not only on elemental symbols that equated unbelievers to noxious animals like snakes, dogs, and scorpions, it also exploited the damnation narrative in the biblical story of Cora, Dathan and Abiron. It turned Maximian, and his followers, into living types in their own time of the disobedient and rebellious men who prefigured them.

As we have already seen in its use by Optatus in the 360s, the story of Cora, Dathan, and Abiron, as told in the biblical book of Numbers, was already central to the vitriolic rhetoric in which dissenters and Catholics condemned each other. It was to become increasingly central to the exemplary models exploited by both sides in their own sectarian battles.[36] The story told how Moses had been commanded by God to make an announcement to His people about remembering and obeying His laws. When Moses tried to do this, Cora the son of Izhar, and Dathan and Abiron, sons of Eliab, assembled two hundred and fifty leaders of the people and rose up against Moses and Aaron. The rebellion against Moses' authority was put to a divine test. Dathan and Abiron refused a summons by Moses, accusing him of having led them out of a land of milk and honey into a wilderness that threatened to exterminate them. When Aaron and Moses consulted God, He told them to separate themselves from the dwellings of Cora, Dathan, and Abiron. Moses advised the elders of Israel to cut themselves off from "these evil men and to touch nothing of theirs lest you be swept away with all of their sins." A day of apocalyptic confrontation between the two sides arrived. Moses appealed to God to demonstrate his authority. "As Moses finished speaking his words, the ground under them [i.e. the dissidents] split asunder. The earth opened its mouth and swallowed them up, with their household and all the men that belonged to Cora and all their goods. So they and all that belonged to them went down alive into Sheol. The earth closed over them and they perished . . . And fire

---

[35] For example, Aug. *Tract. in Joh.* 42.5.2 (CCL 36: 367), exploiting the remark in Matthew (3: 7–9) that the Sadducees and Pharisees were a *generatio viperarum*, "the offspring of vipers" (*progenies viperarum* in the VG).

[36] Numbers 16.1–35; modern translations usually have the names as Korah, Dathan, and Abiram; I use the names as accepted by Africans in their biblical texts.

came forth from the Lord and consumed the two hundred and fifty men who had offered the incense." The rebels had "offered incense." That alone evoked memories of collaborators in the Great Persecution, whose apostasy was condemned by all African Christians for their traitorous behavior on "the day of turification."

The story gave both biblical and sacred authority to the council's condemnation and it legitimized the extermination of heretical dissenters. Within the confines of the dissenting church itself, the power that had long been used for the final lethal damnation of perceived unbelief outside its community was now turned inwards on itself. But the absolute nature of the condemnation, carefully recorded as having been given by 310 bishops – three times the number that met at Cebarsussi in the previous year – had another target in its sights: the civil authorities of the Roman state. With the manifesto of Bagaï in his hands, Primian was now armed with legitimate grounds to defend the use of force, should it be needed. Such a use of the formal decision announced at Bagaï logically entailed a return to the civil courts. The fight was, once again, over claiming back the basilicas, houses, and other properties that were now in the hands of Maximian and his followers.[37]

This is how they acted when they condemned the Maximianists. They brought court actions before the judges [sc. the provincial governors] and they read aloud the decision of their council [i.e. the decree of Bagaï] and displayed their property titles so that they were seen to be bishops of these places. On that occasion, the judge asked: "Who is this other bishop? The one from the Donatist side?" An official from his office replied: "We do not recognize any bishop here [i.e. here at Carthage] except the Catholic Aurelius."

The last words are probably useful fictive additions. Nevertheless, what remains shows that Primian would now be able to use force legally against Maximian to enforce the occupation of the basilica in which the latter was ensconced. Presumably this would have required the mobilization of rough men to accomplish and, almost predictably, there would have been physical resistance from the other side. Augustine later represented this incident as a destruction of the basilica that was accomplished by the kind of mob action from which other dissidents wished to distance themselves: "Of course, now you will say: 'It was the people by themselves who destroyed the basilica or rather the cave' of Maximian – but that they had no authority to do so from any of our people."[38] But the statement

---

[37] Aug. *En. 2 in Ps.* 21.2.31 (CCL 38: 133); note that although Augustine claims to be quoting an official record, one should not make too much about the appearance of the words "the Donatist side."

[38] Aug. *Contra Cresc.* 3.59.65 (CSEL 52: 471): "Numquid et nunc dicturus es: 'basilicam vel speluncam Maximiani populus nullo nostrorum auctore destruxit.'"

that it was nothing other than a mob action involving the destruction of the basilica is a rhetorical statement put into his opponents' mouths by Augustine. Doubtless there was some hard enforcement of the court order, but it is difficult to know what physical violence actually occurred when, as it was later said, Maximian and his supporters were "terrorized, thrown into upheaval, driven out, and shown to be renegades."[39] More probably, it is a repetition of the perspective of one side, the aggrieved one, in the struggle inside the dissident community at Carthage.

THE FATAL NECKLACE

The best-documented incident connected with the enforcement resulting from the decree of Bagaï in regions outside the metropolis of Carthage was an affair that implicated Salvius of Membressa, one of the twelve bishops who had consecrated the bishop Maximian who had been condemned by the council of Bagaï. Membressa was a small but typical village on the Bagrada River, about fifty miles inland from Carthage.[40] This particular incident became more widely known because it was one of the disputes that had been heard by the civil courts at Carthage. Most of the bishops who had been involved in the ordination of Maximian came from centers in Byzacena and Tripolitania. If charges were lodged against them, they would have been heard by the imperial officials governing those provinces. But cases like those of Praetextatus from Assuras and Felicianus from Musti, like that of Salvius – men who were bishops from small towns in the territory of Carthage – would have been heard by the officials of the proconsular province. It is therefore no accident that we know more about the difficulties in which these particular men were involved. Evidence concerning their cases was privileged by the fact that they were in the judicial circuit of Carthage where news was more likely to be known and to be better preserved. Whatever the fortuitous nature of our knowledge of them, these cases reveal the common framework within which sectarian violence occurred.

---

[39] Aug. *Contra Cresc.* 4.47.57 (CSEL 52: 555): "pariter plebibus suis propria conventicula frequentabant, loca et basilicas quas non invaserant cum populis sibi cohaerentibus perpetua possessione retinebant, terrerentur, proturbarentur, expellerentur, renitentes exhiberentur." It must be remembered that Augustine is trying to use the Primianist (that is, orthodox Donatist) treatment of the Maximianists as a parallel to justify the actions of the orthodox Catholics against the Donatists. Importantly, there is an alternative reading for "renitentes" as "retinentes" which would make much better sense and be much less dramatic, with the meaning of "having shown them to be holding on (illegally) to these properties."

[40] On Membressa (Medjez al-Bab), see Lepelley, *Cités de l'Afrique romaine*, 2, pp. 141–44: "L'histoire municipale de cette cité est fort mal connue."

Armed with the decision of the bishops at Bagaï, Primian moved quickly to replace the bishops who had supported his rival Maximian, especially those who had been directly involved in Maximian's consecration. Salvius, the bishop of Membressa, was one of these hated rivals. Some time before December 394, Primian had one of his own men named Restitutus ordained as bishop of Membressa. Faced with this unwanted interloper, Salvius refused to budge or to surrender his possession of the town's basilica. Once again, the battle was to be over property and the same pattern of conflict was repeated. If Restitutus attempted a tentative use of force to assert his claim to the basilica, he soon relented and the issue moved to the civil courts. He probably filed his petition to the court in late 394. Since Membressa was a municipality in the greater urban territory of Carthage, the case was brought before the proconsular governor of Africa. By February of the following year, 395, it was heard by the governor Flavius Herodes.[41] The legal counsel Nummasius who represented Primian's man, Restitutus, held forth, no doubt eloquently, on the "hidden sacrilege" that had been committed by the defendants and on how they were guilty of "the theft of a bishop's name." In response to a command by the proconsul to "read the bishops' decision," Nummasius read aloud the decree of the Council of Bagaï. Herodes, the governor, seems to have accepted the number and authority of the bishops as decisive. Part of the governor's final decision has survived. Using the convoluted language of judicial sentences, he declared: "I utterly reject any attempt to express a view to the contrary. I decree that all churches whose ownership has been legally reclaimed ('vindicated') from certain sacrilegious persons shall be restored to the most holy bishops."[42]

The legal case brought against Salvius of Membressa was only one of a series of court actions lodged against all of the twelve consecrators of Maximian. Two other cases are known in some detail because they also came from the proconsular province and so had been archived at Carthage. The judicial records of the proceedings were therefore readily accessible to interested parties and just as eagerly preserved by them. The cases were filed against Felicianus, the dissident bishop of Musti, and another man, Praetextatus, the dissident bishop of Assuras, both of whom were supporters of Maximian. Musti was about ninety miles southwest of Carthage on

---

[41] This hearing took place some time well before March of 395 when it is referred to as already having taken place and the records from it are cited in the trial before the governor Herodes on 2 March of that year: see, Maier, *Dossier*, 2, no. 59: 97 n. 20.

[42] Aug. *Contra Cresc.* 3.56.62 (CSEL 52: 468): "Exploso omni contradictionis effectu sacratissimis sacerdotibus a profanis mentibus ecclesias vindicatas oportere restitui."

the main highway that led from Carthage to Theveste, deep in the interior of Africa. Assuras was located about thirty miles south of Musti. It was reached by a branch road that forked off the main Carthage–Theveste highway. The confrontations, once again, were over the possession of church properties: basilicas, houses, and furnishings. As before, the petitions were filed at Carthage, this time in the autumn of 394. The cases were heard on 2 March 395 by the same governor, Flavius Herodes. The statements made in the course of this trial, accessible from the official records kept of the proceedings, permit valuable insights into the process of conflict and violence that upset these small local communities.

The petition to the court bears the formal legal title of "Petition for Action Laid before the Governor Herodes": *postulatio apud Herodem proconsulem*. The initial statement given by Titianus, the lawyer representing the side of Maximian, reveals the modes and effects of conflict within the churches in these two small towns in the hinterland of Carthage. The trial record documents a similar breakdown in the normal local power structures around the bishops; and it also reveals the emergence, as at Carthage, of alternative centers of authority to fill this vacuum, especially that of the Elders or *seniores*. The priest Peregrinus and the Elders of the region of Assuras and Musti had mobilized support for Primian. The way in which they expressed their support is important because it is a statement from the dissident Christians in their own voice about *their* view of the situation. Here, as elsewhere, they represent themselves as orthodox Catholics.[43]

Donatus, a man of venerable memory, defended the holiness of the Catholic Church from the error of mistaken belief . . . Donatus, in whose name and worship almost the whole world has gathered in caring reverence. But the poisons of a certain Maximian have polluted the praiseworthy and wonderful ideals of his beliefs.

Praetextatus of Assuras refused to submit to the judgment issued against him by the proconsul Flavius Herodes in March 395. A rival bishop named Rogatus, who had been elected to confront him, had gone to the courts to try to assert *his* claim to the basilica and the other properties in Assuras that were controlled by Praetextatus. The complicated legal proceedings consumed most of what remained of this year and almost all of the year that followed. It was only on 21 December 396 that the proconsular governor Theodorus issued another decision against Praetextatus.[44] But both

---

43 Quoted by Aug. *Contra Cresc.* 3.56.62 (CSEL 52: 467) from the original court record of which it was part.

44 Aug. *Contra Cresc.* 3.56.62 (CSEL 52: 468–69): "quantum ex gestis proconsularibus et municipalibus indagare potuimus, usque ad Theodorum proconsulem, hoc est usque anni alterius diem xi kal. Ian.,

Praetextatus and his colleague Felicianus at Musti continued to ignore the court orders, and obdurately held on to the basilicas and the other church properties that they controlled as bishops. By 398 or 399, the regional group of bishops who had dominated the council of Bagaï were no longer willing to leave matters in the hands of the civil courts and the vagaries of the private execution of the judicial orders of proconsuls. Led by the energetic authority of Optatus, the dissident bishop of Thamugadi, they put great pressure on both bishops – Praetextatus at Assuras and Felicianus at Musti – to re-enter communion with Primian at Carthage. Equal force was brought to bear on Primian to agree to receive the rebellious bishops back into his communion with their rank and status preserved intact.

It is often claimed that the force that the bishop Optatus of Thamugadi wielded was of a gross, brutal, and violent kind, and that in this case it included the mobilizing of an army of sectarian thugs or circumcellions who fronted an armed attack into the heart of the proconsular province to achieve his aims. For such extravagant claims, there is no convincing evidence.[45] Statements that impute the use of real violence are only found in polemical arguments made many years later by Augustine who wished to argue that "the Donatists" themselves had employed brutish coercion, if they found it useful, to oust unacceptable opponents from their churches. In support of his tendentious argument, Augustine claims that an actual military expedition had been launched by Optatus against some "bad bishops" within the dissident church. But his exact words are worth close inspection. First, he considers the order issued by the council of Bagaï. Then, in full rhetorical flow, he states:[46]

Such were the insults against their own schismatics [i.e. the supporters of the bishop Maximian] to the point of calling them both "the dead" and "those left without burial." But they must assuredly have wished that they would have been buried – then there wouldn't have been a multitude of corpses left without burial and cast up on the shores, Optatus the Gildonian would not have advanced with

quo die clerici et seniores agentes sub Rogato episcopo, qui in locum damnati Praetextati Adsuritani fuerat subrogatus, allegaverunt memorati proconsulis iussionem, cum a foris erant a communione vestra et eiusdem communionis vestrae inimici in iudiciis publicis arguebantur et expellendi de locis Deo summo consecratis tamquam sacrilegi petebantur."

[45] The picture offered by Frend, *Donatist Church*, pp. 222–23, is very colorful but, as far as I can determine, it is mostly a fiction not underwritten by the evidence.

[46] Aug. *Contra litt. Petil.* 1.10.11 (CSEL 52: 11): "Ita quidem isti insultant schismaticis suis, ut eos et mortuos et insepultos vocent. Sed certe optare debuerunt ut sepelirentur, ne de multitudine iacentium in litore cadaverum insepultorum Gildonianus Optatus incedens cum agmine militari tamquam rabidus fluctus ultra prosiliens Felicianum et Praetextatum introrsus postea resorberet"; cf. *Contra litt. Petil.* 2.83.184 (CSEL 52: 114): "Ipsa ecclesia Catholica solidata principibus Catholicis imperantibus terra marique armatis turbis ab Optato atrociter et hostiliter oppugnata est."

his armed battle line and would not have swept forward like an enraged storm at sea, and Felicianus and Praetextatus would not have been swallowed up in the waves of this storm.

How is this colorful and emotional replaying of the events that plays on the words of the decree of Bagaï to be understood? Did Optatus of Thamugadi actually advance with real battle lines? Did he actually sail a real fleet through the "avenging waters" of the decree? When the dissident Cresconius later objected to the presentation of Augustine's flights of fantasy as if they were fact, Augustine replied by quoting the words from the passage above and then commented in defense of them:[47]

> The cities of Musti and Assuras themselves are witnesses. They say that it was because of the Gildonian army [i.e. the forces of Optatus of Thamugadi] threatened by Optatus that they [i.e. the mainstream "Donatists"] compelled their bishops to return to the communion of Primian.

This is the full evidence for Optatus having led or sent an armed column to the towns of Assuras and Musti. It is not convincing as historical fact. All that Augustine says is that he had heard from the "Donatist" Catholics at Assuras and Musti that they were afraid because they had been "threatened" by Optatus with "serious consequences," so they had brought pressure on their own bishops to join Primian's church. That seems to be the full extent of what had happened. In other words, by using hard diplomacy, Optatus had compelled the two bishops to return to their original communion and Primian to accept them.[48] The most effective policing was that which was enforced within the dissident religious community itself.

Salvius, the bishop who supported Maximian's side at Membressa, remained intransigent. All that the newly elected bishop Restitutus could do was go back to the courts to present yet another claim to the church property at Membressa. Filed probably in early 397, the matter finally came before the proconsular governor Seranus for a hearing either late in 397 or early in 398. In the little snippets that have survived about the hearing, there are hints of frustration on the part of the secular authorities over this case, as well as of their general unwillingness further to involve themselves in ecclesiastical disputes of a complicated and frustrating kind. The

---

[47] Aug. *Contra Cresc.* 4.25.32 (CSEL 52: 530): "Quod et ipsae civitates Mustitana et Adsuritana testantur, quae se dicunt ex Optati comminatione Gildonianum militem formidantes coegisse episcopos suos ad communionem redire Primiani."

[48] Aug. *Contra litt. Petil.* 2.83.184 (CSEL 52: 113): "utrum ad communionem vestram non invitum Optatus redire compulerit." *Contra Cresc.* 3.60.66 (CSEL 52: 472): "et Optatum quidem Gildonianum graviora exitia comminantem Mustitani et Adsuritani, sicut ab eis quoque praesens audivi, timuisse dicuntur et suos episcopos coegisse, ut ad Primiani communionem reverterentur."

proconsular governor Seranus confronted the parties with the following cautions:[49]

According to the law, a civil suit between bishops ought to be heard by their fellow bishops. The bishops themselves should be making these judgments. Why don't you go back to the whole body of your ancients [i.e. bishops] for the purpose of seeking a settlement? Or better, as you have it in your own holy writings, turn your backs on your persecutors?

Despite his unwillingness to deal with an issue that he perceived, probably rightly, to be one in which it would be best for the civil courts not to be involved, Serenus nevertheless issued yet another judicial order in favor of Restitutus. Salvius and his supporters suggested that there had been *gratia* or corrupt influence on the judge's decision, but it was generally admitted that it was the public reading of the decision by the council of Bagaï that had moved the governor to his opinion. A good three years had now passed since the first order had been issued by a Roman governor and Restitutus had yet to enforce his claim to the basilica and other properties at Membressa. In his remarks, the governor Serenus indicated what he thought ought to be done: the bishop Salvius either ought to return to the general body of bishops of the communion of Primian or he ought to get up and leave Membressa so that, without any opposition, Restitutus could possess all the places that were held by Salvius.

Armed with the new decision by the governor, both Primian and Restitutus – *his* bishop of Membressa – could use force to execute the judgment. Such enforcement would now be legal. It is possible that this time the governor's decision went further by issuing an order concerning the execution of his decision. Knowing that he would not be able to make headway in executing the order within the town of Membressa, Restitutus began to recruit people from the neighboring town of Abitina to assist in enforcing the judgment.[50] Outsiders could be used to do the dirty work: the

---

[49] Aug. *Contra Cresc.* 4.48.58 (CSEL 52: 555–56): "Sic enim in eisdem gestis legitur: 'Seranus pro consule dixit: "Lis episcoporum secundum legem ab episcopis audienda est: episcopi iudicaverunt. Quare non aut sub satisfactione ad chorum reverteris vetustatis aut, ut habes scriptum, terga persecutoribus prodis?"'" Technically, the proconsul's question was a good one: see CTh 16.2.12 (23 Sept. 385) and Const. Sirmond. 3 (SC 531: 480–85) of 384.

[50] This seems to be the sequence of causes suggested by Aug. *Contra ep. Parm.* 3.6.29 (CSEL 51: 141): "si autem dicit nihil aliud impetrasse a proconsule Primianistas, nisi ut per Abitinenses Salvius de basilica pelleretur, illos autem sua sponte fecisse quidquid ei postea crudeliter turpiterque fecerunt." (If one says that the Primianists sought from the proconsul nothing other than the right to use the Abitinians to chase Salvius from his basilica, and that these latter persons had then taken the initiative on their own in all the cruel and shameful actions that they took against him.) For Abitina, see Lepelley, *Cités de l'Afrique romaine*, 2, pp. 56–62. It has now been located, with its proper name of *Avitina* at Chouhoud al-Batel, see Beschaouch (1976), less than 3 miles from Membressa.

local rivalry and the natural contempt that the two towns had for each other could be usefully exploited. The reason for the failure of earlier orders against Salvius now becomes clear: the great majority of Christians in Membressa liked and supported him. No legal records tell what then happened to Salvius, an elderly man who was held in high esteem by his own community. Precisely because such events were located in a post-trial post-legal world, we tend not to hear of them. It was on a journey that Augustine made through the towns of the middle Bagrada valley in mid-summer of 404 that he learned from eyewitnesses the facts of the case – or so he avers – a story that he claimed that he hardly had the heart to retell. Of course, he still told the story because it was a good piece of ammunition that could be used against the dissident church, unmasking the hypocrisies of its actions.[51] The story ties together other elements in the concatenated sequence of violent incidents. In a later letter, Augustine says that a good deal of private violence was involved in driving "illegal occupants" out of their possessions. But in reclaiming them, how much terror was deployed and how much bodily violence? That depended on the circumstances, and in some cases, like that of Salvius at Membressa, things just went too far.[52]

Even in the aftermath of the proconsul's decision against him, Salvius continued to hold on to his basilica and his position. He relied, as much as he could, on the local people of Membressa who were favorably disposed to him. The mob coming from the nearby town of Abitina, however, overcame his local defenders. Salvius was arrested. The invaders did not take him before a court where the issue between the two sides might have been heard. Instead, the victorious Abitinians staged a sordid triumphal parade. A strange merging of *charivari* and ritual humiliation ensued. Driving the aged Salvius before them, the Abitinians tied a necklace of dead dogs around his neck and paraded him through the streets of Membressa, while they danced around the old man and jeered at him.[53] Their celebratory dance steps were accompanied by "shameful words" – obscene ritualistic chants of a sort meant to destroy Salvius' reputation. The singing of other songs added both to the sense of victory of the supporters of Primian and

---

[51] Aug. *Contra Cresc.* 3.60.66 and 4.449–50.60 (CSEL 52: 472, 556–57); cf. Perler, *Voyages de saint Augustin*, pp. 448–49.

[52] Aug. *Ep.* 108.16 (CSEL 34.2: 630).

[53] Aug. *Contra Cresc.* 4.49.59 (CSEL 52: 556–57): "Nam quia eis pro defendendis ex quantacumque parte sedibus suis etiam post proconsulis iudicatum turbae sibi faventis fiducia Salvius repugnare temptaverat, victus aliquando conprehensus est, non iam ducendus ad iudicem, ubi inter partes fuerat prolata sententia, sed pompa miserabili triumphandus. Capto enim seni mortuos canes alligaverunt in collo et sic cum illo quantum libuit saltaverunt."

Restitutus and to the humiliation of the defeated Salvius.[54] While this violent mini-drama succeeded in driving Salvius from his basilica, it also showed the limits of force in changing hearts and minds. The people of Membressa remained steadfast in their loyalty to *their* bishop. Rather than give in to the dictates of force, they built Salvius a new basilica to replace the one that he had lost.[55] And so the struggle was continued at local level well into the next decade. The small town of Membressa would now have at least three Christian bishops, all consumed with hatred for each other.

These were the same Abitinians, we must remember, who felt sad each year, perhaps even wept, on hearing the high moral demeanor and bravery of their martyrs in the Great Persecution. This is what they now did, joyfully, to their fellow dissident Christians. Some years later, the details of the attack on Salvius were too much to bear, especially for Augustine who was given this opportunity to parade his personal *horreur*. That an elderly man holding the rank of bishop, no matter in what church, should be treated in such a disgusting manner was something that was deeply disturbing. Augustine is certain that a respected aged bishop like Salvius would have found it easier to endure the old Etruscan punishment of being tied to the corpses of dead men rather than to be humiliated in public and to be forced to dance obscenely with a pack of human bitches (as Augustine colorfully puts it, meaning to recall, no doubt, the necklace of dead dogs). In adding the gender and transferring the animalization, Augustine succeeds in condemning the Abitinian mob – but his attention was drawn to the animals.[56] Which provokes a question about the specific nature of this terrible denigration: Why the necklace of dead dogs? The ritual was so awful that it caused revulsion in Augustine, who suggests that the dogs had something to do with impurity and contagion.[57]

The dogs were clearly symbolic. But of what? Two generations earlier, in his attack on Parmenian in the mid-360s, Optatus of Milevis had drawn attention to the fact that it was known that a sinner's sacrifice was a dog.[58]

---

[54] Aug. *Contra ep. Parm.* 3.6.29 (CSEL 51: 139): "Salvius, cui tantas Abitinenses plagas et contumelias intulerant, per quos isti meruerant ut de ecclesia pelleretur, ut eius cervici etiam mortuorum canum cadavera colligarent, ut postremo cum illo ad turpes voces cantionesque saltarent."

[55] At least, this seems to be the implication of Aug. *Contra ep. Parm.* 3.6.29 (CSEL 51: 139): "quem sermonem, posteaquam tanta perpessus est, eum putamus habuisse cum suis quos miseros decepit, ut alteram sibi basilicam fabricarent?"

[56] Aug. *Contra Cresc.* 4.50.60 (CSEL 52: 558); more of his outrage in *Contra ep. Parm.* 3.6.29 (CSEL 51: 139): "canina vero humanis et hoc episcopalibus membris nescio utrum quisquam se vel audisse umquam vel legisse commemoret."

[57] Aug. *Contra ep. Parm.* 3.6.29 (CSEL 51: 140): "quem vero canes mortui collo suspensi immundum fecerint non potest expiari?"

[58] Optatus, *Contra Parm.* 4.1.1 (SC 413: 80): "Solus Deus indicet peccatorem, cuius sacrificium sit canina victima."

In making the statement, he was referring to the way in which he glossed certain verses in Isaiah [66: 3] where the prophet refers to the practices of the heathen: "some immolate an ox, some slaughter a man, some sacrifice a lamb, some strangle a dog," and also a passage in Deuteronomy [23: 18] where there is a warning against prostituting the "daughters of Israel," an injunction which was later taken to mean seduction into heretical belief: "You must not bring to the house of Yahweh your God the wages of a prostitute or the earnings of a dog, whatever vow you have made, for both are detestable to Yahweh our God." The dog here was an animal symbol for a male prostitute. This is a sort of animal symbolism that Optatus himself made explicit:

By saying "adulterers" he means heretics and by "adulteresses" those people's churches which Christ rejects and repudiates in the Songs of Songs... and since it is clearly proven by divine evidence that you are sinners... as is seen in that prophet [Isaiah], in whom we read, "the sacrifice of the sinner is like one who makes a dog his sacrifice."[59]

The necklace of dead dogs formed the scarlet letters of Salvius' sexual delict. He was not a bishop of the true church, but rather a detestable adulterer of the Truth.

A STRUCTURING OF VIOLENCE

Beginning with the death of Parmenian around 390, the battles between the supporters of Primian and the supporters of Maximian, all of them notably *within* the dissident church, consumed the better part of a decade, and involved the exertions of the public courts and several Roman governors. The supporters of Maximian remained a large and sufficiently significant community to be recognized at the time of the great conference of 411 that was held between the Catholics and the dissident Christians. The dissenters within the dissident church were sufficiently numerous, in Carthage at least, that special provisions had to be taken to exclude them from the proceedings.[60] Despite the reconciliations of the late 390s, even two decades later, the divisions within the dissident community had not been wholly

---

[59] Optatus, *Contra Parm.* 4.6.7–8 (SC 413: 98–100): "Haereticos dicit *moechos* et *moechas* ecclesias illorum quas aspernatur et repudiat Christus in canticis canticorum... Et quoniam vos esse peccatores divino testimonio manifestissime comprobatum est, etiam illud ostensum est tua auxilia contra te militasse. In auxilium enim addideras prophetam in quo lectum est: *Sacrificium peccatoris quasi qui victimet canem.*"

[60] GCC, 1.10 (CCL 149A: 61; SC 195 has several typographical errors): "Maximianistis etiam edicti huius innotescet auctoritas, qua sibi ab illo concilio intelligant temperandum, quo inter catholicos donatistasque discingi omnem diiudicarique conflictum."

closed. What do these internal fissionings tell us about the nature of violence and the specific role of violent acts?

It must be remembered that this is a story taking place *within* the dissident church: a schism within a schism, a fissuring with a fission. Because of the nature of the construction of large Christian communities (whether the Catholic communion in Africa or the dissident one does not matter) the propensity to such internal fissionings was to be expected. Both churches were built up incrementally of a series of autonomous building blocks, each of which replicated internally the structure of all of the others. When a division struck the church as a whole, there was a considerable probability that the division would be replicated, or echoed, at lower levels of cohesion. Similar forces would have similar effects on the constitutive units, even if they were lower down on the scale of integration. Violent acts would also replicate themselves in much the same patterns. And since there are patterns, it might be useful to understand them in order to understand to what extent they were replayed in the larger conflict. There is every sign in this history that we are confronting a uniform history of hatred. There is a basic sameness of structure everywhere and at every level, so that even if there were divisions within divisions, similar characteristics of violence are found being replicated over and over again.

In later years, when giving a résumé and retrospective of this dispute and its significance, Augustine emphasized this same cycle of church-based decisions, court decisions, and the recourse to gangs of men to enforce the decisions, with different specific results depending on the circumstances in each community. He points to the regular sequence. Specifically in this case they were: the decision made at Bagaï, then the appeals launched by the Primianists in the courts in which they formally requested court orders – *impetrantur iussiones* – and, with these in hand, they gathered the "muscle" or help – *auxilia congregantur* – needed to enforce them. With these enforcers they attempted to eject the "condemned men" from the basilicas. If the sequence was generally similar, the results varied in each case. In those local circumstances where the congregations were strong and supported "the condemned," there was resistance; where the local forces were weak, they were defeated.[61] But much this same pattern – only one of the structures of violence, admittedly – played itself out again and again.

---

[61] Aug. *Gesta cum Emerito*, 9 (CSEL 53: 191): "venitur ad eiciendos de basilicis homines damnatos et in sua pertinacia constitutos. Illis condemnatis populi qui favebant restiterunt; ubi non potuerunt victi sunt, in locum eorum qui victi sunt et expulsi alii ordinati sunt."

A NEW CATHOLIC STRATEGY

By the mid-390s, the severe breakdown within the dissident church drew to the attention of its enemies a rare opportunity, an unusual opening to be exploited.[62] Weakened by internal dissension, it was possible that the dissidents might be vulnerable to a concerted attack on them and their ideas. This opening was paralleled by the emergence of a new and more aggressive leadership in the Catholic Church. The consequences of these basic ground-level shifts and fortuitous coincidences should not be underestimated. A new Catholic primate of Africa, Aurelius, the holder of the First Seat of Africa, was elected as bishop of Carthage, probably in 392. His elevation to power was soon matched by the election of Augustine as the Catholic bishop of Hippo Regius in 395. These two men, and others like them, were representative of a new energetic level of a dynamic leadership: intelligent and driven men who were willing to strike closer links with secular authorities at the highest levels in order to gain their co-operation in the repression of their enemies.

Aurelius and Augustine were intent on pursuing three possible strategies, any one of which might move imperial authorities to more aggressive action. The first step was to get the dissidents categorized as heretics, thereby opening the way to the use of the full force of existing imperial anti-heretical laws against them. This was to be paralleled by the heavy exploitation of the hypocrisies of their treatment of their own dissidents, the Maximianists. The last and the most critical link in this program was to demonstrate that the dissidents harboured a dangerous and violent insurrectionist movement. One can see all three strategies at play in Augustine's writings through the late 390s and in the first years of the fifth century. A dossier of evidence was being prepared that would provide the probative data for the arguments. These were discussed and prepared in the years before they were first given full public expression in the debates of the Catholic council held at Carthage on 25 August 403. At the conclusion of the conference, the Catholic bishops drafted a formal petition to Septiminus, the proconsular governor of Africa.[63] The letter made an appeal for the direct involvement of the imperial authorities in the coercive repression of the dissident Christians and their church. It was pointed out that the ways in which imperial officials had assisted Primian, the

---

[62] De Veer (1965) reviews the essential evidence.

[63] Septiminus is otherwise unknown. He is the recipient of CTh 12.6.29 (20 Feb. 403) and CTh 8.5.64 + 13.1.19 (26 March 403), which attest him as governor of Africa; see "Septiminus (1)," PLRE, 2, p. 991.

dissident bishop of Carthage, in his repression of the supporters of Maximian, showed that Roman governors had accepted the principle that governmental decrees issued against a religious community were fully legal.
Although true, the application of the principle would get the Catholics no
further than the old run-around of court orders confirming their possession
of church properties. What was wanted was something more decisive and
compelling.

More important than ecclesiastical and theological error, therefore, was
the suggestion that the dissident church sheltered men who were not just
holders of different, and unacceptable, Christian beliefs. They had to be
seen as a violent threat to the secular social order. There existed a kind of
threat that the Catholic bishops felt that they could successfully portray
as an apprehended general insurrection fronted by violent men known as
circumcellions. This picture was to be accepted much later by the authority
of the Roman state, in the person of the tribune and notary Marcellinus who
presided over the great hearing between the Catholics and the dissidents at
Carthage in 411:[64]

Or if they think that they possess anything of the truth, let them defend it *not* with
the raging and violent actions of their circumcellions against the public peace, but
with a calm and cool accounting presented in peace and quiet.

This is the first time that the circumcellions, labelled as such, are known
to have entered the formal official public discourse of the state, specifically
as a threat to the social order. The recognition of them as a serious threat,
not just to some individual Catholics, but to the imperial peace itself, had
been laid down by repeated descriptions of circumcellion behavior and
by the careful identification of them as a specific group of violent men
known by this particular name. The statement by the Catholic bishops at
the conference of Carthage of 403, however, was not conclusive and not
yet sufficient to move the heavy power of the state. The reply made by the
Roman governor on this occasion was notably cool and formal. *All* parties,
he said, were to be held responsible for the peace of the empire. Period.

The council that the Catholic bishops held the next summer in Carthage,
on 16 June 404, therefore decided to ratchet up the stakes. A decision was
made to go over the head of the proconsular governor of Africa and to
make representations directly to the imperial court at Ravenna. It is at
this point that the existence of the circumcellions and the record of their
behavior became critical. What might be called a "circumcellion dossier"

---

[64] GCC 3.174 (SC 224: 1120): "Aut si putant se habere aliquid veritatis, non eam furiosis circumcellionum violentiis contra publicam quietem sed tranquilla rationis redditione defendant."

was being assembled for the purpose of convincing the imperial authorities that there existed a real and palpable danger to the social order in Africa. The purpose of the dossier was to provide a history of "the circumcellions" for consumption by the imperial court. The threat of violence – specifically the amorphous and uncontrolled violence of homeless and masterless wandering men – was to become the trump card to be played in this game. The dossier included some of the spectacular horror stories and detailed narratives of violence that later repeatedly resurfaced as typical instances of what were claimed to be indicative of a wave of violence sweeping the African countryside. The Catholic embassy to Ravenna also took along with it some living examples of survivors of "circumcellion attacks" as a show-and-tell for the imperial court. It was hoped that showcase horror stories might move imperial authorities. They were an in-your-own-life demonstration of "what might happen to you." This is the political context in which the mass of the surviving evidence on the "circumcellions" was generated.

The brief given to the Catholic ambassadors Theasius and Evodius in 404 represented a sea change in the type of discourse. Gone are the issues of purity, orthodoxy, the status of scriptures, and concerns with rebaptism as the center of appeals for imperial help. Such religious matters had had a dismal record of failure in efforts to move the imperial court to action. The Catholic discourse now shifts decisively to one about violence, specifically the existence of a sinister threat to public order. And with this shift, the focus of attention moves more decisively from the municipal courts and those of the provincial governor, with their normative concerns with property and civil matters, to connections with the imperial court, a court that could use armed force to repress heresy and sedition. Accordingly, the preamble to the brief or *commonitorium* of the council to Theasius and Evodius is frankly political. It begins by portraying the Catholic Church in Africa as the locus of peace, a communal source of kindness and mercy. From this point onward, the whole of the brief given to the ambassadors was that they were to take concerns about the problem of violence to the imperial court.[65]

---

[65] Acts of the Conference of Carthage of 16 June 404 (CCL 149: 211): "Commonitorium fratribus Theasio et Evodio legatis ex Carthaginensi concilio ad gloriosissimos religiosissimosque principes missis... et illi, qui veritati respondere nequiverunt, ad immanes violentias sunt conversi, ita ut multos episcopos multosque clericos, ut de laicis taceamus, insidiis oppresserint, ecclesias etiam aliquas invaserint, aliquas invadere pertentaverint, ipsorum iam clementiae est consulere, ut ecclesia catholica, quae eos religioso utero in Christo genuit et fidei firmitate nutrivit, eorum etiam prospectione muniatur, ne temerarii homines religiosis temporibus infirmos populos terrendo praevaleant, quoniam seducendo depravare non possunt. Nota est enim et saepe legibus

... those who were unable to reply to the Truth turned to savage acts of violence, with the result that many bishops and many clergy (we shall remain silent about the fate of mere laymen) were attacked in ambushes. They even invaded some churches and were at the point of attempting to invade others... They [i.e. our ambassadors to Ravenna] should suggest that it is within the clemency of the emperors that the Catholic Church – which gave birth to them in the holy womb of Christ and nourished them with unshakable faith – should be defended by their foresight, so that reckless men should not gain power over weak people in a Christian age, since no one is able to pervert things by seduction alone. Gatherings of the circumcellions are raging about – abhorrent gangs that have been condemned repeatedly in sanctions issued by these same emperors. Against this madness we should be able to invoke defense sought in the Holy Scriptures – for example, when the apostle Paul recorded for the faithful in the *Acts of the Apostles* [Acts 23: 16] that he had done away with a conspiracy of gangsters with the help of Roman soldiers. In our case, we ask that such protection be provided for Catholic churches – and without any sham or pretence – by the town councils of all of the cities and towns, and by the landowners in the surrounding rural areas.

The brief concludes with a request that the dissident Christians be branded as heretics and that the requisite fines be levied upon them. But it is the argument based on public violence that is the critical new linchpin to the whole.

In this fashion, violent gangs of circumcellions became a constructed threat that was a necessary part of the power struggle in Africa in the late fourth century. Augustine admits as much in one of his earliest references to them. It occurs in a letter addressed to a certain Maximinus who was the dissident bishop of a parish close to Augustine's at Hippo. In trying to encourage the man to a dialogue, Augustine offered a conciliatory move:[66]

Let us remove from the table between us various hollow objections, of the sort that are accustomed to be hurled against each other in turn by ignorant men who belong to each side – so you won't bring up objections about "the Macarian Time" and I won't bring up objections about "the savageries of the circumcellions."

The deliberate use of the issue of violence by both sides in the struggle is noted. But it is also admitted that it was an element that could be set

conclamata circumcellionum qua furiunt detestabilis manus quae etiam ipsorum religiosissimo- rum supra principum frequentibus sanctionibus condemnata est, adversus quorum furorem non insolita a scripturis sanctis aliena impetrare praesidia, quando apostolus Paulus, sicut in apostolo- rum actibus fidelibus notum est, factiosorum conspirationem militari etiam submovit auxilio. Sed nos illud poscimus ut catholicis ecclesiis ordinum per civitates singulas et vicinorum quorumque possessorum per diversa loca sine ulla dissimulatione tuitio praebeatur."

[66] Aug. *Ep.* 23.6 (CCL 31: 66): "Tollamus de medio inania obiecta quae a partibus imperitis iactari contra invicem solent, nec tu obicias tempora Macariana nec ego saevitiam circumcellionum."

aside by both parties, if they chose to do so. The mobilization of the issue at this point was a planned and deliberate attempt to influence those who held the real instruments of force in their hands. This was just part of an opening gambit in the struggle. Before it could be pressed to a conclusion, other critical parts of this artificial picture of the sectarian enemy, most importantly as dangerous heretics, would have to be carefully put into place.

CHAPTER 4

Archives of memory

> ...for it is a fact that humans shape
> their memories to suit their sufferings.[1]
> (Thucydides)

> ...as is commonly said by people,
> memory must be the guardian of lies.[2]
> (Optatus)

The primal crimes that were the grounds of the division between the two
Christian communities – the betrayals during the Great Persecution –
remained the lifeblood of sectarian conflict throughout the fourth century.
What African Christians at the end of the century knew about this early
history of theirs, however, was rather limited. Their evidence was largely
confined to the stories and the archival documents that had been assembled
between the 340s and the 360s. These writings and the annual replaying
of the stories of the martyrs who had died in the onslaught of the Great
Persecution formed the basis of their knowledge.[3] Even so, the dissidents
shared a special sense of past events that defined their existence. The most
explicit short statement of this history was read aloud to the conference
at Carthage in 411 by Habetdeum, the bullish dissident bishop of Aurusu-
liana. After quoting a barrage of biblical texts to prove that bad Christians
should be separated from good ones, not just in spirit but also in body, he
continued:[4]

---

[1] Thuc. 2.54.3: οἱ γὰρ ἄνθρωποι πρὸς ἃ ἔπασχον τὴν μνήμην ἐποιοῦντο.

[2] Optatus, *Contra Parm.* 2.18.6 (SC 412: 278): "Ubi est quod vulgus dicitur memoriam custodem debere esse mendacis?"

[3] The dissidents might have possessed their own historical *summa* of the struggle in the writings of their great lay exegete Tyconius; but this is only a guess and a tentative one at that. His *De bello intestino* might not have contained an historical summary of the quarrel, although, given the (possible) title, the absence would have been odd.

[4] GCC 3.258 (SC 224: 1216–18): "Illud vero quale est ut, cum nos eis obiciamus persecutiones et inmanes crudelitates quibus ipsi et maiores eorum nos patresque nostros per annos centum vel amplius sine cessatione adflixerint atque vexaverint, illi isto non erubescant... Quis enim nesciat istos traditores

This is so much the case that when we bring up to them [i.e. the Catholics] the persecutions and the horrific cruelties with which they and their ancestors have harassed and tortured us and our fathers without ever stopping through a hundred years and more – why, they don't even blush . . . But who doesn't know that, from the very beginning of their damnable betrayal and in all of their written petitions to the rulers of the age, these traitors and persecutors have begged for our destruction and have attempted to force us into their communion by means of threats and legal charges – all of this against the commands of God? We must speak not just of how much Christian blood was spilled by Leontius, Ursacius, Macarius, Paul, Taurinus, Romanus and the other executioners whom they obtained from the princes of this age for the murder of the saints. There are their other crimes: the great number of venerable bishops killed and others thrown into exile, Christians tortured far and wide, sacred virgins raped, wealthy men proscribed, the poor pillaged, basilicas seized and their bishops forced to flee. There is no one who does not know how many crimes they have committed in our own time. They forced bishops into exile, threw off great heights Christians who were trying to escape their grasp, oppressed congregations, robbed clergy, invaded our basilicas, and rained blows on those who tried to resist them. Finally, at just one village, named Bagaï, they were the cause of the spilling of the blood of many Christians. But not satisfied with this, they have not stopped their terrible acts against us until the present day.

The "hundred years and more" marked out a century of remembered history that had a precise beginning – "their damnable betrayal" – and a long series of events that consisted of the use of the state by the Catholics – "these traitors and our persecutors" – in an attempt to murder the Church of the Truth. And it culminated, in reality and rhetoric, in the slaughter at Bagaï.

For the Catholics, even for highly educated ones like Augustine, history meant the information contained in a work penned by the Catholic writer Optatus. Knowing anything else about the past, even for an Augustine, took time and patience.[5] And mistakes and errors were strewn, like little

---

persecutoresque nostros ab ipso exordio condemnatae traditionis conmenticiis precibus cunctis in nostram necem huius saeculi principibus supplicasse, atque ad suam communionem contra Dei prae-cepta minis et proscriptionibus coartasse? Nam, ut omittamus quantus sanguis Christianus effusus sit per Leontium, Ursacium, Macarium, Paulum, Taurinum, Romanum ceterosque exsecutores quos in sanctorum necem a principibus saeculi meruerunt, quando plurimi venerabiles sacerdotes occisi, alii in exilium relegati, christianitas late vexata, sacrata stuprata virginitas, proscripti divites, spoliati pauperes, ablatae basilicae atque acti in fugam profugi sacerdotes, nostro nunc tempore quanta com-miserint, nullus ignorat. Episcopis ingesserunt exilia, christianis fugientibus praecipitia, oppresserunt populos, praedati sunt clericos, invaserunt basilicas, intulerunt consentire nolentibus plagas; postremo in uno tantum oppido Bagaiensi eorum causa multorum Christianorum sanguis effusus est et, nec sic satiati, in hodiernum cessare contempserunt."

[5] For example, he did not know about something as fundamental to the history of the origins of the dispute as the council of Arles (Arelate) until the late 390s, see *Ep.* 43.2.4; 43.7; 53.2.5; *Contra ep. Parm.* 1.6.1; cf. Monceaux, *Hist. litt.* 7, p. 196.

landmines, through the basic documents. As Catholic bishop of the hill-town of Milevis, some thirty miles northwest of Constantina, Optatus was the sectarian terrier of his age.[6] The polemic that he composed, along with its appendix of proof documents, was part of a running war of tracts between the two churches. He had written to answer an angry broadside that had been fired off by Parmenian, the dissident bishop of Carthage.[7] His five-book attack on the Catholics had been composed in the backwash of the emperor Julian's decree that allowed the dissident bishops to return from exile to their dioceses. The years immediately following the recovery of his former power were ones in which Parmenian moved to reassert the rights of his own people and to brand the Catholics as nothing other than a church of traitors. Coming out of exile, he nursed a hard animus against his enemies that fueled the violence of his verbal attack on them.

The forceful claims made for the restoration of their property involved the dissident Christians in recourse to the courts, in appeals to public authorities, and in the use of private coercion to enforce the decisions issued by judges. The situation also excited a greater awareness of the ways in which these properties had been lost in the great persecution of 347. Rehearsing the wrongs evoked bitter memories of how Catholics had appealed to the power of the state for the use of secular force. A simple decree of one emperor, Constans, had demonstrated the dangerous power of the state. A large part of Parmenian's polemical assault on his enemies focussed on this one core grievance: that the Catholics had been the first ones to deploy the brute physical force afforded by the state against their fellow Christians. The power of the claim was fed by a popular sentiment that the Roman state – once a savage persecutor – ought not to be involved in any way in the maltreatment of Christians. The reply penned by Optatus had to defuse the sting of the damning charge. Throughout his long response, he was careful to address the dissident bishop of Carthage as "my brother Parmenian," *frater Parmeniane*, in an effort, however disingenuous, to dilute powerful negative feelings: the new bitterness between the two

---

[6] On Milevis, see Lepelley, *Cités de l'Afrique romaine*, 2, pp. 438–39, who notes the unusual case of ILAlg 2, 590 = CIL 8.7013 = ILS 1236, the dedication of a bronze statue to the governor Ceionius Italicus (gub. 343) by the town council of Milevis that was set up not at Milevis but rather at Constantina.

[7] Neither of the modern titles given to the work – *De schismate Donatistarum*, which was accepted by Ziwsa for his CSEL edition, or *Contra Donatistas*, the one preferred by Labrousse and Edwards – is likely to be correct. Monceaux was probably on the right track when he argued that the work originally bore the title of *Contra Parmenianum*, as Jerome entitled it, or *Contra litteras Parmeniani*, or something similar. The work belongs to the African tradition of constructing a polemical treatise as a long "open letter," often in reply to one already sent.

sides that went back to the events of 347. His reply quickly focussed on the violent acts committed by the two sides in the 340s and later.

The descriptions of the episodes of sectarian violence offered by Optatus, including the actions of men and women known as circum-cellions, are the only narrative that survives on the relationship between the two Christian communities for the whole period between the original division in the reign of Constantine and events in the later age of Augustine. The immediate context of his work was the unstable situation created by decisions made by the emperor Julian in 362 in which he declared that the *status quo ante* between the two communities was to be enforced. It was in this tense situation that Optatus completed his six-book jeremiad *Against Parmenian*.[8] Circumstantial evidence about its date indicates a year soon after Julian's death, with a good guess placing it close to the year 365.[9] Without doubt, Parmenian had composed his attack on the Catholics in the year or two immediately preceding. Analysis of Optatus' work, however, is complicated by the fact that he later re-edited it and added a seventh book. Evidence for the date of this final version places its composition more than two decades later, sometime between 385 and 390.[10] In it, Optatus took the opportunity to rewrite parts of the first version of the mid-360s and to insert new facts into the original text.

Whatever the interpretive problems created by the revision, a basic and unrevised fact is that Optatus began his work with the problem of the

---

[8] Three pieces of evidence confirm this. First of all, there is the internal coherence of the first six books, with the conclusion of the sixth book matching the program announced in book one; Jerome, in his notice in the *De viris illustribus* (90), knows only of a six-book work; and finally, the first published edition of the treatise (J. Cochlaeus, Mainz, 1549), based on the now lost *codex Cusanus*, shows that there was a smaller six-book version, which must be the original referred to by Optatus himself and known to Jerome.

[9] A precise dating is simply not possible; see Labrousse, "La date du *Traité contre les Donatistes*," in *Optate de Milève: Traité contre les Donatistes*, vol. 1 (Paris, 1995), pp. 12–14. Traditional dating depends on a general statement in Jerome, *De viris illustribus*, 110, who is notoriously unreliable in these matters, to the effect that Optatus wrote his treatise "in the reign of Valentinian and Valens" – a general indication that is surely derived only from internal evidence and whose value cannot be pressed. Optatus himself says (1.13.2; 3.8.3) that he was writing "about sixty years after" the persecution of Diocletian and Maximian in Africa, which would indicate a date around 365. The best indication of date is his own statement in which he refers to Julian's death on 26 June 363 (2.16.19), and, as Labrousse rightly remarks, one has the impression that "il parle des violences qui ont eu lieu sous son règne comme d'événements dont la mémoire est encore très vivante" (p. 12).

[10] See De Veer (1961); one clear example is afforded by his original list of the "Donatist" bishops of Rome (*Contra Parm.* 2.4.5 = SC 412: 248), which originally ended with Macrobius (as would have been appropriate for a work written in the mid-360s). He later added Macrobius' successors, Lucianus and Claudianus. Such re-editing, however, is not consistent. For example, in listing the Catholic apostolic succession to the see of Peter (*Contra Parm.* 2.3.1 = SC 412: 244–46), Optatus only took the succession as far at the papacy of Liberius or Damasus (again, indicating a date in the 360s). He did not update this list.

betrayal that was seen to be the fundamental cause of the division between the two churches. Only when this matter had been dealt with did he advance to the debates over the use of violence, beginning with recent acts committed by dissident Christian communities in Africa following the edict of restoration issued by the emperor Julian in 362.[11]

> It was almost at this time that your madness returned to Africa, when the Devil was released from the prisons in which he had been held . . . You came as deranged men, you came in rage, tearing at the limbs of the Church, subtle in your seductions, horrific in slaughter, deliberately compelling the Sons of Peace to war. You turned many men into exiles from their dioceses when you invaded their basilicas with hired gangs. In so many places that it would take me too long to specify them by name, many of your men engineered bloody slaughters so savage that accounts of the awful deeds were submitted to the secular judges of the time. But the judgment of God intervened and confronted you, causing the death of that profane and sacrilegious emperor who by his command had allowed you to return, and who, in answer to your appeals, had already unleashed a persecution against us – or was getting ready to unleash one.

This description of sectarian violence is significant not only for the precision of the targets – principally Catholic bishops and other clergy who were being harassed and driven from their local dioceses and churches – but also because the damage was allegedly done by hired gangs of violent men. The nexus of gangs of enforcers and the mode of hiring is important to note.

Behind the obfuscating barrage of polemical rhetoric that pictured the emperor Julian as an agent of Satan, something of the actual sequence of events can be discerned. With many of its bishops in exile and having lost possession of numerous basilicas and other properties to the Catholics, the dissident church suddenly found itself restored to legitimate status by an imperial decree issued early in the year 362. This meant that their high-profile leaders, including Parmenian the bishop of Carthage, could now return to Africa and repossess their former seats. Without doubt, not a few of these returns must have been the occasion of conflict. As usual with such writing, the generalities of this violence were not of great interest to

---

[11] Optatus, *Contra Parm.* 2.17.1–3 (SC 412: 272): "Isdem paene momentis vester furor in Africam revertitur, quibus diabolus de suis carceribus relaxatur . . . Venistis rabidi, venistis irati membra laniantes ecclesiae, subtiles in seductionibus, in caedibus immanes, filios pacis ad bella provocantes. De sedibus suis multos fecistis extorres, cum conducta manu venientes basilicas invasistis. Multi ex numero vestro per loca plurima quae sub nominibus dicere longum est, cruentas operati sunt caedes et tam atroces ut de talibus factis ab illius temporis iudicibus relatio mitteretur. Sed intervenit et occurrit iudicium Dei ut ille qui vos iamdudum redire iusserat, imperator profanus et sacrilegus moreretur, qui persecutionem vobis provocantibus iam miserat aut mittere disponebat."

Optatus: he was focussed on explicit examples of atrocities. Although the episodes of violence that he describes are necessarily specific, they nevertheless seem to fall into distinctive patterns. First in this sequence was the intervention of imperial authority embodied in the person of the emperor. Julian's first act was to permit bishops in the eastern Mediterranean who had been sent into exile by his predecessor to return to their home dioceses. In his view, the more distress that he caused the Christians, the better. One of the emperor's more famous observations was that Christian sectarians hated each other with a special odium, a rage that he thought that he could incite to his own advantage. He had decreed that the exiled bishops in the east could reclaim the ecclesiastical properties that had been confiscated by their enemies.[12] The almost certain result, as Julian would have anticipated, was intense internal conflict within Christian communities.

Seeing this opening, the dissident African bishops who were in exile petitioned Julian to offer them the same relief.[13] The formal request to the emperor was drafted by the bishop Pontianus, and was signed by himself and his colleagues Rogatianus and Cassianus.[14] Why would Julian refuse? They were successful in obtaining an imperial rescript that conceded freedom of worship to their coreligionists, the return of their banished clergy, and the restitution of the basilicas and other properties that had been seized by their Catholic enemies.[15] Part of the original decree survives in a later quotation: "In answer to the petitions of Rogatianus, Pontius, Cassianus, and the other bishops, and also the clergy, to bring this matter to completion we add our order to abolish all the measures taken against them, illegally, without any imperial decree, and so to let everything be restored

---

[12] Maier, *Dossier*, 2, no. 39, p. 42, with sources. We know that, under this decree, Athanasius was able to return to Alexandria by 21 February 362: *Historia Acephala*, 3.3; cf. Barnes, *Athanasius and Constantius*, p. 155.

[13] Although their petition is referred to by Optatus only in general terms, some of the specifics were later known to Augustine. The claim made by Maier (*Dossier*, 2, pp. 42 and 42 n. 6) and numerous other scholars (for example, by Labrousse in her edition of Optatus) that the phrase "data ab episcopis partis Donati" comes from the original document is a strange assertion that runs against the facts. There is no good evidence coming from any period that the bishops of the dissident Christian community ever designated themselves as "Donatists." These words, certainly the last two, are either those of Optatus himself or of a Catholic collector of documents who provided the *explicit*.

[14] Maier, *Dossier*, 2, no. 39, p. 42 and nn 5 and 7: citing Aug. *Contra ep. Parm.* 1.12.19 (CSEL 51: 41); *Contra litt. Petil.* 2.92.203 and 205 (CSEL 52: 127, 129–30); 2.97.224 (CSEL 52: 141–43); *Ep.* 93.4.12 (CSEL 34.2: 456); 105.2.9 (CSEL 34.2: 601–02) and *En 2 in Ps.* 36.18 (CCL 38: 359).

[15] Maier, *Dossier*, 2, no. 39, p. 43, who cites, in addition to the sources above, Aug. *Contra litt. Petil.* 2.83.184 (CSEL 52: 113).

to its ancient state."[16] One can hardly overestimate the chaos caused by the emperor's ruling. What it commanded was this: that all matters between the bishops of the two churches were to return to the "old situation," the *status antiquus*. Declaring the actions taken against dissident bishops by the commissioners of 347 to be void, the emperor ruled not only that the dissident clergy in exile were to be allowed to return to Africa, but also that all properties were to be restored to their original owners – that is, to the owners in the years before the great persecution of 347.

The nature of the violence that ensued is understandable. Not only at Carthage, but also in each town and village in Africa dissident basilicas had been seized and occupied by the Catholics in 347 and in the years shortly after. Now there was to be a complete reversal of ownership. The stories of how each Catholic community responded to Julian's order would have been different. Some Catholics would have bowed to the imperial order but others, who had been in possession of their basilicas for the better part of a generation, would surely have baulked. The returns set in motion repeated cycles of enforcement and resistance. The first steps were usually attempts on the part of the dissidents to enforce the emperor's order. If their efforts met with resistance, violence erupted on the spot. In a more typical pattern, the aggrieved party – the dissident Christians who were attempting to reclaim their property, but who failed to get it back on their first attempts to enforce their possession – went to the local courts to contest the issue. With Julian's decree in hand and evidence of their ownership prior to 347, they would hope to obtain a court decision in their favor. Even if the court decision was favorable, however, it was still up to the dissidents to enforce it. It is at this point that the need to acquire a force of strong men, a *manus*, would arise. Only with such "help" could they drive out the current occupants and assert legal ownership of their former properties.

These are the circumstances in which most of the incidents of violence recorded for the year 363 occurred. The current possessors would barricade themselves in their basilicas, while the claimants, with the assistance of a "gang" of enforcers, would attempt "to invade" the church and to claim it as their own. The dissident gangs, or *manus*, were stigmatized as "hired" by the Catholics. The label doubly disparaged the rough men: as hired hands, they were shown as mercenary outsiders who had no genuine stake in the struggle. And the fact of hire itself suggested social inferiority and

---

[16] Aug. *Contra litt. Petil.* 2.97.224 (CSEL 52: 142): "Hoc quoque supplicantibus Rogatiano, Pontio, Cassiano et ceteris episcopis, sed et clericis, accedit ad cumulum, ut abolitis, quae adversus eos sine rescripto perperam gesta sunt, in antiquum statum cuncta revocentur."

the meretricious motivation of doing things for pay rather than for high ideals. The dissident seizures, when they did succeed, resulted in Catholic bishops and clergy losing the basilicas that they had held, often for decades. The Catholics could then claim they they had been made exiles from their own seats, even if not in the same sense that their dissident opponents had been formally and legally exiled from Africa in 347 by the state. These are the parameters of the violence and the "persecution" of Catholics of which Optatus speaks. It was a situation that, as even he admits, was soon brought to an end by the death of the emperor Julian on 26 June 363.

Optatus' polemical account of the violence of 363 helped to create a dossier of specific acts of violence, some of them happening in obscure places. The incidents were probably culled from cases that the Catholics had brought before local municipal judicial authorities in the hope of relief – the incidents that he says were reported to "the secular judges of the time."[17] The first episodes that he narrates occurred in the southern borderlands of the Roman province of Mauretania Sitifensis: at the small towns of Zabi, Flumen Piscium, and Lemellef.[18] All three villages were located in the northern Hodna Basin in what is today north-central Algeria. No doubt it was their proximity to each other that explains the combination of the incidents as a narrative group. In all likelihood, they had been brought to the civil courts of the time as a related group of actions.[19]

---

[17] Mostly municipal ones, one presumes. The term "iudex" *could* refer to a provincial governor or his judicial *legati* and other legal assistants. But since only one provincial governor of Africa held power through the brief period between midsummer 362 and 363, and Optatus is clear on the plural, it seems less probable that provincial authorities were involved.

[18] On Zabi, see Mesnage, *Evêchés*, p. 256, Maier, *L'épiscopat*, p. 243; Lancel, GCC, 4: 1530–31 (Bechilega in Algeria, which, as Lancel states, is perhaps an echo of the Latin "basilica"): this must be the location of *this* Zabi, rather than its homonym in Caesariensis; on *Flumen Piscium*, see Mesnage, *Evêchés*, p. 271; Maier, *L'épiscopat*, p. 142; Lancel, GCC, 4: 1377. Mesnage guessed that it might be Cedi bel Abbas, since it was probably located on the Wed el-Ksob (which is fairly certainly identified as the ancient *Flumen Piscense*) probably about midway between Zabi and Lemellef; on *Lemellef* (the mss. read "Lefellense," but I accept Ziwsa's correction), see Mesnage, *Evêchés*, pp. 353–54; Maier, *L'épiscopat*, p. 160 (Bordj Rhedir in Algeria). It is important to note that by the time of the Conference of 411, both Zabi and Flumenpiscensis were represented only by dissident bishops with no Catholic adversaries (there were apparently no representatives from either side for Lemellef).

[19] Optatus, *Contra Parm.* 2.18.1–2 (SC 412: 274): "Operata est apud loca supradicta in catholicos trucidatio. Memoramini per loca singula qui fuerint vestri discursus. Nonne de numero vestro fuerunt Felix Zabensis et Ianuarius Flumenpiscensis et ceteri qui tota celeritate concurrerunt ad Castellum Lemellefense? Ubi cum contra importunitatem suam viderent basilicam clausam, praesentes iusserunt comites suos ut ascenderent culmina, nudarent tecta, iactarent tegulas. Imperia eorum sine mora completa sunt. Et cum altare defenderent diaconi catholici, tegulis plurimi cruentati sunt, duo occisi sunt, Primus, filius Ianuarii, et Donatus, filius Nini, urgentibus et praesentibus coepiscopis vestris supra memoratis, ut sine dubio de vobis dictum sit: *Veloces pedes eorum ad effundendum sanguinem.* De qua re Primosus episcopus catholicus loci supra memorati in concilio vestro apud Thevestinam civitatem questus est et querelas eius dissimulanter audistis."

In the places that I mentioned above, there was devised a slaughter of Catholics. Recall your attacks on these individual places. Were not Felix of Zabi and Januarius of Flumen Piscium from among your number? And also the others who hurried to the *castellum* of Lemellef? When they saw that the church was barricaded against their savagery, they ordered their followers to climb onto the roof, to strip off the roofing tiles and then to hurl them down [i.e. onto the parishioners huddled in the church below]. Their orders were obeyed without delay. When the Catholic deacons defended the altar, many of them were covered in bloody wounds caused by the falling tiles. Two of them, Primus the son of Januarius and Donatus the son of Ninus, died. All of this happened while your bishops, named above, were present and were urging on the attackers. Without doubt it can be said of you, "Their feet hurry to shed blood." Primosus, the Catholic bishop of the place [i.e. Lemellef], made a complaint about this affair at the church council that you held at Theveste, and you actually pretended to listen to his complaints.

This is a description of a typical episode of sectarian violence from the time: an attack on a church led by dissident bishops returning from long exile, no doubt harboring sentiments of vengeance in their hearts. Not a few persons died in the assault, and centuries later the terrain was still regarded as hallowed ground.[20] The attackers were organized and urged on by the clergy. This fits well with the structural framework that was generally true of these violent episodes: they were not accidental or spontaneous eruptions of inter-communal religious hatreds. There was a specific nexus of cause and effect, and known leaders. The returning dissidents reclaimed the basilica at Lemellef that had been seized from them in the "persecution" of 347. Under the cover of a legal right to take it back, the dissident bishops from the neighboring dioceses had organized forces to help reclaim the church. The Catholics who were in possession of the basilica at Lemellef had barricaded themselves inside it. The attackers stormed the building, climbing onto the roof. Using the roof tiles as ammunition, they rained them down onto the Catholic parishioners below who had taken refuge on the floor-level of the church.

Primosus, the Catholic bishop of Lemellef, later made a formal complaint that he submitted to a dissident church council held at Theveste. He, at least, must have survived the attack. But the fact that he personally filed a complaint with a church council held by his sectarian enemies raises a number of suspicions. His action indicates that at least some Catholic bishops thought that the violent acts were so horrific that even their sectarian opponents would consider them to be deserving of condemnation

---

[20] See Duval, *Loca Sanctorum*, 1, no. 126 (Hr. Akrib), p. 259, for the large number of reliquaries of Byzantine date, one of them mentioning the local ethnic group of the Nicibes (6 October 580).

and reprimand. His petition also suggests that what happened at Lemellef was unusual, odd, or excessive, otherwise he would hardly have bothered to pursue the civil route of bringing the matter to the attention of a church council of his sectarian enemies. If there were dozens and dozens of such cases, this is hardly the way one would have gone about resolving them. The incident at Lemellef therefore seems to have been an exception. It was a case of the forced repossession of church property which, for whatever combination of circumstances in that small town at that time, got out of hand.

The only other incident of violence that Optatus describes in similar detail took place in Tipasa in Mauretania Caesariensis further to the west and involved two men from the towns of Forma and Idicra.[21] His knowledge of the events may have been personal; the information might have been obtained from connections that he had in the town of Idicra, only some sixteen miles southwest of his diocese at Milevis.[22]

When you invaded the cities of Mauretania, the peoples in them were badly shaken. Infants ready to be born died in the bellies of their mothers... Should I not recollect the attack made on Tipasa, the city of Mauretania Caesariensis? Urbanus of Forma and Felix of Idicra came to this city from their home base in Numidia – two firebrands burning with envy and bitterness, men who hurried to throw into disarray the spirits of people who were living in peace and quiet. Helped by the favor and fury of some government officials, and with Athenius the provincial governor present with his military units, the numerous members of the Catholic community were expelled from their seats [i.e. churches] amidst panic and bloodshed. Men were wounded, married women were violated, infants were

---

[21] Of the places named, Tipasa was about 9 miles east of Caesarea (Cherchel), the provincial capital of Mauretania Caesariensis, on the coast of Algeria. Given the fact that men from Idicra and Forma, both towns in Numidia, were involved, one is almost tempted to think that Optatus has made a mistake and that the Tipasa involved was actually the other Tipasa (modern Tifech) in Numidia. Forma is otherwise unidentified, see Mesnage, *Evêchés*, pp. 413–14; but it was almost certainly in the same general region as Idicra, the modern 'Aziz-ben-Tellis, see Mesnage, *Evêchés*, p. 252; Maier, *L'épiscopat*, p. 154; and Lancel, *GCC* 4: 1397. Not only does Optatus say that it too was in Numidia, but at the Conference of 411, the diocese was now represented only by a dissident bishop named Iustus who had fallen ill and had to be registered by the bishop Martialis, from Idicra. Again, therefore, Forma and Idicra appear to have been neighboring communities. The city of Tipasa was some considerable distance, about 155 miles west-northwest, of Idicra.

[22] Optatus, *Contra Parm.* 2.18.3–5 (SC 412: 276): "In Mauritaniae civitatibus vobis intrantibus quassatio populi facta est, mortui sunt in uteris matrum, qui fuerant nascituri... Quid commemorem Tipasam Caesariensis Mauritaniae civitatem, ad quam de Numidia Urbanus Formensis et Felix Idicrensis, duae faculae incensae livoribus, concurrerunt quietorum et in pace positorum animos perturbantes? Nonnullorum officialium et favore et furore iuvante et Athenio praeside praesente cum signis catholica frequentia exturbata et cruentata de sedibus suis expulsa est: lacerati sunt viri, tractae sunt matronae, infantes necati sunt, abacti sunt partus. Ecce vestra ecclesia episcopis ducibus cruentis morsibus pasta est."

killed, and fetuses were ripped from their mothers' wombs. See! It is *your* church, with its bishops as leaders, that feasts on bloody morsels.

The attacks at Tipasa were led by bishops and involved typical kinds of physical violence used in regaining the possession of a church. Although it is couched in an inflated hyperbolic rhetoric, Optatus' account in fact describes an organized attempt to enforce the repossession of basilicas. He also notes the presence of state officials who were present to supervise the use of force in executing the court decisions. The big difference at Tipasa, compared with the small town of Lemellef, was the presence of the governor along with units of the regular army. He was there, almost certainly, to make sure that the violence entailed in the reclaiming of a basilica at a large and important coastal city (as opposed to any nonentity of a hamlet in the hinterland) did not get out of hand. This was especially true at Tipasa given the huge importance of the basilica complex and the associated martyr cult in the city.[23] Each side naturally interpreted the presence of state officials in these repossession operations from its own perspective. If the soldiers were helpful, they saw them as good and vigilant police of the social order. If not, they were portrayed in darker tones: willing participants who aided and abetted their sectarian enemies. The presence of the governor meant that there was more such state power to be claimed and so a heightened value to the claims being staked by either side.

Apart from the dramatic incidents where these confrontations led to violence involving injury and death – all two of them – Optatus outlines typical actions taken by the dissidents during their repossession of basilicas.[24]

In addition, a terrible outrage was committed (which seems to be trivial to you) when the above-named bishops violated everything that is sacred. They ordered the Eucharist to be cast out for dogs to eat. In committing this act, they did not escape divine judgment, since these same dogs, now burning with madness, treated these same masters of theirs as if they were bandits, tearing at them with their avenging teeth as though they were strangers and enemies, guilty, as they were, of having maltreated the Sacred Body. And they also threw the phial that

[23] Lancel and Bouchenaki, *Tipasa*, pp. 45–48, 60–65, 86–96.

[24] Optatus, *Contra Parm.* 2.19.1–2 (SC 412: 278): "Et quod vobis leve videtur, facinus immane commissum est ut omnia sacrosancta supra memorati vestri episcopi violarent. Iusserunt eucharistiam canibus fundi, non sine signo divini iudicii. Nam idem canes accensi rabie ipsos dominos suos quasi latrones, sancti corporis reos, dente vindice tamquam ignotos et inimicos laniaverunt. Ampullam quoque chrismatis per fenestram ut frangerent iactaverunt, et cum casum adiuvaret abiectio, non defuit manus angelica quae ampullam spiritali subvectione deduceret: proiecta casum sentire non potuit. Deo muniente illaesa inter saxa consedit." All of this latter seems to be a deliberate pun on the dissidents' account of the death of Marculus (see pp. 182–83 below).

was used for giving the chrism out of the window so that it would break. Although the action of throwing it should have helped the phial break, an angel's hand accompanied it with spiritual power and support. Hurled to the ground, the phial did not experience any breakage, but, with God's protection, it landed unharmed among the rocks.

Given the repetitive steps involved in reclaiming basilicas, it is hardly surprising that the violence itself became ritualized. Upon seizing the churches, the dissidents had to decide what to do with the sacred utensils that were left behind by the Catholics. Because they were seen to be just as polluted as the people who had used them, the point was to get rid of them permanently. It made sense to throw the glass *ampullae* that contained the olive oil of benediction out of the windows so that they would smash and become useless. So too, the ritualistic throwing of the communion bread and wine to dogs to eat and drink drove home in the most dramatic way that *this* bread and *this* wine was in no way sacrosanct, but was so ordinary that even polluted canines could consume the bread and wine as dog food. Dogs may even have been found for the task. The choice of animal was not accidental. In common Christian discourse, everyone agreed that dogs symbolized satanic unbelievers and heretics.

The rituals of the violence were reinforced by encounters with the sacral things that the attackers were trying to possess and to control. The nature of the violence had more to do with these typologies and less to do with the specifics of a given time and this place. Just so, a case of sectarian hostility from a later age of African history, as reported by Victor of Vita in his description of the "Arian persecution" of Catholics by the Vandal kings in the mid-480s, repeats the standard form. Despite taking place half a century after our conflicts and in the context of different rationales, the violence reveals many of the same structural similarities.[25]

On one occasion, when the festival of Easter was being celebrated, the Arians learned that some of our people, in order to celebrate Easter Day, had opened a church at a place called Regiae which had been shut down. Immediately, one of their priests named Anduit gathered together a band of armed men and incited them to attack the crowd of the innocent. These men seized their weapons and

---

[25] Victor Vitensis, *Hist. pers. Afr. prov.* 1.13.41 (Lancel, 115–16); transl. J. Moorhead (with minor changes): "Quodam tempore paschalis sollemnitas agebatur et dum in quodam loco quae Regia vocitatur ob diem paschalis honoris nostri sibimet clausam ecclesiam reserarent, compererunt Arriani. Statim quidam presbyter eorum, Anduit nomine, congregata secum armatorum manu ad expugnandam turbam accenditur innocentum. Introeunt evaginatis spatis, arma corripiunt; alii quoque tecta conscendunt et per fenestras ecclesiae sagittas spargunt. Et tunc forte audiente et canente populo dei lector unus pulpito sistens alleluiaticum melos canebat; quo tempore sagitta in gutture iaculatus, cadente de manibus codice, mortuus post cecidit ipse."

went in with swords drawn, while others climbed onto the roof and fired arrows through the windows of the church. Just then, as the people of God were listening and singing, a lector was standing on the platform chanting the Alleluia, and at that moment he was struck in his throat by an arrow, the book [i.e. the Bible] fell from his hands and he fell dead.

Here, as elsewhere, when Victor refers to gangs of men who rushed into churches at Tanuzuda, Gales, and the Vicus Ammoniae, and who scattered the sacraments of the Eucharist over the floor and trampled on them with their feet, he is content to have the reader understand that an armed gang of men led by a priest carried out the seizure of the church of a sectarian enemy.

The violent acts were habitually linked to the innately cruel and violent character of the perpetrators. Their unspeakable cruelty manifested itself in other outrageous acts committed against the most defenseless parishioners of the local community: the elderly, young women, and young boys. In the case of these last-mentioned persons, the shadow and stain of sexual misdemeanor was never far away.[26]

Upon their return [i.e. from Tipasa], Urbanus of Forma and Felix of Idicra found mothers whom they turned from sacred and pure women into used women. See, my brother Parmenian, what sort of bishops you are hiding! When you ought to be blushing for your own people, you have the audacity to accuse innocent Catholics! Among the crimes and unspeakable acts committed by the aforesaid Felix, was his seizure of a girl – a girl on whom he himself had placed the headdress and who only shortly before had addressed him as "father" [i.e. as her bishop] – but with whom he did not hesitate to commit a most unspeakable and incestuous act. As if he would make himself holier by committing more sins, he hurried to the town of Tysedi and audaciously robbed Donatus, a bishop and innocent man of seventy years, of the title, rank, and office of bishop. He came as a schismatic against a Catholic bishop, as a criminal against an innocent, as a sacrilegious man against a priest of God, as an impure man against a pure one, as one who was not yet a bishop against a bishop. Yet secure in your desires and conspiratorial connivances, and armed with your laws and decrees, he laid those hands, with which just a little

---

[26] Optatus, *Contra Parm.* 2.19.3–5 (SC 412: 279–80): "Inde revertentes Urbanus Formensis et Felix Idicrensis invenerunt matres quas de castimonialibus fecerant mulieres. Ecce quales, frater Parmeniane, episcopos celas! Et cum pro tuis erubescere debueras, catholicos innocentes accusas. Interea Felix supra memoratus inter crimina sua et facinora nefanda ab eo comprehensa puella cui mitram ipse imposuerat, a qua paulo ante pater vocabatur, nefarie incestare minime dubitavit. Et quasi de peccato sanctior fieret, Tysedim velociter properavit. Sic Donatum annorum septuaginta episcopum, hominem innocentem, spoliare ausus est episcopali nomine et officio et honore. Venit schismaticus ad episcopum Catholicum, ad innocentem reus, ad Dei sacerdotem sacrilegus, incestus ad castum, ad episcopum iam non episcopus. Sed de placito et de coniuratione vestra securus vestris legibus et decretis armatus, manus quas paulo ante peccata gravaverant capiti innocenti iniecit et de illa lingua ausus est ferre sententiam quae iam nec ad paenitentiam agendam vel idonea videbatur."

earlier he had aggravated his sins, on the head of an innocent man and he made bold to pronounce a verdict with that tongue which seemed not prepared to do penance.

Our task is to decipher what is meant by the overwrought words delivered in the sacred language of the time. Apart from the imputation of sexual improprieties, the only other crime that Felix of Idicra engineered on his return from Tipasa was the same outrage that he had already committed there. He was charged with enforcing the repossession of basilicas and churches in the region of Mauretania around his base at Idicra. In that light, one can see the same kinds of events embedded in Optatus' emotional description of them. The perpetrators were armed with laws, that is to say, with the decisions emanating from Julian's imperial decree and similar kinds of local provincial and municipal court judgments. With these in hand, Felix advanced to the use of physical enforcement against the church at the small town of Tysedi near Idicra where he completed a legal repossession of it for his own side.

In the context of the legal procedures of the time, it was up to Felix to enforce possession, and that is what happened. A plaintiff was permitted to use reasonable force to compel the presence of a defendant at court, to seize properties in dispute, to enforce possession, or to reclaim ownership. The results are described by Optatus. The incumbent Catholic bishop Donatus was physically removed from his basilica and his seat of power. This is the only violence actually specified in the text. No physical harm is ever said to have befallen Donatus himself or his parishioners: had any injuries actually occurred, they would surely have been carefully retold. This reading of the incident at Tysedi agrees with our assessment of the contemporary action at Lemellef: it was the repossession of a basilica. Other than the dispossession of Donatus, there is no evidence of gratuitous acts of harm. And this is one of Optatus' model cases of violent behavior.

THE DANGEROUS STATE

Examples of such collective violence, or threats of violence, however, can be found early in the history of the sectarian battles, described in the same coded vocabulary that was later used to describe the circumcellions, ostensibly its most violent practitioners. We see this at Cirta in 305 as recorded in details only revealed much later at a court hearing in December 320 before Zenophilus, the governor of Numidia. One Silvanus had been subdeacon in the church at Cirta during the Great Persecution. On 19 May 305, he had collaborated with the authorities by handing over church properties to them and assisting in finding the Holy Scriptures of the church. Whatever the extent of his personal involvement in the betrayal, a matter that was much debated, the ordinary members of the congregation continued to value Silvanus, supporting his election as bishop in succession to their former bishop Paul.[27] Although he was condemned as a traitor by the Elders of the church at Cirta, Silvanus was able to mobilize the "lower elements" of the people to have himself elected bishop. His enemies portrayed his supporters as denizens of the arena, gladiators, and prostitutes.[28] If true, the charges might suggest the mobilization of rough men and women at Cirta in church battles. But there are good reasons to see the charges as no more than hostile rhetoric. Although there was a threatening atmosphere at Cirta in 305, there is no record of actual acts of physical violence involving these persons; most of the violence was embedded in the words hurled by one side against the other.

And it is important to note that the violent rhetoric of the time was fed not just by Christian clergy; it was also encouraged by the highest authority in the Roman state. The face of the state was everywhere in these disputes, even in their earliest phases. The emperor Constantine's letter of 5 February 330 to the Catholic bishops of the same city of Cirta – now renamed Constantina after the emperor – is a good example. His words on this occasion are significant, since throughout his reign the emperor had purposefully employed rather neutral terms to label the dissident Christians in Africa. It is manifest from the wording of this letter that the emperor had lost the very patience that he had earlier praised. A harsh language now condemns the dissidents as heretics and schismatics, as evil men who are in league with the Devil, and as men possessed by Satan, the evil being who is their father. In addressing the Catholic bishops of Numidia, Constantine continues:[29]

Your Gravities have acted most rightly and wisely, according to the holy precept of our faith in defending the Church against the perverse forces directed against it,

---

[27] See De Veer (1968d), and "Silvanus (1)," PAC, pp. 1078–80, for the basic references.

[28] *Gesta apud Zenophilum*, 192–96 (CSEL 26: 185–97): 192–96; Lancel (1967) argued that the *campe(n)ses* were rough men of the countryside who were, in effect, the same as the violent men who would later be labelled "circumcellions." The hypothesis is rightly contested by A. de Veer (*REAug* 15 [1969], pp. 308–09), who sees in them nothing much more than other men of the arena.

[29] Letter of Constantine to the Numidian bishops ("Donatist dossier" no. 10 = Maier, *Dossier*, 1, no. 33, pp. 248–49; 5 February 330): "rectissime et sapienter gravitas vestra fecit, et secundum sanctum fidei praeceptum ab eorum perversis contentionibus temperando et hisdem remittendo quod idem sibi indebitum atque alienum usurpare contendunt, ne, sicuti est eorum perversitas maligna et perfida, ad seditiones usque prorumperent et inter turbas atque contentus sui similes incitarent atque ita aliquid exsisteret quod sedari vi oporteret."

even being forgiving to the very men who are struggling to get what they think is owed to them and to usurp something which is not theirs. So great is the malignant perversity and disloyalty of these men that they have burst into seditious behavior. With the use of gangs and violence they incite people like themselves. In this way, something is arising that will have to be repressed with force.

From passages later in this same letter, it emerges that the violence to which the emperor is referring was perpetrated by gangs or *turbae* that were involved in the seizure and occupation of the Catholic basilica of Constantina in Numidia.[30] The occupation at Cirta must have been organized by none other than the former traitor and experienced man of violence, Silvanus, the dissident bishop of the city.

All of this is intriguing and provokes questions since, in a long passage in the third book of his polemical counterattack, Optatus provides our first insight into the men who were the main propagators of dissident violence at the time, men whom he calls "circumcellions." The specific naming of them suggests that these violent sectarians first appeared in the decade before Optatus was writing. But is this first reference to them an accident of the survival of source materials or is it reliable evidence for the recent invention of a new term for a novel phenomenon? It is important to note that the third book of Optatus' work is devoted to the problem of appeals to the civil authorities for the use of secular force. The quarrels over this issue were long and sharp. From the beginning of their division, both sides had appealed to government authorities to intervene in deciding their counterclaims. The propensity of municipal and higher government officials was to remain aloof from such disputes, but on occasion they became involved, sometimes with violent results. The ensuing violence gave each party grounds for bitter complaints that were embedded in their social memory. Every case that involved the civil authorities was fraught with difficulty. This was true even where the authorities tried to stand back from the sectarian violence, as in the case of Athenius, the governor of Mauretania Caesariensis. If they served as unbiased arbitrators and witnesses, they were blamed for "doing nothing"; if they acted more forcefully, they were excoriated as agents of Satan. The charge that one side had used secular force provided by the civil authorities was one of the accusations at the heart of Parmenian's five-volume open letter against the Catholics.

---

[30] Ibid. (Maier, p. 250): "Accepta igitur epistola sapientiae et gravitatis vestrae, comperi haereticos sive schismaticos eam basilicam ecclesiae catholicae quam in Constantina civitate iusseram fabricari solita improbitate invadendam putasse."

There must have been some perceived truth in the barb – the charge that the Catholics were responsible for calling in state force – since it rubbed a raw nerve. It is not accidental that Optatus repeatedly refers to the accusation in the introduction to his work, well before he even gets to the substance of Parmenian's claims. He opens his first book with no fewer than five explicit references to *pax* or peace, and proceeds to blame "your side" as the ones responsible for breaking it.[31] He uses the trope of violence to characterize Parmenian's work: "everyone with any reason can see that you have written at such length with no other motive than to administer a shameful beating to the Catholic church with your writings."[32] The assertion is followed directly by Optatus' statement "You say that *we* requested military force against *you*" – a claim that he repeats for emphasis: "You have said nothing against us, except for your ignorant statement that we requested military force. That this statement of yours is a false charge I shall show by irresistible proofs. Take away this false claim of yours and you are the same as we are."[33]

Concerns with mobilizing the forces of the state in support of a sectarian program loom as large in Optatus' mind as do any of the theological differences between the two sides. Violence is mentioned repeatedly in the introduction to his work, and is included as one of the three or four primary items on the agenda outlined in his "table of contents," the others being the origins of the schism, the problem of designating traitors or *traditores*, and a few of the main theological differences between the two parties (like the heavily disputed practice of rebaptism): "Thirdly, that military force was not requested by us, and that the crimes alleged against the architects of unity do not pertain to us."[34] Optatus ends this argument with an explicit statement: "Brother Parmenian, we have openly and manifestly proved to you that the story about us seeking an armed force is an empty slander."[35]

THE GREAT PERSECUTION

What Optatus does, instead, is to show that his sectarian opponents had themselves benefited from the use of force by the imperial state. Since the dissidents had asked for interventions by the government, the Catholic

---

[31] Optatus, *Contra Parm.* 1.1.2–1.2.1 (SC 412: 172–75).
[32] Optatus, *Contra Parm.* 1.5.1 (SC 412: 180–81).
[33] Optatus, *Contra Parm.* 1.5.2 and 4 (SC 412: 180–83).
[34] Optatus, *Contra Parm.* 1.7.2 (SC 412: 184–85).
[35] Optatus, *Contra Parm.* 5.1.1 (SC 413: 180–81).

Church, he argued, should not be the object of hypocritical criticism coming from them. To make his case, he retells stories involving appeals for the use of repressive force by state authorities in Africa. He begins with the pivotal events of the year 347 that involved the activities of the imperial emissaries Paul and Macarius.[36] Although certain knowledge of the links of cause and effect in the traumas of this year is beyond recovery, some of the events are reliably attested. One of these is that the emperor Constans dispatched two fully empowered court officials, Paul and Macarius – in all likelihood as *tribuni et notarii* or their equivalent – and charged them with the task of bringing about the unification of the dissident and Catholic churches in Africa.[37] They came armed with carrots and sticks. The inducements were huge sums of money to be dispensed in assisting with the reunification process. Both in our own time and back then, such a move might be interpreted as outright bribery or as something different and positive, like technical assistance or foreign aid. Since the process was presented as a Christian endeavor, however much undertaken with the enormous resources of an imperial state, the handouts were represented by the state as a benevolent *caritas*.[38] That is to say, if dissident communities and believers moved to the right side, they were to be rewarded by the power of Christian charity.

The origins of the crisis of 347 are not known. The cause that is often asserted, namely that Donatus the dissident bishop of Carthage petitioned the emperor Constans to be recognized as the sole bishop of Carthage, is a modern fiction.[39] Ossius of Corduba, as reported in the proceedings of the Council of Serdica in 343, more credibly stated (and if anyone

---

[36] Optatus, *Contra Parm.* 3.4.1–3 (SC 413: 36–38): "Quicquid itaque in unitate facienda aspere potuit geri, vides, frater Parmeniane, cui debeat imputari. A nobis Catholicis petitum militem esse dicitis. Si ita est, quare in provincia proconsulari tunc nullus armatum militem vidit? Veniebant Paulus et Macarius qui pauperes ubique dispungerent et ad unitatem singulos hortarentur; et cum ad Bagaïensem civitatem proximarent, tunc alter Donatus, sicut supra diximus, eiusdem civitatis episcopus, impedimentum unitati et obicem venientibus supra memoratis opponere cupiens, praecones per vicina loca et per omnes nundinas misit, circumcelliones agonisticos nuncupans, ad praedictum locum ut concurrerent invitavit. Et eorum illo tempore concursus est flagitatus, quorum dementia paulo ante ab ipsis episcopis impie videbatur esse succensa."

[37] On Paul, see, "Paulus (2)," PLRE, I, p. 683, and "Paulus (2)," PAC, pp. 839–41; on Macarius: "Macarius (1)," PLRE, I, p. 524–25 (not to be trusted), and "Macarius (1)," PAC, pp. 655–58.

[38] Cecconi (1990) is the fundamental analysis of the connection between alms, compulsion, and ideological representation, all of it as remembered in the third book of Optatus' attack on Parmenian.

[39] Frend, *Donatist Church*, pp. 177 and 177 n. 2, citing Optatus, *Contra Parm.* 3.1.2 (SC 413: 8–10): "deinde Donato Carthaginis qui provocavit ut unitas proximo tempore fieri temptaretur," and stating that "Optatus' precise description admits of no other interpretation." But the words do not seem to signify very much, other than that Donatus had been trying to bring about the unity of the Church.

ought to have known, it was he) that Catholic bishops from Africa were incessantly at court lobbying the emperor. They had been so insistent in their demands that they had been disregarding the advice of Gratus, the bishop of Carthage, to restrain the number of their petitions.[40] Although many of these men might well have been soliciting Constans for secular or personal advantage, they were surely part of a normal traffic in Catholic bishops who were busy influencing the imperial court in the 340s. It is perhaps not without interest in this regard that the emperor's chief religious advisor suggested that the Church and the petitioners should pay more attention to dispensing imperial funds to the poor and to widows. Constans, furthermore, was himself in a precarious position where he desired to enforce an ecclesiastical unity in his domains. In consequence, at some point towards mid-year 347, Constans issued an edict (the contents of which do not survive) that called for the forced unification of the two churches in Africa. The edict was posted at Carthage in mid-August of the same year. By that time, the court had already dispatched its two officials, Paul and Macarius, to enforce the emperor's edict.[41] This is the point at which their mission of violence and charity, armed repression and imperial-scale alms giving, entered the scene.

The bishops of the dissident church recognized a clear and present danger when they saw one. There was an almost immediate mobilization of resistance in Carthage. After taking what measures they could in the metropolis, Paul and Macarius took to the road, visiting various communities along the main highway that led from Carthage into the interior. The degree of acceptance or rejection that they met with in the early weeks of their mission is not known. As they entered the high plains of southeastern Numidia and approached the town of Bagaï, however, the events, as retold by Optatus, turned violent.[42]

Whatever harsh measures might have been taken in an attempt to bring about unity, you can see, my brother Parmenian, who is to blame for them. *You* say that

---

[40] Concil. Serd. 8 (Hess, *Council of Serdica*, p. 216): "Inportunitas, nimia frequentia, iniustae petitiones, fecerunt nos non tantam habere nec gratiam nec fiduciam, dum quidam non cessant ad comitatum ire episcopi (et maxime Afri qui, sicuti cognovimus, sanctissimi fratris et coepiscopi nostri Grati salutaria consilia spernunt adque contemnunt), ut unus homo ad comitatum multas et diversas ecclesiae non profuturas perferat causas, nec, ut fieri solet aut oportet, ut pauperibus ac viduis aut pupillis subveniatur; sed et dignitates saeculares et administrationes quibusdam postulant."

[41] Their titles, unfortunately, are not noted in any of the surviving sources; it has been speculated, with some reason, that they were *notarii*: see, "Macarius (1)," PRLE, 1, p. 524–25, and "Paulus (2)," PRLE, 1, p. 683, although the editors are right to state that this is speculative.

[42] See n. 36 above.

we Catholics petitioned for the use of military force. If that is the case, why did no one at that time witness units of the regular army in the proconsular province? Paul and Macarius were in fact coming to relieve the poor everywhere and to encourage individuals to Unity. But when they approached the city of Bagaï, that other Donatus . . . the bishop of this same city, wished to place a roadblock in the way of Unity and an obstacle in the way of the above-mentioned persons who were on their way to his town. He therefore sent criers through the nearby villages and to all the periodic markets, summoning those circumcellions who are known as *agonistici* or Holy Fighters to assemble at a prearranged place. The crowds of men that were stirred up and inflamed on this occasion were made up of those whose madness had been incited by these very same bishops only a brief time before.

We are now asked to remember events that took place in southern Numidia in the generation before Julian ascended the throne. Optatus turns to highlight some of the same aspects of violence that he had noted for the events of 363. Groups of men were summoned by local church leaders, primarily bishops, to commit violent acts. But there are real differences. The situation described by Optatus in the mid-340s was not one involving the civil courts or the use of legitimate civil force in property repossessions.

The mechanisms by which Donatus, the bishop of Bagaï, assembled a defensive force are specified: he used public criers or *praecones* who were sent to villages and places in the countryside where periodic markets were held. The men, who called themselves *agonistici* or Holy Fighters, were recruited from a broader category of men known to the locals as circumcellions. This is the first time in the surviving evidence where the men known to Africans of the time as "circumcellions," from which the holy warriors were recruited by the dissident church, are explicitly named as such. Since Optatus says nothing more about them, nothing more can be added here except for a simple point. The term *circumcelliones* – the singular is unattested – was apparently so common to Africans that Optatus did not have to gloss its meaning: everyone knew who the men were. The word was part of African Latin slang. Whoever the circumcellions were, they were an everyday phenomenon in the African countryside. So the imperial commissioners Paul and Macarius approached Bagaï, with Donatus, the dissident bishop of the town, awaiting their arrival.[43]

---

[43] Optatus, *Contra Parm.* 3.4.7–11 (SC 413: 42–45): "Eorum postea convaluerat multitudo. Sic invenit Donatus Bagaiensis unde contra Macarium furiosam conduceret turbam. Ex ipso genere fuerant qui sibi percussores sub cupiditate falsi martyrii in suam perniciem conducebant. Inde etiam illi qui ex altorum montium cacuminibus viles animas proicientes se praecipites dabant. Ecce ex quali

Later their numbers only grew stronger. In this way, Donatus of Bagaï found the means by which he could hire a demented gang of men to lead against Macarius. In the present day, there are also men of this same kind who, driven by a desire for false martyrdom, hire assassins to strike them to death. Also of this same type of men are those who hurl themselves headlong from the peaks of high mountains, so discarding their already cheap lives. You should consider from what sort of men your bishop, that other Donatus, created these armed bands for himself. Thoroughly terrified by such men, the officials who were carrying the funds which they were to distribute to the poor found themselves in such dire circumstances that they asked Silvester, the *comes*, for the help of some armed soldiers. They did this not to use them to commit any acts of violence, but in order to defend themselves from the violence being organized by the above-mentioned bishop Donatus. It is for this reason that the armed soldiers appeared.

For what happened next, consider for yourself to whom responsibility ought to be or can be ascribed. At that place [viz. Bagaï], they [i.e. the dissident leaders] had collected an enormous force of men and all of the necessary provisions. Out of the town basilica, they created, as it were, a public granary, in the expectation of the arrival of those men against whom they would be able to exert their madness and do whatever their crazed state of mind would suggest to them – unless, that is, the presence of the armed soldiers would prevent them. For when the *metatores* [sc. army camp surveyors, who were also used as advance scouts to find suitable terrain] as is customary were sent on ahead of the main body of the soldiers, they were not received as was fitting, but in a manner contrary to the injunctions of the Apostle who says "To whom honor is due, honor; to whom tax, tax; to whom tribute, tribute. You should not be in debt to anyone" [Romans 13: 7–8]. Instead, the soldiers who had been sent on ahead with their horses were cut down by the same men whose names you now spew forth in your lashings of hatred. They were the teachers of the very violence from which they themselves suffered. What they were able to suffer they knew from the injuries that they themselves had already

numero sibi episcopus alter Donatus cohortes effecerat! Hoc metu deterriti illi qui thesauros ferebant quos pauperibus erogarent invenerunt in tanta necessitate consilium ut a Silvestre comite armatum militem postularent non per quem alicui vim facerent sed ut vim a Donato supra memorato episcopo dispositam prohiberent. Hac ratione factum est ut miles videretur armatus. Iam quicquid subsecutum est videte cui debeat aut possit adscribi. Habebant illic vocatorum infinitam turbam et annonam competentem constat fuisse praeparatam. De basilica quasi publica fecerant horrea, expectantes ut venirent in quos furorem suum exercere potuissent et facerent quicquid illis dementia sua dictasset, nisi praesentia armati militis obstitisset. Nam cum ante venturos milites metatores ut fieri adsolet mitterentur, contra apostoli praecepta competenter suscepti non sunt qui ait: *Cui honorem honorem, cui vectigal, vectigal, cui tributum tributum. Nemini quicquam debueritis.* Qui missi fuerant cum equis suis contusi sunt ab his quorum nomina flabello invidiae ventilatis: ipsi magistri fuerunt iniuriae suae et quid pati possent ipsi praerogatis iniuriis docuerunt. Reverterunt vexati milites ad numeros suos et quod duo et tres passi fuerant universi doluerunt; commoti sunt omnes, iratos milites retinere nec eorum praepositi valuerunt."

inflicted on others. The soldiers who had been wounded returned to their units and when it was found that two or three of their comrades had died, all their fellow soldiers were struck with grief. The enraged soldiers were terribly upset and their commanders were no longer able to restrain them.

In this way there occurred, according to Optatus, a massacre for which no one except Donatus of Bagaï and the violent men whom he recruited were responsible. He assumes that the bishop mobilized his forces by means of news bulletins that were sent through the local channels of communication, principally by means of the networks of periodic markets where such men tended to congregate. At the same time, the very normality of this kind of communication is disguised. The technical terminology specifies hiring as the usual means by which the services of such men were acquired.[44] This is not to say that the bishop Donatus actually took these men into his paid employment. Probably not. Because these men normally hung out around periodic markets, waiting to be hired by prospective employers, and because of the stigma of their pay, they could be spoken of as "hired."

The well-known fact that circumcellions were to be found at rural markets for purposes of occasional or seasonal employment allowed a hostile writer like Optatus to play with words to impute the worst of mercenary motives suggested by the need to hire such thugs. It is important to note that these men were *not* circumcellions in general. Rather, they were a select group of such men who thought of themselves as Holy Fighters. They served for free. Unlike the majority of the circumcellions who *were* hiring out their labor at rural marketplaces, these men had volunteered to defend their religious community. The line that Optatus took – that these men themselves were responsible for what happened to them – was one echoed by later Catholic writers. As late as 411, Augustine admitted that the confrontation at Bagaï had come to have great symbolic significance, but he defended what had been done on the grounds that the dissidents had only themselves to blame: they had brought upon themselves the punishment they deserved for breaking the public laws. He regarded it as an outrage that such men should be commemorated when it was clear how little they had suffered in comparison with the violence that they had perpetrated on others.[45] He was parroting Optatus.

---

[44] That is to say, the use of the verb *conducere* strongly suggests as much.

[45] Aug. *Brev. collat.* 3.8.13 (CCL 149A: 281): "sed pro sceleribus quibus violenter saeviunt nefarieque vivunt, per leges publicas disciplinasque patiuntur; sicut etiam de oppido Bagaitano commemorasse ausi sunt, ubi manifestatum est quanta mala commiserint et quam minora perpessi sunt."

COMMANDERS OF THE SAINTS

It was the aim of Optatus' polemic to suggest that the Holy Fighters were to be identified with circumcellions in general. Having fixed this identification in the reader's mind, he was then able to tar the dissidents with the stigma of a separate and rather frightening incident of violence that had happened in the years immediately before 347. For someone like Parmenian to blame the Catholics for having recourse to the civil authorities as agents of violent repression, Optatus objects, was gross hypocrisy. After all, in 347 the local dissident bishop, Donatus of Bagaï, had called on the same type of violent men whom his fellow bishops had condemned not long before. It is to this incident, one that must precede the events of 347 by a few years, that Optatus turns in the midst of his account of the massacre at Bagaï. We are therefore moved back in memory, to events in southern Numidia that are represented as having occurred in the early to mid-340s.[46]

At that time a gathering of those men was whipped up whose madness had apparently been condemned by these very same bishops only a brief time before. For in the time before Unity [i.e. before 347], when men of this kind were accustomed to wander through small hamlets in the countryside, at the time when Axido and Fasir were being called the Commanders of the Saints by these same madmen, no one could be secure in their own possessions. Records of debts had lost their force. At that time no creditor was at liberty to enforce payment. Everyone was terrified by the letters issued by the men who boasted that they were the Commanders of the Saints. And if there was any delay in obeying their orders, a demented mob suddenly flew to their side. As the terror advanced before them, creditors were besieged with threats. In fear of death, persons who deserved to demand repayment of what was owed to them were forced to groveling supplications. Each of them hurried to write off the debts owed to him – even if these were enormous – and reckoned it a profit if he escaped injury at the hands of these men. Even the safest road could not be traveled because masters, thrown out of their vehicles, scampered like slaves before their own slaves who were now

---

[46] Optatus, *Contra Parm.* 3.4.3–5 (SC 413: 38–40): "Et eorum illo tempore concursus est flagitatus quorum dementia paulo ante ab ipsis episcopis impie videbatur esse succensa. Nam cum huiusmodi hominum genus ante unitatem per loca singula vagarentur, cum Axido et Fasir ab ipsis insanientibus sanctorum duces appellarentur, nulli licuit securum esse in possessionibus suis. Debitorum chirographa amiserant vires, nullus creditor illo tempore exigendi habuit libertatem, terrebantur omnes litteris eorum qui se sanctorum duces fuisse iactabant, et si in obtemperando eorum iussionibus tardaretur, advolabat subito multitudo insana et praecedente terrore creditores periculis vallabantur ut qui pro praestitis suis rogari meruerant, metu mortis humiles impellerentur in preces. Festinabat unusquisque debita etiam maxima perdere et lucrum computabatur evasisse ab eorum iniuriis. Etiam itinera non poterant esse tutissima quod domini de vehiculis suis excussi ante mancipia sua dominorum locis sedentia serviliter cucurrerunt. Illorum iudicio et imperio inter dominos et servos condicio mutabatur."

ensconced in the seats of their masters. At the behest and command of such men, the positions of masters and slaves were reversed.

This was a world turned upside down, a violent carnivalesque in which masters and slaves traded places. The same mechanisms at work in creating this jacquerie were found a few years later in the incident at Bagaï. Violent gangs were summoned and quickly assembled in large and frightening numbers. Communication mechanisms, such as those used by the bishop Donatus, are suggested: market heralds, or men like them, were used to bring messages to workers who were known to hang out at rural centers and periodic markets in the countryside. Only this time, instead of a Christian bishop, the leaders were two local men who are otherwise unknown and unattested: Axido and Fasir.

From their names alone, it is surmised, surely correctly, that these men emerged from local African social ranks that were not fully integrated with the Romano-Latin culture of the towns. Although Axido and Fasir were not Christian bishops, it is important to note that their strength was still rooted in religious power. They were popularly known and represented themselves as *duces sanctorum* or Commanders of the Saints.[47] The parallels with certain institutions known from Amazigh ("Berber") social groups in modern-day Morocco are perhaps too suggestive to ignore.[48] It is not even certain that these men were Christians, much less dissident Christians. What strands of holiness or sanctity in local society were being tapped is unknown, but a skein of Christian ideas and beliefs is strongly suggested by the fate of the men who followed them into battle. The incident also reveals the problematic aspects of their followers' Christian status, even in the eyes of the local hierarchy of the dissident Christian church. The reaction of the local dissident bishops to the violence associated with Axido and Fasir exhibited a peculiar hypocrisy that was a source of malicious joy for Optatus.[49]

---

[47] Some, like Vannier (1926), p. 17, have thought that Optatus was anachronistically transferring a later religious element of the circumcellions to this earlier case. I see no reason why this should be so, and take the argument to repose mainly on Vannier's desire to secularize the phenomena.

[48] On the "Commander of the Faithful" or Amir al-Muslimīn in the Maghrib al-Aqsa in more modern times, see Waterbury, *Commander of the Faithful*, with caveats by Gellner, *Muslim Society*, p. 72.

[49] Optatus, *Contra Parm.* 3.4.5–7 (SC 413: 40–43):. "unde cum vestrae partis episcopis tunc invidia fieret, Taurino tunc comiti scripsisse dicuntur huiusmodi homines in ecclesia corrigi non posse. Mandaverunt ut a supra dicto comite acciperent disciplinam. Tunc Taurinus ad eorum litteras ire militem iussit armatum per nundinas ubi circumcellionum furor vagari consueverat. In Loco Octavensi occisi sunt plurimi et detruncati sunt multi quorum corpora usque in hodiernum per dealbatas aras aut mensas potuerunt numerari. Ex quorum numero cum aliqui in basilicis sepeliri

Because of these events, real hostility arose toward the bishops of your party. So it is reported that they composed a petition to Taurinus, who was the Count of Africa at the time, in which they stated that it was not possible to discipline men of this kind within the confines of their church. So it was *your* bishops who demanded that these men be punished by this same *comes* [i.e. the Count of Africa, Taurinus]. In response to their letter, Taurinus ordered armed soldiers to sweep through all of the periodic marketplaces where the demented gangs of the circumcellions were accustomed to wander. At the place known as Locus Octavensis, large numbers of them were killed and many were decapitated. The number of their dead bodies can still be calculated today by counting the whitewashed altars and tables [i.e. for martyrs] set up at the place. When they had begun to bury some of the dead inside the local basilicas, Clarus, who was priest at the village known as the Locus Subbullensis, was forced by his bishop to undo the burials. Following this incident, an express order was issued as to what was to be done – and it was done – since it was expressly forbidden [i.e. by the dissident bishops] for such men to be buried in the House of God.

So the civil authorities knew, as did the bishops of the dissident Christian community, where it was that such men normally congregated: they gathered at the periodic market centers scattered throughout the countryside of Numidia in search of work. At least two of these *loca* or rural villages are named in this account: the *locus Subbullensis* and the *locus Octavensis*.[50] It is likely that the latter place was so-named because it was the eighth place on the round of eight market days that made up a single cycle that linked different locales into a single network of communication.[51] Furthermore, the fact that the burial places of these men were marked by tables or *mensae*, and that the local priest of the *locus Subbullensis* began burying some of the dead inside his basilica, signaled that the men cut down by the Count of Africa's soldiers had achieved a special and exalted status: they were martyrs. Because the hierarchy of the dissident Christian church wished to repress the power and status acquired by these men, the local bishop ordered the priest of Subbullensis to remove the burials from his church.[52]

---

coepissent, Clarus, presbyter in Loco Subbullensi ab episcopo suo coactus est ut insepultam faceret sepulturam. Unde proditum est mandatum fuisse fieri quod factum est quando nec sepultura in domo Dei exhiberi concessa est."

[50] The *locus Subbullensis* is otherwise unattested; the *locus Octavensis* might be the diocese of the "Victor ab Octavu" in Numidia, thereby attesting a Christian community here as early as 256: Maier, *L'épiscopat*, p. 24 no. 78; p. 183.

[51] Shaw (1981) offers an analysis of these peculiar African periodic markets or *nundinae*, and their role in the management of labor by domanial landowners.

[52] This might offer a clue to date, since, if this had been Donatus of Bagaï, it is hard to believe that Optatus would have let the opportunity slip further to blacken this *bête noire* with yet more hypocrisy, if it were possible.

The fact that the dead men were provided with whitewashed altars and sacrificial tables, however, is compelling evidence that the local people regarded the murdered men as martyrs. The hierarchy of the dissident church might be able to control their priest, but the popular response by large numbers of common people in the countryside was another matter.

There is a big problem with contextualizing the events of 347. It is that the historical memory of Numidians had been focussed on this particular event at Bagaï and on its immediate consequences. There were surely other outbreaks elsewhere in Africa of which we know nothing simply for the reason that no literary source commemorated them. Perhaps even more disturbing is the fact that we happen to know of the rural jacquerie that occurred a few years before only because of the accident of its preservation in the polemic of Optatus.

RITUALS OF VIOLENCE

Even apart from these spectacular set pieces, Optatus kept returning to the fundamental problem of violence in other contexts. For example, at the beginning of his sixth book, although he is ostensibly dealing with sacramental errors committed by the dissident church in Africa, he is so taken with the question of violence that he is almost naturally drawn back to it. The mention of disgusting acts committed against the divine sacraments immediately cues his mind to the fate of sacred objects in a Catholic basilica in the aftermath of its seizure by the dissidents. He begins with the altars.[53]

Now we must expose the cruel and stupid acts that you will be quite unable to deny. For what is more sacrilegious than to break, to smash, and to remove the altars of God – the very altars at which you yourselves made your offerings, the place where both the prayers of the people and the limbs of Christ were uplifted, where Almighty God was invoked, where the Holy Spirit descended in response to our prayers, where many accepted the pledge of eternal salvation and the protection of faith and the hope of the resurrection? . . . For what is the altar

---

[53] Optatus, *Contra Parm.* 6.1.1–3 (SC 413: 160–62): "Iam illa ostendenda sunt, quae crudeliter ac stulte vos fecisse negare minime poteritis. Quid enim tam sacrilegum quam altaria Dei, in quibus et vos aliquando obtulistis, frangere, radere, removere, in quibus et vota populi et membra Christi portata sunt, quo Deus omnipotens invocatus sit, quo postulatus descenderit spiritus sanctus, unde a multis et pignus salutis aeternae et tutela fidei et spes resurrectionis accepta est? . . . Quid est enim altare nisi sedes et corporis et sanguinis Christi? Haec omnia furor vester aut rasit aut fregit aut removit . . . ubique tamen nefas est, dum tantae rei manus sacrilegas et impias intulistis."

but the seat of the Body and Blood of Christ? All these altars your madness has either smashed, broken, or removed . . . Everywhere, it is blasphemous that you laid your sacrilegious and impious hands on something so awesome.

His complaint agrees with the descriptions of attacks on churches found in other sources. Much of the violence was directed against physical objects of great symbolic value, like altars.[54] Reports about altars being smashed, sometimes right over the heads of priests who took refuge under them, confirm that they were a special target in the sectarian violence. Force was also used to remove those objects from the church, instruments that had had sacral connections with the congregation of the hated enemy. So Optatus is moved to anger when he reports how chalices and other sacred vessels in a Catholic basilica were removed and sold as items of common commerce.[55]

Yet you doubled this dreadful outrage when you even broke the chalices which had contained the Blood of Christ, chalices whose shape you melted down to bullion metal and then sold, obtaining monies for them in profane marketplaces. When you didn't care to whom you sold them for money, you were sacrilegious, but you were transfixed with greed in that you sold them at all. You even allowed the vessels to be burned [i.e. melted own] which your own hands had held – since before we held them, *you* were the ones who used these same chalices. You ordered all of them to be sold in any place whatever. It is even possible that lewd women purchased them for their own peculiar uses and that pagans bought them to make vessels in which they might burn incense to their idols.

His personal horror at the cleansing operations is conveyed to the reader. We learn something of the personal hurt that accompanied these takeovers, when he reports that "the Donatists," on retaking possession of Catholic basilicas, would have them exorcised and would wash the coverings, the instruments, the curtains, and even the walls of the church as if they had been contaminated by Catholic use.[56] The outrage leads to a long and exaggerated piece of rhetoric in which this obsessive-compulsive cleaning

---

[54] There is a rough parallel with the iconoclastic tendencies of some Reformation violence. See E. Duffy, *The Stripping of the Altars: Traditional Religion in England, c. 1400-c. 1580*, 2nd ed., New Haven and London, Yale University Press, 2005, pp. 407–21, 453–55; S. Michalski, "Iconoclasm: Rites of Destruction," in *The Reformation and the Visual Arts: The Protestant Image Question in Western and Eastern Europe*, London and New York, Routledge, 1993, pp. 75–98, esp. pp. 91–95.

[55] Optatus, *Contra Parm.* 6.2.1–2 (SC 413: 166–68): "Hoc tamen immane facinus a vobis geminatum est dum fregistis etiam calices, Christi sanguinis portatores, quorum species revocastis in massas merces nefariis nundinis procurantes. Ad quam mercem nec emptores eligere voluistis, sacrilegi, dum inconsiderate vendidistis, avari, dum venditis! Passi estis etiam comburi manus vestras, quibus ante nos eosdem calices tractabatis. Eam rem tamen passim vendi iussistis; emerunt forsitan in usus suos sordidae mulieres, emerunt pagani facturi vasa in quibus incenderent idolis suis."

[56] Optatus, *Contra Parm.* 6.5.2–3 (SC 413: 180).

mania is satirized. Catholics share every part of the daily life in the towns and villages with the dissident Christians. Do "the Donatists" therefore wish to begin cleaning even the roads because they might be contaminated with Catholic footsteps, or wash the very water of the public baths because it might have been polluted by Catholic bathers?[57] The words suggest that much of the violence might usefully be categorized under the heading of purifying operations. In the minds of the perpetrators, its purpose was not so much intentionally to injure or to kill as it was to remove all elements of the "other people" from spaces that were to be reoccupied and reused by pure and clean people. The mere use of it by "the others" filled the new occupants with a sense of personal violation, a morbid repulsion, we might say, at the residual presence of the traitors.

Perhaps more important than these notes on violence is a brief aside that follows on Optatus' reference to the ritual smashing of altars: his description of the violent gangs of men, whom he elsewhere labels circumcellions, who were part of these attacks.[58]

Why should I recall your hiring of a host of degenerate men and the wine that you gave them as pay for their evil acts? So that this wine could be drunk warm in sacrilegious drafts by unclean mouths, it was heated by a fire made from the broken pieces of our altars.

The words are of some significance. In his main text devoted to the description of the marshaling of the circumcellions, that is to say the dissident *agonistici* or Holy Fighters, Optatus had described their hiring in the local periodic market centers. Although averring to hire, he had not described their pay. Here he names the pay: it was drink, more specifically wine. The pejorative way in which he fashions the results of consuming this pay, as drunken and uncouth behavior, is to be expected. It is presented as a perverse communion. The alcoholic drink will later recur in Augustine's reports on these same men and we shall see why. It had its own peculiar rationale.

THE DEATHS OF MAXIMIAN AND ISAAC

The memories that the Christians in the dissident church had of the year 347 and its immediate aftermath were rather different from those shared

---

[57] Optatus, *Contra Parm.* 6.6.4–5 (SC 413: 184).
[58] Optatus, *Contra Parm.* 6.1.3 (SC 413: 162–63): "Quid perditorum conductam referam multitudinem et vinum in mercedem sceleris datum? Quod ut inmundo ore sacrilegis haustibus biberetur, calida de fragmentis altarium facta est."

by Optatus. Their recollections were especially painful. To the extent that the Catholics tended to diminish, explain away, or belittle the events of that year, the dissidents carefully cultivated and nourished the memory of a time whose violence they interpreted in a quite different light. The account of the deaths of Maximian, Isaac, and others, on 15 August 347 reflects this different tradition.[59] Macrobius, the author of the account, was perhaps a member of the clergy of the dissident church at Carthage. He recollects that the events of that year were a shock to his church, coming, as they did, after a long period of peace.[60] It was the suddenness of this "second onslaught of the Devil" that caught his community off guard.[61] If the sequence of events as told by this local witness can be trusted, the more violent episodes of what happened in 347 unfolded first in Numidia in regions far to the south and west of Carthage. News of these violent incidents, including the slaughter at Bagaï, filtered back to Carthage, causing great consternation among the dissident Christians in the city. The same account confirms the existence of some sort of "edict of unity" that was subsequently posted in the metropolis, a decree that involved the active participation of the proconsular governor of Africa and his officials in its enforcement.[62]

No news of harsh punishments had yet struck our ears and hearts. Only the consolation of the news concerning you and the countless martyrs of Numidia encouraged the spirits of our brothers ... when suddenly the Devil, raging about

---

[59] For the text, see Mastandrea (1995), in preference to Maier, *Dossier*, 1, no. 36, pp. 259–75, which is based on the older editions of Dupin = PL 8: 767–74 and Mabillon = PL 8: 778–84. On the date, see Appendix E.3; for general context, see Monceaux, *Hist. litt.* 5, pp. 82–97.

[60] The author appears only in the incipit where he bears no clerical rank, but rather the title of "martyr": "Epistola beatissimi martyris Macrobi ad plebem Carthaginis de passione martyrum Isaac et Maximiani." Some have attempted to identify him with the dissident bishop of Rome (see, e.g., "Macrobius (1)," PAC, p. 662. I find this difficult to accept. The tenor of the letter is more of a local writing to fellow locals, and the wording (e.g., § 3: "hic apud Carthaginem") seems strongly to suggest a person in Carthage writing to his fellow Carthaginians, not a bishop in Rome writing to them. He would seem to be a more minor local, not a bishop; perhaps, indeed, the priest at Carthage to whom Gennadius (*De vir. illustr.* 5) attributes a work *Ad confessores et virgines* (despite the negative views of the editors of PAC).

[61] *Passio Isaac et Maximiani*, 3.13 and 16 (Mastandrea 1995: 77): "Siluerat hic apud Karthaginem aliquamdiu saevae persecutionis immanitas, ut longioris temporis cessatione nutriret peiores insidias ... a quibus idcirco reor diutius illum quietum cessasse, quia cunctos exercitus Christi putaverat sibi mancipasse."

[62] *Passio Isaac et Maximiani*, 3.13–18 (Mastandrea 1995: 77–78): "nulla iam poena terribilis aures et pectora quatiebat. Sola de vobis ac martyribus infinitis Numidiae opinionis consolatio fratrum animos erigebat ... cum repente diabolus, iterum fremens ... et insana suae grassationis arma commovit ... et acrioribus stimulis concitatus requirebat cuius aptum sibi deligeret iudicis pectus. Sed nec segnior et proconsul desideriis eius parem se ipsum subiecit et feralis edicti proposito sacrilegae unitatis iterum foedus celebrari, constitutis cruciatibus, imperavit, legem scilicet addens insuper traditorum, ut peregrini, quos Christus pro se mandat recipi, ab omnibus pellerentur nec quasi contra unitatis foedera molirentur."

for the second time . . . moved to arms the weaponry of his insane banditry . . . and, driven by even sharper incitements, He sought out the heart of a judge [i.e. a provincial governor] that he would select as suitable to his own. And not slowly did the proconsul subject himself as a partner to the desires of this One. With the publication of a savage decree, he [sc. the governor] commanded that an edict of sacrilegious unity be publicly announced for a second time, and then set up his torture chambers. He added a measure suggested by the traitors, namely that those very outsiders whom Christ ordered to be received "for his sake" should be driven out from all places forever and that they should not be allowed to work against the compact of unity.

The writer establishes the general context of events at Carthage in 347. What happened had occurred after a long peaceful interlude. But it was the second time that the Devil had been set on the loose, raging against God's people, and it was the second time that an imperial edict enforcing unification had been ordered. His words hint at a deeper level of memory of a first occasion of persecution that is not described in detail by him. He assumes that his listeners will remember the first attack under Diocletian and that they will see it as a typological precursor to what was happening to them in the present. The writer suggests that there were at least two parts to the edict posted by the proconsul. First there was a decree enforcing the unification of the two hostile communities by a forced merger of the dissident church and the existing Catholic Church. Then there was a second measure that the writer especially associates with "the traitors," suggesting that it was at their behest that this supplemental part of the law was added to the main decree. This was a formal measure calling for the banishing of the dissident church leaders from their seats of power so that they would not be able to agitate against the edict of unification. In the words that follow, the writer describes the ways in which Isaac and Maximian came to perish in the events that transpired at Carthage between 14 and 16 August 347. The intensification of the normal hatreds between the two communities in various types of violent acts involved the usual set of actors: the two hostile Christian communities, the forces of the Roman state, and finally those of the administrative officials of local towns and municipalities.

The story begins on 14 August 347, a Friday, with the members of the dissident Christian community celebrating the Eucharist feast in a church, a house of prayer, at Carthage. With this entrée to his story, the author suggests a normality that is broken on the following day by dramatic events that starred Isaac and Maximian, two members of his community at Carthage. The first of these mini-dramas involved Maximian. As he was about to drink the communion wine from a cup, he witnessed it filling up with blood and saw a vision that foretold his martyrdom on the next day. Fired by these visions, on 15 August, a Saturday, Maximian was emboldened to tear down a poster containing the imperial edict or, as he saw it, "the deadly letters" of the emperor. He tore the poster to pieces and threw the shredded pieces to the wind. The act was performed publicly in a manner calculated to be witnessed by imperial authorities and to provoke their anger. Maximian was arrested on the spot, taken into custody, and led before a tribunal for a hearing.[63] The problem with interpreting the significance of this narrative is that it is a replay of a foundational story of Christian resistance. In February 303, at Nicomedia in Bithynia, an anonymous Christian man tore down the decree of Diocletian and ripped it to pieces.[64]

As soon as the decree against the churches was posted in Nicomedia, a certain man of no mean status . . . was moved by his zeal for God and driven by his burning faith. Since it was something unholy and most profane, when the decree was posted in a full public venue, he snatched it and tore it to pieces – this at a time when the two emperors themselves were present in the same city.

The man was arrested, tortured, and burned alive.[65] And so began the first "Great Persecution" of Christians to which the persecution of 347 was manifestly likened. Was Maximian literally re-enacting a story he knew? Or was the writer creating the re-enactment?

As a narrative, what follows is a standard martyr act developed out of a long African tradition that had at its apex the evocative death of a young woman, Vibia Perpetua, a century and a half earlier in the year 203 in the same city of Carthage. Her martyrdom had given birth to a long series of imitations that established the main outlines of one of the major subgenres of the literary type. The model demanded a complex theological preamble to the main narrative by the writer or editor, and other necessary elements such as visions and dreams that supplemented the details of a mandatory courtroom scene in which the Christian defendant confronted the evil persecuting authority. Facing the intransigence of the defendant, the interrogators in the court resorted to the usual horrors of torture. At

---

[63] *Passio Isaac et Maximiani*, 5.26–27 (Mastandrea, 1995: 79): "Callidae mentis celeritate, non pedum, protinus forum certamen ultro provocaturus ascendit et funestos apices, tamquam diaboli ibi membra discerperet, manu rapida dissipavit. Inde confestim raptus ad tribunal infandum, sine ulla dilatione, proconsulis iussu vallatus est effera caterva tortorum."

[64] See Euseb. *HE*, 8.5 (SC 55: 11); in the accounts of Lactantius and Eusebius, the man has no name. He was later provided with one – a Euethius, who was martyred at Nicomedia on 24 February 303.

[65] Lactantius, *De mort. pers.* 13 (SC 39: 91–92).

this point in the story, it becomes difficult to disentangle any background reality from the forefront of the idea-driven narrative. Maximian's tortures are conventional. But so was real judicial torture. The torturers work away at his body with lead-tipped whips. The martyr is able to display superhuman endurance. The torturers continue to work away at his body. They turn to the use of rods to beat him. In the sacral language of martyrdom, the torturers turn his body into "one big wound."

The story line that follows Maximian over the first stretch of the narrative is set aside for a moment in order to introduce the parallel story of a fellow parishioner named Isaac. It is unclear what specific misdeed Isaac had committed that resulted in his arrest and summons before the governor's judicial tribunal. He seems deliberately to have encouraged an attack on himself by the calculated use of insult, by aggressively chanting and shouting at his enemies: "TRAITORS! TRAITORS!" "COME ON! COME ON! TRY TO SAVE THE MADNESS OF YOUR UNITY!" The writer of the narrative claims that the Catholics, hearing the insults, reacted badly. In his view, the traitors of his own time were the congenital descendants of the original traitors who had handed over the Holy Scriptures to the persecuting authorities in the Great Persecution of 303–05. Naturally, the new traitors were just as eager to hand over Isaac to the new persecutors of his own time. Isaac's appearance in the dock of the proconsular governor is construed as so upsetting to the demeanor of the governor that he set aside all his concerns with Maximian in order to turn his full attention to the new defendant. The same scenes of courtroom torture are repeated, only with greater intensity. The highly tendentious narrative, however, reports no penalty inflicted on the men other than that of exile. The two were kept in prison awaiting the imposition of the sentence. The penalty of exile suggests that the two men might have been from the privileged ranks of the clergy.

The writer now passes from the events of Saturday, 15 August, to those of Sunday, 16 August 347. Although the Roman proconsular governor had sentenced the defendants to exile, a worse fate was in store for the others who had been arrested. Although the Roman authorities had accepted exile as the solution for obstreperous and contumacious (and dangerous) rebellious clerical types, the uglier fate in store for the other "brothers" is specifically blamed on the lobbying efforts of "the traitors." Just as they had campaigned to have the penalty of exile added to the imperial edict, they now educated the governor on the nature of Christian martyrdom. They urged the need for him to rid himself once and for all of these evil men, but in a manner that would ensure that their corpses could never be recovered by their brethren, providing bodily material for their veneration as martyrs. The writer now describes, in pathetic words, how all those being kept in detention in the jails in Carthage were gathered together and driven in lines down to ships in the harbour. En route, the living were whipped and clubbed into submission. Once loaded on a boat, they were taken far out to sea, where barrels filled with sand were roped to their necks and hands. They were then thrown overboard to drown. Revulsion at the mode of execution roused a palpable rage in the writer against the "traitors" and "the agents of Satan" who had committed this act of judicial savagery.

Once again, the problem of typology intervenes. The story bears a striking resemblance to two sequential events that took place some four and a half decades earlier in the course of the Great Persecution under Diocletian as recounted by Eusebius and also, notably, by the African Christian rhetor Lactantius. It was at the beginning of this persecution, at Nicomedia, when the first edict was posted in the city. The incident of the man who tore the poster of the edict from the wall and ripped it to pieces was followed by another parallel piece of repression. Those who were enforcing the terms of the imperial decree against the Christians punished other miscreants: "the executioners bound a multitude of other Christians and placed them on boats and hurled them to the depths of the sea."[66] The echoes in the events of 347 at Carthage, and the fact that the writer conveniently situates his story in a Friday to Sunday cycle, must excite some suspicion that the narrative has been crafted to produce a sacred narrative of "history repeating itself" in the minds of the believers who heard it. It is far less an archive of memory than it is a carefully programmed manipulation of sentiment produced by recalling the event in the present. In effect, the preacher is saying to his parishioners: We've been through all of this before. This is a replay of the Great Persecution, and this time we shall win just as surely as we did the first time round.

THE GREATEST OF SAINTS: DONATUS AND MARCULUS

If the horrific events transpiring at Carthage in mid-August of 347 were remembered by the dissidents in sermons and writings, other events were taking place in Numidia to the southwest that were to be so indelibly fixed in the memory and anger of the dissidents that they were not to escape anyone's notice. For many decades that followed his death, the execution of the dissident bishop Marculus was to have a special place in

---

[66] Eusebius, *HE*, 8.6.7 (SC 55: 13).

the dissidents' understanding of their history and of who they were. His execution was one thing that they would never forget. The events involving his death transpired over the summer and autumn of 347 as the imperial agents Paul and Macarius worked their way southwest from Carthage, first to the region around Bagaï and Theveste, and then further to the west along the great trunk road connecting Theveste with the towns of Lambaesis and Thamugadi. The Catholic record of this journey was one of the understandable, if lamentable, killing of large numbers of Africans who had needlessly provoked the soldiers accompanying imperial emissaries who were doing necessary work to effect the unity of the churches. This is not how the dissidents saw this violent incident nor, needless to say, how they understood what followed it.[67]

What was important for the dissidents and what they remembered is what is *not* in Optatus' account – namely, the organized repression that followed the massacre at Bagaï. It is easy to imagine the attitude of Paul and Macarius, plenipotentiaries of the emperor. Their position was not at all like that of the short-term civil proconsul imposing sentences in the mixed urban milieux of the cosmopolis of Carthage. The massacre at Bagaï had created a poisoned atmosphere in southern Numidia, one of great hostility in a land where the supporters of the dissident church were in the huge majority.[68] In entering it, Paul and Macarius were truly alone. Any signs of disobedience would have to be stamped out ruthlessly. Of the death of Donatus, the bishop of Bagaï who was implicated in the resistance to Paul and Macarius, we know little, since so little of the relevant dissident literature has been preserved.[69] But the different assessments of the incident are clear. Roman authorities arrested Donatus, he was lynched, and his body was unceremoniously dumped down a well. He had been executed.[70] In which case, he was a martyr. But Catholics later disputed the fact. They claimed that Donatus had killed himself, that he had voluntarily thrown himself down the well. So they interpreted his death as just another precipitation, another case of "a Donatist" who gratuitously threw himself to his death, just as they were to claim that Marculus was later to do at

---

[67] For the text of the *Passio Marculi*, see Mastandrea (1995), 65–75, which supersedes the older defective text printed in Maier, *Dossier*, I, no. 37, pp. 275–91 (a reprint of Migne, PL 8: 760–66); for background, Quinot (1967d).

[68] I accept this sequence of events. But *if* Paul and Macarius came down the Carthage–Theveste trunkroad and then proceeded westward along the Theveste–Lambaesis road, it is just as probable that they would have arrived at Vegesela first and only after that would they have been involved in the incident at Bagaï which is further to the north and west of Vegesela.

[69] For the known sources on Donatus of Bagaï, see "Donatus (8)," PAC, pp. 304–05.

[70] Aug. *Tract. in Ioh.* 11.14–15 (CCL 36: 120): where the claim is denied and the standard Catholic claim of suicide is proffered instead.

Nova Petra.[71] In this Catholic memory, Donatus was severely censured by a universal condemnation that came to be placed on all self-killers. The extent and impact of this general damnation, however, was only to become fully apparent in the 410s and 420s, half a century later, when the struggle between the two communities reached a fever pitch of intensity.

Part of the reason for the great rage felt by the writers who narrated the subsequent death of Marculus is without doubt rooted in the superior social status of the main protagonist, the bishop Marculus.[72] Unlike Maximian and Isaac, who appear to be two laymen or lower-level clerics of the dissident church at Carthage, Marculus was a convert to Christianity who, like Cyprian earlier and Augustine later, was a man of high social standing and education. In the mini-biography that prefaces the account of his martyrdom, the writer is at pains to emphasize the continuity of his upper-class virtue as a Christian bishop. Like Augustine, Marculus was a highly trained rhetor and expert in the law, but one who had turned his back on "the false honors of worldly knowledge." He had had, it seems, a successful career in the courts before turning to Christianity and becoming a bishop in the dissident church.[73] This image of Marculus as a man of learning and status was rejected by later Catholic interpreters.[74] But in Numidia the dissident church held a prevalent position of power and status that would have been attractive to a man of culture like Marculus who might, in other circumstances, have been drawn instead to the Catholic Church. Throughout his account, the writer highlights the innate aristocratic virtues of Marculus: his lofty demeanor, his probity, his honesty, his dignity, and his brilliance – inner virtues that were manifest in his outer physical appearance. His carriage was noble, his bearing exuded modesty and charm.

As the imperial emissaries in charge of implementing the imperial decree of unity crossed the frontiers of Numidia, violence erupted with the massacre at Bagaï and the death of its bishop Donatus. It was obvious to all that the situation was bad and getting worse. The whole assembly, the most holy *chorus* of dissident bishops from the ecclesiastical province of Numidia, gathered hurriedly to formulate a negotiable position that they

---

[71] Aug. *Tract. in Ioh.* 11.15 (CCL 26: 120): "Ecce Donatus Bagaiensis in puteum missus est! Quando potestates Romanae talia supplicia decreverunt, ut praecipitarentur homines?"

[72] On the martyrological tradition, see Delehaye (1935).

[73] *Passio Marculi*, 2.6 (Mastandrea, 1995: 65): "Ipse namque olim praeelectus et praedestinatus a domino, mox ubi primum beatae fidei rudimenta suscepit, statim mundanas litteras respuens, forense exercitium et falsam saecularis scientiae dignitatem suspensa ad caelum mente calcavit, et a calumniosis tribunalium saeptis ad sanctissimam ecclesiae transiens scholam, dum verum magistrum elegit Christum, sic inter principales Christi discipulos meruit honorari."

[74] Aug. *Contra litt. Petil.* 2.13.32 (CSEL 52: 37): "quanto labore impenso nullo modo probaturi sitis, quod Donatus et Marculus prophetae fuerint aut sapientes aut scribae, quia non fuerunt."

could present to the imperial emissary Macarius, now ensconced on a rural estate at Vegesela, to the west of Theveste.[75] No doubt because of his superior education and status, Marculus was chosen to head a delegation of ten bishops that undertook this embassy to Macarius. If there was anything meriting the name of a rational discussion at the meeting, there is no evidence of it. The confrontation appears to have been summary. The bishops came with "salutary advice" for Macarius, namely that the Roman authorities should "desist from committing such a great crime." Macarius, who had just emerged from the slaughter at Bagaï was in no mood to listen to such "advice" and surely deemed their request a kind of outrageous contempt or *contumacia* towards his office and the imperial law. He immediately had the ten men arrested and put on trial. On their refusal to submit, his queries naturally led to the use of judicial torture.

The observant description of the violent attacks on the bodies of the bishops dilates on small details of the physical assault. Above all, it is the fact that these attacks were vented on the sacred bodies of bishops that raised the greatest anger: that their limbs were stripped nude so that they could be seen in public, that they were bound to a whipping column so that soldiers acting as enforcers could assault them savagely with wooden clubs was shocking. These were the bodies of holy men, men of Christ.[76] The narrator takes comfort in the fact that Marculus displayed such self-control and virtue that he did not have to be tied to the whipping post. He wrapped his arms around the column, knit his fingers together and then hung on by the force of his own will.[77] The bishop's endurance, his superhuman patience, combined with the exhaustion of his torturers and tormenters, were (for the narrator) in themselves evidence of the superior standing of this slave of God.

Precisely what happened after the incident at Vegesela is not entirely clear, but it is certain that Marculus and some of the other bishops survived the savage beatings inflicted upon them. They were taken in a train, hauled along behind Macarius and his entourage, dragged though the towns and

[75] *Passio Marculi*, 3.12 (Mastandrea, 1995: 66): "Nam cum ad eum antiquissimorum patrum sanctissimus chorus et adunatum concilium sacerdotum decem ex numero suo probatos episcopos legationis causa misisset, qui eum salutaribus monitis aut a tanto scelere revocarent, aut certe (quod contigit) priores ipsi ad devotissimi certaminis campum et ad fidei aciem prosilirent."

[76] *Passio Marculi*, 4.15 (Mastandrea, 1995: 67): "Ut seorsum singuli ad singulas columnas vincti, nudatis publice sacerdotalibus membris, acerbis fustium ictibus caederentur."

[77] *Passio Marculi*, 4.18–19 (Mastandrea, 1995: 67): "Circumdant igitur fortissimum Christi bellatorem cruentae latronum manus et barbarae militum classes in carnifices repente mutatae. Cumque eum ad columnam duris nexibus conarentur adstringere, prompte ille continuo tantam occasionem ostentandae dei virtutis adripuit: nam columnam ipsam ita ultro vinculis brachiorum et digitorum nodis instrinxit, ut eum inde nulla valeret poena divellere, nulla posset crudelitas separare."

villages of southern Numidia as the imperial commissioner attempted to complete his mission. Marculus became a prize exhibit put on parade to demonstrate what happened to a Christian bishop who opposed imperial authority. He was, in the words of the narrator of his story, made a "public spectacle of cruelty."[78] The final incident happened at the town of Nova Petra – a place whose very name meaning the "New Rock" or the "New Peter" was nicely symbolic for a Christian believer – where Marculus and the other dissident bishops were held in detention, awaiting their fate. Nova Petra was the site of a fort located at the foot of a great height, a precipice that fell away, steeply, into a great chasm.

Early in the morning of the 29 November, Marculus trudged to the top of the precipice, led to the peak by a guard of Roman soldiers. Depending on one's point of view, one of two things happened that resulted in the death of Marculus. According to the skeptics, that is to say the Catholic doubters, Marculus somehow just fell from the height; it was suggested that he might have deliberately thrown himself off the pinnacle. In this way, Marculus' death could be degraded to a despicable form of self-murder for which only he himself was to blame.[79] For the dissidents, this false claim was a vile lie typical of the ones propagated by their adversaries. What in fact happened was that a Roman executioner marched Marculus to the top of the height and deliberately threw him into the chasm to his death.[80] The mode of execution was quite purposeful. As in the case of the executions at Carthage, the final concern of those advising the authorities (the Catholics) was to deny the dissident faithful the possession of a body with which they would then initiate the veneration owed to a martyr.[81]

Whatever the authorities intended, they failed miserably. Whether or not the actual body parts of Marculus were recovered, believers believed that they had been saved. The narrative of Marculus' death recounts how,

---

[78] *Passio Marculi*, 5.24 (Mastandrea, 1995: 68): "Tunc eum secum per aliquas Numidiae civitates, quasi quoddam crudelitatis suae spectaculum, ducens, nesciens feritas et gentilibus stuporem et Christi hostibus confusionem et fidelibus dei servis incentivum gloriosi certaminis exhibebat."

[79] Attempts have been made to reconcile the two accounts. Thus, for Monceaux, *Hist.litt.* 5, p. 73, the evidence of Optatus (*Contra Parm.* 3.6 = SC 413: 48–50) definitely shows that Catholics close to the time of the death knew that it was not a suicide; therefore, the Romans executed Marculus and then deliberately hurled Marculus' dead body off the cliff to deprive it of proper burial.

[80] *Passio Marculi*, 6.25 (Mastandrea, 1995: 68): "At vero postquam exquisitum atque truculentum genus mortis invenit, statim eum secum ad castellum Novae Petrae, quod ardui montis praecipitio et nomine et vicinitate coniunctum est, sub artissima militum prosecutione perduxit."

[81] *Passio Marculi*, 13.60 (Mastandrea, 1995: 73): once again, as at Carthage, the dissident writer was sure that the "evil counsels" of "the traitors" were advising the Romans authorities about what to do: "Confusa sunt igitur virtutibus Christi persecutorum exquisita ingenia et traditorum iniqua consilia, qui ad hoc tale supplicium cogitaverant, ne umquam in testimonium crudelitatis eorum a populis dei memoria martyris posset honorari."

during his fall from the great height, he suddenly experienced the sensation of a slow-motion glide gently downwards towards the earth and then, simultaneously, an upward airy drift to celestial realms. The next morning, at first light, his body parts were miraculously revealed to searchers by shafts of light piercing the clouds in the sky, interpreted as divine searchlights that picked out his limbs, scattered on the sharp rocks at the base of the mountain. Marculus' death was to be the turning point in relationships between the two churches. As much as later Catholic writers would try to explain away his death, to blame the "excesses" of the Roman authorities, to question the veracity of the "Donatist" account, or to blame Marculus himself, there was born in the heart of this execution an adamantine nodule of hatred that was nourished by the dissidents to the very end of the conflict.

A concrete way in which the memory of what happened to Marculus was kept alive throughout southern Numidia was the church that was constructed at the site of Vegesela, modern Ksar el-Kelb ("Castle of the Dog"), where Marculus and the nine other bishops who undertook the embassy to Macarius were arrested and tortured.[82] The pious shout of the dissidents was celebrated in the letters of an inscription carved on a vaulted arch that stretched over the opening of the apse at the end of the basilica: DEO LAUDES OMNES HIC DICAMUS: "In this place, let us all shout 'Praise to the Lord.'"[83] The additional words unusually appended to the core cry of "Praise to the Lord" have emphatic meaning. *Here* we shall all say "Praise to the Lord," where the "here" and the "all of us" distinguish the congregation from "others" who are "not us" and who are not "in this place."[84]

Remains of the murdered bishop Marculus had been brought back to Vegesela from Nova Petra and had been placed in a memorial built in the extreme southeastern corner of the basilica. One half of the shrine was open to the sight of the congregation. Fixed on the front of this part was a plaque, on which rectangular bands of geometrical designs and an inner circle of convoluted ivy leaves surrounded the inscribed words: MEMORIA DOMNI MARCHULI,[85] *Memorial of Lord Marculus:*

---

[82] Cayrel (1934) and Courcelle (1936). Ksar el-Kelb (Gsell, *Atl.Arch.* f. 28 [Aïn Beïda], no. 165) is approximately at the location, 18 miles from Mascula (Khenchela), where the Antonine Itinerary, 33.5 (O. Cuntz, ed., *Itineraria Romana*, 1, Leipzig, 1929, p. 4) locates Vegesela (at a distance of 19 Roman miles).

[83] Cayrel (1934), pp. 125, 131–32; Courcelle (1936), p. 173.

[84] Cayrel (1934), p. 132: "Sans vouloir exagérer la portée de ce dernier mot [sc. *omnes*], on peut noter que cet accent mis sur l'unanimité des fidèles convient bien à une secte qui trouvait dans l'enthousiasme collectif la force de soutenir un perpétuel combat."

[85] Cayrel (1934), pp. 134–35, and the photograph, plate II, fig. 6.

"Lord" since the bishop was now honored as *dominus*, a term that likened Marculus in formal address to the supreme deity – *the* Lord. His heroic death, his martyrdom, had raised him far above the status of ordinary mortal Christians. The other half of the shrine, a martyr's table or *mensa*, the part that contained the relics of the martyr, was hived off within the *diaconium* to the right of the apse, whose western wall had been extended outwards to incorporate this part of the memorial.[86] The excavators noted that there were nine more burials located in the church – eight in the apse and one beneath the altar itself – fuelling speculation that these were the remains of the other bishops who had accompanied Marculus on the diplomatic mission to Macarius.[87] They too must have been executed, either at Vegesela or later at Nova Petra. Some of them might have been among the "brothers" detained with Marculus at Nova Petra to whom he related the story of his prophetic vision early on the morning before his death.

The memorial of Marculus was set within two contexts: first within a basilica or the House of God and the Hall of Peace that was the physical home of the dissident congregation and their deity in the town.[88] Then again, it was set in the memory of a specific event – an act of violence – and it promised revenge for those who had committed it. Inscribed on the basilica was the following inscription: "By the gift of God, he [i.e. Marculus] created confusion for the enemies [i.e. of God and therefore of the dissidents]."[89] This public notice announced two things: that there were sectarian opponents who were openly declared as enemies and that, echoing the words of the Psalmist, they were going to be thrown into confusion by the heroic acts of a great martyr.[90] More to the point is the embedding in literary memory of the fact that this is just what Marculus achieved: the shrine in the basilica, the epigraphical text, the martyr's narrative, and the acts of the martyr echoed and reinforced each other. The narrator of

---

[86] This was only made clear by Courcelle's subsequent excavation of the site in May and June of 1935; see Courcelle (1936), fig. 1, pp. 167, 176–78; for the earlier discovery of the outer part of the shrine, see Cayrel (1934), pp. 133–36.

[87] Courcelle (1936), fig. 1, p. 167: two were placed in *loculi* hollowed out of the ground; the six others were placed in above-ground sarcophagi; for the burial under the altar, see p. 174; for his speculation, see p. 183 n. 1.

[88] Cayrel (1934), pp. 129–30: two inscriptions were found that had originally stood over the entrance doorway to the basilica. One read *Domus Dei* (House of God) and the other *Aula Pacis* (Hall of Peace). *Domus* or "house" was one of the normal Christian terms for a church, widely attested in the Christian epigraphy of Africa, see Cayrel (1934), p. 129 nn. 4–5, with examples.

[89] Courcelle (1936), p. 181: "[d]e dono / [Dei] iminicis (*sic*) / conf]usionem / [fe]cit."

[90] For Catholics labeled *inimici* or enemies in sectarian inscriptions, see CIL 8.8623–24, commented on by Monceaux, *Hist. litt.* 4, p. 447; for the Psalmist, see Ps. 131: 18: "Inimicos eius induam confusione" (VG and Itala).

the martyrdom notes that as Marculus was paraded from town to town through Numidia, his heroic endurance "raised astonishment among the pagans, confusion among the enemies of Christ and, among the faithful slaves of God, zeal for our glorious struggle."[91]

More than half a century later, when the dissident and Catholic bishops met in the conference in 411 in the Gargilian Baths at Carthage to settle their great quarrel, each bishop stepped forward to identify himself and to recognize his opposite number in the same diocese. There must have been an air of expectant apprehension when Dativus, the dissident bishop of Nova Petra, stepped forward to declare himself. Some of those long-simmering and resentful hatreds must have welled up in the hearts of a few of his fellow bishops who were present. He did not disappoint.[92]

The imperial scribe read out aloud: "Dativus, bishop of Nova Petra." When Dativus had stepped forward, he declared: "I have given my mandate to our authorities and I have signed the protocol. I have no Catholic adversary in my diocese, because Lord Marculus is there, whose blood God will avenge on the Day of Judgment."

On the Day of Judgment. These people were in this for the long haul. Their hopes and expectations, their loves and hatreds, were firmly anchored in that concretely imagined future which, by its very nature, was a boundless field of vengeance.

"THIS BLOODY BUSINESS": THE DISSIDENTS REMEMBER

Something as deep as a terrible act of betrayal formed the point of genesis of the two churches, but for the dissidents the defining moment when the consequences of this division were made manifest was fixed in the terrifying events of 347. The Macarian Time or *Tempora Macariana* as they called this year was a violent watershed that defined a before and an after in their history and in their attitudes. Why did the events of 347 present such a shocking blow to the dissident community? For them, it is no exaggeration to say that this attack on their community was as surprising and as devastating as the Great Persecution under Diocletian had been for an earlier generation of Christians in Africa. The preamble to the narrative

---

[91] *Passio Marculi*, 5.24 (Mastandrea, 1995: 68): "et gentilibus stuporem et Christi hostibus confusionem et fidelibus dei servis incentivum gloriosi certaminis exhibebat." The coincidence was noted by Courcelle (1936), p. 182.

[92] *GCC*, 1.187 (SC 195: 834): "Item recitavit: 'Dativus episcopus Novapetrensis.' Cumque accessisset, idem dixit: 'Mandavi et subscripsi. Et adversarium non habeo, quia illic est domnus Marculus, cuius sanguinem Deus exiget in die iudicii.'"

of the martyrdom of the dissident bishop Marculus in 347 makes manifest that this attack, too, was both sudden and unexpected.[93]

But then suddenly the polluted rumblings of the Macarian Persecution roared out of the tyrannical House of King Constans, from the very stronghold of his palace. Then two beasts were dispatched to Africa: this very same Macarius, and another named Paul.

That is how the dissidents saw the events of that ominous year: as a brutish persecution. The violent dispossessions, the use of the coercive force of the state, the beatings and the killings, were seen as a sudden and terrible depredation on their community that threatened its very existence. But witnesses for the truth had stood up and had been counted: they were the martyrs. If the memory of the events of the 340s for the majority Catholic side were embedded in narrative treatises and polemical *libelli* that refuted claims of dissident suffering, implicating them in the acts of violence and unveiling their hypocrisies, then the dissidents themselves remembered and celebrated their resistance in different literary modes more appropriate to persecution and martyrdom.

Constantine's accession to imperial power and the peculiar conditions of the seating of a new bishop of the Christian church at Carthage had created the conditions under which the fissioning of the church in Africa into two bitterly hostile camps had occurred. Even so, it is clear that by the decade of the 320s the imperial state had resigned itself to bitter rhetorical excoriations of the one side – the so-called Rebaptizers (as the dissidents were called at the time) – whom the court held mainly responsible for the divisive conflict. Otherwise, the emperor's men staged a strategic withdrawal from an intricately complicated and potentially costly regional ecclesiastical struggle to concentrate on the more serious task of stabilizing the emperor's Mediterranean-wide empire. The Catholic church in Africa might well have found itself favored by its legitimate position as the formally acceptable church, but the Rebaptizers could be tolerated and more or less left to their own devices. As far as can be determined from the evidence that has survived, this condition of parity characterized an almost three-decade-long period from the late 310s to the later 340s. The documents that survive from the dissident community of this period reflect on it as an age of prolonged peace.

---

[93] *Passio Marculi*, 3.9–10 (Mastandrea, 1995: 66):. "ecce subito de Constantis regis tyrannica domo et de palatii eius arce pollutum Macarianae persecutionis murmur increpuit. Et duabus bestiis ad Africam missis, eodem scilicet Macario et Paulo."

What actually happened in 347 from the perspective of the emperor and his advisors is difficult to reconstruct. Constantine's policy of benign non-interference had proven rather successful from the point of the state's secular interests. Why and how this attitude was abandoned, and in what way, is difficult to recover. One possible sequence of events (as it has been hypothetically reconstructed) began with an inadvertent action taken by Donatus, the dissident bishop of Carthage – "inadvertent" in the sense that it provoked a series of responses that he surely did not intend or expect. But Donatus' action was itself provoked by another event that he could not have planned: the death of the Catholic bishop of Carthage and Primate of Africa in 346. It is claimed that Donatus took the lead in aggressively petitioning the imperial court to unify all Christian churches in Africa under *his* aegis. Provoked by the arrogance of the request, the emperor Constans reacted badly and ordered the unification, but under the aegis of the Catholic Church. However frequently this hypothesis has been reiterated as an historical fact, there is almost no evidence to support it.[94] It is *possible* that the great Donatus unwittingly caused an unforeseen and unexpected concatenation of events that led to his own demise. The only thing of which we can be reasonably certain is the decree of the emperor Constans that called for the forced merger of the two churches in Africa under the Catholic aegis, and his use of harsh compulsion after his attempts to use enticements failed miserably. The emperor's actions *could* have been a response to lobbying by dissident bishops from Africa, but the court could just as well have decided upon them by itself given its own wider imperial agenda.

OUR DEEPER MEMORY

Also embedded in the events of the Macarian Time, as the dissidents named this period of persecution, is a recollection of an earlier persecution directed against the dissidents that had occurred under the reign of the emperor Constantine. Almost our sole evidence of this earlier spate of violence is a sermon by a dissident preacher, delivered long after the event itself in

---

[94] The case is strongly argued, for example, by Frend, *Donatist Church*, pp. 177–78, based on Optatus, *Contra Parm.* 3.1.2 (SC 413: 8–10): "Donato Carthaginis, qui provocavit ut unitas proximo tempore fieri temptaretur." The phrase is vague and in a painfully committed source. Given that these few words are the sole evidence to burden Donatus with unwittingly causing his own demise, due caution should be shown. Seeck, *Untergang*, 3, pp. 337 and 351, whom Frend finds so convincing, has nothing to add to the case.

order to strengthen and to edify the faithful in their present ordeals.[95] The events that would most likely have provoked a sermon about these past martyrdoms were the traumatic attacks of 347. The earlier events to which the preacher refers, however, took place "at that time, when Caecilian was the false bishop, when . . . Leontius was *Comes* and Ursacius the *Dux*, at the time when Marcellinus was tribune, and when the Devil became their advisor." Since none of the imperial officials is attested independently of this highly tendentious sectarian source, it is difficult to assign a specific date to the events. A reasonable estimate would locate them in the years of the first imperial attempt to compel the unification of the two discordant African churches, a move that seems to date between the end of 316 and an imperial order of toleration of 5 May 321.[96] Since the events seem to follow soon after the posting and implementation of an imperial order at Carthage, probably by the early months of 317 at the latest, then the events might date to this same year. Given the religious language of the sermon, and the allusive nature of its statements, a reconstruction of "what actually happened" and the place of violence in these earlier events is a difficult if not impossible task. It seems that an order, most probably (given the regulation of a highly contentious religious matter) one emanating from the imperial court, was issued for Africa that called for the unification of the two communities into a single Christian church. At least, that is how the dissidents interpreted the posting; or perhaps better, how they later reinterpreted it.

The steps by which the imperial authorities sought to achieve this end in 317 were the two conventional means of the carrot and the stick – the same devices that they were to use again in 347 – hence the great utility of the event as typology. The instrument of authority consisted of the publication of a decree calling for the unification of the churches, compelled by instruments of force and enticement. The enticements were

---

[95] For the text, see Dolbeau (1992) who decisively replaces the antiquated and defective versions in Maier, *Dossier*, 1, no. 28, pp. 201–11 (simply Dupin's text published by Migne in PL 8: 752–58). In general, see Monceaux, *Hist. litt.* 5, pp. 60–68 and cf. Schäferdiek (1989), pp. 176–77. Almost all of Frend's reconstruction of these incidents, *Donatist Church*, pp. 159–60, is fictitious. Brisson, *Autonomisme et christianisme*, p. 310, dates the episode to 318–19, but Maier, *Dossier*, 1, p. 200, dissents and I think rightly: he thinks that the "tunc" or "at that time" in § 1 places these events at some time in the distant past. On the other hand, the threat in § 8 that these events should be remembered "later" (*postmodum*) does *not* provide us with any *terminus ante quem*, despite claims to the contrary. The "episcopatus" is a genitive with the "nomine," so the phrase does *not* read "after his episcopate" as is sometimes asserted; the "postmodum" stands alone and means, simply, "in later times."

[96] For Leontius, see "Leontius (4)," PLRE, 1, pp. 499–500, and "Leontius (2)," PAC, p. 632; for Ursacius, see "Ursacius (1)," PLRE, 1, p. 984 and "Ursacius," PAC, p. 1235; Marcellinus, the *tribunus*, is unknown outside this sermon.

important. According to the preacher, the state used its not inconsiderable fiscal resources to engage in a program of offering money and other sorts of benefactions as rewards to those who would be willing to forgo their attachment to the dissident cause and join the one Catholic Church.[97] The imperial actions, if they actually occurred, directly foreshadowed the repetition of the same tactic of large-scale state bribery that was to be attempted in the repression of 347, precisely three decades later. In the sermon, the two sides are distinguished by the fact that one side is labeled *Catholicus* and therefore acceptable while its opponents were labeled "heretics." The formal naming of the one side as "Catholic" is, of course, contested by the dissident preacher. He nonetheless seems to admit that this verbal labeling had already become a popular distinction between "us" and "them." But when was the preacher preaching? Are we in the world of 317 or of 347?

The steps that led to violence followed the posting of the imperial order. When a sufficiently large number of dissidents refused to be bought off by imperial benefactions – which they, not unnaturally, construed as bribes – it became a matter of the authorities using the alternative of coercion. At this point, the coercive power of the state was directed against material things that could be seized from the dissidents so as to disempower them. These property resources were mainly the basilicas and other houses (i.e. churches) in their possession. The flow of actions involved recourse to local courts to seek court orders on property ownership. When the magistrates had issued their judgments as to which party was the legitimate owner, "muscle" was required to enforce the decisions of the courts. The enforcement agencies were two: public and private. In the former instance, the later preacher refers to the fact that *vexillationes* or military detachments surrounded the churches of his people. In most instances, the role of the imperial military forces was to make manifest the presence of the state, since the actual enforcements were mostly accomplished by the use of private force. It is averred that gangs of "pagans" – so-called since the dissidents denied the label of "Christian" to their Christian enemies – were hired and brought in to do the deed.

The preacher remembers the forcible seizure of the churches and basilicas of his religious community in a language that purposefully exaggerates what had happened. The gangs of "lascivious" young men who seized

---

[97] *Passio Sancti Donati*, 1 (Dolbeau, 1992: 256); for the historical context, see Monceaux, *Hist. litt.* 5, pp. 60–68; taking the phrase "never forgetting the persecution of Caecilianus" (§ 8), he believed that the sermon was to be dated to the time of the Caecilian persecution itself and so dated it to 12 March 317 (p. 61). Almost without doubt, the events of *c.* 317 are the ones to which the writer refers, but the sermon itself seems to have been delivered much later.

the basilicas were joined, he says, by "outcast women," and the two sexes shamelessly transformed the basilicas into drinking bars. These foul men and women were nothing other than "offspring of the Devil."[98] In the overheated language of a dissenter's outrage, he rants on about how the occupiers celebrated a *convivium* or feast of the holy Eucharist in a manner so improper and so outrageous that they turned the church into a low-class dive, or something worse. The role of the imperial soldiery in these enforced possessions was, even as the preacher describes it, rather passive in nature. They might well be portrayed as "servants of the mad acts of the traitors," but they did not do much except stand around and observe what was happening. They acted like interested witnesses – spectators who "gazed on the curious spectacle."[99] The preacher seems not so much to be remembering a discrete series of events as merging different ones into a single burst of outrage. The scene involving the forcible occupation of a basilica with units of the army looking on seems to have taken place in Carthage.

What is involved here is much less reportage than it is an interpretation of the conventions of the involvement of state forces in the seizure of a church or a basilica. In the later fourth century, when this sermon was being consumed in Africa, these assaults, even elsewhere in the empire, had become typical, almost scripted affairs. In Egypt, for example, beginning with assaults in the age of Constantine, the attack on the followers of Athanasius in Alexandria in 356 is replayed in a petition that parades a similar language of outrage. There are the same images of a sudden night-time assault on persons peacefully engaged in prayer, the ensuing chaos and death, and the assaults on women's honor.[100]

We were keeping vigil in the House of the Lord and deep in prayer and reading lessons, when, all of a sudden, around midnight, the most illustrious *dux Syrianus* attacked us in the church with many soldiers... they broke down the doors... many virgins were killed, men were trampled underfoot as they fell over each other when the soldiers rushed in, some pierced by arrows. The soldiers began

---

[98] *Passio Sancti Donati*, 4 (Dolbeau, 1992: 259): "Iam quae dicta vel gesta sint illic inter epulas lascivientium iuvenum et ubi praesto fuerint aspernamenta feminarum, scelus est et dicere, fidelissimi fratres. Quanta repente rerum mutatio! Basilica in popinam, ne turpius dicam, conversa est . . . Quis talia vel filiis diaboli auctoribus gesta negat vel facti auctores christianos appellat, nisi qui aut ipsum diabolum excusatum velit . . . ?"

[99] *Passio Sancti Donati*, 6 (Dolbeau, 1992: 260): "Erat tunc videre militum manus traditorum furiis ministrantes, quae ad perpetrandum tanti facinoris opus memoratorum mercede conductae sunt. Circumstabant denique diligentissima curiositate, inspicientes ne quid illic mitius gerere crudelitati mercennariae licuisset. Quidam illam eorum tam curiosi spectaculi intentionem."

[100] Athanasius, *Historia Arianorum*, 71 (PG 25: 793), translation from Gaddis, *Religious Violence*, pp. 79–80.

to take plunder and to strip the clothes off the virgin women. Some of the dead are buried there in the church. The soldiers were ordered to take away the other bodies and to dispose of them.

In a similar petition made in 395, John Chrysostom complained of an attack on his followers, evoking the same images of chaos, the breaking down of doors, women having to flee unclothed, and so on.[101] It was the way that preachers preached about such things: to incite the emotional response of outrage and anger.

In our African sermon, the preacher's attention jumps, with little notice, to a different scenario in the small town of Sicilibba, some thirty-five miles southwest of Carthage.[102] The same sequence of events unfolded here, but then ran out of control. Unlike at Carthage, they ran so amok that the government forces were compelled to intervene. Catholic attempts to possess the basilica at Sicilibba ran into determined opposition. The repossessions were a civil matter to be enforced by private means. But if there was resistance, the violence that occurred, or which threatened, could justify the intervention by the government. So it was at this point that the Roman soldiery became directly involved. In the resulting mêlée, the dissident bishop of Sicilibba had his throat cut by a soldier's sword. The bishop's parishioners panicked. What then ensued appears to have been a general massacre of the congregation barricaded in their basilica.[103]

The sword of the tribune gashed the throat of our most holy bishop Honoratus, even if it did not run it through... and then the end of this hatred, as always, was sealed with an outpouring of blood, just as in our own time when one never concludes a criminal agreement or oath except with a sealing of blood. There was a general slaughter of persons of every age and sex when their eyes were still closed in sleep, killed right in the middle of the basilica. The same basilica, I say,

---

[101] Chrysostom, *Letter to Pope Innocent*, cited by Gaddis, *Religious Violence*, p. 80.

[102] On Sicilibba (modern Bordj Alaouine), see Lepelley, *Cités de l'Afrique romaine*, 2, pp. 162–63; Lancel, *GCC* 4: 1461–62: 45 km west of Carthage (and only *c*. 20 km from Tunis) along the road to Membressa. For a long time a local community ruled by *undecimprimi* under the aegis of the Carthaginian *pertica*, it transformed into a *municipium* some time in the course of the third century. At the Conference of 411, the town was represented by a dissident bishop who had no Catholic adversary.

[103] *Passio Sancti Donati*, 7–8 (Dolbeau, 1992: 260–61): "quamquam Honorati sanctissimi Sicilibbensis episcopi iugulum tribuni gladius etsi non penetravit, tamen conpunxit;... Denique huius odii exitus semper effusione sanguinis consignatus est, sicut et nunc pactum conventionemque sceleris non aliter quam consignatione sanguinis transegerunt, cum omnis aetas et sexus clausis admodum oculis caesa in medio basilicae necaretur; basilicae, inquam, intra cuius parietes et occisa et sepulta sunt corpora numerosa, ut et illic ex titulationibus nominum persecutionis etiam Caecilianensis usque in finem memoria praerogetur, ne alios quandoque postmodum episcopatus nomine gestae rei expertes deceperit parricida."

within whose walls numerous persons were both murdered and buried. At that very place the epitaphs of their names will preserve till the end of time the memory of Caecilian's persecution, so that *that parricide* will never be able to deceive others who live in later times, and who are ignorant of the facts, about what was done under the authority of his office as bishop.

As that the preacher who was later sermonizing on this incident goes on to make clear, the whole object of the enterprise was nothing other than the seizure and repossession of the basilica. As in other cases, this was no doubt to be done pursuant to the covering terms of imperial law and the favorable decisions of local magistrates.

What happened at Sicilibba was that the use of private force, as witnessed by imperial troops, failed. The efforts to repossess were botched and the soldiers had to move in "to restore order." Taking advantage of the elements of surprise, their attack came either during the night under the cover of darkness or very early in the morning. Most of the parishioners who were with their bishop in the basilica were still asleep when they were cut down. "As an act of even greater madness," declaims the preacher, "after this heinous deed, the murderer thought that he should possess this same basilica, as if he had fallen in love with the place."[104] In this case, as in the possession of the basilica at Carthage described earlier in his sermon, the possession at Sicilibba is presented as a sexual violation or rape: "she" – that is, the basilica and by metaphor the preacher's church – would not prostrate herself to endure this violation of her body." The tribune, the soldiers, and the "false bishop" Caecilian who performed the act are configured as rapists.

In his typical *ex tempore* and associative manner of speaking, the preacher returns to the denouement of this event only after briefly recounting a third incident in this spate of persecution. In the tailpiece to his sermon, he gives some idea of the failure of the act of repossession, at least as he construes it. Somehow, after the murderous mêlée in the basilica, the surviving parishioners and relatives of the people murdered in the church were able to re-enter it to identify the dead and to bury them as martyrs in a *corona* or crown-shaped pattern of tombs encircling the altar in the center of the basilica. Here again, the preacher shows some interest in the sexualizing of the violence: after the deadly assault, men and women were found lying

---

[104] *Passio Sancti Donati*, 10 (Dolbeau, 1992: 262): "Adhuc autem quod dementiae maioris fuit, etiam post tam nefarium factum eandem basilicam possidendam homicida putavit, quasi amore loci subcumberet."

with each other in death in positions that would be "shameful" if the dead had been living.[105]

Another assault, now a different one in a different locale, is recounted next in the same sermon. The preacher passes into it – as he did in the previous incident – with little or no indication of having yet again shifted his focus. As he works on the flow of his delivery, one item in the narrative cues a quick and seamless segue into the next. He is a preacher on a roll. This time he speaks of the arrest of the dissident bishop – who perhaps bore the name of Donatus – of the town of Advocata, located somewhere in the rural hinterland of Carthage.[106] As with the incident at Sicilibba, he knows only the place where it happened and not the bishop's name. So the most that the preacher can tell is that an arrest took place as a result of which this bishop was taken under guard to Carthage "to enjoy Catholic hospitality" as he acidly phrases it. The bishop of Sicilibba was taken to the metropolis, as he says, to be consumed by "the jaws of the traitors."[107] Although the preacher remembers these past events, sometimes in a rather confused and disorganized fashion, the message is clear.

If not everything in the years around 347 was configured by martyrdom and blood, much of it was still consumed with hatred. Even much later memories echo the same deeply hostile sentiments. Such was the case with the response to one Vitellius Afer who, in the reign of Constans, wrote a treatise entitled *Concerning the Reason Why the Slaves of God are Hated by the World*. We do not know who this Vitellius was. Not a single word of this treatise, or others by him, has survived for us to read. Yet in a little

---

[105] *Passio Sancti Donati*, 13 (Dolbeau, 1992: 263): "Interea cum traditorum votis tribuni obsequia paruissent cumque ardorem saevitiae sanguinis copia satiasset, basilicam rursus aliqui fratres ingressi qualia pro tempore poterant obsequia martyribus exhibebant . . . Ubi cum filii parentum, filiorum parentes prostrata corpora repererant, videres alios suorum amplexibus inhaerentes, alios repentino atque insperato visu percussos consedisse semianimes, nonnullos colligendis corporibus pias manus adcommodantes, dum diversi sexus corpora aliter quam decebat iacentia contegunt, dum membra saevis ictibus comminuta et paene discerpta, etiam si non officiis, locis tamen suis reddunt."

[106] On the *oppidum Advocatense* or the *Advocatensis plebs*, see the sane discussion by Lancel (SC 373: 1299); he rightly questions the rush to correct the manuscript reading to "Avioccala" (as suggested by Gsell). The manuscripts of the *sermo* clearly read "oppidum Advocatense," and the existence of an Advocatensis plebs is confirmed by the proceedings of the Conference of 411 (GCC 1: 206 = SC 195: 876). Also against the identification is the fact that Avioccala, deep in the heart of Byzacium, far to the south of the proconsular province, is an unlikely candidate to replace the "Advocata" of the manuscripts. The places mentioned by the preacher of 347 otherwise involve Carthage and Sicilliba. One would therefore expect another place located somewhere in the general region of Carthage.

[107] *Passio Sancti Donati*, 12 (Dolbeau, 1992: 262–63): "At vero memoratus episcopus ex Advocatensi oppido Carthaginiensi hospes adveniens tanta catholicae istius humanitate hospitalitatis exceptus est . . . quam sui sanguinis poculo traditorum fauces avidissimas satiasset." The title of the sermon gives the name "Donatus" to the bishop of Advocata with whom the whole sermon is identified, but the identification appears nowhere in the text itself and may well be spurious or inventive.

book of potted mini-biographies of "Famous (Christian) Men" written by Gennadius of Massilia (Marseilles) about the year 480, which is to say well over a century later, we can sense the abiding animus towards him.[108]

Vitellius Afer, in defending the schism of the Donatists, wrote his work *De eo quod odio sint mundo Dei servi*. If he had just kept his silence about us under the heading of "traitors" in this work, he would actually be thought to have published an outstanding work of theology. He also wrote against the pagans and against us, as if we were traitors in handing over the Holy Scriptures during the great persecution. He also issued many writings pertinent to ecclesiastical discipline.

From this snippet the reader senses that the axial value around which Vitellius' work revolved – as it was to be later in the age of Parmenian and the reply to Parmenian by Optatus – was that of betrayal. But the key word in the book's title is "hatred." The same author triangulated his own group and its hated enemies with a third: "the pagans." In their less generous moments, each side would refuse even the name of Christian to the other, labeling their hated enemies instead as nothing better than mere *gentiles* or worldly denizens, and not celestial people like true Christians. Which raises questions about who "the pagans" were in Africa in this age and what their role, real or imagined, was in this interminable quarrel.

---

[108] Gennadius, *De vir. ill.*, 4 (Richardson ed., p. 62).

CHAPTER 5

The city of denial

Locked inside the world of the Christian texts of the later empire, a reader can easily lapse into the assumption that Christians and their affairs defined and dominated the world in which they lived. From a Christian perspective, there were good grounds for this happy view. They now lived in a Christian state in which they formed a growing part of the whole population. Regions in Africa populated mainly by non-Christian peoples were limited to its "barbarian" peripheries: the marchlands to the south along the edge of the Sahara and, even more so, the mountainous highlands of the Mauretanias to the west.[1] Even so, there were still large and important groups of non-Christians – "pagans" as they had come to be called by Christians – in every town and rural landscape in the heartlands of its most Roman regions.[2] As Christian bishops never tired of reminding these hostile others in their midst, sometimes in a threatening language, the emperors were now Christian. But the impression of a Christian domination of society at large that is suggested by their writings is certainly misleading. Although the imperial state was Christian in the sense that the emperors and the imperial family, as well as significant numbers of appointees to high offices, were Christian, the rulers of the state were driven mainly by a secular agenda and by terrestrial concerns. Emperors, even Christian ones, were primarily concerned with the proper regulation of society, with the revenues of the state, with stabilizing the material and ideological basis of their power, and with the exercise of armed force. As in any other age, imperial rule in Late Antiquity often required the use of brute physical power – the massed deployment of the armament of the state against both external "barbarian" threats and internal enemies.

---

[1] Thouvenot (1964); Février (1976); (1986) *passim.*

[2] O'Donnell (1977) offers a survey of the main hypotheses on the new Christian meaning of the word. As he notes, the first possible African usages are found in Tertullian, followed by a long hiatus. Heavy usage begins again only in our later age – as we shall argue, concurrent with a second wave of anti-heresy interests: see ch. 7, pp. 307–09.

Outside the realm of the imperial court and its officialdom, matters were sometimes different – certainly in Africa. An important social stratum in which traditional non-Christian values predominated was that of the highly cultured notables, the ruling classes of the numerous towns and cities that made up the urban mosaic of local government in the African provinces of the empire.[3] Beyond the confines of the municipal elites, these power networks included local nobles and wealthy grandees on their rural domains outside the cities. The men who made up the curial class – the men who were the town councilors or decurions in the colonies and municipalities – were wedded to a traditional high culture of classical learning. Undergirding it was a professional network of education that was firmly grounded in the complex written codes and spoken discourses of Roman social elites.[4] While it is true that this civic culture was religious because it was seamlessly integrated with a polytheistic world of gods, in practice it was secular in the sense that the pre-Christian social world was firmly anchored in basic and unquestioned assumptions of multiplicity and difference. It is no surprise that in the formal public inscriptions set up by municipal councils in post-Constantinian Christian Africa the Christian religion is simply not mentioned; it is a make-believe *as if* world in which Christians, along with their manifold divisions and disputes, simply do not exist.[5] All of this official public writing "reveals a universe that was worldly, profane, and, as we would say today, secular."[6] It was its own self-contained world in which daily behavior and decisions were not subject to the dictates of the monist religious ideologies of the masses.

If the most important and numerous bearers of traditional culture were the town-centered elites, then we might ask what the relationship was between these scions of traditional culture on the one hand and the Christians on the other. A famous announcement publicly posted in the southern Numidian city of Thamugadi in the year 363 preserves a list of names of the members of the town *ordo* or municipal council.[7] The list of 288 persons connected with the local government – about 190 of whom were town councilors from Thamugadi itself – includes the names of eleven *clerici*

---

[3] Hanoune (1990) on their attachments to "pagan" philosophy.

[4] Brown, "Civitas Peregrina," ch. 7 in *Augustine of Hippo*, pp. 312–29, is essential.

[5] Lepelley, *Cités de l'Afrique romaine*, I, pp. 372–76, and (2002a), pp. 271–72.

[6] Lepelley, *Cités de l'Afrique romaine*, I, pp. 373–75: references to Christianity simply absent from public inscriptions; the life of the city governed by the traditional calendar; cf. (2002a), p. 277.

[7] CIL 8.2403 + 17903 (Thamugadi) has part of the text; for the rest and the whole, see Leschi (1947) and (1948), p. 257, who dates it to 363–65; cf. Chastagnol, *Album municipal*, p. 48, who sustains Mommsen's date of 367 or a year immediately following; further on contents and context, see Piganiol (1955) and Kelly, *Ruling the Later Roman Empire*, pp. 145–48.

who were almost certainly Christian clergy. The suggestion that Christian bishops were normally part of the ruling orders of Roman towns in Africa, however, is misleading. The only reason that they are on this particular list of names is that the emperor Julian had mandated that Christian clergy were not to escape the performance of municipal duties. The Christians are present in a way that was not the case in any year before 363, and that was surely not the case in the decades that followed.

The Thamugadi inscription affords a glimpse of a peculiar and abnormal situation. The Christian clergy would never, save for a specific injunction issued by the emperor himself, have found themselves in this or any other municipal senate. Indeed, the state had established a barrier between men who could be recruited to the Christian clergy on the one hand and those who could be recruited to local municipal senates on the other, limits already put in place by the first Christian emperor by the year 320.[8] However much these injunctions might have been disregarded – and there are signs that they sometimes were – in the mid-320s Constantine re-asserted their force.[9] In legislation accompanied by a letter delivered to the Catholic clergy of Numidia in the year 330, Constantine again confirmed the immunity of Christian clergy from all public duties, including, specifically, service on municipal councils.[10] Although the decree was only protective – not permitting their enemies to insist that Christians engage in public duties – its secondary effect was to create a high sill between the two worlds. Although tinkered with by subsequent emperors, the provisions remained in effect and were further solidified in the late 340s by the emperor Constans. Julian's hostile measures that had mandated that Christian clergy were *not* to escape municipal duties were quickly abrogated by Valentinian in 364. The situation quickly returned to normal.[11]

The families who supplied the pool of men from which local town governments were recruited had been changing their attitudes over the fourth century. But their continued adherence to traditional values and aesthetics was sufficient to maintain a separate world of social superiority. Even where traditional deities are concerned, to think of the values attached to them as constituting an autonomous sphere of religion is misleading. The

[8] CTh 16.2.2 (Constantine to Octavianus, Corrector of Lucania and Bruttium, 21 October 313), and 16.2.3 (Constantine to Bassus, PPO, 18 July 320), the latter a logical continuation of earlier moves of his that forbade decurions and their sons to enter religious orders.

[9] CTh 16.2.6 (Constantine to Ablabius, PPO, 1 June 329).

[10] CTh 16.2.7 (Constantine, from Serdica, to Valentinus, governor of Numidia, 5 February 330); for the letter see the tenth item in the "Donatist dossier" (CSEL 26: 213–16).

[11] CTh 12.1.59 (Valentinian and Valens, from Aquileia, 12 September 364): in effect part of a law abrogating Julian's measure of 13 March of the preceding year.

gods were indeed embedded in the everyday culture of the notables, but the convictions of local elites were different in two senses that are important for a study of secular violence. The aura of authority and the quality of secularity that emanated from traditional institutions was powerful enough that Christians who entered the ranks of local officialdom naturally committed themselves to a set of operative values that were different from those of the Christian churches to which they belonged. These values were so fundamentally different in kind that they were probably not thought to conflict with those of the church in any direct fashion. Christians could be town councilors and could even hold municipal and provincial priesthoods that might once have been viewed as touchstones of "pagan" cult without manifestly sensing a conflict with their Christian values.[12] They held them by a suspension of belief that the religious elements in them were in practice so mundane that they did not seriously threaten Christian faith or practice. The two sets of values functioned in different patterns that formed a bisectorial economy of belief and values.

The continuity of upper-class culture was also supported by the fact that recruitment to its ranks remained exclusive and relatively impervious to the attractions of new institutional statuses. Although there is little doubt that most Christians were from the lower social orders, a few of them were found in the municipal elites and even among men and women of senatorial rank. Although some Christian adherents and converts from the higher ranks of society did enter the hierarchy of bishops in the church, the men who constituted the pool of recruits for the Christian clergy were not ordinarily potential municipal office holders. This isolation was not just a matter of personal choice. As has already been pointed out, the Roman state inhibited the flow of resourceful men out of the curial orders into the ranks of the church. On its side, the church also prohibited such secular involvements.[13] Crossovers from either direction were therefore probably

---

[12] For example, the imperial cult continued right through our age into the subsequent period of Vandal rule, with Christians happily holding the priesthoods because they were, in essence, secular in nature, part of the state's political structure: see Clover (1979–80) and Chastagnol and Duval (1974), with references to the earlier literature. Although there were usually no Christian clergy on town councils (see above), the real question is how many Christians there were on them, or men who had family connections with the clergy. Chastagnol, *Album municipal*, p. 38, argued that such connections existed given common names; but the family names that are the same (Virius, Julius, Sempronius) were so common in the region that arguing for connections on this basis alone seems highly speculative. And some of the known clergy from the list of 363 bear names like Caius Asegmei, Fabricius Apuleus, Aurelius Cresces, and Julius Baric (this last of Punic derivation) that point as much in the opposite direction.

[13] Gaudemet (1958), pp. 142–44; on church regulation, see pp. 146–47; Council of Carthage a. 348, cc. 8–9 (CCL 149: 7–8).

few in number. By mental disposition, by choice, and by default the men in the ruling elites of the towns and cities of Africa were not Christian. They were heirs of a long tradition of privilege and power rooted in the deep past of their world, long before Christians had appeared in it.

Despite the amazingly rapid development of Christian institutions in Africa, the movement and entrenchment of Christian communities was far from uniform.[14] Nevertheless, the faith was more pervasively spread and deeply rooted than in almost any other area of the western Mediterranean. For these reasons, Africans came to assume a pre-eminent position in the development of Latin Christianity: they became driving forces in both its theology and its literature. The rapidity and profundity of this development, however, should not mislead us into conceiving Africa of the fourth century as a fundamentally Christian world. This was far from the case. In the organization and attitudes of belief and cult, African society was strongly dimorphic – Christian and "pagan" – in ways that are relevant to the problem of violence. Hardly insignificant in sustaining this division was the feeling of support and comfort that the local notables derived from their betters. Unlike in the eastern Roman empire of the time, the powerful senatorial aristocracy of the west was thoroughly traditional in its values. Local municipal elites in Africa lived under the penumbral protective cover provided by these powerful superiors of theirs: men and women to whom they could look to for guidance and models. And for the great western aristocrats, the beliefs and cultural practices of their ancestors remained an indispensable core of their high culture.[15]

At the end of the fourth century, African Christians still faced two groups who were not inconsiderable reservoirs of secular non-Christian sentiment and behavior. There were ordinary persons who were either still actively engaged with the traditional world of the gods or who were just latently part of it and had no active interest in Christianity as such – men like Augustine's father Patricius who were busy running their households, managing their farming operations, controlling their slaves, and whose main interests were focussed on family matters, and on public honor and duty. There were also those with no such stake in society who were not greatly concerned with religious matters, some of whom were happy enough to say that there were no gods and go on their way.[16] Even these pragmatically godless persons,

---

[14] On the process of Christianization, see Shaw (2003), pp. 106–14, with bibliography.

[15] See ch. 11 below on the role of the high aristocracy in the western state; see O'Donnell (1979), pp. 70–75, on the religion of Symmachus, one of its best-documented members: "His religion was a matter of convenience, tied rigidly to considerations of class and culture" (pp. 72–73).

[16] There is no need to become involved in a contorted debate over whether or not the pragmatic opinions of such people constituted a genuine "atheism" or something short of this. They were just

however, accepted the cultural milieu all around them that was populated by the multitudinous deities housed in their temples and shrines in every town and city. For such persons, the cultural aspects of cult and practice were just as important, if not more, than any overtly religious ones. The sacred places and occasions, like the seasonal festivals and celebrations in their hometowns, were part of their everyday culture.[17] These special spaces and times were important to them, whether or not the gods existed "as gods." Like the names of the days of the week through which everyone lived, they were basic and normal parts of their day-to-day existence. Christian bishops might rail against the fact that every day was named after a pagan deity – this one after Mercury, that one after the Moon, another after Mars – but the likelihood that these "paganisms" were going to be surrendered for some Christian confection these same bishops knew to be very slight.[18]

The sacred festivities that were a natural and necessary part of the fabric of civic life were a visible and spectacular part of the culture of the Roman city. In all of these religious aspects, it could not function except by continually affirming its individual parts. At the pinnacle of society were men of power and influence who governed it, men who constituted the ranks of its wealthier educated classes. Like Augustine himself in his youth, the educated young men of this social elite naturally placed a greater value on the world of *paideia* – the intricacies of Ciceronian rhetoric, the powerful and (for Africans) emotive poetics of a Vergil, or the skill of the mosaicist recreating a brilliant portrait of the poet himself (or a raucous and joyful procession of the cosmic Lord Dionysus) – than they did on the manifest simplicities, even idiocies, of what passed for Christian learning. To men of education, the shabby skein of low-class superstitions that was Christianity hardly counted as culture. For the scions of the traditional ruling orders in Africa, and those who were imbued with their ideals, the real impediment that stood between them and Christianity was an insurmountable barrier of taste. The aesthetic life that they embraced rejected the elements of Christian education – its writings, ideas, values, and representations – as so inferior and flawed that it would be shameful to be associated with them.

---

dismissive: Aug. *En. in Ps.* 13.2 (CCL 38: 86): there were both "ignorant people" who declared that "there is no god," and also, of course, "pagan philosophers" who dared to say, "There is no God"; *En. 2 in Ps.* 31.25 (CCL 38: 242): again attributed to "fools" (*stulti*) and philosophers.

[17] Brown, *Augustine of Hippo*, p. 312, emphasizes that a lot of "pagan" culture was expressed in ceremonies and spectacles, referring to the *tribunus voluptatum* of CTh 15.7.13 (posted at Carthage on 13 February 414).

[18] Aug. *En. in Ps.* 93.3 (CCL 39: 1302–03): after listing other days of the week: "Quarta ergo sabbatorum, quarta feria, qui Mercurii dies dicitur a paganis, et a multis Christianis; sed nollemus; atque utinam corrigant, et non dicant sic."

Potential crossovers to Christianity from this class, like the young Augustine, whose imagination was excited by Cicero's *Hortensius* (a work now lost to us) embraced the traditional values of their own elite far more than they had any sympathy with the alien simplicity of Augustine's mother. For such men, the creative gateway of allegory was one of the few means by which the manifestly insipid Christian texts could be interpreted to be something more significant and complex than the plebeian confection that they apparently were. On occasion it was a portal through which a few cultured men found themselves able to pass, although still with some difficulty. The creative and magical solvent of allegory, however, was a hard one-way street that exacted its own costs. The device might well save some of the appearances, but it also condemned the man who embraced it finally to reject the most valued core of his own secular education and civic culture as nothing more than a fabrication of demons. While it was true that some of the techniques and skills of traditional *paideia* might be conserved, the content of its classical culture had to be abjured as evil. Taking the decisive step involved the new man in a self-abasement that made taking it improbable and unlikely. The reason was that the one entailed the abjuration of the other, and that was a high price to pay: "for an educated pagan to become a Christian was to lose contact with a glorious tradition."[19] For most of these men – a plain fact suggested by the weight of the evidence – that step was just too dishonorable, and too offensive, to take.

In almost every confrontation by way of discussion and exchange of letters that Augustine had with men and women of elevated social rank, it is not surprising that it was their culture that they regarded as most at risk in any encounter with Christians. They had good reason to be concerned. The perceived threat was only partially concerned with beliefs in the existence or efficacy of specific gods or spirits. Whereas the men of tradition in great metropolises like Rome or Carthage had real depth in their cultural armory, the local town elites lived in smaller and more confined worlds where they directly confronted the gulf between ignorance and learning, between refinement and barbarism. The wealthy decurial landowner Romanianus, the patronal supporter of the young Augustine, and Romanianus' son Licentius, both of them from Augustine's home town of Thagaste, are exemplary representatives of traditional municipal aristocrats and their culture. From displaying the connections that he had with the court and exercising his patronage for the benefit of clients – and

[19] Brown, *Augustine of Hippo*, p. 458, referring to *Sermo* 198.59 (Dolbeau 26; Mainz 62 = *Vingt-Six sermons*, 413): "Am I really going to become what my female receptionist (*ostiaria*) is, and not what Plato was or Pythagoras?"

the consequent rewards of laudatory speeches and statues from the grateful citizens of Thagaste – to the displays of wild beast hunts and ferocious animals for the delectation of all, Romanianus was the conventional great benefactor of "his people."[20]

The most joyous of theatrical applause has always been given to you for staging gladiatorial games furnished with wild bears, and for other spectacles never seen here before [i.e. at Thagaste]. You've been praised to the skies in the shouts and united acclamations of the ignorant, of whom there is an immense multitude. Nobody would dare to be your personal enemy. You have been inscribed on municipal bronze tablets as the patron not only of the citizens of your own town, but also of neighboring communities. Statues have been set up for you. Honors have been poured out on you. Powers have been decreed for you that exceed the community's norms. Rich banquet tables are laid out at your daily feasts for the people. Someone audaciously asks you for whatever he needs and for whatever delicacies he thirsts for – and just as audaciously devours them. You lavish many benefits on those who have not even asked for them. The wealth of your household, carefully and loyally administered by your servitors, has shown itself to be sufficient and ready for such great expenditures. Amid all of this, you enjoy life in the most elaborate of buildings, in the splendor of the baths, in gambling tiles (which even the honest man does not disdain), in hunting and banquets. You are talked about by your clients, by citizens, and by the people more generally as the most cultured, most generous, most refined, and most fortunate of men. If – I say *if* – all of this is true, then I ask you, Romanianus, who would even dare to mention a different kind of happy life to you?

This complete picture of a traditional local big man, the municipal notable who lavishes a river of benefactions on his people, is of a man who, like Augustine himself, was also a Christian (of sorts): he was a Manichee. This classic eulogy of a local grandee, standing at the head of a literary philosophical work dedicated to him, encapsulates better than any other statement of the age the vibrant and living world of municipal politics that had achieved a solid coexistence with the Christian church. The two worlds, like the patterns of a Boolean diagram, could overlap within specific lives of individuals like Romanianus, and yet otherwise have important and quite separate existences.

The lively picture of Licentius in the Cassiciacum dialogues, named after the northern Italian retreat where he shared fellowship with Augustine and his friends in northern Italy in 386–87, reveals the leisured discourse in which these men shared their values. The letters later exchanged between Licentius and Augustine many decades after their hometown friendships

[20] Aug. *Contra Acad.* I.2 (Green: 14); see "Romanianus," PAC, pp. 994–97 and Brown, *Augustine of Hippo*, 9.

were first formed are still marked by civilities of manner and tone that reflect the quality of their relationship.[21] In reply to one of these letters from Augustine, Licentius reciprocated with a long and elaborate poem to his former teacher.[22] The poetic offering was another part of the aesthetics of social dialogue that would normally have occurred between any two educated men. Now, however, Augustine was a Christian churchman. Despite repeated appeals from Augustine for a change of heart in his former pupil, Licentius remained naturally resolute in his superior culture. From his boyhood days in Thagaste, through his association with Augustine and his friends at Cassiciacum, and then after his return to his hometown in Africa, Licentius was a peer of Augustine's who remained confident in his traditional *paideia*. Never once was he moved to exchange it for something less valuable and less elevated. He is a good bellwether of the attitudes of the educated young men of his generation. As late as the generation after Augustine's departure for Italy, we find another student at Carthage, there for its resources of higher learning, who is about to depart the city for wider horizons. In some ways, he replicates the young Augustine, and he reveals no propensities to embrace Christian aesthetics.[23] But then, neither did Augustine when, in the year 383, he left the shores of Africa for Italy.

It is easy to underestimate how powerful and attractive the culture of education remained through the fourth and fifth centuries in the heart of a Christian empire. A few men of higher rank did indeed walk over the threshold of conversion to assume position or office among the Christians – but they were few. One should not be misled by Augustine and his coterie of African friends at Cassiciacum. They were the exceptions. In many ways, they had been provoked to take that step by the greatest living exception of them all: Ambrose, the Catholic bishop of Milan. As a bishop, Ambrose was a wealthy man of senatorial rank, a former Roman governor; in his Christianity, however, he was an avatar of things to come and not typical of his own time. The transition to the rank of a Christian bishop by a man of his elevated status was unique.[24] Armed with his superior social background, with characteristic flair and force Ambrose demonstrated what an imperial bishop might look like. With high-level political experience, he was sufficiently conversant with the practices and rituals of governance

---

[21] Aug. *Ep.* 26.1–3 (CCL 31: 76–86); for Licentius and his background, see "Licentius (1)," PAC, pp. 640–42; and the fine evocation in Brown, *Augustine of Hippo*, pp. 111–12.

[22] On which, see the fine analysis by Cutino, *Licentii Carmen*.

[23] Aug. *Ep.* 117; 118.2 (CCL 31B: 110–11, 113); see "Dioscurus (2)," PAC, pp. 279–80, and Brown, *Augustine of Hippo*, p. 297. The year was 410.

[24] Gilliard (1984) demonstrates that in his age Ambrose is the only known western bishop who can be confirmed to possess senatorial status.

not to be intimidated by the trappings of imperial authority, even those of an emperor. The model of what Ambrose had achieved was a powerful attraction for ambitious young men of Augustine's generation. But the Ambrosian ideal as a norm for Christian bishops was something that had yet to be achieved in practice. When most men of wealth and power in their respective towns and cities in Africa looked at the Christian communities close around them, what their eyes saw was an off-putting confection of ignorance, superstition, low-class language, and even lower ideas that presented a truly frightening perversion of their own high culture. As far as they were concerned, the more the two worlds were kept separate, the better.

In a social order as hierarchical as that in late Roman Africa, it was to be expected that the example set by landed aristocrats and municipal notables would be carefully considered by their inferiors. Men of high rank had real powers of control over the dependants who served in their urban homes and rural villas, and over the larger numbers of peasant farmers who worked their agricultural estates. "If that nobleman were a Christian, no one would remain a pagan," some of these same inferiors were said to have noted. After repeating this common observation twice for emphasis, Augustine adds: "So long as such noble persons do not become Christians, they are like the ramparts of a city that does not believe, a city of denial." He also notes, importantly, that among the "nobles and aristocrats," such men were the norm.[25] The significance that these men had for the problem of sectarian violence is, quite simply, that they existed. Their wealth, rank, and control of the instruments of government at local and provincial level created a late antique social order in Africa that was strangely dimorphic. On the one side, there was a growing popular movement of the Christians and, on the other, the traditional order of the powerful – all of this mix in a "Christian empire." These latter were a serious bulwark against the spread of Christian ideals, as was recognized in sermons of the time.[26] In the division between municipal governments and the organization of Christian churches, it is important that it was the secular elites who managed the instruments of local government. It was they who directed and staffed the municipal courts that adjudicated conflicts that arose in their own communities. In their hands were the powers of investigation and decision-making, as well as some of the effective instruments of enforcement. The central state was

---

[25] Aug. *En. in Ps.* 54.13 (CCL 39: 666): "*Super muros eius*, super munimenta eius, tenens quasi capita eius, nobiles eius. Ille nobilis si Christianus esset, nemo remaneret paganus . . . Quod ergo nondum fiunt Christiani, quasi muri sunt civitatis illius non credentis et contradicentis."

[26] See Lepelley (1998a) on sermon Dolbeau 26/Mainz 62.

linked to each of these different constituencies in quite different ways, but was heavily invested in the local elites for maintenance of order and the steady flow of necessary tribute.

Yet the local "secular" elites must have known, must have sensed, that their world was eroding, that it was under threat. It was palpable. They could see it in the reorientation of public space around them.[27] Although existing temples and shrines still stood, almost no new ones were being built. The municipal elites who were responsible for local construction (often with necessary higher-level approval) must have felt that an end was at hand: a detailed survey of public building relating to traditional cult over the whole of the fourth century reveals "a very rapid decline in the attested number of public buildings for the ancient cults."[28] The reasons for this had far less to do with a fundamental change in the religious sentiments of the local notables, who remained resolutely traditional in their outlook, than it did the overt hostility of the imperial ruling power at the very top. There is a slow but certain effect that can be witnessed in public and private building projects a long time before the first concerted official attacks on the cultic practices themselves. The local elites understood that they could no longer build houses for their traditional gods and shrines for their spirits as functioning public venues or even as cultural ornaments. Those that were built were few and wholly in the private sphere. Some restoration of existing sacral edifices was permitted, but often only with explicit non-religious justifications.[29]

Culturally connected to the municipal elites were the super-rich and the powerful. They were the great landowners, some of whom were of senatorial rank. They were part of a class of men and women endowed with great wealth and authority who lived comfortably in their world of traditional values. There were, it is true, a few Christians among persons of this rank – the Italian woman Melania and her pusillanimous spouse, Pinian, who fled to Africa as refugees in 410, were two of them. But they should not mislead. They, too, were exceptions. Otherwise this class in the western Mediterranean empire remained a weighty reservoir of tradition, filled with men and women who by taste, culture, and disposition had a baleful view of Christians. When Augustine wrote to Pammachius, a great landowner possessing lands in Numidia and a senator who had held proconsular command, he was filled with joy because Pammachius was a Christian who had done the right thing: he had forced the peasants on his

---

[27] The following depends in part on Lepelley, *Cités de l'Afrique romaine*, pp. 344–48 and the revisions in Lepelley (2002a).

[28] Lepelley (2002a), p. 272.   [29] For both of the above, see Lepelley (2002a), pp. 274–75.

estates to convert.[30] But the tenor of the letter suggests that Pammachius, an Italian and a friend of Jerome, was not representative of his class. By the end of his letter, Augustine laments the fact that there were many men of senatorial rank who had no sympathies at all with Christianity. "How we wish," he dreams, wistfully,

that there were many senators and many sons of the Church to perform such good works in Africa as we rejoice at in you. It is dangerous to exhort such men, but safe to congratulate you. They probably will not act and so the enemies of the Church, as if they have already triumphed over us in mind, will set ambushes to ensnare the weak.[31]

The words "dangerous to exhort such men" are telling. These were persons of note and power. They did not wish to have their traditional authority or beliefs or culture mocked or challenged. Capable of demonstrating their anger, they did not want interference from the likes of Christian priests and bishops.

THEY LAUGHED AT ME

One day, while in full rhetorical flow, Augustine could claim that there was not a family in his city of Hippo Regius that was without a Christian in it.[32] Sometimes taken too literally, such sweeping claims depended on what the speaker counted as a family and what families among those would naturally fall under his purview. The tendency to screen out the powerful few, even if they were men of influence, would have been understandable since they were in fact small in number. One could also count base servitors and slaves in their households as making their families "contain Christians." The context in which he made the remark – to his own congregation to reprimand them severely in the aftermath of the lynching of a hated official – perhaps provoked the extravagance of the claim.[33] The bishop wanted to short-circuit any convenient excuse by his parishioners that the

---

[30] Aug. *Ep.* 58 (CCL 31A: 7–8); date is after 405 – the reference to *unitas* – but before 410 (Pammachius' death); for Pammachius, see "Pammachius," PAC, p. 811; and "Pammachius," PLRE, 1, p. 663: it is likely that he was proconsul of Africa some time before 396 (p. 1074).

[31] Aug. *Ep.* 58.3 (CCL 31A: 8): "O quam multorum tecum pariter senatorum pariterque sanctae ecclesiae filiorum tale opus desideramus in Africa, de quali tuo laetamur! Sed illos periculosum est exhortari, tibi securum est gratulari. Illi enim forte non facient, et tamquam nos in animo eorum vicerint inimici ecclesiae, decipiendis insidiabuntur infirmis"; cf. Aug. *Ep.* 58.1 (CCL 31A: 7): "non tibi tam dilecta catholica unitas foret, nec colonos tuos Afros, eo terrarum unde Donatistarum furor exortus est, hoc est in media consulari Numidia constitutos, tali admoneres alloquio, tanto fervore spiritus animares, ut devotione promptissima ad sequendum eligerent."

[32] Aug. *Sermo*, 302.19 (PL 38: 1392). [33] See ch. 1, pp. 28–30.

reprehensible deed had been committed by others and not by Christians like themselves. No family was to escape responsibility. The problem of hatred and violence was not so much a simple matter of numbers as it was one of social location. And if the socially elevated looked down on Christians in their communities as unwanted inferiors, Christians themselves had been systematically imbued with the basic education that these others, even if high and mighty, were bad people, men in a world governed by evil demons who were to be feared and shunned and – should the opportunity present itself – to be dealt with.

Christian dislike of non-Christians did not necessarily have to be artificially inculcated. As late as the mid-fourth century, there were a sufficient number of persons still living who could remember the state-driven persecutions in Africa, conducted by the same kinds of municipal men who were now a recalcitrant reservoir of tradition. And there were those who had heard, in their own lifetime, news of more savage, widespread, and durable persecutions that had been unleashed on Christians in the East. No doubt, the images and words distributed in the West by the adherents of Constantine and his successors guaranteed that such "atrocities" were widely known. As late as the latter half of the fourth century, there were many more who had heard these stories directly from the mouths of their elders, the respected *maiores*. Added to these living memories were the annual replayings of the narratives of the martyrs, fixed into the weekly liturgical celebrations of both churches in Africa. The vivid tableaux reminded parishioners of the horrors of the persecution in virtual reruns of the original scripts. The parishioners who watched and listened were reminded of the divine condemnation of pagans, from the governors who orchestrated the inquisitions to the howling crowds of spectators. Those people had provoked attacks on Christian communities and had eagerly participated in them. Men like them, indeed their descendants, were still around and in power, which was bad.

It was especially bad since things now were supposed to be different. Now the topmost levers of power were firmly in the hands of Christian emperors. In several of the martyr stories to which Christians avidly listened, their ancestors who suffered had promised: "Now we are being attacked by you gentiles, but on that day in the future we shall be avenged." Now us, then you.[34] In saying "then you" the martyrs and those who redacted

---

[34] With much these same words in the *Passion of Perpetua*, 18.8 (SC 417: 166–68): "Dehinc ut sub conspectu Hilariani pervenerunt, gestu et nutu coeperunt Hilariano dicere: 'Tu nos, inquiunt, te autem Deus.'" The sentiment of the impending doom of the future judgment that will hold persecutors responsible for their crimes is found in several of the most popular martyr narratives.

their stories were referring to a future day of divine judgment in which the criminals who had attacked the Christians would be hailed before the court of God's justice. But ordinary Christian parishioners also knew a fact that was constantly reinforced in their minds in weekly sermons: *They* themselves were in power and it was now "the pagans' " turn to have their feet held to the fire. It was true that, as creatures of God the creator, these other persons were also His subjects. But no common grace was shed upon them. They were the godless and the enemies of the church.[35] The words of sermons and tracts remorselessly joined them in an unholy triad who were labeled as the deadliest enemies of true Christians: pagans, Jews, and heretics.[36]

Christians remembered who had injured them and they were ready to behave accordingly. The two great persecutors most closely and intimately identified as the men by whom African Christians had been tried, tortured, and executed in the Great Persecution of 303–05 were not distant emperors but rather men closer to them: Caius Annius Anullinus, the proconsular governor of Africa, and Valerius Florus, the praesidial governor of Numidia.[37] What these men had done to Christians was not forgotten. In later years, their monuments were targets of violence. Almost every inscription set up by Valerius Florus that commemorated buildings dedicated by the emperors in the city of Thamugadi in Numidia was mutilated or otherwise purposefully defaced. There can be little doubt who the perpetrators were.[38] Christians heard the divine condemnations of Anullinus and Florus that were made manifest in the martyrs' stories that were read aloud annually in their liturgical celebrations. Naturally, they imposed memory sanctions on these same men by acts of violence against their physical property that imitated the official violence of *damnatio* that they could witness in official inscriptions of condemned emperors, governors, and others in the fora of the towns in which they lived. This violence was a mimicry of what was perceived to be "what one did" in such cases; it was an acceptable pattern of behavior that had been set as a model by the government itself.

[35] Aug. *Sermo*, 26.4 (CCL 41: 350): "Nam et pagani nascuntur et omnes impii, omnes adversarii ecclesiae eius": commenting on Ps. 100: 3.

[36] For just some of the references, see ch. 6, pp. 273–74; add *Sermo* 71.5.9 (PL 38: 449).

[37] See "Anullinus (3)," PLRE, 1, p. 79; and "Florus (3)," PLRE, 1, p. 368.

[38] Lepelley, *Cités de l'Afrique romaine*, 2, pp. 448–49: nos. 3–5: CIL 8.2347 = 17813 = ILS 631 (dedication to Iuppiter Optimus Maximus); CIL 8.23346 = ILS 632 (dedication to Hercules Augustus, conservator of Maximian); CIL 8.2345 = 17831 = ILS 633 (to Genius Virtutum, Mars Augustus, conservator of Galerius).

In a world where formal powers had been transferred to a Christian state, and where, as Augustine never wearied of emphasizing, pagans feared to criticize Christians openly, the public celebration of non-Christian cult was potentially dangerous.[39] One tactic used by non-Christians to dampen potential Christian hostility was to minimize the apparent differences between their beliefs and those of the Christians. One could, for example, point to the multiplicity of Christian divine beings: the Trinity, the Devil and his agents, angels, demonic spirits, and so on. In principle, this multiplicity did not seem so different from the many gods and spirits of a polytheistic world. Non-Christians could also deny the blunt Christian charge that they were doing nothing other than worshiping deaf, blind, and mute stone and wooden images. Faced with this problem, the creative response was to emphasize not the material image, but the general divine spirit in the multiplicity of the idols. Such concessions, however, were simply not sufficient for Christians. Ultimately the two systems were not compatible.[40] "No," the heathen protests, "I do not worship such objects." "What then?" "I worship the divine spirit that resides in them." Not good enough, says Augustine, citing the words of the Psalmist [96: 5] on the gods of the heathen: in reality, they are demons. Traditional polytheists were caught in a fork: either they were worshiping insensate images or the demonic forces resident in them.[41] Even if they objected that beings as real as the Christian angels were behind the objects that they worshiped, this was met with the riposte that they did not understand the real nature of angels.[42] Everything pagan, the words of the Christian preacher hammered home, was demonic: temples were for demons, priests were there to serve demons, sacrifices were for demons, their prophets were agents of demonic forces.[43] Since physical representations of the traditional deities were either

---

[39] Aug. *En. in Ps.* 79.7 (CCL 39: 1114): "*Et inimici nostri subsannaverunt nos. Et ubi sunt qui subsannaverunt? Diu dictum est: Qui sunt isti colentes mortuum, adorantes crucifixum? Diu dictum est. Ubi est nasus subsannantium? Nonne nunc qui reprehendunt, in cavernas fugiunt, ne videantur?*"

[40] See the analysis in Ando (1996).

[41] Aug. *En. in Ps.* 76.15 (CCL 39: 1061–62); he goes on to imagine further elaborations, but rejects these too; cf. *En. in Ps.* 85.12 (CCL 39: 1186), where the same basic arguments are repeated; *En. in Ps.* 96.11–12 (CCL 39: 1362–65).

[42] Aug. *En. in Ps.* 85.12 (CCL 39: 1186).

[43] Aug. *En. in Ps.* 94.6 (CCL 39: 1335): "*Et tamen gentes omnes sub daemonibus erant: daemonibus templa fabricata sunt, daemonibus arae constructae, daemonibus sacerdotii instituti, daemonibus ablata sacrificia, daemonibus arreptitii tamquam vates inducti. Haec omnia daemonibus gentes exhibuerunt; haec omnia vera non nisi uni magno Deo debentur: templum fecerunt gentes daemonibus; habet Deus templum; sacerdotes fecerunt gentes daemonibus; habet Deus sacerdotem; sacrificium exhibuerunt gentes daemonibus; habet Deus sacrificium. Etenim illi daemones volentes videri dii, non sibi ista exigerent ut fallerent, nisi quia sciunt ea deberi vero Deo.*" See Lepelley (2002c) on the well-known exchange with the Tripolitanian landowner Publicola on "pagan" rituals.

representations of evil demons or were actually inhabited by them, it was right for them to be destroyed: "If I say to a pagan, 'Where is your god?' he will show me his images . . . "There you are," he says, pointing with his finger, "there is my god." I laugh at the stone. I seize it. I smash it. I throw it away. I hold it in contempt."[44]

But it was precisely in these smaller face-to-face venues and micro-levels of divine force that many aspects of traditional belief and practice were still embraced by Christians. The temples, shrines, the cult priesthoods, the statues and the altars, the well-known names and identities of the big deities, could all be abjured, and rightly so, because they were big, they were public, they were named and they were visible. At the level of the anonymous spirits, demons, and the multifarious forces that were there to be manipulated, a murky guerrilla struggle had to be waged against practices that were so localized and yet so pervasive that it was difficult to get Christians to recognize them as "not Christian." They were divine background noise. There was no obvious enemy to fight, no property to be confiscated, no priests to be fined. If Augustine directed much of his *City of God* against "pagan" practices, the first and most prolonged attack was directed against astrology.[45] Practices like these had no public representations, no state supports, no priesthoods, no lands in their possession, and no public images. An ordinary Christian at Hippo could object to his more rigorist fellow Christian: "Why are you so odd? Can't you be just like the rest of us? Use magical spells, good fortune amulets? Consult astrologers and seers? Just like everyone else?" The disciplined Christian made the sign of the cross over his breast to ward off the frightening hybrid.[46] Producing the disciplined Christian represented in this rhetoric, however, was, on Augustine's own testimony, a long and arduous task.

In consequence, the hatreds of non-Christians against Christians were channeled along two lines. First, there was a groundswell of reaction against behaviors and practices that were part of the perceived success of Christians in entrenching the power of their community. Then there were the hostile responses to Christian beliefs that were thought to be so ludicrous and so preposterous that they were moral and aesthetic affronts to any civilized person. Among the former were the acts of charity or the element of Christian love or *caritas* that led Christians to engage in various acts of

---

[44] Aug. *Sermo*, 223A.4 = Denis 2.4 (MiAg 1: 14).
[45] Aug. *Civ. Dei*, the fifth book – as also throughout the *Confessions*, where the connection with its anti-Manichaean message is manifest; cf. Dolbeau (2003b) for the broader significance.
[46] Aug. *En. in Ps.* 93.20 (CCL 39: 1322) "Et tu signas te, et dicis: Christianus sum."

public assistance. Such were the object of "profane remarks" by the "god-less." It was at the level of oral remarks, such as these, that much of the hostility functioned. Most labeling of Christians by non-Christians shared in a common propensity to select bad examples and to attribute them to Christians in general.[47]

Most of the daily confrontations were marked not as much by physical attacks, or by the marshaling of criticisms against specific doctrines, as they were by making fun of Christians and their beliefs. Disdain for Christians was a sentiment that was volleyed at them in humorous put downs, and not just verbal ones: "They mocked me with derisive gestures. They *laughed* at me. They insulted me," says the preacher, getting his parishioners to remember the days of persecution when Christians were beaten, killed, thrown to wild beasts, burned alive, and worse, made objects of mockery. He asks them to remember what fun the spectators got out of Christian suffering. Such persecution has not ceased, even now. It begins with viperish bites:[48]

"They goaded me and they mocked me with their mockings." That is to say, they laughed at me and they insulted me . . . Whenever they run across a Christian, it is their general practice to insult him, to taunt him, to laugh at him, to call him stupid, silly, a person with no heart and no mind . . . so the godless are allowed to insult us, but they are not allowed to use physical violence. But from what their tongue spews out, one can understand what they have in their heart. "They hissed at me through their teeth."

Little vipers, hiss they might, but they were not the only or even the most dangerous of serpents. The differences were less matters of theological dispute than they were matters of culture. More fundamentally, since thought worlds were so different, these included typical accusations of madness or *insania* that peppered the remarks of either side.[49]

To get to the basics: some elements of Christian belief and practice provoked incredulity, derision, and accusations of blockheaded stupidity. Among these beliefs, two in particular were so offensive to non-Christians that they were continually brought up as startling examples of the shameful

---

[47] Aug. *En. 3 in Ps.* 30.11 (CCL 38: 209).

[48] Aug. *En. 2. in Ps.* 34.8 (CCL 38: 317–18): "'Tentaverunt me et subsannaverunt me subsannatione.' Id est, irriserunt me, insultaverunt mihi . . . Ubicumque invenerint Christianum, solent insultare, exagitare, irridere, vocare hebetem, insulsum, nullius cordis, nullius peritiae . . . impius insultare permittitur, saevire non permittitur; sed tamen ex eo quod lingua promit, intelligitur quid gestet in corde. 'Striderunt in me dentibus suis.'" [referring to Ps. 34: 16: "frenduerunt super me dentibus suis"; in the VG: "frendebant contra me dentibus suis"].

[49] Aug. *En. in Ps.* 6.12 (CCL 38: 34): "Nam nunc usque adeo non erubsecunt impii, ut nobis insultare non desinant. Et plerumque tantum valent irrisionibus suis."

and the ludicrous. One was the Christian deity. It appalled the average non-Christian that anyone would actually worship a crucified bandit of base social origin.[50] Those moved to the dislike of Christians found the veneration of a common criminal executed for his crimes, and claims of his miraculous resurrection as a god, too much to swallow. People who embraced this déclassé piece of fraud were so idiotic and so base that they deserved to be removed entirely from the society of rational men. "And don't they say: 'Stamp them out, kill them, all of them, whoever they are, who believe in some unknown who suffered this shameful death'?"[51] To understand this frame of mind is possible. It is much as if we were to take a highly civilized person from another world and show him or her an iconic image in one of "our churches" of the body of a common criminal, convicted of a murderous subversion, slumped in his final death agonies in an electric chair, and then to say: "That's who we worship. This is our god." It was therefore a constant point of derision: "People call you the devotees of an executed criminal, the follower of some dead man."[52] "Whom do you worship?," they say, "A dead Jew, a crucified criminal, a man who was a complete nobody, who wasn't even able to defend himself when he was sentenced to death."[53] The judgments were tied to contemporary attitudes to convicted criminals, and to Jews.[54]

The other big problem for non-Christians was the disturbing image of the resurrection of the dead. In its sheer grossness, the revival of a dead body was such a strange if not bizarre happening that imagining it produced responses of revulsion and ridicule.[55] Some of the combination of humor and disgust can be gained from reading the long defense mounted by Augustine in the *City of God*, beginning with the wondering about what would happen to aborted infants. Would they, too, resurrect?[56] The

---

[50] Aug. *En. in Ps.* 8.6 (CCL 38: 51); cf. *Sermo* 174.3.3 (PL 38: 942): causing "the wise" to "jeer" at Christians: "Denique de cruce Christi nobis insultant sapientes huius mundi, et dicunt: Quale cor habetis, qui deum colitis crucifixum?" It appalled them despite the fact that there were just as many objectionable persons – liars, thieves, adulterers, and murderers – among their gods, as Augustine pointed out at great length in his *City of God*.

[51] Aug. *En. in Ps.* 43.22 (CCL 38: 491): "Dele, occide nescio quos, qui crediderunt in te nescio quem male mortuum?"

[52] Aug. *En. 1 in Ps.* 68.12 (CCL 39: 912): "Opus est ergo ut habeas irreverentiam, quando tibi de Christo insultatur; quando dicitur: Cultor crucifixi, adorator male mortui, venerator occisi; hic si erubueris, mortuus es"; cf. *En. in Ps.* 79.7 (CCL 39: 1114), where almost the same *derision* and *taunts* are recorded (see n. 39 above).

[53] Aug. *En. in Ps.* 40.4 (CCL 38: 451): "Quem colitis? Iudaeum mortuum, crucifixum, nullius momenti hominem, qui non potuit a se mortem depellere."

[54] MacMullen (1986) is fundamental.

[55] Bynum, *Resurrection of the Body*, ch. 2, on the background of Christian debates of the time; cf. Courcelle (1958), pp. 163–70.

[56] Aug. *Civ. Dei*, 22.12 f. (CCL 48: 831–33).

separation of the ways between traditional cult and Christian teaching, however, was focussed on the resurrection of the dead in the flesh.[57] To the unbelievers, the intact state of Christ's body was logically explained by its short time in the grave. "That's not true in our case! When we open our tombs, you don't find even a bone left, nothing but dust. Everything that was flesh has been reduced to powder. How could such a thing, not even able to keep its form, ever be resurrected!"[58] That the rotting corpse would be brought back to life, struggling out of its damp grave, was so revolting an apparition that it was too much even for some Christians to accept.

Every day I'm asked: "Where's your God?" And because I can't show them my God, they mock me as someone who's following a vaporous nothing. But it's not just a pagan who mocks me like this or a Jew or a heretic. Sometimes it's even our own fellow Catholic who grimaces when . . . our future resurrection is foretold . . . "Have you ever seen anyone come back to life?" or "Since I buried my father, I haven't heard him speaking from the grave! God gave a law to his slaves for a limited time, and it is on this time that we must concentrate. Has *anyone* ever come back from the underworld?"[59]

This was the observation that usually provoked ridicule and laughter: "Has anyone ever come back from over there?"[60] The objections raised various scenarios that were by turn revolting, shame-provoking, or just plainly ludicrous.[61] For someone who was contemplating conversion to Christianity, as was one man at Carthage who discussed the matter with the priest Deogratias, this strange thing came immediately to mind. The first and almost insurmountable hurdle that the prospective convert had to overcome was the ghastly apparition of dead bodies coming back to life.[62] It is perhaps not surprising that Augustine's *City of God* culminates with a

---

[57] Courcelle (1958), p. 163: "Le point crucial du divorce entre la pensée païenne et le dogme chrétien, lors même que l'on s'accordait sur l'immoralité de l'âme, est la résurrection de la chair."

[58] Aug. *Sermo* 242A.2 = Mai 87 (MiAg 1: 328).

[59] Aug. *En. in Ps.* 73.25 (CCL 39: 1021): "dicitur mihi quotidie: Ubi est Deus tuus? Et quia non possum ostendere Deum meum, quasi inane sequar insultatur mihi. Nec paganus tantum, vel Iudaeus, vel haereticus, sed aliquando frater ipse catholicus torquet os, quando promissa Dei praedicantur, quando futura resurrectio praenuntiatur. Et adhuc et ipse, quamvis iam tinctus aqua salutis aeternae, portans sacramentum Christi forsitan dicit: 'Et quis huc resurrexit?' et: 'Non audivi patrem meum de sepulcro loquentem, ex quo eum sepelivi. Deus dedit legem ad tempus servis suis, ad quod se avocent; nam quis redit ab inferis?'"

[60] Aug. *Sermo* 157.5.5–6.6 (PL 38: 861–62): "Sed illi ista non credunt, qui dicunt: 'Qui huc inde reversus est? Credituros se volunt videri, si quis parentum suorum revivisceret.'"

[61] For some of these objections, see Courcelle (1958), pp. 165–66; Augustine's discussion of the problems "set the agenda" for later western European debates; see Bynum, *Resurrection of the Body*, pp. 97 f.

[62] Rather than a normal letter, the epistle is in fact a mini-treatise, sometimes entitled "An Exposition on Six Questions Raised against Pagans." Of these, the very first question put by the pagan is on the problem of resurrection: *Ep.* 102.2–7 (CCL 31B: 9–12).

consideration of resurrection. He had to confront the worst thing about it: the ridicule that it provoked. To counter the derision, he assembles what is in effect a judicial dossier of evidence that demonstrated that such miracles were possible.[63]

The hates and sneers did not all flow in one direction. If the *gentiles* or those who were not Christians were remorselessly disparaged, mocked, and belittled in sermons, conversations, pamphlets, and letters, then the Christians themselves naturally assumed an attitude of superiority and condescension. They could sneer and laugh at their neighbours who "worshiped stones." This was the social revenge of the ignorant. It was also the not unpredictable result of having a litany of hatred and harsh disapproval preached at them from one generation to the next. On occasion, bishops chose to countervail their own negative messages and to warn their parishioners not to engage in such disparaging remarks and hostile attitudes since, after all, these same people were potential converts.[64] The bishops might well have uttered such moderations, but by the last decades of the fourth century there was an emerging sense of Christian triumph that not unnaturally encouraged vengeful attitudes. Now it was pay back time. "Those people might have been able to hurt us and to make jokes at our expense, but no one now dares to do such things." This was the new attitude. Christians once had to eat the insults hurled at them and dared not offer any resistance to their persecutors. What Christians were saying was that no one now dared to insult them, at least not in public. If they did, it was done furtively and in fear that they would be found out.[65]

CHRISTIAN TIMES

The people who hated Christians had their own compelling logic of accountability. If Christians now ruled the empire, then they were to be held responsible for its destiny. If things went from bad to worse, then it was obvious who was to blame.[66] The siege of Rome in 410 by the barbarous Alaric was a fearful sign that things were going terribly awry. The pillage of the metropolis of empire naturally provoked widespread elite

[63] Aug. *Civ. Dei*, 22.5 f. (CCL 48: 810–12).   [64] Aug. *En. 2 in Ps.* 25.2 (CCL 38: 143).
[65] Aug. *En. in Ps.* 69.2 (CCL 39: 931); *En. 2 in Ps.* 88.12 (CCL 39: 1242): "Diu continuerunt Christiani opprobria in sinu suo, in corde suo, nec audebant resistere conviciantibus; antea cum crimen videretur respondere pagano, nunc iam crimen est remanere paganum."
[66] See Madec (1975) for a good study of the two faces of this rhetoric, with the insightful analysis of Markus (2000).

and popular recrimination of the Christians and their ideas. The mass rape of Christian women in the siege of the imperial capital was a particular source of satisfaction. The enemies of the Christians did not hesitate to play up the shame and humiliation of these women, which then provoked angry responses in defense.[67] Underlying this joy was the blame assigned to Christians for the fate of a tottering empire: "There you are! We're in Christian Times – *Christiana tempora* – and Rome is being destroyed."[68] Augustine had to expend not a little energy in several sermons, some of them rather intemperate, in attempts to explain to his parishioners that the charges were baseless. In one of his angrier outbursts, he compares the pagan detractors to poisonous scorpions and expresses the hope that they would be pecked to death by an angry hen.[69] He was forced to the defense because the charges had a compelling logic to them. Those who launched the accusations could link the disaster suffered by Rome to the fact that the gods were angry, filled with a terrible rage because their homes – their temples – had been shut down and were falling into disrepair. And also because their living likenesses, their *simulacra*, had been unceremoniously removed from their homes or even destroyed, it was believed, on the authority of Christian emperors.[70]

In the various replies to the pagan accusations, we find ourselves on the road to Augustine's monumental *City of God*. He had reason to fear a growing common ground between the secular elites who dominated the civic life of the towns and the hostile attitudes of the common people: "The well-educated who are devotees of the past are well acquainted with the facts, but they wish to inflame the hatred of illiterate mobs against us."[71] The siege of Rome by the barbaric enemies of Roman civilization was a spectacular refutation of the expectation that all would be better now that the state was Christian. And there were also small but no less influential and mundane problems. Out of the violent events of 410 in Rome and Italy there washed to African shores a flotsam of high-class refugees who embodied the reality of the crisis, who sharpened existing hatreds. They were persons like the one who was celebrated on a funerary stone from Mactaris, which speaks, tragically, of the many disasters afflicting Italy, the

[67] Aug. *Civ. Dei*, 2.2 (CCL 47: 35–36).   [68] Aug. *Sermo* 81.9 (PL 38: 505).

[69] Aug. *Sermo* 105, passim; at § 9.12, he turns on the pagan accusers and labels them blasphemers, and introduces his animal metaphor (PL 38: 623–24).

[70] Aug. *Sermo* 113A.11 = Denis 24.11 (MiAg I: 151–52), where the smashing of the images of the gods is linked (§ 12), with these men remarking: "Look what evils there are in these Christian times."

[71] Aug. *Civ. Dei*, 2.3 (CCL 47: 36–37).

land of his birth, and the fate that has struck Rome.[72] The feelings that the crisis triggered were rooted in a bedrock of ongoing dislikes. Augustine could be appalled by the attitudes held by "the same people whose stupidity had given rise to the popular chant: "THERE'S NO MORE RAIN / THE CHRISTIANS ARE TO BLAME!" If the weather was bad – a hugely consequential matter for the rural economy on which all Africa depended – then Christians were responsible: "God is unleashing downpours on us. Blame the Christians. If God doesn't send rain, we can't sow our crops. When he does, we can't thresh our harvests."[73]

Among those who were not Christian, there was real apprehension over their growing powerlessness, a threat that was manifest even to the most optimistic of traditional exegetes. On every hand, there are signs of a minority, even if a privileged and powerful one, under considerable strain. The surfacing of revindicative prophecies fueled the irredentist hopes of those whose culture was slowly but surely eroding, receding from their grasp. The necessary economic infrastructure was not being developed: few new temples were being built and even fewer repaired.[74] And official pressures that were being exerted upon the bastions of traditional thinking, the walls of denial, beginning in the early 380s, assumed increasing frequency and stridency. As imperial laws began to be enforced and their implications were gradually understood at local level, they contributed to a growing sense of unease, especially since a Christian imperial court seemed to have so little control over its local subjects.

One alarming response was a series of millenarian prognostications that fuelled the growing apprehensions, prophecies of events that were to come to pass in the 390s.[75] One series of predictions foretold the doom of the new Christian capital of Constantinople. Fearful portents, including the earthquakes, shook the city, manifest warnings of the forthcoming cataclysm that had been predicted by the seers.[76] In the late 390s, a divine message sent by way of dream or vision had come to an imperial official in

---

[72] Prévot, *Inscriptions chrétiennes*, no. X.67, pp. 100–02 (figs. 135–36), guessing, correctly I think, that there is a connection here between refugees and the sack of Rome by Alaric: "Italicas multas clades Romanaque fata [. . . .] genuit nos Itala tellus." Dated by consular year to either 414 or 434.

[73] Aug. *En. in Ps.* 80.1 (CCL 39: 1120): "et vetus quidem, sed a temporibus Christianis coepit proverbium: Non pluit Deus, duc ad Christianos. Quamquam priores ista dixerunt. Isti autem modo dicunt et quia pluit Deus: Duc ad Christianos: non pluit Deus, non seminamus; pluit Deus, non trituramus"; see *Civ. Dei*, 2.3 (CCL 47: 36–37), the latter, obviously, also cued by events of 410.

[74] Lepelley (2002a), recapitulating and extending work done in *Cités de l'Afrique romaine*.

[75] On much of what follows, see Hubaux (1948, 1954a, and 1954b); some interesting parallels are offered by N. Cohn, *Pursuit of the Millennium: Revolutionary Millenarians and Mystical Anarchists of the Middle Ages*, rev. ed., Oxford and New York, Oxford University Press, 1970, ch. 1, pp. 19–36.

[76] Philostorgius, *HE*, 11.6–7.

the city, a Christian, about the precise day on which the imperial capital was to be destroyed by fires from heaven.[77] The official was to inform his bishop (which he dutifully did). In the panic that ensued there were mass baptisms and the Christian patriarch and the emperor led the entire population of Constantinople out of the city into the countryside. Apparitions appeared in the heavens. Blood rained from the sky. Only after some days passed and nothing more happened, did some of the braver souls among the huge populace assembled outside the metropolis dare to re-enter the city to inspect their neighborhoods and homes. The fright continued to have a history, even in Africa, where the story was vividly reported in a homily that Augustine delivered to his congregation in the autumn of 410.[78] The long sermon was an attempt to explain to them the nature of divine agency in the vengeful destruction or merciful preservation of great cities – in this case to explain the meaning of the pillaging of the imperial metropolis of Rome by Alaric and his forces in late August 410.

Apprehensive persons in Africa who were not Christians were creating and consuming similar apocalyptic messages. Seers and prophets broadcast the claim that a spell had been cast by Christian magicians who had obtained the Christians' ascendancy for them. One such oracle redacted in Greek verse was specific about the means and the end. The Christians had won empire-wide power by a ritualistic act of black magic in which the apostle Peter had sacrificed a one-year-old child, an *anniculus*, taking the life of an infant boy who was exactly 365 days old. By this act of sorcery, Peter had acquired a grant from the divine powers that controlled the cosmos of a precise time span of earthly power for his master.[79] That period was interpreted as a "long day" in which each day in the life of the sacrificed boy represented one year of terrestrial time – a span of 365 years. Depending on one's point of departure – for when, precisely, had Peter

---

[77] The precise date of the event is difficult to fix. In speaking of the implications of the capture of Rome by Alaric, Augustine places the events in Constantinople "about a dozen years before," which should be about 398. Augustine's formulation, however, seems to suggest a general order of time, and the Chronicle of Marcellinus [Mommsen, *Chronica minora*, 2.64] reports an earthquake that hit the city and a "burning sky" in the year 396.

[78] Aug. *Sermo de Excid. Urb.* 7 (ed. O'Reilly: 68–70); the sermon seems to have been delivered soon after the event became known in Africa.

[79] Aug. *Civ. Dei*, 18.53 (CCL 48: 653): "Cum enim viderent nec tot tantisque persecutionibus eam potuisse consumi, sed his potius mira incrementa sumpsisse, excogitaverunt nescio quos versus Graecos tamquam consulenti cuidam divino oraculo effusos, ubi Christum ab huius tamquam sacrilegii crimine faciunt innocentem, Petrum autem maleficia fecisse subiungunt, ut coleretur Christi nomen per trecentos sexaginta quinque annos, deinde completo memorato numero annorum sine mora sumeret finem . . . Deinde isti dii qui sunt, qui possunt ita praedicere nec possunt avertere, ita succumbentes uni malefico et uni sceleri magico, quo puer, ut dicunt, anniculus occisus et dilaniatus et ritu nefario sepultus est, ut sectam sibi adversariam tam prolixo tempore convalescere."

committed the primal abominable ritual murder? – the exact year of the
end of Christian domination could be predicted and anticipated. If the
original sacrifice was in the year 29, then the end of the Christian order
was due in the year 394.[80] If the murderous black sacrifice took place at the
time of Christ's crucifixion and ascension, in the year 33 – as most seemed
to accept – then the end of Christian ascendancy was to be expected in
398. Whatever the precise calculation (different ones were on offer) the
prophecy indicated an end of Christian Times at some point in the 390s.[81]
A big change was coming. Millennial expectations fueled hopes that the
good old days were about to return. The gods would be worshiped as before
and the Christians would disappear.[82] The end of Christian domination
was at hand.[83] Such apocalyptic utterances gave expression to the hopes
of those who saw themselves as becoming permanent underdogs. Those
who now had the upper hand would be exterminated and those who had
been subjugated to Christian commands would be restored to their former
positions of authority.

---

[80] Augustine set the original blood sacrifice of the child in the year of the consulships of the two
Gemini (in the year 29), which ought to have placed the last year of Christian domination in 394.
Yet (see next note), Augustine clearly accepted the common idea that the end year was 398, which,
in turn, makes the year 33 as the time of the magical sacrifice. Herrmann's (1950) reconstruction of
a "religious crisis" in the year 394, with this particular prophecy anchored in that year alone, is not
entirely convincing.

[81] Aug. *Civ. Dei*, 18.54 (CCL 48: 653–55): calculated from the death of Christ, Augustine says this end of
Christian time should have arrived in the consulships of Honorius and Eutychianus (398), but that
that year came and went, and passed into the consulship of Mallius Theodorus (399) without issue,
and Christianity did not suddenly end, as predicted. In fact, he goes on to say, this was the year when
the idols of the demons were smashed at Carthage (CCL 48: 654–55): "Si autem ut Hierosolymis
sic ad cultum nominis Christi accenderetur tanta hominum multitudo, quae illum in cruce vel
fixerat prensum vel riserat fixum, iam maleficium illud fecerat Petrus, ex ipso anno quaerendum
est, quando trecenti sexaginta quinque completi sint. Mortuus est ergo Christus duobus Geminis,
consulibus octavum kalendas Apriis . . . Tunc itaque nominis illius cultus exorsus est . . . Numeratis
proinde consulibus trecenti sexaginta quinque anni reperiuntur impleti per easdem Idus consulatu
Honorii et Eutychiani."

[82] See G. Bardy, "L'oracle sur la durée de l'Eglise," note 59 in *BA* 36 (1960), pp. 774–75; Aug. *En. in
Ps.* 40.1 (CCL 38: 448): "The time will come when there won't be any Christians and when the idols
will be worshiped as they were in the former days": "Sedent pagani et computant sibi annos, audiunt
fanaticos suos dicentes: 'Aliquando Christiani non erunt, et idola illa coli habent, quemadmodum
antea colebantur . . .'"

[83] Aug. *En. 2 in Ps.* 70.4 (CCL 39: 963), with a promise that the Christians will die out and the idols
will return and "everything will be as it was before" (taking his cue from Isaiah 53: 1): "Quia futuri
erant inimici Christianae fidei qui dicerent: Ad parvum tempus sunt Christiani, postea peribunt,
et redibunt idola, rediet quod erat antea"; at 70.12 (CCL 39: 971), Augustine glosses these claims
for his congregation in rather dark terms: "What they really mean is this: 'The day is coming
when Christians will be done for. There will not be any more of them left.'" "Quando morietur, et
peribit nomen eius: id est: 'Ecce veniet tempus ut finiantur, et non sint Christiani . . .'" Of course,
Augustine is then able to picture for his congregation that future Day of Judgment when it is *they*
who will be tried and punished, "et confundentur qui insultabant, erubescent qui garriebant."

There were nebulous dislikes, some hate, and much fear. But what situations produced more than verbal abuse, rude gesticulations, humorous put-downs, and resentment – even seething resentment? The scenes that cued a move to more physical responses seem to have been two, and both were notably affected by the policies and decisions of the imperial government since the responses of the court to non-Christian practices were one of the main factors that determined the nature of local violence. Although some of these actions did not involve the state directly, they nevertheless produced situations where the recourse to violence became more likely. These were places or times when Christians and non-Christians were involved in public rituals central to the identity of their respective communities. If such celebrations happened in their own times or places, the likelihood of conflict was considerably reduced, but where they overlapped the possibility of violence was enhanced. And the public calendar of public festivities and celebrations remained a traditional ritual one that was separated from and unaffected by the separate Christian calendar.[84] The public nature of the theatrics of confrontation is important: so the outbreaks were mostly centered in towns and cities.

Typical spaces that were mutually shared were large public venues like theaters, circuses or racetracks, and amphitheaters, found in most African towns of any size. Since these entertainment venues were easily distinguished from the ecclesiastical complexes, burial places, or holy shrines where Christians congregated, the two groups could and did gather with little likelihood of conflict. There are no known circus or theater riots in Africa in later antiquity that pitted non-Christians against Christians, even though both groups attended these entertainments in significant numbers. And circus and theater scuffles and riots were known: "The partisan battles of those who take up a cause or a struggle on behalf of some destructive men to the point of open violence, just for some dancer, some actor, some chariot driver, or some wild-beast hunter."[85] On more than one occasion, Augustine admits that many of his parishioners were at the theater, the races, or gladiatorial contests. He even allows that Christians were the majority of spectators at such events – in places and at events that bishops castigated in severe language as the places of the Devil or as the Houses of Demons.[86] Christians did not just attend these entertainments; they

---

[84] See the observations of Lepelley, *Cités de l'Afrique romaine*, I, p. 375.

[85] Aug. *Sermo*, 198.4 (PL 38: 1026).

[86] Criticism of those attending the circus: *En. in Ps.* 39.6 (CCL 38: 429): on the birthday of the city (of which city? Hippo, it seems); for a fuller consideration of the data, see H. Jürgens, *Pompa diaboli: die lateinischen Kirchenväter und das antike Theater*, Stuttgart, Kohlhammer, 1972.

participated with gusto and ardent enthusiasm. In these locales, their presence actually reinforced traditional communal values, a fact that not unnaturally concerned their bishops but which was unlikely to spark sectarian conflict.

Public occasions and venues that had the ingredients for conflict did exist, however. The celebration of the beginning of the New Year on 1 January had long been part of Roman culture in the specific sense that it was part of the festival culture of the city of Rome. The celebration of the day then spread to communities in Italy that came to share the Roman calendar. Other cultural groups in the Mediterranean must also have had their New Year's Day festivities, but theirs did not usually coincide with the Roman celebration. But with the spread of Roman calendrical time throughout the Mediterranean, these local points of time were submerged or were adjusted to the new imperial temporal order. What had once been a simple Roman day, by the late second and third centuries became an empire-wide day of festivity.[87] The day associated with the god Janus and with the beginning of the month of January was, in every sense, not a Christian day. It was a day on which both the civic authorities and common people issued announcements and invitations to join the fun: "Let's raise hell" or "Let's have a good time" or "We don't have to starve ourselves on the First of January festival!" echoed throughout the towns and villages of the empire.[88] The special day exhibited all the elements of a Mardi Gras. As 1 January approached, Christian bishops knew that there was potential for trouble. Christians might be attracted away from their discipline to participate in the "wicked games" and "offensive jokes" that were part of the festivities.[89] The day and its celebrations were marked vividly on illustrated mosaic calendars of the time, such as the one found at Thysdrus (modern el-Jem) that colorfully illustrates the formal clothing – the white angusticlave tunics and formal high-soled shoes – worn for the occasion. The two men engage in the embraces and greetings appropriate to the festive day in front of a table bearing the gifts that were part of the celebrations.[90] These were the *strenae* or good-luck presents that were exchanged by the people of

---

[87] Meslin, *Fête des kalendes*, pp. 23–50, offers a survey.

[88] Aug. *Tract. in Ioh.* 5.17 (CCL 36: 51): "quod solemne est dico, quod quotidianum est dico, quo vocantur omnes dico, et in ista civitate, quando eis dicitur: Alogiemus, bene sit nobis, et tali die festo Ianuariarum non debes ieiunare; ea dico levia, quotidiana." "Alogiemus" was a shout with Greek roots, that was an encitement to disorderly conduct, literally "let's get things out of order" or "let's create some chaos."

[89] Aug. *Sermo* 196.4.4 (PL 38: 1021).

[90] Stern (1981), p. 438 and pl. V.11, citing Foucher (1961): traditionally dated to the third century, but probably a bit later.

Hippo on each New Year's Day.[91] It was the excesses of gift-giving that the bishops criticized and wished to redirect to Christian charity, alms to the poor, precisely because such a redirection would benefit their power and tend to disarm the mutuality of personal connections affirmed between Christians and other members of the community.[92]

The Christian usurpation of 25 December for the celebration of the birth of their god – later called Christmas – created a Christian holiday, artificially invented in the city of Rome in the mid 360s, but soon spread to Christian communities in Africa. Replacing a traditional pagan holiday with a Christian one, the takeover tactic fueled a potential time of confrontation.[93] Christians had also staged a similar temporal takeover with the upgrading of the 24 June from a summer solistice celebration to a feast of John the Baptist. Augustine mentions this promotion in connection with a monitory sermon delivered on Christmas day in warning of the forthcoming January 1 festivities: "On the birthday of John the Baptist, six months ago . . . Christians took part in a superstitious pagan festival by going to the sea and baptizing each other." Unfortunately the bishop had been away from Hippo and had not been able to keep a close eye on his flock, and they had strayed. In his absence, strict discipline had to be imposed by the priests.[94] The big celebration on 24 June was traditionally known the "Day of the Torches" – an occasion of great popular festivity, including the night-time parading of torches that symbolized the power of the sun and the beginning of the summer season and, with it, the all-important reaping of the cereal crops. Now, however, the day was to celebrate the birthday of John the Baptist. Such takeovers were not always clean or clear-cut, and they were far from instantaneous. An African preacher delivering a sermon several generations after the age of Augustine was still busy reconfiguring the imagery and the symbolism of the day in Christian terms, and still teaching his parishioners how it was that they were now to think of the celebration.[95]

But this still leaves New Year's Day, already alluded to by Augustine in his reference to the new Christian John the Baptist day. The Kalends

[91] Aug. *Sermo* 198.2–3 (PL 38: 1025); already condemned by Tert. *De Idol.* 10.3 (CCL 2: 1109) for corrupting relations between students and their teachers; so, likewise, by Jerome in late antiquity, see Meslin, *Fête des kalendes*, pp. 43–44.

[92] Aug. *En. in Ps.* 98.5 (CCL 39: 1382).

[93] The sacred day was recognized rather quickly in Africa *if* a sermon is that of Optatus of Milevis (PLS 1: 288–94); scholars like Wilmart have believed so, but Pincherle thinks it to be "Donatist" and a product of Gaudentius' hand.

[94] Aug. *Sermo* 196.4.4 (PL 38: 1021).

[95] Ps.-Fulgentius, *Sermo* 66; see Dolbeau and Etaix (2003), pp. 256–59 (the text), accepting a date of around 500.

or First of January was a major festival marking the advent of the new year that had achieved a more empire-wide presence and celebration in the late empire.[96] In three surviving sermons, spread over most of his career as bishop, he preached vigorously against the 1 January celebrations in which "the pagans" were excoriated as "worshipers of demons." He noted that the larger-than-usual number of Christians assembled in the basilica represented a counterweight to the raucous singing of obscene songs, the wild dancing and extravagant parading, and the processions that marked "this false feast day."[97] In each of the sermons, the behavior of "the pagans" is condemned in aggressive language as demonic, evil, sinful, and, most of all, dangerous. It was the huge racket and uproar, the frenetic dancing, and the general pleasures of the festivals that evoked most concern.[98] The situation was potentially dangerous because of the unusual compression of large numbers of different people. Even Augustine the bishop had much larger numbers than usual in his church on that day. Many of them had come to town, no doubt, drawn by the other attractions. In all of this, the big, though often silent, player was the state. Its public holidays, its officials, its laws, and its calendar were a constant backdrop to the struggle. If bishops in east and west railed against the 1 January celebrations in their sermons, however, it was not because of any tendency to conflict and hostilities (of which, on the whole, there is little evidence), but because it was a site of competitive attractions for both "pagans" and Christians.[99]

THE PROVOCATIVE STATE

There are many indicators that the imperial state, even if inadvertently, promoted conditions that caused ordinary prejudices and simmering dislikes to be mobilized in the form of public violence. There is little evidence of Christians and non-Christians in Africa being moved on their own to direct acts of violence against their respective communities. Imperial laws that called for the decommissioning of the temples and the icons of the deities formed the watershed. To support a passive prohibition like "please don't sacrifice" was one thing; to tear down the images of the gods and

---

[96] Graf (1998) and Scheid (1998) trace the evidence pertaining to this new power of the festival in late antiquity, especially in eastern Mediterranean venues.

[97] Aug. *Sermo* 197 (PL 38: 1021–24); 198.1 (PL 38: 1024); and 198A (PL 39: 1734–36; *RBén* 84 (1974), nos. 21–23, pp. 259–60); cf. Meslin, *Fête des kalendes*, pp. 73 f. for more criticisms of the wild dancing and leapings about that characterized the day.

[98] Aug. *En. in Ps.* 98.5 (CCL 39: 1382).

[99] In the East, amongst others, John Chrysostom preached a fiery sermon "Against the Kalends" in 387 (PG 48: 953–62), as did Asterius of Amaseia (PG 40: 216–25); cf. Meslin, *Fête des kalendes*, pp. 52–53.

to destroy their homes in the sight of all was quite another. Such injunctions required not just a passive "doing nothing," but concrete actions to carry out acts of physical destruction. The perceived need encouraged the organization and mobilization of Christian gangs, and the desired acts of destruction were committed. "Don't you see his temples – those of the Devil – falling into ruins, his images being smashed, his priests being converted to God?"[100] Critical to this process were imperial laws that *seemed* to sanction attacks on properties, buildings, temples, shrines, and the images in them. For most of the post-Constantinian period, the western imperial court evinced no committed interest in aggressively seeking the deliberate and destructive repression either of non-Christians or of deviants from the true Christian community. The court vacillated back and forth on such issues, pushed by Christian lobbying, but mostly pulled by its own interests. Despite the sometimes violent rhetoric, each situation and incident was negotiable. This mixed and mobile background changed dramatically with Theodosius' ascent to the throne in 379 – a profound imperial about-face took place of which African Christians were well aware.[101]

The way that imperial force was to be mobilized in a campaign directed against unacceptable forms of belief and practice, whether those of pagans or of Christian heretics like the Manichees, was through the usual means by which the state managed civil matters – by legislation. The response of the 390s has aptly been described as a legislative juggernaut whose rulings left an indelible imprint on the pages of the Theodosian Code.[102] Although the trail of this legislation began in the early 380s with measures directed against heretics and Christians who were labeled Manichees, it later grew, by a process of petition and response, into a body of legislation that was specifically aimed at the repression of non-Christian rituals, ceremonial venues, and priestly personnel.[103] This later stream of legislation began on 21 December 381 with a measure directed against "crazed persons" who might

[100] Aug. *Sermo* 15A.6 (CCL 41: 208): "Non videtis . . . simulacra confringi."

[101] Aug. *Civ. Dei*, 5.26 (CCL 47: 162): Theodosius was happier to be a member of the church than to be ruler of the world. He ordered the destruction of the images of the pagans, knowing that wordly rewards are not in the power of demons, but in the power of the true god: "Simulacra gentilium ubique evertenda praecepit, satis intellegens nec terrena munera in daemoniorum, sed in Dei veri esse posita potestate." Augustine connects the emperor's acts to the final conviction of "pagan error."

[102] N. Q. King, *The Emperor Theodosius and the Establishment of Christianity*, Philadelphia, Westminster Press, 1960, p. 54; the place of this religious legislation as law, however, is often exaggerated. It is important to note that all the Christian legislation is segregated from the rest of the Theodosian Code, and that this one book is appended as a separate item to the end of the whole code. The nature of its difference and separateness from the rest of the civil law is manifest.

[103] On anti-heretical legislation, see ch. 11, pp. 533 f.

perform "forbidden sacrifices" by day or by night.[104] When the laws were first issued, they provoked too eager a response. Enthusiastic Christians intepreted the laws as a carte-blanche not just to foreclose "forbidden sacrifices" but also to shut down any place where any sort of traditional sacrifice was offered. In consequence, the emperors had to issue a corrective follow-up decree that made clear that the temples themselves were to be kept open and were to be maintained for cultural and aesthetic reasons. Similarly, they decreed that traditional religious festivals were to be allowed to continue.[105] The Christian responses, however, surely signaled further potential courses of action to the emperor and his advisors.

The zealous response of freelance Christian enforcers caught the imperial court off guard. Their pre-emptive aggression highlighted the problem posed by the combined religious and cultural functions of traditional cult. The challenge for the court was selectively to repress one side, while not harming the other. The cultural significance of temples, shrines, and festivals and other such celebrations, was something on which the cohesion of traditional order and the authority of the state relied. The court was committed, for the time being, to the preservation of an important part of the Roman cultural heritage. The costs of haste in dismantling these institutions, manifested in the disruptions that followed on the heels of the decree of 381, had to be mitigated. In May 385, another imperial measure decreed that certain practices connected with divination were no longer to be tolerated.[106] The attitude, especially of the eastern court, seems to be one of piecemeal tactical strikes at this or that weak element in the panoply of traditional cult, mainly those elements that had always been considered suspect by the imperial state from its origins: the employment of bad magic and the subversive use of occult consultation.

For its own peculiar reasons, the western court at Milan became more aggressive in such matters. A run of imperial laws, beginning in February 391, had a different tone, responding, in part, to Christian petitions. The first law did not simply target forbidden types of sacrifice; it simply forbade all of them *tout court* – it was an absolute prohibition of the ritual of sacrifice

---

[104] CTh 16.10.7 (by Gratian, Valentinian, and Theodosius, from Constantinople, to Florus PPO; 21 December 381): note the specific restriction to *sacrificia vetitia* – not against sacrifices in general, but to certain forbidden ones that were somehow connected with *carmina dira* (horrid chants or songs, and surely, therefore, bad magic).

[105] CTh 16.10.8 (Gratian, Valentinian, and Theodosius, from Constantinople, to Palladius, the Dux Osrhoenensis, 30 November 382): on the specific case of a temple in his jurisdiction, but enunciating general principles about the utility of such temples "in qua simulacra feruntur posita artis pretio quam divinitate metienda."

[106] CTh 16.10.9 (Gratian, Valentinian, and Theodosius, from Constantinople, to Cynegius PPO, 25 May 385).

in any form and in any place, public or private.[107] The ruling was backed up by a heavy penalty against those who knowingly aided and abetted the performance of such rituals. The sanction was to become the normal one used by the court in this struggle: the monetary fine – in this case, one amounting to twenty-five pounds of gold. In November of the following year, a more detailed version of the decree issued from Constantinople made clear the empire-wide scope of the new rule.[108] The main difficulty with the prohibitive legislation on this matter was already foreseen in the terms of the law itself. It was not so much a problem with the emperor's subjects understanding what he was demanding; it was, rather, the difficulty of having his officials enforce the terms of the imperial decree.[109]

This much can be deduced from the terms of the edict of August 395, which not only repeated the content of the earlier law, but also expatiated on the culpability of provincial governors who had not enforced it. Not only were fines of twenty-five pounds of gold to be assessed as a penalty for breaking the law, but the officials who were responsible for enforcing the decree were now also subject to the same fine should they fail in their duty.[110] The additional penalty clause must have generated resentment in local officials who were loath to enforce measures that not only provoked resistance, but also threatened their traditional values and culture. These same laws harbored another danger: they fueled popular pressures for their strict enforcement from the whole spectrum of Christian communities. As with the decree of 381 against "forbidden sacrifices," supplementary orders had to be issued by the emperors that made clear that their decrees were *not* be taken as license for the uncontrolled riotous destruction of public property by private persons.[111]

---

[107] In a sense, this move was not a first, since there is little doubt that Constantine issued a similar decree banning traditional sacrifices. But his measure had been disregarded so long that it was a dead letter by the 390s; our emperors, notably, do not refer to it as a precedent.

[108] CTh 16.10.10 (issued in the name of all the emperors, but clearly Theodosian, from Milan, to Albinus PPO, 24 February 391; cf. CTh 16.10. 11, issued to Romanus the Augustal Prefect and *comes Aegypti*, later, on 16 June, which seems like an interim measure in the East); and CTh 16.10.12.1–3 (the same three emperors, from Constantinople, to Rufinus PPO, 8 November 392).

[109] CTh 16.10.12.4, where terms of enforcement are specifically discussed, placing the burden on *iudices* (i.e. provincial governors), *defensores*, and on municipal decurions.

[110] CTh 16.10.13 (Arcadius and Honorius, from Constantinople, to Rufinus PPO, 7 August 395); a fine of twenty-five pounds of gold would be approximately equivalent to 95–100 *solidi* (precisely, 97); see Kelly, *Ruling the Later Roman Empire*, pp. 140–41, for some equivalents – a substantial amount of money: enough to purchase 25 horses or 20 slaves.

[111] CTh 16.10.15 (Arcadius and Honorius, from Ravenna, 29 August 399): speaking of the ornaments of public buildings, the problem being that certain altars, shrines, and temples were part of existing public buildings or were representative of public authority.

The plain fact is that Christians themselves had been lobbying for an imperial edict calling for the destruction of temples and shrines as legal cover for their actions, and the imperial court had been gradually moving in the same direction. A decree issued by Arcadius and Honorius in 399 was one of a series of laws that for the first time called for the destruction of shrines and temples on rural properties, probably those already owned by Christian landlords.[112] They were to be dismantled so that "the material basis for all superstition will be destroyed." Foreseeing the potential excesses that the measure might provoke from overly zealous Christian enforcers, however, the terms of the same law cautioned that such destruction was to be done "without disturbance or tumult."[113] Separate measures connected with this edict were issued to the senior authorities in charge of Africa. The first, dated to 20 August of the same year, and directed to Apollodorus, the proconsul of Africa, rescinded the earlier general permission that had been granted for the continued celebration of traditional festivals *as religious events*. The celebrations themselves could still take place, as well as the public banquets and other entertainments that were part of the festivities – but now any specific religious aspect of the celebrations, above all sacrifices, had to be removed from them. Whatever their religious agenda, the emperors were good secular politicians. They were not willing to countenance the disruption of joyous festive celebrations that contributed, as they put it, to "the common happiness of our subjects."[114] Wishing to avoid social disruption, what they sought was a workable middle ground. The tactic was the same: the surgical removal of the specifically objectionable religious elements from the larger cultural artifact that they wished to preserve.

More importantly, the same law of 399 was the first one in the western empire that contained specific measures calling for the official physical dismantling of sacred images in public temples and shrines.[115] Given this prompt, it is hardly surprising that popular actions were taken under the

---

[112] CTh 16.10.16 (Arcadius and Honorius to Eutychianus, PPO, posted at Damascus, 10 July 399): "Si qua in agris templa sunt, sine turba ac tumultu diruantur."

[113] CTh 16.10.16 (Arcadius and Honorius, posted 10 July 399 at Damascus): "His enim deiectis atque sublatis omnis superstitioni materia consumetur."

[114] CTh 16.10.17 (Arcadius and Honorius, from Patavium, to Apollodorus, Proconsul of Africa; 20 August 399): "Ut profanos ritus iam salubri lege submovimus, ita festos conventus civium et communem omnium laetitiam non patimur submoveri. Unde absque ullo sacrificio atque ulla superstitione damnabili exhiberi populo voluptates secundum veterem consuetudinem, iniri etiam festa convivia, si quando exigunt publica vota, decernimus."

[115] This much is assured by the actions that Augustine reports of imperial officials in August of this same year, and also by the fact that surviving parts of this same law (see below) contain injunctions against the use of private force in the destruction of temples and shrines. The fact that Catholic councils later in the year were empowered to lobby the imperial court for laws calling for the destruction of temples clearly shows that such laws did not yet exist in July and August 399.

cover of this law in an atmosphere of increasing tension between Christians and non-Christians. In speaking of the end of Christian domination predicted by pagan prophets and seers, an event scheduled to occur in the year 398, Augustine was insistent in pointing out that nothing had actually happened in that year. When the consulship of Mallius Theodorus arrived in 399, not only did the Christian Times not end, the pagan ones did.[116]

> Then the rest of the world passed on into the year of the consulship of Mallius Theodorus, when already, according to the famous oracle of the demons, or the fairy tales concocted by men, nothing of the Christian religion was supposed to survive. What happened in other parts of the world is not necessary for us to consider here. What we do know is that right here in the city of Carthage, the most renowned and eminent city in Africa, on the fourteenth day before the Kalends of April [19 March], Gaudentius and Jovius, *comites* of the emperor Honorius, destroyed the temples of the false gods and smashed their idols.

Christian preachers in Africa, we see, tended to over-represent the force of the law. As with the imperial ruling on parades, the emperors were striking surgically – they only wished to remove the specific element in the temples that was at the heart of their sacral nature: the divine *simulacra*. Christian leaders represented the results in hyperbolically aggressive language as the "destruction" of the temples. In the case of Carthage we know better. Quodvultdeus, who was later bishop of Carthage, where he was a deacon in the 390s, wrote that the temples were "closed" and that their idols had been "removed." He nowhere speaks of their destruction.[117] The violent words of the bishops in their sermons, on the other hand, suggested that a divine imprimatur had been given to Christians to help the government in a broader mission of destruction. But there is nothing to indicate that the imperial officials Gaudentius and Jovius had a writ to do anything more than to remove the statues, the idols, of the gods from the temples. The transfer of the simulacra of divinities from their houses to more mundane locations, thus de-sacralizing them, was what the emperors were willing

---

[116] Aug. *Civ. Dei*, 18.54 (CCL 48: 655): "Porro sequenti anno, consule Malio Theodore, quando iam secundum illud oraculum daemonum aut figmentum hominum nulla esse debuit religio Christiana, quid per alias terrarum partes forsitan factum sit, non fuit necesse perquirere; interim, quod scimus, in civitate notissima et eminentissima Carthagine Africae Gaudentius et Iovius comites imperatoris Honorii quarto decimo Kalendas Aprilis falsorum deorum templa everterunt et simulacra fregerunt."

[117] Quodvultdeus, *Liber de promiss*. 38.41 (SC 102: 568): misdating the episode, however, to the reign of Theodosius, see Lepelley (1994), p. 6; on the identity of the earlier deacon with the later bishop, see "Quodvultdeus (5)," PAC, pp. 947–49, at p. 947.

to countenance.[118] Imperial officials, or those assisting them, as in the city of Caesarea in Mauretania, were permitted to remove statues of divinities from "their unkempt places" (i.e. their temples), as it was phrased, to place them in secular places, like the town baths, which became museums that warehoused images that were now reduced to pieces of art.[119]

Christians expected that something more dramatic would be provoked by imperial decrees. As the bishops who lobbied for the legislation were well aware, in the light of their incessant preaching about the evils of traditional belief and cult, their people might take the laws as a cue to take action on their own. Their sentiment was well founded since crowd behavior was a form of learned and mimetic action that was traditional. People naturally expected that the likenesses of bodies, even if divine ones in stone, would be treated in the same fashion as were the real human bodies of enemies whose existence and memory one wished to expunge. Predictable responses could include a whole range of violent actions that were not just simple "smashing": loud chanting that would accompany and urge the violence on; the mutilation of bodily parts of the simulacrum; the dragging of the statue through the dust, dirt, and muck of alleyways; and the disposal of the unwanted remains in swamps and sewers.[120] In other words, precisely the same kinds of ritual violence that marked sectarian attacks and murders. The analogies are so strong that one must believe that violent sectarian crowds were replicating the same behavior that crowds had exhibited in reaction to the official denunciations in the memory sanctions that the state issued against unwanted persons. The behaviors on both sides were so repetitive, even ritualized, that crowds anticipated the legal "green light" of the state's laws – so that, even as private persons, they could act as the government agents, assisting it in the *damnatio* of an officially condemned individual.[121] In response to perceived legal prompts from the courts or even in anticipation of them, Christian gangs had taken to the streets to destroy temples, shrines, and statues. They, too, had interpreted the imperial law as giving them a "green light" to do the state's good work for it. The connection in the minds of the people was not surprising, since it

[118] Recognized as early as Kunderewicz (1971), cf. Martroye (1921b) and Battifol (1922); see Thornton (1986) on doing God's work; Lepelley (1994), pp. 10–12, on the epigraphical evidence for the *translatio* of statues of "pagan" divinities to secular places in cities, often the baths.

[119] Lepelley (1994), pp. 10–11, citing Stéphane Gsell who early on recognized what was happening: "Aux derniers temps de la domination romaine les thermes étaient devenus une sorte de musée, un asile pour les statues des dieux déchus, anciennes idoles qui n'étaient plus que des objets d'art."

[120] Stewart (1999), pp. 162–67, provides a detailed summary, with examples. For dragging see ch. 15, p. 689; for dumping into the sewer: ch. 3, p. 112; for bodily mutilation: ch. 15, pp. 683 f.; for chanting in the course of violent acts, ch. 10, passim.

[121] Stewart (1999), pp. 162–63.

had been suggested to them all along by their figures of authority that the "destruction of temples, the condemnation of sacrifices and the smashing of statues" were all part of the same unified and beneficent process.[122]

This time, the emperors made a pre-emptive strike against the violent freelancers. In an attempt to prevent the destructive actions that they foresaw resulting from their own words, they issued a warning as part of the edict to Apollodorus, proconsul of Africa, at the end of August 399. In the same decree in which they banned traditional religious content from parades and celebrations, the emperors insisted that temples and buildings were not to be wantonly destroyed nor were the images in them to be smashed or pillaged. The cult statues or idols were to be removed or taken down by officials of the state, and then only after a proper investigation of their history had been completed.[123] Embedded in this same law is a statement that reveals who the agents were who were organizing the bouts of excessive destruction. The men who were interpreting imperial laws to justify a general physical destruction of temples were none other than the bishops of the Christian church. Although the emperors issued their caution in diplomatic terms, their warning was sharp. Bishops were explicitly commanded to confine themselves to issues connected with religion. Other matters, including the enforcement of the law, were to be left to the civil judges and to the framework of the public law.[124] The bishops appear to have taken the emperors' warning seriously. In mid-September, Augustine preached a sermon that was intended to control one such popular recourse to violence.[125] But the same cycle of prompt and response recurred time and again. With every successful lobbying effort with the imperial court that ended in legislation, young Christian men interpreted the result as

---

[122] Aug. *De consensu evangel.* 1.16.24 (CSEL 43: 22): "quod haec eversio templorum et damnatio sacrificiorum et confractio simulacrorum non per doctrinam Christi fiat, sed per discipulorum eius"; cf. Stewart (1999), pp. 179–80, for comment.

[123] CTh 16.10.18 (Arcadius and Honorius, from Patavium, to Apollodorus, Proconsul of Africa, 20 August 399): "Aedes inlicitis rebus vacuas nostrarum beneficio sanctionum ne quis conetur evertere. Decernimus enim, ut aedificiorum quidem sit integer status, si quis vero in sacrificio fuerit deprehensus, in eum legibus vindicetur, depositis sub officio idolis disceptatione habita, quibus etiam nunc patuerit cultum vanae superstitionis inpendi." Lepelley (1994), p. 8, believes that this part of the law was issued in response to lobbying from the ruling orders at Carthage who had witnessed the excesses that followed on the mission of Gaudentius and Jovius in late March of the same year.

[124] CTh 16.11.1 (Arcadius and Honorius, from Patavium, to Apollodorus, Proconsul of Africa; 20 August 399): "Quotiens de religione agitur, episcopos convenit agitare; ceteras vero causas, quae ad ordinarios cognitores vel ad usum publici iuris pertinent, legibus oportet audiri."

[125] Aug. *Sermo* 62.7–8; 17–18 (PL 38: 417–18, 422–23); date is not certain, but cf. Chadwick (1985), p. 11.

permission to engage in violent self-help enforcement of the law – the laws, after all, gave them legitimate grounds for their activities.

It is therefore hardly surprising that imperial laws continued to provoke the kind of behavior that they were trying to avoid. Wherever large numbers of zealous men gathered, the problem became one of controlling the riotous actions that seem to have broken out mainly in the larger cities, including Carthage. A sermon preached in the metropolis by Augustine on Sunday, 16 June 401, attempted to quiet a situation in the city that had involved Christian rioting.[126] The precise events are difficult to discern, but they involved a statue of Hercules, the Roman divine continuator of the old Punic deity Melqart or the "God of the City." A traditional ceremonial had called for the gilding of the statue's beard. An appeal to the new governor by the traditional elites of the city calling for this minor restoration to the statue had apparently met with a positive response from the recently arrived governor, the *novus iudex*, of the province.[127] Although a good "pagan" himself, the governor probably did not respond on any particular religious grounds, but rather on the basis of imperial edicts that called for the maintenance of temples and statuary as part of the cultural heritage of the Roman people.[128] In the atmosphere of the attacks on such shrines during the 390s, the restoration of the statue in the first weeks of June was immediately read by the Christians in the city as a deliberately provocative act. It ignited a violent response in which Christian enforcers "shaved" the gilded beard off the statue. A carefully calculated counter-act designed to punish and to humiliate, it fell precisely short of actually destroying a shrine or statue *in situ*, which would have been clearly illegal. The response by non-Christians to the insult was understandably angry and violent. The governor had become involved, no doubt issuing strong cautionary warnings to the different parties about disturbing the public order.

The Catholic bishops found themselves caught in a gray area between overzealous enforcement and actual illegality. The potential for dangerous violence was high. On 16 June, the Catholic bishops from all Africa had convened in a general council in Carthage, a festive occasion that concentrated popular attention and energies. The Christian people were no doubt

---

[126] Aug. *Sermo* 24 (CCL 41: 326–33); I accept the dating of 401.

[127] For the identity of the judge/provincial governor, one Helpidius, and his actions, see Magalhães de Oliveira (2006), pp. 251–53; if on a normal rota, Helpidius would have arrived in April/May and would have instituted this request by early June – which fits the general chronology.

[128] Aug. *Sermo* 24.6 (CCL 41: 332): "Hic autem etiam barbam inaurata esse voluit . . . Sed qui deaurari eum voluerunt, de raso erubuerunt. Suggestio itaque nescio quae novo iudici obrepsit . . . Fratres, puto ignominiosius fuisse Herculi barbam radi, quam caput praecidi." Note that the official was moved by a "suggestion."

eager to demonstrate to their leaders that their anti-pagan feelings were at a fever pitch and that they were ready not just to shave off a statue's golden beard but for more substantial action. The problem for the bishops was that they had to rein in the excessive fighting zeal. Struggling to get the attention of his restive listeners in the great Restoration Basilica at Carthage that Sunday, Augustine forcefully restated the authority of the people's shepherds, their bishops, against the raucous shouting and chanting of the crowd's contrary views. He was trying to restore order after a failed attempt earlier on the same day by Aurelius, the bishop of Carthage and Primate of all Africa. But violent chanting by the people took over the proceedings: **AS AT ROME! SO AT CARTHAGE!** QUOMODO ROMA! SIC ET KARTHAGO! At Rome all the temples had been closed and the idols had been smashed – or so they believed – so why not at Carthage?[129] The aggressive mood had been set before the sermon with the crowd's chanting of the eighty-third Psalm – the verses gave them a spiritual voice with which to express their anger against "the pagans."[130]

> Lord, do not keep silent or hold your peace!
> Do not be still! Lord! See! Your enemies are in uproar.
> Those who hate you have raised up their heads;
> they are constructing evil plots against your people,
> they are devising plans against your holy people.
> They say: "Come, let's wipe them out as a people,
> let the name of Israel be remembered no more . . . "
> Lord, turn *them* into whirling dust,
> like chaff in the wind. Like fire consumes the forest,
> as the flame sets the mountains ablaze,
> come after them with your storm,
> terrify them with your blasts!
> Fill their faces with shame . . . Let them be humiliated
> and be downcast forever. Let them perish in disgrace.

When Augustine tried to calm the crowd, the congregation broke into angry complaints, denouncing their leaders for their pusillanimity in executing the destruction of pagan idols and their shrines. We cannot know how this volatile and violent situation was brought under control. What we do know is that the bishops, perhaps in fulfilling a public promise to the crowd, passed as one of the central canons of their council in Carthage

---

[129] Aug. *Sermo* 24 (CCL 41: 326–33); chanting and shouting: 24.5 (CCL 41: 330): "apparuit in vocibus vestris . . . Multitudinis animus et voluntas ad quamque rem faciendam istis vocibus poterit apparere . . . Itaque, fratres, quoniam iam quod ad vos pertinebat, implestis acclamando "; and 24.6 (CCL 41: 331): "Utique hoc clamastis: 'Quomodo Roma, sic et Carthago!'"

[130] Psalm 83, vv. 2–5; 13–18 (VG 82).

on that day a measure that called on the imperial government to order the complete and utter destruction of every last element that still survived of pagan cult edifices in Africa.[131] When they reconvened three months later, in September, the bishops empowered their delegates to seek further legal measures on this same matter from the imperial court, with special notice of the need to destroy *simulacra* or statues. One of their requests went well beyond the existing imperial writ on the matter. The desired measures called for the opposite of the emperor's national heritage program: the total destruction of the temple buildings themselves. The wish of the bishops was that not only shrines but all sites of traditional cult should be wholly destroyed.[132] It is also possible that the bishops were seeking legal cover for themselves. If each round of imperial legislation evoked popular violence that went well beyond the bounds of existing imperial law – in fact, wholly against it – then at least calling for the total destruction of shrines and temples would protect the bishops from counter-charges of inciting or planning illegal criminal acts that involved the destruction of public property.[133]

Over the course of the first decade of the fifth century, the emperors issued laws that removed all official support for the final vestiges of traditional public cult. In an edict issued in November 407 – but, importantly, not posted at Carthage until 5 June of the next year – Honorius and Theodosius abolished all revenue sources for pagan temples. The public funds that had been allotted to their upkeep were now to be redirected to the public treasury for use by the army. The emperors ordered that the remaining images still receiving worship in the temples and shrines be taken down from their pedestals. The temple buildings themselves were to be vindicated as public property and used as public places. The altars in them were to be destroyed. Even at this very late stage, the impression given by these laws is of yet more surgical strikes: the images are to be taken out, the altars alone are to be destroyed, but the buildings are to be left standing and confiscated by the state. Striking at the heart of public participation, no convivial banquets or public ceremonials in connection with the temples

---

[131] Concil. Carth. 16 June 401 = *Reg. Eccl. Carth. Excerpt.* 58 (CCL 149: 196): "Instant etiam aliae necessitates a religiosis imperatoribus postulandae: ut reliquias idolorum per omnem Africam iubeant penitus amputari – nam plerisque in locis maritimis atque possessionibus diversis adhuc erroris istius iniquitas viget – ut praecipiantur et ipsa deleri, et templa eorum, quae in agris vel in locis abditis constituta, nullo ornamento sunt, iubeantur omnimodo destrui."

[132] Concil. Carth. 13 Sept. 401 = *Reg. Eccl. Carth. Excerpt.* 84 (CCL 149: 205): "Item placuit ab imperatoribus gloriosissimis peti, ut reliquiae idolatriae non solum in simulacris sed in quibuscumque locis vel lucis vel arboribus omnimodo deleantur."

[133] So Chadwick (1985), p. 12; perhaps part of their motive, I think.

and shrines were to be permitted.[134] A final lethal measure was pronounced in a lengthy imperial decree issued at Ravenna in August 415 by the same emperors.[135] All men holding cult priesthoods in Carthage, as well as in the other metropolitan cities of the Roman provinces in Africa, were ordered to abandon their priestly offices and to return to their municipalities of origin as ordinary citizens. The emperors then reissued the order that all lands that had been assigned to provide revenues for pagan temples were to be confiscated by the state. In like manner, all lands that were possessed by pagan priestly associations for the underwriting of their celebrations, feasts, and festivals were to be vindicated by the state. With the entirety of their financial support removed from them, the ability of the myriad temples, shrines, and religious associations to continue functioning was finally and fatally impaired.

Theodosius and Honorius were therefore especially active in the repression of the public manifestations, the high profile and prominent aspects of pagan cults: the temples, priesthoods, systems of public sacrifices, and the cult images that were integral to their functioning. It is not surprising that several Catholic Christian basilicas at Carthage, and doubtless elsewhere in Africa, were specifically identified with the patronage of these emperors and were named after them. In September 417, Augustine delivered a sermon in one of these, the *Basilica Honoriana*, in which he made it clear that the church had formerly been a pagan temple: "The idols that were here knew how to be fixed in a place, but they did not know how to walk."[136] It seems that several of the confiscated temple properties came into the possession not just of the state but, via its agency, came to be owned by the Catholic Church, which then recorded its thanks for the gift by naming the church in honor of its imperial benefactor.

---

[134] CTh 16.10.19.pr-3 (Arcadius, Honorius, and Theodosius, from Rome, 15 November 407): "Templorum detrahantur annonae et rem annonariam iuvent expensis devotissimorum militum profuturae. Simulacra, si qua etiamnunc in templis fanisque consistunt et quae alicubi ritum vel acceperunt vel accipiunt paganorum, suis sedibus evellantur, cum hoc repetita sciamus saepius sanctione decretum. Aedificia ipsa templorum, quae in civitatibus vel oppidis vel extra oppida sunt, ad usum publicum vindicentur. Arae locis omnibus destruantur omniaque templa in possessionibus nostris ad usus adcommodos transferantur; domini destruere cogantur. Non liceat omnino in honorem sacrilegi ritus funestioribus locis exercere convivia vel quicquam sollemnitatis agitare. Episcopis quoque locorum haec ipsa prohibendi ecclesiasticae manus tribuimus facultatem; iudices autem viginti librarum auri poena constringimus et pari forma officia eorum, si haec eorum fuerint dissimulatione neglecta."

[135] CTh 16.10.20.pr (Honorius and Theodosius, from Ravenna, 30 August 415).

[136] Aug. *Sermo* 163 (Partoens 2005). For the basilica, see Ennabli, *Métropole chrétienne*, p. 31, no. 13; as she points out, Lapeyre (1931) identified the former temple as that of Caelestis, a "fact" then repeated by many others, without any proof – see Partoens (2003), pp. 251–53, esp. 252 n. 4.

Not every decommissioning of a traditional shrine ended with this same fate. If we are not misled by the exaggerations of Christian rhetoric, the temple of Caelestis at Carthage presents one of these alternative cases. There were many shrines, temples, and places of sacred rituals and festivals in the metropolis, but Caelestis had a particular position of pre-eminence. She was identified with Juno, the patron goddess of the city.[137] Through Juno, Caelestis had a continuity of identity with the Punic *Tinnith Pene Ba'al*: the Face of the Lord God of ancient Carthage. About the year 420, the court dispatched officials, including the tribune Ursus, to direct activities against pagans and Manichees. It was under his command that the temple of Dea Caelestis at Carthage and other sanctuaries close around it were razed to the ground. In this case, the site was turned into a Christian cemetery.[138] The demonic cult was ended by an act of violence that created a material symbol of its doom. The victorious Christians could point to the physical destruction of the temple and to the broken cult images: "No craftsman will ever again make the idols that Christ has smashed . . . so consider what power this Caelestis [sc. Goddess of the Skies] used to enjoy here at Carthage. But where is the kingdom of this Caelestis now? The stone hewn from the mountain without hands has shattered all the kingdoms of earth."[139] The talk about the pulverizing done by the hand of God or being God's work was a metaphor. Actual persons with real instruments of destruction had to do the dirty work. In the instance of the destruction of the great temple complex of Caelestis, the violence was legitimized by the presence of an imperial tribune. But what had happened in the 380s and 390s, and not just to shrines and temples, when there was no such convenient legal cover?

There may have been isolated assaults or scattered attacks by Christian gangs on non-Christians, but most of the violence that is reported in this particular period is more focussed. The specific targets were the centers of pagan worship, the temples of the traditional gods, and the images or

---

[137] Rives, *Religion and Authority*, pp. 65–72, 163–66 (Carthage), 189–91.

[138] Aug. *De Haeres.* 46.9 (CCL 46: 315); Possidius, *Vita Aug.* 16.1 (Bastiaensen: 168) on Ursus; Quodvult-deus, *Liber de promissionibus*, 3.38.44 (CCL 60: 185), which incident Quodvultdeus records under the heading of the promise of god concerning the overturning of idols and temples ("promissio impleta in subversione idolorum atque templorum"). For Ursus, see PAC, "Ursus (3)," p. 1236.

[139] Aug. *En. in Ps.* 98.2 (CCL 39: 1379) and 98.14 (CCL 39: 1391–92): "Idola quae fregit Christus, numquam iterum faciet faber . . . Quid est mons unde praecisus est lapis sine manibus? Regnum Iudaeorum . . . Regnum Caelestis quale erat Carthagini! Ubi nunc est regnum Caelestis? Lapis ille fregit omnia regna terrarum, lapis praecisus de monte sine manibus." Cf. Aug. *Civ. Dei*, 2.4 (CCL 47: 37) and *En. in Ps.* 62.7 (CCL 39: 798): "Sunt enim qui, quando famem patiuntur in isto saeculo, dimittunt Deum, et rogant Mercurium, aut rogant Iovem ut det illis, aut quam dicunt Caelestem, aut aliqua daemonia similia," on Caelestis at Carthage.

simulacra of their deities. The terms of the imperial laws focussed attention on places and properties that were singled out as legitimate objects
for decommissioning and destruction. It became legally good, and acceptable, to destroy certain kinds of property. But it had never been legal,
and it was still not, directly to attack undesirable persons. Not random,
indiscriminate, or uncontrolled, the violence involving Christians attacking individual "pagans" was organized, coherent, and conducted by small
gangs of men. And the imperial court, which was reasonably well informed
on these matters by its local officials, firmly believed that Christian bishops
were the organizers of these gangs.

CHRISTIAN GANGS AND "PAGAN" RESPONSES

One of the earliest epistolary exchanges between Augustine and a non-
Christian are letters written in the early 390s between Augustine, who was
still a priest at Hippo, and a man named Maximus, who was a grammarian in the town of Madauros.[140] The letter contains a long discourse
over the status of the traditional gods in connection with a dispute over
a recent violent incident in the town.[141] There had been a riot provoked
by Christian attacks on local shrines. Property and lives had been lost.
The town council had to find someone who would intervene on behalf
of the community to soften impending severe legal punishments. It is
a not unwarranted suspicion that Maximus, now an old man, was chosen precisely because he had once been one of Augustine's teachers. As a
young man between his twelfth and fourteenth years, between 366 and
369, Augustine had been a student at Madauros. If so, Maximus was a
good choice to act as an intermediary with a Christian who was perceived
to be a man of influence.[142] In writing to Augustine, Maximus states that

---

[140] The date of the correspondance is in fact uncertain. It has traditionally been placed before
24 February 391 (based on CTh 16.10.10) but after 388 when he was still returning from Italy
and still resident in Thagaste.

[141] Aug. *Ep.* 16 (CSEL 34.1: 37–39). On the date, the traditional date of 4 July assigned by Baronius does
not withstand scrutiny, see Mastandrea, *Massimo di Madauros*, pp. 27–28, who places it, oddly, in
347 ("furono probabilmente vittime della *persecutio Macariana*"), which seems most improbable.
The attack must have been very recent, the worry being over the impending punishment of
Madauros for the violence. The editors of PAC (p. 733) place it "a une époque sûrement antérieure
aux mesures antipaïennes de l'année 391 – et notamment à la constitution impériale du 24 février
[CTh 16.10.10]."

[142] On Maximus, see R. A. Kaster, *Guardians of Language: The Grammarian and Society in Late
Antiquity*, Berkeley, University of California Press, 1988, p. 311, no. 96; for the argument that the
two already knew each other as teacher and student, see Mastandrea, *Massimo di Madauros*, 12–13.
For details, see "Maximus (3)," PAC, pp. 733–34; and "Maximus (28)," PLRE, 1: 585; he is an old
man at this time (16.1: *seniles artus*), and he already had a regular correspondance with Augustine

he is certain that the town forum of Madauros was populated by a crowd of salvific spirits. He rushes immediately to a chameleon-like mode of defense, a pre-emptive effort to collapse and to paper over the real distance between Christian and non-Christian concepts of deity. Naturally, Maximus suggests, no one would deny that there is a single supreme paternal creator deity lying behind all of the diverse manifestations of godhead sculpted in the forum of Madauros – "as highly educated men like you and me must know" he adds. The concession by Maximus is immediately followed by a gambit grounded on the elite culture that he is sure that both he and Augustine share. "My beliefs and yours," he asserts, "must be close in substance because we are both Romans and both men of Latin culture." His written Latin is leavened with a high formal Ciceronian style affected by the better men of the time and, for good measure, punctuated with verses from Lucan and Vergil.[143] Surely "our values," Maximus avers, are on one side of a cultural ledger whereas those of the men bearing the barbaric-sounding names of Punic-speaking natives are on the other.

In making explicit reference to the barbaric names of the local toughs, Maximus was encouraging Augustine to condemn a recent attack led by a group of Christian gangsters on images of traditional gods found in the temples and in the forum of Madauros. The leader of the pack was named Namphamo. The other men who followed him in committing these acts of destruction included a Miggin, a Saname, and a Lucitas.[144] The last-named man must have died in one of the assaults, since he was now accorded the cultic worship of a martyr by the Christians.[145] Namphamo, who had also

---

(16.1 = CCL 31:38): "Avens crebro tuis affatibus laetificari et instinctu tui sermonis"), so it would not be out of place to imagine him as one of Augustine's teachers during his education in Madauros as a young boy; Baxter (1924), p. 21, points out that ILAlg 1.2209 (Madauros), celebrating a local rhetor of renown whose name has been lost in the inscription, is perhaps our man, especially since his daughter's name was Maxima.

[143] Mastandrea, *Massimo di Madauros*, pp. 39–44, for analysis.

[144] Of these names both Namphamo and Miggin are certainly in correct form, both being Punic. Namphamo, which means something like "good foot," is well attested in the epigraphy of the Madauros region: see H.-G. Pflaum, *L'Afrique romaine*, Paris, Harmattan, 1978, pp. 183–87; Miggin is also Punic and is widely attested in both epigraphical and literary texts from Africa (PAC, 1, pp. 752 f.; Duval, *Loca Sanctorum*, 1, pp. 707–09). Saname(m) is more dubious; it is possible, however, as a variant of a name known in the region: Sanae (ILAlg 1.918), Sanam (919, 1006), Sacnam (1535), Sahnamt and Sahnaim (1901), Sanamt (2315), Sanais (125) and Sene (1575), see Mastandrea, *Massimo di Madauros*, pp. 52–53. Lucitas is clearly problematic. It simply does not look right. The name is probably an error for some other African name; it is otherwise unattested in any African source.

[145] Aug. *Ep.* 16.2 (CCL 31:38): "Quis enim ferat Iovi fulmina vibranti praeferri Migginem, Iunoni, Minervae, Veneri Vestaeque Sanamen et cunctis – pro nefas! – diis immortalibus archimartyrem Namfamonem? Inter quos Lucitas etiam haud minore cultu suspicitur atque alii interminato numero diis hominibusque odiosa nomina." The designation of Namphamo as "archmartyr" was once taken as providing evidence of the first martyr known in African Christianity (and

perished in the same attack, was now honored by the name of "archmartyr" or chief-martyr, assuming in death the quality of primacy and leadership that he probably had in life.[146] These men had been involved in "criminal attacks" on non-Christians and in destructive assaults on the shrines of the gods. The forays had been violent ones and some of the attackers had been killed. In consequence, the men were venerated by local Christians. By contrast, Maximus' reaction to their barbaric actions, to their low social class and to their plebeian values, was one of revulsion. As is manifest in the details of his letter to Augustine, with its heartfelt appeals to the common values held by highly educated men, it was not so much an issue of belief as it was one of culture. A matter of taste. Maximus quotes the poet Lucan, the laureate of social chaos, to portray the attacks as "a second Actium" directed by "Egyptian monsters" who were intent on savaging civilized life.

What especially frightened Maximus was the willingness of the Christian gangsters to sacrifice their own lives in the attacks on traditional places of worship. Seeping out of the underbelly of African society, as he saw it, the young roughs presented the threatening apparition of wild men out of control.[147]

Who can bear to see Miggin held in honor above Jupiter, hurler of thunderbolts, Saname above Juno, Minerva, Venus and Vesta, and that archmartyr Namphamo – who can bear it! – above all the immortal gods? Among these men Lucitas is honored with hardly less a cult – as well as other men, almost without number, whose names are hateful to gods and men. They are men who, in the shared guilt of their unspeakable and evil acts, and for the sake of achieving a glorious death, pile one criminal act upon another and, so defiled, acquire a death worthy of their own characters and deeds. The funerary monuments of these men, as if the matter is to be regarded as worthy of memory, are crowded by mobs of stupid louts who have abandoned the traditional temples and who have forgotten the worship of the spirits of their ancestors . . .

---

therefore dating to the 180s CE). This strange opinion was ably refuted by Baxter (1924), who correctly saw that the events described, and therefore the martyrs themselves, were contemporary with the writer.

[146] On the status of these men as Christian martyrs, see P. Mastandrea "I martiri di Madaura," ch. 3 in *Massimo di Madauros*, pp. 27–31. In 1584, Baronius inserted them into his *Martyrologium Romanum* under 4 July (p. 297: "Madauri in Africa sancti Namphanionis martyris et sociorum, quos ille roboravit ad pugnam et ad coronam provexit"). In the *Martyrologium Hieronymianum*, a saint Namphamo is recorded under xv–xiv kal. Ian. (17–18 December), but there is no way of knowing if he is our man.

[147] Maximus apud Aug. *Ep.* 16.2 (CSEL 34.1: 38): "diis hominibusque odiosa nomina, qui conscientia nefandorum facinorum specie gloriosae mortis scelera sua sceleribus cumulantes dignum moribus factisque suis exitum maculati reppererunt. Horum busta, si memoratu dignum est, relictis templis, neglectis maiorum suorum manibus stulti frequentant, ita ut praesagium vatis illius indigne ferentis emineat: 'inque deum templis iurabit Roma per umbras' [Lucan 7.459]."

This brief note written by Maximus presents a picture from the late 380s and early 390s in which gangs of young men – in his fearful view, almost "without number" – were drawn from the brutish lower elements of the local population, probably mainly rural workers, many of whom still bore Punic names like Miggin, Namphamo, and Saname. They staged organized attacks on "pagan" temples and cultic places, smashing the idols that they found in them. These were Christian gangs and a Christian violence driven by an ideology of martyrdom. Just as the numbers of the gangsters were great, so too the numbers of the ignorant who worshiped them were equally large. The rhetor Maximus is well aware of this when he describes Namphamo as an "archmartyr," which is to say a leading or a chief martyr – no ordinary one, but rather a man of pre-eminent honor and distinction among the thugs. These barbarous men viewed the attacks on pagans and their sacred cult places as a virtuous duty. There must have been armed resistance to them, since members of the Christian gangs were injured and some of them had died in the attacks.

That Maximus wrote to Augustine, a Catholic priest, to complain about the activities of these men of violence is important, as is the fact that Augustine defended the Christian gangsters. But the correspondence is not innocent. They were parts of what Augustine, at least, intended to be a public dossier on the debate.[148] The letters were not just a pleasant private exchange of viewpoints; they were a surrogate for a public confrontation. In his reply to Maximus, therefore, Augustine conceded very little. He began by firmly rejecting Maximus' attempts to create a common ground with Christians.[149] He then pointed out that one might find the names of the multifarious pagan deities to be no less nonsensical than the Punic names of the dead men that Maximus found so offensive. "As one African writing to another," Augustine noted, it was especially hypocritical of Maximus to show disdain for Punic names.[150] In concluding his letter, Augustine drew a distinction between the Catholic Christian community established in Madauros and "these other men." *We* – by which Augustine means "we Catholics" – do not have any special "cult of the dead," he says, referring to the cult accorded to the men who died as martyrs in the assaults launched

---

[148] Mastandrea, *Massimo di Madauros*, pp. 33–34.

[149] See the passage quoted in n. 146 above, which continues Aug. *Ep.* 17 (CCL 31: 40–43).

[150] Aug. *Ep.* 17.2 (CCL 31: 40–41): "Nam quod nomina quaedam mortuorum Punica collegisti, quibus in nostram religionem festivas, ut tibi visum est, contumelias iaciendas putares, nescio utrum refellere debeam an silentio praeterire . . . Neque enim usque adeo te ipsum oblivisci potuisses, ut homo Afer scribens Afris, cum simus utrique in Africa constituti, Punica nomina exagitanda existimares."

against pagans and their shrines.[151] These "other men" were men whom Augustine will later specifically label "circumcellions."[152] Notably, in this case, neither the name nor the concept is deployed.[153] The specific name for the men was to appear first in Augustine's writings in a letter dated two or three years after this event.[154] In polemical replies made later to various dissidents, including the bishop Parmenian, Augustine explicitly stated that it was in fact gangs of circumcellions who were organized by the church to lead attacks on pagan temples.[155] He already knew who they were.

Another incident of violence that happened about a decade later, also at Madauros, provoked the dispatch of a similar diplomatic letter from the town council to Augustine, this time through an intermediary named Florentius.[156] Augustine expresses surprise that the decurions' letter was addressed to him. He wonders aloud, with an acidic mockery, if there "happened" to be any "Catholic Christians" in the ranks of the town councilors. It is mockery because Augustine knew full well of the "superstitious devotion" of the town leaders to their idols. He believed that it would be easier for them to close the temples in their city than to close their hearts to

---

[151] Aug. *Ep.* 17.5 (CCL 31: 43): "scias a christianis catholicis, quorum in vestro oppido etiam ecclesia constituta est, nullum coli mortuorum, nihil denique ut numen adoraris, quod sit factum et conditum a deo, sed unum ipsum deum, qui fecit et condidit omnia."

[152] They are described and condemned in precisely the same language, including references to their *scelera* and *facinora*, as the circumcellions: see Lamirande (1965e) on the strong overlaps in the language.

[153] Lepelley's claim (1980: 266 n. 1) that Baxter is mistaken in identifying these men as being, in effect, circumcellions is based on one objection: "C'est impossible car, dans sa réponse, Augustin prend la défense de ces martyrs, ce qu'il n'eût pas fait s'ils avaient été donatistes, ou pire, circoncellions suicidés." But surely this misunderstands the context of the letter. First, Augustine is mainly concerned with defending Christians *as such* against a scathing attack by a pagan; second, the letter dates to the first year of Augustine's priesthood at Hippo, at a time when he is not very much concerned with, or knowledgable about "the Donatists" and, even less, "circumcellions." Finally, Augustine *does* indicate that this behavior was to be found principally in the "other" Christian community. Baxter was therefore surely right to claim that these men were ones whom Augustine would later label circumcellions. As Mastandrea has noted (*Massimo di Madauros*, p. 30), both men had every reason to try to avoid noting the ecclesiastical membership of the gang members.

[154] Aug. *Ep.* 23.7 of 393/94 (CCL 31: 67), about the same time as his *Psalmus contra partem Donati*, where the term also appears (vv. 144–50: BA 28: 170–71).

[155] Aug. *Contra ep. Parm.* 1.10.16 (CSEL 51: 37): "Cur ergo ipsi ubi possunt templa subvertunt et per furores circumcellionum talia facere aut vindicare non cessant? An iustior est privata violentia quam regia diligentia?"

[156] Aug. *Ep.* 232 (CSEL 57: 511) is Augustine's reply addressed to "Dominis praedicabilibus et dilectissimis fratribus Madaurensibus." For the bearer of the original letter see "Florentius (3)," PAC, p. 471; unfortunately, nothing more is known of him that might assist in dating or contexting the letter (the editors of PAC date it in the decade 400–410); see Mastandrea, "La datazione della Lettera 232," appendice in *Massimo di Madauros*, pp. 81–88 who draws attention to similarities with themes in *Sermo*, 22.4; he places both about 408/09 in the aftermath of Honorius' legislation of 407, but both could be much earlier, around 400.

such worship.[157] It is manifest both from these letters, and from Florentius'
direct testimony, that the membership of the town council at Madauros
was mostly non-Christian and that the attitudes of the councilors had in
no way changed from what they had always been. They were devotees of
the traditional gods. In closing his reply to Florentius, Augustine refers to
the decurions in general as "idol worshipers." The words of his that follow,
piqued by the apparent mockery of his position as a Christian bishop,
are severe. He threatens the councilors with the charges that will be filed
against them in the court of God at his final judgment.[158] He draws their
attention to the fact that their current predicament, including the destruction of temples, had been predicted by early Christians: "Surely you see the
temples of idols fallen, some of them fallen into ruins and not repaired,
some of them thrown down, some closed, some converted to other uses,
and the idols themselves either smashed to pieces or burned or shut off or
otherwise destroyed."[159]

Since the desired physical destruction of pagan shrines was not sanctioned by imperial legislation, freelance enforcement by Christian gangs
and less organized rioters had to be covertly encouraged. Even if the law
explicitly forbade such private enforcement, these men would do God's
work that was *suggested* by the imperial legislation. Both the Catholic and
the dissident churches organized their own gangs.[160] Augustine had to warn
some of his parishioners "not to act like circumcellions," clearly suggesting
that some of them were actually doing so. His warning was specifically
aimed at those Catholics who were going out to smash pagan idols.[161] If
the encouragements to use heavy weapons in breaking images issued by
the bishops might have been metaphoric, rough and less educated Christian men surely took the injunction as meaning to use a more literal axe

[157] Aug. *Ep.* 232.1 (CSEL 57: 511): "Si forte illi, qui inter vos catholici Christiani sunt . . . quorum mihi
superstitiosus cultus idolorum, contra quae idola facilius templa vestra quam corda clauduntur
vel potius quae idola non magis in templis quam in vestris cordibus includuntur, cum magno est
dolore notissimus."

[158] Aug. *Ep.* 232.1; and 7 (CSEL 57: 517): "superbus orbis terrarum et nunc iudicem subiectus expec-
tat; . . . erit testis vobis in iudicio eius, qui credentes sibi confirmaturus est et incredulos confusurus."

[159] Aug. *Ep.* 232.3 (CSEL 57: 513): "Videtis certe simulacrorum templa partim sine reparatione conlapsa,
partim diruta, partim clausa, partim in usus alios commutata, ipsaque simulacra vel confringi vel
incendi vel includi vel destrui."

[160] Augustine seems to hint at this when he speaks of pagans and their idols are now vanquished by
Christians, and that Christians have now turned their assaults (*impetus*) *and* laws (*leges*) against
these same idols (*Ep.* 209.9; CSEL 57: 351).

[161] Aug. *Sermo* 62.17 (PL 38: 422).

against pagan gods.[162] One's specific sectarian allegiance did not matter in doing this good work. Given the nature of the source materials that have survived, the Catholic gangs are rarely mentioned, whereas the actions of dissident roughs are always carefully recorded and highlighted for sectarian advantage. In a tract written some three decades later, Augustine found it easy to refer to the fact that dissident Christians had torn down shrines and temples.[163]

Either it is the pagans who will be filing complaints against you, people whose temples, whenever it was possible, you leveled to the ground and whose places of worship you destroyed – *things that we Catholics also did.* Or is it the musicians of the demons whose flutes and foot-organs you smashed to pieces – *something that we Catholics also did . . .*

Augustine's offhand remarks are testimony to the general operations conducted by Christian gangs of the period, both dissident and Catholic, against pagans – "something that we Catholics also did." Although he claims that the aim was a lofty one (i.e. the repression of error) and he denies that the acquisition of booty or *rapina* was ever the aim of such men, the very fact of the denial strongly suggests what was actually happening. The reality was messy and sometimes ugly. But in the same paragraph in which he details the involvement of Christian gangs in such violent operations, he goes on to name the dissident gangsters as "circumcellions," surely because they were the same kind of men, the same phenomenon, and the same type of violence.[164] Which is to say that in this period of the heavy repression of the pagans, the Catholics had their own circumcellions – never once referred to by this name, of course.

That the circumcellion gangs of the dissident Christians were normally used in attacks on traditional shrines and worshipers is a side to their violence that is not usually highlighted in any detail because it was seen by Christians as acceptable violence. It was a training ground that they shared in common with Catholic gangs of enforcers. Augustine repeatedly hints at these activities but does not elaborate on them, perhaps because

---

[162] Aug. *Sermo* 23B.4 (Dolbeau 6/Mainz 13 = Dolbeau, *Vingt-six sermons*, p. 461): "Et si hoc parum putas, et ascia potest interrogare deum tuum" ("and if you don't think that is good enough, an axe can also 'interrogate' your god.")

[163] Aug. *Contra Gaud.* 1.38.51 (CSEL 53: 250): "aut stabunt contra vos pagani, quorum certe ubi potuistis templa evertistis et basilicas destruxistis, quod et nos fecimus; aut stabunt adversum vos symphoniaci daemoniorum, quorum tibias et scabella fregistis, quod et nos fecimus."

[164] Aug. *Contra Gaud.* 1.38.51 (CSEL 53: 250–51): "In talibus quippe omnibus factis non rapina concupiscitur, sed error evertitur . . . Sed stabunt Catholici non solum adversus gentiles, a quibus veri martyres exspoliati sunt, verum etiam adversus circumcelliones Donatistarum."

the destruction of pagan shrines was not seen by a majority of parishioners of either communion as being a bad thing. Around 405, in developing his response to Parmenian, the dissident bishop of Carthage, he describes the violent activities of the gangs.[165]

We have already spoken at great length about the pagans and also about their demons, and how they were persecuted by the emperors. Or is this also a subject that is displeasing to you? Why then did *they* [i.e. the dissident bishops] have the temples destroyed in any place where they could? Why did *they* not stop from committing such acts, nor desist from getting such acts done through the mad acts of their circumcellions? Is private violence more just than imperial care?

Whether it was or was not "more just" is a rhetorical point that Augustine might have preferred to debate. But it was probably not a big concern for most adherents of each church. They were surely less concerned with the formal justice or legitimacy of such actions than with how effective they were. That Christian gangs normally operated in the destruction of the physical apparatus of traditional cult is also made clear in Augustine's long letter to Bonifatius, the tribune, in 417 – a miniature history presented to the high-ranking imperial official as a beginner's primer on the nature of the Christian conflict in Africa.

After an extended series of remarks on the definition of persecution and the meaning of martyrdom, Augustine proffered a detailed résumé of the types of persons who were responsible for acts of sectarian violence. He claims that there had been a terrible spate of anti-Catholic violence in recent years, but that, given their past history, the behavior of the persons fronting these attacks should not surprise anyone. The past history of these men, he says, is interesting precisely because it did not involve attacks on their fellow Christians, but rather assaults on pagans and their places of worship.[166]

Especially during those years when the worship of idols still took place, huge battle lines of these gangsters came to the most crowded festivals of the pagans, not to smash the idols but to be killed by the worshipers of the idols. If they wished to do

---

[165] Aug. *Contra ep. Parm.* 1.10.16 (CSEL 51: 37): "Sed multa iam etiam de paganis diximus et de ipsis daemonibus, quod persecutiones ab imperatoribus patiantur. An et hoc displicet? Cur ergo ipsi ubi possunt templa subvertunt et per furores circumcellionum talia facere aut vindicare non cessant? An iustior est privata violentia quam regia diligentia?"

[166] Aug. *Ep.* 185.3.12 (CSEL 57: 11): "Maxime, quando adhuc cultus fuerat idolorum, ad paganorum celeberrimas sollemnitates ingentia turbarum agmina veniebant, non ut idola frangerent sed ut interficerentur a cultoribus idolorum. Nam illud, si accepta legitima potestate facere vellent, si quid eis accidisset, possent habere qualemcumque umbram nominis martyrum; sed ad hoc solum veniebant, ut integris idolis, ipsi perimerentur. Nam singuli quique valentissimi iuvenes cultores idolorum, quis quot occideret, ipsis idolis vovere consueverant."

this with the approval of some legitimate power, then, if something happened to them, they would be have been able to claim the shadow of the name of "martyr." But they came solely for this purpose: that, leaving the idols intact, they themselves would be struck down. For there were some particular worshipers of the idols, strong young men, who had the custom of dedicating to the idols any victims whom they killed.

What he is doing here is replaying the one case that he knew so well: the violent attacks on the shrines of Madauros. Were there more? His words hint at a wider sphere of action by Christian gangs during this earlier period of "idol worship."

VIOLENT YOUTH

To cut through this skein of rhetorical claims that were being assembled for the edification and persuasion of an imperial official is perhaps difficult, but necessary, since Augustine is attempting to construct a picture of an irrational drive to self-murder. All the more so, since the author is not averse to repeating this claim as a sound bite aimed at another imperial reader, but written in acerbic reply to the claims of the dissident bishop Gaudentius.[167]

They were the type of men whom *you* persuaded to these evils, men who had had been accustomed to do these things even earlier, especially in the time when the freedom of worshiping idols was still red hot everywhere. At that time these men would rush onto the weapons of pagans who were gathered at their crowded festivals. The pagan youths would then dedicate to their idols whomever of these men they killed. The [Christian men] poured in from all sides in gangs and, like wild animals hunted down by beast-hunters in the amphitheater, they would throw themselves on the sharp spears pointed at them. Raging they died, rotting they were buried; by deceiving others, they were worshiped.

These men, he goes on to say, are none other than the same men whom our own contemporaries call "circumcellions." On his own construal of the past, these gangs of Christian youths who went to crowded pagan festivals did so deliberately to confront the cult worshipers in aggressive and violent ways. They went to the shrines not so much to break or to

---

[167] Aug. *Contra Gaud.* 1.28.32 (CSEL 53: 230–31): "Eorum est enim hominum genus, cui hoc malum persuadere potuistis, qui solebant haec et antea facere, maxime cum idolatriae licentia usque quaque ferveret, quando isti paganorum armis festa sua frequentantium irruebant; vovebant autem pagani iuvenes idolis suis quis quot occideret. At isti gregatim hinc atque inde confluentes tamquam in amphitheatro a venatoribus more immanium bestiarum venabulis se oppositis ingerebant, furentes moriebantur, putrescentes sepeliebantur, decipientes colebantur."

destroy the images, but rather to anger, to rile, and to antagonize pagan youths so much that they would turn on their Christian tormentors and kill them. This claim is then attached to similar actions by these same persons in accosting travelers on the road with terrible threats in order to incite the wayfarers to kill the Christian zealots. These were all willful actions designed to provoke the killing of the attackers who would thereby instantly achieve the status of martyrs.

The assertion that the Christian men in some of the gangs wanted to do nothing so much as to have themselves killed strongly suggests what must have been the usual context in which the gangs were raging. If they had the cover of legitimate state authority under which to operate, and something then happened to them, they could rightly claim the title of martyr. They had a just cause. If the men in the Christian gangs went to pagan festivities and cult places with the express task of smashing idols, then this was construed as legitimate enforcement. This is what was in fact happening. Enforcement actions by Christian gangs happened frequently enough to provoke consistent responses from pagan youths. The ritual of attack and defense had been routinized on both sides. One side knew how to attack and the other how to defend, and they knew on what occasions and in what venues these violent confrontations were likely to occur. The reaction was to fight fire with fire, to organize young men to defend their cult places and cult statues. Local youths protected the home of *their* god against violent Christian forays and then dedicated the body of the enemy as a sacrifice or trophy to their deity, something that they had become accustomed to doing.

Who were these young men who were so ready to defend the traditional cults of their towns? Surely they were none other than the *juvenes* or young elite males who had their own youth organizations in the towns and cities of Africa.[168] Young men are certainly a constant presence in this violence, but then young men always were a problem. They seem always to be the main primary recruitment base for such violence.[169] In his *Metamorphoses*, the second-century African philosopher and writer Apuleius was not inventing out of pure imagination the violent young men found in the towns and cities of empire, including those of his homeland, Africa, and of his own *patria*, Madauros. In the novel, the slave Photis warns the traveler Lucius to show care when returning home at night.[170]

---

[168] Lepelley (1980).   [169] See, in other circumstances, Coogan, *The Troubles*, p. 87.

[170] Apul. *Met.* 2.18.3–5: "Sed, 'Heus tu,' inquit, 'cave regrediare cena maturius. Nam vesana factio nobilissimorum iuvenum pacem publicam infestat. Passim trucidatos per medias plateas videbis iacere, nec praesidis auxilia longinqua levare civitatem tanta clade possunt.'"

Now, take care, she said, and come back early from supper because a crazed gang of noble young men have been upsetting the public peace. You'll see the wounded lying everywhere in the middle of the street. The governor's forces are too far away to be able to protect the city from such internal slaughter.

One way in which Roman towns tried to harness the errant energies of potentially violent young men was by providing a formal organization for them – The Youth or *Juventus* – in which activities that would be useful for the community could be monitored and encouraged. In this way, the aggressive tendencies of young men in their late teens and early twenties were channeled into more acceptable elements of municipal service.[171]

The municipal youth organizations had athletic facilities that encouraged physical training to prepare young men for military or guards service. Such clubs usually functioned under the aegis of Mars, the god of war. In this way, the better sort of young men in any given town would be inculcated with a common elite culture. They would belong to an association of peers in which they would be trained in the cultural norms and military skills that would prepare them for public life. In the town of Mactaris, The Youth boasted of having paid for the construction of a new basilica and two grain storage buildings out of their own funds. They identified themselves as "worshipers of the god Mars Augustus."[172] Since it contains a full list of names of the members in the year 88, the dedicatory inscription gives us an idea of the size of these organizations. In a small town like Mactaris, with a population of two to three thousand, the organization had sixty-five ordinary members, plus two *magistri* or chief officers and two *curatores* – men in charge of the club's operations, projects, and its treasury – for a total of sixty-nine. Large enough to be effective, but small enough to be an elite.

The *Juvenes* also functioned as an informal paramilitary police force for each city and its territory. The Youth of the town of Cuicul were placed under a municipal prefect. A man usually assumed this post only after holding a number of other municipal offices; he would be an older,

---

[171] Jaczynowska (1978), Ladage (1979), Eyben, "Collegia iuvenum," in *Restless Youth*, pp. 112–14, and Ginestet, *La jeunesse*, are the standard treatments. Kleijwegt, *Ancient Youth*, pp. 101–16 offers a convenient survey; for Africa in this period, see Lepelley, *Cités de l'Afrique romaine*, 1, pp. 236–42.

[172] AE 1959: 172 (Mactaris), cf. Charles-Picard (1958), pp. 77–95: "Iuventus civitatis Mactaritanae cultores Martis Aug(usti) solo publico basilica(m) et horrea II p(ecunia) s(ua) f(aciendum) c(uraverunt)." There are other possible indications that young men were connected to religious municipal religious organizations: CIL 8.6970 = ILAlg II.491 (Cirta): for some *iuniores*; and M. Janon, "Cultores Dei Ierhobolis Iuniores," *BAA* 2 (1966–67), pp. 219–30, at pp. 219–20 (Lambaesis). But these seem to refer to a different phenomenon in which the members of a cult are ranked by age groups.

experienced leader.[173] At Cirta, Lucius Iulius Civilis completed the entire run of municipal offices before becoming head of the *Juvenes*.[174] C. Iulius Crescens Crescentianus' prefecture of the Youth at Cuicul similarly came at the end of a long municipal career and before a regular army command in Mauretania.[175] Since The Youth served as town militias, their leaders, like C. Herennius Festus at Thuburnica, were often veteran soldiers, in this case a man who had served as a prefect in charge of army recruiting in Mauretania. After holding his military posts, Festus became chief of The Youth at Thuburnica, and then one of the town's mayors.[176] The Youth honed their skills with weapons by training in the aristocratic pursuit of hunting wild animals. They were also engaged in the culture of the arena, another place where young men could legitimately display aggression and bravado, like the young man from Thigibba who was killed in a bullfight.[177] The links that the elite youth culture had with the world of the amphitheater were ubiquitous. Augustine's statement that Christian gangsters threw themselves on the spears of such men like wild beasts in the amphitheater is not an accidental comparison.

It is important to note that militia-like training was part of the education of the *Juvenes*. That they were mobilized in local emergencies is shown in a poem from Saldae recording the dedication of The Youth to Jupiter and to the patron deities of the *Gens Mauri*. The reason was a recent victory over the Mauri who had attacked the city, but who had been driven back from its perimeter walls.[178] Municipal charters of the high empire show that the town mayors were empowered to conscript groups like the *Juvenes* in the defense of the city.[179] Although evidence for The Youth as a formal organization in the towns and cities of Africa of the later empire is lost to us, there can be no doubt that the organizing of young men continued, whether under this formal name or not.[180] Sons of local elites who were

---

[173] Ti. Claudius Cicero (AE 1912: 22, Cuicul); Flavius Sempronianus (AE 1913: 159, Cuicul).
[174] AE 1942–43: 10 (Cirta).   [175] AE 1920: 114–115 (Cuicul); see Leschi (1927), pp. 400–01.
[176] AE 1921: 21 (Thuburnica): C. Herennius M. f. Quir(ina tribu) Festus, veteranus leg(ionis) X Fretensis honesta missione dimissus, praefectus tironum in Mauretania, praef[ec]tus iuventutis, IIvir bis.
[177] C. 8.11914 (Thigibba); cf. ILAlg 1.3146 (Theveste) for a *iuvenis* who died "on the horns": sum cornuo labsus.
[178] AE 1928: 38 (Saldae), see Leschi (1927), pp. 396, 404–05.
[179] As in § 103 of the Urso charter: CIL 2.5439 = ILS 6087.
[180] The gap in the evidence is almost solely due to the fact that all the data for the *Juvenes* in Africa of the high empire come from municipal inscriptions of a kind that were not produced in Late Antiquity; see Lepelley, *Cités de l'Afrique romaine*, 1, p. 238: he draws attention to the references in Aug. *Ep.* 185.3.2 (CSEL 57: 11) on the *singuli quique valentissimi iuvenes cultores idolorum*; and *Contra Gaud.* 1.28.32 (CSEL 53: 131) on *pagani iuvenes*. Both passages refer to "pagan youths" who dedicated "to the idols" the bodies of the Christian gangsters whom they killed when the latter attacked the shrines of the traditional gods.

attached to the traditional cults of their towns are surely the prime suspects as the "young men" who were violently resisting the inroads of Christian gangs on their turf. Christian youths of this kind certainly existed.

The demographic group of young males, whether specifically organized like the municipal Youth or not, is critical to the forging of this type of civil violence.[181] It is hardly surprising that this same age and gender cohort resurfaces in different guises in different regions of the later empire boasting their own kinds of sectarian violence. Violent young males appear in eastern Christianity, where monks and other ascetic groups of young men were mobilized, allowing both church and state to draw on a pool of readily available enforcers who were inured to hardship and physical discipline, and who were ready to do harm.[182] In late Roman antiquity in Africa, after the apparent disappearance of formal institutions of the *Juvenes*, the aristocratic young men of the time might well have been organized more informally under the aegis of powerful and wealthy families in each town and city. In discussing the destructive anti-pagan activities of Catholic and circumcellion gangs, and their "pagan" counterparts, young males are critical, but so are their organizers. Especially in connection with attacks on shrines, it is interesting to see that the gravamen of Augustine's message is that Christians should not be afraid of powerful and threatening men.[183] His words point to the leading men of the pagan elites in the towns.

THERE'S A RIOT GOING ON

Sometimes, then, the organized gangs of Christian enforcers met with hard violent resistance. All of the named members of the Madauros attack known to Maximus were deemed to be martyrs. We are fortunate to know of the Madauros incident only because Maximus and Augustine knew each other and were involved in correspondence on the matter. These particular circumstances produced the context in which Maximus mentioned the

---

[181] See, e.g., Semelin, *Purify and Destroy*, p. 279: "most of the killers have several common characteristics: they are young, even adolescent, single and male. Most of the potential killers are recruited from among the thirteen to twenty-five year-old age group." He goes on to note (pp. 279–80) that "youth organizations make up the main breeding ground from which authorities select those who will become their devoted servants." In this case, presenting strong analogues with our "pagan" cases, he notes the importance of football clubs (e.g. as in the Tutsi–Hutu massacres).

[182] Compare the role of the gymnasium and its leaders in organizing the anti-Jewish violence in Alexandria in 38 (Philo, *In Flaccum*, 34); see Gaddis, *Religious Violence*, pp. 231, 237: *c.* 375, the emperor Valens ordered monks to be seized and drafted into the army; those who refused were clubbed to death. The monks were used to the violence: their own rules called for disciplinary beatings that appear to have been common.

[183] Aug. *Sermo* 61.11.17 (PL 38: 422).

attack in a dossier of letters that has happened to survive. The normal scope and frequency of these episodes of organized violence are therefore obscured from our view. But the concentrated mass of anti-pagan imperial measures of the 380s and 390s was producing local circumstances in which persons who were not Christian were coming under greater pressure. Many of the inhabitants of these cities, and not just the elite young males, were aware that they were now facing determined efforts to efface their traditions. In this volatile situation, one small incident could ignite a spate of violence – a type of violence that was not likely to occur in the context of organized gang attacks. More probably it would explode out of the generalized resentment that was growing among people who were witnessing their way of life being systematically disparaged, and now finally condemned. And it was more likely to occur in the cities than in the countryside. In the towns there was still a critical mass of persons, both leaders and followers, who shared a culture under imminent threat.

Violence was also more likely to occur at certain flashpoints where one side might openly vaunt its precedence over the other, places where large crowds would gather – for example, at festivals and parades where large numbers would come into direct contact with each other. In May 397, when some Christians stepped in the way of a traditional riverside parade in the valley of Anaunia, the Val di Non, just north of Tridentum (Trento) in northern Italy, three of them were attacked and killed by outraged locals.[184] The reasons for the violent reaction were specific. The Christian missionary clergy were concerned not so much with stopping the parade as they were with preventing recently converted Christians from joining the celebrations. The new Christians, interestingly enough, had not seen anything particularly wrong with participating in festivities which they saw as part of their traditional culture. The Christian clergy thought differently. It could just as well work the other way around. Africa had its own riots incited by the staging of ritual celebrations and ceremonial parades. The combination of local values, cultural norms and behaviors inculcated by religion, and the involvement of state authorities produced the conditions

---

[184] Gaudentius of Brescia, *Tract.* 17 (CSEL 68: 144; dated to 401–02); Maximus of Turin, *Sermo* 105.2 (CCL 23: 414–15); cf. 106 (CCL 23: 417–18), both *c.* 405, but with no more details; and two letters of Vigilius of Trento, one to Simplicianus of Milan and the other to John Chrysostom (PL 13: 549–58; dated to 397–98), are the main sources. On the Christians who were killed and who were celebrated as martyrs, see Chadwick (1985); for background and analysis, see Salzman (2006), pp. 267–73. The incident is important for our purposes because it was known in Africa: Aug. *Ep.* 139.2 (CSEL 44: 152), importantly, in a letter in 412 to Flavius Marcellinus, judge of the great conference at Carthage.

for riot.[185] The final attack on the church, which led to its burning and destruction, was fueled, we are told, by a night of intensely emotional debates and hard drinking.[186] Each group, the Christian and the non-Christian, was attempting to use force to police the boundaries of its respective community – the Christian leaders to prevent new Christians from crossing back to their former life, those who were not Christian to defend the integrity of their own culture. But the move to hard physical violence seems, on the basis of all surviving evidence, to have been a rather unusual thing.

In the year 399, one such incident occurred at the town of Sufes. A small place at the nexus of routes that ran from the proconsular province in the north to the more open lands of the south, Sufes had always been a crossroads of local communication. Through the days of the high empire Sufes remained a simple settlement or *castellum* before it had been raised to the status of a colony in the early third century.[187] The riot that took place on the last day of August was perhaps caused in part by conditions of oppressive heat, and the presence of harvest workers in Large numbers.[188] The outburst had apparently been cued by an attack of the sort described by Maximus at Madauros. In this case, an attempt was made by Christian gangsters to destroy the cult image of the god Hercules in his temple. Hercules was identified with the Punic god Melqart and was, in this form, a Roman version of this God of the City. That is precisely what his Punic name meant: in all likelihood, he was associated with the foundation of Sufes as a Carthaginian outpost in the fourth or third century BCE.[189] In the

---

[185] The analysis here follows the lines of interpretation suggested by Brass, *Theft of an Idol*, outlined in his introduction, pp. 6–9, where he notes that "the transformation [i.e. of precipitating incidents] into caste or communal incidents depends on the attitudes towards them taken by local politicians and local representatives of state authority" (p. 6).

[186] Vigilius, *Ep.* 1–2 (PL 13: 551–54); cf. Salzman (2006), p. 270.

[187] For Sufes, see Lepelley, *Cités de l'Afrique romaine*, 2, pp. 305–07; the modern Henchir Sbiba about 35 km north of Sufetula and 37 km south of Maktar. Its name of Sufes almost certainly reflects its origin as a Punic town under Carthaginian hegemony in the third and second centuries BCE; hence the great importance of Hercules who is identified as the Hellenistic/Roman equivalent of Melqart, the Punic "God of the City."

[188] Aug. *Ep.* 50 (CCL 31: 214). "Ductoribus ac principibus vel senioribus coloniae Sufetanae Augustinus episcopus: Immanitatis vestrae famosissimum scelus et inopinata crudelitas terram concutit et percutit caelum, ut in plateis ac delubris vestris eluceat sanguis et resonet homicidium. Apud vos Romanae sepultae sunt leges, iudiciorum rectorum calcatus est terror, imperatorum certe nulla veneratio nec timor. Apud vos sexaginta numero fratrum innocens effusus est sanguis." The Christians who died at Sufes were honored in the Roman martyrology on 30 August: AASS 2.1, col. 0553C: "Coloniae Suffetulanae in Africa beatorum sexaginta Martyrum, qui furore gentilum caesi sunt." The year is thought to be 399, correlated with the anti-pagan imperial legislation, including the two decrees of Honorius calling for the destruction of temples: see Kotula (1974).

[189] For the identification of Herakles with Melqart, see Bonnet, *Melqart*, pp. 399 f. (with nothing on Sufes, however).

only substantial epigraphical text from the town in late Roman antiquity, Hercules is noted as the town's patron deity.[190] Any attempt to deface and to destroy the image of the god would be going one step too far. The townspeople turned on the Christians in a general massacre. At least sixty of them were killed in the ensuing riot. In the aftermath, there followed the usual response by town leaders to control the political damage done by the rioters. They wrote to Christian bishops in Byzacena, in the proconsular province, and in Numidia to seek protection from possible retaliation by the state.

This attempt to protect the community from legal punishment provoked an angry response from Augustine in a vehement letter addressed to the political leaders of the colony of Sufes. In it, he gave vent to his conviction that the local notables of the city were implicated in the massacre, either by covertly abetting the slaughter or by doing nothing to prevent it. With a sense of sardonic anger, he noted that if a citizen of Sufes had managed to kill even more Christians, he probably would have been feted and exalted by the leading members of the city council.[191] The apparatus of Roman laws and civil courts that had been meant to protect people had simply been forgotten or trampled underfoot. The judges who ought to have been doing their duty had averted their eyes, or worse. From these statements and others like it, it is clear that Augustine assumed that the leading men – the so-called *principes* – in the local curial ranks held steadfast to their traditional religious attitudes.

The ordinary citizens of the town who were becoming more and more anxious about and resentful of Christian inroads into their traditional values and culture might act on these sentiments. If so, they could count on tacit support from the leadership elements in their community. There was little to restrain them from taking matters into their own hands, if they decided to do so. It was this connection that Christians knew and feared. Augustine refers to this attitude of the town elites in an extended argument in his *City of God* that was intended to refute a rising chorus of elite criticisms of Christians as the ones who were responsible for the collapse of the traditional order of the empire. The well educated, he says, know very well that such vile charges are groundless, but they indulge in spreading these ideas about and fixing them in the minds of the common people since "they want to make the mobs of the ignorant very hostile and

---

[190] CIL 8.11430 (Sufes).

[191] Aug. *Ep.* 50 (CCL 31: 214): "et si quis plures occidit functus est laudibus, et in vestram curiam tenuit principatum." Lepelley, *Cités de l'Afrique romaine*, 2, p. 307, seems to take this as fact rather than rhetoric.

dangerous to us."[192] In several aspects, including the centrality of the god Hercules, the incident bears close parallels to the violence (described above) that would erupt two years later, in 401, in the metropolis of Carthage.

For the municipal ruling orders, whether at Sufes or at Carthage, playing the populist card was a dangerous double game. If their aim was to manipulate the mass of common citizens to provide support for what remained of their own secular space, they had to do so with discretion. They wished to protect this space and not to threaten public order so much that the provincial or imperial authorities would come down heavily on them with repressive force. It must have been a delicate game. If fed a continual diet of hostile, disparaging, cynical, and mocking remarks about Christians, in the right circumstances the common people might read a cue from their betters as a "green light" to advance to more aggressive acts. On occasion, these moves simply careered out of anyone's management or control. The members of the town council who were responsible for local law and order were then forced into the more desperate game of damage control. For the Sufes riot, all that survives is the one retort by Augustine, but there are other incidents for which more is known.

DEATH IN CALAMA

The problem of evidence does not bedevil our understanding of the riot at Calama in June of the year 408.[193] The town of Calama (modern Guelma) was on one of the main lines of communication traversed by Augustine. His friend Possidius was bishop there, and it is surely to the latter's autopsy and formal reports that we owe the detailed description of the events that occurred in the early June days of 408.[194] Like the riot at Madauros, the violent outburst at Calama took place in the summer. Again, one must take into consideration the oppressive midsummer heat and the gathering of young men for the completion of harvest as possible contributing factors. But it also followed a normal script for such riots that usually includes the backdrop of longstanding problems, a precipitating event, and a forward rush to violence in which the majority of the violence, an atrocity, was

---

[192] Aug. *Civ. Dei*, 2.3 (CCL 47: 36): "Nam qui eorum studiis liberalibus instituti amant historiam, facillime ista noverunt; sed ut nobis ineruditorum turbas infestissimas reddant, se nosse dissimulant atque hoc apud vulgus confirmare nituntur."

[193] An important analysis is found in Hermanowicz (2004a), who refers to the existing studies; see Lepelley, *Cités de l'Afrique romaine*, 2, pp. 97–101.

[194] Lepelley, *Cités de l'Afrique romaine*, 2, pp. 90–96.

largely one-sided.[195] A mini-dossier of letters exchanged between Nectarius, a "pagan", and Augustine provides the details.[196] Like Maximus of Madauros, Nectarius was acting as an intermediary to plead his city's cause with an influential Christian bishop. Men in the town council of Calama, like Nectarius, hoped to persuade Augustine to intercede for them in softening punishments that might be imposed by imperial and provincial authorities.[197]

In his letter, Nectarius, who, like Maximus of Madauros, was not a Christian and not much in touch with Christian values, similarly founded his appeal to Augustine on traditional core Roman values that he felt they must share. "We all agree," he says, "that we love our home town, our own father, with an affection that surpasses even that which we have as children towards our parents." He then extends these assumed common values into Augustine's Christian world: these ties are much like the bonds that join a Christian bishop to his people, are they not? In his long reply to Nectarius, Augustine not only refutes Nectarius' claims and rejects his overtures, but also, very usefully for an appreciation of that day at Calama, proffers in evidence a detailed step-by-step narration of what happened, an ekphrasis painted with such force that it allowed Nectarius no way to avoid confronting the events themselves. As we follow the path of this narrative, however, it only provokes questions about the sequence of events that led to the riot.

The first day of June 408 at Calama began with expectations among non-Christians and Christians alike, apprehensions that had been provoked by two antecedent events.[198] The first was the existence of what Augustine calls

---

[195] Collins, *Violence*, pp. 115–18, citing Horowitz, *Deadly Ethnic Riot*, pp. 385–86, on the nature of the atrocities that occur under such conditions.

[196] Of this dossier, there now survive four letters: *Ep.* 90 (Nectarius to Augustine: June/July 409); *Ep.* 91 (Augustine's reply: July 409); *Ep.* 103 (Nectarius' second letter to Augustine: sent late July or early August 409, but arrived at Hippo eight months later, on 27 March 410); *Ep.* 104 (Augustine's reply: late March/early April 410). Possidius' *Elenchus* (10.50 = Wilmart, *MiAg* 2: 185) seems to list four letters from Augustine to Nectarius, hinting at a larger body of letters, some of which have been lost. The editors of PAC (p. 778n28) accept the validity of the figure, given the fact that Possidius was bishop of Calama and should have known.

[197] Aug. *Ep.* 90 (CCL 31A: 153): addressed to "Domino insigni et merito suscipiendo fratri Augustino episcopo Nectarius." The riot must be dated to some time after the imperial edict of November 407 (posted at Carthage on 5 June 408) to which Augustine later refers. In addition, in *Ep.* 104.1, which must be dated to some time *after* 27 March 410 (the date Augustine received Nectarius' letter, *Ep.* 103), perhaps early in April, Augustine states that Nectarius' letter had reached him only eight months after Augustine's last letter to him, which therefore would have been in August of 408. For Nectarius see "Nectarius," PAC, pp. 776–79.

[198] Kotula (1974) has made the argument that the recent law was CTh 16.5.43 + 16.10.19 = Sirmond. 12 (issued 25 November 407; see nn. 210–11 below). From the full version in the Sirmondian constitutions, we know that this was not posted at Carthage until 5 June 408. Kotula presumes

"most recent laws" issued by the emperors, measures that banned ritual and religious elements from public ceremonials and parades connected with traditional cult.[199] Whether or not these "most recent laws" actually proscribed the festivities as they were held on 1 June at Calama is debatable – an ambiguity that was a big part of the problems that they caused. The laws were no doubt perceived to be part of a series of imperial measures that were increasingly constraining the ability of persons who were not Christians to continue staging their traditional festivals and parades *as religious events*. But where *was* the line being drawn between popular celebration and religious event? Because of its public and performative nature, parading is a strong irritant in situations of ethnic or religious conflict. Since they both create the spectacle and the participation, parades are fertile grounds for potent reactions by hostile spectators.[200] There are, however, hard questions to be asked about who in Calama actually knew about these laws on the First of June of that year.

The second set of conditions were the firm expectations that were solidly fixed in a long history of the First of June celebrations in Africa. The First of June, as everyone at Calama knew, marked the annual staging of the great end-of-spring summer festival in the town.[201] It was probably a festive harvest celebration connected with the reaping and storing of the cereal crops in the fields around the town.[202] Despite its pagan religious elements, the festival continued to be celebrated because the people of Calama and the members of their council, men like Nectarius, saw nothing particularly wrong with it. Although imperial injunctions already existed against

---

that word of this measure got to Calama before 1 June and was one of the primary causes of the aggravated sentiments. I agree.

[199] This is presumably CTh 16.10.19 (see n. 134 above) issued in November 407, but not actually posted in Carthage until 5 June 408. If so, its terms might not be taken actually to proscribe the sort of public parade held at Calama on 1 June.

[200] Horowitz, "The Occasions for Violence," ch. 8 in *Deadly Ethnic Riot*, pp. 268–25, esp. "A Parade of Processions," pp. 272–77, accounting, he estimates, along with mass meetings and demonstrations, for a third to a half of all ethnic rioting; and in medieval Spain: Nirenberg, *Communities of Violence*, pp. 180–81, noting the element of competition for civic space; as often, too, in sectarian violence in Northern Ireland: Coogan, *The Troubles*, pp. 59, 124; and, especially, where traditional arrangements go awry: pp. 135–36; see also, Bell, *Generation of Violence*, pp. 50–51, 61–62, and 99–101.

[201] Aug. *Ep.* 91.8 (CCL 31A: 157): "Contra recentissimas leges Kalendis Iuniis festo paganorum sacrilega sollemnitas agitata est."

[202] We do not know the nature of this festival in Africa. In Italy, 1 June was the great Bean Festival: Varro, *De vita populi Romani*, 1.21 (ed. B. Risposati, Milan, 1939, p. 285): "quod calendis Iuniis et publice et privatim fabatam pultem dis mactant"; Macrob. *Sat.* 1.12.33: "Nam et Kalendae Juniae fabariae vulgo vocantur." Like the 1 January celebration, this festival might have had a wider imperial presence in late antiquity. The Codex Calendar of 354 places the *Ludi Fabarici* on 1 June: Salzman, *On Roman Time*, p. 92.

traditional sacrifices and other such matters, the notables of the town and many of the townspeople were not interested in a zealous enforcement of these laws. So the two sides arrived at a *modus vivendi*. The festival went on. The Christians did their thing and the other townspeople did theirs. As long as everyone repeated the ritual avoidance year in and year out, as everyone latently agreed, nothing much untoward happened.[203]

On 1 June 408, however, the celebrations developed differently and became violent. The main incitement seems to have occurred when the Christians of Calama came to view the festival differently than they did in previous years. They no longer acted according to script. New and uncustomary modes of behavior appeared – as when "the pagans," no doubt wishing to assert the legitimacy of their traditional practice, perhaps asserted it more aggressively than they had done before. If the parade moved infringe on accepted boundaries, as in other instances of ethnic or religious division, such purposeful movement could have had the appearance of claiming territory for the marchers. In the mixed and indiscriminate neighborhoods and streets of a late antique town, the front of a Christian basilica would form such a manifest boundary.[204] On 1 June 408, the paraders challenged this frontier with an in-your-face attitude, by taking their procession right by this Christian face of the town.[205] The crowd of dancers, says Augustine, with their "insolent daring" paraded through the neighborhood of the city in which the Christian church was located, exaggerating their movements as they danced their way past the front doors of the church.[206] Perhaps. That is how the Christian leadership *later* pitched the behavior of "the pagans," so as to put the blame for the violence on their outrageous and deliberately provocative acts. In the light of the recent restraining legislation, and what seems to have been a traditional practice of mutual avoidance, the fact that "the pagans" took this route was interpreted as a calculated insult. Which it might have been. If so, the provocation had to be met. The resistance was led by the local Christian clergy. When they tried to stop the celebrations, the crowd of dancers stopped dancing

---

[203] In divided communities, parades are performative demonstrations that often compress opposing communities in time and space, enhancing the prospects for violence. For early modern France, see Zemon Davis (1973/1975), pp. 170–72; for modern Northern Ireland, see Moloney, *Secret History*, pp. 44, 65, 86, 89, 100, 167 (for some examples) – many of these, in the circumstances of the late 1960s and onwards, led to violence.

[204] Feldman, *Formations of Violence*, pp. 29–30 for Northern Ireland.

[205] Hermanowicz (2004a), pp. 485–86, who notes the peripheral location of the basilica in the town that might have required some deliberation to march past it.

[206] Aug. *Ep*. 91.8 (CCL 31A: 157–58) "nemine prohibente tam insolenti ausu, ut quod nec Iuliani temporibus factum est, petulantissima turba saltantium in eodem prorsus vico ante fores transiret ecclesiae."

and began hurling stones at the church.[207] This was the story spun by the Christian bishops. Although not quite a lie, it deliberately misrepresents the kinds of misunderstandings involved.

What seems much more probable is that the locals, both the common people and the town officials of Calama, not yet knowing of any imperial restrictions on their festivities, were simply enjoying their usual First of June celebrations.[208] The Christian bishops – including Possidius, the Catholic bishop of Calama – knew better. They knew better because they had privileged advance knowledge of the imperial decree on the subject. News had come quickly down their private pipeline from the court at Ravenna that a decree of the emperors had forbidden the religious elements in local traditional celebrations, like the one at Calama on 1 June. The Catholic bishops in Africa already knew of the prohibitions not many months after the emperors issued their order on 15 November 407.[209] They had a vested interest in lobbying the court on this matter and news of the success of their mission came to them directly through church messengers. What is more, the emperors' language seemed to allow considerable enforcement power to the Christian bishops, speaking of granting them of the use of "church power." The words could easily be interpreted to mean the use of the physical violence of gangs of enforcers.[210] The law certainly gave the bishops the right to call on local agents of the state – the *agentes in rebus* – to see that the law was enforced.[211] What is important in understanding the riot is that Possidius certainly had this decree in hand when he moved to break up the parade on 1 June.[212]

For the court at Ravenna, on the other hand, the law of November 407 was just another piece of legislation. It was surely far from among the most important in its agenda. In consequence, the official copy made its way

---

[207] Aug. *Ep.* 91.8 (CCL 31A: 158): "Quam rem illicitissimam atque indignissimam clericis prohibere temptantibus ecclesia lapidata est." See Horowitz, *Deadly Ethnic Riot*, p. 273: as a Muslim parade passed by a Hindu temple in Ahmedabad (1969), "a minor clash developed, in the course of which stones were thrown at the temple."

[208] The imperial decree was only posted at Carthage on 5 June of this same year. Even given the best communications of the time, the decurions at Calama would only have received the law at some time later in the summer.

[209] Certainly Augustine had a copy of the decree in hand when he wrote his first letter to Nectarius, using key phrases out of it: *sollemnitas agitata est* (Aug. *Ep.* 91.8, CCL 31A: 157); see Hermanowicz (2004a), p. 487.

[210] Const. Sirmond. 12 (SC 531: 518): "Episcopis quoque locorum haec ipsa prohibendi ecclesiasticae manus tribuimus facultatem." The emperors were only granting normal "ecclesiastical force" to the church, but the words *ecclesiastica manus* could easily be taken to hint at more.

[211] Const. Sirmond. 12 (SC 531: 518): "Nam et agentum in rebus executionem Maximi, Iuliani, Eutychi, ut ea . . . impleantur, indulsimus."

[212] So Gaudemet (1992), pp. 187–89.

through the layers of bureaucracy, slowly as usual, to the governor's office at Carthage.[213] Whether the imperial decree actually went so far as entirely to forbid traditional parades, the bishops no doubt interpreted the emperor's words to mean as much. They saw the decree as providing them with the legal basis for direct action. That is why Possidius intervened to stop the parade. The locals, on the other hand, would surely have been perplexed. They did not understand why on earth the Christians were now engaging in these new and offensive gestures. The text of the imperial decree had not yet been officially made public even at Carthage, the metropolis of Africa – at some great distance from Calama. It was not posted by the proconsul Porphyrius in the forum at Carthage until 5 June, four days *after* the first day of rioting at Calama.[214] It probably would not have been delivered to the town council at Calama until some time well after 5 June. The significant fact is that the Christians knew about the law, but the locals did not. The people of Calama naturally reacted with anger and resentment at what they saw as unwarranted Christian interference with their celebrations.

This seems to have been the substance of the first confrontation that took place on 1 June. Probably not much more would have happened if matters had been allowed to remain as they were. But the same clergy who attempted to bring the parade to an end on 1 June were determined to see that the local municipal magistrates enforced the imperial decree that forbade such "pagan ceremonials." In the days following the First of June festival, the bishop Possidius complained to the magistrates of Calama; he demanded that they enforce existing imperial law, drawing their attention to "the most recent decree" issued by the emperor against such pagan processions.[215] This insistence on enforcing a law that was not yet known surely did not move the local town council to action, even if Possidius had his own advance copy of the decree. The magistrates of Calama did consider his demand, but no doubt needed time to inquire into the legitimacy of

---

[213] Const. Sirmond. 12.praef (SC 531: 512): "Impp. Honorius et Theodosius Augg. Curtio Praefecto Praetorii." The edict was sent first to the office of the Praetorian Prefect, whose officials would then have it copied and delivered to the Vicar of Africa to go to provinces like Numidia, and, more directly, to the proconsular governor of Africa.

[214] Const. Sirmond. 12 (SC 513: 518): "Data vii kal. Decemb. Romae, proposita Carthagine in foro sub programmate Porphyrii proconsulis nonis Iuniis, Basso et Filippo vv. cc. conss." See Hermanowicz (2004a), pp. 490–91 on the date: it must be 407, part of legislation including CTh 16.2.38, 16.5.3, 16.5.41, 16.5.43, and 16.10.19. All should be assigned to the same date: 15 November 407.

[215] Aug. *Ep.* 91.8 (CCL 31A: 158): "Deinde post dies ferme octo, cum leges notissimas episcopus ordini replicasset, et dum ea quae iussa sunt velut implere disponunt, iterum ecclesia lapidata est." The laws here are referred to as "very well known," and earlier as "most recent" (see n. 169 above), pointing to months immediately preceding the outbreak of 1 June.

the law before they would enforce it.[216] News of the demands made by Possidius seems only to have stoked an even stronger sense of resentment among the non-Christians who assembled a week later, on 8 June. They began stoning the church. The Christian response was to take the matter back to the civil courts and to insist on the responsibility of the local officials to prevent this attack on them. The cycle of charges and counter-charges began reinforcing and repeating itself, spiraling in intensity. On the next day, 9 June, the Christians tried to file a formal complaint in the public records, but the attempt was rebuffed by the municipal officials. Again, the rejection had good grounds, since the local officials still did not have an official copy of the law.

The reluctance or refusal of the town councilors to deal with the petition lodged by Possidius was interpreted by the non-Christians in the town as a form of permission. They renewed their attack on the Christian basilica, first by stoning it and then by launching firebrands onto the roof in an attack against the people who were huddled inside the church.[217] The last day of rioting was marked by a terrifying downpour of hail. Each side interpreted the divine sign in its own way. The Christians thought that the storm should be taken as a divine warning against more anti-Christian violence. Many of the local people, however, saw it as a sign of the anger of the gods at the sudden interruption of their procession by Christian bishops.[218] The violence now escalated from an attack on a building to assaults on persons. A lone Christian, "one of God's slaves," who happened to be wandering through the town, accidentally ran into some of the rioters and was killed on the spot. Other Christians ran for shelter and hid themselves wherever they could. Rather ignominiously, the bishop, none other than Augustine's close friend Possidius, squeezed himself into a cramped space from which he heard the voices of rioters who were trying to find him so that they could kill him.[219] Cringing in his hiding place, he

---

[216] It is unclear precisely why the submission is called a *replicatio* by Augustine. The problem of knowing if an imperial decree was genuine or not was a real problem for local town administrations: see, e.g., CTh 9.19.3 (9 June 367; Valentinian and Valens, from Trier, to Festus, Proconsul of Africa), where the emperors note the illegal use of writing that imitated the formal imperial script, and where they express fears about the forgery of such documents.

[217] Aug. *Ep.* 91.8 (CCL 31A: 158): "Postridie nostris ad inponendum perditis metum quod videbatur, apud acta dicere volentibus publica iura negata sunt."

[218] Aug. *Ep.* 91.8 (CCL 31A: 158): "Eodemque ipso die, ne vel divinitus terrerentur, grando lapidationibus reddita est, qua transacta continuo tertiam lapidationem et postremo ignes ecclesiasticis tectis atque hominibus intulerunt." See Hermanowicz (2004a), p. 484, for a good estimate of the "pagan" interpretation.

[219] Aug. *Ep.* 91.8 (CCL 31A: 158): "unum servorum dei qui oberrans occurrere potuit occiderunt, ceteris partim ubi potuerant latitantibus partim qua potuerant fugientibus, cum interea contrusus atque

overheard their angry exchanges as they blamed each other for letting him get away. Or so, at least, he later claimed.

The rioting on the last day was as brief as it was intense. The attacks on the church and individual Christians which began in the late afternoon, around four o'clock, continued into the night and then ended abruptly.[220] During all this time, Augustine claims, none of the civil authorities attempted to do anything to stop the violence. According to his account, only one solitary man, a stranger, actually intervened to protect the victims. By his efforts a considerable number of Christians were saved and, Augustine states, perhaps less credibly, a large amount of property was recovered from the looters.[221] This is not to say that the story of the lone helper is untrue, but the interjection of this solitary "good man" into the narrative is in part a rhetorical ploy that enabled Augustine to assert that much of the violence could easily have been prevented if only some of the local people, especially persons in authority, had done anything to halt it. The fact that one man on his own had achieved so much was proof. The Christian response was to use this incident to get the civil authorities involved in punishing the ruling order of the town for their involvement in the crime. Augustine's graphic description of "what actually happened" was meant to put Nectarius and his fellow decurions on notice that they should not expect any mercy. The whole of his presentation has the air of preparation for a court hearing.

Augustine's first letter had prompted a reply by Nectarius.[222] Exercising a patronal interest in protecting his hometown, Nectarius tried to cultivate the bishop's benevolence by comparing him with Cicero, further asserting that he had paid careful attention to Augustine's arguments for the worship of the "most high God." He then developed an argument that the crime of taking things (that is to say, crimes against property) is more serious even than killing. Nectarius then finishes with a rhetorical flourish in which he calls attention to his own sorrowful tears and to the tearful spectacle of the mothers and children of Calama who would suffer from imperial

coartatus quodam loco se occultaret episcopus, ubi se ad mortem quaerentium voces audiebat sibique increpantium, quod eo non invento gratis tantum perpetrassent scelus."

[220] Aug. *Ep.* 91.8 (CCL 31A: 158): "Gesta sunt haec ab hora ferme decima usque ad noctis partem non minimam." Daylight in early June ran roughly from 5:00 AM to 10:00 PM; the "tenth hour" should have been around 4:00 PM.

[221] Aug. *Ep.* 91.8 (CCL 31A: 158): "Nemo compescere nemo subvenire temptavit illorum quorum esse gravis posset auctoritas, praeter unum peregrinum, per quem et plurimi servi dei de manibus interficere conantium liberati sunt et multa extorta praedantibus."

[222] Nectarius, apud Aug. *Ep.* 103 (CCL 31B: 34–36); as Augustine states in the following letter, *Ep.* 104.1 (CCL 31B: 37), he only received this letter on vi kal. April. or 27 March, eight months after he had originally replied to Nectarius.

punishment. Think of the *shame*, he says, of those who return to the town, once freed from detention, who have to display the scars and wounds inflicted by the torturer on their bodies. Even as he was writing his letter, he claims, innocent people who had nothing to do with the riot were being hauled before the court on capital charges.[223] The filing of formal charges against the citizens of Calama had been made by Possidius.[224] In the months immediately after the riot, he had undertaken a diplomatic journey to Italy, via Carthage, in which he probably gave personal testimony about the riot, both to the governor's office at Carthage and to the imperial court at Ravenna, where he lobbied for action.[225]

The riot at Calama speaks more about words than violence. It was a rhetorical goldmine for those who were lobbying the imperial court. In reality, a sectarian urban riot was probably a rather unusual occurrence. In the case of Calama, it was an accident waiting to happen. The triangular links that connected the Christians, the non-Christians, and the imperial government interplayed with each other in sometimes unforeseeable ways. The differential access in communications between the heavily invested petitioners, in this case the Catholic bishops, and the targets of their lobbying efforts, either dissidents or pagans, produced a temporal gap into which private enforcement could move. In this instance, the petitioners had succeeded in their lobbying, but zealous and premature pursuit of enforcement had provoked a violent response. To have gained a real one-off success against the permanently discredited world of "the pagans" was one thing. To get a Christian imperial court to move its heavy machinery against fellow Christians was quite another. This would require a more potent rhetoric – one that would paint a compelling picture of dangerous enemies faced by the state as well as the Church. Beyond the construction of a dire "pagan threat," this would mean inflating the dangerous specter of the Jews and the heretics.

---

[223] Nectarius, apud Aug. *Ep.* 103.4 (CCL 31B: 36): "Iam illud explicari vix potest, quantae crudelitatis sit innocentes appetere et eos, quos a crimine constat esse discretos, in iudicium capitis devocare. Quos si purgari contigerit, cogites quaeso, quanta accusatorum liberabuntur invidia, cum reos sponte dimiserint victi, reliquerint innocentes."

[224] Aug. *Ep.* 104.1 (CCL 31B: 37): "An aliquid audisti, quod nos adhuc latet, fratrem meum Possidium adversus cives tuos... quo plectantur severius impetrasse?"

[225] Aug. *Ep.* 95.1 (CCL 31A: 215).

CHAPTER 6

Ravens feeding on death

That Jews held a central place in the religious conflicts between Christian communities in Africa in the age of Augustine might seem surprising. That there were significant numbers of Jews in a few large communities in Africa during this period is almost certain, but the plain fact is that relatively little is known about them.[1] And much that has been claimed to be known vanishes under close scrutiny. What remains amounts to a few scattered literary references, some archaeological artifacts, and a little nomenclature.[2] And what we can know from these sources is bedeviled by an even bigger problem – a dark figure lurking in the background. That is to say, there were many, if not very many, Jews whom we cannot identify at all simply because, in everything from names to dress, they looked just like everyone else.[3] This singular fact produces a vexatious problem for the historian: just what did Jewish communities in the Maghrib of the Roman period look like when so many of the individuals that constituted them are invisible to our gaze?

---

[1] Old and standard surveys were offered by Mieses as early as 1823, by Monceaux (1904/1970), and then, more recently, the two synoptic overviews by Le Bohec (1981a) and (1981b); and, on literary texts by Castritius (1986) and (1987), and Linder (1985). All of these works are now superseded by Stern, *Devotion and Death*. The problem is that these communities have not left much evidence of their existence. The total number of epigraphical references, including the epitaphs from the cemetery at Gamart (Carthage), is really quite exiguous when compared with the mass of Greek and Latin epigraphy. Much less is known, certainly, than is suggested in the optimistic compilations in the standard textbooks; see, e.g. J. W. Hirschberg, *A History of the Jews in North Africa*, vol. 1, 2nd ed., Leiden, Brill, 1974, pp. 21–86, with full references to earlier work.

[2] For a survey of the material remains, see Le Bohec (1985) and Gebbia (1986); on nomenclature, see Lassère, *Ubique Populus*, pp. 413–26, and the detailed surveys by Le Bohec (1981a and 1994). Le Bohec (1981b: 211) counts exactly 96 persons who he thinks can be known as Jewish or "Judaizers" in the Greek and Latin epigraphy of Africa. Even some of these seem dubious, but even if all are accepted as Jews or Jewish, the whole represents a truly exiguous proportion of all persons known from epigraphical texts. The few literary references of direct relevance to this study will be considered individually in what follows.

[3] It is a signal achievement of Stern, *Devotion and Death*, to have brought this aspect of the problem to the fore in her analysis of "ethnic identity."

Although Jewish communities did exist and could have been the object of Christian violence, most of the hostile "against-the-Jews" polemic that is found in Christian writings does not seem to have served to mobilize gang actions or mob violence against them. There is very little evidence to indicate that Christians in Africa of the period actively engaged in violent attacks on Jews as such or even against Jews in combination with others. Indeed, the most insidious effects (of which we know) of the pictures and language of hate developed in Africa actually took place outside of it in Christian rioting against Jews that took place at Mago (Minorca) in the Balearics in 418.[4] On the bare evidence (as pitiful as it is) this seems to have been the pattern: the words generated for one purpose in Africa assumed a more malign and savage power when exported to new lands where their production was decontexualized and their hate-effect was purified. The urban riots in cities like Carthage, Sufes, and Madauros, and the episodes of rural violence in the towns and villages around Hippo Regius, conversely, are never known to have involved Jews as their principal targets. The silence could be the result of a peculiar blindness in the surviving literary sources, but this seems unlikely given that most of them are the products of Christian writers who had an historical and a theological fascination with Jews. Any significant violent encounters between Jews and Christians, had they existed, would surely have been reported or at least alluded to in their writings.

Although Jewish communities flourished in Africa in Late Antiquity, evidence about their numbers, extent, activities, interests, and contacts is scattered and patchy. It does not permit a fairly focussed picture of Jewish life. That Jewish groups of some importance existed in the metropolis of Carthage is suggested by a number of different indices, including references in Tertullian's treatises from the first decades of the third century. There was a large Jewish cemetery at Gamart, about 4 miles from the center of Carthage, on the northern outskirts of the city.[5] The underground tombs of the Jewish burial ground at this site were hollowed out of the rocky heights facing away from Carthage towards Utica to the northwest. Up to 200 underground chambers provided burial places for about 3,500 persons. The nomenclature and the decorative motifs found in the tombs

---

[4] Van Dam, *Leadership and Community*, pp. 67–68; for more details of the confrontation, see pp. 304 f. below.

[5] Delattre (1895); Leclercq (1924), esp. 610 on size: about 200 underground slots, each with an average of 10–15 burial places: "En définitive c'est une pauvre nécropole juive." For the location, see *DACL* 2.2 (1910), fig. 2109; Stern, *Devotion and Death*, pp. 255–302 is very important for placing this evidence in context. Frend's repeated claims of Christian burials in the cemetery (e.g. 1978, p. 185) are not supported by any evidence.

are evidence of a distinctive ethnic community. The epitaphs reveal a society that was mostly reflective of its western Mediterranean milieu: a few of the inscriptions are in Greek, some are in Hebrew, but most are in Latin.[6] Yet another possible trace of a Jewish congregation at Carthage is provided by six named rabbis, possibly from the city, who are quoted in the Jerusalem and Babylonian talmuds.[7]

From Tripolitania in the east to Tingitana in the far west, however, the sum of all known Greek and Latin inscriptions referring to Jews or "Judaizing" persons amounts to only a hundred items (or so).[8] Most are derived from tombstone epitaphs. With little more than a personal name as evidence, not much can be deduced about the broader community of which each deceased was part. Only a sixth of these persons boasted the formal Roman *tria nomina*, and most of these are from Carthage. Most of them, bearing *gentilicia* like Aurelius and Annius, seem to have lived no earlier than the last half of the second century, but perhaps much later. What little has been reported of the contents of the burial chambers indicates that the main period of use of the cemetery was not earlier than the Severan age – but much later dates are not excluded. Finally, the structure of a single synagogue has been discovered at Hammam Lif (ancient Naro), directly south of Carthage on the Bay of Tunis.[9] The strikingly beautiful floor mosaic of the main prayer hall was provided as a gift to the synagogue: the benefaction of a woman named Juliana. Another mosaic inscription was placed on the floor of the entranceway to the same synagogue by Asterius, son of Rusticus, a jeweller, who held the office of *archisynagogus*. He boasts

[6] Le Bohec (1981a), 170: 42 inscriptions: bilingual: 2: Hebrew: 5 (perhaps 6), Greek: 5; Latin: 29.

[7] Talmud *y. Berakhot* (Aba); *b. Berakhot*, 5.2 (Ada); *b. Baba Kamma*, 114b (Aha); *b. Rosh Hashana* 26a (Akiba); *b. Baba Kamma*, 114b (Hana); and *b. Berakhot* 4.7 and 29a (Isaac).

[8] Le Bohec (1981b): from which the following evidence is taken. He felt confident that he could assemble the names of 96 persons who were either Jews or "Judaïzers"; some of these, however, seem suspect. Even of the total is accepted, however, it is a truly exiguous proportion of all persons known by name in the Greek and Latin epigraphy of Africa. Of these 72 were in Latin, 21 in Greek, and 5 in Hebrew.

[9] Leclercq (1925), pp. 2042–48, with full bibliography; Le Bohec (1985), p. 23; other synagogues are known from inscriptions: at Sitifis (Sétif) where one M. Avilius Ianuarius was *pater sinagogae* (CIL 8.8499 = Le Bohec [1981a] no. 74, p. 192); at Volubilis, where a Greek epitaph records that one Kaikilios was προτοπολίτης, πατὴρ τῆς συναγωγῆς τῶν Ἰουδέων (Le Bohec [1981a], p. 194, no. 79 = AE 1969–70: 748 [Volubilis] cf. Frézouls [1971]); and from literary sources, as, for example, the one mentioned at Tipasa in the mostly fictive *Passio Sanctae Salsae* 3 (Piredda: 74-76) where it is averred to have replaced a pagan sanctuary supposedly devoted to Draco, and was in turn replaced by a Christian basilica. See Stern, "Questioning "Jewishness" in the North African Synagogue: Hammam Lif as a Case Study," ch. 5 in *Devotion and Death*, pp. 193–253, who places the Naro synagogue in the context of other Jewish places of worship in Africa.

of having paid for the tesselation of the *porticus*.[10] The coin finds at the site, as well as the types of pottery and lamps, indicate a date for the synagogue in the late fourth and early fifth centuries.[11] Analysis of the decor of the mosaics provides confirmation: it indicates a slightly later date, in the late fifth and early sixth centuries.[12]

The weight of all this evidence (again, such as it is) suggests an efflo-rescence of Jewish communities in Africa that was later rather than earlier in the long history of Roman domination. The real problem, again, is with that "dark number": the numbers of Jews whom we cannot see in the surviving evidence simply because they looked like everyone else. It is a big shadow that hovers over any analysis. Assumptions about the cate-gories and types of things that must be "Jewish" have both added to and detracted from what has become a canonical corpus of evidence. In the meantime, much, through inadvertence or malice, has been lost.[13] Inso-far as one can take the surviving evidence concerning these communities to indicate their apogee, one would guess that they flourished from the fourth to the sixth century. The few dated epigraphical texts that survive concur: they are from the later empire. The data are signs of a contempo-rary development in Late Antiquity, perhaps fueled in part by immigrants or by a more intense trade emanating from Palestine in the period of the later empire.[14] The known distribution of all texts and archaeological evi-dence demonstrating the presence of Jews or Jewish communities in Africa is heavily skewed towards coastal sites from Oea and Lepcis in the east to the island of Mogador off the Atlantic coast of Africa in the west.[15] Even those local communities that are not technically coastal, like Volu-bilis in Mauretania Tingitana or Cirta in Numidia, were still major inland entrepôts that had close connections with the seaboard. The exceptional

---

[10] For Iuliana, see CIL 8.12457a + ILTun 862 = AE 1996: 1714 (Le Bohec [1981a] no. 13, pp. 177–78), and the illustration in Darmon (1995), p. 9, fig. 3; for Asterius, see Le Bohec (1981a), no. 14, pp. 178–79 = CIL 8.12457b = AE 1996: 1713, and the illustration in Darmon (1995), p. 18, fig. 16.

[11] F. Icard, "Fouilles dans l'antique synagogue juive d'Hammam-Lif," *BCTH* (1910), clxvii f. and 288–89; cf. F. M. Biebel, "The Mosaics of Hammam Lif," *ArtBull* 18 (1936), pp. 541–51, was an early proponent of a much later dating, noting (p. 550) that Frederick Waage dated a Jewish lamp found at the site to the late fifth or early sixth century.

[12] Darmon (1995), pp. 25–26.

[13] Problems rightly highlighted by Stern, *Devotion and Death*, ch. 1, esp. pp. 8–26; there are special cautions about the standard epigraphical "corpora" that have been assembled, from Monceaux to Le Bohec. Real caution must be shown in their use, especially, again, because of the lax "criteria" that have been used to count certain persons as "Jewish," while at the same time large numbers of persons who did not meet artificial criteria of belonging to this textual community simply are not included.

[14] Le Bohec (1981a), p. 170. [15] Le Bohec (1981b), map between pp. 200 and 201; (1985).

finds of the presence of individual Jews at hinterland sites are few, and they are surely that – exceptions. This population migration therefore reveals an east–west pattern from the Levant that seems to parallel the much earlier Phoenician movements, and, one suspects, for some of the same reasons.

TWO COMMUNITIES

There is little evidence to suggest a particularly close or integral relationship between Christians and Jews in Late Antiquity, much less a good body of evidence to sustain the claim that African Christianity developed out of local Jewish communities.[16] Christian knowledge extended as far as the assertion of a selected list of manifest differences: *they* celebrate the Shabbat, *we* the Lord's Day; and when *they* celebrate the Shabbat it is with laziness and luxury, whereas *we* honor the Lord's Day with attention to duty and self-restraint; *they* are forbidden to eat these foods, but for *us* it does not matter, and so on.[17] Christian knowledge of these others in their midst seems to be selective and caricatured in ways typical of ethnic segregation and labeling. A few manifest ritualistic acts that could be publicly observed were known, such as the festival of sukkoth, which is reported in a sort of fragmented and schematic way, from a distance, almost as an anthropological curiosity.[18] And one could gloss Jewish equivalents in Greek or Latin: the Last Supper was known as the *parascuen* (from the Greek *paraskeuein*) "which the Jews call the *cena pura*."[19] But such ethnographic curiosities are significant for their rarity and isolation. They do not justify exaggerated claims about the profundity of contacts and knowledge shared between the two communities. Rather, they suggest the opposite.

There were some hostilities, however, and these ethnic dislikes surely had their own histories as well. The establishment of a Christian state after Constantine was one turning point. Another would have been the growth

[16] Compare Barnes, *Tertullian*, pp. 88–93, and append. 28, "The Jewish Disaspora," pp. 282–85, against Frend (1970a, 1970b, 1978) for different views on the significance of local Jewish communities in the development of Christianity in Africa. I am much closer to Barnes' interpretation.

[17] Anon. *Sermo Caillau-St. Yves* 1.33:4 (PLS 2: 971), from a dissident preacher; Aug. *En. in Ps.* 91.2 (CCL 39: 1280); abstinences from certain foods: *Retract.* 2.37 (CCL 57: 121).

[18] Aug. *Sermo* 133.1 (PL 38: 737) on the *scenopegia*; Aziza (1985), 80–81, interprets knowledge of matters like this as indicating a familiar and probative acquaintance with Jewish life. Based on the evidence in Augustine's large corpus of writings, however, the opposite would seem to be the case. Very little of actual Jewish life is reported, and the little that is reported is almost at the level of caricature found in ethnic stereotyping.

[19] Aug. *Sermo* 221.4 = Guelferb. 5.4 (SC 116: 218).

and flourishing of Jewish communities in Africa that took place through the end of the fourth century. Development assumed a greater pace in the fifth and sixth centuries during the high tide of an ever-increasing commercial exchange between the Levant and the western Mediterranean, especially during that phase of Mediterranean trade when commercial contacts with the region of Palestine began to overshadow former north–south exchanges. It is in this context of a growing Jewish presence and strength, perhaps seen as threatening by Christians, that we find traditional genres of Christian writing being refitted to include specific anti-Jewish themes.

Among these traditional forms was the martyr narrative. In this case the "refitting" was not so radical – anti-Jewish themes had marked some of the earliest of the known martyr narratives of the early second century. But in Africa the first martyr stories of the late second and early third century entered where the main line of conflict was with the forces of the state. The introduction of anti-Jewish elements was a later innovation. The story of the martyrdom of Marciana of Caesarea is a good example of how these new concerns were emplotted within older forms. The original account of Marciana's martyrdom informed the reader and listener of the circumstances of her execution at Caesarea in Mauretania Caesariensis on 9 January 304 in the midst of the Great Persecution.[20] This is the older traditional form of the narrative. In form and purpose, however, the *Acta* in their final form (as we now have them) are manifestly a later redaction, revealing late fourth- or early fifth-century additions. If there was an original version of this martyrdom, it was certainly rewritten with a peculiar emphasis on the aggressive anti-idolatry campaign led by a young girl named Marciana, with emphasis on her virginity and ascetic commitment. Both elements point to concerns in the 380s and 390s. Also embedded within Marciana's story is a new kind of hostility that was added to the old story of Christian–pagan hatreds.

According to the narrative of her martyrdom, Marciana was a devout young Christian woman so filled with zeal for her new faith that she abandoned her parents and her home at Rusguniae, about 80 miles east of Caesarea, and travelled to the provincial capital. In her new home, she immediately displayed an aggressive hostility to traditional forms of civic religion that culminated in a violent attack on a statue of the goddess Diana that stood over a fountain by the eastern gate of the city on the road that led to the neighboring city of Tipasa. Marciana tore the head off the statue and smashed its body to pieces. Irate local citizens arrested her and took

---

[20] *AASS*, 1, Ianuarius, tomus primus, 568–70.

her before the governor's tribunal for punishment. She was made to face a brutal test of her will to defend her sexual purity when she was imprisoned in the local gladiatorial school. In the middle of the account of her travails in this place, however, the narrator brusquely interrupts her story to insert a new episode into it.[21]

But suddenly, rushing out of his home came Budarius, the head of the local synagogue, whose house [i.e. synagogue] was in that neighborhood, along with his daughter and his sons, accompanied by the shouts of other Jews who demanded the most savage punishments for the girl. They did this . . . according to the prophetic voice . . . they demanded divine fire to atone for her insults. "Let this house," she said, "burn with heavenly fire so that it will never be able to be repaired and may it, with all its building stones, lie in ruins. And where it once stood, let there be an eternal ruin."

The next day, Marciana faced punishment in the local arena. She endured the savage punishments vented on her body so bravely that the common people of Caesarea, impressed by her nobility and heroism, were ready to plead with the governor on her behalf.[22] The Jews, however, had other ideas.

But Budarius, along with his sons, and some of the other Jews, who had gathered together for the express purpose of creating an uproar to provoke conditions of riot and disorder, cried out that the governor should order a bull to be set loose upon her.

The bull gored Marciana's breasts, and blood flowed profusely from her wounds. Fainting, she collapsed on the ground. Her body, broken and washed in her own gore, lay on the floor of the arena. She was carried out and allowed to recover.[23] Brought back to the arena the next day for the denouement of her punishment, Marciana finally surrendered her life. She was savaged by a leopard that snapped her neck with a single bite.[24]

---

[21] *Acta Marcianae*, 4 (AASS, 1: 569): "Subito de Budarii Archisynagogi domo, quae in vicino fuerat, ab eius filia vel filiis, vel aliquantorum Iudaeorum vocibus gravissima exacerbatur iniuria, ut prophetica voce cogeretur precari divinas insultantibus flammas: 'Haec domus,' inquit, 'caelesti incendio ardeat, ut in perpetuum reparari non possit, et lapis ipsius ruinae omnibus aedificiis, ubi fuerit, sempiternam praestet ruinam.'"

[22] *Acta Marcianae*, 5 (AASS, 1: 569): "Sed Budarius cum filiis suis et aliquantis Iudaeis, quos ad studium clamoris collegerat, in seditionem vociferantur, ut taurum iudex produci praeciperet."

[23] In several of these elements, Marciana replays the steps also found in the foundational female martyr narrative in the African tradition, that of Perpetua of Carthage, who had been martyred in 203.

[24] *Acta Marcianae*, 6 (AASS, 1: 569): "At ubi devotae virginis exivit spiritus a corpore, eo temporis puncto Budarii blasphemi domus, cum omnibus qui ibidem fuerant, divino arsit incendio. Nam etiam a Iudaeis frequenter domus eadem aedificari tentata est, et semper recidit in ruinam. Multi etiam qui ad structuram saxa collegerant, portare magis sibi visi sunt ad sepulturam. Manet usque hodie de illa domo aeterna martyris beatae sententia, et in aevum mansura perdurat."

The spirit of the devoted girl departed from her body, and at that very moment, the house of the blasphemous Budarius, with all of those who were in it, burned in a divine fire. And as often as the Jews attempted to rebuild the house [i.e. the synagogue], it always fell into ruins. The many persons who collected stones to rebuild it seemed instead to be collecting stones for their own burial. The remains of that house, even to the present day, represent the eternal judgment of the blessed martyr. And so it remains into the ages.

On reading this Christian martyr narrative, however, one must be cautioned that narratives that directly involve Jews in the persecution of Christians are exceedingly rare in African stories of this kind. This one, it is true, does catch some of the enmity that was present between the communities, notably in a coastal city in the late fourth and early fifth centuries when the Budarius episode was artificially inserted into the Marciana story. But it is almost unique in kind. This was not the core of the "Jewish menace" as far as Christians of the period were concerned. And it is unclear when this new element was added to her story. It clearly postdates the second stratum in the story that emphasizes her chastity and her role as a smasher of pagan idols. But by how much? The addition about the hostile Jews was probably made no earlier than the beginning of the fifth century, but perhaps even later.

THE ECONOMY OF GRACE

To the Christians who were much focussed on their own internecine hatreds, "the Jews" were, nevertheless, very important. They were explicitly recognized as central actors in the wars that rent the period. "There are still wars in the present age," Augustine notes, "wars between secular peoples over royal power; there are wars between sects; wars between Jews, pagans, Christians, and heretics; wars becoming more intense, some men fighting for the truth, others for lies."[25] By the late fourth century, there already existed a long and well-developed anti-Jewish literature that emerges, almost full-blown, in the Latin west with Tertullian's pamphlet *Against the Jews*.[26] In addition to the well-defined theological tract, one

---

[25] Aug. *En. in Ps.* 45.13 (CCL 38: 527): *"Auferens bella usque ad fines terrae.* Hoc nondum videmus esse completum: Sunt adhuc bella, sunt inter gentes pro regno; inter sectas; inter Iudaeos, paganos, christianos, haereticos, sunt bella; crebrescunt bella; aliis pro veritate, aliis pro falsitate certantibus"; the subheading comes from Aug. *En. in Ps.* 39.13 (CCL 38: 435): the economy to which the Jews are alien.

[26] I accept that this text is genuine and that it was composed mostly or wholly by Tertullian: see the recent analysis by Dunn, *Tertullian's Adversus Iudaeos*, pp. 6–26, 175–78; for the broader context, Aziza (1977) and Stroumsa (1996), esp. pp. 7–10 on the formal "Adversus Iudaeos" literature.

also finds poems, sermons, and other modes by which the same hostile ideas about Jews were delivered to believers. Writings about how and why the Jews and their practices were bad and had been decisively replaced by Christian ones were important to Christians because they were resources that could be exploited in diverse ways in the sectarian battles amongst themselves. For the purposes of understanding the violent acts by Christians against each other in the streets and fields, however, the narrower *Adversus Iudaeos* tradition is a misleading guide.[27]

The Latin tradition of the texts in Africa that began with Tertullian and continued through Cyprian and pseudo-Cyprian ended with the bishop Quodvultdeus of Carthage in the mid-fifth century. It was specifically concerned – as was John Chrysostom, a priest in Antioch, with his anti-Jewish tirades – with reinforcing Christian identity and with fixing commitments within the Christian community against potential "Judaizing" tendencies. Such tracts or pamphlets usually consisted of two parts. The first was concerned with a list of typical Jewish practices, institutions, and rituals – for example, the keeping of Shabbat, circumcision, or dietary regulations – that were not, and, from the perspective of the writer, should not be part of Christian practice, and the reasons why they were not. Ordinarily, the second part of such "Against the Jews" treatises sought to demonstrate the legitimacy of Christianity not as a mere continuation of its Jewish origins, but rather as a movement that had decisively superseded these false beginnings and which therefore had the right to appropriate the "old" Testament texts for its own new purpose. A catena of texts selected from the Hebrew Bible was arrayed to prove that the supersession had actually been predicted in detail in the Jewish texts themselves.

These theological texts and ones linked to them, like the poetic and pedagogical versions of a Commodian, continued to be produced in Late Antiquity, but they are of little direct relevance to the problem of sectarian violence. Put in different terms, views on the place of "the Jews" in Christian dialogues in this period are streamed into two different kinds of media. It is important to understand the distinction between the two modes of delivery to comprehend the specific function that images of "Jews" had in the sectarian struggles of the time. The division is a tactical one found

---

[27] The "Against the Jews" tracts have their own history – see Williams, *Adversus Iudaeos* and Schreckenberg, *Adversus-Judaeos-Texte* – which, in some ways, parallels the tracts on heresies, in which the late fourth-century function of these writings is different from the one that they had in the second and third century. In the earlier phase, the problem of "the Jews" is principally, indeed almost solely, one of various strands of Judaizing tendencies inside Christian communities. For the similar division of texts on heresy, see ch. 7, pp. 307–09.

in similar situations that involve ethnic, sectarian, or political violence. At one end of the spectrum is a dialogue about ideas and concepts that is conducted at an elevated theoretical level. At the other is the plainer and often cruder language, studded with rough images and caricatures, that is directed towards partisans at ground level. Such a division was evident, for example, in the Protestant and Catholic communications to their own followers during the European Reformation.[28] The same division is seen in the distinction between the street talk in Ballymurphy and the Falls Road in Belfast and the elevated political discourse of high-level Sinn Fein and British government officials.[29] The same was also true of the street-level argot of the Brown Shirts and other ex-Freikorpsmen in Munich in the early 1930s under the leadership of the gangsterish Ernst Röhm and the more diplomatic pronouncements of the high-level NSDAP political leaders who were seeking public office. Here, too, one finds the same consistent division of discourse.[30]

On the subject of "the Jews," there similarly existed Christian theological treatises in different forms – letters, pamphlets, booklets – that must be distinguished in their purpose from the images and messages consciously created for popular audiences. The latter were ordinarily disseminated in sermons, tracts, public debates, posters, verbal pronouncements, or other such modes, most of which were predominantly oral. One is therefore seeking to understand not the elevated discourse of the bishops, but the effects of a street-level understanding of dislike and hatred. It is one matter to understand the theological and historical dimensions of a treatise like Tertullian's *Against the Jews*, but quite another to understand the actual working out of hatreds in the neighborhoods of his own Carthage. He refers to a typical recent case in the city. A man whom he describes as "a deserter of his own faith" had become a circumcised Jew and was hiring out his services. He carried around the streets of Carthage a large picture on which was painted the image of a creature festooned with the long drooping ears of an ass, dressed in a toga, one of its feet with a cloven hoof.[31] The ass was holding a book, doubtless representing the Christian scriptures, in one hand. At the bottom of the placard was an inscription bearing the caption to the libellous cartoon:

---

[28] See, e.g., Scribner, "Printing, Prints and Propaganda," ch. 1 in *Popular Propaganda*, pp. 1–11.

[29] Moloney, *Secret History*, p. 61, also referring to the young Ian Paisley's oratory on the Protestant side.

[30] J. C. Fest, *The Face of the Third Reich: Portraits of the Nazi Leadership*, New York, 1970, pp. 144–45; and esp. R. Evans, *The Third Reich in Power*, Harmondsworth, Penguin, 2005, pp. 21–24.

[31] Since the *Apologeticum* and the *Ad Nationes* seem to date to the summer/fall of 197, the incident probably took place in 196 or early 197.

DEUS CHRISTIANORUM – ONOKOITES

[GOD OF THE CHRISTIANS – ASS FUCKER]

The common rabble, the *vulgus* of the city, says Tertullian, were much impressed with this piece of pop communication, believed "the Jew," and, thus educated, subsequently went around the city shouting at the Christians: ONOKOITAI!![32] If we are to believe Tertullian (or was this just another slander?) propagators of this sort of religious hate, with their mobile billboards and *libelli*, were available for hire.[33] In two literary apologies, Tertullian attempted to avert the slander and to explain its historical roots. But the damage, surely, was already done. So it is this type of communication in which popular images of despised enemies were formed that is our focus, rather than the elevated communications between bishops and their peers.

The same division in communication is also found among the participants in the sectarian disputes in late Roman Africa. The bishops, priests, and lay exegetes carried on an elevated type of discourse with each other in which they were concerned with validating the strategic position of Christianity in a new world order. They wished to propagate correct interpretations, admittedly sometimes of byzantine complexity, of particular theological points of view. It is therefore not surprising to find bishops like Augustine or Quodvultdeus deploying this higher-level discourse when they were embarking on theoretical forays that were intended to establish the legitimacy of their own Christian theodicy or practice against potential contenders. Nor is it surprising that Augustine first deploys this type of critical discourse during his anti-Manichaean phase in his polemical engagements with Manichaean adepts and missionaries. He continued to do so in other contexts in his correspondance with elite exegetes

---

[32] Tert. *Apol.* 16.12 (CCL 1: 116): "Sed nova iam Dei nostri in ista civitate proxime editio publicata est, ex quo quidam frustrandis bestiis mercenarius noxius picturam proposuit cum eiusmodi inscriptione: DEUS – CHRISTIANORUM – ONOKOITHΣ. Is erat auribus asininis, altero pede ungulatus, librum gestans et togatus. Risimus et nomen et formam."

Tert. *Ad Nat.* 1.14.1–2 (CCL 1: 32–33): "Nova iam de Deo nostro fama suggessit, et adeo nuper quidam perditissimus in ista civit<ate>, etiam suae religionis desertor, solo detrimento cutis Iudaeus, uti<que> magis post bestiarum morsus, ut ad quas se locando quot<idie> toto iam corpore decutit<ur> et <cir>cumcidit<ur>, pictura<m> in nos pro<posuit> sub ista proscriptione: ONOCOETES. Is erat auribus cant<herinis> in toga cum libro, altero pede ungulato. Et credidit vulg<us...> Iudaeo. Quod enim aliud genus seminariu<m> e<st> infamiae nostrae? <Inde> in tota civitate ONOCOETES praedicatur."

[33] Although I would not call this "propaganda," some of the same purpose was served; cf. Semelin, *Purify and Destroy*, p. 80: "It falls also to the role of propaganda to create a deleterious climate: it propagates the tone of violence via slogans and images," and noting the importance of these.

like Jerome and with senior bishops like Asellicus of Tusuros.[34] He also used the same tactic in a late treatise cast in the form of a sermon – his own *Adversus Iudaeos*. The aggressive title given to the tracts that represented the most refined version of this higher-level discourse, namely *Against the Jews*, should not mislead. These were types of communication that were least aimed at inciting ordinary hatreds and at disseminating images of dislike that would move ordinary parishioners to commit violent acts. Rather, they were part of an elevated discourse designed for one's peers, which is why they occur in epistolography and in formal theological treatises.

At this end of the spectrum, we find the same hesitation to use a frank and explicitly hostile rhetoric. In the writings constructed to answer dissident bishops and lay exegetes there is an avoidance of violent and crude language, largely because of the context of persuasion in which these replies were being made to high-ranking members of a parallel elite. Their language was conditioned by a voluntary censorship that effectively inhibited the use of the most violent images of the "against-the-Jews" discourse in direct discussions that the bishops and the highly educated on either side had with the other. In the letters, both private ones and the open ones explicitly intended to be part of a public readership, Jews rarely appear and then only in rather anodyne contexts.[35] The point is that "the Jews" were a very useful image deployed specifically in discourses that were most actively involved in the sectarian struggles with others precisely in terms of constructing a hostile attitude towards a "them," whether "they" were pagans, Donatists, or heretics. For other sorts of discourse, such as in contemplative introspections of the self, they hardly appear at all. The two references in Augustine's *Confessions*, for example, are brief, allusive, and hardly relevant to its main arguments.[36]

---

[34] See "Asellicus," PAC, p. 95: bishop of Tusuros (Tozeur) in Byzacena; Asellicus had written first to Donatianus, the primate of Byzacena; the primate then asked Augustine for assistance in forming an answer to Asellicus' concerns. Asellicus was troubled by the "Judaizing tendencies" of one Aptus, otherwise unknown, it seems. It seems unlikely that he is to be identified with the Aptus who was the dissident bishop of Tusuros.

[35] As compared to the sermons, for example, this discourse appears relatively rarely. See, e.g., Aug. *Contra Cresc.* 1.8.10 (CSEL 52: 332–33), where Augustine simply claims that even Jesus was able to discuss differences explicitly with his opponents, namely the Jews and Pharisees, without being castigated as an incendiary agitator or a deliberate provocateur; 1.34.40 (CSEL 52: 358): any reproof of Jews and heretics is for their own good; *Contra litt. Petil.* 2.98.226 (CSEL 52: 144).

[36] Aug. *Confess.* 5.11.21 (CCL 27: 69): a reference to certain men who wish surreptitiously to slip the "law of the Jews" into Christian scriptures; 12.17.24 (Moses); 13.23.33 (CCL 27: 261), which is not even Augustine, but him quoting Paul (Galatians 3: 28): "there will be neither male nor female, that there will be neither Jew nor Greek, nor slave nor free," and so on.

WHO IS NOT WITH ME IS AGAINST ME

For the question before us, the historian must therefore concentrate on the peculiar range of ideas and concepts that were being aired before ordinary people.[37] These images are primarily found in the world of the sermon in all of its variant forms. Here the connections and the parallels suggested by the leaders of the church in which they delineated the most threatening enemies of the Christian community were central to creating the atmosphere in which hostile acts in defense of its interests came to be seen as justified, natural, and necessary. The use of violence and coercive force by ordinary people in part depended on the conviction that one's enemies really were bad people, if not evil, and further (although one is on less compelling ground here) on an understanding of why this or that group deserved to be seen and treated as enemies. The more negative and hostile the images that could be aligned and interconnected, the more they contributed force to the conviction that using violence against such people was a good thing. This imaging, however, was a complex process, since the issuing of these messages assumed an interpretive screen in each listener by means of which he or she could decipher who the "they" actually were.

In his sermons, tractates on the Gospel of John, commentaries on the Psalms, and other comparable homiletic materials, Augustine consistently represents three groups as strongly linked in their hostility to the church and as enemies of the truth: pagans, heretics, and Jews. There is no doubt that the Jews fell into the general category of such hostile persons. They are frequently, and repeatedly, identified as enemies of God.[38] The cross-identification of Jews with dissident Christians is explicitly made in many sermons. In an early homily, after a series of extended remarks against "the Donatists," it is noted that, like them, the Jews (along with Arians and Manichees) will be condemned on the Day of the Final Judgment.[39] In such addresses to the people, the Jews are frequently designated as personal enemies: as "our enemies," "enemies of God," or "enemies of the truth."[40] Christ and the church had many hidden enemies, but the Jews

---

[37] See ch. 9 for the general argument; the quotation from Mtt. 12: 20 is frequently used to delineate the enemies of the people: Aug. *Sermo* 71.4 (PL 38: 446–47).

[38] See, e.g., Anon. *Sermo Liverani* 5 (PLS 2: 1289–90); Aug. *En. in Ps.* 75.1 (CCL 39: 1035); in all of this, however, I am not attempting to construct any consistent "attitude" held by Augustine himself that would count as "anti-Semitic," on which see Alvarez (1966), Bori (1983),

[39] Aug. *Sermo* 5.4 f. (CCL 51: 53–56).

[40] Simply enemies: Aug. *En. in Ps.* 40.14 (CCL 38: 459): "inimici nostri"; *En. in Ps.* 43.14 (CCL 38: 486): "Hodieque non desunt hostes Christi, illi ipsi Iudaei"; *En. 2 in Ps.* 58.2 (CCL 39: 746): "inimici"; *En. in Ps.* 67.2 (CCL 39: 870): "inimici . . . Iudaei . . . inimicitias exercuerunt"; *En. 1 in*

were especially notable for their open and undisguised hostility.[41] If the numbers of pagans had been diminishing and their ability to contradict or criticize Christians had been reduced to fearful things that they only dared utter in private, this was not true of the Jews. They conspicuously and openly rejected the fundamental Christian claim to be a transcendent historical movement that had surpassed and overcome the earlier false start of Jewish practice. Jews were often joined with heretics and pagans in a triad of the most dangerous enemies of the church.[42] All of them were "false brothers."[43] It is a cross-identification that is already found in Augustine's earliest writings because the equation was one that he had accepted and adopted from the existing discourses on the Jews.[44] "They are my enemy," Augustine emphasizes in directly addressing his congregation, "and they are your enemy."[45]

More ominously, these three groups were said to be joining forces to attack the unity of the church.[46] Jews were claimed to be active participants who assisted pagans against Christians and (by implication) aided the

---

Ps. 70.1 (CCL 39: 940): "inimici" (twice); *En. in Ps.* 75.1 (CCL 39: 1035): "solent inimici domini Iesu Christi omnibus noti Iudaei"; *En. in Ps.* 120.6 (CCL 40: 1791): "Non magnum est credere quia mortuus est Christus; hoc et pagani, et Iudaei, et omnes iniqui credunt . . . Si credideris quia mortuus est Christus, quod et pagani, et Iudaei, et omnes inimici eius crediderunt"; *Sermo* 113A.5 = Denis 24.5 (MiAg 1: 145).

[41] Aug. *Sermo* 308A.6 = Denis 11.6 (MiAg 1: 47): "Inimici Christi aperti, qui, nisi Iudaei? Habet enim occultos inimicos Christus."

[42] On the historical development of this triad of enemies, see especially Cracco-Ruggini (1980); for some of the references, see: Aug. *En. in Ps.* 50.1 (CCL 38: 599): "Neque enim loquimur de paganis, neque de Iudaeis, sed de Christianis"; *En. in Ps.* 52.4 (CCL 39: 640): "Hoc dicunt pagani qui remanserunt; hoc ipsum dicunt ipsi Iudaei, qui ad testimonium confusionis suae ubique diffusi sunt; hoc dicunt et haeretici multi"; *En. in Ps.* 73.16 and 25 (CCL 39: 1015 and 1022); *En. 2 in Ps.* 88.13 (CCL 39: 1242–43): "*Quod exprobraverunt inimici tui, domine,* et Iudaei et pagani"; *En. 1 in Ps.* 103.9 (CCL 40: 1481): "Alieni enim omnes a via veritatis, sive pagani, sive Iudaei, sive haeretici, et mali quique christiani"; *Sermo* 15.6 (CCL 41: 197): "Foris tolera haereticum, tolera Iudaeum, tolera paganum. Tolera et intus malum christianum, quia *inimici hominis domestici eius* [Matt. 10: 36]"; *Sermo* 34.6 (CCL 41: 426): "Laus enim non est in synagogis Iudaeorum, non est in insania paganorum, non est in erroribus haereticorum"; *Sermo* 64.1 (CCL 41Aa: 355): "Quotquot remanserunt pagani, quotquot remanserunt Iudaei, quotquot deviantes facti sunt haeretici, numquid non omnes odio nos habent propter nomen Christi?"; *Sermo* 71.6–10 (RBén 75:71–73): repeated no less than three times; *Sermo* 224 (RBén 79: 201): pagans, Jews and heretics compared to bad Catholics; *Sermo* 310.1.1 (PL 38: 1413): "sed plane per Africam totam regiones transmarinasque regiones, non Christianus solum, sed paganus, aut Iudaeus, aut etiam haereticus poterit inveniri"; *Sermo* 349.2 (PL 39: 1530): "et impiorum, id est paganorum, Iudaeorum, haereticorum."

[43] Aug. *En. in Ps.* 109.11 (CCL 40: 1610): "Dominare, dominare in medio paganorum, Iudaeorum, haereticorum, falsorum fratrum."

[44] Aug. *De vera relig.* 5.9 (CCL 32: 194); for development through his Manichaean period, see Fredriksen (1995).

[45] Aug. *Sermo* 56.14 (CCL 41Aa: 166): "*Sed inimicus meus paganus est, Iudaeus est, haereticus est* . . . inimicus tuus est paganus, Iudaeus, haereticus" (quoting Matt. 6: 10).

[46] Aug. *Sermo* 62.12.18 (CCL 41Aa: 312): "Sciatis autem, carissimi, murmura illorum coniungere se cum haereticis, cum Iudaeis. Haeretici, iudaei et pagani unitatem fecerunt contra unitatem."

cause of heretics.[47] By the time of Augustine's attacks on "the Donatists," it was explicitly understood that the unity of Jews with pagans and heretics also included "the schismatics" or the dissident Christians who were the principal object of his polemic.[48] Even more ominously, Jews had nothing to lose. They were utterly damned, permanently beyond the pale of forgiveness: by their actions and statements, they had blasphemed the Holy Spirit.[49] In this, they had committed a mortal sin that had been replicated by "the Donatists."[50] They were explicitly recognized as central actors in the sectarian conflicts that rent the period. In these hostilities, the enmity of the Jews is portrayed as so intense that they rage out of control in their attacks. They had been wild and savage in their attacks on Christ and they remained so against his followers. The "raging Jews," the *Iudaei saevientes*, is the typical and recurrent phrase that conjures up the dominant image of their hatred for Christ and his followers. "As he hung on the cross, the Jews raged madly... they raged wildly, barking around him like dogs, they insulted him as he hung on the cross, like crazed madmen they raged around that one good doctor who had been sent to heal them."[51] Even in the cooler media of historical reflection, the images are no less powerful. In the seventeenth book of the *City of God*, in glossing the words "poor" and "excrement" found in the biblical book of Samuel (1 Sam. 2: 7–8), Augustine says "that as 'excrement' we are permitted to understand the 'Jewish persecutors.'"[52] When preaching on this

---

[47] Aug. *De grat. et lib. arbit.* 20.41 (PL 44: 907), but, according to God's directive by which bad people help good things to happen; *Enchirid.* 26.101 (CCL 46: 103–04); *Ex. Rom. prop. exp.* 62.70 (CSEL 84: 43).

[48] Aug. *Ep. ad Cath. contra Donatist.* 19.49 (CSEL 52: 296), although it is a somewhat diluted linkage, joining pagans and heretics to Jews.

[49] Aug. *Sermo* 71.6, 14 (*RBén* 75: 71 and 79): "Manifestum est igitur et a paganis et a Iudaeis et ab hereticis, blasphemari spiritum sanctum . . . [reiterated at the end of the sermon]: Sed quia non potest 'omnis' intellegi, ne paganis, Iudaeis, haereticis, omnique hominum generi, qui diversis erroribus et contradictionibus suis blasphemant in spiritum sanctum, spes remissionis, si se correxerint, auferatur; restat utique ut in eo quod scriptum est *Qui blasphemaverit in spiritum sanctum, non habet remissionem in aeternum*, ille intelligatur qui non omni modo, sed eo modo blasphemaverit, ut ei numquam possit ignosci."

[50] Already claimed by Optatus in his *Contra Parm.* 7.4.9 (SC 413: 232); and then, later, by Augustine, *Contra Cresc.* 4.8.10 (CSEL 52: 511).

[51] Aug. *Sermo* 284.5–6 (PL 38: 1292): "Adducet Iudaeos, non iam adulantes, sed saevientes: vasa sua possidens clamabit linguis omnium 'Crucifige! Crucifige! . . . Pendebat in cruce', Iudaei saeviebant . . . Illi saeviebant, illi circumlatrabant, illi pendenti insultabant; quasi uno summo medico in medio constituto, phrenetici, circumquaque saeviebant."

[52] Aug. *Civ. Dei*, 17.4.6 (CCL 48: 559): "Inops quippe idem, qui pauper; stercus vero, unde erectus est, rectissime intelleguntur persecutores Iudaei, in quorum numero cum se dixisset apostolus ecclesiam persecutum."

theme, it has been aptly noted, he could be as hateful and vicious as any Chrysostom.[53]

The significance of the similarities of the three great enemies of the church is made manifest in so many of Augustine's sermons that the pattern formed by the repetition could not have been missed even by the dullest parishioner. Insofar as characteristics inherent to, and shared by, these groups could be attached to perceptions of "the Donatists," the latter would be condemned by sharing the same traits that convicted these other enemies of the church. Insofar as they were bad, or evil, and therefore deserving of condemnation and repression, it would be likely that dissident Christians who did not share the views of the orthodox Catholics would be equally deserving of the same treatment. It must be remembered that one of the core aims of the Catholics throughout this period, proclaimed both in local sermons and in the pronouncements of their great church councils, was to affect the policy of the central state of the empire. The goal was somehow to persuade the state to use its considerable power and resources against the dissidents in Africa: to get the state to treat their sectarian enemies as if they were enemies of the state. Following a retrenchment from the very aggressive interventionist responses at the beginning of his reign by Constantine, this proved to be a long and arduous struggle. Imperial authorities were generally loath to move decisively against the dissident Christians by using the instruments of secular force at their command. Both the state, and its agents and representatives in Africa, resisted becoming directly and aggressively involved in repressing the dissenters. By the last decade of the fourth century and the first decade of the fifth, however, these attitudes were changing. New policies were reflected in and implemented by the promulgation of legislation that mobilized imperial resources against the enemies of the orthodox church in Africa.

A constitution issued by the emperors Honorius and Theodosius to Donatus, the proconsular governor of Africa, in November of 408 is typical of this new legislative drive. In it Jews and heretics are linked with "Donatists."[54]

---

[53] Fredriksen (2001), p. 129, referring, rightly, to the work of Efroymson (1999): "On this topic . . . not the least in his sermons on John's Gospel – he can be as hateful, hurtful, and vicious as Chrysostom, Cyril, or any other father of the Church."

[54] CTh 16.5.44 (SC 497: 296; issued at Ravenna, 24 November 408); see Linder, *Imperial Legislation*, no. 37, pp. 239–41: "Donatistarum haereticorum Iudaeorum nova adque inusitata detexit audacia, quod Catholicae fidei velint sacramenta turbare. Quae pestis cave contagione latius emanet ac profluat. In eos igitur, qui aliquid, quod sit Catholicae sectae contrarium adversumque, temptaverint, supplicium iustae animadversionis expromi praecipimus."

Dat. viii kal. Dec. R(a)v(ennae), Basso et Philippo conss.

The new and unusually daring actions taken by the Donatists, the heretics, and the Jews have revealed that they wish to throw into disorder the sacraments of the Catholic faith. You must beware lest this disease should become entrenched and spread more widely by contagion. Against those persons who attempt to do anything that is contrary to and opposed to the Catholic sect, we order that punishments of a just measure must be executed.

Another constitution, issued a few months later, in January 409, by the same emperors to the Praetorian Prefect, Theodorus, makes clear this linkage.[55] The emperors express their almost helpless rage that previous imperial injunctions against the Church's enemies in Africa had not been enforced because of all kinds of "winking" and collusion by local authorities. Suitably harsh measures are decreed to compel the reluctant to act. The decree ends by making it clear that the dissident Christians in Africa are to be counted among the mortal enemies of the true church.

The Donatists and the vanity of the other heretics and those others who are not able to be persuaded to the worship of the Catholic communion, that is the Jews and those gentiles who are commonly called pagans, should not suppose that the provisions of the laws previously issued against them have diminished in force. And let all judges know that the commands of these laws must be obeyed with faithful devotion, and that among their chief concerns must be the execution of whatever measures we have decreed against such persons.

The emperors then go on a rant against local judges and judicial authorities who had connived at seeing that the imperial laws against these groups were not implemented. From this point forward, the emperors warn, the failure of such men to enforce the law will subject them to harsh penalties. What must be recognized, however, is that these laws are only the end point of a lengthy struggle that involved intensive lobbying and the education of the court at Ravenna, a program that had assumed renewed and concerted force from the mid-390s onwards. That the emperors knew precisely how to cast the condemnation of the enemies of the Catholic church in Africa

---

[55] *Const. Sirmond.* 14 (SC 531: 522–31, at 528; issued at Ravenna, 15 January 409) preserves the complete text, which is unusual and permits us to see better the nature of the linkages; see Linder, *Imperial Legislation*, no. 38, pp. 241–55: "Et ne Donatistae vel ceterorum vanitas haereticorum aliorumque eorum, quibus Catholicae communionis cultus non potest persuaderi, Iudaei adque gentiles, quos vulgo paganos appellant, arbitrentur legum ante adversum se datarum constituta tepuisse, noverint iudices universi praeceptis earum fideli devotione parendum et inter praecipua curarum, quidquid adversus eos decrevimus, exequendum."

   On its other manifestations in the codes, see the two fragments in CTh 16.2.31 and 15.6.46; the former was also copied into CJ 1.3.10. There are problems with the dating; see Linder for why the date attached to CTh 16.5.46 is to be preferred to the one attached to the Sirmondian Constitutions (412 CE).

as one that linked them with heretics and Jews is the result of the emperors being told repeatedly that this was the way that they should view the situation.

Because the process of imperial law-making was so responsive in nature, it sometimes seems, as in this case, to be reduced almost to parroting the terms that were demanded of it by the Catholics in Africa. In drafting legislation that sought to regulate the behavior of undesirable religious groups, the court was dependent on the Catholic church to define and to name them. The result was that it tended to repeat the identification of the enemies of the church and their names. On occasion, the legislators express their perplexity at the naming process in the very laws that they were issuing. Such was the case with a group labeled the "Sky (or, Heaven) Worshipers," the *Caelicolae*, who seem from context to be Judaeo-Christians of some kind.[56] More significant here than their precise religious complexion is the fact that they were an African sect who first emerged into public awareness at the end of the fourth century.[57] More important yet is the fact that, other than the emperors, Augustine of Hippo is the only person known to have had any dealings with the Sky Worshipers in Africa. It was at Thubursicu Numidarum that he had tried, without success, to confront the chief votary of the sect, the *maior Caelicolarum*.[58] It is manifest that local knowledge of the sect preceded their "recognition" by the imperial authorities, since we know that Augustine was jousting with the Caelicolarians in the years just before 400. In an imperial decree issued from Ravenna a decade later, on 1 April 409, the emperors Honorius and Theodosius threatened such persons with the severe punishments reserved for heretics if they did not return to true Christian practices within the year.[59]

---

[56] Simon (1978), with reference to Torhoudt (1954), shows, rather persuasively, a long background of syncretistic strands linking the Punic Ba'al and Tinnith Pene Ba'al with Saturn and Caelestis and Saturn, and that pair of celestial deities, in turn, for these "Judaizing" Christians, with Yahweh. They also seem, to my mind, to bear a rather close relationship to the cult of the Theos Hypsistos, which displays very similar characteristics and which also had strong connections between Jews and Christians: see Mitchell (1999), esp. pp. 110–21.

[57] Simon (1978), pp. 509–10; cf. Torhoudt (1954).

[58] Aug. *Ep.* 44.6.13 (CCL 31: 195): "Iam enim miseramus ad Maiorem Caelicolarum quem audieramus novi apud eos baptismi institutorem instituse et multos illo sacrilegio seduxisse, ut cum illo, quantum ipsius temporis patiebantur angustiae, aliquid loqueremur." It is important to note, first, that the letter is part of a pair addressed to "Donatists," and, second, that it probably dates to a year in the late 390s (396 or 397, most probably the former) well before the imperial legislation that mentions the Caelicolae.

[59] CTh 16.8.19 (issued at Ravenna, 1 April 409); see Linder, *Imperial Legislation*, no. 39, pp. 256–62: "Caelicolarum nomen inauditum quodammodo novum crimen superstitionis vindicabit. Ii nisi intra anni terminos ad dei cultum venerationemque Christianam conversi fuerint, his legibus, quibus praecepimus haereticos adstringi, se quoque noverint adtinendos. Certum est enim, quidquid a fide

But the perplexed emperors did not have any idea of who the Sky Worshipers actually were. At the beginning of their decree, they express their sense of consternation over the sudden appearance of yet another bizarre heretical group: "A new crime of superstition has, by some fashion, acquired the previously unheard of name of Caelicolarians." So it is manifest that Honorius and Theodosius did not by themselves initiate such identifications or labels in the process of naming the enemies of the church. Rather, they were dependent on interested parties who brought such enemy IDs to them (including that of the Sky Worshipers) indicating who they were and what sort of repressive legislation was needed.[60] The same communications channels to Italy that connected "the Donatists" with heretics are in evidence here, since the same persons were also feeding information on the Caelicolae to Filastrius of Brescia.[61] These links ran vertically from a small coterie of bishops who were conversant with such matters in the region of Thubursicu Numidarum – that is, Augustine, Alypius, and others – via Carthage to Milan, and then from that communications hub to Brescia. The laws of 408 and 409 in which Jews appear were part of

Christianorum discrepat, legi Christianae esse contrarium. Quam quidam adhuc, vitae suae etiam et iuris inmemores, adtrectare ita audent, ut de Christianis quosdam foedum cogant taetrumque Iudaeorum nomen induere."

    Parts of this law are repeated in CJ 1.9.12. Why Linder translates this term as "God Fearers" escapes me, unless this is linked to some of Simon's arguments; see (1978), p. 574.

[60] They are also mentioned in CTh 16.5.43 = full text in Sirmond. 12 (issued at Rome 15 November 407 to Curtius, the PP, posted in the forum at Carthage by the order of the proconsul Porphyrius, 5 June 408). a law that reasserts the force of earlier decrees that Honorius and Theodosius had issued against Donatists, Manichaeans, Priscillianists and pagans. "Thus the buildings of the aforesaid persons and those of the Caelicolists also, who hold assemblies of some unknown new dogma, shall be vindicated to the [Catholic] churches." Although the law mentions Priscillianists, Maximianists and pagans, it ends by mentioning only Donatists and Catholics or "those who shun the communion of the Catholics under the pretext of a perverse religion, although they pretend that they are Christians." This order was strengthened by another, a year later (CTh 6.8.19 = CJ 1.9.12 + 1.12.2), issued at Ravenna on 1 April 409, to Jovius PP, specifically directed against the Caelicolists alone, in which they are still referred to a "a name hitherto unheard of"; they are branded as a heresy whose members are ordered to return to Christian worship within one year. They are a sect who "compel certain Christians to assume the detestable and offensive name of the Jews." The emperors are stern in the rebuke that they are not going to permit "persons instructed in the Christian mysteries to be forced to adopt a perversity that is Jewish and alien to the Roman empire, after they have adopted Christianity." For "it would be more grievous than death and crueller than murder if any person of the Christian faith should be polluted by Jewish disbelief." The charge for anyone found guilty is that of high treason.

[61] Filastrius Brixiensis, *Diversarum hereseon liber*, 15.1 (CCL 9: 222): "Alia est heresis in Iudaeis, quae Reginam, quam et Fortunam Caeli nuncupant, quam et Caelestem vocant in Africa, eique sacrificia offerre non dubitant, ut etiam prophetae Hieremiae Iudaei tunc dicerent ex aperto, cum moneret eos recedere ab idolis et servire domino, solumque eum adorare eos debere: irati exclamant, dicentes, ex quo illi, inquit, Fortunae Caeli sive Reginae non sacrificant, ex eo cuncta illis mala et pericula contigisse"; cf. Simon (1978), pp. 510–11: he calls them a Jewish sect who adored "the Queen named 'Fortuna of the Sky' who is called 'Caelestis' in Africa."

this same response network. The imperial legislation, specifically aimed at Africa, therefore reveals the prior workings of an African Catholic lobby in the court at Ravenna. The connections ran back through bishop Aurelius at Carthage to the influential coterie of Catholic bishops in Numidia of whom Augustine was the leading member. The target of these specific laws was not so much Jews or heretics against whom there was already a considerable body of repressive legislation, or indeed the Caelicolae, a small odd new sect of Judaizers who happened to be thrown in for good measure.[62] Rather, the need was to join these ideological malefactors to a third culpable party, the dissident Christians in Africa who, in the fashion of these others, were labeled as a small and odd new sect with a name derived from their own heresiarch: "the Donatists."

This linkage of heretics, pagans, and Jews as the three enemies of the established church assumed a fixed geometry of hatred that was repeated more than a century after the social context in which it had originally arisen had fundamentally changed. In a law issued at Constantinople on 1 August 535, in response to a request from the Council of Carthage held earlier in the same year under Reparatus, bishop of Carthage, the emperor Justinian met the request for a harsher repression of the Arian Christians who had held sway in Africa during the previous period of Vandal domination. Again, the matter had primarily to do with the possession of basilicas and church properties. Justinian issued the edict to Salomon the praetorian prefect of Africa.[63] The law called for the restoration of all churches and church properties to the orthodox church without delay and, if necessary, by the use of force deployed by the state. In some of its parts the law legislates against Jews alone, and sometimes against heretics alone, but in several places the normal triad of enemies reappears.[64]

---

[62] For imperial legislation on the Jews, see Linder, *Imperial Legislation* and his more specific essay (1985). Most of the approximately thirty imperial *constitutiones* concerning Jews that survive between Constantine and the laws of 408/09 are repressive in some degree, especially those beginning with Valentinian and Theodosius (his nos. 14–35).

[63] Justinian, *Nov.* 37 (1 Aug. 535); Linder, *Imperial Legislation*, no. 62, pp. 381–89.

[64] Justinian, *Nov.* 37: "Curae autem erit tuae sublimitati, quatenus neque Arianis neque Donatistis nec Iudaeis nec aliis qui orthodoxam religionem minime colere noscuntur aliqua detur communio penitus ad ecclesiasticos ritus, sed omnimodo excludantur a sacris et templis nefandi, et nulla eis licentia concedatur penitus ordinare vel episcopos vel clericos aut baptizare quascumque personas et ad suum furorem trahere, quia huiusmodi sectae non solum a nobis, sed etiam ab anterioribus legibus condemnatae sunt et a sceleratissimis nec non inquinatis coluntur hominibus. Omnes autem haereticos secundum leges nostras quas imposuimus publicis actibus amoveri et nihil penitus publicum gerere concedantur haeretici nec aliquam administrationem quibuslibet subire ambitionibus, ne videantur haeretici constituti orthodoxis imperare, cum sufficit eis vivere . . . Rebaptizatos autem militiam quidem habere nullo modo concedimus . . . Neque enim Iudaeos neque paganos neque Donatistas neque Arianos neque alios quoscumque haereticos vel speluncas habere et quaedam quasi

It shall be the responsibility of Your Sublimity to see that Arians, Donatists, Jews, and others who can barely be said to practice orthodox religion, will have no communion at all with worship in the church. These unspeakably evil persons shall be wholly excluded from sacred rites and places of worship, and no permission at all shall be given to them to ordain bishops or clerics, or to baptize any persons, or to draw these people into their madness, since sects of this type have been condemned not only by us, but by previous laws, and their worshipers are the most evil and polluted of persons. Therefore, according to the laws which we have placed in the public records, all heretics shall be removed [from public office]; heretics shall not be permitted to manage any government office at all or to undertake any administrative duty simply because they wish to do so, lest heretics seem to have been legally appointed to rule over the orthodox, when it is enough for them that they are permitted to live . . . and we do not allow in any way that the rebaptized shall have any public office . . . We do not allow the Jews, the pagans, the Donatists, the Arians, nor any other heretics to have their own caves [i.e. places of worship], nor are they to be allowed to celebrate any rituals whatever as if they were genuine acts of worship of the church, for it is perfectly absurd that such impious men should conduct sacred ceremonials.

The significance that anti-Jewish rhetoric had for intra-Christian violence is important, not only for the role that it played in the politics of the imperial court as part of the lobbying efforts that urged emperors to issue decrees favorable to the orthodox cause in Africa, but also for the longer and deeper history that it already had for conflicts amongst Christians in Africa. The role that the Jews played for Catholics in mobilizing opinion, in forming and fixing attitudes towards "the Donatists," or for the dissidents in configuring negative images of the Catholics, is what was always at stake in the long-term struggle between the two Christian communities. Most important here were the sermons of a large number of bishops and priests who systematically educated their parishioners. It is no accident that in the one great coherent corpus of writings that survives for this period the "against the Jews" rhetoric is overwhelmingly concentrated in sermons and sermon-like materials.[65] It is important to note that Augustine's one

---

ritu ecclesiastico facere patimur, cum hominibus impiis sacra peragenda permittere satis absurdum est."

[65] In Augustine, Jews are mentioned surprisingly infrequently in some categories (only twice and in neutral terms in the *Confessions*, for example), forming a contrast with the emphasis given to them in the sermons. Apart from the obvious locus of biblical exegesis and commentary, the majority of the specific references to Jews/Judaea, etc., are in the sermons and letters: *Enarr. in Psalm.*, N = 628; *Tract. in Ioh.*, N = 490; *Sermones*, N = 735; *Adversus Iudaeos*, N = 12; *Epistulae*, N = 192 (I include the letters as an analogous form of communication). Of course, there are specific treatises, such as the *Contra Faustum* (N = 239), that purposefully contain more of such material. For our purposes, it is important to note how little of this external "labeling" material appears, comparatively, in the specific polemical treatises that the dissidents and the Catholics directed against each other. Since

work specifically devoted to the subject, his own *Against the Jews* (*Adversus Iudaeos*), is of late date, written in the last year or two of his life.[66] In fundamental ways, it is a rather un-Augustinian production, bearing the same hallmarks of artificiality as his *Book of Heresies* of the same time.[67] It is not generically characteristic of the communications against Jews that he had developed and conveyed to his parishioners over the rest of his life. In that lifetime, the sermon, in its various forms, was the main vehicle for propagating these hostile views. It therefore makes sense that his *Adversus Iudaeos* was cast more in the form of a sermon than in that of a theological treatise; the sermon was, after all, the form in which he had habitually worked with this theme over his entire life as a bishop.[68]

Unlike the elaborate theological treatises of the *Adversus Iudaeos* tradition, the weekly sermons put before large numbers of ordinary people, in a common language, simple rhetoric, and with a remorseless repetitiveness, certain basic ideas about "the Jews." These could then be used, by implication, to label "the Donatists" as a similar type: an evil people deserving of coercive repression and, if necessary, punishment by the state. If the fact was accepted as manifest by parishioners that the Jews were evil, even dangerous, because of basic characteristics that they exhibited, it would then be easier to condemn other people who shared similar characteristics. By analogy, it might be suggested, or even stated outright that "the Donatists" were not really Christians at all but rather, like the Jews, mortal enemies of the true church. The anti-Jewish rhetoric that could be deployed by sectarians was already well developed by the fourth century. Any Christian preacher, whether an Ambrose in his imperial seat at Milan or a Chrysostom in his priestly one at Antioch, could reiterate or improvise on the themes present in hundreds of existing sermons and treatises on the subject.[69] The preacher could modulate the power of the message by

---

the interest is specifically polemical, such references are, comparatively speaking, almost entirely absent from all of his early work up to the point in the mid-390s when he begins to engage with "the Donatists." Since Fredriksen's analysis (1995) is concentrated on this early period, it cannot shed much light on the specific history and problem with which I am concerned here.

[66] Zarb's contention that since this work is not specifically mentioned in the *Retractationes*, it must postdate it and must be assigned to either 428 or 429 still seems a good argument. Blumenkranz, *Die Judenpredigt*, p. 207, however, did point out that if the work was considered to be a sermon, then it might not have appeared in any of the works that Augustine reconsidered. The most that he is willing to venture is that, since the arguments seem a much more complexing working out of themes in the eighteenth book of the *De Civitate Dei*, it must postdate 425.

[67] Augustine, *Adversus Iudaeos* (Bazant-Hegemark (1969), pp. 24–63).

[68] Blumenkranz, *Die Judenpredigt*, comes down on the side of the work as a large sermon that later received separate "packaging" as a book; see also Bori (1983).

[69] For Chrysostom, see Wilken, "Chrysostom's Rhetoric and the Judaizers," in *John Chrysostom and the Jews*, pp. 116–27

depressing or ratcheting-up the violence of the rhetoric as the situation demanded. As the Mediterranean-wide distribution of the "against the Jews" rhetoric reveals, the existing body of anti-Jewish sources contained themes that Christians of all kinds could exploit for their own purposes.

A central theme of the conflict in Africa that was much debated by both sides, but which was an absolute issue for the dissidents, was that of betrayal. To be one of those who betrayed one's faith in the Great Persecution, to be a traitor or *traditor*, was one of the worst possible sins – one that irrevocably stained and polluted the sinner and his successors. It is not surprising, then, that the figure of Judas is drawn on time and again. But he does not stand in isolation as a symbolic figure: the fact that he was Jewish is constantly in the background of references to him. Judas is already seen as a member of a fifth column of the Jews within the circle of the disciples. If the rest of the disciples were Christians, Judas is taken as a typological representative of the Jewish people as a whole. In glossing the words of Psalm 109: 5 [108]: "they pay me back evil for kindness and hatred for friendship," the Christian preacher remarks:

> If we understand the evil in this passage to apply to every person, then it does not make much sense; but if we understand this type of evil men to be the ungrateful enemies of Christ, the Jews, then everything becomes clear . . . and in the same way, Judas in general represents the Jews, those enemies of Christ, who at that time hated Christ and now in the present day, through the succession of generations, continue to hate.[70]

It was one of the most powerful mobilizing images in the whole corpus of biblical literature.

THE ECONOMY OF GRACE?

It is difficult to know how this rhetoric specifically affected the Jews who lived in Africa in Augustine's time. Certainly there were some hostilities. There is an allusion to what might have involved a violent confrontation. "See in what great honor the Christian people are now held and in what disrespect the Jewish people are held. Not long ago, when by chance they dared to oppose the Christians, you heard what then happened to them." The incident of daring was probably local, involving the Jewish community of Hippo Regius, and the concluding comment seems both ominous and

---

[70] Aug. *En. in Ps.* 108.1 (CCL 40: 1585), and through the whole sermon to § 18, where he speaks of the Jews as persons who remain pernicious in their hatred of Christ; just as Judas is a figure for the whole people of the Jews, so Peter figures the Church.

menacing.[71] In another sermon that combines Jews, heretics, and pagans as the main groups opposed to the universal unity of the church, Augustine remarks: "because it so happens that the Jews have been disciplined in some places for their misbehavior, they accuse us, suspect, or pretend that we are always getting them treated like that."[72] Such statements hint at the use of force.

The negative images, after they had been thoroughly inculcated in both sides, naturally entered everyday talk. The preacher appealed to the experiences of his parishioners with Jews in Hippo Regius. "Plenty of curses are uttered in these terms, aren't they? 'May you be crucified like him.' Even today there is no lack of enemies against whom we have to stand up to for Christ, including the Jews themselves, who daily say to us: 'May you die in the same way that he did.'"[73] A potential atmosphere of hostility therefore, and Christian preaching must have fueled some of it. Following a discourse on how "lost and seditious Jews" murdered Christ, Augustine explains to his parishioners, "and you still see to this day that the Jews refuse to believe in Christ."[74] This rejection, in the face of the manifest proofs of the church's success over the centuries after Christ's death, was both galling and exasperating. That the Jews "even to the present day ignore the just order of God and wish to establish their own, even in our time, a time of open grace, a present time of a grace made manifest that was previously hidden, in our own day, in a land of manifest grace," was almost too much to understand.[75]

Jewish responses to Christian challenges were taken to confirm an inveterate hatred, and guilt: "Ask a pagan whether Christ was crucified and he exclaims, "Certainly." Ask him whether Christ has risen from the dead (that which distinguishes us from the pagan). He denies it. Ask a Jew whether Christ was crucified. He confesses the crime of his ancestors. He confesses the crime in which he himself has a share."[76] Certainly those occasions when the preacher employed the present tense to accuse the

---

[71] Aug. *Sermo* 5.5 (CCL 51: 53–56): "Videte enim cum quanta dignitate sit populus Christianus, et in quanta defectione sit populus Iudaeorum. Quando forte ausi sunt vel modicum movere se contra Christianos, quae illis contigerint audistis in recenti tempore." The incident, it is true, could have taken place elsewhere, for example at Carthage, and news of it come to Hippo, but it seems that Augustine is addressing his parishioners on something that was of direct knowledge to them in very recent times.

[72] Aug. *Sermo* 62.12.18 (CCL 41Aa: 312).

[73] Aug. *En. in Ps.* 43.14 (CCL 38: 486): adding in what follows: "therefore, brothers, the Jews today are not persuaded to believe in Him . . ."

[74] Aug. *Sermo* 113A.2 = Denis 24.2 (MiAg 1: 143).

[75] Aug. *Sermo* 131.9.9 (PL 38: 733); cf. Anon. *Sermo Caillau-St. Yves* 1.31: 1 (PLS 2: 965), the same from a dissident preacher.

[76] Aug. *Sermo* 234.3 (PL 38: 1116).

Jews – "You Jews *are* the murderers of Christ" – could hardly be construed by the congregation as referring to anything but those Jews living around them.[77] The connection between past and present is always implicit in general statements about Jews in the sermons, but sometimes it is made explicit. In a sermon that begins by outlining the status of the Jews as evil persons and enemies of Christ, Augustine continues: "in this way Judas upholds the general character of the Jews, the enemies of Christ, who at that time hated Christ, whom, because of the obstinate continuity of their impiety, they continue to hate in our own day."[78] So it is no surprise that Jews in Africa continued to name their children Judas, while not a single Christian case is known.[79] It was the primal fact that "the Jews hate us" that was the living force governing these imagined relationships.[80]

But relationships with actual Jews in different communities in Africa do not seem to betoken any special hatred sufficient to incite acts of violence. In a riot that took place in the Christian community at Oea in Tripolitania around the year 402 – an uproar provoked by the reading of Jerome's new translation of the Bible – local Jewish experts were consulted to acquire an idea of what the "correct" translation should be.[81] This sort of distant yet connected relationship seems to have been the norm. That is to say, Jews stood outside Christian conflicts, in this case even being appealed to as unbiased adjudicators of an internal Christian dispute. There might well have been verbal jibes and other unpleasantries exchanged between Christians and Jews in the community of Hippo Regius, but a striking piece of evidence concerning daily relations between them, at least at leadership level, suggests that day-to-day relations were perhaps determined by other, more mundane factors.[82] It is a letter addressed by Augustine to his "brother" Victor, apparently a fellow bishop. The exchange was provoked

---

[77] And not just in sermons; see *Civ. Dei*, 20.30 (CCL 48: 756): "Sed sicut dicimus Iudaeis: 'Vos occidistis Christum,' quamvis hoc parentes eorum fecerint; sic et isti se dolebunt fecisse quodam modo, quod fecerunt illi, ex quorum stirpe descendunt."

[78] Aug. *En. in Ps.* 108.1 (CCL 40: 1585); *En. 9 in Ps.* 118.2 (CCL 40: 1690) for the same sentiments: "et eius a Iudaeis irrisam crucem totamque humilitatis christianae medicinam, qua sola tumor ille sanatur quo inflati cecidimus et iacentes amplius intumuimus, eadem superbia permanente et crescente contemnere?"

[79] Le Bohec (1981a), pp. 166–67.

[80] Aug. *Sermo* 313G.2 = Morin 2.2 (MiAg 1: 594): "Quicumque sunt reprobi Iudaei... ipsi oderunt nos" (along, needless to say, with pagans and heretics)

[81] Aug. *Ep.* 71.3.5 (CSEL 34.2: 253) on Jonah 4.6: "Factus est tumultus in plebe maxime Graecis arguentibus et inflammantibus calumniam falsitatis, ut cogeretur episcopus – Oea quippe civitas erat – Iudaeorum testimonium flagitare. Utrum autem illi inperitia an malitia hoc esse in Hebraeis codicibus responderunt, quod et Graeci et Latini habebant atque dicebant?"

[82] Aug. *Ep.* *8 (CSEL 88: 41–42).

by a complaint lodged with Augustine by a Jew named Licinius. Victor had somehow involved himself in a scam whereby he purchased several plots of land from Licinius' elderly mother-in-law.[83] The problem is that these were pieces of land that Licinius had already purchased from his mother-in-law. They included a piece of land that she had given to him with her daughter when Licinius married her.[84] Victor was asserting his rights of ownership to these properties and rejecting the Jew Licinius' counter-claims. Victor's rude riposte was that if Licinius' mother had sold them illegally, then Licinius should take *her* to court.[85]

Far from assuming a prejudicial view of Licinius' complaints, Augustine wrote a brusque letter of warning to his Christian brother Victor, a letter that was both a paean to the efficacy and correct standards of the Roman law and a demand that Victor make appropriate restitution. Augustine condemned Victor for his ignorance of the law and remarked further that the whole affair was hateful and contrary to the morals expected of a Christian. He ordered Victor to restore the property to its legal owner and to recoup the money that he had paid for it from the elderly woman, quoting the apostle Paul to the effect that a Christian should "give no offence to the Jews or to the Greeks or to the Church of God." The tenor of the letter suggests that there was nothing unusual about the dealings between Licinius and Victor.

Theological or moral statements about Jews in general, however, were quite another matter. It is sometimes claimed that Augustine had some good things to say about Jews. He did. But these probative evaluations appear to be unalloyedly good only if they are torn from context. Restored to context, the apparent approbation only functions because the Jews are so bad to begin with. In one exemplary case, Augustine exhorts his parishioners not to participate in the pagan celebration of the great New Year's festivities that were about to take place in Hippo in the first week of January. "The

---

[83] Madec (1981) denies that Victor was a fellow bishop, but Rougé (1983), 177–83, makes a reasonably compelling argument for the high rank; that Jews and Christians normally involved themselves in such business dealings is not surprising. Compare the case of the two nuns and a Jewish man involved in the leasing of an *exedra* and a cellar at Oxyrhynchus: *POxy.* 62.3203 (June/July 400: the lessee a Jewish man named Aurelius Josê, son of Judas).

[84] Aug. *Ep.* *8.1.1–2 (CSEL 88: 41): "ea quae apud me Iudaeus Licinius deploravit, si verum est, multum me contristant. Provabit quidem mihi per tabulas quas ferebat emisse se nescio quos agellos ab eis quibus mater eius vendiderat et aliquam partem in uxorem suam, quando eam duxit, donatione conlatam."

[85] Aug. *Ep.* *8.1.3–4 (CSEL 88: 41): "quod sanctitas tua ab eadem anicula matre eius omnia emerit et eum qui optimo iure possidebat excluserit et, cum tibi quereretur de te ipso, responderis ei: 'Ego emi; <si> male mihi vendidit mater tua, cum ipsa litiga! A me noli aliquid quaerere, quia nihil tibi dabo.'"

First of January is coming soon. You are all Christians. By God's grace our city is Christian. There are just two (i.e. non-pagan) peoples in it: Christians and Jews ... and do the Jews do this (i.e., participate in these pagan ceremonials)? Let that at least shame you into refraining."[86] The example that Augustine uses to shame his Christians, however, reposes on the understood proposition that if the Jews, of all people, could reject these celebrations, then what about the Christians who were, after all, so much better? It is therefore understandable that Augustine could rail against pagans and Jews, but then say that bad Christians are worse than these other enemies of the church.[87] The Jews served as a useful benchmark of badness. Then again, there is the question of why Jews are evoked at all on this occasion. Part of the reason is their latent identification with pagans and heretics. The shenanigans at the First of January celebrations provoked another tirade against Jews and pagans; the one group was much the same as the other. If the boisterous and joyous celebration of the New Year caused bile to rise in the bishop's gorge, it also provoked a general identification of the enemies of the church who were so enjoying themselves: "The anger of God is rightly directed against the Jews, as it is also against the pagans and the Donatists."[88]

Although much of the rhetoric is directed against a model of "the Jews" taken from biblical texts, it is clear in a sufficient number of instances that the condemnation of the whole people applies to the Jews of Augustine's own day and for the same basic reason: their obstinate rejection of the truth. Such anti-Jewish words could become rather colorful, especially amidst the heightened emotions of the Easter season: "the Israelites, taken captive by the Devil, accomplished their evil deed ... and so still their descendants, belching out the leaven of their ancestors in futile indigestion, go around preening themselves in their arrogant pride."[89] The Jews were so dangerous as enemies, not just because of some personal *refuse de croire*, but also because behind them stood the Devil and his angels. They had been possessed by the demons. Indeed, according to another comestible metaphor, they had actually been devoured by the evil spirits.[90] Jews and

[86] Aug. *Sermo* 196.4.4 (PL 38: 1020–21).
[87] Aug. *En. 2 in Ps.* 30.2 (CCL 38: 203); *En. in Ps.* 50.1 (CCL 38: 599); *De cat. rud.* 7.11 and 27.55 (CCL 46: 131 and 177): note that here it is initiants who are being taught who are the enemies of the church; *De fid. rer. quod non vid.* 8.11 (CCL 46: 19).
[88] Aug. *Sermo* 197.1 (PL 38: 1021; cf. *RBén* 84: 256): "Recte revelatur ira Dei super Iudaeos." This leads to a discussion of pride and arrogance (*superbia*) as a characteristic of all those involved in the First of January celebrations.
[89] Aug. *Sermo* 229C.1 (PLS 2: 723–24); see Nirenberg, *Communities of Violence*, pp. 200–01, for the same seasonal rhythm of sectarian rhetoric in mediaeval Spain.
[90] Aug. *En. 2 in Ps.* 29.11 (CCL 38: 182); Aug. *En. in Ps.* 46.2 (CCL 38: 530).

pagans were enemies of Christ. Jews might be hostile to pagans, but both groups belonged to the Kingdom of Satan.[91] At their best, they were a people saved from extermination by the grace of God, who had allowed them to survive, albeit homeless and wandering about the world, as an example of what Christians should not be.[92] They continued to carry around their holy books, not for themselves, however, but as living proof that Christianity was right and they did so as slaves trudging behind their Christian masters.[93] Again, the imagery of slavery is not accidental or limited to the picture of Jews as servile porters of Christian scriptures. Christ had come as a redeemer, that is as a liberator of slaves, as an emancipator who paid the price of freedom of the enslaved. It was the core Christian metaphor of salvation. The Jews had foolishly chosen, almost beyond belief, to remain slaves, condemned to the lowest ranks of the social order.[94]

CHRIST KILLERS

The core damning characteristic shared by all Jews was that they had murdered God.[95] It is around this pivotal defining act that most of their

---

[91] Aug. *Sermo* 71.4 (*RBén* 75: 68): "Paganus hostis Christi et Iudaeus hostis Christi; divisi sunt adversum se, et ambo ad regnum pertinent diaboli" (and note): "donatista et maximianista ambo haeretici, et adversum se ambo divisi; omnia vitia erroresque mortalium inter se contrarii divisi sunt adversum se: et omnes ad regnum pertinent diaboli."

[92] Aug. *En. in Ps.* 65.4 (CCL 39: 842): "nolite imitare Iudaeos."

[93] Aug. *En. in Ps.* 40.14 (CCL 38: 459): "modo, fratres, nobis serviunt Iudaei, tamquam capsarii nostri sunt, studentibus nobis codices portant"; *En. in Ps.* 56.9 (CCL 39: 699–700): "Proferimus codices ab inimicis, ut confundamus alios inimicos . . . Librarii nostri facti sunt, quomodo solent servi post dominos codices ferre, ut illi portando deficiant, illi legendo proficiant. In tale opprobrium dati sunt Iudaei."

[94] Aug. *Sermo* 5.5 (CCL 41: 55): "Ecce Iudaeus servus est Christiani"; ibid. 5.5 (CCL 41: 56): "Et sparsi per orbem terrarum, facti sunt quasi custodes librorum nostrorum. Quomodo servi, quando eunt in auditorium domini ipsorum, portant post illos codices et foris sedent."

[95] The fact is reiterated so often that it would be useless to compile all of the references; the frequency, as well as the context, of the reiteration of this basic fact is important to note; see, e.g., *Sermo* 10.2 (CCL 41: 153–55); 60A.2 = Mai 26 (PLS 2: 472–75; MiAg 1: 320–24); *En. in Ps.* 59.10 (CCL 39: 762); *En. in Ps.* 72.2 (CCL 39: 987); *En. in Ps.* 73.5 (CCL 39: 1009); *En. in Ps.* 100.9 (CCL 39: 1414); *En. in Ps.* 131.17 (CCL 40: 1919); *En. in Ps.* 138.8 (CCL 40: 1996); *En. in Ps.* 139.18 (CCL 40: 2025); *En. in Ps.* 140.26 (CCL 40: 2045); *Sermo* 45.5 (CCL 41: 519); *Sermo* 152.10 (CCL 42 Ba: 44); *Sermo* 272B.3 = Mai 158.3 (MiAg 1: 382): killed the lamb; *Sermo* 304.3.3 (PL 38: 1396): "usque ad irrisionem populi Iudaeorum, usque ad sputa et vincula, usque ad alapas et flagella, si parum est, usque ad mortem"; *Sermo* 313B.4 = Denis 15.4 (MiAg 1: 74): "Iudaei Christi interfectores"; *Sermo* 375B.7 = Denis 5.7 (MiAg 1: 29): "unigenitus autem Dei Christus multo magis totus extingui non potuit, cum eum se Iudaei extinguere putaverunt"; *Sermo* 375C.4 =Mai 95.4 (MiAg 1: 344): "Viderunt et Iudaei, qui occiderunt"; *Tract. in Ioh.* 47.13 (CCL 36: 412). The idea also appears, of course, in treatises: *Quaest. In Hept.* 2.79 (CCL 33: 110), also on the role of Judas; *Civ. Dei*, 3.15 (CCL 47: 78): "cum Dominus crucifixus est crudelitate atque impietate Iudaeorum"; 5.18 (CCL 47: 154): "Unde etiam, Iudaei qui Christum occiderunt." For an evaluation of these types of statements in the context of the long run of Christian discourse on the subject, see Cohen, *Christ Killers*, chs. 3–4.

other evil characteristics such as blindness, obstinacy, and pride, revolve. The theme is hammered home again and again: "the Jews hated him and committed such an unspeakable crime by killing an innocent, the holiest of the holy."[96] It was shared by both Catholic and dissident preachers.[97] The Jews were moved to contempt at the mere sight of Christ.[98] The evil was described in general anti-Donatist sermons, but reached an annually repeated ceremonial and ritual-like crescendo in the Easter season of each year.[99] The retelling of the events was expected to evoke an emotional response from the listeners. "How can you bear it," agonizes the preacher, as he comments on his congregation's response to the picture of the Jews insulting Christ on the cross.[100] It is not far from saying that it constituted one of the core defining characteristics of sermons preached with a particular intensity during what was for Christians the holiest of all the seasons of the year.

It is not the Jews' murder of Christ repeated as a bare or simple fact of "history" that is so important, but rather the language in which the charge was conveyed to the listeners. A few words from a scriptural text, like those of the sixty-third Psalm, are exemplary: "They sharpened their tongues like swords," prompts a series of comments that guide the listener's attention.[101] "Another Psalm makes the same accusation: 'The teeth of human beings are weapons and arrows, their tongue a sharp sword,' and so here too . . . the Jews have no right to say: 'We did not put Christ to death' since in fact they handed him over to a judge for no other purpose than to make it *appear* as if they were not guilty of killing him. In fact, you did kill him, you Jews. What weapons did they employ? The sword of the tongue, for you sharpened your tongues; and when did you strike him? When you shouted: 'CRUCIFIGE! CRUCIFIGE! CRUCIFY HIM! CRUCIFY HIM!'"[102] The whole sermon continues in this vein, quoting passage after passage from the Psalm and linking each one to the guilt of the Jews for the murder of Christ.[103] The

---

[96] Aug. *Sermo* 4.28 (CCL 41: 41): "inviderunt Iudaei et fecerunt tantum scelus occidendo innocentem, sanctum sanctorum."

[97] For just some examples, see Anon. *Sermo Caillau-St. Yves* 1.28: 1 (PLS 2: 957); 1.29: 1 (PLS 2: 959); 1.32: 4 (PLS 2: 968); 2.85: 1 (PLS 2: 1097–98), and not the present tense in describing them as killers; *Sermo Mai* 189: 1 (PLS 2: 1283).

[98] Aug. *En. in Ps.* 46.9 (CCL 38: 534): "Nam et Christum Iudaei visum contemserunt."

[99] Consider, e.g., the run of sermons at Aug. *Sermo* 218–229 and *Tract. in 1 Ioh.* 1–10.

[100] Aug. *En. in Ps.* 63.17 (CCL 39: 819).   [101] Aug. *En. 1 in Ps.* 68.4 (CCL 39: 904–05).

[102] He rejects the judicial form as nothing more than an attempt by the Jews to exculpate themselves and blame the Roman authorities: see also *En. in Ps.* 56.12 (CCL 39: 702).

[103] Aug. *En. in Ps.* 63.4–8 (CCL 39: 810–12); the idea that the Jews deliberately tried to distance themselves from responsibility for the murder by handing Christ over to the Roman governor is frequently repeated: *Sermo* 223 C (PLS 2: 552–54) offers one of the more detailed expositions.

repetition of the rhythmic shout "CRUCIFIGE! CRUCIFIGE!" occurs frequently in the sermon, no doubt with the intended effect.[104] Such polemical rhetoric reached a crescendo of vitriolic hatred in the Easter sermons where the combinations of words, of nouns and adjectives, seem to have been purposefully selected for their powerful effect. "The godless wickedness of the Jews, observed through their own cruel eyes... they swarmed together in savage violence," the preacher notes in a pounding sermon that uses Jews as a foil for heretics.[105] Or in words that were surely intended as a triumphalist in-your-face aggressive taunt: "But look! Christ our Lord rose again on the third day. Where now is the jeering of the Jews? Where now is the derision of their leaders? Where now is their growling and prowling around? Where now the murdering of their own healer?"[106] So the considerable number of times that Augustine has occasion to repeat the words: "Crucify him, Crucify him," from the gospel of John (19:6) gave him, as a preacher, an opportunity to replay the fervor of the shouting crowds of Jews for his own audience.[107]

There are also the visual images of the Jews that are evoked in the listeners' minds. The serial playing through of the events as if in real time in which the Jews "were powerful enough to treat him with contempt, to arrest him, to bind him, to insult him, to strike him, to spit on him. How far did their power prevail? Up to his death..."[108] Moved by the spirit, says Augustine, this prophet [John] "saw the Lord humiliated, beaten, whipped, punched on the head, slapped by their hands, dirtied with spit, crowned with thorns, and suspended on the cross; saw them raging, him enduring..."[109] These condemnations of Jews were particularly vivid, almost an ekphrasis of the crucifixion itself. "I am speaking of those Jews who crucified the Lord, who attacked him with their hands dripping with blood... whose tongues were made ready like swords: their teeth were weapons and arrows, and their tongue a sharp sword."[110] The same

---

[104] "Crucify!": Aug. *En. in Psalm.* 17.48 (CCL 38: 101).   [105] Aug. *Sermo* 218B.1 (PLS 2: 543).

[106] Aug. *Sermo* 229E.1 (PLS 2: 558–59).

[107] See, e.g., *En. in Ps.* 17.48 (CCL 38: 101): he calls on this cry nearly 200 times (192); apart from the technical discussion in the *de consensu Evangelium*, almost all of the references are in the sermons.

[108] Aug. *En. in Ps.* 68.3 and 6 (CCL 39: 903 and 907): "Praevaluerunt ad contemnendum, ad tenendum, ad ligandum, ad insultandum, ad colophizandum, ad conspuendum. Adhuc quousque? Usque ad mortem..."; *En in Ps.* 56.13 (CCL 39: 703): "Vidit Dominum in spiritu iste propheta humilatum, caesum, flagellatum, colaphis percussum, expalmatum manibus, sputis illitum, spinis coronatum, ligno suspensum; illos saevientes, illum tolerantem"; cf. *En. in Ps.* 38.18 (CCL 38: 419).

[109] Aug. *En. in Ps.* 56.13 (CCL 39: 703); cf. *En. in Ps.* 93.8 (CCL 39: 1309) for another extended description.

[110] Aug. *Sermo* 229G.5 = Guelferb. 11.5 (MiAg 1: 477).

elements are replayed in other sermons, showing that the details were parts of a trope on the way that the crucifixion was conveyed to listeners in the congregation: "How superior the Jews seemed to themselves as they kept on beating the Lord about the head, when they were spitting into his face, when they were savagely beating his head with a rod, when they crowned it with thorns, when they wrapped him in a disgusting cloth. How 'superior' they were then!"[111] "There they stand, opening their mouths wide like a ravenous roaring lion. Listen to them roaring in the evangelist: 'Crucify him! Crucify him!'"[112]

The phrase "mouth wide like a ravenous roaring lion" was well known to parishioners. It was a standard image used to describe Satan.[113] So, accordingly, the leaders of the Jews were lions, and their followers lion cubs.[114] In another sermon, the Jews "gaze savagely at the crucified Christ."[115] Individual incidents of the crucifixion are then glossed allegorically to refer to matters of broader historical significance. So the vinegar given to Christ on the cross is wine gone sour.[116] This is made to refer to the Jews who are represented as a soured and degraded version of the patriarchs and prophets. The image is then used of heretical Christians who are degraded forms of the true blood or wine of the church.[117] Given the normal codes of honorable behavior governing their social relations, the images that are conveyed in the sermons (spitting in the face, and so on) would assuredly rouse emotions of bitterness, distaste, anger, and hatred in the listeners. The fact that the Jews are constantly portrayed as *laughing* at the sight of the crucified Christ was surely one that would provoke rage.[118] So too, the fact that the Jews repeatedly *insulted* the deity, and engaged in making shameful and insulting remarks – *convicia* – at his expense, were, by the canons of that age, such dishonoring actions that they were bound to

---

[111] Aug. *En. 2 in Ps.* 33.10 (CCL 38: 289); *En. in Ps.* 56.13 (CCL 39: 703); cf. *En. 1 in Ps.* 68.3 (CCL 39: 903) for another case.

[112] Aug. *En. 2 in Ps.* 21.8 (CCL 38: 125); see also *En. in Ps.* 40.12 (CCL 38: 457); *En. in Ps.* 95.5 (CCL 39: 1346–47) where the images of the roaring lion is again drawn upon to describe the Jews in the crucifixion scene.

[113] Poque, *Langage symbolique*, pp. 9, 15–18.   [114] Aug. *En. in Ps.* 56.10 (CCL 39: 700–01).

[115] Aug. *En. 2 in Ps.* 33.10 (CCL 38: 289): "crucifixus Christus inter Iudaeos erat saevientes et videntes."

[116] Aug. *Tract. in Ioh.* 119.4 (CCL 36: 659–60); cf. *En. in Ps.* 61.9 (CCL 39: 780) and *Sermo* 218.11 (PL 38: 1086–87).

[117] Aug. *En. in Ps.* 8.2 (CCL 38: 50).

[118] The verb *ridere* and its cognates are regularly used: Anon. *Sermo Morin*, App. 9: 5 (PLS 2: 1356); *Sermo Caillau-St. Yves* 1.33: 2 (PLS 2: 970) and 1.40:2 (PLS 2: 992), all from dissident preachers; Aug. *En. 1 in Ps.* 103.3 (CCL 40: 1475); *En. in Ps.* 46.2 (CCL 38: 530); *En. in Ps.* 49.5 (CCL 38: 578–79): "they were happy when they saw him crucified and had contempt for him"; *En. 3 in Ps.* 103.25 (CCL 40: 1520).

raise sentiments of outrage against the perpetrators.[119] Such remarks were calculated to humiliate.[120]

It is the deliberation and planning, the intention behind the act that is repeatedly emphasized: "this is what the Jews did to him. They laid their foul trap . . . they set up their rat-trap."[121] It is they who planned the arrest, carried it out, and deliberately insulted God.[122] The Jews were the ones who vilely formed a purposeful conspiracy to commit the murder.[123] They deliberately planned the killing.[124] The Jews are "men of blood" who "murdered a just man" in whom there was no fault, men of blood who screamed out "Crucify him! Crucify him!" and then cried out "let his blood be on us and our sons."[125] The refrain "His blood be upon us and our children," is repeated in sermon after sermon as a way of explaining the present condemned status of the Jews.[126] "Men of blood," Augustine repeats in a cadence that hammers home the image of the Jews as bloody murderers. Because this murder was a conscious and absolute rejection of God, the Jews are naturally characterized as mad or deranged for doing it, like, Augustine says, insane patients who injure or kill the doctors who come to heal them.[127] It was the same fundamental lack of reason of an act in which people who are ill attack their own healer; hence, the frequent

---

[119] Aug. *En. in Ps.* 35.17 (CCL 38: 334); "convicia": *En. in Ps.* 62.20 (CCL 39: 807): "insultaverunt"; *Sermo* 8.18 (CCL 41: 98): "obicientes domino convicium Iudaei"; *Sermo* 78.6.10 (PL 38: 487): "ex eo veluti convicio humilitatem ostendit"; *Sermo* 171.2.2 (PL 38: 934) for an earlier use of *convicia*.

[120] Aug. *En. 1 in Ps.* 48.11 (CCL 38: 559–60) is typical: "Quomodo Iudaei viderunt Christum pendentem in cruce, et contemserunt, dicentes: Iste si filius Dei esset, descenderet de cruce"; *Sermo* 88.8 (*RBén* 94: 82): "quod cum magna insultatione persecutores Iudaei domino procurarunt . . . Et cum ei pendenti Iudaeorum caecitas insultaret" (in a sermon on "the two blind men"); *Sermo* 285.2 (PL 38: 1294): "Iudaei contempserunt miracula facientem."

[121] Aug. *En. 1 in Ps.* 34.10 (CCL 38: 306).

[122] Aug. *En. in Ps.* 35.17 (CCL 38: 334), leading, logically, to the role of Judas.

[123] Aug. *En. in Ps.* 63.3 (CCL 39: 809): "Nostis qui conventus erat malignantium Iudaeorum, et quae multitudo erat operantium iniquitatem. Quam iniquitatem? Qua voluerunt occidere Dominum Iesum Christum."

[124] Aug. *Tract. in Ioh.* 49.28 (CCL 36: 433); *En. in Ps.* 81.4 (CCL 39: 1138); *En. 9 in Ps.* 118.3 (CCL 40: 1691): "invenies sedisse principes Iudaeorum, consilium quaerentes quomodo Christum perderent"; *En. in Ps.* 40.1 (CCL 38: 448), in a long sermon on the subject, carefully lays out the deliberation involved; *En. in Ps.* 61.22 (CCL 39: 790–91).

[125] Aug. *En 1 in Ps.* 58.5 (CCL 39: 732): "Erant illi quidem viri sanguinum, qui iustum occiderunt, in quo nullam culpam invenerunt; erant illi viri sanguinum, quia cum vellet alienigena lotis manibus dimittere Christum, clamaverunt: 'Crucifige, crucifige'; erant viri sanguinum, quibus cum iam obiceretur crimen sanguinis Christi, responderunt, propinantes posteris suis: Sanguis eius super nos, et super filios nostros."

[126] Aug. *En. 1 in Ps.* 58.5; 108.20 (CCL 39: 732; 40: 1596); *Sermo* 220F.22 (MiAg 1: 471), 234.3 (PL 38: 1116), and repeatedly elsewhere.

[127] Aug. *En. in Ps.* 77.9 (CCL 39: 1074); again, more vividly, at *En. in Ps.* 96.2 (CCL 39: 1354): "phrenetici saevientes in medicum, et salutem insania repellentes."

references to the insanity, the savage and uncontrolled rage, and the sickness of those who committed it.[128]

THE ORIGINAL PERSECUTORS

The Jews were not just pictured as the murderers of Christ. They killed the deity and the first of his followers, so they were also the *fons et origo* of persecution itself. As the killers of the first martyr, murderers of the man who stood at the head of the long tradition of martyrdom to which the African church was heir – the protomartyr Stephen – they began the whole process of the systematic attack on Christians.[129] Here the same characteristics of savagery, madness, and insanity are the driving forces.[130] In descriptions of the killing of Stephen by stoning, it is again emphasized that the Jews did this because of an essential characteristic of obstinacy and blindness: they refused to see or to hear the truth that Stephen was bringing to them. Blindness is one of the core characteristics that African preachers constantly reiterate as inherently Jewish.[131] The same applies to the fact that the Jews refused, in the face of centuries of evidence against them, to budge from their rejection of Christ. Their obstinacy and hardness of heart or *duritia* is itself an almost inexplicable trait of near-madness.[132] This hardness is represented in their physiological trait of being "stiff-necked" – *dura cervice*.[133]

These characteristics opened the way to the exploiting of the suitable animal images. In a typical, and long, anti-Donatist sermon, the Jews are arraigned as murderers of the first martyr precisely because they

[128] Aug. *Sermo* 223I (MiAg 1: 717): "Hic ille inimicus est, qui adversus dominum nostrum Iesum Christum insanos Iudaeos velut propria vasa et arma commovit"; *Sermo* 229E.1 = Guelferb. 9.1 (MiAg 1: 467): "ubi est insultatio Iudaeorum? Ubi est insultatio circumfrementium et insanientium principum Iudaeorum, et medicum occidentium?"

[129] Aug. *Sermo* 116.6 (PL 38: 660): "insaniant Iudaei, impleantur zelo, lapidetur Stephanus."

[130] Anon. *Sermo Caillau-St. Yves*, append. 1.57 (PLS 2: 1357 = Leclercq [1947], 121): a dissident preacher; 1.36:4 (PLS 2: 981); 1.37:2 (PLS 2: 983); Aug. *Sermo* 278.1.1 (PL 38: 1268–69): "et illius furoris atque insaniae qua pertrahebat Christianos ad necem, qui minister erat furoris Iudaeorum, sive in lapidatione sancti martyris Stephani, sive in ceteris exhibendis et adducendis ad poenam."

[131] Aug. *En. in Ps.* 9.1 (CCL 38: 58); *En. in Ps.* 46.3 (CCL 38: 530–31); *En. in Ps.* 55.9 (CCL 39: 685); *En. 2 in Ps.* 58.2 (CCL 39: 746); *En. in Ps.* 65.5 (CCL 39: 842); *En. 2 in Ps.* 68.10 (CCL 39: 924); *En. in Ps.* 81.6 (CCL 39: 1139): "perversi et caeci principes Iudaeorum"; *En. in Ps.* 109.11 (CCL 40: 1611); *En. in Ps.* 138.8 (CCL 40: 1996): "et excaecati crucifixerunt dominum" (linked to their pride); *Sermo* 165.5.5 (PL 38: 905): "gentes illuminantur, Iudaei excaecantur"; *Sermo* 200.2.3 (PL 38: 1029): "magnum testimonium caecitatis exstitit Iudaeorum."

[132] Aug. *En. in Ps.* 102.11 (CCL 40: 1462): "significans duritia Iudaeorum"; *Sermo* 229I.4 = Mai 86.4 (MiAg 1: 326): "pro duritia cordis sui"; *Civ. Dei*, 14.9 (CCL 48: 427).

[133] Aug. *Sermo* 7.6 (CCL 41: 75): quoting Acts 7: 51 again and again; *Sermo* 49.10 (CCL 41: 622); *Sermo* 90.9 (PL 38: 565); *Sermo* 317.4.5 (PL 38: 1437).

refused to see the light that Stephen was attempting to bring to their dark minds: "beyond these blind poisonous serpents, more obdurate than any stones... their rage was like the rage of a poisonous viper."[134] The murder of Stephen enables the preacher to link the murder of Christ with a general pattern in which the Jews are configured as arch-persecutors of the church precisely because they persecute those trying to bring them a message of truth. The Jews, imitating Saul, persecuted the true David. They were the models of the proto-persecutors.[135] It is a main theme that is repeatedly emphasized: the Jews are especially persecutors of the church since they sought the death of Christ and hounded his students.[136] "We especially understand this of the Jews, who sought to extinguish the life of Christ, because they crucified that very head of ours and because they then persecuted his disciples."[137] After their persecution of Christ's students came that of Paul, who was at the very head of the "modern" church.[138]

Because they stubbornly insisted on their false beliefs, the Jews were also the world's first heretics. And that is why the Church had rightly repudiated them. A visual image frequently deployed to depict heretical Christian groups – the limb snapped off the tree of life – is also used to describe them. The Jews, too, are a branch broken off the true tree of the church.[139] The reason for the break is pride which leads, necessarily, to blasphemy.[140] The animal imagery that was typically deployed in the case of heretics is also used here, since the Jews have allied themselves with Satan, as his servants or slaves, or his demons, or both.[141] The image of the snake conjures up associations with the Devil.[142] So Augustine several times has recourse to John the Baptist's statement castigating the Jews as

---

[134] Aug. *En. in Ps.* 57.8 (CCL 39: 715), repeating the last phrase twice.

[135] Aug. *En. in Ps.* 56.3 (CCL 39: 695).

[136] Aug. *En. in Ps.* 62.18 (CCL 39: 806): "Quotquot persecuti sunt, vel persequi cupiunt ecclesiam, potest de his hoc intellegi; maxime hoc tamen accipiamus de Iudaeis, qui quaesierunt animam Christi perdere, et in ipso capite nostro quod crucifixerunt, et in discipulis suis quos postea persecuti sunt." Aug. *En. in Ps.* 78.2 (CCL 39: 1098–99), after Christ's resurrection the Jews still reject him and then begin killing the martyrs as well.

[137] Aug. *En. in Ps.* 62.18 (CCL 39: 806).   [138] Aug. *En. in Ps.* 35.8 (CCL 38: 327).

[139] Aug. *En. in Ps.* 45.6 (CCL 38: 522); *En. in Ps.* 134.7 (CCL 40: 1943): "proud" branches broken off the tree; cf. Aug. *Sermo* 89.1 (PL 38: 554).

[140] Aug. *En. in Ps.* 134.7 (CCL 40: 1943): "et inde superbi rami fracti sunt; ipse est blasphemus et impius populus Iudaeorum."

[141] Aug. *De cat. rud.* 25.48 (CCL 46: 171): Jews as servants of Satan, in the sense that they try to tempt Christians away from the true faith; *De Gen. ad litt.* 11.11 (CSEL 28.1: 343): but as part of a triad: "Quis enim paganus, quis Iudaeus, quis haereticus non hoc in domo sua cotidie probet?" On other occasions, redemption was considered as possible: Aug. *Ep. Rom. incoh. exp.* 22 (CSEL 84: 177–78).

[142] Poque, *Langage symbolique*, pp. 11–15.

"You brood of vipers." In this case, however, he carefully explains that this does not mean that Abraham was such a viper, for it was by their subsequent evil ways that the Jews had became allied with the demonic forces that opposed Christ. But as for vipers, he is ready to gloss them in greater detail for the listener: John "called them a brood of vipers, not of men, to be sure, but of vipers. He saw the shape of human beings, but he recognized the inner poison."[143] The same sermon identifies Jews and pagans as common enemies of the true church. Although the Jews and the pagans thought that they would be able to exterminate the Christians, the church had flourished and now held the whip hand. No one nowadays, the preacher says, rather menacingly, dares to say a word against Christ in public.[144]

The rejection of the truth by the Jews was founded on an arch sin, that of pride.[145] This pride was not just an ordinary pride; it was implanted by Satan, it was a diabolical pride.[146] This pride created arrogance. More than that, it created an assumed right to aggressive behavior, to act with irrational and ignorant force against another. The images of Jewish savagery and pride are often merged.[147] "Do not let the proud Jew be your model," Augustine warns, meaning: do not be one of those who reject the manifest truth because of some mulish certainty that your view is correct.[148] All of this is patently a parallel to an anti-Donatist rhetoric in which their separation from the true Church was also attributed to obstinacy, blindness, and arrogance, but above all to their pride.[149] Few parishioners would have failed to grasp, even if half-consciously, the suggested lesson. Moreover, prideful persistence in error suggested why coercion was needed to compel

---

[143] Aug. *Tract. in Ioh.* 42.5 (CCL 36: 367); pride: cf. Aug. *En. in Ps.* 16.9 (CCL 38: 93).

[144] Aug. *En. in Ps.* 62.20 (CCL 39: 807): "Quanta iniqua locuti sunt Iudaei? Quanta mala dixerunt, non solum Iudaei, sed et omnes qui propter idola christianos persecuti sunt? Quando saeviebant in christianos, putabant quod possent finire christianos; cum putabant quod possent finire, christiani creverunt, et ipsi finiti sunt... Nemo audet modo publice loqui contra Christum; iam omnes timent Christum."

[145] Pride is a core sin of the Jews that is reiterated so often that a list is superfluous, but see, e.g., *En. in Ps.* 46.11 (CCL 38: 535); *En. in Ps.* 65.12 (CCL 39: 848); *En. in Ps.* 74.12 (CCL 39: 1033); *En. in Ps.* 106.13 (CCL 40: 1578): "superbis, scilicet primo populo Iudaeorum, arroganti et extollenti se de genere Abrahae"; *Sermo* 175.1 (PL 38: 945); *Sermo* 77.7.11 (PL 38: 487–88).

[146] Aug. *En. in Ps.* 81.6 (CCL 39: 1139): "Per diabolicam quippe superbiam factum est" (i.e., the crucifixion, through the power of the Devil).

[147] Aug. *En. in Ps.* 56.9 (CCL 39: 699): "Saevierunt Iudaei in Christum, superbierunt in Christum."

[148] Aug. *Sermo* 163.11 (Partoens 2003: 283): "ne tibi similis sit superbus Judaeus."

[149] Optatus, *Contra Parm.* 7.1.3 (SC 413: 194): it was their *superbia* that caused the dissidents to separate; cf. Lamirande (1965h) for an outline of the constant anti-Donatist rhetoric centered on their pride and arrogance.

change from inveterate ways.[150] Just so, it was Donatus' pride, his willful *superbia* and desire to turn himself into the *princeps* of Carthage, Prince of Tyre, Donatus of Carthage, and the first of all bishops, that was at the origin of "the Donatists'" creation of their little separatist *Umwelt*.[151] The Jews' obstinate refusal caused them willfully to separate themselves from Church and God, a rejection that led them, in the end, to commit violent acts, including murder.[152] It was this linkage between obdurate independence, the potential to violence, and the penchant to wrong belief that the Catholics were to attach to "the Donatists" at the conference at Carthage in 411 that was supposed finally to resolve their differences. And it was with specific reference to Jews.[153]

Rejection of the truth also implicated the Jews in mendacity. Since they had consistently to uphold one great untruth, they were compelled to invent other untruths to mask the greater one.[154] That they were a "people of the lie" is developed in another anti-Donatist sermon, again vividly describing the crucifixion of Christ, but then expatiating on attempts by the Jews to spread lies in the aftermath of the resurrection: "They prefer this lie to the true message."[155] The nets of mendacity which they wove were the result of their rejection of the truth.[156] They are a people who deliberately propagate a lie because the truth would condemn their entire existence.[157] They are "outside." They just do not wish to hear the truth.

---

[150] Aug. *En. in Ps.* 28.6 (CCL 38: 170): "sicut filius Iudaeorum ignorantium iustitiam Dei et superbe iactantium tamquam singularem iustitiam suam." Horowitz, "Selective Targeting," in *Deadly Ethnic Riot*, pp. 124–50, on the targeting of those who are "too proud" or "too big for their britches."

[151] Optatus, *Contra Parm.* 3.3.9 –3.13 (SC 413: 26–28) is a particularly vivid portrait of Donatus' pride, combined with his blindness.

[152] Aug. *En. 2 in Ps.* 58.7 (CCL 39: 751): "Non tantum Iudaeorum dominabitur, sed et finium terrae; quod non scirent, si adhuc in superbia sua essent; in superbia autem sua essent . . . quia comprehensi fuerunt in superbia sua, ex maledicto quod fecerunt, quando Christum occiderunt . . . Mortuus est [i.e. Christus] inter manus Iudaeorum."

[153] GCC, 1.18 (SC 195: 604–06) in the terms of the final Catholic reply to Marcellinus before the inception of the conference. The "calumniae Iudaeorum" and "the Jews who deny Christ" are used as models for the "Donatists" throughout.

[154] At length in *En. in Ps.* 65.8–10 (CCL 39: 846–47).

[155] Aug. *En. 1 in Ps.* 58.3 (CCL 39: 731): "Hoc est vere Christum velle interficere, nomen resurrectionis eius exstinguere, ut mendacium evangelio praeferretur"; *En. in Ps.* 134.22 (CCL 40: 1954): "separando . . . apostolos a Iudaeis mendacibus"; *Civ. Dei*, 15.13 (CCL 48: 470): "Sed cum hoc dixero, continuo referetur illud Iudaeorum esse mendacium."

[156] Lies, often linked, critically, to the false charges lodged against Jesus: e.g., Aug. *En. in Ps.* 71.7 (CCL 39: 976): "occidit per calumnias Iudaeorum"; *En. in Ps.* 134.22 (CCL 40: 1954): "a Iudaeis mendacibus"; *Sermo* 4.11 (CCL 41: 28): mentium Iudaeorum; *Sermo* 293.4 (PL 38: 1329–30): "calumniantes Iudaei domino"; *Serm* 293D.2 = Guelferb. 22.2 (MiAg 1: 511): "Inimici eius . . . denique Iudaei de discipulis Iohannis insultabant discipulis Christi, et calumniabantur."

[157] Aug. *En. in Ps.* 134.22 (CCL 40: 1953): "Ipsa est domus Iacob, quae est domus Israel; qui enim Iacob, ipse est Israel . . . domus Iacob et domus Israel, una gens, una plebs; hanc invitat, et

"They hate the very good news itself. When He was alive they procured false evidence against the Lord in order get him condemned, and after his death they spent money to buy other evidence against him."[158] The passage in this sermon is then followed by an imaginary conversation between a Christian and a Jew in which Augustine construes the latter, along with the Donatists, as typical enemies of the church. The parallel discourses that linked the two as enemies of the church were so close as not to be missed. As repeated statements by their Catholic opponents show, "the Donatists" were regarded as equally guilty of the big lie: propagating false statements, inventing counterfeit documents, and supporting claims that had been proven to be mistaken or invented, or both.

Pride entailed not only rejection, but also innate characteristics of ignorance and stupidity: "just like a son of the Jews, ignorant of the justice of God and proudly boasting about their own unique 'justice'."[159] To persist in this kind of illogical contrarian thinking and behavior was itself a sign of madness or insanity. The conscious decision of the Jews to reject Christ and his message made them the world's first schismatics and heretics: they had deliberately separated themselves from the one true church, the one true message. "That was the first beginning of schism: when among the original Jewish people some proud men separated themselves who wished to make their sacrifices 'outside' [i.e. the true faith]."[160] In the precise sense of a renegade religious group that had willfully set up "one altar against another," the Jews were direct precursors of "the Donatists." By their rebellion, the Jews had become degenerate and had separated themselves from the true root of Abraham.[161] The perhaps bizarre conclusion to which this train of thinking led was that the real Jews or the true Jews were the Christians and the church of Christ, whereas the breakaway Jews, the heretical

---

hanc dimittit. Et nunc iam certe occidisti Christum, o domus Iacob; nam occidisti Christum, iam caput ante crucem agitasti, iam pendentem irrisisti, iam dixisti . . . ", amongst many such references.

[158] Aug. *Sermo* 129.3.3–4 (PL 38: 721–22): "Relinquamus ergo paululum Iudaeos, quibus Dominus tunc loquebatur. Foris sunt, audire nos nolunt. Ipsum evangelium oderunt, falsa testimonia in Dominum procuraverunt, ut damnarent vivum; alia testimonia emerunt pecunia contra mortuum." The sermon leads, by way of the Antichrist, to the subject of the Donatists (129.7.8 = PL 38: 724); fairly closely connected is *En. 2 in Ps.* 58.7 (CCL 39: 751): "in superbia autem sua essent, si adhuc sibi iusti viderentur . . . quia comprehensi fuerunt in superbia sua, ex maledicto quod fecerunt, quando Christum occiderunt."

[159] Anon. *Sermo Caillau-St. Yves* 2.44:3–4 (PLS 2: 1064); Aug. *En. in Ps.* 28.6 (CCL 38: 170).

[160] Aug. *En. in Ps.* 54.16 (CCL 39: 668): "Quomodo replicavit et recolere nos fecit primum illlud schismatis initium, quando in illo primo populo Iudaeorum quidam superbi se separaverunt, et extra sacrificare voluerunt"; cf. *En. in Ps.* 65.5 (CCL 39: 843) for much the same view.

[161] Aug. *En. in Ps.* 84.4 (CCL 39: 1164).

and schismatic Jews, were the enemies of Christ and his church. Therefore they were not really genuine Jews.[162]

More to the point was the "fact" that Jews in Judaea represented only a small part of mankind, a sort of "regional truth" which was not good enough since it was promised that the universal church would be established as a force in the entire known world. The Psalmist had said that the whole earth, and not just Judaea, was to rejoice in God.[163] In both of these patterns, the average parishioner would hear an echo of "the Donatists": separatist rebels who by their obstinacy and blindness had set up their own church in their own little corner of the world. And it was precisely not just the pride and arrogance of Donatus, but his blindness that was the cause of his schism.[164]

The culmination of the argument is that these evil acts by the Jews justified their punishment, a punishment that had been enacted by God through the agency of the Roman state.[165] Just as pagans and heretics were rightly being crushed by the might of the Christian state, so too Jews had been dispersed throughout the world and they had lost their homeland forever, being forbidden to inhabit it by the fiat of Roman authority.[166] Babylon and Jerusalem are two cities, each evoking images of punishment. Because Christ was crucified by the Jews "a terrible punishment" was inflicted upon them – they were uprooted from their homeland and scattered throughout the whole world, and their country was taken over by Christians.[167] The Sallustian tag that they were lost and abandoned

---

[162] Aug. *En. in Ps.* 75.1 (CCL 39: 1035–38).

[163] Aug. *En. in Ps.* 55.2 (CCL 39: 839): "Iubilate Deo. Qui? Omnis terra. Non ergo sola Iudaea. Videte, fratres, quemadmodum commendatur universitas ecclesiae toto orbe diffusae, et non solum dolete Iudaeos qui gratiam istam gentibus invidebant, sed plus haereticos plangite . . . Nemo iubilet in parte. Nemo, inquam, iubilet in parte: omnis terra iubilet, catholica iubilet. Catholica totum tenet: quicumque partem tenet, et a toto praecisus est, ululare vult, non iubilare." The reference to the "heretics" could not be missed.

[164] Optatus, *Contra Parm.* 3.3.12 (SC 413: 26); cf. Aug. *Contra Gaud.* 2.3.3 (CSEL 53: 258); *de Bapt.* 2.3.4 (CSEL 51: 178–79), drawing on ideas in Cyprian, *Ep.* 54.3.3 (CCL 3B: 254–55).

[165] Aug. *Sermo* 374 (PL 39: 1667) at length; *En. in Ps.* 52.4 and 9 (CCL 39: 640 and 644), in a sermon generally devoted to the subject; *Civ. Dei*, 17.18 (CCL 48: 584): "Quis hoc iam neget, qui Iudaeos post passionem resurrectionemque Christi de sedibus suis bellica strage et excidio funditus eradicatos videt?"; *Civ. Dei*, 18.46 (CCL 48: 644): "Iudaei autem, qui eum occiderunt et in eum credere noluerunt, quia oportebat eum mori et resurgere, vastati infelicius a Romanis funditusque a suo regno, ubi iam eis alienigenae dominabantur, eradicati dispersique per terras . . . Et ideo non eos occidit, id est non in eis perdidit quod sunt Iudaei, quamvis a Romanis fuerint devicti et oppressi."

[166] Aug. *En. in Ps.* 55.17 (CCL 39: 691): the justification for the Romans coming and taking their land (viz. property) away from them, quoting John 11: 48 in support.

[167] Aug. *En. in Ps.* 64.1 (CCL 39: 822–23): continuing and developing the message in the preceding sermon (*En. in Ps.* 63) that vividly describes the role of the Jews in the crucifixion, and at length.

men – *perditi* – as well as seditious ones – *seditiosi* – is repeated time and time again.[168]

The Jews are an example of a "true death," the deepest kind of sin into which one can fall: a willful ignoring of the law of God. Although they are the enemies of God, He has, through His divine patience, decided not to exterminate them, but rather to let them survive as a living mirror: a reflection of what Christians should not be. The Jews are descendants of Abraham, marked with the sign of Cain; they survive to teach us that we too should show *misericordia* towards our own enemies.[169] So the Jews might hate God, but they have to fear him. In justifying that punishment and God's revenge against persons who reject him, the preacher proffers verbal images that are calculated to fire the emotions and the anger of his listeners: "The fires of their hatreds sent them puffing up proudly. Their boastful talk was directed to the sky as they shouted "Crucify him! Crucify him!" They mocked him as their prisoner and laughed at him as he hung there on the cross. In their victory they were puffed up with pride and boasting, but very soon they were smashed and blown away." The preacher, indeed, expresses the hope of this people: "Let them fade just as smoke fades away."[170]

It is not just that there had been punishment, but that the punishment was deserved and could be explained. "The Jews . . . deserve to be beaten, deserve to be overrun, deserve to be driven out of their kingdom, for the land that they lost was the land for which they killed the Lord . . . this is why all these calamities befell the Jews."[171] But the preacher often uses a rhetoric that does not put matters in such a calm and objective way. Instead, he creates a visual scene of such visceral revulsion that the hatred of the listener is roused. For example, in a long sermon on vengeance and retribution where God is the God of vengeance and the Jews his object: "The Jews seized him, they whipped him, they mocked him, they beat him, they spat on him, they crowned him with thorns, they hoisted him high onto a cross, and finally they murdered him."[172] The Jews are like wolves

---

[168] Aug. *Sermo* 112A.13 = *Caillau-St. Yves* 11.13 (MiAg 1: 263).

[169] Aug. *En. 1 in Ps.* 58.21 (CCL 39: 744): "Maneat gens Iudaeorum: certe victa est a Romanis, certe deleta civitas eorum; non admittuntur ad civitatem suam Iudaei; et tamen Iudaei sunt. Iudaei tamen manent cum signo." The parallel is that the Jews killed Christ, like Cain killed Abel: *En. in Ps.* 77.9 (CCL 39: 1073–74).

[170] Aug. *En. in Ps.* 67.3 (CCL 39: 870): glossing Ps. 67: 3: Sicut deficit fumus, deficiant (Sicut deficit fumus deficiant: VG).

[171] Aug. *En. 2 in Ps.* 88.7 (CCL 39: 1240); cf. *En. 1 in Ps.* 58.1 (CCL 39: 730) for much the same sentiment.

[172] Aug. *En. in Ps.* 93.8 (CCL 39: 1309–10): "Tenuerunt, flagellaverunt, illuserunt, colaphizaverunt, sputis illinierunt, spinis coronaverunt, in cruce levaverunt, postremo occiderunt."

who took the Lord's blood in fits of rage, Augustine states in a sermon in which he closely links such behavior with the Donatists who had rejected the unity of the church.[173] Just as the Jews were once proud, now they have been humiliated, made humble – and that is a good thing.[174] The victory of Roman emperors over them means that the place where they crucified Christ is free of Jews, it "harbours no Jew," it is free of "the enemies of Christ."[175]

How could this evil exist? How could it happen that any people would consciously reject the manifest truth and reject the manifest God Himself? Deliberately? Willfully? And a people so well endowed with prior knowledge of the true divinity? In a sense, it was not just their own power, but rather the fact that God himself permitted or had brought this to pass. The general argument, frequently repeated, is that He can use evil agents to achieve good. So in a discourse on the synagogue Augustine comments on the Jews' hatred of Christ and their contempt for Him. All of this is understandable, he says, in the light of the fact that the Devil himself is the leader of all of Christ's enemies.[176] What was particularly annoying in the case of the Jews (and that of the pagans and heretics) was that this appeared to be a matter of choice, since it was because of their deliberate and conscious acts that the Jews became "children of the Devil": that is, by imitating his evil nature and not by descent.[177] That the Jews were (and are) instruments of the Devil or his agents is a common theme, explicated in its harshest form in the Easter sermons.[178] The idea that there was an overlap between the enemies of the true church and the Jews is not alien to the other sermons as well where this is expressed: who are the enemies of the church? The Jews, or rather, Satan and his angels.[179] So accepted was this by the congregation that Augustine can say of them: "we are horrified at the Jews, because they said to our Lord Jesus Christ, 'You are possessed by a demon.' And when we heard that part of the gospel being read aloud, we beat our breasts."[180]

---

[173] Aug. *Sermo* 89.1 (PL 38: 554): "Sed nescio ubi tanquam a lupis depraedati latebant in vepribus; et quia latebant in vepribus, ideo ad eos inveniendos non pervenit . . . illi occiderant . . . et credentes sanguinem biberunt quem saevientes fuderunt."

[174] Aug. *En. 2 in Ps.* 58.2 (CCL 39: 746).   [175] Aug. *En. in Ps.* 62.18 (CCL 39: 806).

[176] Aug. *En. in Ps.* 82.8 (CCL 39: 1143).

[177] Anon. *Sermo Caillau-St. Yves* 1.38:4 (PLS 2: 987): on their cruelty, making them a *hostem robustum et immanem diabolum*; Aug. *Tract. in Ioh.* 42.10.4 and 42.15.3 (CCL 36: 369–70; 372–73).

[178] Aug. *Sermo* 223I (PLS 2: 740).

[179] Aug. *En. 2 in Ps.* 29.11 (CCL 38: 182): "Quos ergo inimicos? Iudaeos, an potius diabolum et angelos eius."

[180] Aug., *En. 2 in Ps.* 48.4 (CCL 38: 568): "Horremus Iudaeos, quia dixerunt domino Iesu Christo: *daemonium habes*; et quando audimus evangelium recitari, tundimus pectora nostra."

One of the core messages, elaborated in small details by quotation and reference to scripture and commentary, is that the Jews represent a kind of quintessential evil. They can be identified, in list-like fashion, as "the Jews, those insane men, ragers, scoffers, laughers, insulters, crucifiers."[181] By consciously rejecting God and his truth, and murdering him, they established a model or pattern of behavior that all others must avoid. Not to do so makes one like a pagan or like a heretic. Obdurate rejection of the truth to the point of violence and murder marks one as being like the Jews. In a vivid replay of the crucifixion scene before the eyes of his congregation, Augustine remarks: "The Jews continued to be angry... Don't think, brothers, that this is evident in the Jews alone! Indeed, a primal example is provided in them, so that in that people is made manifest what every man should avoid."[182] By rejecting the truth, the Jews turn themselves into the enemies of God.[183] In this sense, they offer a good parallel to Christian heretics, who behave in precisely the same way. Often this message is left latently in the minds of the listeners, but just as frequently the preacher takes pains to point it out. In their rejection of God, the Jews are condemned along with pagans.[184] "Your undivided attention should be kept focussed on what I have just said, and on what I have suggested to you. Keep this before your minds. Don't let your thoughts wander from it. This Psalm is directed against the arrogance of the Jews... They crucified Christ," he begins in a detailed sermon that works out the full implications of this murderous rejection of the one true God, during which he constantly points out the equation between Jews and heretics.[185] The invocation to the violent repression of the hated enemy, however, can be made more explicit. He begins by quoting the sixty-seventh Psalm: "God will shatter the skulls of his enemies, and the hairy head of those who walk obstinately in their crimes."[186] Not only, he adds, will this happen to the Jews who insulted him while he hung on the cross, wagging their heads

---

181 Aug. *Sermo* 317.2.2 (PL 38: 1436): "Undique enim Iudaeis frementibus, irascentibus, irridentibus, insultantibus, crucifigentibus, ait"; insanity was a normal condition: Anon. *Sermo Mai* 199: 1 (PLS 2: 1285).

182 Aug. *En. in Ps.* 55.2 (CCL 39: 677–78): "Data sunt quidem in illis quasi primitiva exempla, ut in illo populo eluceret quod omnis homo caveret. Aperte illi regem Christum recusaverunt."

183 Aug. *En. 2 in Ps.* 58.2 (CCL 39: 745–46): "Videamus ergo quid restat de hoc psalmo. In hoc enim dimiseramus, cum coepisset de inimicis suis loqui dicens Deo." Who are these enemies? "Nam ecce inimici Iudaei, quos videtur significare psalmus iste."

184 Aug. *En. in Ps.* 94.7 (CCL 39: 1336).   185 Aug. *En. in Ps.* 65.2 and 5 (CCL 39: 839, 842–43).

186 Aug. *En. in Ps.* 67.30 (CCL 39: 890): "Verumtamen Deus conquassabit capita inimicorum, vertice capilli perambulantium in delictis suis." He is quoting the words of the Psalmist (Ps. 68: 21), to which he returns repeatedly in this section of the sermon.

and jeering at him, but to all others who rear themselves up in pride like they do.

Parishioners were reassured that the Lord had raised himself up and avenged himself upon his enemies, and that he would continue to do so. For their rejection of the truth, the final punishment of those Jews who had been permitted to survive was to take place at the final judgment as a kind of divine vengeance.[187] In this world, however, a substantial punishment has already been imposed upon them by the intervention of the Roman state. This is worded in terms of the punishment of Jews in the present: "The Lord shattered the jawbones of lions," not of asps only, the preacher says, commenting on the fifty-seventh Psalm. The vengeance of the Lord is outlined in a long anti-Donatist sermon where the deafness of the Donatists is systematically linked to the deafness of the Jews. They are asps; the Jews are lions, the totemic symbol of Satan. They had shouted "Crucify him! Crucify him!" with the savagery of lions, but the Lord had shattered the jawbones of these lions. Let the Jews try to rampage, he challenges. They would rampage now if they could, but they do not because "the Lord has shattered the jawbones of the lions."[188] The Donatists, like the Jews, deny the true Christ: "the Jews crucified Christ because they saw him, whereas you [sc. Donatists] reject his word because you do not see him; the Jews had contempt for him hanging on the cross, while you have contempt for him enthroned in heaven."[189] The consistent message, whether by the use of biblical citation or by the use of vivid image, is that "the Donatists" are worse than the Jews. The Jews merely stumbled over a stone (sc. Christ) whereas the Donatists stumble over a mountain (sc. the Church). The folly of the one act is somewhat comprehensible, the other not at all.[190]

In the battles over the oneness and unity of the true church that emerged with particular ferocity as the end of the fourth century approached, this rhetoric became particularly useful. A test for the existence of the true church was that it was accepted throughout the known world. The rejection of the church by the Jews was a sign of their peculiarity and their regionalism. In this sense the "mutterings" of the pagans against the one true church echoes those of the heretics and those of the Jews. Their essential characteristics are reiterated, list-like, for the listener: "since weren't the

---

[187] Aug. *En. in Ps.* 47.11 (CCL 38: 547); *En. 1 in Ps.* 48.5 (CCL 38: 555).
[188] Aug. *En. in Ps.* 57.14 (CCL 39: 720).   [189] Aug. *En. 1 in Ps.* 48.5 (CCL 38: 555).
[190] Aug. *Sermo* 147A.4 = *Denis* 12.4 (MiAg 1: 53).

Jews malignant, savage, cruel, seditious, and enemies of the Son of God?"[191]
The heretics, the Jews, and the pagans have united against unity. The fact
that the Jews, along with pagans and heretics, had been disciplined for
their misbehavior, was simply because all three had suffered just penalties
for the wrongs that they had inflicted on the true church.[192] The Jews were
said to be a species of heretic, a particularly virulent one. They were arch-
enemies of the church and were portrayed as such in sermons preached
on typical lists of heretics.[193] They were part of a typology to which "the
Donatists" were assigned. Like the Jews, the dissident Christians are also
portrayed as stupid, obdurate blockheads who blindly refuse to embrace
the manifest truth of the orthodox church. The Jews were one of those
branches severed from the trunk of the true tree of the Church, and so too
were "the Donatists."[194] Some of them, like the bishop Petilian of Constantina, might object that they were not "Jews according to the flesh," did
not worship idols or demons, and so did not deserve the imperial authorities weighing upon them. But the reply was that the similitude was close
enough.[195]

The core characteristics that made the Jews "enemies of God," "enemies of the truth," and "enemies of the church" were the same ones that
made them so useful an instrument with which to construe how Catholic
parishioners should think of "the Donatists."[196] In short, the one side was
accessing an existing discourse about a much-disliked third party, in order
to label and excoriate the other.[197] When Saul is presented as filled with
pride and boasting to his fellow Jews that, emulating ancestral practices
handed down to him by his forefathers, he had persecuted the true church,
the parallel with "the Donatists" could hardly be missed.[198] Above all, there
was the arch-Jew, Judas. It was dinned into the ears of Catholic parishioners
by the means of popular songs that Judas as the arch-traitor represented
those who had betrayed Christ and his Church, and who had therefore

---

[191] Aug. *Sermo* 80.5 (PL 38: 496): "quia non illi Iudaei maligni erant saevi, cruenti, turbulenti, inimici
Filio Dei?"

[192] Aug. *Sermo* 62.12.18 (CCL 41Aa: 312).   [193] Aug. *Sermo* 71.3.5 (PL 38: 447).

[194] Aug. *Sermo* 162A.9 = Denis 19.9 (MiAg 1: 107).

[195] Aug. *Contra litt. Petil.* 2.98.226 (CSEL 52: 144); such explicit references to Jews in the direct
discourse with the dissidents, however, are rare.

[196] The identification is sometimes covert, sometimes only suggested or assumed, but sometimes made
quite explicit either by placing such an image in the context of an explicitly anti-dissident sermon
or by explicitly making the connection: see *Sermo* 202.3.3 (PL 38: 1036).

[197] For this accessing of other religious discourses to fight internal sectarian battles, see Nirenberg,
Communities of Violence, pp. 166 ff.

[198] Aug. *Sermo* 169.9 (PL 38: 920): "Cum [Saulus] saeviret, erectus, iactabundus, glorians apud ipsos
Iudaeos quod secundum aemulationem paternarum traditionum persequebatur ecclesiam."

turned their backs on Him.[199] In other words, "the Donatists" were the new Judases.

BLACK BIRDS

Most often, however, the identification of the Jews and "the Donatists" was conveyed to listeners in striking visual pictures, using images that were deeply embedded in a Christian *paideia* that had roots in times long before the age of Augustine. The constant glossing of the symbols and the connections between them produced a convenient sign language in which enemies of the true faith could be identified. In the metaphorical language identifying humans and their behavior in sermons, animal images are dominant. This is surely not accidental. By using this device, the preacher could tap into the everyday talk of his parishioners and draw on an existing body of oral lore about animals that they already shared.[200] If the Jews were the original persecutors, then it was they who had rejected the lamb and had chosen the wolf.[201] If the Jews are abhorrent as a people, then they are like the very animals, the swine, that they themselves loathe.[202] And because they herd together in synagogues, they are more like cattle than genuine human beings who might constitute a true congregation.[203] Jews call other people dogs because they are filthy, but they themselves are the real dogs.[204] If Jews are lion cubs, it is because they are the offspring of leaders who are lions, lions because these leaders are like Satan, and the seduced common people are like their natural offspring.[205] Similarly, the Jews are sheep, but bad sheep, ones who have arrogantly chosen to ignore the shepherd and to build their own sheepfold. Christ came as a shepherd

---

[199] E.g. Aug. *Psalmus contra partem Donati*, vv. 205–210, 262–64 (Lambot, 1935: 325 and 327): "Habet iam Domini exemplum et in Iuda traditore . . . et posset per illum tradi, etiam si inde exisset ante . . . Non enim peiores errant illo Iuda traditore, / cum quo apostoli acceperunt primum sacramentum cenae, / cum tanti sceleris reum inter se ima scirent esse."

[200] The use of wolves and lambs/sheep are too common from Aesop onward to call for comment; so are ravens (almost always as malign figures). In Baebrius and Phaedrus doves do not occur that often (usually as animals so pacific that they are taken advantage of by the heartless and the vicious: Perry no. 606, for an encounter with a raven); the raven or the crow is usually a bad or malificent character: see Perotti, Appendix, no. 26; Perry, nos. 125, 128, 577, 599, 606, for examples.

[201] Aug. *En. in Ps.* 62.19–20 (CCL 39: 806–07): *partes vulpium erant* are the words of the Psalmist on which Augustine is commenting; *En. in Ps.* 62.20 (CCL 39: 807).

[202] Aug. *En. in Ps.* 79.3 and 11 (CCL 39: 1112–13, 1116).

[203] Aug. *En. in Ps.* 77.3 (CCL 39: 1068): "synagoga Iudaeorum . . . quia congregatio magis pecorum"; *En. in Ps.* 81.1 (CCL 39: 1136): more of the same.

[204] Aug. *En. 1 in Ps.* 58.15 (CCL 39: 741).

[205] Aug. *En. in Ps.* 56.10 (CCL 39: 700–01); cf. *Civ. Dei*, 16.41 (CCL 48: 547): where Jews are identified with the lion and with Judas.

to care for his sheep, but not to those who follow Donatus and certainly not for sheep like the Jews, not for those sheep "unyielding in their cruel hatred and persisting in darkness."[206] Any community, after having been carefully coached for generations in this sort of animal language, would not be too hard pressed to make the equations, even where the preacher did not explicitly spell out the parallel, as Augustine has done above.

Should it be imagined that this preaching had no effect – that it was just so much sectarian polemic or just so much rhetorical invective – one has only to consider the effects of preaching these views about Jews on the island of Minorca in the year 418. The Christian bishop Severus, who lived in the city of Iamo on the western part of the island, was happy that his side of the island was free of noxious animals, like foxes and wolves, like poisonous snakes and scorpions, unlike the eastern side of the island around the city of Mago where the Jews happened to live. That the western part of the island was both free of poisonous and hateful animals and also free of Jews ("they had learned from experience not to live there") were similar parts of the same equation. In the eastern side of the island around Mago, where the Jews lived, on the other hand, the place was crawling with poisonous snakes and scorpions, as befitted the "generation of vipers" that they were.[207] That his own western parts of the island were *judenrein* is portrayed by the bishop as part of a divine plan mirrored in the distribution of the island's noxious animal life. It is manifest that it was preaching laced with this sort of animal imagery, deployed for some time before the actual outbreak of hostilities, that led to the burning of the synagogue on 2 February 418, and the forced "conversion" of Minorca's Jewish population.[208] The net effects were rather nasty; it was "a thoroughly dirty business."[209]

There are simply too many animal metaphors deployed in constructing the Jewishness of the Donatists for them to be considered in detail.[210] One

[206] Aug. *Tract. in Ioh.* 47.4 (CCL 36: 406): "multum enim commendavimus unum ovile, praedicantes unitatem, ut per Christum omnes oves ingrederentur, et Donatum nulla sequeretur . . . Loquebatur enim apud Iudaeos, missus autem fuerat ad ipsos Iudaeos, non propter quosdam immani odio pertinaces et perseverantes in tenebris."

[207] Severus, *Ep. Severi*, 3.3–6 (Bradbury: 82): "Nec hoc fide indignum ducimus, cum etiam vulpes luposque et omnia noxia animalia deesse videamus . . . Illud etiam magnum mirum est, quod colubri atque scorpiones sunt quidem plurimi . . . Cum igitur Iamonam nullus Iudaeorum, qui lupis ac vulpibus feritate atque nequitia merito comparantur . . . Magona tantis Iudaeorum populis velut colubris scorpionibusque fervebat, ut quotidie ab his Christi ecclesia morderetur . . . ut illa, sicut scriptum est 'generatio viperarum' ."

[208] On the connection with preaching, see ch. 9, pp. 436 f. below.

[209] Brown, *Cult of the Saints*, p. 104: he is "describing a thoroughly dirty business, where violence and fear of yet greater violence played a decisive role."

[210] See Poque, *Langage symbolique*, pp. 10–23, for just some examples.

example will have to suffice – a motif centered on bird images that is inter-woven throughout one of Augustine's sermons. The dove, the *columba*, was identified with Christ, the truth, the true Church, and with sunshine and daylight. The dove is white, innocent, good, and peaceful. The raven or *corvus*, on the other hand, is black, guilty, bad, and violent.[211] The evil raven is identified with Satan, and so with darkness and night. Working with this assumed background of symbolic language, the preacher delivers a sermon on the gospel of John (1: 32–33).[212] The preacher begins with the protomartyr Stephen and with the "stiff-necked Jews" who resisted his message of truth, who rejected the presence of the Holy Spirit. Stephen, it is true, reproved them with fiery words, but he is a dove. The Jews are ravens. Although the angry words that Stephen volleyed against the Jews appear so violent that a listener would think that he wished them to be exterminated, nevertheless, he is a dove. They are ravens. They stone him. Stephen is a dove, like Christ on the cross; the Jews are ravens. The dove has the true kiss, the kiss of peace, whereas ravens tear and lacerate when they try to kiss. The dove does not feed on death; ravens do. Those who have lacerated the Church are those who are feeding on death. Who are those who are lacerating the body of the Church? "The Donatists." They too are ravens. The dove is unity; the raven is discord. "The Donatists" are savage birds of prey.[213] So it is only right that they, like the Jews, suffer correction by a Christian state. The sermon was delivered in March of 413, two years after the Conference at Carthage in 411, in a year between the two pieces of imperial legislation meant to repress the dissident church. It manifestly pictures Jews and Donatists in terms which, even if only metaphoric ones, suggest they are both somehow evil and therefore deserv-ing of coercive repression.

Without doubt, however, the dissident Christians also had access to precisely this same anti-Jewish rhetoric and certainly played it, from their point of view, for all it was worth. For them, one of the great themes was less one of identifying bad people who were general enemies of the church than it was one of identifying the ancestry and the lineage of the traitors. The act of betrayal by which Christ was handed over to the Roman authorities by the arch-traitor Judas was the base action that led to the crucifixion and the primal division between us true Christians and

[211] For the place of crows and ravens in Mediterranean proverbial communication, see Foufopoulos and Litinas (2005).
[212] Aug. *Tract. in Ioh.* 6.3–9 (CCL 36: 54–67).
[213] Aug. *Tract. in Ioh.* 6.10 (dove unity, raven discord); 6.12 (birds of prey); and 6.20–25 (on imperial repression of the ravens) (CCL 36: 58–59, 64–66).

those arrogant, blind, prideful segregationists. It was the original deed that separated the Jewish people from the true church. As the dissident bishop of Constantina, Petilian, put it in his circular letter to his own clergy:[214]

We must, I say, grasp and understand how it was that a disloyal traitor must be considered to be dead to life. Judas was an apostle when he betrayed Christ. It was precisely then that he lost his position as apostle and died a spiritual death before he died by hanging himself... After all of that, how can you possibly claim the position of bishop? *You*, the heir of that even more guilty traitor – how? Judas betrayed Christ in the flesh, but in your contempt for the Spirit, you handed over the holy gospel to sacrilegious fires. Judas betrayed the Lawmaker to the unbelievers, but you handed the Law of God, over to men for destruction... What sort of fate awaits you, *you* who threw the most holy Laws of God the Judge into the fires? In his death, Judas at least repented of his crime, while you have not only not repented but, what's worse, you, the evil traitors that you are, have made yourselves our persecutors and executioners – persecutors and executioners of us who keep the Law!

It was this image of Judas and the connection of betrayal that was played on time and time again by dissident preachers.[215] No doubt, the refrain "Let his blood be upon us and our descendants," shouted by the Jews at the crucifixion, could be replayed as another model that would confirm the inherited nature of a primal act of betrayal and rejection of truth. If "the Donatists" were the Catholics' surrogate Jews, then the Catholics easily fit the same role in reverse. But then, the dissidents were only officially to be called "the Donatists" for a very good reason – a good reason that reflected the central place of heresy in the conflict.

---

[214] Petilian, *Ep. ad presb. et diac.* 5–6 (restoration by Monceaux, *Hist. litt.* 5: 312) = Aug. *Contra litt. Petil.* 2.8.17 (CSEL 52: 29–30): "Agendum, inquam, nobis dicendumque est, quatenus perfidus traditor vita mortuus habeatur. Iudas apostolus fuit cum traderet Christum, idemque honore apostoli perdito spiritaliter mortuus est, suo postea laqueo moriturus."

[215] For just some examples, *Sermo Caillau-St. Yves* 1.68: 3 (PLS 2: 1018–19), a detailed screed on Judas as the archetypical *traditor*; 1.App.3: 1 (PLS 2: 1019); 1.App.6: 10 (PLS 2: 1023); *Sermo Mai* 28: 1 (PLS 2: 1126); 29: 1 (PLS 2: 1129); 33: 2 (PLS 2: 1133); 37: 1–2 (PLS 2: 1137–38); 38: 1 (PLS 2: 1139); 79: 1 (PLS 2: 1192); 84: 2–3 (PLS 2: 1198); *Sermo Casinensis* 1: 1 (PLS 2: 1315–16), where his status as a betrayer is particularly emphasized.

CHAPTER 7

Little foxes, evil women

Fascination with bad people has its own fashions. Two centuries before Augustine's time, African Christians had an obsession with the enemies of true belief who obstinately chose their own perverted way to the truth: "heretics" as they had come to be named. These early heretics, however, had a style of their own. The writings of Tertullian, the pre-eminent Christian ideologue in the Africa of his age, a stern Catonian moralizer, are focussed on his struggles with the enemies of true belief. The names that he provides for them are a guide to identifying the most dangerous of these hostiles as they were perceived at the time. Apart from external non-Christian threats like diviners, fakirs, false seers, astrologers, and Pythagoreans, the most threatening internal enemies of the church were heretics who advocated gnostic versions of Christian truth. Like those of other orthodox activists of the time, Tertullian's battles were waged against dangerous persons who advocated a less material and tangible, a less fleshy nature of the Christian deity. The rather satisfying frisson to this story, in the eyes of some, came when the obstinate and feisty Tertullian was caught in his own ideological trap. He was branded a Montanist, an adherent of one of the other big heresies of his age. Then nothing.

A long and strange interlude extended over the remainder of the third century and most of the fourth when this first fascination with heretics faded. New concerns, such as local and then state-driven persecutions, and the forging of a harder ideology of martyrdom, came to the fore. But in the decades of the 370s and 380s, there was a resurgence of interest in heresy and heretics, and this time it amounted to something more than an obsession. In the world of western Mediterranean Christianity, the general history of writings attacking heresies and heretics can be divided into two broad periods. The first great anti-heretical movement, which included the writings of Irenaeus in Gaul, Hippolytus in Rome, and Tertullian at Carthage, as we have noted, was directed against gnostic attacks on the real material substance of Christ's body. After this initial spate of anti-heretical action, the urgent interest in heresy went dormant for over a century. Then, with sudden force, a second great wave of interest in heretics resurged in the third quarter of the fourth century. Very few of the specifics of the first obsession with heretics made it across the great divide between the two movements. In his treatise written in the mid-360s, Optatus, the Catholic bishop of Milevis, accused Parmenian, the dissident bishop of Carthage, of having introduced into his jeremiad many strange ideas and names of men long forgotten and currently unknown in Africa – men like Marcion, Praxeas, Sabellius, and Valentinus.[1] Optatus was right. These men *were* long forgotten. The reason for their presence in Parmenian's writings was his use of old literary texts to construct his attack on the Catholics as the "real heretics" of his age. In consequence, as Optatus claimed – scoring a direct hit on his hated rival – Parmenian had dragged a lot of long-forgotten episodes from ancient history, like so many dead fish, into his argument.

It is the writings of Epiphanius, the bishop of Salamis in Cyprus, in the 370s that especially mark the new phase of energetic concern with heresy that configured much ecclesiastical and theological writing in the later fourth and early fifth centuries. His ideas were to have considerable repercussions in the Latin West.[2] This second anti-heretical movement was characterized by a determined drive to identify heretics: to develop systematic identikits to identify the hated enemies of right thinking.[3] This late fourth-century interest in heresies had its own style. It was different both in kind and extent from the earlier anti-heretical movement. The big concern of the later age was not so much one of internal ideological defense and cleansing of a single threatening idea as it was with the identification of a wide range of various types of external pseudo-Christian enemies. Rather than the extensive and detailed theological treatise, it is the heresy list that is the characteristic document of the second movement devoted to hunting down the enemies of the true church.[4] They were also part of a process of

---

[1] Optatus, *Contra Parm.* 1.9.1–2 (SC 412: 188–90): "et post laudem baptismatis haereticos cum erroribus suis iam mortuos et oblivione sepultos quodammodo resuscitare voluisti, quorum per provincias Africanas non solum vitia sed etiam nomina videbantur ignota." Once again, this demonstrates the point made above about the *relative* rarity of such heretical sects in Africa; also, the fact that they were "long forgotten" and "unknown" shows the long hiatus of interest in such matters.

[2] For our argument, see Altaner (1951).

[3] Schneemelcher (1962) for general background; Pourkier, *Epiphane de Salamine*, esp. pp. 29–52 on his background and pp. 53–76 on the state of pre-Epiphanian heresiology.

[4] As I have already remarked elsewhere (Shaw [2004], p. 258 n. 24), these lists deserve more analysis; in a brief study, McClure (1979) noted their chronological convergence as types of documents, but retreated from offering any explanation for the phenomenon. One such list became attached to the writings of Tertullian, although it manifestly belongs to our later age. Usually referred to as the *Adversus omnes haereses*, it is a discursive discussion of thirty-two heresies. In our standard

labeling and naming in which Christians were imposing a holistic Christian interpretation on their world.[5] It was less the systematic refutation of ideas than it was the identification, pursuit, and arrest of suspects that was at the core of the new movement.

This later tradition produced extensive hit lists of heresies, lists that were meant to provide quick identity profiles by which concerned believers could recognize any one of the variegated host of enemies that the orthodox faced. Involving Epiphanius and similar heretic hunters, the fourth-century resurgence of interest in heresy and heretics did not begin in Africa, but rather in the eastern Mediterranean, and perhaps for obvious reasons. African Christians, to tell the truth, shared only a subdued interest in heretics. By comparison with other areas of the Mediterranean, their religious landscape seemed relatively clean of such ideological vermin. Except for the larger port cities with their trans-Mediterranean contacts that naturally harbored religious adepts and missionaries of all varieties, the heartlands of Africa were not considerable breeding grounds for diversity or for aberrant views of Christianity that could gain traction in a big way. This does not mean that such aberrations were entirely absent in the interior, as is clearly demonstrated, for example, by the presence of Manichaean codices in a remote, if connected, region near Theveste.[6] It is, rather, a matter of emphasis. Africa might well have been the mother of lawyers, but it was not a prodigious generator of heresies. The eastern Mediterranean lands of the empire were another story. Here all kinds of difference, distortion, and divergence flourished and prevailed with an intensity that would have baffled most African Christians, had they ever been aware of the florid menagerie of idiosyncratic oriental Christian ideologies in their fullest flower.

Unlike his African peers, the bishop Epiphanius, a converted Jew, seated at Salamis on the island of Cyprus, found himself located at the epicenter of a vast circuit of lands and heresies that surrounded him.[7] The striking panorama of heretical species that he could spy from this vantage point set his Linnaean instincts alight. With a fervour that helped fire the age, he began categorizing, labeling, and describing them in his *Panarion* – a *Medicine Box* because it was intended to be a doctor's medical bag filled with the medicaments necessary to cure the poisonous infections of wrong belief.

---

texts, it is usually appended to the *De praescriptione haereticorum*; for the text see F. Oehler, *Corpus Haereseologicum, 1: Continens scriptores haeresologicos minores latinos*, Berlin, 1856, pp. 271–79.

[5] Noted by Cameron (2008), p. 105, referring, especially, to the work of Inglebert, *Interpretatio Christiana*.

[6] Stein, *Codex Thevestinus* and (2001); and Merkelbach (1988).   [7] Kim (2006), pp. 241–46.

No such convoluted complexity and diversity was evident in the western Mediterranean lands. Outside Africa, it is true, there were fundamental diversities of perspective and belief in different Christian communities, especially in the most intense foyers of Mediterranean communication: Campania, Rome, regions of southern Gaul around the busy port cities of Massilia and Arelate, in the Ebro valley, and in the still larger valley of the Guadalquivir of Spain. Such concerns are evident in Iberian records, for example, as early as the canons of the Council of Elvira and in the harsh views of Ossius of Corduba at the dawn of the Constantinian age.[8] In such places, the orthodox had real worries. But not in Africa.

A relative disinterest in heresy is evident in all the African Christian writings of the time. There are few signs that the problem greatly bothered Tyconius, Parmenian, or Optatus. The vast range of legislation of the many African church councils also reveals relatively little interest. Very much against his will, Augustine was persuaded, albeit with considerable pressure, to produce a typical Mediterranean handbook of heresies at the very end of his life. In his *Book of Heresies*, his *Liber de haeresibus*, Augustine was working with and adapting an existing handbook on the subject.[9] He would have had every opportunity to add a large number of indigenous African heresies to these already prepared lists, if they had existed. His knowledge of such matters was surely almost without peer. Yet, other than "the Donatists" and "the circumcellions," both of whom were already in the standard lists that he was using, he could only think of one other African heresy to add: it was a bizarre regional group about whom he happened to know. His knowledge of them was both accidental and highly local. Drawing on some personal connections, he was able to describe an odd Christian group that lived on the wild peripheral fringes of his own diocese of Hippo Regius.[10]

And there is also one rural heresy in our countryside, that is to say in the territory of Hippo – or rather there *was* one. For growing smaller little by little it only survived in one small hamlet, in which there were a very small number of such persons, even if they were the sum total. By now, all of them have been corrected and have been made Catholics, so that nothing of that former error now remains. They were called *Abeloîm*, a name derived from the Punic language. Some say that they were named from the son of Ada, who is called Abel – so we can call them *Abeliani* or *Abeloitai*. These men did not have sex with their wives, although

---

[8] For example, Concil. Eliberr. canon 22: "De catholicis in haeresem transeuntibus, si revertantur": Martínez-Rodríguez, *Canónica hispana*, p. 249.

[9] For the degree of his dependence on existing treatises, see Jannaccone (1952).

[10] Aug. *De Haeres.* 87 (CCL 46: 339–40).

it was not permitted for them to live without wives from the same sect in their belief. Therefore males and females, with a public declaration of continence, but living together, adopted a son and a daughter for themselves, and by this sort of agreement they furnished their future descendants. For those removed by death, replacements could be sought on a one-by-one basis, as long as two sexes replaced two in the same household so that they would succeed in it. Indeed, whichever of the two parents died, the children served the surviving one up to the point of his or her death. After that person's death, these persons would then likewise adopt one boy and one girl. Nor was there ever any shortfall among the people from whom they would make these adoptions – that is, from all of the children that were procreated in surrounding and nearby districts – since the poor would willingly give up their own children because of their hope for another's wealth.

These people were an amazing curiosity. Doubtless there were other odd hill and mountain folk like them, isolated communities that had developed their own peculiar Christian beliefs. But this is the only place where Augustine notes the Abelonians, a strange zoo-like oddity thrown into the mix of heresies to show that he had at least one species that he could add to the existing lists. They had never appeared before and never would again. Like the Shakers, and sharing a similar ideology, they were growing smaller and smaller, not bigger and bigger, until they were finally extinguished. They were certainly not the looming and growing heretical threat with which bishops like Augustine were really concerned. The Abelonians were just another microregional blip, one of the thousands of genetic misfires typical of idea systems in growth. But other than this, nothing.

OUR VERY OWN DANGER

The one heresy in which the African Augustine did come to be strongly interested, the error of Pelagius, illustrates the difference. It is therefore important to understand why, in the years leading up to 415, he became so fascinated with a marginal British priest and his ideas. Why would a bishop who had dedicated his life to battling a huge Christian division within Africa become so involved in a dispute entirely outside of it? The answer is failure. Or at least stalemate and the dim prospect of any real success. To understand Augustine's personal interests around the year 415, one also has to understand that he was old. He was now more than sixty years of age, and he had spent almost all the years since his ordination as bishop in 395, the past two decades of his life, struggling with the scourge of "the Donatists." All the lobbying of government officials, the construction of churches and seminaries, the preaching and writing of letters, the church councils aimed at reform and reorganization, and the exhausting hard work was to culminate in the formal hearing held in 411 at Carthage. It was at this critical forum that the Catholic Church finally achieved its long-awaited goal of a formal public condemnation of the rival Christian church in Africa. Imperial laws intended to crush "the Donatists" followed in 412 and 414. This could be interpreted as a tremendous success, and not a few modern scholars have tended to echo the triumphalist claims of Catholic orthodoxy.

A closer look at the facts raises some serious questions. The Catholic bishops in Africa had made huge exertions over generations in the hope of moving a great imperial state to action on their behalf. The great irony is that just as they succeeded in their aim, the imperial state upon which they had counted so much had become too weak effectively to implement the laws that it had made to help them. The state's main concerns were now directed to the urgent and truly dangerous problems that it faced on its northern and western military frontiers. A weakened and distracted imperial court was severely hampered in providing real assistance on the ground in Africa. Despite all their hard work, Augustine and his peers had netted rather little. On a quite different front, but one just as important, writing and preaching against an African threat was only ever going to be a concern to Africans and to no one else (as was openly admitted by Augustine) and so attracted almost no merit in Mediterranean-wide terms. A related problem was that "the Donatists" were of no interest to the whole of eastern Mediterranean Christendom. So the option of entering eastern Christian disputes and making one's mark there was not open either. There were almost no serious ongoing connections between East and West on African matters.[11] Whatever a western bishop might have to say about Arius and his "heresy" was bound to be ignored by eastern bishops as derived from a second-rate source and as having little or no significance to them.

Leading African Catholic bishops, like Augustine, were facing the prospect of irrelevance. This was true on their home ground where they had made little real progress against the dissident church despite decades of hard work. They had few prospects in front of them of gaining any

---

[11] Lössl (2000), pp. 267–72, documents Augustine's ignorance of Greek writers in the original texts and also notes the failure of his writings to make an impact on eastern bishops, referring to the few known letters. Before the publication of the Divjak letters, only one letter of Augustine's (*Ep.* 179) was known to have been addressed to an eastern bishop; the new letters produced two more (*Ep.* 4* and 6*) – all three, notably, were generated by the Pelagian affair: see Dunn (2006), pp. 63–64.

more interest, or action, from the state than the imperial government had already shown. This was just as true on the external front where their main expertise – the description, refutation, and uprooting of "Donatist error" – was of little or no concern to anyone outside Africa. What a bishop like Augustine needed was a western Mediterranean heresy, one that had roots in his own world – a burning controversy that would be played out on his own ground, in his own language, and to which his knowledge and his role would be central. If he wished ever to be known outside of his own small world, as any American businessman would say, Augustine would have to reposition himself in the marketplace. A battle against a Mediterranean-wide heresy would provide the grounds on which his important ideas would finally receive a worthy audience. There was every compulsion for such men, if not actually to invent a heresy, at least to be complicit in creating it. Most unfortunately for Pelagius, he was the wrong man at the right time.

It is not that African bishops, with their wider Mediterranean connections and communications, were not aware of heresies and did not agree that they had to be fought. It was just that within Africa these aberrant Christianities were relatively unimportant. Christianity had grown and developed within Africa differently than it had in other Mediterranean regions. The results had imparted a more monolithically uniform landscape to African Christendom.[12] The most exciting and provocative hostilities that evoked interest and response from African Christians were the ones that they had with each other: dissidents versus Catholics. This was the great game that intrigued them and that consumed their attentions. Religious disputes that happened elsewhere in the Mediterranean did not attract them. So it was difficult for African bishops to make these external heretical disputes seem important to their congregations. Augustine repeatedly attempted to explain to his parishioners at Hippo the differences that he used to identify and to excoriate Arian Christians. In numerous sermons he struggled with them to outline the main diagnostic features of "Arianism," and why it was that they would have to recognize and to reject this brand of Christianity. The almost universal response of his listeners to these sermons was one of rigid boredom. They did not understand what he was talking about, could not grasp the significance of his words, and generally were not interested in a recondite problem that had no real presence or force in their world. The constant pleadings by Augustine for the members of his congregation "to pay attention" or even just "to wake up"

---

[12] Shaw (2003), esp. pp. 106–16, for the argument.

are revealing. Arianism, and dozens of other heresies, might well have been burning issues in Egypt, Asia, Dalmatia, or northern Italy, but the degree to which the two Christian orthodoxies had swept the field in Africa left relatively little room in which such alien aberrations could flourish.

The Pelagian affair might perhaps offer a minor exception, but it was certainly a minor one. And Pelagius had at least visited Africa, including Hippo Regius. Even so, the construction of the Pelagian heresy involved a lot of hard uphill struggle and sweat, and the remorseless education of churchgoers. All the controversies that centered on Pelagius and his ideas came well after the ones that were central to the internal African disputes. They were new, not traditional. Despite the general lack of interest of external heresies to Africans and despite the fact that their land was not one particularly fertile to the production of heresies (no major local ones are known) heresy was central to the dispute between the two Christian churches and to the violence as it escalated through the end of the fourth century and the beginning of the fifth. The reason for the growing significance of heresy was simple: the struggle to impose orthodoxy was long and difficult, a form of sacred trench warfare.[13] The accusation of heresy was a useful charge in Africa precisely because it was not acceptable for one Christian community to persecute another. This was especially true in Africa where the Great Persecution under Diocletian had left an indelible imprint on the collective consciousness of Christian communities in later generations. Any involvement of the state in the harassing of Christians had a very bad name. African Christians had firmly identified the secular state as an evil agent in the service of the Devil. On the other hand, beginning immediately with the reign of Constantine, it was more or less acceptable for the state to serve in an auxiliary fashion in keeping the new House of the Lord clean by removing extreme and generally undesirable interlopers, and to use its considerable resources in doing so. Although a hard line on this issue was laid down early in the reign of Constantine, there had followed a considerable retreat from his inflexible and aggressive position in the last decades of his rule. The reluctance of the imperial court to engage in such house cleaning was manifest in the attitudes of his successors.

In any serious attempt to attack their "Donatist" enemies in Africa, who were numerous and powerful, the Catholics required just such instruments of large-scale repression, which is to say those of the imperial state. Neither municipal court decisions at the lower end of the governmental spectrum, nor imperial laws at the top end, were of much use unless they could

---

[13] Just how long and how difficult is made clear by Cameron (2007).

be put into effect. In both cases, the big problem was to find powerful agents who would actually enforce the orders. Over the mid-decades of the fourth century, the problem facing the Catholic Church was therefore simple: How could it move the Roman state and its resources to decisive action? As long as their opponents in Africa were perceived simply to be aberrant orthodox Christians – and the constant reference to their identity in imperial laws as no more than "Rebaptizers" admits as much – there was not much hope that the Roman state was going energetically to pursue their enemies as long as they were seen as minor ecclesiastical deviants. Heresy was a different matter. But the long period between Tertullian and the age of Augustine had been marked by a lassitude of interest. A connection somehow had to be made with a manifest danger that the managers of state power would recognize and which they would have a real interest in repressing.

AN ALIEN THREAT

In the late fourth century, a more intense interest in heresy was to be revived on a grand scale, and with the revival came opportunity. If the enemies of the Catholics could be classified as heretics, then there would not only be good grounds for attacking them, but also a greater likelihood that the state would act. There were increasing signs that the state might be cajoled into direct action based on charges of heresy. The main developments, however, did not take place in Africa, but elsewhere in the western Mediterranean. About the year 380, a dozen bishops had assembled at Saragossa in the province of Tarraconensis in northern Spain to debate the character of Priscillian and his qualifications to be bishop. Priscillian was an exegete whose roots were local, but whose ideas and education were more cosmopolitan.[14] He survived the inquiry and judgment, and went on to be ordained bishop of Avila. Objections to his views and behavior, however, continued to be made by parties hostile to his ordination, and his status was once again put under question at a council held at Bordeaux, probably in 384, where he was judged to be a Manichee and a heretic.[15] The charge of "being a Manichee" was surely being used by the hostile bishops since a general imperial law had been issued against Manichees only the

---

[14] Although no existing study says so, the precise number of a dozen might show that this was not a general council, but rather a meeting connected with Priscillian's ordination as bishop.

[15] Lieu, *Manichaeism in the Later Roman Empire*, pp. 148–50, reviews the accusations launched against Priscillian by his sectarian enemies. The charges of being a Manichee and of being involved in bad magic were both explicitly denied by Priscillian himself.

year before, in 383, a law whose effects are documented for Africa for this year. The law had been transmitted through the Praetorian Prefect and the Vicars and had been made public in the Spanish provinces. Charges of black magic and unusual sexual practices were added to this toxic mix. In 385, a trial before court officials was held at the imperial capital at Trier.

After matters had been transferred to Trier, it is telling that the charges of sorcery came very much to the fore while those of "being a Manichee" and a heretic faded permanently into the background of accusation. Avoiding the latter charges, the regional Praetorian Prefect, Evodius, found Priscillian guilty of sorcery.[16] When the emperor Magnus Maximus pondered the necessary punishment, he decided that Priscillian and his closest associates were to be executed. They were put to death in 386.[17] Even under the tense, confused, and marginal conditions in the northwest provinces of the empire at this time, the regional state and its local emperor still hewed to a secular-like path, preferring to assist the churchmen in their concerns, but doing so by imposing a capital sentence on the criminal charge of evil magical practice rather than for heresy. No Christian emperor was yet willing to move actually to execute a dissident Christian on the charge of being an unacceptable Christian. But the line between the two was becoming thin, notably in a Spanish context. If the disaffected Iberian bishops could have found a Spanish emperor, someone more like themselves who shared their background and attitudes, the chances of pressing over that line might have been better. They would not have long to wait. It was with a combination of culture and belief from this quarter that the pieces of a serious imperial anti-heretical policy would finally be assembled.

As the case of Priscillian indicates, the accusation of "being a Manichee" had become pivotal to the new wave of anti-heretical action in the west. It is hardly accidental that it was the same time that Priscillian was executed, the year 386, that Messianus, the proconsular governor of Africa, was having accused Manichees hauled before his tribunal for judgment. It was later

---

[16] On the charges as charges of being a Manichee, see Lieu, *Manichaeism in the Later Roman Empire*, pp. 148–49, where he takes them as the basis for the execution, based on Sulp. Sev. *Chron.* 2.51.2–3 (CSEL 1: 104, lines 5–11) and Pacatus, *Panegyricus Theodosio dictus*, 29.3 (ed. Galletier), vol. 3, p. 96. I am more persuaded by the interpretation of Burrus (see next note) since even Sulp. Sev. *Chron.* 2.50. 7–8 (CSEL 1: 103) clearly states that he was convicted of *maleficium*: cf. Chadwick, "Priscillian's End and Its Consequences," ch. 3 in *Priscillian of Avila*, pp. 111–69, at pp. 138–144, and, particularly, Humfress (2000), pp. 138–39, who also accepts that the formal charge was *maleficium*.

[17] This is an almost cartoon-like summary of a very complex and not well-documented series of events: see Van Dam, "The Heresy of Priscillianism," ch. 5 in *Leadership and Community*, pp. 88–117; and Burrus, *Making of a Heretic:*, esp. pp. 81–98.

rumoured that Augustine had been been swept up in the denunciations.[18] These latter "facts" where known to Petilian, the dissident bishop of Constantina, perhaps because of what he knew had happened to Faustus, one of the Manichaean Elect, who came from the nearby town of Milevis. Faustus had been charged by his fellow Christians with being a Manichee, and in 386 he had been convicted on the charge at the court of the proconsular governor of Africa. Although Faustus was found guilty, it is important to note the nature of the governor's enforcement. A capital crime exposed the defendant to various penalties. One was death, but there were other less severe possibilities that were open to the judge. In this case, the governor chose exile to a remote island.[19] Significant matters to note are the date, the general rules of the state that were being enforced, the accusations that were being provoked, and the response of the governor. The Christian state and its officials were not yet willing actually to execute a dissident Christian, even a formally unacceptable one, on the charge of heresy. Up to this point, the state's general attitude to Manichees was that they were nasty pests, but not much more. Having been sentenced to exile on an island, Faustus was released only a year after his sentencing and allowed to resume his activities under the terms of an imperial amnesty.[20] Nevertheless, Manichees were increasingly coming under the scrutiny of the state, and surely Augustine, Faustus, and Priscillian were all becoming liable to accusations in the same years of the mid-380s precisely because of the availability of general state regulations that opened them to attack.[21] It was in this connection that Christians were hailing Manichees before the civil courts – *several* of them, we are told, were in the group of which Faustus was part.

The reason for this special treatment was that the Manichees were Christians who were regarded as so unusual and so strange that they were in a category set apart, clearly defined, recognized, and excoriated by most

---

[18] The accusations were made by Petilian, dissident bishop of Constantina, in his polemic with Augustine: apud Aug. *Contra litt. Petil.* 3.25.30 (CSEL 52: 185), apparently with supporting legal documents; the incident dates to 385 or 386; for the governor, see "Messianus (1)," PAC, p. 750.

[19] Aug. *Contra Faust.* 5.8 (CSEL 25.1: 280): "Faustus autem convictus vel confessus, quod Manichaeus esset, cum aliis nonnullis secum ad iudicium proconsulare productis, eis ipsis Christianis, quibus perducti sunt intercedentibus levissima poena. Si tamen illa poena dicenda est, in insulam relegatus est." See, also, "Faustus (2)," PAC, p. 392.

[20] Aug. *Contra Faust.* 5.8 (CSEL 25.1: 280): "quod sua sponte cotidie servi Dei faciunt se a turbulento strepitu populorum removere cupientes, et unde publica terrenorum principum vota per indulgentiam solent relaxare damnatos. Denique non multo post inde omnes eadem sollemni sorte dimissi sunt." See the editors of "Faustus (2)," PAC, p. 392–93, who argue that the *vota publica* in connection with which Faustus was released were the *quinquennalia* of Arcadius in 387.

[21] The accusations also had force because it was known that these men knew each other well: Augustine, for example, was closely associated as a Manichee with Faustus during the early 380s when the two were in Carthage – Faustus as the senior teacher and Augustine as the more junior student.

other Christians. More important is the fact that being a Manichee was a capital crime, a crime that had been instituted at the beginning of the fourth century by the emperor Diocletian.[22] Early in the year 302, Amnius Anicius Julianus, the proconsular governor of Africa, a scion of the prestigious aristocratic family of the Anicii, had written in Pliny-like fashion to the emperor Diocletian, asking what he was to do with the Manichees and their activities once these had been drawn to his attention.[23] In a rescript to Julianus from Alexandria on 31 March of the same year, Diocletian condemned the Manichees on the grounds that they were establishing new and unheard-of sects. The emperor's words paint them as a foul excrudescence oozing from the earth that produced strange and monstrous portents; they are portrayed as dangerous men, promoting their evils with poisons drawn from the fangs of vipers. The references to poison and evil doing were not accidental. The close association of Manichees with the existing capital crime of being a magician and the manipulation of bad magic was fully intended.[24] The Manichees are pictured as an alien force that threatened the wellbeing of the Roman state and society.[25]

It is an important concern of ours to punish the obstinacy of the distorted minds of these most wicked men – concerning whom Your Carefulness has made report

---

[22] For discussions, see Seston (1940), Volterra (1966), Lieu, *Manichaeism in the Later Roman Empire*, pp. 121–22; for important revisions, see Decret, *Aspects du Manichéisme*, pp. 73, 331–33; he rejects the date of 297 proposed by Seston and others: for the arguments, see Decret, *L'Afrique manichéenne*, I, pp. 162–64; 2, pp. 112–16.

[23] As is clear from Diocletian's reply (see below); on Anicius, see "Julianus (23)," PRLE, I, pp. 473–74.

[24] Decret, *L'Afrique manichéenne*, I, pp. 168–89.

[25] Diocletian and Maximianus Augustuses, Constantius and Maximianus Caesars, from Alexandria, to Julianus, Proconsul of Africa (31 March 302): *Mosaicarum et Romanarum Legum Collatio*, 15.3 = FIRA 3.580–81 = M. Hyamson ed., *Mosaicarum et Romanarum Legum Collatio* (London-Oxford, 1913), pp. 130–33: "Unde pertinaciam pravae mentis nequissimorum hominum punire ingens nobis studium est: hi enim, qui novellas et inauditas sectas veterioribus religionibus opponunt, ut pro arbitrio suo pravo excludant quae divinitus concessa sunt quondam nobis, de quibus sollertia tua serenitati nostrae retulit, Manichaei, audivimus eos nuperrime veluti nova [et] inopinata prodigia in hunc mundum de Persica adversaria nobis gente progressa vel orta esse et multa facinora ibi committere, populos namque quietos perturbare nec non et civitatibus maxima detrimenta inserere: et verendum est, ne forte, ut fieri adsolet, accedenti tempore conentur [per] execrandas consuetudines et scaevas leges Persarum innocentioris naturae homines, Romanam gentem modestam atque tranquillam et universum orbem nostrum veluti venenis de suis malivolis inficere. Et quia omnia, quae pandit prudentia tua in relatione religionis illorum, genera maleficiorum statutis evidentissime sunt exquisita et inventa commenta, ideo aerumnas atque poenas debitas et condignas illis statuimus. Iubemus namque auctores quidem ac principes una cum abominandis scripturis eorum severiori poenae subici, ita ut flammeis ignibus exurantur; consentaneos vero et usque adeo contentiosos capite puniri praecipimus, et eorum bona fisco nostro vindicari sancimus" (15.3.4–6). For discussion of the genuineness of the text, see Seston (1940) and Kaden (1953), pp. 56–57; for a defense of an earlier date of 297 for the edict, see BeDuhn, *Augustine's Manichaean Dilemma*, I, p. 27 n. 24, and the literature cited there. For Mani and his followers seen as a sort of "fifth column" threatening the state, see Brown (1969/1972) and Van der Lof (1974).

to Our Serenity – men who are setting up new and unheard-of sects against our traditional beliefs with the intent (at their own wicked discretion) of discarding the divine things that have been handed down to us from time immemorial. We have heard that these persons have most recently arisen and advanced into our world from among the Persians, a people who are hostile to us. Like new and unexpected monstrosities, they are committing many evils among us, throwing our peaceful people into an uproar and causing serious harm in our cities. Our fear is that with the passage of time (as usually happens) they will try to infect men of more innocent character – the otherwise modest and tranquil Roman people – with their malevolent poisons; and that they will try to infect the whole of our world with the damnable customs and perverse laws of the Persians. Since all the matters that Your Wisdom has explained and documented in your report about their religion are kinds of evil-doing that are carefully constructed and made-up falsehoods, we decree the appropriate and deserved penalties for them.

The Manichees are categorized as a kind of threat to the social order that the Roman state had normally concerned itself with repressing.[26] The penalty was commensurately severe: the authors and chiefs of the cult were to be burnt alive, along with their abominable writings. Ordinary followers, if they remained obstinate in their beliefs, were also to suffer capital punishment and their goods were to be confiscated by the imperial fiscus. The manner in which anti-Manichaean laws were to continue to function over the fourth century – the legislative attack, the public excoriation of the threat, and the penalties – prefigured the type of assault that would be made on other unacceptable Christians beginning in 303.[27] From their inception, therefore, anti-Manichaean laws were being extrapolated to cover analogous cases.

A problem that African churchmen in the later age of Augustine had in assessing the continued validity of Diocletian's law lay in the paradox that, on the one hand, the Manichees were Christians whereas, on the other, Diocletian was the Great Persecutor. So what *was* the post-Constantinian status of the death penalty that Diocletian had imposed on Manichees? In an odd way, the law still lingered on the books. Logically, however, the decree had not been much enforced, if at all, since the Manichees

---

[26] Note that the heading under which the law was originally collated in the Codex Gregorianus was *De maleficis et Manichaeis*; consider anti-magic measures, going back to Bacchanalian "conspiracy" of 186 BCE, see J.-M. Pailler, *Bacchanalia: la repression de 186 av. J.-C. à Rome et en Italie: vestiges, images, tradition*, Paris, de Boccard, 1988, with full bibliography, and for the sense of continuity of this attitude in the late Roman state, see Humfress (2008), pp. 132–24; for connections with Persians seen as magicians, see Lieu, *Manichaeism in the Later Roman Empire*, pp. 143–44.

[27] Decret, *L'Afrique manichéenne*, 1, pp. 167–69, noting, however, the important differences of target groups and precise penalties; the crossover use of the Manichees as a model for attacking Christians, as in the burning of sacred books, began in 303: see Cameron (2007), pp. 2–3, and 10.

were indeed Christians.[28] There was the additional problem that defining who or exactly what a "Manichaeus" was was especially difficult: did they count as Christians or not?[29] Manichees in Africa lived under the threat of this official sanction, and they rightly feared denunciation, arrest, and punishment.[30] This strangely liminal threat was exploitable, especially by those who were well aware of the situation in which Manichees found themselves. If the capital sentence under which they lived could be justified on the grounds that they were heretics and not just alien and seditious Christians (as Diocletian's legislation envisaged them), then it might be the key to getting the state to act against heretics. The Manichees could become the avatars of a new species of dangerous heretic that merited capital punishment.

In the Constantinian and immediate post-Constantinian decades, there was a basic division in the quality of heretics. Most heretics like Eunomians, Photinians, and Arians, although bad, were excoriated mainly for false dogma, false beliefs, and false teachings – doctrines and practices that did not cohere with Nicene norms, for instance.[31] The Manichees, however, were seen in quite a different light. They were a breed apart. They were viewed, fearfully, as a mortal danger to social harmony and as a criminal conspiracy threatening the state itself, a strange cult that was a danger to the secular order.[32] In the early 370s, as part of the new movement against heresy, they became the object of the first anti-heretical legislation that went beyond the passive denial of privileges to bad Christians and moved to the active imposition of harsh punishments on unwanted persons. The teachers of the Manichees were to be heavily fined, and their meeting places

---

[28] A point that is forcefully made, and rightly, by Van Oort (2003), pp. 203–04.

[29] First, the label was external – few known persons actually identified themselves as a "Manichaeus" in these terms; there followed problems of what litmus tests could be used to secure identity: see Lim (2008), pp. 149–50 and 154–58; as he argues, much of the talk about Manichaean "dissimulation" and "mendacity" stems from the the lack of a perceived need on their part to act out the role and the name assigned to them.

[30] That is to say, the situation described by Augustine in *De mor. Man.* 19.69; cf. 19.70 (CSEL 90: 150–51), refers to some period before the first known new anti-Manichaean laws of the mid-370s: Decret, *L'Afrique manichéenne*, 1, pp. 211–13; 2, p. 159.

[31] See, e.g., CTh 16.5.1 (1 September 326) defining *Catholica lex*; 16.5.2 (25 September 326): controlling Novatianists; 16.5.6 (10 January 381): heretics condemned for the *dementia* or madness of their obstinate minds, failing to be of Nicene faith handed down by "our ancestors", and of mistaken doctrines; 15.6.8 (19 July 381): Eunomians and Arians condemned for dogma and doctrines.

[32] Recognized, in part, by Lieu, *Manichaeism in the Later Roman Empire*, pp. 143–44: "The only surviving anti-Manichaean edict issued between the edict of Diocletian and the legislations of Theodosius was clearly actuated more by fear of the harm such a secretive group of people could do to the moral welfare of the state than by intolerance of its heretical doctrines."

were to be confiscated by the imperial fiscus.[33] The more severe penalties that were first set for Manichees could then be extended to other heretics, no doubt in response to the insistent lobbying of the imperial court. Only a few years after this measure against Manichees, its penalties were applied to heretics in general.[34] A new imperial decree issued in the spring of 381 upped the stakes. The Manichees were now condemned as permanently guilty of public crimes.[35] Under whatever particular names they might happen to be lurking, they were to have their meeting places confiscated by the state and, more importantly, as individuals they were to be deprived of the ability to pass wealth on to their descendants: their wills were to be voided. In a truly unusual move, the emperors decreed that the terms of this law were to be made retroactive. It was a move that the emperors themselves recognized as odd, but which they justified on the grounds that it was necessary "to avenge" the lack of past enforcement of the existing laws against the Manichees. In March of the next year, 382, these measures were confirmed, with the additional emphasis that the Manichees were subject to the supreme penalty and that there was to be no statute of limitations in pursuing anyone who was guilty of the crime.[36] It took only one year to extend these anti-Manichaean measures to heretics in general, with the injunction that all of their properties were similarly to be seized by the state.[37]

It was in the year immediately following, at the meeting at Bordeaux in 384, that Priscillian was formally accused of being a Manichee. The hope of his accusers was to use the new legislation to provoke state action. The function of the Manichees was to serve as a leading edge in establishing new ways in which the hardest and most hated enemies of orthodoxy could be treated. The trend was encapsulated in a law issued in November 389. Its terms were harsher yet. The evil men who upset the peace of all society were "to be expelled from this world . . . with which they should share nothing." They were to be deprived of all their worldly possessions and permanently to live under the threat of capital punishment.[38] These harsher measures were brought to Africa with particular force in a specific imperial directive

---

[33] CTh 16.5.3 (2 March 372): Valentinian and Valens to Ampelius: Praefectus Urbi; as Kaden (1953), p. 58 remarked, this was a new interest in Manichees that came after a long interlude. That is true, but the fact is that as such it simply conforms to the broader hiatus in interest in heresy in general.

[34] CTh 16.5.4 (22 April 378).

[35] CTh 16.5.6 (8 May 381): Gratian, Valentinian, and Theodosius to Eutropius PP.

[36] CTh 16.5.9 (31 March 382): Gratian, Valentinian, and Theodosius to Florus PP.

[37] CTh 16.5.11 (25 July 383); cf. 16.5.12 (3 December 383); 16.5.13 (21 January 384); measures reconfirmed in 16.5.14 (10 March 388).

[38] CTh 16.5.18 (26 November 389): Valentinian, Theodosius, and Arcadius to Tatianus PP.

issued by the emperors to Dominator, the Vicar of Africa, in May 399.[39] In their command to the Vicar, the emperors ordered that Manichees were now to be actively hunted down and hauled before state authorities; and they were to be allowed no reprieve from the culpability for their crimes. They were to be cut down by "the most severe correction." In addition, persons who harbored or protected them were to be severely punished. It is no accident that the year 399–400 witnessed a flurry of accusations of "being a Manichee" made in the hope of catching rivals in a lethal trap. In the internecine Christian battles between dissidents and Catholics at Constantina, for example, the Catholic bishops Profuturus and Fortunatus were accused of being Manichees.[40] Dangerous threats. It was also the same year, notably, in which the former Manichee, Augustine of Hippo, began to write his *Confessions*, demonstrating by personal memoir what an orthodox Catholic Christian he had become and the full extent to which he now abjured his Manichaean past. The title of his composition gestures to the world of trials and testimony.[41] The accusations were credible precisely because all three men were good friends who had a close and, possibly, a subversive history going back to shared days at Hippo and earlier.[42]

ORIENTAL SUBVERSIVES

The move to strike a vital connection between Manichees and heresy made sense from views shared by both Christian churches in Africa. In his accusations made against Augustine, including that of being a covert Manichee, Petilian, the dissident bishop of Constantina, was echoing a long-held view among Africans that there was an original source of heresy

---

[39] CTh 16.5.35 (17 May 399): "Arcadius and Honorius: Quapropter quaesiti adducantur in publicum ac detestati criminosi congrua et severissima emendatione resecentur. In eos etiam auctoritatis aculei dirigantur, qui eos domibus suis damnanda provisione defendent."

[40] Aug. *De unico bapt.* 16.29 (CSEL 53: 31).

[41] See Kotzé, *Augustine's Confessions*, for a different view of the work that interprets its pervasive Manichaean elements as protreptic in nature. Although there might be some of these elements in a complex and multi-layered composition, I still read most of them as meant to signal Augustine's decisive separation from his Manichaean past to a more general public.

[42] See De Veer (1968n and 1968o) for background, but "Fortunatus (5)," PAC, pp. 494–96, and "Profuturus," PAC, pp. 928–30, on the chronology of their episcopates; PAC rightly dismisses De Veer's claim that Fortunatus was Augustine's pupil. Profuturus, however, was so close to Augustine that the latter regarded him as his "other self": *mihi est alter ego*; he became bishop at Constantina around 395 and lived to *c.* 400, when he was succeeded by Fortunatus. BeDuhn (2009) wishes to place the beginnings of Augustine's literary palinode on his past in the context of the anti-Manichaean legislation of the 380s; but he misses the law of 399 that is surely most directly relevant to the production of the *Confessions*. More convincing is his explication of the way that Augustine's selective memory of his past involved him in the justification of what I am tempted to call passive mendacity: see BeDuhn (2009), pp. 104–07.

going back to the very foundations of Christianity.[43] In his mission, Jesus had had seventy-two disciples. Of these, only eleven, a select and prestigious elite, had remained with him, loyal to the end. To the dissidents, all those descended from the traitorous sixty, and Judas, who had abandoned Jesus were the fathers of heretics, and Mani must surely have been a descendant of one of them.[44] And, notably, Augustine and a whole coterie of his fellow Catholic bishops had only recently transited out of the ranks of the Manichees.[45] They were fatally exposed to accusations that they were hiding a continuing devotion to the Persian heretic. It was hardly accidental that Petilian launched his accusation against Augustine – namely, that he was still a Manichee – in the same year, 399, that the Vicar and the governors of the African provinces published the emperor's harsh explicit decree against the oriental sect.

The parallel and related idea – that the "Rebaptizers" in Africa might also be successfully labelled as heretics – was in the range of possibilities as early as Constantine. This prospect must have been an active part of Catholic discourse through the mid-fourth century, since detailed conceptions and attitudes about the dissidents as heretics are already present in the writings of Optatus of Milevis, just after mid-century. Although he addressed the dissidents as "brothers," they are nonetheless brothers who run with the Devil and with adulterers, which is to say, as he explains, with heretics.[46] By this time, the Devil or Satan already had a proven track-record of providing irrefutable and absolute moral grounds for condemning unacceptable kinds of deviant Christians as more than just errant believers.[47] Just so, in the African churchmen of our period, including Augustine, the image of Satan not only as the Great Seducer, but also as the Father of Lies, could base their attacks on dissent as a species of heresy – as something more than just innocuous disagreement – by linking dissenters in a palpable way

---

[43] On the accusations launched against him by Petilian, apud Aug. *Contra litt. Petil.* 3.10.11 (CSEL 52: 172) and Cresconius, apud Aug. *Contra Cresc.* 3.79.91; 4.64.79 (CSEL 52: 494–95; 577–78); see Frend (1954), Adam (1958), Lamirande (1965d), pp. 710–11, and Courcelle, *Recherches sur les Confessions,* pp. 238–45.

[44] The appeal for the 72 was to Luke 10: 1; cf. Frend (1954); Brisson, *Autonomisme et christianisme,* pp. 209–10; and see Aug. *Ep. ad Cath. contra Donatist.* 13.33 (CSEL 52: 274).

[45] Known former Manichees in this group, other than Augustine himself, included Alypius (bishop of Thagaste), Profuturus (bishop of Constantina), Severus (the latter's successor as bishop of Constantina).

[46] Optatus, *Contra Parm.* 1.3.4 (SC 412: 176–78): "Sed de istorum fratrum delictis dicam alio loco, qui sedentes adversus nos detrahunt et contra nos scandala ponunt et cum illo fure concurrunt, qui Deo furtum facit, et cum moechis, id est haereticis."

[47] Pagels, *Satan,* esp. chs. 5 and 6 is one of the clearest expositions of this role assumed by the Blocker and the Prince of Darkness.

with Satan, as his offspring or agents.[48] In some senses, for the Africans, the Antichrist was an even more powerful figure. Satan was like an external enemy, but the Antichrist was a powerful internal subversive who threatened the church from within. He was far more applicable to their inside war.[49] If the dissident exegete Tyconius had already laid down the powerful image of the Antichrist as an evil embedded in a Christian believer who, by hating the other, showed that he did not believe in Christ, then Augustine and the Catholic exegetes ran with the theme and developed it as their own.[50] Heretics and, more importantly, inside enemies like schismatics were true exemplars of this danger which was present not so much as a general social phenomenon, but rather as a matter of bad individual behavior.

More powerful than just the label of "heretic" in popular perceptions was the moral baggage that came along with the bad name. As a deviant, the heretic was immediately linked with the main codes of moral depravity as they had traditionally been mapped in Mediterranean societies. This moral language highlighted bad women and bad sex. The sexualization of heresy and heretics in which they are guilty of illicit sex and of the seduction of true believers was already commonplace in Optatus, and he was the heir of a long tradition going back at least to the time of Tertullian. Although nothing as pervasive as the intense regulation found in the canons of the early fourth-century Spanish Council of Elvira can be paralleled in African norms, there is still the same intimate and pervasive identification of heresy and internal dissent with bad sex.[51] The great moralist had already warned wobbly Christians that one day they would have to face the final tribunal of God where they would have to deny that they had ever committed illicit sexual acts against the Virgin (viz. the true church), whom Christ had handed to them in marriage, through the adultery of heresy.[52] Similarly, for Optatus heretics were like prostitutes, women who lack the sacraments,

---

[48] See Russell, "Satan and Saint Augustine," ch. 7 in *Satan*, esp. pp. 109–11, on Satan as the *pater mendacii*.

[49] As argued, with his usual power, by Ratzinger (1958), noting the powerful impact of Tyconius' thinking on Augustine, and the great danger of this inside subversive threat to the well-being of the Church.

[50] See McGinn, *Antichrist*, pp. 75–77, noting the huge importance of Tyconius; both he and, later, Augustine emphasized the particular importance of 1 Joh. 2: 18–27 (on which, see McGinn, ibid., pp 54–56), as evinced in Augustine's sermons on 1 John.

[51] See the extraordinary number of canons at Elvira that are concerned with various forms of adultery: *moechia, lenocinium, extraneae feminae, meretrices, adulteria, alieni viri, stuprum*, and so on: see the "Tituli" in Martínez-Rodríguez, *Canónica hispana*, pp. 233–39, and the contents of the regulations; Laeuchli, *Power and Sexuality*, attempted an initial analysis, but more needs to be done.

[52] Tert. *De praescript. Haeret.* 44 (CCL 1: 223): "Quid ergo dicent qui illam stupraverint adulterio haeretico virginem traditam a Christo?"

the legitimate basis of honorable marriage (i.e. with the Church).[53] With others, he portrays "the Donatists" as *seducing* simple minds. All the pieces were here, but two matters stood in the way. First, the internal conditions in Africa were not sufficient, as they were in the Spanish provinces, to excite a very harsh response within Christian communities.[54] Then again, by the 360s the state had still not moved to the point where it was willing to assume the role of aggressively punishing Christian heretics with capital punishments.

In asserting the close affinities between the dissident Christians in Africa and dangerous heretics, the early Optatus did *not* go so far as to say that the dissidents were in fact heretics, only that they consorted with them. It is a fine line that he wished to maintain. He insists on categorizing his Donatist enemy Parmenian as a *schismaticus*, and emphatically states that heretics had nothing to do with the arguments between himself and Parmenian. The two of them shared the sacraments of the faith in common; the others, the heretics, did not possess the true Gifts of the Church, the *dotes ecclesiae*. But he suggests that Parmenian does.[55] In deciding to follow this path, Optatus was also aware of the harder position that was there, in the background, to be drawn upon if necessary. To be a schismatic was the lesser crime, involving a difference of opinion within the true Christian community. Heretics, on the other hand, were genuinely evil men. They deliberately set about trying to deceive the ignorant and the unlearned with their palpably false ideas.[56] These harder judgments were there to be drawn upon, if needed.

On the dissident side, Parmenian had not been as conciliatory or as forgiving towards his Catholic brother. According to Optatus, he had gone all the way and had simply labeled the Catholics as heretics: "You are branches broken from the vine and, destined for punishment, you are reserved like dry wood for the Fires of Hell."[57] Optatus, on the other hand, had an agenda that was conciliatory in tone, a program in which he insisted on seeing the dissidents as "brothers" who shared all of the same elements of the Christian faith that he himself did as a Catholic. He downplayed their

---

[53] Optatus, *Contra Parm.* 1.10.2 (SC 412: 192): "Interea dixisti apud haereticos dotes ecclesiae esse non posse et recte dixisti. Scimus enim haereticorum ecclesias singulorum prostitutas nullis legalibus sacramentis et sine iure honesti matrimonii esse."

[54] See, e.g., Van Dam, *Leadership and Community*, pp. 103–04, on the differences in practice in the function of the accusation of being a Manichee in Spain and in Africa of the time – differences which he rightly (in my view) ties to internal conditions in the respective societies.

[55] Optatus, *Contra Parm.* 1.9.3 (SC 412: 190).

[56] Optatus, *Contra Parm.* 1.12.1 (SC 412: 196): "Haeretici vero veritatis exules, sani et verissimi symboli desertores . . . ut ignorantes et rudes deciperent," citing 2 Tim. 3: 6–7 in support.

[57] Optatus, *Contra Parm.* 1.10.4–11.2 (SC 412: 192–96).

differences and portrayed the dissidents as nothing more than *schismatici* or breakaway renegades who had willfully divided themselves from the true church, and not as heretics. In this sense, he interpreted the biblical story of Dathan, Abiron, and Cora – as the dissidents themselves were to do at the Council of Bagaï – as indicating a lesser kind of division. Those men, Optatus said, are your ancestors, the men who taught you what to do.[58]

This softer line was tailored as part of an appeal to Parmenian and to the dissidents based on their supposed mutual brotherhood. Optatus did not modify the nature of his appeal through the mid-380s when he produced the enlarged second version of his reply to Parmenian. A good part of the reason for this was context. The attitudes of the imperial court under Julian and his immediate successors did not encourage a harsher attitude on the part of the Catholics. Up to the mid-380s, there was no sign that the necessary coercive force would be forthcoming from the state, so conciliation and diplomacy were the order of the day. The new circumstances of court power in the late 380s and early 390s, the renewed interest in heretics, and the new patterns set by the repression of the Manichees changed this ground entirely. The imperial government of the Theodosian state, driven by an emperor of harder Iberian disposition, revealed itself as ready and able to move decisively against heretics. In this world of different horizons, alluring possibilities of new alliances with the state were now open to Catholic powerbrokers.

BAD SEX

The changed attitude at the political center and the developing possibilities of serious action against the enemies of orthodoxy encouraged plans to attack the dissidents by exploiting the complex repertoire that had been designed to find and to label heretics. The full force of all of the stories, biblical parallels, striking animal metaphors, and other sources of similitude, could now be arraigned in a more consistent polemical campaign. Here, too, the preachers could exploit an expansively developed discourse, also grounded in Epiphanius' typologies, that connected heresy with bad sex.[59] The allusive effect was dramatic and the metaphors powerful: they

---

[58] Optatus, *Contra Parm.* 1.21.2 (SC 412: 216): "et tamen Dathan et Abiron et Core, perditos magistros vestros, sine trepidatione estis imitati"; and 6.1.10 (SC 413: 166): "Sed observate ne veniatis ad inferos et illic inveniatis Core, Dathan et Abiron schismaticos, magistros scilicet vestros."

[59] Cameron (2003b), pp. 354–55; cf. Knust, *Abandoned to Lust*, passim, but esp. pp. 144–58; the attacking language, potentially connected with violence, has more to do with immoral acts injurious to marriage than it does with the threats of intermarriage between the two hostile religious groups:

could be used to sketch the social evil of the heretic and then to identify dissident Christians in Africa not just as ecclesiastical dissenters, but
as the kind of heretic in whom the new imperial dispensation was interested. As with Optatus, Augustine also sexualized the dissident heretics
and their behavior.[60] This rhetoric, like that of some modern purveyors of
the sermon, at times bordered on soft porn.[61] But there was a new harshness, precision, and vividness in the metaphors. In a sermon delivered just
before the great conference of 411 that linked Donatists and heretics, the
preacher joined biblical quotation and exegesis to issue a warning about
the allurements of these bad people:[62]

Unless you know yourself, he says, *beautiful among women* – because however these
other women might be beautiful with gifts from their husbands, they are heresies.
Alluringly attired and made up, they are not beautiful inside. They shimmer on
the outside – on their exterior. They have put on the cosmetics of justice. *The
beauty of the daughter of the king, however, is inside* . . . so you should not be seduced
by the perverse talk of such evil companions.

In a similar sermon delivered in the New Basilica at Carthage on 17 July 410,
on the anniversary of the Scillitan martyrs, less than a year before the great
confrontation with the dissidents, Augustine compared heresies to bad
daughters. Why are they bad daughters? Because they, too, were born from
the same woman (sc. the church); therefore they are daughters. Despite
all of the apparent similarities with their siblings, however, the dissident
Christians in Africa were "bad daughters." He explains: "They are bad
daughters – daughters not in the sameness of their behavior, but in the
sameness of their sacraments. They too have our sacraments, they have our
scriptures, they have our Amen and Alleluia, most of them have our creed,
and many of them have our baptism. That's why they're daughters."[63] But
he goes on to expatiate on them as fallen females. In this case, the kinship
of sameness that Optatus had used to make the dissidents "our brothers"

---

contrast Nirenberg, "Sex and Violence between Majority and Minority," ch. 5 in *Communities of
Violence*, reflecting a situation that could have arisen here, but did not.

[60] Again, this strategy draws on a common repertoire; it was not limited to the time or to Africa. For
some apposite comments, see Burrus, *Making of a Heretic*, pp. 16, 33–35.

[61] See various assessments, for example, of the use of sexual innuendo in the Reverend Ian Paisley's
anti-Catholic sermons, which led one official to dub him "the great pornographer": see Coogan,
The Troubles, pp. 54–55.

[62] Aug. *Sermo* 138.8 (PL 38: 767).

[63] Aug. *Sermo* 37.27 (CCL 41: 469): "Sunt enim malae filiae, quae sunt haereses. Quare filiae? Quia et
illae ex ista natae. Sed filiae malae, filiae non similitudine morum, sed similitudine sacramentorum.
Habent et ipsae sacramenta nostra, habent scripturas nostras, habent Amen et Alleluia nostrum,
habent pleraeque symbolum nostrum, habent multae baptismum nostrum. Ideo filiae."

is used to turn them into bad sisters, bad daughters, bad females. They are doubly bad.

The labeling of the heretic as sexually aberrant was connected with specific perverse acts that characterized individual heretical groups – incest and various kinds of sex with women of protected and honorable status being the most common of the charges of immorality. Other accusations of unusual sexual behavior were perhaps more compelling since they bore the sharpness of specificity and precision. In the hearings at Carthage, probably in the 420s, conducted before the imperial tribune Ursus, for example, confessions were wrung out of two women, Margarita and Eusebia. Since the confessions were extorted from them "with difficulty," it is not out of place to assume the use of threats and, probably, force. Among other things, the two women admitted to being involved in an illicit sexual practice that was specifically Manichaean. They had watched as a couple engaged in sexual intercourse in a room in which flour had been sprinkled on the floor underneath the copulating pair. The reason was to collect the semen as it fell to the floor so that it could be consumed by the Elect of the cult. Augustine was concerned to advertise the shock value of the "depravity" involved.[64] A few years after Ursus' hearings, Quodvultdeus, the Catholic bishop of Carthage, had uncovered more of this same "bad sex" in inquisitions that he had held, at least one of them involving a Manichee named Viator.[65] The difference was that Augustine had been a decade-long Manichee and it is difficult to believe that he had not even heard of such practices. His shock, surely, was feigned.

And so it was that at the primal origins of the divisions – the heresies and the heretics – within the churches, whether Catholic or dissident, were found the activities of vile Eve figures, portrayed in colors as lurid and wicked as those of an evil Sassia in Cicero or the malific Sempronia in Sallust. It was the fatal kiss of the wealthy Spanish noblewoman Lucilla, the *factiosissima femina*, in the disputes in Carthage between Caecilian and Maiorinus in the first decade of the 300s, that lay at the root of the awful and dreadful creation of heresy within the Christian church in Africa.[66] Just so, in the early 390s another such woman was the primal cause, or so it was reported, in the terrible schism that rent the dissident church between Primian and Maximianus in the metropolitan see of Carthage.[67]

---

[64] Aug. *De Haeres.* 46.8–10 (CCL 46: 314–15); cf. van Oort (2000) for contextual comment.

[65] Aug. *De Haeres.* 46.10 (CCL 46: 315).

[66] On Lucilla's kiss, see Optatus, *Contra Parm.* 1.16.1 (SC 412: 206–08): "per Lucillam scilicet, nescio quam feminam factiosam . . . os nescio cuius martyris, si tamen martyris, libare dicebatur"; cf. Shaw (1992/1995), pp. 25–26, De Veer (1968e), and the earlier study by Dölger (1932/1950).

[67] See full references in "Lucilla," PLRE 1, p. 517; and "Lucilla (1)," PAC, p. 649.

In this case, the dangerous woman was unnamed, anonymous (as often), but meriting the sobriquet of "a second Lucilla." Augustine, who notes the role of this other evil woman, surely known from the polemical texts hurled by Primianists against Maximianists, and vice versa, was rightly sceptical of her real existence.[68] Christian aetiologists in Africa were able to piggy-back on existing explanatory stereotypes that were already deeply embedded in Mediterranean tropes that explained decisive events with the intevention of members of the bad sex.

The construal of heresy (and schism) as "bad sex" had other logical correlates. If heresy was a form of adultery, then there existed a host of savage scriptural denunciations of adulterers that could now be deployed. If the use of private lynch justice was accepted by most males (at least) in the society at large to punish the adulterer, then a Christian mapping of just violence onto an existing moral template only added to powerful sentiments. Already in the 360s, Optatus was using the biblical story of Phinehas (Numbers 25: 6–11) as a model to justify the use of violence in quashing heresy as adultery. There might well be a prior biblical injunction "thou shalt not kill," he admits, but the narrative in the book of Numbers justified a clear exception since it showcased the committing of an ostensibly bad act – that is, murdering someone – in the name of a greater good.[69] He makes this argument in justification of the deaths inflicted by imperial officials Paul and Macarius in 347. The use of Phinehas, however widespread it might be among bishops of the church, was nevertheless a matter of debate. One could accept it but, equally, one could simply reject it as a legitimate parallel.[70] Some of the dissidents objected that the model of Phinehas did not apply in present times. The example for their own times was that of the forgiving Christ who restored the ear of the soldier that Peter had cut off. But one can easily see how some of the dissidents could read the same story in the same fashion as the Catholics: Catholic heresy was just like a sexual deviancy, the work of adulterers, and there was good biblical precedent in the Phinehas story to justify the use of extreme violence to punish it.

Since these sins were inherited, birth raised the issue of certain kinds of women as progenitors of evil. In typology and allegory, good Catholics were seen as children descended from the free woman Sarah, while heretics

---

[68] Aug. *Ep.* 43.9.26 (CCL 31: 186) and *En. in Ps.* 36.2.19 (CCL 38: 360): "alia Lucilla corruperit, et forte non inventurus."

[69] Optatus, *Contra Parm.* 3.5.1–3.7.5 (SC 413: 46–56).

[70] Gaddis, *Religious Violence*, p. 329, for a case where church authorities would not put up a monk's violent acts, no matter how often he cited the example of Phinehas (and Elijah).

were the descendants of Abraham's slave woman. And we know that slave women signify no good: "We accept that slave women are among the evil; we accept that free women are among the good. Free women produce good men: Sarah gave birth to Isaac. Slave women produce evil men: Agar gave birth to Ishmael."[71] This model story had bad implications for the people who constituted the other church. For them it was not Mater Ecclesia, Mother Church, who had birthed them. Rather, their church must be an offspring of the Great Whore.[72] A severe caution had to be sounded about a threat that was doubly immoral to the pure body of the Church. The heretics were so sexually impure that it was almost impossible for the preacher to describe the depths of their sexual depravity (as a metaphor, of course).[73]

I advise you strongly, in the love of Christ, to beware of impure seducers and sects of absolutely filthy indecency about whom the Apostle [sc. Paul] says: "But it is shameful for me even to speak about the things that these people do in secret." . . . indeed, there are some evils that no human sense of decency whatever can manage to bear . . . the very ones that occur in unclean bodies . . .

The sexual metaphor could be made more powerful by mixing it with animal images. Ordinary good Christians who were not thinking carefully about their beliefs, or who were more simple-minded, might easily be led astray. They could be seduced. They are cows. The aggressive and predatory heretics are bulls. Like bulls, they are stiff-necked, proud, and refuse to obey. Therefore they are heretics. The identification with "the Donatists" is made all the time in these sermons: the dissidents who "talk frivolously and lead the minds of others astray – the minds of those whom our psalmist calls cows."[74] Unsuspecting Catholic cows are seduced by Donatist bulls.[75] The frank and vivid imagery that would come into the minds of persons who were in much closer contact with rural reproduction than most are today requires no further description. To some extent this was inculcated into believers on both sides. As in Priscillian's case, accusations of being a Manichee were closely linked both with charges of sexual impropriety and

---

[71] Aug. *Tract. in Ioh.* 11.7.1–2; 11.10.1 (CCL 36: 114 and 116).
[72] So Emeritus apud Aug. *Sermo ad Caes. Eccl. Plebem*, 8 (CSEL 53: 177) "publice blaspheman- tem . . . quando dicit, 'nostra est quae in parte est,' quando dicit, 'illa meretrix est.'"
[73] Aug. *Tract. In Ioh.* 96.5 (CCL 36: 572): "Quae cum ita sint, dilectissimi, moneo vos in caritate Christi, ut seductores caveatis impuros et obscoenae turpitudinis sectas, de quibus ait apostolus: *Quae autem occulte fiunt ab istis, turpe est et dicere.* [Eph. 5: 12] . . . Alia sunt mala quae portare non potest qualiscumque pudor humanus . . . ista fiunt in corporibus impudicis."
[74] Aug. *En. in Ps.* 67.38–39 (CCL 39: 896–97), quoting 1 Tm 3: 6–7 on the entrapment of poor women.
[75] Aug. *En. in Ps.* 106.14 (CCL 40: 1581).

with charges of being an educated rhetor who knew just too much for his own good. All were tell-tale signs that pointed the way to the heretic.

So it was with Augustine who was exposed to these same accusations not only because of his known lengthy Manichaean past, but also because of strong suspicions about his current crypto-Manichaean leanings. He, too, was accused of having dispensed poisonous love-philters to seduce beautiful women. As with Priscillian, the moral charges against Augustine stemmed from inside hostilities that were part of the same types of internal conflicts generated by the contentious process of electing a new bishop.[76] What sort of pseudo-Christian was he anyway? The hearings held by Messianus, the proconsular governor of Africa in 386 that involved Manichees, in which Augustine's name was noted in the records, were supposed to have been the real reason for his sudden departure from Africa: to seek refuge in distant Italy. On the basis of the chronology and the records, Augustine was able to present a good alibi and was able to dull the sting of the charges.[77] The connections are not without some force. Strange sexual delicts were constantly suggested about the Manichees and their rituals, sometimes, as we have seen, with quite graphic descriptions in support. They might be entirely untrue, but, as the Manichee Fortunatus commented, the accusations worked. They had a real effect in exciting hatred, maltreatment, and finally persecution.[78] But a harsh imperial order made directly to the imperial official in charge of Africa in early 399 reignited opportunities for the accusers. The metaphors used in these accusations, moreover, were often mixed and not neatly separated as we have seen them here. In his sermon to the newly baptized at Hippo in 394, the same Augustine who had been accused of seducing women warned the new Christians in explicit sexual

---

[76] We only know about these charges because they became news and so were picked up by the dissidents and later reiterated by them, and Augustine was forced to face them in his own replies: Aug. *Contra Cresc.* 3.80.92 (CSEL 52: 495) is merely a general reference to the letter issued by Megalius, the Catholic primate of Numidia, against Augustine at the time of his impending election as bishop; *Contra litt. Petil.* 3.16.19 (CSEL 52: 177): in addition to being an evil "dialectician" and a Manichee, Petilian also charged: "ut amatoria maleficia data mulieri marito non solum conscio, verum etiam credi sibi posse praesumat." The parallels with Priscillian are therefore precise in all respects.

[77] On the nature of the accusations, see Quinot (1967c) and Lamirande (1965d). Courcelle, *Recherches sur les Confessions*, pp. 238–45, provides a detailed review. For Messianus, see "Messianus," PRLE, I, p. 600: not much else is known of him save for what is in CTh 10.1.13.

[78] On the sexual perversions of which Manichees were accused, see pp. 328–29 above; for this incident see Aug. *Contra Fortunat.* 1 (CSEL 25.1: 84), where the Manichee Fortunatus, in a debate with Augustine in midsummer of 392 at Hippo, asked Augustine, as an ex-Manichee – "quia te medium fuisse nostrum scio" – to denounce such charges as untrue: "De conversatione hic agitur, de quibus falsis criminibus pulsamur. Ex te ergo praesentes audiant boni viri, utrum sint vera, super quibus criminamur et adpetimur, an sint falsa." Augustine, notably, sidesteps Fortunatus' request, claiming that he had come to debate matters of faith not morals, and that, as an *auditor*, he never had occasion to witness the doings of the Elect.

language not to be "seduced" by the heretics. But in mid-rhetorical flow he switched to animal metaphors: "you'll find yourselves surrounded by the snarling, yapping wickedness of dogs" – that is to say heretics, of whom dogs were a well-known symbol.[79] The addition of bestial animalism to bad sex enhanced the power of the accusation. What sort of bad people were these men?

ANIMALIZATION

Just as there was a long history of identifying heretics as sexually evil seducers, so too there was an equally long tradition of identifying them with the inhuman or the non-human, above all with bad beasts. Just as human types at the periphery of the world degenerated from true types into bizarre hybrids of animal and human, so too heretics, at the edge of the acceptable idea world, were identified with animal-like threats.[80] As with the elements of proto-racism, which this strategy tapped, the identification flagged the heretic as an aberrant, exotic, and marginal undesirable. The imagery also drew on a long folk and learned tradition that came to be embodied in Christian scripture. The original apostles, indeed, were empowered to grind underfoot noxious and poisonous vermin like vipers and scorpions, because the persons represented by the dangerous life forms were agents of Satan.[81] All of the animal imagery that was central to the popular medium of the sermon could now be used to refer to "the Donatists." In the brief expanse of one sermon, the preacher could coach his listeners on the significance of the wild ass, the ram, the heifer, the nanny goat, sparrows, rabbits, hedgehogs, and lions. The hedgehog, for example, is covered with spines. What does this mean? The answer? Sinners, of course, covered, as they are, with tiny prickles.[82] So, beginning at the base, one can begin with beasts in general. Common beasts of the field represented the illiterate, the uneducated, and the uninstructed in the faith.[83] Such spiritual *idiotae* were easy prey for the purveyors of heresy, because it was known that it was the overly intelligent and self-vaunted learned who invented such outlandish interpretations of scripture. So it was "known," from the Christians' folk knowledge of their own conversion process, that the women were the first

---

[79] Aug. *Sermo* 260C.7 = Mai 94 (PLS 2: 488; MiAg 1: 339).
[80] Isaac, "Brutes and Animals," in *Invention of Racism*, pp. 194–207.
[81] Luke 10: 18–20 (Vulg.): "Et ait illis: Videbam Satanan sicut fulgur de caelo cadentem. Ecce dedi vobis potestatem calcandi supra serpentes et scorpiones et supra omnem virtutem inimici, et nihil vobis nocebit."
[82] Aug. *En. 3 in Ps.* 103.4–5 (CCL 40: 1501–03).   [83] Aug. *En. in Ps.* 134.18 (CCL 40: 1950–51).

to fall to the message of Christian preachers – in the case of bad ones, false prophets and charlatans, they were lured away by evil seducers. That was the sexual connection.

Sermons are filled with negative animal imagery, and for good reason. Such everyday pictures were easily understood. And fables, especially animal fables, were commonplace media for dealing with conflict in their society.[84] So, for Catholic preachers, the Donatists are like savage and ravenous wolves who are set to prey on the innocent sheep of the Lord. A florid imagery of bestial wolves, their sharp fangs dripping with saliva in anticipation of the victim of the hunt, with the innocent blood of lambs trickling from their jaws after the kill, had long been developed by Christian preachers. It had been applied to Apollinarians, Sabellians, Arians, Photinians, and Manichees. Now it could be marshaled against the hated Donatists.[85] These heretics had sharp fangs not just because they raided and harmed the sheep, but because they consumed them. They were ravenous. They threatened to devour the faithful.[86] The trope of the true believers as sheep that were to be guarded by their bishops from the ravenous wolves was attached not just to any heretics, but especially to dangerous ones. So Augustine, averring that he had just managed to escape a terror attack on himself planned by the circumcellions in the summer of 403, could tell his congregation that he has not been unduly frightened: "But *if* these wolves did terrorize me, what will I then say to the one who tells me: 'Feed my sheep'? The wolves bare their ravenous fangs to tear apart my sheep; I bare my tongue to heal them."[87] To Catholics these were "the Donatists." But the sermons of the dissident preachers were also laced with the same venomous tropes. The threatening animalism was just as appealing and just as powerful in their attacking rhetoric: the vile poison could be more than returned in kind. In a sermon of a dissident preacher, the hated Catholics are vividly described as ferocious wolves.[88]

As much as the species of wolves is lower than all other wild animals, just so they are also worse in their evils and cruelties. The craftier and more dangerous they are, the more submissive and craftily they behave. Stealthy in their step, dangerous in deed; innocent in appearance, but savage in their evils; kind in appearance, but

---

[84] For the broader canvass, see Morgan, *Popular Morality*, pp. 13, 35–37, and esp. 68–70, on negotiating relations with friends and enemies.

[85] Aug. *Tract. in Ioh.* 47.9.2 (CCL 36: 409).   [86] Aug. *Ep.* 65.1 (CSEL 34.2: 233).

[87] Aug. *Sermo* 299A.3 = Dolbeau 4/Mainz 9 (Dolbeau, *Vingt-six sermons*, p. 368).

[88] Anon. *Cavete a pseudoprophetis*, ll. 31–35 (Leroy, 1997: 260): "Luporum genus quanto omnibus est bestiis inferius, tanto malitia et crudelitate deterius; quanto subtilius, nocentius, quanto submissius, peius. Incessu humiles, sed actu nocentes, vestitu simplices, sed malitia saeviores, aspectu mites sed inmanitate crudeles. Et tamen lupi, vigilante pastore, ovibus nocere non possunt."

cruel in their outrages. And yet these wolves, as long as the shepherd is watchful, are not able to harm his sheep.

It was a common metaphor of danger for those who palpably felt less powerful and in imminent danger of being attacked. Cued by the words of Jesus in Matthew, "I send you as sheep into the midst of wolves," in a circular letter sent round to his clergy, Petilian, the dissident bishop of Constantina, portrayed the Catholic persecutors as ravenous wolves panting with slaughter for the innocent sheep of his flock, fangs stained with their blood, their mouths exhaling the breath of rage and hate. "O miserable traitors," he concludes, "it is fitting that the scripture is thus fulfilled!"[89] Given the amount of time and energy that Augustine expended in trying to refute the charge, the animalization must have had a powerful effect. It had tradition on its side. A dissident preacher of mid-century had already condemned Catholics as wolves in sheep's clothing. The animal trope was a big favorite with both sides, each of them appealing to the same passage in the Gospel of John.[90] If true bishops were shepherds and true Christians their sheep, then one had to beware of false shepherds: men who were wolves who had disguised themselves as sheep. "Even among the heretics who have endured a certain amount of 'harassment' because of their unjust acts and mistakes, there are those who boast of being martyrs. But they do this only to be able to take victims more easily under the cloak of respectability, since they are dangerous wolves."[91] As with many of the other pictures exploited by preachers, the wolf images worked so well because they were linked to a broader, already existing, and widely used language of animal tales. The wolf in sheep's clothing was a common folkloric proverb, an image constantly used to make moral points about dangers and threats.

The images of wolves were there to evoke danger and fear, but there were other animal images that fed simple disgust and revulsion of these others. The slime, muck, and moistness of the swamps bred this lower and repulsive kind of animal life – and, so too, things as loathsome as pagans and heretics: "Those possessed by demons croak loudly like frogs

[89] Petilian, *Ep. ad Prebyt. et Diacon.* 42 [restoration of Monceaux, *Hist. litt.* 5, p. 322] = Aug. *Contra litt. Petil.* 2.73.163 and 2.74.165 (CSEL 52: 103 and 105): "'Mitto, inquit, vos sicut oves in medio luporum.' [Matt. 10: 16] Lupinam rabiem vos implestis, qui non aliter ecclesiis insidias facitis aut paratis, quam lupi ovilibus inhiantes, pernicie semper atque impetu, suffectis sanguine faucibus, iram anhelantem respirant... O miseri traditores! Impleri scripturam sic decuit."

[90] See Matthew 7: 15 and John 10: 10–13; cf. the preacher of the sermon on the *Passio Sancti Donati*, 1 and 5 (Dolbeau, 1992: 257 and 259): "Proditione ergo luporum latentium sub vestitu ovium... de lupi rapacis faucibus."

[91] Aug. *Sermo* 138.2 (PL 38: 764) in a long sermon playing on the sheep versus wolves theme.

in the swamp; the more raucous they are the more filthy they become from the slime and the mud."[92] The attentive listeners were instructed: the frog stands for a talkative puffed-up emptiness.[93] Their vanity was the stuff of heresy: "the clouds of heaven thunder their witness that God's dwelling is being constructed throughout the whole world, and yet all the while these frogs are croaking in their swamp: 'We are the only Christians!' CROAK, CROAK."[94] The suggestive repellent images that linked frogs and a variety of other creatures of mud and slime were too good to turn down.[95] So other noisome vermin and insects of the swamp and field were used. The Donatists were nothing but bothersome and dirty flies to be swatted and eliminated. The dissidents, in turn, referred to the Catholics as flies, gleefully quoting Ecclesiastes (10: 1): "Dying flies destroy the odor of the oil." In this code language, Catholics were noxious insects that had destroyed the efficacy of baptism. The picture of the repellent household insect must have taken hold, given the amount of time that the Catholic counter-polemicist devotes to refuting the image. No, he says, it is the dissidents who are the real flies. It is not us, but *you* who are the dying flies, says Optatus. You are flies because they perish once and for all. This is the reward of your special kind of sin, he adds, quoting the gospel of Matthew on those who have sinned against the Holy Spirit.[96]

Frogs and flies were an amphibian and insect sideshow. The dog was more important. In everyday lore, even without any specific sectarian purpose in mind, dogs were seen as vile and filthy – rolling happily in the excrement of other animals and marked by the foul habit of returning to inspect and to eat their own vomit (so the Psalmist, as an acute observer of canine life). In a letter to Alypius condemning the excesses of drinking and dancing at the festivals of the martyrs, Augustine compares such excesses – notably *within* the Catholic Church – to the behavior of dogs, given, as they are, to carnal pleasure and sheer filth.[97] Sectarian enemies were no different. They might feel joy on witnessing problems within the Catholic Church, but "if there are those who take pleasure in our suffering then we can compare them to dogs who lick the suppurating sores of beggars."[98] It makes sense, then, that dogs as quintessentially dirty animals were identified particularly with Jews and also with heretics, and for the same reason. Therefore dogs put in

---

[92] Aug. *En. in Ps.* 45.10 (CCL 38: 524): "Arreptitii idolorum tamquam ranae de paludibus personabant, tanto tumultuosius, quanto sordidius de luto et caeno."

[93] Aug. *En. in Ps.* 77.27 (CCL 39: 1087). [94] Aug. *En. in Ps.* 95.7, cf. 95.11 (CCL 39: 1348–49).

[95] See Dulaey (2000) for more of the details.

[96] Optatus, *Contra Parm.* 7.4.1 (SC 413: 228). The harsher imagery occurs, notably, in the new book added in the mid-380s. He quotes Matthew 13: 32 (also said of the Jews, see ch. 6, p. 274).

[97] Aug. *Ep.* 29: 2 (CCL 31: 98). [98] Aug. *Ep.* 78.6 (CCL 31A: 89), referring to Luke 16: 21.

an appearance, repeatedly, in the preaching about the dissident Christians. "Let me not be trampled on by my hate-filled enemies who bark at me, the heretics who went out from me because they have never been truly mine."[99] For both sides in this mud slinging, the canine was always the one who returned to his own vomit, and so was the perfect stand-in animal for the unrepentant heretic.[100] If Jews were dogs, then so were heretics, and by extension the dissidents as well. The preacher warns his congregation: "There will be no kingdom of heaven for them, no heretics will be barking there, no schismatics who set themselves apart." It logically follows: "Don't let anybody tell you false tales. Ignore the heretics rabidly barking from their little corner."[101] Adding madness to canine afflictions, he openly wonders how insane the dissidents, those rabid dogs, can possibly get.[102]

As far as dangerous animals were concerned, the current age was, above all, the age of the viper. If the dissidents in their conference at Bagaï attacked each other by conjuring frightening images of venomous snakes slithering out of their fetid nests to attack the good, then the same serpentine imagery was available to attack heretics. The poisonous viper was at the center of every discussion of hated opponents within the church. Augustine explains why. In the first age of persecution, Satan strode the earth openly, roaring against Christians like a lion. In those early days, the lion raged openly. In the current age, following Constantine's Christian revolution, the Devil had been driven underground. He could no longer attack Christians openly and from the outside. He had to be devious. So now Satan lies hidden in ambush. It is as a poisonous viper that he spreads his venom surreptitiously, producing false Christians who work by scandal and deceit, first saying "Christ is here" and then "Christ is there."[103] A good preacher made the viper's danger so vivid that his listeners could almost feel it.[104] That this was the age of the snake logically set up the equation between Jews and heretics. A saying originally directed against some priests was habitually taken to refer to all of them: "you brood of vipers, who have been shown to flee from the wrath to come."[105] Each side indulged in abundant references

---

[99] Aug. *En. 1 in Ps.* 68.11 (CCL 39: 911), quoting 1 Jn 2: 19.

[100] Aug. *En. in Ps.* 83.3 (CCL 39: 1148), citing 2 Pt 2: 22.

[101] Aug. *Sermo* 229M (MiAg 1: 488) and *Sermo* 238.3 (PL 38: 1126): on Priscillianists and Manichees: as opposed to the Catholic Church, which is to be found everywhere.

[102] Aug. *Sermo* 313E.6 = Guelferbytanus 28 (MiAg 1: 541): "O insani Donatistae! O rabidi!"

[103] Aug. *En. in Ps.* 39.1 and 19 (CCL 38: 423–24 and 439).   [104] Aug. *En in Ps.* 139.6 (CCL 40: 2015).

[105] Aug. *Tract. in Ioh.* 9.16 (CCL 36: 98), quoting Matt. 3: 7–9.

to poisonous snakes: dissidents did this not only of Catholics, but also of dissenting breakaway groups within their own church.[106]

The snake does harm most of all by cunning and craft, especially when it slithers. It doesn't have feet, so that it has no steps to be heard as it advances. It glides along smoothly and quietly in its path, and not in a straight line. In the same way, they [i.e. our sectarian enemies] creep and slither along, concealing a hidden venom that poisons at the slightest touch.

Just so, the dissidents (according to Augustine in this same passage) commonly referred to Catholics as poisonous vipers. The charge is hardly unbelievable. Each side was just as good as the other in constantly assailing its own believers with degrading animal images of the other. Whereas once the gentiles had raged openly against Christians as lions, now the enemies of true Christianity were poisonous asps whose aim is to inject their venom stealthily, to spatter it about, and to hiss. These are heretics, more dangerous by far than the Jews who once raged openly against the Lord.[107] All of these images could be combined to be linked in a critique of violence: the lies of snakes lead to the violence of the lion. In this way the dissident Christians had actually reversed the temper of the times, reviving the old aggressive lionish ways of Satan of an earlier age.[108]

There is nothing they can say in reply, since *God has smashed their teeth in their mouths*. So where they are no longer able to hiss the false slitherings of vipers, they roar open violence like lions. The armed bands of circumcellions spring to the attack and rage about. Let them commit as much slaughter as possible, and as much as they are able – nevertheless *God broke the teeth of lions*.

Comparisons to dangerous beasts were embedded in a common knowledge of rural life, and in a wide range of well-known agricultural similes. Such matters were embedded in the nature of popular lore, oral and written, or what was peddled as "popular" even if composed by elite producers – stories and fables that were often used precisely to delineate and to

---

[106] Aug. *En. in Ps.* 139.6 (CCL 40: 2015): "In serpente maxime adstutia est et dolus nocendi; propterea etiam serpit. Non enim vel pedes habet, ut eius vestigia cum venit audiantur. In eius itinere velut lenis est tractus, sed non est rectus. Ita ergo repunt et serpunt ad nocendum, habentes occultum venenum et sub leni contactu"; cf. Aug. *Contra litt. Petil.* 2.14.32 (CSEL 52: 36–37); see ch. 3, pp. 127–28 on Maximianists and the violent language directed against them.

[107] Aug. *En. in Ps.* 57.7, 13, 15 (CCL 39: 714, 719, 720–21).

[108] Aug. *En. in Ps.* 57.11 and 14 (CCL 39: 717–18, 720): "Non est quod respondeant: *Deus contrivit dentes eorum in ore ipsorum*. Ideoque ubi non possunt lubrica fallacia serpere ut aspides, aperta violentia fremunt ut leones . . . Prosiliunt et saeviunt armatae turbae circumcellionum; dant stragem quantum possunt, quantamcumque possunt. Sed et *molas leonum confegit Dominus*."

negotiate the relationships between the weak and the powerful.[109] Some of these media relied on the use of wild animal surrogates, others on the mundane processes of everyday rural life. Preachers relied on this popular knowledge, even in the towns; after all, most of them were agrotowns where the separation between city and country was never very great. Everyone knew about the process of pressing olives to produce olive oil. The pure olive oil represented true Christians; the refuse and the dregs left by the pressing process: these were the heretics, the pagans, the Arians and the Manichees.[110] And the circle of the true church's enemies could be closed: as difficult as it might be to imagine, heretics were worse than Jews.[111] The interweaving and interdependence of agricultural metaphor, animal imagery, and sexual innuendo culminated in the sly and deceitful little fox. In a sermon that begins by referring to heretics as the "dregs" of humanity, using a metaphor of olive pressing, the preacher passed immediately to the little foxes. They are much like this too, and here is why:[112]

Foxes represent cunning and dangerous people, especially heretics – sly and deceitful persons who hide in winding and hollow lairs and who deceive others, all the while emitting a foul stench. . . . The *Song of Songs* refers to these foxes when it asks: "Please trap the little foxes for us, the ones that ruin vineyards and that live in twisting lairs."

In an extensive treatment of enemies, the preacher could then knit together all of the bad animal life. The evil wrought by little foxes, who are none other than both heretics and dissidents, is then tied into the destruction wrought by adulterous women.[113] They too are sharp-fanged little vixens. With their piercing eyes, they connive, they seduce, and they destroy. A good preacher could ratchet up the metaphoric language of vileness to any degree that he wanted, uniting dissident Christians and heretics in a single violent language of condemnation. The picture of the heretic was still in the making. It had not yet reached the concrete tangibility of a later age when a Roman emperor could set up, in the forum of his capital city, statues of heretics "so that passers-by could 'shit, piss,

---

[109] Morgan, *Popular Morality*, pp. 37–39, 63–68; the latter passage leads to the subject of the delineation of enemies.

[110] Aug. *En. in Ps.* 80.12 (CCL 39: 1127).

[111] Aug. *Sermo* 218B.2 = Guelferbytanus 2 (MiAg 1: 451): heretics are more miserably demented and crazy not only than the Jews who deny Christ now, but also than those who killed him then.

[112] Aug. *En. in Ps.* 80.13 (CCL 39: 1127), referring to Sg 2: 15: "Vulpes insidiosos, maximeque haereticos significant; dolosos, fraudulentos, cavernosis anfractibus latentes et decipientes, odore etiam tetro putentes."

[113] Ps.-Aug. *Sermo* 364.3–4 (PL 39: 1641–42).

and spit' on them."[114] But the language of the preacher was beginning to achieve the same effect. Both breakaway schismatics and heretics were not genuine Christians: they were just so much shit being voided from the body of the church.[115] That put the matter about as succinctly as it could be. Whether being shit or being shat upon was no big difference in the rhetoric of hatred.

CONFESSIONS

The point of attacking heretics was twofold: to eliminate unwanted persons and communities; and, more hopefully, to convert those who were in manifest error. In this two-pronged attack, there was always a problem with the point at which inducements, which were likely, at worst, to insult, would be replaced by threats and acts of coercion that created a situation in which violence was more likely. On a larger scale than normal, substantial offers of inducements and serious threats of coercion that involved the state, as the persecution of 347 revealed, were fraught with danger. The big problem for the African Christians by the end of the fourth century was that conversion was the flip side of betrayal: it was seen as a quintessential evil by those who had been left behind and quintessentially good by the new hosts. To confirm the new status of the crossover and to make sure that he could never re-cross to his community of origin, his betrayal was often marked by a public ceremonial of denunciation in the form of a personal confession. Take the public confession of a "Donatist" who went over to the Catholics at Hippo Regius.[116] The convert stood before the congregation of the Catholic Church and made a long personal testimony containing the following statements.

Thanks be to God, my brothers. Rejoice with me, your brother, *who was dead but who has come back to life, was lost but now is found* [cf. Lk 15: 32] . . . I was held fast by the words of my parents – not by those of the patriarchs, not by those of the prophets, and not by those of the apostles, but by those of my parents in the flesh. But I did not find comfort in flesh and blood. Being overcome, I found comfort in the truth. Having returned, I now find rest in Unity . . . as Saul turned into Paul, the arrogant man into the least of all, the bandit into the shepherd, the wolf into the ram . . . In the same way I, too, was hearing the real truth about the

---

[114] Lim, *Public Disputation*, p. 148 n. 209; cf. Cameron (2003b), 346.

[115] Aug. *Sermo* 5.1 (CCL 41: 50).

[116] Aug. *Sermo* 360 (PL 39: 1598–99). This is not a sermon of Augustine's, but rather a document preserved among his sermons that is exemplary of the public confessions enunciated by the crossover. Note the phrase: "Sic et ego de ecclesia catholica toto orbe diffusa circumtundebar divinarum vocibus litterarum; et me surdum faciebant a parentibus intentata falsa crimina traditorum."

Catholic Church spread throughout the whole world, repeatedly dinned into my ears from all sides by the words of the Holy Scriptures. It was the false charges made against "the traitors" by my relatives that had made me deaf... the peace of Christ opened my eyes, and Charity has covered and enclosed the multitude of my sins.

Enunciating oral confessions like this before the whole assembly of their new community made it commensurately more difficult for the converted – or the traitor, depending on one's point of view – to consider changing his or her decision. The man who delivered the public confession above might well have been Maximinus, the dissident bishop of Siniti (near Hippo), who became a Catholic in 407.[117] On the one hand, the betrayal cost Maximinus heavily, alienating him from his former community and exposing him to danger. On the other, it made him a high-value commodity to his new group. It meant that powerful bishops, like Augustine, went out of their way to support and to protect him. The same action also turned Maximinus into a valuable item for public display. He could be taken around from one community to the next by Augustine in a show-and-tell spectacle, presenting a living witness with his own personal testimony about the good of assenting to the new program of Catholic Unity.[118]

Made in public, such oral self-denunciations were sometimes accompanied by written statements that were posted and verbally announced. Although these signed affidavits served as insurance policies of adhesion to their new community, like the public addresses by the new converts they also created tensions and hatreds in the ranks of those who had been abandoned. A good case is provided by a Manichee who, like Augustine, had crossed over to the Catholic community in his hometown, which happened to be the city of Caesarea in Mauretania.[119]

---

[117] See "Maximinus (2)," PAC, 728; Dolbeau, *Vingt-six sermons*, p. 630 thinks that this public declaration of Aug. *Sermo* 360 is to be attributed to Maximinus.

[118] This is surely the context of Aug. *Sermo* 360C = Dolbeau 27/Mainz 63 (Dolbeau, *Vingt-six sermons*, pp. 311–14).

[119] A. Mai, "Sancti Augustini fragmentum pertinens ad disputationes contra Manichaeos," in *Novae Patrum Bibliothecae*, 1 (Rome, 1852), pp. 382–83 = PLS 2 (1960), p. 1389 (from Cod. Lat. Vat. Reg. 562): "Ego Cresconius unus ex Manichaeis scripsi, quia si discessero ante quam gesta subscribantur, sic sim habendus ac si Manichaeum non anathemaverim. Felix conversus ex Manichaeis dixi sub testificatione Dei, me omnia vera confiteri de quo scio: esse Manichaeos in partes Caesarienses, Mariam et Lampadiam uxorem Mercurii argentarii; cum quibus etiam apud electum Eucharistum pariter oravimus; Caesariam et Lucillam filiam suam; Candidum qui commoratur Thipasa, Victorinum, Hispanam, Simplicianum Antonini patrem, Paulum et sororem suam qui sunt Hippone, quos etiam per Mariam et Lampadiam scivi esse Manichaeos. Hoc tantum scio. Quod si aliud inventum fuerit me scire supra quam dixi, me reum ego ipse confiteor." An alternative text, in a manuscript from Saint-Gervais, Paris, was edited by Baronius (printed in PL 42: 517-18). The text edited by Mai directly follows the text of Augustine's *Contra Felicem Manichaeum* in the

The convert, named Cresconius, had to sign the following personal statement.[120]

I, Cresconius, a member of the Manichees, have written this, because if I depart [i.e. die] before the public records are signed, I will still be held to be one, as if I had not abjured my identity as a Manichee. I am happy that I have converted from the Manichees, and, with God as my witness, I state that I am confessing the whole truth about what I know when I declare that the following persons in the region of Caesarea are Manichees: Maria and Lampadia, wife of Mercurius, the banker – I used to pray together with them at the home of the Elect Eucharistus – and Caesaria and her daughter Lucilla; Candidus, who resides at Tipasa; Victorina, Hispana; Simplicianus, the father of Antoninus; Paul and his sister, who come from Hippo – persons whom I know, through Maria and Lampadia, to be Manichees. This is all that I know. If it is subsequently discovered that I know more than I have declared, I agree that I shall be held liable.

Mr. Happy had ratted on no fewer than eleven of his coreligionists on a matter that exposed them to arrest and capital punishment. It requires no great feat of intelligence to imagine how *they* felt about what Cresconius had done to them. Now he would be more dependent than ever on his new community and permanently alienated from his former friends, who, no doubt, wished him dead or worse. What is significant in this case is that the use of the confession was known to have had a central place in the religious practices of Manichees.[121] In making Manichees confess, hostile Christian bishops were turning back on them the same tool of public declaration that was already at the center of Manichaean self-definition. They hurt them with their own weapon. And now the device of the confession could be extended to non-Manichaean cases.

It was in connection with similar anti-Manichaean hunts at Caesarea that Augustine had written to Deuterius, the bishop of the city and Primate of the ecclesiastical province of Caesariensis, discussing the case of a former member of the Catholic clergy in the church at Malliana, a town about 15 miles directly south of Caesarea, who had covertly become a

---

Vatican manuscript, whereas the text edited by Baronius comes immediately after Augustine's *De Haeresibus*. Both contexts demonstrate the connection that it had not just with the repression of Manichees, but also of heretics.

[120] I accept the argument – albeit not with full confidence – that Cresconius is the subject of the whole document and that the "Felix" beginning the second sentence is not a person but is rather an adjective that signifies that Cresconius is "happy" to have been converted: see Lieu and Lieu (1981). But the suggestion has been rejected by Decret (1990), p. 144 n. 21. From the copy of Cod. Lat. Vat. Reg. 562 reproduced in Decret (2001a), p. 345, it is clear that "Victorinam" rather than "Victorinum" is the correct reading of the name.

[121] See the vivid explication by BeDuhn, *Augustine's Manichaean Dilemma*, 1, pp. 37–40.

Manichee. The problem is that he had been denounced and his current loy-alties exposed. Facing serious consequences, he wished, rather judiciously, to come back to the Catholic Church. He was only to be accepted back not just on the pain of confession and penitence, but also at the price of the denunciation and the betrayal of his former coreligionists. He is *only* to be readmitted to the Church, Augustine emphasizes to Deuterius, so long as he denounces all those persons whom he knows to be Manichees not just in Malliana, but *everyone* whom he knows to be a Manichee in the *whole province*.[122]

The function of the public admissions, however, was more than just a function of the involvement of state judicial procedure. The public "debates" that Augustine staged with Manichees in August 392 and again in December 394 were no ordinary free and open debates about ideas but rather were parts of public court proceedings in which the "orthodox" Christian bishop was involved by the courts to determine the status of the accused.[123] As in Stalin's Russia of the 1930s, the point of the involvement of the state and of the trial was not so much the convic-tion of the defendant as it was his or her confession. The public admission of "wrong" and, by implication, the affirmation of "right" was a large part, if not almost the whole point, of the exercise.[124] So too, the process of hunting the heretic was not as innocent as might appear at first. In the case of the subdeacon from Malliana, for example, the additional facts that he was a doddering old man who commonly liked to ventilate some of his own ideas, perhaps ill-advisedly, to those around him is relevant. The matter can be interpreted as I have just done. Or we can take Augustine's line that these incriminating statements by the old man were unguarded lapses in which he revealed his true sinister self. In any event, the occasional glitches were not enough. The elderly man was set up in a sting operation. Augustine planted false "pretend students" in the old man's circle, young men who got the necessary information from the subdeacon and then acted as witnesses against him. By any measure, this was a dirty business.

NAMING THE NAME

A small quotidian result of the constant dinning of such hatespeak into the ears of adherents of one side in the struggle was the emergence of low-level

---

[122] Aug. *Ep.* 236.3 (CSEL 57: 525); cf. Decret (1990), p. 145.

[123] Humfress, *Orthodoxy and the Courts*, p. 249.

[124] For a series of formulaic written and signed confessions from fifth-century Lycia in which the heretic admits his or her wrong and affirmed orthodoxy – documents that abundantly illustrate the points being made here – see Millar (2004).

apprehensions, fears, and revulsion against contact with the other. The rituals of avoidance in themselves caused great offense. One side might, for example, not engage in the ordinary civilities of daily life. Why, complains Optatus, *they* won't even say "hello" to you or greet you on the street – but then there were good Pauline verses to legitimize and enjoin such behavior: "Don't eat with these people; don't say 'good day' to them, for their speech creeps like a cancer."[125] Precisely the same cessation of daily courtesies marked the turn to violence and hatred in the Christian attacks on Jews on the island of Minorca in 418: "even the duty of greeting each other was cut off." The sudden stopping of the one quotidian custom led to the end of the "customary" *modus vivendi* between the two communities.[126] Such warnings against merely greeting or sharing food with hated others has been a constant in the patrolling of ethnic and religious boundaries.[127] These and a dozen other like practices were at once reinforcements of identity and calculated insults. Just so, the bakers who belonged to the dissident church at Hippo ostentatiously refused to bake bread for *them* – the Macarians, the Caecilianists, the traitors, or whatever the Catholics happened to be called at the moment. It was not, of course, a matter of impetuosity on their part: they had been ordered to do so by the dissident bishop Faustinus.[128] These everyday lines of prejudice might have reinforced and laid the ground for distaste and maltreatment, but show no signs of rising to the level of implicating municipal councillors, provincial governors, or the imperial court in rougher kinds of repression.

At the end of this process of bad talk about heretics and dissident Rebaptizers, however, came one of the most important steps: the process of naming the heretic. Sometimes the naming took the ploy of using a hated thing with which to identify the other. Given the horrors of the persecution of 347, for example, it was to be expected that the dissidents

---

[125] Optatus, *Contra Parm.* 4.5.4 (SC 413: 90–92): noting that "the Donatists" refuse to engage in these ordinary civilities: "Nam et vos ipsi aliqui in perfunctiora salutatione oscula denegatis solita et docentur multi ne 'ave' dicunt cuiquam nostrum... [quoting Paul] 'Cum his nec cibum capere, "ave" illi ne dixeritis; serpit enim eorum sermo velut cancer.'" The quotation is in fact a catena of scriptures: 1 Cor. 5: 11; 2 Jn 10; 2 Tm 2: 17.

[126] *Epistula Severi*, 5.1 (Bradbury: 84): "Denique statim intercisa sunt etiam salutationis officia, et non solum familiaritatis consuetudo divulsa est, sed etiam noxia inveteratae species caritatis ad odium temporale... translata est." Note that Severus recognizes this breakdown as a significant step in the transformation of the former *modus vivendi* into hatred.

[127] As, for example, between Christians and Jews in mediaeval Spain: Nirenberg, *Communities of Violence*, pp. 169 ff.

[128] Or so Augustine claims: *Contra litt. Petil.* 2.83.184 (CSEL 52: 114), saying that a baker who was a renter with one of Augustine's deacons would not bake bread for his own "master," so refusing normal commerce not only in a Roman city, but even in his own house.

would label the Catholics as "Macarians." But the more usual ploy was to impute a series of genetic links of descent that created an aberrant kinship group of the so-and-sos.[129] Donatus, like Arius and the others, came to be branded not just as any dissident church leader, but as an heresiarch – as the founding father of his own peculiar breakaway church or heresy.[130] Like these others, Donatus was a "mountain" of Untruth who stood in the way of Christ's mission; heresiarchs like him were like reefs and crags that caused the shipwrecks of the Christians and communities who foundered on them. If they formed a religious group that could be designated and labeled, and entered into the formal lists of heresies that could be legally proscribed by the state, the heresiarch's followers would have to be designated by a personal name such as was commonly used to delegitimize them as aberrant personal movements. They were to become, not Christians, our fellow Christians, much less "our brothers" in faith, but rather "the Donatists," the *Donatistae*, followers of Donatus the arch-heretic. So it had always been, almost from the beginning of the conflict. Each side called the other names calqued after the name of the supposed founder of the aberrant and unacceptable brand of Christianity. The evil father of each had spawned a spate of adopted sons: *Tertullianistae, Majoriani, Parmeniani, Maximianisti, Donatistae* –Tertullianists, Majorianists, Parmenians, Maximianists, and Donatists. It was a well-known process. The real problem was to get the state to recognize them as "bad persons" against whom it would take official action.

But the labeling and the accompanying hostile imagery also helped unofficial private action that reposed on the legal powers wielded, for example, by private landowners over the peasant farmers or *coloni* who farmed their domains. If force and compulsion were used to convert non-Christians to the worship of the true god, this could be made easier to the extent that it became more accepted that not being a true Christian was *per se* a bad thing. In a letter dating to these years, one African landowner remarked to another, named Salvius, that the latter had turned his peasants, who were riven with "error," to the worship of the one true God. The writer further noted, with some astonishment, that Salvius had managed to achieve this transformation by using "no threats

[129] On the process, and on the Catholics as "Macarians," see Aug. *Contra Iul. Opus Imperf.* 1.71 (CSEL 85.1: 80–84).
[130] Aug. *En. in Ps.* 35.9 (CCL 38: 328): "Erant montes alii, per quos unusquisque cum duceret navim, naufragium faceret. Emerserunt enim principes haeresum, et montes erant. Arius mons erat, Donatus mons erat, Maximianus modo quasi mons factus est."

or terror at all."[131] We cannot know for sure whether or not the man, a landowner in the region of Matar in northern Proconsularis, was acting under a legal cover.[132] Whatever the circumstances, the pervasive discourse of repressing unwanted dispositions in one's inferiors, and the power of the new ideology, created an atmosphere in which large landowners regarded it as part of their prerogative to use force, if necessary, to compel belief. If force did not have to be used (perhaps a surprising thing) then so much the better. But one way or the other, one is considering a kind of law under which superiors could compel inferiors in the most basic matters of the latter's thinking.

The renewed interest in heretics and heresy was therefore not accidental. It arose primarily because a new player, the imperial state, absent from second- and third-century concerns, had entered the field. A Christian empire with an interest in unity and orthodoxy could be persuaded and exploited as a resource to repress diversity and dissent. At first, it seemed as though this aspect of governmental power might be exercised with full force with the advent of Constantine. There were signs that deviants were going to be dealt with using the maximum power of the state. This was certainly true in Africa. For various reasons, however, there was a manifest retreat of the state from this very hard line over the whole last half of Constantine's reign, and during those of his successors. A more variable attitude of emperors, their advisors, and officials to how deviants ought to be dealt with became normal. Sometimes harsh measures were used, but most of the time they were not.

For Christian deviants, Julian's brief reign brought not just a respite, but a complete reversal of the lines of power and repression. After Julian, especially in the 370s and 380s, matters began to shift decisively in ways that connected the state with orthodox Christianity. The problem became more sharply defined. The imperial court had demonstrated its willingness to pursue cases of extreme divergence from true faith, namely outright heresy: so proven and named heretics were now fair game. On the state's side, however, there was still a real hesitation to pursue mere deviance or

---

[131] Lepelley (1989), 265: "Hoc ipsum nos in tuis praeceptionibus admiramur, quod nullis minis, quod nullis omnino terroribus, ad cultum Dei vaesanos animos convertisti, ut confusa mens illud crederet esse rectissimum cum omnibus bene beateque vivere, quam cum paucis iniusta sentire."

[132] Lepelley (1989), pp. 254–55, argues that the verbiage (including the reference to the "submotis erroribus" at the head of the letter) argue that the peasants were not suffering from mistaken "pagan" beliefs as much as from "Christian error" and so that we are facing Catholic enforcement in the aftermath of the conference of 411. This is possible. In that case, local landowners like this man would have legal coverage; but the words are susceptible of different constructions, which only serves to show how the overlaps in vocabulary could serve different kinds of repression.

difference that seemed to be within the broad confines of true and correct Christian belief, or where difference was not so great as to create a palpable and manifest threat to the social fabric of belief and empire. The problem for Christians who wished to persuade the state to act was not to lobby it on minor divergences of belief and practice – on which it was unlikely that real action would be taken – but rather to construct a convincing case for dangerous heresy.

The ploy worked. An internal Christian group within the Christian community in Africa had been distinguished from the right-thinking orthodox by nothing more than their propensity to regard the other church as congenitally impure and therefore to demand rebaptism of its members. They had logically been designated as nothing more than "the Rebaptizers" throughout the fourth century. But this group now came to be designated as a formal heresy. Its adherents were descended from their own heresiarch, Donatus. And now they became a named heresy: the *Donatistae* or those who followed Donatus in his fatal path of error. The dissidents were not just any group of divisive Christians. They were the spawn of an evil genius: a mountain of a man fully comparable with the other great creators of heresy:

> You must not think, dear brothers, that heresies have come into being through the efforts of spiritual midgets. It was only persons of huge stature who began heresies . . . think of Donatus and how remarkable he was. And then Maximianus – there's a wonderful man for you! There was another named Photinus. What a great man! And how about Arius? Without doubt he was very important too.[133]

Preachers could now harp on the connection between a known and named heresy, that of "the Donatists," and the fact that the imperial state was moving decisively against heretics. In long and repetitive sermons against heretics, it is emphasized that they will perish at the end of time in the Final Judgment and that even now the emperors have passed laws against them.[134] That they should be accused of being heretics, and so lumped together with Arians, Sabellians, Pelagians, and others whom they themselves condemned as unorthodox, must have struck the dissidents as strange. It was a dishonorable reproach that they firmly rejected. They were willing to admit to the label of schism, because in a certain sense it was obvious that they had divided and separated themselves from the Catholics for what they felt were justifiable reasons. But to be branded heretics struck them as terribly unfair. They were also, without doubt, well aware of the possible consequences.

---

[133] Aug. *En. in Ps.* 124.5 (CCL 40: 1839).   [134] Aug. *En. 2 in Ps.* 101.9–12 (CCL 40: 1443–47).

In the aftermath of the conference at Carthage in 411, Augustine could speak, with official government authority, of the "Rebaptizers" as "the Donatists." No longer mere schismatics, but full-blown heretics, the dissidents and their leaders now had no alternative left to them except to abandon the errors of their ways or face the consequences.[135]

[135] Aug. *Contra Gaud.* 1.3.4 (CSEL 53: 202).

CHAPTER 8

Guardians of the people

The bishops who directed the affairs of each church presented themselves in public by drawing on images from humble figures of daily life. Among the Christian decorative motifs found on the utility oil lamps that provided household lighting is one such image. It is the picture of a man perched on a platform high up in a tree overlooking a grain field or an orchard.[1] The figure is one drawn from everyday experience. He was the guardian of the cereal crops, the *custos fructuum*, or he was the watchman of the vineyard high up in his *speculatorium vinitoris*. This image of the good guardian was often evoked by bishops. In his abortive debate with Emeritus, the dissident bishop of Caesarea, Augustine defined who a bishop was: he was a man chosen by the people to lead them. Like the Lord himself, the bishop is stationed in a high lookout where he can see everything, high over the vineyards to guard the harvest.[2] The elevated image of the lookout could be linked to the title of *episcopus* given to the bishop, which literally meant someone who oversees the welfare of others. In considering the term, Augustine explains:[3]

He [i.e. the apostle Paul] kept guard; indeed he was a guard. As much as he was able, he kept watch over those over whom he was in charge. We bishops do this

---

[1] Also a biblical type: see, e.g., Is. 1: 8; on the language and formal terminology, see Mohrmann (1977).

[2] Aug. *Gesta cum Emerito*, 7 (CSEL 53: 189): "Fratres mei, si dominum cogitamus, locus iste altior specula vinitoris est, non fastigium superbientis."

[3] Aug. *En. in Ps.* 126.3 (CCL 40: 1858–59): "Custodiebat, custos erat, vigilabat, quantum poterat, super eos quibus praeerat. Et episcopi hoc faciunt. Nam ideo altior locus positus est episcopis, ut ipsi superintendant, et tamquam custodiant populum. Nam et graece quod dicitur episcopus, hoc latine superintentor interpretatur; quia superintendit, quia desuper videt. Quomodo enim vinitori altior fit locus ad custodiendam vineam, sic et episcopis altior locus factus est. Et de isto alto loco periculosa redditur ratio ... et pro vobis oremus, ut qui novit mentes vestras ipse custodiat. Quia nos intrantes vos et exeuntes possumus videre; usque adeo autem non videmus quid cogitetis in cordibus vestris, ut neque quid agatis in domibus vestris videre possumus. Quomodo ergo custodimus? Quomodo homines; quantum possumus, quantum accepimus ... Laboramus in custodiendo, sed vanus est labor noster, nisi ille custodiat qui videt cogitationes vestras ... Tamquam vobis pastores sumus, sed sub illo pastore vobiscum oves sumus. Tamquam vobis ex hoc loco doctores sumus; sed sub illo uno magistro in hac schola vobiscum condiscipuli sumus."

too. For bishops are placed in a higher position precisely so that they can keep watch and can guard their people. The word *episcopus*, from Greek, means one who vigilantly looks over another in Latin, an over-see-er, because a bishop "looks down" from an elevated position. Just as in a vineyard, a watchtower is provided for the worker who is responsible for the vineyard's safety, so that he can keep an eye on the field. Exactly like this, a higher place is given to bishops... we work hard to guard you... We act as your shepherds but, together with you, we are all sheep under the one shepherd. We stand in an elevated position as your teacher, but we are fellow students under the one great teacher...

The theme is elaborated again and again whenever the duties and the powers of a bishop are considered: he is a watchman, a guardian, and a lookout who protects his people and warns them about the dangers that threaten them.[4]

Just as importantly, whether dissident or Catholic, the bishop was also the shepherd of his flock, guarding them against the fangs of wolves and, if necessary, shedding his own blood to protect them. The dissident preacher, remembering the death of the bishop Honoratus at Sicilibba in the persecution of 317, presents this extreme act of the good pastor: "Their shepherd lay fallen there, gathered with him was the flock of his sheep, blood-red from their suffering."[5] Here, too, was the faithful guardian. Like any good guard or lookout, the bishop was at the center of networks of information, always listening and acquiring useful news. As Augustine warned in speaking to his congregation: "After this sermon of mine, people are going to talk. But whatever they might say, in the end some of their talk will reach my ears, from whatever direction the wind is blowing."[6] The image of the caretaker was provoked, in part, because the bishop, like a Roman magistrate, was ensconced in his great seat or *cathedra* on a raised tribunal above the ordinary people who stood lower down, listening to him from ground level. "We are addressing you from a raised place, since we are more honorable than you." It was a frank description of superiority that would not have struck any Christian of the time as anything but right.[7] Since the bishop was literally higher than the common people of the congregation, anyone could see that he possessed a higher status.

---

[4] Aug. *Sermo* 339 (PL 38: 1480–82; MiAg 1:189–200) at length.
[5] *Passio Sancti Donati*, 13 (Dolbeau, 1992: 263): "ubi pastor percussus iacebat, illo et ovium grex de passione purpureus colligeretur."
[6] Aug. *Sermo* 356.12 (PL 39: 1579).
[7] Aug. *En. in Ps.* 66.10 (CCL 39: 868): "De isto loco quasi sublimiore loquimur ad vos"; cf. *Sermo* 94A.5 = *Caillau-Saint-Yves* 2.6 (PLS 2: 426; MiAg 1: 253): "nobis, qui de superiori loco stamus vel sedemus et ad vos loquimur"; *Sermo* 134.1 (PL 38: 742) and 137.13 (PL 38: 761).

With the higher rank came responsibility. Preaching on the anniversary of his own ordination as bishop, Augustine expanded on the duties incumbent on a man like himself.[8]

The turbulent must be corrected, the faint-hearted cheered up, the weak supported, the opponents of the gospel refuted; the community must be guarded against its insidious enemies, the ignorant must be taught, the lazy must be stirred up, the argumentative checked, the proud put in their place, and those who have lost hope set back on their feet.

Note how many of the duties required disciplining others and the use of force. Images were both useful and necessary in carrying out these tasks. The power of most bishops rested, ultimately, on the fact that numbers of quite ordinary people were willing to assent to their authority. The appropriate representations struck the right note: the protector, the caretaker, the guardian, the shepherd. The images evoked the expected responses from the poor, the ignorant, and the weak. They did so because the power represented itself as so consistently beneficent.[9] Among his benefactions, the bishop was responsible both for strengthening his community on the inside and for defending it against its external enemies. The image of the guardian in turn suggested that of the shepherd, warding off attacks on his flock by wolves and other predators. This duty of the good shepherd was interpreted by some bishops as indicating that they should (ideally) be willing to surrender their own lives to defend their sheep from violent predators.[10] In one of his epic sermons, "To the Shepherds," preached in 414, Augustine declaimed at length on the role of the bishop. Here the prospect was less the actual surrender of one's own life in a violent confrontation than it was the normal mundane necessity of facing the day-to-day problems of his people. The good shepherd was required to render an account to his master or owner on what happened to the sheep placed in the power of his crook.[11]

In his more human guise, the bishop was a father figure, commonly addressed as *pater* or *papa*.[12] It was a role assimilated from the pervasive everyday model of the family and the powerful image of the Roman *paterfamilias*. Every secular man of power from the local municipal notable

---

8 Aug. *Sermo*, 340.1 (PL 38: 1484).
9 Foucault, *Security, Territory, Population*, ch. 5, pp. 118–34, esp. pp. 125–26: "pastoral power is, I think, entirely defined by its beneficence; its only *raison d'être* is doing good, and in order to do good. In fact, the essential objective of pastoral power is the wellbeing (*salut*) of the flock."
10 Aug. *Contra Gaud.* 1.16.17 (CSEL 53: 211) where Gaudentius, quoting, as frequently, the trope on the true shepherd as opposed to the *mercenarius* or hired hand (John 10: 11–12), makes the point that the true shepherd should be willing to sacrifice his life to defend his sheep.
11 Aug. *Sermo* 46.21 (CCL 41: 548).   12 Aug. *En. in Ps.* 44.32 (CCL 38: 516).

to the emperor interpreted his power in this same familial mode, and so, naturally, did the bishops. When the dissidents accused Caecilian the Catholic bishop of Carthage of being responsible for a massacre of their own at Sicilibba in 317, they blamed him not only for the murder of his siblings – his "brothers" and "sisters," that is, his fellow Christians – but of a double crime, since he was also responsible for the murders of "sons" and "daughters" – after all, as bishop and primate he was also their father.[13] The assumption of the status of such a "father" could produce odd and dissonant relations: when the son of a layperson became a bishop, he became a father to his own father. This, too, was a normal near-incestuous situation found in some Roman families.[14] The problem is evident in an incident in the mid-340s at Idicra involving a dissident bishop and one of his female parishioners. A hostile source maliciously construed the bishop as engaging in incestuous relations with her since, as a Christian woman, she came under the bishop's authority as his "daughter."[15]

The image of the father figure was developed self-consciously as part of the frame within which bishops were seen as biological descendants of the original twelve apostles of Jesus. The absolute purity required of this priesthood was not an extreme rigorist position held by the dissidents alone. It was as much a central position of the Catholics, which is why they could not escape from the rhetoric about the polluting effects of betrayal.[16] The need for such purity, and its severe regulation, was emphasized by the reforming Catholic council of Hippo in 393.[17] The bishop and indeed all clergy were to be separated from contact with members of the other church. No man was to be ordained unless every member of his immediate family was a Catholic Christian.[18] Theirs was to be a closed order. Clergy were not to emancipate their children: to maintain their moral integrity,

---

[13] *Passio Sancti Donati*, 8 (Dolbeau, 1992: 261): he was a *parricida*.

[14] Aug. *En. in Ps.* 109.7 (CCL 40: 1607); see P. Veyne, *The Roman Empire*, Cambridge MA, Harvard University Press, 1997, pp. 177–85, for similarly striking anxieties produced by slave-holding Roman families – "little Hells," as he calls them.

[15] Optatus, *Contra Parm.* 2.19.4 (SC 412: 280): "Interea Felix supra memoratus inter crimina sua et facinora nefanda ab eo comprehensa puella cui mitram ipse imposuerat, a qua paulo ante pater vocabatur, nefarie incestare minime dubitavit."

[16] On the Catholic position see, for example, Concil. Carth. 390, canon 2 (CCL 149: 12): absolute sexual purity is required of the clergy, even to the point of abstaining from their wives, if they had them.

[17] Concil. Hipp. 393, canon 4 (CCL 149: 21) and canon 28 (CCL 149: 41): "Ut sacramenta altaris nonnisi a ieiunis hominibus celebrentur"; cf. *Reg. Eccl. Carth. Excerpt.* canon 41 (CCL 149: 185); cf. Aug. *En. 2 in Ps.* 36.20 (CCL 38: 362).

[18] Concil. Hippo 393, canon 17 = *Reg. Eccl. Carth. Excerpt.* canon 36 (CCL 149: 38 and 184): "Ut episcopi, presbyteri et diaconi non ordinentur priusquam omnes qui sunt in domo eorum christianos Catholicos fecerint."

children were to remain under the firm control of their father.[19] More than this, the sons and daughters of clergy were not to be married to pagans or to heretics, and the latter included their Christian sectarian enemies.[20] Of the *familia* in its broadest sense – the power and property unit under the control of the ascendant male – no persons and no property were to pass from a member of the clergy by way of donation or will to non-Catholics, especially to pagans or heretics, even if they were blood relations.[21] Clergy were allowed no escape from this requirement: there was no excuse for them not having a valid will. To fail in this respect and to allow property to be transferred to forbidden persons was to earn the punishment of anathema and to have their names struck from the church's list of official clergy.

The clergy of both churches were segregated by a purposeful endogamy and by an inwardly directed circulation of wealth and property. Not just in terms of ideology and belief, but also in the physical world of kinship relations and family property, they were set apart from everyone else. All external links were severely attenuated or severed, especially those with the sectarian enemies of their respective churches. With the standard of behavioral purity set so high and emphatically proclaimed as a hallmark of their priesthoods by both Catholics and dissidents, even minor infractions had a disproportionate effect among parishioners who had such elevated expectations of excellence constantly preached to them. If the bishop was a man of unusual purity, then this both separated him from and raised him above ordinary men and added to his aura of authority. This *askesis* or arid self-control displayed by the bishop was an important source of power, marking him apart from the common herd of the lesser clergy.[22] To fail in either purity of descent or honor was to be stigmatized as a *pseudo* or false bishop, a potentially dangerous and dishonored pretender to ecclesiastical power.[23]

---

[19] Concil. Hippo 393, canon 13 = *Reg. Eccl. Carth. Excerpt.* canon 35 (CCL 149: 37 and 184).

[20] Concil. Hippo 393, canon 12 (CCL 149: 37): "Ut gentilibus vel haereticis et schismaticis filii episcoporum vel quorumlibet clericorum matrimonio non coniungantur."

[21] Concil. Hippo. 393, canon 14 (CCL 149: 37); Concil. Carth. 13 Sept. 401, canon 15 = *Reg. Eccl. Carth. Excerpt.* canon 81 (CCL 149: 204).

[22] Rapp, *Holy Bishops*, chs. 3–4; Elm, *Bild des Bischofs*, emphasizes this moral control, especially in pictures of Augustine's authority. There is some danger of exaggerating its importance *as such* for a history of violence, although its role in marking the more important bishops as "men apart" is significant.

[23] So the dissident preacher condemns Caecilian, the first separate Catholic bishop of Carthage, as *Caecilianus pseudoepiscopus: Passio Sancti Donati*, 1 (Dolbeau, 1992: 257) – for the dissidents the word carried a double condemnation, the sentence of being "a false bishop" already canonized by Cyprian.

Possessing power and authority, bishops were the rulers of their own kingdoms; they were very much "the chiefs and princes of everyone."[24] The temptation for a high-ranking bishop was to see himself in this exalted light. Cautions therefore had to be issued: He was not to call himself the Prince of Priests, the Highest Priest, or anything of that sort.[25] The warning was needed because it was not only material assets that allowed bishops to lead effectively. It was also a collage of images of authority. They were *seen* as men who could get things done, as managers of a beneficent patronage. That is why people came to them.[26]

One man has a business deal to get done, so he tries to get the clergy to intervene. Yet another is being leaned on hard by a powerful man, so he runs to the church. Another wants an intervention on his behalf with a man over whom he has little influence. So one man, so another. Today the church is filled up with such men. Jesus is hardly ever sought for his own sake.

It was especially when they were in trouble that men sought the help of their bishop. If someone felt in peril for his life, he and his friends hurried to the bishop to see what he could do.[27] It was this worship of them by their parishioners and others that created the potential for the abuses of power that both churches tried to control. "There are good bishops and there are bad ones – and why?" Because of the tendency of people to fawn on them. All the bowing and scraping excited the pride of the man.[28] It was openly recognized that high ambition was involved in the rise to power of such men. The rewards were well known: the steps of the tribunal in the apse where the bishop was ensconced on his elevated podium, the elaborate tapestries, the throne on which he sat, the worshiping crowds of holy young women singing and rushing up, gushing, to the great man.[29] This much was tacitly assumed by the bishops themselves, as when Augustine made an insider's remark to Proculeianus, his dissident counterpart at Hippo: "We're all bishops here and we know what's going on."[30]

---

[24] Optatus, *Contra Parm.* 1.13.3 (SC 412: 200): "Ipsi apices et principes omnium."
[25] Concil. Hippo 393, canon 25 = *Reg. Eccl. Carth. Excerpt.* canon 39 (CCL 149: 40 and 185): "Ut primae sedis episcopus non appelletur princeps sacerdotum aut summus sacerdos aut aliquid huiusmodi, sed tantum primae sedis episcopus."
[26] Aug. *Tract. in Ioh.* 25.10.1 (CCL 36: 252).   [27] Aug. *Sermo* 368.3 (PL 39: 1653).
[28] Aug. *Sermo* 340A.8 = Guelferbytanus 32 (PLS 2: 643).
[29] Aug. *Ep.* 23.3 (CCL 31: 63), in a confidential tone, to Maximus the dissident bishop of Mutugenna: "Transit honor huius saeculi, transit ambitio. In futuro Christi iudicio nec absidae gradatae nec cathedrae velatae nec sanctimonialium occursantium atque cantantium greges adhibebuntur." Cf. *En. in Ps.* 106.7 (CCL 40: 1574): the more that clergy are honored, the greater the risk of misbehavior that they run.
[30] Aug. *Ep.* 33.5 (CCL 31: 122–23).

Your people honor us. Our people honor you. Yours swear to us by our crown. Ours swear to you by yours . . . Men wishing to advance their worldly aims through us – as far as we are useful to them – call us saints and slaves of God so they can complete a business deal involving their own land . . . and so we are daily greeted by men with suppliant heads, begging us to settle their quarrels.

But real difficulties arose for reasons other than the fawning of suppliant parishioners. The usual popular accusations against the clergy, bishops in particular, were about their greed for other people's money and property, for improper sexual indulgences, and for the consuming vices of drunkenness and gluttony.[31] Ambition and avarice, however, both vitally connected with the bishop's special access to church property, were believed to be their most common and dangerous faults.[32]

Beyond the leadership in word and deed that bishops and their clergy provided in incidents of violence, there were structurally competitive aspects of their position in Africa that sometimes urged them to more extreme actions. First of all, there were far more bishops compressed into a smaller space than in almost any other region of the empire. It was not just that in many communities there were two (and sometimes more) bishops from hostile churches within the Christian community, but that the large numbers of those who were needed to serve as bishops exacerbated the normal competition for resources and position. Using the best single body of evidence that exists – the full count of the Catholic and dissident bishops who appeared at the great conference of Carthage in 411 – we can estimate that there were approximately 230 bishoprics or sees in Africa in which there were two bishops – one dissident and one Catholic. In addition to these bishoprics, there were approximately another 250 in which either a single Catholic or a single dissident bishop held authority. The total number of dioceses in Africa therefore came close to 500, and the total number of bishops, counting those from both sides, exceeded 700.[33] These numbers are very large and are not matched by those from any other comparable region of the Mediterranean. Before any other factors are considered, some attention must be paid to the serious problems that arose from the need to recruit numbers of bishops on this scale.

A special qualitative aspect of the status of the African bishops added to these quantitative problems. In other areas of the empire – extreme cases are offered by Cappadocia and northern Syria – a relatively small number

---

[31] Aug. *En. in Ps.* 99.12 (CCL 39: 1401): "Rursus qui reprehendunt avaritiam clericorum, improbitates clericorum, lites clericorum, appetentes res alienas, ebriosos, voraces iactant."
[32] Rapp, *Holy Bishops*, p. 217.   [33] See Appendix A.

of elite urban-centered bishops controlled much larger numbers of subordinate and lesser-ranking clergy, including rural bishops or *chorepiscopoi*. In the African churches, on the other hand, whether dissident or Catholic, each and every bishop felt himself to be a little monarch, fully entitled and independent in his own right to command his own diocese and his people. Control of such bishops depended very much on consensus-building mechanisms. Should these fail, as they did on occasion, there were few means that were powerful or effective enough to constrain a rogue bishop against his will. This regal-like position of the bishop provoked deep feelings against having more than one bishop for each church in the same city or community.[34] It was an idea of the unity of the bishop and community that was popularly enforced by mass chanting of the slogan: "ONE GOD! ONE CHRIST! ONE BISHOP!"[35] Each bishop saw himself as a man of rank and power, a conduit through whom God spoke, a man not easily restrained, even by his peers.

RANK AND HIERARCHY

Of the many hundreds of dioceses that constituted the organization of the two churches in Africa, it was the local priestly hierarchy that managed the resources, educated the people, led their activities, represented them, and conducted the most important rituals of their sacral year. Each diocese had a regular set of officials: readers, subdeacons, deacons, and priests. But at the head of each diocese was a single bishop who was, without doubt, the most important and powerful figure in the local politics of his church. Elsewhere in the Mediterranean there was a strict *cursus honorum* for these ecclesiastical offices. The Council of Serdica in 343 had imposed a precise sequence for advancement or promotion: lector, deacon, priest, and, finally, bishop as the *culmen* or peak of the official pyramid.[36] In Africa, an ideal ranking of clergy also existed and was indicated, for example, by the number of peers required to hear cases when disputes arose: twelve for bishops, six for priests, and only three for deacons.[37] Given the greater

---

[34] Chadwick (1980), p. 2.

[35] Euseb. *HE*, 6.43.11 for Rome, and Cyprian, *Ep.* 49.2.3 (CCL 3B: 235–36) for Africa, both already by the mid-third century.

[36] Sabw Kanyang, *Episcopus et plebs*, pp. 19–20; Concil. Serd. canon 13 (L); 10 (G): Hess, *Council of Serdica*, pp. 220–21 and 232–35: "Et hoc necessarium arbitror [sc. Ossius episcopus dixit] ut diligentissime tractetis: si forte aut dives, aut scolasticus de foro, aut ex administratore, episcopus postulatus fuerit, non prius ordinetur nisi ante et lectoris munere et officio diaconii et ministerio praesbyterii fuerit perfunctus; ut per singulos grados (si dignus fuerit) ascendat ad culmen episcopatus."

[37] Concil. Carth. 390, canon 10 (CCL 149: 17).

volatility of recruitment in Africa, however, no such firm hierarchy was pragmatically enforceable all the time. It was not unusual for someone to advance directly from the rank of deacon to that of bishop.

Unlike some other areas of the Mediterranean – again, Cappadocia and Syria are good examples – there was no severe dimorphic hierarchy or leadership, with a few elite bishops under whose authority fell a much larger number of lesser bishops.[38] In Africa each bishop felt himself to be ideally the equal of any other in status and in power. This sentiment was deeply rooted historically, in part because of the wide dispersal and comparatively great numbers of bishops. Already by the Council of Carthage in 256, Cyprian assured his fellow bishops that none of them should ever set himself up as a "bishop of bishops" or use "tyrannical power" to compel any of the others to subservience.[39] Each was a monarch in his own domain, but not over other bishops. This meant that disciplining any given bishop was a most difficult task. The case of the bishop Auxilius of Nurco is paradigmatic. He had excommunicated an entire local family of some importance, including its family head, a powerful imperial official named Classicianus. In appealing to Auxilius to mitigate this penalty, Augustine gave a summary assessment of the authority of the individual bishop: "we have power and we are therefore more prone to abuse it."[40] Despite the best of his rhetoric, however, Augustine was never able to rein in the bishop. Auxilius dug in his heels and would not relent. In the end, having expended his resources of persuasion and influence, Augustine could do nothing more.

There was a difference in each bishop's power and status depending on where he held his appointment. The ecclesiastical provinces, for example, were ranked in prestige: the proconsular province centered on Carthage ranked above Numidia, and Numidia ranked above Byzacena and all of the others.[41] Other factors contributed to ranking within each ecclesiastical province. The most important was the formal one of seniority, but yet other ones contributed to a looser hierarchy of bishops. Augustine explained to one of his correspondents that he tended to rank his colleagues who were bishops as seniors, contemporaries, or juniors.[42] Seniority was counted from the time that a man was "born" as a bishop – the years that he had spent

---

[38] On *chorepiscopi*, see Kirsten (1954) for a survey.   [39] Cypr. *Ep.* 66.3.1–3 (CCL 3C: 436–38).

[40] Aug. *Ep.* 250 (CSEL 57: 593–99): the excommunication was in retaliation for Classicianus' use of force to arrest a man who had sought asylum in the local church.

[41] Concil. Carth. 525 (CCL 149: 262; 271–72).

[42] Aug. *Ep.* *1.2 (BA 46B: 46): "et scio plurimos fratres et collegas meos sive praecedentes sive in episcopatu coaevos sive sequentes."

in his post since his ordination as bishop were what mattered. The day of his ordination was his birthday, which was carefully recorded and celebrated every year.[43] This rank could be strictly determined, but seniority was not always set in such an objective fashion. Authority, wealth, education, prestige, and the size of his diocese cast a more favorable halo over certain bishops. In a circular notice to Catholic bishops in 401, despite his exiguous seniority – only about five years – Augustine was somehow "accidentally" bumped up on the scale to become the third-highest-ranking bishop in Numidia.[44] Such queue-jumping must have caused resentment among the other bishops who were expected to wait their turn. But those who already had wealth, standing, and authority in their lives before entering the hierarchy of the church expected such marks of rank to be preserved, and held in some contempt bishops who were not as socially qualified as themselves.[45]

The extraordinarily large number of bishoprics that covered the whole of urban and rural Africa meant that both churches – with some exceptions – had self-sufficient organizations in most parts of the land. This sufficiency determined another trend in church organization that was peculiar to Africa – one that separated it, for example, from patterns emerging in the northwestern provinces of the empire like Britain, Gaul, and Spain, where the absolute number of bishops was, comparatively speaking, very small.[46] In those lands, faced with a severe shortage of bishops, wealthy and powerful landowners began to step in to fill the gap, becoming bishops themselves. They started to dominate local ecclesiastical politics by building shrines, chapels, churches, and basilicas on their own rural domain lands.[47] In Africa, by contrast, the two social groups, the secular and the ecclesiastical elites, tended to remain separate in recruitment, interest, and influence. This different pattern had real consequences for African bishops. It made

---

[43] Aug. *Sermo* 339.1 (PL 38: 1480), preached on the anniversary of his own ordination, where he speaks at length about the bishop's duties, specifically mentioning his *anniverarius dies*; at *Sermo* 111.4 (PL 39: 1965–66) on 19 January of 413, he preaches on the anniversary of the ordination of Aurelius, the *senex* or Primate of Africa, on his *natalis*.

[44] Aug. *Ep.* 59.1 (CCL 31A: 9): "Deinde ad ipsos Numidas ita perturbato et neglecto ordine scriptum, ut nomen meum tertio loco invenerim, qui novi, quam post multos episcopos factus sim."

[45] See, e.g., Rapp, *Holy Bishops*, pp. 174–75, quoting Basil of Caesarea, *Ep.* 239 (PG 32: 889–94) on his "distaste for bishops who were poor men," in rhetorical attacks on the man who had driven his brother Gregory from Nyssa and who made a slave of an orphan of the bishop of Doara.

[46] See Baumgart, *Bischofsherrschaft im Gallien*, and Heinzelmann, *Bischofsherrschaft in Gallien*, for the Gauls where the process is best understood.

[47] A process noted by Brown, *Augustine of Hippo*, p. 425: "The nexus of bishop and great landowner, which was to be so important for the morale of the Roman populations of Spain, Gaul, and Italy, had plainly not happened in Africa."

the mobilization of secular force a more indirect and a more difficult task for them.

The need for a large number of bishops that was unprecedented for any other Mediterranean land of comparable size produced its own special problems. The evidence for the Catholic Church is clear, but some of the same pressures, no doubt, were also felt by its opponents. From the mid-fourth century to the last decade of Augustine's episcopate in the 420s, there were constant complaints about the lack of qualified men to hold senior positions.[48] The Catholic Church suffered throughout the period from a lack of potential clerics who could be ordained.[49] The problem was a serious one, as Aurelius, the Catholic primate of Africa, reported to the Council of Carthage on 16 June 401:[50]

There is such a great need for clergy who cannot be found, with the result that many churches are so abandoned that they could not be found to have even a single deacon in them – even an illiterate one. As far as the other ranks and higher church offices are concerned, I think that I might as well remain silent since, as I've said, if a person willing to serve in the office of deacon cannot easily be found, then it is even more certain that those willing to serve in the higher ranks cannot be found.

The lack of sufficient numbers of clergy provoked two responses. First, the labor shortage allowed the existing clergy much greater opportunities to move around opportunistically. On the other side, bishops who faced pressures to acquire clergy began to poach on neighboring dioceses to fill positions in their own churches. Regulations were passed again in 390 that clearly defined the boundaries of dioceses and forbade any bishop to invade another bishop's territory in the search for clerical manpower.[51] Both the demographic facts and the difficulties that they caused, however, remained chronic, certainly in the Catholic Church, down to the decade of the 420s and beyond.[52]

Whatever problems the bishops faced, they were the final figures of local authority in the church. They were almost unchallengeable authorities on

---

[48] On what follows see Rousselle (1977), Lancel (1992), and Sabw Kanyang, "Le recrutement des clercs in Afrique. Etat de question," ch. 1 in *Episcopus et plebs*, pp. 7–74.

[49] Concil. Hipp. 393, canon 37 (CCL 149: 43): "Tantum autem inopia clericorum ordinandorum in Africa patiuntur ecclesiae, ut quaedam loca omnino deserta sint."

[50] Concil. Carth. 16 June 401 (CCL 149: 194–95): "maxime quia tanta indigentia clericorum est multaeque ecclesiae ita desertae sunt ut ne unum quidem diaconum vel illitteratum habere reperiantur. Nam de ceteris superioribus gradibus et officiis tacendum arbitror, quia, ut dixi, si ministerium diaconii facile non invenitur, multo magis superiorum honorum inveniri non posse certissimum est."

[51] Concil. Carth. 390, canon 11 (CCL 149: 17).

[52] Aug. *Ep.* *22.1 (BA 46B: 346): "Tanta ibi autem querela fuit de inopia clericorum": his remarks on some of the proceedings at the Catholic council at Mazaci in Numidia on 6 March 420.

their home turf. In their minds, at least, they were the men who made the decisions and who caused things to happen. The extent to which their hands were moved by popular pressures, rather than at their own initiative, is rarely admitted in the sources that the bishops themselves composed. But it is hardly surprising, given their power, that bishops could be bad men. They were seen as the "authors of heresies and schisms." Through their in-fighting, they divided their own congregations and led them astray.[53] Parishioners and church authorities seeking discipline could at least dream of bringing such men under control and holding them to account. Augustine was well aware of one of these apocalyptic visions in which bishops were brought to heel and made to pay for their wrongs, and he did not like it.[54] One of the dreamers, masquerading as St. Paul taking a tour of Hell, found various miscreant churchmen being punished there in rivers of fire.[55]

Then I looked back to the river of fire and there I saw a man being suffocated by hellish angels holding a weapon with three prongs in their hands with which they pierced the innards of the old man. I asked the angel: "My lord, who is the old man on whom such tortures are inflicted?" The angel replied: "The man whom you see was a priest who did not fulfill his office well for, while he was eating, drinking, and fornicating, he made a sacrifice to the Lord on His holy altar." And not far away, I saw another old man whom four evil angels brought forward, running in a great rush. They stood him up to his knees in the river of fire and hit him with stones, lacerating his face like the blows of a storm, not even allowing him to say "Have mercy on me." I asked the angel who he was. The angel said to me "The man whom you see was a bishop, but he did not fulfill his episcopal office well. He accepted a great title, but he did not enter into the Holiness of the One who granted him this title through his whole life. He did not issue just judgments and did not have compassion for widows and orphans. Now he is being paid back in measure according to his own injustice and misdeeds."

Given the centrality of bishops, it is hardly surprising that, when considering the nature of the conflict between the two churches that tore local communities apart, Augustine saw the whole thing as caused by men like himself. The struggle was a dispute between the bishops of the two sides. It was created by them, nourished by them, and sustained by them.[56] On the

---

[53] Aug. *En. 3 in Ps.* 103.5 (CCL 40: 1503): "Nonne episcopi fuerunt auctores schismatum et haeresum?"

[54] Aug. *Tract. in Ioh.* 98.8 (CCL 36: 581).

[55] *Apocalypse of Paul* [Latin vers.] = *Visio Pauli*, 34–36 (Robinson 1893/1967: 29–30 = the Paris ms.; cf. Silverstein 1935: 142–43 = St. Gall ms.); deacons and readers are also included in the list of condemnations of clergy.

[56] Aug. *Ep. ad Cath. de Donatist.* 2.4 (CSEL 52: 234–35): "Afri nempe inter se episcopi confligebant. Si finire inter se obortam dissensionem non poterant, ut sive per concordiam compositis sive degradatis qui male contenderent hi, qui bonam causam habebant . . . restabat utique ut episcopi transmarini,

other hand, it was admitted to be a bad thing, rarely done, to parade the "tyrannical" power that caused these troubles. In their own representations of themselves as the popularly chosen or elected leaders, bishops had to conform to the image of being men who guided their people based on "the consent of all."[57]

The bishops were certainly most attentive to their own rank and privileges. The roll-call of the bishops at the conference of Carthage in 411 provides some of the best evidence. It confirms the impression of the regulatory measures passed by the church councils and their concerns with order, hierarchy, discipline, and the status of the clergy. The matters were ones that especially affected the bishops, men who manifestly saw themselves as bearing a certain elevated status. Only when bishops were infirm, deceased, or unable to function for some other reason, were their peers willing to record the presence of a priest as a replacement. But they were wary about status and took care to note the inferior rank of the man facing them in their own diocese if he was not a bishop. The final straw was to have a lower-ranking clergyman simply assume the position of a bishop. The comments made by Fortunatus, the Catholic bishop of Sicca Veneria, are exemplary. When Victor, the Catholic bishop of the congregation at Migirpa was called forward to identify himself, his opposite number at Migirpa, Gloriosus, admitted that he "recognized him." This alone caused the bile to rise in Fortunatus' gorge. He burst out with an attack on Gloriosus:[58]

Since this conference was sought at the behest of bishops, I am shocked at the sort of outrageous impudence with which this *deacon* here presents himself as ready to usurp the identity of a bishop, thereby upsetting the proceedings that we are ready to begin – by the Grace of God – by his zeal for trouble! He should restrain himself from such behavior. It simply isn't right for him to involve himself unnecessarily in these serious matters.

It mattered little that Gloriosus was the best-qualified person that the dissidents had in the diocese of Migirpa or even that he was a dissident. It was the jumping of rank that rankled Fortunatus. Gloriosus' presence in the august assembly was not to be allowed to pass without a little public disgrace.

---

qua pars maxima diffundebatur ecclesiae Catholicae, de Afrorum collegarum dissensionibus iudicarent."

[57] Rapp, *Holy Bishops*, pp. 28–29.

[58] GCC 1.127 (SC 195: 730): "Cum episcoporum sit petita conlatio, miramur nescio qua impudentia praesentem diaconum episcopi personam velle suscipere, et conlationem quam Deo favente coepimus inchoare studio contentionis perturbare. Unde cohibeat se a tali actione, quia non decet rebus seriis non necessaria commiscere."

Priests were also ambitious, but their ambitions were suppressed – sometimes for what they surely deemed to be inordinate lengths of time – by the single bishop placed in authority above them. And only one of the many priests in any diocese could succeed to the bishop's position. Another option for a priest was first to generate local support for himself in the local community that he served. He would then turn around and support the "popular demand" that the community have its own bishop and, of course, *he* would then be appointed as the new bishop. Such priests were accused of raising a personal lordship, or *dominatio*, and of turning themselves into little tyrants.[59] They were charged with bribing the people by using gifts like public banquets and lavish celebrations. They were accused of being puffed up, bloated with their own vanity, of being vicious and depraved little men. Existing authority made it very clear that such democratic bottom-up movements were unacceptable to the church. Tyrannical power, such as these petty priests incited, was portrayed as *only* popular at its base; that is, it was base and vile and therefore not of much worth. And so the appropriate warning was issued: those who imagined that the people *alone* are sufficient for legitimate power are mistaken. Such men cannot "spurn the love of their brothers" – the collective power of all the bishops. Priests who acted in this way were not only to lose their spurious dioceses, but were to be harshly judged as rebels. Some priests, obviously, pursued this path. The other alternative was outright betrayal.

ALTERNATIVE LEADERSHIP: SENIORITY AND THE ELDERS

Any long and difficult struggle both demands and produces direction and guidance, and sometimes recourse to abnormal types and forums of leadership and decision-making. The Christian communities involved in the long fight in Africa had complex and varied levels of leadership of both their lay and ecclesiastical members. The level about which most is known is that of the bishops. Great caution that must be exercised when reconstructing a picture of leadership based on the surviving evidence. Because

---

[59] For this and what follows, see Concil. Carth. 28 Aug. 397, canon 5 = *Reg. Eccl. Carth. Excerpt.* canon 53 (CCL 149: 189–90): "[Epigonius episcopus dixit]:... At vero quia nonnulli dominatu quodam adepto, communionem fratrum abhorrent, vel certe, cum depravati fuerint, quasi in quadam arce tyrannica sibi dominatum vindicant; quod pleri tumidi atque stolidi adversum episcopos suos cervices erigunt presbyteri, vel conviviis sibi concinnantes plebem, vel certe persuaso maligno, ut inlicito favore eosdem velint sibi collocare rectores... [Aurelius episcopus dixit]:... Sunt enim plerique, conspirantes cum plebibus propriis quas decipiunt, ut dictum est, earum scalpentes aures, blandi ad seducendum, vitiosae vitae homines, vel certe inflati et ab hoc consortio separati... etiam propriis publica careant auctoritate, ut rebelles."

authority, education, wealth, and access to the preserved banks of written records were in the hands of the bishops, it is their own accounts of what was happening that are both the best known and the best preserved by posterity. This fact raises obvious questions about possible alternative sources of power and leadership in both Christian communities, either among the lower clergy or among important lay members of their congregations. There is no doubt that there were influential lay exegetes, like Tyconius and Cresconius among the dissidents, for example, who acquired considerable power in the struggle between the two churches.

Other than the lower levels of the clergy named in the various violent incidents of the time, especially priests and deacons, one of the groups that consistently comes to the fore in the narratives that replay episodes of sectarian violence are the Elders or *seniores*. The *seniores* were an unusual institution found in the structure of African churches, both Catholic and dissident. In both communions, the Elders formed an advisory council that functioned alongside of and parallel to the official ecclesiastical hierarchy.[60] The simple fact that they were elderly was important. The power conceded to these men out of respect for their age or seniority was one of the peculiarities of African social structure where being older or more senior conferred unusual status and authority. The sentiment of age-respect was strongly reflected in mundane matters, such as the much greater frequency, compared to other Mediterranean societies, with which Africans commemorated elderly persons at their death with a formally inscribed tombstone (a practice that has given the false impression to some modern-day historians that Africans of the time were particularly long-lived).[61] The value of seniority was also reflected in the peculiar way in which the formal hierarchies of both churches were organized. As has already been pointed out, the bishops of each church were ranked according to seniority calculated as the number of years that they had been bishop. According to the same principle, the primate or head of the church in each of the ecclesiastical provinces was the senior-most bishop in terms of his "age" as bishop or the number of years that he had held his position. Logically, the primate was formally known as the *Senex* or the Old Man of the province.

This ascendancy of age in the ranking of bishops held true everywhere in Africa, with the notable exception of the proconsular ecclesiastical province of Africa, centered on the great metropolis of Carthage. Here, against

---

[60] On what follows, see Shaw (1982) where most of the earlier bibliography is cited.

[61] See Shaw (1984), pp. 476–81, where I note that this propensity becomes heightened in the period of the later (Christian) empire.

the grain, Roman administrative norms overrode local social values.[62] The primate of this province – and technically of the entire church in Africa (although the claim was always under challenge) – was a bishop who was selected by competition among the most powerful or meritorious candidates, those who perceived themselves as most deserving of holding the top position. This simple division in merit created the great divide in internecine violence in the election of church leaders. For all the ecclesiastical provinces outside the ecclesiastical province of Africa – Numidia, Byzacena, Sitifensis, Caesariensis, Tripolitania – the bishop who was acknowledged as the most senior in rank in terms of the number of years that he had been bishop automatically ascended to the rank of provincial primate. The quite different arrangement for succession to the highest rank at Carthage meant that there was always a potential for dangerous disagreement, division, conflict, and violence. When it occurred, because the violence happened in the largest city in Africa, the repercussions would be felt throughout the whole land.

With seniority came power. Ordinarily lower-ranking bishops were expected to concede to their elders. This system of value naturally conflicted with the notional equality of all bishops and their diocesan organizations. When assembled in a group, however, a manifest sentiment emerged that the new and the young in the ranks of the bishops would be expected to follow the views of those who were more senior. This is perhaps most evident in explicit statements made by new-ranking bishops at the conference of eighty-seven bishops held in September 256 at Carthage. At this conference, the bishop Prudentius from Cuicul, for example, admitted the newness of his episcopate, the *novitas episcopatus*, and the fact that he would probably uphold what the more senior bishops, the *maiores*, had decided. So too, Victor, bishop of Octavensis, also a new man, admitted that he had been carefully watching the views expressed by those who had gone before him in the session and that he too agreed with the *maiores*.[63] It was this profound sense of the power imparted by seniority from which the Elders also derived their authority.

The ecclesiastical institution of the Elders found in both African churches was no doubt derived in part from the parallel and antecedent secular institution of Elders or *seniores* who served as the local headmen of African villages and hamlets. These Elders – the men who governed small towns, villages, and hamlets – had a long history that went deep into

---

[62] See Battifol (1923) on the status of the *primae sedis episcopus* at Carthage.
[63] *Sentent. Episcop. LXXXVII*, 71 and 78 (CCL 3E: 93 and 99).

pre-Christian and pre-Roman times.[64] Whereas these secular Elders had largely been replaced and effaced by formal Roman municipal institutions in the more important towns and cities, they were now found serving in the local ecclesiastical structures of both churches in cities, like Hippo Regius and Carthage, whose local secular governments were thoroughly Roman in form. In his large urban-centered diocese at Hippo, Augustine had a group of Elders with whom he would meet on Sunday mornings to discuss local problems before he went to take care of the rest of his duties for the holy day.[65] Unlike the formal priestly hierarchy of the church, the Elders were a rather homogenous group who worked by consensus rather than the formality of internal ranks and rules.

The long-term history of the involvement of the ecclesiastical Elders in the leadership of the Christian churches in Africa shows that their powers repeatedly surfaced and rose to prominence in conditions of crisis, especially when troubles arose in the selection of new bishops. Any unusual importance or higher profile of Elders in a single incident is a reasonably good test of the presence of formidable pressures bearing down on the normal hierarchy of church leaders. In ordinary circumstances, the Elders tended to confirm the ongoing usual power and authority of the traditional hierarchy headed by the local bishop. Circumstances where the *seniores* suddenly assume the principal role of leadership in a local church were an almost certain sign that the bishop and the formal clergy are in a state of extreme distress and disarray.

The case involving the bishop Maurentius of Thubursicu Numidarum and the Elders of Nova Germani, a nearby village, is a case in point.[66] Whatever the volatile matters in which Maurentius had become implicated, they were serious enough to be brought before the Catholic council of Carthage in June 407.[67] Despite the fact that they had been summoned a second and a third time to appear before the council, the Elders of Nova Germani would not budge from their local stronghold. Maurentius appealed to the council to close the matter and not to allow him to be condemned by false charges. The council diplomatically decided to send a letter to Sanctippus, the Old

---

[64] Shaw (1991) provides an analysis and evidence.

[65] Brown, *Augustine of Hippo*, p. 192, citing Aug. *De Div. Daem.* 1.1 (PL 40: 581) on *fratres laici* who consulted with Augustine in the early morning; they were perhaps not *seniores*, however.

[66] The details of the case are found in *Reg. Eccl. Carth. Excerpt.* 100 (CCL 149: 217).

[67] See "Maurentius," PAC, p. 714. Given Maurentius' rank – 240th – in the Catholic clergy in terms of seniority, he could not have been bishop for more than a year or two – making one suspect that the uproar had some connection with his election as bishop. Since Maurentius was placed in a big Numidian diocese that was critical to Augustine's program, and since he had received support from Augustine's junta, we must suspect that this is another example of a hyper-qualified man who was parachuted into a small town, upsetting the locals and their hierarchies of order.

Man or Primate of Numidia, asking him to hold a hearing at Thubursicu Numidarum.[68] For the ensuing hearing, Maurentius asked to have
Augustine, Florentius, Theasius, Samsucius, Secundus, and Possidius –
that is to say, Augustine's personal mafia – as his jurors. The council
balanced his choice (which they accepted) by requesting the Primate of
Numidia to select the other (six) judges from among the *seniores* or Elders
of Nova Germani. In a situation where there had been a breakdown of
episcopal authority, the Elders could not be ignored. Maurentius, however,
emerged victorious in this conflict. He had the heavyweights on his side.[69]
If the rest of the hierarchy of the church held firm, there was only so much
"damage" that the Elders could do.

EXPERIENCE AND LEADERSHIP

If some of the power of the Elders resided in the fact that they were older and
experienced permanent members of a consultative body, it might be useful
to determine how much experience bishops, the leaders in each diocese, had
in managing their power. This can be measured from the lists of bishops
from the major church conferences, including the one at Carthage in 411.
In constructing the formal attendance records, the bishops who attended
the assemblies were listed according to seniority of rank. The most senior
were recorded first, highest in order of rank, followed by others in order
of their seniority. The checking of identities at the conference in 411 began
with the most senior bishops from both churches: Silvanus of Summa
and Valentinus of Baiana for the Catholics and Januarius of Casae Nigrae
and Primian of Carthage for the dissidents. Seniority of rank depended
on one's length of service as bishop. In the reading of the list of the 266
Catholic bishops, when the name of Emilianus, the bishop of Bennefa, was
read out, and his status was queried, he replied that he had been ordained
only about three years previously.[70] Emilianus was ranked 186th in the list
of the Catholic bishops in terms of seniority. This benchmark reveals an

---

[68] *Reg. Eccl. Carth. Excerpt.* 100 (CCL 149: 217): "promissae sunt litterae ad Senem Sanctippum, ut
noverit iudices, de concilio electos, sine dilatione considerare debere in civitate Thurbursicensi."
Given the location of Nova Germani (i.e. in the ecclesiastical province of Numidia), the Thurbursicu
is probably Thurbursicu Numidarum, which, we know from the proceedings of the council of 411
was Maurentius' seat (GCC 1.143 = SC 195: 792).

[69] So it is not surprising to find him in the elevated position of one of the high-ranking *consiliarii* or
advisors chosen by the Catholic bishops to represent them at the Conference of Carthage in 411
(GCC 1.2, 1.55, 2.2 and 3.2 = SC 195: 670; 224: 924 and 982).

[70] GCC 1.133 (SC 195: 756): "Emilianus episcopus ecclesiae Catholicae dixit: 'Triennium habeo ex illo
quo ordinatus sum. Nullum illic scio.'"

interesting insight. From Emilianus' ranking, we can deduce that at least eighty of the Catholic bishops had served less than three years in their position. That is to say, something like three out of every ten Catholic bishops had only a very modest number of years of what might be called on-the-job experience. The average years of experience in their episcopate of a majority of all bishops could not have exceeded five years at most. Of those who survived to have long tenures, however, the competition for seniority became commensurately intense. Augustine, who had nearly thirty-five years in his position at the time of his death, was still not sufficiently senior to become the Primate of Numidia, the apex of the seniority pyramid in his ecclesiastical province.

Similar rankings for the dissident bishops are less useful, but they also indicate much the same pattern. Victor, the dissident bishop of Villa Regia, had just recently been ordained and was ranked 242nd at the conference.[71] Cresconius of Musti, who was ranked 230th, gives every appearance of being another recent ordination.[72] Victorinianus, bishop of Aquae, had also been ordained very recently – probably within the last year – and was ranked 271st in order.[73] Finally, Victor, the dissident bishop of Hilta, who was also recently ordained (within the last two years or so), was ranked 201st.[74] The net indication of all of these cases is that we can say that about a third of the dissident bishops had less than two years of power in their position. The numbers are roughly of the same order as for the Catholic bishops. They indicate that a few bishops at the top end of the seniority ladder had a lot of experience and longevity in their posts, but that they were exceptions. Most bishops, by far, were relative novices as bishops. This fact alone imparted an unusual degree of authority to the seniormost few, and a greater sense of uncertainty and transitoriness to the rest.

Perhaps more significant than the rather small number of years of power in their posts that most bishops had was the quality of the incumbents. The proportion of more experienced bishops and senior clergy seems to have been higher among the dissidents. Part of the greater difficulty in this regard faced by the Catholics was owed to difficulties with recruiting adequate numbers of competent clergy, a problem that seems to have been a nagging

---

[71] GCC 1.207 (SC 195: 890), and GCC 1.128 (SC 195: 736): "Constat me modo fuisse ordinatum"; cf. PAC, "Victor (55)," p. 1171.

[72] GCC 1.206 (SC 195: 880), and GCC 1.133 (SC 195: 758); "Cresconius nunc ordinatus est contra": indicating a recent ordination; cf. PAC, "Cresconius (22)," p. 244.

[73] GCC 1.297 (SC 195: 894): where it is suggested that he had been ordained while "on the road" to the conference – perhaps an exaggeration.

[74] GCC 1.133 (SC 195: 770): "Modo sum ordinatus, non me novit": clearly indicating a rather recent ordination.

one through the last decades of the fourth century and the first decades of the fifth.[75] It is manifest in the mass of disciplinary legislation passed by reforming Catholic Church councils of the same time; but the problem of the poor, sometimes abysmal quality of the lower clergy must have afflicted both churches. Beneath the elite level of the bishops, the competence of the priesthood in technical terms of literary and other abilities declined, sometimes precipitously. On one occasion, Augustine went to visit an old bishop on his deathbed. Although he was a good man who was praised for his fear of God, it was admitted that he had grown up on a rural farm and that, putting it charitably, he had "little book learning."[76] It is hardly surprising that Augustine could receive letters from other bishops, in which they complained bitterly that their views on complex questions, such as the origins of the soul, were not understood "by the herd of ignorant clergymen" with whom they were forced to work.[77]

There is a necessary caution, however. Whereas "ignorance" and "lowness," especially among the clergy below the rank of bishop, might well have been "true" judged in terms of the aesthetics of culture and learning of those at the top, the judgment did not necessarily have much to do with power. Take, for example, the priest Samsucius. Augustine refers to him as a "brother" at the town of Turris, a distant hamlet in his diocese of Hippo. Samsucius bears an indigenous African name. The portrait of this rural priest is of a rough-hewn sort: a man of not very great literary knowledge, crude in speech, and generally ignorant, although well-grounded in the scriptures.[78] However rustic and uneducated Samsucius might have been, there is no doubt that he exerted real power over his flock. For this reason alone, he was an important man. Samsucius was consulted in the years immediately after Augustine became bishop in connection with the new aggressive Catholic program of reform, and he was called on to deal with internal conflicts in the church in 401–02, and again in similar circumstances in 407.[79] Whatever the level of his upbringing, Samsucius was a man of local power and of some utility. He was the kind of bishop or priest who had good communications with his people and was capable of organizing and directing them to violent or non-violent ends. For the

---

[75] See n. 48 above.

[76] Possidius, *Vita Aug.* 27.9–10 (Bastiaensen: 202); see Brown, *Augustine of Hippo*, p. 264.

[77] Aug. *Ep.* 202A.3.7 (CSEL 57: 306); see Brown, *Augustine of Hippo*, p. 415.

[78] Aug. *Ep.* 34.6 (CCL 31: 126): "Postremo est hic frater et collega meus Samsucius, episcopus Turrensis ecclesiae . . . et eum dominus pro veritate certantem, quamvis sermone inpolitum, tamen vera fide eruditum, sicut confidimus, adiuvabit."

[79] Aug. *Ep.* 83.4 (CCL 31A: 124–25); and Concil. Carth. 407 = Reg. Carth. 100 (CCL 149: 217), where Samsucius is one of the seven *iudices* selected by Maurentius of Nova Germani.

purpose of analyzing violence, however, it must be noted that Samsucius was drawn from the ranks of middle-range bishops who would be good at doing the organizing but who, for the most part, are invisible in our evidence.

RESOURCES AND CONFLICT

The resources that bishops could draw upon as private persons, which they might be tempted to draw upon as bishops, depended on the social pool from which they were drawn. In this respect, Africa can be contrasted with two different regions of the empire. In the eastern Mediterranean, it seems that bishops were largely taken from the same catchment group of men who otherwise served as muncipal councillors.[80] There might well have been some "drift" into the clergy that the state tried to control, but there is no sign that this affected the views of the men concerned or, even less, the attitudes of the men left behind on the town councils.[81] By contrast, a different pattern can be discerned in the northwestern provinces of the empire, in the Spains and the Gauls. In these lands there was such a deficit of bishops from any source that large landowners were gradually drawn into senior positions in the church. Neither of these models was true of Africa. Here the social backgrounds of bishops were polarized between two groups. At the top of each church was a truly tiny aristocratic elite: men like Augustine, Alypius, and Possidius in the Catholic church, and bishops like Emeritus, Parmenian, and Petilian among the dissidents.[82] Not far beneath these upper ranks, every index points to a precipitous falloff in talent, education, and wealth. Unlike other areas of the empire, especially the east, Africa never boasted large numbers of powerful writers of exegesis and theory: only a few bishops wrote. The great majority were readers and followers. This basic divide within the clergy of both churches produced tensions between the mass of plebeian bishops and their elitist leaders. For most of them, the temptation to enrichment and empowerment through a career in the church was a powerful incentive.

While it is not possible to speak about the social catchment of all African bishops, it is manifest that the few men at the top of each church had substantial property interests that gave them power and authority

---

[80] Rapp, *Holy Bishops*, pp. 183–88; I see nothing to sustain her claim (p. 178) that the same was generally true of Africa.

[81] Lepelley, *Cités de l'Afrique romaine*, 1, pp. 279–84, for some of the evidence.

[82] And even Possidius could be represented as "not educated in the liberal arts" (*Ep.* 101.1 = CCL 31B: 3), but see Hermanowicz, *Possidius of Calama*, pp. 5–6.

independent of their rank in the church. Regulations repeatedly issued by church councils confirm that bishops were involved in various kinds of businesses, including landowning, commercial enterprises, and the lending and borrowing of money. General canons forbade the clergy from undertaking secular businesses or procuratorial duties.[83] But other canons from the same period permitted exceptions. Clergy were not to be involved in businesses, for example, "*unless* they have given prior notice or reason."[84] Here was the loophole. And imperial legislation allowed commerce and marketing enterprises to bishops as long as they did not extend their networks into neighboring dioceses or net profits greater than those needed to sustain their households.[85] On the other hand, men who were involved in business enterprises were not to be ordained as clerics. Once again, however, exceptions were allowed. If men of affairs had given prior notice and a reasonable explanation for their involvement in business, then such secular involvements were permitted.[86] Laypersons in the church were similarly to be made aware of the fact that they were not to institute clergy as estate managers, bailiffs, or handlers of accounts.[87] The repeated rules that forbade clergy from involvement in money lending and profit taking, however, suggest that such practices were well enough known to provoke the repetition of the counter-measures.[88]

The official clergy recognized by the state were accorded additional benefits, allowances that were repeatedly confirmed for the clergy of the Catholic church in Africa by imperial constitutions.[89] Some of the privileges were of an important fiscal nature. For example, clerics of the Catholic Church were allowed to be involved in the buying and selling of cereal grains – within certain subscribed limits – "for the use of the church." These purchases were made through a favored link with the imperial *annona* system by which the bishops were exempt from normal taxes on

---

[83] Concil. Carth. 358, canon 6 (CCL 149: 6).

[84] Concil. Carth. 348, canon 8 (CCL 149: 7): such persons are not to be ordained as clerics; also, they cannot serve as *tutores* or *curatores pupillarum*.

[85] Rapp, *Holy Bishops*, pp. 176–78, drawing attention to Concil. Elvir. canons 19 and 20; for the imperial legislation, see CTh 16.28, 15, and 36.

[86] Concil. Carth. 358, canon 8 (CCL 149: 7).

[87] Concil. Carth. 358, canon 6 (CCL 149: 6): clergy were not to undertake secular businesses or procuratorial duties; canon 9 (CCL 149: 7): as *actores* or *ratiocinatores*; the local bishop who is proposing this measure and who bears a Punic name, used different terms, calling the managers *apothecarii* rather than *actores*.

[88] Concil. Carth. 358, canon 13 (CCL 149: 9).

[89] CTh 16.2.29 (Arcadius and Honorius, from Mediolanum, to Hierius, Vicar of Africa; 23 March 395): the emperors confirm the validity of the privileges that they have granted to the "sacrosanct churches" in Africa and to those who serve in them.

these purchases and sales.[90] It was just one of many tribute exemptions and advantages that accrued to Catholic bishops, so it is perhaps not surprising that some men were driven with a great desire to acquire the rank. It was in this same age, at the end of the fourth century, when Sulpicius Severus wrote acerbically – in a comparison that is particularly apt for Africa – that the martyrs of the early Christian church had possibly been driven by a greater ambition for death than the clergy of his own age who were fired with a "crooked ambition" to seat themselves in a bishop's throne.[91] Just possibly. It was not meant to be a nice comparison. It was in line with claims that some men were willing to go as far as committing murder (tempted by Satan, of course) to get a bishop's chair.[92]

Now and then, bits of evidence about the property and wealth of some of the bishops surface, often unveiled by their enemies in circumstances of crisis. In a polemical letter to Crispinus, the dissident bishop of Calama, Augustine claims that Crispinus had forcibly rebaptized Punic-speaking peasants on a landed estate that he had purchased. As a great landowner, Crispinus is compared to a little emperor who rules over others.[93] But Crispinus was surely far from alone in either church. The presence of the almost eighty farmers on his lands, the Mappaliensis, who were forcibly rebaptized, hints at an estate that was not small.[94] The push to acquire wealth in land provoked collusory agreements between bishops and landowners, the details of which are sometimes rather murky. In a letter to Olympius, a powerful imperial official in Numidia, Augustine refers to the case of Bonifatius, the Catholic bishop of Cataquas. He mentions the practice or, as he puts it more politely, "the customary arrangement," by which bishops purchased lands from rich landowners – for the church, it is averred – on the condition that the former owners would agree to continue to pay the taxes on the lands that they had sold to the church. The landowner thereby became a patron to the bishop.[95] The landowners sometimes failed to live up to this gentleman's agreement, leaving the bishop, in this case Bonifatius, owing substantial sums of unpaid taxes

---

[90] CTh 16.2.36 (Arcadius and Honorius, from Mediolanum, to Pompeianus, Proconsul of Africa; 14 July 401).

[91] Sulp. Sev. *Chron.* 2.32.4 (CSEL 1: 86): "multoque avidius tum martyria gloriosis mortibus quaerebantur, quam nunc episcopatus pravis ambitionibus appetuntur."

[92] Palladius, *Dialogus*, 20.579–84 (SC 341: 444); cf. Gaddis, *Religious Violence*, p. 284.

[93] Aug. *Ep.* 66 (CCL 31A: 25–26), dated to 400.

[94] Aug. *Contra litt. Petil.* 2.83.184 (CSEL 52: 114): "Quid nuper, quod ipse adhuc lugeo? Nonne Crispinus vester Calamensis cum emisset possessionem et hoc emphyteuticam, non dubitavit in fundo Catholicorum imperatorum, quorum legibus nec in civitatibus esse iussi estis, uno terroris impetu octoginta ferme animas miserabili gemitu mussitantes rebaptizando submergere?"

[95] Aug. *Ep.* 96 (CCL 31A: 222–23) dated to early September 408.

to the state. But the clergy were certainly normally making money out of such arrangements. The evidence stems mainly from polemical attacks of Catholics against dissidents. Writing to Macrobius, the dissident bishop of Hippo, Augustine repeatedly quotes against him Cyprian's condemnation of bishops who were accumulating considerable wealth.[96] Such instances must have been well known, since Augustine returns to the same theme in his attack on the dissident bishop Parmenian, noting bishops who were piling up wealth, seizing lands, and lending money at interest.[97]

The bishops naturally represented themselves as men of great consequence, sometimes of almost transcendental importance. In dealing with the laity among their parishioners, they cultivated an aura of authority. When it came to many secular aspects of power, however, there can be no disguising the fact that most bishops, even those with the greatest air of authority, were rather powerless. The state managed empire-wide agencies and possessed enormous fiscal and other resources. The state had access to powerful networks of communication and controlled institutions of a pervasive system of civil law. Above all, it had a near-monopoly of large-scale coercive force. Such resources the bishops did not have. In these secular ways, they were weak. Commenting as late as 420 on the lack of attractions of clerical office for young men, Augustine frankly admitted that the powerlessness of bishops and how they were held in open contempt by the powerful were downsides to the office that deterred qualified candidates.[98] The general weakness of most bishops, even the most eminent and exalted among them, meant that their ability to mobilize public force was limited. The deficit explains a pattern that is found everywhere in our sources: if serious force or compulsion was needed, bishops were always compelled to lobby government authorities, both local and central.

A big problem in determining the wealth of the church and assessing the effect that it had on diocesan operations, and the powers of mobilization that these resources gave a bishop, is that this economic aspect was a deliberately hidden element of church life. The church was an organization that paraded its lack of concern with earthly life, advertising its denigration of the secular affairs of the present, declaring its primary concerns with humility and poverty. The logical consequence was the propensity to obscure secular matters, to ignore them in writing and discourse almost as if they did not exist. Augustine's diocese of Hippo is the one on which there exist at least some of the relevant data. But even here it is very

---

[96] Aug. *Ep.* 108.10 (CCL 31B: 73), quoting Cyprian, *De Lapsis*, 4–6.
[97] Aug. *Contra ep. Parm.* 3.2.14 (CSEL 51: 117), cf. 3.4.25 (CSEL 51: 131).
[98] Aug. *Ep.* *22.1–3 (BA 46B: 346–50).

difficult to reconstruct what sort of fiscal recourses a bishop like Augustine had and how he used them. In his biography of the bishop, Possidius goes far out of his way to distance Augustine from any direct connection with church property. Augustine himself, says Possidius, never possessed a key for a storehouse or had a signet ring for authorizing financial transactions. Instead, he allowed all such matters to be taken care of through a manager or *domus praepositus* who was in charge of the church's affairs.[99] Known in the eastern church as an *oikonomos* or household manager, they were usually deacons by rank.[100]

Possidius' chapter in his "Life of Augustine" on the economic affairs of the church at Hippo notably follows a long one devoted to the expenditure of church funds, almost all of which is a record of the sums that Augustine spent on the poor. The firewall built between the bishop and his economic manager is almost absolute. Augustine is said to have trusted everything to the church's manager. The *praepositus* was the man in charge of all valuables that were received and dispensed by the church. Although the accounts were read aloud to Augustine at the end of the year, he trusted the manager and never went so far as to inspect them in detail.[101] Whether true or not, the imputed practice freed the bishop from first-order blame if ugly fiscal improprieties emerged. The normal daily expenditures in the church are reported as being none of Augustine's concern. They were taken care of by the treasurer and the secretary of the church.[102] It is explicitly stated that the bishop himself was never involved in the purchasing of properties. His one big economic task was to decide which of the legacies and bequests that the church had received it would accept and which would be refused.[103] This was an idealistic view of church fiscality that Augustine himself propagated.[104] For one of the wealthiest and largest dioceses in Africa, outside that of Carthage, the bishop is deliberately presented as alien to and consciously uninterested in the wealth that it generated and controlled.

---

[99] Possidius, *Vita Aug.* 24 (Bastiaensen: 188–94).　　[100] Rapp, *Holy Bishops*, pp. 201–02.

[101] Possidius, *Vita Aug.* 24.1 (Bastiaensen: 190): it was the *praepositi* who "cuncta et adcepta et erogata notabantur. Quae anno completo eidem recitabantur, quo sciretur quantum adceptum quantumque dispensatum fuerit vel quid dispensandum remanserit, et in multis titulis magis illius praepositi domus fidem sequens quam probatum manifestumque cognoscens."

[102] Possidius, *Vita Aug.* 24.17 (Bastiaensen: 194): "Sed et de neglecto a fidelibus gazophylacio et secretario."

[103] Possidius, *Vita Aug.* 24.3–6 (Bastiaensen, 190–92).

[104] Aug. *Sermo* 355.2 (PL 39: 1569–70). He represents himself as a man of slender means who had given away or sold what little he had. He did keep some, but only because one of his main duties as bishop was to act as host in offering hospitality to visitors: "Perveni ad episcopatum: vidi necesse habere exhibere humanitatem assiduam quibusque venientibus sive transeuntibus; quod si non fecisset episcopus, inhumanus diceretur."

Augustine certainly knew that his church had considerable assets in land and movables. He says that when he set up the miscreant Antoninus (of whom more, presently) as bishop at Fussala: "For his upkeep and for those who were with him, I gave him a domain, belonging to the church at Hippo, which was located in the territory of this same Fussala."[105] As bishop, he personally disposed of an agricultural estate in a far-flung region of his diocese that was so large that its income could support the new bishop, the clergy associated with him, and the church itself. Augustine later pretended to find fault with the fact that Antoninus rented out these domain lands on a regular five-year lease. But this is surely what most bishops must have done with lands owned by their churches. They certainly did not run them or labor on them personally. Just like Antoninus, they leased the lands out on regular rental contracts to *actores*, *procuratores* or other lessees often generally known as contractors, or *mancipes*, who took the leases on church properties and then managed the farms.[106]

In two embarrassing sermons, both delivered as a form of public accounting, Augustine felt compelled to report to his congregation at Hippo the sordid details of property holdings and disputes among his clergy.[107] If clergy were supposed to divest themselves of all their property before being ordained, or to hand over what they had to the church, such complete divestment had not happened. In presenting his report, Augustine indulges in a bit of rhetorical self-presentation, claiming that he was a man of small means who had given away or sold what little that he did have.[108] He similarly tries to explain and exculpate the rest of his clergy, but the record is long and consistent. The priest Januarianus had substantial money reserves; the subdeacon Valens owned fields and slaves (shared with his brother who was subdeacon at Milevis); the deacon Faustinus had more property; the deacon Severus owned houses, fields, and slaves; the deacon Eraclius – later Augustine's successor as bishop at Hippo – possessed lands and numbers of slaves that produced sufficient wealth to benefit both his close relatives and the church at Hippo on a substantial scale. Even the people in the congregation said: "He's a rich man." And so Augustine's report proceeds, with the priests Leporius, Januarianus, Barnabas – owners of farms, slaves, and holders of hardly derisory sums of property and money. The clergy were

---

[105] Aug. *Ep.* *20.29 (BA 46B: 336): "sed ei dederam propter suam sustentionem et eorum qui cum illo erant fundum Hipponiensis ecclesiae in eodem Fussalensi territorio constitutum."

[106] Aug. *Ep.* *20.29 (BA 46B: 336): "Hunc locavit et quinquennii totius accepta pensione pretium quo emere posset invenit." So the real charge by Augustine is that this is the way that Antoninus acquired a sudden infusion of cash whereby he could go out and buy things. But this was still surely not unusual.

[107] Aug. *Sermo* 355 and 356 (PL 39: 1568–81).   [108] Aug. *Sermo* 355.2 (PL 39: 1569–70).

armed with resources and personal interests. A conflict of some sort within the church at Hippo had unveiled this otherwise hidden underworld of property. These were men of some means who wanted more, a lot more, if they could get it.

DISCIPLINA ET PROBITAS

Different types of normal conflict were built into this system, any one of which had the possibility of escalating into more violent confrontations. As a new priest in the early 390s, Augustine was already struck by the severity of the problems with internal discipline within the church, a matter on which he had a frank confrontation with Valerius, his bishop. He felt that more severe punishments were needed to bring the miscreants into line.[109] In a subsequent letter that he wrote to Valerius on these same problems, he outlined three types of conflict: riotous and drunken behavior; fornication and other kinds of impure sexual delicts; and quarrels and hatreds based on envy. He thought that the church was already rigorously policing the second of these sources of unrest: sex in all of its illicit forms was a difficulty on which action had been taken. The first and the third problems, however, were ones that had been neglected. Sexual lapses were taken as a sufficient basis on which to deny ecclesiastical office to a given individual, even for a single fault that had happened only once in the past, but riotous and drunken behavior were *daily* problems to which little attention had been paid. And the disciplining of the ordinary people was no easy task.

The problems were also divided along structural lines. The first source of conflict, that of drunkenness and violent behavior, was seen as a problem found mainly among the common people, whereas the third area of moral lapse, that of quarreling and envy, was peculiar to the clergy. The first was connected with festivity and joyous excess, while the third was caused by competition for status and power. Ordinary people just wanted to have fun; the clergy were focussed on personal advancement. Consequently, basic causes of conflict internal to the clergy had to be dealt with by different means. In response to the first problem, the popular one where large masses of people were concerned, Augustine argued that the use of physical coercion would be difficult and unproductive. A program of mass education was what was needed. For the latter problem, where the numbers were few and the miscreants specific, more severe measures would be useful.[110] At the end of his second letter to Valerius, Augustine darkly alludes to an affair

---

[109] Aug. *Ep.* 21 (CCL 31: 48–51).   [110] Aug. *Ep.* 22 (CCL 31: 52–57).

involving a priest named Saturninus that had demonstrated the serious problems of discipline about which he was speaking.[111] Understandably, no more was said, but the roilings within the church hierarchy were not just notional ones.

The structure of the local ecclesiastical organization, the pressures involved in the selection of leaders, the problems caused by promotion through the ranks, and the sometimes less-than-honest management of resources provoked quarrels and conflicts well short of violent physical assault. When bishops were elected, the elections involved hard competition and the mobilization of resources. It must also be borne in mind that if bishops were elected, the lower ranks of the clergy that served them were *not*: they were selected and appointed by the successful bishop. In this process, there were always opportunities for enrichment. It was said that Silvanus, the miscreant dissident bishop of Cirta, had received an outright payment of twenty *folles* from one Victor so that Silvanus would appoint him priest.[112] Not only payments were involved. The whole power structure of each church at local level was open to such manipulation. When Silvanus was elected as bishop at Cirta in 305, it was not just that he won, but rather that his opponent, Donatus, and all of his supporters, lost. Over the next years, every new reader, subdeacon, deacon, priest – and doubtless other members of the clergy – was a personal appointee of the new bishop, loyal to him and hostile to others.[113]

And bishops could be as aggressive as any *padrone* in defense of their interests. In his investigation into the misdeeds of bishops (wrongs that might have disqualified them from voting) who gathered in May 306 to ordain Silvanus, the newly elected bishop of Cirta, the primate of the dissident church in Numidia, Secundus of Tigisis, concentrated on the great crime of betrayal. Had any of the bishops been guilty of this particularly heinous act? When he came to make inquiries into the past behavior of Purpurius, the bishop of Liniata, he was met not with fear,

---

[111] Aug. *Ep.* 22.9 (CCL 31: 57).

[112] *Gesta apud Zenophilum*, 16 (CSEL 26: 194): "Nundinarius dixit: 'Viginti folles dedit et factus est presbyter Victor?' Saturninus dixit. Et cum diceret, Zenophilus v.c. consularis Saturnino dixit: 'Cui dedit?' Saturninus dixit: 'Silvano episcopo.' Zenophilus v. c. consularis Saturnino dixit: 'Ergo ut fieret presbyter, Silvano episcopo viginti folles praemium dedit?' Saturninus dixit: 'Dedit.'" How much were twenty *folles* worth? If the single coin, not that much; enough, for example, to buy about five pounds of pork: H. Mattingly, *Roman Coins*, 2nd ed., London, Methuen, 1960, pp. 222–23. But it might well be that the source here is speaking of a purse (*folles*) containing hundreds or thousands of low-value coins: see K. Harl, *Coinage in the Roman Empire*, Baltimore, The Johns Hopkins University Press, 1996, p. 166. The latter would make more sense in the circumstance.

[113] Duval, *Chrétiens d'Afrique*, pp. 181–83.

apprehension, or prevarication, but rather with a brutish honesty and an open counter-threat recorded in a later court transcript.[114]

Secundus said to Purpurius, bishop of Liniata: "It is reported that you killed the two sons of your sister who lived at Milevis."

Purpurius replied: "Do you imagine that you're going to frighten me like you've frightened these others? And *you*. What did *you* do? You who were arrested by the Curator [sc. of the town of Cirta] and the local town council, with the order that you hand over the scriptures. How was it that *you* were somehow "released" by them without handing over anything? Unless, perhaps, you gave them something or ordered something to be given to them? They wouldn't have released you for *nothing*. As for me – OK, I've killed. I kill those who do anything against me or my interests. So don't provoke me or I'll start talking a lot more openly. You know that I don't fool around with anyone. Not me.

After hearing these frank words, and wisely listening to some prudent suggestions made by his nephew, Secundus decided not to pursue these embarrassing matters any further. At least, this is the way that the document presents the matter.

Problems like these fueled personal distrusts and hatreds, which in turn fed into more serious trouble. The chronic lack of sufficient numbers to fill church offices produced a normal condition of the hyper-mobility of men who were ready to exploit any quick route to promotion. It also encouraged the parallel tendency of bishops who needed clergy to poach from a neighboring bishop's personnel. Both factors converged to produce instability in the system. Take the case of Epigonius, the Catholic bishop of Bulla Regia who had fallen into a bad quarrel with Julian, the Catholic bishop of the neighboring town of Vazari. The dispute between the two bishops became so serious that it was brought before the Catholic conference held at Carthage in August 397.[115] The argument centered on a young man who had been a reader in the church at Bulla Regia. He had abandoned his position there – patently without his bishop's permission – and had transferred to the church at Vazari where the bishop, Julian, immediately promoted him to the rank of deacon. The case was complicated because the young man had originally come from Vazari. He might have felt that he had a natural right of return to his home church. Epigonius, the bishop of Bulla Regia, however, saw things very differently. The young man had come to *his* town as a boy and a very poor one at that. It was the diocese

---

[114] Apud Aug. *Contra Cresc.* 3.27.30 (CSEL 52: 436–37); the brutal words of Purpurius were so well known that a version of them was quoted by Optatus, *Contra Parm.* 1.13.3–4 (SC 412: 200).

[115] Concil. Carth. 28 August 397 = *Reg. Eccl. Carth. Excerpt.*, canon 54 (CCL 149: 190–91).

of Bulla Regia that had fed, clothed, trained, and educated the boy at its own expense. As Epigonius saw it, his church had invested a lot in the young man and had a right to his services. Moreover, the youth had served as reader for only two years before running off to the church at Vazari to receive an immediate promotion to the rank of deacon. None of this was entirely unusual (as we shall see).

The other side of this same coin was not the ambition of the rising young man like the anonymous reader from Bulla Regia, but rather the deliberate poaching of competent and promising young men by the bishops themselves – like the actions taken by Julian, the bishop of Vazari. It was a problem that was already apparent as early as the mid-fourth century when the Catholic bishops who convened at Carthage in 348 began to legislate against such hunting sallies made into neighboring dioceses.[116] The problem was also linked to a larger one of the general competitiveness between bishops for numbers: to acquire the "sheep" that would be part of their fold. The incitements and pressures to encroach on the flock of a neighboring bishop were constant. In legislation against the practice, Gratus, the Catholic Primate of Africa, noted that the problem was so serious and so pervasive that it was thought to generate "all the other evils" suffered by the church in Africa.[117]

Bishops could use the existing resources of their own diocese to invade and take over a neighboring diocese that looked richer and more promising. Such was the long story of Cresconius, the Catholic bishop of Villaregensis, a diocese deep in the southern parts of Numidia on the border of Mauretania Sitifensis. Early in the 390s, he had cast greedy eyes on the neighboring diocese of Thubunae and used force to take it over. Bitter complaints about his behavior came to the Catholic council at Hippo in 393, where the bishops ordered Cresconius to return to his own diocese.[118] That was the most that they could do. The church had no instruments of physical force at its disposal to deal with an outright rebel. A full four years later, Cresconius had not moved; he was still illegally in control of Thubunae. Legates from Mauretania Sitifensis once again brought the case before the general Catholic council at Carthage in the summer of 397. Cresconius was ordered, again, to abandon Thubunae and to return to his original

---

[116] Concil. Carth. 348, canon 5 (CCL 149: 6): no bishop is to keep on his staff anyone from another diocese who did not come with an express letter of permission from that person's bishop.

[117] Concil. Carth. 358, canon. 10 (CCL 149: 8): stating that no bishop is to encroach on or seize the congregation of a neighboring bishop, adding: "Quia inde cetera mala omnia generantur."

[118] Concil. Hippo, 8 Oct. 393 (BF.tit. 4.B = CCL 149: 32); for the whole run of evidence on the case, see "Cresconius (3)," PAC, p. 230.

diocese at Villaregensis. The council even demanded that the matter be brought to the attention of the civil governor of the province to get *him* to do something, manifestly because the church did not itself have adequate powers of coercion to compel Cresconius.[119] In response, Cresconius did nothing. Four years later, the Primate of Numidia once again brought the case before the general Catholic conference at Carthage. The miscreant bishop was ordered to appear before the next council.[120] Cresconius treated these demands of his own church with disdain and contempt, and with good reason. The church had no real power to quash his ambitions or even to control him. It clearly did not get any response from the governor of Numidia in 397 or 398. In short, Cresconius won. Should the church get too far in its disciplining of him, Cresconius could defect. He did not. Cresconius was still there in 411 when, at the great conference at Carthage, it was he who held the diocese of Thubunae and was officially recognized by the Catholic church as the bishop of the town. Another man had been appointed as bishop of Cresconius' original diocese at Villaregensis.[121]

The Cresconius incident shows that low-level local violence or use of force, given careful tactical application, could pay off. In the case of Thubunae, Cresconius' little imperialistic venture had succeeded. Salience above local level – that is, for the larger church to get bigger force in its hands to overcome local coercion – meant that it had to go to the state. But appeals to provincial governors, as in this case, were falling on deaf ears. Moreover, incidents like these were not the only or even the usual sources of inside conflicts. Among the many other potential irritants, it was expected that a senior priest or deacon would succeed the bishop upon the latter's decease. Since the bishop held his office for life, however, the wait for the prospective replacements would often be long and agonizing. In the interim years, the jockeying for position not only generated rancor among the lower-ranking clergy, but sometimes enticed those immediately in line for succession to enter into quarrels with their bishop. The problem of contumacious clergy was common. As early as 348, Gratus, the Catholic primate of Africa, had condemned priests who quarrelled with their bishops as "agents of the Devil."[122] Elaborate rules were established for hearing such internal disputes, but it is not known how well they worked.

---

119 Concil. Carth. 28 Aug. 397, canon 1 = *Reg. Eccl. Carth. Excerpt.* canon 48 (CCL 149: 187); that this was the first item on the agenda of the conference is probably some indication of its importance.
120 Concil. Carth. 13 Sept. 401, app. canon 11 = *Reg. Eccl. Carth. Excerpt.* canon 77 (CCL 149: 203).
121 GCC 1.121 (SC 195: 710–12); cf. "Cresconius (3)," PAC, p. 230.
122 Concil Carth. 348, canon 11 (CCL 149: 8).

Among the range of resolutions were other options made possible by the simple existence of the two churches, and these too could excite greater hatred and violence. Neither church had a monopoly of control over the whole community of Christians in Africa. Apart from accepting an internal resolution, the clergyman who found himself under attack or formally condemned had other alternatives. He could – and it seems that more than a few did – take the matter to the secular civil courts.[123] He could decamp to the opposition church. Or he could choose to go it alone. Cases of priests who resisted their excommunication by simply setting up their own independent churches – "setting up one altar against another," as it was put – were common enough to provoke legislation on the problem.[124] Of course, any move to independence was blamed on the ambition and pride of the priest concerned. If he persisted in his rebellion against his local bishop, then measures called for the local church to use force and violence to compel the rebel to stop his activities. He was to be physically driven far from the town where he lived "so that the ignorant and the simple will not be misled by viperish deceit."[125] It is typical that moves to take disputes outside of the community were taken as grounds for more serious measures.

Sometimes conflicts actually became worse because of the attempts made to resolve them, as in cases where contending parties agreed to share a diocese. Such an arrangement was made when a dissident bishop was accepted into the Catholic Church as a crossover, but with the maintenance of his rank. Just such a situation erupted in the diocese of Maginensis where a new bishop, a dissident crossover named Optantius, had been accepted as a co-bishop of the diocese alongside the existing Catholic bishop, Antigonus. The merger did not work. According to Antigonus, no sooner had Optantius been granted the position than he began showering insults and outrages on him, despite the fact that there had been a public handshake and a written agreement concerning the sharing of the diocese. Optantius had been circulating among the congregation, insinuating that it was *he* who had been named "father" or *pater* of the congregation, whereas Antigonus was only its *vitricus* or "step father". The bitterness of this inside fight became so poisonous that it was taken to the council of Carthage in 348 where the assembled bishops resolved to dampen the dispute, chanting in unison: "PEACE BE KEPT! PEACE BE KEPT!"[126] It is not known what finally happened.

---

[123] Concil. Carth. 390, canon 7 (CCL 149: 15).   [124] Concil. Carth. 390, canon 8 (CCL 149: 16).

[125] Ibid.: "Nihilominus et de civitate in qua fuerit longius depellatur, ne vel ignorantes vel simpliciter viventes serpentina fraude decipiat."

[126] Concil. Carth. 358, canon 12 (CCL 149: 9): "Pax servetur! Pacta custodiantur!"

One way of avoiding this type of conflict was to nominate one's successor in a public fashion before the whole *populus* of the church in a manner that gained their prior assent. The record of the diocese of Hippo, however, was not uniform on the success of the tactic. It was attempted in 395 when the aging Valerius had Augustine ordained as his "co-helper" bishop. An outburst of protest and objection coursed through Numidia that was only quieted with great difficulty, and never completely.[127] At the conference at Carthage in 411, the dissident bishop Petilian raised the matter of the irregularities of Augustine's ordination as bishop (and not for the first time). It caused an uproar in the assembly.[128] Augustine had good reason to institute preventive measures when, in September 426, he put forth Eraclius, one of his priests, to his people as his successor. He knew that "after the deaths of bishops, churches are usually thrown into deep disorder by ambitious and combative men."[129] A transcript of the dramatic events in the crowded church at Hippo that day has survived. Impressive, and transcribed verbatim into the church's official record, the words were meant to guarantee a succession free of dispute and violence. But it is not known if the tactic worked this time.[130] Augustine's move had also been prompted by his recent involvement in an upheaval at Milevis. There, the bishop Severus had nominated his successor before his death, but had failed to engage the people of the diocese in any public ceremonial. He had involved only the clergy in his decision, with the result that many of the people were "unhappy."[131] Augustine was called in as an outside mediator. The threat of violence apparently did not involve conflicts within the clergy as much as it did with the people's objection to not being informed and involved.

LEADERSHIP AND VIOLENCE

In most episodes of violence where Catholics were the victims, Augustine invariably points to what he believed to be the decisive involvement of the dissident clergy as the leaders. He frequently employs a standard alliterative

---

[127] For some of the problems with such collegial appointments, see Zmire (1971).

[128] GCC 3.238–47 (SC 224: 1176–86).

[129] Aug. *Ep.* 213.1 (CSEL 57: 373), and extensively (see ch. 10: pp. 453–55, below): "Scio post obitus episcoporum per ambitiosos aut contentiosos solere ecclesias perturbari."

[130] See "Eraclius," PAC, pp. 356–58: nothing is known of him after Augustine's death.

[131] Aug. *Ep.* 213.1 (CSEL 57: 374): "Sicut novit caritas vestra, in Milevitana ecclesia modo fui; petierunt enim me fratres et maxime servi dei, qui ibi sunt, ut venirem, quia post obitum beatae memoriae fratris et coepiscopi mei Severi, nonnulla ibi perturbatio timebatur ... Minus tamen aliquid factum erat, unde nonnulli contristabantur ... et erat inde aliquorum nonnulla tristitia." See "Severus (1)," PAC, 1070–75.

phrase – "your clerics and circumcellions" – to designate those carrying out the attacks. The rhetorical snippet provokes the question of who served as leaders when leadership was required in incidents of sectarian violence. In partial confirmation of the charge, references to the direct involvement of clergy in inciting and managing violence certainly exist. One case is recorded in the minutes of the hearing at Carthage in 411. When the dissident bishop Cresconius of Caesariana declared that he had "no rival bishop" facing him in his diocese, he provoked an angry outburst from the Catholic bishop, Novatus of Sitifis.[132]

He *does* have a Catholic priest facing him in his diocese, as well as many clergy and parishioners [sc. who crossed over] from the congregation of the Donatists. I would also like to note that there is a priest, and a deacon, here, right here in this city of Carthage, whom he robbed, whom he tortured, whom he hung on the rack. This man plundered the Catholic church, stole its money, took away its grain supplies, and seized its wagons – all in a way that makes clear that he knows full well that there is a Catholic church there. This is what I charge.

As much as the objections were denied by the dissident bishop Adeodatus as preposterous claims that had to be documented, cautioning that anyone who lied before a tribunal would be held responsible for such libels, the allegations were never refuted. The imputation is that the bishop Cresconius had been implicated in organizing the violence, most of which involved the seizure of a Catholic basilica and its resources. The same is reflected in a dispute that erupted following the declaration of his presence at the conference by the dissident bishop Cresconius of Pudentiana when he made the aggressive claim that there were no traitors present in his diocese. That provoked a controlled but angry reply from Aurelius, the Catholic bishop who was checking the declarations made by the opposite side.[133]

When you are gotten out of the way, we will ordain one of our own. These men here [sc. the two dissident bishops just named] seized our basilicas, these same men took away the furnishings that belonged to the church. The very man who is speaking now seized no fewer than four basilicas located in one place.

---

[132] GCC 1.189 (SC 195: 840): "Habet contra se Catholicum presbyterum, clericos abundantes et populos ex coetu Donatistarum. Hic est presbyter, et diaconus, hic in hac civitate Carthaginiensi, quem praedavit, quem torsit, quem suspendit. Ecclesiam autem Catholicam praedavit, pecuniam sustulit, frumenta deportavit, carpenta duxit, ut norit iste quia est illic ecclesia Catholica. Hoc sum prosecutus."

[133] GCC 1.201 (SC 195: 864): "Aurelius episcopus ecclesiae Catholicae Macomadiensis dixit: 'Remotis vobis ordinamus. Ipsi deposuerunt basilicas; ipsi tulerunt ornamenta ecclesiae. Ille qui loquitur quattuor basilicas deposuit uno loco.'"

This incident, amongst others, makes it clear that the imperial government, in the wake of its anti-pagan legislation of the 380s and 390s, was faced with a situation in which Christians accepted the state's laws as legitimate cover for private violent enforcement. The gangs of men who attacked pagan shrines and festivals, as far as the imperial government was concerned, were under the direction of Christian bishops. Imperial laws, including that of 399, therefore cautioned bishops that they were to involve themselves with religious matters only; they were to leave the enforcement of the law to the local courts and imperial officials.[134] The state itself was therefore well aware of who the prime organizers of the violence were.

Since both churches had always faced problems of internal organization and discipline, as the bishops saw the matter, they were only developing and extending powers that they had always wielded. The bishop was ultimately responsible for the actions of his subordinates and the parishioners in his diocese. Controlling their behavior and making certain that it fell within the parameters of acceptability was not always an easy task. Augustine might have been exceptional in going so far as to police even the table manners in his monastery at Hippo, where he had a slight piece of verse that he had composed condemning loose talk about absent friends carved into the surface of the dining table.[135] But his attention to the fine details of human behavior was justified. It was the little things that tended to get out of control. Bad talk and gossip led to sentiments of resentment and hostility, and then to worse. Conflict within the churches was a direct source of dissension, and dissent weakened the position of the one church with respect to the other, leading to decisions to cross over to the other side. This constant option in the hands of a resentful cleric constrained the extent to which bishops could use a heavy hand in disciplining him. In commenting on internal conflicts within congregations, Augustine noted that nothing was more dangerous.[136] The lines of dissent within a diocese were potentially manifold, but a number of typical situations seemed to recur. Prime among these were the election of a new bishop, the frustrated expectations of lower-ranking clergy in the process of promotion through the ranks, and the poisonous relations that sometimes developed between a bishop and the people of his diocese.

Good examples, however, could be used to encourage better morals. When he went preaching to small rural congregations Augustine would

---

[134] CTh 16.11.1 (20 August 399); see ch. 5 n. 124.

[135] Possidius, *Vita Aug.* 22.6 (Bastiaensen: 186–88).

[136] Aug. *Sermo* 360C.1 = Dolbeau 27/Mainz 63 (Dolbeau, *Vingt-six sermons*, p. 311): "Nihil est enim dulcius quam studium fratrum, sed nihil est periculosius quam dissensio populorum."

point to the Catholic Christians of Carthage as an example of good behavior. Their model was called on when he encountered parishioners clamouring against their bishops and actively resisting their authority.[137] There is nothing generally unbelievable about the situation that he envisaged: perceptions of better-controlled and more civil behavior might have been found in the more urbane atmosphere of the larger cities and might have been less easily manipulated in the depths of the countryside. It was the small rural dioceses, as we shall see, that were to provide him with some of his worst problems. If there were patterns to these internal troubles, they were still rather unpredictable in detail. Conflicts could erupt within any level of the layers of a local church hierarchy, but for overall discipline and order, those directly involving bishops were still potentially the most dangerous.

Bishops themselves were not always good men. Right from the beginning of his priesthood Augustine believed that many of the most critical problems facing the church were ones of internal discipline. He expressed frank alarm at the way in which bishops, priests, and deacons were not performing their duties; he was able to refer to some notorious examples.[138] Everyone knew the sometimes sordid details of the incidents concerned, although no one wished to say much in public about them. Difficulties like these had a serious impact on the congregation of any given town. Just so, the congregation of Hippo was in "a state of extreme distress" over certain recent events.[139] But Augustine's neat typology that separated intra-clerical disputes, driven by the honorable, if lamentable, vice of envy, from the plebeian problems of riot and sexual license, was somewhat artificial. Clerical power was always founded on the control of people and abuses potentially involved the illicit use of physical force or violence in coercing the uncooperative and in the sexual exploitation of subordinates.

Although surely colored by bias, the reports that the aggressive campaign of preaching and pamphleteering engineered by the Catholic Church against the dissidents produced an equally violent response in their preaching are credible. The dissidents preached, for example, that Augustine was a seducer and a deceiver of souls. They also preached that this dangerous wolf must be killed in defense of their own flock. It is even claimed that they taught their own people to believe that whoever would be able

---

[137] Aug. *Sermo* 359B.5 = Dolbeau 2/Mainz 5 (Dolbeau, *Vingt-six sermons*, p. 331): "ut diceremus minutis plebibus in agro obstrepentibus et episcopis suis resistentibus: 'Ite, videte Carthaginis plebem,' cum ergo de vestro bono exemplo abundantius gauderemus."
[138] Aug. *Ep.* 21 (CCL 31: 48–51).   [139] Aug. *Ep.* 22.9 (CCL 31: 57).

to achieve this violent act would have all of his sins forgiven by God.[140] But the bishops were only being caught in their own machinations; they were not always peaceable men. They were perfectly capable of inciting violence and adducing the appropriate biblical scriptures to justify their incitements: such acts of coercion were good because they were morally necessary and had good precedents.[141] The favorite biblical recourse was to the story of Jesus and the money-changers in the Temple. If the apostle Matthew had Jesus driving the evil men out with nothing more than hard rhetoric and pushing over some tables, then John the Evangelist had Christ arm himself with a whip to get the task done.[142] Which version the bishop selected to emphasize was a matter of tactics.

INSIDE VIOLENCE

In the secular sphere of municipal politics, where elections were vigorously contested, the presence of claques, organized support groups, clamorous supporters, and the use of ritual chanting, popular marches, and parades, all contributed to an atmosphere that could be both joyous and festive, but which could also become disruptive and violent. The selection of the higher officials of the church, especially bishops, in each regional diocese, was a process that similarly caught up the people in fits of democratic participation. It seems that these not infrequently involved highly contentious issues and personalities.[143] Neither church, neither the Catholic nor the dissident, escaped the potentially disturbing effects of these elections.[144] Such conflicts were normal in almost all parts of the Mediterranean where the choosing of bishops was subject to various types of election.[145] In the

---

[140] Possidius, *Vita Aug.* 9.4 (Bastiaensen: 152): "sed irati furiosa loquebantur atque seductorem et deceptorem animarum Augustinum esse … et ut lupum occidendum esse in defensionem gregis sui, dicebant et tractabant, omniaque peccata a Deo indubitanter esse credendum posse dimitti his qui hoc facere ac perficere potuissent."

[141] Gaddis, *Religious Violence*, pp. 251–58.

[142] Matt. 21: 12–13; Jn 2: 14–16. Notably, the use of these passages provoked debates in the Eastern church about what the whip was intended to chastise: just the animals or also the men: Gaddis, *Religious Violence*, pp. 259–61.

[143] On the modes and procedures in electing bishops see Sabw Kanyang, "Le processus d'élection et d'ordination de l'évêque en Afrique," ch. 2 in *Episcopus et plebs*, pp. 75–118, citing the studies by Ganshoff (1950), Gryson (1973), (1979), and (1980).

[144] Aug. *Sermo ad Caes.* 2 (CSEL 53: 169), where he states that the dissidents and the Catholics have much in common, including the whole process of the ordination of bishops. Although he does not explicitly mention the electoral process, it seems to be implied by his remarks.

[145] Norton, *Episcopal Elections*, esp. chs. 3, 8, and 9, on disorderly and disputed elections; Rapp, *Holy Bishops*, p. 47, citing John Chrysostom, *On the Priesthood*, 3.11 on "the fierce competition that often surrounded episcopal elections in his day."

election of the bishop at Cirta in 305, the supporters of the contenders, Donatus and Silvanus, shouted and chanted against each other. The loser, Donatus, and his followers, later castigated the supporters of the winner as nothing more than a mob of gladiators and prostitutes.[146]

Augustine's election as priest at Hippo was marked by similar disputes, but one has to understand how it was that his own interests had created them. On the one hand, wishing to enter the hierarchy of the church, Augustine had to appear to be a disinterested party, and not to exhibit an ambition that would be unfitting for a member of the Christian clergy. He also had to be shown to have been selected by popular acclaim. On the other hand, opportunities for advancement at a level appropriate to an ambitious and talented young man of rank were rather limited in his provincial home town of Thagaste in the mid-390s. And it was here that Augustine was moldering. For a middle-aged man who was highly educated, who had risen to the position of court rhetor at Milan, the desired criteria of a proper location were suitably high. In the back of Augustine's mind must have been the model of the grand imperial bishop whom he had witnessed at Milan, no matter how exceptional he was at the time: Ambrose, who received baptism, all ecclesiastical offices, and ordination as bishop in one week.[147] Augustine might not have hoped for the instantaneous ascent available to a grandee of senatorial rank, but a quick rise to the top from the priesthood was surely what he expected.

Men who came to the church with wealth, power, and education naturally had such expectations of a rapid advance through its ranks, and usually had their expectations met. In 343, the Council of Serdica had specifically targeted these economically and culturally advantaged candidates and the way that they tended to receive special treatment, thereby giving rise to local envies and hatreds. It was ruled that men of wealth and forensic education could not become bishops immediately but, like everyone else, had to rise through the ranks.[148] The problem, however, was that both African churches had the propensity to hurry along promotion in order to get competent and well-connected men to the top. In direct contradiction to the fixed *cursus honorum* required by Serdica, in Africa men not infrequently passed directly from the deaconate to the position of

---

[146] *Gesta apud Zenophilum* (CSEL 26: 194 and 196): "Nundinarius dixit: 'Vidi quia Mutus harenarius tulit eum in collo.' Zenofilus [v.c.] consularis Saturnino dixit: 'Sic factum est?' Saturninus dixit: 'Sic.' . . . Nundinarius dixit: 'Prostibulae illic fuerunt'."

[147] Paulinus, *Vita Ambr.* 9 (Bastiaensen: 64). But we must keep in the forefront how very exceptional Ambrose was at the time; in the western church, as a bishop recruited out of high senatorial rank, he was a solitary figure: see Gilliard (1984).

[148] Rapp, *Holy Bishops*, p. 203, citing Serdica, canon 10 (= Nicaea, canon 2).

bishop.[149] The lack of men not just for the ranks of the clergy in general, but for the bishop's post in particular created a countervailing pressure to disregard the rules or to feign ignorance of them.

Sometimes more violent means were brought into play. If an experienced, talented, and resourceful man was sighted by a needy congregation, press-gang tactics could be used to bag their man. The Pinianus affair, the best-documented incident of inside violence that rocked the church at Hippo, was one such case. Gothic raids into central Italy and the siege of Rome in late August 410 produced a flood of frightened refugees. Two of these, the noblewoman Melania and her husband Pinianus, had fled across the sea to seek refuge on estates that they owned near Augustine's home town of Thagaste.[150] Out of Melania's vast property holdings around the town, the couple bestowed gifts of land on the local Catholic church. When they arrived for a visit at Hippo, the ordinary members of the congregation not unreasonably saw in Pinianus a potential source of similar lavish gifts.

The visit of the grandees, however, quickly degraded into a near-riot that ran out of Augustine's control. Trapped in the church, the noble husband and wife were subject to loud and insistent ritual chanting from the parishioners in which they made manifest their will to appoint Pinianus as priest at Hippo.[151] The scene was frightening. Augustine later reported that he had feared that a few violent men might take advantage of the situation to start a riot; he had to reassure Pinianus' mother, Albina, that her son had no reason to fear death at the hands of the congregation at Hippo (Pinianus or Melania had probably reported exactly this fear to her). Paranoia was exploited to explain the bishop's lack of control over his own people. In yet other attempts at self-exculpation, Augustine hinted at the involvement of "bad monks" and blamed "outside agitators" for the troubles: they had oozed out of Carthage, a known sinkhole of urban sedition.[152] A frightened Pinianus was hemmed in the rear of the church by the chanting mob. The slightest sign of unwillingness on his part to

---

[149] Lancel (1992), p. 336.

[150] *Vita S. Melaniae*, 21, D. Gorce ed. (SC 90: 170–72) Greek life; 20–21, P. Laurence ed. (pp. 192–94): Latin life.

[151] Aug. *Ep.* 124, 125, and 126 (CCL 31B: 178–94) contain the main points.

[152] Aug. *Ep.* 124.2 (CCL 31B: 183–84); *Ep.* 125.5 (CCL 31B: 183–84): "Clericos sane nostros vel fratres in monasterio constitutos participes vel hortatores fuisse contumeliarum tuarum utrum probari possit, ignoro. Nam cum hoc quaesissem, dictum est unum tantum modo Carthaginiensem in monasterio clamasse cum populo, cum illum presbyterum peterent, non cum in te indigna iactarent"; *Ep.* 126.1 (CCL 31B: 185): "nam et nos metuebamus, ne ab aliquibus perditis, qui saepe multitudini occulta conspiratione miscentur, in violentam prorumperetur audaciam occasione seditionis inventa."

become a priest was met by a barrage of verbal insults hurled at him and at Augustine's brother Alypius.[153]

Augustine and his brother were forced to retreat, with Pinianus in tow, to the rear of the church, to find shelter in the apse. The violent crowd moved closer to them, mounting the stairs that fronted the high platform in the apse. Here they set up a continuous frightening racket. They hurled more terrible abuse at Alypius. By scurrying back and forth between the agitated crowd and the cowering Pinianus, Augustine finally managed to strike a deal. He extracted a verbal promise from Pinianus that he would serve as a priest in Hippo. This was not good enough for the crowd. They would not accept Pinianus' mere verbal assent. They demanded that he *swear* their version of an oath. Pinianus, ever the bargainer, wanted an "exit clause" in the agreement: If the "barbarians" invaded Africa, he was to be exempted from his agreement. His wife Melania piped up and wanted another exemption clause added: in case of bad weather. When the people got wind of these prevarications, they set up a terrible uproar. At last, a mutually acceptable agreement was hammered out and written down. A deacon then read it aloud to the congregation. The people finally accepted this modified text, but they demanded that Pinianus sign it in public and that Augustine and Alypius also sign the document.

All of this was not accidental and it was certainly not the result of out-side agitators or subversive monks. Augustine refers, not implausibly, to certain leaders of the people who formed the congregation's demands and controlled the final agreement.[154] Such leaders could have been created out of the tense situation itself – men who rose to the occasion – but more likely they were part of an informal leadership in each community that we rarely hear about. Unfortunately, but perhaps understandably, Augustine does not report the reactions of the people when they learned that Pinianus, despite his sacred oath, had skipped out of town the following day. The Pinianus incident is one example of the ongoing pressures to find and to recruit a few good men. Perhaps one of the more striking of these incidents was the recruitment of Petilian, the dissident bishop of Constantina, one of the most skilled and powerful leaders in the dissident church of Augustine's day. In his youth, however, he was a Catholic catechumen. Then he was kidnapped by dissidents, violently seized, forcibly baptized, and appointed to their clergy, all apparently against his will – which only

---

[153] Aug. *Ep.* 125.1 and 3 (CCL 31B: 180–82); and 126.1 (CCL 31B: 185).
[154] Aug. *Ep.* 126.6 (CCL 31B: 188–89).

serves to demonstrate that any means, even violent ones, could produce a man who was qualified to lead.[155]

The mobilization of violent or near-violent popular demonstrations to compel the denunciation of a sitting bishop or the election of a wanted candidate as bishop was surely not unusual. Here was another potential system for the organization of actions by crowds and gangs. In attempting to legislate against such rude behavior, general church councils reveal the circumstances in which much of it emerged. In the accusations and counter-accusations made by bishops against their critics, and by their opponents against them, the laws speak of "evils" done by violent crowds against one side or the other, including the intimidation of witnesses.[156] No man, the rules held, was to be instituted in a diocese because of popular uproars, upheavals, or seditions, as they were called.[157] The episodes of organized violence occurred within situations of existing conflict, but they were equally possible in circumstances, like the Pinianus episode, where the people were only attempting to compel an appointment. They, too, were competing, it is true, but against other perceived and potential takers.

In a general pattern that is discernible elsewhere in the Mediterranean, and which was also true of Africa, the larger, wealthier, and more presti-gious sees attracted resourceful outsiders who competed for the position of bishop – outsiders who were often more aggressive and better equipped to compete than were those who had risen slowly and painfully within the local hierarchy.[158] That was the problem and the enticement that faced a young man like Augustine. The most prestigious see of Carthage was already held by Aurelius, who was not to be replaced in the foreseeable future. Augustine's choices were limited, so his eyes were logically drawn to Hippo, the next most important diocese in wealth, power, and territory after that of Carthage in the ecclesiastical provinces of Africa and Numidia, if not in all of Africa. He had connections there, a man in the imperial *agentes in rebus* – a man who, like his good friend Evodius, was in the impe-rial communications service and who, it is said, drew Augustine's attention to Hippo Regius.[159] It was a rich and suitable posting, and likely to provide

[155] See ch. 2, p. 88; Norton, *Episcopal Elections*, pp. 192–96, lists other known cases involving reluctance and compulsion.

[156] *Canones in Causa Apiarii*, canon 30 (CCL 149: 144).

[157] Concil. Carth. 13 Sept. 401, canon 9 = *Reg. Eccl. Carth. Excerpt.* canon 74 (CCL 149: 202): "quibuslibet populorum studiis vel seditionibus retinere."

[158] Rapp, *Holy Bishops*, pp. 198–99, citing the study of G. Bardy, "Sur la patrie des évêques dans les premiers siècles," *RHE* 35 (1939), pp. 217–42,

[159] Possidius, *Vita Aug.* 3.3 (Bastiaensen: 138): "quos dicunt agentes in rebus, apud Hipponem Regium constitutus"; for Evodius see Aug. *Confess.* 9.8.17 (CCL 27: 142–43): "consociasti nobis et Evodium iuvenem ex nostro municipio."

its bishop with resources and possibilities. The existing bishop, Valerius, was old and slow. As the sitting bishop of Hippo, he was naturally less than happy to have Augustine appointed as his priest. Almost certainly, he would have preferred not to have an alien competitor on his doorstep.[160] The whole thing had to be staged. The appointment was later portrayed as Valerius demanding that the people provide him with a good priest; the congregation then literally laid their hands on Augustine, who is presented as someone who was unaware of what was about to happen. The people took him to their bishop and raised vociferous rhythmic chants demanding that he be ordained: Pinianus *avant l'homme lui-même*. The candidate, moved by his own humility, is said to have wept profusely.[161] Valerius is presented as old and as a Greek who had less than a good command of the Latin language. He reasonably allowed the priest the right to preach the gospel in his church, despite the fact that this was contrary to the custom of the African churches.[162] The allowance raised the ire of other bishops. But it was done.[163]

The next step was Augustine's appointment as coadjutor bishop with Valerius in 395 after having served only three or four years as a priest. This caused another outburst of resentment. For a long time there would be those who would question the validity of his appointment. Among the angry men was Megalius, bishop of Calama, who was the Old Man or Primate of Numidia. From the beginning, he was suspicious of the sudden intrusion of a too-well-qualified outsider, marked by too much ambition, who was likely to upset the order of things. The fact that the appointment was manifestly illegal had to be countered by a barrage of hyperbolic justifications.[164] Megalius continued to oppose the appointment as illegal. Even after being persuaded on the basis of "examples of churches overseas," he still remained convinced that the appointment ought not to have been made.[165] Feeling deceived by Augustine and his supporters, he

---

[160] Aug. *Ep.* 31 (CCL 31: 108–12), of 395/96, where Paulinus and Therasia, being outsiders to Africa, can speak a little more frankly and openly about the hostility to Augustine's appointment.

[161] Possidius, *Vita Aug.* 4.2 (Bastiaensen: 140): the local *plebs*, "eum ergo tenuerunt et, ut in talibus consuetum est . . . magnoque studio et clamore flagitantibus."

[162] Possidiius, *Vita Aug.* 5.2–3 (Bastiaensen: 142): "cui rei se homo natura Graecus minusque Latina lingua et litteris instructus, minus utilem pervidebat. Eidem presbytero potestatem dedit se coram in ecclesia evangelium praedicandi ac frequentissime tractandi, contra usum quidem et consuetudinem Africanarum ecclesiarum."

[163] Possidius, *Vita Aug.* 5.3 (Bastiaensen: 142): "unde etiam nonnulli episcopi detrahebant."

[164] Aug. *Ep.* 32.2–5 (CCL 31: 113–16) in 395/96 from Paulinus and Therasia.

[165] The appointment violated canon 8 of the Council of Nicaea; Augustine claimed that neither he nor Valerius knew of the provision (*Ep.* 223.4 = CSEL 57: 376); and appeal was made to precedents in Africa (*Ep.* 31.4 = CCL 31: 110).

became very angry and legislated against any other such appointments in the future. The uproar that it caused in the Catholic Church was exploited by Augustine's sectarian opponents.[166] The enduring odor was so bad that Augustine's biographer had to defend him against the resentments that continued decades after the bishop's death.[167] None of the irregularities, or the distaste and rancor raised by them, slowed the ambitious candidate.

Such animosities, big and small, could be found at every level of promotion and succession from the lower clergy, like readers and subdeacons, to the decision about who was to be made primate of the ecclesiastical province. In 397, on the death of Megalius, bishop of Calama and Primate of Numidia, Augustine had to move quickly to cut off any hostilities that might emerge. It was a task undertaken in trying circumstances. He was suffering so severely from hemorrhoids that he could hardly walk. In the midst of his anal pain, Augustine had to contact the main bishops of Numidia to head off the expected violence. "We must be on our guard against such hatreds," he warned. In this case, he wished that Profuturus, the bishop of Constantina, would make sure that his courier, one Victor, would not purposefully travel through Calama.[168] Problems with finding a successor to Megalius were finally sorted out with the appointment of Crescentianus who held his position less than three years, dying in midsummer of 401.[169] Then the whole scene had to be replayed. In a reply to the complaints of a certain Victorinus about the general summons that had been sent to the bishops concerning the appointment of the new provincial primate, Augustine once again referred to problems with ranking and seniority in the province of Numidia. Victorinus claimed that Sanctippus, the bishop of Thagora, had said that the position of the most senior-ranking bishop belonged to him and that many recognized him as such. He complained that, for some reason, the circular letter had failed to mention Sanctippus, whereas it named Augustine, who had only been a bishop from 396, as the third-highest-ranking bishop in Numidia.[170] There was renewed outrage over the apparent special privileges being given to the new man in Hippo.

---

[166] On the objections of Megalius, the Old Man of Numidia, to Augustine's appointment, see Aug. *Contra litt. Petil.* 3.16.19 (CSEL 52: 177); *Contra Cresc.* 4.64. 79 (CSEL 52: 578); *En. in Ps.* 36.3.19 (CCL 38: 380–81); Megalius' letter was known to the dissidents and used by them: Aug. *Contra Cresc.* 3.80.92 (CSEL 52: 495); cf. Lamirande (1965d), p. 713.

[167] Possidius, *Vita Aug.* 8.1–6 (Bastiaensen: 148–50).   [168] Aug. *Ep.* 38 (CCL 31: 156–57).

[169] See "Crescentianus (3)," PAC, p. 226.   [170] Aug. *Ep.* 59 (CCL 31A: 9–10).

MONEY, PROPERTY, AND POWER

However it was done, bishops had access to considerable sums of money, both their own and those of the church. The money was used not only for the expenses involved in the daily running of the church and for the alleviation of the poor, but also for long-term investments. Fines that were levied on miscreant clergy by the state, for example – sometimes not inconsiderable sums – went not to the fiscus of the government, but rather to the church, to be distributed to the poor.[171] And the bishops did the distributing. A potential problem in the management and control of this property was in distinguishing between the bishop as a private person and as officer of the church. Already in the age of Cyprian, the bishop of Carthage had railed against bishops whose incomes were being augmented by usurious loans.[172] The problem was not just an African one. Early in the fourth century, the bishops at the Council of Nicaea were compelled to regulate against such practices that were apparently widespread among the clergy.[173] On the other hand, the canons of the Council of Serdica of 343 ruled that bishops were to be allowed to leave their sees for up to three weeks each year to collect incomes from properties that they owned.[174] The Council of Carthage of 348 again legislated against the practice of clerics involving themselves in making loans that involved the taking of interest.[175] It also forbade them from involving themselves in business dealings outside of the church; and they were specifically prohibited from becoming procurators or managers in charge of running the properties of others.[176] The countervailing personal interests of bishops (and other clergy) and the community claims of their churches naturally produced complaint and conflict.

The priest Abundantius who served the church on an agricultural estate named the *fundus Strabonianensis* in the diocese of Hippo Regius illustrates the complexity of conflicts that emerged under the general rubric of abuses of power, but which are perhaps best viewed in terms of attempts by clerics to use their positions for illicit economic gain. In a letter that he

---

[171] CTh 11.36.20 (Valentinian, Valens and Gratian, to Claudius, Proconsul of Africa; 14 May 369): in the aftermath of the Chronopius case, where the bishop was fined fifty pounds of silver.

[172] Cypr. *De lapsis*, 6 (CCL 3: 223–24).

[173] Council of Nicaea, can. 17 (Pitra I, 428–29; Hefélé-Leclercq, I, 610).

[174] Rapp, *Holy Bishops*, p. 213, citing Concil. Serd. canon 12 (G) = 15 (L); see Hesse, *Council of Serdica*, pp. 222–23 and 234–35.

[175] Council of Carthage, 345, can. 13 (CCL 149: 9): "Abundantius episcopus Adrumetinus dixit: In nostro concilio statutum est ut non liceat clericis faenerari."

[176] Council of Carthage, 345, can. 9 (CCL 149: 7).

wrote in early 402 to Sanctippus, the Primate of Numidia, Augustine reported the results of an inquiry he had made into complaints about Abundantius' behavior.[177] True to his name, Abundantius had been accused of stockpiling monies for himself from funds that belonged to the church. Such accusations, whether true or false, tended to be supplemented by others that were meant to confirm the moral depravity of the delinquent. In the hearing into the misdemeanors of Abundantius, as was often the case, additional charges were ones of moral misconduct. He was accused not only of fiscal malfeasances, but also of sexual ones. He had stopped at a hamlet called Gippe, it was said, where he had stayed in the house of a woman of bad repute. He had actually dined with her. The ideal of priestly conduct in such touchy matters was noted by Possidius in his biography of Augustine: no woman, even his own sister, stayed in his house. He was never seen alone with any woman, even in urgent matters.[178] No suspicion was permitted to arise. It was logical, therefore, that more serious cases, like that of the priest Abundantius, tended to link sex and money to produce a more toxic mix of wrongdoing.

One response of an aggrieved member of the clergy who found himself under threat, like Abundantius, was to improve his position by moving out of the religious community where he was exposed to his enemies – where his career prospects were slim or at a dead end – to one that was more attractive. A lateral movement was an obvious answer to his difficulties. Leaving one church and moving to another was much like *traditio*, although within a given church it never went by such an awful name. Betrayal of one's communion was a more serious matter. In *traditio*, the miscreant cleric did not simply move within his own church to another parish, another diocese, or to another province. Rather, he went all the way, making a permanent break with his home church to join the enemy camp. The cases that fall short of total conversion to the other side, however, are intriguing precisely because they reveal some of the micro-dynamics of power that ran along a spectrum of possible responses. They permit a better understanding of how far an individual could be harassed, threatened or humiliated before he would embrace the cost of crossing over to the other church. Normally, existing ties were strong and outweighed almost all other considerations. For example, in the 370s the dispute between the dissident exegete Tyconius and his own church led to harsh confrontations between himself and Parmenian, the dissident bishop of Carthage and Primate of Africa. The differences were so irreconcilable and the two men so intransigent that, around 380, Parmenian had a general council of

---

[177] Aug. *Ep.* 65 (CCL 31A: 23–24).   [178] Possid. *Vita Aug.* 26 (Bastiaensen: 196–98).

the dissident church remove Tyconius from its communion. Much to the puzzlement and frustration of many Catholics, however, these punishments were never sufficient to provoke Tyconius to cross over to the Catholic Church.[179]

Some of the reasons for Tyconius' hesitation might be found in cases that fell short of full betrayal and which reveal alternatives to this type of *traditio*. These internal decampments were frequent enough to be known. What impelled a monk named Donatus in the Catholic monastery at Hippo, for example, suddenly to leave the church there with another brother and take the road for Carthage? We do not know. The reasons could have been negative ones having to do with discipline at Hippo, but they might have been just the positive attractions of Carthage. After all, Donatus was able to be ordained as a priest in the metropolis. A deeply upset Augustine demanded of Aurelius, the bishop of Carthage, that both the men should be disciplined.[180] At the end of the same year, the pattern was repeated, but this time in reverse. Quintianus, a priest from a small congregation, the *plebs Vigesilitana*, had become entangled in wrongdoings of a kind that merited his being removed from communion by Aurelius, the bishop of Carthage.[181] Whatever it was that the priest had done, the quarrels had risen above the head of his own bishop to arrive at Aurelius who, as Primate of Africa, had found it necessary to intervene directly and with force. There is no doubt that the machinations in which Quintianus had become involved had been very disruptive of local order.

Although he was only a priest, Quintianus was also a man of ambition and personal principle. He spoke of men in a monastery connected with the church of Vigesilita who, having been caught up in the fray, now wished to leave it to seek protection elsewhere. Aurelius advised Augustine not to receive these men, since it would be in violation of recent conciliar decisions that were valid for the whole church in Africa.[182] Finding his own position intolerable, Quintianus had pursued the same option: he appealed to Augustine to accept him into his clergy. Both to help Quintianus with an exit strategy and to help Aurelius to defuse a threatening situation, Augustine replied that he was willing to offer the man a place of refuge at Hippo,

---

[179] See "Tyconius," ch. 5 in Monceaux, *Hist. litt.* 5, pp. 168–70.   [180] Aug. *Ep.* 60 (CCL 31A: 11–12).

[181] See "Quintianus (1)," PAC, p. 939; the editors think that he came from Vegesala (Hr. Rekba in S. Tunisia). The toponym is variously spelled, however, so that it is far from certain that Vegesala is meant.

[182] Presumably Quintianus was thinking of the decisions reached by the Council of Carthage of 13 September 401 (*Reg. Eccl. Carth. Excerpt.*). 80 = CCL 149: 204), one of which states that where any man was received from an outside monastery, the local bishop could not appoint such a person to be head of his monastery or to the clergy of his church.

although *not* as a member of his own clergy.[183] The proffered grounds of his hesitation were connected with Quintianus' reported persistence in reading non-canonical scriptures. Augustine suggested that these writings had Manichaean overtones that would mislead ordinary people. For his part, Quintianus was confidently able to assert that the local congregation would never accept as their bishop a man who had been shipped in by the decision of the council held at Carthage on 13 September 401. He suggested that the impending visit by Aurelius to Vigesilitana, no doubt to lend his considerable authority to the seating of the new bishop, might serve only to provoke the faithful to violence.

Another episode that happened the same year and that involved minor clergy from Hippo provides more insights into similar problems produced by clerical ambition. The story centers on a certain Timothy who was serving as a subdeacon in the small town of Subsana, a hamlet located on the far western mountainous borderlands of the diocese of Hippo. This Timothy was no ordinary subdeacon. In the years immediately preceding the incident that had brought him to the attention of his superiors, he had been shunted around from one small village to another serving in the rank of reader or *lector*.[184] After he arrived at Subsana, however, with the collusion of the priest at the place, named Carcedonius, and with the assistance of another man named Verinus, Timothy finally managed to have himself ordained to the higher rank of subdeacon – all of this without consulting Augustine. He now had the higher rank that he felt that he deserved. It was time to move on and to play the same game again. Without so much as a goodbye to Carcedonius, Timothy relocated to the larger town of Milevis and to its bishop Severus. Here he would serve in the same rank, but now in a much larger and wealthier diocese.

At some point, Augustine and Alypius got wind of this migrant entrepreneur and attempted to call him to heel, demanding that he return to Subsana in his original capacity as lector. Not unnaturally, Timothy did not wish to see his hard work of self-promotion undone and so he refused, claiming that he had sworn an oath not to leave bishop Severus in Milevis. Augustine's final position, as staked out in a diplomatic but forceful letter to Severus, was, simply, that Timothy ought to be returned to Subsana to serve there as reader, that his ordination as subdeacon was not valid, and that his so-called oath was illicit and therefore not relevant.[185] Although

---

[183] Aug. *Ep.* 64 (CCL 31A: 20–22).
[184] Aug. *Ep.* 62 (CCL 31A: 15–16): the other towns were Turres, Cizau (or, Cizan) and Verbalis – so small, notably, that the latter two are never again referred to in all of Augustine's writings.
[185] Aug. *Ep.* 62 (CCL 31A: 15–16).

we have two more letters on this same matter from Augustine to Severus, we cannot be certain what deal Timothy finally managed to strike.[186] The affair was almost certainly the cause of a specific regulation passed by the Council of Milevis on 27 August 402, the year immediately following. The canon forbade anyone who was a reader in a given church to be appointed to a clerical position in another.[187] Such movements were entrepreneurial in nature: men were trying to better themselves by moving to greener pastures. That they might succeed indicated yet another source of conflict, but one that was short of outright violence. Mediating the extremes were the talents of personnel management.

MANAGING CONFLICT

One way of diplomatically controlling violence was to find a creative way to resolve potential causes. The events involving the priest Bonitatus at Hippo in 402 provide as good a case study as any. The quarrel in which he was ensnared had caused a great deal of trouble in the diocese. The problems began to attract the attention and censure of important lay members of the congregation to whom Augustine was compelled to address a letter. Bonitatus had accused a monk named Spes (appropriately named) of various misdeeds. Not to be cowed, Spes struck back and began accusing Bonitatus of misdeeds that would require his removal from the ranks of the priests in the church at Hippo. Faced with the difficult problem of an intractable quarrel within his church, Augustine first tried to investigate the facts, but he could find no reasons for removing Bonitatus from the formal list of the priests of the diocese.[188] The conflict between these two men was not limited to them. Their quarrel mobilized some members of the congregation, while others, who did not wish to take sides, were greatly distressed. Augustine's attempt to defuse the problem (we do not know whether he succeeded) struck along two lines. First he reclaimed the public ground of the congregation by holding meetings in which the sordid details were ventilated in full, as much against convention as such total revelations of "dirty laundry" might be. Then the two men were made an offer that they could not refuse. Augustine shipped the whole problem overseas. He ordered the men to journey to the shrine of the holy Felix at Nola where the saint himself would decide the matter by miraculous revelation. It was

---

[186] Aug. *Ep.* 62 and 63 (CCL 31A: 15–19).
[187] *Reg. Eccl. Carth. Excerpt.* 90 (CCL 149: 208): "Item placuit, ut quicumque in ecclesia vel semel legerit, ab alia ecclesia ad clericatum non teneatur."
[188] Aug. *Ep.* 77 (CCL 31A: 81–82).

to be a final court, without appeal.[189] Whatever substance there was to his accusations, the promotion of Bonitatus to the rank of priest was what most rankled Spes. He felt that he was the equal of Bonitatus and he was not likely to let the matter rest until he himself had been promoted. Until then, there was going to be trouble.

In these model cases, a number of typical causes emerge as well as a number of standard responses. The causes are not surprising: the drive for more power, status, and rank, the need to muscle aside or to frighten a rival, or the rewards of sexual exploitation. Most of these ends required resources. So there is a parallel drive to acquire property, money, access to kick-backs and payments, protection money, and so on. The recourse in most cases was not to physical violence but to the word and the pen: verbal protests and complaints lodged with figures of authority, normally, the local bishop; the compiling of banks of written documents; and the drive to hold ecclesiastical councils, official tribunals, boards of hearing; and even, if only sometimes, recourse to the secular civil courts. The stories of Quintianus, Timothy, Spes, and Bonitatus are all mini-vignettes about these different avenues of ambition and self-assertion in the face of the cloying constraints of ecclesiastical rules. In addition to these cases, the personal narratives of a young reader named Antoninus and a priest named Apiarius might be extreme cases that we happen to know about because their protagonists were unusually troublesome. But their stories are ones that illustrate the real power of small fry to make big trouble. So they are intriguing.

BAD BOY: ANTONINUS OF FUSSALA

It is rather rare that a small-time bad boy from the past comes to life so vividly in a story of Dickensian color as does Antoninus of Fussala in the story of his personal battles within the Catholic Church. It is rarer still that new manuscript discoveries infuse even greater life into a rogue's apparent misdeeds and the not inconsiderable trouble that he caused. But then again, it is clear that Antoninus was no ordinary guy.[190] His story deserves to be retold, and not just for its intrinsic interest. Perhaps more than any other

---

[189] Aug. *Ep.* 78 (CCL 31A: 83–91): note that the general report on the matter is addressed to "Most Cherished Brothers, the Clergy, the Seniores [Elders] and the Whole Congregation of the Church of Hippo."

[190] For existing studies, see Frend (1983c), Lancel (1983), Merdinger, "The Case of Antony of Fussala," ch. 10 in *Rome and the African Church*, pp. 154–82; Munier (1983), (1986–94); and see "Antoninus (3)," PAC, pp. 73–75; as the editors remark, we cannot be certain about his name; it might have been, simply, Antonius.

single narrative from rural Africa of the fifth century, it details the authority and wealth, and the weakness and limitations, of the nominally powerful. The constraints that hedged in the senior bishops who wanted to control their peers considerably influenced what they could and could not do. The adventures of Antoninus also reveal the avenues of power that were open to the apparently lower and weaker to assert their own will, and with some justice from their point of view, given the cards that life had dealt them.

The stories in which Antoninus starred and which created such furor transpired in the mid teens of the fifth century when he was in the monastery at Hippo and in the early 420s when he became bishop of the village of Fussala. At first these events were very small and very local, but by 423 they had reached Pope Celestinus in Rome and the circles of powerful and wealthy persons in the imperial metropolis. But it is best to begin at the beginning.[191] Antoninus was born into a world of rural poverty and deprivation. His parents were so poor that, in the common parlance of the indigent, they did not know the source of the next day's food. As a young boy, Antoninus had come to Hippo with his mother. She had been divorced from his birth father and had remarried. Because of their poverty, she and her new husband, with her small child in tow, had thrown themselves on the good will of the local Catholic community. In response, Antoninus' mother was registered on the rolls of the poor who were sustained by the church.[192] The price tag for this benevolence had been her agreement, along with that of her new husband, to take vows of chastity.[193] So the mother of Antoninus joined the women's monastic establishment at Hippo. In a parallel move, her second husband and her little son were received into the Catholic monastery in the city. Even in the midst of his greatest successes, it was the poverty of his birth, this history of

---

[191] Aug. *Ep.* 209 (CSEL 57: 347–51). The chronology is loose. Augustine addressed this letter to Pope Caelestinus; it cannot date earlier than 423. The hearing at Hippo that took the record of Antoninus' misdeeds is most likely immediately antecedent, so in 422, when Bonifatius was still Pope (see *Ep.* 209.6). How many years before 422 Antoninus was ordained as bishop of Fussala is difficult to judge, but surely not long before, probably *c.* 420. Antoninus would therefore have been born *c.* 400.

[192] Aug. *Ep.* *20.2 (BA 46B: 294): "illa in matricula pauperum quos sustentat ecclesia"; cf. Brown, *Poverty and Leadership*, pp. 65–66.

[193] Aug. *Ep.* *20.2 (BA 46B: 294): "Parvulus cum matre et vitrico venit Hipponem; ita pauperes erant, ut quotidiano victu indigerent ... quod adhuc pater viveret Antonini atque illa se alteri a viro suo separata iunxisset, ambobus continentiam persuasi; atque ita ille cum puero in monasterio, illa in matricula pauperum quos sustentat ecclesia"; *Ep.* 209.3 (CSEL 57: 349): "obtuli non petentibus quendam adulescentem Antoninum, qui mecum tunc erat, in monasterio quidem a nobis a parvula aetate nutritum sed praeter lectionis officium nullis clericatus gradibus et laboribus notum."

resourcelessness, that was later brought up against Antoninus.[194] But one can easily see how it would be central to his way of looking at the world.

These early life steps in which the little Antoninus was involved were not unusual. They were part of a common practice in which churches took in unwanted or exposed children and trained the vulnerable dependants for their own purposes.[195] The monastery was now his only world. He was fed, clothed, and educated within its confines, and, trained with the skills of reading and writing, he was able to serve as a reader or *lector*. All of this transpired, approximately, in the years between 410 and 415. As time went on, the stepfather died, the mother grew old, and Antoninus grew up, gained usable skills, and became more opportunistic. He was a young man of some talent and great expectations. In one of Augustine's lengthy absences from Hippo, Urbanus, the head of the monastery, selected Antoninus to be ordained as the priest of a rural estate in the diocese of Hippo. Although Augustine approved, Antoninus showed himself to be a person of independent mind and judgment. He refused to go – probably for very good reasons.[196] We can only speculate that the assigned hamlet was just too low on the spectrum of his expectations.

The sudden forced transfer of former dissident congregations to the Catholic church in the hinterlands of Hippo in the aftermath of the imperial measures of 412 and 414 faced Augustine with the problem of providing sufficient clergy for the new larger congregations. The pressures provoked him to form a new diocese centered on the *castellum* of Fussala, a small village and territory located in the extreme southern borderlands of the diocese of Hippo, and to furnish the town and territory with its own bishop.[197] Fussala was about forty (Roman) miles from Hippo in a region where hitherto most of the Christians belonged to the dissident church. At Fussala itself, Augustine admitted that before the legislation compelling adherence to the Catholic Church not a single Catholic was to be found.[198]

---

[194] Aug. *Ep.* *20.29 (BA 46B: 336), for example, harps on Antoninus' poverty when he was appointed bishop of Fussala: "homo qui de monasterio episcopus factus est nihil habens praeter quod ipso die vestiebatur"; and again *Ep.* *20. 31 (BA 46B: 340): "et adhuc Fussalensibus dicit ex monacho pauperrimo episcopus."

[195] See the case of the anonymous young man from Vazari (above pp. 376–77).

[196] Aug. *Ep.* *20.2 (BA 46B: 294): The incident must date before *c.* 415 when Urbanus had become bishop of Sicca Veneria: "ut frater Urbanus qui tunc apud nos presbyter et praepositus monasterii, in quodam fundo amplo et in nostra dioecesi constituto eum presbyterum fieri me absente voluerit."

[197] Aug. *Ep.* *20.3 (BA 46B: 296): "ut in quodam Fussalensi castello quod Hipponiensi cathedrae subiacebat aliquis ordinaretur episcopus"; the location of Fussala is not known, but Desanges and Lancel (1983) pp. 92–95 and map, fig. 1, p. 94 "La localisation de Fussala," place it directly south of Hippo, at about 30 miles from the city, and at the very edge of the diocesan boundaries.

[198] Aug. *Ep.* 209.2 (CSEL 57: 348): "Fussala dicitur Hipponiensi territorio confine castellum, antea ibi numquam episcopus fuit, sed simul cum contigua sibi regione ad parochiam Hipponiensis

The problem, therefore, was not just a complex one of merging two hostile religious communities, but also one of finding a new Catholic leader for them.

Not everything ran according to plan. Augustine had an ideal candidate in mind for the new position: a priest who had knowledge of spoken Punic, a skill that was essential for anyone who was to manage the distant posting and its people.[199] Because he feared the local conditions, he was made a better offer by the opposition, or for some other reason, at the last minute the priest bailed on Augustine.[200] It was a situation of some acute embarrassment for the bishop of Hippo. Silvanus of Summa, the Old Man or Primate of Numidia, as well as other bishops, had come all the way to this hamlet in the middle of nowhere for the ordination of a candidate who now did not exist. Faced with the urgent need to find a replacement, Augustine rushed to find an alternative: the youthful *lector* Antoninus. He states that he made this choice because the young man could speak Punic. So, even though he was only twenty years old – well below the minimum required age for a bishop – and had no experience of any higher clerical office, Antoninus was made the new candidate and was promptly ordained bishop of Fussala.[201]

What ensued were the young man's activities as bishop of Fussala, following his ordination. The problem is that Antoninus and Augustine saw these activities in diametrically opposed terms, and without Antoninus' version of the events, it is very difficult to reconstruct a fair version of what actually happened. We do know that complaints made by the locals about certain misdeeds of Antoninus finally led to a formal hearing at Hippo, probably in 422, where he was found responsible for some misdemeanors, but exonerated of others. Of some importance to the judgment of the wrongs is the way in which the new and youthful bishop Antoninus is said to have collected men around him who would do his bidding. Who were they and what did they do? The background of these "bad men" is instructive. One of them was a secretary or *notarius* of the church at

---

ecclesiae pertinebat. Paucos habebat illa terra Catholicos . . . in eodem castello nullus esset omnino Catholicus . . . Sed quod ab Hippone memoratum castellum milibus quadraginta seiungitur."

[199] Aug. *Ep.* 209.3 (CSEL 57: 348): "Quod ut fieret, aptum loco illi congruumque requirebam, qui et Punica lingua esset instructus. Et habebam, de quo cogitabam, paratum presbyterum . . . Quo iam praesente omniumque in re tanta suspensis animis ad horam nos ille, qui mihi paratus videbatur, omni modo resistendo destituit."

[200] Aug. *Ep.* *20.3 (BA 46B: 296): "ad horam nos deseruit presbyter quem mihi habere paratum videbar."

[201] Aug. *Ep.* *20.3–4 (BA 46B: 296–98): "istum qui aderat, quia et linguam Punicam scire audieram . . . Ingressi ergo tantae sarcinae adolescentem non multo amplius quam viginti aetatis annos agentem."

Hippo. He had lost his good reputation by talking too late at night with the *sanctimoniales* or the holy women of the church. Serious sexual improprieties were alleged. The man was severely disciplined: a harsh beating was meted out by the head of the monastery. Not unnaturally, the secretary rebelled against this unfair treatment (as he saw it) and sought refuge in a different diocese where he would be better appreciated or, at least, more fairly treated. He went to Fussala.[202] Having fled there, he was ordained as a priest by Antoninus. It is not too much of a guess to think that the two young men already knew each other from Hippo. Later, it was claimed that Antoninus had another similar "bad man" ordained as deacon. In a later comprehensive list of the bad men that he had serving him, it was claimed that Antoninus had in his entourage the new priest, the new deacon, the local *defensor ecclesiae*, and an ex-soldier, who, it is darkly suggested, was perhaps a deserter. The ex-army man is interesting since he organized some men from the village to serve as a local night watch for the town. These agents and this impromptu militia were the muscle that Antoninus had at his command when he needed "a more numerous force" to coerce or compel others – or, so it was said.[203]

Antoninus, we are told, mobilized the forces of fear and compulsion to suit his own advantage. Accusations against him included a range of petty extortions and seizures: furnishings, building timber, cattle, items of clothing, and building stones, among other minor items. More serious charges concerned the impounding of fields and their crops. Sexual improprieties were also said to have been part of the compulsory favors that Antoninus extorted from his parishioners. Local farmers from Fussala presented *libelli* or written complaints on these and other matters to a formal hearing held by the church at Hippo in 423. Antoninus was found responsible for some of the material extortions and was asked to make restitution for them. He outwitted the intentions of the bishops who placed this requirement on him by borrowing gold coins and quickly paying off the debt.[204] On the brighter side, he was acquitted of the four serious charges of *stuprum* or

---

[202] Aug. *Ep.* *20.5 (BA 46B: 298–300): "Erat in monasterio nostro ex notario meo quidam qui me gemente non bonus evaserat et a praeposito monasterii eo quod inventus fuerit solus hora importuna cum quibusdam sanctimonialibus loquens plagis coercitus contemptibilis habebatur."

[203] Aug. *Ep.* *20.6 (BA 46B: 300): "Per hos duos clericos, presbyterum et diaconum, et per ecclesiae defensorem et per quendam alium sive exmilitem sive desertorem cui familiarius imperabat et per eos quos eiusdem castelli homines ad nocturnas custodias vigiles fecerat eisque, ubi manu aliqua paulo numerosiore opus fuerat, utebatur."

[204] Aug. *Ep.* *20.6–8 (BA 46B: 300–06): objects of theft: "pecuniam, suppellectilem, vestem, pecora, fructus, ligna denique et lapides . . . (7) Multa praeter illa quae comprehensa sunt gestis et nos ex aliqua parte cognovimus . . . (8) Haec sententiam nostram et ipse amplexus est usque adeo, ut neque provocaverit et post paucissimos dies mutatos pro direptis solidos reposuerit."

illicit sexual acts with women that were capital crimes in secular courts.[205] But given the ease of escaping charges of sexual exploitation before all-male hearings composed of fellow bishops, it is just as possible that Antoninus had indulged in these pleasures as well. In any event, it is important to note that even Augustine thought that the latter charges were ones of convenience brought against the young bishop by people who were filled with hatred and envy towards him.

Between the decision made by the hearing at Hippo and what happened next, however, much is unclear. Several months later, Aurelius, the new Primate of Numidia, dispatched a new bishop for Fussala who was to be "chosen" by the people of the town. Having paid back the fines imposed on him, and having been exonerated of any sexual wrongdoing, Antoninus no doubt felt that this penalty – the removal of his diocese and his replacement by another – was definitely *not* something to which he had agreed.[206] Restitution of property was one thing; but a sanction this serious was something to which he had never consented. Augustine disagreed. He claimed that Antoninus was to retain his rank as bishop, but that he was not to be allowed to return to Fussala. Instead, he was to have his seat in one of eight parishes that had once constituted other parts of his diocese. The new bishop sent by Aurelius was to have the town of Fussala itself as his seat. Apparently trying to make the best of a bad situation, Antoninus directly confronted Aurelius, the Primate of Numidia. In addition to the eight parishes promised to him, he demanded an additional one: the rural domain or *fundus* of Thogonoetum. Its importance to him was a symbolic one of saving face: the estate abutted directly on the village of Fussala.

Although the Primate of Numidia himself agreed to this transfer, there were others who stood in his way. They included the peasant farmers of the estate at Thogonoetum. They had a letter of protest written to the owner of the domain, a wealthy woman, in which they objected vociferously to what was being done to them. If she allowed the restoration of Antoninus to happen, they threatened, they would pack their belongings and leave. The letter provoked alarm in the landowner. What she saw was not an

---

[205] Aug. *Ep.* 209.4 (CSEL 57: 349): "Ut cum eo hic apud nos causas dicerent, qui de illius episcopatu suscipiendo tamquam bene sibi consulentibus obtemperaverant nobis. In quibus causis cum stuprorum crimina capitalia, quae non ab ipsis, quibus episcopus erat, sed ab aliis quibusdam obiecta fuerant, probari minime potuissent atque ab eis, qui invidiosissime iactabantur, videretur esse purgatus"; and *Ep.* *20.8 (BA 46B: 306) "quia de magnis et capitalibus quattuor stuprorum criminibus... est veritate purgatus."

[206] Aug. *Ep.* 209.7 (CSEL 57: 350): "Clamat: 'Aut in mea cathedra sedere debui aut episcopus esse non debui.'"

ecclesiastical crisis, but the threat of suddenly losing her labor supply.[207] The same farmers also wrote to Augustine asking him to intervene. Later, both the wealthy female landowner and Augustine wrote to Aurelius, the Primate of Numidia. When Antoninus got wind of these communications, he was understandably very angry. Once again, his superiors were reneging on a deal that they had made with him. What is interesting is not only his knowledge of the options that he had, but also the fact that he acted on them. Taking a formal letter of introduction from the Old Man Aurelius, the Primate of Numidia, with him, Antoninus travelled all the way to Rome to file a formal appeal with Pope Bonifatius.

In Rome, Antoninus had his own supporters. One of them was a wealthy Roman lady, Fabiola, to whom Augustine later wrote a long letter of dissuasion, referring to her support of Antoninus – her too kind loyalty to the young man and the Christian charity with which she supported his poverty-stricken travels.[208] The result of Antoninus' efforts, however, was that he succeeded.[209] Pope Bonifatius himself intervened by calling for a new hearing of all of the facts – a meeting that was to be convened at the church at Tegulata, near Fussala.[210] At this hearing, things did not go well for Antoninus. A priest of the newly ordained replacement bishop of Fussala came armed with a long letter of complaint registered against Antoninus. In refusing to accept the letter as genuine, Antoninus asked Aurelius, the Primate of Numidia, to allow him to take some of his own representatives on a fact-finding mission to Fussala. He did allow that if the complaints against him were confirmed he should not get Fussala back as his seat. But he countered by requesting that he at least be guaranteed the eight parishes that had already been given to him, as well as Thogonoetum, which he had been promised in addition, *and* another five parishes that Augustine had promised him in a verbal statement made "off the record."[211]

---

[207] Aug. *Ep.* *20.10 (BA 46B: 308): "Porro idem coloni, quia eum de vicinitate iam senserant et cum aliis mala illa pertulerant, scripserunt ad dominam possessionis, si hoc fieri permisisset, se continuo migraturos."

[208] Aug. *Ep.* *20.2 (BA 46B: 292): "Filium dilectum et coepiscopum meum Antoninum quam benigna pietate comperi inopemque eius peregrinationem quam christiana fueris humanitate solata."

[209] Aug. *Ep.* 209.9 (CSEL 57: 351): Antoninus made this first appeal to Pope Bonifatius. The hearing at Hippo must therefore have been earlier in 422, with time for Antoninus to put together the appeal that he made to Pope Bonifatius (who died at the end of 422), and for Bonifatius to establish the hearing at the church at Tegulata (also before the end of 422?).

[210] For the location of Tegulata, see Desanges and Lancel (1983), p. 89; all that can be said is that it was somewhere in Numidia, surely well outside of the diocese of Hippo.

[211] Aug. *Ep.* *20.13 (BA 46B: 314): "si Fussalenses de illo suscipiendo referrent, contra voluntatem acciperet plebem Thogonoetensem illis octo additam plebibus quas antea iam tenebat; a me etiam peteret sanctus senex, ut alias de eis quinque, quas illi citra acta promiseram ut Fussalensibus non esset infestus, etiam gestis promittendo firmarem."

He asked that this agreement be entered into the records of the proceedings and that Augustine be made to sign it.

A committee of inquiry set off for Fussala. It is manifest that neither Augustine nor any of those close to him, like Alypius, dared to go near the village. Because of what he had done to them, the people had conceived a virulent hatred for Augustine. They shouted and chanted imprecations against him. In a raucous town meeting, the people demanded the presence of their new bishop. When he arrived the next day, there was more shouting and hectoring, all it carefully recorded by secretaries. It was clear that nothing more could be done at the town itself. The anger of the people was not to be assuaged. Aurelius, as Primate of Numidia, summoned a new meeting at Thogonoetum, some ten miles from Fussala, so that Augustine and others could attend in a less threatening atmosphere. The problem with this meeting was that the Primate Aurelius had already excommunicated the people of this congregation for their violent behavior against Antoninus. The seething resentment against the Primate exploded in his face. At the new meeting, Aurelius had spoken to people through an interpreter in Punic, their first language, but the concession only had a modest impact. The farmers of Thogonoetum began to shout back vociferously what they thought of Antoninus. When asked to put their comments down in writing and to sign their names for the record, however, they refused to do so – "out of fear of what Antoninus might do to them," says Augustine. When Aurelius ordered them to confirm their statements, the parishioners got up and stalked out of the meeting. Aurelius called them back with great difficulty. Being unable to move them, the Primate of all Numidia had to concede the demands of the recalcitrant parishioners of Thogonoetum: he promised that he would not impose an unwanted bishop on them.[212]

On the other side, Antoninus, from his point of view, considered any infringement of the agreements reached concerning the eight parishes *and* Thogonoetum – plus the five others promised "under the table" by Augustine – to be a breach of promise. So when Aurelius summoned him to the hamlet of Gilva for a meeting and informed the young man that he was not to have Thogonoetum, Antoninus naturally responded very angrily. Considering the compromise agreement that he had reached with Augustine to be broken, marching out of the meeting in fury, he returned to his original position that he be restored as bishop of Fussala. From Antoninus' perspective, all the local authority figures, from Augustine to the provincial Primate, were set against him. So he launched another appeal

---

[212] Aug. *Ep.* *20.15–21 (BA 46B: 316–26).

with the Pope in Rome. Despite his origins in poverty and humility, he had powerful supporters, including the lady Fabiola at Rome.[213] He would go back to them.

The final outcome of this sordid little squabble is unknown. We must suspect that the big powers in the Catholic Church in Africa finally prevailed. But by the mid-420s, this local matter was still an ongoing dispute. What the mechanics of the quarrel demonstrate, amongst other things, is that the perceived distance between central and local power, despite the apparent increasing strength and authority of the former, could easily be collapsed. It was possible for a local man of no great status or rank, stuck in the middle of a poor rural parish in a remote hinterland, to take his grievances over the heads of local bishops and the provincial Primate, to the Pope in Rome. Antoninus might have known this could be done because it had been done before, in fact not many years before he first took his own complaint overseas.

THE APIARIUS AFFAIR

At about the same time that the troubles involving Antoninus were beginning to simmer, another case of purely local origin grew to upset the whole of the Catholic Church in Africa. Although this incident, too, had small beginnings, it exploded into a crisis that involved at least two popes at Rome. It became a burning issue that divided African Catholics from the Roman Church over basic issues of ecclesiastical jurisdiction and power.[214] It was precisely because the appeal of the priest Apiarius to the Church at Rome raised significant concerns about the autonomy of the African church and over the delineation of different spheres of authority that we happen to know about this case at all. In other ways, the Apiarius affair reveals factors that were surely at play in many dioceses and about which nothing is known because they never came to have the paradigmatic significance that this dispute did.

Unlike Antoninus of Fussala, who was a bishop, Apiarius was only a priest who was serving under the Catholic bishop of Sicca Veneria in the

---

[213] Delmaire (1983), p. 85; she is already known from Aug. *Ep.* 267 and Jerome (*Ep.* 126 = Aug. *Ep.* 165). Delmaire is surely right to challenge the identification of her with the *clarissima femina* who died in 452 (see "Fabiola (2) and (3)," PLRE, 2, p. 448) since she is already described as old in 422/23.

[214] See Merdinger, "The Case of Apiarius," ch. 8, and "The Return of Apiarius: 'A Pigsty of Vices'," ch. 11 in *Rome and the African Church*, who gives good direction to the earlier studies of this problem.

proconsular province.[215] For some sort of transgression that was characterized as "not a trivial scandal," Apiarius had been disciplined by his bishop Urbanus. The punishment was severe. He was excommunicated. Like the bad boy Antoninus, Apiarius felt that the punishment was unmerited and that he had to find the means to right a personal wrong. As in the case of Antoninus, *traditio* or crossing over to the other church was apparently not considered to be an option. For both men, this might well have been the case in the mid-410s to mid-420s because of the lack of a viable alternative. The dissident church was perhaps in such a weakened and exposed state that it was no longer a viable place of refuge for Catholic clerics who found themselves in trouble. Apiarius had to find another solution. By the time that we pick up the remainder of the story, he had already given up on the support of Aurelius, the Primate of Africa. Aurelius had always been a stickler on the disciplining of minor clergy, and in these years his attitude on such matters had only hardened.

Apiarius therefore appealed over the head of his own bishop and over the head of the Primate of Africa to the See of Rome. Precisely when all of this happened is difficult to say, but the years between 415 and 417 seem probable for the quarrels, the crises, and the internal hearings at Sicca Veneria. It is almost certain that Apiarius made his appeal to Rome early in 418. On 1 May 418, a full Catholic council held at Carthage issued disciplinary rules, one of which explicitly forbade lower-ranking clergy, like priests, to appeal their cases overseas.[216] It is probable that the ruling was made in direct response to the Apiarius case. Apiarius, however, was to find a favorable ear, and leverage, in Rome. Pope Zosimus, who had replaced his predecessor Innocent in 417, accepted his appeal and appointed a commission of three to go to Carthage to hear the facts of the case. The commissioners arrived in Africa in late 418. Their investigations prompted the calling of another plenary conference of Catholic bishops at Carthage in May 419, in which 220 bishops crowded into the Basilica of Faustus. Matters were now complicated by the fact that Pope Zosimus had died in December 418 and had been replaced by a new Pope, Bonifatius, only

---

[215] The case is recounted in the canons of the church of Carthage that will be discussed in detail in what follows.

[216] Concil. Carth. May 418, canon 17 = *Reg. Eccl. Carth. Excerpt.* 125 (CCL 149: 227): "Item placuit ut presbyteri, diaconi, vel ceteri inferiores clerici in causis quas habuerint, si de iudiciis episcoporum suorum questi fuerint, vicini episcopi eos audiant, et inter eos quidquid est finiant adhibiti ab eis ex consensu episcoporum suorum. Quod si et ab eis provocandum putaverint, non provocent nisi ad Africana concilia vel ad primates provinciarum suarum; ad transmarina autem qui putaverit appellandum, a nullo intra Africam in communionem suscipiatur"; both Cross (1961), p. 241, and Marschall, *Karthago und Rom*, p. 167, accept that the rule was a reaction to the Apiarius case; Munier (1983) dissents.

a few months before the conference convened.[217] On hearing the facts of the Apiarius case, the assembled bishops decided to remove the penalty of excommunication imposed on him by Urbanus of Sicca. Although Apiarius' rank of priest was to be restored to him, the bishops thought that he should serve in a diocese elsewhere than Sicca Veneria, a suggestion to which Apiarius not unreasonably agreed.

It was at the Catholic Council of Carthage held in May 419, when the legates of Pope Bonifatius were asked to present their position, that a fundamental conflict broke out between the Catholic church in Africa and the Church at Rome. The dispute centered over which church, and in what circumstances, had the right to hear clerical appeals. There emerged a long battle over what, precisely, the canons of the Council of Nicaea had ruled on the matter. Believing them to be Nicene, Bonifatius had mistakenly cited canons from the Council of Serdica. In any event, the measures passed at Serdica regarding appeals applied only to bishops. The protracted conflict focussed contentious questions about the location of final authority in the western Christian church.[218] The simple structural point for conflicts within Africa was that as long as the Church of Rome provided an alternative source of authority that could decide such matters, it also provided a legitimate point of leverage for lower-ranking clergy against their higher-ranking local foes. In the end, it seems that Apiarius succeeded and was able to clear himself of the charges made against him and was able to return to his clerical duties. He was allowed to retain his rank as priest and was given positive letters of recommendation so that he might seek employment elsewhere.

About 420, Apiarius moved to the northern coastal city of Thabraca to begin his career afresh. Once again, his nefarious activities in his new position provoked accusations against him by members of his congregation. This time, the misdeeds in which he was involved were ones of gross sexual misconduct.[219] Again, he was disciplined and excommunicated by his bishop, and again he appealed the local judgment to the papal See at Rome. Such leverage had worked well for him once, so why not again? As amazing as it might seem, the tactic worked its magic again. On hearing Apiarius' version of the facts, Pope Celestinus restored him to communion.[220] The Pope sent his legate Faustinus back to Carthage to conduct a hearing with Apiarius present and so, late in the year 425, yet another council of the

---

[217] CCL 149: 89 and 157.
[218] See Merdinger, *Rome and the African Church*, pp. 114–20; Munier (1983) and Marschall, *Karthago und Rom*, pp. 173–83.
[219] CCL 149: 170, ll. 25–39.   [220] CCL 149: 169, ll. 19–24.

Catholic bishops of Africa was devoted to the problem. Before this hearing, Apiarius maintained a brave and slightly mendacious front, but under vigorous and persistent cross-questioning by the assembled African bishops, he finally cracked on the third day of the hearings and, in a confessorial outburst, poured forth a detailed litany of his crimes and misdemeanors.[221] As the senior African bishops presented the results of their hearing, Apiarius had condemned himself out of his own mouth of a "pigsty of vices." Although it is nowhere made precise what these crimes were, it is clear that they were of an explicitly sexual nature. The hearing records refer to "so many and such great crimes," "unspeakably shameful acts" "a cesspool of sexual transgressions" "black and putrid excesses," and "unbelievably shameful acts." The miscreant was quickly excommunicated by the decision of the council and nothing more is heard of him.

The importance of the Antoninus and Apiarius cases for the problem of violence is not so much that they furnish evidence on the power that clerics, especially bishops, wielded at local level, as Antoninus surely did. It is rather that they reveal how clerics under extreme duress might behave. In both of these narratives, neither man seems to have seriously contemplated going over to the other side. This is especially manifest in the case of Antoninus who was made bishop over a region that was overwhelmingly populated by adherents of the dissident cause. Since the final outcome in either of these cases is unknown, it is still possible that such transfers did happen. But all evidence that exists concerning Apiarius and Antoninus never indicates that either was thinking or threatening to cross over. As long as the option existed of going to a higher judicial authority to get beyond and to circumvent the perceived bias of local jurisdiction – in these cases by taking appeals overseas to the See of Rome – aggrieved parties, even lowly clerics, preferred to take this road rather than to leave their own religious communities.

In the world of African Christians during the late fourth and early fifth centuries, many priests and other lower clergy who fell into conflict with their bishops had at least one clear alternative in front of them, namely to go over to the other church. After the watershed formed by the great conference of 411 at Carthage, however, it seems that Catholic clergy preferred to move upwards through the internal hierarchy of the church and to find leverage against their bishops and primates by using the increasing interest of the Church of Rome in asserting its primacy in deciding such ecclesiastical disputes. Since the great conflict between

---

[221] CCL 149: 170, ll. 25–39.

the two churches over the preceding century was thought to have been generated, managed, and sustained by bishops and other clergy, the shift in direction is significant. But the change also demands a better understanding of what forces created the new grounds on which these disputes were contested and controlled. This is where the campaign by the Catholic bishops of Africa to assert an apprehended violent insurgency was to bear fruit. The imperial state under Honorius finally moved to action on their behalf, and the move by the imperial court was to produce many of the results that we see in these cases.

Throughout the entire century-long struggle, the main powers that the bishops of each side had in their hands were two. The first basis of their power was the wide range of material supports that they could offer to the poor, the needy, and the not-so-well-off in their dioceses. The role of giving, the ideal of the gift without counter-gift, the ideal of alms, was preached about incessantly.[222] Whatever practice there was of the much-advertised ideals gave real substance to the other basis of their power: the image of a new pastoral care. In their wide range of benefactions, small but dependable, the bishops exercised a different quality of patronal power over their flocks than did their secular peers, the notables of the municipalities, over their clientele. The image of its consistent, pervasive goodness and beneficence set this new social role quite apart from any other comparable kind of political power in antiquity[223] The bishop was guardian and shepherd, the pastor, of his sheep. It is no accident that two of the greatest of Augustine's sermons were entitled "To the Shepherds" and "To the Sheep." But he was also doctor and teacher. Here, too, the bishop was armed with an unusual and new and powerful instrument not known before his rise to eminence. The new instrument paralleled the developing role of pastoral care. With it, the bishop educated, instructed, cajoled, urged, reprimanded, hectored, educated, and guided his flock. It was the sermon.

---

[222] Brown, "'Governor of the Poor': The Bishops and their Cities," ch. 2 in *Poverty and Leadership*, pp. 45–73; cf. Finn, *Almsgiving*, pp. 34–89.

[223] Foucault, *Security, Territory, Population*, chs. 6–9, emphasizes the novelty of a kind of power that presented itself as entirely benevolent.

CHAPTER 9

In the house of discipline

If violence and hatred were as ordinary and as old as Africa itself, they were now urged along in new modes by the novel figure of the Christian preacher. The preacher's sermon is one of those mundane things that is so ordinary in our experience that its invention and impact has often flown beneath the level of our attention.[1] In communicating a mass of new ideas, the Christian sermon had no precursor or equal. Nothing like it had existed. It had to be created.[2] The need for the new vehicle was considerable since in the mass popular communications of the time there was necessarily a constant interplay between the written text, the iconic picture, and the spoken word.[3] There were numerous ways in which these different media could be connected and negotiated, but it was usually assumed that they would somehow be linked. In a world where most persons were illiterate, it was everyday knowledge that there would have to be a constant transcription of the fixed written text, through various channels of oral transmission, to

[1] It took an exceptional and pathbreaking work of the early 1990s, Averil Cameron's *Rhetoric of Empire*, for example, to initiate serious discussion of this specific problem. More is now being done, but still not in any reasonable proportion to the importance of the subject.
[2] When, how, and at what pace as yet seems rather unclear because of the deficit of a clear run of evidence. Although some earlier "sermonic" or homiletic materials are referred to in our sources, it seems that it was only in the decades of the 320s and 330s that the earliest examples of sermons in our sense came into existence: see Edwards, *History of Preaching*, pp. 31 f. for claims about Origen that are not all that compelling; and pp. 51 ff. for the Cappadocians who seem to provide some of the earliest attested continuous examples of the genre. In Africa, the earliest examples known seem to be some sermons attributed to Optatus of Milevis, so, perhaps, in the 350s and 360s.
[3] The following general works have been used: Drobner, *Sermones ad Populum*; Monceaux, " Sermons et autres discours," ch. 5 in *Hist. litt.* 7, pp. 146–88; and "Tableau chronologique des sermons d'Augustin relatifs au Donatisme," *Hist. litt.* 7, pp. 287–92; Barry, *St. Augustine, the Orator*; Banniard, *Viva voce* and (1998); Madec, *Augustin prédicateur*; Mandouze (1968); Van der Meer, "Preaching," pt. 3 in *Augustine the Bishop*, pp. 405–70. The epigraph to the chapter is taken from Aug. *Speculum*, 23 (CSEL 12: 152); "adpropriate ad me, indocti, et congregamini in domum disciplinae"; and from *De Discip. Christ.* 1.1 (PL 40: 669): "Disciplinae domus est ecclesia Christi." In both cases, he was commenting on Eccl. 51: 31: *Accipite disciplinam in domo disciplinae* (Vulgate: "Adpropriate ad me indocti et congregate vos in domum disciplinae").

listeners.[4] It was at the critical juncture between the Holy Scriptures of the faith on the one hand and their transmission and interpretation to large numbers on the other that the figure of the preacher was situated.

To succeed, the preacher had to be an attentive listener, carefully attuned to his audience. It must have been a difficult task in some cases, with an audience so varied and complex in its makeup.[5] In the case of the rules or canons decided upon by African church councils, for instance, it was assumed that the main audience for the decisions would be listeners who would acquire knowledge of the new rules by hearing them.[6] Despite other types of teaching, preaching was the main means by which such important things were to be heard. In speaking of the ways in which the behavior of widows and widowers might be controlled, Gratus, the Catholic Primate of Africa in the mid-350s, remarked that the rules governing these vulnerable women and men were enforced within the Christian community "by unrelenting preaching and by constant verbal warnings."[7] The powerful impact of sermons ran deeper than any text. Even imperial laws had to be proclaimed. No matter how widely distributed and publicly posted, and occasionally read aloud on market days, they were still written texts whose base was the transcribed form. The Christian sermon was a far more effective means of bridging the running space between written and oral. Even when based on written texts, the whole aim of the sermon was focussed on oral delivery. In his letter to the imperial official Bonifatius in 417, Augustine remarked that the sermons of Catholic preachers were trying to persuade in the same manner as imperial laws were trying to convince.[8] The sermons, both Catholic and dissident, were achieving this persuasion in a fundamentally different manner.

In communicating ideas there was always a twofold process of writing and speaking in play. In his war against the dissidents, Augustine battled on two fronts: by writing and by preaching.[9] The practice of writing was worked out in tracts, books, pamphlets, letters, leaflets, and other such

---

[4] Also true of sixteenth-century Europe, see Pettegree, "Preaching," ch. 2 in *Culture of Persuasion*, p. 10.

[5] A critical discussion was initiated by MacMullen (1989) whose views have been modified somewhat by recent analyses, amongst which see, especially, Mayer (1997, 1998, and 1999) and Rousseau (1998). The complexities involved not only the range of social composition of the listeners, but also the control of gender in space (separate entranceways for men and women came into play in the larger churches only in the time of Augustine's tenure as bishop, for example).

[6] Concil. Carth. 348, canon 2 (CCL 149: 4): "auditores percipientes regulam rectam."

[7] Concil. Carth. 348, canon 4 (CCL 149: 5): "tractatu assiduo et commonitione frequenti."

[8] Aug. *Ep.* 185.8 (CSEL 57: 7).

[9] Aug. *Contra ep. Parm.* 1.1.1 (CSEL 51: 19): "Multa quidem alias adversus Donatistas pro viribus quas dominus praebet, partim scribendo partim etiam tractando disserui."

media, as well as in sermons. Sermons were sometimes drafted, sometimes written as whole documents, sometimes dictated, and sometimes were a combination of written and spoken.[10] But the orally delivered sermon was the critical element of the process. It was the interplay between the published tract and treatise, and the verbal sermon that Possidius, Augustine's biographer, emphasized as central to his war against heresy. The books are characterized as completed and finished as opposed to the sermons that were improvised and of the moment.[11] The sermons fed into the wider oral world of the parishioners, among both their immediate neighbors and more distant communities. News was communicated by sermons and then by the rumors spread by Africans about what they had heard.[12] In the case of technically adept and renowned preachers, there was a continuous pipeline of transmission of their ideas to others beyond their own congregation. As Augustine preached, we are told, not only did Catholic shorthand recorders take down his sermons, but the dissidents also had their own shorthand secretaries on hand who then disseminated his speeches as written texts throughout all of Africa.[13] The two sides monitored each other's best men closely. The dissidents at Hippo quickly transferred the notes and excerpts of Augustine's sermons to their own bishops.[14] The transfer then fueled more acerbic exchanges between the two hostile camps.

The Christian practice in Africa of having an authoritative figure (usually a bishop, but sometimes a priest) speak several times a week to an assembly of his people was a hugely significant innovation in the communication of new pedagogies to mass audiences. The bishop was authoritative not just because of his status, but rather because, as a preacher, he was presented as the mouthpiece of God – a mortal conduit through which the supreme deity spoke.[15] The resulting quality of interaction was therefore unique.

---

[10] For some of the creative process as it is known for Augustine, see Deferrari (1915) and (1922).

[11] Possid. *Vita Aug.* 7.1 (Bastiaensen: 146): "Et docebat et praedicebat ille, privatim et publice, in domo et in ecclesia, salutis verbum cum fiducia adversus Africanas haereses maximeque contra Donatistas, Manichaeos et paganos, libris confectis et repentinis sermonibus . . . Et hos eius libros et tractatus mirabili Dei gratia procedentes ac profluentes, instructos rationis copia atque auctoritate sanctarum Scripturarum."

[12] Aug. *Ep. ad Cath. contra Donatist.* 18.47 (CSEL 52: 293): "non in sermonibus et rumoribus Afrorum, non in conciliis episcoporum suorum, non in litteris quorumlibet disputatorum."

[13] Possid. *Vita Aug.* 7.3–4 (Bastiaensen: 146): "ipsi quoque haeretici [sc. Donatistae] concurrentes cum catholicis ingenti ardore audiebant et, quiquis, ut voluit et potuit, notarios adhibentes, ea quae dicebantur excepta describentes. Et inde iam per totum Africae corpus praeclara doctrina odorque suavissimus Christi diffusa et manifestata est." On the role of these *notarii* in the transmission and dispersal of sermons, see Comeau (1932); for the use of similar stenographers in Reformation contexts, see Pettegree, *Culture of Persuasion*, p. 23.

[14] Possid. *Vita Aug.* 9.1 (Bastiaensen: 150): his *dicta et excepta.*

[15] Aug. *Sermo* 82.15 (PL 38: 513); it was a common sentiment, and one also felt, later, by the preachers of the Reformation: Pettegree, *Culture of Persuasion*, pp. 31–32.

That learned or semi-learned persons would communicate complex ideas and narratives with each other, and with select adepts, was not unusual in that world. The bishop or priest was a highly qualified, and sanctified, person who was able to convey the basic messages of the new faith through a combination of narratives and the technical codes that he, as an expert, controlled.[16] That systematic, continuous, and high-quality attention should be paid to persons whom even their teachers, the bishops and priests, considered to be unlearned, ignorant, or even downright stupid was unusual, if not unprecedented. And the sheer quantity of preaching for Africa alone is arresting, and also unprecedented, for this kind of communication. It is possible to provide an estimate for the age of Augustine, the nearly four decades over which he was priest and then bishop of the church at Hippo Regius. During that time he, or persons who stood in for him when he was absent or ill, would have delivered about three to four sermons a week to the congregation at Hippo, or about 6,000 homilies.[17] Given the nearly 750 dioceses, dissident and Catholic, in which bishops and priests addressed their congregations during this time, something on the order of 5 million sermons were preached to various congregations in Africa.[18] The numbers alone are impressive.[19] The impact of the quantities, the consistency, and the repetition were important, but so too was the role played by style and content.

The usual connection between the oral and the written was sensed by everyone. When the Catholic bishop Optatus, in the mid-360s, spoke of the sermons, the *tractatus*, of his enemy Parmenian as being "in the hands" and "in the mouths" of multitudes of people, it is this constant

---

[16] Tilly, *Why?*, pp. 16–22 on the use of stories, codes, and technical accounts in conveying everyday explanations. He refers to "theologians" as a type; in this case they are our bishops. He notes that "specialists" in technical accounts and codes "devote significant effort to either translating from conventions and stories into their own idioms or helping others make the translation" – or the reverse (we might add) as in the case of preaching.

[17] Augustine seems to have preached about three times a week – sometimes more frequently during festival seasons, or periods of travel when he was preaching daily, and sometimes less often in times of absence caused by illness. That average also seems to be true of other preachers, like John Chrysostom, for whom statistics can be assembled; see Mayer (2001). Mandouze (1968), pp. 624–25, estimated "at least" twenty sermons a month, which, if accepted, would yield a somewhat higher overall figure than I am offering here, but the number is based on La Bonnardière's figures for an Easter season, which might well have been a little higher than normal.

[18] Total sermons in Africa: *c.* 750 bishops × 4,500 = *c.* 3,375,000; over the period when Augustine was both priest and bishop = *c.* 4.5–5 million.

[19] The numbers are not unusual. Comparable figures are known from the European Reformation: Luther and Zwingli produced on this same scale. In the forty-four years of his career, Zwingli's successor at Zurich, Heinrich Bullinger, preached over 7,000 sermons; and Jean Calvin at Geneva, preaching twice on Sunday and on weekdays, totaled more than 4,000 sermons over the period of his ministry: see Pettegree, *Culture of Persuasion*, pp. 10–11.

bridging effect to which he refers. The one was always thought to inform the other. So Optatus states that he had patiently "listened" to Parmenian, meaning that he had read his sermons; now it was Parmenian's turn "to listen" to him, that is, to read his reply.[20] But Optatus was less interested in this elite manipulation of sermons than he was in their insistent use to inculcate in Parmenian's flock a hatred of Catholics, to teach them vile and vicious insults that they were to aim at their enemies. His sermons were a pedagogy in hatred, says Optatus, while disclaiming that Catholics did exactly the same.[21] He was being disingenuous, if not mendacious. He and other Catholic preachers were walking this same road. The instruction in hatred through the sermon was one in which the preacher emphasized separation, of having nothing to do with "them" – the enemy. Don't eat with them. Don't greet them in the street. All supported by appropriate biblical citations.[22] The effects might have well have upset Optatus, since he knew that he was preaching the same messages. The persuasiveness of the sermon, however, was perhaps rooted less in this deliberate and conscious persuasion or in charismatic and entertaining storytelling than it was in the less apparent power of suggestion.[23] The words of sermons implanted possibilities in the minds of the congregations and laid down the substrata on which locals could anticipate that something might happen.

The effect of this relentless and ubiquitous teaching of common people was transformative. The good parishioner was envisaged as an assiduously busy ant: rising daily, scurrying to church, listening carefully to the reading, singing the hymns, then ruminating on what he or she had heard, thinking it over at home, and storing that meaning within themselves like wheat collected from the threshing floor.[24] Constant exposure to the Psalms, one of the main biblical texts on which sermons were frequently based, had led many Africans to think of the peculiar Latin of the Psalms as of

---

[20] Optatus, *Contra Parm.* 1.4.4. (SC 412: 178): "Sed quoniam et accessum prohibent et aditus intercludunt et consessum vitant et colloquium denegant, vel tecum mihi, frater Parmeniane, sit isto modo collatio, ut, quia tractatus tuos, quos in manibus et in ore multorum esse voluisti."

[21] Optatus, *Contra Parm.* 4.5.2 (SC 413: 90): "nullus vestrum est qui non convicia nostra suis tractatibus misceat . . . Lectiones dominicas incipitis et tractatus vestros ad nostras iniurias explicatis . . . Auditorum animis infunditis odia, inimicitias docendo suadetis."

[22] Optatus, *Contra Parm.* 4.5.4 (SC 413: 90–92): "salutationis videlicet officium. Nam et vos ipsi aliqui in perfunctiora salutatione oscula denegatis solita"; Parmenian had cited Paul at 1 Cor. 5: 11; 2 Jn 10; 2 Tim. 2: 17: "Don't eat with these people; say goodbye to them; their speech snakes into you like a cancer."

[23] See, e.g., Semelin, *Purify and Destroy*, pp. 80 (although calling it "propaganda" – a term that I would rather avoid), 95 (drawing attention to what Victor Klemperer called "lexical poison"), 194–95.

[24] Aug. *En. in Ps.* 66.3 (CCL 39: 860): where he also speaking of such persons making their way home from church, finding a book, opening and reading it.

a better and higher quality than that of the standard Latin classics.[25] In other words, sermons and their biblical underpinnings had fundamentally changed perceptions of language. Achieving this effect was not easy. To incite energy and to focus composition, one of the comparisons that the preacher set before himself was to envisage the church liturgy, and especially the sermon, as a sacred Christian analogue to the secular spectacles of the stage and the arena.[26] If the attractions of the church were compared with the allurements of the theater and amphitheater, it was admitted that the small numbers sometimes found in congregations were a sure indication that the rest were off to the public entertainments.[27] In attracting audiences, preachers were sometimes implicated in a theatrical zero-sum game.

The standards and expectations set by secular entertainments could conflict with the bishop's mission of education. On more than a few occasions, Augustine noted that his parishioners were beginning to be wearied by the arcane nature of the exegetical materials. The grinding length of his sermons that expounded on fine details of dogma was exhausting for the men and women who were standing in the heat of a confined space.[28] Perceiving fatigue in the listeners, the bishop could cut the sermon short and promise to continue the same theme on the next occasion.[29] But not always. The bishop's sense of his own importance and the significance of his message might lead him to expound his views at great length, causing inattention and drift in the audience.[30] He had to be attentive to cues coming from them. Perceiving boredom in his listeners meant that he should terminate the day's proceedings.[31] Weariness or other diversions led, inevitably, to restlessness. Women were perhaps the least willing to put up with the lengthy and the irrelevant. The shorthand notaries taking down one of Augustine's sermons noted in their comments on the sermon that women began leaving the church through lack of interest. He had entangled himself in a long and boring metaphor on borrowing and lending. The preacher was incensed: "Our sisters who are unwilling to listen, it seems, are unwilling to meet the collector." He then hectored those who remained that they ought to listen more carefully to his important point.[32]

---

[25] Aug. *De Doctr. Christ.* 2.14.21 (CCL 32: 47); cf. Brown, *Augustine of Hippo*, p. 263.

[26] Aug. *En. 2 in Ps.* 30.2 (CCL 38: 203).   [27] Aug. *En. in Ps.* 50.1 (CCL 38: 599–600).

[28] E.g. Aug. *En. 2 in Ps.* 21.21 (CCL 38: 128); *En. 2 in Ps.* 34.16 (CCL 38: 321); *Sermo* 104.4 (PL 38: 618).

[29] E.g. Aug. *En. 1 in Ps.* 33.11 (CCL 38: 281); *En. 2 in Ps.* 33.1 (CCL 38: 281–82): *En. in Ps.* 35.18 (CCL 38: 335–36); *En. 2 in Ps.* 90.1 (CCL 39: 1265–66).

[30] E.g. Aug. *En. in Ps.* 93.30 (CCL 39: 1330).   [31] Aug. *En. in Ps.* 38.23 (CCL 38: 422).

[32] Aug. *Sermo* 32.23 (CCL 41: 408–09).

So the preacher sometimes had to beg for attention, or to demand it, or to call for silence and the suppression of crowd noise arising from boredom.[33] The calls for silence, for dampening down the competing noise and talk, were sometimes successful, sometimes not.[34] On occasion, the preacher's words might be too effective. Wishing further to expound a theme, Augustine had to quieten his congregation when in response to a series of examples, too many of them began muttering aloud: "That's me! That's me!"[35] But a good performance was worth its weight and length. "The dears," as the congregation were called, would return, in even greater numbers and with greater eagerness to hear the next installment of a good story.[36] But larger crowds, even if a good sign of success, had their own peculiar dynamic. It made it difficult for the bishop to be heard, and that alone, if the sermon was long, led to more problems. It was difficult to cope with a large audience. "With all of this talking among yourselves, there are some of you who are trying to listen but who cannot hear, but those persons should not become angry with me, since they are the cause of their own distractions."[37] But there was also the simple factor of chaos. Despite all the planning and preparation, the worst-delivered sermon, a disaster in the eyes of the preacher, turns out to have been particularly well received by his audience.[38]

When sermons worked well, they connected in a special way. They set up a near-physical link with the audience. The people were engaged. We must remember, as one commentator has aptly noted, that "Augustine was not the only one speaking: his listeners talked back, chanted, whispered, and tut-tutted, registering their feelings in manifold ways."[39] When they were with the preacher, on a roll, the audience sensed his message in advance, got ahead of the curve and began applauding and shouting in anticipation of the climactic points that he was about to make.[40] In interpreting this apparent prescience of his listeners, the preacher could draw on Platonic ideas to explain their foreknowledge. They *already* knew what he was going to say because the Great Teacher had already put into their hearts what they knew. In preaching to them, he was not teaching them, but

---

[33] Aug. *En. in Ps.* 50.1 (CCL 38: 599–600); *En. in Ps.* 121.14 (CCL 40: 1813), apologizing for the necessary length.

[34] Aug. *En. 2 in Ps.* 103.2 (CCL 40: 1492–93); *En. in Ps.* 143.6 (CCL 140: 2076–77), calling for attention; for many more examples of this problem, see Mandouze (1968), pp. 622–23, 625–27.

[35] Aug. *En. in Ps.* 145.16 (CCL 40: 2117).

[36] Aug. *Tract. in Ioh.* 12.1.1 (CCL 36: 120): addressing *caritas vestra*.

[37] Aug. *Sermo* 68.1 and 7 = Mai 126 (MiAg 1: 356, 361).

[38] Aug. *De cat. Rud.* 2.4.8 (CCL 46: 123–24).   [39] Pontet, *Augustin prédicateur*, p. 43.

[40] Aug. *Sermo* 131.5 (PL 38: 731).

merely reminding them of their innate knowledge.[41] To listen to the ideas as expounded by a powerful and justly famous preacher was, in a sense, to witness all the rest at work. He was an example to them. The copied and circulated sermon was vital to the better preacher's fellow priests and bishops, significant numbers of whom were only marginally literate. They might be able to preach well, but they needed models and ideas, and these were provided by the master craftsmen.[42]

No matter how much bishops prized their own sermons, these gems of their rhetorical talents, and had them recorded by stenographers and distributed to networks of friends, and to friends of friends, the basic difficulties of communicating with and persuading a crowd of not always attentive parishioners should not be underestimated. It was manifest that many of them came to church for reasons other than to listen to a boring sermon: to hook up with girls (as Augustine did in his youth), to chat with neighbors, or for other social liaisons of this kind. There were those, hopefully, who did "not bring their domestic preoccupations inside these walls and settle down to enjoy some family gossip, coming here only to find people with whom they can chatter about trifles . . . who don't enjoy talking about other people's business when they have failed in their own."[43] Audience inattention, however, was not the only problem. Ignorance and misunderstanding loomed just as large. On some occasions, the audience broke into applause, entirely mistaking the cue that the preacher had given them.[44]

The only large consistent body of sermons that survives from this conflict are the homilies preached by Augustine. Little by little, others are being discovered: some by other Catholic bishops, some by known ones like Optatus of Milevis, and others by more anonymous preachers – and also sermons that were preached by the clergy of the dissident church. The corpus of sermons reliably attributed to Augustine is large and fairly representative. The sermons are spread over all the decades that he was bishop at Hippo Regius, preached on diverse subjects and occasions, and before various types of audiences in different African venues. They were delivered to discerning great crowds in the impressive basilicas of the metropolis of Carthage, to congregations in provincial capital cities like Constantina and Caesarea, to more middling crowds in towns like Thagaste and Calama, and

---

[41] Aug. *Sermo* 131.5 and 9 (PL 38: 731 and 733–34).
[42] Aug. *Ep.* *16.1 (BA 46B: 270); *23A.3 (BA 46B: 376); and the programmatic statement in *De Doctr. Christ.* 4.29.62 (CCL 32: 165–66): "Sunt sane quidam, qui bene pronuntiare possunt, quid autem pronuntient, excogitare non possunt"; cf. Sabw Kanyang, *Episcopus et plebs*, pp. 64–65.
[43] Aug. *Sermo* 32.2 (CCL 41: 398).   [44] Aug. *Sermo* 96.4 (PL 38: 586–87).

to assemblies in small off-the-track villages like Boseth and Chusa.[45] On a rough calculation, about 850–900 of Augustine's sermons have survived, something like one out of five of those that he originally preached as priest and bishop.[46] Not all of them are in a perfect state of preservation. Some are fragmentary, others are notes that were intended for sermons that we do not have in the form that they were delivered orally (if, indeed, they ever were), while still others are more formal literary compositions that are "like sermons." Even with these caveats, this remains a most important body of evidence for our problem since these sermons furnish a long, detailed, and consistent record of the efforts of one bishop to educate his parishioners. Not only did he gradually learn how to preach superlatively well, he could also invent and craft the ideas. In the widespread circulation of his sermons we can reasonably expect echoes, repetition, and development of argument.

With Augustine, as no doubt with many other priests and bishops, especially the less talented, the differences in the rhetoric of the treatises and other written works and the sermons mark the steep learning curve that the bishop had to climb to communicate effectively with his people. Once the responsibility was embraced that average and even less-than-average people were worthy of serious edification, the preacher also had to accept the hard fact that it was his standards of communication that would have to change and not theirs. Although not requiring the extreme adjustments of a popular song, the rhetoric of the sermon demanded of the preacher that he try to convey ideas in a form that he would expect his audience to understand. In Augustine's case – as surely happened with most other priests and bishops – one can actually see the transformation from the

---

[45] Not all of the texts of the Psalms, for example, were actually delivered as sermons. But in his preamble to *En. in Ps.* 118, he makes clear that he had treated all the other Psalms partly in sermons and partly by dictation. He then states that he has decided to undertake Ps. 118 in a series of public sermons that the Greeks call "homilies," precisely because his parishioners will "enjoy the sound of the Psalm when sung, as they do in the case of all of the other Psalms." Whether "dictated" or "preached" therefore, he regarded all of these "talks" as if they were "sermons": See *En. in Ps.* 118.6, 7, 12–13 and 24, where explicit comments to this effect are made.

[46] As bishop, he preached about (35 [years] × *c.* 50 [weeks] = *c.* 1500 × 3 [sermons]) 4,500 sermons. Mandouze (1968), pp. 599–615, estimated at the time he was writing that there were about 509 genuine sermons to the people, 122 sermons on the Psalms actually delivered orally, 124 sermons on the gospel of John, and 34 other items for at total of 789 (see Mandouze [1968], p. 615 n. 1). I am more inclined to count all of the sermons on the Psalms as "sermon-like" materials. With these additional sermons, plus the discoveries of more sermons since Mandouze made his count (including the Dolbeau sermons, the new Erfurt sermons, and so on), I make the count at *c.* 580 sermons to the people, 124 sermons on the gospel of John, 10 sermons on the First Epistle of John, and 207 sermons on the Psalms, or about 920 sermons in total. In which case, we have about one out of five of the original corpus.

comparatively formal, even rigid, delivery of the classical rhetor to the confident Christian teacher who has found that middle-ground between his higher status as a well-educated leader who knew scripture and how it should be interpreted, and the daily language and experiences of his ignorant listeners.[47] The preacher was in a constant process of learning how better to communicate his ideas to his audience. Over his lifetime as a preacher, Augustine improved immensely in this mode, moving from a rhetoric heavily inflected by his elite rhetorical training to one more directly oral in nature in which he paid close attention to the responses of his "dears." It was getting to their level that mattered. In one sermon, he asked his audience to imagine that they might have received a senator to stay in their home. Noticing the lack of empathy in his listeners when he used the comparison of a man of senatorial rank, he quickly adjusted: "OK, OK – *not* a senator – let's say a procurator of some other big shot in this world." This they could understand.[48]

There is also a large body of non-Augustinian sermons known from Africa of this period. In the flotsam and jetsam of Christian writings that floated out of their original home in the fifth to seventh centuries, in response to the Vandal, Byzantine, and Arab invasions, were a large number of sermons whose texts were transported northwards across the Mediterranean to venues in Spain, southern Gaul, and southern Italy. The main problems with these sermons are to fix their origin as African and then to try to identify their ecclesiastical provenience. The difficulties arise because the propensity of persons outside Africa who were collating these often anonymous items was to attach them to writers whom they knew. Since their knowledge of ecclesiastical matters within Africa was slight, and their knowledge of specific writers thin, the overwhelming tendency was to attribute such writings to Augustine who, to externals, was the best-known African bishop of the time.[49] Consequently, the volume of pseudo-Augustinian materials is huge, and, among them, the sermons alone

---

[47] As Mandouze (1968) noted, however, whether by nature or deliberation, he did not "descend" all the way down to the level of his listeners; there was always, to the end, a certain distance even in his most popular talk; cf. Banniard (1998), p. 91: "Ce *sermo humillimus* est aussi près qu'il est possible de l'être dans la bouche d'un évêque lettré du *sermo quotidianus* des Africains. Près, mais non identique. Car ce latin tardif parlé par Augustin garde un caractère soigné . . . la langue parlée par Augustin s'intègre dans le système général du latin parlé d'Afrique, mais sans se superposer strictement à lui. Il en ressort que nous sommes en présence d'une latinité orale ouverte, certes, mais non relâchée."

[48] Aug. *En. in Ps.* 131.6 (CCL 40: 1914): "Si vellet apud te hospitium habere aliquis senator . . . non dico senator, procurator alicuius magni secundum saeculum."

[49] By the same reasoning, if such unattributed sermons or treatises were thought to be from an earlier age, then they were usually assigned to Cyprian.

amount to some two thousand or more items.[50] Even after allowances are made for difficulties in identifying their African provenience, and a time frame out of which such sermons came, there are still a reasonably large number of African sermons of the period not from Augustine's hand – other voices that provide a control over the corpus of sermons delivered by the bishop of Hippo.[51] But it is still often not possible to say whether or not these other non-Augustinian sermons are Catholic or dissident, since there are very few specific details, distinctive themes, and other criteria by which the two can be distinguished.

The simple fact that they are African sermons from the same time, however, means that historians have at their disposal a large bank of material with which to compare the general trends in Augustine's preaching and, in some cases, a few items with which to flesh out the picture of dissident preachers. Examples of these other sermons reveal what we might expect. The lesser talents did not have the logical rigor or theological talents of an Augustine, even in his most popular mode. A good example from an anonymous African preacher of his time shows characteristic modes of presentation: he prefers vivid images to ideas, he does not so much teach and explain as describe in a striking story-like fashion.[52] He personifies and dramatizes. His style tends to the overly dramatic and the overly emphatic. If anything, he strives a little bit too much not to appear simple, and so gets entangled in his own arguments and analogies. Like popular sacred songs of the time, the preacher drives his sentences to endings that are marked with strong accentual rhythms. He is much taken with the coercive devices of repetition and reinforcement. In vocabulary, although somewhat attracted by the poetic diction of the educated, his words are suffused with the juridical and military terms that are typical of African Christian writers of the age. This one sermon demonstrates the wide range of possibilities that were exploited by the literate and text-based preachers who were challenged to transform that material into a popular oral mode.

More important on the dissident side, however, are two discoveries of sermon materials that had previously gone unrecognized. The first is the

---

[50] Frede, *Kirchenschriftsteller*, pp. 263–302, provides an initial list of some 2,064 itemized pseudo-Augustinian sermons. Many are doublets, fragments, and some of doubtful attribution, some not African and others much later and not late antique creations. Nevertheless, the number is large and certainly represents only part of what could be known if more attention were paid to this floating and amorphous body of evidence to which not much is given simply because it consists of items that have been demonstrated to be "not-Augustine."

[51] A list of those consulted is provided in Appendix H.

[52] Leclercq (1947), text at pp. 121–25; analysis at pp. 126–29.

identification of a handbook used by a dissident preacher of the period.[53] This is a particularly exciting discovery since it reveals the kinds of technical aids upon which a preacher of the time would have depended. It seems to be a standardized handbook, and so it is not illogical to assume that many dissident preachers might well have had access to ones like it. It reveals a considerable concern with authenticity of the texts – the number of lines in the accepted authentic version of a text are given so that any preacher could judge for himself whether or not he was in possession of a genuine version. The texts with which the handbook are particularly concerned are those of Cyprian whose overwhelming authority in the dissident church is manifest. The second discovery is a body of sixty sermons that had long been categorized as "Pseudo Chrysostom" or "The Latin Chrysostom." The main manuscripts that have preserved these sermons were found in Spain, a logical provenience since many late Christian texts from the Maghrib would have drifted to Iberian shores, and so it is here that much "lost" African material has been salvaged.[54] It is now reasonably certain that these sermons belonged to a single dissident preacher, perhaps from the region of Byzacena or Numidia.[55]

What the new sermons reveal, given our construction of Christianity in Africa, is much of what one would expect. First of all, the dissident homilies betray few specific differences that would distinguish them from most Catholic sermons. Although these precise points were of great importance to the dissidents, there were actually few major doctrinal or theological differences between the dissidents and the Catholics that could identify the sermons delivered as belonging to one of the two churches. Both sides were orthodox Trinitarians sharing the same conceptions of the nature of God, the nature of baptism, and other core elements of the faith. We should therefore not expect the dissenting sermons to be very different from Catholic ones. Indeed, save for personal style and interests, they share considerable overlaps in content and presentation with the homilies of the Catholic preachers of the age. This is precisely what is evident: most of the sermons of the dissident preacher could be taken to be those of an Aurelius, an Optatus, or an Augustine. They pound away remorselessly at the main themes of Christian narrative, doctrine, discipline, and ethics. The principal concern of the preacher is the education of his parishioners in the recognition of sin and sinful behavior. Only now and then does he

---

[53] Rouse and McNelis (2000).

[54] For all of what follows on these sermons from the Escorial, I shall be citing the standard treatments by Leroy (1994), (1997), and (1999).

[55] For example, the reference to camel herding: Leroy Sermon 14, *De Job* = Leroy (1999), p. 173.

turn to themes that specifically excoriate Catholics. In this, he and his peers were quite typical: the small critical matters of difference were founded on a mountain of sameness.

SPEAKING WITH BLOOD

Whether the preaching was by a dissident or a Catholic bishop or priest, the techniques were much the same and are important to understand. The aim was the same as in other ages: to manipulate and to manufacture emotion.[56] How did the preacher present his materials and with what purpose and with what assumed effect? To understand the place of sermons in the culture of violence, one has also to understand that their main purpose was *not* directed to this end at all, but rather to other more mundane and simple ends. Sermons were intended as an ongoing education in a world of new stories and new morals that were to replace and to supersede the old ones, or they were to confirm Christian rituals and beliefs in those who already shared them. If there are two elements that are important in them, they are the education in the new narratives that anchored the Christian understanding of the world, and, second, the remorseless (and remorselessly repetitive) inculcation within the believer of the elements of personal discipline and behavior expected of him or her. The largest amount of the preaching, whether Catholic or dissident, was directed to the fundamental and primary goals of producing a subject who knew these new directions and who behaved accordingly. It is therefore almost impossible to distinguish most Catholic and dissident sermons from each other. Day in and day out, they were trying to achieve exactly the same things in precisely the same ways. The occasional intrusion into this world of the specifics of this story and the marshaling of hatreds and dislikes assumed this greater mundane background, the daily mountain of the normative Christian thinking and behavior that the preacher had constructed for his parishioners. As good an example as any is the long sermon delivered by Augustine in the great Restoration Basilica at Carthage in September 403.[57] At the end of the sermon, he apologizes for its length, but reaffirms the importance of the homily as a systematic means of educating: the point was not just to come to church, but to hear and to act. Beginning by citing the words of the Psalm that "sinners have been alienated from the womb,

---

[56] For the techniques used, see Comeau, *Rhétorique de saint Augustin*; for some of the comparative effects, see Semelin, *Purify and Destroy*, pp. 72–76, although I dissent with the utility of seeing the means (in our case, at least) as "propaganda."

[57] Aug. *En. in Ps.* 57 (CCL 39: 707–29).

they wandered from the belly, they have spoken lies," he continues in his own voice:[58]

Whoever is separated from the womb of the Church will necessarily utter lies. Again, it is necessary, I say, that anyone who does not want be conceived there or who, having been conceived, is aborted from that womb, will utter lies. This is why the heretics [i.e. the Donatists] raise an uproar against the gospel, so that we will speak about these matters rather than the abortions that we mourn.

He then picks up the next verses of the Psalm: "Their resentment is like the venom of a snake" and glosses the core characteristic of this specific snake as "Like that of a deaf asp" found in Africa. He proceeds:[59]

The Spirit of God uses this snake as an image of a people who do not hear God's word – that is, people who are not merely disobedient to the word, but who are firmly resolved not even to hear it in order to obey... Their disdain is the resentment of the snake. We have to put up with this same kind of people. At first they seemed to hold to the truth... but truth was preached in the church and in that maternal womb their lies were exposed... "Why are you looking for us?" they say "Why do you want us?" they say – "Get away from us!" That is all that they say to us. But to their own people they say: "Let no one speak with them [i.e. the Catholics], let no one associate with them, let no one listen to them." Such is their fury: the resentment of snakes is just like the deaf asp...

Then the preacher picks up the next verse: "God smashed the teeth in their mouths."[60]

Whose teeth? The teeth of those whose resentment is like a snake's, their ears like those of the deaf asp... What did our Lord do to them? *He smashed the teeth in their mouths.* This actually happened. It happened in those early times and it still happens now in our own day. But wouldn't it have been enough, brothers, to say simply, *God smashed their teeth*? Why add, *in their mouths*?

Having answered this rhetorical question, and then others – and we are only a little more than half way through the sermon – the preacher then offers a convenient résumé for his listeners:[61]

---

[58] Aug. *En. in Ps.* 57.6 (CCL 39: 713).   [59] Aug. *En. in Ps.* 57.7–9 (CCL 39: 715–16).

[60] Aug. *En. in Ps.* 57.11 (CCL 39: 717–18): "Deus contrivit dentes eorum in ore ipsorum. Quorum? Quibus indignatio est sicut similitudo serpentis, et aspidis obturantis aures suas... Quid illis fecit Dominus? Contrivit dentes eorum in ore ipsorum. Factum est; hoc primo factum est, et modo fit. Sed sufficeret, fratres, ut diceretur: Deus contrivit dentes eorum. Quare in ore ipsorum?"

[61] Aug. *En. in Ps.* 57.14–15 (CCL 39: 720): "Saeviunt modo Iudaei, si possunt. Non saeviunt. Molas leonum confregit Dominus. Habemus et in haereticis hoc documentum et experimentum, quia et ipsos invenimus esse serpentes indignatione obsurdatos, nolentes audire medicamentum a sapiente; et in ore ipsorum contrivit Dominus dentes eorum."

Let the Jews rage about now – if they can! But they do not rage, do they? *The Lord has shattered the jawbones of the lions.* We have an instructive example of the same thing in our own experiences now in our own heretics, don't we? For we find that they [i.e. the Donatists] too are vipers, deaf, unwilling to hear from the wise about the medicine that would cure them. In their case, too, the Lord has smashed their teeth.

The sermon is a typical dialogue with biblical texts, back and forth, interspersed with questions and answers that cue the listener about how to understand the present force of the typological references from sacred scripture in which "the Donatists" are successively demonstrated to be deaf and dumb, poisonous vipers, aborted fetuses, liars, and persons whose teeth have been smashed in their mouths.

Repetition of basic ideas, the hammering away, time and again, at them, is such a fundamental device, and is found so often, that a few examples of the tactic will suffice. In an acerbic sermon delivered in the immediate aftermath of the conference of 411, the preacher warns against his parishioners accepting any false claims from their sectarian enemies:[62]

Don't let them sell you "smoke," don't let them deceive you! Those men who say, "We are the holy, we don't carry your burdens. That's why we don't communicate with you." Those big men do indeed carry burdens: burdens of division, burdens of exclusion, burdens of schism, burdens of heresy, burdens of conflict, burdens of hate, burdens of lying testimony, burdens of false charges.

The pounding rhythm of the preacher's delivery fixes the basic idea in the listener's mind. The device of anaphora or a feedback loop of iteration replicated the repetitive violent force of the chanting of young men in public entertainments in the very process of condemning them.[63]

For demons delight in vapid songs and chants. They are overjoyed with worthless spectacles, with the manifold shameful acts of the theater, with the madness of the circus, with the cruelty of the amphitheater, with the hateful fights of those men who take their quarrels and battles on behalf of a few disgusting men to the point of open hatreds – all for a dancer, for an actor, for a mime, for a charioteer, for a beast-hunter. When they do these things, it's as if they are offering burnt incense to demons from their hearts. The demon seducers rejoice in their seductions. They feed on the bad morals and on the shameful and disgraceful lives of those whom they have seduced and deceived.

---

[62] Aug. *Sermo* 164.10 (PL 38: 899–900).   [63] Aug. *Sermo* 198.3 (PL 38: 1026).

Repetition was particular useful in a challenge and response form used by the preacher, a question and answer dialogue that coached the audience how to respond with the right answer.[64]

> I ask you, my faithful Christians: Was the mother of Jesus there? You reply: Yes she was. How do you know? You reply: The evangelist says so. What did Jesus reply to his mother? You reply: "Woman, what does this matter to me or to you? My hour has not yet come." How do you know this? You reply: "The evangelist says so."

Of course, most interaction was not at this crude "here is the question, here is your answer" level, but the variants were often just subtler versions of the same device. More to the point, the preacher could hail forth the person of the enemy vividly in front of the eyes of the parishioners – the device of prosopopeia, well known to classical orators – and conduct a virtual dialogue with the vile heretic. We find the device in an important sermon delivered at Carthage in autumn of 403, a small part of which imparts a sense of the mixture of history, demonstration, and dialogue that was used to unveil the dissidents not as descendants of primal traitors but, much worse, as the progeny of primal liars.[65]

> Stupidity! Madness! . . . So it is with *their* offspring – as you remember. There's no chance of just avoiding the matter . . . See how the body of Christ suffers these lying witnesses . . . "Offspring of traitors!" they say. Well, it's *you* who are making a false statement. I'm going to convict *you* of being a lying witness right here and right now by investigating a few of your own words. You say to me: "You're a traitor!" I say to you: "You're a liar!" You'll never ever prove that I am a traitor. But right here, right now, I'll show your lying from your own words! You said that we sharpened our swords? I read out the records of your circumcellions . . . "We only preach the gospel," you say. I quote the many judicial decisions you've used to persecute your own separatists. I read aloud your appeals to that apostate emperor . . . Perhaps you think that Julian is part of the gospel? See how I've caught you being the liar that you are . . .

---

[64] Aug. *Tract. in Ioh.* 8.7 (CCL 36: 86): "Interrogo vos, o fideles Christiani: Erat ibi mater Iesu? Respondete: Erat. Unde scitis? Respondete: Hoc loquitur evangelium. Quid respondit matri Jesus? Respondete: *Quid mihi et tibi est, mulier? Nondum venit hora mea.* Et hoc unde scitis? Respondete: Hoc loquitur evangelium." See Charles (1947), p. 621.

[65] Aug. *En. 2 in Ps.* 36.17–18 (CCL 38: 359): "'Stulta insania! . . . Sic et isti filii eorum, sicut meministis, et praetermittendum ex occasione non est . . . Ecce corpus Christi patitur falsos testes . . . qui dicant: "Progenies traditorum!" Falsum testimonium dicis. Ibi te convinco falsum testem, secutus pauca verba. Tu mihi dicis: "Traditor es." Ego tibi dico: "Mendax es!" Sed tu traditionem meam nusquam et numquam probas. Ego mendacium tuum hic in istis verbis tuis modo probo. Certe ibi dixisti, quia nos acuimus gladios nostros; recito gesta tuorum circumcellionum . . . Certe ibi dixisti: "Nos sola offerimus evangelia." Recito tot iussiones iudicum, quibus a te divisos persecutus es. Recito preces ad apostatam imperatorem, cui dixisti . . . An forte apostasia Iuliani pars evangelii tibi videtur? Ecce mendacem te teneo.'"

Specific enemies are targeted and a bead is drawn on the most subversively dangerous aspects of everyday life. So among "pagans" it is the celebrations and festivals, particularly those of the First of January, that draw fire. It is the time when the consuls and magistrates at Rome pretend to "renew" the year with their annual festivities. But it is God who made the world. Then it is time to make fun of "them" and "their practices." The silly joyfulness, the fasces – those completely meaningless symbols! The laurel fronds – of what good are they? The exchanges of gifts and kisses – what good do they do for anyone?[66] The same cleansing operation was performed for the 24 June celebrations, taken over by the Christians as the Birthday of John the Baptist. It will not be celebrated in the shameful manner of "the pagans" – no ragings or insane rantings, no flowers strewn on temples – no, none of that![67] In the case of the dissidents, Catholic preachers are clear to name them as men who "cut through" the "cloth of unity" – those heretics. The point was to inculcate fear and apprehension: *Ita cavete*! So beware![68]

Sermons by preachers of all sectarian stripes played heavily on a symbolic language in which they conveyed coded messages to their listeners. A dissident preacher can run through a whole list: the roaring lion, the hungry dog, the enticing serpent, the crafty wolf, the wily fox hiding its criminal acts.[69] The identification of Jews with ravens has already been noted. They are black in color and yet pale white with fear and timidity; foul in name, but worldly in their work. The raven covers up its own crimes and then returns to a simulacrum of obedience.[70] The raven, *as we all know*, he says, is a dirty animal and so all that it touches becomes filthy.[71] In order better to persuade, the sermon had to be a carefully modulated thing, not too much given to extremes. The cutting and hostile language of undisguised polemic was naturally counterbalanced by the huge world of normal pedagogy and narration, and the explication of scripture, that

---

[66] Anon. *In Octava Natalis Domini = Sermo Caillau-St. Yves* 2, Append. 15: 1 (PLS 2: 1109–10). For the tone, consider: "Quid nunc, mundana, laetitia, fasces, secures atque infulas, ceteraque bonorum vanissima insignia, plausibili ambitu ostentas? Quid laureas renovando frondescis? Quid reciprocis osculis et pecuniis hunc tibi vendicas diem?"

[67] Anon. *In Natali Johannis Baptistae = Sermo Caillau-St. Yves* 1.55: 5 (PLS 2: 1009) "Frequentemus itaque hunc diem non obscaeno gentilis more erroris . . . Ne ullum in delubris sertum pendeat, aut insanientibus turbis . . . petulantes rotae concurrant."

[68] Anon. *De Octava Paschae = Sermo Mai* 42: 2 (PLS 2: 1142).

[69] Anon. *In natali Sancti Vincentii = Sermo Caillau-St. Yves* 2.64: 2 (PLS 2: 1082).

[70] Anon. *In natali domini = Sermo Caillau-St. Yves* 1.7: 14 (PLS 2: 918): "O . . . corvos . . . nigros in colore, sed candidos in timore; immundos in nomine, sed mundos in opere. Emundavit tandem corvus culpam suam et reversus est ad oboedientiam."

[71] Anon. *De Sancto Helia Propheta = Sermo Mai* 137.2 (PLS 2: 1230–31).

characterized the larger sermon-world in which it was set. Every explicit exhortation to aggression and dislike was more than outweighed by the more numerous exhortations that encouraged self-control, charity, understanding, and love. The tactic of the hostile command was located within this greater strategic communication of love, forgiveness, and benevolence. As it has been well noted of preaching in another age, "it was necessary to maintain a balance of comfort and terror."[72] Although the effect of a specific injunction has to be gauged against this larger normative background, the one did not always effectively control, govern, or cancel out the other. In similar circumstances during the European Reformation, it has been observed that "few really believed that bitter and incendiary denunciations of idols could be balanced by pious warnings to wait on the magistrate." This was because common experience had demonstrated the opposite: that attacks on idolatry from the pulpit led, and sometimes rather quickly, to actual acts of destruction.[73]

Central to all the modes of Christian communication was a new narrative replete with a plenitude of new stories to be told. Some of the most vivid and striking of the sermons are themselves wonderful pieces of storytelling, revealing the talents of the preacher recounting an exciting narrative line. All the preachers drew on the same huge bank of stories, each of which was capable of demonstrating by typology and allegory what the believer was to think in the present age. The same biblical stories provided the necessary foundations of understanding for their analogies – the narratives both exemplified and explained in a memorable fashion. The tale of the terrible fate of Cora, Dathan, and Abiron, who rebelled against the rightful authority of Moses and Aaron, was brought up time and again to frighten those who might consider just such betrayal of their own party and its values. These men were buried alive even before they died. The preacher could be a Catholic condemning the dissidents, or a dissident condemning internal dissidents. It did not matter.[74] The story functioned either way, and just as well. Similarly, the story of the decapitation of John the Baptist provided wonderful fodder for preachers to dwell on the grisly details, the fear and the horror, all of which they artfully inculcated in their listeners.[75] Even more, the effect that narrative evocations of violence had is palpable in

---

[72] Pettegree, *Culture of Persuasion*, p. 36.

[73] Ibid., pp. 30–31; for the same effect of violent rhetoric in Northern Ireland, see Coogan, *The Troubles*, pp. 168–71. Part of the problem, of course, is to separate the "safety valve" function of violent words from the occasions when they lead to physical violence.

[74] E.g. Anon. *De Epiphania Domini* = *Sermo Caillau-St. Yves* 2.42: 3 (PLS 2: 1060); *In natali domini* = *Sermo Caillau-St. Yves* 1.7: 20 (PLS 2: 920).

[75] Anon. *Sermones Caillau-St. Yves* 2.79 and 80 (PLS 2: 1085–88; 1088–90).

the care and devotion that preachers, both Catholic and dissident, devoted to the bloody description of the Slaughter of the Innocents.[76] The theme allowed the dissident preacher, for example, to incite in his listeners a sense of the huge injustice that was being perpetrated upon them, the crime of innocent persons who were being harmed by a persecuting state and an evil king. The pathos of the scene, painted carefully, word by word, surely elicited in the hearer the suffocating effects of heavy persecution, a story-like identification with the murdered infants who "spoke with their blood, since they could not yet speak with their voices."[77]

WHOSE VOICE? WHOSE EARS?

To talk with assumed confidence about the spread of narratives, allegories, and doctrines readily conveyed by oral modes of discourse like the sermon is to speak too glibly. The questions remain: Who was listening? And what were they hearing? Even for Augustine's own diocese of Hippo, with its large urban port that was well connected with the transmarine world, there was at least one large communicative hurdle to surmount. In a letter written to Novatus, the Catholic bishop of Sitifis, we read that Augustine had balked at returning a deacon named Lucilius to him. The reason that he gives is that this particular deacon possessed a language skill that was badly needed. The preaching of the gospel, Augustine noted, was greatly impeded in regions around Hippo because of the people's poor knowledge or ignorance of Latin.[78] Latin and some Greek was spoken in and around the city, but the great language barrier about which Augustine was speaking was formed by those persons whose main or only language was Punic.[79] In challenging the dissident bishop Crispinus to a public debate at Calama, Augustine wanted precise legal form to be followed: the exact words of both speakers were to be taken down in transcript and then signed by each

---

[76] E.g., Anon. *In Epiphania Domini* = *Sermo Mai* III (PLS 2: 1210–13).

[77] Anon. *Sermo Escorial.* 45 (PL 95: 1175–76).

[78] Aug. *Ep.* 84.2 (CCL 31A: 1128): "Sed cum Latina lingua, cuius inopia in nostris regionibus evangelica dispensatio multum laborat, illic autem eiusdem linguae usus omnino sit, itane censes nos saluti plebium domini oportere consulere, ut hanc facultatem illuc mittamus et hinc auferamus, ubi eam magno cordis aestu requirimus?"

[79] That the language was Punic and not some indigenous African language is an almost certain deduction from the evidence, although it has been challenged by Courtois (1950a) and *Les Vandales*, pp. 57–60 (unconvincingly, with much special pleading, I think) and Camps (1994). The bibliography is immense and immensely repetitive – see, *inter alia*, beginning as early as Thümmel, "Die Sprache," ch. 5 in *Beurtheilung des Donatismus*, pp. 63–74: the language was Punic; it was widely spoken; it was the common language of the circumcellions; then Green (1951), Simon (1953), Lecerf (1954), Vattioni (1968), pp. 441–52.

bishop. He realized, however, that much of the oral debate and certainly the transcript would not be understood by its intended audience: the great majority of the local peasant farmers, like the eighty whom Crispinus had forcibly rebaptized, could neither read nor comprehend Latin. For them, the whole of the disputation would have to be translated into Punic.[80] But how were the words of the public debate to be "translated"? Everything of the context at Calama, including the illiterate peasants, suggests that, in the end, the translation would have to be oral. In turn, this suggests the existence of a class of bilingual persons who could act as *interpretes* – who could "speak between" the two worlds of Punic and Latin.

Although Punic had been a written language in Africa, the long history of its existence after the extermination of Punic Carthage in 146 BCE was one of the gradual and then quicker extinction of its written form. While formal public inscriptions in neo-Punic script are found as late as the rule of the emperor Tiberius, by the end of the first century CE and the first decades of the second, knowledge of the written language and its peculiar scripts was rapidly vanishing as the literate classes that sustained knowledge of the language's inscribed forms inexorably became Roman and switched permanently to Latin. In later times, when there was a perceived need to put the language into written form, as in the rural hinterland regions of Tripolitania where the language of the local elites remained Punic, recourse was had to the artifice of writing the language in the letters of the Latin language.[81] The first language of a wealthy landowner in the hinterland of Tripolitania, named Publicola, who wrote to Augustine on a problem of proper ritual was not Latin. It must have been Punic.[82] The persistence is understandable since there is good evidence that the indigenous peasants of the region also spoke a variant of Punic.[83] Even the large cosmopolitan cities of the Mediterranean coast, however, displayed some of these same characteristics. In the city of Oea, as late as the mid-second century CE, members of the local municipal elite still spoke Punic, sometimes to the

---

[80] Aug. *Ep.* 66.2 (CCL 31A: 26): "Quid multa? Si voluntate sua Mappalienses in tuam communionem transierunt, ambos nos audiant, ita ut scribantur quae dicimus, et a nobis subscripta eis Punice interpretentur, et remoto timore dominationis eligant, quod voluerunt."

[81] See Amadasi Guzzo (1990) and Elmayer (1983, 1984), and, in summary, Adams, "The "Latino-Punic Inscriptions," ch. 2.5.6 in *Bilingualism*, pp. 230–35.

[82] Publicola apud Aug. *Ep.* 46 (CCL 31: 198–202).

[83] Arnob. Iun., *Comm. ad Psalm.* 104 (CCL 25: 159): "a Rhinocoruris usque Gadira habens linguas sermone Punico a parte Garamantum"; he implies that the Garamantes spoke Punic, but the text is very schematic; cf. Elmayer (1983), p. 92, but rightly doubted by Courtois (1950a), p. 265, as signifying that much.

exclusion of an acceptable knowledge of Latin.[84] In the grand city of Lepcis Magna, just to the east, where the extinction of written Punic can be traced, we know that it remained the bedrock of oral speech even amongst the uppermost ranks of the local aristocracy well into the third century.[85] Such evidence strongly suggests, *a fortiori*, that Punic must have been the dominant language of most of the lower classes in these same regions, that is the same lowly persons whom Christian bishops were attempting to convert and to mobilize.

In the region of Hippo, well to the west of Carthage, the same language situation is found, so a significant problem of communication was faced by the bishops in both churches. In writing to Macrobius, the dissident bishop of Hippo in 410, Augustine referred to a recent incident in which the violent freelancers and enforcers associated with the dissident church had gone too far in some of their actions with the result that Macrobius was compelled to reprove them. An upset Macrobius had hurled hard words of reprimand at the men, who were stung and angered by his condemnation of their actions. But they were only able to understand the bishop's words because Macrobius had them interpreted on the spot by someone who spoke Punic.[86] In the cities, like Hippo, the language situation was mixed. In one case, when preaching to his congregation, Augustine referred to a well-known Punic proverb that he would tell them in Latin since *not all of them* knew Punic.[87] The suggestion, however, is that many of them did.

The language problem is important because the men whom Macrobius disciplined were none other than the circumcellions who were organized men of violence who sometimes cooperated with the dissident church to enforce its aims. This example shows that a constant effort had to be made to get messages through to them in their own language in the multitude of villages and rural settlements in the countryside. Failure to do so could lead to frustrating, but sometimes humorous, results. An illustrative vignette

---

[84] Apul. *Apol.* 98: in an admittedly rhetorically biased attack on a personal enemy in court, he remarks pejoratively of his son-in-law: "Loquitur nisi punice et si quid adhuc a matre graecissat, enim Latine loqui neque vult neque potest" – but the charge must have carried some weight with those who knew the person.

[85] The sister of Septimius Severus was reputed to have difficulties speaking proper Latin (SHA, *Vita Sev.* 15.7). The claim by Courtois (1950a: 271) that this was just bad Latin and nothing else is not credible. Of the emperor himself, Ps.-Aurelius Victor (*Epit. de Caes.* 20.8) remarks: "Latinis litteris sufficienter instructus, graecis sermonibus eruditus, punica eloquentia promptior, quippe genitus apud Leptim provinciae Africae."

[86] Aug. *Ep.* 108.14 (CCL 31B: 78–79): "Alio tamen die concussi et stimulati [sc. circumcelliones] aculeis verborum tuorum, quae in eos per Punicum interpretem honesta et ingenua libertatis indignatione iaculatus es."

[87] Aug. *Sermo* 167.4 (PL 38: 910): "Proverbium notum est punicum, quod quidem Latine vobis dicam, quia Punice non omnes nostis."

was told, perhaps with some relish, about Valerius, Augustine's predecessor as bishop of Hippo. At a rural venue outside the city, he was speaking with some peasants when he realized that they did not understand a thing that he was saying. At one point, however, they seemed to recognize one of his words, the Latin *salus*. Seeing them light up, he tried to find out what they had understood the word to mean. One of the two, who knew both Punic and Latin, answered: "Three." Making the best of the circumstance, Valerius enunciated his opinion that "salvation" reposed in "the Trinity."[88] This was a different language world that is systematically hidden from us in the mass of written records that have survived only in Latin.

Naturally, the documentation of the Punic language in Punic script disappeared from the record when the connections between its written and oral forms were broken.[89] There are proxy data, however, that indicate the continued power of Punic as a form of oral communication, and they are probative. The villages of Fussala and Thogonoetum, and the troubles involving the errant bishop Antoninus in the early 420s, are as good an example as any. In establishing a new bishopric in this remote part of his diocese to deal with the large numbers of dissidents who were now being forcibly recruited into the Catholic Church, Augustine needed to select competent persons to nominate for the post. The single most important skill that the nominee had to have was the ability to speak the local language – the man had to be "learned" in Punic.[90] The final appointee, indeed, was chosen mainly on the same basis – that he could speak Punic.[91] The skill was not trivial.

When the crisis at Thogonoetum reached a height in 422–23, the Catholic Primate of Numidia himself had to go to the village to speak with the locals who were both disgruntled and very angry with their new and very much disliked Catholic bishop. In a stormy meeting, he addressed them at length and he had the whole of his speech translated, *viva voce*,

---

[88] Aug. *Ep. ad Rom. inchoat. Ep.* 13 (CSEL 84: 161): "Quo loco prorsus non arbitror praetereundum, quod pater Valerius animadvertit admirans in quorundam rusticanorum collocutione. Cum alter alteri dixisset: 'salus,' quaesivit ab eo, qui et latine nosset et punice, quid esset 'salus'; responsum est: 'tria.'"

[89] When the written forms of the language finally disappeared is difficult to say. Roman jurists, for example, enunciated the opinion that *fideicommissa* were valid, even if written in Punic (Dig. 32.1.11.pr). The jurist is Ulpian, but this might not mean much. He seems to be using "Punic, or Gallic, or whatever language" as examples that were probably traditional ones.

[90] Aug. *Ep.* 209.3 (CSEL 57: 348): "Quod id fieret, aptum loco illi congruumque requirebam, qui et punica lingua esset instructus et habebam de quo cogitabam, paratum presbyterum." For further context on this passage and the one that follows, see Opelt (1983).

[91] Aug. *Ep.* *20.3.3 (CSEL 88: 96): "quia et linguam Punicam scire audieram, ordinandum ut offerrem utilem credidi."

into Punic so that the peasant farmers would understand what he was saying.[92] References to the speaking of Punic are made with such ease that we can only deduce that the primary language of many peasants in the African countryside, inland from the coast in northern Numidia and in the hinterlands of Proconsularis and Tripolitania, was Punic. Augustine explicitly states as much when he says that the Punic language shaped the ethnic identity of the speakers: "When our rural peasants are asked what they *are*, they reply, in Punic, 'Chanani,' which is only a corruption by one letter of the alphabet of what we would expect: What else should they reply except that they are 'Chananaei'?"[93] That is to say, they called themselves Chananaei or "Canaanites" as people whom we call Phoenicians actually called themselves in their own language. To themselves, they had never been "Phoenicians." They had been given the name *Phoinikes* or "the Purple People" first by Greeks and then by the Romans.

The problem is that we see so very little of this other large world and the problems of organization and communication that it presented to Christian bishops. It is a huge dark figure in the historian's reconstruction of this part of the African past. The constant transcription of a certain range of materials appropriate to such a population was taking place all of the time. We know that both churches, for example, were producing oral materials like simple chants and songs in Punic.[94] They had to. If they were going to mobilize large numbers of people either for adherence to a faith or for more concerted action, a basic range of educative materials had to be provided for them. Because of a profound illiteracy that was both social (the people were uniformly from the lower social strata of a vast rural world) and structural (there was no longer any Punic writing or literature), all these transcriptions had to be oral ones. The sad result is that they are permanently lost to us.

If the bishops wished to evangelize the countryside and to make uniform the Christianity of the remoter parts of their dioceses, they were sure to encounter such people, for example the Abeloîm who lived in a backwater

---

[92] Aug. *Ep.* *20.21.1 (CSEL 88: 105): "Sed ubi eis de Antonino episcopo sermonem facere venerandus Senex verbis Punicis coepit."

[93] Aug. *Ep. ad Rom. inch.* 13 (CSEL 84: 162): "Unde interrogati rustici nostri, quid sint, punice respondentes: 'Chanani' – corrupta scilicet, sicut in talibus solet, una littera, quid aliud respondent quam 'Chananaei'?" Vattioni (1968), p. 444, rightly remarks of this passage: "la testimonianza più certa che al tempo di Agostino la lingua punica era parlata dai contadini." It simply will not do to try to argue away the effect of this passage by saying that the peasants in the hinterland of Hippo were somehow referring to the standard myth about the Phoenician origins of Africans, as, for example, Courtois (1950a), pp. 278–79, does. The peasants both made their reply "in Punic" and identified themselves, unqualifiedly, as "Chananaei."

[94] See ch. 10, pp. 480–81.

far from Hippo and whose name was a Punic version of Abel's name.[95] But they did exist and the men of violence whom the dissident bishop Macrobius reprimanded in 410 only understood Punic. Their organizers must have been interstitial men set midway between the world of Latin and Punic communication. So too, the circumcellions who were attacking "pagan" shrines in the 390s were men recruited from a rural underclass who bore Punic names, rough men who evoked the disdain and contempt of the educated Latin classes in towns like Madauros and who provoked a lot of rhetorical posing between the philosopher Maximus and Augustine about whether or not "as Africans" they ought to despise such Punic barbarisms.[96] The attitude was embedded in the polemical use of ethnic labeling of the time.[97] On this occasion, Augustine hypocritically protested his innocence to his advantage. On other occasions, however, when Catholics wanted to emphasize their cosmopolitan presence against the narrow geographical constriction of "the Donatists" to Africa, their "African-ness" was marked by the fact that their languages were Latin *or Punic* – "just African" – and nothing else.[98]

It is not surprising, then, that preachers knew enough to link Punic with biblical Hebrew as cognate languages, and that they had a sufficient knowledge of basic items of vocabulary to be able to gloss connections and relations of meaning.[99] It was not just that the preachers' sermons were peppered with explanations that glossed the meaning of words in the bible with equivalents or roots in Punic.[100] It has not unreasonably been suggested that there were at least low-level oral biblical students and exegetes and students in the language.[101] In a discussion of the Punic word for *misericordia*, Augustine suggested to his son, Adeodatus, that there were "those who knew the Punic language better" than he did, which assumes the existence of more fluent speakers who were interested in such matters.[102]

---

[95] See ch. 7, pp. 310–11.   [96] On these incidents, see ch. 5, pp. 236–38.

[97] For example, Julius of Aeclanum's labeling of Augustine as "Punic" and therefore "African" in a pejorative sense: e.g. apud Aug. *Contra Iul. op. imperf.* 1.72 and 78 (CSEL 85.1: 84–85, 405).

[98] Aug. *In. Ep. Ioh. ad Parth.* 2.2 (SC 75: 154–56): "Sic honorant Christum ut dicant illum ad duas linguas remansisse, Latinam et Punicam, id est Afram." Courtois (1950a), 275–76, and others, in making the argument that by "Punic" Augustine really means "Libyan," completely misrepresent the contextual meaning of "id est Afram."

[99] Courtois (1950a), p. 272n40, provides a list.

[100] E.g. Aug. *En. in Ps.* 123.8; 136.18; *Sermo* 113; 162A; 167; 359A; and, of course, in his exegetical works as well.

[101] Cox (1988), pp. 102–05, much of which is only suggestive and speculative, but with some good grounds.

[102] Aug. *De Mag.* 13.44 (CCL 29: 201): "Velut te nuper verbo quodam Punico, cum ego misericordiam dixissem, pietatem significari te audisse dicebas ab eis, quibus haec lingua magis nota esset... nequaquam mihi videretur absurdum pietatem et misericordiam uno vocabulo Punice nominari."

These Punic-speaking Christians had their own terms and words, their own special vocabulary, in which they interpreted the Christian message.[103] In some ways, therefore, the Abeloîm of the remotest hinterland of Hippo were not as unusual as they first appear. They were just an extreme example of a normal language and cultural situation in the countryside.

PAMPHLET WARS

If crossing the frontiers of language was one necessary stratagem, another type of transcription was required that would bridge the space between the elite discourses of the bishop and lay exegete as writers and creators of ideas and the mass of ordinary persons. Streaming alongside the sermon and related to it in form and purpose was the *libellus* or written (and perhaps illustrated) pamphlet. Although no imperial edicts were enunciated against sermons, such measures were frequently reiterated against polemical written pamphlets – called defamatory chapbooks or *libelli famosi* in the laws – whose effects on public order were deemed to be so pernicious that they hailed forth repeated injunctions against them by the imperial government. The pamphlet was the closest written text to the song and the sermon in the popular mass dissemination of ideas in this religious battle – not surprisingly, it was widely employed in other ages of sectarian conflict.[104] The sectarian *libelli* took existing discourses of hate in the more complex literary sources of the time and parlayed them into modes that enabled quicker production, distribution, and consumption of key ideas. Almost all the authors and the contents of the pamphlets have been lost to us. It is only very rarely that we catch a glimpse of the purveyors of the rapid-fire chapbooks. One of them was a dissident layman named Centurius who turned up one day outside the Catholic basilica at Hippo Regius with one of the small books in hand which he placed in the hands of the Catholic clergy of the church. Its contents outlined, with great brevity and force, the main points at issue between the two churches. It was effective enough

---

[103] Aug. *De pecc. merit. et remiss.* 1.23–34 (CSEL 60: 33): "Optime punici Christiani baptismum ipsum nihil aliud quam salutem et sacramentum corporis Christi, nihil aliud quam vitam vocant."

[104] For some of the rich literature on the use of pamphlets in the Reformation and Counter-Reformation, see Ozment (1982) who emphasizes (pp. 85–86) the scale of their production and the degree to which they were addressed to "a non-specialized and often non-literate audience"; and Scribner, *Popular Propaganda*, p. 6 and *passim*, noting the hybridization of forms and the rapid turnover of pamphlets in the communication of ideas; see also Ruff, *Violence in Early Modern Europe*, pp. 17–28, who draws attention to the close connections between pamphlets and song texts, as well as the ever-present use of illustrations; and Pettegree, *Culture of Persuasion*, pp. 133, 149, and esp. ch. 7, "Pamphlets and Persuasion," pp. 156–84.

to alarm Augustine and to provoke him to write an equally brief and sharp reply in the same genre.[105] Not surprisingly, both works are lost. They were from a subliterary world that was entirely functional and, like the pop songs, not deemed worthy of long-term preservation. But their effect was such that they kept being employed, and on a substantial scale, in all the decades of this struggle.

All the popular forms of communication were interconnected and were part of the same violent struggle that marked certain ideas and property as one's own and marked the defects and the humiliation of the enemy. In the aftermath of the imperial legislation of 405 that permitted the occupation and seizure of the church properties and basilicas of the dissidents, Augustine composed a brief squib of this kind, his own pamphlet, that justified the moral grounds of these seizures and excoriated the moral wrongs of the dissidents that made them just and deserving targets of such takeovers. Entitled "The Book of Proofs and Evidence against the Donatists" (*Probationum et testimoniorum contra Donatistas liber*), the pamphlet was another one of these attacking sectarian literary jabs at the enemy. But merely writing it, having it distributed, and read aloud was not enough. To hammer home the message to the dissidents, Augustine ordered the text to be posted, papered on the walls of the enemy's basilica at Hippo that had just been seized by the Catholics.[106] The "Donatists" would get to read, in pithy and pungent form, on the very walls of their former church, the just reasons for its confiscation by their enemies. It has been remarked, aptly, that in this war of pamphlets, obscure and nameless pamphleteers – perhaps deliberately and wisely anonymous – conducted a guerrilla war of intimidation, denunciations, defiance, protests, and harm from the shadows of the literary demi-monde of the conflict.[107]

---

[105] Aug. *Retract.* 2.19 (CCL 57: 105): his reply was entitled *Contra quid attulit Centurius a Donatistis*; later, he composed another similar pamphlet entitled *Contra nescio quem Donatistam* – "Against Some Donatist" (note that the author was anonymous): "Cum adversus partem Donati multa crebris disputationibus ageremus, attulit ad ecclesiam quidam laicus tunc eorum nonnulla contra nos dictata vel scripta in paucis velut testimoniis, quae suae causae suffragari putant; his brevissime respondi"; cf. *Retract.* 2.28 (CCL 57: 113). Given their genre, it is again no surprise that both of these works have also been lost.

[106] Aug. *Retract.* 2.27 (CCL 57: 112–13): "eumque (sc. libellum) sic edidi ut in parietibus basilicae quae Donatistarum fuerat prius propositus legeretur."

[107] Monceaux, *Hist. litt.* 6, p. 240: "Cette guerre de pamphlets . . . des pamphlétaires obscurs, et plus prudents, menaient dans l'ombre la petite guerre d'intimidation, de dénonciations, de défis, de protestations et d'injures." Surely (consider the "protestations") influenced in some part by what he knew of the Reformation and aftermath.

The authors might be anonymous and the texts lost forever, but in their time the pamphlets, like the sermon, were a most powerful medium that had real and immediate effects on behaviors, especially those that tended to public disorder and violence. Right from the beginning of the struggle, but again and again, with almost regular predictability, beginning with Constantine's order to Aelianus, the proconsul of Africa, posted at Carthage on 25 February 315, the emperors issued severe condemnations of those who wrote and distributed such "malicious pamphlets."[108] Constantine's counter-measures were meant to control the perceived impact of these *libelli* in exciting hatred of, and violent action against, Caecilian at Carthage.[109] Constantine had to reissue the same warnings in 319 and then again in 320, clearly in connection with the renewed sectarian battles that emerged again in 317–18, incited by the intrusion of the state.[110] Towards the end of his reign Constantine had to reiterate his warning against the use of such "infamous pamphlets" to the Africans, and his rulings were reiterated by his son and successor Constantius in the year of his succession.[111] There is a long period of lack of concern over the public effects of these pamphlets in Africa until Constans, when another imperial counter order was issued.[112] The worries of the state were well founded because the effects were real. This "combat literature," as it has rightly been labeled, was everywhere a pipeline of hatred that funneled the attacking arguments developed by the literate elites, again and again, into the ears of the parishioners on each side in the battle.[113]

---

[108] CTh 9.34.2 (Constantine to Aelianus, Proconsul of Africa; posted at Carthage on 25 February 315): "Licet serventur in officio tuo et vicarii exemplaria libellorum, qui in Africa oblati sunt."

[109] On these, see Aug. *Ep.* 43.5.15 (CCL 31: 178): "Accessit aliud ut a quibusdam adversus Caecilianum denuntiationis libellus daretur"; 88.2 (CCL 31A: 139–40): quoting a letter of Constantine to Anullinus, the Proconsul of Africa: "qui Caeciliano contradicendum putarent, quique fasciculum in aluta signatum et libellum sine signo obtulerunt dicationi meae... Transmissi libelli duo, unus in aluta suprascriptus ita: *Libellus ecclesiae catholicae criminum Caeciliani traditus a parte Maiorini*: item alius sine sigillo cohaerens eidem alutae"; and 93.4.13 (CCL 31A: 176): another reference to this same pamphlet.

[110] CTh 9.34.1 (Constantine to Verinus, Vicar of Africa; 29 March 319); cf. CTh 9.34.3 (Constantine to Januarius, Vicar of the Prefect; 4 December 320): "cum eosdem libellos flammis protinus conducat aboleri, quorum auctor nullus existit." CTh 9.34.4 (Constantine to Dionysius; posted at Tyre 21 October 328), might well be another of these.

[111] CTh 9.34.5 (Constantius to the Africans; 18 June 338); confirming the rulings of his father on *famosi libelli* (cf. CTh 9.34.4).

[112] CTh 9.34.6 (Constantius to the People; 21 October 355) is possibly another instance; CTh 9.34.8 (Valentinian and Valens, from Marcianopolis, to Florianus, the comes Rerum Privatarum; 9 November 368), might be connected with the aftermath of Julian?

[113] Monceaux, "Anonymes Donatistes: traités, pamphlets, chroniques," ch. 7 in *Hist. litt.* 7, pp. 233–58, at p. 242.

INCITEMENTS TO VIOLENCE

The basic questions still remain: What did the parishioners hear, even if in translation, that might incite more aggressive behavior? And how did they hear it? What we must constantly remember is that each day the preacher built a huge and vast foundation of normality and the ordinary. It deserves emphasis that the fixation of both sides on the inculcation of Christian history and values means that it is not possible to distinguish most Catholic sermons from most dissident ones. The overlap between the two, save for a few critical issues, is almost total. The speakers in both religious communities were most interested in inculcating Christian behavioral values into their flock. Of the whole corpus of Augustine's sermons, two-thirds (or more) were primarily directed to various kinds of biblical exegesis that would be shared by most preachers in Africa, Catholic or not. A similar proportion of his sermons – again, if not more, since both categories overlap – were directed primarily to various kinds of moral or behavioral instruction of his flock in matters of Christian life.[114] Only on the basis of this huge mountain of normative ordinariness did the preacher essay individual points of reference or longer forays that were pointed attacks on specifically designated enemies of the church. His listeners were the more disposed to accept them for the very fact that they were embedded in a huge ocean of ordinary Christian stories and values whose status and worth were beyond immediate dispute or doubt.

Preaching was central to encouraging and inciting all kinds of behavior, good and bad. Whether the purpose was to instill new pastoral values in believers or to prod them to action, it was hard work that required repetition and persistence. Where parishioners were hesitant to take violent action (probably in most cases), the preacher's role was crucial. The connection can perhaps be best observed in the island community of Minorca, with its longstanding connections with Carthage and Africa. Here, from his western perch in the town of Iamo, the bishop Severus preached against the hated community of Jews who lived around the city of Mago, on the other side of the island. In the first week of February 418, the Christians of Iamo made the thirty-mile march across the whole island to attack the Jewish synagogue and to burn it to the ground. Severus presents their actions as the result of a sudden "fiery desire" that had somehow overtaken them after the arrival of the relics of the protomartyr Stephen, delivered to the island by the Spanish priest Orosius, in mid-summer or autumn of 417. But

---

[114] Both are estimates of a very general order made on very general principles by the author; both are probably underestimates.

close inspection of the chronology shows that the assault was not a sudden response to the martyr's presence. It had been prepared by at least a year or more of preaching by Severus on the matter.[115] The bishop's preaching might well have drawn on a long and traditional standard language of invective, laced with vile and hateful images of poisonous and dangerous animals to which the Jews were compared (for example), but it was no less effective for all that.[116] The result was not only the burning the synagogue, but the forced conversion of the island's Jewish population. The preaching therefore had a real effect, which was recorded by the proud bishop in an encyclical letter. The letter was then recycled and turned back into oral communication in a sermon delivered by the Catholic bishop Evodius to his congregation at Uzalis in Africa around the year 420.[117] The letter of the bishop Severus on the anti-Jewish actions of his parishioners, when read aloud to Evodius' flock, was greeted with cheers and applause. Were they not ready to do the same?

The point, therefore, was to derogate from the humanity of "them," of one's sectarian enemies, in such a way that doing harsh things to them – like burning their basilica (or synagogue) or compelling their conversion – would be seen to be doing a good thing. In a long sermon that attacked "the Donatists" as heretics, the preacher urges his flock to love one another just as they love the parts of their own body. But what if something goes wrong with a part of your body?[118]

Donatus . . . couldn't keep his body healthy because he didn't have charity. Those people became so rotten with disease that they simply had to be cut off. As for them saying that they have some limbs of their own, well they're nothing but maggots in a rotting body. The maggots have been cut off. They're incapable of

---

[115] Bradbury, *Severus of Minorca*, pp. 23–25, who sees the chronological problem, and the logical consequences. In my view, the length of the antecedent preaching demonstrates the depth of Severus' commitment to achieving this result (and not much this way or that about the state of mind of his parishioners). For a somewhat happier view, see Fredriksen, *Augustine and the Jews*, pp. 359–60.

[116] For a sample of some the rhetoric, see ch. 6, pp. 293–94, 304 above.

[117] Evodius, *De miraculis sancti Stephani*, 2 (PL 41: 835): "manuum suarum acclamantibus et exsultantibus fidelibus ipse dicere videretur." The incident is reported in a text composed, perhaps, *c.* 424–25, but referring to an earlier sermon that was delivered, surely, not long after the events on Minorca – therefore, *c.* 419; cf. Fredriksen, *Augustine and the Jews*, pp. 361–62, on the Augustinian background. Since five of the seven important manuscripts containing the *Epistula Severi* also contain the *De miraculis sancti Stephani*, one has to suspect that it is mainly through the African connection that the text of Severus' encyclical letter was preserved: see Bradbury, *Severus of Minorca*, pp. 74–76.

[118] Aug. *Sermo* 162A.7 = Denis 19 (MiAg 1: 104): "Donatus . . . tenere non potuit sanitatem, quia non habuit caritatem. Denique ita isti putrefacti sunt, ut necessario praeciderentur; et quod se habere aliquos dicunt, vermes putredinis sunt: praecisi vermes sunt, nec sanitatem possunt admittere. Etenim tandiu membrum admittit sanitatem, quandiu est de corpore non praecisum."

being healthy. A limb can be healthy only as long as it is not cut off from a healthy body.

The metaphor of the surgical removal of bad body parts so that what remained might be healthy was a rather anodyne way of describing doctrinal separation and then punishment and elimination of heretical or dissident belief and behavior. On the other hand, there is no doubt that to some listeners such words encouraged the use of real knives. After all, "they" were only maggots. A long polemical sermon by a dissident preacher sets the boundaries of hatred in a deep historical record for his listeners. They are holy narratives into which he sets his own people. First, the story of Cain and Abel. One brother kills another. Cain – understand the Catholics – is persuaded by Satan. Only Abel – understand the dissidents – persists in his purity. He is the innocent man, the *gloriosus sacerdos*. He is the victim, the sacrifice, the holocaust. Then the story of Jacob and Esau. Esau is simply waiting for the death of his father in order to kill his own brother. These fratricidal narratives prompt the preacher to quote the gospel of John (15: 20): "As they have persecuted me, so they will persecute you." But then, how were the persecuted – obviously his own congregation – supposed to act? So he continues with his pedagogy of hatred:[119]

No one accepts the friend of his enemy into his own friendship. No one would wish that his own friend should have enemies. No one adopts the adversary of his brother as his own friend – unless, driven by an envious rivalry, he would want to violate the basic rules of brotherhood. A slave never befriends the enemies of his master, unless he has been punished with unusual savagery by his owner . . . These are the reasons why you must hate your enemy if you wish to be pleasing to your Lord. Otherwise, if you love His enemy, then, along with that man you will pay the penalty on the final Day of Judgment.

That is to say, the canons of loyalty and betrayal trump the virtues of love and forgiveness. And given how powerful the same preachers had made these latter, the importance of harming the enemy was commensurately greater. There was therefore a huge dialogue of peace, love, conciliation, and forgiveness; but the polemical forays were made from the midst of these virtues: attacks on pagans, heretics, Jews, Manichees, Arians, Pelagians,

---

[119] Anon. *Sermo Escorial.* 46 (PLS 4: 728–29): "Inimici sui amicum nemo in amicitias sumit, nec qui amico inimicos esse voluerit. Nemo adversarium fratri, familiarem sibi arrogat, nisi qui germanitatis iura violare aemulo livore desideret. Hostes domini sui servus nunquam famulatur, nisi a domino atrocissima severitate vexetur . . . Quare aut oderis inimicum necesse est, si domini tui volueris esse charissimus: aut si eius amaveris inimicum, cum eodem in die iudicii mulctaberis."

and others.[120] So, too, there were Catholic sermons in which attacks were directed against "the Donatists." Not surprisingly, in Augustine they out-number all of his other attack sermons.[121] If always couched in a language of love, the sermons were still an education in hostility. The aggressive language and pacing replicated the general context in which the violence itself happened: long periods of peace and boredom, punctuated by sudden and vigorous action. The modulation was largely in the hands of preachers who, in their role as writers of polemical tracts and refutation, could choose to ratchet up or tone down the power of the rhetoric.[122]

A fundamental appeal, on both sides, was to tradition and authority, and none was greater than the example of Cyprian.[123]

What a full sack of plunder! On what results of the hunt, on what a great booty Godless Babylon would have feasted, if the bishop Cyprian, the teacher of the peoples of the world, the smasher of idols, the unmasker of demons, the one who even benefitted pagans and who strengthened Christians, the man who fired the zeal of the martyrs – if the Lord had been denied by such a man, how Godless Babylon would have rejoiced at its kill ... Let them rage, persecute, torture, imprison, shackle, beat, burn, and throw us to the wild beasts: Christ was not denied, the confessor of the Lord was crowned. They lost their savagery. The martyrs found glory.

The towering figure of the martyr-bishop Cyprian was exploited by both sides to assess the validity of martyrdom and the legitimacy of the "others" in the context of self-destruction.[124]

If the heretics and the Donatists, who falsely boast that they belong to Cyprian, paid attention to his record as bishop, they wouldn't separate themselves [i.e. from

---

[120] Again, on my count, there is good evidence for the dominant use of these themes in the following very approximate quantities: anti-pagan (*c.* 65), anti-heretical (*c.* 55), anti-Manichaean (*c.* 25), anti-Arian (*c.* 25), anti-Jewish (*c.* 225), anti-Pelagian (*c.* 20).

[121] On my general estimate, about 100 sermons have this as one of their dominant themes; this is the same order of estimate arrived at by Monceaux, *Hist. litt.* 7, p. 150.

[122] As in comparable situations; see, e.g., Diefendorf, *Beneath the Cross*, p. 105: "The radicalization of Catholic and Huguenot polemics during the first decade of the Religious Wars effected both quantitative and qualitative changes in the willingness of people to act upon their murderous impulses. Popular poetry and placards urged Catholic Parisians to envision violent solutions to their religious quarrels: 'cut them down ... burn them, ... kill them without a qualm.' The unimaginable was first put into words and then acted out ... Catholic preachers in Paris, rather than using their moral authority to quell the tensions caused by religious differences, actually encouraged recourse to violence by describing the extermination of heresy as a necessary purging of the social body."

[123] Aug. *Sermo* 313B.2 = Denis 15.2 (MiAg 1: 72). Note the attacking language: "Saevierint, persecuti fuerint, torserint, incluserint, alligaverint, percusserint, incenderint, bestiis subrexerint: non est Christus negatus, confessor Domini est coronatus. Illi saevitiam perdiderunt, gloriam martyres invenerunt."

[124] Aug. *Sermo* 313E.2 and 5–7 = Guelferbytanus 28 (MiAg 1: 536–37, 539–42).

the Catholic Church]. If they paid attention to his martyrdom, they wouldn't throw themselves off heights. The heretic who is separating himself in heresy or the Donatist who is deliberately jumping to his death is certainly not any disciple of Christ, not any friend of Cyprian . . . I have made these remarks about keeping the peace because of the heretics, who have separated themselves from the Catholic Church and who keep on separating themselves from it every day, and who falsely call themselves Catholics . . . But the Donatists aren't just false Christians, they're not Christians at all . . . "Throw yourself off this height," the Devil said [sc. to Jesus] . . . This is what the Devil is also suggesting to the Donatists, saying "Throw yourselves off, the angels are there to catch you. With this death you won't go to punishment, you'll go to win a crown." They would be Christians if they listened to Christ and didn't believe the Devil. It was he who first separated them from the peace of the Church and later gave them the cliff-jumpers . . . If they had a healthy heart, they would recoil from throwing themselves off cliffs and they wouldn't commit murder [i.e. of themselves]. But this is exactly what they do, what their father the Devil has taught them, and what their teacher Donatus has instructed them to do. Quite unlike this, the blessed Cyprian courageously defended unity and peace.

Being told what to do, even if it is suggested by a figure of authority and in a highly entertaining mode, was one thing. Doing it yourself was quite another. If the preacher's favorite source materials were the Psalms, it was for a good reason. These song and near-song materials were a huge middle ground between the preacher and his audience, and they were filled with violence and retribution as well as kindness and love. When the goal is not as much to understand the preacher's intent as it is to know what his audience heard and understood, and consequently how they behaved, the point of focus shifts. It is what the latter did collectively that mattered. If the preacher crafted an oral presentation that connected with his listeners in whatever popular mode, he was nevertheless always translating his own education into terms that he thought that his listeners would understand and would make them more prone to accept his message. The greatest numbers of his parishioners lived in a world of more persistent oral communication in which the essence of the strongest-felt sentiments and values was summed up in strongly syncopated voices: rhythms, shouts, songs, and chants.

CHAPTER 10

Sing a new song

People who separate themselves from the community
of the holy are not singing a new song.
They are following the music of old hatreds,
not the new music of charity. What is the music
of this new charity? It is peace.[1]

(Augustine)

It is forbidden to kill. Therefore every killer is
punished, *unless* he kills as part of a large crowd
and to the sound of trumpets. That's the rule.[2]

(Voltaire)

Ritual chanting, singing, rhythmic shouting, metrical voices accompanied by bodily gestures like clapping and dancing involved members of
Christian congregations in common ritual practices.[3] These types of bodily participation were also an important part of traditional non-Christian
sacred ritual and ceremony in Africa. One such performance had imprinted
itself vividly on Augustine's memory. As a young man at Carthage he
had heard the chanting and singing of songs at a festival for the goddess

---

[1] Aug. *En. in Ps.* 149.1–2 (CCL 40: 2178): "Quisquis se a coniunctione sanctorum separat, non cantat canticum novum. Secutus est enim veterem animositatem, non novam caritatem. In nova caritate quid est? Pax."

[2] Voltaire, "Droit," in *Questions sur l'Encyclopédie*, Paris, 1770–74 = *Dictionnaire philosophique, 2: Oeuvres complètes de Voltaire*, vol. 18, Paris, Garnier, 1878, p. 425: "Il est défendu de tuer; tout meurtrier est puni, à moins qu'il n'ait tué en grande compagnie, et au son des trompettes; c'est la règle."

[3] The title is derived from Optatus, *Contra Parm.* 2.1.9 (SC 412: 240), who is quoting Ps. 95: 1, which is, in turn, quoted by Aug. *Contra litt. Petil.* 2.47.110 (CSEL 52: 83); and *Contra Gaud.* 1.20.22 (CSEL 53: 219) in condemning the dissidents: "Cantate domino canticum novem, cantate domino omnis terra." Cf. Aug. *Ep.* 142.2 (CSEL 44: 248) and 237.8 (CSEL 57: 8); *En. in Ps.* 97.1 (CCL 39: 1372); and, at length, in *En. in Ps.* 149.1 (CCL 140: 2178). Of course, all of this echoes the threatening coming of the apocalypse: *Revelation*, 5: 9; the actions analyzed here fall under the category of "incorporating practices" that function to reinforce, form, and create social coherence, see Connerton, "Bodily Practices," ch. 3 in *How Societies Remember*, pp. 72, 79–83, where gestures represent an analogue to the movements discussed here; for the Roman analogues, see Horsfall (2003).

Berecynthia – the Mother of Everything – songs that he later castigated as grossly obscene, even if quite effective.[4] Among African Christians it was the same. They knew that song had the power to transform hearts and minds.[5] Their leaders, the bishops, knew from their own personal experiences how much song mobilized emotions by appealing to what they called "pleasure," or *voluptas*, and that singing did this so strongly that they feared its effects, knew its dangers, and were aware of the subversive threats that it posed, especially to the minds of "the weak." They wished, if possible, to ban singing and chanting from the church.[6] But they knew that this was not possible. They knew that this power would have to be managed and controlled.

The unifying and mobilizing drive of chants and songs suggested their utility in sustaining crowd actions, sometimes violent ones.[7] The use of rhythmic repetition and exhortations repeated in unison produces group unity and energy.[8] To understand some of the effects, we might begin by retelling the model horror story of the savage beating inflicted on the Catholic bishop Maximianus of Bagaï, a small town in southern Numidia, around the year 403.[9] One day, as Maximianus stood at the altar in his basilica, sectarian enemies rushed at him with what is described as "a terrifying force and a furious cruelty." His assailants repeatedly struck him with clubs and other makeshift weapons, including jagged pieces of wood that they had broken off the altar when they smashed it to pieces over his head. The terrified bishop had taken refuge underneath it. Getting to

---

[4] Aug. *Civ. Dei*, 2.4 (CCL 47: 37): "et Berecynthiae matri omnium, ante cuius lecticam die sollemni lavationis eius talia per publicum cantitabantur a nequissimis scaenicis."

[5] Anon. *In Festo Translationis Reliquariarum SS. Martyrum = Sermo Mai*, 47: 3 (PLS 2: 1151): "Hoc autem a Christianis longe abesse debet, quia omnis qui ad ecclesiam Catholicam venit, novum se canticum cantaturum . . . Cum enim gentilis fuerit, ut Christianus fiat, sicut mutatur vocabulo, sic debet mente mutari."

[6] See Aug. *Confess.* 10.33.49 (CCL 27: 149), a powerful analysis of the effects of songs and chants on the human mind that deserves far more attention than I can give it here; it was written, notably, some years after the composition of his pop song. It is suffused with Platonic fears about corrupting effects of music and poetry. See Pizzani (2003) and (2007), pp. 27–29, and Richter (2009), pp. 119–20, both of whom draw attention to the significance of this passage.

[7] For but one recent example among the very many that could be offered, consider the case of Simon Bikindi, the renowned Rwandan singer who was put on trial by the International Criminal Tribunal for Rwanda, accused of writing lyrics that were used to incite killings in the 1994 genocide. He was sentenced to fifteen years in prison for composing songs that fueled contempt of the Tutsi and incited Hutus to kill Tutsis. Three songs of his were cited as ones sung by Hutu mobs as they murdered their ethnic enemies (*The New York Times*, Tuesday, 19 September, 2008, p. A8; ibid., Wednesday, December 3, 2008, p. A12).

[8] Collins, *Violence*, pp. 409–12, analyzing the United Airlines Flight 93 case, and noting how "conflict talk is highly repetitive," i.e. analyzing precisely how it is used in order to overcome the impediment to direct violence that is at the center of his model.

[9] This is one of the model "horror stories" that became part of a dossier of violence that was deployed for political purposes; as such, it will be discussed in detail later (see ch. 11, pp. 527–29).

him, one of the attackers stabbed the bishop in the groin with a dagger, presumably cutting a femoral artery since he began to bleed profusely.

Maximianus' life was saved by a fortuitous accident. As his attackers dragged his body along the dusty road outside the basilica, the dirt from the ground clogged the bleeding artery and stopped the outpouring of blood that had brought him to the point of death. When his attackers relented a little, men from Maximianus' side, his Catholic partisans, counterattacked. Grabbing and pulling at the bishop's body, they succeeded in tearing him away from the grasp of his assailants. The attempt to carry Maximianus to safety was done to the accompaniment of the singing of songs by the Catholics who had rushed to their bishop's defense. These actions, especially the singing, provoked a renewed outburst of rage on the part of the original attackers who returned to the fight, violently pulling Maximianus out of the hands of those who were trying to rescue him.[10] What songs were the Catholics singing in the midst of this violent scene? Were they biblical psalms, well known from liturgical readings and from sermons? Or were they singing another kind of song, a hymn for example? And why in the middle of this violent mêlée, providing, as it were, a soundtrack for their rage?

To mobilize attitudes and sentiments, to guide the opinions and actions of large numbers of ordinary people requires forms of communication other than the written letter, a pastoral tract, or even the living message of a sermon. In a polemical sermon delivered in the basilica of one of his great enemies, the dissident bishop Emeritus, in September 418, Augustine claimed that the Church itself was speaking through his mouth in the words of the Psalmist: "I shall persecute my enemies and I shall seize them, and I shall not turn back until they are utterly defeated."[11] Those who heard his words were roused to action. Like an aggressive and fiery sermon, militant song, often modeled on Psalms like this one, could mobilize men for an attack.[12] Some involvement of the body in rhythm, in movement as well as in thought is helpful, and some participation that connected all the members of a congregation in a common act is important. The church

---

[10] Aug. *Ep.* 185.27 (CSEL 57: 26): "Deinde cum ab eis tandem relictum nostri cum psalmis auferre temptarent, illi ira ardentiore succensi eum de portantium manibus abstulerunt male mulcatis fugatisque Catholicis."

[11] Aug. *Sermo ad Caes.* 8 (CSEL 53: 177): quoting Psalm 18: 37: *Persequar inimicos meos et comprehendam illos, et non convertar donec deficiant.* (VG: same text); having already quoted Psalm 100:5 (VG 101:5), with much the same intent.

[12] For a comparison, see Pettegrew, "Militant in Song," ch. 3 in *Culture of Persuasion*, at p. 60: "gangs of Protestants rampaged among the stalls, singing psalms and overturning the wares of Catholic vendors. Iconoclastic attacks on churches and wayside shrines would invariably be accompanied by boisterous singing."

in Africa was hardly alone or the first in this use of song and chant in sectarian conflict. Even so, the singing of hymns was a recent revolution in the Latin-speaking churches of the West, much newer than the sermon.[13] It was precisely in the decades of the late fourth and early fifth centuries when the practice arrived. Novelty added to power.

In the churches of the eastern Mediterranean in the 360s, the mobilization of people by means of hymns had assumed renewed force in the context of Ephraem's polemical attacks on the followers of Bardaisan and Mani.[14] The response made sense, since it was Bardaisan himself who reputedly first developed the medium of sacred songs to battle his sectarian enemies.[15] If the songs excited common dislikes in a popular mode, they were still elite productions. Ephraem wrote them after having observed the success that the songs and rhythmic compositions of his enemies had in mobilizing their supporters. He set himself to learning the rhythms and imitating the form. The utility and apparent success of the songs is suggested by the large numbers that Ephraem composed: the texts of well over four hundred have survived, a number that is probably well below the total that he created. These eastern origins are often noted, but another important one is often not: the centrality of hymn singing to Manichaean devotions, as is manifest from Ephraem's response to the songs already being sung by the followers of Mani.[16] Augustine makes repeated reference to the core place of hymn singing in his religious life as a Manichee. Importantly, he recalled that he could remember the words by heart precisely because he had sung them in songs.[17] The large numbers should also be noted. Like sermons, songs were mass produced for mass consumption.[18] There does not exist any exact record of the numbers composed in our period, but comparison with other ages suggests the possibility of the truly great numbers

---

[13] It was an innovation reaching the western churches in the late 380s and early 390s from the East: Fontaine (1985), p. 161, cf. Richter (2009), p. 117.

[14] T. J. Lamy, ed., *Historia sancti Ephraemi*, 31–32 in *Sancti Ephraemi Syri Hymni et Sermones*, vol. 2 (Machliniae, 1886), pp. 5–90, at pp. 63–70; cf. Sozomen, *Historia Ecclesiastica*, 3.16.7 (GCS 50: 129); see Lieu, *Manichaeism in the Later Roman Empire*, p. 133.

[15] Ephraem refers to about 150 of these songs, suggesting a larger-scale production of them; see Griffith (1986) on the cultural background.

[16] BeDuhn, *Augustine's Manichaean Dilemma*, 1, pp. 57–58.

[17] Aug. *Contra Faust.* 13.18, 15.5–6 (CSEL 25.1: 400, 425–26); *Confess.* 3.7.14, 10.33.49 (CCL 27: 34, 181).

[18] Brown, *Singing the Gospel*, p. 14: "the sheer volume of sixteenth-century hymnal printing provides very strong indirect evidence of the popular diffusion and use of the Lutheran hymns." Brown then demonstrates the significant effects that hymns had for the creation of a new Christian identity and for resistance to opposing religious ideas. Again, it is the scale of the production of the new songs that is evident: Pettegree, *Culture of Persuasion*, pp. 45–46, 58–59. There was no print revolution in the fourth and fifth centuries, but the principles of a mass-communicated medium still apply.

that could be achieved.[19] The total of individual sermons perhaps absolutely outnumbered those of individual songs, but because of repetition and mimicry, songs no doubt involved the participation of much greater numbers.

The hymns sung in church, the Psalms that were chanted or sung as a regular part of the liturgy, were an important part of this engagement. The songs were one of the main repetitive actions that large numbers of ordinary parishioners had in common with their clergy. Singing and chanting were sometimes supplemented by bodily movements, like the hard thumping of the breast with open hands or clenched fists during stirring moments of a sermon, for example, to signify sympathy or contrition. As a preacher, Augustine noted the verve with which a congregation (on one occasion in his home town of Thagaste) engaged in the singing of the psalms.[20] But singing was everywhere used to mobilize emotions and not only in churches. Travelers sang songs in unison to ward off their fears as they moved through a potentially threatening countryside, especially in the ominous dark of night.[21] There is little reason to doubt that Christian songs, once popularized, were sung throughout the same range of venues found in later ages: in private houses, workshops, marketplaces, streets and fields, and even in bathhouses.[22] As with the clutch of fearful travelers, the suggestion is that the singing was frequently done in groups.

Songs were also part of an improvised oral world of abuse and aggression. Ritually chanted insults called *convicia* were the heart of inflicting verbal injury among non-Christians. But they were also powerful verbal weapons adapted by Christians for their attacks on each other.[23] Verbal insults had become the stock-in-trade of polemical assaults by one side on the other, embedded, in their most powerful oral form, in the sermons preached in

---

[19] Brown, *Singing the Gospel*, p. 5, indicates the volume: 2,000 hymn editions, and more than 2,000,000 hymn books and song sheets in circulation in sixteenth-century German-speaking lands. England of the Methodist revival was no different. Charles Wesley alone published more than 4,400 hymns in his lifetime and left more than 2,800 in manuscript: a total on the order of 6,000–7,000 authored by him alone: Rattenbury, *Charles Wesley's Hymns*, pp. 19–20.

[20] Aug. *En. 1 in Ps.* 34.1 (CCL 38: 299–300).   [21] Aug. *En. in Ps.* 66.5–6 (CCL 39: 862–63).

[22] The list of places is for Luther's hymns in sixteenth-century German lands: Pettegree, *Culture of Persuasion*, p. 52; compare Licentius' singing of songs in the outhouse at Cassiciacum: see p. 477 below.

[23] On the use of *convicia* or ritual insults, see, for example, J.-P. Cèbe, *La caricature et la parodie dans le monde romain antique des origines à Juvénal*, Paris, de Boccard, 1966, pp. 157–69; A. Richlin, *The Garden of Priapus: Sexuality and Aggression in Roman Humor*, rev. ed., New York and Oxford University Press, 1992, p. 87 f.; for their purpose in forensic confrontations, see J. M. Kelly, "The Underlying Sanctions of Roman Litigation," ch. 1 in *Roman Litigation*, Oxford, Clarendon Press, 1966, pp. 1–30, at pp. 22–26.

both churches.[24] Whether sung or chanted, the impulses and the materials were already in the popular repertoire.

When by chance it is necessary for a slave of God [that is, a Christian] to reprove drunkenness and debauchery on some rural farm or in a village where God's word has not yet been heard, it's not enough for those being reproved to continue their singing. More than that, they'll begin to invent new songs on the spot, attacking the very Christian who was trying to prevent their singing.[25]

The songs incited bad behavior. Bad boys sang what they wished and they knew full well what they were singing: filthy songs. The dirtier the better and the more they were enjoyed.[26] But the practice went deeper than boisterous singing and chanting at local bars. Ritual insults were part of a traditional world of song and chants, like those used in hard harvest labor.[27] They welled up out of the rhythms of daily work: the "strange rhythmic chant of the laborers in the field."[28]

Understand that you aren't able to express in words what is sung in your heart. It's the same for those men who sing, whether in the harvest or the vintage, or in any other kind of work. They begin their rejoicing with the words of songs, but soon, as if filled with such a great happiness that they are not able to express it in words, they abandon the syllables of actual words and simply sing and shout with sounds that express their joy.

Naturally, songs learned in the theater or other such venues, even unseemly ones, made their way laterally into Christian celebrations, as in the singing and dancing that accompanied the celebrations on the anniversary of Cyprian's martyrdom, every September in Carthage.[29] In trying to discipline Christians at Carthage for the riotous misbehavior in the basilica on the previous day, a critic could remember the bad old days in the humble neighborhood of Mappalia in Carthage when "the noise of disgusting

---

[24] Optatus, *Contra Parm.* 4.5.2 (SC 413: 90): "Nullus vestrum est qui non convicia nostra suis tractatibus misceat, qui non aut aliud initiet aut aliud explicet."

[25] Aug. *En. 1 in Ps.* 68.16 (CCL 39: 914).

[26] Aug. *En. 2 in Ps.* 18.2 (CCL 39: 106); Brown, *Augustine of Hippo*, p. 135; for the salacious songs learned in the theater, see *Sermo* 153.10 (PL 39: 830).

[27] Brown, *Augustine of Hippo*, p. 23.

[28] Aug. *En. 2 in Ps.* 32.1.8 (CCL 38: 253–54): "Intellegere, verbis explicare non posse quod canitur corde. Etenim illi qui cantant, sive in messe, sive in vinea, sive in aliquo opere ferventi, cum coeperint in verbis canticorum exsultare laetitia, veluti impleti tanta laetitia, ut eam verbis explicare non possint, avertunt se a syllabis verborum, et eunt in sonum iubilationis." Cf. Aug. *En. in Ps.* 99.4 (CCL 39: 1394) for another version of the same observations; Brown, *Augustine of Hippo*, p. 255.

[29] Aug. *Sermo* 311.5 (PL 38: 1415): "Aliquando ante annos non valde multos etiam istum locum invaserat petulantia saltatorum . . . locum, inquam, tam sanctum invaserat pestilentia et petulantia saltatorum. Per totam noctem cantabantur hic nefaria, et cantantibus saltabatur."

and sordid songs was heard" on Cyprian's *natalitia*, whereas today it is the singing of hymns that dominates.[30]

Despite obvious overlaps, there might well have been some difference between songs and chants. Distinguishing the two, even in the vocabulary of the time, is difficult.[31] Songs in the sense of psalms were more often, it seems, used in situations of consolidating solidarity in the face of threat. Martyrs facing their final end would engage in the singing of the Psalms, as much to demonstrate defiance as to console each other.[32] So the dissident men and women who were being marched to Carthage to their death in 347 sang psalms and similar songs.[33] And there were the psalms, hymns, and songs, sung by the dissidents celebrating their martyred dead at Carthage in the same year.[34] The distinctions were made and did matter. Chanting was often more aggressive, fueling impending purposeful communal action. Singing or chanting by large numbers, however, suggests the presence of hierarchy and leadership: someone leads and others follow.[35]

Chanting could be also be mobilized to confirm and to express approbation for a course of action. The election of a municipal town official or the announcement of a public course of action mobilized these public demonstrations of collective assent.[36] In fourth-century Lepcis Magna, local municipal decrees were passed into force amidst the loud rhythmic shouts of assent that joined the members of the town council and the ordinary citizens in a collective reverie.[37] Both kinds of loud callings – the

---

[30] Aug. *Sermo* 359B.23 = Dolbeau 2/Mainz 5 (Dolbeau, *Vingt-six sermons*, p. 344).

[31] See Richter (2009) for a useful discussion of the principal terms: *canere, cantare, carmen, dicere, hymnus,* and *psallere.* The argument for real differences between them seems, on balance, to be rather inconclusive.

[32] Pettegree, *Culture of Persuasion,* p. 60: "Psalm singing became the defining activity of the Protestant insurgency . . . condemned evangelicals walked to their execution with the psalms on their lips. The crowd often responded in an embarrassing gesture of solidarity . . . authorities were discomforted: their response was to order that those condemned to die should have their tongues cut out to prevent such communal acts of defiance."

[33] *Passio sanctorum Dativi, Saturnini et aliorum,* 3 (Maier, *Dossier,* 1, no. 4, p. 64): "ac laeti per totum iter hymnos Domini canticaque psallebant."

[34] *Passio sanctorum Maximi et Isaac,* 12 (Mandstandrea, 1995: 84): "Illic tota die cum nocte populi triumphantes psalmos hymnos cantica in testimonium cunctis gloriae Domini decantabant, et omnis aetas et sexus interesse tantis gratulationibus ardenti cupiditate gaudebat."

[35] Aug. *En. in Ps.* 87.1 (CCL 39: 1207–08). There was even a technical parlance: the *precentor* led off and the *succentor* or *succentores* chimed in, following or echoing his lead.

[36] In what follows, note the terms "dignus" and "meritus" from municipal elections: see the electoral graffiti and wall paintings from Pompeii, some of which are referred to by Roueché (1984), p. 183 n. 21.

[37] IRT 131 (Lepcis Magna), amongst a series of such inscriptions, noted by Lepelley, *Cités de l'Afrique romaine,* 1, pp. 148–49, on popular acclamations: dated to 350–60: "ordo . . . cum populo . . . decretis et suffragiis concinnentibus conlocavit."

organized actions of claque-like groups and the more spontaneous vocal-
izations of popular responses – could easily feed on each other. As the
apostle Paul's account of the behavior of hostile silverworkers at Ephesus
in the early 60s shows, chants that were already well known from existing
venues – in this case, a chant that was used to praise Artemis, the patron
deity of the city – could be redeployed in public without much conscious
management. Paul says that at first the anti-Christian chants were disorganized. Only gradually did they coalesce into a unified shout.[38] The chant
GREAT IS ARTEMIS OF THE EPHESIANS! was already well known.
It could easily be exploited to excite a mob and to unite a dispersed crowd.

The practice of chanting was not just a raucous plebeian one. Its ubiquity
was what made it so powerful in communicating sentiment. It was found
from top to bottom in all social ranks. At Carthage, the provincial capital
of the proconsular province, the people would assemble to hear the roll-call
of the tax collectors' names and would chant their approval or disapproval
as each name was read aloud.[39] The bishop Quodvultdeus of Carthage
reports an even more striking occasion where the people, gathered in
the forum of the metropolis to hear the reading of the names of previous
proconsular governors. They chanted their acclamations of the good ones –
in their view, of course – and hissed and whistled at the names of the bad
and unacceptable ones. It was a popular ratification of right and wrong.[40]
It also required a popular historical memory of who had been good and
who bad. The same behavior linked rulers and ruled in local municipal
venues. In a particularly tense situation in Carthage in June 401, Augustine
was called upon to defend the "pagan" money manager Faustinus as a
new convert to the Christian community at Carthage. The parishioners
were very suspicious of his motives and ambitions and so began chanting:
NO PAGAN AMONG OUR LEADERS! NO PAGAN AT OUR HEAD!
NO PAGAN AMONG OUR LEADERS! NO PAGAN AT OUR HEAD!

---

[38] *Acts*, 19: 23–41; for comments see Roueché (1984), p. 181, citing Louis Robert in *CRAI* (1982),
pp. 55–57.

[39] CTh 11.7.20 (Honorius and Theodosius to Eucharius, Proconsul of Africa), on the people's ability
to protest publicly against the appointment of specific tax collectors: "Constituto tempore publice
apud Karthaginem in secretario, admisso populo, exactorum ordinabuntur idoneae strenuaeque
personae, de quibus si popularis accusatio ulla processerit, in eorum locum alios par erit destinare,
ita ut severa indagatione, si in concussione possessorum deprehensi fuerint."

[40] Quodvultdeus, *Gloria Sanctorum*, 15 (CCL 60: 220): "In calculeis eburneis nomina proconsulum
inscripta Karthagini in foro coram populo a praesenti iudice sub certis vocabulis citabantur et
erat sollemnis diei albi citatio. Hi qui avaritiam superantes rem publicam fideliter egerant, suffragiis favoribusque etiam absentes honorabantur. Eos vero quos rapacitas vicerat, populus conviciis
sibilisque notabat." On this, and the item preceding, see Lepelley, *Cités de l'Afrique romaine*, 1,
p. 145.

With some difficulty, Augustine had gradually to persuade them to a different attitude, and with some difficulty finally managed to get them to chant instead: "FAUST-IN-US! FAUST-IN-US!"[41]

The anger of the parishioners was closely connected with the very power of expressing their public approval and disapproval that they had used, first in condemning and then in praising Faustinus. After all, these were the same people who, in this same city, chanted for or against their secular governors and tax collectors. It has been guessed, probably rightly, that Faustinus was a money manager who might also have been an *exactor* or tax collector.[42] When this rich and powerful pagan was introduced in person to them in their church as a new convert, the people were suspicious of his motives. On 23 June 401, they were only a week, or so, away from the incident of the shaving of the beard of the statue of Hercules which had mobilized this same device of violent chanting to rouse anti-Christian hostility in the city.[43] And now this. A man who would need *their* public approval as part of his appointment as a tribute-collecting agent for the state. The effrontery of the man was almost unbearable. The self-interest and ambition behind his sudden transformation into a Christian was patent. So this is the way that the body of the people, whether of a church or of a municipality, made their voice, their vote, their *suffragium* – in this case their disapproval – manifest to their leaders.

Public chanting functioned so well precisely because it was a performance that was understood by the great and the small, and that linked them. The small could look to imitate the model of the great: like the behavior of the senators who governed the Roman empire. On 25 September 233, hearing of Alexander Severus' Persian victory, the senators shouted their approval of the emperor, chanting DI TE SERVENT!...VERE PARTHICUS! VERE PERSICUS! And hailing him repeatedly as PATER NOSTER![44]

---

[41] Aug. *Sermo* 279 = Morin 1 (PL 38: 1275–80; PLS 2: 657–60) of 23 June 401; on what follows, see the important essay by Magalhães de Oliveira (2006), esp. pp. 254–60.

[42] I accept the interpretations of Lepelley, *Cités de l'Afrique romaine*, 2, pp. 41–42, and Magalhães de Oliveira (2006), pp. 259–60.

[43] For the Hercules statue incident, see ch. 5, pp. 230–31; on the probable connection of this incident with that one, see Aug. *Ep.* 279.10 = Morin 1.1 (PLS 2: 657–58; MiAg 1: 589–90), with Magalhães de Oliveira (2006), p. 259.

[44] SHA, *Vita Alex. Sev.*, 56–57, and *Vita Diadum.* 1.6–2.2. The former (56.9–10) is an acclamation by the Senate following Alexander Severus' Persian victory: "Alexander Auguste, di te servent. Persice Maxime, di te servent. Vere Parthicus. Vere Persicus...Iuveni imperatori, patri patriae, pontifici maximo...Dives senatus, dives miles, dives populus Romanus." R. Syme, *Ammianus and the Historia Augusta*, Oxford, Clarendon Press, 1968, p. 45, flatly rejects the "acta Senatus" as genuine. The latter occasion is the accession to power of Macrinus, when Diadumenianus himself was only nine years old, 11 April 217; see Peterson, *Eis Theos*, p. 143; Kantorowicz, *Laudes Regiae*, p. 17 n. 7, points out other cases.

The reports might be thought to be anachronistic, or invented, were it not for that fact that the Acts of the Arval Brethren confirm that similar rhythmic chants were used by the senators in 213.[45] Mosaics and inscriptions from Africa confirm comparable shouts of VIVA! or VIVAT! LONG LIFE! – in popular affirmations of the power of a wealthy notable.[46] The chant of EXAUDI! or HEAR US! addressed to deities was also shouted to Roman emperors, as in the chants shouted by the senators at Rome following the assassination of Commodus.[47] Here are some of their acclamations, shouts of truly bloodcurdling verbal violence.

> ASSASSIN BE DRAGGED!
> WE IMPLORE, AUGUSTUS.
> ASSASSIN BE DRAGGED!
> HEAR US, CAESAR!
> INFORMERS TO THE LION!
> HEAR US, CAESAR!...
> HEAR US, CAESAR!
> BUTCHER BE DRAGGED BY THE HOOK!
> BUTCHER OF THE SENATE
> BE DRAGGED BY THE HOOK!
> AS OUR ANCESTORS!
>
> PARRACIDA TRAHATUR!
> ROGAMUS, AUGUSTE!
> PARRACIDA TRAHATUR!
> EXAUDI CAESAR!
> DELATORES AD LEONEM!
> EXAUDI CAESAR!
> . . .
> EXAUDI CAESAR!
> CARNIFEX UNCO TRAHATUR!
> CARNIFEX SENATUS
> MORE MAIORUM
> UNCO TRAHATUR!

These are only a few lines excerpted from a lengthy series of murderous chants shouted in unison by the highly educated and refined political and

---

[45] CIL 6.2086 = ILS 451 (Acta Fratrum Arvalium); see Peterson, *Eis Theos*, pp. 143–44; and Kantorowicz, *Laudes Regiae*, pp. 66–67; cf. Klauser (1950) for general background.

[46] *CRAI* (1920), p. 270 (Timgad); ILS 8982 = de Pachtère, *Inventaire des mosaïques de l'Algérie*, p. 20 n. 77.

[47] On the *exaudi*, see Aug. *En. 1 in Ps.* 101.3 (CCL 40: 1427–28) where the *clamor meus* is meant to reach the ears of God. The source is SHA, *Vita Commod.* 18.10–11; 19.2; but see all of 18–19; cf. Dio 74.2.1–4: a series of horrific violent chants. R. Syme, *Emperors and Biography: Studies in the Historia Augusta*, Oxford, Clarendon Press, 1971, p. 117, accepts the chants as genuine, the information being derived, he thinks, from the imperial biographies of Marius Maximus.

cultural elite of the empire. To speak of any one set of elite and popular influences is misleading. In daily life, there was a constant dialectic between them, as well as between civil and ecclesiastical practices, both directed at the mobilization of important decision-making.[48]

The rhythmic shoutings need not have been orchestrated. The same people who learned chants in one venue, like the theater or the hippodrome, could easily mimic them in another, like the church. In Augustine's Hippo Regius, crowd-song had a known role in provoking pandemonium. On the First of January celebrations, the loud and disgraceful songs accompanied by much leaping about and dancing unified the crowds in actions that were sometimes riotous.[49] Church congregations indulged in the same behavior – and not surprisingly, since they were the same people singing and dancing on holidays like the First of January. The near riot that occurred in one of the great basilicas of Carthage when Augustine preached there in the early 400s is a good example. The crowd, gathered in the church for the festival of the martyr Vincentius of Tarraco, proved difficult to control. To make himself better heard above the din, Augustine had decided to preach from high in the apse rather than from the altar at ground level in the center of the basilica, as was then the custom. The people who had crowded around the altar were insulted and raised a chant to have him come down to the area where they were standing.

In the ensuing pushing and shoving, Augustine refused to budge. In a huff, he ostentatiously sat down and refused to preach. This only further infuriated the groundlings who now raised a threatening series of chants: MISSA FAC! MISSA! MISSA FAC!: GET ON WITH THE MASS! THE MASS! GET ON WITH THE MASS! The riotous behavior provoked a long and angry sermon by Augustine on obedience that he delivered on the next day.[50] In reproving the congregation, Augustine labeled the chants that fueled the sedition that he had faced on the previous day as the work of the Devil, linking the chants to the emotions of anger, hatred, and the desire to provoke. He saw the chants as calculated insults or *convicia*, a theatrical practice, and warned the congregation that they must distinguish

---

[48] Kantorowicz, *Laudes Regiae*, pp. 65–66.
[49] Aug. *Sermo* 198.1 (PL 38: 1024); and cf. *Sermo* 198.3, on the violence that occasionally erupted.
[50] Aug. *Sermo* 359B.20 = Dolbeau 5 (Dolbeau, *Vingt-six sermons*, p. 342): "Serpens ille ... coluber ille ... excitavit seditionem. Agnoscant et doleant qui ei suas linguas ad ministerium praebuerunt. Quid enim sibi volebant voces illae: 'Missa fac; missa, missa fac.'" See Brown, *Augustine of Hippo*, pp. 455–56, for further comment.

the Church of God from the world of the stage.[51] In the theater such things might be proper, but here, in the church, "God forbids us to surge forward in waves, to roar out, or to dominate."

VOICE OF THE PEOPLE, VOICE OF GOD

The warning should not be seen as a general prohibition, especially since the lordship or *dominatio* of the people had to be measured and witnessed in tense and volatile situations. The democratic power of the people was disguised or conveniently reconfigured as giving voice to the will of God. Their mortal words embodied the divine judgment of God.[52] The bishop as preacher was one voice of the divine, but the powerful collective enunciations of the people counted in the same way. This holy chanting had a long tradition in the African church, especially where the choice of God's men on earth, the shepherds of the people, were involved.[53] In the election of bishops, the chants are detailed, for example, in the account of the electoral contest to be bishop of Cirta in 305 between Donatus and Silvanus. The sides supporting each candidate were crammed into the close confines of the basilica, shouting imprecations at each other. The Elders led the chanting on behalf of Donatus, who was an "honest man" (in their view) unlike the "bad" Silvanus. A participant in the chanting reported: "I shouted along with the people. We were asking for our fellow citizen, a good man."[54] Their rhythmic shouts supported one side and condemned the other.[55]

---

[51] Aug. *Sermo* 359B.23 = Dolbeau 5 (Dolbeau, *Vingt-six sermons*, p. 344): "Tamen potentes non nobis possetis displicere, quomodo displicuistis succensentes: 'Missa fiant'... si non videtur a petitione convertite vos ad obtemperationem; in iram tamen, in convicium, in lacessionem eorum qui vobis in Christo cum tanta sollicitudine serviunt, si erumpere voluistis... Nolite, fratres, rogamus vos, obsecramus vos; discernatis ecclesiam Dei a theatris... Hic surgere, hic reboare, hic dominari avertat Deus et a cordibus vestris et a dolore nostro."

[52] Sabw Kanyang, *Episcopus et plebs*, pp. 55–59, on the *suffragium* of the people as expressing the *iudicium Dei*.

[53] MacMullen, "The Democratic Element," ch. 1 in *Voting About God*, pp. 12–23, esp. pp. 13–18, with numerous striking examples of the role of the acclamations in all kinds of decision-making assemblies of the time, from low to high.

[54] *Gesta apud Zenophilum*, 13 (CSEL 26: 192): "'Vos seniores clamabitis: Exaudi, Deus, civem nostrum volumus. Ille traditor est'... Zenophilus v. c. consularis Victori dixit: 'Clamasti ergo cum populo, quod traditor esset Silvanus et non deberet fieri episcopus?' Victor dixit: 'Clamavi et ego et populus. Nos enim civem nostrum petebamus, integrum virum.'"

[55] See the questions of the governor Zenophilus and the answers by the petitioner Nundinarius in the *Gesta apud Zenophilum*, 16 (CSEL 26: 194): "Utique veniat, de quo clamavit populus biduo post parem: 'Exaudi Deus, civem nostrum volumus.' Zenophilus v. c. consularis Nundinario dixit: 'Certe clamavit hoc populus?' Respondit: 'Clamavit.' Zenophilus v. c. consularis Saturnino dixit: 'Traditorem clamavit Silvanum?' Saturninus dixit: 'Utique.'"

HEAR US, GOD! WE WANT OUR FELLOW CITIZEN!
SILVANUS IS A TRAITOR! SILVANUS IS A TRAITOR!

EXAUDI DEUS! CIVEM NOSTRUM VOLUMUS!
SILVANUS TRADITOR! SILVANUS TRADITOR!

It was the "EXAUDI!" – the invocation to God to listen to them, to their shouting – that struck a direct connection between the chanting populace and their almighty deity.[56] As African preachers made clear, Christians took the prompt from the Psalms.[57] Their chants therefore had something sacred about them. They were not just interested celebrations but pleas for divine action.

In the critical choice of their new shepherd, the demand of the people was to be heard by their God.[58] Nearing the end of his life as bishop at Hippo, Augustine wished to avoid some of the ugliness and scandal that had marred his elevation as coadjutor bishop to the aged Valerius in the year 395. The illegalities and insider arrangements had provided rich fodder for his enemies and much embarrassment for himself. It was a bad situation to be avoided. In September 426, he nominated the priest Eraclius to be his successor. The choice had to be seen to be a popular one, wholeheartedly supported by the people of God. Their assent was made manifest by ritual chanting during the course of the public announcement. We are fortunate to have the verbatim secretarial minutes, the *acta ecclesiastica* of the meeting of the congregation held on Sunday, 26 September of that year, no doubt kept as another form of public record to confirm the choice.[59] When Augustine introduced Eraclius to the crowded church, his name was greeted by a series of loud acclamations:

THANKS TO GOD! PRAISE TO CHRIST! [repeated 23 times]
HEAR US, CHRIST! LIFE TO AUGUSTINE! [repeated 16 times]
YOU OUR FATHER! YOU OUR BISHOP! [repeated 8 times]

---

[56] Compare CIL 8.11629 and 11270 = ILTun 304 (Thelepte) for the shout of: "Exaudi Deus or[a]tionem meam. Au[ri]bus percipe ber[ba] (=verba) oris mei"; cf. Duval, *Loca Sanctorum*, I, no. 38, p. 86; and AE 1909: 118 = ILCV 1842 = Leschi, *Etudes*, p. 309 (Aïn Ghorab): "hic exaudietur omnis q(u)i invocat nomen D(omini) D(e)i omnipo[tentis]"; cf. Duval, *Loca Sanctorum*, I, no. 70, p. 152.

[57] Anon. *In Festo Translationis Reliquiarum SS. Martyrum = Sermo Mai* 47: 2 (PLS 2: 1150) where the African preacher draws attention to the fact, commenting at length on "Cantate Domino canticum novum, laus eius in ecclesia sanctorum" (Psalm. 149:1) and "Clamavi in toto corde meo: Exaudi me Domine" (Psalm. 118: 145).

[58] So in the election of a bishop in the eastern church, attacking one of the candidates: see J. P. G. Flemming, ed., *Akten der Ephesinischen Synode vom Jahre 449* (Berlin, Weidmannsche Buchhandlung, 1917), pp. 14–16; cf. Gaddis, *Religious Violence*, pp. 268–69.

[59] For all of what follows, see Aug. *Ep.* 213 (CSEL 57: 372–79).

DEO GRATIAS, CHRISTO LAUDES (xxiii)
EXAUDI CHRISTE, AUGUSTINO VITA (xvi)
TE PATREM, TE EPISCOPUM (viii)

As in the number of their shouts, the enthusiasm of the crowd diminished in a decrescendo from the initial outburst. Silence was restored. Augustine resumed speaking. He made specific reference to the formal record that was being kept of the occasion. This excited further rhythmic chanting from the people of God, the *plebs Dei*, increasing both in fervor and duration:

THANKS TO GOD! PRAISE TO CHRIST! [repeated 36 times]
HEAR US, CHRIST! LIFE TO AUGUSTINE! [repeated 13 times]
YOU OUR FATHER! YOU OUR BISHOP! [repeated 8 times]
IT IS WORTHY! IT IS JUST! [repeated 20 times]
HE'S DESERVING! HE IS WORTHY! [repeated 5 times]
IT IS WORTHY! IT IS JUST! [repeated 6 times]

DEO GRATIAS, CHRISTO LAUDES (xxxvi)
EXAUDI CHRISTE, AUGUSTINO VITA (xiii)
TE PATREM, TE EPISCOPUM (viii)
DIGNUM ET IUSTUM EST (xx)
BENE MERITUS, BENE DIGNUS (v)
DIGNUM EST, IUSTUM EST (vi)

Silence was restored once more, this time with difficulty. The fervor of the chanting was itself riling the crowd. Augustine addressed his people again, emphasizing the nature of the agreement that was being struck between him and them. His words provoked further chanting:

THANKS FOR YOUR DECISION! [repeated 16 times]
MAY IT BE! MAY IT BE! [repeated 12 times]
YOU OUR FATHER! ERACLIUS OUR BISHOP! [repeated 6 times]

IUDICIO TUO GRATIAS AGIMUS (xvi)
FIAT, FIAT (xii)
TE PATREM, ERACLIUM EPISCOPUM (vi)

Augustine then glossed the events of his own elevation to the bishop's seat, thereby trying to ensure that his own earlier appointment would be viewed in a proper historical perspective. More chanting erupted.

THANKS TO GOD! PRAISE TO CHRIST! [repeated 13 times]
DEO GRATIAS; CHRISTO LAUDES (xiii)

Augustine reminded the people, again, of the nature of the arrangement that he had made with them concerning Eraclius. His words provoked a prolonged outburst of chanting, as if the people were confirming the agreement with their intensity:

> THANKS FOR YOUR DECISION! [repeated 26 times]
> IUDICIO TUO GRATIAS AGIMUS (xxvi)

When Augustine asked the people to signal their assent to the pact by signing it, his words are greeted with an extended series of rapturous and clamorous rhythmic shouts.

> LET IT BE! LET IT BE! [repeated 25 times]
> IT'S RIGHT! IT'S JUST! [repeated 28 times]
> LET IT BE! LET IT BE! [repeated 14 times]
> LONG WORTHY! LONG DESERVING! [repeated 25 times]
> THANKS FOR YOUR DECISION! [repeated 13 times]
> HEAR US, CHRIST! PROTECT ERACLIUS! [repeated 18 times]
>
> FIAT, FIAT (xxv)
> DIGNUM ET IUSTUM EST (xxviii)
> FIAT, FIAT (xiv)
> OLIM DIGNUS, OLIM MERITUS (xxv)
> IUDICIO TUO GRATIAS AGIMUS (xiii)
> EXAUDI CHRISTE, ERACLIUM CONSERVA (xviii)

The public agreement signaled by the shouting in unison confirmed the pact between the bishop and his people. There was real power in those shouts. They energized the people and the bishop was happy, no doubt, to have the force of the unified shouts as a manifest sign of popular assent and of divine approval. The dissident church was no different. Its leaders, its bishops, were hailed by its faithful with chanting as well. "With clarion voices shouting, these words are sung aloud for Donatus":[60]

> WELL DONE! WELL DONE!
> OUR GOOD LEADER!
> OUR BRILLIANT LEADER!

But the chants were not invented on occasions such as these. The people were well educated in their own culture. Like the combatants of Caesarea, they already knew what to do. Some of the chants had been transferred to the church from municipal elections, others from the arena and the theater.

---

[60] Aug. *En. in Ps.* 69.5 (CCL 39: 935): "Apertissimis vocibus Donato dicuntur ista cantata: 'EUGE, EUGE, DUX BONE, DUX PRAECLARE.'"

The extent to which these ritual chants were orchestrated, or directed by so-called claques, has been much debated.[61] Certainly, it was a known part of popular repertoire by which a good bishop could be praised and a bad one condemned. In this way, about two decades later at Edessa in the east, an official report was issued to imperial authorities that detailed the use of popular chanting to condemn the current Nestorian bishop Ibas.[62]

> LET NO ONE ACCEPT THE NESTORIAN IBAS!
> GIVE US ANOTHER BISHOP!
> HE PILLAGES THE HOUSE OF GOD!
> LET HIM GIVE BACK TO THE CHURCH AND
> TO THE POOR WHAT HE HAS STOLEN!

The people matched these rhythmic shouts with ones that praised their own hero and choice for bishop, the holy Rabbula:

> HOLY RABBULA! HOLY RABBULA! HOLY RABBULA!

Here we find the use of the same rhythmic device. It was a Mediterranean music of social, political, and ecclesiastical condemnation and approval of actions and of men. Whatever the answer to the problem of the deliberate orchestration of the music, there was certainty among contemporaries in Africa that chants by partisans in the theater and amphitheater cued violent behavior. It was a form of popular education.[63] It is hardly surprising, then, that one of the best descriptions of customary chanting is found in the writings of a Christian bishop on basic teaching for the uneducated.[64]

---

[61] More in favor of organized responses as the norm: Cameron, *Circus Factions*, pp. 186 f., 274 f.; in some respects, Rouché (1984), pp. 186–89, 274–78, is more skeptical, for good reasons.

[62] Gaddis, *Religious Violence*, p. 269.

[63] As in the circuses and amphitheaters in general, see Hugoniot (2002b), pp. 182–83, 187–88.

[64] Aug. *De cat. rud.* 16.25.9–10 (CCL 46: 150): "Studiis autem spectaculorum fiunt daemonibus similes, clamoribus suis incitando homines, ut se invicem caedant, secumque habeant contentiosa certamina qui se non laeserunt, dum placere insano populo cupiunt: quos si animadverterint esse concordes, tunc eos oderunt et persequuntur, et tamquam collusores ut fustibus verberentur exclamant, et hanc iniquitatem facere etiam vindicem iniquitatum iudicem cogunt; si autem horrendas adversus invicem inimicitias eos exercere cognoverint (sive sintae qui appellantur, sive scenici et thymelici, sive aurigae, sive venatores, quos miseros non solum homines cum hominibus, sed etiam homines cum bestiis in certamen pugnamque committunt) quo maiore adversus invicem discordia furere senserint, eo magis amant et delectantur, et incitatis favent et faventes incitant, plus adversus se ipsos insanientes ipsi spectatores alter pro altero, quam illi quorum insaniam insani provocant, et insaniendo spectare desiderant. Quomodo ergo sanitatem pacis tenere animus potest, qui discordiis et certaminibus pascitur? Qualis enim cibus sumitur, talis valetudo consequitur"; almost the same verbiage is used by him in *En. in Psalm.* 149.10 (CCL 40: 2184); and *Sermo* 198.3 (PL 38: 1026): "Etenim illa daemonia delectantur *canticis* vanitatis, delectantur nugatorio spectaculo, et turpitudinibus variis theatrorum, insania circi, crudelitate amphitheatri, certaminibus animosis eorum qui pro pestilentibus hominibus lites et contentiones usque ad inimicitias suscipiunt, pro mimo, pro histrione, pro pantomimo, pro auriga, pro venatore." The whole of which is presented as a seduction of their spirit and their soul.

In their furious zeal for spectacles these men become like demons. By their chanting, they incite men to slaughter each other and to hurl themselves into enraged fights. Even if the men themselves have not been harmed, they do this as long as they wish to please the demented crowd. And if the people notice that the fighters are colluding, they hate them and harass them. On the grounds that the men are agreeing to fake the fight, the crowd cries out that they should be beaten with clubs. They even urge the referee, who is supposed to correct unfairness, to this contorted view of theirs. They know when men have vented terrible hatreds against each other, whether these are the men who are called "maulers," or actors or singers, or chariot drivers, or beast-hunters, inciting the wretched men to action, not only men against men, but also men against beasts. The more that they sense that the men are unleashing their hatreds against each other, the more they love them and are pleased with them. They incite the maddened fighters with their shouts and by their shouting they incite them. Then the spectators themselves become enraged against each other – some in favor of such and such a man, others in favor of another – more enraged than the men whose madness they provoke and whom they wish to gaze at in their own madness. How is a mind that is fed on such quarrels and fights to keep its sanity? The sort of food that one consumes produces a commensurate state of health.

The recruitment to these groups, again according to this same description, was not always from the better off.[65]

There are the sort of men who don't seek riches and who have no desire to advance to the hollow parade of offices and honors, but who just want to have fun and lie around in bars, whorehouses, theaters and to enjoy common shows that they can have for free in big cities. In this way, they either consume their own slender resources in this luxurious living and then, because of their poverty and need, they advance to robberies, breaking and entering, and even to brazen banditry. Suddenly they are filled with many great fears: those who only recently sang songs in the bars are now sleeping in the noisy din of the prison.

Through the heavy moralizing, it is possible to see the association between the raucous bonding of young males and paths that led to various kinds of collective violence. The consistent point of reference is young men, *juvenes*.[66]

I'll omit mention of those youths [i.e. among the Manichees] whom we used to see involved in riots on behalf of actors and charioteers. This alone provides no

---

[65] Aug. *De cat. Rud.* 16.25.7–8 (CCL 46. 149–50): "Sunt autem homines, qui nec divites quaerunt esse nec ad vanas honorum pompas ambiunt pervenire, sed gaudere et requiescere volunt in popinis et in fornicationibus et in theatris atque spectaculis nugacitatis, quae in magnis civitatibus gratis habent. Sed sic etiam ipsi aut consumunt per luxuriam paupertatem suam, aut ab egestate postea in furta et effracturas et aliquando etiam in latrocinia prosiliunt, et subito multis et magnis timoribus implentur; et qui in popina paulo ante cantabant, iam planctus carceris somniant."

[66] Aug. *De mor. eccl. Cath. et Manich.* 2.72 (CSEL 90: 152–53).

small indication of how they would be able to control themselves in private, since they were not able to control the desires that revealed their real character to the eyes of the Hearers, making them blush and run away.

The transfer of these chants from the public arenas or politics and entertainment to the church was to be expected because they were such a useful means of mobilizing mass opinion and of creating a public legitimacy for the choice of a particular individual to hold a governmental office or for the passing of a municipal decree. Since analogous things had to be done within the structure of the Christian church – the choosing of a man to hold a position in the ecclesiastical hierarchy or the support of a measure decreed by an ecclesiastical council – it is to be expected that similar forms of Christian popular legitimation would emerge. They would be learned more quickly and would become part of a popular repertoire more easily because they would only have to be transferred from existing spheres of public behavior and imitated from them. In these other venues, whether the Senate in Rome or the amphitheater in Carthage, the rhythmic affirmation of group solidarity was enacted to efface individual caution and fear, and so to forge bonds that would incite public bravery and daring: the courage to act with greater aggression.

THE MODEL OF MILAN

Since support and legitimation achieved by means of mass mobilization were the purpose of these chants, it is hardly surprising that their deployment was especially important where physical conflict threatened. A good case from outside Africa, but one well known to African bishops, is provided by the bitter conflicts that emerged within the church in Rome during the mid-360s.[67] The structural elements of the conflict have similarities with those found in the religious battles in Africa, raising issues of betrayal and loyalty. In Rome, it was a period of persecution, this time of Arians against orthodox Catholics. In 355, when Liberius, the bishop of Rome, and other bishops refused to support imperial orders repressing Athanasius, they were sent into exile. The exile opened an opportunity that Felix, Liberius' own archdeacon, exploited to have himself ordained bishop in the place of the absent Liberius. The role of the assembled Christian people of the city in these events was critical. It was claimed that at the time of Liberius' exile they had sworn a public oath that they would have no bishop other than

---

[67] For what follows, see the *Collectio Avellana*, *Ep.* 1.1–4, "Quae gesta sunt inter Liberium et Felicem episcopos" (CSEL 35.1: 1–2); for background, see Barnes, *Athanasius and Constantius*, pp. 117–18.

him. When the emperor Constantius returned to Rome two years later, in 357, the people made a public appeal to him, probably in May of that year, on behalf of Liberius and they were successful in gaining the emperor's assent to the bishop's return.[68] On his return from exile, Liberius was met on the road by a joyous people. The people, as a crowd, were instrumental in having his enemy Felix driven from the city. The role of an organized and supportive Christian *plebs* was powerful and decisive.

The problem for Liberius was how to respond to those clergy who had supported Felix and who had betrayed him. His policy was one of forgiveness, with an attempt to reintegrate them into the church hierarchy. It is clear that those who had remained loyal to Liberius constituted a core power group who regarded themselves as deserving of controlling affairs in the church at Rome. When Liberius died in 366, these priests along with the deacons Ursinus, Amantius, and Lupus, led the "holy people" into the Basilica Julia in order to appoint one of their number, Ursinus, as the successor to Liberius. An armed battle then emerged, for which the account of only one side survives. According to this version, Damasus, who was supported by those who had "forsworn" themselves in the earlier conflict, was able, for a price, to incite all of the "charioteers" and the "ignorant multitude." Arming them with clubs, they broke into the Basilica Julia, and there raged a battle that lasted over three days with "a great slaughter of the faithful."[69] A week later, with the help of the "forsworn men from the arena" whose services he had "purchased at a great price," Damasus seized the Lateran Basilica where he had himself ordained as bishop of Rome. He then arranged with the civil authorities, Viventius, the Praefectus Urbi, and Iulianus, the prefect of the annona, to have Ursinus sent into exile.

Once he had succeeded in this aim, Damasus employed his private muscle to bring compulsion to bear down "with clubs and fire" on those who had opposed his election. He had seven priests loyal to Ursinus seized and held under arrest in order to expel them from the city. "Ordinary people" from the other side, however, were able to free them and then without delay repaired to the Basilica of Liberius which they used as their defensive headquarters. Damasus responded by marshaling his men, not only those from the arena and the hippodrome, but also gravediggers and the minor clergy from within the church. He armed them with axes, swords,

---

[68] Barnes, *Athanasius and Constantius*, appendix 9, p. 222, for the chronology: Constantius entered Rome on 28 April 357 and remained there till the end of May.

[69] *Collectio Avellana*, *Ep.* 1.5 (CSEL 35.1: 2): "quod ubi Damasus, qui semper episcopatum ambierat, comperit, omnes quadrigarios et imperitam multitudinem pretio concitat et armatus fustibus ad basilicam Iuli perrumpit et magna fidelium caede per triduum debacchatus est."

and clubs. In the early morning of 26 October, he laid siege to the basilica. In the attack that followed, it is said that 160 or 137 men and women inside were killed and many more were wounded (and many of these later died from their wounds).[70] But the battle was not over. Three days later the people gathered together in great numbers and began chanting verses from the New Testament and from the Psalms against their so-called "master." They chanted from the gospel of Matthew (10: 28):

> DON'T FEAR THOSE WHO KILL THE BODY!
> THEY ARE NOT ABLE TO KILL THE SOUL!

And then, in a single loud voice, they chanted verses from Psalm 78:

> THE REMAINS OF YOUR SLAVES
> ARE EATEN BY THE BIRDS OF THE SKY
> THE FLESH OF YOUR SAINTS
> BY THE BEASTS OF THE EARTH!
> THEY POUR OUT THEIR BLOOD LIKE WATER
> THERE'S NO ONE TO BURY THEM!

And often, it is reported, this same Christian populace assembled at the Basilica of Liberius would shout out in unison:

> EMPEROR OF THE CHRISTIANS!
> THERE'S NOWHERE YOU CAN HIDE!
> DAMASUS HAS FOUGHT HIS FILTHY WAR
> LET THE MURDERER BE CAST
> FROM THE SEAT OF PETER!

In this way, it is said, the "voices of the people" were carried to the emperor Valentinian.

More directly relevant to Augustine's experience was the influence exerted on him by the image of the imperial-like power displayed by Ambrose, the great bishop of Milan, especially in the sectarian struggles that rent the northern imperial capital, conflicts to which Augustine himself was witness. In December 374, Ambrose had become the bishop of Milan when, as Roman governor of Liguria-Aemilia, he had brought imperial troops into the city in order to quell the violence that had broken out

---

[70] Amm. Marc. 27.3.12–13: who relates the incidents under his reportage of events in the city of Rome under the rubric of "Praefectus Urbi." When Viventius succeeds Lampadius in that post, he cannot control the *discordantis populi seditiones . . . cruentae*. He then recounts the battles of Damasus and Ursinus, telling of the deaths of 137 people in one day in the basilica of Sicinnius (the former Basilica of Liberius in the fifth region). On the different numbers, see McLynn (1992), pp. 16–19.

between the Catholic and Arian factions in the city.[71] The violence had been escalating since the death of Auxentius, the Arian bishop of the city, who had taken the position of bishop in 355 by driving out his Catholic opponent. In the mid-380s, Augustine was living in a city that replicated the structure of the dyadic religious division that he was later to confront in Africa. But intra-Christian violence was not the only place where song was being exploited to provoke sentiment and action. In the year just before the outbreak of the hostilities in which Ambrose was a central player, an anonymous Christian writer penned what has rightly been called "a vicious Christian diatribe" against a high-ranking pagan official, probably Praetextatus, the Praetorian Prefect, who died in December of 384.[72] The *Poem Against the Pagans* – the *Carmen contra paganos* – probably composed by pope Damasus immediately before his own death, is another instance of the use of verse to influence opinion, although it was still the traditional convention of classical verse and traditional anti-pagan rhetoric that were deployed.[73] The Christian innovations in hymn singing by Ambrose must therefore be seen in the context of a combative milieu in which several writers were moving to singing, recitation, and chanting to mobilize mass opinion.

To grasp Augustine's perspective, it is important to understand the events that he witnessed in Milan in the mid-380s. Sometime in the first months of 385, Ambrose, the bishop, was summoned to the imperial court to be informed that the court would require the use of one of the basilicas in Milan.[74] The court intended a meeting at which the bishop would be ordered to do his duty. The problem was that the common people of the city were mobilized on a large scale. Crowds of Catholic Christians suddenly appeared in such huge numbers that a threat to the court was manifest. When soldiers that were part of the force protecting the emperor tried to disperse the Christian demonstrators, they offered to have themselves killed.[75] The question is how were large numbers of ordinary people like

---

[71] I generally accept McLynn's reconstruction of Ambrose's sentiments and actions in this episode: *Ambrose of Milan*, pp. 1–13.

[72] See McLynn, *Ambrose of Milan*, pp. 165–66 (the quotation is his words) who accepts the identification of the target made by Cracco Ruggini, *Il paganesimo*, and Dolbeau (1981). The authorship, and therefore date, is now confirmed by Alan Cameron, "The Poem Against the Pagans," ch. 8 in *The Last Pagans of Rome*, Oxford University Press, 2011, 273–319, at pp. 305–17.

[73] Text is found in D. R. Shackleton-Bailey, ed., *Anthologia Latina*, 1.1 (1982), no. 3 (= Riese, no. 4), pp. 17–23.

[74] Ambr. *Sermo contra Auxent*. 29 = *Ep*. 75A.29 (CSEL 83.2: 101–02).

[75] Ambr. *Sermo Contra Auxent*. 29 = *Ep*. 75A.29 (CSEL 83.2: 102).

this moved? What was to direct them or to give them a sense of cohesion?[76] Although this first incident was a successful standoff for Ambrose, the next year, 386, brought a renewal of the same hostilities.[77]

The new crisis came to a head in the tense atmosphere of the Easter season. It began on Friday, 27 March, when a demand came from the court that the Basilica Nova should be made available for imperial use. In a concession, however, the imperial court relented and asked instead for the provision of the Portian Basilica. Ambrose rejected the new request in his Palm Sunday sermon, a refusal backed by a mass popular occupation of the basilica on the same day. This time, the government threatened to send in troops to barricade the church. Ambrose used the counter-threat of martyrdom: he was willing to suffer imprisonment or death rather than allow this to happen.[78] Before dawn, on Wednesday of the following week, the court sent troops to surround the basilica. In response, Ambrose conducted a service at the Old Basilica, where his remarks were greeted by repeated acclamations or rhythmic shouts that were used as a means of mobilizing the congregation: the people shouted that they should march *en masse* to the Portian Basilica to support the people barricaded inside it. It was a move that Ambrose opposed for his own tactical reasons. And hymns and psalms had their place, too. In his sermon, improvised on the spot, Ambrose reminded the people of their "fearful chanting" of the seventy-ninth Psalm.[79] One has only to recite the verses of the Psalm to get a sense of the emotional atmosphere in the basilica.[80]

O GOD, THE PAGANS HAVE INVADED YOUR HERITAGE,
THEY HAVE DESECRATED YOUR HOLY TEMPLE;
THEY HAVE REDUCED JERUSALEM TO A PILE OF RUINS,
THEY HAVE LEFT THE CORPSES OF YOUR SERVANTS
TO THE BIRDS OF THE AIR FOR FOOD,
THE FLESH OF YOUR DEVOUT FOR THE BEASTS OF THE EARTH.
THEY HAVE SHED BLOOD LIKE WATER
THROUGHOUT JERUSALEM, NOT A GRAVEDIGGER LEFT.
WE ARE NOW INSULTED BY OUR NEIGHBOURS,
BUTT AND LAUGHINGSTOCK OF ALL THOSE AROUND US.

---

[76] McLynn, *Ambrose of Milan*, p. 180: "Ambrose did not explain how the populace had 'learnt' of his appointment at the palace. It nevertheless seems highly likely that the bishop had himself a hand in organizing these reinforcements for his case ... The gradual process of mobilization must have been largely invisible [i.e., to the court]."

[77] The three critical original sources are all authored by Ambrose: *Ep.* 75, the *Sermo contra Auxentium* (*Ep.* 75A), and *Ep.* 76; see McLynn, *Ambrose of Milan*, p. 185, for some of the problems of interpretation.

[78] Ambr. *Ep.* 76.8 (CSEL 82.3: 112).   [79] Ambr. *Ep.* 76.13 and 20 (CSEL 82.3: 114–15; 119–20).

[80] Psalm 79 (Jerusalem Bible translation).

HOW MUCH LONGER WILL YOU BE ANGRY, YAHWEH?
  FOREVER?
IS YOUR JEALOUSY TO GO ON SMOULDERING LIKE A FIRE?
POUR OUT YOUR ANGER ON THE PAGANS
WHO DO NOT ACKNOWLEDGE YOU
AND ON THOSE KINGDOMS
THAT DO NOT CALL OUT YOUR NAME...

WHY SHOULD THE PAGANS ASK: 'WHERE IS THEIR GOD?'
MAY WE SOON SEE THE PAGANS LEARNING WHAT
  VENGEANCE
YOU EXACT FOR YOUR SERVANTS' BLOOD SHED HERE.
MAY THE GROANS OF THE CAPTIVE REACH YOU;
BY YOUR MIGHTY ARM RESCUE THOSE DOOMED TO DIE.

PAY BACK OUR NEIGHBORS SEVENFOLD, STRIKE THEM TO THE
  HEART
FOR THE MONSTROUS INSULT PROFFERED TO YOU, O
  LORD...[81]

The words, especially if one imagines them being shouted in unison by a large crowd, as Ambrose says, "with a fearful chanting," pack a terrible force. Behind the willingness to die or to have oneself killed, there was anger, if not rage; there was an implacable hatred for one's enemies and an almost unquenchable desire for vengeance. This martyrdom was not patient or enduring. It was violent and aggressive.

It is not accidental that a verse that they shouted aloud – "Holy faithful Master, how much longer will you wait before you pass sentence and take vengeance for our death on the inhabitants of the earth?" – was embedded in the Christian vision of the Apocalypse.[82] The threatening words of the seventy-ninth Psalm had been made part of the Apocalypse of John and in that context it assumed a new and propulsive force.[83] In singing these songs, the Christians at Milan were also surely recollecting a range of

---

[81] Revelation 6: 10 (Jerusalem Bible translation), and the note following. The point is not only that it echoed the sentiments of the Psalms, but also of many other biblical passages known to these same persons, e.g. Deut. 32.

[82] Compare the importance of "the Fifth Seal" and the following passage from the Book of Revelation (6: 9-11) to David Koresh and his followers at Waco, Texas: "And when he had opened the Fifth Seal, I saw under the altar them that were slain for the word of God and for the testimony which they held; and they cried out in a loud voice, saying 'How long, O Lord, holy and true, doest Thou not judge and avenge our blood on them that dwell on earth?'": see Shaw (2009) with citation of the relevant studies.

[83] Apoc. 6: 9-11: "Et cum aperuisset quintum sigillum vidi subtus altare animas interfectorum propter verbum Dei, et propter testimonium, quod habebant. Et clamabant voce magna, dicentes: Usquequo, Domine, sanctus et verus, non iudicas et vindicas sanguinem nostrum de iis, qui habitant in terra? Et datae sunt illis singulae stolae albae, et dictum est illis ut requiescerent tempus modicum donec compleantur conservi eorum, et fratres eorum, qui interficiendi sunt sicut et illi" (VG).

similar biblical injunctions and divine promises that joined the contents of the Psalms with the Apocalypse.[84]

> I LIFT MY HAND TO HEAVEN
> AND SWEAR: "AS I LIVE FOR EVER,
> WHEN I HAVE SHARPENED MY FLASHING SWORD,
> WHEN I HAVE SET MY HAND TO JUDGEMENT,
> THEN I WILL PUNISH MY ADVERSARIES
> AND TAKE VENGEANCE ON MY ENEMIES.
> I WILL MAKE MY ARROWS DRUNK WITH THEIR BLOOD,
> MY SWORD SHALL DEVOUR THEIR FLESH,
> BLOOD OF SLAIN AND CAPTIVES,
> THE HEADS OF ENEMY PRINCES."
> REJOICE WITH HIM, YOU HEAVENS,
> BOW DOWN, ALL YOU GODS, BEFORE HIM;
> FOR HE WILL AVENGE THE BLOOD OF HIS SONS
> AND TAKE VENGEANCE ON HIS ADVERSARIES;
> HE WILL PUNISH THOSE WHO HATE HIM...

So God Himself had declared in the second book of his laws, prefiguring the words of the seventy-ninth Psalm.

Inside the besieged basilica songs became an important unifying ritual. Augustine, as he later remembered the occasion in his *Confessions*, was much impressed:[85]

It was not long before that the church of Milan had adopted this practice, a kind of consolation and exhortation, in which our brothers, with the unified resounding of their hearts and voices, celebrated with great enthusiasm. It was only a year – certainly not much more – since Justina, the mother of the boy emperor Valentinian, set about persecuting your man Ambrose for the sake of her heresy, into which she had been seduced by the Arians. The pious people kept watch and mounted a defense in the church, ready to die with your slave, their bishop. My mother, your slave woman, was there as well, holding the first place in concern at her nightly guard post, living by her prayers. We ourselves, freezing from the cold, far from the warmth of your spirit, were nevertheless on edge,

---

[84] Deuteronomy 32: 40–43 (NEB translation, with minor modifications).

[85] Aug., *Confess.* 9.7.15 (CCL 27: 141–42): "Non longe coeperat Mediolanensis ecclesia genus hoc consolationis et exhortationis celebrare magno studio fratrum concinentium vocibus et cordibus. Nimirum annus erat aut non multo amplius, cum Iustina, Valentiniani regis pueri mater, hominem tuum Ambrosium persequeretur haeresis suae causa, qua fuerat seducta ab Arrianis. Excubabat pia plebs in ecclesia mori parata cum episcopo suo, servo tuo. Ibi mater mea, ancilla tua, sollicitudinis et vigiliarum primas tenens, orationibus vivebat. Nos adhuc frigidi a calore spiritus tui excitabamur tamen civitate attonita atque turbata. Tunc hymni et psalmi ut canerentur secundum morem orientalium partium, ne populus maeroris taedio contabesceret, institutum est: ex illo in hodiernum retentum multis iam ac paene omnibus gregibus tuis et per cetera orbis imitantibus."

sensing that the city was thunderstruck and in a state of turmoil. It was on this occasion that the practice of singing hymns and songs according to the custom of the eastern regions was established, to prevent the people from becoming wearied by sadness and tedium, a thing which, from that day to this, has been maintained, with almost all Your flocks throughout the other parts of the world who now imitate this practice.

Note the impact of Ephraem and others: "according to the customs of the eastern regions." Augustine and other Africans had witnessed the power of Ambrose's hymns and, no doubt, had heard from the bishop himself the reasons for the innovative place that he had given to the composition of hymns. They were part of the network of communications that spread this innovative practice to "to other parts of the world," including their own. Augustine records, with approval, the fact that a whole people or congregation, so moved, might gather together with their bishop in a basilica and be prepared to die with him. In an emotional sermon delivered against his Arian rival Auxentius, the court bishop at Milan, Ambrose elaborated on the ways in which vivid images and themes of a simple and forceful kind were produced to affect the heart rather than to appeal to the mind – images that would be more easily impressed on memory.[86] This sermon, delivered in the full heat of sectarian struggle, on Palm Sunday, 386, in the second part of the struggle over the basilicas, is itself a political and polemical *tour de force*. In it, Ambrose noted the power of songs and singing:

They say that the people were quite taken with the singing of my hymns. Obviously, I am not about to deny this. It is a great song. Indeed, nothing is more powerful. For what is more powerful than an open confession of the Trinity, which is daily celebrated in the mouths of the whole people? They all strive to outdo each other in confessing the faith. Armed with my verses, they know how to preach the Father, the Son, and the Holy Spirit. All of those people are thereby transformed into teachers, who previously were scarcely able to be students.

"Those who were scarcely able to be students." These were "the stupid" and "the idiotic" with whom Ambrose had to communicate. The use of a simple form of metrical verse, iambic dimeters, rather than Vergilian-pastiche hexameters, facilitated both learning and memory. In Ambrose's case it was the sectarian struggles with Arians and the imperial court in the

---

[86] Ambrose, *Sermo contra Auxentium de basilicis tradendis* = *Ep.* 75A.34 (CSEL 82.3: 105): "Hymnorum quoque meorum carminibus deceptum populum ferunt. Plane, nec hoc abnuo. Grande carmen istud est quo nihil potentius. Quid enim potentius quam confessio Trinitatis, quae cottidie totius populi ore celebratur? Certatim omnes student fidem fateri: Patrem et Filium et Spiritum Sanctum norunt versibus praedicare. Facti sunt igitur omnes magistri, qui vix poterant esse discipuli."

mid-380s and the demand that he make a basilica in the city available for the court that provoked recourse to a new mobilizing strategy.[87] It might be noted that Augustine had participated in and witnessed the innovation. As in other ages, no special technical knowledge was required. As the hymn-writer of a later age remarked: "We know *from experience* that singing has the power to enflame the hearts of men so that they praise God with an ever more vehement zeal."[88] He knew this, just like the African bishops did, from personal experience.

SINGING AND CHANTING

If chants were one important means of producing group cohesion, songs were another. Chants could readily be used simply by minimally altering their context or content. But Christians perceived *Christian* songs as different in kind than their secular analogues. Hymns were not just more songs. "Hymns are praises offered to God in song; hymns are songs containing the praise of God. If there is praise, but not praise of God, it is not a hymn . . . for there to be a hymn, three elements are required: there must be praise, it must be for God, and it must be sung."[89] It was frequently remarked that the singing of Psalms as part of the liturgy had just been completed, and the fact that the congregation responded "together" or "in unison" or "with one voice" was important. Voices united in a single powerful sound not only symbolized the unity of the church, but also enacted that powerful sentiment and imparted to each singer a sense of belonging and of participating in making that unity.[90] The questions were: What was to be sung, by whom, and to what purpose? After all, there were bad singers and bad songs: "We know and we are pained by how many evil and debauched men sing in this manner things worthy of their own ears and hearts. The singers themselves are worse for the very fact that they are not ignorant of what they are singing. They know that their little

[87] A judicious account is found in McLynn, "Persecution," ch. 4 in *Ambrose*, pp. 158–219, esp. pp. 181–208.

[88] Pettegree, *Culture of Persuasion*, p. 41, quoting Theodore de Bèze, from the mid-1560s: note that the effect was learned from experience.

[89] Aug. *En. in Ps.* 72.1 (CCL 39: 986): "Hymni laudes sunt Dei cum cantico; hymni cantus sunt continentes laudem Dei. Si sit laus, et non sit Dei, non est hymnus . . . si sit hymnus, habeat haec tria: et laudem, et Dei, et canticum"; cf. *En. in Ps.* 148.17 (CCL 40: 217–77) to much the same effect on defining what is meant by a hymn, and in which he assumes that they are sung rather than chanted.

[90] So frequently in his sermons that it is unnecessary to annotate all instances here; see, e.g., *Sermo* 14.1; 16B.1: "though we are many, we have been singing with one voice"; and, *inter alia*, *Sermo* 17.1; 19.1; 31.1; 40.1; 47.1; and 311.1.

songs are about disgusting things, and yet, the filthier the song, the more joyfully they sing; the more shameful they are, the happier they consider themselves."[91]

In a long, thundering sermon delivered at Carthage in 403 on the subject of obedience, and in support of the reforms that Aurelius was attempting to enforce in the metropolis, Augustine refers to the bad past of recent memory: "If we remember the things that used to happen in the church at Mappalia at the shrine of our blessed bishop and martyr Cyprian, we will perhaps find ourselves pained over them... where in those days disgusting and sordid songs were bellowed out, now it is hymns that lift off the roof."[92] Aurelius, the bishop of Carthage, had been in the forefront of this movement, instituting new songs or hymns that were to be sung in the church at Carthage. The innovation met with opposition, so Augustine rushed to the help of Aurelius with a defense of the new practice.[93] The same applied to dancing, since the mobilizing of certain repetitive body movements was closely associated with ritual chanting and singing. All these practices were connected with collective behavior that was potentially a precursor to aggression and violence. As such, he argued, the bishops *were* concerned (despite the criticisms) to control the venues and the performances.[94]

The concern of the critics was justified. There was a common ground between the world of popular secular songs and the singing at uncontrolled events like the anniversary festivities of the martyrs. These celebrations had developed by means of a lateral transfer of existing forms of secular public celebration into the sphere of the holy. The songs and dances performed at these festivals were considered to be bad and potentially subversive

---

[91] Aug. *En. 2 in Ps.* 18.1 (CCL 38: 105): "Et quam multi mali et luxuriosi sic cantant digna auribus suis et cordibus, novimus et dolemus. Eo enim peiores sunt, quo non possunt ignorare quod cantant. Sciunt enim se cantare flagitia, et tamen cantant tanto libentius, quanto immundius; quoniam tanto se putant laetiores, quanto fuerint turpiores."

[92] Aug. *Sermo* 359B.5 (Dolbeau 2/Mainz 5 = Dolbeau, *Vingt-six sermons*, p. 65): "In ecclesia Mappaliensi memoriam beati episcopi et martyris Cypriani, quanta fieri solebant, si meminerimus, fortasse dolebimus... Ubi tunc impudicae cantiunculae perstrepebant, nunc hymni personant."

[93] Aug. *Contra Hilarum* referred to in *Retract.* 2.11 (CCL 57: 98). This work, now lost, appeared about 398 concerning the objections of one Hilarus, a *vir tribunitius* and a Catholic layman. He was a gadfly who was habitually irritated with the clergy at Carthage. In this case, he was angered by the "custom" initiated at Carthage in which hymns taken from the book of the Psalms were sung before the offering or when the offering was distributed to the people.

[94] Aug. *Contra ep. Parm.* 3.6.29 (CSEL 51: 139–40): All three behaviors are noted in connection with the ritual humiliation and punishment of the Maximianist bishop Salvius of Membressa. It is specifically in this connection that Augustine notes: "Notum est omnibus nugaces et turpes saltationes ab episcopis solere compesci; quis umquam meminit ab hominibus, quos in auxilium episcopi petiverunt, cum episcopis esse saltatum?"

matters; so they came under intense scrutiny by the Catholic hierarchy in the 380s and 390s. Their aim was to impose tighter controls on perceived erratic behavior to produce a community that was leaner, fitter, and more disciplined for sectarian conflict. The festive days of the martyrs were marked by a particular conviviality that involved drinking and singing of a type that threatened to contravene the norms of controlled behavior that were thought to be appropriate for a martyr. In an early letter to Alypius, bishop of Thagaste, Augustine remarked on the need to control excessive drinking and other forms of wild behavior at the *natalitiae* of the martyrs. The drunkenness at these festivities was linked with singing and with the presence of women. It was a point where Catholics distinguished themselves from "the Donatists." Augustine says that he himself had heard the loud celebrations in "the church of the heretics," where crowds continued to sing hymns until nightfall.[95] Their energy was disturbing. It was a quality of singing that produced a different type of cohesion or *dominatio*, one that was inimical to the discipline that Augustine and his peers were seeking.

In a long letter to the layman Januarius, Augustine dealt with a series of disciplinary practices that should and should not be followed. In noting the way in which Easter and Pentecost were to be celebrated, he commented on the problem of different customs in liturgical practice followed in different regions of Africa. He says that so long as they are not harmful, they should be permitted.[96]

Not only should we *not* condemn such practices, we should support them with praise and by imitation, as long as the weakness of a few persons is not an impediment. If this obstacle is only a small one, such that a greater gain for the devout is to be hoped for than harm from the evil-minded is to be feared, then, without doubt, the custom should followed. These include practices that can be

---

[95] Aug. *Ep.* 29.11 (CCL 31: 105): "acta sunt vespertina, quae cottidie solent, nobisque cum episcopo recedentibus fratres eodem loco hymnos dixerunt non parva multitudine <utri>usque ad obscuratum diem manente atque psallente"; so, too, in the Reformation, Roman Catholics could identify Lutherans from the hymns that they sung: Brown, *Singing the Gospel*, p. 20.

[96] Aug. *Ep.* 55.18.34 (CSEL 34.2: 208–09): "non solum non improbemus, sed etiam laudando et imitando sectemur, si aliquorum infirmitas non ita impedit, ut amplius detrimentum sit. Si enim eo modo impedit, ut maiora studiosorum lucra speranda sint quam calumniatorum detrimenta metuenda, sine dubitatione faciendum est, maxime id quod etiam de scripturis defendi potest sicut de hymnis et psalmis canendis, cum et ipsius Domini et apostolorum habeamus exemplum et praecepta, de hac re tam utili ad movendum pie animum et accendendum divinae dilectionis affectum varia consuetudo est et pleraque in Africa ecclesiae membra pigriora sunt, ita ut Donatistae nos reprehendant, quod sobrie psallimus in ecclesia divina cantica prophetarum, cum ipsi ebrietates suas ad canticum psalmorum humano ingenio compositorum quasi ad tubas exhortationis inflamment. Quando autem non est tempus, cum in ecclesia fratres congregantur, sancta cantandi, nisi cum legitur aut disputatur aut antistites clara voce deprecantur aut communis oratio voce diaconi indicitur?" On Januarius' identity, see "Januarius (9)," PAC, pp. 584–85.

defended by scriptural authority, such as those concerning the singing of hymns and psalms – especially since we have the example and the injunctions of our Lord Himself and of the apostles concerning a practice that is so useful in moving the spirit piously and in the firing of divine love. The practice is admittedly different and many members of the church in Africa are somewhat lazy in its performance, so that the Donatists reproach us because we sing the divine songs of the prophets in too sober a manner in church, while they fire up their drunken ravings by singing songs composed by human talents as if incensed by trumpets of exhortation. Whenever our brothers congregate in a church, there is therefore no inappropriate time for the holy act of singing *except* if a reading is being made, a sermon is being delivered, priests are intoning in a loud voice, or common prayer is being directed by the voice of the deacon.

Differences of style had come to distinguish the two churches. The singing heard in the "other church" seemed to move the singers "to dominate" the service. In a struggle between congregation and clergy, the power of song to unite and to mobilize was threatening. What Aurelius of Carthage and his cohorts wanted was to put the threatening genie back in the bottle. The control would not have been required were it not for the fact that congregational singing of a certain emotional type actually infringed on the time, space, and authority of the clergy. And what was true within one church was even truer in the struggle between them.

PRAISE TO GOD! PRAISE TO GOD!

Singing of songs and shorter forms of rhythmic affirmation, such as the rit-ualistic chant, were closely linked, the two often being performed together on dramatic occasions of intense emotion. Like the PRAISE BE TO GOD! – the *Deo Laudes* that the enemies of the Catholics would chant at the top of their lungs.[97] It is difficult to catch the full force of the repeated rhyth-mic shocks in English. DEO LAUDES, DEO LAUDES, DEO LAUDES. The rhythmic shout to a trochaic beat, but almost spondaic in perfor-mance, that was particularly identified with "the Donatists" was perceived to be a most effective battle cry. The feeble THANKS BE TO GOD or GRATIAS DEO of the Catholics was a weak affirmation, with no strong attacking syllables.[98] The words sounded wimpish, and were mocked by the

[97] For *Deo Laudes* as the dissident war cry, see Martroye (1914b), col. 1703 n. 4 for a full set of references to both literary and epigraphical sources; see also Leclercq (1920a) and Monceaux, *Hist. litt.* 4, pp. 439–43.

[98] Leclercq (1920a). The phrases were perhaps less exclusive to either side than the polemical literature might suggest. See Aug. *Civ. Dei*, 22.8 (CCL 48: 826): "Procedimus ad populum, plena erat ecclesia, personabat vocibus gaudiorum: 'Deo Gratias, Deo Laudes'! Nemine tacente hinc atque

dissidents. The chant lacked power and drive.[99] In a sermon on the festivals of the martyrs, for example, the celebration was tied to the basic memory of betrayal of brother by brother. The dissident preacher moved to the theme of God as the "Lord of the Martyrs" and urged his parishioners to go out and to shout DEO LAUDES during the joy of the festival.[100] In a long sermon on the festival day of Saint Cyprian's martyrdom, Augustine noted the atmosphere of fear that the shout of DEO LAUDES created in those who heard it.[101]

The blessed Cyprian stands, he confesses Christ, he does not agree to what is forced upon him. He accepts the judgment of the temporal court to act as judge with Christ in eternity. He accepts his sentence, *Deo Gratias*, and rightly so, since he had honestly confessed. You mad and deranged Donatists! Crazed men! *Deo Gratias*. They say that they are celebrating the birthday of Cyprian. But all Christian men fear their shout of DEO LAUDES. The Donatists are gathered together to commit all their crimes, so that they might throw themselves off heights, shouting DEO LAUDES. DEO LAUDES. "Praise to God, Praise to God" on their tongues, but "hateful to God" in their deeds. So any Catholic Christian standing far away and hearing DEO LAUDES is already afraid and considers where he can hide lest he witness their suicidal jumpings. See how the Donatists have made bitter the words DEO LAUDES.

These shouts and chants were not created by the sectarian struggles of the late fourth century. They were inherited. In each case, they were so highly valorized because they were embedded in a long tradition of violence

---

inde clamantium." That is to say, when a cult was introduced and became successful (i.e., it *worked* for its petitioners) then despite the fact that it was introduced by Catholics and for Catholics, there was little to impede other Christians from taking advantage of its powers as well, as, clearly, they did.

[99] Aug. *En. in Ps.* 132.6 (CCL 40: 1930): "Et tamen vos 'Deo Gratias' nostrum ridetis. 'Deo Laudes' vestrum plorant homines. Sed certe reddidistis rationem de nomine, quare appelletis agonisticos."

[100] The sermon is normally thought to have been composed by Augustine and it is therefore catalogued as Aug. *Sermo* 64 (*RBén* 51: 14). Clearly it is not his. The emphasis throughout on betrayal, as well as the metaphors and language that it uses to parse betrayal, are nowhere else to be found in Augustine's existing sermons, and its injunction to shout "Deo Laudes" is absolutely un-Augustinian. The characterization of God as *martyrum dominus* is found elsewhere only once in Augustine (if the sermon is his); see *Sermo* 335G = Sermo Lambot 15 (PLS 2: 804): "dominum martyrum," in a long standard list.

[101] Aug. *Sermo* 313E.6 = Guelf. 28.6 (MiAg 1: 541): "Stat beatus Cyprianus, Christum confitetur, non consentit ad id quod cogitur; accipit iudic<i>ariam sententiam temporalem, fit cum Christo iudex in aeternum. Accipit sententiam, et DEO GRATIAS recte, quia recte confessus est. O insani Donatistae! O rabidi! DEO GRATIAS. Cypriani celebra<re> se dicunt natale; DEO LAUDES ipsorum omnes viri Christiani formidant. Congregati enim sunt Donatistae ad omnia scelera sua; ut se praecipitent, DEO LAUDES clamant, in ore DEO LAUDES, in factis DEO ODIBILES. Itaque quisquis tunc stans a longe Christianus Catholicus audierit DEO LAUDES, iam contremiscit, iam quaerit qua fugiat, ne praecipitationes ipsorum videat. Ecce quomodo Donatistae amaricaverunt LAUDES DEI."

and resistance, in the actions of the martyrs who had resisted overbearing and illegitimate authority and who had surrendered their lives, happily. Parishioners, whether Catholic or dissident, had heard the stories, year after year, in which the Christian martyrs having just been sentenced to death by the Roman governor would shout THANKS TO GOD! or PRAISE TO GOD! depending on one's preferred version of the past. Such shouts rang out not only the gratitude and defiance of the present, but echoed the same sentiments from the most highly valued episodes of their own past.

No wonder the rhythmic shouts of the opposition were dreaded. In his reply to the dissident bishop Petilian, Augustine notes how often the "gangs of your armed men" have infused great grief into the words DEO LAUDES.[102] In a letter addressed to "our beloved Lord and Brother Macrobius," on the occasion of Macrobius' ordination as the new dissident bishop of Hippo, Augustine drew a striking picture of the formal entry of the new bishop, his triumphal *adventus* into the city – a kind of military parade in which Macrobius was accompanied by an array of armed men marching in formation. Augustine begins by quoting a verse, a great favorite with both sides in the struggle – "with their feet hurrying to shed blood" (Rom. 3: 15, see Is. 59: 7) – and he continues.[103]

Indeed we have experience of such things in the outrageous acts of banditry of your circumcellions and clergy, who, after our human bodies have been raked with the most atrocious slaughter, have stained so many places with our blood – whose generals escorted you with their massed formations when you made your entry into this hometown of ours, shouting out in unison LAUDES DEO! Praise to the Lord! among their other songs, men whose voices blare out like the trumpets of battle in the midst of all their brutal acts of brigandage.

What the other battle songs were that the armed men sang on this occasion is not specified, but one must suspect the existence of a set repertoire of hymns and psalms that were well known to them. Augustine goes on to state that the leaders of the Holy Fighters embellished the bishop's honor with their cries of DEO LAUDES! shouted out amid their other chants,

---

[102] Aug. *Contra litt. Petil.* 2.65.146 (CSEL 52: 98): "Augustinus respondit: Considerate paululum quam multis et quantum luctum dederint 'Deo Laudes' armatorum vestrorum."

[103] Aug. *Ep.* 108.5.14 (CCL 31B: 78): "*Veloces pedes eorum ad effundendum sanguinem.* Nos potius ista in tantis latrociniis circumcellionum clericorumque vestrorum experti sumus, qui corporibus humanis caede atrocissima laniati tot loca nostrorum sanguine cruentarunt, quorum duces, quando te ingredientem in hac patria cum suis cuneis deduxerunt, DEO LAUDES inter cantica conclamantes quas voces velut tubas proeliorum in suis omnibus latrociniis habuerunt."

and he specifically links the war cry to the shedding of their enemies' blood.[104]

There seems little doubt that, whether intended or not, as with any formulaic battle cry, like the Elder Cato's war face, or the *barritus*, the battle roar of Germanic savages, the loud rhythmic shouting of the words created fear. "Oh would that such men were really soldiers of Christ," laments Augustine, "and not soldiers of the Devil, men from whom the shout DEO LAUDES! is more to be feared than the roar of a lion.[105] The reference to their shout as "like the roar of a lion" is no innocent metaphor. When the Jews repeated their rhythmic chant CRUCIFIGE! CRUCI-FIGE! CRUCIFY HIM! CRUCIFY HIM! before a Roman governor, they were castigated as roaring *like a lion* because this is how the voice of Satan sounded.[106] In a sermon on the subject of the celebration of the birthdays of the martyrs, it is with this gloss from the apostle Paul that Augustine begins: "Don't you know that your adversary is the Devil who goes around roaring like a lion, seeking the one whom he will devour?"[107] It is easy to underestimate the importance of these shouted rhythmic chants to the problem of real violence. But the terror that they excited by way of association with the fearful expectation of what was to happen, was central to the notation of the violence itself. The phenomenon was widely recognized in the Mediterranean of the time. In the East, violent gangs of monks would preface their attacks, and accompany them by chanting hymns. In 386, at Antioch, the Roman governor Tisamenus, hearing the fearful chanting of the approaching monks jumped out of his seat, abandoned his tribunal, and fled the city.[108]

That chanting and singing were involved in the mobilization of Christians for violence, there can be no doubt. The phenomenon is found in almost all ages of Christian violence, as in the Protestant cries of the

---

[104] Aug. *Ep.* 108.18 (CCL 31B: 82) "et in ipso scelere principibus agonisticis confessoribus vestris, qui ad DEO LAUDES ornant honorem vestrum, ad DEO LAUDES fundunt sanguinem alienum." Note that the word *canticum* is often used to designate a popular song from the theater that is satiric or libellous in nature: *Pauli Sent.* 5.4.15; Apul. *Met.* 75.

[105] Aug. *En. in Ps.* 132.6 (CCL 40: 1930): "Quia sunt qui certant adversus Diabolum, et praevalent, milites Christi agonistici appellantur. Utinam ergo milites Christi essent, et non milites Diaboli, a quibus plus timetur DEO LAUDES quam fremitus leonis."

[106] See ch. 6, p. 290.

[107] Aug. *Sermo* 328 (RBén 51: 20): first quoting 1 Peter 5: 8: "*Nescitis quia adversarius vester Diabolus tamquam leo rugiens circuit quaerens quem devorat*"; he then confirms its message to his parishioners: "Sicut leonem rugientem circumeuntem et quaerentem aliquid de ovili tollere vel lae<dere> descripsit Diabolum."

[108] Libanius, *Or.* 30.5 and *Or.* 45.26, in passages that are, of course, rhetorically inflected; cf. Gaddis, *Religious Violence*, pp. 210, 216–17.

Apprentice Boys' parade on 12 August of every year as they marched above the Catholic Bogside in Derry.[109]

> SLAUGHTER, SLAUGHTER, HOLY WATER
> SLAUGHTER THE PAPISTS
> WE WILL TEAR THEM ASUNDER
> AND MAKE THEM LIE UNDER
> THE PROTESTANT BOYS WHO FOLLOW THE DRUM

Once again, there is the drum beat. Like the circumcellion *agonistici* who marched to their own drum beat, accompanying the dissident bishop Proculeianus into Hippo, shouting out their sectarian battle cries. Another compelling instance found in the ambit of persons and situation with which the Catholic bishops of Africa were connected was the anti-Jewish violence on the island of Minorca in 418. On 2 February of that year, the Christian bishop Severus led his parishioners on a long trek across the island to confront the Jewish community at Mago. In the resulting mêlée, the synagogue was burned down and the Jewish population was subjected to fearful threats of an order that led to the forced "conversion" of all of them.[110] At every significant step in the process, the singing of hymns and songs, and the chanting of refrains was part of the violence. In the first confrontation, which ended with the throwing of stones, both sides engaged in the singing of the Psalm (9: 6–7) "Memory of them has perished with a crash, but the Lord remains forever." That both sides could sing the same song might be interpreted as a sign of a happy *modus vivendi*, but perhaps more pointedly that each side could exploit the same repertoire of vocal exhortations for their own purposes.[111] The preceding verses of the Psalm give some sense of what it meant to the singers to sing them and to the hostiles to hear them:

> I WILL PRAISE YOUR NAME IN PSALMS,
> YOU, MOST HIGH, WHEN MY ENEMIES TURN BACK,
> WHEN THEY FALL HEADLONG AND PERISH AT YOUR SIGHT,
> FOR YOU HAVE UPHELD MY RIGHT AND MY CAUSE,

---

[109] Bell, *Generation of Violence*, pp. 61–62, who notes, further: "The marchers in bowlers and Masonic gear were easy in their superiority, militant, arrogant, cruel and crude, bussed into the city to intimidate and to celebrate."

[110] See ch. 6, p. 304 above for details.

[111] *Epistula Severi*, 13.1–2 (Bradbury: 92): "Pergere igitur ad synagogam coepimus et hymnum Christo per plateam ex multitudine canebamus. Psalmus autem, quem mira iucunditate etiam Iudaeorum populus decantabar, hic fuit, 'Periit memoria eorum cum strepitu et Dominus in aeternum permanet' [VG, Ps. 9.7–8: Periit memoria eorum cum sonitu: et Dominus in aeternum permanet]." See Brown, *Cult of the Saints*, pp. 103–05, for a somewhat happier view.

SEATED ON YOUR THRONE, YOU, THE RIGHTEOUS JUDGE,
YOU HAVE CONDEMNED THE FOREIGNERS
AND YOU HAVE OVERTURNED THE GODLESS,
YOU HAVE BLOTTED OUT THEIR NAME FOR ALL TIME!
THE STRONGHOLDS OF MY ENEMIES ARE THROWN DOWN
    FOREVER;
YOU HAVE LEFT THEIR CITIES IN RUINS,
ALL MEMORY OF THEM HAS PERISHED . . .

So, the burning of the synagogue itself was followed by the singing of
hymns, the Christians chanted THEODORE, CREDE IN CHRISTVM
at the Jew Theodore, monks chanted at the site of the burned out synagogue, and the Christian attackers sang more hymns on the way back
to their basilica at Iamo.[112] The words of the Psalm that they chanted
emphasized that their enemy's extermination would be permanent.

In their formal mandate issued in June 404 to the representatives they
were sending to the imperial court, the Catholic bishops noted that circumcellion gangs had been designated and listed for punishment "many
times" in earlier imperial laws. More important, they stated that the "loud
shouts of the circumcellions" had been designated in the imperial laws
themselves.[113] The chants were that important. We do not know who was
providing the psalms sung by the dissident gangsters who attacked Maximianus at Bagaï, but we do know that Parmenian, the dissident bishop of
Carthage, was in the forefront of efforts to provide his people with new
psalms. In the late 380s or early 390s he had composed a series of popular
songs that were successful in mobilizing anti-Catholic sentiments among
his parishioners.[114] It is unfortunate that the texts and the contexts of these
songs of sectarian battle have been lost. But it is fortunate that at least one
example has survived to show what the genre was like. The song survives in
the works of Augustine, who composed it among the earliest of his polemical writings against the Donatists.[115] Written to confront the popular songs

---

[112] *Epistula Severi*, 14, 16.4, 16.11 and 20 (Bradbury: 94, 96, 98, 100).

[113] Council of Carthage, 16 June 404 = *Reg. Eccl. Carthag. Excerpt.* 93 (CCL 149: 212): "Nota est enim
et saepe legibus conclamata circumcellionum qua furiunt detestabilis manus." From what follows,
it is clear that these are imperial and not just local laws.

[114] It was one of the literary efforts for which Parmenian had gained some repute, even outside Africa:
"Praedestinatus," *Liber de haeresibus*, 1.44 (Oehler, *Corpus haereseologicum*, 1 [Berlin, 1856], 247):
"Parmenianos a Parmeniano, qui per totam Africam libros contra nos conficiens et novos psalmos
faciens circumibat, contra quem noster scripsit Optatus."

[115] Lambot (1935) and Anastasi (1957) are the basis for the modern standard editions; they supersede
the defective edition of Petschenig in CSEL (51: 3–15). For some early studies, see Daux (1903),
Engelbrecht (1908), Ermini (1931), and Vroom (1933) – all based on defective versions of the song,
however; subsequently, see Baxter (1952), Springer (1984), and, especially, Pizzani (2007), for a good
analysis of background and content.

that had already been composed by Parmenian, it emerged from the series of strategic and tactical plans that were developed at the conference held at Hippo Regius in October 393.[116] Composed in the immediate aftermath of that conference, his *Song Against the Donatists* was part of a series of texts that mark a sea change in Augustine's function, from his early role as an anti-Manichaean hit man to the front ranks of the battle against "the Donatists."[117] The pop song was his own ABCer.[118]

MY VERY OWN SONG

Augustine's little song has long been despised and dismissed as unworthy of the great bishop – a piece of low doggerel.[119] The great Paul Monceaux remarked of the body of Augustine's anti-Donatist writings: "It is strange indeed that the series of treatises begins with a poem, as bizarre as it is." He opined that the author had only himself to blame for the composition of "this odd piece of poetry." Monceaux was at pains to emphasize that there is nothing original in the song, that it "certainly suffers from a fatal flaw as a poem: it's just so banal. As with other great writers, Augustine was not a poetic writer, except in prose."[120] These are some of the kinder remarks made about the song. One feels that the pedants would prefer that this effort, like Cicero's poems, had somehow been lost in the messy process of textual transmission. In their view, the song reveals, unfortunately, that even

---

[116] For what is known of the developing tradition, see Monceaux, "Les débuts de la poésie chrétienne en Afrique: poésie a tendances populaires," *Hist. litt.* 3, pp. 451–97.

[117] For the date of composition, we can only argue from the serial order of works listed in the *Retractationes* (1.20 = CCL 57: 61), where it is placed after the text of the *De fide et symbolo* (1.17), the developed text of his address to the conference at Hippo; after one of his last anti-Manichaean works of the period, *De Genesi ad litteram* (1.18), and after his first substantial anti-Donatist work, the *De sermone Domini in monte* (1.19) and just before another one of his first anti-Donatist works, *Contra epistulam Donati haeretici*, the text of which has been lost (1.20). Therefore, a date late in 393 or early 394.

[118] The formal title usually given to it is "The Song Against the Donatists," *Psalmus contra partem Donati*, but his own biographer and bibliographer could refer to it in his list of Augustine's works as "The A-B-C Song": Possidius, *Indiculus*, 6.1: Psalmum abecedarium (Wilmart, 1931: 168).

[119] Van der Meer, *Augustine the Bishop*, p. 104: "doggerel," "a sort of ballad of very slender merit, an interminable didactic poem." Bonner, *Augustine of Hippo*, p. 253: "It must be confessed that not even the most devoted of the saint's admirers is likely to make any great claim for the *Psalmus* as a piece of literature." Even those who studied it have felt it necessary to make public abjurations of its worthlessness: so Tréhorel (1939), p. 309, states that it has no doctrinal or literary value, "Le chant populaire, oeuvre de circonstance et de vulgarisation."

[120] Monceaux, *Hist. litt.* 7, p. 81: "On peut trouver singulier que la série des traités s'ouvre par un poème. Si bizarre qu'elle soit, cette fantaisie de classification n'est pas imputable aux éditeurs; elle remonte à l'auteur lui-même"; p. 83: "Comme oeuvre littéraire, le Psalmus est d'une valeur fort inégale. Ce poème a certainement un défaut grave pour un poème: c'est d'être prosaïque. Ainsi que d'autres grands écrivains, Augustin n'était poète qu'en prose."

the great Augustine could slum around in the lowest levels of unculture. Since the song is unique and comes early in the corpus of Augustine's writings, it can easily be dismissed as being atypical of the bishop as he later developed. Such judgments reveal the connections between the power of certain theological and ecclesiastical traditions and their aesthetic requirements, but little about the importance of songs in the sectarian confrontations of the time. For the historian, the song is significant for the very reasons that have provoked many to denigrate and to marginalize it.[121] Like other men of education, the use of his talents for this genre was condemned.[122] But it is precisely the fact that it was *not* a piece of literature and that the man who composed it recognized it as "not poetry" that is its importance. That it was *not* original but rather that it attempted to convey a series of received theological positions – most of them already apparent in the writings of Optatus of Milevis a generation or two earlier – to a large and varied audience of "uneducated" persons is a signal of its significance.[123]

Entitled *Song Against the Donatists*, it is, in important ways, the western world's first known pop song. The song, 297 lines long, is organized into twenty stanzas of twelve verses each, prefaced by a five-verse introduction and a conclusion of thirty verses. The song begins with the refrain line: ALL YOU WHO REJOICE IN PEACE NOW JUDGE THE TRUTH – which is repeated twenty-one more times in the intervals between the stanzas that make up the song. The title of "song" or *psalmus* is important since it is *not* a hymn or *hymnus* in the classic terms defined by Augustine himself. It is not addressed to God or in praise of Him. It is, rather, a song that directly addresses the ordinary person in explanation of a contemporary conflict. To understand better the place that the song had in the sectarian battles of the period, it is fortunate to have the author's own reflections on its making, written some three and a half decades after its composition.[124]

---

[121] Lancel, *Saint Augustin*, pp. 244–47, is a marked exception.

[122] So it was similarly remarked, for example, of Charles Wesley: his conversion created a hymn writer, but destroyed a poet: Rattenbury, *Charles Wesley's Hymns*, p. 32.

[123] Monceaux, *Hist. litt.* 7, pp. 82–83, is hardly alone in such judgments: "L'essentiel était donc, ici, le résumé historique. D'ailleurs, ce résumé n'avait rien de bien nouveau. L'auteur s'était contenté de mettre en vers un sommaire de l'ouvrage d'Optat, sa source unique. Peu familier encore avec les choses du Donatisme, il avait tout emprunté à son prédécesseur . . . Aussi, comme oeuvre de controverse, le Psalmus n'a rien d'original."

[124] Aug. *Retract.* 1.20 (CCL 57: 61): "Volens etiam causam Donatistarum ad ipsius humillimi vulgi et omnino imperitorum atque idiotarum notitiam pervenire, et eorum, quantum fieri per nos posset inhaerere memoriae, psalmum qui eis cantaretur per Latinas litteras feci, sed usque ad V litteram. Tales autem abecedarios appellant. Tres vero ultimas omisi; sed pro eis novissimum quasi epilogum adiunxi, tamque eos mater alloqueretur ecclesia. Hypopsalma etiam, quod respondetur, et prooemium causae, quod nihilominus cantaretur, non sunt in ordine litterarum; earum quippe ordo incipit post prooemium."

Wishing to bring the case against the Donatists to the awareness of the lowliest of the common crowd, especially to the ignorant and the uneducated, and, as far as it was in our power, to fix it in their memories, I composed a song which was to be sung to them based on the letters of the Latin alphabet, but only as far as the letter "V" – the sort of song that they call an "ABC" song. I omitted the last three letters of the alphabet and in their place I attached an epilogue right at the end in which Mother Church addresses them directly. And there is a refrain, used as a response, which also serves as an introduction to the case [i.e. against the Donatists]. It is also to be sung, but not following the order of the letters of the alphabet. The regular order of the letters of the alphabet begins after the introduction.

That is to say, Augustine was concerned to use devices that would cause ideas to become fixed in memory and which would make it more likely that the words and ideas would be repeated and absorbed by the minds of persons whom he called "ignorant" and "stupid," but whose sentiments and attitudes he wished to influence. The forces that induced a highly trained rhetor like Augustine to condescend to this level of communication are apparent. So too are some of his models. It is not without significance that some two decades earlier, Augustine's talents were sufficient in this regard for him to have entered a competition for the composition of a theatrical song, a *carmen theatricum*. It was either on this occasion, or another like it at Carthage, that Augustine actually won the contest and received a crown from no less grand a personage than the proconsular governor of Africa.[125] During his stay in Italy, and his time at Cassiciacum, accompanied by his African boyhood friends, we find the same impulses. Licentius, son of Augustine's patron from Thagaste, the wealthy Romanianus, was "an enthusiastic poet" who was "obsessed by the unaccustomed rhythms of the Ambrosian chant." Nor was this young man above offending the proprieties of Augustine's mother, Monnica, by singing psalms while in the lavatory.[126]

By the year in which he composed his song, Augustine was already aware of the fundamental adjustments that he would have to make to be able to communicate in a popular style. His anti-Manichaean works, dating from 386 and the years immediately following were composed in the formal Latin of the most cultured circles in Carthage and Rome. The problem was that "the idiots" whom he was trying to persuade could not read, much less understand, these works, so their intended effect was being lost. The decisive shift in Augustine's understanding of what was required had

---

[125] Aug. *Confess.* 4.2.3 (CCL 27: 41): "Recolo etiam, cum mihi theatrici carminis certamen inire placuisset" (the case where a haruspex promises him victory, for a charge); and 4.3.5: (CCL 27: 42) "Erat eo tempore vir sagax, medicinae artis peritissimus atque in ea nobilissimus, qui pro consule manu sua coronam illam agonisticam imposuerat"; cf. Brown, *Augustine of Hippo*, p. 134.

[126] Aug. *De ord.* 1.8.22–23 (CCL 29: 99–100); cf. Brown, *Augustine of Hippo*, p. 111, for comment.

come earlier, with his work "On Genesis against the Manichees," *De Genesi contra Manichaeos*, composed in 389, about four years, or so, before the song. It was written in a looser form of Latin that abandoned the elevated diction, rhythmic clausulae, and the structured periods of the high style. Augustine felt that he had to defend this descent in aesthetics to those who had identified him so much with the proper Latin of a court rhetor. So he wrote a preface to this work in the cultivated Latin of his social peers, a preface that is worth quoting for its programmatic statement.[127]

If the Manichees choose those whom they would ensnare, then we too must choose the words by which we reply to them, since they pursue both educated men with their writings *and* the uneducated with their error. And since when they promise the truth, they attempt to avoid it. Their emptiness must therefore be crushed not with ornate and polished words, but with plain ones. That's why the opinion of certain Christian men, learned in liberal literature, persuaded me. When they read the other books against the Manichees that I had published, they said that the ignorant either could not understand them at all or could only understood them with great difficulty. They very kindly advised me that I should not deviate much from the common and customary way of speaking if I wished to drive out these extremely dangerous errors, especially from the minds of the ignorant. For the learned understand this ordinary and simple language, whereas the ignorant do not understand the other [i.e. the high] style.

At a general level, the popular songs that were sung by the *imperiti* and the *idiotae* at the festival celebrations on the birthdays of the martyrs were an effective means of producing a group cohesion, sometimes a frightening or threatening cohesion that was already being made the object of coercive controls. The anti-Manichaean struggle, in which Augustine was seen to be the church's local expert, also had a popular side. There were educated men within the church who, in the late 380s, were drawing to Augustine's attention that the sort of style he was using in his anti-Manichaean works was itself an impediment to the aim of persuading the common people about the grave dangers presented by Manichaean beliefs. The education of the *imperiti* was always problematic. If the educated took the low road, they were open to the charge of social condescension. If they remained at

---

[127] Aug. *De Genesi contra Manichaeos*, 1.1 (CSEL 91: 67): "Si eligerent Manichaei quos deciperent, eligeremus et nos verba quibus eis responderemus; cum vero illi et doctos litteris et indoctos errore suo persequantur et, cum promittunt veritatem, a veritate conentur avertere, non ornato politoque sermone, sed rebus manifestis convincenda est vanitas eorum. Placuit enim mihi quorundam vere Christianorum sententia qui, cum sint eruditi liberalibus litteris, tamen, alios libros nostros quos adversus Manichaeos edidimus cum legissent, viderunt eos ab imperitioribus aut non aut difficile intellegi et me benevolentissime monuerunt ut communem loquendi consuetudinem non deser- erem, si errores illos tam perniciosos ab animis etiam imperitorum expellere cogitarem. Hunc enim sermonem usitatum et simplicem etiam docti intellegunt, illum autem indocti non intellegunt."

the higher level, they could be accused not only of placing themselves above the level of the "unlearned" whom one ought to be teaching the simple unvarnished truth, but also of being professional rhetors who were seeking to use superior technology to manipulate the minds of the ignorant.[128]

In the sectarian wars in Africa, bishops in the dissident church were already composing songs that were specifically produced for fighting. Parmenian, the dissident bishop of Carthage, was one of these. And why not? As the study of other sectarian conflicts has shown, hymns and songs "spread ideas more effectively than any kind of... literature."[129] It was known that they worked. Augustine was well aware of the success that Parmenian's songs were having among the masses of believers. But it is important to note that Augustine's *Song Against the Donatists* was not intended to be sung by the *idiotae* alone. It was a dialectical response form that encouraged acclamatory chanting on the part of the unlearned as part of a song. The stanzas of the song were to be sung *to* the assembled people. The point of the simple language and the mnemonic devices was to help the ordinary parishioners to remember and to assimilate the content that they were hearing. Their active role was to respond between the stanzas being sung to them with the rhythmic refrain line. So the function of the song was actually located half way between a popular song and a chant. It was not the first or the last time that a move to the colloquial and rhythmic would be made in order to get a fundamental religious message across to the unlearned.[130]

The simple A–B–C form had a long history. Even as a novice preacher Augustine must have been familiar with those *Psalms* of the Hebrew bible that were organized according to this alphabetical form.[131] The fact that he called song a "psalm" points to the genre of singing that Augustine envisaged. The Psalms had a core place in his creative writing, certainly in the words of his sermons. The same series of prompts are found in other

---

[128] Cresconius apud Aug. *Contra Cresc.* 4.2.2 (CSEL 52: 498–99): "Ac primo illud, quod tibi ipse contrarius eloquenter eloquentiam vituperare voluisti, tamquam esset veritatis inimica et patrona potius falsitatis, ut eo modo me quasi eloquentem cavendum atque fugiendum ostenderes imperitis."

[129] Brown, *Singing the Gospel*, p. 9; cf. p. 30 where he remarks how songs were absolutely central to the success of Luther's mission in the town that he studies.

[130] See the case of Ibn Tumart in twelfth-century Morocco, the Maghrib al-Aqsa. Unlike high Islamic theologians in their high ivory towers, like al-Ghazali, Ibn Tumart consciously aimed at the use of the Berber language rather than Arabic. When he wrote, always in Berber, it was small pamphlets or treatises of which we have a few examples. And he perfected mnemonic devices which, although they might appear simple-minded, took into consideration the people with whom he was attempting to communicate: Ch.-A. Julien, *History of North Africa: Tunisia, Algeria, from the Arab Conquest to 1830*, ed. J. Petrie, transl. C. C. Stewart, New York, Praeger, 1970, pp. 98–99.

[131] See Psalms 9–10, 25, 34, 111, 112, and 118.

ages.[132] This much makes sense of the paradigms already being propagated by his enemies: Parmenian was renowned for traveling around Africa, propagating the new psalms that he was composing. In the course of preaching on one of these alphabetic psalms, Psalm 118, Augustine commented on the new ABC songs:[133]

If I have said nothing about the Hebrew alphabet [sc. in this psalm], where groups of eight verses are placed beneath individual letters of the alphabet and in this way the whole psalm is constructed, this would not at all be surprising since I have found nothing which especially pertains to this psalm, for it is not the only one that is arranged by letters of the alphabet. I must explain this to those who read the scriptures in Greek and Latin, since this practice is not conserved in these versions and so they are not able to find groups of eight verses in the Hebrew codices under the letters which are placed at their head – as the persons who know this language have informed us. The author of this psalm therefore brought much more care to his composition than do our writers who are accustomed to compose songs that they call ABCers in Latin or Punic. For a stop does not close the end of every verse – rather, they only begin the first verse with a letter of the alphabet, which they place at the very beginning of the verse.

Augustine refers to "our people" who compose A–B–C songs in Latin or in Punic (and hence some of the utility of the Hebrew originals). Being popular, the form not only had to be simple, it also had to be in a language that would be understood. For many Christians in the heartlands of Africa, whether Catholic or dissident, this meant that the pop song had to be in Punic – either that or in a Latin that could be more easily understood by most persons. The move towards a more popular form of communication was more radical than just the use of the mnemonic device of the abecedarian format. It logically suggested other innovations in the use of language. These other novelties included a new kind of meter and rhythm that was meant to make the tune catchy and its contents memorable. The African Christian writer Commodian moved in this same direction with

---

[132] Pettegree, *Culture of Persuasion*, pp. 40–41, cf. 45: Luther, for example, was moved by the model of the Psalms, "to make vernacular psalms for the people, that is spiritual songs, so that the Word of God, by means of song may live among the people."

[133] Aug. *En. 32 in Ps.* 118.8 (CCL 40: 1775–76), dated to 418 by Hombert: "Quod autem de alphabeto hebraeo, ubi octoni versus singulis subiacent litteris, atque ita psalmus totus contexitur, nihil dixi, non sit mirum, quoniam nihil quod ad istum proprie pertineret inveni; non enim solus habet has litteras. Illud sane sciant qui hoc in graeca et latina scriptura, quoniam non illic servatum est, invenire non possunt, omnes octonos versus in hebraicis codicibus ab ea quae illis praeponitur, littera incipere; sicut nobis ab eis qui illas noverunt litteras indicatum est, quod multo diligentius factum est, quam nostri vel latine vel punice, quos abecedarios vocant psalmos, facere consueverunt. Non enim omnes versus donec claudatur periodus, sed solos primos ab eadem littera incipiunt, quam praeponunt." See, also, *En. 21 in Ps.* 118.2 (CCL 40: 1733) where he also explains the nature of the acrostic as used in this Hebrew psalm.

his polemical and pedagogical verses. Composed in hexameters with end rhymes, and characterized by the frequent use of acrostics to mark the line beginnings, his poems were designed to inculcate ideas. According to Commodian's preface to his own verses, they were of a simplified kind precisely because they were intended to instruct the simple and uneducated: "Our preface reveals a way to the errant soul... I grieve for the common crowd, ignorant because it wanders in search of empty gods. For this, I, a learned man, am instructing the ignorant in the truth."[134]

Not being sure in what genre such rhythmic productions should be placed, Gennadius of Massilia later categorized them as "sort of" poetry, *quasi versus.*[135] Augustine also admitted that his song could not be categorized as a poem, a *carmen,* and explains why: he did not wish to be constrained in any way by the requirements of formal quantitative metrics. More important for him was the communication of basic ideas to common people and the implanting of these ideas in their minds. In his own words:[136]

Therefore I did not want this to be any sort of "poem" in type, so that metrical necessities would not force me to use specific words that are not usually spoken by the common people.

The point was effective communication, not high art. So his popular song emphasized the stress accents of everyday speech as opposed to the rhythmic alteration of longs and shorts that created the quantitative verse patterns of the poetry of the high culture. For his song, Augustine apparently preferred a longer line of eight feet, with a strong break or *caesura* marking an internal division between the two halves formed by the hemistichs. It is somewhat a matter of preference as to how one arranges the verses or prints them on a page.[137] In effect, they reduced to trochaic tetrameters: a pounding on and off beat that was like that of marching feet. Like the chant DEO LAUDES, for example. Other innovations, like the use of end-of-verse rhyming patterns, further emphasized the connectedness of the ideas and made their memorization easier.

We do not know how many of these songs were in the repertoire of either side. The numbers need not have been great. A limited number

---

[134] Commod. *Instructiones, Praef.* 1, 7–9 (CSEL 15: 5): "Praefatio nostra viam erranti demonstrat... doleo pro civica turba / inscia quod pergit periens deos quaerere vanos; / Ob ea perdoctus ignaros instruo verum."

[135] Gennadius, *De vir. illus.* 15 (PL 58: 1068); cf. Tréhorel (1939), p. 314.

[136] Aug. *Retract.* 1.20 (CCL 57: 61): "Ideo autem non aliquo carminis genere id fieri volui, ne me necessitas metrica ad aliqua verba quae vulgo minus sunt usitata conpelleret."

[137] As Rose (1926–27) pointed out long ago.

of well-known ones might have sufficed. The dissident Christians around their bishops like Parmenian were composing their new songs. Augustine and men of the reformation of 393 began providing equivalents for their own side. This song is one of them. It probably had some success, since it was imitated by the Catholic bishop Fulgentius of Ruspe a century later in his battle song against the Arian Christians who were backed by the authority of the new Vandal state.[138] With its hemistichs of eight metrical feet, rhymes at the ends of the lines, a refrain line, a prologue, and an epilogue, it faithfully reproduces all the salient structural aspects of Augustine's song. However effective these songs were in moving ordinary believers, their authors and those who preserved their works discounted these minor efforts, dismissing them as unworthy of notice.[139] In Fulgentius' case, we have his pop song only because of the good fortune that it was preserved along with Augustine's *Song Against the Donatists* in the same manuscript. None of his biographers or commentators ever deigned to mention its existence.

Underlying these innovations was a bedrock of cultural assumptions that indicated even to highly educated men like Parmenian, Augustine, and their fellow bishops, what popular communication, speaking with the *imperiti*, had to be like. They had knowledge of devices in verse that were popular, but that were also part of educated Latin culture in Africa. For example, the device of the acrostic, heavily used by Christian poets like Commodian to communicate complex ideas to the ignorant, was, to judge from its frequency in Latin epigraphical texts from Africa (including many examples from Late Antiquity) a stylish and attractive form of poetry.[140] Someone thinking of how to communicate a verse message to everyday people would naturally think of this form. So it is not accidental that Augustine employed the device in one of the few pieces of his poetry that have been preserved. It is also important to note that the context was violent

---

[138] For the text, see J. Fraipont ed., CCL 91A: 877–85 = Lambot (1936); and Bulst, *Hymni Latini antiquissimi*, pp. 147–55; for commentary and a full revision of the text, see Bianco (1980) and Isola (1983). Fulgentius' song was explicitly entitled an "Abecedarius."

[139] In Fulgentius' case, for example, none of his later recorders, neither Ferrandus in his biography of the bishop nor Isidore in his *De Viris Illustribus*, has a word to say about this song and for an obvious reason: it was deemed to be beneath the authorial dignity of the bishop. Had it not survived on its own, we would not know of its existence. And it survived precisely because it was later attached to its model, Augustine's song, and was preserved along with it in the same Leyden manuscript.

[140] See J. N. Adams, "The Poets of Bu Njem: Language, Culture and the Centurionate," *JRS* 89 (1999), 109–34: both poems are acrostics spelling out the centurions' names. Note line 17 of the Iasucthan inscription: hard labor was done to rhythmic shouts: "cum voce militum" in the building of the turret.

and sectarian.[141] The commonest of these cultural devices only required the memory of the bishops for their own childhood. For at one time, they too were *imperiti* when, as young children, they knew nothing of how to read or write. And how did they learn? By beginning with the alphabet and by repeatedly, if agonizingly, copying and repeating first the letters and then lists of words arranged in alphabetical order. Only two and a half years after composing this song, Augustine began writing his *De Doctrina Christiana*, a handbook on Christian education. Although it is intended to instruct a Christian learner at much higher technical levels than those that we are considering here, it is interesting to witness the fundamental importance that Augustine attributes to the alphabet. No less than four or five times in the preface to this work, he mentions learning the alphabet as a paradigm for learning in general.

KEEP IT SIMPLE: A–B–C, 1–2–3

As for educating the stupid and the unlearned, the *stulti ac imperiti*, what did the song say to those who sang it? It was a new style, a new song. In an early sermon, Augustine already castigated the Rebaptizers for not singing a new song.[142] His new song focussed the conflict between the two sides as a dispute over the truth of what had happened, a disagreement that was subject to a judicial process of proof and refutation. The refrain line of the song, to which the singers returned no less than twenty-two times, put the matter clearly.[143]

> ALL OF YOU WHO REJOICE IN PEACE,
> NOW *JUDGE* WHAT IS TRUE.

Here the word peace, *pax*, was as heavily loaded ideologically as the word "what is true," *verum*. The dominant image of the song construes the singers and listeners as judges or jurors in a court. The first verses that form the prologue to the song proper, the lines just before the first stanza headed by the letter "A," make this manifest.[144]

---

[141] See ch. 13, p. 624 below.

[142] Aug. *Sermo* 33.5 (CCL 41: 415): at length, but note: "Nec se arbitrentur rebaptizores Donatistae ad novum canticum pertinere."

[143] Aug. *Psalmus contra partem Donati*, 1, 7, 20, 33, etc. (Lambot, 1935: 318–19 = BA 28: 150–54): "Omnes qui gaudetis de pace, modo verum iudicate." Lambot reads "omnes" instead of "vos." Although it flies in the face of the prosody, it seems to be guaranteed by what Augustine himself lists as the first line of the song in his *Retractationes*; so, a hypermetric verse.

[144] Aug. *Psalmus contra partem Donati*, 2–5 (Lambot, 1935: 318 = BA 28: 150): "Foeda est res causam audire et personas accipere. / Omnes iniusti non possunt regnum Dei possidere. / Vestem alienam

> IT'S A DIFFICULT THING TO HEAR A CASE
> AND TO ARRAIGN THE PARTIES.
> BUT ALL THE UNJUST MEN CANNOT
> POSSESS THE KINGDOM OF HEAVEN.
> IF NO ONE CAN BEAR THAT
> ANOTHER'S CLOTHING IS TORN,
> HOW MUCH MORE WORTHY OF DEATH
> IS ONE WHO HAS RIPPED TO SHREDS
> THE PEACE OF CHRIST?

The judicial metaphor is important because it is the way that the sectarian struggle is construed for an audience of the ignorant who were, nonetheless, expected to be reasonably well acquainted with Roman trial process as a model for arbitrating disputes. The song tells the listener that those who have torn up the peace of Christ, his contract with them, are worthy of a death sentence: it is parsed as a just or legal penalty for them to suffer. The point of the verses that follow is that an inquiry must be made into who committed this capital crime. The process is presented as one that will give a sure result: the judicial investigation will be made *sine errore*.[145]

The initial stanza of the song, led off by the letter "A" for *abundantia*, begins by implanting in the listener's mind a theme to which it will return and that will remain at the core of the Catholic defense: the world is made up of the good and the bad persons, and everyone should endure this less-than-happy fact until the coming of the End of Time. The biblical image of the fisherman's net catching both good and bad fish, a favorite motif of Catholic preachers, is used to anchor the theme and to make it vivid.[146] But the "B" to "F" stanzas move quickly to the heart of the matter: the primal act of betrayal. The song's lyrics translate into terms readily comprehensible to ordinary people the complex argument in Optatus' six-book reply to Parmenian, written in the mid-360s. One moves from images of peace and the unity of the Church disturbed by bad people to the historical core of the dispute, the emotive issue of the traitors.

The song carefully makes its basic points. The enemies of the Catholics are haughty and arrogant men – *homines multi superbi* – who (like the Jews)

---

conscindas nemo potest tolerare: / quanto magis pacem Christi qui conscindit dignus {est} morte." Compare the verses of the "I" stanza on Justice (*Iustitia*) – verses 112–123 – for another concentrated run of judicial metaphors.

[145] Aug. *Psalmus contra partem Donati*, 6 (Lambot, 1935: 318 = BA 28: 150): "Et quis est ita qui fecit quaeramus hoc sine errore."

[146] Augustine later has echoes of almost these very words: e.g., *En. in Ps.* 49.9 (CCL 38: 582–83): "Significabat enim illa captura hoc tempus; retia rupta significabant conscissiones et conscissuras haereticorum et schismaticorum."

falsely claim that they are the right, the just, the righteous. But it is *they* who deliberately cut themselves off from the True Church and who "set up one altar against another." In making such a great furor about a supposed act of betrayal, it is actually *they* who were the real betrayers.[147]

> ALTHOUGH THEY BATTLE ABOUT BETRAYAL,
> IT IS THEY WHO BETRAYED THEMSELVES TO SATAN,
> AND THE CRIME THAT *THEY* COMMITTED
> THEY WISH TO SHIFT ONTO OTHERS.
> *THEY* BETRAYED THE HOLY BOOKS,
> YET THEY DARE TO ACCUSE US OF THE CRIME!

The theme and the problem of betrayal is brought up incessantly throughout the song, matched in importance only by the heavily freighted problem of the use of the secular force of the state to settle church disputes.[148]

> THEY HEAR ABOUT "TRAITORS,"
> BUT THEY DON'T KNOW HISTORY,
> AND IF I SAY "PROVE IT,"
> THEY HAVE NOTHING TO SAY.
> THEY SAY THAT THEY BELIEVE THEIR OWN;
> I SAY THAT THOSE MEN ARE LIARS,
> BECAUSE WE BELIEVE OUR OWN
> WHO SAY THAT *YOU* WERE THE TRAITORS.

The whole vexatious matter of betrayal, traitors, and who handed the holy books containing the Word of God over to secular authorities is treated in the "D" and "E" stanzas.[149] Words referring to traitors and betrayal occur repeatedly, only to be refuted by appeals to the real history of the matter known by our ancestors or *maiores*. The "F" stanza completes the picture of Catholic innocence and "Donatist" guilt in this matter. It was because of their *blindness* that the princes of the "other side" did what they did.[150] Imperial judges attempted impartially to assess the dispute. The big deceit,

---

[147] Aug. *Psalmus contra partem Donati*, 24–26 (Lambot, 1935: 319 = BA 28: 152–54): "Diabolo se tradiderunt, cum pugnant de traditione / et crimen quod commiserunt in alios volunt transferre. / Ipsi tradiderunt libros et nos audent accusare."

[148] Aug. *Psalmus contra partem Donati*, 39–42 (Lambot, 1935: 319 = BA 28: 156): "Audiunt enim 'traditores': et nesciunt quid gestum est ante. / Quibus si dicam 'Probate,' non habent quid respondere. / Suis se dicunt credidisse: dico ego mentitos esse; / quia et nos credimus nostris, qui vos dicunt tradidisse."

[149] E.g. Aug. *Psalmus contra partem Donati*, 49, 57, 62, 66 (Lambot, 1935: 320 = BA 28: 156–58): "Erant quidam traditores librorum de sancta lege ... dicunt ordinatorem eius sanctos libros tradidisse ... Crimen nobis quis probavit antiquum de traditione? ... Quia fama iam loquebatur de librorum traditione."

[150] Aug. *Psalmus contra partem Donati*, 73 (Lambot, 1935: 321 = BA 28: 160): "Fecerunt quod voluerunt tunc in illa caecitate."

the big lie is that, while claiming to be pure and innocent, it is *they* who tolerate evil men in their midst, men worse than any supposed traitors.

The theme of "Donatist hypocrisy" is the bridge to the following "G" to "N" stanzas in which the history of "the Donatists" is described in detail. It is *they* who are actually the betrayers, the violent, and the deceitful, the real enemies of Truth and the Church. The "G" stanza begins with the critical events of the recent Maximianist division within the dissident church. The core point here is that they have many evil men among them whom they find odious and hateful, but whom they haven't separated from *their* communion. And, the words of the "H" stanza declare, it was *your* founder who was intent on riot and revolution. Emotive and loaded words like uproar, *tumultus*, and phrases like "wishing to upset everything," *totum vellent turbare*, are suggestive of political insurrection. Donatus, the Prince of this Evil, after whom *your* side is named, wished to rule all of Africa. The following "I" stanza refers to an entrenched evil attitude: the enemies of the Church prefer their Kingdom of Error so much that they pretend not to know the Truth; it is pride that locks them into the "seat of their disease."

There follows another allusion to the recent Maximianist controversy at Carthage, in which the hypocrisy of the dissidents is made manifest by their appeal to "overseas judges" and the acceptance of secular authority. You are blind (again, echoes of Jews), whereas we see. We embrace peace and unity, but you reject it. The main point of this part of the song, however, is to point out the hypocrisy of "the Donatist" use of government forces to repress their "heretics," the Maximianists, while blaming the Catholics for this same tactic. The dissidents' hypocrisy on this score is double since they not only solicited state force, but also sustained their own purveyors of partisan violence, of whom the men called "circumcellions" – although not named as such in the following verses – were emblematic.[151]

> YOUR PEOPLE DON'T WANT PEACE,
> YOUR MEN THREATEN WITH THEIR CLUBS . . .
> BUT WHO GAVE ORDERS TO THEM
> TO RAGE IN THIS WAY THROUGH ALL AFRICA?
> NEITHER CHRIST NOR THE EMPEROR

---

[151] Aug. *Psalmus contra partem Donati*, 147, 154–62 (Lambot, 1935: 323–24 = BA 28: 170–72): "Vos enim non vultis pacem. Illi minantur de fuste . . . Quis enim praecipit illis per Africam sic saevire? / Non Christus, non imperator haec probatur permisisse, / fustes et ignes privatos et insaniam sine lege. / Quia scriptum est *Reconde gladium*, scelus non putant in fuste, / non ut homo moriatur, sed ut conquassetur valde / et postea moriatur inde, iam cruciatus in languore. / Sed tamen si miserentur, occident et uno fuste. / Fustes Israheles vocant quod Deus dixit cum honore, / ut plus vastent ipsum nomen quam corpus quod caedunt inde."

CAN BE SHOWN TO HAVE ALLOWED THIS:
THE PRIVATE USE OF CLUBS AND FIREBRANDS,
AND THIS ILLEGAL MADNESS.
BECAUSE IT'S WRITTEN: "SHEATHE THE SWORD"
THEY THINK THERE'S NO CRIME IN USING CLUBS!
NOT SO THAT SOMEONE SHOULD BE KILLED (OF
    COURSE)
BUT SO THAT THEY MIGHT BE BADLY BEATEN
AND THEN LATER DIE,
HAVING SUFFERED FROM LONG TORTURE.
BUT IF THEY HAD PITY, THEY COULD KILL
WITH ONE BLOW OF THEIR CLUBS.
THEY CALL THEIR CLUBS "ISRAELS"
BECAUSE GOD HELD THIS NAME IN HONOR,
BUT THEY SHAME THE NAME
MORE THAN THE BODIES THEY HAVE BEATEN.

In the "L" to "M" stanzas, at the center of the song, sectarian violence becomes the core of the problem. The message is that if Macarius, the imperial commissioner of 347, committed some "excesses," he at least did so under the aegis of Christian law. I won't deny that he did some bad things, admits Augustine, but your people are worse by far.

At this point, the song restates its common theme. The Church embraces the good and the bad. Just because some men are bad does not mean that they should be cut off from Mother Church. The verses presents its core message, as did thousands of Catholic sermons of the age, with a harvest metaphor filled with everyday images that would have been familiar to African listeners. Christ is the winnower who will separate the good grains from the bad chaff, but only at the time of the Final Harvest at the end of time. Both good grain and bad weeds will grow together until then. There is no reason in the present time to label any person a *traditor*, or traitor, or to condemn his descendants as evil men. The "R" and "S" stanzas turn to the reason why there is no justification for the practice of rebaptism. Finally, "T" and "V" restate the case for Unity, and with the letter "V" the abecedarian part of the song ends.

An epilogue of twenty-nine lines closes the song and directly addresses "our brothers": the verses adjure them to listen to what the speaker has to say and not to become angry. What does Mother Church herself have to say? In a striking prosopopoeia, *Mater Ecclesia* Herself addresses the listeners.[152] The dominant image is that of a family and of a *matrona* addressing her

---

[152] For more detailed analysis, see Springer (1987); I have emphasized the elements that are most pertinent to an aggressive polemical discourse.

children. Some of them have hurt her by their false accusations against their siblings and by their rebellious actions. I am called Catholic, she says, while you are "from the party of Donatus." What follows is an approbation of the violent repressive actions taken by the imperial commissioner Macarius in 347. God gave him gifts to dispense and *you* rejected them. By doing this *you* forced Macarius to seek retribution for the personal insults and injuries done to him. Mother Church then reiterates the message that she tolerates those bad men whom she cannot expel before the end of time. If you hate bad men, she says, then *you* ought to seek what kinds of bad men you have among yourselves. And if you actually tolerate such bad men, then why not do so from inside the Unity of the One Church?

But whatever other devices are used, it is the atmosphere of the courtroom and of judicial process that infects the whole tenor of the song. The verses of the "F" stanza can be taken as exemplary of this judicial refrain that suffuses all the verses of the song.[153]

> A GREAT MANY BISHOPS DID NOT SIT
> AS JUDGES IN THE USUAL WAY,
> MEN WHO, HAVING ASSEMBLED, ARE ACCUSTOMED
> TO JUDGE GREAT CASES.
> NO ACCUSOR AND NO DEFENDANT
> STOOD IN THE COURT,
> NO WITNESS, NO DOCUMENT BY WHICH
> THE CHARGE COULD BE PROVED,
> BUT ONLY MADNESS, DECEIT, AND UPROAR
> THAT REIGN IN UNTRUTH.

Court metaphors and legal references occur repeatedly throughout the song.[154] It is hardly surprising, therefore, that the song also ends with a judicial metaphor: with an announcement that it was difficult to conduct a court case and to hear all of the evidence. This is precisely what the A–V stanzas of the song had tried to show. The metaphor encompasses the appearance of Mother Church herself who makes her appeal like an

---

[153] Aug. *Psalmus contra partem Donati*, 74–78 (Lambot, 1935: 321 = BA 28: 160): "Non iudices consederunt tot sacerdotes de more / quo solent in magnis causis congregati iudicare, / non accusator et reus steterunt in quaesitione, / non testis, non documentum, quo possent crimen probare, / sed furor dolus tumultus, qui regnant in falsitate."

[154] Take the stanzas "C" and "D" as examples: Aug. *Psalmus contra partem Donati*, 45, 47–48 (Lambot 1935: 319–20 = BA 28: 156): this court case has been decided long ago: *olim causa iam finita est*; our ancestors judged this case, which they were able to investigate thoroughly because the facts were recent: *dixerunt maiores nostri . . . qui tunc causam cognoverunt quod recens possent probare*. Such legal language pervades the whole of the song from beginning to end.

emotional and tearful entreaty directed to jurors in a secular court. But the
concluding words of the song, if still judicial in tone, are more ominous.[155]

> WE HAVE SUNG TO YOU, OUR BROTHERS,
> ABOUT PEACE – IF YOU WISH TO HEAR.
> BUT THAT JUDGE OF OURS IS COMING.
> WE PAY THE PENALTY, HE EXACTS IT.

The song ends with a threat. The death penalty awaits those who are found
guilty of the crime. But it also construes the battle as a dispute between
brothers who are children of the same mother. It is to these "brothers" that
the contents are addressed, the implied point being that both Catholics and
dissenters ought to be singing the same song.[156] But the song encouraged
the betrayal of the values of the dissidents' community as much as it
confirmed the correct beliefs of the Catholics. Already in late 393, in one
of the earliest interventions by Augustine in this war of words, the song
reveals that almost all of the main lines of the battle were already matters
of a deep ancestral heritage. In part because both sides kept feeding the
conflict with inflammatory verbal ammunition, and inventing new ways
in which to communicate them, like this one, it promised to be, in the
evocative words of the song, a *rixa sine fine* – a quarrel without end.[157]

---

[155] Aug. *Psalmus contra partem Donati*, 296–97 (Lambot, 1935: 328 = BA 28: 190): "Cantavimus vobis,
fratres, pacem si vultis audire. / Venturus est iudex noster: nos damus, exigit ille."

[156] Aug. *En. in Ps.* 95.11 (CCL 39: 1350): "lingua tua sonat quod sonat mea."

[157] Aug. *Psalmus contra partem Donati*, 141 (Lambot, 1935: 323 = BA 28:): "Quibus si et nos non
credamus, erit rixa sine fine."

CHAPTER II

Kings of this world

One of the few verbatim statements attributed to the bishop Donatus of Carthage, the founding father of the dissident church, was a verbal volley issued in the crisis of 347 – angry words spoken during a hostile confrontation he had with Paul and Macarius, emissaries of the emperor Constans. When they arrived in Carthage, Donatus demanded of them, *Quid est imperatori cum ecclesia*? – "What does the emperor have to do with the Church?"[1] With this provocative rhetorical question, he was suggesting that the emperor was a secular official whose writ was to manage the earthly affairs of the Roman state and nothing else. For all his power, the emperor was *not* a bishop of the church and so ought to keep out of its affairs. Whether Donatus liked it or not, however, any reasonable answer to his question "What does the emperor have to do with the church?" would have to be an emphatic "almost everything."

The state created, defined, and sustained the material, institutional, and ideological order of the secular world in which the bishop Donatus and the people of his church lived. Christian churches and the Roman state existed, as it has been well expressed, "in a permanent state of mutual dependence." Even if Christian communities were closely integrated with and dependent on the state, however, this did not guarantee the government any easy or ready control of Christian behavior.[2] Despite the fact that empire commanded immense, mostly unchallengeable resources of wealth, authority, and force, elements of both interest and pragmatic politics meant that the court's ability to manage ecclesiastical affairs at local level was limited. Despite these limitations, and whether the Catholics or

---

[1] Optatus, *Contra Parm.* 3.3.22 (SC 413: 20–22): A question that Optatus claims was issued "with his usual violence": "Qui [i.e. Paulus et Macarius] cum ad Donatum, patrem tuum, venirent et quare venerant indicarent, ille solito furore succensus in haec verba prorupit: Quid est imperatori cum ecclesia?" The chapter title is taken from Petilian's remark recorded by Augustine: *Contra litt. Petil.* 2.58, 132, 2.92.203, and 210; 2.92.212 (CSEL 52: 93, 126, 135, 137).

[2] Millar, *Greek Roman Empire*, p. 133.

the dissidents wanted it or not, the state was a constant player in their game. Both sides were therefore incessantly involved in a long-term game of trying to persuade the emperor and his officials to see things their way – to mobilize the state's considerable resources of property, law, and coercive power for their side. However hypocritical their objections might have been, what made the dissidents most angry was their conviction that the force of the state had been unjustly used by their opponents to compel them against their will.[3]

THE BITTER DEBATE

The first years of the reign of the first Christian emperor were marked by aggressive interventions by the state in Church affairs in Africa. The language of Constantine's letters and other documents dispatched to imperial and church officials in Africa in years immediately after his accession to power in the West is marked by the violently assertive language of a man who was personally certain of the difference between good and evil belief, and who was ready brutally to enforce his version of the good. Constantine's policies aimed at achieving a unity that identified the one true church with the one true state. For disturbing the singular relation with the one supreme deity that was beneficial to the state, the dissidents in Africa were castigated in severe terms by the emperor, from the beginning of his reign, as agents of Satan.[4] Such harsh interventions by the imperial court only encouraged ever more powerful fissionings in provincial Christian communities. Some unity was achieved, but at the cost of creating even larger and more coherent units of hostility and opposition. Backfiring of this kind was not in the interest of the state. Consequently, there soon emerged a tendency on the part of the rulers of the western empire to retreat from direct heavy-handed coercion of local ecclesiastical factions.

Less than happy experience had taught the emperors, including Constantine, that aggressive actions of theirs often caused more problems for the court than they solved. In fact, the interventions of the emperor and his advisors in the internal African church factionalism in the 310s was

[3] Aug. *Ep.* 129.4 (CCL 31B: 209): letter of Aurelius, Silvanus, and all other Catholic bishops to Flavius Marcellinus just before the conference of 411 at Carthage, noting that this was the greatest grievance of the dissidents who quoted biblical prophecies (perhaps Psalms 101: 23 and Daniel 7: 27) on the subordination of the kings of this world to God.

[4] See Euseb. *HE*, 10.7.1–2 on the dissidents' upsetting proper *religio*; for their castigation as agents of the Devil, see Const. *Ep. ad Episc. Cath.* (Maier, *Dossier*, 1, no. 21, 167–71, at p. 169: spring 314): "Quid igitur sentiunt maligni homines officia, ut vere dixi, Diaboli?", although the same sentiment is found throughout the whole letter (this is the fifth document in the dossier appended to Optatus' polemic against Parmenian).

instrumental in creating the permanent hostile division between the two churches that continued to cause difficulties for the imperial state over the remainder of the fourth century. A realization emerged that the government's agenda differed fundamentally from that of the bishops. Almost instinctively, emperors and court officials recoiled from this counterproductive game and left punishment to a higher authority. When the emperor Constantine withdrew from the field of sectarian conflict in Africa in 321, in one of his letters to the Africans he quoted holy scripture to the effect that vengeance was to be left to God. If left to Him, he said, the punishment wrought on one's enemies was only going to be all the more savage.[5] Up to the watershed of the emperor Julian's actions in the early 360s, there was only one other serious coercive intrusion by the state into Christian affairs in Africa. This was the sudden decision by Constans in 347 to intervene directly to force the dissidents to rejoin the Catholic Church. The ways in which this intervention unravelled and the similar results of Julian's meddlesome actions were lessons not lost on their successors.

The standoffish attitude of the court was consistent with the structure and behavior of the imperial state from the earlier Principate. No less than their predecessors, the leaders of the late Roman state tended to react in response to pressures and petitions coming from sources outside the court. From the age of Constantine, the most forceful representations to the state in matters of religion were those organized by church councils for the systematic lobbying of the emperor and the court. Since they represented the collective views of large numbers of bishops, the councils exuded a peculiar power. The device of voting on specific issues imparted legitimacy and force to requests or demands for action.[6] The result was that any Christian faction was compelled to lobby the court intensively for actions that it might want the state to take. The court would sometimes be willing to respond with legislation, but was much less inclined to use the military forces at its command to enforce the wishes even of its own orthodox Catholic church. The violent verbiage of imperial decrees, barking and snarling with vitriolic denunciations of its sectarian enemies, was intended to frighten them into submission. But the vanity of action behind the words revealed the court's unwillingness to do much more than to engage in verbal scare tactics and to issue decrees to be enforced by others.

---

[5] Constantine, *Ep. ad Cath.* (Maier, *Dossier*, 1, no. 30, 239–42, at p. 242): "vindictam enim quam Deo servare debemus"; and Constantine, *Ep. ad Episc. Numid.* (Maier, *Dossier*, 1, no. 33, pp. 246–52, at p. 249): "At ideo cum vindicta Deo permittitur, acrius de inimicis supplicium sumitur." Both passages refer to Paul, *Rom.* 12: 19. (This is the tenth document in the dossier appended to Optatus' polemic against Parmenian.)

[6] See MacMullen, *Voting About God*, for the most compelling analysis of this problem.

Whatever the caveats, from the first months of rule of the first Christian emperor Constantine, the Roman state became one of the central players in the long-running quarrel between the two Christian communities in Africa. Under the influence of the powerful bishop Ossius of Corduba, it became the aim of the imperial court to create a single orthodox church in the land. The active involvement of the Christian emperor became critical to determining the course of Christian affairs in Africa. But Constantine's interventions, often clumsy in nature, tended to exacerbate existing problems.[7] In part, this was because any direct coercive interference in the affairs of the church by the state was a highly charged matter. The episodes of severe persecution in the decade immediately preceding the Constantinian settlement had implanted sentiments of resentment, suspicion, and fear of the state in African Christians. The sudden official acceptance of the Christian church by the emperor, the imperial court, and a few members of the upper aristocracy was not enough to erase this profound sense of unease. Historical apprehensions were especially heightened in Africa, where the intervention of Constantine on the side of one Catholic faction only confirmed and fuelled a permanent divorce between the two Christian communities. Although Constantine remained firm in his decision and continued to issue decrees couched in savage rhetoric against "the Rebaptizers," he nevertheless retreated from further direct action. The rhetoric is therefore no sure guide to the government's behavior.[8] The same pattern has been noted of the late Roman state in other circumstances: "the state deployed much heavy rhetoric," but its terroristic declarations were usually followed by "the relatively tentative application of quite restricted official measures."

However Christian it might be, the state had its own agenda and its own pressing concerns, and these did not involve sorting out religious differences in the African provinces. Likewise, from the viewpoint of most African Christians the involvement of the state in their affairs, even the new state of Constantine and his successors, was not seen as a good thing. Government interventions were located somewhere along a spectrum between undesirable and evil. Even when they were argued to be necessary, they were rarely seen to be wanted or good. When measured against the long

---

[7] This often remains true even of modern states, where the forces involved are so much greater: see, e.g., Stern, *Terror in the Name of God*, pp. 72 f.

[8] On what follows, see Millar, *Greek Roman Empire*, p. 167; he continues: "this was true even of those who were the most determined enemies of unity and true doctrine . . . " They most frequently merely went off into exile where they continued to write. Throughout, he rightly cautions that we should not be misled by the violent power of the imperial rhetoric.

history of state persecution of Christians, the heavy handed intrusions by the court were portrayed by the victims as the betrayal of a shared Christian heritage. This negative view of state intervention was certainly shared by the minority dissident community in Africa. The fact that they themselves were deeply embroiled in lobbying the new Christian court was somehow lost to sight and memory, and for good reason. For the dissidents, the whole post-Constantinian age was one in which parts of the imperial state had come to be transformed into an evil force.[9] In 347, the resources of the imperial government were deployed against them again: money and armed violence were used to attract and to compel dissident believers into union with the Catholic Church. The acts of violent coercion were seen as proof of persecution. They excited a visceral and permanent anger in their community.

By the 390s, the dissidents had come to harbor long and deep resentments over any liaison between the church and secular power: they saw shadows of the Antichrist in the guise of imperial agents. The fact that the Catholic apologist Optatus dedicated no less than the first half of his reply to Parmenian – three of six books – in an attempt to refute the specific charge that the Catholics had solicited state intervention, is a measure of dissident apprehension and anger. He would never have expended the effort had the accusation of Catholic collaboration with the state fallen on deaf ears. The angry charge made by the dissidents had hit home. It had struck a common vein of hostility to the state that had deep roots among African Christians. Optatus' defense was nervous and guarded. He admitted that the charge was terrible and was made with such bitter resentment that if this one issue could somehow be resolved, then all other impediments between the two churches could easily be removed.[10] Optatus was not referring just to the sentiment that the forces of the state had been aligned with the Catholics, but to the specific charges concerned with the violent events of 347: "You say that military force was requested by us." Fully aware that this was a great issue that divided the two communities, Optatus devoted the whole of the second book of his work to an investigation of who was responsible for calling in the state authorities in 347.

Parmenian's hard attack on the Catholics in his *The Church of the Traitors* had reverberated among Christians in Africa, reviving vivid memories of the great persecution of 347. No Christian community, he argued, would have

---

[9] Again, a pattern found in other, modern, cases where each side tends to exaggerate the enemy's capabilities, as in Indonesia in the 1990s where each side believed that the other was trying to seize the state to turn it into its own creature: Stern, *Terror in the Name of God*, pp. 79 f.

[10] Optatus, *Contra Parm.* 1.5.5 (SC 412: 182): "Tolle hanc calumniam et noster es."

associated itself with such despicable actions. How could the Catholics have done it? On the grounds of having solicited state violence alone, the Catholic Church was no church at all. The bishop's words were blunt: "That thing cannot rightly be called a church which is fed with bloody morsels and which grows fat on the blood and flesh of martyrs." Referring to the events of 347, he angrily asserted that his enemies were men who had "dined on the blood of the martyrs." A refutation of his charges was necessary because the angry denunciation had struck a strong and responsive chord. In response, Optatus devoted the whole of the third book of his reply to Parmenian to painting a different picture of who was responsible for the intervention by the army in 347.[11] His answer was not to deny the bare facts of the events themselves, but rather to construe them in a frame where the acts of violence were justified.

In Optatus' view, even if Paul and Macarius, the emperor's "Workers of Unity" in 347, had done a *few* bad things, they were not necessarily evil men. Good men in pursuit of good things can do things that *appear* to be bad. A bandit is a bad man who does bad things, but a judge in his court is someone who does a bad thing, such as killing a criminal, in order to achieve a good: the protection of society. He argued that Paul and Macarius were like Phinehas in the Book of Numbers. Whereas it is true that there is a general injunction from God not to kill, when Phinehas came across a pair of adulterers in the midst of their immoral copulation, he cut them to pieces. God is for marriage, which is to say unity. We are all against schism (which is a kind of adultery) just like that punished by Phinehas.[12] The people who were killed by Paul and Macarius were no more martyrs to the Christian faith than were the polluted adulterers who were rightfully executed by Phinehas. According to the laws of God, both deserved to die. And, like Phinehas, Paul and Macarius were His agents. Otherwise, the dissidents were responsible for what happened to themselves. Paul and Macarius were just enacting good typological roles. Their true predecessors were not state persecutors, but rather Moses, Elijah and Phinehas. Moses had killed 3,000 heretics, Elijah had killed 450 false prophets, Phinehas had killed two adulterers. Just so, Macarius had also killed two bad men, Donatus and Marculus. Like Phinehas and the prophets of old, he was punishing those who had disobeyed the laws of God: he was God's agent

---

[11] Optatus, *Contra Parm.* 3.1.1 (SC 413: 8): "tertio, quis fecerit ut miles mitteretur armatus?"

[12] Optatus, *Contra Parm.* 3.5.1–3 (SC 413: 46–48; 49–50), with reference to the Phinehas episode in Numbers 25: 6–11; and 3.6.1–2. Like others of his time, Optatus construes the intercourse between the Israelite man and the Midianite woman that moved Phinehas to action as a kind of adultery.

in the apostle Paul's sense: "a minister of the will of God" like Elijah who killed so many false prophets.[13]

Part of Optatus' argument on violence is interesting, since it did not wholly rule out the possibility of a necessary, legitimate, and therefore good Christian violence. Parmenian's argument was that violence against Christians was no longer justified at all since the context of Africa in the 370s and 380s was different. "We do not live in violent times like those where such things were justified. Our model was set by Christ, who restored the ear that Peter cut off."[14] But for Optatus an appeal to force from the Christian state was justified if it was to achieve a patent good like the Unity of the Church. So there was nothing inherently wrong with petitioning Christian emperors to do God's work. A subject that Optatus does not broach is: Why, if this was the case, did the emperors apparently do so little of the Lord's urgently needed good work? The answer (which he does not give) is that they did not do so because the late Roman state in the west was not particularly well structured to deal with such matters in an easy and decisive fashion.

INTERESTS OF STATE

The late Roman state was not just an emperor and his court, or indeed the emperor and his big men: the vicars and praetorian prefects and provincial governors. Nor was the state the emperor and these men plus minor officials, bureaucrats, and servitors. Nor was it all of these plus the army. The imperial government was a peculiar mix of personal monarchic beneficiaries and servitors, court intriguers and spin-doctors, bureaucratic functionaries, and competitors holding armed forces: congeries of high and low civil and military powers, both central and local. Just as the Christian church in the empire at large and in Africa in particular was divided and subdivided, both internally and externally, so too the late Roman state was made up of different, sometimes conflicting and confusing levels and admixtures of power and authority. In the late fourth century, the basic division in imperial power was between a western and an eastern empire. But even this divide was fluctuating and uncertain. After the mid-360s, it is true, no eastern or western emperor, save for brief exceptions, wielded any real power in the other half of the empire. Although imperial decrees were issued in the names of the ruling emperors and so maintained the fiction that both

---

[13] Optatus, *Contra Parm.* 7.6.5–6 (SC 413: 240).
[14] Parmenian apud Optatus, *Contra Parm.* 3.7.7–8 (SC 413: 54–56).

emperors ruled everywhere in the empire, in reality it was only the western court that effectively ruled in the west.[15] Every crisis of empire, however, threw into question the position of Africa between east and west. Even in normal conditions, the emperor, the central court, provincial governors, army commanders, high and low aristocrats, decurions and local notables, and others, all had their own interests and agenda that affected the ways in which the instruments of authority worked and in which the effects of state power were experienced.

In the formal structure of the state, there were at least three principal levels of decision-making and action. Each of these had its own peculiar powers, its own structures of operation and, more important, its own agenda. Yet, since all were involved to one degree or another in the episodes of sectarian violence, each of them, with its own perspectives and interests, must be understood. At the acme stood the emperor and his court, often on the move, present in two or three capital cities of empire. In the late fourth and early fifth century, the western court that most directly concerned Africa was located first at Trier, before it retreated southwards to Milan in 381 and moved, finally, in 402, to the safe haven of Ravenna. The successive relocations of the court are one element in understanding the factors that conditioned the emperor's relationship to Africa. When the court was sited on the distant northwestern frontier at Trier, it was physically and mentally furthest removed not only from Africa, but also from the western aristocratic elite in Rome and Italy that provided most of the high-level governing officials for the western empire. Like the senator Symmachus, many members of this senatorial elite had substantial landed interests in Africa. And, like Symmachus, there are good reasons to presume that many of the wealthiest and most powerful of these senators were absentee owners, mainly resident in Rome and Italy.[16]

Furthermore, the implosion and fragmentation of the frontiers and the forced retreat of the imperial court first to Milan and then to Ravenna had two precise consequences that affected Africa.[17] The retreat brought the military court and the civil senatorial aristocracy in Rome and Italy into closer and more direct proximity. At the same time, the moves also focussed the court's concern more urgently on its African provinces. Africa

[15] Errington, *Roman Imperial Policy*, pp. 1–3, 91–92: what he calls "the existential constitutional myth."

[16] See CTh 11.1.13 (Valentinian and Valens, from Paris, to Dracontius, Vicar of Africa; 18 January 366): which assumes that a significant number of such African landowners and taxpayers were resident in Rome.

[17] No one has documented and analyzed this process better than Matthews, *Western Aristocracies*, esp. pp. 203 f.; and see Errington, *Roman Imperial Policy*, p. 195, on the effects of the move from Trier to Milan.

was one of the few remaining peaceful regions of the western empire on which the emperor could depend for strategic supplies. Naturally, a heightened awareness of this basic fact emerged at Milan and Ravenna. A land that had once been a quiet, dependable, almost assumed resource in the background of empire was now critical to the survival of the state. More intense communications between Africa and the court, and therefore increased opportunities to lobby the emperor, arose as a by-product of this new orientation.

Perhaps paradoxically, despite its growing dependence on Africa, the court remained almost as remote from the region as it had ever been. The western emperors recursively toured the Rhine and Danube lines along the armed northern frontiers of the empire. Never once did they go to Africa. Not a single emperor, eastern or western, in the whole of the period had any direct or personal knowledge of the African provinces. Everything that the court knew about Africa was the result of facts and ideas fed to it by state officials or by interested private parties, especially members of the great landowning classes. As they became more intensely involved, the influence of these latter persons, mostly of senatorial status, grew in importance. In this circumstance, emperors tended to react to the most compelling representations made to them: demands that penetrated the inner circle at Milan or Ravenna and that convinced them of the orders that they had to issue to imperial officials in the African provinces. Africa was simultaneously caught up in a sense of remoteness and a heightened awareness of its strategic importance. In a situation in which imperial agents in Africa were commanding some of the most important resources of empire and yet most information directly supplied to the court was coming from intensely interested parties physically close to the emperor, Africa was now perceived as seedbed of pretenders to imperial rule.

At the middle or second level of governance, the most important and prestigious civil representatives of the imperial state resident in Africa were the provincial governors. Other high ranking officials existed, such as the great military commanders of the frontier sectors and the army, but the likelihood of their involvement in day-to-day civil affairs was remote. The state reserved the army for its own most important secular interests in enforcement. Units of the imperial army in Africa were rarely directly involved in incidents of sectarian violence. Although some soldiers might be delegated from the proconsul's limited forces, or a few assigned to serve special imperial emissaries, there was never any ongoing policy to involve the regular army in any large-scale enforcement against Christian dissenters. Lower-level police functionaries were far more important in sectarian conflicts.

Violent incidents that occurred at places almost on the southern frontier itself, where the army was stationed, as in the incident in the early 360s at Lemellef, were never sufficient to provoke the involvement of the regular armed forces of the state. In almost any circumstance, the men who held the office of the commander-in-chief of Roman military forces in Africa, the Count of Africa or *Comes Africae*, or the generals or *duces* in command of the sectors of the frontier, would only move their forces to action if there were serious military threats, real or perceived, that imperiled the state's interests in Africa. Even in these cases, such as the Firmus "war," the central court was reluctant to draw units of the standing army in Africa off the line of the frontiers, preferring instead to send special expeditionary forces from overseas to deal with specific large-scale threats as they arose.

The civil governors were the men who had to deal with lower-level kinds of violence, but the senators who held these governorships were caught up in the complex web of official links between themselves and the court. They usually held their position for just a year or two, only exceptionally for longer. It was expected that the governor would, ideally, leave Rome in March (at latest by mid-April) to arrive at his post in April and remain in it until the end of April of the following year.[18] Exigencies of life, however, from the death of an incumbent to massive dislocations in imperial power at the center could create the need for a sudden replacement or for the extension of the term of a sitting governor. Although he was one of a number of men at this level (there were about 120 of them empire-wide) the temporary nature of their tenure generated peculiar kinds of knowledge and interests.[19] The governor was mainly tasked with the maintenance of peace and order, but since his term of office was brief, he had to avoid acting in a manner that would cause unwanted disturbances or unnecessary upheavals, especially ones that could threaten the regular flow of tribute or that might raise questions at court about his competence or loyalty.

Being a transient figure, the governor was not always well versed in local affairs. He often came from outside Africa and would face a myriad of local problems that were peculiar to the region and about which he would have to be educated. What is more, most governors were involved in public career paths that were unlike those of their peers in the high empire. Their main interests were in their larger social careers, in which the holding of official power was a rare and more occasional thing than it had been for aristocrats

[18] Barnes (1985a), p. 144, with reference to (1983), 256–60; and *New Empire*, pp. 168–70.
[19] For the total number of governors, see Slootjes, *The Governor*, p. 19, who estimates 116, based on the numbers attested in the *Notitia Dignitatum* (a source of rather mixed value on this matter, however); for the more pressing problems, however, see Carrié (1998).

in the Principate. The amateurishness and slightness of the role of governor is illustrated by the typical figure of Quintus Aurelius Symmachus who was governor of Africa in 373–74. It has been noted that during the forty years that Symmachus was a senator he only held three official imperial posts that required any serious hard work. Each of these assignments had lasted no more than a year and each one was separated by a decade of private life.[20] Although a governor like Symmachus was an important focus of decision-making at provincial level, given the brevity of his tenure of office, most of the permanent operative power was in the hands of the local bureaucrats and servitors who staffed the governor's headquarters, such as those at Carthage and its satellite offices in the proconsular province.

The central office of the proconsul of Africa, for example, had something on the order of 400 appointed officials salaried by the court.[21] But this number did not include the very much larger numbers of permanent service personnel drawn from lower social ranks who accomplished the business of government in each town and rural district. Unfortunately for us, these lower-level provincial bureaucrats are almost as unknown and undocumented as they were faceless in their own time. As ground-level servitors, they were both important and unimportant. Important in that they controlled the day-to-day application of imperial administration that was concerned with record keeping, tribute collection, and the maintenance of provincial courts. Their perspective was rooted in the local conditions of the *status quo* that would allow them to get along with people with whom they had to deal to get their job done with a minimum of hindrance. Conversely, they were unimportant. They could not form any significant policy initiatives or make new laws. Such decisions had to come from the imperial court or from the governor's office. The higher-level officials were open to "suggestions" coming from below, but they alone decided. Further, despite imperial rules against local recruitment, most of these lower-level permanent bureaucrats were long-term residents of the places where they served.[22] They had little incentive to upset local power networks.

---

[20] Matthews, *Western Aristocracies*, p. 12.

[21] Jones, *LRE*, I, pp. 592–93, citing CTh 1.12.6 (Arcadius and Honorius, from Mediolanum, to Victorius, proconsul of Africa; and to Dominator, Vicar of Africa; 21 May 398) to Victorius, Proconsul of Africa and Dominator, Vicar of Africa) assigning a maximum of 400 apparitores to each *officium*; one can also add CTh 1.15.5 (Valentinian, and Valens, from Mediolanum, to Dracontius, Vicar of Africa; 25 January 365), setting the upper number at 300 for the vicar's *officium*. Alas, the "400" figure is often read (as Jones does) with an exactitude that I think that it does not have – and, even so, the emperors were attempting, in vain it seems, to impose an upper limit; cf. Palme (1999) on the upper levels of this administration; see p. 100 n. 80 on this item.

[22] Brown, *Power and Persuasion*, p. 22.

The court's interests and those of the governors were not local but rather Mediterranean-wide ones that affected the empire's general condition. It was precisely in this sphere that there was a long-term disjunction between the governors in Africa and the court in Milan or Ravenna. The imperial court's interests were mainly military and tributary, and, directly related to these, the maintenance of the administrative, legal, and bureaucratic mechanisms that underpinned the economic and ideological infrastructure of its rule. Where the evidence can be tested, however, we find that almost all of the consular governors of the provinces of Numidia and Byzacena, and the proconsular governors of Africa, were drawn from the traditional senatorial aristocracy centered in Rome and Italy.[23] The interests of these men who, like Symmachus, were only occasional high-level servitors of the state, were more in the economic, cultural, and status demands of their own class than in the urgent military and political pressures that were bearing down on the imperial court. The Africans in the senatorial elite were men much like Symmachus. They were members of a civil aristocracy of wealth and power who were remote from the emperor's inner circle. And this elite, especially among the members of it especially oriented to African matters, was still mainly non-Christian in makeup.[24] They rarely held permanent administrative appointments at court.[25] The main priorities assigned to the governor by the state were the maintenance of peace and order and the collation of the imperial tribute. As in the high empire, the first of these duties engaged him, or his legates, in a circuit of annual assizes in which he traveled to the principal urban centers of his province in order to hear cases that rose to a level above local jurisdiction.[26]

Between most provincial governors and the imperial court there were several possible levels of administration, but the province of Africa ranked

---

[23] Matthews, *Western Aristocracies*, p. 14, referring to the work of Chastagnol (1966), which has been confirmed by subsequent discoveries and research.

[24] See Barnes (1995) who, in criticism of the faulty analysis of von Haehling, argues for an earlier and more pervasive Christian membership in the high elite; but see also his important remarks on appointments to high office concerning Africa in the reign of Constans (p. 144). A more traditional perspective is sustained by the analysis of Salzman, *Christian Aristocracy*; on Africa, see pp. 94–96. The figures, such as they are, are subject to the many caveats on fixing identity and problems with valuing the source materials. They seem to indicate a sustained impetus of patronage of Christians under Constantine, but much less so by his successors up to the last decades of the century. The position taken here is basically that esposed at the beginning of these debates, first by Brown (1961a/1971a) and then by Eck (1971) based on prosopographical analysis, with the exception that the research done by Barnes and Salzman has demonstrated an early phase of the appointment of officials to high office under Constantine.

[25] Matthews, *Western Aristocracies*, p. 16: how little normal contact these men had with the court is manifest from Symmachus' correspondence and writings.

[26] On the impressions made by the judicial *legati* of the governor, see Hugoniot (2002a).

apart as an exception, as it always had in the past. In the high Roman empire it stood, with Asia, at the pinnacle of the senatorial administrative career. In late antiquity, it remained one of the three highest-ranking civil provinces of the empire. Its governors held the rank of proconsul. In an exception to the norm of imperial appointments, these men were selected by the western Senate from its own members, by agreement or sortition, and they governed their province for one or two year terms, rarely longer.[27] Unlike the governors of the other provinces, the proconsuls were directly responsible to the emperor. In consequence, many imperial decisions and directives of the period were issued directly to the proconsul of Africa. The governors of all the other imperial provinces in Africa – Tripolitania, Byzacena, Numidia, Mauretania Sitifensis, and Mauretania Caesariensis – fell under the jurisdiction of the Vicar of Africa.[28] After the emperor and the Praetorian Prefect of the western empire, the Vicar was responsible for all civil administration in the provinces of his region and the governors reported in the first instance to his office. Normally resident, like the proconsul of Africa, at Carthage, the Vicars could hold their positions for anything from one to four years. In the case of these other African provinces, imperial edicts were delivered via the Praetorian Prefect of Italy and Africa, to the Vicar of Africa, and thence to the governors.[29] The governors of these other African provinces were also senators who were directly appointed by the emperor himself. Holding the title of *praeses*, they normally governed their provinces for one or two year terms, only exceptionally longer.[30]

The administration of imperial law at gubernatorial level faced several problems that affected the nature of sectarian violence. For most normal day-to-day disputes that had to be decided and administrative tasks that had to be done, there were no great difficulties. There was the permanent administrative structure of tax officials, imperial procurators, imperial freedmen and slaves, who carried out these tasks from one year to the next. The bigger problem was with extraordinary or specific measures that had to be enforced. Here difficulties are found at all levels, sometimes exacerbated by the more complex channels of communication between court and province for the lower-ranking provinces. Local administrators were either not competent to undertake such tasks, had no experience with them, or

[27] PLRE, I, pp. 1072–74 (AD 257–95); 2, p. 1274 (394–429).

[28] PLRE, I, pp. 1079–80 (AD 303–95); 2, p. 1275 (392–445); see the still useful study by Pallu de Lessert (1916).

[29] On the governor's office and staff, see Barrau (1987); Pallu de Lessert (1901 and 1916), pointed out that it is possible to see the two distinct flows of information in the imperial constitutions regarding the dissident church.

[30] PLRE, I, pp. 1086–89; 2, p. 1277.

did not see them as falling in their sphere of responsibility. On the other hand, the governor, who had the formal power and the mission to undertake such special enforcement measures, was generally hesitant to do so since the year or two that he administered one of the African provinces was only a moment in a sporadic public career. The logical propensity for most senior administrators was to perform their duties in such a way as to provoke the fewest disturbances and to draw the least possible attention to anything other than matters that would reflect favorably on their term of office.

Anullinus, Proconsul of Africa in 303–04, and later reputed as the arch-persecutor of Christians, an almost satanic figure, found himself in just this sort of bind between local politics and the central court.[31] The so-called "first edict" against the Christians posted at Nicomedia on 24 February 303, must have arrived in Carthage around the end of April or beginning of May of the same year. Anullinus was then faced with the problem of enforcing an order that, on almost any assessment, would most likely provoke serious dissent and resistance. If he rigorously enforced the decree, what would be *his* reward? Would the emperors back a governor who might not be able to maintain conditions of peace and order? More to the point, Anullinus simply did not have in his own hands the means to enforce such an extraordinary measure. He would have had to rely substantially on local powers by passing on the primary enforcement duties to local municipal officials. And how much would *they* cooperate in enforcing such a measure on their fellow citizens, people with whom they had face-to-face relations in their own towns and villages? There is good evidence that Anullinus, like many earlier Roman governors who found themselves in the same position, attempted to find creative ways to satisfy both his constituencies: to convince the emperor and the court that he was enforcing the decree and the local citizenry, including Christians, that he was doing his job only to the limited extent that was necessary and not in ways that would permanently impair their most valued relations.[32]

Facing a deficit of sufficient infrastructure, it was expected that governors and their assistants would often be compelled to use harsh measures. In lobbying Apringius, the proconsular governor of Africa in 412, concerning the punishment of circumcellions, Augustine observed that administering a province was different from running a church in that the former had to

---

[31] See "Anullinus (3)," PLRE, I, p. 79.
[32] On earlier governors, see Tertullian's remarks, and detailed cases, offered to Scapula, the proconsular governor of Africa in 212–13: *Ad Scap.* 3.4–4.8 (CCL 2: 1129–31).

be ruled by a deterrent fear.[33] Without discussing any high-flown theories of the relationship between church and state, let us say that Augustine was not innovating. When he spoke of the nature of the exercise of state power in this fashion, he was surely echoing common sentiments. The state had to return evil for evil. Even if Christians judged the role of the state differently (as the dissidents surely did) they did not disagree with the nature of its strict functioning.[34]

Let those who say that the teaching of Christ is set against the state produce such an army and such soldiers as the teaching of Christ demands; let them produce such subjects, such husbands, such wives, such parents, such sons, such masters, such slaves, such kings, such judges, and finally, such payers and collectors of tributes owed to the state treasury as Christian teaching commands.

Everyone, somehow, had to fulfill a specific role of obedience in this layered and sometimes conflicting series of loyalties. It might have been just so much rhetoric when Augustine wrote to Macedonius, the Vicar of Africa, in 415, to protest the Vicar's reprimand that Augustine should mind his own business as a bishop of the Christian church and not interfere with the state's punishment of criminals, but his reply drew on the image of a great ladder of power founded on fear, a picture with which neither the imperial official nor his subjects would tend to disagree.[35] Apringius, and other imperial officials like him, however, were not alone in feeling that there were too many clerics and bishops meddling in the state's interests and business.[36]

The description of this complex pile of bureaucracy and power helps to explain why so little happened in terms of state intervention and sectarian violence in Africa. All these various levels of the state were set, by nature and structure, against any effective interference by the central court in local matters like religious disputes. If there is one thing that is manifest about the intersection of state and sectarian violence in Africa it is that, to get anything accomplished, the emperor had to cut directly through all of the intervening layers of administration and officialdom. To achieve this end he had to appoint special plenipotentiary agents who were empowered to get a specific task done, shielded from the unwanted interference and the

---

[33] Aug. *Ep.* 134.3 (CCL 31B: 246): "Sed alia causa est provinciae, alia est ecclesiae: illius terribiliter gerenda est administratio, huius clementer commendanda est mansuetudo."

[34] Aug. *Ep.* 138.15 (CCL 31B: 285).   [35] Aug. *Ep.* 153.3.8–4.11, esp. 5,16 (CSEL 44: 404–08, 413–14).

[36] Humfress (2008), p. 133, noting that as late as 439 in the West, a quaestor could make the complaint (see NovVal. 3).

lethargy of provincial governors, local notables, and the like. These special officials were called tribunes and notaries, *tribuni et notarii.*[37]

It is not by accident that *tribuni et notarii* were used on the occasions in our age when the hand of the emperor reached deeply and directly into African sectarian struggles. First in 347, Paul and Macarius, whether by name or not, were clearly such fully empowered emperor's men. There followed the appointment of the tribune and notary Flavius Marcellinus to hold a great conference at Carthage in 411, for which task he was given specific powers and directives that enabled him to hold the hearing without any interference from local authorities, even imperial ones. Finally, in the enforcement of the state seizure of dissident churches and basilicas in the years after 415, the same officials are seen at work – like the *tribunus et notarius* Dulcitius, for example, in southern Numidia. In using these plenipotentiaries, the involvement of the court became doubly difficult. On the one hand, such intervention involved the downward salience of imperial power through its various levels of governance to mobilize force at local level. On the other, the managers of institutions at local level were less than eager to engage in internal disputes among Christians. In this specific sense, the power of the tribune and notary was unnatural, driving roughshod through the balances of authority that normally characterized local social and power relations.

LOCAL GOVERNMENT, LOCAL COURTS

The lack of official enthusiasm for involvement in Christian conflicts is important because the town and city elites were the next critical link in the loosely concatenated chain of imperial power. Lowest in hierarchy, they were the face of Roman administration that most inhabitants of most communities in Africa confronted. In Africa they were more omnipresent than in any other region of the western empire except perhaps Campania and central Italy. These urban-centered governing classes were the embodiment of Roman law and order. Each town had an *ordo* or town council that was responsible for the same two critical functions of imperial administration as were governors: maintaining civic order and managing the state's tribute. In their mandate to maintain order, the magistrates of the towns, who were ordinarily elected to annual terms of office, were directly responsible for the dispensing of Roman law. The town mayors or *duumviri*, along

---

[37] See Teitler, *Notarii and Exceptores*, pp. 19–21, for some comments. While noting a "vast gap," to my taste he still conflates this office too closely with that of an ordinary *notarius*. The title indicates, rather, something like a plenipotentiary "military/civil" administrator: Lengle (1937).

with their assistants, ran the local courts that had jurisdiction over a wide range of delicts valued below certain sums and criminal acts short of capital offenses such as homicide. Very importantly for our purposes, these included a wide range of property disputes that concerned reasonably significant values. Even where some property cases might eventually have to be put before the governor, municipal magistrates, like provincial governors in miniature, acted as judges and would hear the particulars to determine if the facts of the case placed it in their jurisdiction or if it needed to be transferred to a higher level of authority.

Elsewhere in the empire, men who formed the curial classes were a huge reservoir of qualified persons of privilege from whom Christian clergy were recruited. In these regions, Christians were substantially represented in the local municipal *ordines* or town councils that governed the cities.[38] If this permeability existed in other provinces of the empire, especially in some of its eastern ones, it was certainly untrue of Africa. Every item of evidence concerning the membership and the leadership of the local town councils in Africa indicates that they mimicked the senatorial and aristocratic hierarchy above them. They were almost wholly non-Christian. The best-preserved membership list available for a fourth-century African municipality, that of Thamugadi (Timgad) in Numidia, reveals a normal situation in which Christian clergy and municipal officialdom functioned in their own spheres.[39] The ordinary situation through the fourth and early fifth centuries in Africa was that of an almost complete separation between the recruitment base and membership of the hierarchy in the two Christian churches and the ranks of state officials at all levels, including the municipal.

In the incidents of sectarian violence that marked the history between the two Christian churches in Africa over the fourth and early fifth centuries, these structural aspects of the state suggest the following consequences for action by its officials. First, the front-line policy officials of the state, the governors, had little or no interest in getting involved in Christian affairs. Quite apart from their brief tenure of office, almost all of them were members of a traditional ruling elite whose cultural and other ideals were the antithesis of the low and common culture shared by the Christians of both churches. Even if the state issued central directives against "pagan" worship or in favor of any given Christian party, these measures were likely to be disregarded or pursued with less than full enthusiasm. A further

---

[38] Rapp, *Holy Bishops*, pp. 184 f., drawing attention to the work of Paul Petit on Antioch.
[39] See ch. 5, pp. 196–97 for a discussion of the Timgad inscription.

consequence, which is also consistent with the surviving evidence, is this: if Christians wanted the state to enforce dictates favorable to them, they would have to bypass local and provincial officials and bureaucrats to appeal directly to the court at Milan or Ravenna. And even if the African bishops might finally have some success at court and acquired the desired imperial directives to the Praetorian Prefect, to the Vicar of Africa, or to the proconsular governor, they would find themselves back at square one. They would still be faced with a host of local officials who had little or no desire energetically to implement such measures, which, in the end, might only endanger the one year that they were responsible for their office.

The problem was that the separation of the municipal elites and the secular nature of their institutions of power (and their frank disinterest in Christians and their quarrels) ironically provoked the opposite of the expected reaction amongst Christians. Although excoriating their ideas, their education, their beliefs, and their deities, the Christians of all factions constantly had recourse to the civic institutions of local governments for adjudication precisely because they were seen to be neutral or disinterested.[40] The state at all its levels represented a polarizing force towards which they could orient themselves. As it weakened and drained from their midst, however, the paradox is that the contending parties would be put more directly into confrontation with each other.[41] Still, Christians who attempted to place copies of their complaints against each other in the official records of a town or city, or who tried to bring charges before local courts, had to overcome the resistance of local officials who did not wish to become entangled in internal Christians disputes. When Augustine tried to register a complaint against Proculianus, the dissident bishop of Hippo, he was met with an outright refusal from Eusebius, the procurator of the city, who stated flatly that he did not wish to act as judge in a matter between bishops.[42] Here was the heart of the problem for both the Catholic church leadership and the imperial court: local enforcement. In lobbying Olympius, an imperial official, in an attempt to get him to compel local authorities to enforce the laws on the books against "heretics," Augustine complained that these local men of power were able to spin certain laws as not applicable or as somehow illegitimate. They thereby incited "the ignorant" in their communities to a hostile attitude to Christians.[43]

---

[40] Lepelley (2002a), p. 278.   [41] See Brubaker (2004), pp. 89–90, who analyzes a similar case.

[42] Aug. *Ep.* 34–35, esp. 35.1 (CCL 31: 124–29; 127): "Non ego recusanti voluntati tuae iudicium, sicut dicis, inter episcopos subeundum, molestus exhortator aut deprecator imposui."

[43] Aug. *Ep.* 97.2 (CCL 31A: 224–25). All of which takes place in the context of Augustine's involvement by correspondence with persons in Rome concerning imperial policy: "quo noverint inimici ecclesiae

If appeals could theoretically be made all the way up the chain of government to the imperial court, disputes and conflicts, even violent ones, were habitually negotiated first through the agency of the local courts. The fact that the town decurions who staffed the tribunals and heard the cases were largely non-Christian encouraged the keeping of the Christians and their ecclesiastical or theological disputes at arm's length. But it also meant that the courts, not being usurped or controlled by either of the two sides, represented a relatively neutral forum of adjudication. So it was to the civil courts that both sides went first and, naturally, images of trial hearings and judicial metaphors permeate much of their writing and speaking.

THE MOTHER OF ALL LAWYERS

In these circumstances, and more often than not, Christian disputes were normally first dealt with by municipal governments and by local town courts. At this face-to-face level, there was a similar hesitation if not out-right resistance to deal with matters involving quarreling among Christians. It bears repetition that the notables who governed the towns and cities of late Roman Africa were largely secular in their orientation. Their religious values were embedded in a traditional classical education that was inter-woven with their everyday behavior as urban elites. To deal with Christian squabbles was to implicate themselves in distasteful low class superstitions that were so déclassé that involvement with them might risk degrading social standing. To mix base superstition and the imperial law was some-thing that surely ran counter to their values and attitudes. It would sully the high culture of rhetoric with which the law was so closely identified. And there were the unnecessary dangers to be faced. Mutually hostile Christian groups might wish to use the civil courts as a form of impartial adjudication of their differences. But the decurions who sat as judges or assessors could easily see that to decide one way or the other in such cases was to become embroiled in intractable ecclesiastical disputes that might later harm their own interests.

It is probably in this context that the claims and counter-claims of the two sides – complaints about biased court decisions or, more frequently, about the inaction of the local courts – can be best understood. In the year 401, when Augustine defended the Catholic use of the courts to get

leges illas, quae de idolis confringendis et haereticis corrigendis vivo Stilichone in Africam missae sunt, voluntate imperatoris piissimi et fidelissimi constitutas; quo nesciente vel nolente factum sive dolose iactant sive libenter putant atque hinc animos inperitorum turbulentissimos reddunt nobisque periculose ac vehementer infestos."

decisions against the dissidents, he suggested that the other side acted no differently, and that they were able to get court decisions that favored them because of the connivance of judges and local authorities with whom they had relations of "friendship."[44] But many more of his complaints concern the inaction of local judges and courts on issues put to them by Catholic petitioners. Whatever the problems, both churches consistently went to the courts to resolve problems. One such incident arose within the Catholic Church at the hamlet of Germanicia in the region of Hippo. Disaffection had arisen over the conduct of a priest named Secundinus, and charges were leveled against him by disaffected elements within the church. Some of these disputes revolved around claims to church property, and it was this part of the wrangle that was taken before the local courts.[45] The problem was that such cases, including this one, could become long, entangled, expensive, and wearing on the participants. The patience of the petitioners could give out or they could reject the court's verdict, situations that might provoke recourse to violence. So it was in this case, where Augustine pleaded with the locals not to drag the bishop from his house, or to pillage and destroy it.

That is to say, the very common recourse to the civil courts might excite sectarian violence for two reasons: one was the simple failure of one's own point of view to persuade the judges. The other was more subtle: the continual grinding away in the courts recursively fed bad sentiments back into the participants and heightened the value of what was at stake in the quarrel between them. Such disputes tended to be resolved at local level, however, simply because Africa was a profoundly peaceful and civil society that had rapidly developed a deep interest in and commitment to the law, in its profession, as well as in the rhetorical and theatrical displays of the civil courts.[46] It was in the Africans' cultural blood. It is no accident that, as early as the first decades of the second century, Juvenal could satirize Africa as "the mother of lawyers."[47] It is also no accident that the one extensive piece of rhetorical prose that has survived from Africa of the high empire is the *Apologia*, the speech made in 158 CE before Claudius Maximus, the

---

44 Aug. *Contra litt. Petil.* 2.83.184 (CSEL 52: 114): "Quis autem possit enarrare omnia, quae nulla amicitia iudicum aut aliquarum potestatum quisque potuerit in locis vestris propria dominatione committitis?"

45 Aug. *Ep.* 251 (CSEL 57: 600): "ut eiusdem prebyteri domus non diripiatur neque vastetur"; Augustine suggests that the accusations might have been prompted by "heretics," but the whole conflict is manifestly within the Catholic community; see "Secundinus (3)," PAC, p. 1050.

46 On the technical side of this legal culture, see Liebs (1989); for the teaching and the law schools, especially at Carthage, see Vössing (1996), p. 127 n. 3.

47 An approximate rendering of Juvenal's *Africa, nutricula causicidorum*: Juv. *Sat.* 7.148 f.; see Vössing (1996) for a glossing of African legal culture in the light of this satirical cut characterizing Africans.

governor of Africa, by Apuleius who was defending himself on the capital charge of bad magic. Both for these practical reasons of experience and also because it represented a common mode of communication, judicial and court language is strewn throughout the writings and sermons of Christian bishops of the time, including those of Augustine.[48]

Not surprisingly, judicial culture profoundly affected the African Christian construction of legitimacy and power. Examples of the general impress of the law can be found on every hand. Because the Roman governor of the later empire was a civil official who was as much construed as a judge or *iudex* as he was a governor or *praeses*, all normal government was seen as bureaucratic and judicial in nature. Africa's rich court culture produced not only eminent Roman jurists, but also several of the more important legal texts of the time.[49] Perhaps the most significant impact of this court culture on the Christian ideology of the Africans was the idea that God was in the final instance not a general or a soldier, a businessman, a ship captain, or a doctor – although all these were possible – but a stern and authoritative judge seated with his court.[50] It is the final judgment that mattered, not some putative piece of divine combat or healing. So, too, God's son, Jesus, is configured as a lawyer, a *iurisperitus* or an *adsessor*, who argues our case before his father, the judge, and who, as in the case of the governor as judge, sits as an advisor on the judge's judicial council.[51] The divine court was usually compared favorably with any terrestrial Roman court: it would be fairer, quicker, allowing no influence peddling or patronal intervention other than the intercession of Jesus and his martyrs.[52] Naturally, all of this

---

[48] Poque, *Langage symbolique*, 1, pp. 117–50, provides a survey for Augustine's preaching.

[49] Liebs (1992), pp. 201–03, and *Römische Jurisprudenz*, pp. 23 f. on the *Sententiae Pauli*. Although doubts have rightly been expressed by Vössing, *Gnomon* 68 (1996) and *Schule und Bildung*, pp. 286 f. on the relevance of much of the evidence for legal profession as such, this does not impair my argument about the profound impact of Roman legal institutions, procedures, and writing on the broader African culture of the time. Vössing also disagrees with Liebs on the significance of the approximately dozen jurists attested (eleven for Liebs, ten for Vössing) in the evidence for Africa: Liebs sees them as evidence of a special significance of lawyers and legal culture, Vössing not. Again, I do not think that a count of known lawyers is important to an assessment of the general impact of Roman legal culture.

[50] The number of references in Augustine is so large that it is not possible to cite them here. Aug. *En. in Ps.* 9.9 (CCL 38: 63) is a particularly striking description of the divine judge and his court; *En. in Ps.* 102.26 (CCL 40: 1472) is yet another; and *Tract. in Ioh.* 22.5. (CCL 36: 225); *Ep.* 52.4 (CCL 31: 220) are typical.

[51] Liebs (1992), p. 205, citing, among other texts, Aug. *En. in Ps.* 142.6 (CCL 40: 2064) and *Tract. in Ioh.* 7.10 (CCL 36: 72).

[52] Aug. *En. 1 in Ps.* 103.19 (CCL 40: 1491): no *excusatio* in the court of God, unlike in the civil courts; *Sermo* 9.2 (CCL 41: 107–08): in *that* court, there will be no tricky lawyers with their clever tongues, no ability to bribe the judge; so too in *Sermo* 47.7 (CCL 41: 577–78): "No opponent can corrupt this judge (i.e. God), no lawyer can twist him around his little finger, no witness can play fast and

worked its way into how the churches organized themselves and conducted their affairs. The whole panoply of procedure of the great church councils staged by both churches was modelled directly on the formal procedures of local town councils and of the Roman Senate.[53]

As frustrating and difficult as the institutions of local government were, the images and standards of its daily operations nevertheless greatly influenced how non-governmental organizations, like the Christian churches, conducted their business. By mimicking official power, they lent to their own dealings a sense of authority and legitimacy. The aggressive verbal confrontations between bishops were carefully recorded in written documents that copied the official style, including the formal notation of place and date. In this vein, the record of the *Proceedings with Emeritus*, or *Gesta cum Emerito*, that Augustine had with the dissident bishop Emeritus in Caesarea in 418 begins sententiously: "Gloriosissimis imperatoribus Honorio duodecimum et Theodosio octavum consulibus, duodecimo calendas Octobris, Caesareae in ecclesia Maiori... [In the twelfth consulship of Honorius and the eight consulship of Theodosius, Our Lord Emperors, on the twelfth day before the Kalends of October (20 September), at Caesarea, in the Great Church...]."[54] Again and again, we find this drive to keep archives of documents and to produce official-looking records, often with one eye looking forward to possible court proceedings. Official culture continued to dominate the way things were done by collective groups that wished to appear to be legitimate. Whatever parallel institutions might be in the process of development, official state power was the gold standard of power by which local variations or manifestations were judged.

Given that the greatest number of sectarian disputes either began or ended not in violent acts, but in civil law suits in the courts, it is hardly surprising that one of the main protagonists could picture the sum of the conflict as one great legal dispute.[55]

We are like brothers and sisters involved in a legal litigation. Why are we embroiled in this legal quarrel? Our father did not die intestate. He died and rose again. Contention begins with the legacy of one who has died only when the will has been accepted. But when the last will and testament is finally produced in public, everyone falls silent. The documents are opened and read aloud. The judge listens intently, the lawyers are silent, the court heralds maintain order, and everyone is

---

loose." Cf. *Sermo* 113.2 (PL 38: 649), at length on the problems of corruption and influence in the secular courts that will not be found with Christ the judge.

[53] Battifol (1913); MacMullen, *Voting About God*, pp. 20 f. on the secular model; Hermanowicz, *Possidius the Bishop*, pp. 12–13.

[54] Aug. *Gesta cum Emerito*, praef. (CSEL 53: 180).   [55] Aug. *En. 2 in Ps.* 21.30 (CCL 38: 132).

on tenterhooks waiting for the words of the deceased to be read aloud . . . Why are we locked in this court battle? Why are we pursuing this sectarian rivalry? Come on! You will lose your case . . . so why are you still acting as accusers?

The courts themselves were not just venues where disputes were settled, but, as Apuleius' speech for his own defense made clear, one of the few monumental places in the African town, besides the theater and the hippodrome, of mass public entertainment. The courts have rightly been described as a form of spectator sport, where crowds in the provincial metropolis of Carthage, for example, could "listen for hours on end in the forum as the fate of a man "hung in the mouth" of a skilled defender."[56] That Christian churches in Africa tended to mimic the modes and inculcate the values and behaviors of this "hard-headed and relentless" legal culture in their institutions is hardly surprising. This is precisely what we witness in the long record of the infighting between the Catholic and dissident parties. So it has been observed: Augustine's fight against his sectarian enemies "shows little trace of oecumenical moderation. It drew its strength from the bitter obstinacy of small men committed, as it were, to a long family lawsuit."[57] It was like a spiteful ecclesiastical riff on Jarndyce and Jarndyce.

Why were the courts and all the legal talk so meaningful to the Africans? Because out of the whole range of matters that composed the Roman repertoire that the scions of this local culture might have absorbed, it was the law and the courts that particularly fascinated them. In part it was because Africa was the most civil of the Latin lands of the west; and also, with its protective isolation, that this particular civil mode of discourse increasingly became the norm. It is no accident that Africa was renowned as the home of lawyers. It is not that Africans did not also absorb Horace and Vergil, the style of the Roman forum (but there, too, the connection with law cannot be avoided), or styles of domestic architecture and public building. But it was the living drama and role of the law that held a central place in the making of their vision of imperial culture. Its profound impact on the rhetorical construction of their version of Christianity is not to be doubted. Although the official state-sponsored persecutions were relatively few, ending earlier than almost anywhere else in the so-called Great Persecution, nowhere else did they leave such a profound effect in their telling and retelling, and in the permanent embedding of them in Christian

---

[56] Brown, *Augustine of Hippo*, p. 457, citing Aug. *En. in Ps.* 136.3 (CCL 40: 1965): "'Advocatum esse,' inquit, 'magna res est, potentissima eloquentia; in omnibus habere susceptos pendentes ex lingua diserti patroni sui, et ex eius ore sperantes vel damna, vel lucra, vel mortem, vel vitam, vel perniciem, vel salutem.'"

[57] Brown, *Augustine of Hippo*, pp. 11 and 222.

culture in the various forms of martyr stories: personal diaries of trial and punishment, formal court *acta* or records, and judicial narratives. It is a discourse, it has been noted, in which the Roman civil trial was at the center.

Even if African Christians were deeply implicated in this legal culture, and filed complaints and petitions against their sectarian adversaries with local municipal courts, it is worth repeating there was a deep reluctance on the part of secular court administrators to become involved. Take the case of the circumcellion attack on Possidius, the Catholic bishop of Calama, in the fall of 403. Instead of filing the usual charges against his attackers for "violence" or "injury," Possidius proceeded to charge Crispinus, the dissident bishop of Calama, under the imperial laws on heresy. Local officials were clearly reluctant to become involved in something that was neither a property nor a personal injury dispute. The case was eventually heard by the proconsul, before whom Crispinus denied emphatically that he was a heretic. At this point, the very official who was in charge of overseeing the application of imperial laws governing the Catholic Church, in support of its legal interests, the *defensor ecclesiae*, withdrew from the case, one suspects, from the same reluctance to become involved in arbitrating a dispute that threatened his own community.[58] The result was that the local Catholic bishop had to file the charges, and become the prosecutor, on his own. In the meantime, Augustine was encouraging the two parties to arbitrate their dispute. No less than three meetings were held to this end, while everyone awaited the decision of the proconsular governor. Far from resolving matters, the intervention of the governor made them worse. He decided that Crispinus was in fact "a heretic," and that he was therefore subject to the heavy fines in gold that were established by the imperial decrees of 392 and 395.

The decision might seem to be a happy thing from the Catholics' point of view, but along with the decision came a lot of bad things that they wished to avoid. The same laws under which Crispinus was convicted also automatically held local municipal officials responsible for inaction and on the same penalties as the condemned heretic himself. So the local town mayor, who should have acted aggressively as judge in the case, and all of the judicial officials in his advisory council, were now held to be just as guilty as Crispinus and liable to the same harsh penalties. Whatever hostilities had once existed between two Christian communities now threatened to career out of control, creating a furious resentment in the men who controlled

---

[58] Possid. *Vita Aug.* 12.5–6 (Bastiaensen: 158).

the secular affairs of Calama. Unless they wished to face open hostility from this powerful social group, Possidius, Augustine, and the Catholics had to back down. And so they did. An appeal was made to the governor and to the emperor on the basis of "Catholic charity," that the fines should not have to be paid. The request was granted. To put the best possible face on the turnabout, Catholic forgiveness and leniency were highlighted. Just how complex and dangerous these matters could become had been thrown into high relief. When leading men of the local town suddenly found themselves charged as criminals and subject to huge monetary fines because of the doings of a local Christian bishop, they would not be pleased.

An old hypocrisy ruled here as well. It was created by the existence of an apparent anomaly, even paradox: a terrestrial Christian state. A great deal of previous history and Christian ideology had inveighed against the possibility of such a beast. Ideally, as Donatus held, the state was supposed to have nothing to do with God or the Church. But it always did. According to a longstanding Pauline injunction, Christians were supposed to settle their disputes among themselves and not ventilate their sordid internal affairs in the public spectacle of the civil courts.[59] Given the overt hostility between the two during the whole period up to the Great Persecution under Diocletian, the advice carried added conviction. The advent of a Christian state, however, seemed to suggest that a natural barrier had been broken. It certainly always had been in actual behavior. Christians in Africa who were attempting to enforce a more uniform internal discipline were caught in a crux. On the one hand, they preached that the public courts were not to be the arbiters of any serious conflicts within their community. But as soon as any internal conflict outran their abilities to contain it, they ran to the courts. The canons issued by the Catholic council held at Carthage in 390 – a critical part of the drive to internal discipline in the Church – illustrate some of the difficulties. It speaks of men who had been driven from communion, presumably for what had been judged to be bad behavior. These men had then "jumped" (as it is colorfully phrased) to the public courts to settle their grievances with the Church. The internal disciplining of them was severe. Not only were such miscreants to be thrown out of the Church, so too was any bishop or other member of the

---

[59] 1 Cor. 6: 1–4; referred to by Aug. *En. 24 in Ps.* 118.3 (CCL 40: 1745), admitting, somewhat wearily, that this is one of the reasons that he has to hear such cases in his "episcopal court," rather than allow them to be taken to the public courts.

clergy who dared to receive them.[60] Still, the public courts were always there as external leverage for the discontented within each community.

The constant presence of dissident and Catholic parties as petitioners before courts, at both municipal and provincial levels, raised a question in the minds of the judges who were to allow the cases to be heard, or not. What types of cases were the courts willing to entertain? Although the judges shied away from matters that were manifestly religious or ecclesiastical, it seems that they were willing to hear the kinds of cases that the civil courts had normally heard and which they regarded as falling within their jurisdiction. In most disputes involving the two hostile churches, such "hearable" cases ordinarily came down to ones that centered on counter-claims to ownership of property: to houses, farms, lands, other such goods, but, above all, to church buildings. This sort of Christian-state interaction had a long history. Once emperors granted Catholic Christians the right to the ownership of churches, any group could rush to file its *bona fides* as "Catholic" and therefore its right to certain properties. So, for example, armed with the emperor Theodosius' laws on observing Catholic rites, a group of "Luciferian" Christians, in a long and vitriolic *libellus* addressed to the emperor in 383, complained bitterly that many adherents of other heretical groups were claiming to be "Catholic" precisely so that they could file for possession of churches and other properties.[61] The Roman court system, moreover, was ideally suited to deal with this particular aspect of church quarrels.

In one of his prolonged attacks on the dissidents, Augustine makes clear that property was the object on which many Christian court actions were focussed.[62]

In all of these cases, having failed to demonstrate anything and finding nothing else to say, what do they now charge us with? "They have seized our estates and buildings, they have seized our farms." They bring forth the wills of men.

---

[60] Concil. Carth. 390, canon 7 (CCL 149: 14–15): "aut ad iudicia publica prosilire." These men were presumably bishops or men of such standing; one needed influence and money to go to court.

[61] The so-called *Libellus precum*, 114 (A. Canellis ed., *Supplique aux empereurs*, Paris, SC 504, 2006: 224–26) offers a parallel: it is a long *libellus* to the court with the brief reply of the emperor Arcadius attached, notably, on the matter of the possession of churches: "nihilominus hi omnes de vestris gloriantur edictis et sibi ecclesias vindicant, cum has impias sectas patres nostri apostolica semper et evangelica auctoritate damnaverint." Cf. Hermanowicz, *Possidius the Bishop*, pp. 90–91.

[62] Aug. *Tract. in Ioh.* 6.25 (CCL 36: 66). Note the hard challenge: "Vultis legamus leges imperatorum, et secundum ipsas agamus de villis? Si iure humano vultis possidere, recitemus leges imperatorum; videamus si voluerunt aliquid a haereticis possideri. 'Sed quid mihi est imperator?' Secundum ius ipsius possides terram. Aut tolle iura imperatorum, et quis audet dicere: 'Mea est illa villa'." Faustinus was the dissident bishop of Hippo at the time of the donation: see "Faustinus (3)," PAC, p. 386: bishop before 395; Aug. *Contra litt. Petil.* 2.83.184 (CSEL 52: 112–15).

"Look here where Gaius Seius [viz. our "Jones"] gave his farm to the church over which Faustinus presided." But of which church was Faustinus the bishop? What is the church? "To the church," he said, "over which Faustinus presided." But Faustinus did not preside over a church but rather over a faction . . . "See, there are country villas." Under what law do you claim these villas? By a divine or a human one? . . . "This rural villa is mine, this house is mine, this slave is mine." By human law, then, by the laws of the emperors. Why? Because God has granted these human laws to humankind through the rulers and the kings of this world. Do you want us to read the laws of the emperors and have us act according to them concerning the rural villas? If you wish to possess by human law, let us read aloud the laws of the emperors. Let's see if *they* wish anything to be possessed [i.e. owned] by heretics. "But what has the emperor to do with me?" Well, it's by *his* law that you own the land. Remove the laws of the emperors and will you still dare to say "That's my villa, or that is my slave or that's my house"? If men have received the laws of kings so that they can have their possessions, do you wish us to read these laws aloud so that you can rejoice in the fact that if you possess so much as one garden, you can credit it to the generosity of the dove that you are even allowed to stay on it? For manifest laws have been made in which the emperors have ordered those who usurp for themselves the name of "Christian," but who are outside the communion of the Catholic Church and who do not wish peacefully to worship the creator of peace, are not to think that they should own anything in the name of the Church. "But what do we have to do with the emperor?" you say.

In saying the words "but what has the emperor to do with me?," Augustine willfully threw a variant of Donatus' famous words in the face of his adversaries. After all, they were quite willing to use imperial laws, the emperor's law, to get their way. The long riposte was delivered in the aftermath of the imperial laws of 405 that labeled the dissidents as "the Donatists" and stripped them of their property rights. Faustinus was the dissident bishop of Hippo at the time.

The whole struggle was one that was centered in the civil courts. In the aftermath of the imperial decrees of 414 that were to be the final word of the imperial court on the matter, Augustine directly confronted his opponents with their loss as a matter that had been finally decided judicially.[63]

You prisoners, you – once upon a time it was certainly you that found fault at the beginning of your rebellion with betrayers who condemned the innocent, you who sought the emperor's judgment, who did not accept the decision of the bishops, who appealed so often after losing your case, you who kept the litigation going so insistently at the emperor's court. Where's that arrogance of yours now? Where's that tongue of yours? Where's that *hiss*? . . . You say that you have court records to produce. Well, I have court records to produce too . . .

---

[63] Aug. *Sermo* 46.29 (CCL 41: 555), in the massive sermon "To the Shepherds." Note the verbal taunts at the end: "Ubi est cervix tua? Ubi lingua tua? Ubi sibilus tuus?"

It was not just that conflicts within the church were configured as forensic struggles. There was also a pervasive impact of the modes of literacy employed by the state for ruling others and of the use of documentation in the courts. So in this conflict the written document assumed a special place in the legitimation of evidence and action. One of the more striking examples is found in the dossier of written records assembled by Augustine to document the miracles associated with the holy remains of Stephen, the protomartyr, imported into Africa by Catholic bishops in the later 410s.[64] The compulsion, everywhere, was to compile and to archive documents to be used as forensic evidence and as court-like proofs. The attitude was a normal one: Possidius, the bishop of Calama, and later biographer of Augustine, kept "meticulous records" for his diocese.[65]

LOBBYING THE COURT

Whatever either side pretended or professed about dragging the secular state into the business of Christians, both labored remorselessly to get various levels of government to respond to their wants. Quite apart from the petitioning of the court in notorious *causes célèbres*, there was a constant drive to petition the imperial court at Ravenna. Awareness of these lobbying efforts was well known to all the power players. The stream of messengers bringing news to the court is compared to the function served by senses in the human body.[66] The Catholic lobbying of the court in the years 404 and 405 was so intense that the court asked the Catholic Church in Africa to stop dispatching so many embassies to Italy and to Ravenna.[67] These concerns of the court about being lobbied too intensely and in too partisan a fashion by African bishops were not new; on occasion the appropriate penalties and costs had been imposed to discourage the too diligent.[68] Priests and bishops performed such lobbying efforts both in concert with conciliar decisions but also, sometimes dangerously, on their

---

[64] Aug. *Civ. Dei*, 22.8 (CCL 48: 815–27).

[65] Hermanowicz (2004b) and *Possidius the Bishop*, p. 8; cf. Aug. *Civ. Dei*, 22.8 (CCL 48: 824): "Calamae vero, ubi et ipsa memoria prius esse coepit et crebrius dantur, incomparabili multitudine superant."

[66] Aug. *Sermo* 159B.5 = Dolbeau, 21.5 (Dolbeau, *Vingt-six sermons*, p. 283).

[67] Concil. Carth. 23 Aug. 405 = *Reg. Eccl. Carth. Excerpt.* 11.94.d (CCL 149: 214): "Recitatae litterae papae Innocentii, ut episcopi ad transmarina pergere facile non debeant: quod hoc ipsum episcoporum sententiis confirmatur."

[68] See, e.g., CTh 16.2.15 (Constantius and Julian, from Mediolanum, to Taurus, PPO; 30 June 359): on the lobbying done by bishops from Spain and Africa; and CTh 12.12.6 (Valentinian, Valens, and Gratian, from Trier, to Claudius, Proconsul of Africa; 2 February 369): bishops who came to court with unnecessary requests and on objectionable matters were to return to the province at their own expense and by using their own animals.

own as individuals. On his way to the court in the autumn of 408, in the course of this same mission, Possidius visited Memorius, the father of Julian of Aeclanum and Paulinus of Nola. It has been guessed that he also managed to acquire formal introductions to Anicius Auchenius Bassus and to Mallius Theodorus, one the consul of the year and the other an ex-consul, both friends of Augustine's from his time in Italy.[69] That is to say, the lobbyist was currying favor with persons of potential utility.

In pursuit of his aims, Possidius was armed with a large dossier of information on the urban riot that had erupted in his own town of Calama in June of the same year. His claim would be that "the pagans" had willfully broken the emperor's decree on holding religious ceremonials. For this part of his embassy, he was perhaps filled with an excess of personal animus and zeal. It was not without good grounds that Augustine pleaded with Paulinus of Nola to intervene. He rightly feared that Possidius was about to make a case against his fellow townsmen in a vengeful spirit inappropriate for a Catholic bishop.[70] But Possidius and the other Catholic lobbyists were not going to Ravenna for the Calama riot alone. In the council held on 13 October in the Basilica Restituta at Carthage (the church that had been "restored" to their possession), the Catholic bishops empowered Restitutus and Florentius to undertake an embassy to the court "against the pagans and heretics." In this case, the primary data were to be violent acts committed against members of the church. The bishops Severus and Macarius had been murdered. The bishops Evodius, Theasius, and Victor had been savagely beaten.[71] And there were Possidius' own experiences at Calama. Over this period of lobbying, in fact, we can witness the deliberate swing away from issues of religion to ones that emphasized the existence of a violent threat to the imperial social order.

The modes by which officials at the court were approached, given information, persuaded to respond, and managed so as to achieve the appellant's purpose are largely hidden from us. Official church documents present the process as a regular and anodyne administrative process that functioned by the simple means of showing up, presenting information, and patiently waiting for responses. On occasion, a crack appears in this smooth edifice of description and we get to see something of what was actually happening. Catholic bishops appealing to Catholic emperors did not go to court

---

[69] For some of the arguments, see Hermanowicz (2004a).

[70] Aug. *Ep.* 95 (CSEL 31A: 215–21), adding, not inconsequentially for our argument, that his disagreement with Possidius over this matter was harming their friendship.

[71] Concil. Carth. 13 Oct. 408 = *Reg. Eccl. Carth. Excerpt.* 14 (CCL 149: 219): "In hoc concilio susceperunt legationem Restitutus et Florentius episcopi contra paganos et haereticos, eo tempore quo Severus et Macarius occisi sunt, et propter eorum causam Evodius, Theasius et Victor episcopi caesi sunt."

with empty hands; they were regularly filled with all kinds of "gifts." The diplomacy was rather costly. On one of his embassies to the imperial court, Alypius brought with him more than 80 prize Numidian horses, raised to the finest form on church lands throughout all of Africa. These were to be "gifts" for high-ranking officers, tribunes, at the court, who were expected to look kindly upon Alypius' petition.[72] This is pretty low-level stuff when compared with the evidence of the massive "gifts" and "blessings" – in other words bribes – that were funneled through the agency of Christian bishops to the imperial court in the East in the early fifth century.[73] There is no doubt that more wealth and power was being contested in the East, and that the "gifts" were accordingly much larger. But the process was the same at the western court.

Why, in all of this, did the Catholic bishops not have the help of a large class of landowners in Africa, some of whom must have supported their cause? Some probably did, but there were not enough of them. Augustine lamented the inaction of Catholic landlords in not forcefully converting the peasant workforces under their control. Perhaps, as Catholics, they did support their church's views. But as large landowners they simply took the expedient and useful course for themselves of provoking the least resistance from their workers. Melania and her family were longstanding Catholics, but they had clearly tolerated the existence of churches of both sides on her domain lands near Thagaste.[74] Her interests, and those of her procurators, were in the peaceful work of her tenants, not in causing trouble both locally and at court by involving themselves in the wars of the bishops.

The connections between churches that had few instruments of coercive force at their disposal – other than gangs of men using low-level instruments of violence – and various levels of the state were therefore constant. Most of the dealings went on at local level where the membership of municipal town councils tended to inhibit much involvement above the level of the use of the civil courts and the archiving of records of the disputes. To acquire serious coercive assistance, the bishops had to get matters to provincial level, before provincial governors and, above that, to the imperial court at

---

[72] Aug. *Contra Iul. op. imperf.* 1.42 (CSEL 85.1: 30–31): in an accusation made by Julian, as quoted by Augustine: "Vociferans cum feminis cunctisque calonibus et tribunis, quibus octoginta aut amplius equos tota Africa saginatos collega tuus nuper adduxit Alypius." Augustine retorts that either Julian does not know what he is talking about or he is lying; see Brown, *Augustine*, p. 364 for comment. The lobbying in this case was against the Pelagians. Accusations of civil violence notably played a similar forerunner role in this case too.

[73] See, e.g., Brown, *Power and Persuasion*, pp. 16–17.

[74] *Vita sanctae Melaniae* (L) 21.4 (Laurence: 194): "Quae possessio maior erat etiam civitati ipsius habens . . . et duos episcopos, unum nostrae fidei et alium haereticorum."

Ravenna. Far from being able to coerce hostile enemies in the other church, the Catholic bishops did not even have the force at their disposal forcibly to expel an unwanted member of their own clergy from his position. The Cresconius case had demonstrated the real power of a local bishop to hold out against rulings and injunctions issued against him (and, in this case, in fact, to succeed in his personal aims). In cases like these, the church had to run to the state. In attempting to answer the problem of priests who used their local power and influence over local communities to set themselves up as bishops, the church not only condemned the practice, but ruled that such men were to be removed from their dioceses. Councils had held, in fact, that these men were to be removed by public or state authorities. These unwanted men were designated by the politically loaded secular term of "rebels."[75] These cases of internal discipline provided training in the modes and channels by which the church's external enemies could be handled.

THE RAVENNA DOSSIER

It is against this background of a pervasive legal culture and central state power that much of the evidence on sectarian violence must be read. Accounts of violence were not disinterested historical accounts or even just more ecclesiastical polemic. Rather, they were affidavits attached to cases involved in judicial hearings, parts of dossiers that were carefully collated and filed in court depositions. The critical task to be played by these narratives of violence was to convince imperial authorities that there was a threat to civil order in the African provinces of the empire, a threat that required action on their part. If some of these stories are truly striking narratives, it is because they were forged in the process of preparing to tell and retell them in court, and then to submit them for the record as coherent and compelling proof stories. Judicial processes encourage the production of stories from their human participants, especially in cases where violence and contention are involved.[76] The tales of violence adduced in this case were being used to demonstrate the reality of the violent acts committed against

---

[75] Concil. Carth. 28 Aug. 397, canon 5 = *Reg. Eccl. Afr. Excerpt.* canon 53 (CCL 149: 190): "Aurelius episcopus dixit:... ut etiam auctoritate publica reiciantur, atque ab ipsis principalibus cathedris removeantur... non tantum dioceses amittant sed, ut dixi, etiam propriis publica careant auctoritate, ut rebelles."

[76] There are many studies, but my favorite is Natalie Zemon Davis, *Fiction in the Archives: Pardon Tales and their Tellers in Sixteenth-Century France*, Stanford, Stanford University Press, 1987. Following her excellent preliminary discussion of the problem, ch. 2, "Angry Men and Self-Defense," pp. 36–76, bears most directly on our problems here.

Catholic properties and persons, and hence the real danger to the peace of the state. As a collection of exemplary stories of violence, the purpose of these mini-histories was to make an archive of them for purposes of lobbying. At first, they were proffered to the judges who directed the municipal courts, then to the governor's *officium* at Carthage and to the governor himself when he made his judicial tour of his province. As time went on, however, they were increasingly used to petition the imperial court at Ravenna and the high-ranking plenipotentiaries of the state sent to Africa.

In their final form, the following cases were collated as part of a concerted political campaign to get the court at Ravenna to act, so it is perhaps simplest to refer to the compilation of stories as "the Ravenna dossier." One of the purposes of assembling this collection of cases for consumption by the court was to put a human face on the violence. In discussing circumcellion attacks in the years immediately after the embassy to Ravenna in 404, Augustine repeatedly drew on the contents of the dossier to provide specific and striking examples of what this violence meant at ground level. One of the most extensive narratives drawn from it was included in his *Contra Cresconium* of 406. In it, Augustine prefaces the extensive discussion of violence with specific reference to incidents involving the circumcellions. He states that he will omit the many earlier crimes committed by these men that finally led to the laws intended to repress them. Instead, he will use the device of citing recent striking cases of their violent actions.

The tactic is a perfectly understandable way of conveying the essence of the struggle more immediately to imperial officials. Standing, as they did, for a greater whole, a few alarming stories would have much greater persuasive power. But one might reasonably wonder if a much larger record of violent acts ever existed. Since the cases that detailed circumcellion violence always seem to be the same small number of instances, the vigilant must at least suspect that the total number might never have been very large. The claim that there were many earlier incidents of violence and numerous earlier imperial laws designed to repress them, unfortunately has to be taken at face value, since there is no independent evidence for either. We must therefore question how many of the "many" cases actually existed. Once we eliminate the corpus of "horror stories" assembled for the Ravenna dossier, other cases of circumcellion attacks where any details are known such as specific places, times, or the names of the persons involved, are almost non-existent. The suspicion therefore arises that the number of other cases that were known and recorded was not very great. And even if there were many other violent incidents, they remained anonymous and faceless. Hence the political importance of the following stories.

Servus Dei: Catholic Bishop of Thubursicu Bure (c. 403)

The following violent incident involved Servus or rather, more fully, Servus Dei, the Catholic bishop of Thuburscu Bure.[77] The situation was one of the typical internecine battles within the Christian communities that were found in the small towns of Africa of the time. The dissident Christians in the town of Thubursicu had managed to gain control of a church or *locus* that had once belonged to the Catholics. In Augustine's words, *"your people* had invaded it."[78] No doubt, the "invasion" was made under imperial legislation that called for the return of such church properties, perhaps as long before as the reign of the emperor Julian. Servus Dei was only attempting to reassert Catholic control over and ownership of the basilica.[79] It is suggested that Servus Dei was doing this by some legal means, and that the procurators or representatives of either side were waiting for the investigation of the issue by the proconsular governor.[80] The presence of procurators is significant, because it suggests that both sides were accustomed to taking such property disputes before the civil courts. In this particular case, they were awaiting the arrival of the governor who was on the judicial rounds of his provincial assizes. It was while the two sides were waiting in a tense situation that surely contributed to a heightened sense of apprehension, that armed men rushed into the town and attacked Servus Dei and the persons with him. He was barely able to escape alive. His father, a priest of old age and burdened with illness also suffered a severe beating from which, it is reported, he died a few days later.[81]

Augustine of Hippo: a virtual attack (late summer 403)

The propensity to collate details about known cases and to increase the number of incidents in the dossier encouraged the production of more such

---

[77] Aug. *Contra Cresc.* 3.43.47 (CSEL 52: 454–55); see De Veer (1968j), pp. 814–15. There has been some dispute over the location of his episcopal seat, since there are several Thubursicus known in Africa. Whereas it is true that the manuscripts offer variants, in at least one place they are specific in reading *Thubursicubure* or equivalent (the addition of "bure" is a correction that is unlikely to have been made by a later scribe) which leaves little doubt that the modern Téboursouk was meant – which location was in the proconsular province, as is required by the narrative: "et utriusque partis procuratores proconsulare praestolarentur examen."

[78] The Latin only says *locus*, which would ordinarily just mean "place"; but in Christian parlance this had become a technical term meaning "holy place" or church.

[79] Aug. *Contra Cresc.* 3.43.47 (CSEL 52: 453): "Episcopus Catholicus a Thubursicu Bure, Servus nomine, cum invasum a vestris locum repeteret."

[80] Aug. *Contra Cresc.* 3.43.47 (CSEL 52: 453): "et utriusque partis procuratores proconsulare praestolarentur examen, repente sibi in oppido memorato vestris armatis inruentibus vix vivus aufugit."

[81] Aug. *Contra Cresc.* 3.43.47 (CSEL 52: 453): "A quibus pater eius presbyter aetate ac moribus gravis ea caede, qua vehementer adflictus est, post dies paucos excessit e vita."

exemplary cases. One suspects that it also created an atmosphere where it was expected that such attacks *might* have taken place in which one *might* acquire heroic merit for having faced such an attack. Inside the rhetoric in which the acts of violence were reported, it sometimes becomes difficult to distinguish which acts of violence had actually occurred as opposed to those that were imputed to have happened. Opportunities were taken to encourage a merging of the actual and the possible in the minds of listeners. Since he did not fit the principal target profile of the normal victims of sectarian assaults, Augustine was not likely to be the object of a circumcellion attack. Nevertheless, it could be imagined that threats of violence might lead him to police his criticisms of the dissidents and to curtail activities of his that might be construed as encouraging betrayal. Some members of his own congregation believed that he had been toning down the sharpness of his sermons for precisely this reason. The reality of the threat that he faced could be demonstrated by detailing how he had *almost* been attacked.

The "almost" incident involving Augustine was therefore repeatedly replayed. It was good enough to make it into the little handbook or *Enchiridion* on the core basics of Catholic faith written in the early 420s. The value of retelling the "almost attack" on himself was that the *Handbook* was written for Laurentius, brother of the imperial official Dulcitius whom Augustine was urging at the time to hard enforcement action against the dissidents. Although the incident was used to illustrate a moral point – that sometimes God's grace helps us by having us choose what is seemingly the "wrong" way – it is retold with the same liveliness of the original.[82]

It even happened to us that we made a mistake at a place where two roads met, with the result that we did not pass through the place where an armed band of Donatists lay in wait for our passage. Yet it still came about that I arrived at the place where I was going, albeit by an out-of-the-way circuitous route. And after I heard about the ambush set by those men, I congratulated myself on my mistake and on that account gave thanks to God. Now, who would not hesitate to place the traveler who made a mistake like this above a bandit who made no mistake?

The incident was finally enshrined in Possidius' biography of Augustine, where it was embedded in the deeds or *facta* of the bishop's life – his *res gestae* as opposed to his rhetorical accomplishments. The great bishop's acts

---

[82] Aug. *Enchirid.* 5.17 (CCL 46: 57): "Nam nobis ipsis accidit ut in quodam bivio falleremur et non iremus per eum locum ubi opperiens transitum nostrum Donatistarum manus armata subsederat, atque ita factum est ut eo quo tendebamus per devium circuitum veniremus, cognitisque insidiis illorum nos gratularemur errasse atque inde gratias ageremus Deo. Quis ergo viatorem sic errantem sic non erranti latroni praeponere dubitaverit?"; cf. 6.19 (CCL 46: 59–60) for the further playing out of this same incident.

are conceived by Possidius as a struggle against the enemies of the Church, beginning with the Manichees and then passing to "the Donatists." At the heart of Possidius' description of Augustine's campaign against the dissidents, is a lengthy narrative of the circumcellions and their activities that culminates in Augustine's "almost encounter" with them. Possidius ends his treatment of the violent men by stating that many Catholic priests and clerics who were in the front line of suffering attacks from the circumcellion gangs were those who were struggling on behalf of Unity. The observation sets the stage to construe Augustine as someone who (almost) shared in the terrible injuries of the same physical danger. Possidius places the incident immediately before the vivid account of the attack launched on himself by the gang led by the dissident priest Crispinus at Calama, thereby suggesting that the two were part of the string of violent attacks that took place in autumn 403 in response to Catholic pressure to engage the dissidents in a forced dialogue.[83]

Sometimes these same armed circumcellions even set ambushes on the public roads for Augustine, the servant of God, when he happened to go on the road after he had been asked to visit, to instruct, and to exhort various Catholic congregations – something he was accustomed to do rather often. On one of these occasions, it happened that these armed men, with full reinforcements, just missed laying hold of him in the following way. By the providence of God – that is, by a mistake of his guide – it happened that Augustine and his companions arrived at their destination by a different route. It was by this mistake, which he only became aware of later, that he escaped their impious hands and so, with everyone, gave thanks to God the Liberator.

When reading repeated versions of this almost attack, it is important to remember that it never happened. Augustine was not actually attacked by anyone, and it is impossible for the historian to reconstruct the truth of the claim: Was Augustine told the truth and did he believe what he was told had "almost happened"? Possidius ends the same paragraph with a sentence that suggests the reality of the attack: "According to their custom, they spared neither laypersons nor clergy, as the public records witness."[84] But in this case, no one was actually "not spared."

---

[83] Possid. *Vita Aug.* 12.1–2 (Bastiaensen: 156): "Aliquotiens vero etiam vias armati iidem circumcelliones famulo Dei Augustino obsederunt, dum forte iret rogatus ad visitandas, instruendas et exhortandas Catholicas plebes, quod ipse frequentissime faciebat. Et aliquando contigit ut illi subcenturiati hactenus perderent captionem; evenit enim Dei quidem providentia sed ducatoris errore, ut per aliam viam cum suis comitibus sacerdos quo tendebat venisset, atque per hunc quem postea cognovit errorem manus inpias evasisset et cum omnibus liberatori Deo gratias egisset."

[84] Possid. *Vita Aug.* 12.2 (Bastiaensen: 156–58): "Et omnino suo more illi nec laicis nec clericis pepercerunt, sicut publica contestatur gesta."

Possidius: Catholic Bishop of Calama (later autumn 403)

Possidius could speak so forcefully and credibly on Augustine's behalf since he actually had been attacked. The circumcellion assault on Possidius had roots in different circumstances of local conflict. Unlike the Servus Dei case, it was not a dispute over the possession of a basilica, since each church in Calama had its own. Following the decisions made by the Catholic Council of Carthage on 25 August 403, Possidius, the Catholic bishop of Calama, had issued several invitations to his opposite number at Calama, the dissident bishop Crispinus, to attend a joint conference at Carthage. In response to his repeated rejection of these overtures, Crispinus (the dissident) was made the target of frequent abuse and insults from the Catholics. In response, a relative of Crispinus – a lower-ranking priest who bore the same name of Crispinus – decided to take revenge for these grievous insults to his kinsman.[85] He set an ambush for Possidius as he was making his way to a domain near Calama called the Fundus Figulinensis.[86] Possidius claims that he had to run for his life and seek shelter with his followers in a farmhouse on a neighboring estate, the Fundus Olivetensis ("Olive Tree Farm"). Augustine suggests that had Possidius not made it to this refuge, he would have been killed.

As it was, Possidius had the good fortune to spot his attackers in advance, and was able to take refuge in the villa-like house on the rural estate. The house was soon besieged by armed men who launched stones and firebrands at it. Although Possidius and his people fought back, they were surrounded and had to beat off repeated attacks. In the midst of the mêlée, they tried to put out the firebrands that were causing various parts of the house to catch fire. After repeated assaults on the main doorway of the house, the attackers broke in and began killing the animals that were in the ground-level courtyard of the villa. They then rushed into the upper part of the house, dragging the bishop out, raining blows and insults on him. Augustine suggests that Possidius would surely have died in the assault, had it not been for the interventions of Crispinus, the dissident priest, with the armed men. His aim, apparently, was to punish and to terrorize, but not actually to go to the full extent of homicide.

---

[85] There is a brief allusion to the incident by Possidius himself in his later biography of Augustine: *Vita Aug.* 12 (Bastiaensen: 154 f.); and another by Augustine himself written about 406: *Contra Cresc.* 3.46.50–51 (CSEL 52: 456–59). For these details: "nihil adversum veritatem posse probaretur [sc. Crispinus the bishop], subito post paucos dies iter agenti Possidio alius Crispinus eius presbyter et ut perhibetur propinquus tetendit insidias armatorum."

[86] The precise location of the Fundus Figulinensis is unknown. It was so named, probably, because it contained important *figulinae* or clay beds that were exploited by its owner.

The incident became well known at Calama where, Augustine claims, the people watched to see what would be the response of Crispinus, the dissident bishop of the town. The Catholic response to the incident was to file a protest that was filed in the town archives. In this way, a written description of this violent episode was produced. This was, no doubt, the narrative of the violence that was kept by the Catholics and which was later repeated for the record. There were various attempts to charge Crispinus, the dissident bishop of Calama, and to get him embroiled with the civil authorities, but it might well have been that it was not possible to prove any actual collusion of Crispinus the bishop in the incident, or to demonstrate the passing of orders from him to Crispinus the priest, the leader of the gang of men who attacked Possidius. Not being able to make this charge stick to the dissident bishop himself, charges of heresy were filed against him with the governor of the proconsular province as a surrogate means of getting at him with a charge that *could* be proved.

The assault was turned into a narrative of a classic type, probably in connection with writing up descriptions of the incident for the purpose of filing it with the courts. It is reported again, at length, by Possidius in his biography of Augustine written in the mid-430s. In a seamless sequence, the story immediately follows the account of Augustine's personal narrow escape from a circumcellion ambush.[87]

It is necessary not to pass over in silence how much was done and accomplished for the praise of God by the devotion of this man [i.e. Augustine] who was of such illustrious standing in the Church, and by the zeal of the House of God against the aforementioned Donatist Rebaptizers. By chance, one of those men whom he had raised in his monastery from his clergy to be bishops of the church was visiting the diocese of the church of Calama. He was preaching against that heresy what he had learned for the peace of the church. In the middle of his journey he ran into an ambush staged by these men. They attacked him and all of his companions. Taking away his animals and all of his baggage, they inflicted serious injuries and violence on him and his men. So that the progress of the Peace of the Church should not be impeded any further by this matter, the Defender of the Church was

---

[87] Possid. *Vita Aug.* 12.3–5 (Bastiaensen: 158): "Interea silendum non est quod ad laudem Dei per illius tam egregii in ecclesia viri studium domusque Dei zelum adversus praedictos rebaptizatores Donatistas gestum et perfectum est. Cum forte unus ex his, quos de suo monasterio et clero episcopos ecclesiae propagaverat, ad suam curam pertinentem Calamensis ecclesiae diocesim visitaret et quae didicerat pro pace ecclesiae contra illam haeresim praedicaret, factum est ut medio itinere eorum insidias incurrisset et pervasum cum omnibus illi comitantibus, sublatis illis animalibus et rebus, iniuriis et caede cum gravissima affecissent. De qua re ne pacis amplius ecclesiae provectus impediretur, defensor ecclesiae inter leges non siluit. Et praeceptus est Crispinus, qui iisdem Donatistis in Calamensi civitate et regione episcopus fuit, praedicatus scilicet et multi temporis et doctus, ad multam teneri aurariam publicis legibus contra haereticos constitutam."

not silent before the bar of the law. It was ordered that Crispinus, who was bishop of these same Donatists in the city and region of Calama, a much-vaunted man, advanced in years, and very learned, should be subjected to the penalty assessed in gold that had been established in the public laws against heretics.

There is no need to follow the details of the case further, except to note that the advocate who was charging Crispinus the bishop of Calama does not, as one might logically expect, link the physical attack on Possidius and his men with the judicial charges. In that case, one would expect him to file charges under *de vi, damnum iuria datum, iniuria,* or some such heading. Instead, the court charge brought against Crispinus had no direct connection whatever with the violent episode itself: the Catholic advocates had him charged and fined as a heretic.

Maximianus: Catholic Bishop of Bagaï (October 3, 403)

Having already considered this episode in connection with the social ritual of singing and chanting, we now return to it as an exemplary case of sectarian violence.[88] The circumstances are almost the same as those in the Servus Dei case at Thubursicu: a dispute over the possession of a basilica, this time in a rural locale not far from Bagaï in southeastern Numidia.[89] Maximianus, the new Catholic bishop of the town of Bagaï, had gone to court to claim ownership of a basilica that had once been his. He had obtained a favorable judicial decision that awarded him the basilica on the Fundus Calvianensis, an agricultural domain not far from Bagaï.[90] The problem was that the dissidents had already held this basilica for some time; in effect, they felt that it was their church. Although Maximianus went

---

[88] There are problems with the possibility that two different bishops are involved: a Maximianus of Vaga and another at Bagaï, but I accept that they are one and the same (see De Veer [1968k], pp. 816–17; cf. "Maximianus," PAC, pp. 723–24); the date of 3 October for his "martyrdom" recorded in the *Martyrologium Romanum*, I take to refer to the date of the attack on him – his "passion" (as is clearly suggested by the words "iterum atque iterum saevissima *passus*") – and not to his later death and deposition: AASS Octobr. 2, pp. 160–61 ("In Africa sancti Maximiani episcopi Bagaiensis, qui a Donatistis iterum atque iterum saevissima passus, ex alta denique turri praecipitatus et pro mortuo derelictus, gloria confessionis illustris postmodum quievit in Domino").

[89] Aug. *Contra Cresc.* 3.43.47 (CSEL 52: 453); the same case is trotted out again at *Ep.* 185.7.26–27 (CSEL 57: 25–26) in a series that had gradually been built up into a veritable casebook that Augustine could present to imperial authorities to educate them (in this case Bonifatius in 417). In the latter report for the eyes of an imperial official, Augustine tones down the lurid details of the original: the pile of excrement becomes a "heap of something soft"; Maximianus happens to be discovered by "someone with the aid of a light of a passer-by," and so on.

[90] Aug. *Contra Cresc.* 3.43.47 (CSEL 52: 453): "Maximianus episcopus Catholicus Bagaïensis dicta inter partes iudiciaria sententia basilicam fundi Calvianensis evicerat, quam vestri inlicite aliquando usurpaverant."

to occupy the basilica and did so with the manifest support of the law, it provoked a violent response on the part of the dissident Christians. Gangs of rough men entered the bishop's principal church at Bagaï and smashed the altar to pieces over his head. In some considerable fear, the bishop had taken refuge under it. Armed with pieces of wood from the broken altar, with wooden clubs, and with some iron "weapons," his assailants began to beat Maximianus. Blood flowed from him, covering the floor of the sanctuary. He then received a severe wound in the groin. The blood began pouring from his body in rivulets. He might have died then and there had it not been for a quirkish bit of fate that resulted from the further cruelties vented on the man by his attackers. At this point, Maximianus had been stripped of his clothes, and was being forcibly pulled out of the church. As he was dragged, face down through the dirt on the road outside of the church, the blood from the wound and the dust from the road congealed and prevented further bleeding.[91]

There ensued a tug-of-war over the body of the beaten man. Some of "our men," says Augustine, managed to pull him away from his attackers as they sang and chanted, which only further enraged the dissidents. The latter men mounted a second foray. Getting hold of Maximianus, they dragged him out of the hands of his Catholic supporters and beat him again severely. In this same assault, the church itself was burned down and its holy books thrown into the fire. This attendant material destruction, however, was often omitted from the core narrative that stressed the extent of the personal injuries suffered by the bishop.[92] In all of this, it is important to note that the attackers did not kill Maximianus with a sword, a dagger, or a knife, something that would have been easy to accomplish under the circumstances. Instead, they were content to beat him. Even in the aftermath of the second attack and the new beating that they administered to the Catholic bishop, they still did not kill him. What happened next was something different. His attackers chose instead to drag him up flights of stairs to the top of a nearby high tower and, once they got him to the top of it, they threw him off its height. In other words, they hoped that

---

[91] Such accidental survivals in episodes of sectarian violence are not without parallel. For a comparable instance, consider the case of one Gerard McLaverty, a Catholic attacked by members of the Shankill Butchers and left for dead: "Instead of using a meat cleaver or an axe on McLaverty, after the customary torture, they tied a bootlace around his throat to silence him and then slashed his wrists with knives and threw him in an alleyway where his blood congealed in the cold so that the bleeding stopped and saved his life": Coogan, *The IRA*, p. 346.

[92] These incidents are always connected with the attack on Maximianus at Bagaï: see Aug. *Brev. Collat.* 3.11.23 (CCL 149A: 288), and *Ad Donatist. post Collat.* 17.22 (CSEL 53: 118–19).

he might perish by precipitation. And this is the way that the Catholic martyrology presents his suffering: as a precipitation.

Very fortunately for Maximianus, a large mound of human excrement had accumulated at the bottom of the tower. Apparently the town's people and travelers relieved themselves at the base of its walls. The deep heap of human ordure broke the force of Maximianus' plunge from the tower.[93] He survived the fall. Fading in and out of consciousness over the next hours, Maximianus barely clung to life. By another good stroke of fortune, there occurred one of those little human dramas that reveal something of daily routines in a late antique town. Later that same night, a poor man, a pauper, and his wife happened to be passing by the tower in the dark. The man made a detour off the road in order to defecate. Apparently, it was known that such acts of personal relief were performed at the foot of this particular tower. (With all that the practice suggests about ordinary sanitary conditions in rural towns like Bagaï.) When the man got to the pile of shit in order to relieve himself, he found the half-dead Catholic bishop of Bagaï on top of it. Immediately recognizing who the man was, he shouted to his wife who, obedient to the normal canons of shame, was waiting for him back on the main road. He called out to her to come quickly and to bring the lantern that she was carrying to light their way in the night (another item that allows us to picture this dimly-lit scene in miniature). The two of them then shouldered the body of the wounded bishop and carried him to their home – "Out of pity," remarks Augustine, "or because they hoped for a small reward." Whether he was alive or dead, they would at least be able to show the Catholics in the town that they had found the bishop and that they had tried to rescue him. After his body was recovered by the Catholics, Augustine reports, Maximianus made a miraculous recovery, although his body "had more scars on it than it had limbs."[94] Those scars were to prove very useful.

Once this basic dossier of violent cases, all of them ones coming out of the specific confrontations of the year 403, was compiled, it was then used for the Catholic mission that was dispatched to the court at Ravenna in June 404. But additions kept being made to it, thus deepening the record of acts of circumcellion violence that could serve to confirm the threat posed by the dangerous dissidents to the public order.

[93] Aug. *Contra Cresc.* 3.43.47 (CSEL 52: 454): "rursus inruentibus violenter extortus est graviusque mulcatus et de excelsa turri noctu praecipitatus subter cinere stercoris molliter iacebat exceptus, sensu amisso vix extremum spiritum tenens." This is a dirty equivalent of the death of the dissident martyr Marculus who lands softly on the rocks beneath his precipitation: see ch. 16, pp. 751–53.

[94] Aug. *Contra Cresc.* 3.43.47 (CSEL 52: 454): "Quid plura? Mirabili curatione sanatus est, vivit, plures in eius corpore cicatrices quam membra numerantur."

Restitutus: Catholic Priest of Victoriana (c. 405–06?)

This case, and the one that follows, must be seen as Augustine's personal later contributions to the dossier. Restitutus was a priest of the dissident church in a rural settlement named Victoriana in the hinterland of Hippo Regius.[95] He had come to "see the light" and had decided to transfer his allegiance to the Catholics. When the fact of his crossing over became known, a force of "Donatist" clerics and circumcellions dragged him out of his home in broad daylight and took him prisoner to a nearby *castellum* or village. With a large crowd looking on and with no one daring to object, Restitutus was systematically beaten with wooden clubs and dragged through a muddy stream, clothed in a special garment of reeds known as an *amictus iunceus* that was part of the ritual of shaming and degradation. Those who witnessed Restitutus' distress, we are told, laughed all the while at the humiliated cleric and at the awful circumstances in which the "traitor priest" now found himself. His attackers then took him away to another place, where he was kept in confinement until he was finally released, some twelve days later.[96] This is how Augustine told the story:

A certain Restitutus who was one of your priests in the region of Hippo Regius...was dragged from his home by your clerics and circumcellions, and in the broad light of day he was taken to a nearby village. With a large crowd of people looking on and not one of them daring to resist, he was beaten with the bloody wooden clubs of his self-appointed judges. He was then dragged through a muddy swamp, and humiliated by being clothed in a reed jacket. After he had thus tortured the eyes of those onlookers who suffered in sympathy with him and had satisfied those who laughed at him, he was taken to another place – a place which none of our own people dared to approach – and was only released from it twelve days later.

As in the Maximianus incident, it is important to note that Restitutus was not murdered in the attack. The violence was modulated so as to produce

---

[95] In chronological order, the dossier on Restitutus includes *Ep.* 88.6 (CCL 31A: 143); *Ep.* 105.3 (CCL 31B: 50–51, containing the reference to his position at Victoriana); *Contra Cresc.* 3.48.53 (CSEL 52: 460–61); *Ad Donatist. post Collat.* 17.22 (CSEL 53: 118–19); see "Restitutus (6)," PAC, p. 972; Victoriana was a hamlet about thirty miles from Hippo (*Civ. Dei*, 22.8 = CCL 48: 820): "Victoriana dicitur villa, ab Hippone regio minus triginta milibus abest."

[96] Aug. *Contra Cresc.* 3.48.53 (CSEL 52: 460–61): "Restitutus quidam in regione Hipponiensi vester presbyter fuit... de domo sua raptus est a clericis et circumcellionibus vestris, luce palam in castellum proximum ductus et multitudine spectante nihilque resistere audente ad furentem arbitrium fustibus caesus, in lacuna lutulento volutatus, amictu iunceo dehonestatus, posteaquam satis excruciavit oculos dolentium ridentiumque satiavit, inde ductus ad alium locum, quo nemo nostrorum audebat accedere, duodecim vix die dimissus est." In fact he was the priest of a small village or settlement known as Victoriana: see *Ep.* 105.2–3 of c. 409 (CCL 31B: 50–51), with more on the violence that he suffered. The incident is also recounted in *Ep.* 88.6 of c. 406 (CCL 31A: 143).

a humiliating display of Restitutus' body and, in this way, to make a contemptible public example of him.

Marcus: Catholic priest of Casphaliana and Marcianus: Catholic Bishop of Urga (c. 405–06)

Marcus was the priest of a village called Casphaliana, located in the region of Hippo. He had earlier been a subdeacon under Marcianus, the priest of the town of Urga, which was also located close to Hippo.[97] Marcus and the priest Marcianus, along with Marcianus' new subdeacon, had gone into hiding to protect themselves from threats that were being made against them, but Marcus' hiding place was discovered by his sectarian enemies. He was dragged out of it and was severely beaten. Augustine reports that he would have been killed had not some passers-by stopped and jumped into the fray to protect him. He also claims that Marcianus' subdeacon was beaten and stoned "to the point of death" and that he, too, had barely survived the attack. What most identified these three men is precisely the same characteristic that marked most of the other objects of violent circumcellion assaults that are noted above. All were seen by their attackers as traitors. All three men, Augustine tells us, had crossed over to the Catholic Church "of their own free will." From the dissidents' point of view, they had to be punished. As with the others, an example had to be made of them.

COMPELLING EVIDENCE

The importance of this dossier of cases in the lobbying of the court at Ravenna is manifest. It collected in a compact form a limited number of spectacular cases that made more vivid and striking the violence that Catholic bishops were facing. Who was doing the collating is also manifest. Note the cases: a priest from Thubursicu Bure, Possidius, Augustine (almost), a bishop from Bagaï, two priests and a deacon from villages in the hinterland of Hippo Regius. And all the cases in the first version of the dossier came from the year 403 or the early months of 404. Important for our purpose is how often this limited number of instances – Servus Dei, Possidius, Maximianus, Rogatus and Marcus – was brought up again

---

[97] Aug. *Ep.* 105.2.3 (CCL 31B: 50–51); for the characters involved, see "Marcus (1)," PAC, p. 697 and "Marcianus (4)," PAC, p. 693.

and again as paradigmatic of a general Africa-wide crisis of violence. Additions were made to the dossier, but in the lobbying of court officials, it is instructive to see how often the same few cases were repeated. In his brief to the military commander Bonifatius upon his arrival in Africa in 417, Augustine again refers to the same few stories.[98] By removing the specific names of the victims, he achieves the effect of suggesting that they were typical.[99]

In places like this, trouble still exists and Catholics, but especially Catholic bishops and clerics, have suffered terrible and harsh things, which would take very long to enumerate, since some had their eyes blinded, and a certain bishop had his hands and tongue cut off, and some were even slaughtered.

The same rhetoric continued to the end. As late as 419, it could be suggested to the imperial agent Dulcitius that certain men raging round the African landscape thought that they were doing a service to God by killing Catholics. But the specific cases of the violence remained the same paradigmatic ones.[100]

If the Donatists had not destroyed the churches of the Catholics, if they had not burned Catholic basilicas, if they had not thrown the holy books of the Catholics into these same fires, if they had not inflicted the bodies of Catholic persons with horrible injuries, if they had not blinded their eyes and, finally, if they had not cruelly slaughtered Catholics.

That is to say, right down to the last lobbying between Catholic bishops and imperial officials, not just any violence but the same named violent incidents played a vital role of exemplarity.

A CLEAR AND PRESENT DANGER

The state might move, but it had to be persuaded to do so. One avenue of persuasion that had been attempted from the beginning of the conflict

---

[98] See "Bonifatius (2)," PLRE, 2, pp. 231–40: his rank is uncertain; he seems to have come to Africa in 417 as "tribune." Statements that he was *praepositus* over a sector of the Numidian *limes* are only guesses that are not backed by any evidence. He was formally *Comes Africae* at least from 423 onward.

[99] Aug. *Ep.* 185.29.30 (CSEL 57: 27–28): "Ex his sunt, in quibus adhuc laboratur, in quo labore multa catholici et maxime episcopi et clerici horrenda et dura perpessi sunt, quae commemorare longum est, quando quorundam et oculi extincti sunt et cuiusdam episcopi manus et lingua praecisa est, nonnulli etiam trucidati sunt."

[100] Aug. *Contra Gaud.* 1.22.25 and 1.23.26 (CSEL 53: 223–24): "Si catholicorum domus Donatistae non diripuissent, si catholicas ecclesias non incendissent, si catholicorum codices sanctos in ipsa incendia non misissent, si catholicorum corpora non immanissimis caedibus afflixissent, si catholicorum membra non praecidissent, si oculos non extinxissent, si denique catholicos non crudeliter occidissent."

between the two churches in the teens of the fourth century was to appeal for direct state intervention into the heart of the ecclesiastical controversy. This kind of appeal had had variable success: a little, initially, under Constantine, was followed by a long retreat. The dramatic intervention by Constans in 347 provoked consequences that were far from those for which the court had hoped. The catastrophe was followed, in the next decades, by a withdrawal by the government from such direct action. It has been rightly observed that "Augustine continually impressed upon his audience that the Catholics always had numerous legal options to prosecute the Donatists." But it has been pithily noted that "the assertion is false."[101] In the 390s, a different strategy suggested itself to the most energetic of the Catholic bishops. By now, the imperial state was committed by a series of pieces of legislation in the mid-380s to use the instruments of force at its command to combat heresy and heretics. The different strategy that now logically suggested itself was to exploit existing imperial legislation, to which the court was firmly committed, to get it to act under this new rubric. Another line of attack could also be used to reinforce the first. The latter lobbying efforts were meant to convince an increasingly nervous and apprehensive court that "Donatist heretics" were linked with violent threats to the imperial political order. It was suggested that the dissidents had forged links with dangerous men in Africa like Firmus and Gildo whom the court had branded as usurpers of imperial power, and that they were allied with dangerous gangs of violent men known as circumcellions who were a threat to the social order of the countryside and therefore to the property and production that underwrote critical imperial revenues.

The first tactic became available in the aftermath of the Theodosian regime's reformation and the issuing of an imperial law against heretics in mid-June 392.[102] Under its terms, heavy fines were to be imposed on the clerics of heretical sects, on those who ordained them, and those who owned or leased lands on which heretical practices took place. Catholic attempts to have this law applied to the clergy of the dissidents were made almost immediately and they were directly connected with incidents of violence. The first known target was Optatus, the dissident bishop of Thamugadi. Imputations were made that he had directed armed gangs against Catholic

---

[101] Hermanowicz, *Possidius the Bishop*, pp. 100–01.
[102] CTh 6.5.21 (15 June 392): the uniform fines were ten pounds of gold; for an approximate idea of its value, see n. 111 below.

churches.[103] The specific incident involved an attack on a church at Asna which was occupied and its altar smashed.[104]

The first big success in the campaign happened, almost accidentally, in 403–04, notably in connection with the incident of violence retailed above involving the attack on Possidius, the Catholic bishop of Calama. In its aftermath, Possidius had filed complaints with the municipal courts to force Crispinus, the dissident bishop of the city to discipline his priest Crispinus who had led the attack. Both the local town officials and Crispinus, the bishop, did nothing. In frustration, Possidius took an alternative route. Going over the heads of the local authorities, he went before the court of the proconsular governor to charge Crispinus (the bishop) with being a heretic and made subject to the penalties laid down by Theodosius' decree of 392, confirmed by Honorius on his accession to full power in 395.[105] Success in this case was critical since it was the first time that a formally empowered official of the Roman state had decreed "a Donatist" – and, by implication, all such persons – to be a heretic and therefore subject to imperial laws on heresy.[106] In the local hearing held at Calama, the Catholics, with the assistance of their official *defensor ecclesiae*, succeeded in having Crispinus declared a heretic, in the face of the man's denial of the charge and his affirmation that he was simply "a Catholic."[107] Crispinus then appealed the decision to the proconsul of Africa, where he once again denied that he was a heretic and affirmed that he was "a Catholic."[108] The same *defensor ecclesiae* was supposed to take the case on appeal for the Catholics, but his intervention was not accepted by the proconsul who wished to hear the two men state their cases directly. Great crowds of Christians gathered at Carthage to hear the trial and its outcome, which was eagerly awaited,

---

[103] Aug. *Contra litt. Petil.* 2.83.184 (CSEL 52: 114): "Ipsa ecclesia Catholica solidata principibus Catholicis imperantibus terra marique armatis turbis ab Optato atrociter et hostiliter oppugnata est."

[104] Aug. *Ep.* 29.12 (CCL 31: 105). The incident seems to date to some time while Augustine was still a priest at Hippo, therefore *c.* 393–94 (probably).

[105] Aug. *Contra Cresc.* 3.47.51 (CSEL 52: 458–59).

[106] Aug. *Contra litt. Petil.* 2.92.203 (CSEL 52: 126–27); *En. 2 in Ps.* 36.18 (CCL 38: 359); for the ongoing, central role of Possidius in all of this, see Hermanowicz, "Donatists, Catholics, and Appeals to the Law: 392–404," ch. 3 in *Possidius the Bishop*, pp. 97–131.

[107] A first hearing at Calama seems to be the only way of making sense of the sequence of events, see Possid. *Vita Aug.* 12.5 (Bastiaensen, 158): "defensor ecclesiae inter leges non siluit. Et praeceptus est Crispinus . . . ad multam teneri aurariam publicis legibus contra haereticos constitutam."

[108] Possid. *Vita Aug.* 12.6 (Bastiaensen, 158): "Qui resultans, legibus praesentatus, cum apud proconsulem se negaret haereticum, recendente ecclesiae defensore . . . convinceretur eum esse quod se fuisse negaverat." Possidius then avers that "the heretic was perhaps believed to be 'a Catholic bishop, but only by the ignorant'"; cf. Aug. *Sermo Denis*, 19 (MiAg 1: 108): "Quod dixisti in iudicio proconsulis? 'Catholicus sum.' Vox est ipsius. De gestis recitatur."

we are told, throughout all Africa.[109] The proconsul affirmed Crispinus' condemnation as a heretic – a decision announced from his tribunal and posted throughout the province – and imposed upon him the fine of ten pounds of gold as required by the Theodosian law of 392.[110] It was a considerable amount, even for a large landowner.[111]

The results revealed the potentially dangerous consequences of the new strategy. They put in danger the position of the African Catholic bishops in relation to the local men of power who controlled the towns and cities, and the rich agricultural lands around them. Catholic representatives were sent to the court at Ravenna to soften the penalty imposed on Crispinus as a heretic. They argued that they did not wish uniform penalties to be applied to all "Donatists" as the legal logic of the situation seemed to demand, but only to the clergy of places where the Catholics had actually suffered from violence. But their brief for this carefully tailored imperial response was trumped by another delegation to the imperial court that happened to get to Ravenna before them. This embassy featured the in-person theatrics of Maximianus, the bishop of Bagaï. The display of his "fresh and shocking" scars so moved the emperor Honorius, we are told, that he moved immediately to pass general laws against "the Donatists" compelling them out of heresy and back to the true Church.[112]

The importance of this decision was at once sensed not just by Crispinus, but by all the dissidents. An appeal was made to the emperor Honorius. The Catholics, having acquired the fundamental decision that they

---

[109] Possid. *Vita Aug.* 12.7 (Bastiaensen, 158, 160): "ad controversiam ambo illi Calamenses episcopi venerunt, et de ipsa diversa communione tertio conflictum secum egerunt, magna populorum Christianorum multitudine causae exitum et apud Carthaginem et per totam Africam exspectante."

[110] Possid. *Vita Aug.* 12.7 (Bastiaensen, 160) "atque ille est Crispinus proconsulari et libellari sententia pronuntiatus haereticus." Cf. Aug. *Contra Cresc.* 3.47.51 (CSEL 52: 459): "intercedente Possidio non est conpulsus exsolvere" (i.e. he was not compelled to pay the fine of ten pounds of gold set by Theodosius against heretics); the violence embodied by "the private madness of the raging circumcellions" is purposefully introduced as a rhetorical counterpoint to the Catholics' peaceful recourse to the instruments of the civil courts.

[111] To get some idea of the scale, compare the terms of CTh 11.17.2 (21 March 399) to the Comes Sacrarum Largitionum. The Count of Africa, Gaudentius, requests 7 solidi of gold to cover expenses for horses and their upkeep for cavalrymen; earlier in the same law, the value of cavalry horses is commuted at 2 solidi per horse. Ten pounds of gold or 720 solidi would be enough to buy a very large herd of horses.

[112] Aug. *Ep.* 88.7 (CCL 31A: 414): "Sed cum legati Romam venerunt, iam cicatrices episcopi Catholici Bagaitani horrendae ac recentissimae imperatorem commoverant, ut leges tales mitterentur"; *Ep.* 185.26 and 27 (CSEL 57: 25–26): "praecipue horrenda et incredibilis caedes Maximiani Catholici episcopi ecclesiae Bagaiensis effecit . . . iam enim lex fuerat promulgata . . . quo posteaquam venit et vita eius inopinatissima apparuit, cicatricibus suis tam multis, tam ingentibus, tam recentibus non frustra famam mortuum se nuntiasse monstravit." And, again, at length: *Contra Cresc.* 3.43.27 (CSEL 52: 454), with lurid reference to the *recentissimae cicatrices*.

wanted – that is, the "the Donatists" were now officially to be categorized as "heretics" – were not interested in the application of the fine and
petitioned the governor as a favor not to impose it. The chronology of
these events is difficult to establish. The appeal to Ravenna was certainly
no earlier than mid-404. Whatever its precise date in later 404, however,
there is no doubt about Honorius' decision on the appeal. He upheld the
decision of the proconsular governor, with the result that Crispinus (and
hence all "Donatist" clergy) was deemed to be a heretic and subject to the
fine of ten pounds of gold. The emperor went further than the Catholic
bishops had expected or wanted in severely reprimanding the proconsular
governor and his staff for remitting the penalty decreed by Theodosius. For
this willful abrogation of an emperor's law, the proconsul and his whole
staff were made subject to the same fines. The Catholics reacted vigorously
by supporting the proconsul and his staff: they petitioned the emperor to
remit the fine as an act of imperial indulgence.[113] The emperor's decision
on this matter was issued, it seems, in 405. It was followed later in the same
year with a general order from Ravenna, on 8 December, issued to Diotimus, the proconsul of Africa, that any persons who either admitted to the
fact or who were convicted of being "heretics of the Donatist superstition"
were to "pay the full penalty of the law without delay."[114]

The additional lethal weapons in the arsenal of anti-heresy legislation
were the existing laws directed against Manichees. These were imperial
decrees dating from the early 380s that not only condemned Manichees
as heretics, but which formally imposed the penalties upon them of not
being able to accept property through last will and testament or by gift, and
which forbade them to give or to bequeath their property to others by these
same means. Any attempt by a known Manichee to maintain such property
made the whole of his or her holdings liable to seizure by the imperial fisc.[115]
These were matters of which Augustine, himself a former Manichee, must
have been well aware. It is therefore hardly accidental that he discusses this
connection and echoes the words of these same laws in a work that was
composed in the prelude to the Catholic conference held in June 404.[116]

---

[113] Possid. *Vita Aug.* 12.9 (Bastiaensen, 160).

[114] CTh 16.5.39 (the three Augusti to Diotimus: 8 December 405): "Donatistae superstitionis haereticos
quocumque loci vel fatentes vel convictos legis timore servato poenam debitam absque dilatione
persolvere decernimus."

[115] CTh 16.5.7 (Gratian, Valentinian, and Theodosius to Eutropius PP on the Manichees; 8 May 381)
and 16.5.9 (the same Augusti to Florus PP, also on the Manichees; 31 March 382).

[116] In *Contra ep. Parm.* 1.12.19 (CSEL 51: 41), Augustine refers to a case involving an appeal to the
emperor by a noble, whose sister was "a Donatist," over receiving under a last will and testament.
In his description, Augustine uses elements of the same verbiage found in the original imperial
decree.

In considering the lobbying mission that the council would undertake to the imperial court, the bishops empowered their representatives, Evodius and Theasius, to make a request to the imperial court that the emperor reconfirm the law by which heretics could not transfer property.[117] In doing so, the instructions given to the legates repeated words and phrases taken directly out of the existing anti-Manichaean legislation. The tactic was the same. If "the Donatists" had been decreed legally to be heretics, existing anti-heretical legislation, such as the laws against the Manichees, could be applied to them as well. And the particular utility of the template of the anti-Manichaean legislation, as the emperors themselves were at pains to point out, was that, unlike other laws, they were to be applied retroactively.[118]

By the end of 405, the state had been mobilized in ways for which the Catholics had hoped. As the years immediately following rolled by, however, nothing much happened. It is clear that the dissidents remained largely untouched by the pronouncements of the court at Ravenna. The emperor Honorius had declared them to be heretics and he had emphatically supported heavy penalties against them. Why was so little done against them? The main reasons appear to be two. The first had to do with local conditions. Despite the Edict of Unity and the imperial edicts declaring the dissidents to be heretics, the fragmented and disjointed nature of the state meant that there were few local authorities who were willing to enforce imperial legislation against heretics on their home ground. The attitude of local apathy, if not passive resistance, is confirmed by another imperial decree that was issued by the court at Ravenna in November 407, almost certainly in response to Catholic complaints about inaction. In it, the emperor fulminated about the lack of the application of existing imperial laws by local authorities in Africa.[119] Despite the harsh imperial warning, the situation of local inaction remained unchanged, and further imperial decrees, filled with threatening language, had to be addressed on

---

[117] *Reg. Eccl. Carth. Excerpt.* no. 93 (CCL 149: 213): "Petendum etiam, ut lex quae haereticis, vel ex donationibus vel ex testamentis, aliquid capiendi aut relinquendi denegat facultatem, ab eorum quoque pietate hactenus repetatur: ut eis relinquendi vel sumendi ius adimat, qui pertinaciae furore caecati in Donatistarum errore perseverare voluerint."

[118] CTh 16.5.7.1 (as above): "Nec in posterum tantum huius emissae per nostram mansuetudinem legis forma praevaleat, sed in praeteritum etiam, quidquid talium personarum aut proprietas reliquit aut successio habuit, usurpatio fiscalis commodi persequatur. Nam licet ordo caelestium statutorum secuturis post observantiam sacratae constitutionis indicat neque actis obesse consueverit, tamen, quoniam quid consuetudo obstinationis et pertinax natura mereatur, in hac tantum quam specialiter vigere volumus"; all of this in justification of the quite unusual application of the law to acts performed before the legislation even existed.

[119] Const. Sirmond. 12 (SC 531: 512–18).

the matter of enforcing laws against heretics, specifically "the Donatists."[120] But the locals who wielded power, both in town councils and as owners of large landed estates, had neither the taste nor the will to execute imperial sanctions against heretics.

The intransigence was partly due to local interests. But the hesitation was surely also owed to the diminishing authority of the court and uncertainty concerning its status in African affairs. How would the decree of a boy king and his court in distant Ravenna be treated when local power interests were at stake? The reasons were rooted in the inherent instability of the court and the precise status of the power beside the throne, the general Stilicho. Although lines of power at court were sharpened with the fall of Stilicho in August 408, the general situation of uncertainty only worsened. With the depredations of Alaric and his appointment of his own alternative emperor, Attalus Priscus, in Rome, the Ravenna court effectively lost control over central Italy. Given these conditions, it is no wonder that officials in Africa were not sure what to do. While they might be willing to see that normal judicial and administrative procedures were carried out, they were less willing to execute a whole host of imperial commands that might only make matters worse for themselves by exciting local hatreds and hostilities.

It is therefore hardly surprising when the Ravenna court complained bitterly again in January 409 that its orders were not being enforced in Africa.[121] The problem was a longstanding one. Part of the reason, surely, was that many of the senior officials of the state who were in charge of applying the laws against the dissidents were traditional religionists who had no interest in seeing that the anti-Donatist laws were strictly enforced. As early as 376–77, the Vicar of Africa, Flavianus Nicomachus, who was in receipt of an imperial edict that condemned the dissenters in Africa, was so disinterested that Augustine later remarked of him that he was, in effect, "one of *your* party."[122] In these later years, however, local imperial officials had the additional problem of locating their own interests in the balance between local realities and an increasingly exposed central court. Toward the end of 409 and the beginning of 410, this situation became more unstable. High imperial officials in Africa must have been informing the court that it had to do something to temper measures taken by it that

---

[120] CTh 16.5.44 (Honorius and Theodosius to Avus, Donatus, and other *carissimi*: 24 November 408); 16.5.45 (Honorius and Theodosius to Theodorus PP; 27 November 408); and Const. Sirmond. 14 (SC 531: 522–30).

[121] Const. Sirmond. 14 (SC 531: 522–30); cf. CTh 16.2.31 (Honorius and Theodosius to Theodorus PP; 13 January 409) and 16.5.46 (Honorius and Theodosius to Theodorus PP; 15 January 409).

[122] See Birley (1987), p. 34; the law was CTh 16.6.2; cf. Aug. *Ep.* 87.8 (CCL 31A: 136–37): "partis vestrae homini." The identification of this law and the official, however, is problematic.

were needlessly creating hostility to the government – hostilities that were dangerous not just for the court, but also for themselves.

In response, in the late spring of 410, Honorius issued an edict rescinding all punitive imperial legislation directed against "the Donatists."[123] By June of the same year, the court at Ravenna went even further in assisting the position of its administrators and governors in Africa by ordering general tax remissions.[124] Alaric's actions in Italy throughout this period, including the sacking of the city of Rome in August, provoked a large number of aristocrats and other persons of wealth and status to seek refuge in Africa. This first large-scale, direct confrontation that Africans had with the effects of "barbarian raids" north of the Mediterranean certainly inflected their picture of the standing of the imperial government in Rome and Ravenna. Yet by September 410, with Alaric's departure from Rome, the great crisis in Italy suddenly abated. The court at Ravenna returned to its old attitudes, and the emperor and his advisors happily acted as if nothing had happened in the interim. Perhaps to emphasize "normality," they determined to return not just to the status quo ante, but to something even harder. On the very day that Alaric entered Rome, on 25 August, the court issued an edict that confirmed the continuing power of imperial legislation against heretics.[125]

HEARING THE LAW

It must be borne in mind that the effect of these laws, as well as of many others, depended not only on local enforcement by officially sanctioned state officials down to the level of town decurions, but also on how the mass of citizens *heard* what the emperors had to say. In the case of anti-heresy laws, this popular hearing was complicated by the special language in which the laws were couched. Surely part of the reason that some of the more zealous members of Christian communities reacted emotionally to imperial laws, rushing off to break and to maim, was that they heard the tenor of the law as much as they did its strict bureaucratic content. The problem of properly grasping this critical element is a technical one.

---

[123] The law was issued before the Catholic Council of Carthage of 14 June 410 which sent a legation specifically to get the measure repealed: see Maier, *Dossier*, 2, no. 92, pp. 170–71: "In hoc concilio legationem susceperunt contra Donatistas Florentius, Possidius, Praesidius et Benenatus episcopi, eo tempore quo lex data est ut libera voluntate quis cultum Christianitatis exciperet"; see De Veer (1966).

[124] CTh 11.28.6 (Honorius and Theodosius to Macrobius, Proconsul of Africa; 25 June 410).

[125] CTh 16.5.51 (Honorius and Theodosius to Heraclianus, comes Africae; 25 August 410); cf. Maier, *Dossier*, 2, no. 93, pp. 171–73.

The texts of the laws as we have them (in the Theodosian Code, for example) are shorn of the all-important preambles that set up the announcement of the emperor's decisions.[126] A striking exception, notably not found in the Code, but preserved separately, namely Diocletian's decree against the Manichees, shows how much of the emperor's violent rhetoric was a vital part of the impact of the law as it was enunciated and heard. We ordinarily miss this critical context in reading the stripped-down edited versions of imperial laws preserved in later codifications.[127] What remains – by intent of the Roman editors of the law codes – is the operational essence of the law drained of its emotional packaging. The texts of the laws in the codes are the abbreviated, cleaned-up, and anodyne products of jurists and legal scholars. They are *not* the original pronouncements, certainly *not* the ones that were publicly announced. To those who heard the laws read aloud – the vast majority – it is this heightened volume of hatred in the emperor's voice that they would hear. Further exciting these hostile tones was the fact that the person reading the law to them was usually an interested party, say a local bishop, who might not even bother to emphasize the bare legal core of the law. Take the emperor Constantine's letter to the governor of Numidia dated 5 February 330. Here is the law as it appears in the Theodosian Code.[128]

Readers of the divine scriptures, as well as subdeacons, and other clerics who through the unjust act of heretics have been summoned to serve on municipal councils, are to be absolved from such service. And in the future, according to the practice of the Orient, they shall by no means be summoned to the municipal councils, but they shall possess the fullest exemption from such service.

Lectores divinorum apicum et hypodiaconi ceterique clerici, qui per iniuriam haereticorum ad curiam devocati sunt, absolvantur et de cetero ad similitudinem Orientis minime ad curias devocentur, sed immunitate plenissima potiantur.

In terms of effects on human behavior, the differences between this neatly trimmed and edited version of the law that appears in the law code that we read today and the original words that were *heard* by the Africans are fundamental. The text of the original is too long to be quoted at full

---

[126] Millar, *Greek Roman Empire*, pp. 166 f.   [127] See ch. 7, pp. 318 f. above.

[128] CTh 16.2.7 (Constantine, from Serdica, to Valentinus, governor of Numidia, 5 February 300). There are notable differences between the text of the law as it appears in the CTh and the parallel document in Optatus. Note the following: "readers of the divine scriptures" = "readers of the Catholic Church" (CTh); "who through the unjust acts of heretics" = "who, at the instance of the aforesaid persons have, on account of certain customs" (CTh).

length, so a sample of the expressions from its introductory passages must suffice.[129]

There is no doubt that heresy and schism come from the Devil who is the source of all Evil. So there is no doubt that whatever is done by heretics happens at the instigation of The One who has seized hold of their senses and reason. For when He has brought such people under His power, He rules over them in every way. So what good can be done by a person who is made traitorous, impious, sacrilegious, hostile to God and an enemy of the Church? What good can by done by one who withdraws from the Holy, the True, the Righteous and the Most High God who is the Lord of All... and who rushes headlong with error into the Party of the Devil? Once a mind is seized by evil, it must necessarily follow the work of its teacher... and it is for this reason that those who have been taken by the Devil follow his lies and evil... I am not at all surprised that men of no shame would avoid good since, as the saying goes: "like attracts like." When people are infected by the evil of an impious mind, they should separate themselves from our company. "An evil man," as the scripture says, "brings from his evil treasury evil things" and... as I have said, heretics and schismatics abandon good and chase after evil things that are not pleasing to God, and commune with the Devil who is their Father... Their depraved intention is always in need of the Devil's work to perform... But... God... condemns by his patience and endures all things that come from them. He promises to be the avenger of all, and so when vengeance is left to God a harsher penalty will be exacted from one's enemies.

All of this – and there is much more in the same vein – is a long and emotional preamble to the simple point of the law in which the emperor finally gets around to stating, simply, that he was granting the Catholic community at Cirta funds from the imperial purse to build their own basilica to replace the one that had been occupied by the dissidents. As with other political leaders, the emperor might well have been using heavy language to distract attention from the little that he was actually going to do or from the unexpected course that he was going to take.[130] But in the real situation at local level, what large numbers of people heard read aloud by their bishops and other authorities was not some cool and brief bureaucratic statement of policy on providing funds for the building of a

---

[129] Optatus, *Contra Parm.*, append. 10 (CSEL 26: 213–16): the text of the letter sent by the emperor from Serdica, also on 5 November 330, to the Catholic bishops of Numidia. First part of the overlapping section: "Lectores etiam ecclesiae Catholicae et hypodiacones, reliquos quoque [qui] instinctu memoratum quibusdam pro moribus ad munera vel ad decurionatum vocati sunt, iuxta statutum legis meae [= the edited portion in CTh 6.2.2] ad nullum munus statui evocandos. Sed et eos, qui ducti sunt haereticorum instinctu, iussimus protinus molestis perfunctionibus absolvi."

[130] Compare revisionist interpretations of apparently racist statements made by Abraham Lincoln as "politically useful tactics": J. McPherson, "What Did He Really Think About Race?," *NYRB* 54.5 (29 March 2007).

church, but rather the emperor of Rome calling their enemies his own, and marking them, repeatedly, as evil men and as agents of Satan upon whom the cold vengeance of God will surely fall.

The process was a simple but important one. As in the case of the lobbying of the court to repress "pagan" festivities and to decommission their shrines and temples, the Christian bishops constantly and purposefully over-read and over-interpreted the strict point of imperial laws, so as to suggest that the impact of these laws was more general and all-encompassing than it actually was and so as to encourage more proactive aggressive actions by their parishioners.[131] The tactic was encouraged not only by their own interests, but also by the violent verbiage of the imperial pronouncements themselves.

THE STATE AND VIOLENCE

The agency of the state was therefore critical. At every point in the conflict, its intervention marked the escalation of sectarian violence to levels of hyper-violence that did not exist before and after its deep reach into local Christian affairs.[132] The state's role alone accounts for most of the roller-coaster ride of ups and downs in passivity and action in successive waves of sectarian violence. When Constantine ended his heavy-handed coercion in Africa in 321, there is no further record of acts of violence between the churches meriting notice until 347, the year in which the emperor Constans decided on another hard and direct intervention by the imperial government. Indeed, there is almost no religious history of any sort in this long intervening period for the simple and plain reason that nothing was happening. All of this changed in the last decades of the fourth century. And state intervention had to be forcefully driven by the imperial court since local holders of power were generally unwilling to do anything serious in the way of hard enforcement.

Long efforts by Catholic bishops to force a decisive official confrontation with their enemies finally succeeded in the last months of 410 when

---

[131] A more general phenomenon, as Gaddis, *Religious Violence*, pp. 203–05, shows, referring to the legislation that was interpreted in the East as abolishing the Olympic games and gladiatorial contests; and pp. 208–09, on Ambrose's similar over-interpretation of the significance of Theodosius' decrees on Jewish synagogues. For similar exaggerations and fictions concerning sectarian violence indulged in by modern-day politicians in India, see Varshney, *Ethnic Conflict*, p. 91.

[132] A conclusion that concurs with Tilly's observation, *Collective Violence*, p. 9: collective violence does sometimes occur quite outside the range of governments; however, above a very small scale, collective violence almost always involves governments as monitors, claimants, objects of claims, or third parties to claims. The same importance of the state is, of course, observable in parallel modern instances: e.g. Semelin, *Purify and Destroy*, p. 69.

the imperial court at Ravenna decreed that both sides were to meet at Carthage finally to resolve their differences. On 14 October 410, the emperors Honorius and Theodosius issued a constitution that charged the tribune and notary Flavius Marcellinus with the task of convoking the hearing.[133] Among the greatest concerns of their rule, the emperors noted the *reverentia Catholicae legis* as the first and foremost. It had been a good thing, the emperors opined, to fill the Donatists with fear – "persons who are staining and shaming Africa, the greatest part of our empire that is loyally submissive to our civil rule, with their hollow error and meaningless divisions" – and to terrorize them with stern warnings.[134] But the threats had not had the desired effect. The emperors therefore confirmed the abrogation of all earlier measures that had offered toleration of differing religious views. Since there was only one true Catholic law that had been confirmed by long practice and imperial decisions, they had decided to assent to the request of an embassy of Catholic bishops that they and the Donatist bishops should gather in the most resplendent city of Carthage. In this hearing, bishops selected by either side were to enter into a debate in which, as the emperors saw it, "reason would utterly refute heretical superstition." The aims of the hearing were manifest. But what was going to happen when the little monarchs of the Church who had created this conflict were assembled in their hundreds in the great metropolis of Africa, finally to confront each other?

---

[133] GCC 1.4 (SC 195: 563–69), cf. 3.24 and 29; CTh 16.11.3; Maier, *Dossier*, 2, p. 174, nos. 1–9, outlines the series of measures and official communications involved in the arranging of the hearing that took place before the first session 1 June 411, of which this is the first.

[134] GCC 1.4 (SC 195: 562–64): "Ut etiam Donatistas vel terrore vel monitu olim <iam> implere convenerat, qui Africam, hoc est regni nostri maximam partem et saecularibus officiis fideliter servientem, vano errore et dissensione superflua decolorant."

CHAPTER 12

We choose to stand

> "The question is," said Alice, "whether you *can* make
> words mean so many different things."
> "The question is," said Humpty Dumpty, "which is to
> be master – that's all."[1]
>
> (Lewis Carroll)

> "It would be best for us not keep our silence."[2]
>
> (Petilian)

On the first day of June 411, at Carthage, the resplendent imperial metropolis of all Africa – second only to Rome as the great city of empire in the West – two bitterly hostile groups of Christians met in a confrontation that was intended finally to settle the differences between them.[3] As if to heighten the sense of occasion, the First of June was also a traditional day of midsummer festivity.[4] If this were not enough, the city had also experienced the upheavals created by the flotsam and jetsam of refugees who had fled across the sea to Africa to escape Alaric's armed incursions, driven by the panic caused by the "barbarian" plundering of Rome and Italy. The great interest stoked by the heat of controversy meant that the only public venue large enough to contain the numbers on either side were the monumental Gargilian Baths, the *Thermae Gargilianae*, in the

---

[1] L. Carroll, *Through the Looking-Glass, and What Alice Found There*, New York, Thomas Y. Crowell, 1893, p. 132.

[2] GCC 1.167 (SC 195: 812): "Nobis hoc salvum sit quod non debuimus reticere."

[3] The primary source for the conference, the minutes of the proceedings, has received a masterful edition by Serge Lancel: *Actes de la Conférence de Carthage*. The version of the minutes of the conference that survives is not a direct and unmediated report, however. It is derived from a copy kept by one Marcellus, an otherwise unknown person, who held the rank of *memorialis*. There are no obvious signs of deliberate tampering with the manuscript as he had it, with the exception of the "table of contents" that he prefaced to the whole (see Lancel, *Actes de la Conférence de Carthage*, 1, pp. 357–63). In what follows, I have used an earlier investigation of my own, Shaw (1992), and I have benefitted from several other studies, but especially Hermanowicz, "The Conference of 411," ch. 6 in *Possidius of Calama*, pp. 188–220.

[4] See ch. 5, p. 253.

center of the city.[5] The baths had been selected by the government not just to provide a place sufficiently large for the meeting, but also to furnish a public venue equal to the grandeur of the occasion.[6] Often, as with debates between sectarian factions in the past in Africa, the town baths were the only structures large enough to provide a numerous and interested crowd with reasonable conditions of shade and acoustics.[7] The atmosphere in such baths might be imagined as a humid hothouse that was hardly conducive to reasonable and rational debate. But in fact the rooms of the great Gargilian Baths in which the bishops congregated in 411 were – so we are assured – cool, bright, and spacious.[8] The reason was that the bishops and the government officials met not in the *thermae* proper, but in the *secretarium*, a large general-purpose building that was attached to the baths as a place of public assembly.[9] From the late 390s, it had been one of the principal aims of the Catholic Church to compel the dissidents to a combined meeting of both sides.[10] Seeing nothing to gain from such a common meeting, the dissidents had consistently rejected the self-interested overtures from their sectarian enemies. But now it was happening, under compulsion.

[5] The remains of the baths have not been located at the modern site of Carthage. Augustine, *Brev. Collat.* 1.14 (CCL 149A: 268) and *Ad Donatist. post Collat.* 25.43 (CSEL 53: 144), places them *in urbe media*. Lancel, *Actes de la Conférence de Carthage*, 1, pp. 50–53, reviews the literature and wisely chooses the course of agnostic prudence. For the injunction to the bishops to meet in the Gargilian baths, see Marcellinus' *mandatum* on the organization of the debates: GCC 1.10 (SC 195: 578): "Erit autem conlationi aptissimus locus thermarum Gargilianarum, in quem die kalendarum iuniarum eosdem episcopos solos qui designati sunt oporteat convenire."

[6] Aug. *Ad Donatist. post Collat.* 25.43 (CSEL 53: 144): "Qui loquantur pro omnibus eliguntur ab omnibus, locus etiam re tanta dignus in urbe media procuratur." There is some evidence that Marcellinus shifted from his initial choice of place for the conference to the Gargilian Baths, precisely for reasons of publicity: Aug. *Brev. Collat.* 1.14 (CCL 149A: 268): "In loco ergo collationis, hoc est in thermis Gargilianis, quia ipse postea locus placuerat."

[7] So the debates between Augustine and Faustus the Manichee took place in the August heat of the year 392 in the Baths of Sossius at Hippo Regius: Aug. *Contra Fortunat.* praef. (CSEL 25.1: 86): "Sexto et quinto Kalendae Septembris Arcadio Augusto bis et Q. Rufino viris clarissimis consulibus actis habita disputatio adversum Fortunatum Manichaeorum presbyterum in urbe Hipponensium Regionum in Balneis Sossii sub praesentia populi."

[8] Aug. *Ad Donatist. post Collat.* 35.58 (CSEL 53: 161): "Sed quomodo dicamus iniuriam, quando in tam spatioso et lucido et refrigeranti loco nos fuisse recolimus?"

[9] GCC 1.1 (SC 195: 558): "Post consulatum Varanis, viri clarissimi, kalendis Iuniis, Karthagini in secretario thermarum Gargilianarum." Christian churches also had these *secretaria*: for a building complex that is probably the *secretarium* of a basilica at Carthage, see H. Dolenz, D. Feichtinger, and N. Schütz, "Der dreischiffige Saalbau," in Dolenz, *Damous-el-Karita*, pp. 21–39, figs. 3 and 5 – that is to say a large meeting room or hall, as is often found attached to modern-day churches. See Lancel, *Actes*, 1, pp. 52–53 and 52 n. 4, for examples of *secretaria* known for other Christian basilicas at Carthage and elsewhere in Africa.

[10] The idea had been in the air for some time. One can see some of the ideas already in Optatus, *Contra Parm.* 1.4.2 (SC 412: 178): "Cuius dictis cum respondere veritate cogente compellimur, erit inter nos absentes quoquomodo collatio." Lancel, *Actes de la Conférence de Carthage*, 1, p. 9, is right to see the conference as the proximate result of the program of lobbying efforts by the Catholic Church from the later 390s, pushed in large part by Aurelius and Augustine.

THE WAR OF KISSES

One of the pacific tactics that could be employed by the Catholic bishops in approaching their sectarian enemies was to play the "brotherhood" card. Seen as alternatives to the use of the imperial stick, offers to meet peacefully to discuss and to talk over one's differences were presented as a generous act of Christian charity. Suffused with a language of generosity and forgiveness, apparently open and conciliatory gestures of this "let's kiss and make up" kind did not usually elicit positive responses from the dissidents. Instead of kind advances, they saw false, deceitful, deceptive traps. Riven with suspicion, they feared a monster that was set to devour them whole. As one dissident bishop expressed his attitude frankly in a polemical tract:[11]

In this way, in *this* way, you – you wicked persecutor – however *you* might try to cover yourself with the veil of goodness, however you wage this war with kisses in the name of peace, however you seek to entice humankind with words of unity, you who deceive and mislead this much – in reality you are the son of Satan. By your behavior, you reveal who your true father is.

In speaking of a war of kisses, the bishop surely meant bring to mind the hard-edged saying of the Proverbs: "The wounds inflicted by someone who likes you are better than the fraudulent kisses of someone who hates you."[12] This loving deceit was part of the concerted strategy deployed at the end of the fourth century by Catholic bishops to urge, to entice and, if need be, to compel the dissidents to a plenary meeting between the two sides in which their differences would finally be adjudicated. Since the dissidents saw the endgame in which they would be implicated, they were justly fearful of the kisses. The move to a policy of direct engagement happened by a series of steps in the 390s and early 400s that not only proffered a conciliatory hand, but also enticed the involvement of the state. In councils held at Carthage in 397 and 401, the Catholic bishops decided to send ambassadors to the overseas churches at Rome and Milan to draw them into the new program of reform. Although this involved the idea of striking connections with churches in the important centers of imperial power in the West, the negative responses from the sister churches in Italy pushed the Africans' attention to a different alternative: the imperial court. There had already been earlier moves to send ambassadors to the imperial court but, as with

---

[11] Petilian apud Aug. *Contra litt. Petil.* 2.17.38 (CSEL 52: 41): "Sic, sic, improbe persecutor, quocumque te velamine bonitatis obtexeris, quocumque nomine pacis bellum osculis geras, quolibet unitatis vocabulo hominum genus inlicias, qui hactenus fallis ac decipis, vere Diaboli filius es, dum moribus indicas patrem"; cf. Brown, *Augustine of Hippo*, pp. 227–28.

[12] Proverbs 27: 6: "Meliora sunt vulnera diligentis, quam fraudulenta oscula odientis" (VG).

the embassy to the court dispatched by the Catholic council of 399, these representations were on rather routine matters that did not have direct significance for the serious sectarian conflicts of the time in Africa.[13]

Serious moves to engage the state began with the second plenary council held at Carthage by the Catholic bishops on 13 September 401. The minutes of this conference are filled with matters to be taken by Catholic emissaries to the imperial court at Ravenna – on everything from pagan idols and festivals to the control of actors and slaves.[14] The main decision taken by the Catholic bishops at the session was to initiate a program by which the dissident bishops would be compelled to attend a combined discussion and debate over the differences between the two churches.[15] It was in this context that the council requested the intervention of the provincial governors in Africa to provide records out of the public archives, the *gesta publica*, that would convince the dissidents of the truth of the Catholic claims.[16] Nothing was left to chance. The proceedings of the council were packed with large numbers of official-looking documents: the formal minutes of the council itself, a series of church canons (six of them concerning the dissidents), a letter of Pope Anastasius, the formal decision of a council, copies of letters to the governors of the African provinces, copies of instructions to the Catholic bishops who were to serve as messengers and representatives of the council, and copies of records from municipal courts and council proceedings. The final dossier of the council was marked with a heavy patina of technical and official language.

This whole process was repeated, only with greater rigor, in the Catholic council held at Carthage on 25 August 403. Once again, it was decided that each Catholic bishop would directly invite the dissident bishop opposite him in his diocese to a general common hearing between the two churches at Carthage. Once more, a conciliatory pacific line was followed. The formal invitation was filled with the language of brotherhood. "Blessed are the peacemakers," the invitation went, trumpeting: "You are our brothers."

---

[13] Concil. Carth. 27 April 399 canon 1 = *Reg. Eccl. Carth. Excerpt.* canon 56 (CCL 149: 194): "In hoc concilio legationem susceperunt Epigonius et Vincentius episcopi, ut pro confugientibus ad ecclesiam, quocumque reatu involutis, legem de gloriosissimis principibus mereantur, ne quis audeat eos abstrahere."

[14] Concil. Carth. 13 Sept. 401 = *Reg. Eccl. Carth. Excerpt.* e.g. canons 58–64, 82–84 (CCL 149: 196–98, 204–05).

[15] Concil. Carth. 13 Sept. 401 = *Reg. Eccl. Carth. Excerpt.* canons 66, 69, and 85 (CCL 149: 199–201, 205).

[16] Concil. Carth. 13 Sept. 401 = *Reg. Eccl. Carth. Excerpt.* canon 67 (CCL 149: 199): "Ita placuit, ut ex concilio nostro litterae darentur ad iudices Africanos"; cf. canon 68 on the involvement of the overseas church: "Deinde placuit, ut litterae mittantur ad fratres et coepiscopos nostros et maxime ad sedem apostolicam" (CCL 149: 200).

Such fraternal spirit pervades some parts of the document, but other parts of it were peppered with provocative words – "we shall rejoice in your correction," for example – that were bound to be taken as calculated insults.[17] Since it was foreseen that the request was likely to meet with responses on a spectrum ranging from indifference to outright rejection, recourse was now had to the civil authorities of the state for more direct action. Governors and municipal officials were no longer just to provide copies of records; they were to become agents involved in forcing the dissidents to the table. Letters were sent to the provincial governors in Africa requesting them to send orders to the municipal councils to have *them* guarantee that the invitation process would be enforced in each town and village. The magistrates in each municipality and the elders who governed the hamlets and villages were to be responsible for compelling the invitation.[18]

The impressive dossier produced by the council was meant to suggest the gravity of an official pronouncement of the state. An impression of its administrative weight is signaled by its contents: a detailed transcript of the whole proceedings, a close record of all the verbal interventions, all properly signed; canons and decrees issued by the council, including copies of documents read into the record; a model framework of the way the forthcoming joint council with "the Donatists" would be conducted (a copy of which was sent out to each Catholic bishop); a copy of the order to assemble; and copies of synodal letters sent to the Proconsul of Africa and to the other governors of the African provinces. This was the core of the record. To it was also appended a large dossier of supporting documentation: copies of the edicts issued by the Proconsul of Africa and the Vicar of Africa in response to the council's requests; copies of official records drawn from the proconsular governor's archives and those of the Vicar of Africa relevant to the disputes between the Catholics and dissidents; and documents from municipal archives preserved in different towns of Africa relevant to these same sectarian disputes. The notary Laetus read into the record of the proceedings that each bishop was to bring the matter to the attention of the municipal authorities in his town, noting that the governor had issued an order or *mandatum* to the town councils on the matter. The bishops, in turn, were to demand that a copy of it be placed in the municipal archives, the *gesta municipalia* of his own town or

---

[17] Concil. Carth. 25 Aug. 403 = *Reg. Eccl. Carth. Excerpt.* canon 92 (CCL 149: 210): "de vestra correctione gaudere cupientes...*Beati pacifici, quia ipsi filii Dei vocabuntur...Fratres nostri estis.*"

[18] Concil. Carth. 25 Aug. 403 = *Reg. Eccl. Carth. Excerpt.* canon 91 (CCL 149: 210): "ut pariter eos in singulis quibusque civitatibus vel locis per magistratus vel seniores locorum conveniant"; and Aug. *Brev. Collat.* 3.5.6 (CCL 149A:): "Obtulerunt ergo Donatistae gesta proconsularia et vicariae praefecturae, ubi Catholici petierant eos actis municipalibus conveniri."

city. Once it was there, as often as they wished, Catholic bishops could refer to the existence of this written record in making requests to local officials to enforce it.

There was more, but the enumeration of these contents is sufficient to indicate the heavy deployment of an official tone that was calculated to give the document "governmental" authority. On 13 September, the Catholic primate of Africa, Aurelius, was able to put the whole of this record and his formal request before the governor of Africa.[19]

We file this formal Petition with Your Equity, Septiminus, Vir Clarissimus, Most High and Sublime of Proconsuls:

Against the justice of both human and divine laws, the Catholic Church has suffered many attacks on it by the heretics of the party of Donatus. If we were to file a formal petition under earlier or more recent imperial edicts that commanded their repression or punishment, they could not possibly dare to complain about our court actions. They know full well that, not even having the support of any general law of this kind, they nevertheless prosecuted their own schismatics, the Maximianists. With the decisions of judges [i.e. provincial governors] in hand, they drove them out or expelled them from the churches and the buildings that they [i.e. the Maximianists] had occupied. On the other hand, we only desire their well being; we are mindful of our reputation for peace and also of that Charity because of which we are Christians. For these reasons, we wish to admonish them in all gentleness so that, by reflecting on and recognizing their error, they will not hesitate to correct it. If they believe that they possess any truth that they can defend, then let them do it not with the crazed and violent acts against the public peace committed by their circumcellions, but rather by a reasoned accounting.

Wherefore, we formally ask of Your Sublimity:

To order – everywhere where we wish to notify them of this proposal through the agency of the appropriate magistrates either in cities or in the rural regions that are attached to them – that the resources of publishing formal records shall be made available to us. And that you command them honorably to convene for a meeting in response to our written representations to them. For this favor, we offer overflowing thanks to God for Your Excellence.

---

[19] The document is preserved in the acts of the later conference of 411: GCC 3.174 (SC 224: 1118–22 = Maier, *Dossier*, 2, no. 69, pp. 121–23).

> Issued by all the Catholic bishops of the Council of Carthage, in the con-
> sulships of Our Lord Theodosius, Father of the Fatherland, Augustus in
> Perpetuity, and Rumoridus, Vir Clarissimus, on the Ides of September,
> at Carthage.

This time, the confrontation of a conciliar decision and governmental
power had the desired effect. The proconsular governor of Africa, Septiminus, responded positively to the request put to him by the council, ordering
that a conference be held between the bishops of the two churches. His
decision was confirmed and was even recorded in the archives of the Vicar
of Africa, presumably because it was to have Africa-wide application. The
Vicar's office would make sure that the order was circulated to the other
provincial governors. The Catholics had finally succeeded in eliciting a
favorable response from the state, albeit at provincial level, helped, perhaps, by the official-like nature of their petition. The other critical element
in their petition was that it drew attention, for the first time, to the men
called circumcellions who were considered to pose a violent threat to the
general public order. This threat was made palpable by giving the "dangerous men" a specific official-sounding name.

The focus of all of the annual Catholic conferences, since 393, had been
the mobilization of official power. Here, at last, was success. An order was
to be issued by the governor announcing a general assembly of the two
churches, and the order was to be effected locally in the province by municipal officials in the towns or by elders in charge of villages and hamlets.[20]
The culmination of this process took place in the following year at the
conference held at Carthage on 4 June 404. The intervening year had been
marked by the outright rejection of the invitation by the dissident bishops and also, it was claimed, by an efflorescence of circumcellion violence
by dissident gangs who were policing the invitations and terrorizing both
the importuners and potential "traitors." The lack of power exercised by
provincial governors and the level of the violence encouraged salience: the
need to jump the appeal to a higher official level – to the imperial court
at Ravenna – to get decisive action. The Catholics could now petition
the court for imperial protection from an insurrection that threatened the
provincial peace and for the punishment of their sectarian enemies. The
council therefore selected two bishops, Theasius and Evodius, as envoys to
take these requests to the imperial court at Ravenna.[21]

[20] Concil. Carth. 25 Aug. 403 = *Reg. Eccl. Carth. Excerpt.* canon 91, cf. n. 13 above.
[21] All that survives from this council is the lengthy brief issued to its legates: Concil. Carth. 16 June
404 = *Reg. Eccl. Carth. Excerpt.* canon 93 (CCL 149: 211–14, at 211): "Commonitorium fratribus

The aims of their embassy, however, were to be trumped in advance by a show-and-tell demonstration at the Ravenna court of the ravages of circumcellion violence: principally the star performance of the bishop Maximianus of Bagaï and the display of the impressive scars on his body. An aggressive Numidian faction (one suspects the hand of Possidius) had struck pre-emptively on the council's agenda. The imperial response was more than had been hoped for. Far from just issuing edicts that required the protection of Catholic churches or the repression of violence, on 12 February 405 the emperor Honorius issued an edict that called for the wholesale forced unification of the two churches. He ordered the abolition of the dissident church and commanded its bishops and adherents to merge with the existing Catholic Church.[22] The "Rebaptizers" were condemned as heretics, and their churches subject to confiscation. There must have been differential access to and enforcement of the decree. Catholic ambassadors to the court, including Thesasius and Evodius, would have known of its contents immediately and would have transferred them rather quickly to Africa via internal church channels. But the imperial decree was not posted at Carthage until 26 June, when the first acts of "persecution against the Christians" occurred in the city.[23] The gap in knowledge between Catholic bishops and the dissidents surely led to premature efforts at enforcement by zealous Catholics, provoking violent resistance by the dissidents who must have felt that the Catholics had no legal basis for their actions.

Since the Catholic councils of 404 and 405 had achieved what was wanted from the imperial government, it is logical that the drive to continue to hold great annual conferences for all of Africa began to dissipate. The "brothers" were beginning to feel fatigued and exhausted by the effort that was needed to organize them. The sentiment was widely felt and voiced among the Catholic bishops. In the Catholic council held at Carthage in 407, the matter came to a head. Specific reference was made to the requirement of the council of Hippo in 393 that the Church hold large annual councils for all of Africa. Sentiments were strongly expressed that such massive efforts made for every year were no longer required and that the omnibus conferences were now deemed to be "too onerous" for "the brothers."[24] It was moved that the fatiguing and draining annual councils

---

Theasio et Evodio legatis ex Carthaginiensi concilio ad gloriosissimos religiosissimosque principes missis."

[22] We do not have the original text; only fragments of it survive, dispersed through the Theodosian Code: the order to post referred to in a later law of 5 March (CTh 16.11.2) and other parts excerpted (CTh 16.5.38; 16.6.3–5); cf. De Veer (1968i), pp. 810–14 for a detailed discussion and outline.

[23] *Liber genealogus*, 626–27 (Mommsen, *Chronica minora*, MGH 9: 196 = Maier, *Dossier*, 2, no. 82, p. 149): "Stilichone iterum consule . . . ipso consulatu venit persecutio Christianis vi kal. Iulias data pridie kal. Febr. Ravenna."

[24] Concil. Carth. 13 June 407, canon 1 = *Reg. Eccl. Carth. Excerpt.* canons 94–95 (CCL 149: 214–15).

should be abandoned and that general councils should henceforth be held only when events demanded. The age of the great annual councils held by the Catholic Church in Africa, it might be noted, had coincided precisely with a specific interest in mobilizing state power. This interest was also paralleled by an internal disciplining within the church itself that was construed as a reform program. The two were vitally interconnected.

The main difficulty with continuing the annual conferences was that their one big ostensible aim had been gained: the imperial decree of February 405 that demanded the unification of the two churches. The real problems now lay elsewhere, namely with the enforcement of the terms of the decree. In the events that followed in the years between 406 and 409, it is reasonably clear that the local authorities who were to compel the unification either did not wish to do so or did not have sufficient force at their disposal. The rotating provincial governors were no more enthusiastic. The Catholic council held at Carthage in 407 again sent ambassadors to the imperial court to petition action from the courts against "pagans" and "heretics."[25] The same petitions were repeated by the Catholic councils held at Carthage on 16 June and 13 October of 408.[26] The reason for holding two conferences in one year, both of them concerned with sending urgent petitions to the imperial court, was the inflammatory issue of violence. Some time after the June meeting, there had been violent confrontations between dissidents and Catholics. In these incidents, two Catholic men named Severus and Macarius had been killed, and the bishops Evodius, Theasius, and Victor had been severely beaten.[27] The repetition of the embassies also hints at the lack of effectiveness of the government, which is understandable given the more pressing secular concerns of the Ravenna court in these same years.

The year 410 brought a dramatic reversal of court favor, as the emperor Honorius, surely under the lobbying pressure of the dissidents and the fearful condition of the state itself in the face of Alaric's incursions, decreed not a forced unification of the two churches, but rather the opposite: a general edict of toleration in which each Christian was to be free to

---

[25] Concil. Carth. 13 June 407, canon 4 = *Reg. Eccl. Carth. Excerpt.* canon 97 (CCL 149: 215): "Placuit etiam ut petant ex nomine provinciarum omnium legati perrecturi, Vincentius et Fortunatianus, a gloriosissimis imperatoribus."

[26] Concil. Carth. 16 June 408 = *Reg. Eccl. Carth. Excerpt.* canon 106 (CCL 149: 219): "In hoc concilio legationem iterum suscepit Fortunatianus episcopus contra paganos et haereticos"; Concil. Carth. 13 Oct. 408 = *Reg. Eccl. Carth. Excerpt.* canon 106 (CCL 149: 219): "In hoc concilio susceperunt legationem Restitutus et Florentius episcopi contra paganos et haereticos."

[27] Concil. Carth. 13 Oct. 408 = *Reg. Eccl. Carth. Excerpt.* canon 106 (CCL 149: 219): "eo tempore quo Severus et Macarius occisi sunt, et propter eorum causam Evodius, Theasius et Victor episcopi caesi sunt."

follow his or her own worship.[28] The Catholics now had two precise goals that they had to achieve. They had to undo Honorius' panicked and ill-considered grant of freedom of worship, and they had to force the issue of the direct invention of the imperial court. The latter would require the emperor himself to cut through the multiple layers of local and provincial inaction to get the big central state to move its resources without delay or prevarication. The best way to produce these two aims this was to return to the idea of a combined meeting of the two churches. It had to be a meeting that would be configured as a court hearing with an imperial judge sitting in judgment. In it, one side would win and the other would lose. And the consequences of losing would be serious. Since the judge deciding the issue would be hearing it in the place of the emperor himself, the full weight of the imperial state would be brought directly to bear in punishing the guilty.

Events in Italy aided the new Catholic agenda. Quickly recovering from his fright at the armed intrusions of Alaric and his premature edict of tolerance granted to African Christians, Honorius regained his composure and rescinded the general grant of toleration that he had issued earlier in the year.[29] Perhaps compensating for the panic that led to his granting of freedom of religious worship to the dissidents, or perhaps exasperated by long inaction at local level in a manner that questioned the status of the imperial court's power, Honorius acceded to the petition. On 14 October 410, he issued a decree setting up the great judicial hearing. It was to take place in the metropolis of Carthage in the summer of the following year.[30] Using the harsh language that imperial edicts of the time could sometimes assume, the emperor condemned outright the *superstitio* of "the Donatists" who were declared to be heretics. Some modern historians have been surprised by the law's lack of fairness or objectivity.[31] It was not meant to be fair. In his instructions to the president of the meeting, the emperor declares that "the Donatists" were to be brought to heel by the use of stern threats or by sheer terror, and that he was to remember to implement the *mandata* or orders given to him on the matter.

THE GRAND CONFRONTATION

The great meeting at Carthage in 411 was not a church conference in the normal sense of church councils that had previously been held in Africa.

---

[28] This decree does not survive; we can only guess at its existence from its later repeal by Honorius in an edict dating to 25 August 410 (CTh 16.5.51).

[29] CTh 16.5.51 (25 August 410): issued to Heraclian, the Count of Africa.

[30] The decree was twice read into the records of the council of 411, which is our main source for its text: GCC 1.4 (SC 195: 562–68) and 3.29 (SC 224: 998–1004).

[31] Lancel in his preface to the GCC (SC 194: 29): "Tant de partialité nous confond . . . Or les donatistes étaient d'avance déclarés hérétiques!" (his exclamation mark).

All of them, apart from this gathering in 411, had been internal to each of the two churches.[32] Of the councils that had taken place between the age of Cyprian and the early fourth century, all of those that are known or documented were held in order to manage matters internal to the Church, even when it was under the extreme duress of persecution. There had been about forty, or so, of these councils over the previous century, and then more of them between Constantine and the conference of 411.[33] With the exception of the flurry of conciliar meetings that took place in 312–14 that were connected with the original division between the two churches, the record of what survives for the rest of the fourth century indicates that councils were occasional in meeting and that they were usually summoned in response to immediate crises or internal matters that concerned each church. And most of these intervening councils were factional in nature or regional in scope, being restricted mostly to provincial concerns.

The general profile and rhythm of church councils shifted dramatically beginning in the early 390s, and in two ways. First, on the Catholic side, and also in some factions of the dissident church, councils seem to have been held more frequently. In fact, from 393 onward the Catholic Church held regular councils on an annual basis. In addition, the large annual meetings were now plenary councils that assembled the sum of all bishops of the church in Africa (or, at least, pretended to do so). The second change, manifest in the records surviving from the Catholic councils held during this period, is that there was a shift in them to the constant and intentional lobbying of the imperial state. The holding of the great council at Carthage in 411 was itself a direct result of the lobbying of the imperial court by Catholic councils through the early 400s.[34] It was in the 390s that general church councils became integrated with the state in a way that had not previously been the case: the bishops were no longer reacting as much to decisions by the court and its officials as they were proactively setting an agenda that *they* wished the court to pursue. In this sense, the new councils laid particular emphasis on unity, the weight of numbers, and their representative force in promoting specific aims with the court. Like the secular provincial councils headed by provincial priests, and other such conciliar bodies, the ecclesiastical councils had become institutionalized

---

[32] Monceaux, "Les actes des conciles donatistes et antidonatistes," *Hist. litt.* 4, pp. 321–436; cf. *Hist. litt.* 2, pp. 41–66 and 3, pp. 205–37, provides lists and commentary.

[33] Monceaux, *Hist. litt.* 4, pp. 322–23, counts thirty-seven councils, the caution being that some of these were local, specific to a given crisis, or provincial in scope.

[34] As is clear from the emperor's own words in his instructions to Flavius Marcellinus in his edict of October 410 (GCC 1.4 = SC 195: 564): "studio <tamen> pacis et gratiae venerabilium virorum episcoporum legationem libenter admisimus."

non-governmental organizations that aimed to be "governmental" in their impact.

Furthermore, the conference at Carthage in 411 was less a church council than it was a legal hearing that reflected a new integration of the Catholic Church and imperial state in Africa. The two hostile churches were summoned not by their primates, but rather by the emperor before an imperial official, the tribune and notary Flavius Marcellinus, who was informed that he would hold his position as *iudex in loco principis* – judge in place of the emperor himself. The position of tribune and notary made him an imperial plenipotentiary for this specific mission. A tribune and notary was a special imperial official delegated directly by the emperor with full powers to take care of a specific item of official business.[35] Just so, Marcellinus was to achieve the aim of his mission by cutting through all the existing bureaucratic levels between the provincials and the court at Ravenna. By bypassing all intervening figures of authority – in this case in particular the proconsular governor, the Vicar of Africa, and the Praetorian Prefect – to report directly to the emperor, the judge was empowered to get the particular task done without any undue external interference. The court accordingly informed its higher officials in charge of Africa to place their resources at his disposal.

Above all, the emperor Honorius made it clear that Marcellinus was to issue a final decision against the dissidents: if "the Donatists" attended they were to be judged; if they did not, they were to be subject to punishment for contumacious behavior. If Marcellinus decided that the Catholic Church was the sole legitimate Christian community in Africa, then the dissidents, whether they wished it or not, were to be forced to belong to it. In certain senses, the whole thing was not far short of a "kangaroo court" in its officious rubber-stamping of a decision already made by the state. There are frequent attempts to argue for the supposed "lack of bias" or "fairness" of the judge in his management of the hearing. Quite apart from the bias already evident in such claims, they have little to do with the real position in which Marcellinus found himself at Carthage. As with other such plenipotentiary officials, his aim, surely, was not as much one of

---

[35] Marcellinus was to function "in the place of the emperor himself": "Cui quidem disputationi principis loco te iudicem volumus residere – quicquid etiam ante in mandatis acceperis, plenissime meministi" (GCC 1.4 = SC 195: 566). For the historical background, see M. Peachin, *Iudex Vice Caesaris: Deputy Emperors and the Administration of Justice during the Principate*, Stuttgart, Steiner, 1996, for the development of the procedure, especially under the Severan emperors in the high empire; in those cases, he argues that it is for more efficient government. In the case considered here, as well as those of other *tribuni et notarii*, the emphasis seems to be more on the ability to exert a full and direct imperial power in a specific local situation.

fairness as it was one of emerging from his assigned task by causing the least local distress and the least collateral damage to himself. Given the problem that Marcellinus faced – to fulfill the emperor's blunt command (find the dissidents guilty) and to achieve this end with a minimum of overt hostility and humiliation – his even-handed and punctilious management of the proceedings, even if it failed, was entirely rational.

The form and procedures of the meeting followed those of the civil courts and public deliberative bodies. The atmosphere was that of a super-court, buzzing even more than normally with the comings and goings of lawyers and legal experts. The judge was formally seated with the court advisors, the notaries, the secretaries, and the rest. As it was later remembered:[36]

We see the presence of those who had been chosen by all to speak on behalf of all – a place worthy of a magnificent occasion chosen in the middle of the city – the assembling of both sides – the judge is present – the official books are opened – the hearts of everyone beat in anticipation of the beginning of such a great gathering. Then all the most eloquent and leading men through whom this great endeavour was to be accomplished strove mightily to see that nothing would be accomplished! They began to debate and to analyse these matters in the usual manner of lawyers – arguing about who, precisely, were the accusers and who the defendants – matters such as litigators are accustomed to grind away at for years in the law courts.

Even if the emperor Honorius had transferred his full judicial powers to hear the matter to Flavius Marcellinus, to exercise these powers he still had to get to Africa in the full rigors of the winter sailing season. It seems that he did not make it to Carthage until December 410 or even early January 411. On 19 January, he posted his own decree at Carthage that went some way to softening the brutal language of the emperor's peremptory condemnation of "the Donatists." Instead of the "hollow error of the sterile schism," Marcellinus spoke in a more anodyne language of "religious differences." He also emphasized that he had not come to Carthage to coerce anyone but rather "to bring peace."[37] To assist in getting all the bishops of both parties to Carthage, he ordered all imperial procurators, municipal magistrates and town councillors, all private managers of rural domains, and the elders who governed hamlets and villages, to see that the bishops who lived in their various communities responded to his summons.[38] If we listen

---

[36] Aug. *Ad Donat. post Collat.* 25.43 (CSEL 53: 144).

[37] GCC 1.5 (SC 195: 568–74); for the softening of language, see GCC 1.5, lines 6 and 9–10 (SC 195: 570).

[38] GCC 1.5, lines 35–38 (SC 195: 572): "Universos etiam cunctarum provinciarum curatores, magistratus et ordines viros, necnon et actores, procuratores, vel seniores singulorum locorum pari admonitione convenio."

to the summons, we hear the same words issued and approved by the Catholic council of 403 coming out of the mouth of a high imperial official. Hearing these sectarian and biased echoes, the dissident bishops were surely somewhat suspicious of Marcellinus' guarantees of protection and of safe passage. But he had indeed sworn an oath on the name of the Day of the Final Judgment that he meant exactly what he said.[39] For the judge himself, the oath was to be doubly auspicious.

On 18 May, while the Catholic bishops were still continuing to arrive in small separate groups, the bishops of the dissident church, having assembled in force outside the city, made an impressive grand entrance into Carthage. In the same week, the tribune and notary Marcellinus published his second edict concerning the technical format of the hearing and the procedures to be followed in the forthcoming meeting. He set the date for the beginning of the assembly at 1 June. Since only seven representatives of each side were to be permitted into the hall actually to debate the matters before the hearing, Marcellinus required all the bishops of each side to sign a contract that mandated the specific bishops whom they selected to represent their side in the proceedings. In compensation for the fact that the great majority of bishops on either side would not to be allowed to attend in person, he promised to have a written record of each day's proceedings made public. He also required that each side provide him with formal letters signed by their respective Primates, confirming their agreement to the procedures that he had outlined.[40]

IPSISSIMA VERBA

The verbal contents of the proceedings, the debates and discussions in the Gargilian Baths in June 411, have survived in surprising detail. In large part, this is because the precision of every recorded word mattered greatly to the participants. For one thing, they had every reason to fear manipulation and forgery by their enemies. Both sides therefore went to extraordinary lengths to ensure that their exact words would be recorded. Because of the minute notarial precautions and because of the historical importance of the debates for the ecclesiastical battles of the time, much of the word-by-word record of what the participants said over the days between 1 and 8 June of 411 has

---

[39] GCC 1.5, lines 73–74 (SC 195: 574): "quod me et per tremendum iudicii diem et per sacramenta superius memorata ita facturum esse polliceor."
[40] GCC 1.10, lines 125–35 (SC 195: 586).

survived intact.[41] Indeed, the detailed description of the painstaking scribal and notarial provisions made for this conference furnishes one of the best pictures of how such official records were kept in the Roman world.[42] The verbatim record is not without its peculiar technical problems and biases; but the plain fact remains that the transcript was systematically checked by both sides in the confrontation, and it is extensive and detailed.

First of all, heading the notarial team taking down the minutes were six secretaries or *scribae* attached to the *officia* of various imperial officials in Carthage. They were assisted by two secretaries or *notarii* from each church.[43] The actual note-taking was assigned to four stenographers or *exceptores* from official sources, plus four stenographers assigned by each church. The final ecclesiastical stenographic teams were deliberately "mixed" and were composed of four persons, two selected from each side. These teams were then rotated through the day as each day's proceedings were recorded. Since each team had both dissidents and Catholics on it, the opposing members acted as a check on each other's record-taking. When each scribal team left the conference room, its notes were counterchecked by a team of *custodes codicum, custodes chartarum,* or *custodes tabularum* – guardians of the books, papers, documents – as they were variously called, again composed of both dissidents and Catholics, who placed their seals on the documents in the presence of Flavius Marcellinus himself.

In this way, each speaker had his own words carefully recorded. Additionally, there was a team of scrutineers from each side who then checked the records. At the end of the day, each speaker was asked to authenticate, to sign and to notarize, that his words had been accurately taken down. He did so by writing in his own hand the word *recognovi* ("I have reviewed") at the end of the transcript of what he had said in the conference session, signaling that he had inspected and certified that these were exactly his own words. There might have been some minor editing of the transcripts, but any study of the syntax and grammar of the Latin reveals that the minutes faithfully reflect the oral character of the proceedings. Men who were otherwise renowned as artful writers and skilled rhetoricians fell

---

[41] Even for this detailed document, it is clear that part of the proceedings of the third session – those that transpired on 8 June – are missing; the *capitula* at the head of the document indicate that chapters 282–585 (303 chapters in all, or a little more than the last half of the original) have been lost. What remains is a detailed verbatim record of what was said for all of the first and second sessions, and a portion of the third.

[42] Tengström, *Die Protokollierung*, is fundamental to an understanding of the technical arrangements for recording the proceedings; cf. Teitler, *Notarii and Exceptores*, ch. 1, pp. 5–16; for a synopsis of Tengström's findings, see Lancel, *Actes de la Conférence de Carthage*, I, pp. 342–53.

[43] For what follows, see Tengström, *Die Protokollierung*, esp. pp. 9–16 and Teitler, *Notarii and Exceptores*, pp. 5–15.

back on a limited real-time vocabulary, marked by repetitions, rhetorical interjections, and the sudden lapses and shortcut expressions that are characteristic of live talk.[44] The result is that in this transcript we possess a verbatim recording of almost unprecedented quality for the ancient world. A gem of hard reportage. What does it tell us?

The position of the participants in the confrontation broadly reflected the main powers and forces on each side, and also the directives under which the conference operated. The record also mirrored, in miniature, the general power situation in which either side had found itself over the previous decades. The Catholics entered the hearing with all the authority of the imperial state behind them. The man whom the emperor Honorius appointed to preside over the conference and to direct it to its end, the tribune and notary Flavius Marcellinus, was a faithful orthodox Catholic and a friend of Augustine, one of the most prestigious of the Catholic bishops.[45] Augustine had an intimate correspondence with Marcellinus. Not long afterward, he was to dedicate the grandest of all his works, *The City of God*, to the imperial official.[46] What is perhaps most striking about the nature of bias in the conference is the staggering disparity between the brutish partiality of the emperor's directive and the minutiae put in place to guarantee fairness in recording its proceedings.

These detailed arrangements were less a façade of legitimation than they were an enacted theater of legal correctness that was meant to counter the gross unfairness that undergirded the whole hearing.[47] The structure of

---

[44] Lancel, "Etude linguistique", ch. 4 in *Actes*, 1, pp. 289–335, esp. pp. 309 f.

[45] There seems no good reason to doubt Marcellinus' inclinations in this matter, although, given both his behavior in the matter, and the chronology of Augustine's dealings with him, we might be cautious in accepting too total a pre-commitment on his part. Augustine's correspondence with him does not begin until the time of the conference itself, and much follows in the aftermath (including the dedication of *The City of God*). A compelling case could be made that Marcellinus was heavily "lobbied" by Augustine from the inception of the conference, and that much that followed between them is better read in the light of his successes in that regard. Marcellinus' behavior should therefore be read in a more narratological manner. His attempts at moderation and impartiality were, no doubt, in part a response to his recognition of the "realities" of the situation he faced when he got to Africa, when he surely realized he could not crudely impose the mission in the stark terms presented in the imperial edict. Moreau (1973a) has the full record, the chronological sequence of which is significant.

[46] See, "Fl. Marcellinus (10)," PLRE, 2, pp. 711–12; and the extensive notice, "Flavius Marcellinus (2)," PAC, 1, pp. 671–88. Augustine dedicated the first three books of the *De Civitate Dei*, which he composed and published in the immediate aftermath of the Conference, to Marcellinus by summer of 413. He temporarily discontinued the rest when Marcellinus was executed: see Barnes (1982), pp. 70–71.

[47] Despite his commitments in such matters, even the Catholic historian Paul Monceaux, *Hist. litt.* 4, p. 393, was repelled by what he saw: "cette partialité naïve ou cynique, non moins que le ton de l'exorde et la confirmation intempestive des lois de proscription, ne laisse pas que de surprendre un peu dans un document officiel destiné à préparer un jugement arbitral."

apparent fairness was arranged in such a fashion that merely participating was to implicate oneself in the appearance of justice. A monumental double bind therefore confronted the leaders of the dissident church. If they refused to attend, they were guilty. If they did attend, they were still going to be found guilty. And in either case, the surrounding judicial apparatus would make either result seem just. The Catholics already knew as much. Although it was important for them to maintain the appearance of an open discussion, it was not for any decision to be arrived at as the result of free debate that they wanted the conference, but rather for reasons of public show. It was the ceremonial display of power, the witnessing and seeing of it all, that mattered. "Therefore," as Augustine puts it with his characteristic frankness, "in seeking this conference with you, we are not looking for yet another 'final decision' on this matter, but rather to have what has already been settled made known, especially to those who seem to be unaware that it is so."[48]

The laws or regulations by which the meeting was to be conducted were ground-rules that set the constraints within which a game was to be played for public consumption. The dissidents' expectations and desires, their assumed model of what a church conference should be like – which they expressed for the record – meant that they saw these procedural rules as unfair. Their natural expectation of a church conference was one of more democratic and egalitarian dimensions, a meeting in which each bishop would be allowed to speak and to have his say in turn.[49] Instead, the elaborate rules established by Marcellinus for the confrontation, apparently according to the prior wishes of the Catholic side, were intended to restrict both discussion and membership. Each side was to select only seven representatives or agents who were to be empowered to speak on behalf of all the bishops of their church. Each group of seven was to have access to a further group of seven bishops who were to act as advisors, but who were not to be allowed to speak in the sessions. In addition to these fourteen persons, each side was to be permitted to appoint a team of four persons who were to act as inspectors of the verbatim transcript of the proceedings. Each side, therefore, was to be represented in the debates themselves – from which the great majority of the bishops were to be barred – by its own team of eighteen bishops, and no more.

To the Catholics – whatever the nature of the official arrangements or how they were achieved – this was the long-awaited final verbal

[48] Aug. *Ep.* 88.10 (CCL 31A: 146): "Sed ideo vos conferre volumus, non ut causa iterum finiatur, sed ut eis, qui nesciunt iam finita monstretur."
[49] Frend, *The Donatist Church*, pp. 280–81.

confrontation in an official court or hearing. The local leaders of the dissident community, on the other hand, had no reason to see the conference as anything more than yet one more battle in a century-long fight against attempts to humiliate them, and to outlaw their version of Christianity and their proper defense of a centuries-old African tradition. They came knowing full well the purpose of the conference and its avowed aim. But they could ignore its pre-ordained end and join the battle in the trenches over symbols and display, over the assertion of labels and words and what they were to mean. The Catholics could be confident what the final judgment of the court's judge would be, but the result of the conference would be a dubious victory if it was perceived by too many Africans as imposed by force, as the coercive act of an imperial and secular power, as just another in the long line of attempts by "the Catholic side" to use the government of the empire to force its view of the Christian Church on them. It was precisely in the minutiae of legal procedure that the dissidents had some hope.

What would happen between the opening scenes and the finale of the conference was to be a grand theater of great importance. The dramaturgical aspects were not lost on Augustine. As we have seen, he later vividly remembered the dramatic aspects of its inception, the atmosphere of suspense and great expectation that surrounded its launch.[50] On that first day of June in the Gargilian Baths, the bishops of both churches gathered in force. Flavius Marcellinus, the president of the imperial hearing seated high on his tribunal, was surrounded by his resplendent *officium* of twenty-three judicial advisors. The struggle was to be a great public contest, a battle between the best and the brightest on both sides.

WE ARE NOT DONATISTS!

When the bishops finally assembled in the Gargilian Baths on 1 June, Marcellinus began the proceedings by having the edict of the emperors Honorius and Theodosius issued on 14 October 410 read aloud to them. The imperial edict emphasized the emperor's concern with the maintenance of "Catholic law." Honorius thought it good that "terror and dire warnings" had been used against "the Donatists" whose "hollow error and sterile disagreements have polluted Africa, the greatest part of our empire." The words of the edict labeled the opposition as "Donatist bishops" and foresaw only one possible result of the arguments at the council: "the refutation of

---

[50] Aug. *Ad Donatist. post Collat.* 25.43 (CSEL 53: 144).

superstition by manifest reason."[51] There followed a reading of Marcellinus'
edict of 18 January which identified the two contending legal parties at the
hearing as "the Catholic" and "the Donatist."[52] The dissidents came to
the conference with the almost certain knowledge that its conclusion was
foreordained, but from their behavior during the hearing they manifestly
did not come to it depressed by a defeatist attitude. Rather, they came
armed with the determination to demonstrate their separate identity and
the justice of their cause. Knowledge of the required tactics came from
their careful cultivation of the remembered past of persecution.[53]

The extensive and detailed table of contents, the *capitula gestorum*, that
prefaces the surviving record of the conference identifies the two sides as
the party of the Catholics, the *Catholici* or the *pars Catholicorum*, on the
one side, and party of "the Donatists," the *Donatistae* or the *pars Donatistarum* on the other.[54] The problem is that this table is a later addition to
the verbatim record and is manifestly a biased gloss or guide to the contents of the original transcript prepared by one Marcellus at the behest of
some Catholic bishops.[55] It cannot be used for any purpose other than to
demonstrate the obvious: that the Catholic Church and the imperial court
identified their opponents as "the Donatists" and used that particular per-
sonalizing label as the means of identifying their opponents. By contrast, in
the verbatim text of the conference the individual speakers on either side are
not identified in this way. The Catholic bishops are clearly marked as such –
for example, "Augustinus, episcopus ecclesiae Catholicae", "Aurelius, episcopus ecclesiae Catholicae," or "Alypius, episcopus ecclesiae Catholicae."
But their opponents never identify themselves as "the Donatists," "bishops
of the Donatist Church," or anything of the sort, but merely as this or that
Christian bishop – for example, "Emeritus, episcopus" or "Petilianus, episcopus." The only thing that the dissident bishops assented to being called
was simply "bishop" – that is to say, they identified themselves as bishops of
the Christian church and not as members of any special "Donatist church."
However it was done, the dissident bishops managed to enforce their own
perception of themselves throughout the entirety of the official transcript.
But not wholly and not without effort. When the matter was raised again at
the beginning of the third day's proceedings, the power of defining words

---

[51] GCC 1.4 (SC 195: 562–68).   [52] GCC 1.5 (SC 195: 568–74).
[53] Mainly, I think, through various modes of "re-enactment"; see Connerton, *How Societies Remember*,
pp. 61f.
[54] Lancel, *Actes de la Conférence de Carthage*, 2, pp. 420–557.
[55] For this capitulation, see Lancel, "L'édition de Marcellus," in *Actes de la Conférence de Carthage*, 1,
pp. 357–63; for an analysis of his method, see Alexander (1982).

became apparent. The judge declared that he could only call those persons "Catholics" whom the emperor had already designated as such.[56]

The matter of who was being identified as whom became a critical focus of dispute on the opening of the second day's proceedings in the Baths on 5 June, because by then the dissident bishops had had the opportunity to read the label used for them in the official record. The descriptive introduction in the proceedings of the first day specifies the two men, Ianuarius and Vitalis, who were the secretarial team of the "Catholic Church," the *notarii ecclesiae Catholicorum*, and Victor and Crescens, who were the team of "the Donatist Church," the *notarii ecclesiae Donatistarum*.[57] The introduction of the debating teams assigned by either side is marked by a similar identification. From one side, the bishops of the Catholic Church, the *episcopi ecclesiae Catholicae*, entered, and from the other, those of "the Donatist side," the *episcopi partis Donati*.[58] Logically, the conference general secretary, the *exceptor* Martialis, informed the president Flavius Marcellinus of the notice that "the Donatist bishops" had presented to His Nobility on the previous day.[59] Martialis' words provoked an immediate response from Petilian, bishop of Constantina, the leading spokesman for the dissidents, in which he made the matter as clear as he could: he and his fellow bishops were not prepared to accept this identification.

We are simply bishops of the truth of Christ, our Lord – so we call ourselves and so it is usually noted in the public records. As for Donatus of holy memory, a man of a martyr's glory, although it is obvious that he is our predecessor and an embellishment of the church of this city, we only accord him the sort of honor and status that he deserves.[60]

The requested correction – that the dissident bishops simply be called "bishops" or "bishops of the Catholic Church" and not "Donatists" – struck at the heart of the Catholics' attempt to label their enemies and so provoked a sharp response from the usually hyper-aggressive and proactive Catholic bishop Possidius: "Bishops of the Truth! That's something they need to prove, not just to boast!"[61] The critical objection made by the dissident Christians was a watershed in the proceedings because they made it stick.

---

[56] Aug. *Brev. Collat.* 3.3.3 (CCL 149A: 272): "interlocutus est cognitor se interim sine cuiusquam praeiudicio non posse aliter appellare Catholicos, quam eos appellavit imperator a quo cognitor datus est."

[57] GCC 2.1 (SC 224: 922). [58] GCC 2.2 (SC 224: 924). [59] GCC 2.8 (SC 224: 926–28).

[60] GCC 2.10 (SC 224: 928): "Episcopos nos veritatis Christi domini nostri et dicimus et saepe actis publicis dictum est. Donatum autem sanctae memoriae, martyrialis gloriae virum, praecessorem scilicet nostrum, ornamentum ecclesiae istius civitatis, loco suo meritoque veneramur."

[61] GCC 2.11 (SC 224: 928): "Episcopos veritatis probare opus est, non iactare."

The president of the court, Marcellinus, accepted that the statements "of either party," in these neutral terms of reference, were to be recorded.[62] From that point on in the record the so-called "Donatists" are never so labeled again. Henceforth, whenever Marcellinus referred to the two groups he was careful to refer neutrally to "either side" in the dispute.[63] Martialis, the court notary who had made the reference to "the Donatists" that provoked the original objections by Petilian, now corrected the record to read "bishops and defenders of the church of the Truth."[64] It was probably with this incident fresh in mind that the dissident bishops insisted on their legal right to re-read and to correct the transcripts of the first day's proceedings.[65] They were becoming eagle-eyed in the pursuit of small matters that they perceived to be important to a truthful representation of themselves.

DEMOS AND DRAMATICS

Rather than seeing the dissidents as defending what had been presented to them as a lost cause, it might be more useful to try to understand their reactions as the deployment of small tactics of resistance often assumed by the weak. In their own terms, the behavior of the dissident bishops summoned to the confrontation in the summer of 411 was a pedagogy of the persecuted. Their responses were far from the acts of men who regarded themselves as already defeated. Improvisation, the gaining of space, the insistence on the exact meaning of words, the refusal to concede automatic obedience – all of these tactics, and more, worked and worked well against legitimizing the final verdict of the hearing precisely because they contested the grounds for which Aurelius and the Catholics had demanded the conference: the legitimation of their cause through ceremonial public advertisement.[66] The dissident bishops, it must be remembered, still had

---

[62] GCC 2.12 (SC 224: 928): "Utrarumque partium prosecutiones gesta retinebunt."

[63] E.g., GCC 2.19, 2.24; there were some apparent deviations from this standard practice, but these seem to be notarial lapses.

[64] GCC 2.12 (SC 224: 928): "episcopi et defensores ecclesiae veritatis."   [65] GCC 2.25 (SC 224: 934).

[66] The same approach was utilized, for example, by defendants in the trial of the "Chicago Eight" in 1969, where the charges of "conspiracy" were manifestly casuistic means used by the formal powers of the time which were guaranteed (so they thought) to rid them of political undesirables. The reaction of certain of the defendants was to reject the basic legitimacy of the court itself by turning it into counter theater: "For Abbie [Hoffman] and Jerry [Rubin] . . . the courtroom was a new theater, perhaps a purer kind of theater than anything in previous Yippie history. More than any of the other defendants, they wanted to create the image of a courtroom shambles." The proponents of such tactics accepted that the final verdict would go against them (as it did): "as Abbie said, the trial would be 'a victory every day until the last.' Tom Hayden disagreed with these tactics ('Then we

the support of great numbers of the local people, so their own audience was more than worth the effort.

One stratagem was to win the battle of public opinion, the *mentes publicae*: to make a decisive visual impact on the large numbers who would be in Carthage to witness the exterior effects of the conference. Since the great mass of ordinary people could not participate in its inner workings, efforts to fulfill their desire to know what was happening would profit whichever side could better manipulate the flow of information. That process could begin with a public demonstration of power outside the physical confines of the conference proper within the walls of the Gargilian Baths. There were many potential spectators in Carthage, the metropolis of all Africa and one of the largest cities in the empire. Even if we cannot know its precise extent, such a great event must have had a large popular audience.[67] And there are many signs that the organizers expected a huge popular response. The Catholics strongly feared that a tumult might break out among the common people in the city. They insisted that the bishops should enter the city in small groups precisely to avoid inciting such an occurrence. No uproar could then be blamed on their machinations.

The orders of Flavius Marcellinus that governed the technical aspects of the debate, including the means by which the bishops were to assemble in the Gargilian Baths, similarly emphasized that no assembly of the people was to be permitted in connection with the conference. No persons other than the representatives selected by either side were to appear at the venue itself. Such measures were being taken to prevent "catervic" misbehavior on the part of the crowds in the city.[68] Anyone who had anything to say on the matter, other than the officially sanctioned representatives, was required

---

would be sentenced for contempt. We could strip away the authority of the judge and prosecution but not their power'), but he was finally constrained to admit that they worked: 'In the end, Dave [Dellinger] and Abbie [Hoffman] were right in their argument that a symbolic stand would move people'": T. Hayden, *Trial*, New York, Holt, Rinehart and Winston, 1970, pp. 69–72. These tactics were castigated by supporters of the power status quo at the time as "silly", "a waste of court time," "absurd," "needless delaying tactics," "comic," "childish antics," "nihilistic," and so on – that is to say, much the same sort of formal charges leveled by Catholics against the actions of the dissident bishops who faced them at Carthage in 411.

[67] The presence of crowds and the possible tumult that they might cause are occasionally referred to: e.g., GCC, 2.72 (SC 224: 968).

[68] GCC, 1.10 (SC 195: 580): "Ex quo illud profecto perspicuum est, eo nullum penitus populi fieri debere conventum quo nec ipsos universos confluere sinatur episcopos. Nam cum patientia disputandi, quae soli amica silentio est, omnem catervatim agminis strepitum perhorrescat, nihil interest utrum eam congestio populorum an episcoporum turba praepediat"; Aug. *Brev. Collat.* 1.7 (CCL 149A: 263): "cum tamen illic ex Catholicis episcopis illi soli adessent, quos edicto suo cognitor definierat ut, si aliquis tumultus existeret, quod Catholici valde metuebant, non illis imputaretur qui paucissimi adessent, sed eis potius qui multitudinem suam praesentem esse voluissent."

to communicate with them by letter only. Further provisions in the order of assembly made clear that no person, whether lay or clergy, was to enter the peaceful place of the council in greater numbers than were permitted. Furthermore, both sides were encouraged to convey these measures and requirements to their own congregations with exhortations to peace and quiet by preaching this message in their respective churches before the beginning of the conference itself.[69] In their final response to Marcellinus' edict, however, the Catholics again gave voice to their fear that tumult and uproar might erupt in the city; they suggested that such violence was being deliberately provoked by their enemies in order to destroy the meeting.[70]

On the first day of the conference, a demand arose from the dissidents that there should be a formal roll call of all of the bishops. Since this would require the presence of more than 500 senior men and their support staffs, rather than fourteen representatives, fears of disorder and tumult kept resurfacing in the discussion of these new plans.[71] The request and the response by the president of the conference led to a series of prolonged remarks on the likelihood of riotous acts that would be caused by the presence of such large numbers of men. Although Augustine expressed his fears of a "tumult," Emeritus, the dissident bishop of Caesarea, drew the judge's attention to the fact that the first day was almost at an end and that, despite the presence of a large number of clergy, no disorders had broken out. There were no signs of brawls, harsh words, or scurrilous language that were commonplaces of everyday quarreling.[72] Augustine remained fearful

---

[69] GCC 1.10 (SC 195: 580): "Nullus ergo vel laicus, vel episcopus ultra numerum praestitutum in illum tranquillissimum concilii locum contra prohibitum moliatur accedere; quin potius etiam plebes suas pia quietis ac modestiae commonitione conveniant, hoc per ecclesias proprias ante tractantes, quatenus a die disputationis ac loco omnis se multitudo contineat, ut religioso patientiae magisterio delinitum christianae paci populum parent." In their formal notification to Marcellinus, the Catholics insisted that they had met the requirement of preaching a message of calm to their congregations, insisting that they should stay away from the conference site: GCC 1.16 (SC 195: 592).

[70] GCC 1.18 (SC 195: 604): "ne forte, etiamsi non omnes, aliqui tamen eorum per multitudinis tumultum seu strepitum conlationem quae pacifica et pacata esse debet, impediant"; (SC 195: 614): "Nam, etiamsi clamor non sit, solus susurrus ipse multorum satis magnum strepitum faciet quo impediatur illa collatio."

[71] GCC 1.71–74 (SC 195: 682): Marcellinus, in response to the request, states: "Evitandae quidem multitudinis causa ad hunc locum de quorum numero dubitatur minime convenisse dicuntur"; to which the Catholic bishop Aurelius adds: "Nos evitamus tumultum." And when Marcellinus finally accedes to the request, Aurelius objects: "Quid opus est turbis?" and Augustine soon contributes his viewpoint (1.78; SC 195: 686): "Tumultus ne fieret cavendum fuit."

[72] GCC 1.80 (SC 195: 688–90): "Paene iam peracto solis curriculo totus transactus est dies, et nullus adhuc exortus tumultus, cum tanta sacerdotum Dei multitudo consistat . . . Nullus strepitus, sermo nullus . . . Unde hic tumultus publicus de privatis scurrilibusque sermonibus quibus <est> facile strepere, aut ex ipso usu rixa cottidiana metus iudiciorum non timens possit exsurgere? . . . tumultu superfluo et quadam rixa turbantes."

that street violence was a real threat, claiming that it had not broken out only because there was no convenient scapegoat to blame by those who were secretly desiring to incite riot.[73] The judge Marcellinus was especially concerned with any kind of collective or gang behavior. Foreseeing the real possibility of sectarian violence sparked by the conference, he attempted to insist on conditions of law and order in the city. He issued strict rulings that forbade the involvement of the crowds of common people close to the place of assembly.[74]

The forbearance required for the proceedings, for which only peaceful conditions are a good companion, recoils at every gang-like (*catervatim*), uproar of the battle line. For this reason, dense congregations of common people and the crowds of bishops are very worrying.

The imperial official used the concept of the *caterva*, an evocative and emotive one, to describe riotous internecine violence that the bishops might excite in the streets of Carthage

A counter-argument, put by Adeodatus, the dissident bishop of Milevis, was that such riots were unlikely to occur as long as *all* the bishops were in the same venue, inside the baths, and not outside on the streets of Carthage where they would have the motive and the opportunity to excite violence.[75] The fears appear to have had some real basis. As arguments dragged on through the second day of the conference, on 5 June, and it appeared that there might be further delays with the proceedings, Alypius remarked that false rumours had provoked popular unrest that had taken place two days before, on 3 June, presumably in response to "news" coming out of the Gargilian Baths.[76] Marcellinus cautioned the bishops that they should not be affected by what the public was saying in the streets outside the venue. He nonetheless persevered with his intent to publish the daily proceedings.[77] The strong dialectic between what was happening inside the baths and in the streets outside of them marked almost every move at this early stage in the debates and discussion inside the Baths.

That popular demonstrations and riotous uproars that were feared as part of the conference show the critical role of the general populace as the

---

[73] GCC 1.81–83 (SC 195: 690–92).

[74] GCC, 1.10 (SC 195: 580): "Nam cum patientia disputandi, quae soli amica silentio est, omnem catervatim agminis strepitum perhorrescat, nihil interest utrum eam congestio populorum an episcoporum turba praepediat."

[75] GCC 1.84 and 88 (SC 195: 692–94).

[76] GCC 2.72 (SC 224: 968): "Alypius, episcopus ecclesiae Catholicae, dixit: 'Multa nudiustertiana die falsa iactata sunt. Ne huiusmodi inlusionibus populus perturbetur . . .'."

[77] GCC 2.73 (SC 224: 968): "Marcellinus . . . dixit: 'Ea quae populus loquitur sanctitatem vestram permovere non condecet. Tamen, sicut edicto meo definitum est, gesta proponentur.'"

audience of the theatrics staged by the bishops. They were the real objects of the debates. This much is manifest in Marcellinus' statement that he was going to publish the proceedings so that "the truth" would become available to public opinion. This was just a larger stage for the hundreds of micro-struggles being carried on in each diocese. As Victor, the Catholic bishop from Libertina, was later to assert of the small neighboring town of Aptuca: "We have Unity in that place. That much cannot be hidden from the public awareness."[78] After receiving the written responses of both parties to his initial edicts that established the venue, time, and terms of the conference, Marcellinus stated, a second time, his intent to publish the results of the hearing as widely as possible in public so that "all the people" would be able to be informed of the contents of the *acta*.[79] With his formal praise of the judge on the first day of the proceedings, Petilian, the head of the dissident team, highlighted the noble judge's role as a popular agent in his duties toward the "listeners in the general public."[80]

On Thursday, 18 May, about two weeks before the conference actually began – a day deliberately chosen for its political significance – the dissident bishops turned the popular element in the whole confrontation to their advantage by staging an ostentatious parade of their bishops and priests, along with their attendants, into Carthage and through the city's streets and avenues.[81] When they submitted their formal notification of acceptance to Marcellinus one week later, on 25 May, they took care to include in their written record an account of their *adventus* into the city, noting that everyone in Carthage had been witness to it and that His Sincerity was also not unaware of its significance.[82] The parade of the bishops into the metropolis was so impressive that Augustine was later vividly to recollect

---

[78] GCC 1.201 (SC 195: 864): "Unitas est illic, publicam non latet conscientiam."

[79] GCC 1.17 (SC 195: 602): The key phrases in his declaration are "in publicam transmissurum," "offerendum publicis obtutibus iudicavi," and "ubi totius populi considerarit agnitio"; they show that "all people" were the object of the information campaign.

[80] GCC 1.10 (SC 195: 588): "Egisti partes tuas, vir nobilis, ut et partibus te iustum futurum esse promiseris, et auribus publicis popularem."

[81] The reason for choosing 18 May for the demonstration was that the dissidents believed (or, more likely, were trying to emphasize their belief) that the following day, 19 May, was the day on which the conference was *supposed* to begin (i.e. exactly four months following Marcellinus' public notification of 19 January). That the conference actually began much later, on 1 June, was a contentious matter to which they were to return in the proceedings themselves.

[82] GCC 1.14 (SC 195: 590): "Notum facimus Sinceritati Tuae nos edicto tuo conventos ex diversis partibus Africae convolantes, ingressos fuisse Carthaginem XV kalendarum die Iuniarum, cuius nostri adventus et omnes quos Carthago continet testes sunt, et Tua Sinceritas non ignorat"; cf. 1.29 (SC 195: 622) and Aug. *Brev. Collat.* 1.7 (CCL 149A: 263). There were, perhaps, elements in this *adventus* that captured, for the bishops, some of the divine elements embedded in the parousia of the emperor and other high-ranking officials: S. G. MacCormick, *Art and Ceremony in Late Antiquity*, Berkeley and London, University of California Press, 1981, pp. 18–22, 41–50 (*adventus* and

the parade, commenting on the event with a sarcasm that betrays the real impact that it made: "So many bishops gathered from every part of Africa! They entered Carthage with the great pomp and ceremony of a parade, with the appearance of a battle line, so that they turned the eyes of inhabitants of the great city, intently, on themselves."[83] In other words, the plan to affect public sentiment worked. Even before the first words of the conference had been uttered, the dissident bishops had struck their first collective blow.

In estimating the significance of events like the parade through the streets of Carthage, we cannot confine our gaze to the highly artificially defined world of the conference itself. Rather, our line of sight must be raised above and beyond the walls of the Gargilian Baths. The views of the bishops, mostly rather elderly males, cannot be taken to define the limits of this power.[84] Such a failure would be owed to a kind of historian's myopia. There was a vast and numerous audience outside the Baths. Whether or not *they* were persuaded by the highly regulated proceedings inside them was what was at issue. That audience included very large numbers of Christians – young and old, male and female – who were not permitted to attend the conference itself. This huge audience cannot be overlooked. They and their actions were to be as decisive as anything that happened within the confines of the baths.

THE NUMBERS GAME

The decision as to which side deserved recognition as *the* Christian church in Africa also hinged on a demonstration that each was not just some odd fringe sect, but rather that it had a numerous and widespread representation in all parts of Africa. The great importance of numbers was recognized by both sides. The problem was not just to make this point with those in Africa who knew the strengths of each church, so much as it was to persuade the

---

procession identified with succession to power), and 64–66 (on new Christian elements), as well as echoing parades for local deities, see ch. 10, p. 441.

[83] Aug. *Ad Donatist. post Collat.* 25.43 (CSEL 53: 144): "Congregantur ex universa Africa tot episcopi, ingrediuntur Carthaginem cum tanta speciosi agminis pompa, ut tam magnae civitatis oculos in se intentionemque convertant."

[84] Just how old and decrepit is difficult to say, but probably older in Africa than elsewhere; see Shaw (1982) and (1984), pp. 457–97, on the factor of seniority in African society in general and in the Christian churches in particular. The roll call of the bishops themselves seems to guarantee as much; extraordinary numbers, up to about a third from either side, were absent because of sickness, other weaknesses of old age, or death itself, not a few of the deaths occurring en route to the conference.

imperial court and a host of lesser authority figures.[85] Following the first
long roll call of the Catholic bishops, Marcellinus wished to get out of
repeating the lengthy and time-consuming procedure for the dissident
bishops. But since an impartial count could be used to dramatic effect
by them, they insisted on the procedure. Petilian objected that the whole
purpose was to give each bishop a chance to make his own declaration,
making quite clear publicly where there existed no Catholic bishop opposite
him and thereby demonstrating the absolute numerical superiority of the
dissident Christians in Numidia. He further argued that the distribution
revealed by such a roll call would be a manifest way of showing that the
dissidents had maintained their numbers by peaceful means, whereas the
Catholics had achieved theirs by force.[86]

Public demonstrations of quantity were part of the purpose of the great
parade of dissident bishops that preceded the conference itself, as Augustine
recognized.[87] That is why the dissidents had persevered with tactics that
displayed their numbers. When the Catholic bishops, in obedience to the
orders of Marcellinus, came to the Gargilian Baths on the morning of 1 June
with only eighteen bishops who were permitted to represent their side, the
dissidents decided to turn up *en masse*. Marcellinus could have demanded
that all except the deputized speakers and their assistants should leave the
venue of the Baths. But he was trapped by the ensuing arguments that led
to demands to check, by way of public declaration, the actual presence of
the bishops who had signed the mandate by which they empowered their
respective deputies.[88] The number of dissident bishops actually present
according to the facts in the record itself amounted to 277 bishops, six
additional representative bishops, and five others somehow "not counted"
by the official court record, for a total of 288. The Catholics objected to
including the absent dissident bishops in this count, including one of them
who was dead. The Catholics then declared 266 subscribers. That still left
them in a manifest minority.

The bishop Alypius was hurriedly sent out on an urgent mission to
drum up another twenty Catholic bishops who would at least be capable
of walking into the Baths. Once recognized, and written into the record,

---

[85] So Petilian complained that the Catholics constantly "lied" about the smallness of dissident numbers
to "imperial ears" (GCC 1.61 = SC 195: 674): "ut de numero nostro primo constaret quem esse
parvulum semper imperialibus auribus mentiuntur."

[86] GCC 1.165 (SC 195: 810–12): this is the substance of Petilian's objection at this point in the
proceedings.

[87] Aug. *Ad Donatist. post Collat.* 24.41 (CSEL 53: 143): "Hoc erat videlicet optimum in causa, ut ingens
eorum numerus appareret."

[88] GCC 1.186 (SC 195: 828).

they brought the Catholic total to 286. That number is significant for, despite having 288 bishops present at the conference, the official record credited the dissidents with only 279 plus six additional representative bishops who were not counted among these, for a total of 285.[89] The Catholics had officially ended up with exactly one more.[90] It was a critical, even if the smallest, margin of difference.[91] It is difficult to understand how the Catholics were credited with such a large number: the total number of Catholic bishops that ever appear in the Acta amount to 230; if one adds the seventeen representatives and the additional twenty rounded up by Alypius, the total number is still only 267.[92] By whatever fictive means and however it was done, the Catholics had ended up with one more officially recognized bishop than did the dissidents.

The whole point of the struggle over who was present and who was not was in the numbers themselves. Church councils were like quasi-official organs of state, running themselves according to the regular norms of other bodies like the senates in Rome and Constantinople, and like local municipal town councils. The voting and the numbers gave the real appearance of a substantial sanction that was important to the state; and, within the church, they were also critical in deciding between the validity of one council and its decisions and another. The bishops represented the collective voice of their peoples.[93] So the hugeness and size of that voice mattered. As organizations that functioned parallel to those of the state, councils were the representative bodies in which the state could ground the legitimacy of its actions, if it so wished. That is surely the reason both for the vaunting of numbers and for advertising their significance.[94] It remained the point after the conference was over and the spinning of its message began. In his polemical little book addressed to "the Donatists" after the conference, Augustine harped away on the 279 dissident signatories, clearly

---

[89] That is, the secretary of the court counted the names of the dissident bishops who signed the mandate that empowered their seven representatives to speak for them; one of the seven, however, the Primate Primian of Carthage, was already on the list of mandatories: hence the total number of 279 + (7–1) = 285. There are even problems with this number, when it is checked against the numbers that are actually attested in the *acta*: see Lancel, *Actes*, pp. 111–13.

[90] See Lancel, "La représentation des deux églises à la conférence de 411," ch. 2 in GCC I, pp. 107–90, esp. at pp. 111–14, with a thorough rehearsal of all of the problems, caused mainly by the maneuvering of each side to "get the numbers."

[91] For the numbers, see Lancel, *Actes de la Conférence de Carthage*, 1, pp. 110–18; each side claimed about 400+ bishoprics in total in Africa.

[92] Lancel, *Actes de la Conférence de Carthage*, 1, p. 115; seventeen instead of eighteen because the Primate of Africa, Aurelius, had already been otherwise accounted.

[93] MacMullen, *Voting About God, passim*, but esp. see pp. 20–23.

[94] Which is why Chalcedon claimed that with 636 bishops in attendance, it had doubled Nicaea's number of 318: cf. Gaddis, *Religious Violence*, p. 324.

suggesting that this was the total number of their bishops present at the conference or recognized by it. If the number of 279 signatures was a "truth" of sorts, the basic claim was false, as he well knew.[95]

It was at the point that the mandate signed by the Catholic bishops was submitted to the court and that Petilian challenged the genuineness of the Catholic signatures. He wanted to see each Catholic bishop in person. He was able to cite cases from personal experience of the creation of shadow bishoprics by his Catholic adversaries.[96] Moreover, by forcing an in-person parade of bishops of either side, the dissidents could demonstrate that they too had the "big numbers" and were not just any minority church.[97] The challenges and counter-challenges over numbers and identities ultimately played into the hands of the dissidents because they provoked another bit of drama. In effect, there was to be a second parade of bishops in the city. In order to match names against signatures, the claims of bishoprics against actual bishops, the judge Marcellinus agreed to a systematic roll call of all the bishops from either side. It was assumed that within their small face-to-face communities each side had such an intimate knowledge of the other that such identifications would pose no great difficulty.[98]

In fact there were to be no end of problems, since the dioceses of each church did not line up in an easy one-to-one pattern. In some cases, a single Catholic or dissident bishop might face up to two or three competitors from the other side in his one see: the other church had simply configured its dioceses differently.[99] In the face of this difficulty, the agreed-upon procedure was that the name of the Catholic bishop would be read out first. He would then confirm his presence by declaring: *Praesto sum* or "I am present." Then his opponent in the same diocese would declare his presence, normally by saying *Agnosco illum* or "I recognize him" – that is to say, he recognized his opposing number, the bishop of the other Christian community in that particular town, village, or rural place. Beyond merely

---

[95] Aug. *Brev. Collat.* 1.14 (CCL 149A: 268); *Ad Donatist. post Collat.* 24.41 (CSEL 53: 142), while at the same time emphasizing that hundreds of "our bishops" were missing.

[96] GCC 1.59 and 61 (SC 195: 672–74): a demand to know precisely who signed the mandatum of the Catholics.

[97] GCC 1.89–93 (SC 195: 694–96).

[98] GCC 1.64 (SC 195: 676): where Petilian remarks: "Singuli quique sedium nostrarum adversarios facile possumus agnoscere."

[99] GCC 1.65 (SC 195: 677–78), where this is recognized by the dissident Petilian who says that he faces two Catholics in his diocese: one, Fortunatus, at Constantina itself, and another, Delphinus, at another location; he also notes the case of the nearby diocese of Milevis where his colleague Adeodatus faces a Catholic bishop at Milev, another at a place called Tucca, and a third at a place called Ceramussa.

signaling recognition of the person, the bishops confronting each other also took advantage of the occasion to add some not-so-gratuitous comments about each other. Often these were of an equally formulaic nature. Sometimes, for example, they made clear that they had sole possession of their diocese by emphasizing the fact that "I have no bishop facing me" or "I have no adversary."[100]

But there was often more to these remarks. Each side also had its own battle cries or ritual shouts that were thrown in as additional punches to the simple declaration of presence. A typical Catholic one was *Unitatem habeo!* meaning "I have Unity in my diocese."[101] Sometimes the "I have Unity!" slogan was glossed, as when Alypius, Augustine's friend and Catholic bishop of Augustine's hometown of Thagaste, declared his presence and added for good measure: "I hope that as much as Thagaste has rejoiced in its old-time Unity, so we will be able to rejoice at it in other places!" Thus provoked, the dissident Petilian coldly remarked that "It is an evil unity that forcibly joins the innocent and the criminal, two things that cannot be mixed with each other."[102] In response to the Catholic bishop's declaration of his presence, the dissident bishop could say simply that he "recognized" him, but the acknowledgment could be made sharper, more pointed, as when Marcianus, the dissident bishop of Sitifis, said of his opposite number: "I recognize my persecutor."[103]

NAME-CALLING

Our interest in these one-on-one confrontations is less in the checking of the numbers and identities of bishops on either side than in the dramatic way in which each bishop walked forward to the center of the hall, made a declaration of his identity, and then placed that identification within the context of his relationship to his opponent. Each confrontation became a mini-drama of self-assertion. Bishops who had driven all opposing clergy who had contested their authority from their dioceses could boast of the fact when they came forward to identify themselves, as in the case of Aptus, the Catholic bishop of Tigias: "Present. I have not had nor do I

---

[100] Amongst many such instances: GCC 1.120 (SC 195: 710): "Praesto sum, sed adversarium non habeo" and "Praesto sum, sed non contra me habeo episcopum."

[101] Amongst many such examples, see the run of declarations at GCC 1.124–126 (SC 195: 720).

[102] GCC 1.136–37 (SC 195: 784): "'Utinam, quemadmodum Tagastis antiqua unitate gaudet, ita etiam de ceteris locis gaudeamus.' Petilianus episcopus dixit: 'Mala est unitas innocentiae et criminis; non possunt utraque iuxta misceri.'"

[103] GCC 1.143 (SC 195: 790): "Agnosco persecutorem meum."

presently have any Donatist bishop in my diocese."[104] Or, Innocentius, the Catholic bishop of Germania: "Present. I have no adversary."[105] Urbicosus, the Catholic bishop of Igilgili, could declare, belligerently, if proudly: "Present. My town has been entirely Catholic from ancient times."[106] One can compare similar sentiments loudly declared by other Catholic bishops, such as "Totally Catholic," "My community has been Catholic from the very beginning," or, "I have no competitors, no heretics [in my diocese]."[107]

Denigrating the status of your opponent was another favorite tactic. So, Privatus, the Catholic bishop of Usila, noted with precision: "Present. I don't have any bishop opposing me – just a priest."[108] In fact, one side or the other might have had only a priest to point to as the head of their church in this or that diocese. That, too, was a cause of caustic comment. The bullish bishop Habetdeum who was acting as a spokesman for the dissidents, remarked of the diocese of Turuzi: "We do have a priest there, one Cattus." The reply of Serotinus, the Catholic bishop of the place? "Sure he's there, and he's perfectly useless."[109] Having no parishioners was a repeated accusation, such as in this acidic exchange between two rival bishops:[110]

Likewise [the court scribe] read out: "Victor, bishop of the Catholic church at Libertina."

He made the same statement: "Present."

Januarius, bishop of the aforementioned place said: "I do recognize him – but the diocese is mine."

Victor: "But he has no one in his congregation!"

Januarius: "I say the diocese is mine."

[104] GCC 1.120 (SC 195: 710): "Aptus episcopus plebis Tigiensis. Idem dixit: 'Praesto sum. Nec habui, nec habemus episcopum Donatistam.'"
[105] GCC 1.120 (SC 195: 710): "Innocentius episcopus ecclesiae Germaniensis. Idem dixit: 'Praesto sum. Sed adversarium non habeo.'"
[106] GCC 1.121 (SC 195: 714): "Urbicosus episcopus plebis Igilgilitanae. Idem dixit: 'Praesto sum. Sed Catholica est omnis ex vetustate.'"
[107] GCC 1.126 (SC 195: 720): "Benenatus episcopus plebis Simittensis. Idem dixit: 'Praesto sum. Nec habeo alium, nec haereticos.'; . . . Adeodatus episcopus plebis Belalitanae. Idem dixit: 'Praesto sum. Non habeo nec episcopum, nec haereticos; unitatem habeo.'"; 1.128 (SC 195: 732): "Adeodatus episcopus plebis Bencenensis. Idem dixit: 'Praesto sum. Catholica est ab origine.'"
[108] GCC 1.126 (SC 195: 726): "Privatus episcopus plebis Usilensis. Idem dixit: 'Praesto sum. Non contra me habeo episcopum; presbyterum illic habeo.'"
[109] GCC 1.133 (SC 195: 754): "Habetdeum diaconus dixit: 'Presbyter est illic, Cattus.' Serotinus episcopus ecclesiae Catholicae dixit: 'Illic est, sed superfluo.'"
[110] GCC 1.116 (SC 195: 706–08): "Item recitavit: 'Victor episcopus ecclesiae catholicae Libertinensis.' Idem dixit: 'Praesto sum.' Ianuarius episcopus loci suprascripti dixit: 'Agnosco illum; dioecesis mea est.' Victor episcopus ecclesiae catholicae dixit: 'Neminem illic habet.' Ianuarius episcopus partis Donati dixit: 'Dioecesis mea est.' Victor episcopus ecclesiae catholicae dixit: 'Cum neminem illic habeat, neque ecclesiam, neque aliquem communicantem, frustra mentitur quod sit eius dioecesis.' Ianuarius episcopus dixit: 'Communicarunt tibi ante vim tuam?'"

Victor: "Since he has no parishioners, and no church, and no one in communion with him, he is vainly lying about whose diocese it is."

Januarius: "Where was the congregation that was in communion with you before the recent violence?"

Other similar cases provided fodder for assertion, as when Adeodatus, the Catholic bishop of Vazari, came forward to identify himself. "Present," he declared, and then added: "There was a actually a certain Calipodius who was physically present in the diocese, but when he saw that his whole congregation had been converted to the Catholic Church, he simply left the place."[111] And so it went on.

There were also frank admissions meant to frighten, and ones that referred to the normal small-scale violence that marked relations in each small town, like the statement made by Trifolius, the Catholic bishop of Abora: "Present. If anyone in my diocese is called a Donatist, he is stoned."[112] Another is the case of Vegesala, which, given its past history as the epicenter of the bloody events of 347, was, like Nova Petra, almost certain to be a special case of tense relationships between the two hostile communities. Here Privatianus the Catholic bishop declared his presence. This provoked Donatus, the dissident bishop of Cillium to walk forward and state: "I have deacons there, the neighboring congregation manages its affairs, and I regard it as my diocese." Privatianus then became aggressive: "Tell me where this congregation of yours meets." Donatus shot back: "It's you who have forbidden us access to the places and shrines of our martyrs. I at least have a priest Candidus there, don't I?"[113] From this brief exchange, it emerges that the Catholics had seized possession of the basilica at Vegesala that housed the all-important memorial to Marculus, the great martyr of 347, and that they were forcefully preventing the dissidents from getting access to the martyr's shrine and from celebrating the liturgy in the basilica there. Given the great symbolic importance of Vegesala, it was obviously a special case where force had been used to prevent the parallel existence of a dissident church organization.

---

[111] GCC 1.129 (SC 195: 740): "Adeodatus episcopus plebis Vazaritanae idem dixit: 'Praesto sum. Est quidem in corpore constitutus Calipodius; sed, cum videret universum populum ad ecclesiam Catholicam fuisse conversum, discessit.'"

[112] GCC 1.133 (SC 195: 750): "Trifolius episcopus plebis Aborensis . . . idem dixit: 'Nomen si illic auditum fuerit Donatistarum, lapidatur.'"

[113] GCC 1.133 (SC 195: 756): "Et accedente Donato Cillitano episcopo, idem dixit: 'Diaconos illic habeo, vicina plebs agit, diocesis mea est.' Privatianus episcopus ecclesiae Catholicae dixit: 'Ubi conveniunt?' Donatus episcopus dixit: 'Et loca et memorias martyrum tamen prohibuisti. Candidum non habui presbyterum inde?'" Which only elicited another provocative remark from Privatianus: "Well, then, where *does* he celebrate his services?"

There were other cases where force surely accounted for the lack of any opposition, as in the town of Hospitia, where the Catholic bishop Benenatus was able to declare: "In my locale there is no other bishop," only to face the riposte of the dissident bishop Lucullus: "Because your persecution has continually hounded me out of it."[114] The situation in the small town of Marazana evoked an exchange of words that gives a more detailed picture. The dissident bishop Habetdeum stated that his predecessor in the diocese was forcefully driven out after his ordination. In reply, Eunomius the Catholic asserts that Habetdeum himself was never "seated" as bishop. The angry Habetdeum had to admit that this was true, but gave as the reason that he was not even allowed to enter into the town proper and so he had to set up shop three miles outside the place. To this the Catholic Eunomius replied: "There *never* were Donatists, there are not now, and they have never held the bishop's seat." But the hard Habetdeum was not about to relent, and clarified: "That's because we've just been driven out of the town."[115]

The force deployed at Vegesala and Marazana was of the kind that we have already seen. It centered on the seizure and permanent occupation of basilicas. On occasion, this is made specific, as in the case of Gorgonius, the Catholic bishop of Liberalia, who declared, "The heretics (i.e. the Donatists) have 'handed over' their basilica to me, so I am alone in the town."[116] Or, in another case, Publicius, the Catholic bishop of Gratianopolis, could aggressively declare: "Opposing me is Deuterius, alone and without any congregation!" To which Deuterius coldly remarked: "Because you threw us out of our places of assembly and led a persecution against me!"[117] Another dissident bishop claimed to have been driven from his seat by violence. "With God as my witness, he's lying," replied the Catholic. "It's simple terror and nothing else that's driven everyone out," retorted the dissident. "He's lying" was the persistent and angry reply.[118] Sometimes we

---

[114] GCC 1.133 (SC 195: 758): "Quo recitato, idem dixit: 'In loco meo alius non est episcopus.' Lucullus episcopus dixit: 'Persequutio semper me fugavit.'"

[115] GCC 1.133 (SC 195: 758–60): "Habetdeum episcopus dixit: 'Praecessor meus ad Marazanensem locum ordinatus est. Is postquam cathedram sedit, expulsus est.' Eunomius episcopus ecclesiae Catholicae dixit: 'Numquam sedit.' Habetdeum episcopus dixit: 'Ego etiam non admissus, in tertio miliario in civitate conquievi.' Eunomius episcopus Catholicae dixit: 'Numquam fuerunt Donatistae, nec sunt, nec aliquando sederunt cathedram.' Habetdeum episcopus dixit: 'Modo oppressi sunt.'"

[116] GCC 1.133 (SC 195: 768): "Quo recitato, idem Gorgonius dixit: 'Basilicam mihi deposuerunt haeretici, solus sum.'"

[117] GCC 1.135 (SC 195: 774–76): "'E diverso Deuterius est, solus sine plebe.' Deuterius episcopus dixit: 'Quia et domos deiecisti et persecutionem mihi fecisti.'"

[118] GCC 1.134 (SC 195: 772): "'Omnis ab origine Catholica est ibi; numquam ibi fuerant Donatistae.' Adeodatus episcopus dixit: 'In plebe mea est; per violentiam inde exclusit omnes <clericos> et

also learn that secular officials had been involved, as in the case of Victor, the dissident bishop of Hippo Diarrhytus. On hearing the name "Victor" called out by the secretary of the hearing, and thinking (mistakenly) that it was he who was being referred to, this Victor ran from the adjoining room, where he was serving as one of the *custodes chartarum*, into the main meeting room where he broke into an angry rant against Florentius, the Catholic bishop of Hippo Diarrhytus. "I'm here! It ought to be written into the record that if this Florentius recognizes me so well it's because he personally persecuted me, an innocent man whom he had arrested and thrown into the public prison to await execution, a prison where I spent three years of my life!"[119]

In other cases, such as the claimed demise of the dissident bishop of Quiza "in the persecution," it is difficult to know how violent his end actually was.[120] On occasion, however, more than the seizure of property and forced expulsion is on record. When Victor, the dissident bishop of Rotaria, came forward to confirm his presence, his brief notation that he had "no adversary" in his diocese was met with a bitter remark by Aurelius, the Catholic bishop of Macomades: "We once had a bishop there. You murdered him and invaded his church." Adeodatus leapt in with a quick defensive note: "He says that their bishop was murdered. Let him file a formal accusation, let him prove it, let him undertake a court action." But no one denied the claim.[121]

Of course, dissident bishops could use the identity parade to make their point. So Honorius, the dissident bishop from Vartani, in identifying his Catholic counterpart Victor: "I have had the pleasure of making his acquaintance recently because of the harm that he has done me."[122] Or one could combine denigration and the icy hatred of personal betrayal. Donatus, the dissident bishop of Vamacurra, said of his opposite number:

presbyteros.' Severianus episcopus ecclesiae Catholicae dixit: 'Mentitur, teste Deo.'... Adeodatus episcopus dixit: 'In plebe mea est, circa meum est totum. Etiam mei terrore succubuerunt omnes, qui in eodem loco constituti erant.' Severianus episcopus ecclesiae Catholicae dixit: 'Mentitur.'"

[119] GCC 1.142 (SC 195: 790): "'Adsum. Scriptum sit si ipse Florentius bene me agnoscit, qui me persecutus est innocentem, quem apprehendit et in custodiam officii dedit necandum, ubi triennium temporis feci.'"

[120] GCC 1.143 (SC 195: 792): "Episcopus noster Quiziensibus succubuit in persecutione." Was he murdered? Worn down and exhausted by fighting? Forced out of his basilica and died outside the city?

[121] GCC 1.187 (SC 195: 838): "Aurelius episcopus ecclesiae Catholicae Macomadiensis dixit: 'Episcopum illic habuimus. Occidistis illum et invasistis.'" Lancel, *Actes de la conférence*, 2, p. 839 n. 2, however, doubts the veracity of Aurelius' claim.

[122] GCC 1.126 (SC 195: 724): "Honorius episcopus partis Donati civitatis suprascriptae dixit: 'In mala quae mihi fecit modo illum didici.'"

"I recognize him. He was once my priest."[123] This was a clear marking of the act of betrayal which, whenever it occurred, was carefully noted for the record. Spotted throughout the proceedings were repeated reminders of the most hateful and detested act of the *traditor*.[124] The very word "traitor" recalled the primal origins of their quarrel. It formed one of the standard replies when it came to the turn of the dissidents to put forth their bishops for identification. As when Colonicus, the dissident bishop of Tinisti or Januarius, his colleague from the town of Numidia, made their similar declarations: "I have no traitors in my diocese."[125] Or the outburst of Veratianus, dissident bishop of Carpi: "I have given my mandate and I have signed. I who am the successor of Faustinianus, who in the Unity of the Truth was ordained by Donatus. It was only later, in the Macarian Times, that the traitors first emerged in our place."[126] It is in small statements and admission like this that we discover that, in some places at least, the Catholic repression of 347 had worked. Or the elaboration of the standard declaration by Donatianus, the dissident bishop of Lamzelli: "I have no traitor in my diocese, I did not have any nor will I have any."[127] The Catholics, on the other hand, noted such crossovers from their own side to that of the dissidents by labeling them as men who had been "rebaptized."[128]

One could also rub in an insult with a dash of humiliation: "I have Felix opposite me. But he only has one parishioner!"[129] One could pinch

---

[123] GCC 1.128 (SC 195: 736): "Donatus episcopus civitatis suprascriptae dixit: 'Agnosco illum. Presbyter meus fuit.'"

[124] See ch. 2, pp. 86, 93–95, for several of the examples; rarely, but on occasion, the side betrayed would admit to losing a crossover, as did Habetdeum of an unnamed bishop the dissidents once had at Culusi who had "recently gone over into communion with *them*" (GCC 1.138; SC 195: 786): "Habuit, sed modo communicavit ipsis."

[125] GCC 1.180 (SC 195: 822): "Colonicus episcopus Tinistensis... idem dixit: 'Et mandavi et subscripsi, et traditores apud me non habeo.'"; 1.188 (SC 195: 838–40): "Ianuarius episcopus Numidiensis... idem dixit: 'Mandavi et subscripsi. Et traditores non habeo.'" Cf. 862 (SC 195: 862): by Donatus, bishop of Arae.

[126] GCC 1.187 (SC 195: 830): "Mandavi et subscripsi, qui sum successor Faustiniani, qui in unitate veritatis fuerat ordinatus a Donato; postmodum vero, temporibus Macarii, illic emerserunt traditores." For other cases, see Cresconius of Pudentiana (GCC 1.201; SC 195: 864); Cresconius of Silemsilensis (GCC 1.201; CCL 195: 870); Crescentilianus of Lambiridi (GCC 1.206; SC 195: 878); Burcaton of Gemellae (GCC 1.206; CCL 195: 878).

[127] GCC 1.206 (SC 195: 878): "Mandavi et subscripsi; traditorem autem nec habeo, nec habui, nec habiturus sum."

[128] E.g. GCC 188 (SC 195: 838) of the bishop of Rotaria: "Et rebaptizaverunt illum hominem nonagenarium episcopum"; 197 (SC 195: 848): of the bishop of Thibilis: "Iste est episcopus qui rebaptizatus est et factus est audiens"; and 198 (SC 195: 858) of the bishop of Rusticiana: "Iste rebaptizabat post partem Donati. Rebaptizatus est postea, et sic est ordinatus."

[129] GCC 1.135 (SC 195: 774): "Domnicus episcopus plebis Bullensium Regiorum... idem dixit: 'E diverso mihi est Felix, sed unus est qui illi communicat.'"

the element of recognition by feigning ignorance, as did Fortunatius, the Catholic bishop of Sicca Veneria, who asserted: "I know there is Unity in the church at Sicca, but I've never heard of any bishop by such a name."[130] Or, to play a final card, one could simply deny the very existence of the other. Asterius, the Catholic bishop of Vicus: "In this place there is no other bishop but me." But Urbanus, his opposite number in the dissident church, could trump that: "God Himself sees that I don't even recognize this man."[131] The same matter could be put more bluntly: "I don't know him any more than he knows me!" shouted another.[132] Such game-playing might finally exasperate the presiding judge. Following another such nihilistic standoff, Marcellinus, the president of the hearing, finally blurted out: "Well, do you at least recognize his face?"[133]

Such repartee could exploit familiar themes, like threats of vengeance. In one of his usual feisty retorts, Petilian drew the Catholics' attention to the fact that one day there would be revenge for the harm they had done to his community. This, too, was another way of putting such matters "on the record," to be remembered for a later time.[134] Earlier, in his personal identification routine with his Catholic opposite number, Fortunatus, Petilian had made the point in an angry exchange about the violent persecution that had been vented on himself and his followers. "There he is," he said, pointing at Fortunatus, "the man himself, the persecutor of the Church in the same city where I am bishop." Aurelius the bishop of Carthage leapt in to defend a high-ranking colleague, cautioning Petilian to be careful: "Just a little earlier, you hurled an insult at another in a case where you had not received one." Fortunatus himself added: "In our same city, all of the altars have been smashed by the heretics!" Petilian angrily retorted: "Let the transcript of these proceedings record that you are a persecutor. In the right time and place you will hear what you deserve."[135] Such pointed

---

[130] GCC 1.139 (SC 195: 786): "Unitatem ecclesiae Siccensis novi; episcopum quidem tantum nomine audivi."

[131] GCC 1.143 (SC 195: 794): "Asterius episcopus plebis Vicensis . . . idem dixit: 'In ipso loco mecum alius episcopus non est.' Et accedente Urbano episcopo, idem dixit: 'Deus videt quia non illum novi.'"

[132] GCC 1.133 (SC 195: 744): "Innocentius episcopus Lamiggigensis . . . idem dixit: 'Praesto sum.' Iunianus episcopus dixit: 'Nec ego illum novi, nec ipse me.'"

[133] GCC 1.178 (SC 195: 820): "Marcellinus, vir clarissimus, tribunus et notarius, dixit: 'Vultum tamen ipsum esse cognoscis?'"

[134] GCC 1.169 (SC 195: 814): "Petilianus episcopus dixit: 'Iniuriam facis vane, reponetur tibi. Et quamquam reponere non liceat, tecum habeto.'"

[135] GCC 1.139 (SC 195: 786): "Petilianus episcopus dixit: 'Ipse est! Ecclesiae persecutor, in eadem civitate ubi ego episcopus sum.' Aurelius episcopus Catholicae Carthaginiensis dixit: 'Et paulo ante iaculatus es iniuriam et non recepisti.' Fortunatus episcopus ecclesiae Catholicae dixit: 'In eadem

references to a future time and place of reckoning were intended to make the adversary realize that, although he might have the upper hand now, one day there would surely be divine retribution. So the air in the meeting must have been filled with apprehension when Dativus, the dissident bishop of Nova Petra, a small town northwest of Diana Veteranorum in Numidia, came forward to identify himself. Nova Petra, as every bishop standing in that assembly knew, had been the site of one of the worst atrocities that was carefully nurtured in their memory by the dissidents. "I do not have any adversary," Dativus stated coldly, "because it is at that place where our Lord, the martyr Marculus lies, for whose spilled blood God will exact vengeance on the Day of Judgment."[136]

The identification parade also opened up other possibilities for labeling the opposition, such as the deployment of the collective slur. If a dispute was to be made over numbers, then the quality of those numbers could be drawn into question. Half way through the dissidents' declarations of their bishoprics, Alypius, the Catholic bishop from Thagaste, Augustine's hometown, objected that most of them were only rural domains or mere farms. In raising this point, Alypius was not just making a technical point about the location of these bishoprics, but he was playing on a deeply rooted prejudice of the time among cultured men against the countryside and a near-racial bias against those who lived in rural idiocy as somehow manifestly and permanently inferior to city-dwellers. Given the pervasive nature of those assumptions, the moral stain of having most of your bishops coming from the pure countryside was a near-impossible one to refute. Petilian did his best. The Catholics, he said, had many rural bishops of their own. And they shouldn't talk too much. Too bad, he added, that *they* had almost no parishioners in theirs.[137] And so things went on, until the whole of the first day was consumed until early evening, all eleven hours of the proceedings, by the arduous and painstaking task of identifying the signatories of the mandates given to the representatives of either side, carefully faced off and counted, one by one.[138]

---

civitate ab haereticis omnia altaria confracta sunt.' Petilianus episcopus dixit: 'Persecutorem te esse acta contineant. Loco suo audies quae mereris.'" This was a very testy relationship.

[136] GCC 1.187 (SC 195: 834): "Dativus episcopus Novapetrensis . . . idem dixit: 'Mandavi et subscripsi. Et adversarium non habeo, quia illic est domnus Marculus, cuius sanguinem Deus exiget in die iudicii.'"

[137] GCC 1.181–82 (SC 195: 822–24).

[138] GCC 1.219 (SC 195: 906): "Rufinianus scriba dixit: 'Exemptae sunt horae undecim diei.'" It would therefore be about seven or eight o'clock in the evening.

WE REFUSE TO SIT

Only the written record survives and so there are caveats. The transcript catches very little of the gestures and expressions, especially facial ones, and of the verbal tone that must have marked the confrontations. Only a small part of this world of movement and appearance is available through a few chance remarks in the record. Such acts of refusal to recognize could be publicly signaled in such small acts. For example, take the simple ritual of making the body obey implicit orders. Rational people will sit down together to discuss their differences. The mere act of sitting down together, as the dissident bishops recognized, was already to surrender to the organization of space by their opponents. So, in their little war, they began by challenging the minutiae of the organization of space itself. During the first day's proceedings, at the mid-point in the identity parade, when the review of the Catholic bishops had just been completed, the presiding judge Marcellinus issued what must have seemed to him a quite innocuous formal invitation: that the participants should be seated. The dissident bishops at once objected. They would not sit. They would stand.[139] There was a compelling precedent. Christ had stood before his persecutors. So would they.[140]

The whole body language of sitting and standing had always had a long significance in the history of the African church. The elite and the privileged sat, while the plebeian stood. The bishop sat on his throne when he preached or held assembly or conducted his episcopal hearings, while the common people stood and listened. When a new clergyman was ordained, he was spoken of as being "seated." The bishop possessed his "seat," and the primate of the province held the First Seat, the *Prima Sedes*. The same bodily protocol determined by sitting and standing was followed in the councils of the church in which bishops, clergy, and the people assembled. Already in the time of Cyprian, in the church councils held at Carthage, the bishops were seated together around the altar. The priests were permitted to sit with them. But the lower clergy and the people were required to stand outside this circle.[141] These protocols of sitting and standing continued to characterize all collective meetings of the church. By the fourth century, when the people had finally been excluded once

---

[139] It was, again, a political management of space. Just as on the twenty-fourth day of their trial the Chicago Eight ostentatiously refused to stand and so used their bodies to deny the legitimacy of the court.

[140] GCC 1.144–45 (SC 195: 796).

[141] Cyprian, *Ep.* 1.1.1, 39.3.2, and 45.2.2 (CCL 3B: 1 and 218); cf. Hess, *Council of Serdica*, p. 21.

and for all from such proceedings, there was now a pervasive and manifest distinction between the privilege of being seated that was identified with the elite and having to stand which identified the plebeian.

So when the meeting of the second day brought another formal invitation from the president of the court for the participants to be seated, the response of the dissidents was both predictable and significant. Once again, they ostentatiously refused to sit. They would stand. They were "the people." After all, they had biblical authority on their side. The righteous should not sit down with sinners.[142] Did not the Psalmist say, "I have not *sat* among worthless men, nor do I mix with hypocrites. I hate the company of evil men. I refuse *to sit down* with the wicked" (Ps. 26: 4–5)? What was Marcellinus, the presiding judge, to do? To get the proceedings under way, he conceded. The dissidents quite literally stood their ground.

OUR LITTLE WAR

All the rhetorical and behavioral micro-rebellions of the dissidents had the disruption of the normal course of the conference as part of their objective. Theirs was a little war meant to challenge the legitimacy of the proceedings. In this, they succeeded.[143] These little actions proved to be a source of immense frustration, both to the civil authorities charged with conducting the hearing (above all to Flavius Marcellinus) and to the Catholic bishops who had hoped for a quick and decisive final confrontation. Marcellinus finally had to use his superior authority to declare an end to the conference, bringing proceedings to an abrupt halt on the third day, calling the bishops back together later the same evening to hear his final sentence. Rather dramatically, if eerily, it was pronounced in the lamp-lit darkness of the Baths. That matters did not proceed smoothly to their foreordained end was something that had a great impact on the participants. Augustine, who provided the most extensive set of post-conference debriefings in his subsequent writings relevant to the meeting, repeatedly labels the actions of the dissidents as nothing more than purposeful and perverse delays, as *delationes*, *morae*, and so on. This was how he and his side "spun" these moves; to the dissidents, their prolonged inteventions with the judge clearly had quite rational purposes.[144] These were, it was claimed, obstructions,

---

[142] GCC 2.3–4 (SC 224: 924–26).

[143] The contempt charges issued by Judge Julius Hoffman in the trial of the Chicago Eight for having brought the court into disrepute were a confession that the contumacious tactics of the defendants had in fact succeeded to some extent in delegitimizing the authority of the court.

[144] For more on the use of these delaying tactics, see Tilley (1991), esp. pp. 14–18.

roadblocks, and actions intended to do nothing other than to waste time and to distract the proceedings from their proper course.[145] Delays and deliberate obfuscations there were, to be sure, but to what end? Had the dissidents been summoned merely to be condemned as bit-players in a piece of theater staged by the imperial state and the Catholic Church?

Augustine had earlier declared the purpose of the Conference from the Catholic point of view. It was a machine designed even before it started to achieve two ends: the persuasion of the undecided and the achieving of a final unassailable imperial law that would compel the merging of the dissidents with the Catholic Church. That the dissident Christians would do everything possible to delegitimize the proceedings in the Gargilian Baths is surely both rational and understandable. From their point of view, the more the debates were reduced to chaos and a shambles, the better. It appears that far from being thwarted in this aim, they largely succeeded in it.[146] That was why the judge in charge of the hearing, Marcellinus, was constrained to bring the whole show to a sudden halt. He cut off further proceedings, dismissed the two parties from the room, and composed his final decision, his *sententia*, in the growing darkness of the night of the evening of the third day of the proceedings.[147] The dissidents later complained bitterly about this unusual night-time sentencing. Had not persecutors come in the night to arrest the Lord?[148] The judge, however, realized that matters were not going to be improved, especially for himself, by extending the hearing any further. He had the representatives of either side summoned back to the *secretarium* and had his decision read out aloud to them.[149]

To acquire a sense of what were the most loaded issues for either side, one has to wait for the proceedings of the third day, after all of the arguments over procedure and tactical maneuvers had been exhausted. Unfortunately, the verbatim record that permits a close understanding of the

[145] For example, Augustine's recapitulation of his view of matters in the *Brev. Collat.* 1.9, 2.3 (twice), 3.2.2, 3.3.3, 3.5.6–6.7, and 3.8.10 (CCL 149A: 264–65, 269–75, 274–76, 278) – a point that he frequently reiterated elsewhere, e.g., *Ad Donatist. post Collat.* 24.42 (CSEL 53: 143).

[146] As William Kunstler, the defense attorney in the trial of the Chicago Eight, remarked: "The significance of the trial is that it showed . . . for the first time how ingenious defendants can use a courtroom to get their point across and not to be afraid of authority." Which is true, except for the claim about "the first time."

[147] Aug. *Brev. Collat.* 3.25.43 (CCL 149A: 305); *Capit. Gest.* = GCC 3.585 (SC 195: 556); *Ad Donatist. post Collat.* 35.58 (CSEL 53: 161).

[148] Aug. *Ad Donatist. post Collat.* 12.16 (CSEL 53: 112–13). Augustine was unmoved: if the dissident bishops had had anything of the truth to say, the night did not stop them from saying it; the darkest night was the one to be found in their minds.

[149] Aug. *Brev. Collat.* 3.25.43 (CCL 149A: 305).

verbal volleys is lost from about half way through the proceedings of the third and final day.[150] It is important because from about the point that the detailed record of the jabs and counter-jabs is lost, it is clear, from the summary "table of contents" that have survived, that the debate turned to the critical problem of violence. The Catholics raised the point that "the Donatists" had not actually suffered any persecution, but rather that it was they who had inflicted precisely this kind of suffering on the Catholics through the violence of their circumcellion gangs. Although the dissidents tried to deny that whatever the circumcellions were doing had very little to do with their clergy, the Catholics countered with lurid stories about actual acts of violence. It was the Ravenna Dossier all over again. To them, anyone who used such rabid and barbaric men to gouge out other men's eyes, for example, had surpassed the Devil himself in doing evil.[151] The dissidents, after hearing more such remarks, countered with the assertion that their churches were still full of bloody corpses.[152] The thread of discussion about violent acts inexorably brought up accusations of betrayal.[153] This highly charged accusation led, once again, to the lengthy reading of original documents to determine whether or not there had indeed been a primal act of betrayal committed in the time of Caecilian.

The tribune and notary Marcellinus had the bad luck to be in Africa at this time to preside over the colloquium between the dissident and Catholic bishops held at Carthage. In the aftermath of the purge of Heraclian, Marcellinus and his brother Apringius, who was proconsular governor of Africa in 411–12, were imprisoned and then executed in September 413. Their fate and the general course of the violence shows the fundamental divide between this kind of state-driven conflict and sectarian battles. The actors in the two fields followed different imperatives. There was little overlap between the two. If Marcellinus had been sent to Carthage by the emperor Honorius to adjudicate the conflict between the Catholics and dissident Christians in Africa, he was executed for different suspected connections. Living in the midst of the most intense time of sectarian conflict, and also of this state violence, Augustine has not a word to say

---

[150] In the short "table of contents" or *capitula* for the third day, we have the record of 585 verbal exchanges, of which the original verbatim record survives as far as number 281.

[151] GCC, *Capitula*, 3.296–98 (SC 195: 502–04): "Catholicorum ad ista responsio . . . quod persecutionem non patiantur ipsi (sc. Donatistae), sed faciant. Ubi dicunt Donatistae quod circumcelliones faciunt ad sacerdotes minime pertinere. Prosecutio Catholicorum, quod Donatistae, oculos eruendo, Diabolum superaverunt."

[152] GCC, *Capitula*, 3.303 (SC 195: 504): "Prosecutio Donatistarum, ecclesias suas cruentis adhuc plenas esse corporibus."

[153] GCC, *Capitula*, 3.309 (SC 195: 504): "Ubi dicunt Donatistae traditores, id est malam arborem, ex factis suis, id est, ex fructibus, posse cognosci."

about Heraclian and his redeployment of the African grain supply and the army in Africa. His silence is explained in part by his fears of being too closely identified with Marcellinus and Apringius, and a desire not to alienate the court at Ravenna from enforcing the hard-won results of the conference of 411.

The problem for the Catholics was that they knew that the results of the conference and the judgment of the imperial *cognitor* would be insufficient to persuade their enemies. So in the immediate aftermath of the conference, their spin machines were thrown into overdrive. Letters were written. Sermons were delivered. Posters were prepared. The entire contents and summaries of the transcript were read aloud to church congregations, with suitable commentaries. Brief versions of the conference proceedings were written so that the interested could "without hard work" get access to its "essence." Augustine's own *Brief of the Conference* is full of the usual prevarications. Since each side had access to the official transcript, outright lying, of which there is some, could not form the weight of the spin. Instead, there are strategic omissions: Habetdeum's long statement of the dissenters' position, for example, or the uproar caused by questions about Augustine's ordination as bishop (to name a few); or insertions of strategic additional comments – lurid descriptions of circumcellion violence, for example; or misleading interpretation of the dissidents' arguments – on the definition of Catholic, for example; or insistence on a loaded vocabulary that was not in the official transcript – like calling the dissidents "Donatists" or the "party of Donatus" throughout.[154] And on and on.

This program of "interpretation" might have had some effect. But the dissident bishops were already well prepared by the history of the vicissitudes in their treatment by the state, which they had embedded in the long memory of Christian persecution. They were strengthened, too, by a robust ideology of martyrdom in resisting whatever the state might direct against them. Finally, as in earlier episodes of hostile declarations by the imperial state, including those issued by the first Christian emperor Constantine almost exactly a century earlier, it was really a question of how such decrees would – or would not – be enforced in each locale in Africa. With the manifest exception of the use of specially empowered tribunes and notaries, the provincial governors had not usually involved themselves in campaigns of enforcement. In that light, the dissidents might expect the reality to dissolve, once again, into a fragmented series of local confrontations. The

---

[154] These are a few items that I have noted; for others, see Monceaux, *Hist. litt.* 7, pp. 118–19; Lancel, *Actes de la conférence de Carthage*, 1, pp. 353–57; and Alexander (1973).

question was one of how the state would interpret Marcellinus' decision and how it would mobilize its resources in support of his judgment. Despite their apparent victory, there must have been some apprehensions among the Catholic bishops. The imperial decisions issued between 411 and 414 had disturbing echoes of similar decrees favorable to them that had been issued by the state in earlier times, and these had provoked not unity but further outbreaks of violence. What would happen this time?

CHAPTER 13

Athletes of death

The blood of the martyrs was the vital force, the kinetic energy powering Christian life in Africa. For believers, the blood sacrifice of their noble men and women was the foundation of Christian truth. The blood of the martyrs was collected, remembered, venerated, worshiped. The spilled blood of the Christian witness was liquid soul. Possessing the blood of the martyr was like having the DNA, the code to a higher existence.[1] The sanctified blood of martyrs had been shed by Florus, the praesidial governor of Numidia in the Great Persecution, in 304, when he murdered Christians at Milevis in "the days of turification." Their gore was taken up, preserved, and carefully distributed to nearby towns, like Mastar, some fifteen miles to the southeast, where it was deposited to mark the place as holy ground made sacred by the martyrs' blood.[2] The days when the governor came to towns like Milevis with the demand that the Christians turificate – to burn incense to the gods – were traumatic ones. True Christians would have to refuse. In the hearing held by Secundus, the Primate of Numidia, in May 306, concerning the status of the clergy who had ordained the bishop Silvanus at Cirta, the stark division for people in these local communities was between the martyrs who had remained loyal and the traitors who had not.[3]

---

[1] So Gillian Clark in *JECS* 7 (2000), p. 370; cf. Sizgorich, *Violence and Belief,* p. 58.

[2] CIL 8.6700 + 19353 = ILAlg II.3 1303a (Mastar, Hr. Rouffash): "Tertius idus Iunias deposi/tio cruoris sanctorum marturum / qui sunt passi sub pr(a)eside Floro in civ/itate Milevitana in diebus turifi/cationis"; see Duval, *Loca sanctorum,* 1, no. 117, p. 245; cf. Optatus, *Contra Parm.* 3.3–5 and 8 (SC 413: 56–58).

[3] Aug. *Contra Cresc.* 3.27.30 (CSEL 52: 436): "Secundus Donato Masculitano dixit: 'Dicitur te tra-didisse.' Donatus respondit: 'Scis quantum me quaesivit Florus ut turificarem, et non me tradidit deus in manibus eius, frater; sed quia deus mihi dimisit, ergo et tu serva me deo.' Secundus dixit: 'Quid ergo facturi sumus de martyribus? Quia non tradiderunt, ideo et coronati sunt.' Donatus dixit: 'Mitte me ad deum; ibi reddam rationem.'" This purports to be a transcript of the hearings held by Secundus at Cirta on 4 March 303. The year must be in error; see Appendix B, where I argue that the date is probably May 306.

Secundus to Donatus from Masculula: "It is said that you betrayed." [i.e. handed scripture to the authorities]

Donatus: "You know how often Florus asked me to turificate [i.e. to burn incense to the gods] and, my brother, God did not betray me into his hands. And since God Himself has released me, I ask you to save me for God's judgment.

Secundus: "In that case, what are we to do with the *martyrs*? Because they did not betray [i.e. the Word of God], they were crowned."

Donatus: "Send me before God and I will give a full accounting to Him of my actions."

If traitors like Donatus were to be excused, the bishop Secundus wondered aloud, then what was to become of the martyrs? After all, it was their blood that had laid down the marker, the standard of courage required of true believers.

As living witnesses who had bled and died for the immutable laws of God, martyrs were set on a plane that elevated them permanently above all other ordinary Christians. They lived with God in the present, they spoke with Him, and they would judge with Him. For generations before the great fourth-century divide between dissidents and Catholics, the African church had proclaimed itself the church of the martyrs. It had good reason to do so. As the realm of a long historical empowerment of human sacrifices, Africa's connection with Christian martyrdom was unusual, indeed very special. The foundation piles of Christian martyrdom had been sunk deeply and powerfully into African soil. The broader reasons are manifest: killing and sacrifice were at the heart of Christian cult when it first came to Africa. And at the time of its arrival, Africans already had a pervasive cult of human blood sacrifice that had been deeply embedded in memory and practice for nearly a millennium, and maybe more.[4] The sacrifice of infants and children to the one deity Ba'al and his consort Tinnith for centuries of Carthaginian hegemony in Africa was continued in similar practices for the great god Saturn in the age of Roman domination. There was a gradual shift, perhaps, from the blood sacrifice of humans to the use of substitutes or *vicarii*, usually lambs, in these great nocturnal rites. The substitution, as was noted in inscriptions marking the awful sacrifices, was spirit for spirit, blood for blood, life for life.[5]

---

[4] For a résumé of the history and some details, see Shaw (forthcoming).

[5] As is specifically spelled out in the famous Saturn inscriptions from Nicivibus: see Leglay, *SAM*, 2, no. 75: "N'gaous, Nicivibus," pp. 68–75; see, especially, AE 1931: 59–60 and CIL 8.4468 = 18.630, where the great nocturnal sacrifice, the *molchomor*, is said to be "anima pro anima, sanguine pro sanguine, vita pro vita," with the sacrificial lamb being a substitute, "agnum pro vikario."

The history of the original Christian joining and empowerment of this tradition is one that we cannot know. What we do know of the story begins suddenly in the year 180 in the middle of nowhere. It happened in the tiny village of Scilli, a nothing of a place about 150 miles up the Bagrada Valley from Carthage.[6] Seated in the rough borderlands of Numidia, its smallness, remoteness, and presence on the stage on this one occasion is a sign of the anywhereness of the new religion. The Christians at Scilli were the first known government victims of anti-Christian attacks in Africa. The record of their arrest, torture, and execution marked the earliest knowledge that the Africans themselves had about their own history.[7] The narrative of the Scillitan martyrs was *the* foundational story of the Christian church in Africa. The memory that African Christians had about their past converged retrospectively on this one apical point of origin: the five women and the seven men who were executed on 17 July 180 by the governor Publius Vigellius Saturninus.[8] The dozen martyrs replayed the number of the original apostles. In remembering this one episode, martyrdom appeared to later Christians in Africa as *the* meaning embedded in their beginning: these men and these women were *their* apostolic foundation, and all of them had shed their blood. Subsequent sporadic fits of accusations and arrests, such as the ones in 203 that led to the execution of the young noblewoman Perpetua and her servile companion Felicitas, continued to nourish the primal vision of the church as a community forged and commanded by its martyrs. By Perpetua's time, however, the featured actors in this holy drama were no longer the rural and the ignorant, but persons of more exalted status. The stage was no longer a hamlet in the hinterland, but metropolitan towns closer to Carthage, like Thuburbo Minus. The whole movement was going upmarket and upstyle. Even if she was a woman, the new "it" martyr, Perpetua, was a person of high social rank. The low-class

---

[6] On Scilli [?], see Lancel, "Scilitana Plebs" in *Actes de la Conférence de Carthage*, 4 (SC 373: 1456–57): it was so inconsequential that little is known of it; even its proper name is uncertain; cf. Birley (1992), p. 57 n. 15, who draws attention to the existence of a *vicus Scillitanorum* at Carthage (*Passio sancti Felicis*, 31 = Knopf–Krüger–Ruhbach, pp. 90–91); he seems undecided as to whether it was the home-town of the martyrs as opposed to the place at Carthage where they were buried and memorialized. I think the latter more probable.

[7] For a recent edition, with commentary, see Ruggiero (1991). Tertullian thought that Saturninus was the first governor of Africa to execute a Christian: "Vigellius Saturninus, qui primus hic gladium in nos egit" (*Scap.* 3.4 [CCL 2: 1129]). The memory reflects, within a generation, this same sense of a primal beginning.

[8] The numbers and the names of the martyrs vary slightly between the different versions. For a discussion and bibliography, see Ruggiero (1988) – it is just possible that the number of twelve was reached by later hagiographical manipulation but, despite the problems, I think that twelve was the original number. For P. Vigellius Saturninus, see Thomasson, *Fasti Africani*, no. 90, p. 71, and Birley (1992), pp. 37–39.

woman involved with her arrest and execution, the slave Felicitas, was a bit actor in the greater drama of a noble family.

The empire-wide persecutions provoked by orders of the emperors Decius and Valerian a generation later, in 250 and again in 258, only served to confirm the central place of the martyr in the African church. This time both sides in the confrontation – the imperial state and the local community – moved finally upscale. On the one side, it was now the emperors themselves, Decius and Valerian, who initiated the persecutions; on the other, it was the local monarch of the Christian community, the noble bishop himself, who suffered. It was a powerful convergence. In Cyprian, the bishop of Carthage, the persecution of 258 produced its domineering and heroic father figure. The founding ideologue of the African church, Cyprian was also the first man of such exalted rank in the church – a bishop and the Primate of all Africa, and also a man of elevated status in his pre-Christian life – to be martyred for the faith. High social rank added luster and value to his death. The poor nonentities of Scilli might have been the first to die, but it was Cyprian's death that was to count.

These violent assaults by the imperial state on Christians became the big story that they had to tell about themselves. It was troubling, of course, that more than a few of the attacks were provoked *not* by frightening official dragnets, but by accusations and betrayals from within their own communities. The assaults, and the responses to them, generated acerbic debates in oral and literary media over the role and the disturbing significance of the martyr. At the turn of the third century, the Carthaginian ideologue Tertullian produced a series of treatises on the martyrs of his time, contesting their rank and status, as well as the whole vexed question of whether deliberate provocation or reasoned retreat was the best moral response to be taken by Christians under attack.[9] In the mid-third century, the letters and treatises of Cyprian are vivid, if partial, evidence of the intensity of disputes over the status of martyrs and almost-martyrs (those who were imprisoned, but who had not yet died, the "confessors" as they were called) in the power structures of the African church of the time.[10] All these opinions, and many more that have been lost, were part of debates distilled in writing that nourished the high status conceded to

---

[9] Frend, *Martyrdom and Persecution*, pp. 361–74; Barnes, "Martyrdom," ch. 12 in *Tertullian*, pp. 164–86; among his treatises are *Ad Martyras* (197), *Scorpiace* (203–04), *De Corona Militis* (208), *De Fuga in Persecutione* (208–09), *Ad Scapulam* (212), although the subject is pervasively debated in his other treatises as well.

[10] Hummel, *Concept of Martyrdom*, is important, demonstrating that the fine line between "confessor" and "martyr" was in fact blurred all the time; Frend, "Decius," ch. 13 in *Martyrdom and Persecution*, pp. 389–439, esp. 415 f.

martyrs in each subsequent generation. They helped fuel potential reservoirs of resistance that could be drawn upon, should defenders of the faith
be needed. More importantly, the constant remembrance and replaying of
the martyrs' stories in weekly sermons and annual celebrations kept alive
a catechism of exemplary behavior that could teach others how to resist
an attack on their community. Dissident preachers, especially, realized the
power of repetition in setting a model for behavior.[11]

THE FIRST GREAT PERSECUTION

It was not so much these first generations of suffering, as it was the Great
Persecution under Diocletian, in the first years of the fourth century, that
left an indelible mark on later Christian communities in Africa. This
onslaught was to fix, once and for all, the special elevated rank or *dignatio*
of the martyr and the image of the state as a satanically driven persecuting
force.[12] Which is perhaps odd, since, on any reasonable computation of
quantities, African Christians experienced much less harm and damage
in this persecution than did many of their compatriots elsewhere in the
empire. Compared to Christian communities in the eastern Mediterranean,
for example those in Egypt or Palestine, the enforcement of Diocletian's
anti-Christian edicts in Africa was relatively brief, if intense.[13] Which is
not to say that the attacks were bloodless or that they did not deeply scar
the small worlds in which they took place, often traumatically. As much
is manifest in the ekphrases of suffering, the horrific visual replaying of
the deaths of the martyrs in the narratives that have survived from the
Great Persecution in Africa. The greatest majority of these stories were
anonymous oral narratives of local significance only, which makes them
incommensurate with the few ones that are "known": the stories that made
it into written form and to widespread circulation.[14] We can only guess at
what these events meant to the specific African communities in which they
occurred.

In a much later age, a single church at Ammaedara in the deep central
hinterland of the province of Byzacena was able to remember the names

---

[11] *Passio sancti Donati*, 1 (Dolbeau 1992: 256–57), echoing the introduction to the passion of Perpetua
in his own introduction.

[12] On the Diocletianic persecution, see, in general, Frend, "The Great Persecution, 303–312," ch. 15 in
Martyrdom and Persecution, pp. 477–535 (to be used with caution, however).

[13] For a good summary of some of the eastern history, see De Ste. Croix, pts. 4–5 (1954) = *Christian
Persecution, Martyrdom, and Orthodoxy*, pp. 59–68; and Barnes, "Persecution," ch. 9 in *Constantine
and Eusebius*, pp. 148–63.

[14] Duval, *Loca sanctorum*, 2: 613.

of thirty-four persons from the town who had been executed during the persecution.[15] Ammaedara was a reasonably important town in size, but even so it could not have harbored more than 4,000 or 5,000 persons or so at the height of its urban development. The number of family members, relatives, and acquaintances in the Christian community, indeed in the community at large, who would have been directly affected by the execution of thirty to forty persons would not have been insignificant. On 23 May, at the small town of Vol, about twenty miles southwest of Carthage, the proconsular governor Anullinus heard charges against a number of Christians, including a priest named Pellegrinus, and had all of them executed.[16] A week later, following trials held on 31 May 303 at Thimida Regia, another small village in the same region as Vol, twenty-six Christians were sentenced to death in June of the same year by Anullinus.[17] A few days later, at the modest town of Uthina, only some five miles to the south of Thimida Regia, the same governor sentenced another fifteen Christians to death.[18] And on 18 January 304, at Abitina, a village about forty-five miles west of Carthage on the Bagrada River, the town magistrates and the local detachment of soldiers arrested forty-six Christians, including seventeen women. The criminals were dragged to the town forum for assembly, booking, and to have the formal charges against them read aloud in public.[19] From here they were hauled off in chains and forcibly marched

---

[15] Duval, *Loca sanctorum*, 1, no. 52, p. 109: ILTun 470b, c, d; *AB* 54 (1936), 312–14; AE 1966: 526; for the physical location, the Basilica II (the so-called Basilica of Candidus), see Duval, *Eglises africaines à deux absides*, 2, pp. 204–06, fig. 112. Although the inscription is fragmentary, thirty-four seems to be the total number of the martyrs celebrated. But this is only one of several large basilicas at Ammaedara, so there is no certainty that the thirty-four martyrs noted in this one church were the only ones who suffered in the Diocletianic persecution. The chapel is specifically claimed to be a memorial only for those whose bodies were buried in this particular church: *quorum corpora hoc loco deposita*.

[16] For the location of Vol (or Bol, as it is sometimes called), see Lancel, *Actes de la Conférence de Carthage*, 4: p. 1525, s.v. "Volitana Plebs": probably to be identified with the town that Ptolemy locates between Maxula and Thimida Regia in the lower valley of W. Miliana. For the text, see Chiesa (1998); it is a heavily rewritten martyr story that survives only in late manuscripts found at Aquileia and at centers in the Friuli. Not much more can be rescued from it than the fact that a martyr, perhaps called Pellegrinus, was executed at Vol. The Calendar of Carthage mentions martyrs from Vol, but dates their festival to 17 October (*Kalendarium Carthaginiense*, AASS II.1, pp. lxx–lxxi). There is perhaps an error in the date, however, since Augustine's sermons on these same martyrs (*Sermones* 150 and 156) clearly suggest a date in the third week of May: see Chiesa (1998), pp. 39–40.

[17] *Passio sancti Gallonii*, 1, 10, 38–39 (Chiesa, 1996: 265–67 = Lancel, 2006: 245 and 247).

[18] *Passio sancti Gallonii*, 42, 54–57 (Chiesa, 1996: 267–68 = Lancel, 2006: 247–48).

[19] *Passio sanctorum Dativi, Saturni, et aliorum*, 4 (Franchi de' Cavalieri [1935], pp. 1–71, at p. 35 = Maier, *Dossier*, 1, no. 4, pp. 59–92); in addition to the text by Franchi de' Cavalieri, it is now necessary to consult the revision of the manuscripts by Dolbeau (2003a). For the location of Abitina at Chouhoud el-Batin, about 4 kilometers from Membressa (Medjez el-Bab) on the Bagrada, see

the entire distance to Carthage where, on 12 February, they faced a hearing before Anullinus, the governor.[20] They were tortured and then executed.

The rounds of the proconsular governor in these small villages and towns near Carthage suggests that many centers like them felt the hard enforcement of the imperial edict against the Christians. The experiences of the Christians in these towns also suggest that beyond those who suffered the final penalty of execution, there were others, indeed many others, who were threatened, or imprisoned and tortured, but not executed. In addition to the dozens from small centers like Abitina who lost their lives and whose names were carefully remembered, there were many others whose experiences were no less painful for themselves and for those who knew them, but who are unknown to us – there are no surviving martyr acts for them. Whereas it cannot be said with certainty how representative towns like Ammaedara, Vol, Thimida Regia, Uthina, and Abitina were, they were surely not alone. If the governor Anullinus was uncovering similar numbers of Christians in each of the assize towns at which he stopped to hold his judicial hearings – and we know that he was busy at many, such as Vol close to Carthage and Theveste in the extreme southeastern corner of his province – the total numbers would have been large enough. But a larger and simpler fact deserves emphasis.

The impact on Christian communities found in each town and village made by the arrest, imprisonment, torture, and execution of numbers on this scale in a short period of time would almost certainly have been traumatic.[21] Adding to the shock was the fact that this persecution had come on suddenly and unexpectedly after half a century of peaceful relations in which two generations, and more, of Christians had become accustomed to an acceptable *modus vivendi* in the communities in which they lived. Each little trauma, however, is only worth so much. In contrast to many of the eastern provinces of the empire, the enforcement of the edicts against the Christians in Africa was a brief episode that lasted no more than two years, from early 303 to the early summer of 305.[22] The harsh enforcement of the anti-Christian measures in Africa was later identified

---

Beschaouch (1976); Lepelley, *Cités de l'Afrique romaine*, 2, pp. 56–57. I accept Dolbeau's suggestion (2003, pp. 282–83) that the date of 18 January (perhaps, actually 16 January) in the F[1] tradition probably refers to the date of the arrests at Abitina.

[20] As Dolbeau (2003), p. 280, has noted, this is the consistent date in the F[2] family of manuscripts, and he guesses that it is probably the date of the hearings before the proconsul at Carthage.

[21] So the persecution of 347, as the dissidents saw it, was similarly traumatic, having come suddenly in the midst of a long period of peace: for the *tempora pacis*, see *Passio sancti Donati*, 2 (Dolbeau, 1992: 258).

[22] See Appendix B: the so-called fourth edict of Diocletian's was being enforced in Africa in December of 304, and, in all probability to the early summer of 305.

with two governors only: Valerius Florus in Numidia and Gaius Annius Anullinus in the proconsular province. In later Christian lore, of these two men it was Anullinus who was transmogrified into a fearful apparition, an arch-persecutor of nightmarishly evil dimension.[23] Anullinus was especially hated not only because of his actions at the time, but also because he was a local who was well known: his family were Africans and large landholders with close links to their peasants. He was close to these people, he knew them and they knew him with a peculiar familiarity. His mythical stature derived not just from his position as governor of the largest and most populous of the African provinces, but also because a second governor also named Anullinus came to play a critical role in the first years of the Constantinian crackdown on the dissident church.[24] The names and identities of the two men converged to produce an overdetermined view of an "Anullinus," the arch-persecutor. Such pictures were nothing but imagined fictions.

Frightful experiences, however, are a relative and personal thing, and so comparisons of dimension, although useful for historical perspective, are frequently meaningless in any community's perceptions either at the time itself or later in memory. In later generations, it was these remembered realities of the Roman governors and officials, their actions, and responses to them, that informed current values and behavior. For African Christians, there is no doubt that the official attacks on their communities in 303–05 were a shock, a greater emotional wound than for Christian communities in some other parts of the empire. Several reasons might be offered in explanation, perhaps the best of which is that Africa was, by and large (and it must be emphasized that the judgment is comparative) an isolated and protected Mediterranean environment that harbored one of the most consistently peaceful, civil-oriented, and legally directed of local societies in the empire. Africa had largely escaped the real dangers and destruction of the so-called Third-Century Crisis and the attendant violence that afflicted many of the northern and eastern provinces of the empire. The suddenness of the onslaught under Anullinus, following the directives of a brutish northern military emperor, issued from a distant eastern Mediterranean source, was harsh and unexpected when set against the background of normal experiences and expectations shared by the generation of Christians that faced this sudden assault on their community.

---

[23] On some of this later myth, and on what follows below, see Chiesa (1998), pp. 34–38, Lancel (1999) and Le Blant, *Actes des martyres*, pp. 81–83.

[24] See "Anullinus (2)," PLRE, I: pp. 78–79; and "Anulinus (2)," PAC, pp. 80–81: proconsul of Africa in 313; suspicions are excited by their homonyms; but they seem to be different men.

One effect of the shock – the disorientation and fragmentation caused by the trials and executions – was a peculiar emphasis that came to be placed upon loyalty. The monumental inscriptions, set up in commemoration of Ammaedara's Christian martyrs two and a half centuries after the Great Persecution in which they died, in the age of Byzantine rule in Africa, remembered precisely that these persons were *not* traitors and that their loyalty to biblical strictures was the reason why they had suffered and had been killed. They had surrendered their lives to defend the Holy Scriptures, God's holy laws.[25] Those who had not stood firm in defense of the community were perceived by many to have betrayed not only these fellow believers and their beliefs, but the very Word of God. It was an attitude that had been formed, in part, by Jewish practice and behavior, an ethos and a tradition that had been embraced and exalted by Christian communities in Africa.[26] The Jewish historian Josephus had remarked that for Jews a peculiar benefit of conducting one's life according to divine laws was that living by them and (if demanded) dying for them was rewarded by eternal life after death.[27] Even in the direst of circumstances, he says, "we have therefore never been *traitors* to our laws."[28] He continues in the same vein.[29]

Has anyone ever heard of cases among our people – I don't say very many, but even just two or three – who were *traitors* to the laws or who were afraid of death? I'm not speaking about that easiest of deaths, the kind that happens to those fighting on a battlefield, but death caused by torture of the body, which is rightly considered to be the most terrible of all. I myself am of the opinion that some of our conquerors have exposed us to such a death, not out of hatred for those who are subject to them, but rather because they desire to witness the spectacle of men who believe that the only evil is to be forced to do anything or to say anything that is against the law. One should not at all be surprised, therefore, that we bravely face death on behalf of our laws . . .

This is exactly what the martyrs of Ammaedara were praised for doing: for not having betrayed the divine laws, but rather having died for them: *divinis legibus passi sunt*. The transcendent value of surrendering one's life to protect the integrity of the "divine laws" is repeated time and again through the narrative of the deaths of the Christians from Abitina.[30] The

---

[25] ILTun 470b.1–2 (on the monumental stone inscription) and 470c.1–3 (repeated on the mosaic inscription where the names of the martyrs are recorded): "Gloriosissimis beatissimisq(ue) martyribus qui persecutionem Diocletiani et Maximiani divinis legibus passi sunt" (a combination of both texts).

[26] See Firpo (1990), on the Maccabees. [27] Josephus, *Contra Ap.* 2.218–19.

[28] Josephus, *Contra Ap.* 2.228. [29] Josephus, *Contra Ap.* 2.232.

[30] For example, see *Passio sanctorum Dativi, Saturnini presbyteri et aliorum*, 6, 11, 12, 13, 17, 19, 20, 23 (Maier, *Dossier*, 1, pp. 68, 73–74, 76, 78, 82, 84–85, 86, 91).

link between the principle of "no betrayal" and martyrdom was explicit, not only in the deaths of the Christians at Ammaedara in 303, but also in the later remembrance and celebration of their deeds. This specific memory about them was kept alive in public for more than two and a half centuries – into an age long after the death of Augustine. The martyr narrative of the men and women from the small town of Abitina, who perished in the same persecution, made a similar connection manifest. The records of their deaths are spoken of as "inscribed in the indispensable archives of memory, so that the glory of the martyrs and the condemnation of the traitors will not be forgotten with the passing of the ages."[31] Note the hard contrast. It is not between the martyrs and their state persecutors. It is between them and those of their fellow Christians who surrendered to an evil injunction. More than once, the record of their deaths returns to the distinction between the martyrs, who gave their lives to defend the scriptures, and the bishop of the town, Fundanus, the vile traitor who surrendered the scriptures to the authorities to be burned in public. As the martyr Tazelita is being tortured by Anullinus at Carthage, the difference between the secular laws of the empire and the divine laws of God is enunciated.[32]

As Tazelita's sides were badly shaken by the iron claws of torture ploughing into them, as waves of blood poured forth in raging torrents, he heard the proconsul saying to him: "You are only *beginning* to feel what you ought to suffer." Tazelita continued: "To your glory, I thank You, God of all kingdoms. May your eternal kingdom come, your incorruptible kingdom. Lord Jesus, we are Christians. We serve you. You are our hope, you are the hope of Christians. God most holy, God most high, God omnipotent, we give praise to you, for your name, omnipotent God." To the one who was praying this prayer, the Devil, through the judge [i.e. the proconsular governor], said: "You should take care to obey the command of

---

[31] *Passio sanctorum Dativi, Saturnini presbyteri et aliorum*, 1 (Maier, *Dossier*, 1, p. 60): "acta martyrum legat quae necessario in archivo memoriae conscripta sunt ne, saeculis transeuntibus, obsolesceret et gloria martyrum et damnatio traditorum."

[32] *Passio sanctorum Dativi, Saturnini prebyteri et aliorum*, 6 (Maier, *Dossier*, 1, no. 4, pp. 67–68): "Et cum ictibus ungularum concussa fortius latera sulcarentur profluensque sanguinis unda violentis tractibus emanaret, proconsulem sibi dicentem audivit: 'Incipies sentire quae vos pati oporteat.' et adiecit: 'Ad gloriam, gratias ago deo regnorum. Apparet regnum aeternum, regnum incorruptum. Domine Iesu, christiani sumus, tibi servimus. Tu es spes nostra, tu es spes christianorum. Deus sanctissime, deus altissime, deus omnipotens, tibi laudes. Pro nomine tuo, domine deus omnipotens.' Cui talibus oranti cum a diabolo per iudicem diceretur: 'Custodire te oportuit iussionem imperatorum et Caesarum.' Defatigato iam corpore, forte atque constanti sermone victrix anima proclamavit: 'Non curo nisi legem dei quam didici. Ipsam custodio. Pro ipsa morior. In ipsa consumor. In lege dei praeter quam non est alia.'" Probably something has gone awry with the orthography of the personal name of the martyr: see Dolbeau (2003a), pp. 285–88, who suggests that the spelling "Tzelica," found in some epigraphic texts, might be the original.

the Emperors and the Caesars." From a body now tortured, a victorious spirit proclaimed in a strong and unshakable voice: "I respect only the law of God which I have learned. I keep it. I die for it. I am consumed by it. I am consumed by the law of God, for there is no other."

It was to safeguard and to remain loyal to the *leges divinae* that the thirty-four martyrs at Ammaedara died. Those laws, God's own words, were literally embodied in the scriptures that the bishop Fundanus had handed over to the authorities to be burned in the forum of his own town.

Another consequence of the long debate in Africa over persecution and martyrdom, and the constant remembrance of martyrs, was an emphatic distrust of the secular state and its involvement in matters having to do with Christian belief and practice. There had come to be embedded at the center of such thinking in the African church a pervasive wariness of the imperial court and its unusual power. Any closeness between what had once been a persecuting state and the Christian church was potentially suspect. When the dissident bishop Parmenian was trying implicate the Catholic church in the persecution of his community in the 360s, as a simple matter of fact he angrily stated that: "that thing cannot be called a church which feeds on bloody morsels and fattens itself on the blood of the saints."[33] In saying this, Parmenian was comparing the Catholic Church to a traditional view of the state. By definition, the state was "not a church" precisely because its cruel actions, archived in the public memory of the true church, had shown that it was not such. There was a pervasive image of the state among African Christians: a bloody beast that had savaged the body of Christ. As a bloody beast, it was another precursor of the Antichrist. It was an image that had been sustained for a century and half before Constantine, and much of the same sentiment was still pervasive in the generation of Augustine, despite the presence on the throne of Christian emperors. The new Christian emperors, and their local agents, stood in a potentially dubious place. There was a hard African Christian line that official persecutors were to suffer divine punishment for their actions. Lactantius, the rhetor renowned as the African Cicero, had made this manifest at length in an attacking and lurid pamphlet written in the course of the Great Persecution entitled, no less, *On the Deaths of the Persecutors*.[34]

---

[33] Optatus, *Contra Parm.* 2.14.1 (SC 412: 268): "Neque enim illa ecclesia dici potest quae cruentis morsibus pascitur et sanctorum sanguine et carnibus opimatur."

[34] Monceaux, *Hist. litt*, 3, pp. 287–97, 340–44; and the edition and comments by J. L. Creed.

THE USE OF THE MARTYRS

As closely tied as it was to the post-Constantinian state, the Catholic Church had to represent state-driven persecutions of Christians as a thing of the past. In its view, there had been ten persecutions that could be enumerated, ending with the Great Persecution under Diocletian. There remained only one more that was yet to happen, to be led by the Antichrist Himself. But it was yet to happen in some unknown age yet to come, and the time of this future persecution had not been revealed to any human being.[35] There was also a grander theodicy that assisted in the strategic reinterpreting of martyrdom. In this larger view, there were three great ages of persecution. In the first age, the evil forces arrayed against Christians had tried to use physical force and violence to dissuade Christians from their beliefs. This age of violence was in the past. It had formally ended with Constantine's ascent to the throne of empire and with divine direction of the state. The second age of persecution that followed was the present age in which the Africans now lived. The new age of persecution was not like the first one at all. The second age was dominated by a covert struggle in the present in which Satan used his devilish tactics of seduction to tempt individual believers away from the Truth. Having been defeated on the field of open battle, the Devil was now compelled to wage a covert guerrilla war against personal souls. The only age that remained beyond this present one was the final battle against the Antichrist.[36]

By contrast, the dissident Christians had their own chronology and list of persecutors according to which the first age of persecution was not yet finished – although they too had to take the new fact of Christian emperors into account. If persecutions were still ongoing, how were they to be squared with the fact of a Christian state? Easily. The emperors as individual Christians were one thing, the whole state and its servitors were quite another. African Christians had peculiarly apposite grounds on which to make the distinction. Sectors of the imperial state at both provincial and local level in Africa were not controlled by Christians. There were objective reasons to separate the well-meaning intentions of a good Christian emperor from his less well-meaning, sometimes hostile officials. The dissidents agreed with the list of official persecuting emperors, from Nero to Diocletian. But after Constantine, the first Christian emperor, their list shifted to focus on lower-level imperial officials whose actions were directly experienced in Africa itself: Leontius, Ursatius, Paul, Macarius,

---

[35] Aug. *Civ. Dei*, 18.52–53 (CCL 48: 650–53).   [36] Aug. *En. in Ps.* 9.27 (CCL 38: 70).

Taurinus, Romanus – so the list ran.[37] These were the new persecutors. The later ideology of the good Tsar and his evil servitors is already present here. For the dissidents, state persecution continued; it was just that the official persecutors were present in a manner consistent with an age of Christian emperors.[38] For them, there were still genuine martyrs in the old-fashioned sense. It was not the emperors themselves who were directly to blame, however, but rather their evil servants.

If only in their social memory of an earlier age, the weekly reprise of the martyrs in the sermons of Catholic preachers constantly set before their listeners a complex road map for survival in conditions of extreme duress: praise for Christians who resisted public authorities and exultation over their ultimate victory. Some powerful figures in their ranks, like Aurelius and Augustine, it is true, were urging the imposition of institutions of managerial control over the "excesses" of the worship of martyrs as if they were quasi-divine figures in their own right. But these same men otherwise preached a message that portrayed the suffering and courage of the martyrs as having a real effect in confronting a persecuting state, openly suggesting that they were heroic figures. The martyrs were shown succeeding in their aim and causing the persecutor to fail in his. This powerful message was preached even by those who were critical of the "cult" of the martyrs and who tried by every means at their command to control and restrain the power of the martyrs that was being created and deployed by their parishioners. In this preaching, militant imagery was present everywhere. The same texts that presented the parishioners with the fearsome apparatuses of the state's power and the suffering of the martyrs also emphasized the armed power of Christ: "Recall the King of the Martyrs, equipping his soldiers with spiritual weapons, pointing out the wars to be waged, coming to assistance with reserves, and promising rewards."[39]

---

[37] For the dissidents' lists of persecutors, see: Optatus, *Contra Parm.* 3.1; 3.12 (SC 413: 8–10, 74–78); Aug. *Contra litt. Petil.* 2.92.202 (CSEL 52: 125): "Ut relinquam Neronem, qui primus persecutus est Christianos, Domitianum similiter Neronis maximam partem, Traianum, Getam, Decium, Valerianum, Diocletianum, perit etiam Maximianus... Perit Macarius, perit Ursatius cunctique comites vestri Dei pariter vindicta perierunt"; 3.25.29 (CSEL 52: 185); GCC 3.258 (SC 224: 1216–18): "Nam, ut omittamus quantus sanguis Christianus effusus sit per Leontium, Ursacium, Macarium, Paulum, Taurinum, Romanum, ceterosque exsecutores quos in sanctorum necem a principibus saeculi meruerunt"; and the *Liber Genealogus*, 621–26 (MGH AA 9: Chronica Minora, I, pp. 195–96).

[38] *Passio sancti Donati*, 2 (Dolbeau 1992: 257): persecution is the work of the Devil in combination with Catholic bishops and civil authorities.

[39] Aug. *Sermo* 276.1 (PL 38: 1256): "Recolite martyrum regem cohortes suas armis spiritualibus instruentem, bella monstrantem, adiutoria ministrantem, praemia pollicentem"; and *Sermo* 284.5 (PL 38:

The core lesson taught by the martyrs was that resistance founded on a range of mini-strategies of heroic endurance and patience had succeeded in the long run.[40] As Augustine preached to one of his congregations:[41]

Were the apostles whose memories we are celebrating today not arrested, were they not butchered, were they not whipped, were they not killed, were they not crucified, were they not burned alive, did they not fight with wild beasts? . . . the martyrs were killed and the persecutors *thought* that they had won. But the persecutors triumphed only in a false appearance. The martyrs were, in reality and even if in secret, crowned as the winners.

Augustine called this the "hidden payoff of God's providence." If Catholic preachers like him could emphasize time and again the real success of these strategies, dissident preachers surely did the same. These stories served, especially, to confirm identity and behavior.[42] And these latter were under no constraint to explain away or to derogate from the status of the martyrs in the present time. They did not have to engage in the constant defusing of power to which Augustine and his peers in the Catholic Church had committed themselves. Dissenting speakers could go at these themes full bore because, for them, Satan was still in league with government agents, and the officially powerful could still persecute.

The constant message, even in Catholic rhetoric, was that the kind of resistance that martyrs exemplified was enduring and long-suffering; it did not depend on instant success. The prospective martyr and believer in the power of the martyrs was taught, time and again, that the apparent successes of the persecutors were irrelevant. The martyrs were engaged in a struggle of long-term, if not cosmic, dimensions. If Catholic bishops and priests kept pounding this message into the minds of their parishioners, it does not take much imagination to understand what the dissident Christians were being taught and upon what principles they would be willing to act.

1291) for the African martyrs Marian and James, where Christ is called the *dux martyrum*: "General of the Martyrs"; cf. ch. 4, p. 168–69 on the African *duces sanctorum*.

[40] On *patientia*, or endurance, and its connections with martyrdom, see Shaw (1996a); for Augustine, this kind of humility was still *the* Christian virtue preached to his parishioners; see, e.g., Aug. *En. in Ps.* 31.2.18–20 (CCL 38: 238–40); *En. 3 in Ps.* 32.13 (CCL 39: 267–68); *Sermo* 299.8 (PL 39: 1374); *Sermo* 311.1 (PL 39: 1414); *Sermo* 335C.1 = Lambot 2 (*RBén* 46 [1934] 399–406), although heavily modified for martyrdom by his specific treatise, the *De patientia* (CSEL 41: 663–91) on the same virtue, in which he attacks the voluntary martyrdoms of the dissidents as not being true "patience" and therefore as not constituting martyrdom.

[41] Aug. *En. 2 in Ps.* 29.5–6 (CCL 38: 177–78): "Non sunt comprehensi apostoli, non sunt caesi, non sunt flagellati, non sunt occisi, non sunt crucifixi, non sunt incensi vivi, non ad bestias pugnaverunt, quorum memorias celebramus? . . . occisi sunt martyres, quasi vicisse se arbitrati sunt persecutores; illi in manifesto falso triumpharunt, illi in occulto vere coronati sunt."

[42] Generally, that is, and not just in Africa: see, e.g., Sizgorich, *Violence and Belief,* pp. 48–49.

Despite the attempt by Catholic preachers to relegate blood martyrdom to a completed age of the past and to transmogrify witnessing in the present age into a regimen of personal self-discipline, even the dullest parishioner in a Catholic congregation could not have missed absorbing a depiction of martyrdom as an effective and successful stratagem of Christian resistance. The parishioners in dissident congregations no doubt heard this same message, only without the controls imposed on it by the Catholic bishops. For them, not only was an aggressive martyrdom *not* a relic of some bygone age and *not* restricted to a purely personal realm of self-control, it was a living strategy against a real and threatening persecution.

To understand what was being heard by the preacher's audience, it is necessary to listen to details of the pedagogy that they were absorbing. It was an education in how to endure chains, squalor, prison, torture, fire, wild beasts, and different kinds of terrifying deaths.[43] The cardinal lesson that they were to learn from the martyrs was the paramount importance of the virtue of patience or endurance. One's enemies might *appear* to have the upper hand at the moment, but, with the assistance of God, the martyr could perdure, not only through the punishments and tortures inflicted on him or her, but collectively through time. In the end, they would win.[44] By braving the tortures inflicted on his or her body, the martyr acquired a very special elevated status or *dignatio*. He or she entered into an aristocracy of Christian rank.[45]

All these actions present to us the truly authentic princes of the church, the people who are worthy to lead us, the ones worthy of imitation, worthy of high honors, I mean the martyrs, who hold the highest rank in our churches and who are pre-eminent on that pinnacle of holy dignity.

Martyrs acquired a glory to which no earthly fame could be compared.[46] The martyrs are spoken of as being especially radiant, handsome, or beautiful. In a future Christian time, they will be resplendent and will glow

---

[43] Aug. *Sermo* 113A.4 = Denis 24 (MiAg 1: 141–55); *Sermo* 299D.5 = Denis 16 (MiAg 1: 74–80); 299E.2 = Guelferb. 30 (MiAg 1: 550–57).

[44] Amongst many cases, since it is an understanding undergirding almost every sermon on the subject, see: Aug. *Sermo* 158.8 (PL 38: 866); *Sermo* 277A.2 = Caillau 1.27 (MiAg 1: 244), in a sermon on Vincentius, the whole of which is devoted to patience; of a strikingly witnessed performance: "Vidimus martyrum inmania tormenta patientissime tolerantum: sed Deo se subiciebat anima eius, ab ipso enim patientia eius"; *Sermo* 283 (PL 38: 1286–87); *Sermo* 284.1 (PL 38: 1288): patience is what enables the martyrs to overcome pain.

[45] Aug. *En. in Ps.* 67.36 (CCL 39: 895): "Quae omnia verissimos nobis insinuant principes ecclesiarum, dignos ducatu, dignos imitatione, dignos honoribus. Martyres namque in ecclesiis locum summum tenent, atque apice sanctae dignitatis excellunt."

[46] Aug. *Sermo* 335C.11 = Lambot 2 (*RBén* 46 [1934]: 405).

with a special light that will distinguish them from the ordinary.[47] Since their cause is higher, indeed the highest, and their marriage is with God, martyrs were right to reject family, marital spouses, kin, and friendship ties in this world, isolating themselves in order to perform the one great task before them.[48] Moreover, they were right to turn their backs on "the present age," and to despise its values as utterly worthless by comparison with the great rewards that awaited them.[49] So it was also right that they should have little regard for their fleshly bodies, to disregard the effects of punishment, torture, and even execution; for them, there would be a new glorious body in the afterlife.[50] What is more, armed with their fortitude and patience, the martyrs will always ultimately win. They will always be victorious over the leadership of the Devil and his agents.[51]

The special *dignatio* or rank of the martyr had been enshrined in African thinking in the words of the noble bishop Cyprian.[52] In his writings, it is manifest that death was rewarded by a series of special honors bestowed on the martyr. First among these was immediate access to eternal life. Upon sacrificing his or her life in a final baptism of blood, the martyr was instantly snatched from this world and taken directly to the kingdom of heaven.[53] The heavenly rewards of martyrs vastly exceeded those of the ordinary believer: they reaped these benefits by the hundredfold compared to others.[54] And since martyrs went directly to heaven, and did not have to await the final judgment or the decision of the court of God, they acquired another highly elevated mark of high rank. Not only was the martyr *not* to be judged in that final court at the end of time, the reverse was to be true: he or she was to sit with God in judgment over others. They acquired real judicial power. The martyrs became like the *adsessores* or legal assistants who sat with the Roman governor or magistrate on his tribunal, and helped him in hearing legal cases: they were to sit with God in His court.[55] They

---

[47] For example, *Sermo* 277.1 (PL 38: 1258) on Vincentius; *Sermo* 280.5 (PL 38: 1283) on the martyrs Felicitas and Perpetua.

[48] A striking formulation is found in Aug. *Sermo* 272B.7 = Mai 158 (MiAg 1: 385); *Sermo* 335G.1 = Lambot 15 (*RBén* 51 [1939]: 23–24).

[49] Aug. *Sermo* 335A.1 = Frangipane 6 (MiAg 1: 219–21) on Perpetua, Victoria and Primus.

[50] Aug. *Sermo* 335F.2 = Lambot 14 (*RBén* 51 [1939]: 21–23).   [51] Aug. *Sermo* 32.26 (CCL 41: 410).

[52] These ideas were being picked up and elaborated later in the fourth century; see Reitzenstein (1914) and Koch (1932) on the pseudo-Cyprianic work *Sermo de centesima, sexagesima, tricensima* (PLS 1: 53–67).

[53] Hummel, *Concept of Martyrdom*, pp. 124–27, 138–39.

[54] Hummel, *Concept of Martyrdom*, pp. 132–37; the nature of this hundredfold reward is never made entirely clear, however.

[55] Hummel, *Concept of Martyrdom*, pp. 140–43; for *adsessores*, see Behrends (1969), with reference to earlier works.

became agents of judicial vengeance. The agents of Satan who had harmed them would now pay the price for their sins against God.

Since courtrooms were the principal venue for adjudicating serious civil disputes, the potential martyr was able to project a mental image of a more powerful parallel of the earthly one that they themselves were about to experience. The image perhaps explains the attitudes that Christians who were put on trial displayed towards the authorities who sat in judgment of them. For example, in the execution of the Christian woman Perpetua in the arena at Carthage in 203, when the Christians who were about to die faced the governor Hilarianus, they used gestures and motions to signal to him: "You [judge us] now, but then God [will judge] you."[56] Even though it was doubtless part of their sentiments, there was more than simple revenge here. The martyrs were asserting that they themselves would sit as judges with God and would be able to hold the Roman governor directly responsible for his treatment of them. A spirit of divine vengeance and the righting of present secular wrongs was built into the role.

The heroic status of those who endured torture and suffered death was considerably abetted by the machinery of the Roman legal system. The good argument has been made that the concept and practice of martyrdom within the Roman world was created in the dialectic between the prosecuted and the authorities in Roman courts of law.[57] The theatrical nature of the trial and the sometimes spectacular nature of the punishments staged in the arenas of the big cities further ensured a celebrity status for the condemned.[58] They became popular in more than one sense. The ways in which the machinery of the state created the publicity that advertised the identity of the condemned are well known. State officials sometimes made a public display of the condemned to create a deterrent effect in the spectators who gazed on them. The governor would drag condemned persons around with him on his rounds, displaying them at his various assizes, finally to execute them only at the end of the road.[59]

---

[56] *Passio Perpetuae et Felicitatis*, 18.7–8 (SC 417: 166–68); see Straw (2000) on the continuing theme of "settling scores" (as she puts it) in the ideology of martyrdom.

[57] Bowersock, *Martyrdom and Rome*, pp. 27 f., has analyzed the role that the Roman civic court system had in the creation of the Christian ideology of martyrdom.

[58] A line of analysis initiated by Barton (1989), and continued by others.

[59] Aug. *En. 2 in Ps.* 101.2 (CCL 40: 1439): "Nonne catenati potius quam compediti? Ductores enim sanctos Dei martyres post iudices, per provincias circumeuntes, in catenas novimus missos, in compedes non novimus." Compare the treatment of the dissident martyr Marculus in 347: "Tunc eum [sc. Marculum] secum per aliquas Numidiae civitates, quasi quoddam crudelitatis suae spectaculum, ducens" (*Passio Marculi*, 5.24 = Mastandrea [1995]: 68).

Were the martyrs not chained together rather than shackled? For we know that
these holy men of God were dragged along in chains, following behind the judges
[i.e. the provincial governors] as they traveled around their provinces [i.e. on their
assizes]. They were not shackled.

The opposite of the government's desired effect sometimes resulted. The
public display turned the condemned man or woman into a celebrity, an
honored person of reputation and elevated status.[60] It was on this pre-
existing popular strand in public punishment on which Christian martyrdom drew. The analogies drawn by Christian ideologues between martyrs
and popular fighters, gladiators, charioteers, and athletes, men who suffered
and won in their competitions, fed this attractive image.

   So the reading of the acts of a martyr as part of the liturgy was almost
invariably followed by an exhortation to imitate the martyr, who was
often portrayed as an athlete struggling on behalf of the Lord.[61] The Lord
trained his athletes and set the prizes for them as they exercised for the
great struggle.[62] The memory of the martyrs was there as an education, to
encourage imitation of endurance. Should the Christian have to face a trial,
he or she would know how to persevere right to the end. The troubles that
the Christian would face are not always reconfigured as internal personal
problems, but rather as the physical torture inflicted by state agents of
repression.[63] When celebrating the anniversary of an individual martyr – his
or her birthday, or *natilitia*, into real or eternal life – the ordinary Catholic
parishioner, and no less the dissident believer, received an education in
how to resist threats and violence, of how to despise persecutors and to
be rewarded with crowns of victory.[64] However much Catholic bishops
wished to reconfigure martyrdom in the present age as a different kind of
personal struggle over disease or temptation, the martyrs' narratives that
were read aloud in the liturgy on their birthdays, and the sermons that
were delivered in combination with them, portrayed and commented on

---

[60] A fact noted for the effects of public punishments in early modern Europe by many historians.
   Instead of terrorizing, public hangings became mass entertainments: among many studies, see the
   classic analysis by Pieter Spierenberg, "The Watchers: Spectators at the Scaffold," ch. 4 in *The
   Spectacle of Suffering: Executions and the Evolution of Repression*, Cambridge University Press, 1984,
   pp. 81–109.
[61] The Catholic council at Hippo in 393 allowed that it was permissible to read the passions of the
   martyrs on the anniversary days of their martyrdoms: Concil. Hippo 393, canon 36 = *Reg. Eccl.
   Carth. Excerpt.* canon 46 (CCL 149: 43 and 186): "Liceat etiam legi passiones martyrum, cum
   anniversarii dies eorum celebrantur" – notably in a rule that also established the legitimate canon of
   biblical scripture. The text seems to have been the canon 5 of the original proceedings: (CCL 149:
   21): "Ab universis episcopis dictum est: Omnibus placet ut scripturae canonicae quae lectae sunt,
   sed et passiones martyrum, sui cuiusque locis, in ecclesiis praedicentur."
[62] Aug. *Sermo* 64.1–4 (CCL 41Aa: 353–60).   [63] Aug. *Sermo* 64A.1 and 3 = Mai 20 (MiAg 1: 310–13).
[64] Aug. *Sermo* 65.1 and 8 (CCL 41Aa: 375–76 and 384).

arrest and detention, inquisition and torture, and trials before judges and courts.[65] The replaying of just one of the birthdays, that of the martyr Vincentius, and the preacher's comments on it, is sufficient to illustrate the point.[66]

In the passion that we have had read aloud to us today, my brothers, we are clearly shown a ferocious judge, a bloodthirsty torturer, and an undefeated martyr. His body having been ploughed with different instruments of torture, there were no tortures left to vent on him and yet his limbs still held out . . . the governor Dacian's crazed words, his wild and maddened eyes, his threatening facial expression and the movements of his whole body betray the inner presence of that One [i.e. the Devil] who had taken up residence inside him, and through these visible signs revealed . . . what had filled him up.

The basic message that was dinned into the parishioners by repeated performative readings of martyr narratives throughout the whole liturgical year was that the state is an evil entity, that its agents are agents of the Devil, and that Christian martyrs are just men and women of great courage who oppose its evil actions and so reap a deserved reward of a vastly enhanced spiritual status. It might be all fine and well to say "well, now, this is in the past and it no longer applies in our present age," but the messages and performances were all living and current. They were not cast in some definite past tense. The calendars of the annual liturgy revealed an ecclesiastical year that was filled with celebrations of the martyrs.[67]

"Many are those who persecute me and punish me, but I have not turned away from witnessing for you" [Ps. 119: 157]. This is a fact. We know it. We remember it. We recognize it. The whole earth is made dark red with the blood of the martyrs. Heaven is flowering with the martyrs' crowns. Our churches are adorned with memorials of the martyrs. Our own times are marked with the festivals of the martyrs. Cures due to the favors of the martyrs are becoming ever more frequent.

Note the words: "our own times." It did not matter which of the two churches was concerned. The utility of a grievous experience from the past was extended in its annual repetition. So the dissidents remembered the massacre at the church of Sicilibba and made the Catholic primate Caecilian responsible for the fate of the martyrs there: The preacher proclaimed that

---

[65] Aug. *Sermo* 94A.1 = Caillau 2.6 (MiAg 1: 252).

[66] Aug. *Sermo* 276.1 (PL 39: 1255–56): "In passione, quae nobis hodie recitata est, fratres mei, evidenter ostenditur iudex ferox, tortor cruentus, martyr invictus. In cuius corpore poenis variis exarato, iam tormenta defecerant, et adhuc membra durabant . . . Per furiosas enim Daciani voces, per truces oculos et minaces vultus et totius corporis motus ille habitator eius interior monstrabatur, et per haec signa visibilia . . . quod impleverat."

[67] Aug. *En. 30 in Ps.* 118.5 (CCL 40: 1768–69), in a sermon delivered at Hippo as late as 418.

the memory of Caecilian's misdeeds was maintained to the present day, and that the deaths of the martyrs caused by his actions were to be honored and celebrated.[68]

Each of the *natalitiae* or birthday celebrations of the martyrs' deaths was an occasion when large numbers of the populace in any given community would converge on the martyr's shrine or church, coming from the surrounding countryside and town neighborhoods. The popularity of the festivities is signaled by the ways in which news and participation were generated by ordinary street communications.[69]

If by chance the day of a festival of one of the martyrs arrives, and some holy place and a set day is named on which all are to assemble to celebrate the solemn rites, can't you recollect how the crowds incite one another, how the people encourage each other, saying: "Let's go! Let's go!" Others say: "Where are we going?" And they are told: "To the place! To the holy place!" So people talk to each other in turn and catch fire with enthusiasm. And all of the separate little fires unite into a single great conflagration.

Of course, the higher the earthly social rank of the martyr, the greater was his or her celestial *dignatio*. This accounted in large part for the absolute pre-eminence of Cyprian. The remarks about the noble woman Crispina, martyred in the Great Persecution, also make the same point.[70]

The persecutors raged against Crispina, whose birthday we are celebrating today. They unleashed their savagery against a weathy and refined young woman ... Is there anyone in all of Africa who does not know about these events? Scarcely, because she was of brilliant rank, of noble lineage, and very wealthy ...

The call to martyrdom preached by the Catholics was indeed so powerful that Catholic parents could still pray that their own children would "be crowned as martyrs." A majority, of course, would be content with the mere survival of their children, but some would hope for, and solicit, something higher, something of greater value.[71]

If a Catholic preacher, like Augustine, wished to confine and restrain the admiration and mimicry of martyrs to a domain of personal inner discipline, what was actually preached was surely perceived to be a more direct imitation. Not unlike Tertullian in the earlier age of "real" martyrdom, Augustine spoke of "the righteous blood that was spilled, blood

---

[68] *Passio Sancti Donati*, 9 (Dolbeau, 1992: 261): "Nam et anniversalis dies religiosa devotione non inmerito celebratur. Est enim honorandus iste dies in quo et omnis ecclesia Dei confessa et post eius Christi domini aeterni iudicis dextera coronata est."

[69] Aug. *En. in Ps.* 121.2 (CCL 40: 1802).   [70] Aug. *En. in Ps.* 120.13 (CCL 40: 1799).

[71] Aug. *En. in Ps.* 108.17 (CCL 40: 1592).

from which, like seed sown throughout the world, sprang the crop of the church." He continues:[72]

The blood of the just is scattered and from this blood, as if from seed sown through the whole world, the crop of the Church rises . . . the deaths by which the pagans vented their savagery are the same ones with which we today are refreshed. We are celebrating the birthdays of the martyrs, we set the examples of the martyrs before us, we contemplate their faith, remember how they were hunted down, how they were dragged off, how they stood before their judges . . . We place all these things before our eyes and gaze at them. We hope to imitate them. These are Christian spectacles. God watches them from above. He exhorts us to join them, He helps us in them, He offers the prizes for the contests and He distributes them to the winners.

The consciously wrought directive of the bishop was that blood martyrs were a thing of the past and that martyrs today were those who endured bodily affliction and rejected the spiritual seductions of the Enemy. Famously, Augustine further urged the critical argument that it was the just cause and not suffering alone that made a martyr.[73] But this was a radical position to which he had been compelled for polemical purpose. Unfortunately for his new view, the dense texts that supported the self-conscious enunciations were replete with real resistance to actual persecutors. The frequency with which Augustine had to reiterate his mantra that it was only the "just cause" and not "suffering" that made a true martyr – and the manifold ways in which he elaborated and expounded this peculiar viewpoint – is a small measure of the extent to which the opposite view was widely prevalent, even among his own Catholic parishioners.[74]

---

[72] Aug. *En. in Ps.* 39.1 and 16 (CCL 38: 423 and 437–38): "et sparsus est sanguis iustus, et illo sanguine, tamquam seminatione per totum mundum facta, seges surrexit ecclesiae . . . Mortes in quas pagani saevierunt, in illis hodie reficimur. Natalem martyrum celebramus, exempla martyrum nobis proponimus, adtendimus fidem, quomodo inventi, quomodo adtracti, quomodo steterunt ante iudices . . . Haec omnia proponimus nobis, et intuemur illa, et optamus imitari. Haec sunt spectacula Christiana, haec videt desuper Deus, ad haec hortatur, ad haec adiuvat; his certaminibus praemia proponit et donat." The first phrase obviously had its roots in Tertullian's famous dictum, and was a staple of sermons; see *Sermo* 22.4 (CCL 41: 294) and *Sermo* 360B.19 = Dolbeau 25/Mainz 61 (Dolbeau, *Vingt-six sermons*, p. 71).

[73] Congar (1963b) and Lamirande (1965h) cite some of the relevant materials.

[74] See, e.g., Aug. *Ep.* 89 (CSEL 34.2: 419–25; *Ep.* 185.2.8–9 (CSEL 57: 7–9); *Sermo* 94A.1 = Caillau 2.6 (MiAg, 1: 252); *Sermo* 138.2 (PL 38: 764); *Sermo* 275.1 (PL 38: 1254); *Sermo* 285.2 (PL 38: 1293–94); *Sermo* 306A.1 = Morin 14 (MiAg 1: 644–46); *Sermo* 325.2 (PL 39: 1448–49); *Sermo* 327.1–2 (PL 39: 1450–51); *Sermo* 328.4 (PL 39: 1453); *Sermo* 331.2 (PL 39: 1459–60); *Sermo* 335.2 (PL 39: 1470–71); *Sermo* 335C.12 = Lambot 2 (*RBén* 46 [1934] 399–406); *Sermo* 335G.1 = Lambot 15 (*RBén* 51 [1939]: 23–24); *Sermo* 335I.4 = Lambot 27 (*RBén* 62 [1952]: 104–07); *En. 2 in Ps.* 34.13 (CCL 38: 320) at length; *En. in Ps.* 43.1 (CCL 38: 481) at length; *En. 1 in Ps.* 68.9 (CCL 39: 909–10); *Tract. in Ioh.* 6.23.2; *Tract. in Ioh.* 88.3.1–2;; *Ep.* 185.2.9–11 (CSEL 57: 8–10); *Ep. ad Cath.* 20.53 (CSEL 52: 301);

The new aberrant position also required the retooling of the fundamental values that underlay resistance, the most important of these being
endurance or patience – the ability to hold out under threat or torture.
Patience was no longer seen as a univalent virtue: it was one that might be
bad – if not directed to a just cause – or good, if it was.[75] Even if it was
loudly asserted that "in most parts of the world" people did not bring sacrifices, celebrate meals, and perform other kinds of adoration at the shrines
of the martyrs, treating them as living and powerful spirits, the fact is that
these vociferous claims only served to show how often Catholic Christians
in Africa did these very things.[76] The status of the martyrs, even within the
Catholic Church, was constantly exalted as a special one, elevated above
all others. Ordinary parishioners lived in a world in which thousands of
martyrs gazed back on them, men and women who were vaunted as "true
and perfect lovers of justice."[77] This justice might be Christian, but the
sentiment was surely not absent that it should be normal justice as well. In
one sense, the martyrs could be seen as just other dead on the rolls of any
given church's deceased. But they were different. They were *not* prayed for
in the daily liturgy like the other deceased. The reverse was expected: the
martyrs would, it was hoped, pray for and commend the ordinary believer
in need.[78]

The visual images of the martyrs in the Catholic Church that were teem-
ing everywhere in a multitude of words, just beneath the deliberate attempt
to craft a new attitude, were those of just fighters for the truth who were
willing to surrender their own lives in defense of the Christian faith against
persecutors who were agents of Satan in secular guise. The dissident clergy,
on the other hand, had no motive to tone down the insistent message of a
vibrant and living martyrdom of blood. Quite the reverse. They had every
reason to ratchet up their verbal exhortations on the compelling power of
the martyrs. For them, there were few incentives to impose controls on
their descriptions of the dynamic power of the martyr's resolve. One can
understand the confusion of Augustine's parishioners when – measured
against the weight of his own preaching on the normal behavior, the meaning and the value of the martyrs – he tried to tell them that they were *not*
to regard the persecution, arrest, torture, imprisonment, and executions

---

Contra Cresc. 4.46.55–56 (CSEL 52: 552–54); *Post Coll. ad Donat.* 17.21–23 (CSEL 53: 119–22); *Sermo
ad Caes.* 7 (CSEL 53: 176); *Contra Gaud.* 1.20.23 (CSEL 53: 220–21).

[75] New views that are argued, at length, in Augustine's *De Patientia*, composed, probably, in the late
410s (text in CSEL 41).

[76] Aug. *Civ. Dei*, 8.27 (CCL 47: 209–10).   [77] Aug. *Sermo* 159.7.8 (PL 38: 871).

[78] Aug. *Sermo* 159.1.1 (PL 38: 868); an idea frequently repeated: *Sermo* 284.5 (PL 38: 1291).

of the dissidents, when bravely endured, as a kind of martyrdom.[79] What *were* they to think? It was confusing.

But no such contradiction in ideology or presentation bothered the dissident preacher or believer. They were living martyrs in an age of martyrdom, and they knew it. The useful images that could be exploited were created not only by means of the recursive replaying of literary texts that recorded the courageous acts of the martyrs, but also by oral memories that were passed down through other channels of community and kinship: ones that produced traditions of heroic behavior. In the mid-third century, in the age of Cyprian, such traditions were already in place. In praising the heroic deeds of the confessor Celerinus, Cyprian was also able to praise the heroic traditions of the man's family: his grandmother, Celerina, had been martyred, as had both his paternal and maternal uncles, Laurentius and Egnatius. All three, Cyprian says, were commemorated every year in the festivities for martyrs celebrated by the church at Carthage.[80] So, too, in later sectarian battles, the importance of family and tradition continued to bear great force. In the year 329, at Castellum Tingitanum, to the southwest of Caesarea, a memorial was dedicated by parents to their four sons, all martyrs.[81] Such memorials were the scenes of monthly and annual meetings of families and friends who ate and drank at the table, the *mensa*, of the deceased hero.

Eating and drinking were worship. But they were more powerful when performed at the tables or *mensae* of the martyrs. Even in the rituals for the ordinary deceased, we can catch the practice of telling tales of praise and narratives of deeds about him or her of a kind that nourished the memory and the power of the more heroic dead.[82] The plain fact remains that we do not know much about the vast majority of these local men and women of power. Only in the cases just mentioned are we able to see one means – the memory of family history – by which the fame was maintained. So inside one of the more democratic forms of

---

[79] Aug. *Sermo* 325.2 (PL 389: 1448): "Non te commoveant supplicia et poenae malefacientium, sacrilegorum, hostium pacis, et inimicorum veritatis. Non enim illi pro veritate moriuntur."

[80] Cyprian, *Ep.* 39.3.1 (CCL 3B: 189): "Avia eius Celerina iam pridem martyrio coronata est. Item patruus eius at avunculus, Laurentius et Egnatius... palmas Domini et coronas inlustri passione meruerunt. Sacrificia pro eis semper, ut meministis, offerimus, quotiens martyrum passiones et dies anniversaria commemoratione celebramus."

[81] Février (1970), pp. 201 f. and Duval, *Loca sanctorum*, 1, pp. 377–80; cf. MacMullen, *The Second Church*, p. 57, for comment.

[82] MacMullen, *The Second Church*, pp. 57–59, who draws our attention to a wonderful inscription from Satafis (mod. Aïn Kebira) about a family gathering at a *mensa* to remember their mother, Aelia Secundula, by telling stories about her (CIL 8.20277 = ILCV 1570; AD 299). The phrase "eating and drinking was worship" is his.

power in antiquity, there developed lineages of power that structured local memory. We might presume, conversely, that connections with Carthage, the metropolis of all Africa and administrative center of the proconsular province, ensured that these more urban martyrs were more likely to make the record and more likely to be remembered and celebrated. This pattern is confirmed by two separate bodies of evidence. Of the 130 or so sermons that Augustine preached on martyrs, it is manifest that those delivered in churches at Carthage or in nearby towns, and on the martyrs of the metropolis, have been disproportionately better preserved.[83] Similarly, in the Calendar of Carthage, the general official record of liturgical days of the years for the whole church in Africa, of the forty-eight days marked for African martyrs, the great majority of entries are for martyrs from Carthage or from towns in its vicinity.[84]

This skewing manifestly obscures our view of the real historical function of martyrdom through most of Africa in the great sectarian struggle of the fourth century. Most Christian martyrs were particularly identified with a small village or rural region, and they were often unknown beyond it. In mentioning individual towns of modest importance like Thizika and Thuburbo Maius, it could be remarked that certainly not everyone in Africa knew of them, and very many in the proconsular province did not either.[85] Each place was like a little island with its own important people. There were very large numbers of martyrs who were not even once recognized outside their own town or valley. They were not noted among the celebrated martyrs recognized at metropolitan level in the uniform registers or calendars of the Church's spiritual heroes.[86] And beyond both of these were still others: the many who lived on in local worlds of oral communication, who had left no written records at all. They were the most numerous and the most powerful. The thirty-four martyrs of the Diocletianic persecution celebrated at Ammaedara, with which this chapter began, finally appear, as if in a photographic plate coming into focus, in

---

[83] Lapointe, *Célébration des martyrs*, pp. 76–77.

[84] Lapointe, *Célébration des martyrs*, ch. 2, pp. 59–70, esp. pp. 66–67.

[85] Aug. *Ep. ad Donat. post Collat.* 22.38 (CSEL 53: 140): admittedly in full rhetorical flow: "immo vero ipsarum in quibus fuerunt civitatum nomina nec universae Africae nota sunt aut fortasse nec universali proconsulari provinciae?"

[86] Duval, *Loca sanctorum*, a work that considerably sharpens and corrects the old, but still useful lists in Monceaux, "Martyrs et reliques mentionnés par les documents épigraphiques africains," appendix 1 in *Hist. litt.*, 3, pp. 530–35; and "Martyrs et confesseurs africains mentionnés par les auteurs, les actes des martyrs, le calendrier de Carthage et les martyrologes," appendix 2 in *Hist. litt.*, 3, pp. 536–51. Important for our purpose is the simple fact that the two lists of names overlap so little: the epigraphy speaks to the prevalent local stories, the literary sources more often to the larger province-wide African stage.

a permanent written text on stone set up in the sixth century. Somehow their names had been preserved over the three preceding centuries. Every one of them is otherwise unknown.[87] They had no existence in the general calendar of saints for Africa or in the elite literary martyr narratives. To comprehend the imitative behavior of violent sectarian fighters, one has also to understand that it was more to these immediate, but anonymous examples that they related – martyrs like those whose deaths were marked by the dozens and dozens of whitened tables or *mensae* found in the countryside around Bagaï that celebrated the martyrs of the repressive violence of 347. The shrines were there in the 360s, and they were still there later in the 380s to worry the Catholic bishop Optatus.

The memorialization of martyrs and their educative value are forces whose dimensions are difficult to estimate. The sum of the surviving evidence indicates several important parameters worth noting. First, the material evidence that is one dimension of collective memory and cult indicates specific limits and concentrations. Almost all of this type of evidence is concentrated in the provinces of Africa Proconsularis, Numidia, and Mauretania Sitifensis. Although more westerly extensions are found in Caesariensis they are limited almost solely to some coastal cities and to the valley of the Wadi Chelif. And the great weight of known sites is located in the ecclesiastical province of Numidia.[88] Even within these parameters – what we have elsewhere called Augustine's Africa – there are manifest communicative nodes: concentrations along the northern flanks of the Aurès mountains or down the main highway connecting Carthage with its hinterland, for example. There is little evidence of a dominant presence of relics of the cult of the martyrs elsewhere, say in the entire region of Byzacena. Then again, whereas some of the permanent memorials from the time, mainly in stone, contain written texts naming the martyr, the greatest numbers are uninscribed. We have no idea who the dead were. They were famous martyrs in their own village or valley, but nowhere else.[89]

---

[87] Duval (1995), p. 105.

[88] Duval, *Loca sanctorum*, and end map. The statistics that I have compiled out of Duval's evidence – the general trends of which have surely not been altered very much by subsequent discoveries (her additional evidence, for example, does not alter the general picture already evident in Monceaux's summation of the evidence as of 1905 – see n. 86 above) – indicate the following distribution by ecclesiastical province: Tripolitania 1 (even this one is Tacapae; so, in reality, none); Byzacena 27 (but 20 of these instances are sites located very close to Proconsularis; so, in essence, only 7); Proconsularis: 30; Numidia: 80; Mauretania Sitifensis: 27; Mauretania Caesariensis: 30 (almost all in coastal sites or sites in the Chéliff River valley). Note the signal paucity of martyr sites in the region of Byzacena–Tripolitania.

[89] Duval, *Loca sanctorum*, 1, pp. 458, 480, 491.

There is a related problem in interpreting the significance of martyrs for African Christians in the late fourth century, one that is rooted in the evidence itself. On the one side, there are a fair number of detailed literary texts that both record the martyrdoms themselves and, more frequently, that preach about, extol, or debate the status of the martyrs and their acts of self-sacrifice. On the other side, there are archaeological data and epigraphical texts, inscriptions written on grave markers, commemorative stone lintels, celebratory mosaic pavements, and ritual tables or *mensae* that attest a large number of martyrs in various locales in Africa and that consecrate the places of their veneration. The problem is that these two sets of evidence overlap only by a little.[90] At some specific points, and with regard to a few martyrs, the literary and epigraphical texts speak to the same cult – for example, the worship of the martyr Perpetua and her companion Felicitas or the great bishop Cyprian. But such convergences are unusual. It is not a question of trying artificially to force these two disparate kinds of texts together, but rather of understanding what each is saying and how that difference affects the relationship of the martyr to violent acts of resistance in each locale. The more extensive written sources – the martyr *acta* and the church calendars marking the festivals of the martyrs – are therefore enormously misleading. They name only a tiny proportion of all the martyrs, and the names are disproportionately dominated by bishops and elite clergy.[91] By far the greatest numbers of known martyrs are attested by a single instance in a small locale, or they are not known at all. The few whose names made it onto the calendars of the official celebrations of the church were the rich and famous. The big problem in connecting beliefs in martyrs with sectarian violence is that it was in the rural, the nameless, and the unknown that the reservoirs of imitative behavior were found.

DISSENT AND PERSECUTION

As one community construed the deaths of their partisans as a great good – as the deaths of martyrs – the other side resolutely refused such an elevated status to them. In long and repetitious sermons preached to his congregation, Augustine never ceased to harp remorselessly on the line that "it is the cause and not the act that creates the martyr." The same objection was

---

[90] See Duval, n. 88 above. [91] Duval, *Loca sanctorum*, 1, p. 158 n. 21.

reiterated in treatises, dialogues, and letters. In a typical passage, he begins by citing the gospel of Matthew (5: 10):[92]

"Blessed are those who suffer persecution for the sake of justice." This last addition separates the martyr from the bandit. Even the bandit suffers persecution for his evil acts, but he is not competing for a crown; he's just paying the penalty that he owes. The punishment does not make a martyr, but rather the cause. So the martyr chooses the cause first and then, unconcerned, suffers the punishment. In that single place there were three crosses when Christ suffered: He in the middle, with a bandit on either side of him. Consider the punishment. Nothing was more the same in each case. Yet one of the bandits found Paradise on the cross. In making his judgment, the One in the middle condemned the proud while He came to the help of the humble. For Christ, the cross was his judicial tribunal.

The logic is impeccable. If it was suffering and enduring violence alone that made one a martyr, then the murderer, the violent robber, and any number of other bad types, including those who were tortured or executed for their crimes, would be counted as martyrs.

What is equally manifest is that this logic was not shared by most Christian believers, even Catholic ones. The counter-arguments, despite their constant repetition, had to overcome serious hurdles that would be very difficult to efface from prevailing values. The first and perhaps the most significant was the idea that suffering ennobled to some degree no matter the status of the sufferer or the deserved nature of his or her suffering.[93] It was a sentiment that was so widespread that efforts to make ordinary people reject it faced a natural resistance. The idea was popularly accepted that the gladiator or the criminal, or even a person of the lowest status like a slave, could display or achieve a kind of honor and acquire a more elevated status or rank by nobly enduring punishment and pain.[94] The idea that they necessarily had to be suffering for "a just cause" was a high-flown formal moral objection not generally shared by large parts of the general populace, Christian and non-Christian. They thought that an

---

[92] Aug. *Sermo* 53A.13 = Morin 11.13 (MiAg. 1: 634; *RBén* 34 [1922]: 12–13; PLS 2: 634–35), a passage that highlights his classic refrain: "Martyrem non facit poena, sed causa."

[93] Barton (1994), with consideration of the connections between "pagan" and Christian ideas; Aug. *En. in Ps.* 129.11 (CCL 40: 1897), is one of the many places where he notes the strict parallel in suffering between martyrs on the one hand and robbers and criminals on the other.

[94] The deaths of gladiators and beast-hunters, for example, were taken in popular values to ennoble, see Barton (1989), *passim* and *Sorrows of the Ancient Romans*, pp. 17–18; esp. p. 19 n. 17 on the use of the arena metaphor by Paul, 1 Cor. 4:9 and by Cyprian, *Ep.* 10.5; cf. p. 20 nn. 32–33 and pp. 31 f.

aristocracy of suffering was gained by the brave sufferer, almost regardless of all other factors. It was difficult to contest this popular model of courage and ennoblement.[95]

What will there be for those who share the sufferings of Christ if charity is not present? Cannot bandits be found who have such great bodily courage under torture that some of them not only refuse to betray their accomplices, but disdain to reveal even their own names? In suffering and torture, their sides raked, their innards almost destroyed, their spirit remains evilly obstinate to the very end.

The problem – clearly seen in this example – is that most persons saw endurance under torture as a kind of real courage. Augustine could list a host of judicial punishments – prison, chain-gangs, mines, deportation, beheading, being thrown to wild beasts, being burned alive, and more – and then had to admit that men and women who suffered such punishments did in fact acquire a measure of glory.[96]

Relying on this popular logic of honor, the dissidents could draw on the power of the martyrs, and, naturally, they emphasized their continuity with the great examples set by the martyrs of the past. For the dissidents, the current age was an age of persecution and they were the persecuted. Even their harshest critics had to admit a number of objective facts. There was little doubt that the dissidents had suffered bodily punishment, imprisonment, confiscation of property, fines, exile, and other penalties, and that "the emperor had persecuted their flesh," even if this "harsh discipline" might be represented as nothing other than the "just correction of the Lord."[97] It was also recognized by their opponents that the dissidents had laid claim to the Christian entitlements of persecution. One could reject, even mock, the basis of their claims:[98]

These men even dare to say that they are accustomed to suffer persecution from Catholic kings and Catholic emperors. What persecution do they endure? Some distress of the body. Even if they have sometimes suffered... even if the party of Donatus has sometimes suffered something from Catholic emperors, it has suffered in the body, not in some deception of the spirit.

---

[95] Aug. *Sermo* 169.11.14 (PL 38: 923): "Quid autem erit in communicationibus passionum Christi, si caritas non erit? Nonne invenientur torti latrones in tanta fortitudine corporum, ut quidam eorum non solum conscios prodere noluerint, sed nec nomina sua confiteri dignati sint; inter cruciatus, inter tormenta, effossis lateribus, et paene perditis membris, manserit animus in obstinatione nequissima?"

[96] Aug. *Contra ep. Parm.* 1.8.13 (CSEL 51: 34); he tries to deny that this should be so, and that only a good man (*bonus*) who suffers thus and not a bad one (*malus*) who deserves his suffering, should acquire honor, but manifestly he is arguing against the popular grain.

[97] Aug. *Tract. in Ioh.* 5.12 (CCL 36: 47). [98] Aug. *Tract. in Ioh.* 11.13 (CCL 36: 118).

But there was no denying the fact that attacks had been made on them, even if they were construed as only a little bothersome rather than truly violent: "Among the heretics [i.e. the dissident Christians], who have endured a little bit of harassment because of their mistakes and their errors, there are some who boast of being martyrs."[99]

Martyrs and their powers were so tightly woven into the fabric of everyday life that common everyday actions were centered on them:

To the present day it's the custom in Numidia to adjure the slaves of God (that is, Christians) like this: "If you win." You see that it's not without some grounds for fighting that this kind of oath is made. For even when we speak about the situation here, at Carthage, or in the whole proconsular province and in Byzacena, or even Tripolitania, the customary way for slaves of God to adjure each other is "By your crown!"[100]

In referring in this way to the *victor* and the *corona*, these Christians accepted the elevated status of their saints. They were swearing by the symbols of the martyrs rather than those of God Himself, surely because the martyrs were a more accessible form of high popular power in the church. As the preacher says in speaking directly to his parishioners:[101]

For many of your number offered the greatest service of suffering, many who were not bishops and not clerics: young men and young women, elders and juniors, many married men and women, many mothers and fathers, heads of families, serving Christ, have also laid down their lives in witness of Him. Our Father has honored them. And they have received the most glorious of crowns.

That is to say, persons who were *not* bishops or clerics – almost every sort of ordinary person, short of slaves – are included in this list. For them, martyrdom was a real source of power, a palpable ideal. It was a career open to all. No great talents were needed, only fortitude and endurance. Cyprian might well have been elevated to a pre-eminent *dignitas* or rank, but his case was almost unique in his age. In most other places, there were a host of ordinary persons, such as those named by Augustine, who set a new model of power in behavior. It is just that we do not know their names. But the locals surely did.

With the partial exception of the Diocletianic persecution – and mostly even then – this loneliness of the ecclesiastical elite remained true. Bishops

---

99 Aug. *Sermo* 138.2.2 (PL 38: 764): "Nam et apud haereticos, qui propter iniquitates et errores suos aliquid molestiarum perpessi fuerint, nomine martyrii se iactant."
100 Aug. *Sermo* 94A.6 = Caillau 2.6 (MiAg 1: 255).
101 Aug. *Tract. in Ioh.* 51.13 (CCL 36: 445); cf. *Tract. in Ioh.* 96.1 (CCL 36: 569), where he repeats the same idea in almost the same words; at *Sermo* 143.5.5 (PL 38: 787), women, and boys and girls, are involved, as well as men.

were ordinarily moved out of the way of the forces of persecution. They were not placed in harm's way. Although the days of their *depositiones* or burials, following a natural death in bed, might be added to the calendars of the martyrs, the real thing was constantly anchored among more prosaic people. And the people who went to the shrines of the martyrs and engaged in rituals of cult made it manifest that, in some important sense, they were worshiping the martyrs themselves. Despite a long crusade by Augustine to educate his parishioners in the idea that this should *not* be so – that is to say, that Christians were not supposed to worship the martyrs themselves but only God *through* the martyrs – it is almost certain that the direct veneration of martyrs remained the widespread practice. External observers of the time – which is to say non-Christians – had no trouble in identifying these cultic practices with common pre-Christian rituals and could justly claim that they presented manifest evidence that Christians were in fact polytheists.[102]

Attempts to remove the trump card of martyrdom held by the dissidents merely by questioning its status were therefore not likely to have much effect. There had to be more effective strategies of containment to cope with the power of martyrdom. As early as 348, sanctions were already being put into place by the Catholic Church against the worship of those who were deemed "unworthy" to be counted as martyrs. The measures were manifestly a response to the appearance of a new raft of dissident martyrs in the Great Persecution of 347. Part of the new internal disciplinary drive of the Catholic bishops in the early 390s centered on the cult of the martyrs. The fifth rule of the council held at Hippo in 393 stated that only canonical scriptures were to be read as part of the liturgy; but, even so, allowance had to be made for reading the "passions of the martyrs."[103] That the Catholic Church had to do this surely was not just a mark of establishing internal markers for the sake of definition, but for the control of Catholics who were themselves likely to be convinced by the power of such deaths.

Catholic orthodoxy emphasized that Satan's attacks were now personal and individual, and came in the form of false ideas propagated by heretics and by attacks on the body in demonic possessions that created illness. The martyr in this new age was not someone who died by the sword or by the claws of wild animals, but someone who patiently sustained faith, like Job, while lying sick in bed or who patiently held out against the

---

[102] Aug. *Sermo* 198.47 = Dolbeau 16/Mainz 26 (Dolbeau, *Vingt-six sermons*, p. 402): "Nec vos itaque seducant, cum vobis dicunt: 'Si vos martyres colitis et per illos putatis adiuvari apud deum, quanto magis nos virtutes Dei colere debemus, per quas nos apud Deum adiuvari.'"
[103] Concil. Hipp. 393, canon 5 (CCL 149: 21).

allurements of false prophets and lying doctrines. The Christian who bore up under these assaults was the true martyr of the new age, and won his or her crown of victory no less certainly than did the martyrs of old. This is the way in which the exemplary behavior of the ancient martyrs, heard by church congregations on dozens of *natalitiae* throughout the year, were understood and acted upon.[104] If one was lying in sickness in one's bed and bravely held out with the help of the Lord, if one was being tempted to commit an immoral act and refused to do so, if one was being seduced to believe in a false teaching and rejected it with the help of the Lord, one was being a true witness, or martyr, to the Lord in a way appropriate to the new age.[105]

The problem with this new interpretation of martyrdom was that it was not likely wholly to convince. The new idea might be added as a supplement to an existing backbone of martyrdom, but it almost certainly had little chance in fully replacing the primal significance of blood witnessing. The contemporary living performance and textual life of the Church featured martyrs as if their sufferings had a real and powerful presence. To confine them to a distant past was a very difficult task. The martyrs were just not that dead. Beyond having these living traditions, whether they liked it or not, most Catholics could actually witness the self-sacrifice and endurance of fellow Christians, even if the sufferers were construed as their enemies. The whole strategy was intended to remove this aggressive sting of the martyr, the attacking power of an active martyrdom, and so to affect behavior. In speaking about metaphors of weapons and the armed service of Christ, Augustine takes a swipe at the martyrs of the dissidents: "Armed with these weapons, the army of Our King is unbeatable. The soldiers of Christ, girt with these arms, triumph. They triumphed *not* by saving the limbs of their own bodies but by having them torn to pieces, *not* by killing but by dying."[106] This re-reading of meaning is frequently found in Catholic sermons of the time. But the power of aggressive militant death was not something that could easily be countervailed by words alone. What might be more effective would be to mimic the form and then to control access to the artificially created center of power – to enter the martyr game,

---

[104] Aug. *Sermo* 4.36–37 (CCL 41: 46–48); note that it is specifically set against "the Donatists" and their men of violence.

[105] See, e.g., Aug. *Sermo* 286 (PL 38: 1300–04); 318.2 (PL 39: 1438–30), ill in bed; *Sermo* 335D (PLS 2: 778–80); *Sermo* 306E.7 = Dolbeau 18/Mainz 50 (Dolbeau, *Vingt-six sermons*, p. 215): ill in bed.

[106] Aug. *Sermo* 282 auct.3 (Erfurt 1: 262): "His armis exercitus nostri regis invictus est, his armis accincti milites Christi non conservatis sed trucidatis corporis membris nec occidendo sed moriendo triumpharunt."

but on one's own terms. It was more a matter of channeling than of outright prevention.

The new strategy entailed a more direct management of martyr cult and attendant miracles. One could do this by preaching and instruction. A better tactic was the artificial insertion into the local system of a new martyr so that the whole process of locating the shrines, the forms of cult, the happening of miracles, and the resulting power could be reoriented around a new controlled center. To trump the superior position of the dissident claims to the legitimacy of martyrs, a decision was made to import a martyr whose inherent superior status could not be denied, even in the face of the large number of local martyrs whose claim on local sentiments would have been almost irrefutable. The remains of the protomartyr Stephen, the First Martyr at the very origins of Christian blood witnessing, would provide the necessary power and ammunition. In December 415, by means of a vision a priest named Lucian who was travelling in Judaea discovered the remains of Stephen in a tomb north of Jerusalem. The Spanish priest Orosius, who had been sent by Augustine to visit Jerome at Jerusalem, returned to Hippo in midsummer 416, bringing news of the dramatic discovery and, more important, bearing some of the actual remains of the martyr.[107] Orosius intended to take some of the relics to Spain, but in the dangerous circumstances of the time he did not go that far; he stopped at Minorca and deposited the relics at Iamo.

The importation of the relics of Stephen must be deemed to be one of the success stories of the Catholic campaign in the sectarian struggles in Africa. The locations of the shrines that were subsequently built as memorials to Stephen indicate the mode of organization: cult centers were constructed at Hippo Regius, and at Castellum Sinitense and the Fundus Audurus in the rural territory of Hippo, at Calama, Uzalis, and at Aquae Thibilitanae.[108] The geographic distribution of sacred remains is like the chemical reaction that lights up and reveals the location of Augustine's coterie of friends. The bishops of these dioceses at the time of the introduction of Stephen's relics were Augustine, Possidius, Evodius, and Praeiectus: a powerful and well-connected clique. Just like Severus on Minorca, the Catholic bishops in this

---

[107] On the vision, see *Luciani ad omnem ecclesiam de revelatione corporis Stephani marytris* (PL 41: 807–18); for the mission of Orosius and the return of the relics, and the establishment of the cult, see, *inter alia*, Aug. *Ep.* 166.1.2; 169.4.13; 172.1; 175.1; 202A.1; *Sermo* 317.1; 318.1; 319.2; and 323.2; *Tract. in Ioh.* 120 (at length); and *Civ. Dei*, 22.8 f. (CCL 48: 821 f.), again at length. An overall perspective is offered by Bradbury, "St. Stephen, the Discovery of his Relics, and the Voyage to Minorca," section 4 in *Severus of Minorca*, pp. 16–25.

[108] Aug. *Sermo* 61A.5 = Wilmart 12.5 (MiAg 1: 708–09; *RBén* 79 [1969]: 182); cf. *Civ. Dei*, 13.8 (CCL 48: 390–91).

circle could now exploit the power of the relics in their long struggle. In 419 or 420, Evodius had the inflammatory cyclical letter of Severus recounting the destruction of the Jewish community read aloud to his congregation, to their enthusiastic applause. For African Catholic bishops, like Evodius, the letter revealed not so much the power of Stephen in destroying Jews as it did the power that the protomartyr might have in destroying "Jews," and how the "use of violence and the fear of violence" might well succeed.[109]

Stephen was not the only external martyr imported into Africa. The Catholic Church in Africa also celebrated the *natalitiae* of Protasius and Gervasius. A memorial to them had been built in Hippo Regius. The idea that one could deliberately manipulate the creation of a constellation of martyr shrines had been demonstrated by Ambrose in Milan when he "discovered" the remains of these two martyrs on 17 June 386.[110] In Africa, the connections used to manage these imports were the same group of bishops as had managed the import of Stephen. Augustine himself provided personal eyewitness testimony to their power:[111]

Today we are celebrating, brothers, the memorial of the saints Protasius and Gervasius, martyrs of Milan, that has been set up in this place. Not the day on which it was set up here, but the day we are celebrating today is the day when the death of these saints, precious in the sight of the Lord, was discovered by bishop Ambrose, that man of God. Of that great glory of the martyrs I myself was a witness. I was there. I was in Milan. I know the miracles that happened there . . .

So the fabricated and invented martyrs of Milan, the fictitious Protasius and Gervasius constructed by Ambrose, were brought to Africa. It is not difficult to see how this discovery, the event in Milan to which Augustine was both participant and witness, provoked in his mind, and in the minds of the close-knit group of men around him, a useful tactic for countering the force of local martyrs.[112] It had worked well for Ambrose, so why could it not also be made to work equally well at Carthage and Hippo?

There was also a concerted attempt to marshal the presence of the earliest of the apostolic martyrs, Peter and Paul. Again, these martyrs would link

---

[109] See ch. 6, n. 209 above, with the remarks of Peter Brown there.

[110] McLynn, *Ambrose of Milan*, pp. 215–16, 229–30, and 284.

[111] Aug. *Sermo* 286.5.4 (PL 38: 1299), perhaps somewhat surprising to us is his emphasis at the beginning of this sermon on the distinction to be made between true martyrs and false ones. Note also the words: "cuius tunc tantae gloriae martyrum etiam ego testis fui. Ibi eram. Mediolani eram. Facta miracula novi."

[112] Apparently, it was only later, after his return to Africa, that the importance of this staging took hold in his mind: Zangara (1981), pp. 124–25; in *Sermo* 318.1 (PL 39: 1437–38), on the *natalis* of Stephen, he makes the connection specific, noting the parallel with Protasius and Gervasius: "Sic ante aliquot annos, nobis iuvenibus apud Mediolanum constitutis, apparuerunt corpora sanctorum martyrum Gervasii et Protasii."

the cause of the Catholic Church to the Mediterranean-wide presence of these holy figures and to the metropolitan imperial city of Rome, and would enable a claim to be made of superior tradition and chronology. But it was a hard sell in Africa where the popular identification with these men as martyrs was slight. In a typical response, in a sermon preached on the feast of these "great martyrs" Augustine noted only a few souls who appeared in his church for the occasion. He was in a mood for reprimand:

we really should have been celebrating the festival of such great martyrs . . . with a much bigger crowd than this . . . in saying all of this, my beloveds, I am happy but at the same time a little sad because I don't see as big a gathering of the faithful as ought to have been assembled for the birthday celebration of the martyrdom of the apostles.[113]

Peter and Paul were a big thing in Italy, and in other parts of the eastern Mediterranean, but as a late import to Africa they failed to have the same allure.

Some of the holy transplants took root better than others. The Roman and Italian martyrs struck Africans as inferior versions of their own holy witnesses. The feast day of Laurentius, a big event at Rome, was imported to Carthage and Hippo, but with little success. In a sermon preached on the *natalitia* of the martyr, Augustine noted the patience of his parishioners at Hippo. Despite the fact that the festival of Laurentius was a tremendous occasion at Rome, and the preacher could visualize the "great concourse" in the metropolis, the occasion did not move his own flock. They presented a tableau of such boredom and restlessness that the sermon was on the verge of being cancelled. The bishop insisted on continuing to preach "out of respect for the martyr." He therefore offered a compromise: a sermon that was much cut down so as not to tax the disinterest of his audience.[114] Several decades later, matters had not improved. Augustine was compelled to note that although the martyrdom of Laurentius was famous, it was at Rome and not at Hippo. He expressed some perplexity as to why this was so, but noted, and not for the first time, the smallness of his congregation. "So," he pleads with them, "the few of you that *have* come here today please listen to just these few words."[115]

---

[113] Aug. *Sermo* 295 (PL 38: 1348–52); esp. 298.1–2 (PL 38: 1365).

[114] Aug. *Sermo* 305A.1 = Denis 13.1 (MiAg 1: 55–56).

[115] Aug. *Sermo* 303.1 (PL 38: 1393): "Beati Laurentii illustre martyrium est, sed Romae, non hic: tantam enim video vestram paucitatem. Quam non potest abscondi Roma, tam non potest abscondi Laurentii corona. Sed quare adhuc istam civitatem lateret, scire non possum. Ergo pauci audite pauca: quia et nos in hac lassitudine corporis et aestibus non possumus multa."

The Protomartyr Stephen, on the other hand, was a different matter. Laurentius was only known as a local person in Rome and central Italy. Stephen was already well known to African Christians from the holy scriptures themselves. He was *the* First Martyr of all Christianity, acceptable to all species of Christians in Africa as a martyr who arguably had a status equal to any of their own. Who knew who Laurentius was? But to know Stephen one had only to have read or to have listened to his story in the Acts of the Apostles – a tale filled with resistance, violence, and a tragic pathos.[116] And that pointed the way to another mode of refutation and management. If the Catholic Church was to claim worldwide dispersal and power as one of its core legitimating aspects, something that proved its status as the true church and which distinguished it from the severe regional peculiarity of the dissidents, then the emplacement of martyrs that unquestionably represented the universality of the Church could parallel and underwrite the claim.

The introductions of the cult of the martyrs Peter and Paul, and of John the Baptist, were surely part of this same movement. Augustine's sermons on Peter and Paul logically emphasized the worldwide nature of their cult. They were geographically located all over the Mediterranean, as opposed to the very local nature of African martyrs, where local was construed as less worthy or even bad in the same sense that "Donatism" was construed as a purely local and isolated version of Christianity. It could not be the true faith precisely because it had not implanted itself throughout the entire Mediterranean world. The same is true of the cult of John the Baptist. Catholic sermons on John also emphasize the Mediterranean-wide nature of his sainthood.[117] The new confections experienced variable success. When preaching on some of these immigrant "world martyrs," Augustine could only remark, once again, on the very low attendance of his congregation. They simply did not identify with some of the imports, including Peter and Paul, despite their good scriptural pedigree.[118] Some transplants worked while others did not. What seems to be different in the case of Stephen is the organized program by a closely linked coterie of bishops to make the cult succeed: the preaching, talking, labeling, the

---

[116] That Stephen's martyrdom had scriptural authority, as opposed to the mere human court records of "ordinary martyrs," is emphasized by Augustine, *Sermo* 315.1 (PL 39: 1426): "Hoc primum primi martyris meritum commendatum est charitati vestrae: quia cum aliorum martyrum vix gesta inveniamus, quae in sollemnitatibus eorum recitare possimus, huius passio in canonico libro est. Actus apostolorum liber est de canone scripturarum." Cf. *Sermo* 318.1 (PL 39: 1437–38).

[117] Aug. *Sermo* 293C.1 = Mai 101 (MiAg 1: 351–52).

[118] Aug. *Sermones*, 295–299C on Peter and Paul (PL 38: 1348–76); esp. *Sermo* 299.1 (PL 38: 1368) on the small audience.

recording of miracles, the production of *libelli*, and the reading of these testimonials in public, produced a communicative world in which a large number of ordinary persons could share.

Managing the successes once you had created them, however, was another matter. Success bred its own problems. The real world was never quite as the bishops represented it or as they wanted it to be. In the end, who actually controlled the agenda? Take the case of the healings at the shrine of Stephen at Hippo and the responses to them. Directing the power of the new martyrs to personal matters of the individual's salvation in spirit and body only partially succeeded. As news of the success of the martyr and his shrine spread, more and more Africans came to it to be healed, and then, in turn, spread the good news to yet others. More people came and more power accrued to the reputation of the saint. In their wild exultation after a particularly dramatic healing, people rushed into the church at Hippo and began shouting **DEO GRATIAS! DEO LAUDES!** THANKS TO GOD! PRAISE TO GOD![119] The latter words and chant, as we are repeatedly told by Catholic sources, were the well-known dissident battle cry. Were Catholics becoming dissidents? Or were dissidents becoming Catholics (This shrine really works!), but still celebrating in their old fashion? Or, more likely, was Christian behavior just much less polarized than preachers like Augustine would have us believe? Probably. There was a significant overlap of ideas about the powers of the martyrs that were shared by all Christians, and once they had plugged into them on their own, no one could prevent them from seizing upon them in their own peculiar ways.

The endurance and deaths of the martyrs were not just contemplated, memorialized, preached, and thought about. Exemplary actions were imitated. The life-story form of the narratives that told of the martyrs' suffering and triumph enabled further mimicry. Because of their narrative presence and biographical significance, the retellings and rewritings of the experiences of arrest and interrogation have been described as central to more than one culture of violence.[120] Here was the problem for the Catholic Church as it tried (and sometimes succeeded) to mobilize the instruments of state repression on its side. In his account of the violence that swept through dissident Christian communities in Africa after the mission of Macarius in 347, Optatus pinpointed its cause in the mimicry of the acts of the dissident martyrs Donatus and Marculus. Even if these men of violence were nothing but rabid dogs barking against the good call for Unity

---

[119] Aug. *Civ. Dei*, 22.8 (CCL 48: 826): "Procedimus ad populum, plena erat ecclesia, personabat vocibus gaudiorum: Deo gratias! Deo Laudes! Nam nemine tacente hinc atque inde clamantium."
[120] Compare, for example, Feldman, *Formations of Violence*, p. 85, for Northern Ireland.

and were imitators of false martyrs, their behavior caused real difficulties for the Catholic Church.[121] It was no small part of the problem that the same message of imitation was incessantly preached by the Catholics themselves, in an age that was supposedly no longer one of hard and bloody martyrdom.[122]

FACTS ON THE GROUND

The large numbers of pamphlets, debates, sermons, and canon laws about martyrs in the renewed conflict beginning in the 390s constitute a huge bank of proxy data indicating numerous and widespread sectarian deaths and martyrdoms in the conflict between the two churches. Between 390 and 430, there are reports of specifically named persons who were wounded, hurled down wells, who were blinded, who had tongues and fingers cut off, who were beaten, sometimes savagely, and brought to the point of death. For such a great conflict, however, the number of known named dead is painfully small. Allegations of much larger numbers are found throughout the literature of the period – extremists among the dissidents, for example, were said to have leapt to their deaths in mass suicides. But the enormous gap between the insistent mountain of rhetoric on death and martyrdom and the facts on the ground must cause some concern. Lists have been compiled of attested named martyrs in Africa.[123] They suggest the orders of magnitude of the numbers of named persons remembered for the persecutions between the beginning of the third century and Diocletian: about 30 in the Decian persecution of 250; about 45 in the Valerianic persecution of 258–59; and about 70 in the Great Persecution under Diocletian.[124] By contrast, for all sectarian violence in Africa of the next century and more, from Constantine to the death of Augustine, only about *fifteen*

---

[121] Optatus, *Contra Parm.* 3.6.1 (SC 213: 48–50). [122] Aug. *Sermo* 64A.1 = Mai 20 (MiAg 1: 310).

[123] The lists assembled by Monceaux are used here, despite the caveats that the literary sources systematically included by him certainly include dubious instances. Although the epigraphical cases are better catalogued by Duval, *Loca sanctorum*, and they record martyrs whose year-dates are mostly unknown, it is Monceaux, "Martyrs et confesseurs africains mentionnés par les auteurs, les actes de martyrs, le calendrier de Carthage et les martyrologes," appendix 2 in *Hist. litt.* 3, pp. 536–51, that is used here. Despite the flaws and criticisms, the general picture that emerges is sufficient for our purpose.

[124] The numbers, as I count them, are: Septimius Severus (12 certain + 4 possible) 16; Decius: 30; Valerian (33 certain + 11 possible): 44; Maximian: 11; Diocletian (50 in 303–04 CE; + 13 in other years + 8 possible): 71. Of course, these numbers are subject to criticism (many suspect cases might be deleted; the cases are surely only the known and reported ones, and so on), but the *order* of the violence suggested by the reportage is reasonably clear.

such cases are known.[125] More importantly, for the entire period between 390 and 430 covered by this study, a meager *five* named instances are on record.

When speaking of deaths and lethal injuries inflicted in the sectarian conflicts in the period, it must be borne in mind how very little evidence there is concerning either. What we in fact are dealing with are current debates and a severely constrained localization of memory that in no fashion left a record behind that was of a quality similar to the pre-Constantinian state-driven persecutions of Christian communities. There is no doubt that each side had its martyrs. But the four martyrs in our period on the dissident side are ones whom we know about only because a local event in the town of Madauros happened to leave a trace in Augustine's letters.[126] Much emphasis is placed on dissident deaths and cult, but there were martyrs on the Catholic side and they too must have been made the object of local memory and worship. We happen to possess one of them because of the accidental preservation of another small piece of Augustine's poetry. Some years after composing his *Song Against the Donatists*, he returned to the powerful device of song and verse, and to the mnemonic and stylish device of the acrostic, to preserve in memory the death of a Catholic martyr. The verse was meant to mark the gravesite of the deceased, a deacon named Nabor who had been killed by his sectarian enemies.[127]

> **D** onatists with cruel slaughter murdered this man.
> **I** nterred here, with pious praise, is the body of Nabor.
> **A** little time before he had been with the Donatists.
> **C** onverted, he loved the peace for which he died.
> **O** n his body, clothed with purple blood, for the best of causes
> **N** ot for error did he die, not in madness did he kill himself.
> **U** nder the banner of true piety, he proved his true martyrdom.
> **S** elect the first letters of these lines – there you find his rank.

> **D** onatistarum crudeli caede peremptum
> **I** nfossum hic corpus pia est cum laude Nabori

---

[125] This also closely matches the total numbers claimed by Duval, *Loca sanctorum*, 2, pp. 487–89: "On connaît en tout, pour les deux églises et toutes sources confondues, qu'une dizaine de noms entre 317 et 434!" (note her exclamation mark).

[126] That is the Miggin, Saname, Lucitas, and Namphamo attested in a circumcellion attack on "pagan" shrines at Madauros at some time in the early 390s: see ch. 5, pp. 235–38.

[127] ICUR 2.461; ILAlg 1.88; cf. Duval, *Local sanctorum*, 1, no. 89, pp. 182–83. Knoell (CSEL 33: 1) wishes to date the poem much later (to the sixth or seventh centuries), but I can see no reason, given the language and the context, to doubt the ascription – *versus s(an)c(t)i Augustini episcopi* – found at the head of the poem.

A nte aliquot tempus cum donatista fuisset
C onversus pacem pro qua moreretur amavit.
O ptima purpureo vestitus sanguine causa.
N on errore perit non se ipse furore peremit
V erum martyrum vera est pietate probatum
S uscipe litterulas primas; ibi nomen honoris.

In his attempt to popularize the name of the martyr Nabor, Augustine used a pop verse-song form, as he had in his song in the early 390s against "the Donatists," that he knew would draw the eyes and be retained in the memory of large numbers of ordinary people. The acrostic of the name of Nabor's rank, that of deacon – **D – I – A – C – O – N – U – S –** would assist the memory of those who wished to sing the song and wanted to remember their own Catholic martyr. Nabor was certainly a victim of circumcellion enforcement. He was another crossover: he had converted. He was a marked man – someone who was seen by them as a traitor. The cruelty of the slaughter with which they murdered him is marked. But almost the same words of praise could be used by the dissidents of their own heroes.[128] Our problem, given the lack of evidence, is to say how many Namphamos and Nabors there were, as opposed to how much rhetorical construction of them and their numbers.

EXEMPLARY BEHAVIOR?

Imitation was at the core, imitation that was constantly encouraged not just in Christian ideals, but also in general cultural values. The insistent comparison of the martyr with the athlete or the competitor who had struggled and who had emerged victorious was a powerful simile. Young men behaved according to the models set by both. The *agonistici* or the dissident fighters who struggled on behalf of their faith were surely part of this system of values. The virtues required by the contests in which they fought were not substantially different from those of secular games: striving, winning, dying, and then eternal glory. The overpowering presence of the hippodrome and the amphitheater, and their factional organizations, for Christian youths fed directly into parallel kinds of behavior. The competitive virtues were so deeply ingrained that African poets celebrated them for well over a century after Augustine's death. In the later Vandal age in

---

[128] Compare the description of the death of dissident holy woman Robba in 434, "caede...vexata": ch. 17, n. 75.

Africa, the poet Luxorius praised the feats of one Olympius, a *venator* in the arena at Carthage.[129]

> O Beast-hunter – you who brought us great joy and
> whose skill against wild animals often pleased us –
> powerful, swift, charming, brave, and daring – you who,
> as a boy, had not yet advanced to the age of a youth,
> finished all your hard work with a grown man's skill.
> You could easily win popular praise for your own feats,
> but you offered the chance to others to share in your victory.
> So great were the rewards of your wonderful form that
> after your death your companions still stand in awe and praise you.
> Now this tomb holds you, suddenly carried off by envious death – you
> whom, with your triumphs in the amphitheater, the walls of Carthage
> itself could not contain.
> You have lost nothing to the underworld with this bitter death!
> The fame of your glory will last after you forever!
> Carthage will always speak you name!

An honorable death that produced eternal fame and glory: this was *the* great reward open to every talent. It only required the will to suffer and to die in a stylish cause and in a public venue. A death in sectarian struggle was one that bestowed great honor on the deceased; his or her death in holy battle was to be recompensed not just by eternal life, but eternal life *with power*. They were like the Constantinus, a Christian man from the town of Mactaris, who died "overcoming the madness of his enemies with the victory of the faith," through his spirit, his mind, and his body.[130] The enemies that he had beaten were not just any ones: they and their hatreds were deeply *personal*. So, his epitaph announces, Constantinus will rule with Christ through the ages.

Because suffering and death in the name of the truth automatically made one a martyr, this power was even more democratic than the fame of the arena. The peculiar merging of popular and transcendent values and behavior created a problem with the coercive repression of religious

---

[129] Luxorius, 68 (Rosenblum: 150–52) = *Anthologia Latina*, 1.1, no. 349 (= Riese, 354 = Shackleton-Bailey, no. 349, pp. 274–75); the power of the ideal might well have been more imaginary than a matter of practice in the Vandal age, see Miles (2005). This poem is presented as the tombstone inscription of Olympius, who is lauded for his bravery, speed, and the palms of victory that he won in *Anth. Lat.* 1.1, no. 348 (= Riese, no. 353 = Shackleton-Bailey, no. 148, pp. 273–74).

[130] Prévot, *Inscriptions chrétiennes*, no. II.1, pp. 22–27 (figs. 12–13) = AE 1946: 115 (Mactaris): "Animo, mente, corporeque Constantinus ... / rabiem inimicorum tropeo fidei vincens, / cum Chr(ist)o fidelis per s(a)ecula regnaturus." The inscription is part of a mosaic embedded in the floor of the nave of Basilica II.

dissent. If physical violence was used to break the back of resistance, it ran the real risk of creating more martyrs. Acutely aware of the problem, Augustine and his fellow-bishops several times backed off supporting the full rigor of anti-heretical laws applied to dissident Christians in Africa. The imperial laws that were issued in the aftermath of the great council of Carthage in 411 had called for the coercive repression of the dissident church. In a letter to Marcellinus' brother, Apringius, in 412, Augustine was openly concerned about the death penalties that would be inflicted on circumcellions who had been arrested and held liable for their acts of violence against Catholic clerics. He urged, instead, a careful manipulation of the convicted: their confessions were to be put on the record and these court records were to be read aloud to audiences throughout Africa to prove their guilt. Beyond this, Augustine preferred that the "savage men" would be set free to demonstrate the mildness and charity of the Catholic Church.[131] In a later letter to Marcellinus, he stated that if the tribune should decide to behead the guilty, Augustine still wanted his own letters appealing for clemency to be placed in the court record, thereby constructing a firewall between the desires of the Catholic Church and the secular authority carrying out the punishments.[132]

The blood witnessing for God and his laws was embroiled in a continuous debate over meaning and action. How aggressive could potential martyrs become before some persons, even within the Christian community, would be moved to condemn them as a species of vain self-murderers? Just where along that spectrum could the active use of violence against others be justified by the larger concerns of defending not just God's laws in time of persecution, but the integrity and core values of one's own community? If aggressive suicidal attacks that would cause casualties among sectarian enemies were envisioned, there were biblical texts, such as the story of Samson, that could have been produced in support. But there are few indications that they ever were so used.[133] The avoidance must have been deliberate, since the story of Samson was well known. Ambrose had

---

[131] Aug. *Ep.* 134 (CCL 31B: 245–48); cf. *Ep.* 133.   [132] Aug. *Ep.* 139 (CCL 31B: 291–94).

[133] Augustine does not seriously consider the Samson episode (Judges 16: 23–31) in the course of his analysis of suicide in Book One of the *Civ. Dei* (1.21), other than to claim, derived in part from the Platonic Socrates, that his death was only permitted because of a divine directive (for which, alas, there is no evidence), nor does he connect Samson's death with behavior that he was confronting in Africa. In any event, the "excuse" or "reason" was rational, in the sense that the emperor, too, could provide precisely such exemptions based on a direct order.

commented on it favorably.[134] One of the pervasive criticisms of Christian martyrdom was that it could seen as nothing other than a willful self-destruction, a kind of murder.[135] As early as about 200, in the aftermath of some of the first broadly celebrated martyrdoms, Clement of Alexandria represented a more skeptical and critical point of view, condemning those persons who did not merely resist the inroads of persecutors, but actually solicited their attention and ostentatiously confronted authorities so as to goad them into inflicting death on themselves. In his eyes, these "athletes of death," as Clement named them, were not martyrs, but rather accomplices with the persecutors. They were not genuine Christians, but immoral poseurs who "only borrowed the name" (i.e. of martyr).[136]

But almost all martyrdoms did involve some element of voluntary assent on the part of the martyr himself or herself: they chose consciously not to do things that otherwise would have saved themselves. That element of complicity, on which Clement chose to focus, was always a potential source of debate over what was reasonable behavior on the part of a Christian. The potential martyr must not be seen to be courting death too eagerly. To be agonistic in this sense was a bad thing, and yet it is precisely by this name – *agonistici* – that the dissident circumcellions, and others like them, named themselves. And there is the category of suicide, to which Augustine avers several times, that was very frightening for those who were its object: deliberate aggressive assaults – on imperial and local officials, wayfarers, and others – whose purpose was to get the person who was confronted to return the violence and in so doing to kill the attacker. Such debates whirled about the violent Christian enforcers of the period in both churches and represented one face of the struggles over power and property. The other face was a more calculating series of plans about the

---

[134] Ambrose, *Ep.* 62.31–32 (CSEL 82.2: 141). In a long letter attempting to dissuade a bishop from permitting a marriage between a pagan and a Christian, Ambrose praises the nature of Samson's death: "tamen in mortem se ipsum vicit et insuperabilem gessit animum, ut contemneret et quasi nihilo haberet vitae finem omnibus formidolosum."

[135] There have been many recent treatments of the subject, some of them used by Droge and Tabor, "The Crown of Immortality," ch. 5 in *A Noble Death*, pp. 129–65, esp. pp. 138–52 on "voluntary martyrdom"; but the analysis by de Ste. Croix, "Voluntary Martyrdom in the Early Church," ch. 4 in *Christian Persecution, Martyrdom, and Orthodoxy*, pp. 153–200, is still fundamental in its systematic laying out of the evidence. His two basic points are that the practice was not found just in Africa, but in all regions and periods of early Christian history, and that it occasioned debate at least from Clement onwards.

[136] Clement, *Strom.* 4.16.3–17.3 (GCS, ed. O. Stählin, rev. L. Früchtel, Berlin, 1960), 256: εἰσὶ γάρ τινες οὐχ ἡμέτεροι, μόνου τοῦ ὀνόματος κοινωνοί, οἳ δὴ αὐτοὺς παραδιδόναι σπεύδουσι τῇ πρὸς τὸν δημιουργὸν ἀπεχθείᾳ, οἱ ἄθλιοι θανατῶντες. Clement goes on to say that they give themselves to a vain death in the manner of the Indian gymnosophists; cf. Droge and Tabor, *Noble Death*, pp. 141–44.

uses to which the sanctified violence of the *agonistici* could be put. Just as relenting on the capital punishment of sectarian murderers could be spun as a new mode of Christian charity, the very existence of the violent men like these could be used to move the state to action. The sectarian fighters themselves, however, were moved neither by the debates nor by the lobbying, but rather by deliberate provocation, a sense of duty, and the call to action

CHAPTER 14

Bad boys

As far as Catholics were concerned, the most feared agents in the sectarian violence of the time were wandering bands of men and women whom they called "circumcellions."[1] The involvement of circumcellion gangs in the religious violence of the age is a well-documented phenomenon. These armed enforcers damaged and destroyed property and physically harmed the persons of their hated sectarian enemies, sometimes even killing them. The circumcellions were emblematic of violence not only for their contemporaries, but also for historians of our own day. The modern literature on them has accumulated into a mountain of scholarly invention.[2] The circumcellions have been variously seen by historians as peasant revolutionaries, as the spearhead of a late antique jacquerie that swept the countryside of Africa, or as wandering ascetic monks of violent disposition who worshiped at the shrines of their models, the martyrs of the dissident cause. More generally, they are seen as simple religious fanatics who were devoted to violent, sometimes suicidal, attacks on their enemies or, worse, who engaged in mad mass suicidal self-killings of themselves. Whatever the construal of their motives or origins, circumcellions are usually

---

[1] There exists a considerable body of ancient primary source material on the circumcellions. A significant part of the corpus of evidence that has been used by modern historians, however, was produced by writers from outside of Africa. I have argued that all of this external evidence is largely fictitious, and that it is sometimes highly misleading on the nature of the circumcellions (Shaw, 2004 and 2006). In no case where these external sources contain dependable data do they have any authority independent of the original African sources. Any use of these external sources is therefore avoided in making the present arguments. Finally, there is a long historiography on the problem of the circumcellions which I do not wish to repeat here; for a *summa* of these earlier interpretations, see Appendix F.

[2] The bibliography on this aspect of the sectarian violence is considerable and continues to grow. The main treatments are: Frend, *Donatist Church*, passim, but esp. pp. 171–78 and 248–63; (1952), (1969); Büttner (1956) and *Circumcellionen*; Brisson, *Autonomisme et christianisme*, pp. 325–55; Diesner (1957), (1959), (1960a and 1960b), (1962e); Tengström, *Donatisten und Katholiken*, pp. 24–78; encyclopaedic surveys have been offered by Byrne (1997), Ferron (1953), Julicher (1899), Lancel (1994), Lepelley (1992b), Martroye (1914b), and De Veer (1968k), among others.

portrayed as wandering groups of hardened men closely attached to the dissident church who vented their sectarian hatreds in violent attacks on Catholics.

Despite these confident modern pictures (some of them elaborate and detailed) and as central as the circumcellions are to the reconstruction of the sectarian violence of the time, there are severe limits on what can be known about them. Were it not for literary sources, mainly Augustine's rhetorical attacks on them, and a single lone reference in our legal sources, the cold fact is that little or nothing would be known about them.[3] If we depended on these other sources, they would not be in our histories of the time. They have left no discernible trace in any material remains – that is, in the archaeological record – or in the many kinds of written texts that have been preserved from the period that are strewn with references to the religious life of the age. In the rich mother lode of tens of thousands of Latin epigraphical texts from Africa, for example, the circumcellions simply do not exist.[4] The plain fact is that from the very beginning these sectarian gangsters were an ideological construct which lived on in precise kinds of writings and nowhere else. The way that they exist in these specific texts, and in no others, makes sense, since name-calling was central to the quarrels of the time. To label any group of persons as "circumcellions" was most of the point of writing about them. An equally significant aspect of the problem is that the violent men never once referred to themselves as circumcellions or conceived of themselves as such.

WHO WERE THE CIRCUMCELLIONS?

Because of basic factual difficulties like these, the general picture of the circumcellions has come to assume different classic guises. Some have said that they were large bands of unemployed and landless men who were produced by the increasing immiseration of late Roman Africa. Their ranks

---

[3] The other literary sources, the specifics of which will be noted as required, include some references in the records of the African church councils, a notice in Optatus, and another in Possidius' biography of Augustine. There are a fair number of other non-African literary sources, but, as stated above, I have argued elsewhere that these are quite undependable and so their evidence will not be used here: see Shaw (2004) and (2006).

[4] There is a single possible epigraphical text to which reference is frequently made. It is an inscription of a *Donatus mile(s) X* [Christi?] (Henchir Bou Saïd, *NAMS* 17 [1909], p. 172) – the caption above the relief sculpture of a man whose right hand is in chains and above whose left side there appears a baton-like object (Martroye [1914b], p. 1705, fig. 2975). I do not know quite what to make of the tombstone relief, but I do not think that it has any connection with circumcellions. Further, see Appendix G for a refutation of Frend's claim that archaeological and epigraphical evidence exists for circumcellion suicides.

were swelled with impoverished peasants who had lost their land. Men who were poor and resourceless, runaway slaves, along with the odd criminal or social outcast, are said to have constituted the core of their ranks. As the down-and-outs of their age, it is only natural that they were attracted to the rebellious schismatic brand of Christianity represented by the dissident church. In the increasingly harsh conflicts that developed between the two churches over the course of the fourth and early fifth centuries, they coalesced into violent gangs led by the priests and bishops of the dissident church. In various descriptions, they are "the strange revolutionary fringe of Donatism" – men who would be regarded as "terrorists" today, having much the same structural relationship to a rebellious movement as the Irgun had to the Zionist movement in Palestine in the late 1940s.[5] Frequently referred to as "religious fanatics" and in more colorful terms as the "storm troopers of Donatism," they are portrayed as the violent arm of "the Donatist church" – in much in the same way that the IRA Provos have been related to Sinn Fein, or other such dimorphic liberation movements that divide into armed and political wings. From the beginning of the division of African Christians into two hostile camps, these rough men provided armed force for the dissidents in their sometimes violent confrontations with their Catholic adversaries.[6] This is one modern picture of the circumcellions.

For others, the sectarian aspects and actions of the circumcellions are interpreted as surface expressions of more fundamental forces that are believed to have created them. It is frequently argued that they constituted a great groundswell of a mass social movement of the impoverished and resentful rural lower classes.[7] They are likened to other movements of popular revindication that are believed to have proliferated across the landscape of the western provinces of the later empire in its final crisis. Frequent comparisons are made with the Bagaudae of late Roman Gaul, who are similarly interpreted as proto-social revolutionaries fighting for a more just social order.[8] If the circumcellions were religious fanatics driven, on occasion, by a suicidal rage to seek self-inflicted martyrdom, this behavior is interpreted as a form of extreme personal transcendence through which they protested the injustices and social outrages of the age. Despite their apparent religious motives and culture, their desperate acts of violence are

---

[5] Frend, *Donatist Church*, pp. 171–72.

[6] Frend, *Donatist Church*, p. 173: "storm troopers"; Warmington, *The North African Provinces*, p. 86.

[7] Popular circumcellion "movement": Baldwin (1961), pp. 3, 5; Atkinson (1992), p. 489.

[8] For example, Martroye (1914b), col. 1694–95; Baldwin (1951), p. 3; Brisson, *Autonomisme et christianisme*, pp. 341 n.1, 350 n.1; Rubin (1995), pp. 137–56, and the argument that follows; and, more recently, Wickham, *Framing the Early Middle Ages*, pp. 530–32, and Cacitti, *Furiosa turba*, p. 5.

interpreted to be a kind of inchoate rage directed against the oppression of the powerful and the wealthy. The circumcellions, it is argued, linked their oppression with Catholic landlords because these landowners were identified with the imperial order that enabled the exploitation of the poor. Attacks on the possessions and property of rich Catholic landowners were therefore attempts to enforce social revindication and to institute a new and more just social order.[9]

Beyond the religious interpretations of the circumcellions as sectarian fanatics on the one hand and secular explanations of them as primitive rebels on the other (or some combination of the two) there is not much more that has been offered by historians. These convenient interpretations, however, seem to be rather suspect. Although some of these characteristics are true of the sectarian gangs of late antique Africa, for the most part this broad-brush general picture of them is misleading. There are other aspects of this complex phenomenon that beg for closer inspection. In what way were they connected with the power struggles of the time? More precisely, how were they located in the intricate and complicated factors that linked local episodes of collective violence with the politics of Christian churches and the Roman state? Attention to these questions immediately reveals the process of labeling to be as important as any social reality in which the identity of the circumcellions was anchored. Like "the Donatists" with whom they were so closely identified, "the circumcellions" appear and disappear from the historical record and from perceived realities in ways that provoke questions about who they were and about their relationship to the sectarian violence of the age.

WHAT'S IN A NAME?

Despite all the detailed historical work that has already been done, it is still worth posing a basic question: Who were the circumcellions? An approach to an answer is helped by making a simple but fundamental difference between a special sectarian use of the word "circumcellion" and the wider more general phenomenon to which the word normally referred in the African Latin of the time. The word *circumcellio* was a term of popular origin that was common in the spoken Latin of the African countryside, but which suddenly surfaces for the first time in our existing written sources

---

[9] For example, G. E. M. de Ste. Croix, *The Class Struggle in the Ancient Greek World*, Ithaca NY, Cornell University Press, 1981, pp. 480–82.

in the 360s.[10] That the word is only found in the Latin spoken in Africa is hardly surprising since the specific combination of characteristics that created circumcellions was peculiar to the region.[11] Many guesses have been made about the origins of the word. Needless to say, even if agreement could be reached on a true etymology, it would not necessarily tell us very much about contemporary usage. All that can reasonably be claimed is that the word began to assume a new and special meaning over the latter part of the fourth century. In the religious discourse of the time, it came to be used to designate certain persons, always acting in groups or gangs, who were implicated in the organized sectarian violence of the age. But the wider normal existing use of the word in the language of the Latin speakers in Africa must be understood if we are to see how it came to be selected and to be used in a special sense in the religious-speak of the fourth century. At the core of this meaning was the coordination of labor, whether normal or violent.

The earliest instance of the term "circumcellion" that survives in our written records is found in Optatus' description of the violent events of the 340s, including the mission of Paul and Macarius in 347. This is their first appearance in the events of the age.[12] Importantly for our purposes, these first notices of the term suggest a wider antecedent non-sectarian meaning of the word. It is manifest that the word "circumcellions" (here, as later, always in the plural) was used by Latin-speakers in Africa to designate laborers who gathered at rural periodic markets in search of seasonal agricultural employment. Even for the first attested usage of the word, a number of aspects can be noted. It is a term in the local argot that is never found outside of Africa. The word was coined locally either

---

[10] Other external labels are sometimes used for these men, such as *cotopitai* or *cutzupitae* (see Shaw [2004], pp. 252–55, with reference to earlier bibliography); the Greek translation of the canons of the Catholic Church of Carthage refers to them as *parasyagontes* (*Codex canonum ecclesiae Africa*, 93 [ed. Hardouin]: *Conc. Coll*, t. 1, p. 916); the term was usually used to designate an "illegal gathering" of some kind: see H. Stephanus, *Thesaurus Graecae Linguae* 6, Paris, Firmin Didot, 1842–47, p. 399.

[11] Aug. *Ad Cath. contra Donat*. 16.41 (CSEL 52: 286): "quam in turbis inquietis furiosorum circumcellionum, quod malum Africae proprium est!" (in the context of the discussion of the nature of Africa).

[12] The efforts by Lancel (1967) – accepted, for example, by Cacitti, *Furiosa turba*, pp. 11–13 – and others, going back to Monceaux, *Hist. litt*. 4, p. 179, to find earlier appearances of the circumcellions in our records going back to the very beginning of the schism do not convince; the same applies to the efforts of Diesner (1962c) to provide a periodization of circumcellion activity, beginning with phases before the early 340s. They might well have been mobilized earlier in the inter-church struggle, but there is no evidence. Mastandrea has edited part of the text of the *Passio Isaac et Maximiani* (3.18; Mastandrea [1995], pp. 77–78) to read *peregrini* rather than *perenne*, and Cacitti, *Furiosa turba*, pp. 9–10, has argued that these 'peregrini' were wandering circumcellions. I am not convinced.

as a Latin translation or equivalent of an indigenous term, or one that was simply constructed from the Latin elements *circum* ("around") and *cella*. In the single most explicit passage concerning the name, Augustine states:[13]

Nevertheless, they [i.e. the heretics/the Donatists] have been accustomed to say: "Why would anyone want the name of 'monk' for himself?" Then how much better is it for us to say: "Why would anyone want the name of *circellion* for himself?" "But no," they say, "they are *not* called *circellions*." Perhaps we're calling them this name because we are mangling the pronunciation? Do we have to be told by you the full and correct form of their name? Perhaps they *are* called "cir*cum*cellions" and not "circellions." Plainly, if they are called by this name, then let them explain what they are. They are called "circumcellions" because they wander "around *cellae*": they are accustomed to go here and there, having no fixed homes. What they *actually* do, you know full well. And *they* know it too, whether they want to or not.

A little later in this same sermon, Augustine expatiates on the name of "circumcellion" as it was used to label the violent enforcers of the dissidents, revealing that it is a derogatory term, and that, because of its nasty connotations, the sectarian fighters never used this name of themselves.[14]

What do those people say who insult us about the name of "monks"? Perhaps they will say: "Our men are *not* called 'circumcellions' – it's *you* who call them by this insulting name. *We* do *not* call them by this name." Then let them say what they do call them and you'll listen. They call these men "fighters" – *agonistici*. So let's agree to call them by this honorable name, if it fits the facts. But in the meantime let Your Sanctities [i.e. the members of Augustine's congregation] consider this:

---

[13] Aug. *En. in Ps.* 132.3 (CCL 40: 1928): "Sed tamen dicere consueverunt: Quid sibi vult nomen monachorum? Quanto melius dicimus nos: Quid sibi vult nomen circellionum? Sed non, inquiunt, vocantur circelliones. Forte corrupto sono nominis eos appellamus. Dicturi sumus vobis integrum nomen ipsorum? Forte circumcelliones vocantur, non circelliones. Plane si hoc vocantur, exponant quid sint. Nam circumcelliones dicti sint, quia circum cellas vagantur; solent enim ire hac illac, nusquam habentes sedes; et facere quae nostis, et quae illi norunt, velint, nolint." He repeats much the same definition in *Contra Gaud.* 1.28.32 (CSEL 53: 231): "maxime in agris territans, ab agris vacans et victus sui causa cellas circumiens rusticanas, unde et circumcellionum nomen accepit, universo mundo paene famosissimum Africani erroris opprobrium?"

[14] Aug. *En. in Ps.* 132.6 (CCL 40: 1930–31): "Quid ergo dicunt illi qui nobis de nomine monachorum insultant? Fortasse dicturi sunt: Nostri non vocantur circumcelliones: vos illos ita appellatis contumelioso nomine; nam nos eos ita non vocamus. Dicant quid eos vocent, et audietis. Agonisticos eos vocant. Fatemur et nos honesto nomine, si et res conveniret. Sed interim illud videat Sanctitas Vestra: qui nobis dicunt: Ostendite ubi scriptum sit nomen monachorum, ostendant ubi scriptum sit nomen agonisticorum. Sic eos, inquiunt, appellamus propter agonem. Certant enim; et dicit apostolus: *Certamen bonum certavi*. Quia sunt qui certant adversus Diabolum, et praevalent, milites Christi agonistici appellantur, utinam ergo milites Christi essent, et non milites Diaboli, a quibus plus timetur, Deo Laudes, quam fremitus leonis . . . Sed certe reddidistis rationem de nomine, quare appelletis agonisticos. Ita fiat, ut appellatis; ita fiat, omnino favemus. Praestet Dominus ut illi contra Diabolum certent, et non contra Christum, cuius persequuntur ecclesiam. Tamen quia certant, dicitis agonisticos; et invenistis unde appelletis, quia dixit apostolus: *Bonum agonem certavi*."

To those who say, "Show us where the name 'monks' is found in the scriptures," let *them* show us where they find the name "fighters." If they say, "That's what we call them because of their fight – because they fight and the Apostle [sc. Paul] says: 'I have fought the good fight.' Because they are the ones who fight against the Devil, and prevail, those who, as soldiers of Christ, are called fighters" . . . Well, you certainly have offered a good explanation of their name, of why you call them "fighters." So let it be as you say. Let it be. We wholly support you. The Lord Himself has so called those who fight against the Devil, but not [sc. those who fight] against Christ, whose Church *they* persecute. Nevertheless, because they fight, you call them "fighters" and you have found a source to quote because the apostle has said, "I have fought the good fight."

So the word "circumcellion" was a part of colloquial African Latin, and it had a rather bad ring to it. It makes sense that the dissident sectarian enforcers did not wish to use the word to describe themselves, but preferred to be called *agonistici*. The pejorative meaning of "circumcellion" explains their preference in part. In the language of the settled and civilized persons in the towns, to say that someone was a *circumcellio* immediately raised unpleasant connotations, much as if today one were to call someone a panhandler, a vagrant, or a drifter – that is, homeless transients with no fixed resources.

In his discussion of the word *circumcellio*, Augustine makes it reasonably clear what he understands the term to mean. Circumcellions had come to have this name because they "hung out" around *cellae* and because they migrated or traveled from one *cella* to another. They did this in order to acquire their sustenance or the basics of their daily maintenance.[15] The dispute is over the precise nature of the *cellae* around which the circumcellions circulated and from which they took their name. It has been claimed that these *cellae* were either granaries or storage places associated with holy places or martyr shrines, or that they were in fact the martyr shrines themselves.[16] If true, it would mean that the circumcellions in general were primarily a religious phenomenon, persons who were defined by special sacral interests and that they derived their name from the fact that they tended to "hang out" around holy places like the sacred shrines of martyrs. But there is absolutely no warrant for such a view in the sources that are absolutely consistent in the meaning that they attribute to *cellae*.

Apart from two mentions in Optatus, the one large body of evidence on the circumcellions is provided by the voluminous writings of Augustine,

---

[15] Aug. *Contra Gaud.* 1.28.32 (CSEL 53: 231): "ab agris vacans et victus sui causa cellas circumiens rusticanas, unde et circumcellionum nomen accepit . . ."
[16] Frend (1952), pp. 87–89.

and his consistent use of the word *cella* is to designate a storage room. A *cella* is *never* used by him to designate a separate granary building, but rather for a structure that was part of an existing villa or rural habitation. Furthermore, the African writer who is the main source for the technical term "circumcellion" *never once* uses the word *cella* in the sense of a martyr's shrine. Although the word might on occasion mean nothing more than a room in a house, Augustine's use of the term assumes that the listener or reader understands a *cella* to be a storage room ordinarily used for the stocking of wine.[17] Sometimes the form *cellarium* (like the modern "cellar") is used, but with the same meaning of a storage chamber or room, only a smaller one.[18] He also assumes that on larger farms and villa complexes these *cellae* or cellars were often under the charge of a *cellarius*, the man who was in charge of the wine stores of the household.[19] When Augustine uses a word to designate a storage place for grain or grain-type foodstuffs, his usage is quite consistent and different: he designates such barns, silos, and granaries as *horrea*. So far as *cellae* are concerned, he several times specifically separates them from *horrea*, stating that *cellae* are for the storage of wine whereas *horrea* are for the storage of cereal grains.[20] The question then becomes more precise: Why would seasonal laborers "hang out" around wine cellars? The question is easily answered and the answer makes perfectly good sense given the usual terms and conditions according to which such laborers were employed. Occasional or seasonal workers of the kind to which the circumcellions belonged were often colloquially named after their place of employment or pay, as, for example, the *kolōnetai* of classical Athens were men who were hired on a daily basis at the *agora kolōnetos*.[21] This raises the question of what work and what pay were normally involved so as to give the circumcellions their name.

The nature of the work in which circumcellions were normally engaged has long been debated, but it is surely beyond reasonable doubt that they

---

[17] The following are only exemplary: as a room in a house: *En. 2 in Ps.* 48.7 (CCL 38: 571); wine storage: *Quaest. in Hept.* 2.109 (CCL 33: 123); *En. in Ps.* 8.1–2 (CCL 38: 50): "quo vel frumenta in horrea vel vina in cellas segregentur . . . velut quodam lacu excipiatur . . . tamquam de lacu in cellas"; storage room: *Sermo* 32 (CCL 41: 482); *Sermo* 169 (PL 38: 924): metaphoric; *Sermo* 231 (SC 116: 256): metaphoric.

[18] Aug. *Confess.* 1.19; cf. 9.8 (CCL 27: 10 and 24); *Ep.* 36.13 (CSEL 34.2: 61); *Spec.* 27 (CSEL 12: 189): "considerate corvos quia non seminant neque metiunt, quibus non est cellarium neque horreum"; as only a small cupboard or storeroom: *En. in Ps.* 62.10 (CCL 39: 800).

[19] Aug. *Ep.* 211.12–13 (CSEL 57: 365–68); *En. in Ps.* 62.10 (CCL 39: 800); *Reg. Tert. seu Praecept.* 139, 182, 186 (PL 32: 428, 432).

[20] Aug. *En. in Ps.* 8.1 (CCL 38: 49): "quo vel frumenta in horrea vel vina in cellas segregentur" (the difference being reinforced in the details of the preceding parts of the passage).

[21] See, e.g., Fuks (1951) on the *kolōnetai* at Athens.

were habitually engaged in labor that made sense of their name. They were mainly itinerant harvesters and persons who performed other kinds of seasonal rural labor. On the basis of not much more than some reported places of their activities – deep in the high plains of Numidia – and the use by the sectarian circumcellions of wooden clubs as instruments of violence, it has been postulated that their employment was specifically the harvesting of olives.[22] No source explicitly says as much, and both of the bases used to reach this conclusion can easily be challenged. First of all, there is the range of environments in which circumcellions were normally found. They were found in locales distributed across the face of Africa. Attested examples of their activities come from locales around the metropolis of Carthage in the east to lands near Calama and Sitifis in the west – and from coastal ports in the north to villages and rural lands in southern Numidia. There is plenty of evidence for their presence in locations throughout the diocese of Hippo, most of these places being in close proximity to the Mediterranean coast.[23] There is no good reason to think of circumcellion work peculiarly or necessarily restricted to southern Numidia or to any one agricultural crop. The clubs that they used to beat and injure their sectarian enemies might well have been harvesting implements. But there is no suggestion in any source that these were the normal or the only tools of their work. Nor were they necessarily the same as the long thin rods, called *baculae*, that were used for harvesting olives for which, again, there is no evidence.

HARVESTERS OF THE LORD

As seasonal harvest workers, circumcellions might have been involved in harvesting grapes and olives, but the main crops that they reaped were cereal grains like wheat and barley. Augustine confirms as much in his sermons when he indulges in agricultural metaphors in which it is clear that he and his listeners knew the basic identity of these men. His casual references assume that the normal work done by the circumcellions was taking off

---

[22] Tengström, "Die Circumcellionen," ch. 1 in *Donatisten und Katholiken*, pp. 24–78, at pp. 48–52; for a good critique, see Schulten, *De Circumcellionen*, pp. 6–26, arguing, correctly I think, against both Tengström and Saumagne, that one cannot read the CTh law too literally to argue that all of them were of free status (i.e. some of them might well be recruited from the ranks of *coloni*); the analysis is marred, however, by too ready an acceptance of evidence said to come from Tyconius (on which, see Shaw [2004], pp. 251–55).

[23] Diesner (1960b), pp. 497–508 = *Kirche und Staat*, pp. 78–90, assembled the specific data.

the cereal harvest. In a circular letter addressed to "you Donatists," he drew the precise parallel.[24]

He [sc. Jesus] Himself said: Allow both to continue to grow until the time of the harvest. He did not say: Let the weeds grow, let the cereal grains not grow. He said: The field is this world. He did not say: The field is Africa. He said: The harvest is the end of the age. He did not say: The harvest is the age of Donatus. He said: The harvesters are the angels; He did not say: the harvesters are the foremen, the *principes*, of the circumcellions.

In a later sermon, he reiterated this same description of the circumcellions as gangs of hired harvesters.[25]

He [the potential Christian convert] finds the Lord in the parable of the field of weeds when he says: *The field is this world.* Note: the field is not Africa, but this world. The grain is found throughout the whole world, weeds are found throughout the whole world – nevertheless, *the field is the world, the sower is the Son of Man, and the harvesters, the* messores, *are the angels*, they are *not* the foremen, the *principes*, of the circumcellions. Both grain and weeds are to grow until the time of the harvest, not the weeds to grow and the grain not to grow, but both are to grow until the time of the harvest. What is the harvest? Hear the Lord himself (say): *The harvest is the End of Time.*

Delivered to everyday listeners, the sermon employed a homely agricultural metaphor. It assumes that the parishioners knew, from their own experience, who the circumcellions were. The preacher's words work with the idea that they were harvesters or *messores* who worked in groups under foremen or *principes*. So too, in a detailed discussion of circumcellions in his response to the dissident Parmenian in 403–04, Augustine speaks of the labor bosses of the circumcellions and the kinds of punishments that the circumcellions and their leaders deserve. The punishments should be calibrated according to responsibility: "so, under just regulations, the labor contractors of the circumcellions deservedly suffer more severe penalties than the types of harm that the circumcellions themselves have inflicted

---

[24] Aug. *Ep.* 76.2 (CCL 31A: 78–79): "Ipse [sc. Christus] dixit: *Sinite utraque crescere usque ad messem*; non dixit: Crescant zizania, decrescant frumenta; ipse dixit: *Ager est hic mundus*; non dixit Ager est Africa; ipse dixit: *Messis est finis saeculi*, non dixit: Messis est tempus Donati; ipse dixit: *Messores angeli sunt*, non dixit: Messores principes circumcellionum sunt."

[25] Aug. *Sermo* 47.18 (CCL 41: 590): "Invenit deum etiam in ista similitudine ziziorum dicentem: *Ager est hic mundus* [Matt. 13:58]. Non ager est Africa, sed hic mundus. Per totum mundum frumentum, per totum mundum zizania – tamen, *Ager est mundus, seminator filius hominis, messores angeli*, non principes circumcellionum – crescere utrumque usque ad messem, non crescere zizania et decrescere frumenta, sed utrumque crescere usque ad messem. Quam messem? Ipsum audi: *Messis est finis saeculi* [Matt. 13: 37]."

on others."[26] The bosses of the circumcellions are understood to be men who acted as professional contractors of seasonal labor, and these *mancipes* or labor contractors are mentioned several times as the "leaders" of the circumcellions.[27]

There is another indication that the ordinary work engaged in by the men called circumcellions was the harvesting of cereal grain crops. It is a subtle hint resulting from a loose association of thoughts. Not infrequently when Augustine uses the circumcellions as an example in his arguments, the mention of the men is provoked by his use of a biblical passage from Psalm 125 on the "wheat and tares." We have considered one such example above. The Psalm highlights the role of the angels as the harvesters of the crop: the souls of humanity that are to be harvested at the end of time.[28] The text had become a standard one in African sectarian disputes, since it neatly encapsulated one of the central points of dispute between the two churches as seen by Catholic ideologues: was the Christian community a pure one, cleaned of "weeds," or was it more inclusive, allowing the good (wheat or barley) and the bad (weeds) to exist together in the same field to grow to maturity and to await the final harvest?[29] The way in which circumcellions repeatedly figure in the aftermath of the deployment of this metaphor strongly suggests a mental cueing of real harvesters by the metaphorical ones.[30]

The repeated use of this metaphor throughout Augustine's lengthy attack on the dissident bishop Parmenian was first provoked by a mention of the circumcellions and a realistic description of harvest conditions. One of the most extensive uses of this same metaphor in this reply appears in direct connection with circumcellions.[31] The parallels are even more pronounced in Augustine's verbal barrage written in 401 and directed against

---

[26] See Aug. *Ep.* 76.2 (CCL 31A: 78–79) and *Sermo* 47.18 (CCL 41: 590); the presence of contractors is assumed by the imperial laws of 412 and 414 that were issued to repress circumcellion activity: CTh 16.5.52.1 (SC 497: 308) and 16.5.54.5-6 (SC 497: 314), both of which reflect the terms of an edict issued by the *cognitor* of the hearing of 411 which specifies *domini*, *actores*, and *conductores fundorum* as responsible for enforcing the decree (CCL 149A: 178).

[27] Aug. *Contra ep. Parm.* 1.11.18 (CSEL 51: 40): "Unde merito constitutionibus iustis graviora patiuntur circumcellionum mancipes quam faciunt circumcelliones."

[28] Another harvest metaphor, parallel to this one, cited from Matt. 3: 12 and 13: 30, on the winnowing of grain to separate weeds and straw from the "good" grain, also serves to cue discussion of circumcellions.

[29] Bavaud (1964), pp. 608–09.

[30] In addition to the texts mentioned below, see, e.g. *Ep.* 43.21–24 (CCL 31: 182–85).

[31] Aug. *Contra ep. Parm.* 1.6.12 (CSEL 51: 33) cues a series of discussions of circumcellions. The pattern is evident in the following passages: 2.2.5, 2.3.6, 2.4.9, 2.6.11, 2.10.22, 2.11.25, 2.15.34, 2.17.36, 2.20.39, 3.1.2, 3.11.11, 3.2.15, 3.2.16, 3.3.18–19, 3.4.24, 3.4.25, 3.4.26, 3.5.27, 3.5.28, and so in, in this treatise alone.

the dissident bishop Petilian. On at least three consecutive occasions in this treatise the harvesting metaphor of the "wheat and the tares" directly precedes a specific mention of the circumcellions.[32] A reader or listener of any reasonable sensibility comes to expect a mention of the circumcellions following the introduction of the biblical metaphor on sowing and harvesting. The comparison of circumcellions with the angels who were to come as harvesters at the end of time was not accidental. In sermons and treatises that were meant to appeal to the expectations of everyday listeners, the connection was manifest – which is why the preacher made it in the first place. From much circumstantial detail, it is clear that the harvesters or *messores* that Augustine had in mind were the normal reapers of cereal crops.

The picture of the circumcellions as a secular workforce also matches the earliest and most detailed account that we have of them in the writings of Optatus. Writing in the mid-360s, and reflecting on events that took place two decades earlier, he gives us a brief glimpse into the social world of hired rural labor in which the circumcellions first appear as holy fighters for the dissident cause.[33] He describes the approach of the emperor's emissaries Paul and Macarius to the town of Bagaï deep in southeastern Numidia in the momentous year of 347. When they took to the main highway leading southwest from Carthage into the African interior, in their attempt to persuade local dissident communities to Unity, the imperial emissaries met with more than verbal resistance. As they approached Bagaï, Donatus, the dissident bishop of the town, marshaled the men who were normally recruited to provide strong arms for the dissident community in their sectarian conflicts. To do this, he sent market-criers, *praecones*, around the circuits of the local periodic markets, the *nundinae* as they were called, to issue a call for these men to assemble. The criers announced that the men known as holy fighters or *agonistici*, drafted from the ranks of the circumcellion laborers, should assemble at a pre-arranged place.[34] It was from the seasonal laborers who congregated at local marketplaces, Optatus states, that Donatus "hired" the "deranged mob" of men with whom he then confronted the Roman soldiers commanded by Paul and Macarius.[35]

---

[32] Aug. *Contra litt. Petil.* 2.10.24 (CSEL 52: 33–34): the parable on harvesting is followed by remarks on men who have all the hallmarks of being circumcellions, although they are not named as such; cf. 2.22.46, 2.39.93–94 (CSEL 52: 76–77): two specific mentions of circumcellions preceded by the harvesting parable; 2.47.110 (CSEL 52: 83–84): again, the harvesting metaphor leads directly to a mention of the circumcellions.

[33] On the problem of dating this incident, see Alexander (1998).

[34] Optatus, *Contra Parm.* 3.4.2 (SC 413: 38). [35] Optatus, *Contra Parm.* 3.4.8 (SC 413: 42).

Gatherings of men seeking occasional work were normally found at rural marketplaces throughout the Mediterranean. Such men were day laborers who wandered around and congregated at the fora of towns and villages where they waited to be hired for day work or by the day for longer periods. In the eastern Mediterranean they were typically known as *agoraioi* or "market men" from the fact that they tended to gather in groups at the local *agorai* or marketplaces. Just so, in Africa it was known that circumcellions tended to congregate at the local periodic markets where they could be hired or contracted for their work. The general reputation of such men was a bad one.[36] Their lack of permanent attachments, absence of proper skills, low social status, lack of fixed places of residence while on the move, and their dependence on hard manual work, cast a malign and servile penumbra over them. Their uncontrolled movements and wanderings tended to associate them with loose and potentially criminal elements in the society who had no permanent homes, people like itinerant entertainers, pastoral nomads, or bandits. Related to these men were larger and more permanent gangs of seasonal workers who were hired not on a daily but on a task-specific basis, usually in connection with seasonal work. Where larger quantities of manual labor were required for a specific task, most often for the harvesting of cereal crops, the required workers would be gathered together by a contractor who would then hire out his gang, or *turma*, to take off a crop at a specific price.

By good fortune, we know of one such a contractor of harvest labor who lived in this same age of late fourth-century rural Africa. Known from a long verse epitaph on his tombstone that recapitulated his rags-to-riches life story, the Maktar Harvester – so named after his hometown of Mactaris where his tale was preserved in a long Latin inscription – was a contractor who gathered together large numbers of men on a seasonal basis for the purpose of providing much-needed additional harvest labor. He took these men for hire on the rounds of the high plains of Numidia in great annual cycles of seasonal work. The profits were good. From being a landless agricultural worker, the harvest contractor from Mactaris became a comparatively well-off municipal gentleman and an important notable in his hometown. In an unpoetic word not used in the verse ode that he had written to celebrate his life, the anonymous man states that he was technically known as a *manceps* or a contractor of hired laborers.

In legal terms, the *manceps* was the middleman who organized and collected the workers and who then hired them to the person who contracted

---

[36] Acts 17:5: for τῶν ἀγοραίων ἄνδρας τινὰς πονηρούς καὶ ὀχλοποιήσαντες ἐθορύβουν τὴν πόλιν.

with him for their labor services. Much of this organization must have been strongly repetitive: establishing predictable routes that the gangs of reapers would follow and building up the same clients whom the contractor would serve year after year. The men who contracted with the *manceps* would have been the larger landowners, *domini* or, more frequently, their agents – the *vilici, procuratores,* and *actores* – the bailiffs, caretakers and agents who managed their farms for them.[37] Because of the much higher demand for labor in the harvest season, seasonal workers tended to be recruited from regions where such labor was in surplus, from reservoirs of agrarian underemployment in the more heavily urbanized regions in the northeastern parts of the proconsular province. They moved in an organized fashion, in groups, to the more thinly populated high plains regions mainly dedicated to the growing of cereal grains where the intensive harvest labor was required.

Not all seasonal labor was organized in this fashion. As confirmed by a host of modern cases, occasional work of this type tended to fall into two broad categories. There were the large organized groups that were sought on a regular basis by larger landowners, as opposed to the more *ad hoc* numbers of individual workers, sometimes traveling in groups of three or four, who were picked up on a more casual basis by smaller landholders. The latter men, who usually negotiated and sold their own labor, tended to congregate at marketplaces, at the agora or at *panēgyreis* in eastern locales of the empire, and in the *fora* or the *nundinae,* the periodic marketplaces, in the western Mediterranean. These were the types of occasional laborers to whom Optatus refers in his narrative of the violence around the town of Bagaï in southeastern Numidia in the mid-340s. From what he says, it is clear that they habitually gathered at the cyclical market centers because these markets also functioned as labor exchanges where landowners or their agents came to pick up men for contract work on a daily basis.[38]

The single piece of legal evidence on the circumcellions – the constitution issued by Honorius and Theodosius on 30 January 412 that ordered the harsh repression of the dissident church in Africa – sheds valuable light on the assumed status of these seasonal workers.[39] The law is one that sought to enforce earlier orders issued against "the Donatists," this time

---

[37] CIL 8.11824 (Mactoris) for the contractor from Maktor; in general, see De Robertis, *Lavoro e lavoratori,* pp. 217 f.

[38] Cato the Elder, *De Agr. Cult.* 5, 144, 147; J. Macqueron, *Le travail des hommes libres dans l'antiquité romaine,* Aix, 1958; reprint: Aalen, Scientia Verlag, 1964, pp. 68–90, and, in more detail: Shaw, *Bringing in the Sheaves,* ch. 2.

[39] Atkinson (1992), pp. 488–99.

by imposing severe fines on recalcitrant members of the dissident church, or their supporters, gradated in proportion to their social rank. Senior-ranking imperial officials or *illustres* were to be fined 50 pounds of gold, *spectabiles* 40 pounds of gold, and senators 30 pounds of gold. The fines worked their way down to the level of town councilors or *decuriones* who were to be fined 5 pounds of gold. In the ranks immediately below men of curial rank, the "less honest" persons of the social order, we find business men or *negotiatores*, fined 5 pounds of gold, as were also the ordinary free citizens or plebs. Beneath these men in rank, in the dregs of society, came the circumcellions, who were to be fined 10 pounds of silver.[40] Beneath all of the above categories were persons of even lower status: slaves and *coloni*. With these men at the bottom, we are no longer dealing with penalties set in terms of monetary fines, but rather with corporal punishments that were to be inflicted on the body.

From the specific nature of the penalties imposed by this law, a series of reasonable deductions can be made. From the perspective of the imperial authorities who drafted the law, like all other groups listed in it, the circumcellions are presented as a distinct legal class or *ordo* of persons.[41] They are listed immediately below the plebs but above slaves and *coloni* in order and they are to pay a fine rather than to be beaten or physically punished. It follows that circumcellions were seen as free men of some status. They were not the same as *coloni*, slaves, or other such dependent persons. Although the ranking of these groups in the imperial decree is informative, it is most improbable that the circumcellions formed anything like a permanent legal *ordo*.[42] The term was obviously a lawyers' convenience used to designate them as a group for the purposes of the law: it likened them to similar legally defined groups and so was able to designate them under the terms of the law. Such a direct connection between label and reality is neither necessary for our argument, nor does it reasonably follow from the whole run of the legal evidence. All that is necessary to understand from the perspective of the imperial drafters of the law is that circumcellions were above slaves and *coloni* in status, but below *negotiatores* and plebeians. The fact

---

[40] For the approximate buying power of 25 pounds of gold, see ch. 5, p. 225 n. 110.

[41] Saumagne (1934), pp. 353–54, was the first to argue that they were a formal "ordo"; the argument was subsequently accepted by Brisson, *Autonomisme et christianisme*, p. 336, among others.

[42] Schindler (1984), for example, sees this point – i.e., that the court at Ravenna drafted a law (CTh 16.5.52: 30 January 412) based on the "final assessment," the *sententia cognitoris*, issued by Marcellinus at the conclusion to the great conference at Carthage in 411. Since he named a class of persons called "circumcellions" who were to be sanctioned, the legal advisors at the court had to draft a law that somehow included them as a "class" of persons to be punished. Much this same point of the dependence of the drafter of the law on the prior wording of Marcellinus' statement is made, at length, by Gottlieb (1978), pp. 12–14.

that circumcellions were thought to be free men who were able to pay a fine, even if the lowest in value of all the groups concerned, and that they were explicitly excluded from the kinds of corporal punishments that could be inflicted on slaves and *coloni*, shows that they were located at the bottom end of the spectrum of persons of free status that ended with traders and plebeians.

The fine to be paid by the circumcellions, 10 pounds of *silver* rather than gold, indicates a person worth about a tenth of a plebeian – rather low indeed, although still above that of a *colonus* or a slave. They were therefore generally thought to be poor, but nevertheless persons who were *free* to contract their own labor as they wished. That the circumcellions were rural seasonal workers and that their hiring was done by labor con-tractors makes sense of other parts of the imperial constitution of 412. Besides punishing the circumcellions themselves, the same law held other specified persons responsible for their behavior. The terms of the imperial edict, indeed, echoed and directly replicated earlier specific suggestions of Catholic lobbyists who had held that the *principes* or *mancipes* of the circumcellions ought to be subject to more severe penalties than the gang members themselves.[43] The category of hiring agents also included the *actores* and *procuratores* who were the domain or farm administrators of wealthy landowners, including the managers of lands owned by the emperor and the state. Following the description of the penalties that were to be paid by those who obstinately remained unrepentant in their adherence to "the Donatist party" and the penalty of 10 pounds of silver imposed on circumcellions, the edict states that the state's enforcer, the *executor* of the law, was to exact the same penalty from the *conductores* or the *procuratores* under whose authority the circumcellions worked.[44]

In the general use of the technical terms *conductor* and *procurator*, both in epigraphical and literary sources on agricultural work regimes in Africa, a distinction is generally drawn between the bailiffs or managers of private domains as opposed to imperial farmlands.[45] Since, by the terms of the same law, the circumcellions were neither slaves nor *coloni*, they must have been free persons who were working under contracts whose terms were enforced by the *conductor*, the private person who was hiring their

[43] See Aug. *Ep.* 88.7 (CCL 31A: 144).

[44] *CTh* 16.5.52.1 (SC 497: 308): "Qui nisi a conductoribus, sub quibus conmanent, vel procuratoribus executori exigenti fuerint praesentati, ipsi teneantur ad poenam, ita ut nec domus nostrae homines ab huiuscemodi censura habeantur inmunes." For a discussion of the "ipsi" and its referent, see the discussion in Rey-Coquais (1998), pp. 448–49.

[45] See Carlsen (1991) on the functions of *actores*, *procuratores*, and *vilici* in estate management in Africa.

services or the imperial *procurator* who was doing the same for imperial or state lands in Africa.[46] The law specifically states that the circumcellions tend "to remain" or "to stay" under the authority of these persons, in the clear sense that they were "temporarily resident" on lands owned or managed by them.[47] Again, this requirement of the law fits the picture of circumcellions as men grouped in bands or *turbae* who contracted to work seasonally on the domains of larger landowners. That the managers of these domains formed a front line of state control and enforcement was already signaled in the sentence issued a year earlier by the judge Marcellinus at the end of the conference held at Carthage. In his decision, he specifically made landlords who knowingly harbored bands or *turbae* of circumcellions on their lands liable for them: their bailiffs were held responsible for restraining and repressing the "insolence" of the violent men. Should they fail to do so, the lands managed by them were to be confiscated by the imperial treasury.[48] Marcellinus' edict envisaged the principal hirers of gangs of seasonal agricultural laborers as the ones who would normally be involved with the management and discipline of the workers. In referring directly to these same laws, Augustine provides a valuable clue about the connection.[49]

Whence deservedly under those just laws of the emperors the labor contractors of the circumcellions, the *circumcellionum mancipes*, suffer more seriously [i.e. have heavier penalties inflicted upon them] than do the circumcellions themselves.

The *mancipes* of the circumcelliones were the men who were engaged in the contracting for the labor of seasonal harvesting gangs. And if they suffered

---

[46] The terms of this law were repeated, almost verbatim in places, in the repressive law issued by the Vandal king Huneric in 484. Here, too, following the listing of the penalties, one gets specific reference to the agency of *procuratores* and *conductores* who are to be held liable for those in their control: Victor Vitensis, *Hist. pers. Afr. prov.* 3.10–11 (Lancel: 179): "circumcelliones argenti pondo dena: et si qui forte in hac pernicie permanerent, confiscatis omnibus rebus suis exilio multarentur. Ordines autem civitatum, sed et procuratores et conductores possessionum tali poena videbantur affligere . . . conductoribus etiam regalium praediorum hac multa proposita ut quantum domui regiae inferrent, tantum etiam fisco poenae nomine cogerentur exsolvere." This passage cannot be taken as independent evidence for the continued existence of circumcellions in this later period, however, the officials in the chancellery of the Vandal kings were simply copying the earlier law.

[47] The verb is *commanere*, which is nicely glossed by Gottlieb (1978), pp. 9–11 (based on other usages in the CTh) with the technical meaning of "to remain with someone" for a specific period of time for some contractual purpose (like billeting of lodging, for example).

[48] *Edictum cognitoris* (CCL 149A: 179): "Hii autem qui in praediis suis circumcellionum turbas se habere cognoscunt, sciant, nisi eorum insolentiam omnimodis conprimere et refrenare gestierint, maxime ea loca fisco mox occupanda; siquidem tam Catholicae legi quam quieti publicae, ut eorum conquiescat insania, in hac parte consulitur."

[49] Aug. *Contra ep. Parm.* 1.11.18 (CSEL 51: 40): "Unde merito constitutionibus iustis graviora patiuntur circumcellionum mancipes quam faciunt circumcelliones."

more serious penalties, then they must have belonged to the ranks of business persons, *negotiatores*, or even the ranks of the *decuriones* specified in the same law. In a legal case at the town of Thubursicu Bure in the year 404 where Catholics were trying to repossess a place that had been seized by sectarian enforcers, both the dissidents and the Catholics had to await the arrival of the governor at the local assize for the hearing of the case.[50] Notably, it was the procurators who were managing the lands owned and leased by each church who were held responsible for the actions of the men under their direction who had been involved in the violence. The contractual links were between the managerial agents of the landowners on the one hand and the *mancipes* or contractors of the labor gangs on the other. The landowners' bailiffs could do double duty as the organizers of violent work as well as work in the fields. The legal case at Thubursicu makes explicit the nature of the ordinary working relations in which *some* of the circumcellions were involved. That is to say, the procurators of each church were required to be present because the men involved in the violence were normally employed by them as landowners' agents.

In a later discussion of incidents of civil violence, the details of this case were rehearsed, with specific mention of circumcellions and of the fact that Crispinus, the dissident bishop of Calama, was a lessor of imperial lands in the region. It was in this role that Crispinus was attempting to force the *coloni*, the emphyteutic or long-term lessees of imperial lands, to become adherents of *his* church.[51] The position that Crispinus held either as a lessor or an owner of lands was surely not unusual for many bishops: they either had their own incomes either as landowners or, as in the case of Crispinus, as renters of lands, or both. In either case, the bishop had two roles to play: one as head of the local church and the other as the manager of lands worked by his peasant farmers. In the latter role, he would have had his own *procuratores* or *actores* who were his agents and who were in charge of farming operations, but who were capable of managing the men whom they hired for purposes other than farming. These are the circumcellions whom Crispinus acquired for the attack on Possidius.[52] Far from being some special outside force, they were the same seasonal laborers whom Crispinus' procurator normally hired through a *manceps* or contractor. The procurator who performed this managerial task was therefore one of

---

[50] Aug. *Contra Cresc.* 3.43.47 (CSEL 52: 453–54): presumably they were awaiting the arrival of the governor on the annual rounds of his assizes of the province, and his decision that would be made under the terms of the new imperial laws.

[51] Aug. *Contra litt. Petil.* 2.83.184 (CSEL 52: 112–13).

[52] See Aug. *Ep.* 88.7 (CCL 31A: 144) where he names them as such.

the responsible parties from whom the provincial governor would take testimony in the inquiry that he would hold in the assize at Calama.

What we happen to learn about Crispinus in this case must also have been true of many priests, bishops, and other clergy.[53] This makes sense of the terms of Augustine's verbal assault on Proculeianus, the dissident bishop of Hippo Regius: "I pass over the drunkenness, your loans and the interest on them beyond the limits of the loans themselves. I pass over mentioning the herds and the mad acts of your circumcellions."[54] The imputed links between drunkenness, money loans, and circumcellions are probably not accidental. The first two relate to the pay owed to the last named. In 347, when Donatus, the dissident bishop of Bagaï, sent runners around to the local periodic markets to acquire circumcellions, he was therefore doing what he and other landowners, some of them clergy like himself, were normally doing all the time. He knew where to go to acquire the workers. His actions were no impulse of the moment.

Landowners either had usual annual contacts with the same *mancipes* of harvest gangs or they would go out to acquire occasional labor on a daily basis by going to nearby marketplaces where they knew that workers habitually congregated to be hired. A standard modern handbook on agriculture in colonial north Africa affirms the routine, namely that "indigenous workers," arriving in large bands on the day of the work – often coming from very far afield – were paid by day rates. They would sleep in the rough, under the open skies. Sometimes the reapers even included women.[55] The mention of the involvement of women in these seasonal labor gangs might seem to be a modern innovation but, as we shall see, it was not. Nor is the reference to these field laborers as "ouvriers indigènes" a surprising modernism. The procurator of the dissident bishop of Calama, who was involved in the recruiting of circumcellions, was managing local farm workers for his boss. When Augustine challenged Crispinus to a public debate in the early autumn of 401, he also insisted that the words of their debate be translated orally into Punic so that the local peasants would be able to understand them.[56] That is to say, culturally and socially the workers came from an under-Romanized stratum of local society.

[53] Shaw (1981), pp. 70 f.; cf. Leone (2006), pp. 100–02.

[54] Aug. *Sermo* 47.17 (CCL 41: 588): "Omitto ebriositates vestras, fenus et usuras super usuras. Omitto greges et furias circumcellionum."

[55] C. Rivière and H. Lecq, *Traité pratique d'agriculture pour le Nord de l'Afrique*, vol. 2, nouv. ed., Paris, Société d'éditions géographiques, maritimes et coloniales, 1929, p. 345.

[56] Aug. *Ep.* 66.2 (CCL 31A: 26): "ita ut scribantur, quae dicimus, et a nobis subscripta eis Punice interpretentur."

What sort of men filled up the ranks of the gangs of wandering laborers whom the landlords or their agents hired, either directly or through the agency of a contractor? They were not slaves. There is never any imputation that theirs was slave labor. They were free persons of low status. In the punishments set by the imperial law of 412, the assumption was that the circumcellions were free men who could be expected to pay fines if they were found to be guilty. Beyond these few certainties, however, it is not possible to say much. And even this much leaves unanswered the question of why violent sectarian enforcers were habitually found among this particular group of young men and women. A possible answer that logically suggests itself is that the work of sectarian violence was just as occasional in nature as that of harvesting. The preprogrammed mobility and gang-like organization of the workers made them a natural source of hired enforcers.

The circumcellions received their name, colloquially, from a normal annual activity – that of harvesting gangs moving in great annual sweeps across the face of the high plains of Africa. Their activities, like those of countless gangs of harvesters known from many different times and places, would probably have encompassed a wide range of normal violence. They were a faceless part of the regime of manual labor not only in Africa, but also the Mediterranean – a great annual cycle that has left very few traces in our literary sources. Some of these men appear in Augustine's writings only because of a peculiar convergence of action and subject: a few of them, who called themselves "holy fighters," had been mobilized as participants in a sectarian conflict. Since these references are polemically determined, however, the reliability of the evidence must be considered with more than ordinary skepticism. The description of circumcellions as "bandits," for example, is easy to decipher as a standard Roman means of labeling a violent and chaotic threat to the social order. On the other hand, the description of circumcellions as moving in herds or *greges* is perhaps both pejorative and accurate at the same time. Sallust was the historian most admired by Augustine, and it is possible to trace many purposeful echoes of the historian in his description of the circumcellions as a dangerous threat to social order.[57] Since a good part of the texts of Sallust has been lost, there are probably more such literary borrowings that have escaped our notice.

---

[57] These will be pointed out as they occur; cf. Aug. *Confess.* 2.4.9 and 2.5.11 (CCL 27: 22–23) for some echoes of Catilinarian images used for dangerous men.

The ranks of the seasonal harvest laborers, out of which the dissident *agonistici* were recruited, no doubt drew on the lowest class of freemen and agricultural dependants who needed this kind of work to supplement their incomes. In Numidia, and elsewhere, they were not infrequently culled from the ranks of the rural social classes whose culture was less Latinized than that of the towns. Many of them still spoke a form of Punic as their first or their only language. This placed the elite of Christian bishops, whether dissident or Catholic, on one side of a cultural divide within their own society. This was true even in the urban heart of Hippo Regius where Augustine refers to the dissident bishop of the city, Macrobius, who attempted to discipline these violent men by addressing them through an interpreter in Punic, their native language.[58] But it was still equally true, many years later, when Silvanus, the Primate of Numidia, tried to placate an assembly of angry peasant farmers at a village deep in the hinterland of Hippo Regius. Here, too, he had to have them addressed in Punic, the language that they normally spoke.[59]

If we consider the names of the men who were members of one of the gangs of Christian "fighters" involved in anti-pagan violence in the town of Madauros in the early 390s – Miggin, Saname, and their leader Namphamo – we see the same cultural profile.[60] Constant interpretation not only of language, but also of culture and belief, was required in the formation and disciplining of these gangs. But we should not be too misled by the name. Although the word circumcellion was used in general for religious gangsters, the recruitment to the groups drew on a wide range of marginal persons. The need for violent actors opened up new careers for men with talents for enforcement. As one UDA man observed of the emergence of violence in Northern Ireland, "Candlestick makers and bakers were made generals and toilet attendants were made colonels. People who never had any military experience... came... for some form of aggression – because they could dig [sc. hit] somebody a wee bit harder."[61] So it was in our age for free peasants and landless men, runaway slaves, down-and-out freedmen, various and sundry urban workers, and out-of-control women. The sectarian battles between Christians and "pagans," and then between the hostile Christian churches, presented all of them with new opportunities for employment.

---

[58] See n. 162 below.
[59] See ch. 8, pp. 236–38; an ability to speak Punic was one of the main reasons why Antoninus had been made bishop of the place.
[60] See ch. 4, pp. 236–38.   [61] As quoted by Feldman, ch. 2.8 in *Formations of Violence*, p. 32.

WOMEN ON THE LOOSE

As for recruitment, we know that modern rural labor gangs in the Maghrib have included women. For the *turmae* of harvesters in the Roman period, the evidence is unclear, but for the sectarian gangs it is manifest. The presence of women in the gangs was one of the aspects of the wandering bands of circumcellions that perhaps most excited Augustine and, no doubt, many of his episcopal peers. Although the acts of violence that typically defined circumcellions are usually associated with males, ordinarily aggressive young men armed with wooden clubs and similar implements, it is certain that the wandering bands often included women. The fact is not unknown in comparable instances of violence.[62] One of Augustine's earliest descriptions of circumcellions tells the story of a Spanish subdeacon Primus who abandoned the Catholic Church in hostile reaction against disciplinary measures that were about to be imposed upon him. Primus took with him two young females who were dedicated holy women or *sanctimoniales* (along with some *coloni* from the estate on which he lived). Augustine wrathfully fulminates that the women were rebaptized, and "along with the herds of circumcellions, they are found among those other wandering herds of women who shamelessly do not wish to have husbands so that they will not be subject to any discipline." The claim is followed by details of inebriation and worse.[63]

Narrative incidents like this suggest that the wandering bands sometimes offered a haven for women who did not wish to marry and who wanted to live a freer life on the road. At first, the assertion seems to conflict with the direct evidence of these women as *sanctimoniales*. It might be nothing much more than vituperative rhetoric, a way of condemning circumcellion women as "loose" and "out of control." On the other hand, both churches always had a deep concern with holy virgins who were separated from their families. They were to be put firmly under the control of bishops and priests precisely because they might cause great trouble for the church by – as it

---

[62] See, e.g., Semelin, *Purify and Destroy*, p. 281, who notes, however, that their known involvement in violence is as passive onlookers; but they also fill an important "supervisory role" of encouraging and egging on the participants.

[63] Aug. *Ep.* 35.2 (CCL 31: 128): "Duas etiam sanctimoniales concolonas suas de fundo Catholicorum christianorum sive idem transtulit sive illum secutae etiam ipsae tamen rebaptizatae sunt, et nunc cum gregibus circumcellionum inter vagabundos greges feminarum, quae proterve maritos habere noluerunt, ne habeant disciplinam." Note that Augustine alludes to other such cases, so our man was not alone in committing such delicts.

was put – *wandering around* uncontrolled.[64] In the light of this evidence, it is unfortunate that more cannot be understood of a clause that survives from the repressive imperial edict of 412 that calls for the punishment of the wives "of these men," who seem, indeed, to be the spouses of the circumcellions. The heavy fine that would have to be paid by their wives was surely a way in which the difficult-to-locate wandering male laborers might be brought to heel by an additional imposition on their family.[65] If so, the law presumes that many if not most circumcellions not only had freedom and property, but families – and further that their wives did not wander with them (as did some women), but rather that they were settled in more fixed habitations where they could be easily targeted by imperial repression.

Whatever one's moral views there is no doubt that there were female circumcellions. When describing the ritual religious ceremonies in which they celebrated the deaths of their own as martyrs, Augustine notes that women were ordinary members of the gangs.[66] He begins by listing the slaughter and murders staged by circumcellions and then continues that the men were "not satisfied with such bestiality at the tombs of their dead, celebrated with their women, who are mixed in indiscriminately with the gangs, against the natural order of divine and human affairs, with whom they wander around both by day and night." In another negative description, he again emphasizes that these were women who

---

[64] Concil. Hippo 393, canon 40 = *Reg. Eccl. Carth. Excerpt.* canon 44 (CCL 149: 42 and 186): "Ut virgines sacrae, cum parentibus, a quibus custodiebantur, privatae fuerint, episcopi vel presbyteri . . . se custodiant, ne passim vagando ecclesiae laedant existimationem." Perhaps significantly, the last phrase appears to have been added after the Hippo Council in 393.

[65] CTh 16.5.52.2 (SC 497: 308): "Uxores quoque eorum maritalis segregatim multa constringat." The problems proliferate. Who are the *eorum*? Because the text has been severely edited, it is difficult to say. If the editors kept the sequence of clauses, it cannot be the "wives" of all penalized classes, since slaves and *coloni* follow in order and the latter of these two categories, surely, could have *uxores*. That would seem to limit the *eorum* either to the procurators and *conductores*, or to the circumcellions. Why *even* the wives (*uxores quoque*) of procurators and *conductores* should be held liable to the same penalties as their husbands is unclear, unless it is the fact that they alone of all the named categories were held vicariously responsible for the behavior of others, and this brought additional pressure to bear on them. Depending on how one construes the meaning of the preceding clause on procurators and *conductores* largely determines whose wives you think they are. So Saumagne (1934) and Brisson, *Autonomisme et christianisme*, p. 335, took them to be the wives of the circumcellions, whereas Tengström, *Donatisten und Katholiken*, p. 30, thinks the opposite. It seems more probable that the wives of the circumcellions were being held separately liable to the same fine as their husbands as another way of helping to bring "wandering men" under control. See Rey-Coquais (1998), pp. 448–49, who seems to accept this interpertation, against Cataudella (1991), pp. 333–38.

[66] Aug. *Contra ep. Parm.* 2.3.6 (CSEL 51: 50): "nequaquam in tanta immanitate satiantur, ubi per busta cadaverum eorum cum feminis, quae cum illis passim commixtae contra ordinem rerum divinarum et humanarum diebus et noctibus evagantur."

did not have husbands and who were therefore free to engage in all-night drunken celebrations. Being "husband-less," they had the freedom of having companionship, wandering, joking, drinking, and generally having a good time.[67]

In describing the dramatic entry of the dissident bishop Macrobius into Hippo in 410, Augustine notes that Macrobius went about the town hedged in by "formations of dissolute persons of both sexes" – persons whom he elsewhere calls circumcellions. The women, apparently, were involved with the men in the use of force to reclaim and reopen basilicas that had been closed by landowners in obedience to imperial laws.[68] Naturally, Augustine suggests the worst about the behavior of the women, emphasizing that they were not married and that they were therefore guilty of *stuprum* or having sex outside the bounds of matrimony. In his blustering outrage, he wildly asserts that the immoral acts committed by these women were "countless."[69] They engaged not only in the drinking that was characteristic of circumcellions, but also in all kinds of lewd and sexually permissive behavior that were both degrading and shameful.[70] The charges were credible, in part, because aggressive sexual marauding was believed to be generally true of harvesting gangs. In the biblical book of Ruth, read and commented on by both bishops and laymen of the age in Africa, and heard by congregations, Ruth's mother and prospective husband comment on the likelihood that a young woman going to work in the harvest would be molested by the men who were doing the reaping.[71]

Once the obvious allowances are made for the heavy moralizing, what does the normal presence of women signal? If the recruiting of the sectarian enforcers was normally made from the members of seasonal harvesting gangs, the presence of women makes perfectly good sense. Although some harvest gangs in different historical epochs were predominantly male, others, such as the gangs of Irish harvest laborers who worked their way through the fields of England in the nineteenth century, sometimes came

---

[67] Aug. *Contra litt. Petil.* 2.88.195 (CSEL 52: 120): "Nam inter vinulenta convivia et cum feminis maritos non habentibus liberam comitandi vagandi iocandi bibendi pernoctandi licentiam non solum fustes tornare, sed etiam ferrum vibrare et fundas circumagere didicerunt."

[68] Aug. *Ep.* 139.2 (CCL 31B: 292): in a formal letter to Marcellinus, probably in 412: "Modo Macrobius, episcopus eorum, stipatus cuneis perditorum utriusque sexus hac atque illac circuit, aperuit sibi basilicas, quas possessorum quantuluscumque timor clauserat."

[69] Aug. *Contra ep. Parm.* 3.3.18 (CSEL 51: 122).

[70] Aug. *Contra ep. Parm.* 2.9.19 (CSEL 51: 64–65): "An cum moechis particulam suam forte non ponunt, qui greges ebrios sanctimonialium suarum cum gregibus ebriis circumcellionum, die noctuque permixtos vagari turpiter sinunt?"

[71] Ruth 2: 8–9; 21–23.

in quasi-familial groups, with women who could assist in reaping, and who were frequently employed in the back-end operations of the harvest like binding and gleaning.[72] If the sectarian gangs were recruited out of an existing reservoir of seasonal laborers, how was that recruiting done and who directed them to the more religious work of violent attacks on their sectarian enemies? The fact that there were *any* women on the loose who were associated with circumcellions only served to nourish the rhetoric that could be directed against "the Donatists" in general. In condemning the dissident bishop Optatus of Thamugadi, Augustine first connects him with circumcellions and then advances to describe them as bandits, parricides, and sexual predators.[73] He strongly suggests ways in which the circumcellions were like brigands and sexual deviants. The lateral connection is repeatedly made between the "herds of circumcellions," mobs of drunken revelers, and the countless sexual excesses and transgressions of their women.[74] It is a bad picture of truly bad people.

TIME AND PLACE

The full extent of circumcellion violence is difficult to map. Despite exaggerated rhetorical assertions that their violence extended to "all of Africa," there are several regions, in fact large parts of Africa, for which there is no evidence at all of their activities.[75] Nothing is attested for the most westerly region of Africa (the Roman province of Mauretania Tingitana) that covered the northernmost parts of modern-day Morocco. Nor is there any evidence for their presence in the whole of the province of Mauretania Caesariensis. The absence of this particular form of violence in Mauretania is probably correlated with the difficulty that local leaders in the dissident church, like Rogatus of Cartenna, had in accepting any legitimate role that such men could have within their church. Augustine noted that "the Rogatists" seemed "less dangerous" to Catholics "since you do *not* rage about with wild herds of circumcellions."[76] Nor is there any evidence for circumcellions in Tripolitania in the far eastern parts of Africa. Finally, although there were incidents of sectarian violence in the province of Byzacena, there is no known involvement of circumcellions from this

---

[72] See Shaw, *Bringing in the Sheaves*, ch. 1.   [73] Aug. *Contra ep. Parm.* 2.9.19 (CSEL 51: 64–65).

[74] Aug. *Contra ep. Parm.* 3.3.18 (CSEL 51: 122): "Unde ergo tanti greges circumcellionum? Unde tantae turbae conviviorum ebriosorum et innuptarum sed non incorruptarum innumerabilia stupra feminarum?"

[75] Aug. *Contra ep. Parm.* 1.11.17 (CSEL 51: 39): "per totam Africam vagantur et saeviunt."

[76] Aug. *Ep.* 93 passim; cf. 93.3.11 (CCL 31A: 174): "mitiores quidem esse videmini, quia cum circumcellionum immanissimis gregibus non saevitis."

region. Despite broad-brush statements, such as that of Augustine's biographer Possidius, that circumcellions were to be found in almost all regions of Africa, the surviving evidence does not sustain such comprehensive claims, even given Possidius' qualification of "almost."[77] What writers like Augustine and Possidius probably meant by these claims is that such men were found in almost all the regions of Africa familiar to them, namely the swath of lands from Mauretania Sitifensis in the west to the proconsular province in the east, including Numidia along its southern span.

The time period during which the circumcellions operated in their classic form is even more difficult to determine. The earliest specific reference that we have to groups designated as circumcellions comes from Optatus' account of events of the year 347. Since we know little about the nature of his sources, however, it is not possible to say with certainty that this designation was being used currently in the 340s to label sectarian gangs, or whether Optatus himself was using the term when he was writing, a generation later, to label the type of violent men whose identity had become more fixed in the interim. On one occasion, Augustine suggests that circumcellions had been mobilized by the dissidents from the very origins of the schism, and therefore as early as the decade of the 310s.[78] But the passage is rhetorical and, strictly speaking, Augustine is enumerating various kinds of violent acts that he finds typical of circumcellion behavior, and it is these typical "circumcellion-like" actions rather than circumcellions as such that he claims go back to the beginnings of the divison.

The last contemporary reference to the circumcellions is contained in Augustine's rhetorical joust with Emeritus of Caesarea in 418. In his summation, Augustine contrasts a picture of Catholic long-suffering at the hands of their enemies: "Therefore we sweat, we struggle, we are facing the great dangers of their weapons and the bloody madness of their circumcellions – but with the patience given to us by God, even now we are still enduring, as best we can, what is left of them."[79] With this, the final polemical attack by Augustine on "the Donatists," we have the last contemporary reference

---

[77] Possid. *Vita Aug.* 10.1 (Bastiaensen: 152): "Et erant in ingenti numero et turbis per omnes paene Africanas regiones constituti."

[78] Aug. *Contra litt. Petil.* 2.14.33 (CSEL 52: 37–38): "quas . . . non tantum ediderint ab initio schismatis vestri, sed omnino edere non desinant strages." The best argument that can be made about possible origins of circumcellion gangs this early has been made by Lancel (1967) – but it has been rejected by most.

[79] Aug. *Gesta cum Emerit.* 12 (CSEL 53: 195–96): "Ideo sudamus, ideo laboramus, ideo inter eorum arma et cruentas furias circumcellionum periclitati sumus et adhuc reliquias eorum qualicumque donata a Deo patientia toleramus."

to circumcellions.[80] But the rhetoric is suspect. He could not be referring to activities of circumcellion gangs in Mauretania, for which there is no other independent evidence. Finally, we must keep firmly in mind that Augustine never literally means *all* circumcellions or harvest laborers in Africa when he uses the word. He is exploiting a negative connotation of the popular term used for these workers in general and is applying it to the gangs of sectarian enforcers. It was a useful name. The sectarian circumcellions, therefore, were a rhetorical construct of fourth-century religious conflict. They are not found under this name earlier or later. So the basic question persists: Who were the circumcellions and why were they labeled with this pejorative name by their enemies?

BEING A CIRCUMCELLION

It is possible to construct a fairly coherent picture of the special sectarian circumcellions, or *agonistici* as they called themselves.[81] From repeated emphasis on certain core characteristics in the descriptions of their activities, primarily in Optatus and Augustine, a fairly standard image emerges of what they were believed to be. First of all, "circumcellion" was primarily a behavioral category. These persons acted so as to earn, and what they earned through their actions was high honor. For example, by dying in one of their operations, the individual *agonisticus* became a martyr. Their violence might be construed as criminal and illegal, but even these hostile observers noted the link between violence, death, martyrdom, and hero worship.[82] One became or was a sectarian circumcellion because one did circumcellion-type things. In speaking of the supposedly large numbers of dissidents who crossed over from "the Donatist side" to that of the Catholics after 412, Augustine makes this explicit: "Those men of that kind who are now constrained by the good order of discipline and who now cultivate fields, having abandoned the work and the name of 'circumcellions,' now serve God, preserve their chastity, and cling to unity."[83] That is to say, if

---

[80] As noted above, later reference to them in the law of the Vandal king Huneric in 484 is certainly a deliberate anachronism; the writers in his chancellery were simply copying the terms of the edict of Honorius of 412.

[81] The claim is frequently made – e.g. by Frend, *Donatist Church*, p. 176, citing Monceaux (1909), pp. 116 and 132; and by Cicatti, *Furiosa turba*, p. 49 – that they called themselves "soldiers of Christ" or *milites Christi*. The *only* evidence in support is Aug. *En. in Ps.* 132.6 (see n. 14 above), which seems to be so much Augustinian rhetoric.

[82] E.g. Aug. *Ep.* 88.8 (CCL 31A: 145): they live as bandits or *latrones*, they die as circumcellions, they are honored as martyrs.

[83] Aug. *Contra Gaud.* 1.29.33 (CSEL 53: 231): he is speaking of those who have abjured the *dementia* and *furor* of Donatus.

one stopped behaving in a certain fashion then one simply lost the name and status of being a circumcellion. Being a circumcellion was not like belonging to an organization or having membership in a status group, but rather being someone because one did certain things.[84] The presumption is that this was not a permanent occupation or status, but rather a fluid and changeable way of behaving.

If there are two characteristics that perhaps most marked the general nature of circumcellions, it is their collective or group behavior and their status as rootless and wandering men. Except for theoretical references in lists of vocabulary, or lemmata, the word *circumcellio* is unknown in the singular. In everyday language use, circumcellions always existed in the plural. By definition and by name their behavior was collective.[85] The frequent use of pejorative words to label them is not only hostile, but surely reflects a certain reality. For example, they are frequently referred to as collected in herds or *greges*, suggesting an element of animality or bestiality that matched their erratic and violent acts and their seemingly aimless wanderings across the African countryside.[86] They are also described as gathering in bands or *turbae*; or in gangs that were called *catervae*.[87] On occasions when these men are not mentioned by the technical name of "circumcellion," bands of men in *turbae* or *catervae* are designated who are clearly understood to be circumcellions.[88] Sometimes images of the men as animal herds or human gangs are combined in the same picture of them.[89] The castigation of the circumcellions as beasts is linked to the savagery that

---

[84] Schindler (1984), pp. 240–41, emphasizes this fluidity of identity as one of the two basic points that he makes about the name.

[85] The collective labeling is surely related to the fact that, like the Bagaudae in late Roman Gaul, they were being constructed as a threat to the social and political orders.

[86] Aug. *Ep.* 35.2 (CCL 31: 127–28): the case of the Spanish subdeacon and his women: "et nunc cum gregibus circumcellionum inter vagabundos greges feminarum"; *Contra ep. Parm.* 1.11.17 (CSEL 51: 39): "per furiosos ebriosorum iuvenum greges"; 2.9.19 (CSEL 51: 65): "qui greges ebrios sanctimonalium suarum cum gregibus ebriis circumcellionum die noctuque permixtos vagari turpiter sinunt?"; *Sermo* 47.17 (CCL 41: 588): "Omitto greges et furias circumcellionum."

[87] See *Contra Cresc.* 3.45.49 (CSEL 52: 456): "crebrius et audacius circumcellionum vinolentiis turbisque furentibus"; *En. in Ps.* 57.15 (CCL 39: 721): "Prosiliunt et saeviunt armatae turbae circumcellionum"; *Ep. ad Cath. contra Donatist.* 16.41 (CSEL 52: 286): "quam in turbis inquietis furiosorum circumcellionum"; for circumcellion bands as *catervae* see: *Contra litt. Petil.* 2.14.33 (CSEL 52: 37–38): "quas furiosi vestri principes circumcellionum et ipsae catervae vinulentorum atque insanorum"; 2.47.110 (CSEL 52: 84): "ad furiosas catervas circumcellionum."

[88] For example, *Contra litt. Petil.* 2.96.222 (CSEL 52: 140): "Respicite paululum catervas vestras, quae non antiquo more parentum suorum solis fustibus armantur, sed et secures et lanceas et gladios addiderunt."

[89] Aug. *Ep. ad Cath. contra Donatist.* 19.50 (CSEL 52: 297): "ebriosi greges vagorum et vagarum permixta . . . sit ista omnis turba palea eorum nec frumentis praeiudicet, si ipsi ecclesiam tenent."

they vented on their victims.[90] Their raging or madness is then connected
with their supposed willingness to involve themselves in acts of collective
suicide.[91] Such group behavior is certainly not accidental.[92] Given the
difficulty with which humans are moved to actual face-to-face personal
acts of violence, the degree of social cohesion required for communal
self-killings like the ones committed by the *agonistici* is considerable.

The other core characteristic of the circumcellions was their propensity
to constant movement. Their mobility is usually described in words that
suggest an aimless, if not chaotic, wandering. In brief descriptions of
circumcellions, this characteristic is usually associated with their violence:
"men who, under the most notorious name of 'circumcellions' wander
and commit savageries throughout all of Africa."[93] The verb "to wander,"
vagare, and forms derived from it are most frequently used to describe the
free-floating world of the circumcellion bands in the African countryside.[94]
They were the gypsies and vagrants of their day. They are described in
the same words as the pastoral nomads pictured so evocatively in one
of Augustine's favorite authors, Sallust, as "going here and there, never
having fixed abodes."[95] Likewise, the sectarian gangs of wandering men
and women are said to be so restless and homeless that they wander both
day and night.[96] A Spanish subdeacon who took up the circumcellion style
of life is said to have entered a floating world of mobile persons lacking
fixed places of residence, people who wandered about the countryside
like animals seeking pasture.[97] In other descriptions of the circumcellions,
however, the constant wandering is seen as purposeful, since they "wander"

---

[90] Aug. *Ep.* 23.6 (CCL 31: 66): "saevitiam circumcellionum"; 88.1 (CCL 31A: 139): "in nos saeviunt."

[91] Aug. *Contra Cresc.* 4.64.77 (CSEL 52: 577): "Negas furorem circumcellionum et praecipitatorum."

[92] Both Tilly and Collins have noted the phenomenon; for a more specific consideration of modern
historical cases, see Semelin, *Purify and Destroy*, pp. 239–42, emphasizing the critical nature of the
"prior ideology"; and pp. 262–64, emphasizing the role of perceived "traitors" in forming group
cohesion.

[93] Aug. *Contra ep. Parm.* 1.11.17 (CSEL 51: 39): "qui circumcellionum notissimo nomine per totam
Africam vagantur et saeviunt."

[94] Aug. *Contra ep. Parm.* 2.19.19 (CSEL 51: 65): "die noctuque permixtos vagari turpitus sinunt?";
Contra Cresc. 3.42.46 (CSEL 52: 453): "namque horrendis armati cuiusque generis telis terribiliter
vagando"; *En. in Ps.* 54.26 (CCL 39: 675): "et ista [sc. arma] portantes ubique ea qua possunt
evagantur."

[95] Aug. *En. in Ps.* 132.3 (CCL 40: 1928): "Nam circumcelliones dicti sunt, quia circum cellas vagantur:
solent enim ire hac illac, nusquam habentes sedes"; cf. Sall. *BJ*, 18.1–2, of Gaetuli and Libyes at the
earliest stage of African history: "vagi palantes quas nox coegerat sedes habebant."

[96] Aug. *Ep. ad Cath. contra Donatist.* 19.50 (CSEL 52: 297): "aut quod ad eorum sepulcra ebriosi greges
vagorum et vagarum permixta nequitia die noctuque se vino sepeliant."

[97] Aug. *Ep.* 35.2 (CCL 31: 128): "et nunc cum gregibus circumcellionum inter vagabundos greges
feminarum."

from one *cella* or cellar to the next in the African countryside in search of sustenance.[98]

Mobility and movement was not all that characterized them. Core aspects of their religious identity must be raised. In his summation of them as a category of bad men, Possidius states that they "wandered around *as if* subject to the *professio* of ascetics."[99] Although he intends to demean the claim, it seems reasonable to assume that some of these men subscribed to some sort of rigorist ethic that separated them from their community's enemies. In comparisons of circumcellions with genuine "good" monks, their movements are unfavorably contrasted with the settled life of a true monastic community.[100] The closest that Augustine comes to treating this subject is in his commentary on Psalm 132, a biblical source that frequently generated comment, approving and disapproving, on the behavior of monastics. At least in terms of the mutual insults that they exchanged, both sides, the dissidents and Catholics, drew a rough parallel between circumcellions and wandering monks. Augustine says that no one should launch insults against Catholics because of their monks, whereas the dissidents are rightly attacked because of their circumcellions. Catholics should not waste any words on a comparison that did not exist: "Are drunkards to be compared with the sober, suicidal precipitators with the normal, the deranged with the stable, wanderers with those who are settled in a congregation?"[101] It was the bad behaviors sometimes associated with monks not of wandering, but rather of consumption and of violence that come to the fore.

EXCESS: WINE AND VIOLENCE

One of the pervasive characteristics associated with the wild behavior of the circumcellions was the excessive drinking of alcohol. The correlation between violence and drinking, however, is no simple one. The argument here does no more than suggest that drunkenness was an attendant cause, perhaps exaggerated by the literary purveyors of circumcellion violence.[102]

---

[98] See, for example, Aug. *En. in Ps.* 132.3 (CCL 40: 1927–28) and *Contra Gaud.* 1.28.32 (CSEL 53: 231): "ab agris vacans et victus sui causa cellas circumiens rusticanas."

[99] Possid. *Vita Aug.* 10.1 (Bastiaensen: 152): "velut sub professione continentium ambulantes."

[100] Aug. *En. in Ps.* 132.3 (CSEL 40: 1928): "comparentur ... vagantes cum congregatis?"

[101] Aug. *En. in Ps.* 132.3 (CCL 40: 1927–28): "Ex voce huius psalmi appellati sunt et monachi, ne quis vobis de isto nomine insultet Catholicis. Quando vos recte haereticis de circellionibus insultare coeperitis, ut erubescendo sal ventur; illi vobis insultant de monachis ... Quid opus est verbis vestris? Comparentur ebriosi cum sobriis, praecipites cum consideratis, furentes cum simplicibus, vagantes cum congregatis?"

[102] A analysis critical of the possible links between intoxication and violence is provided by Collins, *Violence*, pp. 263–69, who points out, with detailed statistical evidence, the near obvious: most

It was a fault noted from the earliest to the latest descriptions of the gangs by the repeated references to the "raging gangs of drunken young men" or similar derogatory phrases.[103] A standard type of name-calling usually denotes them as "gangs of drunken and mad men."[104] The drunken ragings often took place during the evening hours or the night. The bouts of drinking were sometimes linked to actions that led to "insane" acts of self-destruction.[105] Their drunken "bacchanals" were reported to be celebrated following incidents in which some of their fellows engaged in acts of collective ritual suicide by means of precipitation or hurling themselves to their deaths off great heights.[106] When linked with the presence of women in these gangs, it was said to excite licentious acts that are luridly described as bacchic in nature.[107] The inebriation was contrasted with the model of sober behavior set by the founding bishop of the dissident church: "Of what use is the sobriety of Donatus to you, when you are polluted with the drunkenness of your circumcellions?"[108] References to alcoholic drink appear frequently in lists of the kinds of loutishness that typified the circumcellions. Perhaps significantly, it is sometimes linked with the loaning of money. But how are violence, drinking, and money to be related?[109]

The descriptions of alcoholic binge drinking can be dismissed as exaggerations or fictions invented by Catholics to slur the reputation of wild men attached to the dissident cause. But there might well have been a factual basis for the charge that drunken excesses were characteristic of the circumcellions. Even so, inebriation was certainly not limited to them: the

---

    alcoholic drinking does not lead to violent acts; of course, the link is not necessarily universal, unilinear, or monocausal, but seems to be present in some fashion, see Semelin, *Purify and Destroy*, p. 267.

[103] Aug. *Contra ep. Parm.* 1.11.17 (CSEL 51: 39): "per furiosos ebriosorum iuvenum greges"; cf. 2.3.6.

[104] Aug. *Contra litt. Petil.* 2.14.33 (CSEL 52: 37): "et ipsae catervae vinulentorum atque insanorum."

[105] Aug. *En. in Ps.* 132.3 (CCL 40: 1928), comparing monks with circumcellions: "Comparentur ebriosi cum sobriis," followed by remarks on suicides.

[106] Aug. *Ep. ad Cath. contra Donatist.* 19.50 (CSEL 52: 297): "aut quod ad eorum sepulcra ebriosi greges vagorum et vagarum permixta nequitia die noctuque se vino sepeliant flagitiisque corrumpant."

[107] Aug. *Ep.* 35.2 (CCL 31: 127–28): the case of the Spanish deacon and women: "ne habeant disciplinam in destestabilis vinolentiae bacchationibus superbus exultat"; *Contra ep. Parm.* 2.9.19 (CSEL 51: 65): "qui greges ebrios sanctimonalium suarum cum gregibus ebriis circumcellionum"; 3.3.18 (CSEL 51: 122): "Unde tantae turbae conviviorum ebriosorum et innuptarum, sed non incorruptarum innumerabilia stupra feminarum?"; *Contra litt. Petil.,* 2.88.195 (CSEL 52: 120): the association of drinking with the free unmarried women who are attached to these wandering gangs; *Contra Cresc.* 4.63.77 (CSEL 52: 577): (in a standard list of accusations) the *bacchationes ebrietatum* that are associated with *circumcelliones*.

[108] Aug. *Contra litt. Petil.* 2.39.94 (CSEL 52: 77): "Quid vobis prodest sobrietas Donati, cum circumcellionum ebriositate polluamini?"

[109] Aug. *Sermo* 47.17 (CCL 41: 588), where reference to "drinking bouts" is not only paralleled by "hordes of circumcellions and their rampages," but also by "the loaning of money at interest."

excessive imbibing of alcohol, mainly as wine, was a general problem in the society as a whole, one against which Christian bishops, including dissident ones, had to struggle. It was an accepted part of festive behavior that had a long history of association with traditional religious celebrations in which the common people engaged.[110] The intoxication could be interpreted as good, something that was akin to the inspiration experienced by the martyr in his or her final passion. In one sermon, commenting on the verse "And my intoxicating cup, how excellent it is!" (Ps 22 [23]: 5), Augustine remarked.[111]

The martyrs were drunk with this same cup when they went to their death, their passion, not even recognizing their own family members. What could be more like being drunk than not even recognizing your weeping wife, your children, or your parents? But the martyrs didn't even perceive them right before their own eyes. Don't be surprised. They were drunk. How were they so drunk? Understand this: they became drunk from drinking the cup that they accepted.

The transfer of intoxicated celebrations at religious cult celebrations, a matter of ancient custom, to the anniversary days of the martyrs' deaths, from one sacred festivity to another, was to be expected. It was a practice that the Catholic Church tried to restrain with particular vigor beginning in the early 390s – not just because of the excessive dancing and exaggerated body movement that it excited, but also because of the tendencies to violent acts.[112] As circumcellions died in sectarian battles, they were worshiped, as were other martyrs, with sacred intoxication. One of the earliest inscriptions attesting to the cult of martyrs in Africa reads: "This is the mensa of Januarius the martyr. Drink up! Live Long!"[113] An anonymous African preacher of the time railed against the widespread practice of binge drinking at the festivals of the martyrs, so powerful that it turned women, even decent ones of high rank, into near-alcoholic lushes who destroyed the moral foundations of good homes.[114] The noble woman, he thunders,

---

[110] For drunkenness as a common problem, see Aug. *Serm* 17.3 (CCL 41: 237–38), 151.4 (CCL41 Ba: 18–20); *Tract. in Ep. Joh.* 4.4 (SC 75: 226); *Tract. in Joh.* 5.17 (CCL 36: 50–51); as a part of normal martyr celebrations: Aug. *Ep.* 29.5 (CCL 31: 100). Repeated sermons of his against such drinking (already in 395) had met with hostility or disinterest, since the celebrations were deeply embedded in local social practice as old customs. See *Sermo* 65.8 (CCL 41Aa: 384) where the move from celebration of the martyr's feast to violent behavior is noted; *En. 3 in Ps.* 103.14 (CCL 40: 1512) notes this same movement to violence.

[111] Aug. *En. in Ps.* 135.14 (CCL 38: 333). "Et calix meus inebrians quam praeclarus est" (VG).

[112] Aug. *Sermo* 311.1, 5–6 (PL 38: 1414–16), 335D.1–2 (PLS 2: 277–78), 367A.3 (PL 39: 1650–52) are exemplary.

[113] Février (1970), pp. 209 f. and Duval, *Loca sanctorum*, 1, pp. 413 f.; cf. MacMullen, *The Second Church*, p. 57.

[114] Ps.-Aug. *De sobrietate et castitate*, 3 (PL 40: 1110–11): "Vinolentia igitur dominae subtractis locorum clavibus, omnia tentantur: cellariorum plenitudo furtis quotidie servilibus inanitur, indisciplinatae

stumbles homewards from the martyr's festival, drunk out of her mind, propped up by her loyal servile *pedisequa*.

The transfer of alcoholic enthusiasm from one holy venue to another is part of the explanation for some circumcellion inebriation. Naturally, they drank in celebration after the mass suicides of fellow dissidents since the latter had become newly born martyrs of the cause. But the drinking of the circumcellions might well have had less to do with celebrations at martyr shrines or their birthdays, than it did with their normal propensity to drink. It had been noted by observers how, in days of the harvest season, it was common for "many" to get drunk and to get involved in "shameful and brutal" fights.[115] It was part of their work. The plain fact is that rough young men had acquired their name from their place of employment, from the fact that they hung out around *cellae* or wine cellars. For them it was less their place of employment, than it was their source of recompense or pay. Harvest laborers in premodern societies were habitually paid in three currencies: in kind, in coin, and in alcoholic drink. In Gaul, and the other northwestern provinces of the empire, the liquid recompense was paid in the local drink, namely beer. And so it remained well into the early twentieth century in these regions of western Europe when "beer money" was the currency of the itinerant harvester. In the other provinces of the empire, including Africa, this supplementary work pay was in wine. Naturally, it was consumed at inordinate rates.

But the imbibing of wine in drunken revelries, in which the circumcellions participated, was linked to the incidents of sectarian violence; it was seen as fueling the hatreds and exciting the action. The atmosphere, the sheer intoxicating rush, impossible to reconstruct, could have been like that shared by sectarian killings in conditions of internecine conflict.[116]

When the militia men killed their victims, the atmosphere was often that of a party or even an orgy. Wounded prisoners and corpses were dragged through the streets by men who were singing, screaming, playing lutes, and stamping their feet. The militia men sometimes took drugs or even made love before the ceremony to give the collective feast an even more jubilatory meaning. Taboos were broken in these orgies of blood as a combination of alcohol, dancing, and drugs heightened the pleasures of cruelty.

---

quae familiae clamoribus domus omnis perstrepit. Lanificiii vero aut negligens, aut nulla, aut abominibilis efficitur cura...et non vestium faciendarum, sed vini quaerit allatam mensuram. Non tuendae castitatis causa telas ad texendum erigit, quae usum telae olim de domo per ebrietatem amisit; et telas quas ancillis otiantibus subtraxit, texendas araneis dedit."

[115] Aug. *Sermo* 230.1 (PL 38: 1103–04): note its connection with harvest: see Shaw, *Bringing in the Sheaves*, ch. 5.

[116] Khosrokhavar, *Suicide Bombers*, p. 145.

And so on: some scenes from the Lebanese Civil War of the late 1970s. What is clear as that the so-called "taboos" were already broken long before the violence came along. "Drinking" or "dancing" or "making love" or "stamping one's feet" in jubilation were already parts of a known repertoire of life. In late Roman Africa, some of them were already present in all kinds of festival celebrations that had been partly transferred to the birthdays of the saints, days and nights given to the remembrance and the celebration of the blood-based heroes. Others, surely, came out of the normal work routines and lives of the men themselves.

The drunken loutishness and violence of harvesting gangs was not just an imaginary moral reproach or rhetorical disrespect, but a reality, some-times a sordid one. It can come as no surprise that the men who were sectarian enforcers, and who were recruited from these seasonal workers, continued to be paid as they had always been paid, partly in alcohol. A report of the destruction of altars in Catholic basilicas in the mid-360s by sectarian gangsters, speaks of the hiring of "ruined and desperate men" and the paying of them with wine.[117] These are the same hired gang-men, the *conducta manus*, who were involved in campaigns of violent enforcement organized by the dissidents to reclaim their basilicas in the aftermath of the emperor Julian's restoration of their legal status.[118] Although Opta-tus does not yet designate them with the name, these are the same men who would later be called circumcellions. What Optatus describes for the 340s and 360s, is confirmed by Augustine in the early 390s in his *Song Against the Donatists* when he speaks of the "bad men" tolerated by the dissidents "for bad pay."[119] Linked to drunkenness was the claim that the demented behavior of the circumcellions was characterized by a raving that bordered on a frenzied madness.[120] The two aspects were exploited to propagate a view of circumcellions as wild men who were running amok, out of control.[121] Their behavior was portrayed as irrational in the sense

---

[117] Optatus, *Contra Parm.* 6.1.2 (SC 413: 162): "ubique tamen nefas est dum tantae rei manus sacrilegas et impias intulisti. Quid perditorum conductam referam multitudinem et vinum in mercedem sceleris datum?"

[118] Optatus, *Contra Parm.* 2.17.2 (SC 412: 272): "De sedibus suis multos fecistis extorres, cum conducta manu venientes basilicas invasistis"; cf. 6.1.2 where he also speaks of the element of hiring (n. 117 above).

[119] Aug. *Psalmus contra part. Donat.* 294 (BA 28: 190): "Malos tantos toleratis, sed nulla bona mercede."

[120] Aug. *Contra litt. Petil.* 2.14.33 (CSEL 52: 37), where these factors are linked: "quas furiosi vestri principes circumcellionum et ipsae catervae vinulentorum et insanorum non tantum ediderint."

[121] Aug. *Contra ep. Parm.* 1.10.16 (CSEL 51: 37): "Cur ergo ipsi ubi possunt templa subvertunt et per furores circumcellionum talia facere"; 1.11.17 (CSEL 51: 38): "vel etiam faciunt per furorem circum-cellionum"; 2.3.6 (CSEL 51: 50): "quorum et catervae gregum furiosorum huc et illuc armatae"; 2.3.7 (CSEL 51: 52): "Nam ipsi vere sanguinem non solum corporaliter per furias circumcellionum"; *Ep.* 105.2.5 (CCL 31B: 52), where the circumcellions are not explicitly named.

that it was insane or demented when measured against the rationality of normally acceptable actions.[122] Their deranged state of mind was contrasted with the moderate simplicity of true monks.[123] On the other hand, it was thought to be a peculiar fault to which their immediate leaders in the dissident church, local parish priests, were particularly liable.[124] It is not unlikely that the men behaved in such a fashion, but the reason was a simple one that had no direct connection with being either mad or demented.

THEY CLOTHE THEMSELVES IN A DREADFUL CRUELTY

Although the sectarian circumcellions were capable of violent acts, they are never portrayed as heavily armed, even properly armed by the standards of the private retinues or public militias of the time. The violent acts are usually described only in general terms, usually as torching properties and doing bodily harm to persons.[125] Their cruelty was renowned, but their weapons never reached even the lower level of brigand gangs in the empire that possessed at least the rudiments of body armor, an array of swords, spears, daggers, shields, bows, and other such armaments.[126] The typical weaponry of the circumcellion consisted of not much more than a wooden club, referred to simply as a *fustis* or *lignum*. In a parody of the biblical injunction that those who live by the sword will die by the sword, the word "sword" is purposefully changed to "club" to make the phrase fit the standard reality of the circumcellion.[127] The wooden club was closely identified with the fearful figure of these men, echoing traditional uses of the club for enforcement. The circumcellions themselves viewed their wooden clubs in symbolic terms: they named them their *Israels*, their particular instrument of divine retribution.[128] The name echoed the biblical

[122] Aug, *Ep.* 105.2.5 (CCL 31B: 52): "Quae est ista dementia" (probably circumcellions – Augustine speaks of *latrocinia*); *Contra ep. Parm.* 1.11.18 (CSEL 51: 39): "vel per insaniam circumcellionum"; 2.3.6 (CSEL 51: 50): "ubi potuerint stragibus nequaquam in tanta immanitate satiantur, ubi ... tanta fervet ebrietas, ut inde insaniam cotidianam non solum alios insectandi."

[123] Aug. *En. in Ps.* 132.3 (CCL 40: 1928): "Comparentur ... furentes cum simplicibus."

[124] Aug. *Sermo* 293A.14 = Dolbeau 3/Mainz 7 (Dolbeau, *Vingt-six sermons*, p. 393): where Augustine passes over adultery and usury as faults typical of the "Donatist" priest to settle on that of excessive drinking: "est apud te aliquis presbyter vel ebriosus ... vel ebriosus presbyter est apud te."

[125] Aug. *Ep.* 43.8 (CSEL 34.2: 106) is typical, speaking of *incendia* and *caedes*.

[126] Aug. *Sermo* 229A.3 = Dolbeau 4/Mainz 9 (Dolbeau, *Vingt-six sermons*, 513–14); for the subtitle of this section, Aug. *Sermo* 164A = Lambot 28 (*RBén* 66 [1956]: 156): "Haec verba quemadmodum accipienda sint non intellegentes, detestabili crudelitate induuntur."

[127] Aug. *Contra litt. Petil.* 2.88.195 (CSEL 52: 120).

[128] Aug. *Psalmus contra partem Donati*, vv. 161–62 (BA 28: 172): "Fustes Israheles vocant quod Deus dixit cum honore / ut plus vastent ipsum nomen quam corpus quod caedunt inde"; cf. *En. in Ps.*

significance of the name Israel as "fighter for God" – an allusion, surely, to their name of *agonistici* – with all of its implications of the enforcement of the justice and therefore the vengeance of the Lord.[129] They knew from their Bible that Jacob, the good brother of the two brothers, Jacob and Esau, involved in fratricidal struggle, was named Israel.[130] They were like him. And the mere sight of these instruments of justice terrified the targets of their attacks.

Despite claims to the contrary, there is no support in the existing evidence for the claim that there was a gradual escalation to swords, lances, spears, and body armor as typical circumcellion weaponry. In one of the earliest of Augustine's references to them, we already find insinuations of a move to real weapons: "[your circumcellions] at first were armed only with clubs, but now have even begun to arm themselves with swords."[131] Such dark imputations were part of a calculated rhetoric of fear. We find the same discrepancy between facts-on-the-ground and rhetoric in the conflict between Christians and Jews on the island of Minorca in 418. In the heat before the final battle, the Christian bishop Severus challenged the Jews: "We brought books to teach, you brought swords and ammunition to kill."[132] The statement is an intentional rhetorical contrast between the pen and the sword, since elsewhere in the same account, it is clear that the Jews were accused of stockpiling not much more than rocks, staves, and other kinds of objects to throw at people.[133] Serious salience in weaponry *can* happen in sectarian conflicts, creating whole new orders of violent men in the process.[134] But in almost all other references to their weapons, dated both to this year, and to all subsequent times, no such permanent escalation of the armament of the circumcellions takes place: the wooden club remained their characteristic armament: it was their weapon

---

10.5 (CCL 38: 78): "et terribiles fustes Israheles vocare, quae homines qui nunc vivunt, quotidie vident et sentiunt."

[129] See Schulten, *De Circumcellionen*, p. 96 and 164 n. 12, where he draws attention to the meaning of the word.

[130] Gen. 32: 27–29, where Jacob is renamed *Yisra'el* meaning something like "he who struggles with God." The trope of the brothers Jacob and Esau was constantly used as symbolic for "the brothers" – the dissidents and the Catholics – involved in the struggle. Both sides, of course, saw and presented themselves as Jacob, the good brother.

[131] Aug. *Contra ep. Parm.* 1.11.17 (CSEL 51: 39).

[132] *Epistula Severi*, 12.9 (Bradbury: 92): "Nos codices ad docendum detulimus, vos ad occidendum gladios ac vectes."

[133] *Epistula Severi*, 8.5 (Bradbury: 86): "Itaque non solum libros revolvere, sed etiam sudes, saxa, iacula omniaque telorum genera ad synagogam conferre coepere."

[134] Comparable moral effects of this sort of armed salience is found in the move from the "hardman" to the "gunman" in "the Troubles" in Northern Ireland; see Feldman, *Formations of Violence*, pp. 46–56.

of choice.[135] Sometimes they also packed "iron" or cutting instruments of some type, including knives. Only when he wishes to emphasize rhetorically the extent of the danger faced by his fellow Catholics does Augustine suggest that a change in the weapons borne by the circumcellions was imminent: a departure from their customary wooden club was about to take place. As he retorts to the dissident bishop Petilian: "Your bands, your *catervae*, are no longer armed in the matter of their ancestors, with just wooden clubs; now axes, spits, and knives have been added."[136] This might well be so, but a careful consideration shows that these "new weapons" were not formal armaments either.

Whenever means of inflicting harm appear beyond wooden clubs, they are of very primitive means of destruction that would be ready to hand in the immediate environment. Most consisted of natural objects, such as rocks and stones, or natural forces such as fire in the form of torches and firebrands.[137] As just noted, whenever one advances beyond basic weaponry, it is to a range of devices including slings, axes, spits, and other pointed instruments.[138] In short, a collection of weapons that would not greatly exceed the normal range of farm tools.[139] It is a kind of improvised weaponry typical of similar situations and rural insurrections in other historical periods: "weapons" of the kind used by rebellious agricultural slaves in Sicily in the late Roman Republic or by peasant enforcers "armed" by their landlords in the same period in rural Italy.[140] The same profile in personal armament is true of modern cases of "sectarian"-type violence in

---

[135] It is an instrument often simply "picked up" by persons involved in sectarian violence – see, e.g., Philo, *In Flacc.* 66 on the riots in Alexandria in 38 CE. For more on these "associations" of young men in the context of mobilizing violence, see Seeland (1996), pp. 113–14.

[136] Aug. *Contra litt. Petil.* 2.96.222 (CSEL 52: 140): so it must be noted that most references dating to after 401 still portray the wooden club as their principal weapon.

[137] Aug. *En. in Ps.* 10.5 (CCL 38: 78): "cum in vestris castris privati fustes ignesque sic saeviant"; *Ep.* 43.24 (CSEL 34.2: 106): "caedes et incendia circumcellionum."

[138] Aug. *En. in Ps.* 54.26 (CCL 39: 675): "Adtende armatum, si vir pacis est, et non sanguinis. Si fustem saltem solum ferret; sed fert fundibulum, fert securim, fert lapides, fert lanceas; et ista portantes ubique possunt evagantur sanguinem innocentium sitiunt."

[139] K. D. White, "Knives, Sickles, Hooks and Scythes," ch. 3 in *Agricultural Implements of the Roman World*, Cambridge University Press, 1967, pp. 69–103, provides a survey of normal harvesting implements, any one of which might easily serve as a weapon.

[140] See Diod. Sic. 34/35.2.1: in addition to the regular arms the slave leader Eunus provided his followers with in the First Sicilian Slave war (*c.* 135–130 BCE), the men who first joined him out of the countryside were armed with axes, hatchets, slings, sickles, fire-hardened sticks and even cooking spits; compare Ruff, *Violence in Early Modern Europe*, p. 124: "much early modern violence was the result of an assailant wielding some more common weapon: a walking stick or peasant's staff; tools of a trade, like a butcher's cleaver, or a hammer; axes, and a mass of hastily chosen instruments, including iron bars, billiard cues, whips, and furniture."

north Africa.[141] The perpetrators used weapons of convenience, instruments that lay to hand that any rural worker could readily turn to purposes other than agricultural ones. In most instances where such gangs of rural workers were mobilized and armed, however, it was not by themselves, but rather by rural landlords who ordinarily used the men both for armed defense and, where required, for aggressive attacks on threatening or defenseless neighbors.[142]

In the only case where Augustine is specific about a new device used by circumcellions in their attacks, it was not the addition of a new type of manufactured weapon to which he refers, but rather the use of a concoction of vinegar and lime to produce an acidic liquid which they threw into the eyes of their victims.[143] Although this might indeed have been "a new and horrible" innovation, it was still produced out of products that were readily to hand in the rural environment in which these men lived and worked.[144] The impression of the circumcellions is not one of men who were armed or trained in any fashion with formal weapons, but rather one of men who picked up and used as weapons whatever assorted tools were commonly available.[145] As the violent men themselves were persons being mobilized and transferred from one task to another, so too their weapons were usually agricultural implements put to new and violent uses. Both the violent energies and the instruments could easily melt back into their normal world of ordinary uses.

---

[141] It is perhaps surprising how little change in this respect there was between incidents separated by sixteen intervening centuries. Although the perpetrators of the massacres in Algeria in the 1990s did have guns, most of the severe personal injuries and deaths were inflicted with a range of sharp objects: knives, axes, machetes, saws, swords, hatchets, and with "weapons" capable of inflicting blunt-force trauma: clubs, metal bars, spades, picks. See Aït-Larbi *et al.* (1999), p. 126; the defenders armed themselves in a similar fashion: *ibid.*, p. 119.

[142] See the typical case reported in Cic. *Pro Caec.* 21.60: "Si glebis aut saxis aut fustibus aliquem de fundo praecipitem egeris"; cf. Brunt (1971) for a survey of this type of rural violence in late Republican Italy.

[143] Aug. *Contra Cresc.* 3.42.46 (CSEL 52: 453): "Insuper novo et antehac inaudito sceleris genere oculis eorum calce aceto permixto infundentes et infercientes, quos evellere conpendio poterant, excruciare amplius eligunt quam citius excaecare. Nam primo tantum calce ad hoc facinus utebantur, sed posteaquam illos, quibus hoc fecerant, cito salutem reparasse didicerunt, acetum addiderunt." Cf. *Ep.* 88.8 (CCL 31A: 145); Possid. *Vita Aug.* 10.6 (Bastiaensen: 154): "Aliquibus etiam calcem cum aceto in oculos miserunt."

[144] *Calx* or lime was widely produced on rural estates, not only for "liming" soils, but also for use in building: Cato, *De Agr. Cult.* 16 (production); 18.7 (use in paving and foundation courses of a pressing room); Pliny, *NH*, 36.55.177 (use as mortar and stucco); Vitruvius, *De Architect.* 7.3.2 f. (in stuccoing buildings). *Acetum* or soured wine, used to produce vinegar, was also a standard by-product of vinting: Varro, *LL*, 9.66.

[145] Aug. *Contra Cresc.* 3.42.46 (CSEL 52: 453).

LEADERS AND FOLLOWERS

The question of the membership and formation of the gangs naturally raises other ones about the entrepreneurs, managers, and directors of violence. The circumcellions are frequently described as a kind of "external instrument" being manipulated by the leadership of the dissident church.[146] If potential enforcers existed, then what was the balance between self-motivation and outside organization? The hostile phrase "your clerics and circumcellions," a constantly repeated mantra, fixed the connection in the minds of readers and listeners.[147] In recounting lurid stories of attacks on Catholic clergy, churches, and clerics, more than once Augustine portrays the circumcellions as acting under the direct orders of the dissident clergy, even claiming that the dissident bishops appointed the leaders of the violent gangs.[148] Optatus already made assertions about much the same situation in his description of the acts of sectarian violence of the 340s and 360s. Yet the problem of leadership is not so easily resolved. In almost as many other places, Augustine refers to the leaders of the circumcellions, their *principes*, in a way that suggests that they had their own hierarchy of leadership independent of and different from the bishops who sometimes incited and led them.[149] And the laws meant to repress these men were direct responses to charges raised by Catholic bishops that were part of their rhetorical counterattack against dissident claims of persecution. How could the dissidents possibly be so hypocritical was the counterclaim.[150]

---

[146] Admittedly in rhetorical flow, Aug. *Contra ep. Parm.* 1.11.18 (CSEL 51: 39), says that the dissident leadership used "barbarian kings" to inflict damage on "the Rogatists," provincial governors to harm "the Maximianists," and the circumcellions to harm everyone; the connections between circumcellions and the dissident church were part of the official Catholic rhetoric of the age: see Lamirande (1965e) for some standard references.

[147] "Clerici (vestri) et circumcelliones (vestri)" *vel sim.*: Aug., *Ep.* 88.1 (CSEL 34.2: 407), 88.6 (CSEL 34.2: 412), 88.7 (CSEL 34.2: 413), 105.2.3 (CSEL 34.2: 597): clerics as their *duces*; 108.5.14 (CSEL 34.2: 627–28): twice noted, once it is the "brigandage" of both that is involved; 111.1 (CSEL 34.2: 643); 133.1 (CSEL 44: 80); 134.2 (CSEL 44: 85); 185.7 (CSEL 57: 24); *En. in Ps.* 10.5 (CCL 38: 78): bishops and priests are their leaders; *Contra Cresc.* 3.42.46 (CSEL 52: 453); 3.43.47 (CSEL 52.455): circumcellions are *satellites* of the clerics; 3.47.51 (CSEL 52: 459): "inter manus circumcellionum clericorumque vestrorum"; 3.48.52 (CSEL 52: 460): the Crispinus affair; 3.63.69 (CSEL 52: 475): against the Maximianists; 4.50.60 (CSEL 52: 558): "a clericis et circumcellionibus vestris"; 4.51.61 (CSEL 52: 558): again, they are the *satellites* of the clerics; *Brev. Collat.* 3.11.21 (CCL 149A: 287): "cum eorum circumcelliones ducibus clericis"; 3.11.22 (CSEL 53: 71): "a clericis et circumcellionibus eorum."

[148] Aug. *Contra ep. Parm.* 1.11.17 (CSEL 51: 39): "per furiosos ebriosorum iuvenum greges quibus principes constituunt."

[149] Aug. *Contra litt. Petil.* 2.14.33 (CSEL 52: 37–38): "quas furiosi vestri principes circumcellionum et ipsae catervae vinulentorum atque insanorum non tantum ediderint ab initio schismatis vestri, sed omnino edere non desinant strages."

[150] Aug. *Brev. Collat.* 3.11.21 (CCL 149A: 287): suggesting that this might have been part of the debate on the third day of the conference (for which we lack the original record), but it is more probably

It's not *their* place, surely, to speak of "persecution" on the grounds that the Catholics asked for something from the emperors on behalf of their own Church, when at the same time their circumcellions were committing such horrible crimes under the command of *their* clergy. To which charge they vainly object that their *bishops* had nothing to do with this since, they [i.e. the bishops] assert, such terrible things were done under the leadership of the (lower) clergy.

The imputation that the leaders, the *duces* or generals, were provided by the clergy of the dissident church was followed by a list of the usual cruelties: the blinding of eyes with acidic solutions, the torture of the bodies of clergy and bishops of the Catholic Church.[151] The problem is that the connection of circumcellion violence with the leadership provided by the clerics of the dissident church is in part real and in part imputed. The imputations were the deliberate links that Catholic lobbyists were attempting to forge between the two in the minds of imperial administrators like Flavius Marcellinus, despite the vociferous denials of the bishops of the dissident church.

One of the critical functions that circumcellion stories played in the Catholic–dissident struggle was to incite public authorities (in the end, the court at Ravenna) to action through fear of an apprehended rural insurgency. But this function tended to come to the fore later in the conflict. The original function of the stories was internal to the religious struggle: it was to counter the dissident claims that they were suffering persecution and suffering martyrdom at the hands of the Catholics. The narratives of circumcellion violence were a dramatic way of showing that it is *we, the Catholics*, who are really suffering persecution. Although this line of argument did not appear in the debates of the conference at Carthage in 411 (or, at least in the parts of it that survive), Augustine's *Brief Account of the Conference*, produced in its immediate aftermath, emphasized this very point, as did his public letter "to the Donatists" written and circulated at this same time and for the same reason.[152] Here, too, the vivid references to individual acts of circumcellion violence, the horrors committed by them, are specifically meant not to excite official action, but rather to counter "Donatist" claims of persecution and martyrdom.

an Augustinian gloss: "nec de persecutionibus, quod aliquid ab imperatoribus pro ecclesia Catholici peterent, cum eorum circumcelliones ducibus clericis tam horrenda mala committerent. Ubi frustra responderunt nihil hoc ad sacerdotes pertinere, cum clericis ducibus illi talia fecisse asserebantur."

[151] Aug. *Brev. Collat.* 3.11.22 (CCL 149A: 287): "Ibi etiam cum dictum esset quod calce et aceto humanos oculos persecuti sint, in quo scelere Diabolum crudelitate pervicerunt, qui hoc in sancti viri carne non fecit quam in potestatem acceperat affligendam . . . quasi Catholici aliud quam passiones suas dixerint immanissima a clericis et circumcellionibus eorum." Note that keywords that evoke persecution are used throughout.

[152] Aug. *Ad Donatist. post Collat.* 17.22 (CSEL 53: 121).

It was of use to Catholic bishops, of course, to suggest that circumcellions were a strange new kind of men who had arisen because they had been instructed to do what they were doing by "evil teachers."[153] Such assertions were repeatedly met with denials from the dissident clergy.[154] Beyond the problem of sectarian rhetoric is the real difficulty of specifying the role played by the primary controllers of seasonal laborers: the landowners, their procurators, and the other agents and bailiffs who managed these gangs on an ordinary basis, the persons whom the imperial laws of 412 and 414 specifically targeted as the ones who were primarily responsible for the employment of the circumcellions. There are repeated hints that such persons were involved in managing at least some of the violence. A man who was under the authority of a powerful man named Celer, on his lands outside Hippo, was making overtures to Catholics, probably about the possibility of crossing over.[155] Augustine remarks that Celer had a reasonable fear of violence from certain "rough characters," but he expressed the hope that since Celer controlled them they would not prove to be a serious hurdle to his conversion. The fear was justified, given the fact that one of the main tasks of circumcellions was to make "the traitor" suffer.

THE PROBLEM OF VIOLENCE

In general summaries of the gang members from the last decades of reportage on the circumcellions, Augustine and his biographer Possidius state that more than a few "Donatists" wished to separate themselves from the violent excesses of these men. When recounting their more extravagant forms of violence, including the intentional blinding of their enemies by using an acidic solution of lime and vinegar, Possidius remarked that "it was for this reason that these particular rebaptizing Donatists came to be hated *by their own people*."[156] Possidius was reiterating a point of view that Augustine confirmed at the end of his life in the general definition of circumcellions. In his handbook on the identification of heresies and heretics,

---

[153] So Possidius, *Vita Aug.* 10.1 (Bastiaensen: 152): "Habebant etiam iidem Donatistae per suas pene omnes ecclesias inauditum hominum genus perversum ac violentum . . . qui circumcelliones dicebantur . . . Qui malis imbuti doctoribus audacia superbia et temeritate illicita."

[154] E.g. Aug. *Contra ep. Parm.* 1.11.17 (CSEL 51: 39): "Quorum scelera cum ad eos deferuntur, fingunt se ignorare tale hominum genus vel omnino ad se non pertinere contra quam omnes homines norunt ore impudentissimo affirmant . . . si licet in ipsa Africa Donatistis episcopis Donatistarum circumcellionum vel facta nescire vel dicere ad se non pertinere."

[155] Aug. *Ep.* 57 (CCL 31A: 5–6), cf. *Ep.* 56; see, "Celer (1)," PAC, pp. 202–03.

[156] Possid. *Vita Aug.* 10.6 (Bastiaensen: 154): "Unde etiam suis iidem Donatistae rebaptizatores in odium veniebant."

he outlined the violent acts committed by these men, but added: "Never-theless such actions are displeasing to many of the Donatists."[157] Although some purposeful rhetorical exculpation was involved, in his most direct approach to his opposite number at Hippo regarding circumcellion vio-lence, Augustine suggested not only that the dissident bishop was not himself directly involved – after all, he had tried to control the excesses of these men on one occasion – but rather that the gangs were usually controlled by rural priests.[158] Indeed, these same priests are portrayed as having been the primary beneficiaries of the seizures of lands and basilicas in the countryside of Hippo.[159] Many bishops of the dissident church, it seems, either deliberately or for the purpose of cover, kept a significant distance between themselves and the violent actions of the *agonistici*.

This pacific attitude among some of the dissidents who were hostile to the excesses of the violent gangs is one that Augustine notes as early as his tract against Parmenian, written in 400, where he deals at length with the circumcellions as a manifest example of the deep involvement of the dissident church in acts of illegal private violence. But he admits that there were those in the other church who rejected any association with the men of violence.[160]

When the crimes of these men are brought up to them [i.e. the leaders of the dis-sident church] they *pretend* that they don't know any such men or, with shameless effrontery, they emphatically state that these events, which all men know about, have nothing at all to do with them. When these outsiders assert that they do not know what is happening in Africa, whether it is being done by the party of Donatus or against the party of Donatus, they don't wish to accept the united voice of the whole world whose claim is much more likely and true. But how is it possible for Donatist bishops in Africa itself not to know the actions of the Donatist circumcellions or to say that these actions don't belong to them?

---

[157] Aug. *De Haeres.* 69.4 (CCL 46: 332): "Verumtamen plerisque Donatistarum displicent tales, nec eorum communione contaminari se putant."

[158] Aug. *Ep.* 108.5.18 (CCL 31B: 82), where he says that Macrobius wished, because of popular hatred of their actions, to return to their owners the properties taken by the circumcellions, but that he could not do so because it would risk alienating his priests: "ne illorum audaciam, quam sibi putaverunt vestri presbyteri necessariam, nimium cogamini offendere."

[159] Aug. *Ep.* 108.5.18 (CCL 31B: 82): "Iactant enim praecedentia circa vos merita sua demonstrantes et enumerantes . . . quot loca et basilicas per eos presbyteri vestri vastatis nostris fugatisque tenuerunt, ut, si eos volueritis esse severi, beneficiis eorum appareatis ingrati."

[160] Aug. *Contra ep. Parm.* 1.11.17 (CSEL 51: 39): "fingunt se ignorare tale hominum genus . . . neque hanc saltem vocem totius orbis accipiunt, multo probabilius veriusque dicentis nescire se quid in Africa gestum sit sive a parte Donati sive contra partem Donati." But it is a known fact that was repeated in his descriptions of circumcellions, including the classic definition in his *De Haeres.* 69.4 (CCL 46: 332), which ends: "Verumtamen plerisque Donatistarum displicent tales" (note that such men displease *many* of "the Donatists").

This rejection of violence was a claim repeated by some, if not many, of the leaders of the other church. In a letter to Emeritus, the dissident bishop of Caesarea, that discusses the justification for the use of state force to protect Catholics, Augustine refers to the lawless, secretive violence of the sectarian gangsters, but then hastens to add "something over which you, who do not do such things, grieve and lament."[161] In a long letter to Macrobius, his dissident opposite at Hippo, he first notes the threatening behavior of circumcellions who escorted the bishop into the city, but then admits that Macrobius himself explicitly separated himself from their excesses, severely reprimanding them in public and even angering them.[162]

> On the next day, however, they were shaken and stung by the sharp barbs of the words that you hurled at them through an interpreter who spoke the Punic language – moved, as you were, by the honest and inborn indignation of a free person. You were more angered by their actions than thankful for their services. In response, they rushed out of the middle of your congregation, gesticulating with angry gestures – as we've heard from some people who were present and who reported this to us.

In a still earlier reply to Cresconius, in 406/07, Augustine had already taken this line, stating straightforwardly: "You deny the madness of the circumcellions and the sacrilegious cult, impious as it is, offered to the cadavers of the suicide jumpers. But you cannot deny the fact."[163] Yet, deny it they did. Cresconius and other dissident leaders *did* reject imputed associations with the circumcellions. Their denial raises a problem about their relationship to this strand in the sectarian violence of the time. Were they genuinely denying connections with the men of violence, wishing to cut the links between themselves and the popular gangs over which they had no control? Or – as Augustine asserts – was their denial a pretence – a necessary and carefully crafted part of their public face while they covertly supported and cooperated with the men of violence?[164] The dissident bishops' views were put on record at the conference at Carthage in 411.

---

[161] Aug. *Ep.* 87.8 (CCL 31A: 137): "Nostri autem adversus illicitas et privatas vestrorum violentias, quas et vos ibi, qui talia non facitis, doletis et gemitis."

[162] Aug. *Ep.* 108.5.14 (CCL 31B: 78–79): "Alio tamen die concussi ac stimulati aculeis verborum tuorum, quae in eos per Punicum interpretem honesta et ingenua libertatis indignatione iaculatus es factis eorum irritatus potius quam delectatus obsequiis, se de media congregatione, sicut ab eis, qui aderant, narrantibus audire potuimus, furibundis motibus rapuerunt."

[163] Aug. *Contra Cresc.* 4.63.77 (CSEL 52: 577): "Negas furorem circumcellionum et praecipitatorum ultro cadaverum cultus sacrilegos et profanos."

[164] See Aug. *Ep.* 34.4 (CCL 31: 125) for one example amongst many, where he takes the denial of condoning violence as a piece of hypocrisy. The dissident bishops, like Proculeianus, feign their rejection of violent behavior.

The Catholics objected that "the Donatists" were not suffering a persecution, but rather that *they* had been inflicting this kind of suffering on the Catholics by means of their circumcellion gangs. The dissident bishops replied that whatever it was that the circumcellions were doing, it had very little to do with them.[165] Finally, in his persuasive brief to the imperial official Bonifatius in 417, Augustine affirmed that there were "very many persons rooted in this same heretical superstition who were horrified by such deeds, who thought that their innocence in such matters was plain because they were so upset by them."[166]

The claim is not all that unbelievable. The rhetorical charges of Augustine, and his peers, who constantly connected the dissident bishops, priests, and the circumcellions in a fixed unholy triad, simply ignore the fact that many of the gangs were freelancers – Christian gangsters who, from the days of their attacks on "pagans" and their shrines, had mobilized and committed acts of violence on their own. And even if there was a hard core of circumcellions, there were "others like them" who committed similar violent acts, but who were distinct from them.[167] In some cases, such as the seizure of basilicas, there is not much reason to doubt the direction to violent acts offered by priests and bishops. In other cases, the priests and bishops of the dissident church manifestly did not direct or control these men. It is probably better to understand "the circumcellions" as an amorphous and mixed phenomenon. In some cases they were sectarian men of violence who were self-directed, recruited, and motivated; in other circumstances they were not much more than the group of men who happened to be recruited in an *ad hoc* manner to be used as enforcers; in still others, they appear to have been more permanent religious gangs mobilized and activated by a given dissident priest or bishop.

A basic point that must be emphasized about these gangs, Catholic or dissident, is that the recent phase in which they had been activated was in the anti-pagan campaigns of the late 380s and early 390s in which they had been used to attack traditional temples, shrines, sacred images, sacrifices, and ceremonials. As such, they naturally received encouragement

---

[165] GCC, *Capitula*, 3.296–97 (SC 195: 502): "Catholicorum ad ista responsio . . . quod persecutionem non patiantur ipsi (sc. Donatistae), sed faciant. Ubi dicunt Donatistae quod circumcelliones faciunt ad sacerdotes minime pertinere."

[166] Aug. *Ep.* 185.16 (CSEL 57: 15); in his letter to the tribune Dulcitius, in a year soon afterwards, he noted that the self-killings of some of the dissidents were "hateful and horrible even to many of their own people whose minds have not been possessed by this great insanity." (*Ep.* 204.5; CSEL 57: 320).

[167] Aug. *Ep. ad Cath. contra Donatist.* 20.56 (CSEL 52: 305): "non tantum talia, qualia vestri circumcelliones et eorum similes ubi possunt membris eius infligunt."

from their religious leaders, again whether dissident and Catholic. It is precisely in the context of warning his parishioners against taking violence into their own hands against powerful "pagans" and their idols that Augustine states that such illicit private violence is characteristic of men like the circumcellions.[168] In a discussion where he debates the distinction between private violence and public authority, he explicitly points to the fact that circumcellion gangs had been organized to destroy "pagan" temples and to enforce their ideas of justice.[169] As we have already seen, there is good evidence to show that these leaders systematically and liberally over-interpreted and extended the specific meaning and intent of more restricted imperial laws so as to encourage a broader enforcement that encompassed the destruction of "pagan" temples, shrines, and simulacra. Sometimes these holy initiatives met with collusion, acceptance, and even active support by imperial officials, like the Praetorian Prefect Cynegius in the East, which only served to propagate the conviction that such free-wheeling agents of self-help were simply helping the government in the enforcement of imperial law.[170] Once again, the transfer from anti-pagan to anti-Christian violence was a lateral one that was made easier by the construction of certain heretical Christians as no different than pagans, or Jews.

[168] Aug. *Sermo* 62.13 (PL 38: 421), probably from the late 390s; the linkage between circumcellion violence and Catholic attacks on pagan shrines is surely not coincidental.

[169] Aug. *Contra ep. Parm.* 1.10.16 (CSEL 51: 37): "Cur ergo ipsi ubi possunt templa subvertunt et per furores circumcellionum talia facere aut vindicare non cessant? An iustior est privata violentia quam regia diligentia?"

[170] Libanius, *Or.* 30.25–26; cf. Gaddis, *Religious Violence*, pp. 218–19.

CHAPTER 15

Men of blood

And I will execute great vengeance
upon them with furious rebukes;
and they shall know that I am the Lord,
when I shall lay My vengeance upon them.[1]

(Ezekiel)

Just how violent were the sectarian circumcellions? How eager were they,
in the much-quoted biblical parlance of the time, to rush with their feet
to shed blood?[2] In the context of the types of violence that characterized
late Roman Africa, the episodes of circumcellion violence did not amount
to anything much above the level of hard street-fighting – the mayhem
of fisticuffs, stabbings, beatings, and the occasional homicide ordinarily
indulged in by gangs of harvester workers. Their violence was not remotely
close to a war, to "barbarian incursions" – even where these latter were
smaller interpellations of wandering bands – or, much less, to the systematic violence of slavers whose attentions in these years were turning more
intently to exploit the "inside supply" offered by vulnerable rural peoples
in Africa.[3] Nor was circumcellion violence comparable to the large regional
upheavals of the kind that involved a Firmus or a Gildo. In terms of scale,
their destructiveness was at the distal end of a grid of violence, close to
individual acts of physical aggression. A standard list of acts of sectarian
violence in Africa of the period includes assaults on basilicas, the forced
ritual cleansing of sacred sites, sacrileges committed against holy objects,

---

[1] Ezekiel 25: 17 (KJV). The chapter title comes from Aug. *En. in Ps.* 138.26 (CCL 40: 2008), referring
to vv. 18–20 of Ps. 138, where he comments: "Who are the men of blood? John says: 'everyone who
hates his brother is a murderer'" (1 Jn 3:15); cf. *En. in Ps.* 54.26 (CCL 39: 675).

[2] "Their feet rush to shed blood" (*veloces pedes eorum ad effundendum sanguinem*: VG): Romans 3: 15,
referring to Isaiah 59: 7 – a verse frequently quoted in these struggles: e.g. Aug. *Contra litt. Petil.*
1.27.29 (CSEL 52: 22), although he suggests especially by the dissidents against the Catholics: *Ep.*
108.14–15 (CCL 34.2: 628–29).

[3] For the operations of these slavers, and their armed gangs, in late Roman Africa, see, e.g., Lepelley
(1981) and (1983), Rougé (1983), and Woolf (2004).

injuries inflicted on persons and attempts on the lives of clergy.[4] What was the place of circumcellion actions in these and similar actions? Rather than rushing to exaggerated claims about rural jacqueries or social rebellions, questions need to be posed first about the modes and styles of circumcellion violence and about the specifics of their targeting practices. Most circumcellion violence, by far, was rural in nature, taking place in small towns, rural villages, and in the full countryside around market centers or on farms. Their violence was the opposite of the "pagan"–Christian riots that were mainly urban in nature.[5]

The social and work background out of which these men emerged has been mostly imputed and generally misunderstood. A fairly standard picture of the behavior of itinerant seasonal labor gangs out of whose ranks the sectarian circumcellions were recruited is one of men who always had a potential for violence. Migrant mobility, the lack of local family attachments, the dynamics of young men in groups, the physical nature of the work – all of these factors, and others, conduced to occasional outbreaks of violence. Beyond and behind these specific links was the fact that young men were always a problem.[6] When added to the pressures and inducements of work on the road, the catalyst of alcohol encouraged violence inside and between itinerant harvesting gangs, and between them and local communities. Whether or not violence erupted on any specific occasion or harvest season, locals were nevertheless apprehensive, and they were prepared for the worst.[7] But the reaping gangs on the move were not the only armed men associated with the harvest who were capable of violence or prone to it.

Given the economic importance of the harvest, there were other normal risks of damage, from the purposeful burning of grain fields (a typical crime in Africa) to the thieving of crops, that fed heightened expectations of trouble.[8] In these circumstances, it was normal for landlords to hire men to serve as protectors of the crops: harvest guards, or *custodes fructuum*, as they were called. The harvests had to be carefully watched in the vulnerable

---

[4] Brisson, *Autonomisme et christianisme*, pp. 243–44.

[5] On "pagan"–Christian riots, see ch. 5, pp. 247 f. above; Augustine, for example, routinely characterized circumcellion violence as "rustic" (see, for example, the typical *rusticana audacia* of *Ep.* 108.6.18, see ch. 17, p. 782 below). This pattern of sectarian violence seems to be the opposite of the communal Hindu–Muslim violence in India where most violent acts, including killings, have been concentrated in urban riots: Varshney, *Ethnic Conflict*, pp. 94–95.

[6] As always in sectarian violence of this type; see ch. 5, pp. 243f.; and, by comparison, in Northern Ireland: Coogan, *The Troubles*, pp. 87 ff.

[7] Shaw, *Bringing in the Sheaves*, chs. 1 and 5.

[8] The firing of crops standing in the fields was known to be a crime typically found in Africa: *Dig.* 48.19.16.9

stage between reaping and storage. The men who performed this task were tough and, ordinarily, they were armed.[9] They were rough young males who were prepared to patrol and protect on behalf of a landlord or patron. Even if there was a lot of normal potential for violence surrounding such men – reapers, harvest guards, and others like them – their usual behavior and the ordinary objects of their violence would not normally have anything to do with sectarian matters. If *some* of these men, including the reapers who were known as "circumcellions," were to be mobilized to protect and to attack in the new context of sectarian loyalties, then they had to be oriented to new targets. Associated with these new targets, there were, broadly speaking, two kinds of violence: attacks directed against property – principally basilicas, shrines, houses of the clergy, and other ecclesiastical properties – and attacks directed against persons, mainly certain types of "bad" clergy.

Although the violence of the sectarian circumcellions was sometimes aimed at objects of property, frequently their assaults were connected in some fashion with hostile persons. The typical form of personal violence engaged in by circumcellions was the physical beating, especially that administered with wooden clubs. Persons who were dragged from their homes, who were stopped while they were traveling on the public roads, or who were trapped inside churches, were detained, physically threatened, and beaten with wooden staves. The wooden club, indeed, was their iconic and single most feared weapon.[10] But was this use of the club a practice peculiar to them – something new that they had adopted – or was it part of an existing social repertoire of punishment? Given the propensity to social mimicry, the fact that men whose normal occupations were not those of permanent police enforcers began behaving in this new role raises the possibility that they were imitating others, namely their legitimate betters. If there is one standard picture of circumcellions, it is that they were bands of men armed with wooden clubs who acted in concert or unison, and who often formed marching units that reminded observers of *turmae* and

---

[9] The classic instance of these *custodes* or field guards for Africa is Aug. *Ep.* 46.2 (CCL 31: 199); cf. *Ep.* 93.2 and 11 (CCL 31A: 168, 174–75); they are referred to in the standard regulations for the management of *coloni* on large domain lands in the high empire: see CIL 8.25902: III.14–16 = FIRA², I: 100 (Hr. Mettich, AD 116–17); for their presence elsewhere in the Mediterranean, see Pliny, *Ep.* 9.37.3; cf. Cato, *RR*, 33; Columella, *RR*, 7.3.25; Jerome, *Ep.* 106.57; and legal texts such as *Dig.* 34.1.15.1 and 32.92.pr.

[10] Aug. *En. in Ps.* 10.5 (CSEL 38: 78); *En. in Ps.* 95.11 (CCL 39: 1350): "an forte hic obtinebunt et dicent se regnare a ligno, qui a fustibus circumcellionum regnant?"; *Contra litt. Petil.* 2.64.144 (CSEL 52: 97): "nam de vestra mansuetudine non tuae voces, sed circumcellionum fustes interrogentur"; for other typical references, see, e.g., *Contra ep. Parm.* 1.11.17; 2.3.6; *Contra litt. Petil.* 2.47.110, 2.63.144, 2.88.195.

cunei – that is, of regular units of the state's militia. Both these terms have military denotations, which raises the suggestive parallel of modes of official enforcement. Were the circumcellions not just *like* the "wing" and "wedge" formations of the army, but men who constituted themselves as legitimate enforcers in the same mode?

When examples of dissident writings from the time are considered, the parallels found in them are hardly without significance. In these narratives, which surely reflect common attitudes of the time, dissident Christians are repeatedly portrayed as subject to beatings with *fustes* or wooden clubs by the legitimately empowered officials of the state. In the acts of the Abitinian martyrs, for example, the narrator reports the confrontation between the Christian Felix and the Roman governor Anullinus on 12 February 304.[11] Driven to distraction and anger by the recalcitrant Christian defendant, the governor ordered him to be beaten with wooden clubs – *fustibus caesum*. This man was followed by another, likewise named Felix, who made a similar confession and suffered a similar fate. He too was beaten with wooden clubs – *ipse fustium illisione quassatus*. A third man, called Quintus, was also subjected to a brutal beating – *caesus fustibus*. Then a man named Felix "the younger" came forward proclaiming the "hope, salvation, and day of the Christians" and he was similarly savagely beaten with clubs –*similiter ipse fustibus caederetur*.[12] Even putting aside the fictive elements in the narrative, including the verbal taunting by the martyrs, savage beatings with clubs appear as one of the standard elements of normal judicial enforcement.

From these incidents involving the tribunal of the provincial governor, which are quite typical, a few logical conclusions follow. First, beatings with clubs were routinely administered by soldiers who were part of the enforcement personnel accompanying the governor on his annual round of provincial assizes. And, just as important, these beatings were disciplinary in nature. Christians who listened to the readings of the stories of African martyrs would hear this message time and again: Christian defendants were beaten with wooden clubs to bring them into line with the demands of authority.[13] Beatings administered with wooden clubs were a constant part of a disciplinary regime in which the victim was not meant to be killed by his or her official assailants, but rather to be disciplined to see reason and to

---

[11] *Passio sanctorum Dativi, Saturnini presbyteri et aliorum* (Maier, *Dossier*, vol. 1, no. 4); there are both Catholic and dissident versions. For critical evaluation, see the indispensable study of Franchi de' Cavalieri (1935a) with the review by Delehaye (1936) and, especially, Dearn (2004).

[12] *Passio sanctorum Dativi, Saturnini presbyteri et aliorum*, 13–14 (Maier, *Dossier*, vol. 1, pp. 77–78).

[13] Beating with rods and clubs is found in earlier African passions that were likely to affect later perceptions and practices; see e.g. *Passio Perpetuae et Felicitatis*, 6.5 (SC 417: 124).

admit the truth. In the drama of public justice that Roman courts replayed in the hundreds of municipalities, villages, and rural domains, both as part of local courts and as the judicial assizes of the governor, the basic message was inculcated into the minds of imperial subjects: this is how you punish contumacious behavior and this is how you enforce obedience.

These scenes of judicial discipline were normal and typical. The account of the martyrdoms of Maximianus and Isaac record that at the end, when the bodies of the martyrs were being brought back to Carthage, the excited and angry crowd of dissident believers was repressed by exactly these types of men and methods: "Then soldiers and local militiamen, the *triviarii*, who were armed with wooden clubs, came to the prison, and driving the people down the road in a general slaughter, wounded almost all of them."[14] Similarly, the passion account of the martyr Marculus repeatedly refers to the public beatings with wooden clubs inflicted by the bands of soldiers who accompanied the imperial emissaries Paul and Macarius in 347.[15] When Macarius arrived at Vegesala, he arrested the dissident bishops whom he discovered assembled with Marculus. The bishops were stripped of their clothing, bound to pillars, and beaten with wooden clubs:

Among the men who came there was the most holy Marculus. When they had been discovered on a certain estate that had the name of Vegesela, they were immediately arrested because of the "humanity" of the man [sc. Macarius] who had been placed in command of the sacrilegious campaign of Unity. They were bound to individual columns, their priestly limbs were stripped bare in public, and they were beaten with the savage blows of wooden clubs.

The author of this account wishes to draw attention to the fact that the soldiers similarly beat Marculus with wooden clubs: "A large number of the executioners raged against one man, lacerating his sacred arms and raining down on him the harsh blows of wooden clubs."[16]

The actions of public enforcers and soldiers were witnessed by crowds of ordinary people who came out of interest or who had been summoned to watch the trial and disciplining of defendants in the town square.[17] Beatings with clubs and rods were the normal means of coercion used,

[14] *Passio Maximiani et Isaac*, 13.90 (Mastandrea 1995: 85): "Venerant ergo ad carcerem militum cunei et triviarii fustibus onerati, et vi caedis populos repellentes cunctos paene fecerant vulneratos."
[15] *Passio Marculi*, 4.14–15 (Mastandrea 1995: 67): "Inter hos igitur sanctissimus Marculus venit: qui cum eum in quaddam possessione repperissent, cui Vegeselae nomen est, statim hac eius qui sacrilegae unitati praeerat humanitate suscepti sunt, ut seorsum singuli ad singulas columnas vincti, nudatis publice sacerdotalibus membris, acerbis fustium ictibus caederentur."
[16] *Passio Marculi*, 5.20 (Mastandrea 1995: 67): "Saeviebat itaque contra unum multiplex carnificum numerus et sacratos confitentis artus dura fustium poena laniabat."
[17] Grasmück, *Coercitio*, p. 123 n. 636, on the normal use of the beating with clubs by the armed attendants of the governor's or judge's enforcement entourage.

for example, by Flavius Marcellinus in 412 in his judicial inquiries into circumcellions who had been accused of assault and murder. It was a form of punitive violence that was found in all basic units of social discipline: "a form of restraint that is customarily used by the teacher of liberal arts, by parents themselves, and by bishops in their courts."[18] The soldiers who are described by the author of the passion of Marculus as possessing the "bloody hands of bandits" – a phrase meant to delegitimize their violence – presented a vivid model of armed officials that was fixed in the minds of the onlookers. In the Christian iconography of the time, militiamen are pictured in typical scenes of arrest, either of Jesus himself, or often the apostles, who are portrayed as prototypical martyrs. The scenes, carved in high, detailed, and dramatic relief on the sarcophagi of Christians of the fourth and fifth centuries, contemporary with our events, show groups of soldiers, dressed in military attire in the manner of a civil militia: crowned with pillbox hats and armed with wooden clubs.

For Africa, the evidence is more specific. The *stationarii* or police units were seen as the normal local enforcement detachments by the inhabitants of Roman towns and cities like Carthage and Hippo Regius. Men in militia units in other locales, like Caesarea in Mauretania, were normally shown proudly displaying their wooden clubs in public monuments of their service.[19] And the highway patrolmen or *triviarii* who enforced the arrests, imprisonments, and savage beatings of the dissident martyrs at Carthage in the great persecution of 347 were also typically armed with clubs.[20] Closer in type to the sectarian circumcellion gangs in context, soldiers who served as enforcers who disciplined workers on the rural domains also habitually used clubs and rods. The regulatory inscriptions of imperial agricultural domains make specific reference to them in the formal complaints lodged by *coloni* against the physical discipline used against them.[21] These same instruments of enforcement were also enshrined in the imperial laws that determined the punishments of "the Donatists" who were determined to

---

[18] Aug. *Ep.* 133.2 (CCL 31B: 242): "non extendente eculeo, non sulcantibus ungulis, non urentibus flammis sed virgarum verberibus eruisti. Qui modus cohercitionis et a magistris artium liberalium et ab ipsis parentibus et saepe etiam in iudiciis solet ab episcopis haberi"; cf. *Ep.* 134.2 (CCL 31B: 245): "non tormentis ungularum atque flammarum sed virgarum coherciti." Surely these men were not the only dissident *agonistici* who had faced these kinds of physical inquiries in Roman courts; Augustine is careful to say that Marcellinus did not use iron hooks or fire as means of torture.

[19] Speidel (1993), who emphasizes that the club or *fustis* was the symbol and reality of day-to-day enforcement or policing.

[20] *Passio Isaac et Maximiani*, 13.90 (Mastandrea, 1995: 85): "Venerant ergo ad carcerem militum cunei et triviarii fustibus onerati, et vi caedis populos repellentes cunctos paene fecerant vulneratos." For the precise meaning of *triviarii*, see Mastandrea (1992), 340–42.

[21] Khanoussi (2000).

be heretics: elite persons were to suffer monetary fines, but persons from the poorer servile dregs were to be beaten with clubs before being exiled.[22] Anyone wishing to form a group of men in an official fashion – to behave and to appear like a police unit – would have good models to imitate, ones whose style and organization they would have had generations to absorb. The imitators were rough young men who, without doubt, had already had encounters with local militiamen who were tasked with controlling drunken rowdies, village brawlers, and ordinary criminals.

Mimicry of formal secular authority explains only so much. There were other analogies between the gangs of sectarian circumcellions and the bands of soldiers who were used as police, enforcers, and agents of punishment of the state. When it came to arms and organization, soldiers of the army were another model that was impressed on everyone's experience. The annual rotation of the governor and his entourage through the provincial assizes – or, as more modest extensions of his authority, the circuits of the legates nominated by him who toured smaller centers and heard less impressive cases – brought the theater of trial and punishment to a large number of provincial venues. When it came to the acts of sectarian enforcement, it was a matter of putting these models of authority into action. Dissident enforcers were not just interested in a passive mode of "how to organize and to present ourselves" Instead, they asked the question: What are we to do to these people, our enemies, so that they will understand, so that they will get the message? If the circumcellions were acting *like* normal militias, then their main function suggested by this mimicry was to police not a civil society but a religious community. Their normal work – to intimidate and to frighten – could be interpreted as a good thing, as a kind of discipline – or as a bad thing, as a kind of terror. If the former, the violence was legitimized as part of the defense of the dissident church; if the latter, it offered just the sort of bad thing that Catholic lobbyists were seeking in the late 390s and early 400s.

WHERE THERE IS TERROR, THERE IS SALVATION

One of the main aims of Christian lobbyists in Africa, both Catholic and dissident, was to get the imperial court to engage in the physical destruction of temples, shrines, and images of the traditional gods. In the pursuit of this goal, every piece of relevant imperial legislation was taken

---

[22] CTh 16.5.21 (15 June 392): "si servili faece descendens paupertate sui poenam damni ac vilitate contemnit, caesus fustibus deportatione damnabitur." Compare the terms of the laws of 412 and 414, ch. 14, pp. 644–45 above.

as a cue for freelance Christian enforcers to take to the streets to do some of the destructive work for the government. As a form of volunteerism, it would feel good. It was holy work. Whatever dangers the enforcers had to confront, including from angry defenders of "pagan" holy places, there would be compensation because their work was virtuous and the rewards divine. For this reason, the official churches skated a fine line in their attitudes towards the violent gangsters. On the one hand, they were doing God's work; on the other, they had to be formally condemned because they were going far beyond what the imperial state officially condoned or tolerated. As early as the first decade of the fourth century, the Council of Elvira in southern Spain ruled that persons killed while breaking and destroying idols were not to be counted as martyrs.[23] The prohibition perhaps had more to do with the deliberate courting of martyrdom than it did with a deliberate intent to violate imperial law, although the two might well have been closely related in the minds of the critics of deliberately sought martyrdoms.

In the anti-pagan rages of the 390s, the targets were manifest: most Christians agreed that idol-smashing and the destroying of temples were virtuous actions. Which raises the question of against whom or what were they going to vent their rage.[24] Only a few persons at the time openly labeled such good destruction specifically as "circumcellion" violence. As in the attacks at Madauros, violent Christian men were defended as doing the right thing.[25] So what were the targeting practices of Christian gangs that *were* labeled as circumcellions? The objects of their attacks sometimes included property as well as persons. As for property, the principal targets of their assaults were the churches of their opponents, including the most important utensils and objects of ritual in the church, above all the altar. In one of the earliest attacks recorded by Augustine, which happened at the village of Asna "where our brother Argentius is priest," the circumcellions attacked the basilica and smashed its altar.[26] In this, as in other such instances, the law courts were never far away, indicating that the circumcellions were probably none other than the men who were accused of being the "hired muscle," the *conducta manus*, involved in battles over the repossessing of basilicas. So it was in this case. The dispute at Asna had

---

[23] Concil. Eliberr. canon 60 (Martínez-Rodríguez, *Canónica hispana*, p. 261).

[24] Quotation at subheading, see Aug. *Sermo* 279.4 (PL 38: 1277): "Ubi terror, ibi salus. Qui faciebat contra nomen, patiatur pro nomine. O saevitia misericors" – wondrously, of God's actions towards mortal men.

[25] See ch. 5, pp. 236–38.

[26] Aug. *Ep.* 29.12 (CCL 31: 105): "Apud Asnam, ubi est presbyter frater Argentius, circumcelliones invadentes basilicam nostram altare comminuerunt."

already been before the civil courts.[27] In this context, circumcellion attacks on other properties, including farms and houses, were often part of a larger rationale of civil court procedure.

But it was circumcellion assaults on the bodies of persons that evoked the greatest, often irrational, fear. In all reports of this type of violence, one thing is manifest. Despite much rhetorical talk about murder and lethal slaughter, ordinarily anything but outright homicide was involved. Most attackers were not interested in killing the person whom they attacked, but rather, if we might put it in polite terms, in reshaping the body (and therefore the mind) of the enemy. When he is speaking directly with dissident clergy or spokesmen, Augustine most often does not talk about killings, but rather about persons severely beaten or cut up but who are then "thrown out" while still "half alive."[28] That is to say, there was a map of body parts that signified different things of value to the attackers. For example, the eyes. Late in the year 411, circumcellions attacked the priest Innocentius in the Hippo diocese, dragging him out of his house, chopping off one of his fingers and then gouging out one of his eyes.[29] Attacks like these raise the history of specific acts of violence, in this case one finger and one eye. The objects were purposefully chosen. The gouging-out of eyes, for example, is a well-attested practice with its own history. In Africa, the punishment was almost inflicted on the young female martyr, Perpetua, in 203, by her angry father: he was disappointed, humiliated, and frightened by his daughter's disobedient adherence to Christianity and the trouble and danger to which it exposed her and his family.[30] The response had wider Mediterranean dimensions and its own history. Nor was it not necessarily a déclassé thing associated with violent underclasses. No less a figure than the emperor Augustus himself had physically assaulted a man of praetorian rank and had gouged out the man's eyes with his own fingers.[31] The common theme linking all of these attacks is that of betrayal, indeed a sharp sense of personal betrayal.

[27] Aug. *Ep.* 29.12 (CCL 31: 105): "Causa nunc agitur."

[28] Aug. *Contra Cresc.* 3.47.46 (CSEL 52: 453) is typical: "Fustibus tonsos ferroque concisos semivivos abiciunt."

[29] See "Innocentius (8)," PAC, p. 603; Aug. *Ep.* 133.1 (CCL 31B: 241): "et de caede Innocentii, alterius Catholici presbyteri, atque de oculo eius effosso et digito praeciso fuisse confessos." The men who attacked him and another priest, Restitutus, had been taken from Hippo to Carthage in 412, where they were to be tried. Augustine refers to the same case in a letter to the governor Apringius in the next year: *Ep.* 134.2 (CCL 31B: 245–46), by which time they apparently had still not been punished.

[30] *Passio Felicitatis et Perpetuae*, 3.3: "Tunc pater motus hoc verbo mittit se in me, ut oculos mihi erueret."

[31] Quintus Gallius, the praetor, was suspected of hiding a weapon with which to attack Augustus: "et Quintum Gallium praetorem . . . servilem in modum torsit ac fatentem nihil iussit occidi prius oculis eius sua manu effossis" (Suet. *Aug.* 27.4).

Attacks on the eyes cannot be separated from another type of sectarian assault that particularly horrified Augustine who referred to it, when he first heard of the practice, as "a new and unspeakable kind of violence, a piece of cruelty deserving of the Devil Himself." The horror to which he referred was the use of a liquid concoction made of vinegar and lime, a caustic substance which the dissident *agonistici* threw into the eyes of their enemies in order to blind them.[32] They did not kill, but rather maimed. What was the meaning? One cannot rule out an element of mimicry of the kinds of torture invoked by the state itself, picked up as learned experiences by onlookers as the sort of things that one did to one's enemies. For example, there is the account of the deaths of Isaac and Maximianus, a narrative produced by the dissident Christians in Africa at some point in the latter half of the fourth century, but reflecting on events that happened in the mid-340s. The narrator reports that after having been subjected to savage tortures Isaac went into shock. He lapsed into a torpor from which he had a vision in which he engaged in a physical struggle with ministers of the emperor.[33]

When he had overcome these men in a day-long contest, he [i.e. Isaac] spotted the emperor himself suddenly coming towards him. When the emperor tried to force Isaac to obey his order, Isaac bravely refused the order of the sacrilegious command and disregarded the savage punishments that the emperor threatened. Rather, it was by means of repeated threats of his own that Isaac promised that *he* would tear out the emperor's eye. The two men engaged in a fierce and prolonged combat with each other. Isaac could no longer endure holding off becoming a great victor. Seizing hold of the emperor with great force, he put an end to any delay in his threat. Violently gouging out the emperor's eye, he emptied out the socket, leaving a face bereft of eyesight.

It is a subversive text, frankly threatening to the established political order. The emperor of Rome is reduced to the level of street brawling with a low-class Christian. Not only that, the scene is set as a violent athletic

---

[32] Aug. *Brev. Collat.* 3.11.22 (CCL 149A: 288): "Ibi etiam cum dictum esset quod calce et aceto humanos oculos persecuti sint, in quo scelere Diabolum crudelitate pervicerunt, qui hoc in sancti viri carne non fecit quam in potestatem acceperat affligendam, hic Donatistae quaesierunt, utrum qui faciunt filii essent Diaboli an qui patiuntur; quasi Catholici aliud quam passiones suas dixerint immanissimas a clericis et circumcellionibus eorum."

[33] *Passio marytrum Maximiani et Isaac,* 8.59–61 (Mastandrea 1995: 82): "quos cum diuturno certamine superaret, ipsum quoque imperatorem respexit subito venientem: qui cum ad complendam iussionem ab eodem cogeretur, fortior refutabat sacrilegae iussionis imperium, et minanti saeva supplicia, ipse quoque oculum se illi pariter eruturum frequenti comminatione terribilis promittebat. Cum his diu certationibus inter semetipsos ferocius dimicarent, non passus est tantum se differri victorem, sed iniecta fortiter manu moram suae communationis irrupit et oculum violenter eliciens, viduata facie, sedem luminis evacuavit."

contest found in the amphitheaters and arenas of the empire. Both Isaac's framing of the contest in a dream and his configuring of it as a violent one-on-one battle with a force of evil evoked memories of the images in the passion of Perpetua, the charter martyrdom that was annually read aloud in churches throughout Africa, both dissident and Catholic. Perpetua had fought a no-holds-barred fight, a pseudo-*pankration*, with a dark figure who signified the Devil Himself. Just so, the implicit identification of the emperor as Satan in Isaac's combat would not be missed.[34] The pattern was bounded by the nature of the contest itself, since in a *pankration* the gouging out of the opponent's eye was one of the few holds that was actually forbidden.[35]

Both the scene in the dissident martyr act and that in Perpetua's earlier model martyrdom are overseen by a divine figure who acts as the *editor* of the contest. In our case, he rewards Isaac with the crown of the victorious athlete. The plucking out of the eye is the blinding of someone who was already blind to the Christian message.[36] It is surely not accidental, given the theodicy of divine vengeance embedded in martyrdom, that the fate suffered by the first Roman governor to execute Christians in Africa, Publius Vigellius Saturninus, was to be struck blind.[37] Attacking the eyes of sectarian enemies marked the person as one who was "blind to the truth" and then linked them to heretics and to the ultimate "blind people": the Jews. These links open onto other possible avenues of cause and effect.[38] Augustine and a learned opponent of his, the dissident bishop Petilian of Constantina, had been debating the meaning of blindness just before the first reported cases involving the new mode of attacks made by the circumcellion gangs armed with their lime and vinegar concoction. But Augustine himself was just as happy to draw on the words of Cyprian according to which his opponents, "blinded by their pride had lost the light of the Truth."[39] Were the gangs taking cues from virulent debates

---

[34] *Passio Felicitatis et Perpetuae*, 10.9–11 (SC 417: 138–40), for her pankration with the Devil; cf. Shaw (1993), pp. 28–29.

[35] M. B. Poliakoff, *Combat Sports in the Ancient World: Competition, Violence, and Culture*, New Haven and London, Yale University Press, 1987, p. 54 – a debated point, however.

[36] *Passio martyrum Maximiani et Isaac*, 10.67–68 (Mastandrea 1995: 82–83): "Namque pugnasse se contra ministros regis sic in nocte sibi soli conspexit, sicut per diem nobis postmodum demonstravit, sic lumen imperatori eruisse, sicut eum habebat per diem vincendo caecare."

[37] Tert. *Ad Scap.* 3.4–5 (CCL 2: 1129–30).

[38] See Gaddis, *Religious Violence*, pp. 128–29, esp. p. 128 n. 10, with reference to the peculiar Christian significance of blindness.

[39] Aug. *Contra Gaud.* 2.2.3 (CSEL 53: 258): "et dum insolenter extollunt, ipso suo tumore caecati lumen amittunt" = Cypr. *Ep.* 54.3 (CCL 3B: 253–55); see Augustine's use of imagery of blindness and gouging out of eyes, cited in n. 125 below.

occurring among their leaders and teachers? They would make their enemies literally blind in the way that they were already spiritually wounded: in the disfigurement of their bodies others would see what they themselves could not.

The language of body provokes the question of why the priest Innocentius had one of his fingers cut off in the attack made on him. This, in turn, raises a whole series of connected questions about this whole body language: Which parts are connected in which fashion for these people? What is absent in this repertoire? Some parts, the nose and anus to select two at random, are never involved.[40] This act of violence is also one that had its own context, its own history. For this, we should consider the attack on another dissident crossover: Rogatus of Assuras. Rogatus was the dissident bishop of Assuras who had replaced Praetextatus in the Maximianist crisis in the mid-390s. When Augustine mentioned this case in 418, he described Rogatus' turning to the Catholic Church as recent, probably in the aftermath of the imperial legislation of 414.[41] When the circumcellions attacked Rogatus, they cut out his tongue and then cut off his right hand.[42] In this case, the meaning is clear enough, since both the tongue and hand were joined in punishment. They were the instruments with which Rogatus, as bishop, preached the gospel. His tongue spoke the words, his right hand made the typical gestures of the rhetor, as well as of benediction and of consecration. Innocentius' finger is surely to be seen in this same light.

Not just bishops, however, but also ordinary Christians were not to be prevented from speaking their truth. As with blinding, the punishment was not just a Christian one, but rather one whose Christian analogues were suggested by current secular practices. When the allies of the Count of Africa, Romanus, were found guilty and were thought to be lying, the appropriate punishment was cutting out their tongues.[43] The Rogatus episode, however, led to more violence. When some of the men who attacked him were arrested and sent to Carthage for trial, other circumcellions attacked and inflicted a serious beating on an *agens in rebus*, an imperial official who had

---

[40] See, for example, Groebner, "Saving Face," ch. 3 in *Defaced*, pp. 67–86, on the defacing of appearance by attacks on the nose, with interpretation of what this means in certain western European milieux in the later "Middle Ages."

[41] See "Rogatus (6)," PAC, pp. 991–92, citing *Gesta cum Emerito* 9 (CSEL 53: 192), of 418, where Rogatus' crossing-over is referred to as *modo* (see note following); cf. *Ep.* 185.7.20 (CSEL 57: 28).

[42] Aug. *Gesta cum Emerit.* 9 (CSEL 53: 192): "Rogatus, qui modo Catholicus est, cui exercitus istorum, id est agmen circumcellionum, linguam et manum praecidit." The case is also cited in *Sermo* 356.8 (Lambot, *Sermones selecti duodeviginti* = SPM 1 [1950], 137).

[43] For Romanus, see ch. 1, pp. 36–38; Amm. Marc. 28.6.20, 28 on the cutting out of their tongues.

been put in charge of investigating the case.[44] The punishments inflicted on Rogatus were simply part of a long tradition of sectarian enforcement in Africa. In the later Vandal persecution of Catholics in Africa, the Arian bishop of the town of Tipasa in Mauretania reported to the Vandal king Geiseric that the Catholic Christians of the town were holding their own services. In response, Geiseric dispatched a Count from the court with orders that the guilty persons were to be rounded up and gathered in the forum of the city. He was then to excise their tongues and cut off their right hands.[45]

The symbolic connection between the indication of the finger and the speech of the tongue is noted earlier on in the mid-fourth century by Optatus in his criticisms directed against various modes of violence. He begins by noting that the tongue is a sword that is sharpened against one's opponents.[46]

But you – *you* don't fear God and you don't recognize your own brothers. Rather, you have sharpened the razors of your tongues on the whetstone of hatred and, trampling on God's commands, you have mounted an attack on the persons of the unfortunate in order to take these blind and ignorant people prisoner, after you have murdered their leaders.

He continues in the same vein, discussing the difference between murdering by the use of a real sword or some other instrument and killing by other means. "What difference does it make," he says, "if you strike with a sword or with your tongue?"[47] The point is made to lead the reader to understand the special physical punishment inflicted on Catholic priests by their attackers.[48]

Deuterius, Parthenius, Donatus, and Gaetulicus, who were bishops of God – these men you slashed with the sword of the tongue, pouring out the blood not just of their bodies but of their honor. These men did subsequently live, but you had murdered them in their positions as priests of God.

---

[44] Aug. *Ep.* *28.7 (CSEL 88: 136–37): "Olympius graviter illic ipsis perditis caesus est," notably not naming the *perditi* specifically as circumcellions.

[45] Victor Vitensis, *Hist. pers. vand.*, 3.6.30 (Lancel: 191): "linguas eis et manus dextras radicitus abscidisset."

[46] Optatus, *Contra Parm.* 2.25.5 (SC 412: 296–97): "Vos nec Deum timetis nec fratres agnoscitis; in cote livoris acuistis novaculas linguae et divina praecepta calcantes miserorum properastis in capita, ut in captivitatem caecos et imperitos populos iugulatis ducibus traheretis."

[47] Optatus, *Contra Parm.* 2.25.8 (SC 412: 298–99): "quid interest an gladio an lingua percutias?"

[48] Optatus, *Contra Parm.* 2.25.10 (SC 412: 298–300): "Deuterium, Partenium, Donatum et Getulicum, Dei episcopos, linguae gladio iugulastis, fundentes sanguinem non corporis sed honoris. Vixerunt postea homines, sed a vobis occisi sunt in honoribus Dei sacerdotes."

The cutting out of the tongue and the removal of the priests' ability to speak the word of God from the position of his formal office are merged. And here, it is to be noted, the punishment was inflicted with "the sword of the tongue."

Perhaps one of the oddest punishments inflicted upon victims of sectarian violence is one where an implement was used against their hair and they were "scalped." It must have been a painful and brutish punishment. Even the descriptions are painful to read.[49] But the apparently gratuitous nature of the violence is not random. It was part of the language of these assaults – acts that were intended to send a message to one's enemy by marking the body. Victims were transformed into living, walking advertisements of their immoral ideas. The explanation goes back to some words in Optatus that note the physical appearance of priests and bishops in the dissident church. It was an artificial physical trait that was striking, and on which he comments, mockingly.[50]

You, on the contrary, try to despise God's commands with the same insistence that those who fear God show when they try to fulfill his orders. So show us where it is commanded to shave the heads of priests and bishops, when there are so many examples on the other side of the argument to show that this should *not* be done.

Optatus objects that there is no biblical authority for shaving the head and, obviously, the practice was not followed in the Catholic Church. Sectarian physical attacks on Catholic priests and bishops therefore physically inflicted upon them a "clean head" as a sort of mockery of what they pretended to be and were supposed to be. It was a bloody shaving. Once again, the act was symbolic.

The lower parts of the body were not exempt. Kneecapping in sectarian violence is no new thing, and perhaps for much the same reasons. In Christian culture in Africa, the tradition reputedly went back to the Great Persecution. The punishment was connected with certain rituals that were demanded of Christians by the third edict of Diocletian. This law required that the individual Christian involve himself or herself in acts of performing sacrifice and obeisance to the gods of the state. This involved the bodily act of kneeling. The requisite punishment was therefore to attack the knees.[51]

---

[49] Gaddis, *Religious Violence*, p. 120, rightly, I think, takes this to be a violent form of shaving rather than the actual scalping a live person.

[50] Optatus, *Contra Parm.* 2.23.2 (SC 412: 290–91): "Et tamen vos contra isdem viribus conati estis praecepta contemnere quibus qui Deum timent mandata conantur implere. Docete ubi vobis mandatum est radere capita sacerdotum, cum e contrario sint tot exempla proposita fieri non debere."

[51] Optatus, *Contra Parm.* 2.25.10 (SC 412: 300–01): "Multis notum est et probatum persecutionis tempore episcopos aliquos inertia a confessione nominis Dei delapsos turificasse, et tamen nullus

It is well known, indeed proved, that in the time of persecution some bishops, through lack of backbone, lapsed from the confession of God's name and involved themselves in the ceremony of offering incense. Nevertheless, none of those who avoided this ceremony physically attacked the lapsed or ordered the piercing of their knees. But you today, after Unity, do what no one ever did in the aftermath of the ceremonials of offering incense.

The piercing of the knees was clearly connected with the ritual act of "bending the knees," *genibus flexis*, while engaged in either the act of supplication of sacrifice in traditional cult, or in the act of obeisance and prayer for Christians. The destruction of the knees would simply make impossible the physical act by which one was able to approach the deity on an earthly plane.

The common ground underlying all these punishments was that the body was a habitus, a domestic site of decor and clothing that was capable of modification. It was part of a larger set of symbols available to the attacker to exploit. One such assault, the attack on the priest Restitutus, highlighted the special clothing into which the victim was dressed after he had been denuded and savagely beaten: a vestment called a *buda*.[52] But what was a *buda* and why were those being punished clothed in it as part of the violence vented upon them?[53] The same garment reappears with a different name in another version of the attack on Restitutus. He was denuded, beaten with wooden clubs, dragged through and rolled about in mud, and clothed in something called the *amictus iunceus*.[54] The earlier description of this same case was sent in a circular letter from the Catholic clergy of Hippo to Januarius the dissident bishop of Casae Nigrae and Primate of Numidia in the year 406.[55]

When a certain priest of his own free will chose to join the Unity of our communion, they dragged him out of his home, and beat him savagely as they wished.

---

eorum qui evaserunt aut manum lapsis imposuit aut ut genua figerent imperavit. Et facitis vos hodie post unitatem quod a nullo factum est post turificationem."

[52] See "Restitutus (6)," PAC, p. 972; this "horror story" is told by Augustine, without naming the victim, in *Ep.* 88.6 (CCL 31A: 143); he is surely the same as the Restitutus of Victoriana whose story is recounted in *Ep.* 105.2.3 (CCL 31B: 50–51).

[53] There are no entries for the word either in Lewis and Short or in the new *Oxford Latin Dictionary*; obviously it was not standard classical Latin. Souter cites only Claudius Donatus, *In Aeneida*, 2.135 (sedge plant) and *Anth. Lat.* 85.2 (SB = 95.2 Riese) (a garment made of reeds): "Ut devota piis clarescant lumina templis / Niliacam texit cerea lamma budam."

[54] Aug. *Contra Cresc.* 3.48.53 (CSEL 52: 460–61); Talmud, Tractate Berakhot 3, might offer a clue.

[55] Aug. *Ep.* 88.6 (CSEL 34.2: 412): "Presbyterum etiam quendam, quia propria et libera voluntate unitatem nostrae communionis elegit, de domo sua raptum et pro arbitrio immaniter caesum, in gurgite etiam caenoso volutatum, buda vestitum cum quibusdam dolendum, quibusdam ridendum in pompa sui facinoris ostentassent, abductum inde, quo voluerunt, vix post dies XII dimiserunt."

Then, having clothed him in a *buda*, they dragged him through a muddy pool – a matter of sadness to some, but of humor to others. Next, as if to brag about this crime of theirs, they displayed him in a public parade of their crime. After holding him for about a dozen days in a place where they wished, they finally let him go.

No precise garment of this type is attested elsewhere, but its name must signify something like a "reed jacket." Other African authors offer very little in the way of help, although a letter in the Cyprianic corpus refers to a man whose occupation was that of *budinarius*.[56] Did he make such garments? A possible clue comes from the martyr narrative of Marciana of Caesarea. In a substory that was added to the main tale of her martyrdom, it is a specifically Jewish threat that Marciana repels. The arch-villain in the story is the *archisynagogus* of the city who happens to bear the occupational name of "Budarius."[57] From context alone, it is clear that the clothing of the harassed and beaten victim in a *buda* or *amictus iunceus* was intended to humiliate. Someone in the attacking party must have provided the jacket for the occasion.

CAVE CANEM

In the Restitutus story we have the element of publicity that was one possible side of this violence – which should not close our eyes to the hidden violence that certainly occurred as well. The two faces of sectarian killing recall the political and sectarian killings in the Lebanon in the Civil War of the late 1970s and early 1980s.[58]

People now died in one of two ways. Some deaths were theatrical, solemn, and orchestrated for the media; others were clandestine, and no one knew precisely where or when the executions took place. In the first case, the captives were paraded through the streets, sometimes in chains, mistreated, and sometimes tied to vehicles. Onlookers applauded, insulted them, screamed at them and even hit the condemned men. The bodies were sometimes burned and left by the roadside. In many cases, killing was not enough. The killers enjoyed their victims' deaths, humiliating and torturing them before executing them.

The difference with our cases of sectarian violence is that killing does not seem to have been the main aim. Rather, it was all of the other publicity that mattered much more: the humiliation, the insulting and the spectacle of degradation that elsewhere attends the execution in a murderous internecine conflict. What happened to Restitutus was not Beirut in the 1970s, but rather Membressa in the 390s: like the aged bishop Salvius,

---

[56] Cypr. *Ep.* 42 (CCL 3B: 199).   [57] *Passio sanctae Marcianae*, 6 (AASS 1: 569): "Budarii ... domus."
[58] Khosrokhavar, *Suicide Bombers*, p. 143.

pummeled and pushed through the streets of his hometown, with a necklace of dead dogs tied around his neck. Nevertheless, he was allowed to live.

Not only body parts and clothing were elements of this language of violation – so were actions involving other parts of the natural and social world. These point to the presence of a *paideia* of violence that was peculiar to the participants who had to learn it. And the symbolic language could be extended as was fit to suit each assault. The men staging a personal assault might supply the accoutrements with which the core punishment could be accessorized. If their enemies could be construed as wolves whose dripping fangs threatened, then they could also be likened to dogs. One of the actions taken in attacks on basilicas of the opposition was to seize the sacred instruments of ritual and to abuse them in specific ways. One was to sell parts of the communion plate and vessels on the open market as if they were so many items of common commerce, to be bought and sold. In a final, gross insult, however, the attackers were said to have fed the communion bread to dogs. At first glance this seems a trite observation, perhaps a metaphorical expression of the disdain in which one held the other's sense of the sacred.

There are strange incidents that indicate other parts of this same repertoire of canine punishment. These were charivari-like humiliations vented on the person whom one was punishing. Take the example, already mentioned, of the bishop Salvius of Membressa who, driven and beaten, was symbolically paraded through the streets of his town with a necklace made of dead dogs tied around his neck.[59] Although dogs had symbolic values attached to them in the various local cultures of the empire, there is not much evidence to sustain a concerted and exclusive use of them as a derogatory symbol. In both Jewish and Christian cultures, on the other hand, the dog was a heavy symbol. With few exceptions, in the books of the Old Testament dogs are regarded as repugnant and vile animals, to be classed along with the dangerous and the dirty hyena.[60] This cultural significance was selected and emphasized by the writers of the New Testament books for whom the dog represented not only baseness and vileness, but also dangerous, hostile, and evil forces that threatened the good orthodox community of believers.

In the Book of Revelation – a powerful text in African Christianity – the eschatological city of God includes the good, while those on the outside

---

[59] See ch. 3, pp. 131 f.
[60] For this and what follows see Thomas (1960), and S. Pedersen, "κύων, κυνός, ὁ," *EDNT* 2 (1989), p. 332.

are dogs and false prophets: "These too must stay outside: dogs, poisoners, prostitutes, murderers, and idolaters, and everyone of false speech and false life."[61] The dog is also, most significantly, used as a metaphorical designation for heretic. The author of 2 Peter describes a sinister process in which "false teachers" insinuate themselves into the Christian community. These men propagate bad ideas that pervert and seduce believers to "disown their Master" and to follow the false prophets to their destruction. The author rails in anger against them. Such persons, he says, "are not reasoning beings, but simply animals born to be caught and killed." The writer then turns on people who are enticed and convinced by such false teachers: it would be better they had never known the way of holiness than that they knew it and then *betrayed* it: "What such a person has done is exactly as the proverb rightly says: *the dog returns to its own vomit*, and when the sow has been washed, it wallows in the mud." The identification of dogs with heretics is made explicit in Philippians, where the writer warns the Christian: "Beware of dogs."[62] Similarly, the author of Matthew repeats Jesus' dictum: "Do not give dogs what is holy; and do not throw your pearls in front of pigs, or they may trample them and then turn on you and tear you to pieces."[63] The words could be construed as a command not only to those who read the words when they were first written, but also as an injunction by African Christians who wished to signal that something was "not holy" to them. The command was a memorable one. That the communion bread of the opposition church was deliberately thrown to dogs was not accidental, but the result of a long engagement with a new Christian culture and its system of symbolic meanings.

But the practice of such symbolic acts and their meanings is not always easily contained. Reports on the widespread mutilations, killings, and massacres that were part of the violence in Algeria in the 1990s provide a good example.[64]

The bodies of the dead are reportedly hacked, mutilated, disfigured, dismembered or burned. The perpetrators of the massacres use parts of their dismembered victims for spectacularly ghoulish effects. There are reports of children crucified

---

[61] Rev. 22: 15: ἔξω οἱ κύνες καὶ οἱ φάρμακοι καὶ οἱ πόρνοι καὶ οἱ φονεῖς καὶ οἱ εἰδωλολάτραι καὶ πᾶς φιλῶν καὶ ποιῶν ψεῦδος.

[62] Philippians, 3: 2: βλέπετε τοὺς κύνας – where the warning is clearly anti-Jewish, but it was later easily read out of context to designate any similar threat to orthodoxy.

[63] Matthew, 7.6: μὴ δῶτε τὸ ἅγιον τοῖς κυσίν, μηδὲ βάλητε τοὺς μαργαρίτας ὑμῶν ἔμπροσθεν τῶν χοίρων, μήποτε καταπατήσουσιν αὐτοὺς ἐν τοῖς ποσὶν αὐτῶν καὶ στραφέντες ῥήξωσιν ὑμᾶς.

[64] Aït-Larbi *et al.* (1999), p. 127 (with sources) who describe such acts as "necromaniac."

on trees and heads spiked on stakes, put on doorways or on the road. Survivors of the massacre of Had Chekala in Relizane reported that they had found "the head of a man on the decapitated body of a donkey" and, in the October 1997 massacre of Hamadi, the perpetrators "beheaded a man and a dog before attaching the man's head to the dog's body and vice versa... In the November 1996 massacre in Douaouda, in Tipaza, men were castrated before their throats were slashed. In the January 1997 massacre of Haouch El Hadj, in Blida, one of the female victims was reportedly found with one of her severed breasts in her mouth. In the January 1998 Relizane massacre, a baby was reportedly found with his extirpated heart in his mouth. In this same massacre, a foetus was reportedly extirpated from an eviscerated woman and slaughtered. The perpetrators' passion for tearing apart living structures and terrorizing extends also to animals. In December 1997 massacre in Sidi Senoussi, in Tlemcen, 500 sheep were slaughtered along with the six shepherds to whom they belonged.

In discussions of the causes and meanings of such acts, recourse is had both to rationalization – somehow, for example, the state through the agency of the army is either causing or doing these things – or to the castigation of such acts as "strange" or "demented" or "manic." The problem here, as with the violent acts of circumcellions, is that the causes of many of the most horrific localized acts of violence were never direct – that is, falling under the rubric of so-called "Islamist fanatics" committing the acts for sectarian and political purposes. A further complication is that the symbol that had some original significance had lost this meaning: the violent symbol was enacted, but not necessarily in its original context of meaning. On not a few occasions, a peculiar reshaping of the body was now done simply because this is the sort of violence that one enacted.

Violence inscribed on the body and made part of its exterior in late Roman Africa was similarly part of a range of symbolic acts, all of which, as represented, had some biblical authority and meaning. It was part of a new narrative of how things were done. When the dissidents seized or repossessed a basilica or church and made it their own again, it was never simply a matter of the use of force and the act of repossession. They systematically cleansed it of all of the polluting effects of its previous occupants. A house of God that had been occupied by *them* had to be cleaned. The floors were washed with salt to take away the stain imparted by the footsteps of the previous Catholic parishioners.[65] Then the inside

---

[65] Optatus, *Contra Parm.* 6.6.1 (SC 413: 182) where the scrubbers were surely connecting salt with ritual purity: 2 Kg 2: 20–22; cf. Mt 5: 13, Mk 9: 50 and Lk 14: 34; Aug. *Ep.* 108.5.14 (CCL 31B: 79): "ad effundendum sanguinem ulla aqua pavimenta salsa lavistis, quod post nostros clerici tui putaverunt esse faciendum."

walls of the church were whitewashed, and the curtains and even the codices containing holy scripture were washed to clean them of the toxic contamination deposited on them by Catholic worshipers.[66] How far is this sectarian cleansing to be taken? Almost in a parody of these other acts, it was claimed that the dissenter was not even to walk on the same neighborhood roads and mainstreets where *their* (i.e. Catholic) feet had left poisonous imprints.[67] These responses were part of acts of ritualistic avoidance in which one did not sit with, eat with, or provide food or other services for *them*.

RATIONAL VIOLENCE

If circumcellion assaults had their own language, they also had their own underlying logic.[68] In defending and defining their community, the armed men provided the force needed to assert or reassert control over church properties, especially basilicas. Each basilica represented not only the community of the living, but also the community of the dead, including the martyrs and saints. In part, the possessory invasions of basilicas were made in order to gain control over burial grounds and for a double reason. The ownership of the burial places reasserted one's own claim to the past, but it also prevented access to proper burials for the other side.[69] As one side attempted to take over lands and settlements belonging to the other, holy fighters were called to action in defense. When speaking of the remote village of Fussala on the borderlands of the diocese of Hippo in the early 420s, Augustine notes there were hardly any Catholics in the town. When the church at Hippo responded following the imperial legislation that compelled the unification of the two churches, the priests who were first sent there to Catholicize the district were stripped and robbed, badly beaten,

---

[66] Optatus, *Contra Parm.* 6.6.1 (SC 413: 182): "Iam illud quale est quod in mutis locis etiam parietes lavare coluistis et inclusa spatia aqua salsa spargi praecepistis?"; cf. 6.5.2–3 (SC 413: 180): "velamina et instrumenta dominica extorsistis quae iamdudum fuerant in commune possessa; extorsistis cum codicibus pallas. Iudicio superbiae vestrae utraque arbitrati estis esse polluta. Nisi fallor, haec omnia purificare properastis. Lavastis procul dubio pallas." It is tempting to see an antecedent to this in Optatus, *Contra Parm.* 1.2.1 (SC 412: 174) and its point of reference in Ezekiel 13: 10–11.

[67] Optatus, *Contra Parm.* 6.6.3 (SC 413: 186), deliberately exaggerating: "Si Catholicorum vestigia et in vico et in platea calcavimus! Quare non omnia emendatis?" He then advances to say that the dissidents could go so far as to clean the water in the public baths in which the Catholics bathe.

[68] Some of what follows picks up on Blok (2001), especially on the underlying rationales of apparently "senseless violence."

[69] Optatus, *Contra Parm.* 6.7.1 (SC 413: 184–86): "quia ad hoc basilicas invadere voluistis ut vobis solis cimiteria vindicetis non permittentes sepeliri corpora Catholica? Ut terreatis vivos, male tractatis et mortuos negantes locum."

blinded, and even murdered.[70] From this series of incidents, it is manifest how the issuing of enabling legislation, requiring enforcement on the one hand and encouraging betrayal on the other, excited violent behavior. In the years in the aftermath of the imperial laws of 405, sectarian gangs moved into action. After years of hard enforcement, they provoked a long plea by Augustine in 409 to Macrobius, the newly appointed dissident bishop of Hippo, to do something about the worsening situation.[71]

> Unity is vanishing, and so we ask for public laws against the evil actions of your people – I do not say *your* bad acts personally. The result is the circumcellions are armed against these same laws. Indeed, they despise these laws with the same madness that they raised in their ragings against you. Unity is vanishing, and so rural rebels are roused up against their landowners and, against apostolic teaching, fugitive slaves are not only alienated from their owners, but are even threatening them. Not only do they threaten their masters, but, headed by agitators and leaders, they pillage their properties in assaults of extreme violence. In this very crime it is your *agonistici* who are the admitted leaders – the men who to the tune of **PRAISE TO GOD** embellish your honor, who to the words **PRAISE TO GOD** spill the blood of other people.

The imputation was that civil society was facing not just occasional incidents of sectarian violence, but rather a generalized social insurgency. The most detailed description of this fearful aspect of the circumcellions is contained in the general brief that Augustine presented to the imperial official Bonifatius soon after his arrival in Africa in 417. Having outlined their suicidal tendencies, Augustine turned to the enforcement tactics used by the sectarian circumcellions and the wider social threat that they presented – a matter that would surely be a serious concern to a high-ranking imperial official:[72]

---

[70] Aug. *Ep.* 209.2 (CSEL 57: 348): "ita ut ibi presbyteri, qui eis congregandis a nobis primitus constituti sunt, expoliarentur, caederentur, debilitarentur, excaecarentur, occiderentur." The violent men who committed these acts were clearly circumcellions, although Augustine does not use the technical term here.

[71] Aug. *Ep.* 108.18 (CCL 31B: 82): "Fugitur unitas, ut nos adversus vestrorum (nolo enim vestras dicere) improbitates quaeramus publicas leges et adversus ipsas leges armentur circumcelliones, quas eo ipso furore contemnant, quo in vos eas, cum furerent, excitarunt. Fugitur unitas, ut contra possessores suos rusticana erigatur audacia et fugitivi servi contra apostolicam disciplinam non solum a dominis alienentur, verum etiam dominis comminentur nec solum comminentur, sed et violentissimis aggressionibus depraedentur auctoribus et ducibus et in ipso scelere principibus agonisticis confessoribus vestris, qui ad 'Deo Laudes' ornant honorem vestrum, ad 'Deo Laudes' fundunt sanguinem alienum." The precise date of Macrobius' election as dissident bishop of Hippo is not known, see: "Macrobius (2)," PAC, pp. 662–63.

[72] Aug. *Ep.* 185.4.15 (CSEL 57: 14–15): "cum tamen apud illos perditorum hominum dementissimi greges in diversis causis quietem innocentium perturbabant. Quis non dominus servum suum timere compulsus est, si ad illorum patrocinium confugisset? Quis eversori minari saltem audebat

... at that time ... demented herds of these degenerate men threw into utter chaos the peace of innocent persons for different reasons. For what owner was not driven to fear his own slave if the slave had fled to the protection of these men? Who dared to threaten the man who destroyed his property or the one who instigated such actions? Who could discipline the men who pillaged the contents of his storerooms? Who could demand back anything from a debtor once he had asked for their help and protection? Through fear of their wooden clubs and threats of fire and impending death, the records of the very worst kind of slaves were destroyed so that they were able to walk off as free men. Notes of credit were extorted from creditors and given back to the debtors. Whoever showed disregard for their harsh words was forced by harsher whips to do what they ordered. Innocent men who somehow offended them had their homes torn down to the ground or set on fire. Household heads, well-educated men of superior birth, were dragged off hardly alive after one of their savage beatings. Or they were tied to the gristmill and forced by the whip to turn it in a circle as if they were nothing more than contemptible draught animals. Of what worth was help from the public laws of civil powers against these men? What imperial official so much as breathed a word of protest in their presence? What collector collected if *they* did not wish it? And who ever attempted to punish these men who were murdered by their own self-killings – unless, being so insane, he sought his own destruction at their hands? By threatening death, some of these men provoked the swords held by others against themselves in order that these other persons might kill them. Others devoted themselves to voluntary self-inflicted deaths by throwing themselves off cliffs, others by water, and still others by fire. In these ways, they condemned their savage souls to the punishments that they had brought upon themselves.

The destruction of records of debt, the unjust freeing of slaves, the contempt for legally established authority, the role reversal of lords and peasants, owners and slaves – all of this, and more, was the traditional language of social revolution, much of it on display in Augustine's favorite historian,

---

aut auctori? Quis consumptorem apothecarium, quis quemlibet poterat exigere debitorem auxilium eorum defensionemque poscentem? Timore fustium et incendiorum mortisque praesentis pessimorum servorum, ut liberi abscederent, tabulae frangebantur. Extorta debitoribus chirographa reddebantur. Quicumque dura illorum verba contempserant, durioribus verberibus, quod iubebant, facere cogebantur. Innocentium, qui eos offenderant, domus aut deponebantur ad solum aut ignibus cremabantur. Quidam patres familias honesto loco nati et generoso cultu educati vix vivi post eorum caedes ablati sunt vel iuncti ad molam et eam in gyrum ducere tamquam iumenta contemptibilia verbere adacti sunt. Quod enim de legibus auxilium a civilibus potestatibus adversus eos aliquid valuit? Quis in praesentia eorum officialis anhelavit? Quis, quod illi noluissent, exactor exegit? Quis eos, qui eorum caedibus extincti sunt, vindicare temptavit, nisi quod propria de illis poenas poscebat insania, cum alii provocandis in se gladiis hominum, quos, ut ab eis ferirentur, morte terrebant, alii per varia praecipitia, alii per aquas, alii per ignes se in mortes voluntarias usquequaque mittebant et animas ferales a se sibi inlatis suppliciis proiciebant?" Cf. Aug. *Ep.* 108.6.18 (CCL 31B: 82) where the same elements of social disorder are stressed, and where he specifically raises the circumcellions as a spectral threat to law and order. The involvement of the *agonistici* in attacks on properties, and also the threat that they posed to the discipline of slaves, is made clear.

Sallust. Only here the finale is capped with a lurid reference to the anarchic self-murders that were claimed to be characteristic of circumcellion violence.

But things were not simple, especially since, as the circumcellion attacks listed by Augustine readily shows, one person's act of threatening social insurgency was another's strike against social injustice. Even their most severe critics were compelled to admit that the circumcellions sometimes attacked persons who merited coercion or punishment. In this case, the objection to their violence was not so much that their victims were not bad people, but that the circumcellions were not a duly and legally constituted police who possessed the public authority to use force in coercing others. One of these offhand admissions comes in the middle of a verbal attack on them: "we rightly condemn the chaotic outrages and arrogant madnesses of your [i.e. the dissidents'] circumcellions, even if they commit violent acts against some very bad men."[73] In making this concession in a circular letter addressed to Catholic communities in 401/02, Augustine was admitting that, from the perspective of ordinary persons, even those of his own religious communion, it was admitted that the circumcellions sometimes directed violence against "bad" persons who deserved to be punished. Who were they? Augustine might well have been thinking of the history of Axido and Fasir in the 340s documented in Optatus, or about recent actions to which he refers in his brief presented to the official Bonifatius in 417.

There is no doubt that the construction of the sectarian circumcellions or *agonistici* that we have was the one formed in the circumstances of the struggle between the dissidents and the Catholics. Here it was the *image* of circumcellion violence that was central, and in this image it was the *threat* of violence that they represented that was as important as actual acts of damage and harm. One of the most evocative pictures that is offered of circumcellions, perhaps from a personal eyewitness, is of the night on which they escorted Macrobius, the new dissident bishop of Hippo Regius, into the city accompanying him in a regular military formation, their voices shouting rhythmic chants. Like war trumpets, it is said, they chanted the dissident battle cry "LAUDES DEO! LAUDES DEO!" No actual violence was done, but the parade of men marching in formation

---

[73] Aug. *Ep. ad Cath. de secta Donat.* 20.54 (CSEL 52: 301–02): "Proinde circumcellionum vestrorum inordinatas licentias et superbas insanias iuste reprehendimus, etiam cum aliquibus pessimis violenti sunt, quia illicita illicite vindicare et ab illicitis illicite deterrere non est bonum, cum vero et innocentes vel causa incognita vel iniquissimis inimicitiis persequuntur, quis eorum sceleratissima latrocinia non perhorrescat?"

accompanied by raucous chanting produced a threatening effect.[74] When discussing the circumcellions under their own name of *agonistici* or holy fighters, Augustine likened them not to "soldiers of Christ, but to soldiers of the Devil." Even as soldiers of Satan, he did not find their acts of physical violence as frightening as the ritualistic and rhythmic chanting of LAUDES DEO, "with a roar more frightening than that of a lion."[75]

This makes sense, both of the threats and of the targets of the violence. The aim of much of the violence was not so much to destroy property (or to acquire it) or to kill, as it was to intimidate: to police the frontiers of the religious community. Circumcellions existed to prevent desertion from "our side" by severely punishing those who crossed over in a manner that would stop others by achieving a terror effect.[76] In a word, deterrence. Creating an exemplary fear. This function is confirmed by Augustine when he rails against the circumcellions as "men of blood." It was not so much the shedding of real blood and actual homicide that he was thinking about as it was the invisible murder of souls they effected by discouraging crossing over to the side of the truth and by protecting the false practice of rebaptism.[77] If the club was their main weapon, it was effective enough against internal unrest if not against outsiders: "They don't spare the flesh either: they beat to death as many as they can, sparing neither their own or those who are not their own." It is notable that force was deployed as much against "their own" as against others, surely to enforce sanctions against desertion.[78] It was behind the protective wall of their violence that Catholic crossovers could be shielded from retribution and dissident clergy could perform the necessary rebaptisms. Augustine complained bitterly of forty-eight cases alone on the day before he dictated his letter of complaint in 409 to Macrobius, his opposite number at Hippo.[79]

Circumcellion violence was also aimed at a closely related target: effective propagators among the clergy of the other side whose messages were

---

[74] Aug. *Ep.* 108.5.14 (CCL 31B: 78): "circumcelliones . . . quorum duces, quando te ingredientem in hac patria cum suis cuneis deduxerunt, Deo laudes inter cantica conclamantes quas voces velut tubas proeliorum in suis omnibus latrociniis habuerunt."

[75] Aug. *En. in Ps.* 132.6 (CCL 40: 1930): "Quia sunt qui certant adversus Diabolum, et praevalent, milites Christi agonistici appellantur. Utinam ergo milites Christi essent, et non milites Diaboli, a quibus plus timetur, Deo laudes, quam fremitus leonis."

[76] Aug. *Ep.* 108.6.19 (CCL 31B: 82–83).   [77] Aug. *En. in Ps.* 54.26 (CCL 39: 675–76).

[78] Aug. *Tract. in Ioh.* 5.12 (CCL 36: 47): "Et tamen nec carni parcunt: quotquot potuerunt caedendo necaverunt, nec suis nec alienis pepercerunt."

[79] Aug. *Ep.* 111.1 (CCL 31B: 92–93): "Depraedantur etiam domos aliquas et incendunt, fructus aridos diripiunt, humidos fundunt et talia ceteris comminando multos etiam rebaptizari compellunt. Pridie, quam ad te ista dictavi, ex uno loco per huiusmodi terrores XL et VIII animae mihi rebaptizatae renuntiatae sunt."

intended to break down the coherence of dissident communities by presenting arguments that encouraged crossing over to the Catholic Church.[80] Some of the intimidation seems to have worked. In a sermon delivered at Carthage in 404, Augustine noted that the local brethren had perhaps been surprised, given the need and the opportunity, that he had said so little about the heretics, which is to say the dissidents.[81] They were not surprised and they were right. Threats had been made against the type of preaching which was intended "to entice and to cajole our brothers back to the fold and out of their error." He adds in explanation of his apparent silence: "It has come to my ears that those pitiable and ever to be pitied people have been saying that it was fear of the circumcellions that imposed silence on me. It is indeed true that they never stop trying to deter me by terror from preaching words of peace."[82] They probably did try to achieve precisely this effect, and succeeded on occasion.

It was well known that in the late summer of the preceding year Augustine had "barely escaped" a circumcellion attack.[83] The perception was that, in the aftermath, he had been unusually reticent about condemning "the heretics" and about encouraging "unification." Augustine hastened firmly to deny that any such thing had happened. Helped by the prayers of his parishioners, he would continue to face danger and to persevere in preaching the word of God. A main aim of circumcellion violence, at least as it was perceived by some of its targets, like Augustine and his parishioners, was to achieve this specific terror effect. In the aftermath of the initiatives of 403–05, Catholics firmly believed that the dissidents were actively using circumcellions as a means of deterring Catholic priests and bishops from preaching in favor of the imperial order for the unification of the two churches.[84] So it was not against preaching in general that the violent gangs were mobilized, but rather against the kind of proselytizing preaching that attempted aggressively to advance the program of unification of the two

---

[80] Possidius, *Vita Aug.* 10.3 (Bastiaensen: 152), saw this as one of the main functions of their violence.

[81] Aug. *Sermo* 299A.3 = Dolbeau 4/Mainz 9 (Dolbeau, *Vingt-six sermons*, p. 413): "Fortassis fratrum nonnulli mirabantur quod, cum sit nobis magnum studium lucrandi et recipiendi ab erroris exitio fratres nostros, per sermones quos anteriores habuimus nihil de haereticis diximus." He had already referred to his miraculous escape from this attack in a huge sermon preached on the great day of "pagan" festivity: 1 January 404: *Sermo* 198.45 = Dolbeau 26/Mainz 62 (Dolbeau, *Vingt-six sermons*, p. 401).

[82] Aug. *Sermo* 299A.3 = Dolbeau 4/Mainz 9 (Dolbeau, *Vingt-six sermons*, p. 413): "et perlatum est ad nos illos quoque miseros miserandosque dixisse terrore circumcellionum nobis inpositum est silentium. Est quidem revera quod illi nos <a> praedicatione verbi pacis terrere non cessant."

[83] Possid. *Vita Aug.* 12.1–2 (Bastiaensen: 156–58): notably, in connection with his preaching and exhortation in the rural parts of his diocese.

[84] Aug. *Contra Cresc.* 3.43.49 (CSEL 52: 456): "solito crebrius et audacius circumcellionum violentiis turbisque furentibus nos a praedicanda Catholica veritate."

churches. The threats certainly helped the dissident cause. Between 405 and 410, for the whole of the five years after the emperor Honorius' edict of unification, no real progress was made towards the goal of compelling the dissidents to rejoin the imperial church. From the perspective of the Catholics, the situation in 410 was almost as pessimistic as it had been in 405.

Given the goal, it is easier to understand the configuration of the attacks on persons and the specificity of the targets. The assaults were modulated so as to intimidate. Their main targets and the symbolic ways in which the body was harmed were meant to signal a message to witnesses of the violence and to those who heard accounts of it. Just as important, however, the force of containment also had a strong internal face. Given the small number of crossovers in the whole conflict, this might well have been the most powerful and effective part of the policing, namely the internal intimidation and control of the dissident community itself.[85] Unlike physical attacks on Catholics and Catholic properties, there was no great need or impetus for the Catholic sources, largely the only surviving ones, to report on these inside incidents. There was even less impetus for the dissidents to report on acts of violence and intimidation. Yet surely they did exist. In 407, the year that saw the dissident bishop Maximinus of Siniti, a village near Hippo, cross over to the Catholic side, it was reported that the dissidents sent heralds and criers to the village make public announcements of threats to burn down the houses of any persons who dared to communicate with the traitor.[86] There is little doubt about how or by whom the deed would be done, if necessary. The essential point was the inculcation of the fear that was imposed by the presence of the circumcellion threat.

WHAT IS THIS VIOLENCE?

These observations do not mean to understate the real effects of circumcellion violence. Their attacks tended to be direct, physical in a brutish fashion, personal, and elemental. The apparent sporadic and random nature of their assaults added to the fear that they created. A standard image of their

---

[85] Compare Brubaker (2004), 99, referring to the practices of "necklacing" in the South African townships during the anti-Apartheid struggles and "kneecapping" in Northern Ireland during the Troubles; as for the latter, a significant proportion of IRA deliberate hits were on internal persons either known or suspected of betrayal.

[86] Aug. *Ep.* 105.2.4 (CCL 31B: 51): "Quid amplius dicamus? Modo praeconem misistis, qui clamaret Siniti: 'Quisquis Maximino communicaverit, incendetur domus eius.'"

attacks was one of them springing on their victims unawares, waylaying them unexpectedly "in the manner of bandits."[87] When staged under the cover of the darkness of night, their ambushes shared the same characteristics of the terrifying inroads of brigands.[88] It was an age when bandit attacks were not uncommon. It was also one in which the raiders feeding the demands of the slavers were staging attacks "like bandits" in which the vulnerable and largely defenseless inhabitants of rural villages and hamlets were being kidnapped and dragged off to a life of slavery.[89] Fear was not an unreasonable response to attacks that looked similar in kind. It was this frightening image, one of violent men closer to bandits than to common criminals, that Augustine wished to fix in the minds of his listeners and readers.[90] In stating that circumcellion violence was a kind of banditry or *latrocinium*, Catholic lobbyists construed them as a frightening menace, as a general insurgency that threatened the whole fabric of the social order.[91] In constructing circumcellion violence as mad, deranged, and not fixed anywhere, but as erupting from amorphous and nameless wandering packs of near-animals out there somewhere, Catholic writers and preachers heightened the fear of a generalized and unknowable threat.

It was a common strategy used by both Christians and non-Christians to castigate the quality and nature of a violent threat, specifically when speaking the government's own language in order to persuade it.[92] It is difficult to know to what degree they believed their own hard line. But one has to have some sympathy for the Catholic priest in Italy who, in 409, wrote to Augustine in real fear of the widespread violent forays of

---

[87] Attacks are *more latronum*: Aug. *Ad Donatist. post collat.* 17.22 (CSEL 53: 121): "sed pro apertissimis facinoribus et sceleribus suis, quae more latronum inmani furore et crudelitate comittunt"; *Ep.* 105.2.4 (CSEL 34.2: 598): "Cui ambulanti viam suam latronum more insidiati sunt" (the attack on Possidius of Calama; although the term *circumcelliones* is not used, it is clear that these are the same men). For further references, see *Ep.* 43.24; 108.14; 111.1; *Contra ep. Parm.* 2.9.19; *Contra Cresc.* 3.42.46; 3.48.52; and *Sermo* 299A.3 (Dolbeau 4 = Mainz 9), amongst others.

[88] Aug. *Contra Cresc.* 3.42.46 (CSEL 52: 453): "cum cotidie vestrorum incredibilia patiamur facta clericorum et circumcellionum multo peiora quam quorumlibet latronum atque praedonum . . . nocturnis adgressionibus."

[89] Aug. *Ep.* *10, esp. *10.3 (CSEL 88: 46–51, 47): "Nocte enim dixit huiusmodi irruisse praedones"; on the involvement of the *mangones* with local violence see Lepelley (1981), Rougé (1983), Szidat (1985), and Gabillon (1986).

[90] Aug. *Contra ep. Parm.* 2.9.19 (CSEL 51: 64–65): "Eos sane cum fure concurrisse non dico, quia fure peior est raptor, quod esse undique conclamabatur Optatus."

[91] Aug. *Ep.* 43.8.24 (CCL 31B: 184): "Parco iam dicere singularum per Africam regionum et civitatum et fundorum tyrannicas potestates et publica latrocinia"; *Ep.* 108.5.14 (CCL 31B: 78): "Deo laudes inter cantica conclamantes quas voces velut tubas proeliorum in suis omnibus latrociniis habuerunt."

[92] So Libanius, for example, on the behavior of violent Christian monks in the east: see Gaddis, *Religious Violence*, p. 211.

larger-scale "barbarian" attacks that were penetrating deeply into Gaul and Spain, and who was in terror of Alaric and his army of Goths making savage and pitiless inroads into Italy. Basically, Augustine's response was: "That's nothing, we have *real* violence here in Africa."[93]

Just look, right here in our region of Hippo Regius – I admit that it is a fact that barbarians have not reached it – the brigand attacks of Donatist clerics and the circumcellions are so devastating our churches that the deeds of barbarians would perhaps be milder.

Although it is good to have the conviction of one's own fictions, to paint a picture of circumcellion violence as that of real bandits and as bad as full-scale "barbarian" raids was a political necessity. The assertion is not underwritten by any objective evidence. Rather, the construction of circumcellions as a threat that presented serious parallels with "barbarians" was central to an agenda that was attempting to persuade an imperial court that was daily faced with real "barbarian" inroads into its empire.[94] In some of his earlier writings on the problem, Augustine had come to realize that the identification of circumcellions with bandits was a useful analogy: brigands had always been a benchmark of comparison for political purposes, for raising the specter of social anarchy.[95]

Whatever circumcellion violence might have been like, and however widespread, it almost certainly did not rise to the level of war, brigandage, or even a serious crime wave. Despite repeated references to the horrors of their acts of violence, in relatively few of the specific cases (that were reported) was death a result. Since Augustine and others on his side wished to suggest that homicidal violence was the norm, the relative absence of reported deaths seems to be significant. In a sermon delivered in January 404, Augustine launched a hard attack against "the Donatists," asserting that Catholic clemencies and rewards offered to the dissidents as encouragements to reunite with a Mediterranean-wide church had only evoked hateful responses from them. The dissidents lashed out against manifest

---

[93] Aug. *Ep.* III.I (CCL 31B: 92): "Ecce in regione nostra Hipponiensi, quoniam eam barbari non attigerunt, clericorum Donatistarum et circumcellionum latrocinia sic vastant ecclesias, ut barbarorum fortasse facta mitiora sint."

[94] Aug. *Contra Cresc.* 3.48.52 (CSEL 52: 460): "Haec qui faciunt quid aequos dicam latronibus, piratis, truculento alicui generi barbarorum, quando nec ipsi omnium crudelitatum magistro Diabolo conparandi sunt?"; *Contra litt. Petil.* 2.85.189 (CSEL 52: 117): "Vestri circumcelliones quiescant, et nolo nos de barbaris terreas."

[95] Aug. *Sermo*, 299A.3 = Dolbeau 4/Mainz 9 (Dolbeau, *Vingt-six sermons*, p. 514): How I have to spend my time among the furious assaults of men who are no better than bandits: "Credimus enim quod, cum auditis de periculis nostris quemadmodum inter furores latrocinantium deversemur, oratis pro nobis."

truth: "that is why they hate us and, if they get the chance, have us murdered at the hands of their circumcellions."[96] On the basis of the existing record, this is an exaggerated threat made mainly to police one's own congregation by instilling fear in them. Circumcellions did not strike at random nor, as far as specific cases indicate, did they normally aim at homicide.

Details in the surviving records – both the occasional references to violent episodes and the more detailed descriptions of specific attacks – suggest that most often cold-blooded murder was *not* the main purpose of circumcellion assaults. In the general summary of the problem offered by Possidius, the description is not that of men who were so murderous that their normal intent was to kill, but rather of youths who might in some cases be driven to this extreme: "and if someone did not obey them, they had serious damage and wounds inflicted on them. Armed with different sorts of weapons, these men raged through fields and rural villas, not fearing to go so far as the shedding of blood."[97] The possibility that they might shed blood is suggested as one extreme of their actions. So too, Augustine could wax hot on the circumcellions as "men of blood," but then hasten to point out that although they might well have indulged in some physical murder, it was much more the "murder of souls" in which they excelled.[98] The rhetorical contrast is especially significant, since he could actually wish that people *would* be slaughtered by the circumcellion weapons rather than be rebaptized.[99]

Acts other than the outright murder of their sectarian enemies seem to have been more usually the case. The deaths that are recorded in connection with circumcellion activities are more usually their own: death inflicted upon them by imperial authorities or death inflicted on themselves in acts of ritual self-killing. If there had been large numbers of murders of Catholics that had resulted from circumcellion attacks, Augustine would surely have highlighted them. He does not. Even in his worst horror cases, it is various

[96] Aug. *Sermo*, 198.45 = Dolbeau 26/Mainz 62 (Dolbeau, *Vingt-six sermons*, p. 125): "propter hoc oderunt nos et, si facultas detur, occidunt manu circumcellionum." The statement seems to be qualified somewhat; the phrase "si facultas detur" would seem to indicate a contrary-to-fact condition (i.e., "if the opportunity would offer itself, they would kill us").

[97] Possid. *Vita Aug.* 10.2 (Bastiaensen: 152): "et nisi oboedissent, damnis gravissimis et caedibus affliciebantur – armati diversis telis, bacchantes per agros villasque, usque ad sanguinis effusionem adcedere non metuentes."

[98] Aug. *En. in Ps.* 54.26 (CCL 39: 675): "*Viri sanguinum et dolositatis.* Viros sanguinum propter interfectiones dicit; atque utinam corporales, et non spiritales. Sanguis enim de carne exiens, videtur et horretur; . . . Quamquam et de istis mortalibus visibilibus non quiescant armati ubique circumcelliones. Et si istas visibiles mortes adtendamus, *viri sanguinum* sunt."

[99] Aug. *Contra litt. Petil.* 2.86.191 (CSEL 52: 118): "Et utinam innocens frater in vestrorum potius circumcellionum tela trucidandus quam in vestram linguam rebaptizandus incurrat!"

types of physical harm that are inflicted on the victim, usually by way of a severe beating – but the victims usually survived. The purpose of the violence was not to kill, but rather to enforce a sort of disciplinary regime and to intimidate so as to deter. The targets of circumcellion violence were rather limited, either properties of the Catholic Church or specific persons. Their violence was neither random nor chaotic, but purposeful and rational. In his later summation of Augustine's involvement with the circumcellions, Possidius suggests that they staged attacks on Catholic bishops and their assistants, and against property in general.[100] What he omits to say, critically, is *which* bishops and clerics were targeted and why.

DISCIPLINE AND PUNISH

The omission is important because the men who were attacked were not just any random sample of Catholic parishioners. The targets of circum-cellion violence that are most frequently named were members of their own dissident community who converted and who (certainly in the eyes of the circumcellions) had betrayed their church to cross over to join the Catholics. Attacking persons for this reason was part of a deliberate policy of preventative violence that involved the active policing of the frontiers of one's own community to ensure its internal cohesion.[101] This kind of violence was sustained by the long discourse on betrayal and traitors that formed the critical watershed between the two Christian communities. The instances were apparently few and striking enough to form a canon of typical cases. Augustine recounts three of them in a letter of 409. They include Marcus, a priest of Casphalianensis, who "of his own free will" decided to become a Catholic. He was attacked and beaten, and might well have died had not a gang or "a force" from the Catholic side intervened to beat off his attackers.[102] The second was Restitutus of Victoriana, a dissident who also crossed over of his own free will. He was dragged from his home, beaten, "clothed in the *buda*," and held in captivity for a number of days.[103] A

---

[100] Possid. *Vita Aug.* 10.5 (Bastiaensen: 154): "ipsisque Catholicis sacerdotibus et ministris adgressiones diurnas atque nocturnas direptionesque rerum omnium inferebant."

[101] Again, this behavior was not *as such* peculiar to Africa. For the labeling of traitors and betrayers, and the attacks on and executions of such crossovers in the East, see, e.g., Sizgorich, *Violence and Belief*, pp. 62, 66, 73, and 109.

[102] Aug. *Ep.* 105.2.3 (CCL 31B: 50): "Marcus presbyter Casphalianensis a nemine coactus propria voluntate Catholicus factus est; qua re illum vestri persecuti sunt et paene occidissent, nisi Dei manus per homines supervenientes violentias eorum compressisset."

[103] Aug. *Ep.* 105.2.3 (CCL 31B: 50–51): "Restitutus Victorianensis ad Catholicam nullo cogente se transtulit; qua re raptus est de domo sua, caesus, in aqua volutatus, buda vestitus, et nescio quot dies in captivitate retentus est, nec libertati propriae fortasse restitutus esset."

similar violent incident involved Marcianus of Urgensis, a bishop whose subdeacon had crossed over with him. The subdeacon was pummeled and stoned almost to the point of death. Their home was looted and plundered as punishment for the bishop's "crime."[104] This policing function was not the monopoly of Christians. Jewish gangs, we might suspect, were just as busy using intimidation and violence for precisely the same purpose: to prevent crossing over to the other side.[105]

We know that as late as 411, the Restitutus beating was still referred to as an exemplary case, although others had been added. In the proceedings of the conference at Carthage, Restitutus is simply referred to as a Catholic priest who happened to suffer a violent attack. If only this later source existed, we would not know, very importantly, that *the* reason for the attack on him was not just because he happened to be a Catholic priest, but because he was a special kind of priest: one who had switched sides from the dissidents to the Catholics. It was purposefully misleading innocuously to label him simply as "a Catholic priest." That was certainly not how his attackers saw him. To them, he was a traitor. And what is more, they did not forget. The physical attack made on him in 404 was provoked, one must suspect, by the immediate pressures and hostilities arising from the Catholic campaign for unification. He survived, but the renewed campaign of the 410s, the conference of Carthage of 411, the subsequent decision by Marcellinus, and the renewed legislative drive for unification, excited memories. This time, Restitutus did not escape. He was murdered in the immediate aftermath of a renewed campaign of repression that revived and concentrated old hatreds on this emblematic figure of betrayal.[106]

The same rationale is probably behind the attacks made on an Innocentius who is also presented simply as another Catholic priest. Again, it is the ritualistic nature of the violence that is striking. In the latter case, one of the man's eyes was gouged out and one of his fingers was cut off.[107] Precisely one eye and one finger indicate care and deliberation. But Augustine avers

---

[104] Aug. *Ep.* 105.2.3 (CCL 31B: 51): "Marcianus Urgensis catholicam unitatem propria voluntate delegit; qua re subdiaconum eius, cum ipse fugisset, prope usque ad mortem caesum clerici vestri lapidibus obruerunt, quorum domus pro suo scelere eversae sunt."

[105] See CTh 16.8.5 (Constantine, from Constantinople, to Felix PPO): issued on 22 October 335 from Constantinople; posted at Carthage on 8 May 336: against Jews who attack or intimidate Jews who are converting to Christianity.

[106] Aug. *Ep.* 133.1 (CCL 31B: 241, cited below), see also *Ep.* 134.2 (CCL 31B: 245–46) and *Ep.* 139.1 (CCL 31B: 291), where Augustine suggests that the bishop Macrobius was instrumental in this murder.

[107] Aug. *Ep.* 133.1 (CCL 31B: 241): "de homicidio quod in Restitutum, Catholicum presbyterum commiserunt, et de caede Innocentii, alterius Catholici presbyteri, atque de oculo eius effosso et digito praeciso fuisse confessos."

that Catholic clergy in general were the victims of attacks: their houses are ravaged, the men themselves are dragged out of their homes and then beaten with clubs and iron instruments and then thrown away, as he says, left half dead.[108] Since such men in the priestly hierarchy of the Catholic Church were regarded as traitors to begin with, forming the organizational backbone of the "church of the traitors," they were liable to attack on this ground alone. But the polluting sight of a living crossover, a man like Restitutus, who embodied in his own person the terrible stain of betrayal, was a hypervalued example of the type and so was more likely to attract retribution.

Another such case is mentioned by Augustine in his faux-debate with Emeritus, the dissident bishop of Caesarea in Mauretania. In this instance, both the forces leading to betrayal and the rationale behind the subsequent enforcement are manifest. If the full narrative behind the violence was not known, Rogatus of Assuras would be just another Catholic bishop who was subject to vicious and wanton attacks by circumcellions, who seized him, cut out his tongue and then hacked off one of his hands. But the full story is more complex and it provides the grounds for understanding the nature of the attack and the violence. The whole matter began within the ranks of the dissident church and involved the Maximianist dispute within it. As a result of this dispute, Praetextatus, the sitting dissident bishop of the town of Assuras, found himself declared to be an enemy by his own church and no longer the bishop of Assuras. In his place, another man, named Rogatus, was elected as bishop of the town. In the sometimes quite sordid politicking that emerged by which this whole division within the dissident church was papered over, a deal was struck whereby the "errant" bishops could mend their ways and, before a given date, be formally accepted back into the ranks of the bishops of the dissident church and reclaim their bishoprics.

The result was that Praetextatus was rehabilitated, received back into the dissident church, and re-ensconced in his seat at Assuras. Rogatus, on the other hand, had had every expectation that *he* would be the bishop of Assuras, especially since he was replacing a man who had been condemned by a formal council of the church and who was part of the losing side in this little civil war between the supporters of Maximian and those of Primian. Because of his superior patronal connections, however, and the support of Optatus, the powerful bishop of Thamugadi, the former criminal was

---

[108] Aug. *Contra Cresc.* 3.42.46 (CSEL 52: 453): "nocturnis adgressionibus clericorum Catholicorum invasas domos nudas atque inanes relinquunt, ipsos etiam raptos et fustibus tunsos ferroque concisos semivivos abiciunt." The *domus* in these attacks could be churches or basilicas.

now reappointed and restored to his old seat. The sense of disappointment in Rogatus must have been acute. To construe his response as feeling that he had been "stabbed in the back" or betrayed would not be out of place. Out of a sense of dishonor or anger, or both, Rogatus took the only rational course of action open to him. He struck back by crossing party lines. He went over to the Catholics and became their bishop of Assuras, preserving his honor, maintaining his rank, and avenging himself on his former coreligionists.

It was at this point that the circumcellions entered the picture. Someone guilty of this gross and public act of betrayal (whatever the reasons) had to be turned into an example. Rogatus had to be punished physically. They cut out his tongue and cut off one hand precisely because these were the public sources of power of a bishop who stood before his congregation and preached, and who wrote, gestured, and blessed with his right hand.[109] In a letter to Vincentius, a dissident bishop at Caesarea in Mauretania, in the aftermath of the measures of 405 that were meant to encourage the mass abandonment of the dissident church by its adherents, Augustine noted that there would have been many more such crossovers from the dissident church if it had not been for the presence of the circumcellions.[110] In making the observation, he reveals one of their main purposes. The primary role filled by the circumcellions was the policing of their own community, mainly to prevent and to discourage acts of betrayal. In this function, they appear to have been reasonably successful. In the aftermath of the conference of 411, Augustine complained that not many dissidents were crossing over to join the Catholics. "Why?" he asked. His answers were two: The force of tradition and the effectiveness of enforcement: "the frenzied ones are . . . roaming about, insane, raving, and armed, looking for people whom they can kill, people whom they can blind."[111] Although he does not use a formal label for these men, the cumulation of adjectives leaves no doubt that these are the same persons whom he elsewhere describes as "circumcellions."

---

[109] Aug. *Gesta cum Emerit.* 9 (CSEL 53: 192): "Nam in loco unius ipsorum Praetextati Assuritani alium iam ordinaverunt nomine Rogatum, qui modo Catholicus est, cui exercitus istorum, id est agmen circumcellionum, linguam et manum praecidit"; and, again, in *Ep.* *28.7 (CSEL 88: 137): "Venit enim quidam ex fratribus Carthaginiensibus qui eum dixit adhuc latius disponere pergere propter causam episcopi Rogati cui linguam et manum haeretici praeciderunt," showing that the case had still not been dealt with in 417/18.

[110] Aug. *Ep.* 93.2 (CCL 31A: 168).

[111] Aug. *Sermo* 356.8 (PL 39: 1596): "Phrenetici . . . et insani atque furiosi armati vagantur hac atque illac, quaerentes quos occidant, quos excaecent."

Furthermore, the circumcellions were neither raving nor insane. They had their own compelling logic and manner. Take, for example, the attack on the Catholic bishop Maximianus of Bagaï that has already been described in detail. Maximianus was no innocent in the eyes of his attackers. He had once been the bishop of the dissident church at Bagaï before he crossed over to the Catholics. In the eyes of his attackers, he was a traitor. He was perhaps even more open to violent counterattack than other bishops. The circumstances in which he crossed over to the Catholic Church, some time in the 390s, are not known, but he was not a great success with his new Catholic parishioners. In fact, things became so bad that at the council of Milevis, in 402, it was decided that a letter had to be sent to Maximianus to the effect that he should vacate his position, and to his congregation that they should elect another man as bishop.[112] The urgings were a failure. No replacement was made. Maximianus clung on to his position and survived the attack in 404 to become a celebrity exhibit at the imperial court at Ravenna in 405. Making himself an international star, in fact, was perhaps provoked by the need to compensate for his bad local image. But the beating itself, and the punishment, as terrible as it was, fell short of direct killing. It surely would have been quite possible to kill him at any point in the mêlée that broke out in his church and in the dusty streets outside of it in the autumn of 403. Yet his life was preserved, so to speak, so that his attackers could haul him to the top of a tall tower in the town and hurl him off it. Augustine recognized the symbolism involved: Maximianus' fall from grace was a kind of precipitation.[113]

THE UTILITY OF VIOLENCE

Another function of the circumcellions was to offer protection to dissident communities and their bishops against organized Catholic violence. In a letter of 409, Augustine reports two cases. The first is that of Rusticianus, the subdeacon, who, having been excommunicated by his priest, sought refuge with Macrobius, the dissident bishop of Hippo.[114] Augustine mentions another Catholic deacon who crossed over to the dissidents and was rebaptized by Proculeianus. The reasons for his leaving were normal: he

---

[112] Concil. Milev. 402, canon 2 = *Reg. Eccl. Carth. Excerpt.* canon 88 (CCL 149: 207): "et ad eum et ad ipsam plebem placuit de concilio litteras dari, ut et ipse ab episcopatu discedat, et illi sibi alium requirant."

[113] Aug. *Contra Cresc.* 3.43.47 (CSEL 52: 454): "et de excelsa turri noctu praecipitatus subter cinere stercoris molliter iacebat exceptus."

[114] See "Rusticianus (2)," PAC, p. 1011; Aug. *Ep.* 106 (CCL 31B: 63) and 108.6.19 (CCL 31B: 82–83).

had been excommunicated by his Catholic priest. This man did not just cross over. He became one of the violent men who joined the dissident circumcellions in pillaging and setting fire to the properties of their enemies. In the end, he was killed in a counterattack led by Catholic defenders.[115] Incidents like these open up wider questions about the extent to which the dissident holy fighters, in whatever guise they appeared, were in some significant sense a response to and a replication of existing Catholic gang violence. The flipside was the exploitation of descriptions of episodes of their violence as rhetorical sound bites to be used against the dissident claim to be the church of the peaceful, the community of the beatitudes.[116] This Catholic propensity provides a large number of our references to "circumcellions," so a large problem with the details concerning this aspect of sectarian violence is that they all come from one side in the dispute. It is the distribution of the evidence that happens to survive with which we are condemned to work.

This patterning of the evidence is not just fortuitous; the selection of what has survived was quite deliberate. The gross imbalance logically raises questions about the nature of Catholic enforcement. Catholic communities must have organized in a similar fashion, at least to defend themselves. Certainly "pagans" in this same period did. However slight it might be, the evidence indicates that anti-pagan gangs were Christian, both Catholic and dissident. They were not drawn solely from "Donatist" youths. Fronting systematic attacks on pagan shrines and temples in the 380s and 390s – perhaps also in earlier decades, for which the evidence is truly thin – they were an aggressive Christian response to executing imperial orders against "pagan" ritual sites. Some of these men were Catholics who saw themselves as doing the good work of Catholic emperors. As we have just seen in the case of Marcus, the Catholic bishop of Casphalianensis, the attempt by circumcellions to attack this man, whom they saw as a traitor, was beaten back by an organized force of Catholics. The same applies to the attack on Maximianus of Bagaï, where Catholic men rushed to the defense of their bishop. In a letter that Augustine wrote to Emeritus, the dissident bishop of Caesarea, in which he justified the use of state force to defend Catholics against dissident gangs, the possibility was contemplated: "If any of our men act in this way, with an unchristian lack of control, it does not please us." This and other such notices more than just hint at the existence of

[115] Aug. *Ep.* 108.19 (CCL 31B: 82–83).
[116] See, for example, Augustine's series of uses of them in his replies to the pacific claims made by Petilian: *Contra litt. Petil.* 2.63.141–2.65.245 (CSEL 52: 97–98).

Catholic enforcers, however unpleasing the prospect might have been to bishops like Augustine.

Paralleling the response of many dissident church leaders to their holy fighters, the actions of such violent men were rejected by Catholic bishops as proper Christian conduct.[117] In their attempt to control circumcellion attacks in Numidia in 405, Catholic clergy appealed to Januarius, the dissident primate of the province.[118] They knew full well that their heartfelt appeal would appear to be hypocritical and would fall on deaf ears if they did not admit what Januarius himself knew to be true: that Catholic gangs were similarly engaged in violent actions against his people. So they admitted that there were indeed some cases where dissidents had been captured and held by "our people," meaning the Catholics. But, they claimed, these clergy did nothing other than use normal techniques of "education" and "persuasion" on the dissidents whom they held in detention. If this were the end of the matter, the use of force by Catholic bishops and priests is admitted. But there is more. In their appeal, the Catholics further allowed, by way of exculpation, that there were ordinary Catholics who seized dissidents, in which case the treatment of the detainees was not so anodyne. We urge these people, says Augustine, not to hurt their captives but to bring them in to us to be "instructed" and "educated." The words are euphemisms. He confesses that such ordinary Catholics listen to the advice "if they can," but that they often deal with their captives "as they deal with bandits." That is to say, lynch justice could be imposed, and was. The Catholic enforcers are nonetheless construed as brave men. Their code of honor surely paralleled that of the dissident holy fighters, and so it is logical that Augustine used words that would apply to both cases: "They do not abjure the behavior of bandits, but they expect the honor due to martyrs." It would be good to know more about these Catholic sectarian gangs, but the nature of the surviving sources prevents this: we are only informed about the dissident gangsters in any detail. From our picture of them, we must suppose a mirroring of purpose, style, values, and organization.

The reason that we do not hear about the Catholic gangs has nothing to do with their non-existence, but rather with the utility of carefully crafted and archived notices of "circumcellion violence." When Optatus began writing his counterattack against the dissident bishop Parmenian in the mid-360s, the circumcellions were already beginning to fill a vital role in

---

[117] Aug. *Ep.* 87.8 (CCL 31A: 137): "Postremo etiam si aliqui nostrorum non Christiana moderatione ista faciunt, displicet nobis"; cf. *Ep. ad Cath. contra Donatist.* 20.55 (CSEL 51: 304).

[118] Aug. *Ep.* 88 (CCL 31A: 139–47): with attendant documentation, it might be noted.

sectarian rhetoric that was as significant as their violent acts. Augustine was well aware of the fact. In the violent conflicts that pitted Catholics against dissenters in the fourth century, both behavior and words had assumed a ritual-like repetitiveness.[119]

> You confront us with our betrayal,
> We say: "You did it too!"
> You shout about the Macarian Time
> We about your circumcellions.

These verses from his *Song Against the Donatists* recapitulate Augustine's own views and those of Optatus: one type of violence was offset by the threat presented by the other. "We might have made mistakes in the use of secular violent force in the Macarian Time, but what about you and your circumcellions?" This perspective on their place in the rhetoric of the time was forged, in large part, by the events of 347. In his detailed description of the violent episodes of that year that form the backbone of his reply to Parmenian, Optatus helped to construct the charter explanation that the deployment of the forces of the Roman state on behalf of the Catholic Church was justified by the violent excesses of the other side. It was the violent acts of the circumcellions – in this case the men marshaled by Donatus, the dissident bishop of Bagaï – that both caused and legitimized the use of state force. It was a theme that was to be picked up and played upon heavily by Augustine in the years leading up to 405, and then in the immediate aftermath of state-driven pressures for unification that elicited protective enforcement from the dissidents. Writing in the immediate aftermath of the unification decree of 405, he condemned the dissidents' men of violence for destroying the peace not just of the Church but of civil society itself.[120]

In a letter from the early years of his pop song, Augustine wrote to Maximinus, the dissident bishop of the village of Siniti, near Hippo, to dissuade him from rebaptizing a Catholic deacon. In the letter, the same balance of violence is proffered: If you don't bring up the Macarian Time, then I won't talk about the savagery of the circumcellions.[121] At the same

---

[119] Aug. *Psalmus contra partem Donati*, 143–44 (BA 28: 170; Lambot [1933]: 323): "Obicitis traditionem: / respondemus vos fecisse. / Clamatis vos de Machario / et nos de circellione."

[120] Aug. *Contra Cresc.* 3.42.46 (CSEL 52: 453): "Namque horrendis armati cuiusque generis telis terribiliter vagando non dico ecclesiasticam, sed ipsam humanam quietem pacemque perturbant." The reference is certainly to men whom he would otherwise have labeled circumcellions.

[121] Aug. *Ep.* 23.6 (CCL 31: 66): "Tollamus de medio inania obiecta, quae a partibus imperitis iactari contra invicem solent, nec tu obicias tempora Macariana nec ego saevitiam circumcellionum." See "Maximinus (2)," PAC, p. 728 where the editors identify this Maximinus as a crossover who later converted to the Catholic side.

time, Augustine noted that secular state force was present in the town and could still be used if necessary. He speaks of fear, but he promised his interlocutor that "I shall not take any action while the military are present in Hippo in case any of your people might think that I wish to use force rather than more peaceful ways." He said that he would wait until the army departed before he did anything. From our side, he emphasizes, "Terror caused by the use of temporal power has ceased on our side, so on your side let there be an end to the terror created by your gangs of circumcellions."[122] He repeats: "There is no doubt that you said that we sharpened our swords, but I can read aloud the records of the deeds of your circumcellions."[123] Throughout, there is the same consistent linkage between the dissidents' use of circumcellion violence and Catholic justifications for their use of the forces of the state. The threat of the one legitimized the use of the other.

The important role that the circumcellions served for the Catholics was much the same as that played by the Maximianists: they provided a stellar example of the hypocrisies of the dissidents. The dissidents construed themselves as a church of the pure, members of a body "without spot or wrinkle." It was on these grounds that they condemned the Catholic conception of a universal church that was inclusive of both the good and the bad. It was not by chance that the biblical parable of the "weeds and the grain" frequently cued a mention of the circumcellions as a striking example of "bad men" who were tolerated within the ranks of the dissident church – often in lists of the other bad men harbored by their church, like Optatus of Thamugadi, suicidal martyrs, greedy and rapacious clerics, rapists, usurers, and others.[124] Playing on the violence of the circumcellions served to turn the ideological tables on the Catholics' adversaries. It was not the dissidents who were being persecuted by the state, but rather the Catholics who were being persecuted by the violence of the circumcellion gangs. As early as 400, Augustine was taking the line that the dissidents

---

[122] Aug. *Ep.* 23.7 (CCL 31: 67–68): "Neque id agam cum miles praesens est, ne quis vestrum arbitretur tumultuosius me agere voluisse quam ratio pacis desiderat, sed post abscessum militis . . . Cessavit a nostris partibus terror temporalium potestatum; cesset etiam a vestris partibus terror congregatorum circumcellionum."

[123] Aug. *En. 2 in Ps.* 36.18 (CCL 38: 359): "Certe ibi dixisti, quia nos acuimus gladios nostros; recito gesta tuorum circumcellionum."

[124] Aug. *Ep.* 43.8.24 (CCL 31: 184): "Ad summam se ipsos interrogent! Nonne tolerantur ab eis caedes et incendia circumcellionum, veneratores praecipitatorum ultro cadaverum, et sub incredibilibus malis unius Optati per tot annos totius Africae gemitus?"; *Ep. ad Cath. contra Donatist.* 20.56 (CSEL 52: 305); *De unico baptismo,* 8.14 (CSEL 53: 15): "Ipsos quoque non arbitror tam esse inpudentes, ut audeant dicere tam multis malis et sceleratis, qui in eorum parte sunt manifestis flagitiis et facinoribus perditi et inquinati, hoc est avaris atque raptoribus sive truculentis faeneratoribus sive cruentis circumcellionibus."

could hardly complain about any legal penalties that they suffered from duly constituted government authorities, given the fact that they were guilty of having violent bands of young men commit savage acts on their sectarian enemies.[125]

If they suffer some "difficulty" in this world imposed through the agency of a fully legitimate and duly established order of power – all this while they themselves inflict much more serious harm everywhere on a daily basis with their private armies of madmen, with no royal and no ecclesiastical law giving them the authority to do so – then *they* call us "persecutors" of their bodies. While not calling themselves murderers of souls, they allow themselves the private right not to spare our bodies as well. Because of our Christian charity, the gouging out of an eye in a quarrel is punished more severely than making a soul utterly blind by schism . . .

The circumcellions inverted the whole ideology of persecution. Theirs was "a new kind of persecution of hitherto unheard of cruelty"; they and their clerical leaders created a violent repression that Catholics had to endure.[126] "It is your persecution of us," asserts Augustine, "it is our passion."[127] If the dissidents made so much of persecution, especially the Great Persecution of 347, circumcellion violence became part of the evidence formally arrayed against claims of the uniqueness of their suffering. This use of the circumcellions had to do with a theodicy of Christian suffering. On the other hand, references to the circumcellions in the proceedings of the conference of 411 before the judge Flavius Marcellinus, who was to make a final decision on the status of the dissident church and on the mobilization of state resources, had a different, secular, purpose.[128] To have this beneficial effect with officials of the state, in their rhetoric Catholic leaders had to blind themselves to the widespread existence of their own enforcers whose presence and actions would have cancelled out the apparent uniqueness of the threat of dissident men of violence. Important and influential figures in

---

[125] Aug. *Contra ep. Parm.* 1.8.14 (CSEL 51: 35): "Et si quid temporalis molestiae passi fuerint per certissimum et rectissimum ordinem potestatum, cum ipsi privatis furiosorum agminibus multo graviora passim atque cotidie nulla regia, nulla ecclesiastica lege committant, nos corporum persecutores vocant, se animarum interfectores non vocant, cum privata licentia nec corporibus parcant, sed quia per mansuetudinem Christianam multo severius vindicatur oculus evulsus in lite quam animus excaecatus in schismate."

[126] For example: Aug. *Ep.* 88.1 (CCL 31A: 139): "Clerici et circumcelliones vestri novi generis et inauditae crudelitatis persecutione in nos saeviunt."

[127] Aug. *Ep.* 108.5.14 (CCL 31B: 77–78).

[128] Aug. *Brev. Collat.* 3.8.13 (CCL 149A: 281): "De persecutionibus etiam, quas perpeti se queruntur, multa in suis litteris posuerunt nec tamen respondere ausi sunt ad illud quod in mandato Catholicorum dictum est . . . <in> invidiam Catholicorum exaggerantes sive mortes, quas eorum circumcelliones sibimet ipsis inferunt."

the Catholic Church preached and wrote incessantly about "circumcellion violence," but almost always for political purposes.

Which is hardly surprising. From the beginning, the significance of expatiating on the circumcellion threat and exaggerating its nature was starkly political. For nearly a century, the Catholics had been attempting to move the imperial authorities at Carthage and the court at Ravenna to use the considerable resources of violent force at their disposal finally to crush their sectarian enemies. But the agents of the state, both centrally at the court and locally in the municipalities, were reluctant to enter a sectarian fray. On the occasions on which they had done so, as in 347, the results had been rather unhappy. As long as African disputes remained local and religious in nature, the men who governed the state were not overly interested in a policy of hard intervention; they had much to risk and little to gain from direct involvement. Caught in this trap, the circumcellions offered just what the Catholics needed: an apprehended violent threat to the imperial civil order. If the imperial and civil authorities could be persuaded about the reality and seriousness of the threat and, more specifically, the direct links of the men of violence with the dissident church, then the likelihood of state intervention would be enhanced. Whereas emperors, prefects, vicars, governors, imperial procurators, and others might not be attracted to intervene in an ecclesiastical quarrel where intervention had no special consequences for the interests of the state, they might become involved if they were persuaded that the conflict was affecting the well-being of the political commonwealth. Hence the persistent implication of "the bishops and clerics" of "the Donatists" in a rhetorical language that contrasted circumcellion violence with the legitimacy of state power.[129]

We do not presume anything about the power of humans, although we do presume that what is much more honest comes from the emperors than from the circum-cellions, from laws rather than from riots. And we remember that it is written: "Let all be cursed who place their hope in man."

Statements like these deliberately contrasted the violent acts of the circum-cellions with the probity and stability of the state and its public laws.[130] This line of persuasion was developed very early. It became an ongoing part of the repertoire of appeals to the imperial government, emphasized at certain moments in the struggle, but soft-pedaled, downplayed, or avoided at others. In the renewed offensive of the late 390s, the argument came to

---

[129] Aug. *Ep.* 105.6 (CCL 31B: 57). The quotation is of Jer. 17: 5.
[130] Aug. *Ep.* 108.6.18 (CCL 31B: 82): "Fugitur unitas, ut nos adversus vestrorum – nolo enim vestras dicere – inprobitates quaeramus publicas leges et adversus ipsas leges armentur circumcelliones."

the fore again, as can be seen in the arguments in Augustine's *Against the Letter of Parmenian* written around 400. How could the dissidents complain of persecution when they used private gangs to attack Catholics? How could they complain of state-directed penalties when they themselves had appealed to the state? Did the state therefore not have a right to intervene in this instance too?

These same notes were struck in a letter written to Flavius Marcellinus, the high judge of the hearing at Carthage in 411. In reciting the same limited number of model horror stories (those of Restitutus and Innocentius) Augustine harped away on "the circumcellions and clerics of the Donatist party," men whom "in our concern for public order, we had escorted from Hippo to court for their misdeeds, whose cases were heard by Your Nobility – most of them on the charge of murder."[131] In a letter of 412 addressed to Apringius, the elder brother of Marcellinus who was now proconsul of Africa, the same construction of the circumcellions and their commanders, the "Donatist clerics," as a serious threat to the public order, the *publica disciplina*, is found.[132] In his résumé of the results of the conference, Augustine struck the connection between the threat of circumcellion violence and the just use of secular force to repress them, and the dissident church of which they were part.[133]

And they should not complain about persecutions, about anything that the Catholics seek from the emperors on behalf of the church, when their circumcellions commit so many terrible evil acts under the leadership of their clergy.

The presence of circumcellion violence was the critical plank in the campaign to justify the use of state force in the repression of the dissident church with which they were closely allied. The subject of violence perpetrated by the dissident church on Catholics, indeed, appears to have been the high point of the Catholic case presented to the hearing at Carthage in 411, replete with the conventional tales of horror and terrible innovations – like the blindings with the acidic mix of vinegar and lime.[134] The story

---

[131] Aug. *Ep.* 133.1 (CCL 31B: 241): "Circumcelliones illos et clericos partis Donati, quos de Hipponiensi ad iudicium pro factis eorum publicae disciplinae cura deduxerat, a tua nobilitate comperi auditos et plurimos eorum de homicidio."

[132] Aug. *Ep.* 134.2 (CCL 31B: 245–46).

[133] Aug. *Brev. Collat.* 3.11.21 (CCL 149A: 287): "nec de persecutionibus, quod aliquid ab imperatoribus pro ecclesia Catholici peterent, cum eorum circumcelliones ducibus clericis tam horrenda mala committerent."

[134] Aug. *Brev. Collat.* 3.11.22 (CCL 149A: 287): "Ibi etiam cum dictum esset, quod calce et aceto humanos oculos persecuti sint, in quo scelere Diabolum crudelitate pervicerunt... hic Donatistae quaesierunt, utrum qui faciunt filii essent Diaboli an qui patiuntur; quasi Catholici aliud quam passiones suas dixerint immanissimas a clericis et circumcellionibus eorum."

was pitched not only to imperial officials who had to be persuaded to take action, but also to the congregations of their own followers. These defenses of the use of normal state compulsion to restrain violence are set up with discussions of the ordinary use of force to discipline.[135]

Every day we witness a son who thinks of his father as a persecutor – and a wife her husband, a slave his master, a *colonus* the one who owns his land, a defendant his judge, a soldier or a subject his general or king – although these authorities, through the fear inculcated by light punishment, are often seeking to restrain and to divert these persons, who are under their authority by virtue of a hierarchy of ordered power, from committing even more serious evil acts.

Such evocations of the function of normal constraints and fears as deterrents in quotidian social relations framed the arguments against the circumcellions and their violence to justify state intervention. "It is only right," says Augustine, "to hold those men responsible who rush forth in mad and anarchic bands to coerce people whom no law has placed under their power." And it was manifest who was mobilizing the raging and disorderly gangs.[136]

Therefore we justly condemn the chaotic disorders and arrogant madnesses of your circumcellions, even if they do their acts of violence to some very bad people, because to punish illegalities unlawfully and to deter by using illegal means is itself a bad thing. But when they persecute innocent persons without hearing their case or with most unjust hatreds, who then is not utterly horrified at their repellent acts of banditry?

The theme was developed in Augustine's replies to his dissident critics, including Cresconius, the grammarian from Constantina. In these replies, he construes circumcellion violence not just as the acts of men who have in mind some specific and limited goal in localized sectarian disputes, but rather as a kind of violence that was a threat to the general social order, a violence that was illegitimate. It was both private and unlawful because it usurped the kinds of authority that ought to be in the hands of state officials. If the dissident bishop Crispinus was to be punished for his involvement

---

[135] Aug. *Ep. ad Cath. contra Donatist.* 20.53 (CSEL 52: 301): "Nam cotidie videmus et filium de patre tamquam de persecutore suo conqueri et coniugem de marito et servum de domino et colonum de possessore et reum de iudice et militem vel provincialem de duce vel rege, cum illi plerumque ordinatissima potestate sibi homines subditos per terrores levium poenarum a gravioribus malis prohibeant atque compescant."

[136] Aug. *Ep. ad Cath. contra Donatist.* 20.53–54 (CSEL 52: 301–02): "Item iure culpandi sunt, qui turbide atque inordinate in eos cohercendos insiliunt, qui nulla sibi lege subiecti sunt. Proinde circumcellionum vestrorum inordinatas licentias et superbas insanias iuste reprehendimus, etiam cum aliquibus pessimis violenti sunt, quia illicita illicite vindicare et ab illicitis illicite deterrere non est bonum. Cum vero et innocentes vel causa incognita vel iniquissimis inimicitiis persequuntur, quis eorum sceleratissima latrocinia non perhorrescat?"

in organizing the attack on the Catholic bishop of Calama, it was because "laws were not lacking," even if they would not be fully enforced because of Catholic charity and good will. The Catholic Church was portrayed as having more than enough power against its enemies, and so it did not need to make too much of the circumcellions who with their "heretical presumption were raging about with their *private* violence."[137] But the opposite was the reality. The initial decision made by Flavius Marcellinus on the third day of the hearing at Carthage in 411 already made specific the relationship between circumcellion violence and the repression of the dissidents.[138]

As for those persons who know that they are harboring gangs of circumcellions on their lands, let them know that – unless they act to repress and restrain the aggression of these men by every means possible – their lands will be immediately confiscated by the state treasury. It is as much a part of respecting Catholic law as it is of the public peace that a stop should be put to the madness of these men.

In terms of the feedback connections between the local enforcement and the imperial court, it is surely no coincidence that the emperor Honorius used exactly these same words in his edicts of 412 and 414. An earlier part of the same edict of the judge Marcellinus relevant to more general enforcement reveals the extensive range of this mimicry or copying.[139]

Gross falseness has been unmasked and bows its head to the manifest truth. Therefore, by the authority of this edict, I enjoin upon all men of municipal rank, and also landlords, agents, lessees and managers of both private lands as well as those of the Divine Household, and the Elders of all rural places – being mindful of the law, their rank, their reputation, and their wellbeing – energetically to strive to prohibit gatherings of Donatists in all towns and rural places. They must also hurry, and without any delay, to return to the Catholics all those churches which – by my sense of humanity alone and without any imperial order – I permitted to the enjoyment of the Donatists up to the day of the final sentencing – that is,

---

[137] Aug. *Contra Cresc.* 3.47.51 (CSEL 52: 459): "quid adiutorio Christi ecclesia Catholica in suos inimicos posset et nollet, non secundum haereticam praesumptionem privato furore circumcellionibus saevientibus."

[138] GCC, *Edictum Cognitoris* (SC 224: 978): "Hi autem qui in praediis suis circumcellionum turbas se habere cognoscunt, sciant, nisi eorum insolentiam omnimodis comprimere et referenare gestierint, maxime ea loca a fisco mox occupanda. Siquidem tam Catholicae legi quam quieti publicae, ut eorum conquiescat insania, in hac parte consulitur."

[139] GCC, *Edictum Cognitoris* (SC 224: 974–76; CCL 149A: 178): "Declaratae igitur veritati detecta falsitas colla submittat. Unde universos ordinis viros, dominos etiam fundorum, actores, con-ductores tam domus divinae quam etiam privatarum possessionum senioresque omnium locorum huius edicti auctoritate commoneo quatenus memores legum, dignitatum, aestimationis salutisque propriae, donatistarum conventicula in omnibus civitatibus et locis prohibere contendant, ita ut ecclesias quas eis humanitate mea absque imperiali praecepto usque ad diem sententiae constat indultas catholicis tradere sine ulla dilatione festinent, ni malunt tot sanctionum laqueis inretiri; quas quidem, si unitati catholicae consentire voluerint, eorum esse sat certum est."

unless they wish themselves to be caught up in the snares of great punishments. Which churches would certainly be theirs [i.e. the Donatists] had they wished to assent to Catholic Unity.

It was this hierarchy of local authority and enforcement – municipal decurions, private great landlords, agents, managers and lessees of private and imperial lands, and finally the Elders of villages – that the imperial laws activated and worked through to achieve their desired effect. More important is the question: In what was supposed to be a hearing over doctrinal and ecclesiastical matters, why did Flavius Marcellinus drag in the circumcellions for special attention and official action in his final judgment? The reason, surely, is that they were one of the true causes hovering offstage that provoked the real interest of the imperial government in repression. They were presented as an apprehended social terror. That is why Marcellinus paid particular attention to the *turbae* or gangs of circumcellions in his final *sententia*, and why his words were picked up and echoed in the anti-Donatist edict issued by Honorius at the end of January 412. When the supplementary and less harsh decree of June 414 was issued, the circumcellions had disappeared from its terms.[140] They were no longer necessary to make the case for the hard imperial intervention of the state. That had already been decided. The frightening image of the circumcellions had served its purpose and could easily be retired from sight.

INSIDE VIOLENCE

For all the talk about their attacks on others, their destruction of property, and their incitement of social rebellion, one of the most frightening, terror-provoking aspects of the violence of the dissident holy fighters was the violence that they freely inflicted on themselves, often to the point of death. It was turned inwards in self-provoked and self-inflicted wounds, and in self-killing. These self-inflicted deaths were construed as a suicidal terroristic threat to the general social order. These sacred deaths were the trump card that was to be played in the portrait of an apprehended social insurrection of truly frightening aspect. The self-killings were taken by the perpetrators and their own community to be a species of martyrdom. The firm denial by the Catholics that these self-inflicted or self-sought deaths transformed the deceased into martyrs only served to confirm that

---

[140] The absence has puzzled many, and led Diesner (1959), p. 55, to postulate that the emperors and the law had succeeded in abolishing the existence of the circumcellions as an *ordo* – a strange extremity rightly rejected, amongst others, by Gottlieb (1978), pp. 11–12.

the dead were popularly regarded as sacred heroes by many of the dissident believers.[141] The relationship between "circumcellions" and the phenomenon of ritual self-killing, however, was a various and complicated
one. Because of the insistent rhetorical presentation of these men and their
violence, it is difficult to separate fact from fiction.

The suicides themselves, even the mass ones, were probably not invented,
but the relationship of the dissident *agonistici* or holy fighters to this self-
destructive behavior is partial and unclear. In his own "heresy book,"
Augustine seemed to take such self-inflicted deaths as at the core of the
definition of circumcellion identity.[142]

And the men who are called "circumcellions" also belong to this same heresy [i.e.
of "the Donatists"] in Africa. They are a rough and primitive type of men of
notorious daring not only in committing terrible crimes against others, but also in
not sparing even themselves from their mad ferocity. For they are accustomed to
kill themselves by various kinds of deaths, especially by throwing themselves off
heights, by drowning, and by fire. And they seduce others of both sexes whom they
are able into this same madness, sometimes even threatening others with death if
those people do not agree to kill them.

This disturbing picture, however apparently clear-cut it appears to be, is not
without its difficulties.[143] Some but not all circumcellions were involved
in these self-killings, and the suicides involved many dissident believers
who were not circumcellions. The difference between the two, if it was
at all significant, is difficult to understand because the whole ideological
construction of "the circumcellions" was purposefully intended to collapse
the distinction between suicidal acts of violence, ritual self-killings, and
the circumcellion violence towards others. The *agonistici* might well have
been in a vanguard of dissident self-killings (although even this much is
far from certain) but they were hardly alone.[144] But the mass suicides are

---

[141] Denial that the circumcellions were martyrs: Aug. *Sermo* 313E.7 = Guelferbytanus 28.7 (MiAg 1: 542): "Dicimus et nos: non esse haereticos martyres, non esse martyres circumcelliones."

[142] Aug. *De Haeres.* 69.4 (CCL 46: 332): "Ad hanc haeresim in Africa et illi pertinent qui appellantur circumcelliones, genus hominum agreste et famosissimae audaciae, non solum in alios immania facinora perpetrando, sed nec sibi eadem insania feritate parcendo. Nam per mortes varias, maximeque praecipitiorum et aquarum et ignium, seipsos necare consuerunt, et in istum furorem alios quos potuerint sexus utriusque seducere, aliquando ut occidantur ab aliis, mortem, nisi fecerunt, comminantes."

[143] Not the least of which is how much of it was actually written by Augustine and not simply copied from an existing "heresy handbook" of non-African derivation: see Shaw (2004), pp. 232–38.

[144] Aug. *Ep. ad Cath. contra Donatist.* 19.50 (CSEL 51: 297), where he seems to separate the circumcellions "among them" (i.e. the "Donatists") from those "among them" who commit these gross acts of self-murder; but see Aug. *Contra litt. Petil.* 2.92.204 (CSEL 52: 129): "et miramur quod se circumcelliones vestri sic praecipitant?," where the two are merged; cf. Aug. *Ep.* 48.24

presented in a vocabulary that suggests the involvement of persons who were very much like the holy fighters.[145] If Augustine felt that he could deny that the *communio Donati* was part of the Church of Christ it was because of the traitorous behavior of their own bishops, because they had lost their judicial appeals before emperors:

Whether because they have among themselves the leaders of the circumcellions, because the circumcellions themselves have committed such terrible acts, or because there are among them those persons who throw themselves off high cliffs, who throw themselves onto burning pyres which they themselves have set afire, and who compel their own slaughter by terrifying unwilling men to do this to them – all of these persons seeking so many voluntary and deranged deaths in order to receive worship from men . . . [146]

The horror of the suicidal deaths was a core element in the Catholic rhetoric intended to countervail dissident claims of persecution. By connecting the violence inflicted by the dissident gangsters on others with the violence that they inflicted on themselves, the specter of a terrifying social threat was created.[147] The self-killings became officially significant. By analogy, the horror-power of the self-killings was added to the murders of others. The self-killers, on the other hand, saw such self-inflicted deaths as martyrdoms. If martyrdom in general was a matter of choice, then at one end of the spectrum of personal practice stood the ultimate voluntary act: the decision of absolute renunciation, the final act of self-sacrifice – the purposeful killing of one's self. If only for its peculiar consequences, this was a separate kind of violence that merits its own focus and special attention.

(CCL 31: 184–85). Such rhetorical claims have led to the unwarranted assumption that all such sectarian suicides were circumcellions: see, e.g., Cacitti, "*Per vacua liquidi aeris spatia*: il carattere 'suicidiario' del martirio circoncellionico," ch. 4 in *Furiosa turba*, pp. 81–101.

[145] For example, Aug. *Contra ep. Parm.* 3.6.29 (CSEL 51: 138): "natalicia celebrentur magno conventu hominum furiosorum, quorum e numero illi sunt, qui etiam nullo persequente se ipsos ultro per montium abrupta praecipitant"; cf. *Contra litt. Petil.* 1.24.26 (CSEL 52: 20), which both separates the phenomena but also suggests their connection: "omitto furorem circumcellionum et praecipitatorum ultro cadaverum cultus sacrilegos et profanes"; it is suggested that circumcellions imitate Marculus in throwing themselves off great heights: *Contra litt. Petil.* 2.20.46 (CSEL 52: 46), where such deaths are said to be shared by the *teachers* of the circumcellions, *magistri circumcellionum*, rather than the men themselves. But other passages, like *Contra litt. Petil.* 2.32.73 (CSEL 32: 62), clearly state that circumcellions "burn" to throw themselves off heights to their deaths.

[146] Aug. *Ep. ad Cath. de secta Donat.* 19.50 (CSEL 52: 297): " . . . aut quia tales sunt apud eos circumcellionum principes, aut quia tanta mala committunt circumcelliones, aut quia sunt apud eos, qui se per abrupta praecipitent vel concremandos ignibus inferant, quos ipsi sibimet accenderunt, aut trucidationem suam etiam invitis hominibus terrendo extorqueant et tot spontaneas et furiosas mortes, ut colantur ab hominibus, appetant."

[147] For example, Aug. *Brev. Collat.* 3.8.13 (CCL 149A: 281).

CHAPTER 16

Divine winds

After following a long and sometimes contradictory path, Augustine was finally to condemn the taking of one's own life as an absolute sin, an inexpiable crime against God. Born at Mondovi, a village only some 12 miles south of Augustine's Hippo Regius, Albert Camus began his *Le mythe de Sisyphe* with the declaration:

There is only one serious philosophical problem: it is suicide. To judge whether life is or is not worth the pain of living is to answer the fundamental question of philosophy. All the rest – if the world has three dimensions [we must admit that Camus was not a physicist], if the soul has nine or a dozen categories – all these follow. This is the game. We must make a reply.[1]

But Camus' suicide was very different from Augustine's. For Camus, suicide is provoked, ultimately, by a growing sense of the absurdity of existence. He construed a typical scenario as follows. The stage props of a person's life are present on each ordinary day: "Get up, catch the train, four hours at the office or workshop, dinner, streetcar, four more hours of work, eat, sleep, Monday, Tuesday, Wednesday, Thursday, Friday, Saturday, according to the same rhythm. This path is easily followed most of the time. Only, one day, a 'why' arises."[2] A process of the disintegration of the familiar stage-sets of one's life begins, life becomes a stranger to the one living it, and all normal meaning drains from existence.

This is the pathology of one type of self-killing – a peculiar kind of modern despair. But it is not my suicide problem. Nor was it Augustine's. Camus, who wrote his master's dissertation at the University of Algiers on Augustine and Plotinus, examined by no less a figure than Louis Gernet,

---

[1] A. Camus, *Le mythe de Sisyphe: essai sur l'absurde*, Paris, Gallimard, 1942; reprint: 2000), p. 17 (my translation); for Camus' birthplace and origins, see P. Thody, *Albert Camus*, London, Macmillan, 1989, pp. 1–2.
[2] Camus, *Le mythe de Sisyphe*, p. 29 (my translation).

knew this too.[3] His novel *La mort heureuse* – *A Happy Death* – shows that
he was alert to these differences, indeed opposites, between his world and
that of Augustine – the contrast with the latter's *De beata vita*.[4] Perhaps
because of this awareness, Camus appended a footnote to his text, admitting
that *his* problem of suicide was, after all, historically contingent: "We will
not miss the opportunity," he says, "to note the specific character of this
essay. Suicide can in fact be linked to more honorable considerations. One
example: political suicides of protest."[5] It is precisely this type of suicide,
relegated by Camus to a footnote, that is our concern here: a kind of
honorable self-killing that was motivated *not* by a sense of "the absurd" or
by the meaninglessness of existence, but rather by the precise opposite. It
was a self-inflicted death that was interpreted as full of meaning and one
that embraced life, indeed a better one without end.

This distinction in self-killing is precisely the divide that separates the
two parts of Durkheim's classic study: the historical and social watershed
between his "altruistic" (and "fatalistic") and "egotistical" types of suicide.[6]
And it is Durkheim's treatment of the former kinds of self-killing that is
most problematic, a strange "historical" foray in which he relies on snippets of classical literature from the Elder Pliny, Athenaeus, Aelian, among
others, and on odd collations of nineteenth-century ethnographic observations, some of them culled from Frazer's ever-present *Golden Bough*.[7] Like
Camus, Durkheim had his own footnote to which he relegated suicides
peripheral to *his* interests. His footnote was for a kind of self-killing that
bore strong analogies to his "altruistic" type: the "fatalistic suicide" of slaves
and of women, for example, in desperate circumstances.[8] So each writer

---

[3] J. McBride, *Albert Camus: Philosopher and Littérateur*, New York, St. Martin's Press, 1992, contains
an English translation of Camus' *Diplôme d'études supérieures*; cf. O. Todd, *Albert Camus: une vie*,
Paris, Gallimard, 1996, fig. 25, and ch. 9, "Saint Augustin sans Marx," pp. 101–09: Camus had read
and heavily annotated his copy of the *Confessions* (p. 104).

[4] S. E. Bronner, *Camus: Portrait of a Moralist*, Minneapolis, The University of Minnesota Press, 1999,
p. 14; although, as we have been warned, we should perhaps not make too much of his knowledge of
Augustine: Archambault (1969).

[5] Camus, *Le mythe de Sisyphe*, p. 19 n. 1 (my translation).

[6] See Davis and Neal (2000), but perhaps most clearly put by A. Giddens, *Durkheim*, London, Fontana,
1978, p. 47: "He was . . . convinced that suicide in the simpler societies is distinct from that in the
more advanced, and tried to document this at some length in *Suicide*. If in modern society people kill
themselves because life is meaningless, in traditional society they do so because death is meaningful:
values exist which make self-destruction, for certain categories of individuals, an honourable or even
an obligatory act."

[7] Durkheim, "Altruistic Suicide," ch. 4 in *Suicide*, pp. 217–40; Pliny the Elder, Athenaeus, and Aelian
(the latter two misspelled in the translation): p. 222 nn. 18–20; Frazer: pp. 218 n. 8, 220 n. 16, etc.

[8] Durkheim, *Suicide*, p. 276 n. 25; cf. K. Thompson, *Emile Durkheim*, London and New York,
Tavistock, 1982, p. 113; cf. p. 110, for a schematic representation of the model that Durkheim was
using; cf. Hill, *Ambitiosa Mors*, pp. 13–14, who makes much the same point.

or researcher has his or her own preferred types.[9] Such ideal categories affected by personal choice must be confronted with an historical analysis of facts on a whole range of self-killings in different types of social order. Such a factual and more statistical approach to the problem of suicide in late antique Christian Africa is difficult, if almost impossible, to achieve. Research therefore demands the recourse to what can be known more precisely.

The majority of the large number of modern studies on suicide rates, patterns, and trends have a sameness to them because they are set within Jewish, Christian, and Muslim moral regimes of self-killing that have heavily conditioned modern thinking and behavior. These data therefore reveal expected parameters: low or lower rates in the more heavily religious niches of these societies and standard patterns of such deaths; the suicides of males, especially young males, for example, usually outnumber those of females by a factor of several orders. The problem is to get outside these societies and to consider other ones governed by family and kinship networks, informed by values that have not been ordered by monotheistic moral regimes but which have been governed by traditional codes of honor and shame, and by a heavy patriarchy of the kind found in the Roman empire. Take modern China, Japan, and India. Suddenly the Jewish–Christian–Muslim social rules of suicide vanish. Japan, for example, has consistently had some of the highest suicide rates in the world. The same is true of China and the southern regions of India, both of the population in general, but especially of young women who proportionately take their own lives much more frequently than men.[10] Within these societies, despair, poverty, humiliation, dishonor, and other such factors, are freely admitted as reasonable and defensible grounds of taking one's own life and so the social parameters of self-killing assume entirely different dimensions.[11]

Observations such as these raise the question of the assumed background against which the historian can assess the value and practice of self-killing

---

[9] And not just Camus or Durkheim – Murray, in his large study of medieval suicide, makes clear that he, like Camus, is dealing with a "normal" kind of suicide that rules out other types of self-killing, such as the *endura* of the Cathars: *Suicide in the Middle Ages*, 1, pp. vii–viii; Murray's self-killing is therefore a suicide, like that of Camus, marked by a peculiar kind of despair: "A wish to die can only result from the strongest negative impulses from life: loss, incapacity, failure, and pain."

[10] For southern India, Kerala has produced rates of 32 per 100,000 per annum. In some regions of Tamil Nadu rates for women have been as high as 148 per 100,000 per annum as opposed to 58 per 100,000 per annum for men; these are some of the highest suicide rates in the world: *The New Scientist* 14.30 (2 April 2004). General rates for India in the 1990s ran at about 10 per 100,000 per annum, with the lowest rates in the north (3 to 5) and the highest in the more traditional societies of the south (15+ to 18+).

[11] Chang and Lee (2000), pp. 39–41, with Table 2.1; in "Western" lands male suicides tend to outnumber female ones by factors of 3:1 to 5:1: see Cantor (2000), pp. 16–18, esp. p. 17, Table 1.1.

in late antique Africa. There is little doubt that the impact of Catholic Christian and Islamic ideology has had a long-term depressing effect on self-killing in populations that subscribe to their value systems. Suicide rates in Islamic lands and in more traditional less-modernized Mediterranean populations have hovered around very low rates of about 1 to 5 per 100,000 per annum. Secular western European lands where the power of religious prohibitions has loosened considerably have witnessed much higher suicide rates of between 15 and 25, even as high as 45 per 100,000 persons per annum.[12] These rates mirror those found in Asian countries whose populations have not labored under the weight of repressive moral systems of a Judaeo-Christian type, where higher suicide rates run at about 25–30 per 100,000 persons per annum.[13] A significant problem with establishing a "violence quotient" for suicides, however, is that the relationship between self-inflicted deaths (suicides) and deaths deliberately inflicted (homicides) varies, sometimes radically, from one society and time period to another. In some societies, murder rates greatly exceed suicide rates, but frequently the complete reverse is true.[14] If self-killing in late Roman Africa was conditioned by value judgments different than those in modern societies and if it affected social, gender, and age groups differently, then the context for analyzing the practice is shifted considerably out of the frame of most of our modernizing assumptions and social studies.

The self-killings that were such a dramatic element in the dissident–Catholic struggle were shaped by a peculiarly unstable mix of traditional values and the new mass ideology of Christianity. The self-killer who most tested the limits of the old and the new values was the martyr. For some Christians, distress was provoked by the martyr who welcomed or sought out death in a way that was felt to be too eager, too aggressive. In an earlier age in Africa, both Tertullian and Cyprian had already faced this problem. In fourth- and fifth-century Africa, the suicide problem that Augustine had to face had emerged because of the central place of martyrdom in the resistance both to Catholic orthodoxy and to the coercive measures used by the Roman state. He had already confronted one facet of this

---

[12] Cantor (2000), pp. 12–13, and p. 17, Table 1.1; the unusual high rate of 45 per 100,000 has been set by the depressive Finns.

[13] Chang and Lee (2000), p. 40, Table 2.1.

[14] Based on WHO statistics for 2000–2008: suicide rates considerably exceeded murder rates in e.g. Lithuania, Russia, Hungary, Belgium, Finland, Italy, China, and Japan, whereas homicide rates greatly exceeded suicide rates in El Salvador, Mexico, Venezuela, Brazil, Jamaica, Peru, and the Dominican Republic. Again, if there is any broad division that might be discerned, it is perhaps to be explained by moralizing religious ideologies that succeed in repressing certain kinds of tendencies to self-killing.

problem as early as 395 in his work *On Lying* in which he debated the moral status of the person who chose to lie rather than to sacrifice to the gods of the Roman state. This in turn raised the problem of the person who told the truth knowing that he or she would die at the hands of the state's executioner. Following other hardliners who were trying to confine the power of the martyr, his answer was that the person who knowingly did this was murdering himself.[15] It was part of an old problem. The extremes of death wishes encouraged by martyrdom had provoked debates among Christian ideologues about where the line was to be drawn between the noble death of the martyr and the execrable death of the man or woman who sought the celebrity of their own demise. Among Africans, there are signs of this debate in terms relevant to the fourth-century sectarian struggle as early as the writings of Lactantius, reactions provoked by the terror of the Great Persecution.[16] Hewing a very hard line on homicide that held that the killing of another human being was always wrong, Lactantius extrapolated this to the case of self-killing. He seems to have been the first explicitly to connect a Christian injunction against self-killing to the Fifth Commandment: "Thou Shalt Not Kill." The Commandment meant, he said, that you were not only not to kill others, but also not to kill yourself.[17] The fullest argument of his position in the *Divine Institutes* lays out self-killing as a form of homicide that is as absolutely forbidden as murder of another.[18] The long peace after the Great Persecution, however, tended to allow Lactantius' connection of self-killing and sin to lapse into a background of ideas that would only be revived with the resurgence

---

[15] Aug. *De Mendac.* 9.13 (BA 2: 274): "Expedit hoc pati potius quam illud facere? Et utrum recte ille thurificare quam stuprum pati? Et utrum mentiendum est potius, si ea conditio daretur, quam thurificandum. Sed si talis consensio pro facto habenda est, homicidae sunt etiam qui occidi maluerunt quam falsum testimonium dicere, et quod est homicidium gravius, in seipsos." Augustine is discussing a specific situation raised by the examples discussed in the Great Persecution of Diocletian. He is not yet making any claims about self-killing in general; he is specifically concerned with those persons faced with potential martyrdom (a matter much discussed before him) and his remarks rest on the observation that the persons who killed themselves were also, in some sense, murderers (which idea also had a long pedigree). For a different view of this text, see Hofmann, *Suizid in der Spätantike*, pp. 53 f.

[16] Especially emphasized by Hofmann, *Suizid in der Spätantike*, pp. 50–51.

[17] Lact. *Epit.* 59.5 (SC 335: 230): "Vetus praeceptum est non occidere: quod non sic accipi debet, tamquam iubeamur ab homicidio tantum, quod etiam legibus publicis vindicatur, manus abstinere, <sed> hac iussione interposita nec verbo licebit periculum mortis inferre nec infantem necare aut exponere nec se ipsum voluntaria morte damnare." The problem is that there is some dispute over whether or not the epitome of the *Divine Institutes* was actually written by Lactantius. It does, however, reflect his detailed argument in the *Divine Institutes*. For his longer argument against homicide or the killing of humans in any fashion whatsoever (including infanticide or child exposure), see *Div. Inst.* 6.20.15–26 (SC 509: 316–22).

[18] Lact. *Div. Inst.* 3.18.6–9 (CSEL 19: 237–38).

of another intense episode of martyrdom and persecution. It is in this later context that Augustine was to replay his African forebear's words and arguments.

In the extreme hard core of last-line resistance to the measures taken against the dissenters in the fourth century, Christians could interpret the deliberate courting of a death at the hands of state authorities as a bad death – one that would later come to be castigated as "an act of suicide." But deliberate self-killings could also be construed as a kind of martyrdom, although this, too, was a response that was, by almost any possible measure, also an extreme.[19] Whether accurately or not, the dissident self-killings by immolation, drowning, and precipitation were represented by the Catholics as frequent, and, on some occasions at least, as mass group acts of self-destruction.[20] If so, the collective self-inflicted deaths would surely be one measure of a crisis, an indication of the dissidents' conviction that they lived under imminent threat and that they were hard-pressed on all sides by the heavy legal and military force of the Roman state.[21] At the time – as by certain historians today – recourse was had to an easy explanation: the suicidal dissenters were "religious fanatics," just like those of any other age, like the so-called Old Believers of seventeenth-century Muscovy, for example.[22] This is a judgment frequently levied on Gaudentius, the dissident bishop of Thamugadi, who had an important role to play in one of the collective suicide stories.[23]

To support the interpretation of a perception of a dreadful imminent threat, there is no doubt that the dissidents saw the coercive measures undertaken by the forces of the Roman state in 314–17, in 347, in 405, and again in 412–414, as persecutions directed against them by their Catholic enemies. The collective self-killings could then be interpreted as symptoms

---

[19] Murray, *Suicide in the Middle Ages*, 1, p. 9: "Suicide, I take it, marks an extremity of human experience." Just how extreme it is in terms of violence, however, depends very much on the precise historical circumstances.

[20] See Combès (1948) and Lamirande (1965i), with a selection of texts.

[21] The question must be posed: did these self-killings actually take place? Some, like Butterweck, *Martyriumssucht*, pp. 129–39, have taken a possible point of view: that the claims of such mass suicides were Catholic inventions. Although there is legitimate debate about numbers and frequency, however, it is difficult to believe that the phenomenon is a pure fiction.

[22] Brisson, *Autonomisme et Christianisme*, p. 321 n. 6, and text. It is a frequent similitude; see Shaw (2009) for problems with the historical comparison.

[23] For example, van der Lof (1967), while rejecting the judgments of Duchesne and Labriolle that Gaudentius was simply a fanatic, and seeing him as slightly more moderate in his actions, nevertheless portrays him as a "theological extremist"; Monceaux, *Hist. litt.* 6, pp. 197–98, opines that the man was only modestly fanatical, if also naïve, bull-headed, and mediocre – typical of an inward-looking, narrow-minded bishop who was "raised in a fanatical environment" that was "devoid of any intellectual life."

of a despair in which the dissidents saw themselves increasingly hemmed in by their enemies – necessary sacrifices that were martyrdoms in their eyes. Certainly by the 390s self-killing formed an irreducible core of sectarian resistance. The tactic especially recommended itself because the willingness voluntarily to surrender one's own life for community and belief was something against which few counter-measures, threats of deterrence, or official enforcement had much effect. The giving up of one's own life came to be valued as the pinnacle of martyrdom by the dissidents, but was condemned by Catholics as the criminal act of a deranged person. For the person who killed himself or herself it was the culmination of a great good, the ultimate self-sacrifice, a final altruistic act. For the persons who were the witnesses of the self-murders and who were, in part, the objects of this final statement of human existence, it provoked only the most troubling of responses: disgust, derision, denial, fear, hatred, and anger.[24]

THE BIRTH OF SUICIDE

These sentiments lead us to a work that was to become one of the central monuments of Western civilization – Augustine's imposing 22-volume *Concerning the City of God against the Pagans*, the *De Civitate Dei contra Paganos*.[25] This great work is most often read as a grand visionary statement of a new Christian order. It is easy to forget that a contemplation of suicide is placed at its inception and that it ends with the dual problems of martyrdom and resurrection. Already in its first two books, completed by 413, the author had arrived at a point of view that not only separated him from the prevalent views of his own classical past, but which itself would help to create a new attitude, a novel hard line on self-killing, a position that would define norms that would be legally enforced in the Western world until the mid-twentieth century and later.[26] Before Augustine, and even

---

[24] Murray, *Suicide in the Middle Ages*, 1, p. 12, again, reflecting the huge impact of Augustine's thinking.

[25] The bibliography on this aspect of the *City of God* is too large and unwieldy to be repeated here, even briefly; only items necessary to the argument will be referenced in what follows. For the dates, see Perler, *Voyages de saint Augustin*, p. 321 and Barnes (1982), pp. 65–66: the first book was probably published by September 412, books two and three before September 413; Marcellinus, to whom these books were dedicated, was executed on 14 September 413; all three were circulated as a group.

[26] On Augustine's innovative role, see Droge and Tabor, "The Augustinian Reversal," ch. 7 in *A Noble Death*, pp. 167–83, and the earlier survey by Bels (1975); both treatments, however, are marred by superficiality and significant errors of fact. The survey and analysis by Baudet (1988), esp. pp. 135 ff., is important because he notes the huge change of attitude since Augustine's writing of the *De libero arbitrio* (esp. 3.7.21) where he accepted the existence an innate human desire to die in order to be with God and at peace, an attitude that made sense of self-killing. So up to the mid-390s, his views on self-killing were still largely informed by non-Christian debates, especially those

within Christian circles, the moral status of self-killing had been disputed and debated; it had been an evaluated, criticized, and lauded act.[27] What Augustine did was to abolish the debate. His firm conviction was that the voluntary taking of one's own life in any circumstances was an evil: an horrific crime and an unforgivable sin.[28]

If it is clear that if there is no private empowerment to kill even a guilty man – and no law allows the right of such a murder – then certainly the man who kills himself is a murderer. When he kills himself he is as guilty [of his murder] as he is innocent of the reason for which he thought that he had to kill himself. For if we rightly detest that act of Judas, and truth itself judges that when he hanged himself with a rope he made worse the act of that criminal betrayal rather than expiating it . . . how much more ought that man to refrain from killing himself who has committed no act for which he must inflict on himself such a punishment . . . and it is not for nothing that in the sacred canonical books there can nowhere be found any injunction or permission to kill ourselves either to acquire immortality or to avoid or to escape any evil . . . killing oneself is therefore a damnable sin and a detestable crime, as truth itself manifestly proclaims.

The new attitude was forged in the throes of the violent sectarian conflicts in Africa, culminating in the first decades of the fifth century, in which self-killing had a prominent role. As the decade advanced in which *The City of God* was written, Augustine's new concept of self-killing began to coalesce with other ideas into a mutually reinforcing structure of new values. In drawing attention to Judas, and in claiming that his self-killing

within late Platonism on good and happiness. Augustine's attitude and the influence of his views on subsequent doctrine marked a watershed in Christian views of suicide in the West. Origen, for example, was explicit in the denunciation of suicide, but his veiws had little or no impact in the West; his commentary on the Gospel of Matthew only became readily available to Western thinkers in a Latin translation that dates to *c*. 390/400. Augustine can only be regarded as "exceptional" in this regard (the argument of Hofmann, *Suizid in der Spätantike*, pp. 210–12) if one expects an immediate sea change visible in both canon and public law. This is to expect too much. The effects of his views were persistent and long-range, and they were powerful in helping to create a new permanent stigmatization of self-killing *as such* as "suicide."

[27] Amundsen's critical survey (1989) makes this clear; after a thorough review of the evidence he concludes, rightly, that, apart from the debates over martyrdom, suicide had not been seen as a central problem by Christian writers.

[28] Aug. *Civ. Dei*, 1.17, 20, and 25 (CCL 47: 18, 22, 26): "Nam utique si non licet privata potestate hominem occidere vel nocentem, cuius occidendi licentiam lex nulla concedit, profecto etiam qui se ipsum occidit homicida est, et tanto fit nocentior, cum se occiderit, quanto innocentior in ea causa fuit, qua se occidendum putavit. Nam si Iudae factum merito detestamur eumque veritas iudicat, cum se laqueo suspendit, sceleratae illius traditionis auxisse potius quam expiasse commissum . . . quanto magis a sua nece se abstinere debet, qui tali supplicio quod in se puniat non habet . . . Neque enim frustra in sanctis canonicis libris nusquam nobis divinitus praeceptum permissumve reperiri potest, ut vel ipsius adipiscendae inmortalitatis vel ullius cavendi carendive mali causa nobismet ipsis necem inferamus . . . Verum tamen si detestabile facinus et damnabile scelus est etiam se ipsum hominem occidere, sicut veritas manifesta proclamat."

compounded his earlier sin of betrayal, Augustine was drawing not on African tradition but on the extreme views of Jerome, an exegete from whom he was otherwise loath to borrow.[29] But he probably also drew on his African forebear, Lactantius, who had also condemned all forms of self-killing. As the uniform condemnation of taking one's own life formed in Augustine's mind, so the other values on which Christian martyrdom had been built had to be reinterpreted, most important amongst these being that of patience or endurance. In his reassessment of the fundamental value espoused by the Christian martyr in the *De patientia*, written towards the end of the decade, taking one's own life is condemned outright as a crime worse than parricide.[30]

The determinate power of sectarian violence in the forging of this new idea must be noted, since Augustine himself had not always held such hard views, even in the case of fellow Christians. In making suicide the axial question around which some of the most important problems in the first books of his *City of God* turned, Augustine was ostensibly answering pagan critics who were blaming Christians for the shocking events that transpired during Alaric's occupation of the city of Rome in August 410. But this is only partially true. There was also an important internal Christian audience.[31] Among the most violent acts of Alaric's plunder of the imperial metropolis was the rape of the women of the city. Not a few of them, it seems, had sought to escape fearful dishonor and shame by taking their own lives. Augustine debated the problem by recourse to all kinds of historical and quasi-historical examples, above all the foundational example of Lucretia.

In this realm of extremity, a man like Augustine had to face his own limits. In all his internal debates over women and suicide, he never once broached the female self-killing that would have immediately come to the

---

[29] Jerome, *In Jonam prophetam* (CSEL 76: 390): "Non est enim nostrum mortem arripere, sed illatam libenter accipere. Unde et a persecutionibus non licet propria manu perire, absque ubi castitas periclitantur"; *In Matthaeum*, 27.5 (CSEL 77: 264): "ut non solum emendare nequiverit proditionis nefas, sed et prius scelus etiam proprii homicidii crimen addiderit." The commentary on Matthew dates to 398: see J. N. D. Kelly, *Jerome*, London, Duckworth, 1975, pp. 222–24, and was taken west in March of that year by Eusebius of Cremona; the commentary on Jonah dates from the year immediately preceding (ibid., pp. 220–21).

[30] Aug. *De patient.* 13.10 (CSEL 41: 674). He states that the true martyr, like Job, endures suffering and does not accept the option of death: "Et augeret potius quam evaderet poenas, qui post sui corporis mortem sive ad blasphemorum sive ad homicidarum vel etiam plus quam parricidarum supplicia raperetur . . . sine dubio peior est, qui se occidit, quia nemo est homini se ipso propinquior." Those persons who murder themselves, he goes on to say, surely would not have the gall to lay claim to the glory of the martyrs.

[31] Brown, *Augustine of Hippo*, p. 511, who cites the important study by Barnes (1982) and draws attention to the "Divjak letter" to Firmus: *Ep.* *2. Furthermore, the dedication to Marcellinus makes the connection with a certain type of committed Christian audience reasonably certain.

mind of any cultured African, especially one who had been educated at Carthage. He could not, because it was too painful. He had loved and still loved Dido.[32] He would only discuss other cases. Even so, the prolonged and (to our eyes) extremely insensitive discussion of the suicides of the women of Rome led Augustine to the conclusion that Christians have no authority to take their own lives under any circumstances whatsoever. His conclusion was based on scriptural authority. He managed, with some difficulty, to explain away many of the classical *exempla* that presented the taking of one's own life as a virtuous and honorable course of action. But he realized that in the cases where women's honor was at stake, even Christians had traditionally recognized the great moral virtue of a woman surrendering her life rather than her sexual purity. "But," they say, "in the times of persecution there were holy women who escaped those who threatened their chastity by throwing themselves into rivers so that the current would carry them off to their death. After such a death, they were venerated as martyrs in the Catholic Church and crowds thronged to their tombs."[33]

Provoked by a new wave of dissident self-killings, some of them mass self-killings, in the aftermath of 405, Augustine eventually arrived at a position that absolutely condemned the act of taking one's own life as an evil, as a manifest sin. But he had not always held this view. The extent and nature of the change can be sensed by replaying two scenes in which Augustine himself participated, two scenes that bear for the most part a symmetry and sameness that make them good examples for comparison. Both incidents involve the identical structural elements of a Christian bishop facing an imperial order to surrender his basilica, and the decision by the bishop to barricade himself in his church along with his congregation in order to confront the imperial authorities who were attempting forcibly, if legally, to expel him. The first scene took place in northern Italy in 385–86; the second in Africa, some thirty-five years later, in 419–20. Augustine was witness to and a participant in both incidents.

---

[32] As is manifest from Aug. *Confess.* 1.13.20–21 (CCL 27: 11–12): "she killed herself for love": "quia se occidit ab amore"; and from the parallel that he constructs between himself and Aeneas, between Monnica, his mother, and Dido. Early in his career, he had delivered a speech on the anger of Juno, for which he won a prize: *Confess.* 1.17.27 (CCL 27: 15).

[33] Aug. *Civ. Dei*, 1.26 (CCL 47: 26): "Sed quaedam, inquiunt, sanctae feminae tempore persecutionis, ut insectatores suae pudicitiae devitarent, in rapturum adque necaturum se fluvium proiecerunt eoque modo defunctae sunt earumque martyria in Catholica ecclesia veneratione celeberrima frequentantur."

TWO SCENES: AMBROSE AND GAUDENTIUS

In the opening months of the year 385, Ambrose, the orthodox Catholic bishop of Milan, had been summoned to the emperor's seat in the city to be informed that the court required the use of one of his basilicas.[34] The court assumed that the bishop would do his duty. What muddied the waters for the authorities was the mobilization of the common people of the city, who expressed their outrage at the imperial request. Crowds of Catholics suddenly appeared in such large numbers that a threat to public order was apparent. When the emperor's soldiers tried to disperse the demonstrators, the Catholic supporters of Ambrose offered to have themselves killed.[35] It has been suggested that the bishop and his assistants had somehow provoked the popular response and they must have been aware of the potential of the crowd's devotion. This is possible, but various forms of self-mobilization are perhaps just as likely. A perception of an imminent danger to their church and their bishop might well have been met by a popular insurrection. That Ambrose both knew and approved of what was happening, however, is not in doubt.

Although this first incident was a success for Ambrose, the next year brought a renewal of the same hostilities.[36] The crisis came to a head in the tense atmosphere of the Easter season. It began on Friday, 27 March 386, when a demand came from the court that the Basilica Nova should be made available for imperial use. Ambrose again refused, construing the handing over of the basilica as a betrayal or *traditio* that would turn him into a betrayer or *traditor* of holy things to a secular power. Such heavily loaded terms raised the ghost of the Roman government's record of complicity in its persecutions of Christians. In a concession, the imperial court relented and asked, instead, for the provision of the Portian Basilica. This request Ambrose also rejected in his Palm Sunday sermon, a rejection that was backed by a mass popular occupation of the basilica on the same day. This time, the government threatened to send in soldiers to seize the church. Ambrose then deployed the useful counter-threat of martyrdom. He stated publicly that he was willing to suffer imprisonment or death rather than to allow this to happen.[37] Before dawn, on Wednesday of the following week, the court sent in troops to surround the Portian Basilica.

---

[34] Ambr. *Sermo contra Auxent.* 29 = *Ep.* 75A.29 (CSEL 83.2: 101–02).   [35] Ibid. 29.
[36] The three critical original sources are all authored by Ambrose: *Ep.* 75, the *Sermo contra Auxentium* (*Ep.* 75A) and *Ep.* 76; see McLynn, *Ambrose of Milan*, p. 185, for some of the problems of interpretation.
[37] Ambr. *Ep.* 76.8 (CSEL 82.3: 112).

In response, Ambrose conducted a service at the Old Basilica, where his remarks were greeted by repeated acclamations and rhythmic chanting: the people shouted that they would march *en masse* to the Portian Basilica to support their brethren who were barricaded inside it – a move that Ambrose opposed for his own tactical reasons. Hymns and psalms had their place, too. Sermons and the singing of songs were linked in inciting insurgency, insurrection, and resistance to authority. Sacred songs, as we have seen, were core to the polemics of sectarian conflict. The more intense the conflict, the greater the recourse to this useful device. Typical is a mid-sixteenth-century Protestant "translation" of the fortieth Psalm by Théodore de Bèze.

> Who will rise up for me against the evil doers?
> And he shall bring down upon them their own iniquity;
> And shall cut them off in their own wickedness;
> Yes, the Lord our God shall cut them down!

Not without good reason has it been called "a veritable hymn to violence."[38] The same description could be used for the Psalms sung by Ambrose's people. In a sermon, improvised on the spot, Ambrose reminded the people of their "fearful chanting" of the seventy-ninth Psalm.[39]

When this powerful experience, with its evocation of the occupied basilica as an armed camp, was vividly recalled about a decade and a half later in his *Confessions*, Augustine manifestly placed a high probative value on the willingness of a bishop and his congregation to surrender their lives voluntarily in the impending storming of the basilica by imperial troops, soldiers who, it might be noted, were enforcing a legitimate imperial order by a Christian emperor. Augustine did not just approve of the actions of the Christians holed up in the basilica. Rather, he set them in the context of an elevated form of goodness in which the quintessential exemplar of his own mother was offered as one of those barricaded inside the basilica, voluntarily awaiting death at the hands of the emperor's soldiers.

The second incident took place at Thamugadi in southern Numidia in the year 419. In this year, a plenipotentiary imperial agent, the tribune and notary Dulcitius, had been dispatched by the central government to enforce the imperial edicts against "the Donatists." One of the principal aims of these edicts was to effect the seizure of basilicas that belonged to the dissident church. The dissident Christians construed the handing over of their churches to secular authorities, no less than did Ambrose before them, as a betrayal or *traditio*. If necessary, Dulcitius was to use force to have

---

[38] Pettegree, *Culture of Persuasion*, p. 66.   [39] Ambr. *Ep.* 76.13 and 20 (CSEL 82.3: 114–15; 119–20).

the churches handed over to the officially recognized Catholic Church. In the pursuit of this mission, he had undertaken a campaign of rigorous enforcement in southern Numidia. At Thamugadi, the great center of the dissident church in southwestern Numidia, he met with determined resistance from Gaudentius, the bishop of the city. Gaudentius planned to take the same course of action that Ambrose had in Milan. He would follow the actions of those bishops whose resistance he no doubt knew from the martyr narratives of his own church. Faced with an imperial order to surrender his basilica to government authorities, he barricaded himself in the church and, like Ambrose, he threatened to surrender his life along with those of his parishioners rather than to betray his basilica to the military.

As the tribune in charge of the operation, Dulcitius had every reason to be concerned. Seizures of dissident basilicas were highly charged events. No differently than in 313 or 347, the seizures of the basilicas at Carthage in the aftermath of the imperial orders of 412 and 414 had produced resistance, and violence, even if, as Augustine claimed, no actual deaths had occurred.[40] As a Catholic, Dulcitius might draw both on his biblical knowledge and on some help from the most prestigious bishop of Numidia, to encourage Gaudentius to obey the law or, at least, to give up his position and to flee. Gaudentius saw his duty as bishop differently. Referring to the gospel of John, he said that the Lord had said that, unlike the absentee owner of a flock of sheep or a mere hired hand, men interested only in their own wellbeing, and who flee at the first sight of a marauding wolf, the true good shepherd is willing to surrender his life for his flock.[41] Should the bishop fail in his duty, the wolves would seize his sheep and devour them. Any suggestion simply to get up and to leave his post, Gaudentius objected, was dangerous and foolish advice given, as it was, in the threatening circumstances of a state-driven persecution in which ordinary people naturally feared to harbor Christians. In the oppressive atmosphere of fear not only do common people not offer safe haven to

---

[40] Aug. *Contra Gaud.* 1.6.7 (CSEL 53: 204): "quandoquidem id agere ignibus praeparas? Haec est innocentia partis Donati, ut hoc faciatis adiunctis mortibus vestris, quod etiam apud Carthaginem in invidiam nostram de basilicis, quae vestrae fuerunt, sicut potuistis et cum quibus potuistis, fecisse asserveramini sine mortibus vestris."

[41] Gaudentius apud Aug. *Contra Gaud.* 1.16.17 (CSEL 53: 211): "Nam audi et dominum dicentem quia 'pastor bonus animam suam ponit pro ovibus suis, mercenarius autem et cuius non sunt oves propriae, videt lupum venientem et fugit et lupus rapit eas et dispergit.'" See John 10: 1–14 for the background; he is quoting (probably in his African version) verses 10–11; the Vulgate reads: "bonus pastor animam suam dat pro ovibus; mercennarius est qui non est pastor cuius non sunt oves propriae; videt lupum venientem et dimittit oves et fugit et lupus rapit et dispergit oves." The passage was a favorite of Christian bishops on both sides, frequently used by Augustine, for example (see ch. 8, p. 350).

people like him, they are even afraid to look at them.[42] The bishop must remain resolute as their true guardian.

The seizure of the dissident basilica at Thamugadi would have been a difficult undertaking by any measure. The city itself was the great regular-planned Roman colonial settlement that dominated the southwestern frontier of Numidia. The basilica held by Gaudentius had been constructed on a rise of land overlooking the southwestern quarter of the colony, on the far side of a large ravine. It dominated the southern skyline of the city. Not only did the basilica present a looming silhouette, it was by far the single largest and most imposing structure of the entire city.[43] Within a large and impressive outer quadrangle of circuit walls built of rough-hewn stone, its complex of buildings comprised, in addition to the large church itself, a huge forecourt atrium area, a baptistery, a special residence for the bishop himself (constructed by Gaudentius' famed predecessor Optatus) and a large number of ancillary reception facilities and storage rooms.[44] One of the craftsmen who had been involved in the construction and decoration of the basilica had placed a written record of his own pride embedded in the building that he had helped to construct: "I completed this work at the order of Optatus, the Priest [i.e. bishop] of God."[45] The storming of such a complex, and its potential destruction in the process – especially if those barricaded within it carried out their ostensible threat to set fire to it – would have considerable repercussions in a large military colony like Thamugadi, and from there throughout Numidia and Africa.

This time, Augustine's attitude was not at all so happy. He restated, but with a hardened resolve, the position on self-killing that he had staked out in the first book of *The City of God* published some six or seven years earlier. Why this novel position was taken, and how it came about, is a partial clue to the important role that suicidal deaths had assumed in sectarian resistance. Which raises the critical question: What was meant by suicide? Here, there are difficult and significant problems with words. Living under what might be called an Augustinian regime of suicide, it is difficult for us

---

[42] Gaudentius apud Aug. *Contra Gaud.* 1.18.19 (CSEL 53: 213): "nunc vero Christianorum receptores proscriptionibus territi pericula formidantes non solum non recipiunt, verum etiam videre timent quos tacite venerantur."

[43] Monceaux, *Timgad chrétien*, p. 29: "L'enceinte chrétienne du faubourg Sud-Ouest . . . occupe une superficie de 18,700 mètres carré, supérieure, et de beaucoup, à celle du Forum et du Capitole, ou de la citadelle, ou des plus grands thermes. Il n'y a pas d'ensemble aussi considérable à Timgad, ni pour l'étendue, ni pour le nombre et la variété des édifices, ni pour la complexité du plan et contenu."

[44] Courtois, *Timgad*, pp. 72–75, and endmap.

[45] Albertini (1938), p. 101: "Haec iubente sacerdote Dei Optato peregi," is the inscription placed in a mosaic by the mosaicist himself.

to conceive of a broader world in which there existed no term loaded with the permanently pejorative sense of our word "suicide."[46]

KILLING ONESELF

There was never a single word in Latin to define the act of suicide as we now think of it. Rather a wide variety of circumlocutions were drawn on according to the moral, aesthetic, and literary demands of the speaker or writer to describe the taking of one's own life. The word "suicide" itself is a strange modern coinage that appeared first in English in the mid-seventeenth century and in French almost a century later. But it was not in common use in either language until the latter part of the eighteenth century.[47] By this time, the term was a technical one that recapitulated a long Christian history in which the modern state and its apparatuses had become involved in the criminalization of various immoral activities. So Augustine, in his reply to Gaudentius on self-killing, used a whole range of periphrastic phrases for killing oneself: *ad mortem festinans* ("hurrying to one's death"), *se ipsum occidere* ("to kill oneself"), *mors spontanea* ("a voluntary death"), *interitus voluntarius* ("a voluntary end"), *mors voluntaria* ("a self-willed death"), *ipsum necare* or *ipsi necem inferre* ("to kill oneself"), and other words and phrases that had normally been used to describe what we call suicide.[48]

It has therefore been reasonably suggested that there was no such thing as a monolithic suicide regime in antiquity. Rather, there was a spectrum of discrete types of self-killing. It was these acts, taken under precise circumstances, that occasioned value and debate. Bayet broadly divided these types into an aristocratic model that forefronted the freedom or unfettered power of the elite male to control his own destiny and therefore his own life and death; and a popular model where the taking of one's own life was

---

[46] For what follows, I have depended, in part, on recent accounts, primarily those of Van Hooff, *Autothanasia to Suicide*, and Grisé, *Le suicide*; and the standard studies by Daube (1971) and (1972); cf. Murray, *Suicide in the Middle Ages*, 1, pp. 38–40. Van Hooff notes that the word *suicida*, meaning a self-killer, existed as early as 1177; but the fact it that no further interest was shown in the neologism until the mid-seventeenth century is what is significant for our argument.

[47] Grisé, *Le suicide*, pp. 21–23, esp. p. 23 nn. 4–5, referring to Bayet, *Le suicide*, pp. 586–88.

[48] Bels (1975), p. 165, seems to think that they are somehow unusual and has even persuaded Murray, *Suicide in the Middle Ages*, 2, p. 107, that they are Augustinian neologisms. Nothing could be further from the truth. They have known precursors in the long list of descriptors drawn up by Grisé, "Liste des principales formules employées dans les textes Latins pour exprimer l'idée de suicide," in *Le suicide*, pp. 291–97, which even she admits is only an exemplary and not a complete list of the phrases in existence; a more extensive list has been drawn up by Van Hooff, "Suicidal Vocabulary of Greek and Latin," Appendix C in *Autothanasia to Suicide*, pp. 243–50, but even it is not complete.

generally disapproved, since, by definition, it was usually taken without proper authority.[49] If there is some truth to this opposition, the polarities are in need of nuance and revision. In day-to-day life, given the examples witnessed in the literary sources of the time, as well as in theory, which is to say in philosophical justification, the taking of one's own life was normally provoked by any one of a number of standard causes: the unbearable consequences of an illness, the unbearable infirmities of old age, the unbearable circumstances of extreme poverty. Any of these were real conditions and acceptable grounds for taking one's own life. It was generally agreed that most self-killings were personal decisions of this type. In this range of honorable self-killings, it was recognized that there were sacrifices of one's life that were made for altruistic purposes, both to save and to defend supreme values or even to register what we might call political protest.

Even so, the actions that Gaudentius was contemplating are somewhat unclear, since the motives and aims ascribed to him impute a more belligerent, aggressive, and proactive behavior than might actually have been the case. According to the hostile sources, the official and Catholic ones that is, Gaudentius was threatening to burn himself and his congregation alive inside his church in a typical "Donatist" act of self-immolation. The mise-en-scène can be understood from Augustine's later summation:[50]

> Gaudentius, bishop of the Donatists at Thamugadi, was threatening to burn himself alive in his church along with some of the demented persons who were attached to him. The *vir spectabilis*, tribune and notary, Dulcitius, to whom the most pious emperor had given the task of enforcing his laws for the sake of bringing Unity to a completion, was acting with gentleness – as was only right, of course – towards these madmen. First, he sent a peaceful letter to this same Gaudentius. Gaudentius then replied to him with two letters.

If all that we had to assess the situation at Thamugadi was this brief summary of Augustine's, we would be right to deduce a deliberate plan

---

[49] Bayet, *Le suicide*, pp. 272 f. and pp. 307 f. for the two types; much the same points are reiterated by Hill, *Ambitiosa Mors*, pp. 18–20.

[50] Aug. *Contra Gaud.* 1.1 (CSEL 53: 201): "Gaudentius Donatistarum Tamugadensis episcopus cum se ipsum in ecclesia quibusdam sibi adiunctis perditis incendere minaretur, viro spectabili tribuno et notario Dulcitio, cui piissimus imperator leges suas exsequendas cura perficiendae unitatis iniunxit, agenti, ut oportebat, cum furentibus mansuete et prius ad eundem Gaudentium litteras pacificas danti duas rescripsit epistulas, unam breviorem et perlatoribus, sicut indicat, festinantibus festinantam, alteram vero prolixiorem, in qua secundum scripturas se respondisse diligentius arbitratur."

This was still the same view that Augustine offered in the *Retractationes*, 2.59.86 (CCL 57: 137): "Per idem tempus Dulcitius tribunus et notarius hic erat in Africa exsecutor imperialium iussionum contra Donatistas datarum. Qui cum dedisset litteras ad Gaudentium Tamugadensem, Donatistarum episcopum . . . exhortans eum ad unitatem Catholicam, et dissuadens incendium, quo se ac suos cum ipsa in qua erat ecclesia consumere minabatur."

by the bishop to burn himself and his parishioners alive in his church. Augustine further claims that the authorities had charged that Gaudentius was holding his parishioners in a suicide pact against their will.[51] The detailed correspondence to which Augustine averred, and some of which survives, reveals a rather different story. In his first letter to the dissident bishop at Thamugadi, Dulcitius had taken a possible Christian line of attack: he had advised Gaudentius "to flee persecution" – that is, to walk away and to abandon his basilica. In his reply, Gaudentius tried to explain the actions taken by himself and his partisans barricaded in the basilica, as *he* understood their meaning.[52]

We, the living, shall remain in this church as long as it might be pleasing to God, a church which in the name of God and of his Christ – as even you yourself have said – has always been crowded in worship of the truth. As is only right for the family of God, we shall set a measure to the end of our life here in the army camp of our Lord. But only on this condition: only if you begin to use violence [against us] will this then happen. No one is so devoid of reason [i.e. demented] that he would rush to death with nothing compelling him to that end.

In uttering the words, "here in the army camp of the Lord," Gaudentius was echoing the words of Cyprian, words that had been written over a century and a half earlier to a fellow African bishop to explain the exhortations needed to encourage Christians who were facing an impending apocalyptic battle with the forces of persecution.[53] Gaudentius' perspective was founded on a more basic dissident belief: the free will of each believer to decide his or her own actions. It was a belief founded on the fact that human beings had been created by God as imperfect beings and that they were free to make their own mistakes.[54] This attitude to surrendering one's own life, as seen

---

[51] Aug. *Contra Gaud.* 1.5.6 (CSEL 53: 203): "eos . . . quos a te ad exitium teneri dixit invitos."

[52] Gaudentius apud Aug. *Contra Gaud.* 1.6.7 (CSEL 53: 204): "In hac autem ecclesia . . . in qua Dei nomen et Christi eius, ut etiam ipse dixisti, in veritate semper est frequentatum, nos aut vivi, quamdiu Deo placuerit, permanemus aut, ut dignum est Dei familia, intra dominica castra vitae exitum terminamus, sub ea scilicet condicione, quia, si vis fuerit operata, tunc id poterit evenire. Nemo enim tam demens est, ut nullo impellente festinet ad mortem." The phrase *familia Dei* ("family of God") appears to be typical dissident usage to describe themselves: cf. Aug. *Contra litt. Petil.* 2.91.201 (CSEL 42: 123).

[53] Cypr. *Ad Fort.* 2 (CCL 3: 183): "et exercitum in castris caelestibus constitutum adversus Diaboli tela et iacula exhortationibus adsiduis praeparare."

[54] Gaudentius apud Aug. *Contra Gaud.* 1.19.20 (CSEL 53: 215): "Per opificem . . . rerum omnium dominum Christum omnipotens Deus fabricatum hominem ut Deo similem libero dimisit arbitrio. Scriptum est enim: *Fecit Deus hominem et dimisit eum in manu arbitrii sui.* Quid mihi nunc humano imperio eripitur, quod largitus est Deus?" Gaudentius is quoting Eccl. [Sirach] 15: 14: "Deus ab initio constituit hominem et reliquit illum in manu consilii sui" (VG); it was, apparently, a standard dissident text; Ecclesiastes is also referred to by Petilian apud Aug. *Contra litt. Petil.* 2.84.185 (CSEL 52: 115): Eccl. [Sirach] 15: 16–17: "Si volueris mandata conservabunt te et in perpetuum fidem

through Gaudentius' eyes, seems not much different from that of Ambrose and his parishioners in Milan in 386: a willingness to be killed if the forces of authority launched an assault on the church in which Christians had gathered. Gaudentius does not envisage himself or his flock as dangerous provocateurs or as violently aggressive persons who were going out of their way to challenge or to confront imperial authorities. Gaudentius was apparently no less willing than Augustine to castigate as "mad" or "deranged" any persons who would gratuitously kill themselves. In fact, in the conclusion of his first letter to Dulcitius, Gaudentius took some pains to emphasize the completely voluntary nature of the commitment of the Christians who were holed up with him in the basilica.[55]

> As for those who are with us, I call upon God as a witness, as well as on all of his sacraments, that I have exhorted and urged with the greatest vehemence possible that anyone who wants to leave us can say so publicly and without any fear. Nor would we be able to restrain such persons against their will – we who, of all people, have learned that one must not force anyone to believe in God.

The decision to surrender one's own life was a voluntary act involving the free decision of a free person; it fell well within the parameters of the noble and honorable self-killings of Roman tradition. The cause was great and just, indeed the most just. We must also remember that as late as 400 Augustine himself had embraced this position: that defending one's church and community was a praiseworthy form of witnessing and not at all an execrable kind of self-murder. Not very long after he penned this evaluation, Augustine experienced what can only be called a *volte-face*. Having had some time to gather his thoughts, Gaudentius was able to compose a longer reply to Dulcitius. His arguments are important because they reveal some of the received and traditional wisdom within the dissident church after generations of conflict that had involved various kinds of voluntary death. It was a complex set of ideas worked out in dialogue with local tradition and biblical texts. The forthcoming attack by the forces of the state on Gaudentius' basilica was naturally understood to be a persecution.

placitum facere adposuit tibi aquam et ignem ad quod voles porrige manum tuam" (VG). It is important to note, however, that the combatants depended on different translations of this critical text, and that the ones used by Augustine were not the same as those appealed to by Petilian: see A.-M. Bonnardière, "Quelques remarques sur les citations scripturaires de *De gratia et libero arbitrio*," *REAug* 9 (1963), pp. 82–83.

[55] Gaudentius apud Aug. *Contra Gaud.* 1.7.8 (CSEL 53: 205): "Eos autem qui nobiscum sunt . . . testem Deum facio eiusque omnia sacramenta, quod exhortatus sum et impensissime persuasi, ut, qui haberet voluntatem egredi, securus publice fateretur. Nec nos enim invitos retinere possimus, qui didicimus ad Dei fidem nullum esse cogendum."

Moreover, Gaudentius had prepared his parishioners with a heavy diet of texts that reinforced the idea that the current age bore only hatred for them and that, as slaves of Christ, they could only expect what the Lord Himself had foretold: "If the age hates you, know that it hated me first, before you. And if they persecuted me, they will persecute you too."[56] To endure such persecution only made one better. It was therefore necessary to undergo the test.[57] Living in the bishop's palace that had been constructed by the powerful Optatus, his predecessor, Gaudentius would have been aware that he was treading in the footsteps of his great forebear.[58] He would have been conscious of the fact, as were his parishioners, that his predecessor had been arrested and had died in prison at Carthage in 398. Optatus had sacrificed his own life in defense of his community. His model was direct, immediate, and compelling.

The hostile view of dissident suicides is that they were intended to create an atmosphere of fear and terror, much as, in our own day, suicides of persons under detention can credibly be described as acts of "asymmetric warfare."[59] Perhaps so. But the most extreme statement on self-killing that we have in any surviving dissident text, that of the bishop Dulcitius, does not indicate any such motive. Nor does the core biblical text that he arrays, the story of Razis from Second Maccabees, point in this direction. Nevertheless, the self-killings did create a real sense of apprehension and fear, probably out of all proportion to their actual effect; and, after a while, those killing themselves apprehended this effect and played upon it.[60] At any rate, the Catholic Church had early on condemned these specific

---

[56] Gaudentius apud Aug. *Contra Gaud.* 1.26.29 (CSEL 53: 227): "Odio ... saeculi gaudeamus, in eius pressuris non succumbimus, sed laetamur, mundus hic non potest servos Christi diligere, qui Christum cognoscitur non amasse, domino ipso dicente: *Si saeculum vos odit, scitote quia me primum odio habuit quam vos. Si me persecuti sunt, et vos persequentur*" (Gaudentius is quoting John 15: 18 and 20).

[57] Gaudentius apud Aug. *Contra Gaud.* 1.20.22 (CSEL 53: 218), citing Matt. 5: 11–12, 2 Tim. 3: 12, and Joh. 16: 2–3.

[58] For the bishop's house, located at the juncture of the large chapel and the main basilica, see Courtois, *Timgad*, p. 72 and plan, p. 73.

[59] As Rear Admiral Harry Harris, commander of Joint Task Force Guantánamo, declared of the self-killings of men detained under his remit: "They have no regard for life, either theirs or our own. I believe this [i.e. the suicides of three prisoners at Guantánamo] was not an act of desperation, but an act of asymmetrical warfare waged against us" (BBC News: Sunday 11 June 2006). I thank Aislinn Melchior for drawing this item back to memory.

[60] Whatever actual combat results were expected of the Japanese *Shimpu* ("Divine Wind") aviators in the Second World War, there was a firm conviction that they would at least have a profoundly detrimental psychological effect on the enemy. In the field, this fear effect appears to be much less than expected. On the home front, however, where apprehensions played on imagination, these fears seem to have been considerable, affecting debates and judgments, for example, on whether or not to use the atomic bomb against the Japanese; see D. McCullough, *Truman*, New York, Simon and Shuster, 1992, pp. 394 f. and pp. 438 f.

kinds of self-killings and their glorification. Following the dissident martyrdoms in the great persecution of 347, the Catholic Council at Carthage in the following year condemned "evil" deaths of this kind as not meriting martyrdom.[61]

THREE DEATHS

In all his discussions of the self-inflicted deaths among the dissidents, Augustine habitually specified three kinds of suicide: death by burning oneself alive (immolation), death by water (drowning), and death by hurling oneself off a great height (precipitation). In an arid environment like Africa, suicide by drowning would have been difficult. Most likely, one must envisage not throwing oneself into a river or lake, but rather into a well or cistern.[62] In this form, such a death had echoes of precipitation. Following a lengthy consideration of dissident suicides in his small handbook on sectarian violence that he addressed to the imperial official Bonifatius in 417, Augustine noted:[63]

> Then it became a daily sport, a *cotidianus ludus*, for them to kill themselves by jumping off sheer cliffs or by fire or by water. The Devil taught them these three kinds of death, so that, when they wished to die and could find no one to frighten into killing them with a sword, they would hurl themselves from precipices or expose themselves to fire or to water. Who else could have taught them this, possessing their hearts, except the One who challenged Our Saviour to hurl himself down from the pinnacle of the Temple . . . they have made a place in their heart for the Devil, and so they perish in the same manner as that herd of swine whom the band of demons made hurl themselves from the mountain into the sea.

The striking description of manic self-inflicted deaths, Satanic in origin, was made in a brief sent to a high-ranking official of the state. No doubt,

---

[61] See Council of Carthage, 348, canon 2 (CCL 149: 4): against precipitators (see n. 104 below).

[62] As in suicides documented in medieval Europe, see, e.g., Murray, *Suicide in the Middle Ages*, 1, p. 181.

[63] Aug. *Ep.* 185.3.12 (CSEL 57: 11–12): "Iam vero per abrupta praecipitia, per aquas et flammas occidere se ipsos cotidianus illis ludus fuit. Haec enim eos tria mortis genera diabolus docuit, ut mori volentes, quando non inveniebant, quem terrerent, ut eius gladio ferirentur, per saxa se mitterent aut ignibus gurgitibusque donarent. Quis autem illos haec docuisse credendus est possidens cor eorum nisi ille, qui et salvatori nostro, ut se de pinna templi praecipitaret . . . Sed quia in se diabolo potius dederunt locum, aut sic pereunt quem ad modum grex ille porcorum, quem de monte in mare daemonum turba deiecit." The passage ends with the plea to the imperial official that he has a responsibility to protect such people from the demonic forces with which they are afflicted. The reference to the incident involving Jesus and the Devil is drawn from Matth. 4: 5–7 (¶ Luke, 4: 9–13) and the one involving the swine is drawn from Matth. 8: 32 (¶ Luke 5: 13).

Augustine was attempting to use such frightening self-destructive acts as evidence of a kind of threat to the social order that he hoped would compel imperial functionaries to a more active enforcement of the existing laws against his sectarian enemies.

In direct communications with such imperial officials, Augustine repeatedly emphasizes that the self-killings were *intended* to create an atmosphere of fear.[64] The actual numbers of such suicides might well have been small, but the terror that they created among the much greater numbers who might be saved was to be a factor in persuading the authorities to use coercion.[65] Not only were the numbers small, making the suicides an aristocratic elite of death, but the death-cult was limited in its ecology to the heartlands of Numidia, to the "Africa" that Augustine knew best. Given the importance of mimicry or imitation, it is significant that the communicative networks of symbols and ideas that formed the background in which such acts were committed were ones limited to this region. Augustine admitted that in most other parts of Africa the phenomenon was unknown. It existed only where, in his words, "the insane" and "the useless" happened to live.[66]

Dulcitius, the tribune and notary at Thamugadi, was therefore faced with a volatile situation in which a bishop and his congregation, barricaded in their basilica, presented the threat of a mass suicide. The prospect rattled his composure and caused him to have second thoughts. The extremity of the dissidents' response, however, was largely of the government's own making. Gaudentius and his flock had every good reason to view their situation in terms of desperate extremes. In his first official decree issued against them, Dulcitius had used strong and frightening language: "Let them be well aware," he announced, "that they will pay with their own

---

[64] The calculated terror effect is claimed by Augustine in many places, but is perhaps most systematically argued in his letter to Dulcitius in which he argues that it was a deliberate aim of dissident suicides to create a sense of terror in those who beheld them: Aug. *Ep.* 204.1 (CSEL 57: 317): "suo nos exitio terrere se credunt aut suam laetitiam quaerentes de mortibus nostris aut nostram tristitiam de mortibus suis . . . Cum enim sua pernicie terrendos nos putant, non dubitant nos timere, ne pereant."

[65] Aug. *Ep.* 185.3.14 (CSEL 57: 13): "Si autem se ipsos occidere voluerint, ne illi, qui liberandi sunt, liberentur, et eo modo liberantium terrere pietatem, ut, dum timetur, ne quidam perditi pereant, non eruantur perditioni."

[66] Aug. *Ep.* 185.3.14 (CSEL 57: 13): "Gratias autem Domino, quod et apud nos non quidem in omnibus sed valde in pluribus locis et per alias Africae partes sine ullis istorum insanorum mortibus pax Catholica currit et cucurrit. Ibi autem illa funesta contingunt, ubi est tam furiosum et inutile hominum genus, qui et aliis temporibus eadem facere consuerunt." It is an admission that he made perhaps because he was aware that an imperial official like Bonifatius had come to know the approximate regional parameters of the phenomenon.

deaths the debt that they owe to the law."[67] The dissidents in the basilica not unnaturally interpreted this decree to mean that he was threatening to put to death those who would be captured in the assault on their church.[68] In his later letter to Dulcitius, Augustine attempted to re-read entirely the harshness of these words, telling the tribune what it was that he must have meant. Of course, he coached the official, you didn't really *mean* to say that you would kill them; after all, you are not armed with the *ius gladii* or power to execute by the terms of the law under which you are operating. What you *really* meant to say, says Augustine, is that these persons were bringing a richly deserved self-inflicted death upon themselves.[69]

The very extremity of the situation in the first decades of the fifth century, especially the enforcement measures after 412, might well have provoked recourse to more extreme models. In his letter to Dulcitius, Augustine claims that in many of his writings and sermons he had already refuted the dissident claim that self-inflicted deaths were martyrdoms. But he had to admit that he had never confronted the specific example of Razis that was drawn from the second book of the Maccabees, the example that had been used by Gaudentius as a model for his behavior.[70] Given the extent of the suicide phenomenon in the preceding decades, the response seems strange. It might signal a lack of communication between the two churches. Perhaps the example of Razis had never been written about in the letters and *libelli* that marked normal communications between the bishops of the contending sides. Perhaps it was more the stuff of preaching and so not a part of dissident discourse that had reached Augustine's ears before 419. It raises the whole question of the role of the model set by the Maccabees for either church. It might well be that a general reference to the specific example of Razis was indeed a new thing. A history of the Maccabean texts in African Christianity would repay closer scrutiny.[71] Despite writing widely on martyrdom and persecution, and coming from a harder line,

---

[67] Dulcitius apud Aug. *Ep.* 204.3 (CSEL 57: 318): "Noveritis [i.e. Dulcitius is addressing Gaudentius] vos debitae neci dandos."

[68] Aug. *Ep.* 204.3 (CSEL 57: 318–19): "putaverunt, sicut eorum rescripta indicant, hoc te fuisse comminatum, quod tu illos adprehensos fueras occisurus."

[69] Aug. *Ep.* 204.3 (CSEL 57: 319): "non intellegentes de illa nece, quam sibi ipsi volunt ingerere, te locutum. Non enim tu in eos ius gladii ullis legibus accepisti aut imperialibus institutis, quorum tibi iniuncta est executio, hoc praeceptum est, ut necentur."

[70] Aug. *Ep.* 204.6 (CSEL 57: 320–21): "Verum tamen, quod fatendum est, de isto Raxio [sic] seniore, quem summa exemplorum inopia coartati se in Machabaeorum libris quasi ad auctoritatem sceleris, quo se ipsos perdunt, perscrutantis omnibus ecclesiasticis auctoritatibus vix aliquando se invenisse gloriantur, adhuc eis numquam respondisse me recolo."

[71] Duval, *Loca sanctorum*, 2, pp. 618 f., notes that the cult of the Maccabees became widespread in the Christian world in the last quarter of the fourth century, but that in Africa most of the evidence seems to relate to a time later than c. 420.

Tertullian was simply uninterested in the Maccabees. Cyprian's interest was not much greater: one extended passage in the *Ad Fortunatum* is practically the sum. For him, it was the Seven Brothers and the paramount example of Eleazar who set examples for Christian martyrs.[72] Razis is nowhere to be found. No wonder Augustine was surprised and that he had never been provoked to formulate a condemnation of this example in any one of his extensive replies to the dissidents on the subject of martyrdom.

The peculiar relevance of the Razis story for men in the position of Gaudentius is not difficult to see. Eleazar and the Seven Brothers were renowned for surrendering their lives because of their refusal to sacrifice or to obey royal orders that contravened the laws of God. They were therefore good exemplars for those who faced the early persecutions of the Roman state. The story of Razis, found in a different part of Second Maccabees, was surely more pertinent to a persecution that was centered on the violent seizure of basilicas, as the dissident churches were in 315 and 347, and as was the one at Thamugadi in 419.[73] Unlike Eleazar or the Seven Brothers, when Razis faced arrest, he found himself trapped in his stronghold residence, encircled by 500 soldiers of the Syrian monarch. The siege by the soldiers bears all of the hallmarks of the siege of a basilica: the syrians assaulted the main doors of the Razis' fortified villa and they ordered firebrands to be brought up. It was in the desperate situation in which he was encircled by the king's forces that Razis chose "a noble death" – first by falling on his sword, then by throwing himself off the heights of the parapet of his castle, and at the end, in a final act of extreme resistance, by tearing out his innards and hurling them at his persecutors.

The story of Razis was an extreme in the exaltation of human sacrifice that had been canonized for Africans in the example of Cyprian, whose writings, other than the Bible, are the texts most frequently quoted by Gaudentius in his answers to Dulcitius and Augustine. By envisaging deaths like those suffered in the sieges of basilicas as sacred martyrdoms rather than as contemptible self-murders, the dissidents had constructed an impenetrable firewall between such heroic deaths and ordinary secular self-killings.[74] The highly dramatic vignette of Razis is isolated in the middle of the narrative of Second Maccabees. Augustine might have tried to gainsay the nature of its explicit message, but it was embedded in a series of stories, and

[72] 2 Macc. 6: 18–31 (Eleazar) and 7.1–41 (seven brothers and their mother).   [73] 2 Macc. 14: 37–46.
[74] As has been true, again and again, of such self-killings, see, e.g. Hopgood in Gambetta, *Suicide Missions*, p. 74: of the LTTE fighters or so-called Tamil Tigers in Sri Lanka; and Khosrokhavar, *Suicide Bombers*, pp. 50–52, on Iranian martyrs in the Iraq–Iran war of the 1980s.

attached firmly to a name, that of the Maccabees, whose actions as martyrs Augustine had elsewhere lauded to his own parishioners.[75]

> The glory of the Maccabees has made this into a very special festival day for us. When the marvelous account of their sufferings was read out aloud to us, we not only heard about them but we even saw and, like spectators, gazed at them.

Augustine had written favorably on the Maccabees. To deny the applicability of Razis' example to Christian behavior, he now had to refer the relevance of Razis' response to the history of Razis' own age, that of the Jews, but not to the new age of the Christians. He was innovating under pressure.[76]

For reasons like these, the Catholic condemnation of self-killing came to be founded on the critique of false martyrdom. In both cases the acts were intrinsically evil and prompted by the same agent of evil, the Devil. No persons in their right mind would involve themselves with either the evil act itself or its provocateur: by definition, they were outside the scope of reason. As with the agents of circumcellion violence, the actors were driven by *furor* or mental rage and by sheer *dementia* or madness.[77] The Catholic critique also evoked the same range of values that crosslinked the dissidents and Jews, namely arrogance and pride. This united them with the Jewish arch-villain, Judas. His suicide was the same sort of self-killing that they were inflicting upon themselves. Just as Judas was driven by Satan to exacerbate his primal crime of betrayal, so the dissident suicides re-enacted the same folly of pride, and in the same sequence.[78] Since the suicide was a deliberate murderer of God's creation, the crime of

---

[75] Aug. *Sermo* 300.1 (PL 38: 1376–77): "Istum diem nobis solemnem gloria Macchabaeorum fecit: quorum mirabiles passiones, cum legerentur, non solum audivimus, sed etiam vidimus et spectavimus," beginning a long sermon that lauds the Maccabees as precursors of Christian martyrdom; indeed it was Christ, who was yet to die, who made them martyrs; cf. *Sermo* 301 (PL 38: 1380–85) and 301A = Denis 17 (MiAg 1: 80–89) also on the same theme and with the same strong laudation. All these sermons were delivered on 1 August, the festival day of the Maccabees.

[76] Aug. *Ep.* 204.6 (CSEL 57: 321): "Sed, quod tuae caritati et prudentibus quibusque sufficiat ad istos redarguendos, si ad vitam Christianorum de Iudaea gente atque illis litteris parati sunt omnium factorum exempla transferre, tunc et hoc transferant ... qui cum esset apud suos nobilis et multum in Iudaismo profecisset, quae sibi in comparatione iustitiae Christianae damna et stercora fuisse dicit apostolus."

[77] Aug. *Contra Gaud.* 1.6.7; 1.29.33; 1.28.32 (for *dementia*); and 1.6.7; 1.28.32, 1.29.33; and 1.31.40 (for *furor*); noted by Bels (1975), p. 166, among others; in the earlier text of the *Civ. Dei* 1.22 (CCL 47: 23–24), the contrast was between the *sana ratio* of the ordinary person and the *mens infirma* of the suicide; cf. *Ep.* 185.3.12–14 (CSEL 57: 10–13), where the contrast is *amentia–furor*; and *En. 2 in Ps.* 36.3 (CCL 38: 34), where armed ferocity is connected with madness.

[78] Aug. *Contra Gaud.* 34.49 (CSEL 53: 248–49); *Ep.* 185.2.11 (CSEL 57: 10): such persons who "so love homicide" that they kill themselves are afflicted with madness (*furor*) which the love, the *caritas*, of the Church must control.

self-killing was an unforgivable sin that, by definition, barred self-murderers permanently from a future in paradise, and condemned them forever to the eternal fires of Hell.[79]

The way in which the dissidents interpreted these self-killings must be seen within the context of the great value that was placed on martyrs as heroic agents of resistance. In clearly definable ways, self-killing was a logical extension and end-point of strands already embedded in the nexus of martyrdom. The ideology of the martyr emphasized a willingness to meet death, if necessary. The vital defining force had always been the willingness to surrender one's own life when faced with the overwhelming forces of persecution. Even in this latter case, there had been debate. In the sporadic persecutions of the pre-Decian age, it was rare, if not unprecedented, for Roman authorities of their own volition to stage general proactive investigative sweeps through the whole of a provincial society. The general rule laid down by the emperor Trajan was that Roman governors and their assistants were *not* to engage in such general hunts for Christians or to be overly zealous in accepting denunciations.

Since merely falling under "the name" of "Christian" was a capital crime, however, what if one denounced oneself and suffered the supreme penalty? This was an ever-present possibility and it produced debates within Christian communities about the moral status of the willful solicitation of one's own death. Opinions varied. Already by the early third century, some, like Clement of Alexandria, had rejected the possibility. As the African Lactantius later did, they condemned such an act as a species of self-murder. It was condemned with biblical authority, based on the Decalogue: "Thou shalt not kill" (that is, especially yourself). But a consistent and rational viewpoint emerged that was certainly widespread throughout the dissident church in the fourth century, one that was also based on biblical authority. The dissidents founded their ideas on an appeal to the Maccabees, and specifically to the example of Razis. Although Augustine attempts to reject the story as having any value, as belonging to "the Jews" whose values he says, quoting Paul's letter to the Philippians (3: 8), are just so much "ruination" and "excrement," it is manifest that this story had long been regarded

---

[79] Aug. *De patient.* 13.10 (CSEL 41: 673–74); *Civ. Dei,* 1.17–30 (CCL 47: 18–31); cf. *Ep.* 173.4 (CSEL 44: 643): "in cuius desertione mors aeterna metuitur. Quamquam in ista morte, quam tibi tu ipse inferre voluisti, non solum ad tempus, sed etiam in aeternum morereris"; cf. *Ep.* 185.14 (CSEL 57: 13): "Quid agit ergo fraternum dilectio? Utrum, dum paucis transitorios ignes metuit caminorum, dimittit omnes aeternis ignibus gehennarum . . . ne quidem voluntario moriantur interitu . . . ut eos doceant quocumque tempore secundum consuetudinem doctrinae diabolicae ad eas, quae in illis modo timentur, mortes voluntarias festinare?"

as an exemplary one in the dissident church. Whatever the general significance of Razis as a model, the three specific types of self-killing especially identified with the dissident resistance – self-immolation, drowning, and precipitation – had another element of Christian tradition in them: an imitation of common examples that the enactors followed. The fundamental problem of mimicry was clearly understood, even by hostile persons like Augustine. The problem is: an imitation of what? A replaying of what?

Of the typical self-killings, those by burning alive or immolation were probably the least common and most directly reflected a political script taken both from the Great Persecution of 347, from the events of the immolations of believers trapped in basilicas under siege.[80] Augustine suggests that the modes of death were so outrageous that the Devil himself must have taught them to the dissidents martyrs. Apart from the moralizing, this is not necessarily true. A survey of all known modes of self-killing noted in a wide range of Greek and Roman literary sources (nearly a thousand such cases) reveals four dominant styles of self-inflicted death: hanging, drowning, precipitation, and self-immolation.[81] Hanging had been rejected by African Christians for the obvious reason of its close association with betrayal. Once hanging was ruled out as a mode of self-killing, the remaining modes were neither outrageous nor exotic methods that required special instruction by the Devil. They were the normal means that were typical in Graeco-Roman antiquity. Other than avoiding one mode of self-killing for reasons of belief, the dissenters acted according to long-established patterns of behavior in their own culture. Along with drowning, self-immolation is one of the least-attested modes of suicide attributed to their enemies by Catholic critics.[82] But jumping was *the* mode.

FALLING

Almost every era of martyrdom has had its own standard forms of death and punishment, ranging from the self-starvation of Cathar purists to the self-immolation of Buddhist monks or Czech political

---

[80] In terms of comparative reportage in modern times, for example, suicides by fire have been a very rare thing; almost all of those attested in a period between 1790 and 1971 in major British news sources were concentrated in the decade between 1963 and 1972: Crosby, Rhee, and Holland (1977), pp. 61–63. These were largely suicides of political protest that were so strongly determined by mimicry of striking exemplary cases that they constituted mini-epidemics of sorts.

[81] Van Hooff, "960 Cases of Self-Killing," Appendix A in *From Autothanasia to Suicide*, pp. 198–232; for some perceptive criticisms on the limitations of this catalogue, see Murray, *Suicide in the Middle Ages*, 2, p. 527.

[82] Admitted by Augustine: *Contra Gaud.* 1.28.32 (CSEL 53: 231): "aquis et ignibus rarius id [sc. voluntariam mortem] agebant, praecipitis greges consumebantur ingentes."

activists.[83] Here, too, one can see the same impact of fashionability and style, imitation in such concentrated packets of individual cases that produce wave-like patterns.[84] Although self-immolation and drowning were apparently known modes used by the dissident Christians, precipitation – deliberately hurling oneself off a precipice or, where this was not possible, into a chasm or deep pit – was regarded as the characteristic mode of ritual suicide in which they engaged. "You will see others so ready to go to their deaths that, even though there is no persecutor, they hurl themselves to their deaths," Augustine noted, in a typical reference.[85] Jumping off heights to their deaths was thought to be the normal dissident death-style. Augustine could preach in one of his anti-Donatist sermons that they should beware of having heads that were too heavy, puffed up with a misguided sense of rightness, so that if they went near the edge of a cliff it was their heavy heads that might cause them to fall off.[86] It was meant to be a joke.

The self-killings so rattled and unnerved those who witnessed them or heard about them, that the worst motives had to be attributed to the suicides by their sectarian enemies. Obviously the precipitators regarded themselves as martyrs. The whole critique of their behavior was therefore directed to disarming the glory and the status that they acquired not only among dissident Christians, but also among ordinary Catholics who shared just as strong a sense about extreme acts of heroism that created martyrs. "Those martyrs who suffered in the time of persecution acted out of love. They did this out of love. But these men act out of a puffed-up arrogance and out of pride. For although there is no persecutor, they hurl themselves to their death."[87] The lack of Christian *caritas* was the one critical element that was said to remove this type of death, self-killing, from martyrdom. Lacking this element of Christian love, it was reduced to an ordinary and despicable human act.[88]

---

[83] Murray, *Suicide in the Middle Ages*, I, pp. 189–90, provides an introduction; for self-immolations, see Crosby, Rhee, and Holland (1977) as cited in n. 80 above.

[84] See Biggs (2005), pp. 188–90 and fig. 5.1, p. 183.

[85] Aug. *Tract. in 1 Ep. Ioh.* 6.2.1 (SC 75: 280): "videbitis alios paratos ad suscipiendam mortem, ita ut desistente persecutore, seipsos praecipitent: isti sine dubio sine caritate hoc faciunt."

[86] Aug. *Sermo* 266.8 (PL 38: 1229): "Si caput grande fecisti, cave pondus capitis, ne in praecipitium perducaris." It seems to be an odd bit of levity. *Sermo* 354.5 (PL 39: 1565) might be a similar reference to precipitation as a humorous aside: "et cum ingemescis, curaris, humilis eris; tutior ambulabis, non praecipitaberis, non inflaberis."

[87] Aug. *Tract. in Ioh.* 6.23.3 (CCL 36: 65): "Caritate fecerunt martyres illi, qui in tempore persecutionis passi sunt; caritate fecerunt; isti autem de tumore et de superbia faciunt; nam cum persecutor desit, seipsos praecipitant."

[88] Aug. *Sermo* 162A.1 = Denis 19.1 (MiAg I: 99): "Si prophetiam quisquis habens nihil ei prodest, si non habuerit caritatem . . . Et tradere corpus suum ut ardeat? Plerumque hoc faciunt temerarii praecipites."

In attempting to refute the dissident's claims to martyrdom, it was the voluntary suicides of the men and women who threw themselves off heights that represented a limit case of senselessness which, in its very extremity, demonstrated once and for all the falsity of their claims to the status of martyr. If the dissidents founded their legitimacy on the example of Cyprian, then the manner of his martyrdom was a condemnation of their gold standard: "The heretics, though, and the Donatists, who falsely boast that Cyprian belongs to them ought to pay attention to the way that he went to his martyrdom. If they did so, they wouldn't throw themselves off cliffs. The heretic breaking away in heresy, the Donatist jumping deliberately to his death, is certainly not one of Christ's disciples, certainly not one of Cyprian's comrades."[89] These deaths were constantly glossed as the acts of the deranged, the mad, and the insane; they were construed as a kind of senseless violence, an illogic of self-destructiveness that were symptoms of a mass hysteria. The images of the cliff-jumpers pictured by the modern reader evoke in them something like the (false) popular image of the maddened animal-like rush of lemmings. That is not far from the pictures that the ancient critics used. The favorite biblical parallel was the story of the demons that possessed a herd of swine which then rushed en masse down a precipice to drown themselves in the lake at Gadara.[90] Which also suggests that such acts were collective responses, and not a series of isolated individual performances. In a long sermon delivered in September 410 at the *mensa* of Cyprian where Augustine discussed dissident suicides at length, he concluded with reference to the precipitators.[91]

The Donatists have gathered together in crowds to commit all their evil deeds; as they hurl themselves off cliffs they shout "Praise to God" in their mouths. "Praise to God" in their mouths, but so hateful to God in their deeds. Any Catholic standing there at the moment, who hears "Praise to God" from afar, immediately starts trembling and looks for a means to get far away lest he have the misfortune to witness their cliff-jumpings.

---

[89] Aug. *Sermo* 313E.2 = Guelferb. 28.2 (MiAg 1: 537): "Haeretici autem et Donatistae, qui se ad Cyprianum falso iactant pertinere, si episcopatum eius attenderent, non se separarent; si martyrium, non se praecipitarent. Non est omnino discipulus Christi, non est comes Cypriani, haereticus in haeresi separatus, aut Donatista in morte praecipitatus."

[90] Aug. *Contra Gaud.* 1.27.30 (CSEL 53: 228): "mittebat in aquam, aliquando in ignem, ipse et illum gregum porcorum praecipitem fluctibus mersit" in obvious reference to the dissident mass suicides, and comparing the Gadarene swine (Matt. 8: 32 and parallels).

[91] Aug. *Sermo* 313E.6 = Guelferb. 28.5 (MiAg 1: 541): "Congregati enim sunt Donatistae ad omnia scelera sua; ut se praecipitent, Deo Laudes clamant; in ore, 'Deo Laudes,' in factis Deo odibiles. Itaque quisquis tunc stans a longe christianus Catholicus audierit 'Deo Laudes,' iam contremiscit, iam quaerit qua fugiat, ne praecipitationes ipsorum videat."

What might have been some of the ideological parts of the general behavior? In a prolonged refutation of the practice, Augustine perhaps provides some clues. In a long anti-Donatist sermon preached at Carthage on the *natalis* of Cyprian's martyrdom, he insists that his listeners should think carefully about what the Lord had to say about martyrdom, and that they should contemplate his teaching when they heard of "the Donatists" who "throw themselves off precipices." The biblical incident to which he appealed was the incident where the Devil, after he had taken Jesus to a high pinnacle of the temples, challenged him: "If you are the Son of God, throw yourself down" (Matt. 4: 6). When the Devil spoke these words to tempt Jesus, Augustine says, he was saying precisely the same thing that he has to "the Donatists": "Hurl yourselves down and the angels will be there to catch you. With such a death you don't go to punishment, you go to win a crown."[92] Furthermore, in this same sermon, although belittling the imagined reply from his sectarian enemies, Augustine showed that some means of suicide were to be avoided, and others preferred.[93]

We ask them, and say to them: "If a voluntary death delights you and you consider it a beautiful thing to die by your own hand, without any enemy hounding you, without any enemy pursuing you, why do you rush so quickly to the precipice and never to the noose? It's so easy, this other kind of death. And hanging from a noose preserves the body of the person dying far more intact than the precipice method that you have chosen. So why don't you hang yourself with a rope when you wish to die?"

The answer to his rhetorical query was one word: Judas. "Far be such a thing from us, a curse on the rope. After all, Judas the traitor, hanged himself with a rope." And, for the dissidents, the indelible stain of betrayal, and the mode of death chosen by the arch-traitor Judas, absolutely ruled out that sort of imitation in death.

But why precipitation? Generally, of course, it must have been because this kind of voluntary death was somehow connected with martyrdom and

---

[92] Aug. *Sermo* 313E.4 = Guelferb. 28.4 (MiAg 1: 538): "Videamus autem et de martyrio quid dicit Dominus; commemorare debemus, et propter Donatistas, qui se praecipitant, magisterium commendandum est Domini. Ait enim Diabolus Domino, cum eum temptaret . . . Assumserat enim eum super pinnam templi; dominum suum non agnoscebat, et tamquam hominem praecipitium docebat, quod falsis Christianis persuadere praeparabat."

[93] Aug. *Sermo* 313E.4 = Guelferb. 28.4 (MiAg 1: 538): "Quaerimus ab eis, et dicimus: 'Si mors voluntaria vos delectat, et pulcrum putatis nullo urguente inimico, nullo adversario occidente sponte mori, quare ad praecipitium cito curritis, ad laqueum numquam? Est in facili alia mors, magisque suspendium laquei servat integra membra morientis, quam praecipitium quod eligitis: cur ergo non vos in laqueo suspenditis, quando mori vultis?' Respondent: 'Absit a nobis, anathema sit laqueus; Iudas enim traditor laqueo se suspendit.' O miseri et infelices, quae est ista dementia, nolle facere quod traditor fecit, et facere quod magister traditoris Diabolus eos docuit?"

its rewards. In the parts of the sermon that follow, Augustine ridiculed the fact that those who committed suicide reject Judas, but embrace what Jesus rejected when the Devil urged him to jump. He then reports behavior among the dissidents that shows the connection.[94]

"Get behind me Satan!" Donatist, that's what you should say to the Devil when he suggests jumping off a cliff to you – the One who fills you with the desire to worship the one who throws himself off a great height. Yes indeed, my brothers, and consider this: they both throw themselves off heights and they are urged on and taught to do so by their own perverted people. These latter persons are the greater murderers, those who collect the bodies of the jumpers, and who carefully gather up their blood, who honor their graves, and who get drunk at the tombs of their heroes. When they see honors of this kind offered to the jumpers, then they too burn with the desire to throw themselves off great precipices. The former are drunk with wine because of them [i.e. the suicide jumpers], the latter are inebriated with madness and the worst possible error.

Whatever the theological problems, there is no doubt that large numbers of ordinary Christians saw in these self-sacrifices a type of martyrdom and behaved accordingly towards them. They treated the self-killers as martyrs, carefully collecting the body parts, keeping samples of their blood, and turning the *tumulus* of the heroic suicide jumper into a martyr's shrine, a place of hero worship. The great honor shown to these persons, Augustine emphasized, and not unbelievably, was part of the motive that excited other men and women to leap to their deaths.

In the course of explaining the reasons for the rejection of hanging as a standard mode of suicide used by the dissident Christians, Augustine provides hints about why some modes were rejected (in this case, the association of hanging with Judas), but not, alas, why being burnt alive, drowning, or jumping off a cliff were to be preferred. But the circumstantial details of such deaths might provide us with some clues. In the case of the deliberate aggression shown to the municipal youths, the *Juvenes*, who were defending the shrines, temples, and cult images of their hometowns, or the deliberate goading of government officials, there can be little doubt

---

[94] Aug. *Sermo* 313E.5 = Guelferb. 28.5 (MiAg 1: 539): "'Redi retro, Satanas.' O Donatista, hoc hic Diabolo, quando tibi suggerit praecipitium; qui etiam vos implevit, ut praecipitati colamini. Revera enim, fratres, et ipsi se praecipitant, et a suis perversis populis praecipitantur. Illi sunt homicidae ampliores, qui corpora praecipitatorum cum honore colligunt, qui praecipitatorum sanguinem excipiunt, qui eorum sepulchra honorant, qui ad eorum tumulos se inebriant. Illi enim videntes huiusmodi honorem praeberi praecipitatis, inflammantur alii ad praecipitium; illi super eos inebriantur vino, illi inebriantur furore et errore pessimo." Note the use of the technical term *tumulus* and not just *sepulcrum* for the tomb: it is the purposeful employment of the traditional language for the burials of heroes.

that the persons who engaged in such provocative acts were deliberately seeking a violent response from figures of authority, a type of death that the provocateurs could then interpret as martyrdom. Such an aggressive threat, even if it courted a response of lethal force, precisely because the killing was actually done by others might plausibly relieve the self-killed of the stigma of actually having murdered themselves.[95] General statements made about the dissident suicides by Catholic observers show how the specific instances just mentioned were part of a wider range of similar behavior. It was clearly understood, even by hostile spectators, that an aura of martyrdom attended such deaths. But what was it about being burnt alive, drowning, or jumping off a precipice that excited such ideas and conceptions in the first place?

MIMICRY AND DEATH STYLE

In the cases of drowning oneself or throwing oneself off a great height, the answer seems immediately to hand. As with many such cases of martyr behavior, a species of imitation or mimicry was involved. These particular types of self-inflicted deaths were historically attached to earlier martyr-doms, especially to the ones that occurred in Africa in the Great Persecution of 347. Drowning is specifically attached to the martyrdoms and the sub-sequent narration of the deaths inflicted on dissident Christians in the violent repressions that took place at Carthage in midsummer of 347. The horrific deaths by drowning that were inflicted on the dissidents by Roman authorities left an indelible mark in their memory. To die *like* those people had died for the faith would surely be a mark of the highest honor. Simi-larly for precipitation. The other events of 347 that made a greater impact on the dissident memory were the deaths of Donatus, the bishop of Bagaï, in midsummer of 347, who was drowned in a well, and of Marculus, the bishop of Vegesela, at Nova Petra in November of the same year. According to the version of the story that one accepted, the dissident bishop Marcu-lus, who was arrested and tortured at Vegesela, was either thrown off the great precipice at Nova Petra by a Roman executioner or – according to the

---

[95] Although difficult to measure, by almost any measure the proportion of all police killings that are in effect victim-precipitated suicides is much higher than one might suspect: Parent, *Victim-Precipitated Homicide*, pp. 7–15; 93–95, at p. 8: citing Marvin Wolfgang's work as early as 1958: 26% of police homicides studied in Philadelphia for that year; Parent and Verdun-Jones (1998), pp. 436–37, indicated that almost half of the lethal police shootings in the Canadian province of British Columbia between 1980 and 1994 fell into the category of police-assisted suicidal deaths. Of course, such deaths are a truly tiny proportion of all suicides, but the point of comparison with our cases is that they, too, were truly unusual – an extreme form of self-killing.

more hostile view – he threw himself off the height. Whichever scenario was "true," his death provoked the production of martyr narratives and a large number of cult sites in Numidia, including the one at the basilica at Vegesala. His undisputed elevated status as "Lord Marculus" only strengthened his memory among the dissident faithful as *the* great martyr of the age.

Marculus' martyrdom was not only a matter of memory and cult, but also of active imitation. The narrative of his death, read aloud every year as part of the liturgy on 29 November, the anniversary of his martyrdom, highlighted certain aspects of his death that likened it both to the encounter between Satan and Jesus at the Temple (hence the later debates over the precise meaning of that text) and to the death of the African martyr Perpetua. In the one case, the Devil said to Jesus that if he threw himself off the pinnacle of the Temple he would be caught at the bottom by angels who would soften and mutate the impact of his physical death and, simultaneously, assist in the ascent of his spirit to the heavens. Perpetua reported a dream sequence of a fellow martyr, Saturus, that foreshadowed their deaths and in which they were similarly borne aloft to Paradise by angels. That this is what happened to Marculus is manifest from what is reported of his last day on earth. In the following narration of his death, one can sense the replication of sensations – descent, speed, exhilaration, and lift-off – expected by the divine suicide.[96]

Then the monstrous executioner, with his double cruelty, armed with the punishments of precipitation and the sword, brandished this twin death in his hands. With his cruel right hand, he hurled the martyr headlong off the height. The executioner thought that he had plunged into the terrible void a man to whom was owed the sublimity of the heavens. But Marculus' holy body, separated from the solidity of earth, falling from the heights to the depths, was borne through the empty expanses of liquid air. Not encountering any resistance in the void,

---

[96] *Passio Marculi*, 12.55–59 (Mastandrea, 1995: 72–73): "Tunc immanissimus carnifex, qui duplici crudelitate, et praecipitio armatus et ferro, geminam mortem gestabat in manibus, crudeli dextera in praeceps impulit martyrem, et cum in taetrum chaos demersisse se credidit, cui caelorum sublimitas debebatur. Sed enim sacrosanctum corpus terrae soliditate subducta a celsitudine ad ima descendens, per vacua liquidi aeris spatia ferebatur, neque quicquam offensionis in illa inanitate reperiens, velocitatem sui cursus ipso impetu duplicabat, quia pernicitate itineris [spatii] vertigo nutrita est. Inter commoti aeris concitos strepitus, tanta divinitus moderatio procurata est, ut immunia cunctis asperitatibus membra supra ipsam saxorum duritiam, velut super mollissimos toros ac sinus placidissimos, ponerentur. Tunc victrix anima naturali cursu velocius caelum petit quam descenderat corpus ad terram; ut scilicet passione perfecta utraque substantia antiquissimis originis suae principiis redderentur omnipotentis Dei manibus, circa totum martyrem suum clementer operantibus: qui et spiritum eius adiuvantibus angelis ad aeternas sedes iussit imponi, et corpus iactatum, auris blandientibus cinctum et famulantibus ventis leniter supportatum, in media petrarum crepidine collari."

the impetus of his fall, fed by the swiftness of his trajectory, doubled the speed of his course to earth. Amidst the clashing uproars of the rushing air, such great control was divinely procured that his limbs, freed from all harshness, were placed as if on the softest of beds and in the most peaceful of folds. Then his victorious spirit sought the skies with a speed swifter than the natural one with which his body plummeted earthward so that, manifestly, with his passion complete, both his essences [i.e. body and soul] would be returned to the primal principles of their origins by the hands of all-powerful God, His hands folding mercifully around the wholeness of his martyr. It was God who ordered that Marculus' spirit be lodged in its eternal home by the assistance of angels, and that his intact body, wrapped by softly blowing breezes and borne gently aloft by friendly winds, be placed at the base of the rocky cliffs.

The account of the mystical journey of the saint from earth to heaven, levitating through the medium of the air, imparted to the listener a giddy sense of flight and redemption that surely elicited sympathetic sensations in the believer. A death like this one was not just spectacular and heroic. It also possessed elements that made it more aesthetically attractive than drowning or being burnt alive.[97] Repeated statements that jumping off a height was the favored kind of self-killing engaged in by the dissidents make sense. In these sentiments and presentations, it did not matter whether the sacred container was a person or an object. Recall Optatus' description of the cleansing of a Catholic church by the dissidents. A glass ampoule used for the Catholic liturgy was thrown (like Marculus), it fell through the air (like Marculus), and, like Marculus, it landed on the crags below but was not broken because, like him, angelic breezes wafted it to a safe landing on the rocks.[98] This was a Catholic, not a dissident story. In it, that ampoule, like Marcellus, was a holy vessel.

Mimicry of Marculus, the most eminent of the martyrs, rather than the many anonymous persons drowned in the ships off Carthage, would have been a more alluring finale. The observation draws attention to the overpowering function of style in death, especially in deaths that were deliberately chosen. It is no different with modern-day self-killings. The greater the celebrity, the more widespread the media coverage, the greater the imitation. In our own age, the example and celebrity of Marilyn Monroe, and her 1962 suicide, excited, provoked, and enticed a wave of self-killings that

---

[97] That is to say, in the longer history of Roman self-killing and public purpose, the linkages connecting entertainment, the manipulation of mass sentiment, and the role of aesthetics were never far away, as Plass, *Game of Death*, has demonstated for the Principate.

[98] Optatus, *Contra Parm.* 2.19.2 (SC 412: 278): "Ampullam quoque chrismatis per fenestram ut frangerent iactaverunt, et cum casum adiuvaret abiectio, non defuit manus angelica quae ampullam spiritali subvectione deduceret: proiecta casum sentire non potuit. Deo muniente illaesa inter saxa consedit."

were seen as beautiful and aesthetically satisfying.[99] The impulse to kill oneself and to take one's own life in a particular style comes in fashion waves.[100] A stylish figure establishes a vogue for imitation. For the dissidents in the years after 347, Marculus was a great celebrity and the mode of his death much admired.

As the sudden spread of certain styles of self-killing has been measured for our modern world, we are certainly facing a death fashion that spread quickly by imitation and the power of style. A powerful modern instance involving the same mode of preciptation is provided by the self-killing of a beautiful young nineteen-year-old Japanese woman, Kiyoko Matsumoto. On 12 February 1933, she threw herself to her death off the heights of Mount Mihara-Yama on the island of Izu-Oshima. The romantic story of her death, spread rapidly as a narrative by the popular media of the time, evoked an epidemic of mimetic self-killings. Following her suicide, in the remainder of 1933, another 143 people took the boat to the island and threw themselves off the great height; and in 1934 another 167 persons followed her example.[101] The authorities were horrified, and only by concerted and hard official action was the situation on the volcanic island brought back to some semblance of normality and the "suicide epidemic" brought to an end, rather suddenly, in 1935. As in the case of Marculus and the cliff at Nova Petra, the heights of Mount Mihara on the island quickly became a location of pilgrimage. To this day, special boat tours and tourist expeditions take both sightseers and suicides to the site of the crater-cliff off which Ms. Matsumoto jumped.

That such imitation, provoked by the death of Marculus, was an immediate popular response amongst the dissidents seems almost certain from two pieces of evidence. First of all, in his reply to the dissident Cresconius, Augustine specifically refers to the *tradition* that the action of throwing oneself off a height to one's death was known to be an imitation of Marculus' death in 347. He says this in such a way that presumes that the

---

[99] Gladwell, *Tipping Point*, pp. 217–220, in the case of a sudden "suicide epidemic" in Micronesia; and pp. 222–27, based on the studies by Phillips (1974) and (1979) whose claims and results have been replicated and confirmed by many subsequent studies.

[100] See, for example, Khosrokhavar, *Suicide Bombers*, pp. 101–104, who points out the obvious with respect to the "suicidal" martyrdoms of the Iranian Bassidj: "The vogue for martyrdom can also be analysed in terms of fashion: the desire to imitate the other in death was a constant feature of young people in the revolutionary movement..." He emphasizes the importance of "fashionable figures" whose deaths set "a real vogue for martyrdom," producing the typical features of a fashion world: competitiveness, stylishness, and the will to outbid.

[101] Fedden, *Suicide*, pp. 296–97; although the "epidemic" soon subsided, over the following years 944 people (804 men and 140 women) imitated her example, not counting the 1,386 failed attempts.

basic fact would not be denied by Cresconius.[102] Elsewhere, he links the self-killings of the cliff-jumpers to both example and teaching:

those men concerning whom you are accustomed to have the greatest envy, Marculus and Donatus – I can say about them without fear of contradiction that it is uncertain whether they hurled themselves off heights, your teaching does not fail to provide us with daily examples of such behavior, or whether they were hurled off the heights by the command of some secular power.[103]

The attitudes of the dissidents who reacted in this fashion in the distress of 347 were seen to be so extreme by some members of their own community that their own bishops condemned their acts in church councils (or so, at least, Augustine avers). The other response that confirms the presence of this early wave of dissident self-killings during the great crisis of 347 is found in the canons issued by the Catholic Council of Carthage of 348, the year immediately following Marculus' death. They include the first explicit condemnation of suicides of this kind, as well as the practice of the self-killers being treated as martyrs.[104]

It is difficult to know how early imitations of Marculus' death by precipitation began. In the narrative of the female martyrs Maxima, Donatilla, and Secunda, there is a case of literary imitation, but it comes in a story that was later grafted onto an earlier and different version of their story. The women were executed on 30 July 304, and the earliest form of the *acta* dates to soon after their execution. But these proto-*acta* were later modified in versions that became more fictional and featured ever more gross caricatures of the Roman governor Anullinus.[105] In its earliest versions, the narrative of the trial and execution included only two women, Maxima and Donatilla. By some point in the later fourth century, it was thought

---

[102] Aug. *Contra Cresc.* 3.49.54 (CSEL 52: 461–62): "Unde quid prodest, quod conciliis suis hoc vestri episcopi prohibuisse et damnasse se iactant, sicut ipse commemorasti, cum tot rupes et abrupta saxorum ex Marculiano illo magisterio cotidie funestentur?"

[103] Aug. *Contra litt. Petil.* 2.20.46 (CSEL 52: 46): "Illi autem, de quibus maximam invidiam facere soletis, Marculus et Donatus, ut moderatius dixerim, incertum est utrum se ipsi praecipitaverint, sicut vestra doctrina non cessat cotidianis exemplis, an vero alicuius potestatis iussu praecipitati sint."

[104] Concil. Carth. 348, canon 2 (CCL 149: 4). This canon forbade the honoring of unworthy persons as martyrs, including those who killed themselves by throwing themselves off great heights: "Martyrum dignitatem nemo profanus infamet, neque passiva corpora quae sepulturae tantum propter misericordiam ecclesiasticam commendari mandatum est redigant, ut aut insania praecipitatos aut alia ratione peccati discretos, non ratione vel tempore competenti, quo martyria celebrantur, martyrum nomen appellent, aut si quis iniuriam martyrum claritati eorum adiungat insano." Since these specific kinds of self-killings, as a mimcry of the death of Marculus, were surely a response to the events of 347, this is another indication that the council must date to 348.

[105] *Passio sanctarum Maximae, Secundae et Donatillae*: Maier, *Dossier*, 1, no. 5, pp. 92–105, who reprints the version of de Smedt (1890).

provident to add a new female martyr to their number, a young woman who was given the not very imaginative name of Secunda.[106] Her story, unlike theirs, was not centered on the refusal to sacrifice or to burn incense during the Great Persecution. It was, instead, a tale of ascetic purity. The specific concerns of her story and the manner in which her narrative is told date this addition to the backwash of the heated debates over virginity and celibacy in the mid-370s. It was a movement that produced a series of young female virgin martyrs in poetic and other writings of the time, including Agatha in Sicily and Eulalia in Spain. The rabid concern with female purity was not a particularly African phenomenon and the artificial second woman, "Secunda," is one of the rare cases known in the Christian literature of Africa where the theme of virginity is problematized in this extreme fashion. The insertion reads:[107]

There was in that place a certain girl, Secunda by name, about eleven years old, who had been the subject of many marriage arrangements, but who had spurned them all because she loved the one God alone. When she saw them departing [i.e. Maxima and Donatilla who had been sent to Thuburbo by the governor], looking out from the high balcony of her house, she threw herself down from the place. She did not have before her eyes any image of her parents' riches. She utterly disdained, as it is said, all the squalor of this world and she despised all its riches. She desired only the One whom she hoped to find in eternity.

Like Marculus, Secunda never hit bottom. As she plummeted earthwards, her precipitation enabled a magical transformation by which she was able to enter the company of her fellow saints, Maxima and Donatilla. The Secunda episode, a late purity tale artificially embedded into an earlier martyr narrative, has a parallel in the story of the Abitinian martyrs.[108] Once again, this martyr narrative includes a woman's martyrdom that was later inserted into the existing story. It, too, celebrates female chastity: "And lest the most devoted sex of women and the brightest band of holy virgins be deprived of the glory of such a battle, all of the women, with the help

---

[106] CIL 8.25958 = ILAlg 1.3670 = ILCV 2043 = AE 1906: 139 (Hr. Rouis) where Faustinus, bishop of Theveste, put up an inscribed table to the women, "v idus april. [9 April] indict xiii"; they are listed, in order: Maxima, Donatilla, Secunda.

[107] *Passio sanctarum Maximae, Secundae et Donatillae*, 4 (Maier, *Dossier*, 1, no. 5, p. 100): "Cumque illae surgerent et ambularent, erat ibi quaedam puella, nomine Secunda, annorum circiter duodecim, cui multae condiciones sponsales evenerant et omnes contempserat quia unum tantum diligebat deum. Cumque eas proficisci videret, per maenianum domus suae nimis excelsum respiciens, exinde se praecipitavit nullum habens ante oculos intuitum divitiarum parentum: omnes utique mundi huius, ut dictum est, squalores comtempsit, divitias despexit, unum concupivit quem in aeternum invenire meruit."

[108] *Passio Dativi, Saturnini et sociorum*: Maier, *Dossier*, 1, no. 4, pp. 57–92, who reprints the edition by Franchi de' Cavalieri (1935a), with minor revisions.

of Christ, were brought in and crowned with victory." This portentous introduction provides the writer with a bridge to the little vignette of Victoria, "that holiest of the women, the very flower of virgins." As with the heroines of the other virgin-martyr stories, she too was of high birth.[109]

Already from her infancy, manifest signs of her sexual purity shone forth and in the years of her education there appeared that steely resolve of mind and a certain dignity pertaining to her future suffering. Finally, after she had spent the whole time of her years growing up in complete virginity, and although the girl herself was unwilling and reluctant, she was forced into marriage. Her parents gave her a bridegroom against her will. To foil the plunderer of her shame, the girl secretly threw herself off a cliff. Supported by kindly breezes, she was received unharmed in the lap of the earth. She would not later have to suffer again for Christ the Lord, since she died then for the sake of her sexual purity alone.

But the story of Victoria's precipitation, her suicide for the sake of her purity, was a later fiction clumsily shoe-horned into earlier versions of the story of the Abitinian martyrs. The original Victoria, as is made clear by the events that follow immediately in the narrative, actually survived to face trial by Anullinus, who found her guilty, not of any sexual transgressions, but rather simply of being a Christian and sent her to prison to await execution on that charge. Once again, we have a story fabricated and added, probably in the 380s or 390s, to the original story of the Abitinian martyrs. It is a story that reflects some of the new concerns of the age in which a young woman's sacrifice of her bodily sexual purity was seen as a terrible death and its defense by self-killing a genuine martyrdom to be compared with the deaths suffered by Christian women in the old days of the great persecutions.[110] But Victoria's death by precipitation, including the soft-landing aided by friendly breezes, was manifestly derived from the model of Marculus.[111] He is the ghostly primal martyr who hovers behind both of these purity tales. All these African materials make Augustine's rejection of the suicides of the women of Rome in defense of their purity

---

[109] *Passio Dativi, Saturnini et sociorum*, 17 (Maier, *Dossier*, 1, no. 4, p. 81): "Huic namque ab infantia iam clara pudicitiae signa fulgebant et in rudibus adhuc annis apparebat rigor castissimus mentis et quaedam dignitas futurae passionis. Denique postquam plena virginitatis adultum aetatis tempus explevit, cum puella nolens et reluctans in nuptias a parentibus cogeretur invitaeque sibi traderent sponsum parentes, ut praedonem <pud>oris urgeret clam sese per praeceps puella dimittit aurisque famulantibus supportata incolumis gremio terrae suscipitur. Neque fuerat postmodum etiam pro Christo domino passura, si pro sola tunc pudicitia moreretur."

[110] It was precisely these female suicides, amongst them Lucretia, that Augustine had to condemn, somehow, in *The City of God*.

[111] The celebration of death by precipitation makes sense in the context, since the narrative of the Abitinian martyrs, in the final version that we have, is manifestly a dissident confection; see Dearn (2004).

in 410, only a few decades later, move doubly against the grain of local sentiment.

BURNING WITH ZEAL

But why burn oneself alive? What was meant by self-immolation? Here one is on more speculative grounds, since no specific cases are mentioned in the surviving sources: no actual incidents are mentioned that might provide clues about motives. Some kinds of imitative martyrdom relate to specific incidents in the Great Persecution of 347, but immolation is not obviously one of them. One is reduced to speculation. Perhaps immolation might not be related to specific historical incidents. It might have been modeled on a more generic pattern that was especially significant to the dissidents. The story of the three young men in the fiery furnace in the Book of Daniel is one such template that received a lot of play in the sources, especially in Augustine's many attempts to re-read the story and to deny the significance that it had for martyrdom in the eyes of the dissidents. One strongly suspects that this story formed a consistent part of the pattern, just as the Jesus and the Devil story did in the case of precipitation. But there might have been model events unknown to us in the existing records: for example, heroic defenders in a basilica under forced repossession being burned alive in the assault rather than surrendering their church to the authorities. In such attacks, firebrands were sometimes used, with the potential for a disaster.[112] This was the type of circumstance in which Gaudentius and his parishioners, barricaded in the basilica at Thamugadi in 419, were threatening to re-enact. It is the only specific type of circumstance to which Augustine alluded when he spoke of the conscious decision by a dissident (in this case Gaudentius) to burn himself alive. Further, there is no doubt that, as with Ambrose at Milan in 386, such an act of resistance would be interpreted as an heroic deed conferring the status of martyr on those who voluntarily suffered incineration. This also makes sense of references to immolation that never mention it being done by individuals in isolation. References to self-burning are always general in nature and seem to be best covered by an explanation of this kind.

---

[112] There are structural parallels between these cases and the well-documented one at Waco. Indeed, almost all the structural elements are here as well, up to the final immolation of the besieged. Such results were possible in instances where the state intervened with force against a barricaded community: see Shaw (2009) for a more detailed discussion of the main factors involved in this and two other historical cases.

If this interpretation is correct, then the appearance of suicide as a sanctified guerrilla tactic would have begun in the events of 347 and their aftermath when the examples of the martyrs of the great persecution endured by the dissidents in that year became widely known – part of their education as examples to be absorbed and to be acted upon. Is this so? The earliest records of violent acts of this type are not found in any of the documents from the early decades of the internecine conflict between the two Christian communities, but rather in Optatus' long reply to Parmenian in the mid-360s. In one passage, he seems to indicate that such extremist self-killers already existed. In describing the type of men whom Donatus of Bagaï recruited in 347 to oppose the advance of Paul and Macarius, he suggests that such suicidal responses existed in the local repertoire.[113]

In this way Donatus of Bagaï found the mad mob of men whom he could hire against Macarius. They were recruited from that kind of men who were hiring professional hit men to engineer their own destruction in their hope for a false martyrdom. They were from the same origins as those men who, discarding their cheap lives, were hurling themselves off the peaks of high mountains. See from what sort of men this other Donatus recruited his cohorts!

Optatus states that in 347 Donatus of Bagaï was recruiting enforcers from the same pool of desperate and extreme men who were hiring other men to kill them and who were throwing themselves off high precipices. If true, it means that these kinds of suicides were already part of the repertoire of behavior in the 330s and 340s. His statement has a certain persuasive force because of context. The men who died in the confrontation with Paul and Macarius' forces were treated as martyrs. The response does not seem to be an innovation, but rather a tradition, and it suggests the existence of a near-suicidal ethos among persons who deliberately faced well-trained and armed Roman soldiers. But this is still different in kind from a deliberately self-inflicted murder. It might be that Optatus had good evidence that such suicides existed well before the mid-340s, but his statement has all the feel of a later rhetorical gloss taken from the writer's contemporary times, that is in the mid-360s or later. Optatus wished to suggest that the men who supported Donatus were as deranged as the persons who later voluntarily threw themselves off heights to their deaths.

These extreme examples were only likely to be acted upon in circumstances where the dissidents came under renewed attack, which points to

---

[113] Optatus, *Contra Parm.* 3.4.8 (SC 413: 42): "Sic invenit Donatus Bagaiensis unde contra Macarium furiosam conduceret turbam. Ex ipso genere fuerant qui sibi percussores sub cupiditate falsi martyrii in suam perniciem conducebant. Inde etiam illi qui ex altorum montium cacuminibus viles animas proicientes se praecipites dabant. Ecce ex quali numero sibi alter Donatus cohortes effecerat."

the critical watershed period beginning in the 390s. Concordant with this explanation, no earlier suicide attacks or aggressive assaults are attested for intervening times, between the 350s and the 390s. They are not attested, most strikingly of all, in Optatus. His silence on this matter is significant, since he spends much time and effort to condemn grossly unacceptable acts of the dissidents, above all the record of their violent behavior. Although he treats these subjects at length, he never once mentions suicide as a typical mode of behavior of his sectarian enemies. Not once. This indicates that through the mid-360s and, almost as certainly, still by the mid-380s (the time of the revised version of his work), such forms of self-killing were not common. The condemnation by the Catholic Council of 348 of suicidal self-killers who were counted as dissident martyrs does point to imitative self-killings that went well beyond the isolated models of Donatus and Marculus. If they followed the style modes set by these suicides and their causes, however, they would not have long outlasted the end of the Great Persecution of 347. The revival of the tactic would only be provoked by a new situation felt to be a serious and threatening persecution by the dissidents.

Although precipitation was the most unnerving and unsettling of the suicides, these self-killings were not directly connected to incidents of violent assaults. The witnessing of such suicides, or hearing them, no doubt created a volatile mix of emotions, including fear. Augustine later claimed, perhaps speciously, to a high-ranking imperial official, that by killing themselves in these ways the Donatist suicides were deliberately trying to create an atmosphere of terror.[114] Although they were not the cause of direct physical violence, they were part of a behavior in which the willingness to surrender one's own life produced a pool of volunteers that could be exploited for violent acts.[115] While precipitation remained the most spectacular means of suicide, as well as the one described in the

---

[114] Aug. *Ep.* 185.3.14 (CSEL 57: 13): "Si autem se ipsos occidere voluerint, ne illi, qui liberandi sunt, liberentur, et eo modo liberantium terrere pietatem, tu, dum timetur... praesertim cum illi, qui suas mortes voluntarias et furiosas minantur." Of course, Augustine was deliberately emphasizing the "regime of fear" factor in order to justify the repressive measures that he was hoping to evoke from Bonifatius.

[115] A rough comparison would be the manner in which an existing high valuation, the practice, and the images and symbols of *suppuk* or ritual self-killing in Japanese culture could create a general pool of values from which warrior versions of self-sacrifice could be created in attacking a hated enemy, as in the *shimpu* or "Divine Wind" aviators of the Second World War. However, the case here is rather complex, since many such actions were also interpreted by the men themselves within a European culture of sacrifice, based on readings of everything from Plato and Xenophon (on Socrates) to Nietzsche and Kierkegaard: see Ohnuki-Tierney, *Kamikaze, Cherry Blossoms, and Nationalisms*, esp. pp. 19–20, 261–78.

most vivid detail, there was a different mode in which dissidents armed themselves and confronted officials in public venues such as fora or the public roads. The purpose was to threaten them so that the accosted official would turn on the threatening "attackers" and kill them. The problem is that even detailed analyses of dissident suicides do not provide more information than these bare claims. In the long sermon delivered at the *mensa* of Cyprian in 410 in which Augustine attacked these suicides as misguided and as not constituting martyrdom, he lingers on precipitation. But he also mentions this other mode of self-killing in passing.[116]

> The Donatists, though, don't just hurl themselves [off cliffs] of their own accord, but they accost people and say to them: "Kill us!" While these people reply and say: "We're not going to kill *you*." How insane and perverse can you get? This is the point at which you people have arrived: the reason that you are going to call yourself a martyr is that you either commit a murder or create a murderer. So these men come up to people, arming them against themselves, and compel them by the use of terror to kill them. If they were in their right mind, they wouldn't commit murder. But this is what they do, this is what their father, the Devil, has taught them and what their teacher Donatus has instructed them to do.

Notices like these suggest not just individual self-killings, but collective acts that had a more active and aggressive aspect to them.[117] From what source did the model for this type of confrontational suicide derive? And what relationship did it have to non-sectarian types of self-killing?

If the three most commonly mentioned modes of self-killing engaged in by some of the dissidents were drowning, self-immolation, and precipitation, then the least frequent and (apparently) least given to mass self-killings were those acts of aggression in which an individual deliberately provoked figures of authority to kill them. This, too, had a genealogy with martyrdom. At the center of Christian debates over the legitimacy of martyrdom going back at least to Clement of Alexandria were the cases of Christians who so deliberately affronted established figures of authority that they were in fact courting their own death. Did these extreme persons still count as true martyrs deserving of the name or rather were they mere

---

[116] Aug. *Sermo* 313E.5 = Guerlferb. 28.5 (MiAg 1: 540): "Donatistae autem ultro se praecipitant, et veniunt ad homines, et dicunt: Occidite nos. Illi dicunt: 'Non vos occidimus.' O insani! O perversi! Ad hunc arti<cu>lum venis: martyrem te esse ideo dicturus es, et eos in se arment, et terrendo occidere cogant. Qui si sanum cor haberent, et praecipitium horrerent, et homicidium non facerent; sed hoc faciunt, quod eos pater suus Diabolus docuit, et magister suus Donatus instruxit."

[117] For example, Aug. *Ep.* 185.3.12 (CSEL 57: 12): "Sed quia Diabolo potius dederunt locum, aut sic pereunt quem ad modum grex ille porcorum, quem de monte in mare daemonum turba deiecit," repeating earlier comparisons of the suicide precipitators to the Gadarene swine (Matt. 8: 32; Luke 5: 13).

self-murderers? For the dissidents in Africa, such aggressive suicides were rooted in the violent events of 347. Among the men mobilized by the dissident bishops in southern Numidia were those who, it was said, were intent on self-destruction.[118] It is not entirely clear, however, if these men are to be identified with those who "threw themselves off great heights," and not with those who threatened others so as to cause their own death. The control legislation subsequently passed in 348 by the Catholic council at Carthage makes no explicit mention of this extreme type of eagerly sought-out death.[119] This particular form of self-killing was first noted in connection with the attacks led by Christian young men in gangs on traditional shrines, at festivals and other such occasions. The Christian men knew that by threatening to smash the idols they would incite the youths who were protecting the gods in their shrines to kill the attackers. This form of self-killing was explicitly connected with other incidents in which Christian youths used violent threats to Roman officials to provoke orders from them that court guards or soldiers should cut them down.[120] The general statement is followed by an exemplary story of an imperial official (unnamed) who exercised sufficient control and pretended to arrest the threatening dissident to execute him, but instead simply left the man bound and subject to less severe punishment. He was not lured into providing the person with the desired martyrdom.[121]

In partial understanding of them, it must be said that these self-inflicted deaths bear some relationship to the modern phenomenon of "death-by-cop" (as it has been called) in which a person deliberately antagonizes or threatens an armed police officer in order to have the officer kill him. As such, these suicides are related in type to ones in which the self-killer purposefully solicits his or her killing by another agent, for example, by deliberately driving an automobile into oncoming traffic. These self-killings, too, follow patterns encouraged by style and imitation.[122] Detailed studies of the phenomenon have revealed a number of structural similarities. Persons who take this course of action are overwhelmingly young males aged 18–30 who have a prior history of violent or negative involvements

---

[118] Optatus, *Contra Parm.* 3.4.8 (SC 413: 42): on the hiring of "hit men" – "conducebant... percussores" – who were intent on their own destruction: "in suam perniciem."

[119] Concil. Carth. 358, canon 2 (CCL 149: 4).

[120] Aug. *Ep.* 185.3.12 (CSEL 57: 10–11): some caution must be exercised with this particular account, since it is a long brief directed to the persuasion of an imperial official, Bonifatius, that mixes and compresses a wide range of different incidents and cases, in order to persuade an imperial official to act.

[121] Aug. *Ep.* 185.3.12 (CSEL 57: 11).

[122] See Phillips (1979) for the first study that was able to sieve this self-killing effect out of the background of general statistics of automobile fatalities; cf. Gladwell, *Tipping Point*, pp. 222–23.

with public law enforcement.[123] The protagonist knows who possess lethal force and how they are likely to react. In general, these suicides are drawn from the rougher lower orders of society who often have an adversarial relationship with police authorities.[124] The perhaps surprising fact is that these vicarious self-killings constitute a high proportion of all deaths inflicted by police officers in advanced post-industrial modern countries.[125] By contrast, however, they represent a painfully minute proportion of all suicides in any given year. The location of these suicides is therefore specific. They are commonly found in situations where death penalties inflicted by state authorities are enacted as public rituals that involve the victim in mini-theatrical displays of power. Conversely, they are a truly rarified, extreme, and exalted form of self-killing.

THE PROVOCATION TO SELF-KILLING

The dominant impression that one gets is that suicide entered the repertoire of the dissident church not in its early years, but as a result of the traumatic experience of 347. Dissident martyr acts that were re-drafted and rewritten in the mid-370s to mid-380s were using one form of self-killing, that of precipitation, as the characteristic type of self-killing. But these were literary replayings designed to serve an ascetic agenda and not specific sectarian hostilities. By the time of Augustine's early letters and treatises, we are faced with the much more frightening reality of pervasive and frequent waves of dissident self-killings. His references to these suicides as "numerous," "a daily occurrence," "a sport," and as "found everywhere", and similar phrases, are marked, to be sure, by an element of rhetorical exaggeration. Even so, they seem to reflect a resurgent trend to the extremes of self-killing as a form of martyrdom among the dissidents.

In the short guide to the dissident threat that Augustine provided for Bonifatius, the tribune, in 417, he discourses at length on the problem of martyrdom and its meaning, and the "false claims" made about martyrs by his sectarian opponents. He reports that they are in love with self-murder and he details the ways in which they continued to commit ritual suicides, causing alarm and fear among the general populace. But, he asks,

---

[123] Lindsay and Lester, *Suicide-by-Cop*, pp. 12–14, citing Vivian Lord's study (2000): 95% males; 84% between 25–40; Kennedy, Homant, and Hupp (1998): typically males between ages 16–35.

[124] Lindsay and Lester, *Suicide-by-Cop*, pp. 13–14; cf. Kennedy, Hormant, and Hupp (1998).

[125] Lindsay and Lester, *Suicide-by-Cop*, pp. 11–12: citing Parent and Verdun-Jones (1998): of Canadian cases: 54% of lethal shootings by police in British Columbia (Canada) in a fifteen-year test period between 1980 and 1995.

rhetorically, how can one be surprised at this behavior of theirs in the present, given their actions in the past? He then refers back to events that had taken place during the time of the destructive attacks on pagan temples and idols in the 380s and 390s.[126]

Especially during the time of the worship of idols, they used to come in great hordes to the crowded ceremonies of the pagans, not to break the idols but to be killed by the worshipers of the idols. If they had received authority to break the idols and had tried to do it, and if anything happened to them, they might have had a claim to a shadow of the name of martyr, but they came solely to be killed, leaving the idols themselves intact. They did so because there were some worshipers of idols, rough young men, who had the custom of dedicating to the idols any victims that they killed. And in order to be killed, others mingled with armed travelers, making horrible threats of striking them if the travelers did not kill them. Sometimes, too, when judges were passing through [i.e. on their assize rounds], they used violence to extort commands from them that they should be struck down by the executioners or by an officer of the court. In this connection, a story is told of a certain man who fooled them by ordering them to be bound and handed over as if for corporal punishment, and in this way he escaped their attack, unbloodied and unharmed.

Such deliberate confrontations with armed figures of authority, with challenges to kill the challengers, if rare, were not unknown outside Africa. In the spring of 40, for example, Philo reported that leading men among the Jews in Judaea, with a huge popular crowed following them, went to meet Petronius, the Roman governor, at Ptolemaïs on the coast. They did so in a supreme final effort to dissuade him from following through Caligula's request to have a statue of the emperor himself placed in the Holy of Holies in the Temple at Jerusalem. In a scene reported to be one of extreme emotion, the Jewish elders proclaimed:[127]

---

[126] Aug. *Ep.* 185.3.12 (CSEL 57: 11): "Maxime, quando adhuc cultus fuerat idolorum, ad paganorum celeberrimas sollemnitates ingentia turbarum agmina veniebant, non ut idola frangerent, sed ut interficerentur a cultoribus idolorum. Nam illud si accepta legitima potestate facere vellent, si quid eis accidisset, possent habere qualemcumque umbram nominis martyrum; sed ad hoc solum veniebant, ut integris idolis ipsi perimerentur; nam singuli quique valentissimi iuvenes cultores idolorum, quot quis occideret, ipsis idolis vovere consueverant. Quidam etiam se trucidandos armatis viatoribus ingerebant percussuros eos se, nisi ab eis perimerentur, terribiliter comminantes. Nonnumquam et a iudicibus transeuntibus extorquebant violenter, ut a carnificibus vel ab officio ferirentur. Unde quidam illos sic inlusisse perhibetur, ut eos tamquam percutiendos ligari et dimitti iuberet atque ita eorum impetum incruentus et inlaesus evaderet." A variation of the last story came to be known in the eastern Mediterranean where it was picked up by Theodoret of Cyrrhus, either from Augustine or, more probably, from African refugees in the East: Shaw (2004), pp. 242–44.

[127] Philo, *Leg.* 32.225–242, at 233–34 (the speech is a fine piece of rhetoric composed by Philo which, we hope, reflects the actual sentiments of the occasion); cf. Frend, *Martyrdom and Persecution*, pp. 51–52; Josephus later provided a parallel description of the incident: *AJ*, 18.8.3.

We are surrendering ourselves to destruction, unless, remaining alive, we would be called upon to witness an evil worse than death itself. We have learned that infantry and cavalry forces have been made ready against us, should we oppose the raising [sc. of the statue]. No one is so mad who, being a slave, would oppose a master. But we readily put our throats at your disposal. Let your men kill, butcher, and then cut our flesh without any knife used or blood spilled by us, accomplishing all the deeds of those who lord it over others. But what need is there of an army? We noble priests will accomplish these sacrifices ourselves!

Even so, this is not quite the same as rushing aggressively at "pagan" youths and state officials with arms in order to confront and to threaten them in such a manner as to incite them to kill you.

There are similar behaviors in late fourth-century Africa, but probably no direct textual influences. Philo or Josephus might or might not have been common reading materials among Christian dissenters in late antique Africa, but a common set of conditions – an apprehended threat to the most basic foundations of belief, a strident monotheistic commitment, and a determined persecuting authority – might have elicited the same responses. There is, for example, the well-known case of the confrontation between Christians and the Roman governor of Asia, a case that must have been well known to Africans, since it was reported and remembered by their own Tertullian.[128] In the year 185, all the Christians of a certain city in the province where Arrius Antoninus had gone on his judicial rounds presented themselves to him with the demand that he execute them. He obliged a few of them, but finding too many more lined up for the same treatment, he dismissed the rest with the comment that there was plenty of rope that they could use and more than enough cliffs for them to jump off of if they so wished.[129] Hanging and precipitation. Note the latter.

Augustine refers to the precipitators, and on more than one occasion, as when he refers to "those who venerate the corpses of those who willingly throw themselves to death off great heights."[130] The last phrase was a standard, occurring repeatedly, sometimes specifically in connection with the deaths of circumcellions. It often frames the context of other irrational

---

[128] Tert. *Ad Scap.* 5.1 (CCL 2: 1131-32): "Arrius Antoninus in Asia cum persequeretur instanter, omnes illius civitatis Christiani ante tribunalia eius se manu facta obtulerunt. Tum ille, paucis duci iussis, reliquis ait: ὦ δειλοί, εἰ θέλετε ἀποθνῄσκειν, κρημνοὺς ἢ βρόχους ἔχετε." The name of the city involved has been lost in the accounting. For Arrius Antoninus, proconsul of Asia in 184-85, see PIR A 1088: SHA, *Vita Commod.* 7.1; MAMA 6.122 = AE 1940: 192 in addition to the Tertullian.

[129] Frend, *Martyrdom and Persecution*, p. 293: "...and here was the Montanist equivalent of the Donatist Circumcellions of two centuries later"; a view accepted by Droge and Tabor, *A Noble Death*, p. 160 n. 35. I find both assertions to be rather dubious, as does Barnes, *Tertullian*, pp. 146-47.

[130] Aug. *Ep.* 43.8.24 (CSEL 34.2: 106): "veneratores praecipitatorum ultro cadaverum."

or outlandish behavior of theirs – for example, "madness," "fury," "drunk-enness" – so as to castigate the deaths themselves as "sacrilegious" and "profane" rather than as sacred and holy.[131] The whole valuation that was given to these deaths was very much one of opinion and perspective. Augustine wished to brand such self-killings as "mad" and lacking in purpose or reason and therefore a species of false martyrdom.[132] He dilates on the problem of these "false martyrs", arguing that to behave obstinately under a just king or to suffer by burning in the flames of hell is not enough to make one a martyr:[133]

[those kinds of people who] shout "Bravo! Bravo!" and swear oaths by the white hairs of those men who do not even have a sane head, and by the shoes of men *who have not found the road of peace*, much less walked on it. They themselves turn away such crowds from the unity of Christ and wish to convert them to their own name. Having suffered some civil punishments for their schism, they have the audacity to confer on themselves the passions of martyrs, so that the anniversaries of their punishments are celebrated with great gatherings of mad men to whose numbers they themselves belong. With no one at all persecuting them, they throw themselves off the sheer heights of mountains so that they might end their evil lives by an even worse kind of death. But on that day [i.e. the day of the Final Judgment] there will not be any such stupid people about whom it will be said "we are just men who suffered persecution."

That these self-imposed deaths were modeled on the ideal and noble deaths of martyrs is made clear by Augustine's constant attempts to refute the claim. In his rejection of the assertions of Petilian, the dissident bishop of Constantina, about persons who had been killed by Catholics, he states:[134]

---

[131] For example, Aug. *Contra litt. Petil.*, 1.24.26 (CSEL 52: 20): "omitto furorem circumcellionum et praecipitatorum ultro cadaverum cultus sacrilegos et profanos," and he then moves to the subject of their drunkenness, in a series of interlinked claims that was meant to cast doubt on the status of deaths achieved in such deranged states of mind.

[132] Aug. *Contra ep. Parm.* 2.3.6 (CSEL 51: 50): "ut inde insaniam cotidianam non solum alios insectandi, sed etiam se ipsos praecipitandi concipiant? . . . Istis non fiunt tenebrae, dum sustinent lumen in falso martyrio?"

[133] Aug. *Contra ep. Parm.* 3.6.29 (CSEL 51: 138): "dicentes 'euge, euge' et iurantes per canos eorum, qui caput sanum non habuerunt, et per compagos eorum *qui viam pacis non agnoverunt* (Is. 59: 8). Quales turbas isti avertentes a Christi unitate et ad suum nomen convertere cupientes interim temporalia supplicia schismatis sui conferre audent passionibus martyrum, ut eis poenarum suarum natalicia celebrentur magno conventu hominum furiosorum, quorum e numero illi sunt, qui etiam nullo persequente, se ipsos ultro per montium abrupta praecipitant, ut malam vitam peiore morte consumant. Non erunt in illa die stultae plebes quibus dicatur, *nos sumus iusti qui patimur persecutionem.*"

[134] Aug. *Contra litt. Petil.* 2.20.46 (CSEL 52: 46): "Illi autem, de quibus maximam invidiam facere soletis, Marculus et Donatus, ut moderatius dixerim, incertum est utrum se ipsi praecipitaverunt, sicut vestra doctrina non cessat cotidianis exemplis, an vero alicuius potestatis iussu praecipitati sint. Si enim incredibile est magistros circumcellionum solitas mortes sibimet intulisse, quanto incredibilius potestates Romanas insolita supplicia iubere potuisse."

And as for those men, concerning whom you are accustomed to raise the greatest hostility towards us, Marculus and Donatus, we don't know for sure (if we are to use our words carefully) if they didn't in fact throw themselves off great heights of their own free will, following the usual pattern of which your teaching doesn't cease to offer daily examples – or if they were hurled to their death by the order of some person of authority. If it is hardly believable that the leaders of your circumcellions inflict on themselves the deaths that are usual for them, then how much more unbelievable is it that Roman authorities were able to order punishments contrary to their customs?

In sermons to his own people, Augustine continued to condemn the link between Marculus' precipitation and the voluntary deaths of other dissidents.[135] Although he had his own agenda that he wished to impose on Petilian, it is no accident that it happened to be the deaths of Donatus and Marculus that repeatedly resurfaced in Augustine's discussions of the value of the dissident self-killings. First of all, it is clear that certain deaths suffered in peculiar fashions counted much more than others, almost as if they had to be suffered in a particular manner in order to be recognized. Our evidence for deaths suffered by the dissident church in the period before mid-century is insufficient to permit certainty, but the special value that precipitation had for them is manifest.

The meaning of self-killing was essentially contested: necessary and highly valued to one party, irrational and criminal to the other. We might consider the case of a dissident priest named Donatus, from the small hamlet named Mutugenna in the region of Hippo Regius. In a letter that Augustine addressed to this priest in 416, we learn that force had been used against him in connection with the imperial laws of 412 and 414 that had proscribed the dissident church and its clergy. The letter is notorious for the way in which Augustine argued that one is allowed *not* to tolerate another's beliefs and in which he argued that one is permitted to use force and compulsion against such persons if it is for their own good. If salvation is at stake, then coercive means, if lamentable, are justified. It was not a view held by Donatus who, even in Augustine's reportage, is reputed to have objected to the use of such "kindly force" against himself on the ground that "no one should be forced to do what is good." The views of the dissident priest were not simple ones; they were rooted in a contrarian theodicy. "God gave man a free will and therefore men ought not to be compelled, even to do good." It was in the context of his arrest and physical

---

[135] Aug. *Tract. in Ioh.* 11.15 (CCL 36: 120): "Ecce Marculus de petra praecipitatus est! Ecce Donatus Bagaiensis in puteum missus est! Quando potestates romanae talia supplicia decreverunt ut praecipitarentur homines?"

removal from his church that Donatus resisted. "As for the fact that you received a slight bodily injury," says Augustine, "why, you are to blame for that yourself, for you would not make use of the mule that was brought for you and you dashed yourself to the ground with violence."[136]

Donatus had attempted more than just throwing himself to the ground. At some later time just after his arrest, he had tried to kill himself: "Recently, when you threw yourself down a well in order to kill yourself, you certainly did that of your own free will . . . You threw yourself into the water. My men lifted you out, so that you would not die. You did this according to your own free will, but in order to destroy yourself, while they did this contrary to your will, but to save you."[137] From all of what follows, however, it seems that a large part of the valuation had less to do with free will or, indeed, in any simple sense with suicide, than it did with concepts and valuations of martyrdom. Augustine had to refute Donatus' clear conviction, supported by Pauline scripture, that his attempt to kill himself was justified as a kind of martyrdom. Augustine countered with the objection that such a death had merit only if it met the Pauline injunction "If I have not charity, it profits me nothing." He then asks Donatus, rhetorically.[138]

To that charity you shall be called, by which charity you are not permitted to kill yourself. And yet you think that to throw yourself headlong to your death profits you somehow, although even if you suffered death at the hands of another person while you are still an enemy of charity, it would profit you nothing. Indeed, as long as you stand outside the Church, separated from the seams of Unity and the links of charity, you will still be penalized with everlasting punishment – even if you were burned alive for Christ's sake.

What is interesting, again, is the choice of killing oneself, by precipitation, in imitation of the death of Donatus in 347, and Augustine's remorseless castigation of this self-killing as counting for nothing. The priest Donatus manifestly did not see matters in this light. He was a member of the clergy of the dissident church who felt that death by precipitation in defense of the truth was a meritorious death, a sacrifice that not only had its own rationale, but also its own particular glory.

[136] Aug. *Ep.* 173.1 (CSEL 44: 640): "Quod autem aliquantum in corpore laesus es, ipse tibi fecisti, qui iumento tibi mox admoto uti noluisti et te ad terram graviter conlisisti."

[137] Aug. *Ep.* 173.4 (CSEL 44: 642–43): "Modo quod te in puteum, ut morereris, misisti, utique libera voluntate fecisti . . . Et tamen tu te volens in aquam misisti, ut morereris, illi te nolentem de aqua levaverunt, ne morereris; tu fecisti secundum voluntatem tuam sed in perniciem tuam, illi contra voluntatem tuam sed propter salutem tuam."

[138] Aug. *Ep.* 173.6 (CSEL 44: 644): "Ad istam caritatem vocaris, ab ista caritate perire non sineris et putas tibi aliquid prodesse, si te ipse praecipites in interitum, cum tibi nihil prodesset, etiamsi alter te occideret caritatis inimicum. Foris autem ab ecclesia constitutus, et separatus a compage unitatis et vinculo caritatis aeterno supplicio punireris. Etiamsi pro Christi nomine vivus incendereris."

A NEW KIND OF DEATH

Augustine's intervention in this problem was compelled by the extremity of the situation in which he found himself. His equally extreme response was to have a long-term transformative power. Unlike many of his forebears in the classical tradition in which he had been educated, he did not restrict his moral purview to an elite or to the condemnation of this or that kind of self-killing as good or bad because of motive, value, or cause. Instead, he created a new kind of bad death. In this new totalizing moral universe, he defined the new death as "suicide" whereby any kind of self-killing was by the very fact an evil thing. He removed it completely from debates over whether it was good or bad according to the circumstance. The kinds of sectarian self-killings that Augustine faced from the 400s to the 420s were such powerful and frightening acts of violence that he preferred to embrace a scorched-earth policy against all forms of self-killing rather than entertain an exception for self-sought martyrdom. After the creation of this new evil, it could be usefully exploited in condemning, for example, the beliefs of a heretic, like Pelagius, as being a kind of spiritual suicide – as willingly leaping to one's eternal death.[139] In doing so, Augustine took the first critical first steps towards creating a special kind of death that was, per se, quintessentially bad. The new immoral person whom he condemned was first named as "a suicide" in the twelfth century. The new absolute category of death was refreshed and finally provided its own specific name of "suicide" in the sixteenth and seventeenth centuries. Both transitions, both sharpenings, of the concept, it should be noted, were not innocent or accidental. They both occurred in times of heightened sectarian violence.

The widespread recourse to self-killing was a symptom of the most intense phases of the sectarian conflict between Catholics and dissidents in late Roman antiquity. In this history, there were phases of the extreme practice of self-killing. As a response or a confrontational practice it had a precise and limited shelf life. No descriptions of the religious wars among Africans after the Vandal incursions of the 430s make any mention of suicide as a sectarian tactic. The most vivid descriptions of the Arian "persecutions" of non-Arian Christian communities in Africa over the remainder of the fifth century, especially the events of the 480s, provide no notices about suicide as a standard response. Like the more organized suicidal responses in other historical epochs, the self-killings that were part of the intense

---

[139] Aug. *Tract. in Ioh.* 81.2 (CCL 36: 530). Note the language: "praecipitatores liberi arbitrii, ex alto elationis per inania praesumtionis, in profunda submersionis... Ite nunc per abrupta, et non habentes ubi figamini, ventosa loquacitate iactamini."

struggle between the Catholics and the dissidents were practiced only as long as the elements of this particular conflict and the organizational forces driving it remained in place. Once these basic structures changed, so did the values informing behavior and the impetus to take one's own life according to certain styles. Self-killing became outmoded, passé. Sectarian self-killings were a specific type of protest that had their own specific miniature history; they were not part of continuing long waves of individual responses to general social forces. They were event-driven. For this reason, they were assiduously avoided by Camus and by Durkheim, but had to be confronted by men like Augustine.

CHAPTER 17

So what?

The Caterpillar and Alice looked at each other for some time
in silence; at last the Caterpillar took the hookah out of its
mouth, and addressed her in a languid, sleepy voice.
"Who are *you?*" said the Caterpillar.[1]

(Lewis Carroll)

Faust: "Well, then, who are you?"
Mephistopheles: "Part of that power which
always wills evil and always does good."[2]

(Goethe)

Who are you? The question had been at the center of the crisis in African
Christianity, as bishops and priests, deacons and lay persons, landowners
and tenants, fishermen and money-changers, craftsmen and civil servants,
and itinerant gangs of young men and women mobilized the full panoply of
memory, knowledge, and emotion that guided their actions as Christians.[3]
As the partisans of each side exerted themselves to enforce their communal
identities, specific types of violent acts were excited at the peripheries of
the struggle, creating more particulars of the world in which they lived.
But given the plurality of identities from which an individual might choose
or have activated in a given situation, being Christian was only one. And
certain elements of identity were more permanent and powerful than
others; some of the most important, like language, were fixed at a very
early age. Identity, in itself, is not an adequate approach to the problem.[4]

[1] Lewis Carroll, *Alice's Adventures in Wonderland and Through the Looking-Glass*, New York, Macmillan, 1897, p. 59.
[2] J. W. von Goethe, *Faust*, Pt. I, Act 2, Scene ii: Faust: "Nun gut, wer bist du denn?"; Mephistopheles: "Ein Teil von jener Kraft, Die stets das Böse will, und stets das Gute schafft," as commented on by Mikhail Bulgakov in his *The Master and Margarita*.
[3] It would be pleasant to claim that the words of the chapter title were inspired by a source as elevated as Miles Davis. In fact, they issued from a Horse's Ass in Philadelphia in October of 2005. Almost oracular in their unexpected appearance, they set me to thinking about mendacity and meaning.
[4] As much, for example, seems to be suggested in the work of Amartya Sen, *Identity and Violence*, when he repeatedly emphasizes the plurality of identities in a given self, with the suggestion that individual

In the sectarian confrontations of the long fourth century, the reported incidents of violence rarely, if ever, emerged from identity alone. There were the additional, and necessary, elements of the mobilizing powers and capacities of large formal organizations like the Roman state and its armed forces, municipal councils and law courts, local and provincial church hierarchies, and the patronal resources of large landowners.

What is more, in disputing and defining their individual and collective identities, the Christian dissidents and Catholics behaved in certain ways, but mostly in stable normal day-to-day relations, only occasionally breaking into episodes of violence against each other. All of these behaviors, including the violent acts, were a game played according to certain rules. The elaborate conventions depended on the continued existence of a complex set of social behaviors and institutions which required deliberation, constant attention, and energy to keep in place. Then, suddenly, almost everything in this set of social regulations was irrevocably changed by a massive armed incursion. In the spring of 429 – or was it 428? – a large war band, whose leadership and ethnic core were composed mainly of Germanic Vandals, crossed the Strait of Gibraltar from southern Spain into the isolated remnant of Roman rule in the far west of Africa around the town of Tingi.[5] Gaining a foothold in north Africa through its vulnerable back door, they began making their way eastward in fits of plundering and killing that forever changed the economic, social, political, administrative, and religious face of lands that had been among the most important provinces of the Roman empire.

Perhaps ironically for the fate of the empire, it is possible that the Vandals had been invited into Africa. The most powerful locally resident imperial official at the time, the *comes Africae* Bonifatius, held the resources of the Roman army in Africa in his hands. In the increasingly chaotic and uncertain situation of the late 420s, he found himself in the same political trap that Romanus and Heraclian had fallen into before him. Perceived by a nervous court as a potential rebel, he was isolated and at risk of suffering their fate. Facing this threat, Bonifatius had an option that his predecessors as Counts of Africa did not have, but one that had frequently been taken up

choice offers a way out of undesired effects of certain kinds of religious-based identity politics. For broader objections, see Brubaker and Cooper (2000), esp. pp. 6–14.

[5] Courtois, *Les Vandales*, pp. 155 ff.: the dates 427, 428, and 429 are attested in our sources, and all seem possible. Scholarly consensus has settled on 429 – see, e.g., Lancel, *Saint Augustine*, p. 473: May of 429, accepting Possidius, *Vita Aug.* 28.4 as decisive – although 428 seems to be as possible. Much reposes on guesswork about how long it took the Vandals to fight their way across the face of Africa finally to arrive at Hippo Regius in May/June of 430 to begin their siege of the city.

by high-ranking state officials along the northern edges of the empire.[6] The so-called barbarians of the northern frontier whom those men had adopted as allies were now close to Africa. The collapse of the Rhine frontier in 406 – or was it in 405? – involved multiple bands of armed invaders that moved southwards through Gaul and into Spain.[7] Centered on a core of Vandals, the armed influx was in fact a congeries of ethnic groups, each parasitic on the other and on what remained of the Roman state in the West. Faced with two bad alternatives, it was said that Bonifatius chose self-preservation. He struck a deal with the Vandals to have them cross the Strait of Gibraltar into Africa.[8] It was the end, one of the last chapters of the western empire's agonizing suicide.

The struggle between the mutually hostile Christian communities in Africa that had occupied the long century before the Vandal invasion was different from the war violence brought to Africa by the northern conquerors. It was sanctified violence in the specific sense that it was the direct result of commitments and quarrels of a religious nature. Its aims and forms were shaped and enacted through the sacred rhetoric and narratives of its participants.[9] At the opposite end of the spectrum of violence from war were small-scale acts of harm that affected individuals or small communities. There is still a contrast to be made between sectarian confrontations and these other smaller-scale conflicts. The latter type of conflict is perhaps best illustrated by the peasant jacquerie in southern Numidia in the early 340s captained by the insurgent leaders, Axido and Fasir. Understanding the relationship between these two broadly similar but still different kinds of small-scale violence – the sectarian and the secular – is necessary since the violent incidents of the peasant insurrection

---

[6] See Shaw (1999), pp. 151 f. for some examples of the pattern.

[7] The date depends on the accuracy of Prosper Tiro, *Epitoma Chronicon*, 1230, s.a. 406 (MGH AA 9: 465) – a source that has sometimes proven less than dependable; see M. Kulikowski, "Barbarians in Gaul, Usurpers in Britain," *Britannia* 31 (2000), pp. 325–45, at pp. 328–29, reviving an argument of Norman Baynes, in favor of 31 December 405; and the rejoinder by A. R. Birley, *The Roman Government in Britain*, Cambridge University Press, 2005, pp. 455–60, at pp. 457–58, who defends the generally accepted date of 31 December 406.

[8] Courtois, *Les Vandales*, p. 156 and 156 n.1, discusses the problems with Bonifatius' "invitation" which perhaps has the air of a later eastern Greek piece of personal polemic; for a skeptical view, and bibliography, see Lancel, *Saint Augustine*, pp. 471–73; see also "Bonifatius (3)," PLRE, 2, pp. 237–40, and "Bonifatius (13)," PAC, pp. 152–55, for reviews of the primary sources, with Diesner (1963). There are problems with Bonifatius' rank in 416–17 (that of tribune?) that hinge on the dating of Aug. *Ep.* 185, and the back references contained in the much later *Ep.* 207.7. It is certain that he was *comes Africae* at least from 423–24, and that it was in the year 427–28 that he ran into problems with the central court.

[9] In this sense, the argument comes close to that of Denis Crouzet in his *Guerriers de Dieu* on the nature of sectarian violence in Reformation France.

were reported to have involved the same subaltern class of mobile seasonal workers, called circumcellions, who were said to have formed the core of the sectarian gangs of the dissident Christians.[10] Even if the nature of manpower was the same, the structure and quality of the two kinds of small-scale violence betray fundamental differences.

The rural unrest of the 340s involved classic forms of social inversion typical of servile and peasant upheavals of the time: the destruction of notes of credit, threats directed towards wealthy landowners, the freeing of persons held under bond or constraint, the end of maltreatment, and demands for fairness in economic transactions, with the rich and powerful being forced to exchange places with their slaves and servants.[11] A classic world turned upside down. These elements, and their combination, had little in common with the sectarian struggles at the end of the fourth century. Neither the rhetoric nor the typical acts of harm and destruction were the same in action or purpose. The constant undertow of interpretation that seeks to identify either stream of violence (or both) as a surge to local autonomy has been rightly rejected.[12]

Like these incidents of peasant mobilization, sectarian violence was also a small-scale phenomenon that emphasized the motives of individual claims and losses. In that light, we might consider a contemporary observer's remarks on what he considered the main drives leading to individual acts of violence in his own time.[13]

This is the same in the case of evil acts where the desire is to hurt, whether by verbal abuse or by doing actual physical harm, or both. This can be done for the sake of vengeance, as when a person inflicts harm on his personal enemy, or for the sake of taking another's things as when a robber assaults a traveler; or for the

---

[10] For a convenient synopsis of claims about these violent links with the dissident church, see Lamirande (1965e).

[11] This violence as a type therefore shares characteristics with many episodes of local premodern rural violence, like the "Swing" riots that swept the counties of southern England in the early 1830s: see Hobsbawm and Rudé, *Captain Swing*, esp. pp. 97–98, 116–17, 124, 195–96, and the facsimiles on pp. 204, 206, 208, and 210 (e.g. of threatening letters).

[12] Brisson (1956) and *Autonomisme et christianisme*, made this case in some detail – cf. Piganiol (1956–57); against which, see Mandouze (1960) and (1976), and Février (1966a) and (1976) – although the last item is more concerned with pre-Christian forms of "religious resistance," the point remains. The classic "refutation" of variants of this view in English-language scholarship was that by Jones (1959/1974), although the refutation only served to show that this was probably the wrong question to ask.

[13] Aug. *Confess*. 3.8.16 (CCL 27: 35), in a discussion of the nature of individual sins and the *libidines* that incite them: "Item in facinoribus, ubi libido est nocendi sive per contumeliam sive per iniuriam et utrumque vel ulciscendi causa, sicut inimico inimicus, vel adipiscendi alicuius extra commodi, sicut latro viatori, vel evitandi mali, sicut ei qui timetur, vel invidendo, sicut feliciori miserior aut in aliquo prosperatus ei, quem sibi aequari timet aut aequalem dolet, vel sola voluptate alieni mali, sicut spectatores gladiatorum aut inrisores aut inlusores quorumlibet."

sake of avoiding an evil, as when one does harm to someone whom he fears. Or from envy, as when a poor man does harm to another who is more fortunate than himself, or the well-off man harms someone who he fears is becoming his equal or whose equality he already resents. Or, again, it might be done solely for the sheer pleasure of seeing others suffer, as is the case with those who are spectators of gladiators or those who mock or make fun of anyone.

The base causes are seen as desires for revenge or material gain, fear and defensiveness, envy and resentment, or the sheer joy of seeing and sensing others being maimed or killed. These same emotions and motives were at play, in some fashion, in our incidents of violence as well. But these drives cannot be neatly calibrated to take into account the actions of psychopathic or sociopathic torturers and killers who were not just spectators but a different kind of person who simply enjoyed killing and torturing and for whom sectarian violence offered another opportunity.[14] Consider the young men, of whom Augustine was one, who found a centipede, cut it in two with a writing instrument, and then were fascinated to observe the sliced-up pieces writhing in agony.[15] What was this? Adolescent curiosity and normal behavior set along a spectrum where others would share in this mode, only on a more dangerous human plane? And what had set the normal model of violence for these adolescents? The savage beatings inflicted upon them by their teachers – more feared than any other aspect of "education"?[16] Or the whippings inflicted on them by their own fathers?[17] Or terrible beatings inflicted on their mothers by their own fathers?[18] Or the beatings and bullying of soldiers whom they witnessed taking what they wanted – from provisions to horses – from their terrorized parents?[19]

As for doing the actions themselves, an understanding of motives, sentiments, and drives, such as the ones outlined by Augustine above, requires

---

[14] The cases from Northern Ireland are sufficient: the Shankill Butchers (just one case, among others): see Coogan, *The Troubles*, pp. 333–38; Moloney, *Secret History*, p. 145, and esp. 221; or the related case of the violence of the hopeless – what Augustine calls the "gladiator mentality" of the man who injures and kills because this is the *libido* of someone who has nothing to lose; see *Sermo*, 20.3 (CCL 41: 264): "Omnino animo quodam gladiatoricio."

[15] Aug. *De anim. quant.* 31.62–63 (CSEL 89: 208–20); cf. Brown, *Augustine of Hippo*, pp. 112–13.

[16] On beatings by teachers, see Aug. *Conf.* 1.9.14 (CCL 27: 8), *Sermo*, 213.11 (MiAg 1: 450), among many examples.

[17] For which there are a large number of references in the writings of Augustine and his peers, and not all of it is simply metaphorical: see De Bruyn (1999).

[18] Dossey (2008), esp. pp. 10–15, for evidence on north Africa from our time.

[19] Physical impositions by soldiers: *En. in Ps.* 136.3 (CCL 40: 1965) and *De div. Quaest.* 79.4 (CCL 44A: 229): see Brown, *Augustine of Hippo*, pp. 23 and 425. And none of this encompasses the conventional beatings and whipping of slaves – but these might well not have been felt as harsh and invasive by those who were not slaves.

complex sets of data not available to us.[20] Even more dangerous are imputed motives. Either in ignorance of local causes or because of the political need to create a social danger, uniform aims were attributed to circumcellion behavior. The danger with accepting these imputed motives, as has been noted, is that the "man hit with a random snowball assumes, only too readily, that it is deliberately aimed at himself."[21] But perhaps the reasons for the social cohesion of their actions are within reach, since there was manifestly a critical additional element present in the sectarian actions of late antique Africa. In almost all of them, a higher and beneficial divine purpose was shared by the community of those who were engaged in the violence.[22] Like the cutting of a centipede presented as needed for "philosophical research," it made the gratuitous cutting of a living being in two with a stylus understandable and acceptable. So too, dissecting one's own religious community in two was worth the pain and suffering. The appropriate metaphors provided the reasons and the justifications.[23] In making seizures of property, in defending their communal groups, in warding off evils and inflicting punishment and physical harm on others, the Christian men of violence were doing good not just for themselves and for others, but for the cosmic order in general. It was surely as true then, as now, that the larger cause was a necessary ingredient, and that "when leaders express grievances in religious or spiritual terms, they give contestants the feeling they are fighting over eternal, spiritual values, rather than fleeting material ones such as natural resources or territory."[24] But how did the competing agendas and legitimations, religious and secular, communitarian and personal, fit together or relate to each other?

Since parties to the religious struggles of the time insisted that the same persons, called circumcellions, were involved in both the sectarian and

---

[20] For just two modern cases where some of this detail can be seen and understood, see, for example, Oliver and Steinberg, *Martyrs' Square*, for Palestine; Collins and McGovern, *Killing Rage*, and White, *Provisional Irish Republicans*, for Northern Ireland.

[21] Brown (1964b/1972b), p. 410/333, in criticism of Diesner, adding that "one is constantly tempted to argue backwards, from the impingement of their [sc. the circumcellions'] activity on organized provincial life, and, so, to assume without question that the origin of such activity must be in a reaction to Roman society."

[22] Of course, it is a surplus but not absolutely different, since parents punish their children in the name of a higher good (or so they say), and soldiers are said to punish others for the greater good of their own country.

[23] One surely does not have to rerun here the very large number of references in treatises, letters, and sermons of the time to the metaphor of the "surgery" (sometimes presented with vivid examples) that was "necessary" to cure a "diseased body."

[24] Stern, *Terror in the Name of God*, p. 84; and Semelin, *Purify and Destroy*, p. 256, who points out why the process of committing the violence itself leads the perpetrator almost to "believing that he is the instrument of the hand of God."

secular violence, we must ask: Were there strong common grounds between the two types of conflict? Did violence in the one sphere incite actions in the other, forming a larger threat to the social order? The problem is that evidence for linkages between the two types of violent action is perilously thin. The data that do exist concerning the involvement of the sectarian men of violence and their bishops with the violent peasant protests of the mid-fourth century in Africa suggest some nervous connections between them. But the potential feedback between the two seems to have been effectively truncated at the level of leadership – sanctified ethnic leaders on the one hand and bishops of the Christian church on the other. Within the dissident church itself, bishops constantly distanced themselves from incidents of secular violence that involved the circumcellions – actions such as protests against the grinding destructiveness of rural debt. Whether in the case of the bishops of southern Numidia in the early 340s or that of Macrobius, the dissident bishop of Hippo in the early 400s, the bishops emphatically separated themselves from this violence.[25] In the case of Macrobius in 409, Augustine speaks of the circumcellion ragings against the dissident bishop himself, and he mentions Macrobius' actions to restore to victims the properties that had been damaged or taken from them by the violent men.[26] This continual formal distancing of dissident bishops from the secular acts of violence committed by circumcellions, including their own *agonistici*, was said to be pure hypocrisy by their Catholic critics. But the dissident bishops continued to assert, to the end, that they were not directly involved with such violence, but that such acts sometimes involved the lower clergy (whom they could not wholly control?).[27] There is enough consistency in the record to show that the dissident bishops did make the distinction, drawing a critical line between holy enforcement and the secular seeking of social and economic revindication.

In measuring or estimating the flows between the two types of violence, emphasis must be placed on the degree of salience and the consistency of the connections. Otherwise, in the on-the-ground mess of violent acts, it was and is difficult (perhaps not even possible) to disentangle individual motives from general effects. At the base level of the priests, holy men, itinerant monks, harvesting gangs, and local roughs, the mêlée of violent

---

[25] For the response of the bishops to the circumcellion violence of 347, see ch. 4, pp. 169–70; more generally, see the section on "Leaders and followers" in ch. 14, pp. 668 f.

[26] See pp. 782–83 below.

[27] Aug. *Brev. Collat.* 3.11.21 (CCL 149A: 287): "cum eorum circumcelliones ducibus clericis tam horrenda mala committerent. Ubi frustra responderunt nihil hoc ad sacerdotes pertinere, cum clericis ducibus illis talia fecisse asserebantur." Note the distinction between the bishops (*sacerdotes*) and the lower priesthood (*clerici*).

acts interlocked in ways that made motives and adherence in individual cases a rather eclectic matter. As in the ground-level relationship of incidents of local and secular violence to so-called Russian "Old Belief" in seventeenth-century Muscovy, another much-studied case of sacred violence, the closer one penetrates to the level of the myriad actions in precise locales, the more the relationship between specific violent entrepreneurs and faith becomes murky and mixed. Especially in incidents of sectarian violence that are well documented and studied from the Karelia region in the 1670s and 1680s, a general association of violent men with sectarian dissent is discernible.[28] At the micro-level, however, the distinction between individuals involved in one type of violence – that is incidents that were tightly connected with religious dissent *as such* – as opposed to another – private entrepreneurial extortion, terror, injury, and executions made in the pursuit of individual gain – is often difficult to discern or to distinguish. Most cases involved a more occasional and fortuitous intersection of violent actors in peasant communities with religious dissent than any systemic connection between the two. Perhaps the same was true of Africa in late antiquity.

Although individual circumcellions and violent entrepreneurs might well have moved from one form of conflict to the other, there seems to have been little salience between the two types of violence *as such*. At the other end of the spectrum, there is little evidence for any serious connections between *these* forms of violence – that is, religious conflicts and peasant uprisings – and the recurrent abortive state-incited regional *coups d'état* that occurred sporadically through the fourth and early fifth centuries. Here the separation is manifest. The wielders of state force and authority, including local commanders in the army as high in rank as the *comes Africae*, had little interest in the bishops and even less in their sectarian agenda. Bonifatius offers the strongest case for potential connections between Christian bishops and holders of state power, and here the sum adds up to almost nothing.[29] There is not a single known instance where he responded to a request from a bishop with the use of the state's armed forces. Earlier Counts of Africa had even less interest. The strident claims made by opposing sides in the religious conflict that their enemies were involved either with rural peasant rebels or with rebellious army commanders designated as enemies of the imperial state must be discounted. The claims are not confirmed by the facts-on-the-ground. The

---

[28] See Michels, *At War with the Church*, pp. 180 ff. and 201–16, and, especially his detailed study (1992), pp. 213–19; and Crummey (2004), esp. pp. 73–76; for general contexting with our problems, see Shaw (2009).

[29] For the connections, see Diesner (1963b).

alarmist assertions were rather part of a rhetoric of fright deployed by both religious factions, but mainly by the Catholic bishops when lobbying the state for its support.

The different spheres of violence do not *seem* to have been linked in a substantial way, much less did they coalesce to form a continuous stream of social rebellion fueled by religious ideology. The reasons for the absence of connective feedbacks are perhaps related to the power interests shared by the specific groups involved in the violence. The aims of the peasant insurgents were primarily secular and economic. For the high-ranking state officials, the concerns were mainly matters of power politics and the maintenance of social prestige and status. Neither of these goals related directly to the ecclesiastical and moral concerns of the sectarian fighters. Priests, and other lower clergy, might well have engaged – indeed, we know that they sometimes did – in fights for economic fairness. But most of the bishops did not. Furthermore, the incidents of religious violence were small-scale events that were restricted in number and extent. They were a minuscule proportion of all incidents of attacks on property and persons, including homicides, in the African provinces of the empire of the period. As far as the context of sectarian violence is concerned, the paradox is that by far most of these other everyday acts of damage and harm have been entirely forgotten. Since the makers of Christian discourse were the only significant recorders of ordinary life events, these other violent acts were mentally discarded into the trash bin of history, never to be accounted for again. The violent actions in the surviving written documents are the truly exiguous number that mattered to Christians, the ones that were recorded and were remembered for sectarian purposes.

It might be objected that it is strange that there were not more overlaps between the different strands of violence, especially in the case of the peasant protests. After all, there was a manifest religious undertow in imagining the justice of their struggle as having something holy about it and in the sacral nature of their leadership. Their dead were treated as martyrs; their leaders were called Commanders of the Saints. Christian ideas were a new language in which the peasants thought and acted, but the aims of their resistance, even if couched in a Christian discourse, were not ones that divided Catholics from dissidents. Millenarian hopes, if they had existed, could have been given voice in Christian texts, if there was a wish to exploit them: "then the first will be last and the last will be first."[30] If Christian texts and sermons produced an underlying discourse of fairness

---

[30] Mark 10: 31 (one of the source "sayings" of Jesus): ¶ Matt. 19: 30, Luke 13: 30; see Arendt, *On Violence*, pp. 20 ff., drawing attention to the work of Franz Fanon; the best recent argument made in favor of such a radical circumcellion socio-religious ideology is Ciccati, *Furiosa turba*, pp. 41–51,

and hope that the peasant leaders and their followers used, why are the connections between their economic programs and the mobilization for sectarian causes not more manifest? The merging sometimes did occur – or, at least, was averred to have happened. Churchmen like the abbot Shenute from Atripe in fifth-century upper Egypt, was one of several such figures who made part of their careers, either actually or rhetorically, by opposing the wealthy and by demanding fairer treatment, including the rescission of debts.[31] They acted as holy tribunes of the people. Given what these men were attempting to achieve, it is not surprising that they themselves had a reputation for violence.[32] But it is also notable that they were mainly indigenous figures found in the ranks of monks and holy men, and therefore more like the *duces sanctorum*, Axido and Fasir, in type than bishops of the church.

For the sake of understanding violence, the complexity of the relation-ship between the secular social and the sectarian violence of the age must be faced. One problem for any such assessment is that our primary source, Augustine, could argue both sides of the question, depending on the point that he was trying to make. If he and his Catholic peers were trying to use the circumcellions and their violence to countervail dissident claims of persecution and martyrdom, then he emphasized the close connections between circumcellions and the dissident clergy, and between their vio-lence and sectarian goals. On the other hand, he could just as easily argue the opposite. These violent men were not holy warriors in any sense at all. They were just common criminals who did not have any connection with the dissident church. The violent acts were the common acts of common criminals in search of gain.[33]

---

and ch. 7, "*Violenti rapiunt Regnum*: L'escatologia dei Circoncellioni," pp. 135–42; but his arguments depend on untested speculation, supposed comparisons with eastern monastics that fail to carry conviction, and appeals to dubious evidence, such as the verses of Commodian.

[31] See Frankfurter (2000) for a valuable introduction, with more consistent emphasis on the sectarian side of Shenute's activities, however; on attacking the wealthy and powerful, see Brown, *Power and Persuasion*, pp. 140–41. Again, so-called holy men were more likely to engage in such activities, including men like Habib and John the Sleepless in John of Ephesus: see Susan Ashbrook Harvey, *Asceticism and Society in Crisis: John of Ephesus and the Lives of the Eastern Saints*, Berkeley, University of California Press, 1990, p. 44.

[32] See Tambiah, *Leveling Crowds*, pp. 231–32, on various species of holy men as mobilizers, some of them looking not much unlike Axido and Fasir.

[33] Notably in a circular letter addresssed to the dissidents themselves: Aug. *Ad Donatist. post Collat.* 17.22 (CSEL 53: 121): "Si quando enim morte multantur, aut ipsi se occidunt aut eorum cruentae violentiae dum resistitur occiduntur, non pro communione partis Donati nec pro errore sacrilegi schismatis, sed pro apertissimis facinoribus et sceleribus suis, quae more latronum inmani furore et crudelitate committunt."

If these men are sometimes punished with the death penalty, or kill themselves, or are killed in the course of committing their bloody acts of violence, they don't suffer these things for the communion of the party of Donatus nor on behalf of the error of that sacrilegious schism, but rather merely to commit barefaced crimes and evil deeds, which they commit with the savage madness and the cruelty of bandits.

In other words, they were just common criminals pursuing their own gains and had no connection with the dissident church or its causes. The other problem is that overly general or schematic interpretations of violence that suggest widespread peasant movements or social revolutions are too much. What is required are measured terms of just how much violence and how much continuity there was in the connections between the two. Alas, these demands are perhaps too high to be met by the surviving data. There are only three relevant pieces of evidence of the requisite quality: the narrative of Optatus on the rural unrest of the early 340s, and two letters of Augustine. In his account of the rural jacquerie led by the Commanders of the Saints, Axido and Fasir, composed in the mid-360s, Optatus gives a vivid account of the actions of laboring circumcellions against the landowning classes of Numidia that had taken place more than two decades earlier.[34] The main, indeed the sole provocation to violence that he mentions is the problem of debt. Creditors were "besieged with threats" from the wandering gangs of men; no creditor could enforce the payments of sums owed to him or her; in fear for their lives and property, creditors rushed to write off debts that were owed to them. It is in this context that Optatus tells of the positions of masters and slaves being reversed. The whole context, which speaks of nothing else, excites the strongest suspicion that these slaves were not chattel slaves (persons owned as property) as is normally thought, but rather debt-slaves who were seeking freedom from the unjust treatment imposed on them by the terms of debt-bondage.

In his lengthy brief to the tribune Bonifatius, written in 417, Augustine placed the same struggle against debt at the forefront of circumcellion actions.[35] The attacks on landlords and their properties, indeed, seem to be concerned almost solely with this problem. Augustine describes all of the actions *as if* they were contemporary, but the sense of his *libellus* to Bonifatius is more historical in tone. Was he replaying the actions of the 340s or was he actually reporting current events? If the latter, then we are faced with a concatenated series of rural jacqueries over most of the long

---

[34] See ch. 4, pp. 168–70 above.
[35] See ch. 15, pp. 695–97 above – presumably one of the reasons why Sallust was such a congenial writer for him.

fourth century centered on violent rural protests against indebtedness. It is, he says, by the threats and violent acts of the circumcellions that both the landlords and their agents are being prevented from debt enforcement against debtors. The one reference to "slaves" going free surely has nothing to do with manumission of chattel slaves (as the reference has constantly been parsed by modern historians) but rather with the release of men who had become slaves to debt.[36] Such persons, technically known as *addicti*, were called "slaves to the debt" or "debt servitors" and were conventionally grouped along with chattel slaves and called *servi* or "slaves" in common parlance. Since the whole of the passage speaks of nothing but debt and debt collection, it is most probable that the documents, the *tabulae*, that were being destroyed were records of debts owed by peasant workers to landlords. It was in the consequence of the destruction of these that they "were able to walk away as free men."[37]

The other letter by Augustine was perhaps not as much subject to spin. It is a letter, written in late 409 or early 410, to Macrobius the dissident bishop of Hippo. Although Augustine and Macrobius, and the members of their communities, knew each other very well, and blatant misstatement was perhaps unlikely, nevertheless such letters were intended for broader public consumption and their language was cast accordingly.[38]

Unity is vanishing, and so we ask for public laws against the evil actions of your people – I do not say *your* bad acts personally. The result is the circumcellions are armed against these same laws. Indeed, they despise these laws with the same madness that they raised in their ragings against you. Unity is vanishing, and so rural rebels are roused up against their landowners and, against apostolic teaching, fugitive slaves are not only alienated from their owners, but are even threatening them. Not only do they threaten their masters, but, headed by agitators and leaders,

---

[36] For what is still one of the better introductions to this problem in Roman imperial society, see De Ste. Croix, *Class Struggle*, pp. 165–70 and *passim*.

[37] These *tabulae* seem to be equivalent to the *chirographa* or receipt-records of debts owed referred to in the next sentence of this same passage.

[38] Aug. *Ep.* 108.6.18 (CCL 31B: 82): "Fugitur unitas, ut nos adversus vestrorum – nolo enim vestras dicere – inprobitates quaeramus publicas leges et adversus ipsas leges armentur circumcelliones, quas eo ipso furore contemnant, quo in vos eas, cum furerent, excitarunt. Fugitur unitas, ut contra possessores suos rusticana erigatur audacia et fugitivi servi contra apostolicam disciplinam non solum a dominis alienentur, verum etiam dominis comminentur nec solum comminentur, sed et violentissimis aggressionibus depraedentur, auctoribus et ducibus et in ipso scelere principibus agonisticis confessoribus vestris, qui ad 'Deo laudes' ornant honorem vestrum, ad 'Deo laudes' fundunt sanguinem alienum, ut vos propter hominum invidiam collectis vestris atque discursis promittatis praedas eis, a quibus ablatae sunt, reddituros nec tamen et hoc velitis ut valeatis implere, ne illorum audaciam, quam sibi putaverunt vestri presbyteri necessariam, nimium cogamini offendere; iactant enim praecedentia circa vos merita sua demonstrantes et enumerantes ante istam legem, qua gaudetis vobis redditam libertatem, quot loca et basilicas per eos presbyteri vestri vastatis nostris fugatisque tenuerunt, ut, si in eos volueritis esse severi, beneficiis eorum appareatis ingrati."

they pillage their properties in assaults of extreme violence. In this very crime it is your *agonistici* who are the admitted leaders – the men who to the tune of **PRAISE TO GOD** embellish your honor, who to the words **PRAISE TO GOD** spill the blood of other people. It's because of the hatred of other men towards your gangs and their raids that you promised the people who had had things taken from them that their properties would be returned. You really don't wish to do this as much as you *could*, lest you condemn the outrageous acts committed by the violent men too much, deeds that your priests think to be so necessary. They boast of their earlier meritorious acts that were committed before that law in which you rejoiced because of the freedom it restored to you. Your priests point out and enumerate how many places and churches they took possession of by means of these men, after they had plundered our places and had caused us to run for our lives. The result is that if you turned and dealt harshly with them, you would appear to be ungrateful for the favors that they have done you.

The letter goes on in the same vein and uses the same rhetoric to list various acts of purely sectarian violence. Both Optatus and Augustine claim a continuity between the persons who committed the sectarian acts of violence and those who were organized and led in violent protests against the scourge of rural indebtedness and its effects on the poor. The imputed relationship between the dissident priests and bishops and the violent men was one of personal patronage, which in turn mirrored the relationship that the circumcellion leaders had with their own rank and file. And yet, as Augustine reveals in this same passage, this patronage had its limits. As far as the bishops were concerned, it did not extend as far as supporting grossly violent attacks on legally constituted property. So, apart from the role of the constraining ecclesiastical structures, what *was* the role of belief?

The problematic and plain fact is that shared sacred texts and ideas fed different scavengers. They were insufficient to create singularly specific forms of violence. Christian images, narratives, and moral injunctions could be used to underwrite divergent agenda. The other factors that impeded the formation of links – like social status and naked economic interest – were more powerful and consistently overrode potential connections between the different violent groups, despite their apparent proximity. If this was so at the level of local knowledge, it was even truer in the formation of links that would have led to salience between these movements and the secular agencies of the state. Neither the peasants nor the priests and bishops had sufficient access to the state's resources to affect its interests, nor did the government have much direct concern with the issues that were said to be at stake in the religious struggle. In the end, the bishops were able to move the state to action only by suggesting that there were serious *secular* threats to its interests and to the stability of its social order.

This was the only pragmatic option available to the Catholic bishops in Africa. They pursued it vigorously and, on occasion, they met with some success.

Larger-scale secular outbreaks of violence within the empire's frontiers were caused and sparked by specific political or structural crises. Sectarian conflicts and their occurrence shared some of the same stings and urges, but they usually happened in a sphere of their own and were contested according to different rules. Political violence was defined, concerted, and focussed in a fashion that made its beginning and its termination specific – this particular man and his supporters had been defeated in this place, which was then the end of it. Whether it was the threat of a Firmus, a Gildo, or an Heraclian, the matter had been decided. The causes of these local breakdowns in formal power were specific to the fragmenting and attrition of the late Roman state and imperial court in the West. The resources with which these internal conflicts were fought and decided were the conventional armed forces of the state. Apart from rhetoric, no substantial data show that persons who were acting *as Christians* and who were motivated primarily by religious belief were habitually recruited *as such* by the political agents. In fact, there is no evidence of any ideational imagination that consciously linked the two. By contrast, the religious conflicts of the long fourth century were never so clearly defined or terminable. They were fed by a vast reservoir of durable and persistent daily thoughts and practices that shaped identity – an habitual behavior of individuals formed by family, friends, and figures of authority – that made their eradication difficult.[39]

Each sphere of violence tended to remain distinct from the other and each had its own repertoire or characteristic forms of physical harm and damage. It is therefore necessary to grasp the violence not just in the context of its intrinsic meaning, but also in its strict historical reality as specific acts of damage done to property and harm done to individuals.[40] Some of the acts of violence were analogues of normal forms of aggression that were allowed, tolerated, and even abetted by the state's legal system. These were the kinds of regulated self-help needed by the courts. The seizures of basilicas in the aftermath of court decisions, for example, are similar but

---

[39] Compare G. M. Fredrickson, *Racism: A Short History*, Princeton University Press, 2002, pp. 147 ff. on the relative power of ethnic and racial, as opposed to religious identities in conflict (with appeal to the ideas of Dickie Clark on Northern Ireland).

[40] See Groebner, *Defaced*, p. 13, who is equally bewildered by what he sees "as a tendency to concentrate on semiotics and to view physical violence abstractly."

exaggerated forms of self-help because they were collective actions and ones fueled by more social animus, one suspects, than the recovery of ordinary pieces of property. The policing operations of the sectarian gangs were not much different in kind, save for motive and animus, from the rural violence organized by landlords and their agents in the Italian countryside of the late Republic. These episodes of violent enforcement did not constitute rural social jacqueries, but rather the opposite. Far from questioning or undercutting the fundamentals of the existing order of social relations and power, they played inside it and formed their expectations within its norms. They were demanding more of *this* justice. It is hardly accidental that the powerful bishops and priests on both sides who strove to control the ideas and the actions of their parishioners were, in the first instance, highly trained rhetoricians and lawyers. This observation leads inexorably to the fact that the courts, municipal and provincial, were fundamental elements in the struggle. Appeals to courts and judicial decisions contributed to acts of sectarian violence; indeed, they were often a direct prelude to them.

Within the self-contained sphere of sectarian violence, the specific modes of the violent acts committed against persons, their "languages" as I have called them, point to the existence of an enclosed and isolated world of conflict whose types and styles were largely determined by the new rhetoric of sacred Christian narratives. In this sense, the manufacturers and purveyors of the ideology – the bishops and the other high clergy, and the interested lay exegetes – had an important role to play in the violence. It took immense and untiring efforts to maintain continuity, and history, memory, and ritual, all of whose elements had to be constantly taught and inculcated into each new generation of believers. The violent acts themselves were an active part of this larger narrative, but they were in constant danger of being forgotten, downplayed, sidelined, or mutated into something different. The expenditure of energy required to maintain the memory in terms of the construction of sites, the copying and production of texts, the imaginative creation of new ideas relevant to the struggle, the mobilization of action, and the telling of stories was not inconsiderable. For the dissidents, at the heart of this African Christian message were the stories of the martyrs and the primal crime, and sin, of betrayal. The problems with these stories, and others in the struggle, are the fictional and feedback effects. The narratives that the participants told about these events so close to them, above all the incidents of violence connected with them, emerged in a way that is truly disturbing – that is to say, the mind creates coherent stories as modes of explanation, no matter what experience or knowledge the participants have of the actual events.[41] The canonized versions of these stories, as propagated by figures of authority, are just as likely to be wildly untrue as not.

Just so, the related picture much promoted among the bishops, the teachers, and the principal bearers of the ideology – that high-ranking Christian clergy controlled matters of significance to them, including violent enforcement – if difficult to assess, is equally difficult to accept. On the one hand, their own writings show that crowds incited by them sometimes went well beyond the control of the clergy in their destructive actions. Such reports seem to point in a direction opposite to the assertions of episcopal power and authority. In 418, the bishop Severus on Minorca explicitly said as much. A situation that began with provocative name-calling, confrontational challenges, hymn-singing and chanting, escalated to rock-throwing, and from that to a full-blown attack on a synagogue. It may well have been, as Severus averred, that his flock disregarded his injunctions to peaceful action and exceeded the exhortations of their shepherd.[42] On the other hand, as with other bishops, Severus might well have been (rhetorically) protecting himself against charges that he was inciting illegal actions – which he was. He was concerned to emphasize that none of *his* people had engaged in theft or pillage, that there had been no intent to steal among the Christians (save for one "bad slave"), that the synagogue had somehow just burned down, and that holy writings and silver valuables had been returned to the Jews. The purpose of Severus' encyclical letter was not just to vaunt the achievements of the bishop and his martyr, but also to signal to imperial authorities that nothing grossly illegal or threatening to the imperial order had happened. The people on Minorca were living on the geographical and chronological brink of the disintegrating imperial state in the West, and yet the Christian bishop still took great care to construct this self-protective front. His response points to the ever-present state and to the power of its legal norms more than it does to any ability of priests and bishops to do as they pleased.

A problem with neat categories is that violence organized for one rational purpose – like the repossession of a basilica or the destruction of a Jewish

---

[41] Pandey (1992), esp. pp. 34–46; Zimmerman (2006), esp. pp. 352–57, drawing attention to Susan Sontag's *Regarding the Pain of Others*, New York, Farrar, Straus and Giroux, 2003.

[42] *Epistula Severi*, 13.6 (Bradbury: 92): "Omnes siquidem frustra reclamantibus nobis saxa corripiunt, et pastoris commonitione posthabita . . . . lupos cornibus impetendos censuerunt, quamvis hoc illius qui solus verus et bonus pastor est nutu factum esse nulli dubium sit." That is to say, that if their earthly shepherd could not be held responsible, since he tried to prevent the violence, it did not matter in the end because the greater authority of *the* true Good Shepherd surely permitted their actions.

synagogue – could draw in freelancers who joined for their own ends, like the easy taking of available plunder. Such parasitic grazing is typical of both animals and humans. It probably happened frequently, as is attested for the Christian attack on the Jewish synagogue at Mago where there were certainly freelance looters. The bishop's account reduces them, tactically, to one miscreant slave.[43] As we have seen, the claim provided legal cover for the bishop. If there was any rapine or looting, then it was due to "bad elements" that were not part of the Christian congregation. But the report hints at the reality of an uncontrolled surplus of violence that existed in addition to what was planned, intended, or envisaged as on their agenda by the bishops.[44] Why should we expect the bishops to be so good, or so competent as to control it? Their resources and powers of command were less than those of the authorities of the state who were no better at exerting full control over their violent men. When forced into the alien difficulties of sectarian policing, even highly trained army units – like the Parachute Regiment of the British Army in Northern Ireland – if sufficiently provoked, can run beyond the immediate control of their officers.[45] This too, is material to our problem, as when regular Roman army soldiers, compelled to serve as public enforcers in sectarian disputes, after having been goaded and hurt, ran amok in the massacre at Bagaï in 347. Even as soldiers, these persons had their own agenda, ranging from vengeance to psychopathic joy, that had to be disciplined.

There was always a deeper substratum of cause and effect that escaped the direct action or control of the bishops. Bishops, dissident and Catholic, were found almost everywhere across the face of Christian Africa, but the sectarian violence in the modes that we have considered – from individual beatings and the violent seizures of basilicas to mass suicidal self-killings – was not. Like dominant economic and social modes of living, there seem to have been peculiar environments in which these episodes flourished. This kind of sectarian violence was found in the core regions of the ecclesiastical provinces of Africa and Numidia, but not in regions outside of them. In the surviving source materials, for example, dissident circumcellion-type deaths resulting from mass self-killings are not attested for the entire swath of lands including Tripolitania and Byzacena to the east, or the whole of the western Maghrib, including the ecclesiastical province of

---

[43] *Epistula Severi*, 13.9–11 (Bradbury: 94).
[44] As is made clear by the bishop Severus' claims: *Epistula Severi*, 13.11–12 (Bradbury: 94): the Christians looted nothing.
[45] Coogan, *The Troubles*, pp. 158–59, in an attempt to control a protest march to the Magilligan Prison Camp on 22 January 1972.

Caesariensis, where attitudes towards and involvement in these specific types of sectarian violence were markedly different.[46] This was so even within the confines of the dissident church where bishops, like Rogatus of Cartenna, separated themselves from the attitudes of their peers in the core zone. In other words, there was a prevalent ecology of violent sectarian action – a living space in which the conditions of work, social organization, networks of communication, and modes of belief were better adapted to sustaining peculiar kinds of communal hatreds. The Christians involved were therefore a smaller subset of all Christians in Africa. For every statement on sectarian violence in the period, it must be borne in mind that only *some* Christians were involved in these types of actions, and that no combination of specific backgrounds or incitements, from martyrdom and sacrifice to general kinds of mobilization, are sufficient to explain why *these* particular people did *this*.

As for the violent acts themselves, their leading edge at the individual or micro-level, whether in the seizure of a basilica or in the ragged lines of gangs fighting each other, was almost invariably chaotic. No matter how rigorous and intense the organization in the regular and more predictable training, supply, and mobilization stages before forces were sent into battle (and there was plenty of this) – the realm of the bishops that seems so rational to us (because it was) – the combat itself, as one came nearer and nearer to the site of the action, was erratic, hit-and-miss, and unpredictable. The mirage of control and singleness of purpose was made more difficult when the availability of existing bands of violent men could be mobilized for different purposes. Successful entrepreneurs of violence in one sphere, for example sectarian enforcement, were able to be redeployed to provide violent force in other cases.[47] The erratic nature of individual acts of violence and the reluctance of all but a few to become directly involved in them provoked the need for planned organization and the remorseless inculcation of discipline and pictures of the enemy. In the provision of the logistical and ideological infrastructure, the bishops of both sides were able to draw on a vast and growing pool of biblical and post-biblical labels that they held in common. Having this repertoire-in-common could open roads to cooperation and grounds for a quotidian *modus vivendi*. When both sides drew on a shared

---

[46] At least in some cases, this regional concentration of sectarian violence is typical. For Northern Ireland, see the discrepancy, for example, between Counties Fermanagh and Derry, and Armagh and Tyrone: M. Sutton, "An Index of Deaths from the Conflict in Ireland,": www.cain.ulst.ac. uk/sutton; and for the Indian subcontinent, see Varshney, *Ethnic Conflict*, pp. 97–98.

[47] For example, the lateral deployment of elements of the FARC guerrilla forces in Colombia, Taliban groups in Afghanistan, or Protestant militias in Northern Ireland into the parallel world of the lucrative drug trade.

script, however, it could just as readily be used to stoke common hatreds. Biblical stories that the two sides interpreted, typologically or allegorically, to refer to their external non-Christian enemies, were readily useable to label close sectarian foes. The closeness of each side to the other, with almost no real differences between them, was recognized by the proponents at the time. But the increased intimacy of knowledge of the other only made the violence all the closer. As in similar sectarian conflicts, mimicry played its role. If the militant Protestant loyalists of Northern Ireland were characterized by their aggressive marching bands, then by the 1980s a "new beast had emerged – the republican marching band, complete with pipes and drums, and the same limited repertoire of aggressive and intimidatory sounds possessed by their loyalist counterparts." And if colorfully militant wall murals began as republican boundary identifiers, they were soon copied in Protestant districts.[48] Likewise, in the sectarian conflicts of late Roman Africa, if no serious matters of belief or practice separated the two sides, the violence was fueled by common boundaries and copy-cat modes. In consequence, explanations for why it continued became more difficult and came to be attributed to "eternal truths."[49]

Of the larger discourses available to the two sides, it is notable that the language specially devised for heretics acquired more power over the late fourth century as interests in heresy developed along new lines. Manichees, above all, came to be reconfigured as a wholly unacceptable kind of Christian that the state was successfully persuaded to hunt down with increasing vigor. On these grounds, persons who were *like* Manichees were now made subject to the hard sanctions of state power. This criminalization of heresy (and the individual heretic) by the state was one of the great legal innovations of the age.[50] It opened up the full use of the central government's power, where it could be mobilized, against sectarian enemies who could successfully be labeled as heretics. Piled on top of this newly created cosmos of hate was a long and deeply developed anti-Semitic discourse that was

[48] Noted by Collins in Collins and McGovern, *Killing Rage*, p. 7; but this mimicry and therefore convergence is found in many similar cases: it is a main theme in Sizgorich, *Violence and Belief*, for example, on the shared themes of asceticism and martyrdom on the early Christian–Muslim frontier in the East.

[49] Monceaux, *Hist. litt.* 4: 167, for example, admitting that there was little of substance that divided the two sides, could not understand the persistence of the resistance and the violence of the dissidents, and so reverted to the convenient trope of racism: "Son intransigeance théorique était en harmonie avec l'intransigeance naturelle du tempérament africain."

[50] See Humfress (2008), p. 141, at the conclusion of a study on the great importance of the law, which had, as she points out "significant social and economic as well as more narrowly religious implications." An earlier study of the same process by Barnard (1995), from a more strictly legal background, is also useful.

also accumulating increasing power and virulence in this same age. All of the talk, however, rarely led to the actual doing of physical harm to other humans or to their property, without doubt because of a natural propensity on the part of most people to hesitate to do such things to each other at close quarters.[51]

Just as the leading edge of the violence at the level of the individuals directly involved in doing it was formally chaotic – witness the pushing and shoving, grasping and dashing in and out, rush and counter-rush, in the struggle over the bleeding body of the bishop Maximianus at Bagaï – so too were the smaller events themselves. If the broad contours of the sporadic occurrences of violence over the long fourth century display discernible patterns – years of heavy violence separated by long periods of relative peace – this was never so in the localized arena in which individuals acted. This is not to say that the violent acts were irrational or lacked understandable causes. It is just that there is no sign that they were planned, intended, or even desired – or that as individual events they were part of, or replicated, the larger patterns of violent action.[52] They were morally surprising. They just happened, catching the people involved off guard, and hailing forth a long series of justificatory and explanatory narratives produced after the fact. At this level, narratives of violence are no different from ordinary-life narratives.[53] The problem for the historian of the tiny microcosms of violence is how to get behind the creative mendacity to half-decent explanations of what actually happened.

The tortured story telling is more heavily freighted in accounts of attacks that involved direct harm inflicted on human bodies, perhaps because they resulted in the shedding of blood. The presence of gore, carefully collected and preserved, indicates the strong tradition both in Christianity and in the deep background of African belief that hypervalued the ritual shedding of human blood. Africans had long embraced this heightened impor- tance of sacrifice. Human blood sacrifice, or an explicitly acknowledged system of ritual substitution, was embedded in their core beliefs and prac- tices. Even if it is not specifically or consciously proclaimed in the terms of

---

[51] Here broadly accepting the general arguments that have been proffered by Collins, *Violence*, passim; in saying this, I also reject (with Collins) a popularly accepted picture of humans as natural predators; compare the same conclusions, reached from a different angle, by Semelin, *Purify and Destroy*, pp. 239–41, drawing attention to the propensity of humans to commit these actions in gangs or groups – as with our circumcellion enforcers.

[52] Blok (2001) catches some of the obvious objections, although mine are rather broader in kind.

[53] Zizek, *Violence*, p. 47: "The experience that we have of our lives within, the story we tell ourselves about ourselves in order to account for what we are doing, is fundamentally a lie – the truth lies outside, in what we do." Not "a lie," I think – which leads back to Frankfurter's *On Bullshit*, on the nature of these narratives or stories which are not quite lies, but rather other kinds of fictions.

the new Christian religion, this peculiar regional and cultural background must be integrated into any explanation of sectarian violence. Despite the ubiquitous presence of the ideology of martyrdom in the Christian empire, it assumed a particularly strong and virulent form in Africa that was very difficult to control by those who wished to contain its effects, but ready to be mobilized by those who wished to use its power. Even its strongest opponents – the rational Catholic secularists at the end of the fourth century, Augustine a leader among them – were forced to come to terms with the power of the ideology. Rather than abolishing the beliefs and the practices or successfully placing their effects in a superseded past phase of Christian history, they had to use them to their advantage and to work within this ideological context. The dissident bishops themselves could not control these same urges, and could only partially direct them. They, too, could only hope to influence behaviors once the heavy effects of martyrdom had been kick-started by state intervention.

The pervasive and powerful ideology of human sacrifice underwrote the supreme values attributed to individual deaths suffered in the cause of defending God's laws. The mass self-inflicted deaths found at the extreme end of the spectrum of sanctified violence were made possible by this extraordinary valuation of martyrdom. The activation of the ideology required a community that not only subscribed to it and was thoroughly imbued with the idea, but which was also suffused with a real and present fear of persecution. But modeling was also important for all types of martyrdom, including self-killing. Exemplarity not only presented such self-inflicted deaths as noble and good, but also as aesthetically pleasing – as an impressive and stylish mode of death that was worthy of esteem and honor by other members of the community. It is also manifest that some of the emotional response attached to these deaths was connected with the libidinal pleasures of gazing at gladiatorial and other secular entertainment violence, an effect that is attested by personal observers of the time.[54] But this pleasure was just as evident in smaller matters, such as the rush of watching a cock-fight in a neighborhood street.[55] The libidinal

---

[54] Salomonson, *Voluptatem spectandi,* esp. pp. 42–54 and 79–90; Barton (1989) and *Sorrows of the Ancient Romans,* pp. 49–72; and Frankfurter (2009). I would only add the obvious to the latter's conclusions: there is no reason why this same *voluptas* or *libido* should not also be found in Christian violence, as well as in the Roman arena and in the narratives of the martyrs. On the matter of personal observation see, famously, Augustine in *Confess.* 6.7.11–8.13 (CCL 27: 80–83) on the effects on his friend Alypius of witnessing gladiatorial violence and the flowing of blood.

[55] Aug. *Confess.* 2.2.2 (CCL 27: 27) lays out the intensity of the connection between the seeing of harm and the feeling of pleasure or *voluptas,* but it was already evident to him much earlier: see the example of the cock-fight (*De Ord.* 1.8.25–26 = CCL 29: 101) and the power of the *voluptas spectaculi.* The feedbacks in psychological effect have been explicated by Coleman (1990) and (1998).

effect of witnessing suicides, however, would have been extreme, since an edgily exalted form of martyrdom like that of self-killing hailed forth an extreme of devotion and worship that surely excited a narcissistic urge in the martyr and a mixture of fear and pleasure in the spectator. The power required to repress this drive, once it was activated, was something that the enemies of the dissidents did not have in their hands. To achieve this degree of repression, the collaboration and intervention of the imperial state with its instruments of fiscal pressure and monetary bribery, bodily threats and legal sanctions, was required. Even so, the mobilization of the state's resources was, at first, only likely to provoke more self-killings.

Although this kind of extreme resistance stemming out of the ideology of martyrdom was possible, it was insufficient in itself to produce violence. Evidence on the various phases of the struggle indicates that the ideology could remain dormant or inactive for long periods of time, a thing of memory used, at most, to provoke spiritual emulation. It is nonetheless significant for our purposes that the narratives of the martyrs' heroism and deaths continued to be preached, celebrated, and re-enacted on a weekly basis, from one year to the next. Nevertheless, ordinary daily confrontations between one church and the other only occasionally produced martyrs of the struggle. The original connection between the unusual power of the martyrs and state-driven persecution, and also with betrayal, was never forgotten and remained the decisive force in our period. The one factor which tended to activate the ideology in widespread practice was the heavy, armed intervention of the state, especially the intrusion in 347, as well as the ones after 405 and 414. This basic fact imparted an imbalance to the rewards. In the logic of this resistance, by definition the dissidents always held the higher ground; the state's resources were directed against *them*, making them martyrs for a glorious and just cause.

To sustain any kind of violence, especially in sectarian struggle, was a difficult matter. Long periods of desuetude or peace characterized the general history of daily relations between the two religious communities. These were its defining moments, and so these long peaces deserve more attention than they have received in attempts to understand the violence.[56] The

---

[56] The strong analogy here, I think, is with Averil Cameron's call for more attention to the formation of orthodoxy: Cameron (2008); it is the basis, also, of Varshney, *Ethnic Conflict*, and his project to understand which conditions do *not* produce sectarian conflict in the subcontinent. As he says, scholars have concentrated too much on the riots and the violent acts to the exclusion of the normal peaceable conditions that form their context.

episodes of violence, by contrast, were sporadic and concentrated in time. Maintaining longer strings of violent acts depended largely on two internal impetuses: the constant availability of organizers provided mainly by the lower clergy, including the lower-ranking bishops, and the manipulation of specific elements of what might broadly be called a Christian education. In this teaching, all forms of oral communication were important, but nothing was more significant than the Christian sermon. Sermons, it is true, did not create the complex of ideas and narratives that informed daily attitudes, nor did they develop the networks of rules and regulations by which the churches governed themselves. What they did do was to take all these other norms and inculcate them into their listeners as norms of expected behavior. Sermons taught more effectively than anything else, not one-on-one or even in small groups, but to the general mass of the whole congregation. The venue served to increase the power of the lesson, since the sermon was received by each individual in a crowd atmosphere that tended to reinforce the communal nature of the commitments entailed by the bishop's message.

But there was never any one-to-one correlation between sermonizing, even the most hate-filled preaching, and violence. Millions of sermons, many of them filled with broad polemic or little hateful stings were preached regularly throughout the decades of the long fourth century, whereas incidents of violence were clustered in time and space. What the sermons did was to provide images and points of focus embedded like little seeds in a much larger and more constant discourse of pedagogy, moralizing, catechismal instruction, and pastoral care. Like the more specific treatises against heretics, pagans, and Jews, and other enemies of the truth, they provided resources that could be drawn upon when needed. The violent words in sermons, much like the threatening language in the imperial pronunciamentos of the emperors, did not automatically produce violent reactions from listeners. From descriptions of responses to the rough language in political venues and in the entertainment theaters of the time, every response from laughter and anger to the enjoyment of a certain *frisson* at the expense of one's enemies was possible. The words only provided real incitement to action when other factors that compelled collective action came into play: the organization of groups, the personal direction of agents, the provision of large resources, and the sensation and fear of mortal peril.

For all the reasons of this complex mix of necessary inputs, religious or sacred violence was not a stand-in for "more important" matters like economic revindication. For these same reasons, despite the heartfelt cries for a history of violence in itself, such an ideal does not seem even remotely possible.[57] Everything strews out into context, in this case Christian and religious ones. The targeting, the modes of violence, and their specific words and symbols were Christian. As noted for many other sectarian struggles, the violence translated specific biblical prototypes into ritualistic violent acts.[58] Labeled circumcellions by their Catholic enemies, the *agonistici* or holy-fighters of the dissidents – armed with their "Israels," named for the very "struggle-for-God" in which they themselves were engaged – were no different. There were concerted efforts by Catholic bishops to present them as an apprehended rural insurgency that threatened the social and economic welfare of the Roman order in Africa. At very few points in the evidence can we see continuities between the actions of the *agonistici* and the incidents of secular violence in which persons named "circumcellions" were involved. The distinction between the "holy fighters" of the dissident church and the wider and general mass of seasonal laborers called circumcellions is manifest, as were the modes of violence when the latter actually moved to enforce a violent inversion of social roles to demonstrate their unhappiness with their daily roles in production and consumption.[59] The single incident of this kind of violence on which there survives a good report by the bishop Optatus refers to characteristic kinds of revindicative demands typical of other social "world-turned-upside-down-let's-return-to-the-good-old-past" jacqueries of antiquity.

The sectarian *agonistici*, by contrast, beat their opponents as a form of personal punishment and discipline, burned their churches to the ground or seized and ritually cleansed them; they scalped the heads of the hated clergy of their sectarian enemies, and ritually dragged them through water and mire, clothed in a *buda*; they beat, dragged, and precipitated former members of their own community who had betrayed it, cutting off their fingers and cutting out their tongues so that the enemy gospel could not be preached; breaking their knees so that they could not abase themselves before the Lord, and blinding their eyes so that the spiritually blind could be seen to not see. In suicidal waves of despair, they threw themselves to their deaths off great heights in imitation of their arch-martyr Marculus; and

---

[57] A good example is Pandey (1992), p. 27, who, after calling for a history of violence in itself and noting that: "The 'history' of violence is . . . almost always about context – about everything that happens around violence," then proceeds to present the reader with nothing but context.

[58] The classic study is that by Natalie Zemon Davis (1973/1975), and her findings have been replicated elsewhere: e.g. Tambiah, *Leveling Crowds*, pp. 230–31, 310–11.

[59] Diesner (1960a), pp. 72–73, was perhaps the first to emphasize the possible polymorphous nature of "circumcellions," i.e. between poor peasants fixed on domain lands as opposed to wandering young men who were *transeuntes* (although these are not the modes of difference that I am distinguishing here), but with no analysis of the differences that he was suggesting.

they drowned and burned themselves alive in mimicry of other martyrdoms of the traumatic year of 347 that took place in the sea off Carthage. Like hanging necklaces of dead dogs around the necks of hated religious enemies, these acts were part of a vocabulary of Christian sacred violence. By contrast, the circumcellions who were at the forefront of the secular rural violence in the early 340s destroyed credit receipts and debt accounts, and made landowners exchange places with their slaves and servants. In doing so, they were dramatically emphasizing defining elements of *social rank* in the here and now. Of course, it was convenient and strategically advantageous for the Catholics to represent the dissident *agonistici* as one and the same as the socially dangerous circumcellions. But they were not. The reaction of the dissident bishops in southern Numidia in the early 340s to circumcellion violence was neither surprising nor hypocritical. As landowners and property managers, and as pillars and leaders of local society, they genuinely feared and abhorred the laborer circumcellions, and they did not hesitate to call in the army to repress them.

Assaults on "pagans" on the other hand, which were also part of this same sacred violence, were precursors to the violence of the dissident *agonistici* and the Catholic sectarian gangs of the 400s. Their attacks were mainly directed against physical locations – temples, shrines, and the simulacra of the statuary – that were centers of traditional cult; or, occasionally, against persons who were engaged in egregious and flagrant public demonstrations of cultic practices, like parades or other such festivities. These somewhat distinctive characteristics might be thought to problematize this kind of violence, although here the category of sacred violence seems to hold. It is just that in this case it did not divide the Catholics and the dissidents, and set them against each other. Rather, this sacred violence united them in a common cause. It joined the violent men of the hostile churches in shared action. The anti-pagan violence of the 380s became a common training ground for the sectarian gangs of both parties in the conflict. The two sides learned to hone tactics and modes of violent action that they would soon use against each other.

Despite all the documented episodes of violence, however, it was the condition of peace and order in which the two sides lived side by side that was the dominant theme of the age. When violence did occur, it happened in irregular eruptions and discontinuous waves. The transformation from individual violent acts into continuous wave-like patterns required immense pressures to be exerted by the larger organized forces of the society: by church and state, by ethnic groups and civic communes. And in such complex mixtures of force, since no planning was perfect, violence sometimes just happened. It did not necessarily require a specific logic of planning or premeditation. Some violent incidents, like the urban riots at Sufes and Calama, were fueled by the appropriate conditions and types of organization, but they were ignited, in at least one case, by ignorance and misunderstanding. They occurred almost by accident, one might say, and not by any rational and knowingly planned actions designed to achieve some specific effect. The more concentrated environment of the town or city, it is true, heightened the probability of encounters and therefore of accidents. But even here the surviving evidence concerning this factor seems to show that it was no automatic predictor of violence.

Some of the factors that provoked acts of sectarian aggression were always in play at local level, but it usually required the special incitements of the state's presence and pressures to activate wave-like crests of harm. This seems to be a common feature of the salience in this type of violence.[60] However weak and fragmented the western Roman state was by comparison with its modern analogues, it was the single large holder of compulsive power that could create the special conditions that might provoke the extraordinary reaction of physical violence directed at persons and property. Such an assertion in something as ground-level and highly localized as sectarian riot and murder seems overblown because of a tendency to underestimate the presence and effect of the imperial state and of local adhesion to its various civil modes. The Christian communities were not heavily armed; they did not have access to significant resources of physical coercion. Nor did they have the requisite modes of formal organization and training for concerted long-term violent action. Even in the final decade of its existence, the Roman state was the only substantial holder of such resources and authority.

The military and police forces, the system of law and the courts, its rules and modes of arbitration, the governance of municipalities, the mechanisms of tribute collection, and the attendant ideology were powerful forces. Since Christian traditions had been created and had matured within a civil empire, it is hardly surprising that the propensity of combatants was to conduct public debates, to compile archives of documents, to file charges, and to go to the civil courts with their problems. Through the persistent lobbying of the Catholic Church, however, the central state was increasingly moved to a heightened awareness of sectarian violence. In 399 injunctions were sent to Sapidianus, the Vicar of Africa, against those who were failing

[60] See, e.g., Semelin, *Purify and Destroy*, pp. 69, 167; on the other hand, it can have a restraining role, if it so wishes, p. 100.

to respect the privileges of the Catholic Church and who were committing acts of violence – glossed as sudden ambushes – against its clergy.[61] But this pattern was present from the beginning of state intervention. Constantine's actions in 314–16 led to struggles to reclaim churches, basilicas, and other church properties. The emperor sent an order to Catullinus, the Proconsul of Africa, to exert more control over the resulting incidents of manifest violence, ordaining full capital punishment and not mere exile for those found guilty.[62] A long period of relative quiescence was followed by another eruption in wave-like patterns of violence caused by the interventions of Constans, which again required the ruling of the emperors against the use of private violence to settle property disputes.[63] The aftermath of Julian's interventions created another such outbreak, and the need for imperial repression of violence connected with property seizures.[64]

Other than occasional violent incidents, no waves of violence are known other than those that occurred after the heavy involvement of the state. The record of the central government's on-and-off direct involvement and its coercive use of legal and administrative force is closely coordinated with rising levels of religious violence. At the beginning, the state was not using its superior force to repress sectarian violence. But it was aware of the fact that if it took specific actions to compel unification of the churches, to force dissident bishops to transfer to the Catholic Church, and to have dissident basilicas seized, a not infrequent consequence would be waves of violent resistance. Violence was the result because dissident enforcers

---

[61] CTh 16.2.34 (25 June 399). Anyone who violates these privileges was to pay a fine of five pounds of gold: "Si quid igitur contra ecclesias vel clericos per obreptionem vel ab haereticis vel ab huiuscemodi hominibus fuerit contra leges impetratum, huius sanctionis auctoritate vacuamus."

[62] CTh 9.10.1, cf. CJ 9.12.6 (Constantine, from Serdica, to Catullinus, Proconsul of Africa; 17 April 317); cf. CJ 9.12.6 (although in this text the place of issuance is given, mistakenly, as Aquileia: see Barnes, *New Empire*, p. 73): "Qui in iudicio manifestam detegitur commisisse violentiam, non iam relegatione aut deportatione insulae plectatur, sed supplicium capitale excipiat nec interposita provocatione sententiam quae in eum fuerit dicta suspendat, quoniam multa facinora sub uno violentiae nomine continentur, cum aliis vim inferre temptantibus [*certantibu*s: CJ], aliis cum indignatione repugnantibus [*resistentibus*: CJ] verbera caedesque crebro deteguntur admissae. Unde, placuit, si forte quis vel ex possidentis parte vel ex eius qui possessionem temerare temptaverit interemptus sit, in eum supplicium exeri [*exerceri*: CJ], qui vim facere temptavit et alterutri parti causam malorum praebuit."

[63] CTh 11.36.14 (Constans and Constantius to Flavianus, Proconsul of Africa; 3 August 357): ruling against the use of violence in property conflicts in Africa. The edict begins: "Gravis ista conmotio est ac non ferenda iracundia iudicis, quae effusione humani sanguinis expiatur." Since the emperor refers specifically to his father's regulation just noted above, this intervention must have something to do with continued problems of sectarian violence, and serious ones involving "the spilling of human blood," a decade after Constans' intervention in 347.

[64] This one is almost certainly sectarian in background: CJ 3.16.1 (Valentinian and Valens to Festus, Proconsul of Africa; 25 May 366): once again, the violence involved the assertion of countervailing claims to property.

would both protect their churches and punish traitors who tried to cross over to the Catholic side, and they would do so at serious cost, if necessary. The events of 406–08 fit this pattern. They led to insistent Catholic requests that the agencies of the state in Africa be used to punish the wrongdoers. The imperial edict of 15 January 409 directed through the office of Mallius Theodorus, the Praetorian Prefect, reported acts of civil violence against the Catholic Church and its clergy, specifically speaking of men who had invaded basilicas and inflicted outrages on priests. In consequence, the emperors ordered that the governors were not to wait for complaints to be filed by Catholic bishops, but were to confront the sectarian armed gangs with the militia units at their command. If their forces were insufficient, then they were to ask for help from the regular army. The Count of Africa was to provide soldiers out of the forces of the line in Africa.[65]

This directive is revealing of the connections between the imperial state, the Catholic Church impetrating it, and the occurrence of sectarian resistance to state measures. The emperors begin by railing against "judges" and the fact that they had done very little to apprehend and punish those committing the crimes. What had the emperors learned? They had learned about the outrageous behavior of certain lawless persons throughout the province of Africa. Their actions threatened not just the ecclesiastical well-being of their own Catholic Church, but also the local social order of the state. Naturally, they responded. The decision by the court, however, was part of a long series of dialogues between emperors and Catholic bishops in which the replies by the imperial court answered sequentially to a series of cases put to it by the bishops. It was a perfect echo chamber.[66] The court was behaving in the same "response mode" typical of the high Principate. To what, specifically, were the emperors reacting? They were responding to what I have called "the Ravenna dossier." Point by point, their orders refer to the specific individual stories of violence that had been drawn to their attention by Catholic lobbyists at court.

Why, then, had so little been done before this time? According to the emperors – again, based on what they were being told by the Catholic bishops – despite the fact that reports had been filed with municipal authorities and with the *stationarii* or militia posts, nothing had been accomplished by the local authorities in Africa in the way of enforcement. As the Catholic bishops pointed out to the emperors, this put them, that

---

[65] *Const. Sirmond.* 14 (15 January 409, to PPO Theodorus); cf. CTh 16.5.46 + 16.2.31.

[66] Studies that have documented the legal responses of the state, although not usually intended to highlight this aspect of the state's role in the struggle, nevertheless clearly demonstrate *the pattern* (which is our concern); see, for example, Leclercq (1920b), Martroye (1921a), Congar (1963d), Quinot (1967e), De Veer (1968i), and Morgenstern (1993).

is to say the bishops, in a bad position. By constantly harassing the local authorities to take action, they appeared to be the aggressive and violent men that they, as holy bishops, were not supposed to be. Accordingly, the emperors ordered the local authorities, including the provincial governors, actively to hunt down the persons responsible for these acts, to find them guilty, to confiscate their property, and to sentence the guilty culprits either to the mines or to exile. Their words repeat the nature of the violent crimes and what the response to them was to be.[67]

If any persons break out into these types of sacrilegious acts and in the course of invading Catholic churches they do any kind of harm to the priests [i.e. bishops] and to their assistants, to the worship itself or to the place of worship, what happens shall be brought to the notice of the authorities. This must be done by means of reports made by the town senates, by the municipal magistrates and curators, and by the reports of the officials who are called *stationarii*, so that the names of those who have been identified can be published. If the act is reported to have been committed by a mob, then, if not all of them, at least *some* of them can be identified and, through confessions of these persons, the names of their accomplices can be made known.

The emperors emphatically point out to their officials that *they* and *not* the Catholic bishops are to find these persons and to prosecute them.[68]

If it is not possible to bring to court a violent mob by the hard work of imperial civil servants, together with the assistance of municipal senates and the landowners – in the instances where such persons protect themselves with arms or by the difficulty of the terrain – the African governors shall prefix the essentials of this law to the letters which they send to the *vir spectabilis*, the Count of Africa, and they shall demand units of armed soldiers so that the perpetrators of such crimes shall not escape.

This time the armed forces of the central state were to be drawn upon. Upon request, the Count of Africa was to provide armed soldiers. The court was, no doubt, in part motivated by the desire to deny the right of such armed mobilization to bishops and the leaders of sectarian gangs.

---

[67] *Const. Sirmond.* 14 = *CTh* 16.2.31 (SC 531: 526; Honorius and Theodosius to Theodorus PP, Ravenna, 15 January 409: "Ut, si quisquam in hoc genus sacrilegii proruperit, ut in ecclesias Catholicas inruens sacerdotibus et ministris vel ipsi cultui locoque aliquid importet iniuriae, quod geretur, litteris ordinum, magistratuum et curatoris et notariis apparitorum, quos stationarios appellant, deferatur in notitiam potestatum, ita ut vocabula eorum, qui agnosci potuerint, declarentur. Et si per multitudinem commissum dicitur, si non omnes, possunt tamen aliquanti cognosci, quorum confessione sociorum nomina publicentur."

[68] *Const. Sirmond.* 14 = *CTh* 16.2.31 (SC 531: 526–28; Honorius and Theodosius to Theodorus PP, Ravenna, 15 January 409: "Et si multitudo violenta civilis apparitionis exsecutione et adminiculo ordinum possessorumve non poterit praestari, quod se armis aut locorum difficultate tueatur, iudices Africani armatae apparitionis praesidium, datis ad virum spectabilem comitem Africae litteris praelato legis istius tenore deposcent, ut rei talium criminum non evadant."

Given the whole past record of the conflict, however, it was an almost certain guarantee of more holy violence.

In another way, too, the state provided more fuel for sectarian fires, if only inadvertently by the normal means by which its legislative system worked and by the presentation of its rhetoric. The late antique court at Milan and Ravenna functioned according to much the same system of petition and response that characterized the Principate of the high empire.[69] Right from the beginning of the division between the two churches in Africa, the court was besieged by churchmen from both sides as lobbyists.[70] Equally, right from the beginning, the court tended to parrot the words and phrases provided to it by the very same petitioners from the side that it ended up supporting. So the violent sacred language in Constantine's letter to the *consularis* of Numidia of 330 is surely, for the most part, an echo of the language that the Catholic petitioners wanted to have emphasized in their original petition.[71] The funneling effect was enhanced by the presence at court of arch-lobbyists, like Ossius of Corduba, who were responsible not only for the packaging of the legislation, but also for the bundling and communication of documents and information.[72] The process created a boomerang effect, but one that was greatly amplified by the fact that what had gone up to the court in the hands of a few bishops now flew back to be broadcast loudly in the emperor's own voice, and to be repeated and posted throughout his realm. Now the "other side" would get to hear their sectarian enemies' own words propelled back at them with imperial force. The desired effect was to cow the other side into obedience, but, in lieu of effective enforcement, resentment must also have been part of the response.

[69] Millar, *Emperor in the Roman World*, is the classic study; see, especially, ch. 9, "Church and Emperor," pp. 551–607, demonstrating the fundamental continuities of the mechanics.

[70] Millar, "Petitions, Disputes and Accusations: The Donatist Controversy," ch. 9.5 in *The Emperor in the Roman World*, pp. 584–90, at p. 588: through 315, Constantine refers to the huge number of daily petitioners from the dissenters who were at court on the Felix of Abthugni case; see Aug. *Ep.* 88.4 (CCL 31A: 142): "ut illis, qui in praesentiarum agunt atque diurnis diebus interpellare non desinunt." As Millar notes, these same petitioners relentlessly followed and harried the emperor on his various peregrinations.

[71] CTh 16.2.7: see ch. 11, pp. 540–41 above. Millar, *Emperor in the Roman World*, p. 590, notes that Constantine was replying to the complaints filed by bishops from Numidia (the document number ten in Optatus' appendix: von Soden, *Urkunden*, no. 30 = Maier, *Dossier*, 1, no. 33, pp. 246–52): the law and the letter to the bishops date to 5 February 330, and both were issued from Serdica.

[72] See Declercq, *Ossius of Cordova*, pp. 161–80; 195–205; and chs. 5 (Nicaea) and 6 (Serdica) on this aspect of his career. He was involved in not only the receipt of existing packages of documents compiled in Africa (as in Optatus) but the transmission of others, like the documents appearing in Eusebius. See Carotenuto (2002), missing, however, what must have been Ossius' role in their transmission to the East. Men like him would make sure that the wording of imperial edicts contained the right language.

The reasons for the shape of the violence are partly understandable. Africa was only a part of a much larger imperial state ruled by the imperial courts of the time, courts that had Mediterranean-wide competing interests pressing on their attention and resources. The internal sectarian struggle in Africa, precisely because it had almost no effect on economic production, on the status or condition of the army, or on the functioning of the tax-tribute system, was not high on the agenda of urgent items that the court had to face. If direct interventions were made and the excessive costs became evident, the state tended to retreat from a losing situation. This was how Constantine reacted, as had his successors, including Constans, and as Julian would have, had he lived long enough. Only constant, persistent, and intense lobbying of the imperial court might find an accommodating emperor on this or that occasion. But the real costs to be faced by the state were destructive violence and the disruption of the ordinary affairs of government. The resources of the imperial state could be used for several purposes. One was the restoration or the transfer of property from one side to the other, for which the state provided formal legal cover and encouragement but often no enforcement. The result was the recourse to violence by the opposing sides who were trying either to block such transfers or to effect them.

To accomplish another of its aims – the formation of a unified Christian church in Africa – the state once again offered formal legal cover and encouragement (and sometimes actual enforcement) for the transfer of bishops, other clergy, and their parishioners, from the dissident church to the Catholic community. To the extent that such actions succeeded, they only produced manifest "traitors" who excited violent responses from the dissidents because of their hard policing against the "vile Judases," as they were perceived to be. Should the state decide, in the final instance, on the use of its military forces in direct enforcement, as it did in 347 and again in the years after 414, the harshness of its intervention provoked recourse to all the forms of resistance up to the extreme of suicide martyrdom. The formal despair of the dissidents was provoked by the attacks by the state on them, assaults that they modeled on the trope of persecution. The brutishness and immediacy of the use of state power signaled an extreme, making it manifest that there was no Tsar left to whom appeal was possible. The naked reality of the state was revealed. And it was just at this point that state power sometimes failed to work. In the long term, deeply entrenched dissent prevailed on occasion because few ancient states, even imperial Rome, could sustain the micro-level presence of hard power in peripheral parts of its regime to repress widely spread local disturbances that were rooted in a mass popular ideology.

QUARREL WITHOUT END?

In ending the song with which he had begun his lifelong battle against the dissident Christians in Africa, Augustine had foreseen that the sectarian conflict might become a "quarrel without end," a *rixa sine fine* – as, indeed, it already had become at the time that he composed these words. Failing the willingness or the ability of one side or the other to make basic concessions that would, in effect, destroy their own identity, the conflict would push the relations to violence. So he and others expected. The aftermath of the great hearing at Carthage in 411 was supposed to bring an end to the quarrel and in the Catholic side an optimism was born of the seemingly triumphant result of the conference. But the events that then transpired, as long as Augustine remained deeply interested and implicated in them – to the early 420s – tended to confirm his more realistic view. There is enough evidence to show that nothing internal to the identity politics engaged in by either side shifted the ground on which the battles were fought as much as did the sudden and unforeseen intervention of a tidal wave of large-scale violence: the Vandal incursions into Africa. The Vandal war bands worked their violence across the face of Africa, reaching the walls of Hippo Regius and laying siege to the city in the late spring of 430.[73]

The difference was that the Vandal rulers of Africa were quite willing to use the instruments of their new state in a much more direct and brutal way to enforce their acceptable brand of Arian Christianity. It was a Christianity that was rejected and excoriated by both the Catholics and the dissidents in Africa. And both parties were suddenly blindsided by forces that were beyond their understanding, comprehension, awareness, or control. All at once, everything for which they had been killing and maiming, hating and hurting each other was suddenly and violently swept away and counted for little. For the Vandal rulers of Africa, unlike the Roman emperors in Milan and Ravenna, Africa was the sum total of their concern. Its confines *were* their kingdom. They had no other distracting agenda. Nothing impeded them from using the military force of their new state to enforce the degree of internal discipline that they desired on their home ground. What they unleashed was a true religious war that had few internal or external brakes on it.[74]

The dramatic events of 429–430 transformed the homeland of the Africans, rudely awakening them to a larger world of which they had

---

[73] See Lancel, *Saint Augustine*, pp. 473–76: they arrived before the city walls in May or June of this year.

[74] For which, the careful studies of Modéran (1998) and (2003) are unsurpassed guides.

always been part. The invaders forced them to confront and to engage with the huge forces that were transforming the empire outside of Africa. The appearance of the Vandals, however, did not immediately transform old hatreds. The backwash of chaos and disruption that followed in their wake provided new opportunities to settle old scores. As, for example, in the far west of Caesariensis, where dissidents of various stripes had been dominant, but where violent and unsettled conditions set in after 430 that created a new chaos of authority. An exemplary case is furnished by a woman named Robba. A holy woman in the dissenting church and a sister of Honoratus, the dissident bishop of Aquae Sirenses, Robba was attacked by local Catholics and died from her wounds on 35 March 434. The words on her gravestone noted that she had been slaughtered by the hands of "the traitors."[75] She was buried in a sacred place in the crypt of a church that was subsequently built on the site to honor her. Her underground place of burial was provided with a viewing window for the pilgrims. Robba had earned the rank, the *dignitas*, of a martyr.

But Robba was an exception. In the new world of the Vandal overlords, Africans could no longer afford the luxury of their inside quarrels. The entire ground on which their struggles had been fought was being radically redrawn. Africa was no longer governed by imperial administrators dispatched, controlled from, and oriented towards, an external imperial court in Rome, Milan, or Ravenna. Vandal kings now ruled their own autonomous local state from Carthage. The priests and bishops who were put in charge of the churches throughout their realm were Arian clergy approved by the new state. The rest, Catholic or dissident, were driven from their churches and parishes, or sent into exile. The nature of the struggle now careered vertiginously into something new – a quite different kind of religious war which, although it might have drawn on some of the same tropes from the past, even to the point of deliberately re-enacting them, was nevertheless not the same conflict. Tax and tribute now circulated internally to undergird a Vandal kingdom whose limit and core was that of Africa itself. The whole elaborate support structure that had sustained the sectarian violence of the previous century, and more, had simply collapsed.

[75] ILCV 2052 + 1108 n + 1705 n (Ala Miliaria, mod. Benian); see Duval, *Loca sanctorum*, 1, no. 194, pp. 408–11 and fig. 265: "Mem(oria) Robbe sacra Dei. Germana / Honor[ati A]qu(a)esirens[is] ep(i)s(cop)i, c(a)ede / tradi[tor(um)] vexata, meruit digni/tate(m) martiri(i). Vixit annis L et red/didit sp(iritu)m die VIII kal(endas) apriles (anno) pro(vinciae) CCCXCV." Her name is unclear. It could be Bobba. Her brother Honoratus, the dissident bishop of Aquae Sirenses, was particularly devoted; he was one of the very few dissident bishops from Caesariensis at the conference of Carthage in 411 (GCC: 1: 188 = SC 373: 838). Aquae Sirenses (mod. Bou Hanifa) was about 35 km NNW of Ala Miliaria.

We should not be lulled into a false sense of continuity, given the extent to which the servitors of the new Vandal kingdom deliberately re-enacted the past as part of the present.[76] These sometimes bizarre replayings of the past completely mislead us in our reconstructions of the history of sectarian violence in what *seems* to be "the same" environment.

The caution is that this story is only one narrative of a type of violence that happened in Africa in the age of Augustine. The narrative made sense of specific kinds of violent acts. But as the wider history of the circumcellions makes manifest, it could not possibly explain all or even a majority of the physical harm and the murder. Like *La Violencia* in Colombia from the 1940s to the 1960s, or the murderous inside wars, the bloody massacres and killings in Algeria in the 1990s, the main story, whether of Liberals versus Conservatives or of the armed forces of the Algerian state committed against so-called "Islamist" insurgents, tells only one part of a larger series of effects.[77] The reasons are obvious. Violence created by the "big actors" and explained by their narrative only "makes sense" of violence that is directly caused by those forces. But these causes of violence create other ones that are only incidentally, not narratively, related to them *as causes*. So other sorts of violence, sometimes a lot of it as in these cases, appears to be chaotic, nonsensical, illogical, mad, or insane. The external epithets always vary within this range, but they always indicate the same pervasive sense of confusion. It is because the new violence has no logic or sense in terms of the big narrative. Some persons might have killed your brother as a suspected "Islamist," but *you* see the killing as done to your brother, or your neighbor, or your fellow villager by someone else's cousin or community. So you gather an armed gang together and massacre the entire village of those people as an act of personal vengeance. And you kill them in ways that they will understand as revenge. The story line is now entirely different,

---

[76] For our purposes, one of the most striking of these is the Vandal king Huneric's law of 25 February 484 on the repression of orthodox Catholics. The penalty clauses in it repeat almost verbatim terms in Honorius' laws of 412 and 414: Victor Vitensis, *Hist. pers. Vand.* 3.10 (Lancel, pp. 178–79). Its reference to the continued existence of sectarian circumcellions has been taken too seriously by modern historians. If anything, the coincidence only serves to demonstrate the truth of the opposite of George Santayana's supposedly revealing dictum about history. Contrary to his claim, in situations like these it seems that the more that humans know about the past, the more likely they are to repeat it.

[77] There is not, as yet, a comprehensive historical study of either case; in the interim, see G. Sánchez and D. Meertens, pref. E. Hobsbawm, *Bandoleros, gamonales y campesinos: el caso de la Violencia en Colombia*, 2nd ed., Bogotá, El Ancora, 1986 (Engl. transl. *Bandits, Peasants and Politics: The Case of "La Violencia" in Colombia*, transl. A. Hynds, Austin, University of Texas Press, 2001); and Aït-Larbi *et al.* (1999), for some of the basic "facts." Both episodes of violence have been glossed as "civil wars" or "virtual civil wars" with which category, admittedly, they share characteristics, although the label (in my view) allows one to avoid the substantial differences.

and it rarely gets told. And sometimes, as in Colombia and Algeria, there is a lot of this other violence that cannot be contained by the "big story."

This observation confronts us with the problem of the conditions under which the one kind of violence – the religious or sectarian – was begun, developed, and sustained. The onset of violence of the quality and kind associated with civil-oriented religious communities can be sudden and almost unforeseen. Using a familiar example from more recent times, it might be pointed out that in terms of violent homicides, until the year 1971 Northern Ireland was more peaceful than Wales, Scotland, or England. It was the intrusion of the state with armed force, the polarization produced by a new agenda, and then the spark of a violent incident that provoked a sudden escalation of sectarian violence throughout the last three decades of the millennium. If the Bloody Sunday of 30 January 1972 was a threshold event, it was so because the central state had already created the conditions under which it could happen. The Paras and other units of the British Army had been put in place and had already created a hated face of external force. Any schematic picturing of the course of homicidal violence in Northern Ireland between the late 1960s and the late 1990s shows the same, apparently inexorable shape of a warped bell-like curve of rising, cresting, and falling to reach a final dissipation of the murderous side of sectarian violence.[78] As this case also indicates, different types of sectarian violence can take off and then end almost as surely as they have begun.[79] The violence experienced the sudden take-off of any style, fashion, or similar spread of ideas and actions with its own epidemiology. This is not to say that it was nothing other than an infectious disease, or that its rising and falling off was generated, in some predictable fashion, by purely internal impulses. It could be brought to an end by the more overwhelming violence of external circumstances or outside forces.

Augustine himself lived just long enough to witness this larger violence destroy his life's work in Africa.[80] As he lay bedridden in old age, dying in the midsummer heat of August 430, reading the Psalms fixed to the wall close to his failing eyes, the world that he had struggled so hard to shape was permanently changing in ways that he would not live to see. In gazing at the Psalms, did he perhaps read the one that sang about

---

[78] P. Richards, "Homicide Statistics," *House of Commons*, Research Paper 99/56 (27 May 1999): graph: "National Homicide Rates, including Northern Ireland," p. 15; see also, "The Troubles" in Wikipedia: graphs and charts under § 7, "Casualties."

[79] Between 1999 and 2006, the average number of homicides connected with "The Troubles" had fallen to about 9-10 per annum (source: Wikipedia, "The Troubles," 10.4, "The Casualties: Chronological Listing").

[80] Brown, *Augustine of Hippo*, p. 429.

the absolute brevity and transience of human life?[81] Over the long fourth century, from the first Christian emperor's reign to the fragmentation of the empire in the West, African Christians had enacted their own story, in the myriad doings of their daily lives as they lived them from one generation to the next, with whatever expenditure of blood and coin was demanded. The big struggle between their two churches was their human drama. These conflicts were part of a long and complex game, one that mobilized the most profound sentiments and beliefs. It was a struggle whose ideas were to have significant consequences not in Africa where it was played out, but elsewhere. Otherwise, on the stage where the Africans of this age loved and hated, every living element in their story was to be permanently effaced, without a trace.

[81] Psalms 103: 15–16: "And as for man, his days are like grass. / He will flourish like the flowers of the field; / but when winds pass over the field, they will not last, / and their place will know them no more." Augustine, of course, had commented on these very lines: *En. in Ps.* 102. 22–23 (CCL 40: 1470–71). His text is close to, but not the same as the VG: "Homo tamquam fenum dies illius [or, eius] / sicut flos agri, ita florebit. // Quoniam spiritus pertransibit in eo, et non erit, / et non cognoscet amplius locum suum."

Bishops and bishoprics in Africa:
the numbers

The best analysis of the numbers of bishops who represented both sides at the Conference of Carthage in 411, and of the total number of dioceses that each church had in Africa in the first decades of the fifth century, has been provided by Lancel.[1] The treatment of the same subject here is offered as an exposition and extension of his data, with a few minor modifications and additions. The record of the conference, however, is only a partial guide to the numbers of bishops and bishoprics in Africa at the time: it only records the count of the bishops who happened to be alive, healthy, and able to make it to the conference site at Carthage. It cannot therefore be taken to be a complete report that would permit the reconstruction of distribution maps that neatly contrast "Donatist" as opposed to Catholic sees. Quite apart from the problem of the not insignificant number of dioceses whose location is not even approximately known and which therefore cannot be put on any map, there is the persistent problem of the existence of an opposing religious community that is simply not mentioned in the record. It is difficult to believe, for example, that there was no Catholic community whatsoever at Lepcis Magna, Sabratha, and Oea, especially since we know from Augustine's letters that, as we would expect, they did in fact exist. There were simply good reasons why Catholic bishops from these places did not make it to Carthage in May and June of 411. Secondly, there are many cases where there might not exist an bishop from the opposing side present in Carthage, but where the internal record of the conference proceedings attests the existence of an opposing community, often headed by a priest in the absence of a bishop who was ill, recently deceased, or otherwise not able to be declared at Carthage. Then again, it was occasionally the case

---

[1] Lancel, "La représentation des deux églises à la conférence de 411," ch. 2 in *Actes de la Conférence*, 1: 107–90.

that a recent act of "betrayal" suddenly left no head for one of the two communities to declare their presence at Carthage. The existence of a sole declarant in such a case surely does not mean that there did not exist a Catholic or dissident community in the town. When all these factors are taken into account, the actual number of cases where neither church had any representation in any given African community is appreciably reduced. The map then looks rather different from the conventional ones that signal the presence (or not) of bishops at the meeting of 411.

There has been much historical prognostication about the numbers of bishops but, as Lancel has pointed out, the total sum of bishops that was formally announced by each side in the secretarial record of the conference cannot be made to match the total numbers of bishops who actually declared their presence in the roll call in the same document. In his reconstruction of the numbers, Courtois claimed 303 Donatists and 269 Catholics at the Conference.[2] In his count, he arrived at 127 bishoprics where Catholics were alone, 167 where dissidents were alone, and 142 dioceses that had both Catholic and Donatist bishops. None of my counts, however, has been able to confirm these numbers. Courtois also claimed 142 absent, for a total of 430 bishops. But it is generally conceded that the total number of bishops and bishoprics in Africa must have exceeded the total attested for the Conference of 411, and by a rather significant number. Courtois guessed that a third were not present and therefore accounted for, and so he set the grand total of all Catholic and dissident bishops in Africa at about 690; Morcelli set it at a higher number of 720 and Ferrère at a much lower number of 500 – again, all guesses.[3] Most of the bishops who declared their presence were from provinces other than Caesariensis, which alone represents the huge shortfall. On other lists, the bishops from this province alone represent about a fifth of all bishops ever known. They should have numbered something like 120 of the total attested for 411; this number, more or less, is confirmed by a later list of African bishops dating to the year 484. That would add something like 70–80 bishops to the potential of all bishops in the lists of 411 and would indicate a grand total that would indeed be in the range of 675–700 for all Catholic and dissident bishops at the beginning of the fifth century. That is perhaps the best general estimate that can be achieved on the basis of the surviving evidence.

---

[2] Courtois, *Les Vandales*, pp. 110–11.   [3] See Lamirande (1965b).

Total Number of Dioceses Attested for the Conference of Carthage of 411

	Trip	Byzac	Proc	Num	Sitif	Caes	x	Total
Shared	3	34	64	62	11	16	8	198
Dissident only	3	29	18	28	14	16	41	149
Catholic only	1	21	33	14	3	3	7	82
Total	7	84	115	104	28	35	56	429

Abbreviations: As in all the tables that follow: Byzac = Byzacena; Caes = Mauretania Caesariensis; Num = Numidia; Proc = Proconsularis; Sitif = Mauretania Sitifensis;
Trip = Tripolitania; x = unknown

Bishops at the Conference of Carthage of 411

A: Geographical Division of All Bishops Mentioned at the Conference

	Trip	Byzac	Proc	Num	Sitif	Caes	x	Total
Catholic	4	53	97	73	13	18	15	273
Dissident	6	59	70	87	25	32	52	331
Total	10	102	167	160	38	50	67	604

B: Bishops Who Were Unopposed in their Dioceses in Any Fashion

	Trip	Byzac	Proc	Num	Sitif	Caes	x	Total
Catholic	1	22	36	14	3	3	7	86
Dissident	3	28	17	28	14	15	42	147
Total	4	50	53	42	17	18	49	233

C: Bishops Who Were Opposed in their Dioceses only by Priests

	Trip	Byzac	Proc	Num	Sitif	Caes	x	Total
Catholic	0	3	7	2	0	1	0	13
Dissident	0	0	0	3	1	2	0	6
Total	0	3	7	5	1	3	0	19

D: Bishops Absent from the Conference (for any cause)

	Trip	Byzac	Proc	Num	Sitif	Caes	x	Total
Catholic	0	0	3	11	1	3	0	18
Dissident	1	9	12	16	2	5	6	51
Total	1	9	15	27	3	8	6	69

E: Bishops Absent from their Dioceses Because of Death

	Trip	Byzac	Proc	Num	Sitif	Caes	x	Total
Catholic	0	0	1	5	0	0	0	6
Dissident	0	6	7	3	0	3	1	20
Total	0	6	8	8	0	3	1	26

F: Bishops Actually in Attendance at the Meeting (= A – D)

	Trip	Byzac	Proc	Num	Sitif	Caes	x	Total
Catholic	4	53	94	62	11	15	15	254
Dissident	5	50	58	71	23	28	46	281
Total	9	103	152	133	34	43	61	535

CATHOLIC AND DISSIDENT BISHOPRICS: TOTAL NUMBERS EVER ATTESTED

Region	Number	As a percentage of those of known location	As a percentage of all cases
Tripolitania	6	1	1
Byzacium	135	21	18
Proconsularis	150	23	20
Numidia	174	27	23
Sitifensis	52	8	7
Caesariensis	130	20	17

(cont.)

Region	Number	As a percentage of those of known location	As a percentage of all cases
Unknown	99		13
Total	746		

Percentages to the closest 1%

Sources: Lancel, *Actes de la Conférence*; S.-M. Pellistrandi, "Fastes de l'Eglise d'Afrique," PAC, pp. 1243–1300; and the discussions by Duval (1980) and (1984). Note that the number of "unknowns" reflects the element of uncertainty in the identification of some of these bishoprics. For the majority, however, the regional identification is either certain or reasonably certain. From the testimony of Victor Vitensis, *De pers. Prov. Afric.* 1.29 (Lancel: 110), it appears that the number of bishops for the provinces of Zeugitana and the old proconsular province totaled 164 in the late fifth century.

Origins of the division: chronology

The pace and the order in which events occurred that led to the emperor Constantine's intervention in the affairs of the African church, and the ensuing permanent division in the Christian community in Africa, are matters of dispute. The differences can be outlined briefly. Traditionally, a "compressed" chronology has been preferred. The compressed chronology places most of the significant causal steps close in time to the emperor Constantine's involvement in the dispute that led to the separation of the two churches. This chronology compacts the events leading to the division within the church in Africa into the years between 311 and 313. By contrast, others have argued for a "long" chronology that spreads these events out over a greater span of time, in some cases to years well before the time of Constantine's intervention.[1] The long chronology is clearly to be preferred. In fact, I shall argue for a slightly longer chronology than that proposed by some revisionists. Here are the facts.

EVENTS AT CARTHAGE BEFORE AND DURING THE PERSECUTION OF 303–305

We might begin with a brief mise-en-scène. Events involving Mensurius, the bishop of Carthage, just before and during the years of the persecution of Diocletian and Maximian in 303–05, are essential to an understanding of the sordid infighting that erupted within the church immediately after the end of the persecution. Of the many events, there is one that is central to what happened afterwards. It involved three actors: Mensurius, the bishop of Carthage, an old trusted woman who was a parishioner of the church, and, finally, the powerful body of Elders or *seniores*. The church of Carthage

---

[1] Favoring the short chronology: Monceaux, *Hist. litt.* 4, ch. 1; Frend, *Donatist Church*, pp. 15–21; Frend and Clancy (1977), indeed, almost all of the standard publications on the subject before Barnes and Lancel assume this short chronology. Arguing for a longer chronology, see Barnes (1975) and Lancel (1979).

possessed not only many landed properties and buildings, but also valuable chattels in the form of thesaurized wealth, including a large number of objects in gold and silver. As the persecution began, it was Mensurius' reasonable fear that the authorities would begin to seize church property, not just taking copies of scriptures or seizing its fixed assets in churches and basilicas. If its movable wealth could be protected and hidden, it would be able to be recovered when the persecution ended. Accordingly, before he was summoned to a hearing before the Roman authorities, Mensurius placed these valuables in the hands of the Elders. In order to provide a back-up check on the whereabouts and precise nature of this wealth, Mensurius also placed a separate accounting of the items and their whereabouts, in the form of a *commonitorium* or written memorandum, in the hands of a certain trusted old woman. Just in case he did not return from his encounter with the Roman authorities, and did not outlast the forces of the persecution, the *seniores* would have the wealth to be re-assembled for the use of the church and, as a backcheck, the old woman would have a separate full list of the hidden items.

In what year was the bishop Mensurius hailed before the governor? During the great persecution of 303–05, or much later, as the traditional historians have had it, in 311? Any answer has to begin with the context provided by the account in Optatus, our sole good source. He leaves no doubt about when these events were happening. His account of the summons to Mensurius takes place the *middle* of his narrative of the great persecution of 303–05. The specific incident, involving a deacon in the Carthaginian church named Felix, is directly preceded by events that were part of the Diocletianic persecution of 303–05, and it is directly followed by more events in this same persecution. It is part of an unbroken sequence in the flow of this narrative.[2]

Isdem temporibus Felix quidam diaconus qui per famosam nescio quam de tyranno imperatore tunc factam epistulam reus appellatus est, periculum timens apud Mensurium episcopum delituisse dicitur.

When was "this same time" – *isdem temporibus* – and who was the "tyran-nical emperor" about whom Felix wrote the defamatory letter, the *famosa epistula*? The standard answer in most modern histories, encyclopedias, and prosopographies (including PAC) is that this happened in 311 and that the "tyrannical" emperor was Maxentius. These are improbable answers. They run against the natural meaning of the whole of Optatus' text and against the context in which he places the events. Although Optatus can

---

[2] Optatus, *Contra Parm.* 1.17.1 (SC 412: 208).

at times be a little loose with chronology, the plain fact is that up to the point that he begins narrating the incident that involved the deacon Felix, he has been narrating the events in the first stages of the persecution of 303–05. He then begins this paragraph with the words *isdem temporibus* – "at this same time." Moreover, he *follows* his account of the Felix incident directly with more narrative concerning the same persecution of 303–05. It is therefore manifest that *he* regarded the phrase "at this time" to signal events taking place within the context of the persecution of 303–05, and not many years later.

So who is the "tyrannical" emperor against whom the deacon Felix wrote his inflammatory letter? To Christians, the term "tyrant" signaled a delegitimized and therefore persecuting emperor. Optatus signals that the history of the persecution in Africa was marked by two great persecutions, each of which he sees as managed by a doublet of persecuting emperors. The first, the persecution of "the lion," was that associated with Decius and Valerian (250/258). The second persecution, that of "the bear," was the persecution of Diocletian and Maximianus (303–05). The tyrannical emperor against whom the deacon Felix wrote his letter, therefore, is most probably Maximianus, although it cannot be completely excluded that he might have issued a condemnatory letter against Diocletian, the original issuer of the edict of persecution. The story then continues:[3]

> Quem cum postulatum Mensurius publice denegaret, relatio missa est. Rescriptum venit ut, si Mensurius Felicem diaconum non reddidisset, ad palatium dirigeretur . . . Profectus causam dixit. Iussus est reverti, ad Carthaginem pervenire non potuit.

From this it seems that Mensurius was summoned either to the court at Rome or to the governor's palace at Carthage – *palatium* could refer to either – where he faced a judicial proceeding. Mensurius was ordered to go back home, but he was not allowed to return to his seat at Carthage. In either case, there is no evidence about who the emperor or governor was. There are therefore no independent grounds for arbitrarily shifting the whole mise-en-scène from that clearly indicated by Optatus to the imperial court of Maxentius at Rome in 311. In Optatus' account, all of the happenings at Carthage are firmly placed *before* Maxentius' edict that restored freedom to the Christians, and that edict must surely be dated to a time soon after Maxentius' elevation to imperial power in Rome on 26 October 306.[4]

Furthermore, none of the narrative as we have it makes any sense if Mensurius, the bishop of Carthage, had returned to Carthage after the

---

[3] Optatus, *Contra Parm.* 1.17.1–2 (SC 412: 209–10).   [4] Barnes (1975).

persecution to resume his position as primate of Africa, simply to tarry on there for another five or six years, until 310 or 311, waiting for the Felix episode to happen. Mensurius was either exiled, probably right at the beginning of the persecution in 303, or he was executed, or he died while in detention or in the process of exile; or he might even have died a natural death at the time of his return to Carthage or very shortly afterwards. In any event, he did not return to Carthage to resume his position as bishop of Carthage following the persecution. If he *had* returned there would have been no need of a huge dispute or brouhaha over the document, the *commonitorium*, that he had placed in the hands of a certain old woman in the Christian community at Carthage. There would have been no need, since Mensurius himself knew the whereabouts of the treasure in gold and silver objects that had been placed for safekeeping in the hands of the Elders, the *seniores*. This is *not* the situation that Optatus portrays as emerging in Carthage after the persecution. These events, marked by a refusal of the *seniores* to surrender the church's wealth that they had in their hands, and the need to consult the *commonitorium* of Mensurius in the hands of the old woman, could not have happened if Mensurius had returned to Carthage in mid- to late 305 to resume his position as bishop of Carthage. He himself would have known who possessed the valuables and they would have been reclaimed from the *seniores*. The struggle to appoint a successor to Mensurius must therefore have occurred immediately following the end of the persecution. It took place precisely because there was no bishop in the *prima sedes* at Carthage, so one had to be found and quickly.

The first question, therefore, is: When did the persecution end or when was it later *perceived* to have ended. Trials were being conducted at least until mid-305, so one must strongly suspect that the persecution was coterminous with the governorships of Anullinus in the proconsular province and Florus in Numidia. Their terms would have ended some time in late spring or mid-summer but, ordinarily, no later than April/May of 305. It was the end of persecution that cued the infighting among various factional leaders in the church at Carthage. By the autumn months of 305 – at latest by the early months of 306 – the struggle for the succession would have emerged in Carthage, first led by factions around men named Botrus and Caelestius, of whom we know very little, and then, subsequently, by supporters of Caecilianus and Maiorinus. The appeal to the Numidian bishops must also date to this same period, more precisely to the second phase of the struggle when Botrus and Caecilius had fallen out of the running and the main contention now shifted to a struggle between Caecilianus and Maiorinus. The appeal of the *seniores* to external sources of support for their position was surely an immediate part of the struggle between them and Caecilianus over access to the gold and silver valuables of the church that had been placed in their hands. This struggle was surely well underway by the early months of 306. This is the approximate dating of events as they were transpiring at Carthage. The way that these events proceeded further, however, was connected with other events that were taking place about this same time at Cirta, far to the west in Numidia.

THE MEETING OF NUMIDIAN BISHOPS AT CIRTA

The main problem with dating a meeting of a dozen Numidian bishops at Cirta is that the document, the "ancient parchment" in the hands of the Catholic bishops at the Conference of Carthage in 411, was in error concerning the date.[5] As his opponents eagerly pointed out when Augustine held the document in his hands at the time of the great conference, the date in it could not be correct. Augustine later admitted the flaw. The date on the document that the Catholics had in their possession at the Carthage conference – which specified 4 March 303 – was manifestly impossible.[6] The dissidents immediately pointed to the mistaken date as evidence that the document was a forgery. On the problem with the date, they were right and they knew it. If the document itself *was* genuine, however, then the copyist had somehow made an error or had copied the wrong date from another document in the same dossier. The enforcement of Diocletian's (first) edict had not even begun in Africa by the first week of March of that year. Augustine also recognized this. He therefore suggested an emendation of the date to the year 305.[7] This new date was nothing more than an educated guess on his part. It was known that the persecution generally had ended some time in the year 305, and there is no reason why the sitting governors

---

[5] For the text of the so-called "Council of Cirta," see Maier, *Dossier*, 1: no. 7, pp. 112–18; for the debates, see Fischer (1986); the different positions are reviewed in detail in Duval, *Chrétiens d'Afrique*, who, agnostically, returns to the conventional date of 305, also preferred by Fischer's (1986) resurvey of the problem.

[6] Aug. *Brev. Coll.* 3.17.32 (CSEL 53: 81): "consulibus facta sunt Diocletiano novies et Maximiano octies pridie Idus Februarias, gesta autem episcopalia decreti Cirtensis post eorundem consulatum tertio nonas Martias." For a brief overview of the problems, see De Veer (1968c).

[7] It has traditionally been accepted that there were four edicts of persecution issued by Diocletian. This formula, however, does not seem to work very well for the African evidence. It has therefore been proposed by Vita-Evrard (1989), following suggestions made by Kolb (1988), that there was in fact only one edict, followed by three mandates on its specific application, and that governors in the western provinces, certainly in Africa, applied tests of sacrifice and turification right from the beginning as part of their process of "testing" Christians. However one parses the details, it is certain that western governors were working only on the basis of the first edict of 23 February 303: see Barnes, *Constantine and Eusebius*, p. 23.

would have ceased and desisted from their activities while still in office.[8] If the document is genuine, then the date on the copy that Augustine and his Catholic peers had in their possession at Carthage in 411 was wholly in error. It had been miscopied from some other source and must be dismissed. Not only the year, but also the month and day are probably erroneous.

If we accept the testimony that the meeting, a gathering of twelve Numidian bishops assembled to ordain Silvanus as bishop of Cirta, was held "after the persecution" – *post persecutionem* – and people generally accepted when this was (as seems probable), then another possibility must be sought.[9] That it was soon after the formal end of the persecution is made clear by another statement that the meeting was held *before* the arrangements had been made for the formal return of their church properties, including basilicas, to the Christians. These restorative actions must have been part of decrees issued by Maxentius soon after his accession on 26 October 306, decrees that were quickly conveyed to the western provinces. Optatus (1.16) speaks of Maxentius as "the restorer of Christian freedom." It is clear that (1.18) these actions were meant to signal the end of the persecution in Africa and that they were co-ordinated with a subsequent decree of Maxentius that formally restored freedom to the Christians.

Tempestas persecutionis peracta et definita est. Iubente Deo indulgentiam mittente Maxentio Christianis libertas est restituta.

The only good date that we have for the meeting is that offered by the writer who is the earliest person to make explicit reference to it, Optatus of Milevis, who sets it on 13 May, but who does not mention the year. If the meeting actually took place, and if its records are genuine, then there are good reasons to believe that Optatus, from the city of Milevis, just to the west of Cirta, was a person who was likely to have had access to the correct date. The year, therefore, must be 306. Augustine's guess of 305 is just possible as a guess, since the successors to Anullinus and Florus *could*, just possibly, have been in Africa as early as May of that year but, given the normal rotation of governors, this seems unlikely. The year

---

[8] Vita-Evrard (1989) and others have postulated an end of the persecution by the summer of 304, claiming that persecutions did not extend beyond the governorships of Anullinus and Florus (1989, pp. 311–12). This claim, however, requires the redating of the death of Crispina to 5 December 303, in the face of explicit manuscript testimony as to the year (i.e. 304).

[9] Optatus, *Contra Parm.* 1.14.1 (SC 412: 202): "Hi et ceteri ... post persecutionem apud Cirtam civitatem, quia basilicae necdum fuerant restitutae, in domum Urbani Carisi consederunt, die III Idum Maiarum, sicut scripta Nundinarii tunc diaconi testantur et vetustas membranarum testimonium perhibet"; it is also stated by Augustine: "post persecutionem codicum tradendorum" (*Contra Cresc.* 3.26.29 = CSEL 52: 435), but it must be suspected that he is dependent on Optatus.

307, on the other hand, is simply too late for the events that were rapidly unfolding at Carthage and with which the Numidian bishops, including the newly elected Silvanus, became implicated *after* the meeting at Cirta.[10] The meeting in the house at Cirta probably took place on 13 May 306.

THE FINAL EVENTS AT CARTHAGE

The sequence of events that subsequently transpired at Carthage is then reasonably clear. In a battle between Caecilian and Maiorinus, Caecilian was at first chosen and ordained as the bishop. Questions then arose concerning his ordination. But the main problem was not really with the nature of his ordination – although serious accusations were later to be made about it – but rather the ensuing battle between Caecilian and the *seniores* over the latter's possession of the church's wealth that had been left in the hands of the Elders by Mensurius before his departure. The Elders were more supportive of factions hostile to Caecilian than those in support of him, although they might well have had other grounds on which they did not wish to transfer the church's wealth into his hands. Accordingly, the *seniores* sent an appeal to the bishops of Numidia. For the timing of this appeal, and the answer to it, there are some reasonable parameters. It must have been part of the chain of events of 305–06, and yet it could not have been earlier than May 306 since it is known that some of the bishops involved in the meeting at Cirta in May 306 were in attendance at Carthage *after* that meeting – surely in the summer or autumn of that year. It is logical, however, that it would not have been long afterward. The struggle between Caecilian and the Elders must have come to a head fairly soon after his election, and their appeal for help must have been part of this quick succession of events, probably in the summer of 306.

The single biggest problem with this longer chronology – as recognized by all sides to the debate – is the relatively long time interval between the first stages in the quarrel, which must have been settled with the election of Caecilian by 306, and the subsequent appeals by the opponents of Caecilian that drew Constantine into the internecine struggles within the African church in the spring of 313. On the long chronology, one is left with a period of six to seven years in which no specific events are known, but during which there must have been incidents that further fueled the internecine hatreds and that provoked the drawing of ever harder battle lines within the church. Why were appeals not made to Maxentius, for

---

[10] Although this is the date preferred by Barnes, *Constantine and Eusebius*, p. 55, accepting Lancel (1979).

example? Why the long wait for Constantine? An answer that logically suggests itself is that both sides might well have appealed to Maxentius, but that he or his officials showed no interest. Or it could be that the two sides were waiting for a regime change. Maxentius had perhaps decided to support Christian factions as they stood, although he appears to have made more decisive moves at Rome itself in 311 to restore basilicas and other properties to the Christians. By the time it came to a fight with Constantine in 311–12, both parties in Africa were awaiting the outcome to appeal to the victor.

The Catholic conference of 348

The Council of the Catholic Church held at Carthage under the aegis of Gratus, the bishop of Carthage and primate of Africa, has been variously dated to years between 345 and 348. Cross and Crespin, indeed, have argued for a date as early as 345.[1] A rather different construction of the date has been proffered that rejects the corrected reading of "Constanti" for "Constantio" in the manuscripts, which would therefore open the possibility of a date *after* Constans in the reign of Constantius.[2]

1. The acts of the conference refer to current acts of the emperor Constans; therefore the latest possible date is 349. Because of the pragmatic reason of Constans' death in January of 350, that year is ruled out. Therefore, one of the years between 345 and 349.

2. Importantly, the first words of the council that are recorded attribute the move to unity and the dispatch of the emissaries Paul and Macarius to the emperor Constans: "qui imperavit religiosissimo Constantio [corr: Constanti] imperatori, ut votum gereret unitatis et mitteret ministros operis sancti, famulos Dei Paulum et Macarium."[3]

3. In Canon 5 of the proceedings of the conference, Gratus mentions an earlier decision that had been taken at the Council of Serdica: "Gratus episcopus dixit: Haec observata res pacem custodit; nam et memini sanctissimi concilii Sardicensis similiter statutum ut nemo alterius plebis hominem sibi usurpet..." (CCL 149: 6). The Council of Serdica most probably took place in the late summer or autumn of 343 (see Appendix E). This is of little help in dating our conference, however, since, despite

---

[1] Going back to Dupin and Tillemont, the dating received renewed discussion in Cross (1949), pp. 198–200; Crespin, *Ministère et sainteté*, pp. 32–33 n. 5.

[2] Mastandrea, "La data del *concilium Carthaginiense sub Grato*," pt. 3 in (1991), pp. 34–39; see the note following.

[3] *Acta Concil. Carth.* 348 (CCL 149: 3). Most of the manuscripts do read *Constantio*, but this has been corrected to *Constanti* by almost all editors; for a dissenting view, however, see Mastandrea (1991).

repeated claims to the contrary, Gratus does *not* indicate how long before the conference of Carthage the Council of Serdica took place. He merely refers to it as antecedent and no more.[4]

4. According to the preamble to the canons of the council, God had ordered "the most religious emperor" Constans to effect the unity of the church. To achieve this end he would dispatch the ministers of the Holy Word, slaves of God, Paul and Macarius. Although the preamble is phrased in a prophetic mode – as if all of it had yet to happen – it is clear that all of it was composed after the fact, and that Paul and Macarius, who are specifically named and noted, were already engaged in their mission in Africa. It is the supposed unity achieved by their mission to which the general church council is a response. The present time is already specifically labeled as "the time of unity," the *unitatis tempus*, and this unity is spoken of in the past tense as something already achieved (e.g., "qui *dedit* malis schismaticis finem"). The one big problem is with the manuscript reading of the emperor's name.[5] It has been amended by almost every authority since Baronius to read *Constanti* rather than *Constantio* which is found in all of the mss. Was the emperor, therefore, Constantius rather than Constans? The argument has been made, but it does not carry conviction.[6]

5. Since the mission of Paul and Macarius is to be dated to 347 (see Appendix E), the council at Carthage "under Gratus" must date to some time immediately *after* their mission. It could have been held very late in 347, but it would seem unlikely that the conference would have been staged right in the middle of the violence and other disturbances that marked their mission that continued at least through November of 347, the time of the execution of Marculus at Nova Petra in Numidia. It seems much more likely that the conference would have taken place in the year immediately following – most probably in the summer of 348.

---

[4] There are no grounds in the Latin for holding that the Carthage conference "fut de peu postérieure au concile de Sardique": Crespin, *Ministère et sainteté*, p. 2 n. 5.

[5] Mastandrea (1991), p. 38 n. 55.

[6] See Lancel (1988), pp. 340 f. – not the least of which are the objections that Paul and Macarius are known to be in action by the year 347 (see Appendix E).

The Edict of Unity and the
Persecution of 347

THE DECREE ISSUED BY THE EMPEROR CONSTANS

Often labeled by modern historians as the "Decree of Unity" of 347, the text of the imperial constitution issued by the emperor Constans has not survived. Basic questions arise about its dating, its place in the sequence of events of that year, how it reflected the intentions of the emperor, not to speak of its actual contents. Given the importance of the violence that resulted from the decree, it might be a useful first step to list the testimonia in chronological order.

1. *Passio Isaac et Maximiani*, 3.18 [Mastandrea (1995), pp. 77–78]
   Sed nec segnior et proconsul desideriis eius parem se ipsum [sc. Dia-bolum] subiecit et feralis edicti proposito sacrilegae unitatis iterum foe-dus celebrari constitutis cruciatibus imperavit, legem scilicet addens insuper traditorum, ut peregrini, quos Christus pro se mandat recipi, ab omnibus pellerentur ni quasi contra unitatis foedera molirentur.

2. *Passio Marculi*, 3.10 [Mastandrea (1995), p. 66]
   Et duabus bestiis ad Africam missis, eodem scilicet Macario et Paulo, exsecrandum prorsus ac dirum ecclesiae certamen indictum est, ut populus Christianus ad unitatem cum traditoribus faciendam nudatis militum gladiis et draconum praesentibus signis et tubarum vocibus cogeretur.

   [All of the above events are portrayed as having taken place in sequence *before* the mission of the ten bishops is sent to Macarius.]

3. *Concilium Carthaginiense* a. 348, praef. [CCL 149: 3]
   Gratias Deo omnipotenti et Christo Iesu, qui dedit malis schismaticis finem et respexit ecclesiam suam, ut in eius gremium erigeret universa membra dispersa; qui imperavit religiosissimo Constantio imperatori, ut votum gereret unitatis et mitteret ministros operis sancti, famulos Dei Paulum et Macarium. Ex Dei ergo nutu congregati <sumus> ad

unitatem ut per diversas provincias concilia celebraremus et universas provincias Africae hodierno die concilii gratia ad Carthaginem veniretur. Unde considerantibus vobis cum mea mediocritate tractentur tituli necessarii, de quibus necesse est nos memores praeceptorum divinorum et magisterii scripturarum sanctarum, contemplantes unitatis tempus, id est de singulis definire quod nec Carthago vigorem legis infringat nec tamen tempore unitatis aliquid durissimum statuamus.

4. Optatus, *Contra Parm.* 3.1-4 [SC 213: 8–10, 20–22]
   3.1.1: Ab operariis unitatis multa quidem aspera gesta sunt, sed ea quid imputatis Leontio, Macario vel Taurino? . . . deinde Donato Carthaginis qui provocavit ut unitas proximo tempore fieri temptaretur . . . 3.1.3: Venerunt tunc cum pharetris armigeri. Repleta est unaquaque civitas vociferantium. Nuntiata unitate, fugistis omnes. Nulli dictum est: Nega Deum. Nulli dictum est: Incende testamentum. Nulli dictum est: Tus pone, aut: Basilicas dirue; istae enim res solent martyria generare. Renuntiata est unitas . . . 3.1.4: Timuistis omnes, fugistis, trepidastis . . . Fugerunt igitur omnes episcopi cum clericis suis; aliqui sunt mortui, qui fortiores fuerunt capti et longe relegati sunt.

5. Optatus, *Contra Parm.* 3.3.2 (SC 213: 20–22): Aut quis negare potest rem cui tota Carthago principaliter testis est: imperatorem Constantem Paulum et Macarium primitus non ad faciendam unitatem misisse sed cum eleemosynis quibus sublevata per ecclesias singulas posset respirare, vestiri, pasci, gaudere paupertas? 3.3.3: Qui cum ad Donatum, patrem tuum, venirent et quare venerant indicarent, ille solito furore succensus in haec verba prorupit: Quid est imperatori cum ecclesia?

Other later statements found on these events, for example those in Augustine's writings, are vaguer and dependent on the types of sources already encapsulated in Optatus. The testimony of Optatus is particularly valuable since it is less couched in the obscurities of allegory and in the religious language of theodicy. Perhaps because he had to reply directly to the forthright claims of Parmenian, the dissident bishop of Carthage, who was attacking Catholics on the contentious issue of the armed intervention of the Roman state, Optatus had to stick, more or less, with the known facts. He indicates the following sequence of events:

1. He explicitly claims that Paul and Macarius were *not* initially sent to Africa to forge any "Unity," but simply to dispense charitable donations of the emperor to the poor and the destitute (i.e., to entice them to the Catholic side).

2. It was this first imperial intervention that was denounced by Donatus, the dissident bishop of Carthage, with the provocative question, "What does the emperor have to do with the Church?"

3. There were incidents of violence, perhaps many of them, connected with this process. Optatus admits even injuries and deaths. But it was the incident at Bagaï that seems to have been the catalyst of a harsher phase in the use of armed force and coercion against the dissident leaders in Numidia. We know that this harsher enforcement in southern Numidia was taking place by the end of June and in July of 347. The meeting of the bishops of southern Numidia to plan their confrontation with the imperial emissaries took place on 29 June 347. And we know that the execution of Marculus took place at Nova Petra on 29 November.

4. Only *after* the sequence of events leading up to Bagaï, did the imperial "Edict of Unity" come into play, apparently in answer to the hostile response of the dissidents to the earlier, more benign policy of using material inducements to entice unification.

5. In this case, it was the initial dissident opposition and blow-back against the state's attempt to use the heavy weight of its patronal resources "to bribe" dissenters back into the one approved church that caused a frustrated imperial court to have recourse to the heavier instruments of force. The "Edict of Unity" followed upon the initial events and the massacre at Bagaï. These events occurred perhaps in June and early July of 347; the Edict of Unity was probably issued in early August and was posted at Carthage on 15 August.

The preamble to the Catholic Council of Carthage held in 348, although closer to the events themselves, collapses all of these stages and portrays the emperor as having been moved by the command of God to seek the reunification of the Church from the very start. The dispatch of Paul and Macarius follows the emperor's "vow of unity" and, right from the beginning, the commissioners are sent to Africa specifically to execute the imperial order. In the same way, the martyr acts do not see the events in as finely grained and sequential a fashion as does Optatus. In fact, they portray the local governor, the proconsul – whose name is not given to us – as central to the execution of the imperial orders. The problem for the historian is that there is nowhere any indication of what the emperor Constans himself was intending to do, nor is there any surviving record of the terms of the edict itself. But the account in Optatus agrees with the sequence of events that is suggested by the dissident martyr narratives of this same year.

The mission of Paul and Macarius

The mission of Paul and Macarius was undertaken in the aftermath of the decree issued by the emperor Constans – at some time in the course of his reign, between 9 September 337 and January 350 – concerning the settlement of ecclesiastical confrontations between the two churches in Africa.[1] Given the very broad chronological parameters set by Constans' reign, the following items hold:

I. THE EVIDENCE OF AUGUSTINE

According to Augustine, the mission of Paul and Macarius occurred some time *after* the Council of Serdica: Aug. *Ep.* 44.3.6 (CCL 31: 190), which can now be dated with reasonable certainty to the late summer or autumn of 343: see Barnes, "The Council of Serdica," ch. 8 in *Athanasius and Constantius*, pp. 71–81. It seems improbable, given Augustine's wording, and the time by which events would have become known in Africa, that their mission could have been undertaken as early as the winter months of 343. The earliest probable date of their mission to Africa would therefore have been in the spring months of 344. Since Constans died in January of 350, the latest date for their mission is 349.

2. THE DATE OF THE MARTYRDOM OF MARCULUS

Whatever dates are assigned for the death of the dissident bishop and martyr Marculus, they must be in the reign of Constans (*Passio Marculi*, 3.9), later than the Council of Serdica, but no later than 349. Since the months concerned are August [§ 3 below] or November, the year 350 itself is excluded, since Constans died in January.

---

[1] For some of the basic facts, see Congar (1963a); in what follows, the challenging views of Mastandrea, "I tempora Macariana," pt. 2 in (1991), pp. 23–34.

A. Whatever precise date it was on which he died, Marculus died on a Sunday (*Passio Marculi*, 7.29)

B. The incipit of the "S" (Zurich) manuscript reads: "Incipit passio benedicti martyris Marculi die viii kal. decembrium," which is echoed by the "C" (Corbei) manuscript, which reads: "Incipit passio benedicti martyris Marculi quae est octavo kal. decembris," or 24 November. The "P" manuscript (*Parisinus* 5643), on the other hand, reads: "Incipit passio benedicti martyris Marculi iii kl. decemb.," or 29 November; the incipit of "g" reads: "Passio sancti Benedicti qui et Marculus dicebatur, quae est septimo Calendas decembris," or 25 November. Therefore, whatever the specific day, all agree on the month of November.

C. The "g" manuscript is a much later one (from Paderborn, but now lost) that was used by the Bollandists. It seems most likely that its copyist simply misread his source. The only serious contenders are therefore the "S and C," and the "P" manuscripts. The date must be in:

(a) a year between 344 and 349 on which 29 November (S) falls on a Sunday. The only possible year is 347.

(b) a year between 344 and 349 on which 24 November (S&C) falls on a Sunday. There are *no* such cases, so the scribes of texts S and C appear to have produced a mistaken date.

3. THE MARTYRDOM OF ISAAC AND MAXIMIANUS

A. The incipit of the "C" manuscript from Corbei reads: "Incipit passio sanctorum martyrum Isaac et Maximiani quae est vii kl. septembr." This would indicate that their execution fell on 26 August, which day would have been a Sunday (the day *after* the evening Vigil, which began on a Saturday, see § 3B following). Between 344 and 349, a 26 August on a Sunday does not correspond to any possible year. The obvious correction of the date in the incipit would be from "vii" to "xvii," and *xvii kal(endarum) Septembr(ium)* would be 16 August, and a 16 August that was also a Sunday corresponds to only one possible year between 344 and 349, namely 347. The incipit of "S" reads: "Incipit passio sanctorum martyrum Isaac et Maximiani quod est viii die kalendar. sept." which would be 25 August; a similar correction to "xviii die kalendar. sept." would indicate 15 August, but there is no year between 344 and 349 in which 15 August fell on a Sunday.

B. The narrative itself, when it comes to the point of their martyrdom (12.82) offers only two alternatives:

(a) "ut xvii kal(endarum) sept(embrium) die sabbato ad instar Paschae permitteret populis vigilias celebrare" (SP; T reads: "septimo decimo kalendas septembris") = 15 August

(b) "ut xviii kal. Septembr." (C) = 14 August

This notice indicates that the day *before* their execution, either 14 (SPT) or 15 August (C) fell on a Saturday.

The only year between 344 and 349 in which 15 August (SPT) fell on a Saturday was the year 347.

For whatever reasons, the convergence of dates reported by the SPT tradition is superior to that in the Corbei manuscript.

For purposes of limiting the dates to the period "post-Serdica" and before the death of Constans, I have limited the variables above to 344–49, but it might be noted that there are no other possible matches for the dates and days involved for the whole period between 342 and 350 other than those noted above. The balance of the evidence, therefore, favors the traditionally assigned year of 347 as the year in which the imperial emissaries Paul and Macarius began to inflict harsh penalties under the terms of an imperial decree issued by Constans.[2] Contrary to repeated scholarly claims, it is very unlikely that the imperial decree dates to 15 August of the same year. Some time towards the middle of the August is the first time we hear of penal measures being undertaken by authorities in Africa (i.e., arrests, hearings, and punishments) *in the aftermath of the posting of the decree* at Carthage for the first time in all of Africa. The imperial decree must have been issued some time before mid-August of 347.

Of course, all of the above calculations depend both on the validity of the incipits as independent evidence and on religious imperatives not having skewed the deaths of the martyrs specifically to a Sunday.

[2] Mastandrea (1991), pp. 32–33, rejects the reading of the "P" tradition in favor of the Corbei manuscript in view of the superior quality of the latter. On this basis, he places the martyrdom of Marculus on 24 November 345 (ignoring the problem of the Sunday) and proposes the following chronology: 344–34: Paul and Macarius arrive in Africa; 24 November 345: death of Marculus; 345–46: violent events at Bagaï; 16 August 346: deaths of Isaac and Maximianus at Carthage. In my opinion, this reshuffling of the dates involves too much special pleading, especially about the priority of the death of Marculus in sequence (Mastandrea 1991, p. 27).

Historical fictions: interpreting the circumcellions

Modern historians have placed the men and women known as circum-cellions at the heart of a rural rebelliousness – I purposefully use general words – a movement of resistance which, it has been claimed, swept through the African countryside in the fourth and fifth centuries. For centuries by now, beginning before any modern historical interest in them, their violent activities have been catalogued, analyzed, and theorized. Most of the earliest interest in the circumcellions, going back to the sixteenth and seventeenth centuries, was generated by the Protestant Reformation and the interest of its theologians and churchmen in the early history of resistance to the Catholic Church. Works by Friedrich Staphylus, Gustavus Dietz, and others, published in the course of the Lutheran movement in Germany, marked the modern origins of this research.[1] As a result, many details have been assembled and overwrought narratives written about them, but these efforts have not led to much understanding. In a review of the methodological and factual difficulties that bedevil analyses of the circumcellions, Joachim Diesner, an historian of late antiquity who devoted

---

[1] One of these early studies was by theologian Svante Gustavus Dietz – his *Dissertatio historica* of 1690, written in the full context of the Protestant Reformation, as were many of the other more general works on the Donatist movement that effloresced at the time. Throughout, Dietz's work reveals an interest in movements of religious protest: he also wrote a work, for example, on the Bacchanalian "conspiracy" of 186 BCE. One of the earliest of these works produced in the Reformation is that of the Lutheran (then Catholic) reformer Friedrich Staphylus: his *Disputatio circa circumcelliones* was published in 1568 when he was still in his Protestant phase. Nineteenth-century scholarship was rich in specific treatments, amongst which Nathusius, *Cirkumcellionen*, published in 1900, is one of the most important – but its main arguments were already summarized by Julicher in his 1899 entry for Pauly-Wissowa. In many ways, Monceaux, *Hist. litt.* 4, published in 1912, represents a summation of this line of research. The more comprehensive studies of modern times are those of Aguiar Frazão, *Os Circunceliões* in 1976, and Schulten, *De Circumcellionen* in 1984; since they are in Portuguese and Dutch, however, they have had little impact on the debates, which is a shame, particularly in the latter case. Of all the modern studies, few can match the systematic research program of the East German scholar H.-J. Diesner (1959–62). Mazzucco, *Ottato di Milevi*, pp. 122–29 and Lepelley (1992b) offer good bibliographical guides to the historiography.

much time and effort to understanding their activities rightly remarked that the circumcellions are "one of those historical phenomena of which we know many things, but about which we really don't know very much."[2] Because of the peculiar condition of the evidence, this precarious state of affairs remains true. Partly for the same reasons, there have been a number of basic shifts of perspective on the circumcellions, as one dominant historical paradigm has succeeded another in interpreting them, including Marxist approaches that highlighted the "rebels" as prime bearers of the class conflict in late Roman Africa.

If there is any one thing that has fundamentally shifted our understanding of the circumcellions in more recent years, however, it is not any of the new interpretive paradigms about *them* as such, but rather our profoundly altered knowledge of the general economic circumstances in which their violent actions occurred. Among the continuing verities, there is still no real disagreement with the basic fact that over the long fourth century the Roman empire, especially its western parts, was caught up in a process of military and political disintegration. It was a process that began with the crisis of the mid-third century and the "empire of the Gauls," and ended with the widespread breach of the Rhine frontier on the last day of December of 406 (but perhaps a year earlier in 405). This general truism, however, disguises significant, indeed critical, regional differences in the general pattern of the disintegration, and of its economic consequences. Finally, it risks imposing a general schema of remorseless "decline" on the African provinces of the empire that more recent archaeological work has demonstrated, once and for all, to be fundamentally untrue. In the 1970s and 1980s, the archaeological investigation of Roman Africa underwent a major shift from the detailed collation of materials from urban-centered sites, their architectural elements and modes of artistic production, to broad surface surveys of entire rural regions.

Connected networks of detail in these rural surveys are still rare and some of the subregions subjected to these new kinds of material inquiries have been small and are sometimes aberrant from the standpoint of the investigation of the ecclesiastical conflicts analyzed in this book. In the general picture that has emerged, however, one important fact stands out. By the standard of any of the conventional measures used to analyze the material production of the ancient world, fourth- and fifth-century Africa was prospering and not at all in any kind of economic doldrums or

---

[2] Diesner (1959/1964), p. 1009/53: "Circumcellionentum ist eines der historischen Phänomene, über die wir vieles, aber nicht eigentlich viel wissen."

decline.[3] In comparison with most other regions of the western empire of the time, late antique Africa remained an economic success story.[4] It might well be an exaggeration to claim that the local economy was booming, but in comparative terms this would not be an entirely misleading picture. Although it is not yet possible to draw all the significant causal strings together, some of the general attendant conditions are reasonably clear. The African provinces had already achieved a level of prosperity in the high period of the second-century empire. Cities flourished, wealth was accumulated and lavishly spent, all of it based on the intensive and extensive development of the resources of a rural economy. The countryside provided surpluses not only for enhanced local markets, but also for export to centers of mass consumption elsewhere in the empire, above all to the urban metropolis of Rome. Africa therefore entered the fourth century as a highly developed region of empire, and one that had suffered significantly less from the problems that had afflicted the rest of the empire through the middle decades of the third century.

The reason why the African provinces continued to prosper amidst conditions that so badly afflicted the northern Mediterranean regions of the western empire is tied to its peculiar historical ecology. The ancient Maghrib was insulated in a peculiar fashion that both protected it from many of the negative impacts of the Mediterranean world outside its shores, and yet which permitted the land to benefit from external developments, by both importing and developing them rapidly and on a large scale.[5] These insulating effects proved advantageous in the dangerous circumstances of the late fourth-century Roman West, and for a time, at least until the Byzantine invasion in the early sixth century, allowed Africa to continue to prosper.[6] The fragmentation of central rule and the loss of significant parts of the empire in other regions, especially along the northwestern frontier, was a boon for the Africans. They lived in a geopolitical cocoon, mostly

---

[3] Mattingly and Hitchner (1995), esp. pp. 189–96, 198–204, and 209–213, for our period, offers the most convenient synopsis. The first suspicions were fired by the profusion of African Red Slip (ARS) wares in the Mediterranean.

[4] It is important, however, not to exaggerate. Several measurements of the African economic recovery of the fourth century still place it at a level significantly below the levels of the high empire of the late second and early third centuries.

[5] See Shaw (2003) and *At the Edge*, for the general argument.

[6] Although I accept "invasion paradigms" as having a peculiar applicability in Maghribi historiography, my main historical grievance is that the Roman case is always viewed by western historians as an exception and is never interpreted for the Maghrib within this paradigm ("the Roman invasion") but rather as some sort of different phenomenon: "us" rather than "them," with a certain pervasive blindness, not to say bias, that results for historical interpretation. Other invasions are always "bad," whereas this one is always "good."

isolated from the larger external troubles. Their economy continued to produce under conditions of relative peace.[7] As lands in the northwest were lost to Roman control or were so severely disturbed that their economic communications were impeded, and as the military demands of the central Roman state rose, Africa was ideally positioned to benefit from the new situation. It was therefore *relatively* better off in these respects. All of this is reflected in the new archaeological record that has been assembled from the large-scale surface surveys of the last decades: Africa was doing better economically – more sites were more densely occupied, and more frontier and marginal lands were being brought under cultivation. The surplus production was exported in massive quantities all over the Mediterranean in containers, especially African Red Slip (ARS) wares and typical African transport amphorae, that have been identified on hundreds of sites all around the Mediterranean.

The importance of this new paradigm for the interpretation of social movements in Africa of the fourth and fifth centuries cannot be understated. It is a fundamental alteration, almost a total reversal of perspective. As far as the circumcellions are concerned, the new evidence has entirely shifted the ground beneath earlier models of the problem. Almost all previous interpretations of circumcellion violence came under the rubric of one of a limited number of traditionally pessimistic paradigms. Generally speaking, these interpretations fell into three broad categories. First, there were studies written from the perspective of theologians or church historians – from Paul Monceaux in the 1920s to Golven Madec in the 1990s. As noted above, this approach had a long history going back to an early modern interest in the circumcellions that was part of the broader intrigue with "the Donatist Church" that emerged in the course of the Reformation.[8] Studies made in the context of German theological schools and universities in the nineteenth century were especially influential in this tradition. Wilhelm Thümmel's "assessment" of Donatism published in 1893 was important in that it refuted widely disseminated and accepted ideas that the circumcellions were violent monastics or ascetics and that they had a special "organic" connection with "the Donatist Church."[9] His main argument that the circumcellions were not Christians at all, but

---

[7] It is on these grounds, and others, that I reject *internal* "armed resistance" paradigms as particularly useful for understanding the history of the Maghrib during this period.

[8] See n. 1 above; studies of this type continued at least down to Thümmel's *Zur Beurtheilung des Donatismus* of 1893.

[9] Thümmel, "Die Circumcellionen," ch. 7 in *Beurtheilung des Donatismus*, pp. 85–94; he rejected as "mistaken" the idea of them as violent monastics that was being propagated, for example, by Daniel Voelter, *Ursprung des Donatismus*, p. 10, and others.

rather "pagan" votaries attached to Punic and Berber traditions was a truly unusual point of view for the time. It was refuted, in turn, by Martin von Nathusius' detailed study published seven years later.[10] Nathusius felt that the sources underwrote three main characteristics of circumcellions, each of which had a Christian aspect to it: they had pronounced tendencies to commit suicide, they shared a fanatical urge to do harm to Catholics, and they had a "socialist-communist" aspect to their ideals and actions.[11] This final characteristic was confirmed in Nathusius' mind by a study that he had completed three years earlier on "socialist-Christian" ideas in the Reformation.[12] The circumcellions were therefore precursors of the radical Hussites and the Wycliffites, the Lollards, and the followers of Wat Tyler.

All these religious curiosities in the circumcellions, as just remarked, were provoked by Protestant historical interests in an earlier history of dissent or protest against the Catholic Church.[13] But these religious approaches were succeeded in the nineteenth and early twentieth centuries by analyses written from critical "socialist" perspectives, including varieties of classical Marxism. These studies included studies over a wide range, from those composed by François Martroye in the early 1900s to those written by the East German scholar Joachim Diesner in the 1960s.[14] These approaches basically tried to "secularize" circumcellion violence by reconfiguring its basic and "real" causes as economic rather than religious in nature.[15] Finally, a combination of these two approaches emerged, as, for example, in the

---

[10] Von Nathusius, *Charakteristik der Cirkumcellionen*, pp. 5–6.

[11] Von Nathusius, *Charakteristik der Cirkumcellionen*, p. 12, and pp. 27–33 on the last characteristic.

[12] M. von Nathusius, *Die Christlichen-socialen Ideen der Reformationszeit und ihre Herkunft*, Gütersloh, C. Bertelsmann, 1897 (Beiträge der Förderung christlicher Theologie, Bd. 1, Heft 2).

[13] In Germany, most of the nineteenth-century studies took as their point of departure Ferdinand Ribbek's *Donatus und Augustinus, oder der erste entscheidende Kampf zwischen Separatismus und Kirche: ein kirchenhistorischer Versuch*, Elberfeld, Verlag der Bädeker'schen Buch- und Kunsthandlung, 1858, pp. 122–24, and his views of the circumcellions. The Reformation also produced similar items of comparison in English-language scholarship, of which one of the more interesting was the parallel drawn between Elizabeth I and the Lucilla whose fatal kiss was said to have provoked the schism in the African church: *Lucilla and Elizabeth, or, Donatist and Protestant Schism Parallel'd*, London, Henry Hills, 1686; these works were embedded in a context of more general works like Thomas Long's *The History of the Donatists. Mutato nomine de te, Anglia, narratur*, London, Walter Kettilby, 1677.

[14] See Konstantine Sheppa's *Circumcelliones* of 1930. Nikolai Mashkîn (1938) and (1949), Anatoli Dmitrev (1948), and German Diligenskii (1957) are reasonably representative of three decades of three generations of classic Marxist approaches of a fairly orthodox sort. For context, see Gacic (1957). The work of Diesner is so extensive and detailed that it will be quoted in each instance as applicable. Baldwin (1961) might be added since at that time he was a student of E. A. Thompson's, and very much under his influence. Martroye (1904) and (1905) is a good example of early French scholarship in this same general vein.

[15] See Pandey (1992), pp. 39–40, and his objections to a similar strand of argument that emerged in interpreting Hindu–Muslim violence in the subcontinent.

wide range of studies that William Frend published on "the Donatist Church" over the last half of the twentieth century – research informed by both ecclesiastical and social-critical agenda.[16] In effect, Frend's work greatly expanded a synthesis of the religious and the social that was already surfacing in the late nineteenth century, in which interpreters were moving away from "religious appearances" to underlying "social realities" as the main explanation for circumcellion violence. However, these scholars also wished to keep both streams on interpretation in their analyses.[17] All of these historians, and many more subsequently, have appealed to the supposed parallel of the "social revolutionary" movement of the Bagaudae in Late Roman Gaul.[18] This has only succeeded in marrying one unproven theoretical construct to another.

The problem is that *both* the fundamental approaches, and their amalgam in the third, shared assumptions about the prevalence of the decay and decline of the later Roman empire – a general malaise in which Africa also was caught up. In this collapse of empire, either the triumph of Christianity or the collapse of the traditional economic and political order (or both) was the result. This paradigm enabled bold statements such as: "In the fourth century general conditions in Roman Africa were ripe for social revolt... the position of the *coloni* or tenant farmers worsened rapidly... largely as a result of repressive legislation by the emperor Constantine that paved the way for feudalism."[19] In these circumstances of oppression, the circumcellions were the vanguard of a "peasant movement" and were the human fires of a rural rebellion that swept through Africa in Late Antiquity.[20] For Marxist historians, in particular, the situation in Africa in the fourth and fifth centuries bore all the hallmarks of a classic economic and political crisis: the increasing immiseration of the underclasses of peasant farmers and slaves, the greater exploitation imposed by

---

[16] Frend, *Donatist Church* (1952, reprint: 1971), esp. pp. 172–78, 257–68; other more detailed studies by Frend will be noted below.

[17] Approaches that combined the idea of the circumcellions as religious fanatics *and* social revolutionaries can be found, for example, in Leclercq, *L'Afrique chrétienne*, 1, pp. 345–49, who was summarizing approaches adumbrated over the last half of the nineteenth century that are also apparent in Nathusius, *Cirkumcellionen*, published in 1900: "L'insurrection n'eut de religieux que l'apparence, elle fut en réalité une révolte sociale" (p. 346); under Axidus (sic) and Fasir "Il y eut, à la nouvelle des excès auxquels ils se livraient, une terreur comme il s'en répandit au moyen âge, en France, lors de la Jacquerie et des Tard-Venus, ou encore au temps de la domination romaine, lors de la révolte des Bagaudes" (pp. 348–49); and as "moines-communards."

[18] See Rubin (1995) who accepts the comparison and who details most of the earlier research. The parallelism has to rely on assertions about the nature of the Bagaudae that are highly disputed and mostly unproven. This trend, too, shows no sign of dissipating: see Cacitti, *Furiosa turba*, p. 5, who provides the circumcellions with the required radical ideology: see chs. 4 and 7 of his work.

[19] Baldwin (1961), pp. 4–5.   [20] E. F. Gautier, *Geiséric, roi des Vandales*, Paris, Payot, 1932, p. 148.

the class of landlords, and the oppressive demands of a tyrannical state, sparked peasant jacqueries throughout the land. Such claims, tantamount to firm beliefs, then formed a general substratum of accepted ideas from which others, and not just Marxists, drew their interpretations.

This perspective was linked to one in which the "economic stagnation and impoverishment, depopulation of town and country, the increased pressures of high taxes and high rents, and continuing polarization of rich and poor were among the factors contributing to the mounting social conflict that in the fourth and fifth centuries loosened the grip of Roman hegemony in Africa."[21] Perhaps not surprisingly, these same assumptions characterized Russian scholarship on the subject through the mid-twentieth century.[22] But it was also a position adopted by Odette Vannier in an analysis that was, for its time, rather iconoclastic in its denial of a religious explanation for circumcellion violence. She rejected claims of a close connection between the dissident church and the circumcellions that were asserted by most other interpreters of the time. In her opinion, the collaboration between the circumcellions and "the Donatists" was a short-term phenomenon. In her view, it was much more a fortuitous coincidence of interests than anything else. She argued that the circumcellions basically had to be understood as a peasant jacquerie, "an episode of the economic decadence of Africa" of the time, men who "must therefore take their place in an economic history of the province much more than in its religious history."[23]

In Vannier's work we find the flip side of the religious argument. In secularizing the circumcellions in an anti-clericalist mode, she appealed instead to the secular forces of the age – in short, the economy – as providing the basic causes of circumcellion violence. Historians who accepted Optatus' and Augustine's views of the circumcellions as violent religious fanatics were, in Vannier's view, accepting a superficial ideological presentation of what was in fact a deeper, truer economic reality. That is to say, in interpretations like hers, "the circumcellions" *as a whole* were being placed into an either–or situation in which the reader was asked *either* to embrace them as religious fanatics *or* as peasant rebels. The end of this type of approach to the circumcellions can be found in Lepelley's work in which he states

---

[21] Wood (1986), p. 41, and see (1985), which links this interpretation to Augustinian ideology.

[22] See n. 14 above.

[23] Vannier (1926), p. 28: the revolt of the circumcellions was "un épisode de la décadence économique de l'Afrique et elle devrait avoir sa place dans une historie économique de cette province bien plus que dans son histoire religieuse."

that the social revindicative or social revolutionary aspects of the circum-cellions was only apparent in the circumstances of 347, but seems to have disappeared subsequently.[24] Within the purview of interpretations such as these, if "the circumcellions" are to be regarded as a one-dimensional phenomenon (presumably because they share the same name), then the historian is compelled to drop some aspects of the core definition and to embrace others, and to attribute the differences between the two as changes that took place over time.

The interpretations of the circumcellions as religious fanatics of one type or another was usually founded on a quite uncritical reading of the sources, usually through a committed religious or colonialist lens. To this toxic mix, elements that were not far from racist in type were added: "Can we imagine them, even as natives of that Africa, whose remote descendants still furnish the most grotesque examples of American revivalism?" intoned Ronald Knox, following what can only be described as a rather biased viewpoint in which he labeled the Axido and Fasir episode as "a kind of communist crusade."[25] This sort of colonialist paradigm dominated certain strands of scholarship, especially in the interwar and immediate postwar period from the 1930s to the 1950s. Typical is the analysis offered by Beaver in 1935 on "the Donatist Circumcellions," in which "Africa" (the factor of "African-ness" is stressed throughout) is very "native" because, we are reassured, "the Romanization of Africa had never been more than a thin and partial veneer."[26] In consequence of this fact, "one must remember the character of African Christians . . . the fanatical expression of their devotion," that is the devotion of "the native masses" that were made up of "natives of the Punic and Berber races." The problem only grew as European (sc. Roman) controls over the natives weakened: "Racial friction had never entirely sub-sided, and now in the period of the Empire's decline it worsened." The last words cued the reader to the idea that the circumcellions, who represented the worst of an innate African ferocity, barbarism, and fanaticism, were to be tied in to the dangerous immiseration of the peasantry as the empire entered the final throes of its collapse.[27]

The post-war work by East German scholars, including the broad comparative analysis proffered by Theodora Büttner and Ernst Werner,

---

[24] Lepelley, *Cités de l'Afrique romaine*, I, p. 240: "Nous pouvons affirmer que la jacquerie ne se poursuivit pas au delà de ces années (345–347) et que la dimension explicitement sociale du mouvement des circoncellions disparut ensuite." His ideas have had a real impact on subsequent thinking; see, e.g. Schulten, *De Circumcellionen*, pp. 4, 80–81.

[25] Knox (1950), pp. 61–62; and indulging, later, in using "Africanism" to explain not just circumcellions, but also "Donatism," attributing their persistence to "the African temperament" (p. 69).

[26] Beaver (1935), pp. 123–24.   [27] Beaver (1935), esp. at pp. 130 ff.

presented more nuanced Marxist explanations. Their view was still one that saw the circumcellions as symptoms of social upheavals in a social order that was experiencing profound crises caused by the decline and disintegration of the economy. From the very start, however, and citing an authority no less than Engels, Büttner and Werner held that almost all premodern social movements were inevitably religious in nature. So now the interpretive circle was rejoined, only from the "secular" side of the argument. The social and economic context that they provided for understanding the circumcellions was that of the so-called Third Century Crisis and its aftermath. In their view, the crisis produced the different forms of the class struggle that marked the fourth century.[28] Amongst these manifold forms of resistance that were also symptoms of this crisis, they claimed, were the greater military threats now posed by episodes of violent inroads of various indigenous ethnic or "tribal" groups along the frontier zones.[29] These episodes were then linked to the more pervasive presence of bandits and brigandage within the lands still controlled by the Roman state.[30] Much the same linkages were presented in English-language Marxist scholarship, where the religious language or structure in which social ills were expressed was combined with real revolutionary impulses against the dominant classes of the age. The circumcellions were seen not only as "the militant wing of the Donatists" and "a kind of lunatic fringe, bent on religious suicide," but also as social revolutionaries – men who "waged war on occasion not only on the Catholic Church in Africa, but also upon the class of large landowners from which that Church derived its main support."[31]

In the end, the approaches of the historians of Christian dogma or church history were not much different from those of the social historians. Frend's work, in particular, showed how the two interpretations could converge quite nicely. Much the same assumptions were made about a Christian

---

[28] Büttner (1956) and *Circumcellionen*; in her analysis, the elements of the "sharpening social-economic crisis" of the third century are outlined (pp. 8–18) followed by the "different forms of the class struggle in the third century" (pp. 18–20). To a certain extent her model is based on Rostovtzeff, together with what were then received ideas on the "curial class" and the decline of cities (for which works like Jacques Toutain's otherwise excellent study *Les cités romaines de la Tunisie* of 1902 is cited); along with standard selections of the primary data (Frontinus, Melania the Younger) on the growth and domination of large estates. The rest is a rehearsal of quite stereotypical evidence relating to provincial rural economy in north Africa (e.g., the great domain inscriptions from the Bagrada Valley) combined with some quite misleading literary evidence on the supposed growing importance of slave labor.

[29] Büttner, *Circumcellionen*, pp. 18–19.   [30] Büttner, *Circumcellionen*, pp. 20–21.

[31] De Ste. Croix, *Class Struggle*, pp. 481–82; he makes clear, however, that he regards the "Donatist church" primarily as a religious movement and not one of social protest: pp. 445–47, based on Jones' 1959 article, although it is also here (p. 445) that de Ste. Croix designates "Donatism" as one of those "one or two exceptional cases" where religion did intersect with class position.

church that was emerging from a decaying and disintegrating imperial economic and political structure, and was beginning to replace it. It was within this framework of decline and fall that the circumcellions were seen as the violent last-gasp of regional expressions of a local autonomy within the empire – a resurgence of persistent local traditions and particularisms against a uniform, if oppressive, imperial culture. These movements, it was argued, tended to vilify a universal church that was too closely identified with this same central order.[32] There have been exceptions to these views, but they have remained exceptions, thoroughly marginalized in the general debates over the significance of the phenomenon. A strongly related interpretation, that circumcellions were a species of violent monastic or wandering monks of revindicative disposition, is part of this same perspective. It too has no basis in fact, but continues to be reiterated as if it were a well-founded piece of historical analysis.[33]

This standard picture was modified principally because of the work of two historians: Charles Saumagne in the 1930s and, two decades later, Emin Tengström who, in the 1960s, wrote a detailed analysis of the circumcellions in the context of his larger re-examination of social and economic aspects of the ecclesiastical struggles in Africa. By concentrating on the legal details of an imperial constitution of 412 issued by the emperor Honorius that was directed at repressing the dissidents, Saumagne demonstrated that imperial administrators assumed that circumcellions were mainly persons of free status, above slaves and *coloni* in rank, who had to be dealt with by legal means that included fines but not brute physical punishment.[34] Saumagne hypothesized that the main recruitment base for circumcellions must therefore have been amongst free persons of some property or means, however modest, who were engaged in activities that would account for their propensity to wander in search of employment. He therefore postulated that they were seasonal agricultural laborers. Tengström pressed further along this same path by attempting to eke out of the meager source materials some indication of the specific kind of work in which the circumcellions were engaged, finally opting for the harvesting of olive crops.[35]

[32] Monceaux, *Hist. litt.* 4, p. 165: "La dernière cause ... est dans l'état social de l'Afrique, ou la misère était grande depuis le milieu du IIIe siècle; où le parti de la misère était acquis d'avance à tous les mécontents, où ce parti trouvait des réserves inépuisables dans une population indigène restée barbare, et souvent, ignorante même le latin."

[33] The bibliography is long, but most of it has been recapitulated by a recent believer: Cacitti, *Furiosa turba*, esp. pp. 66–70.

[34] Saumagne (1934), pp. 351–64.

[35] Tengström, "Die Circumcellionen," ch. 1 in *Donatisten und Katholiken*, pp. 24–78, who at pp. 24 f. states baldly his view that Saumagne's article placed the analysis of the circumcellions on an entirely new level of analysis.

There were two clues, he argued. First, when they were armed, circum-cellions were habitually spoken of as bearing clubs. These wooden clubs, Tengström claimed, were nothing other than the *baculae* or long poles that olive harvesters used to beat the branches of the trees to cause the olives to fall to the ground where they were collected. Second, the areas of Africa that were typically associated with circumcellion violence were the high plains of Numidia where olives were the pre-eminent cash crop.

To secular historians like Saumagne and Tengström, who founded their analysis on the perspectives offered by the late imperial law codes, the cir-cumcellions appeared to be not much more than itinerant seasonal laborers. Given the places of origin of the circumcellions and their main theaters of work, these historians postulated that most of them were probably "Donatist" by sympathy and allegiance. Even so, their principal quotidian activities were substantially misrepresented and obscured by Catholic bish-ops like Optatus and Augustine. Historians should understand that they were mainly seasonal agricultural laborers. This strand of argument found favor with some interpreters on "the left" for whom the circumcellions were seen primarily as oppressed landless laborers, *coloni*, and slaves who were "always a violent revolutionary force outside the law [and who were] only brought into religious issues by unscrupulous Donatist clergy."[36]

To judge from the balance of subsequent critical scholarship on the subject, however, this wholly secularist approach to explaining the circum-cellions appears to have had only a marginal effect on modern interpreta-tions of their identity and purpose. The main problems seem to be two. Most obviously, there were the manifest connections that existed between persons called circumcellions and the dissident Christian community in Africa. The detailed reports on the actions of the circumcellions given by the primary sources describe violent actions that bear little manifest relation to the normal tasks of harvest workers. As one commentator has put it, to interpret circumcellion clubs as nothing other than olive-harvesting imple-ments was "rather like concluding that a riot-squad armed with pickaxe handles was a gang of road menders."[37] It was a typical category error. The second problem was that a strong internal ethos was asserted by contem-porary writers in antiquity to characterize circumcellion behavior, and this ethos was marked by propensities to certain kinds of aggressive and violent action. Some of this extreme violence, according to repeated specific asser-tions in the primary sources, was turned inwards on themselves in suicidal

---

[36] Baldwin (1961), p. 11.   [37] Brown (1965), p. 282.

urges that culminated in episodes of self-sacrifice and mass self-killings – a behavior that seems irrational in the context of normal agricultural work.

The characteristics that were reported in Late Roman antiquity as core identifying elements of circumcellion identity point to an important religious dimension to the phenomenon that must be integrated into any acceptable explanation of who these violent persons were. Revisionists therefore tended to marry the religious and social elements in the circumcellions to produce a radical social-religious type. In this view, the circumcellions were a movement of social protest, a primitive form of peasant jacquerie, or a more dangerous harbinger of social revolution.[38] This picture can be oriented slightly more in the direction of the ecclesiastical politics and theological battles of the age, in which case the circumcellions become "gangs of religious fanatics" who were allied with "the Donatist church" in its struggle for domination in Africa, and with other assertions of regional autonomy such as the rebellions led by Firmus and Gildo.[39] It is this most recent interpretation of the circumcellions that is contested by my work; specifically, I reject most of the connections postulated by this model. Among these is the claim that the circumcellions were violent monks, volatile ascetics, or various kinds of dangerous holy men, and that it was in this mode that they were integrated with the dissident church.[40] All of these particular reconstructions of them are based on evidence that is non-African in origin. They are external fictions foisted on the circumcellions that must be rejected in modern reconstructions of who they were.[41] This claim and the parallel one – that the sectarian Holy Strugglers or *agonistici* are to be identified with circumcellions in general (rather than separated from them) – are, I think, to be rejected in favor of a more complex picture of the recruitment and definition of the *agonistici* and their relation to a larger pool of men called circumcellions. From here, we must work ourselves towards a new model of a truly complex social phenomenon.

[38] For example, Pleket (1978), pp. 143–57; and Gotoh (1988), pp. 303–11.

[39] For example, Rubin (1995), pp. 129–87, at pp. 156–79, who also offers aspects of the "social revolutionary" explanation as part of his picture.

[40] It is a constant theme, for example, in Frend's work: see (1952), (1969), (1972a), and *Donatist Church*, p. 173. The idea has early roots, but it was later developed in some detail by scholars like Calderone (1967) who summarizes much of the earlier work on the circumcellions as wandering violent ascetics. And it remains a dominant theme that seems in no danger of dying out – see, e.g. "*Nusquam missi?* Un fenomeno di radicalismo itinerante,*" ch. 3 in Cacitti, *Furiosa turba*, pp. 63–80, where the author, for example, accepts certain passages in Augustine's *De opere monachorum* as "transparent" references to the circumcellions.

[41] For example, Tyconius, whose original words, it is falsely claimed, are preserved in the eighth-century text of the Spanish priest Beatus of Liébana; the fantasy is repeated by Cacitti, *Furiosa turba*, pp. 66–71. For the details of this argument, see Shaw (2004) and (2006).

The archaeology of suicide

Since the suicides or, better, the self-killings by the dissident Christians, especially the "circumcellions," were reputed to have been widespread and terrifying in effect, it would nice to be able to find some evidence of them in the material record – some hard "on the ground" data relative to the practice. This turns out to be a version of parallel problem of attempting to find *any* material evidence, either in the archaeological record or in epigraphy, relevant to either the circumcellions or the *agonistici*. Since the self-killers were regarded, and worshiped, as martyrs, such memorials must have existed. The memorial to the dissident martyr Marculus could be argued to be a variant of this kind of material memory, but the nature of his death, and the fact that one is speaking of a record at Vegesala, the site of his bishopric and not at Nova Petra, the site of his death, means that we do not have any direct evidence of a suicidal death.

The problem is that it is precisely the connected meaning between their life and death and our evaluation of it, namely as "suicide," that is lost in the commemoration. Such deaths would be those of martyrs and would be celebrated as such – as those of any martyr (like Marculus, for example). If they exist, they are not distinguishable from the rest. Unfortunately, there is no identifiable material evidence of these suicides or of their celebration or memorialization.

It has been claimed that a series of Christian tombstones from the Aïn Mlila region in southern Algeria are the memorials of just such a series of suicides found in the region of Djebel Nif en-Nser, some thirty miles south of Constantine.[1] The archaeological data were claimed by their discoverers

---

[1] See Logeart (1940) and Leschi (1940) for the first reports of the stones. The claim that these are the records of suicidal jumpers has been made consistently by Frend – see, e.g., *Donatist Church*, pp. 175–76; and 1982b, p. 162 – where he claims to have seen the grave markers and reports "the situation of these stones at the bottom of a cliff." He later claimed actually to have seen some of the stones with the word NAT(ALICIA) inscribed on them, which would clinch the fact that they were martyrdoms. But none of the 65 published stones (and these are the only ones to which Frend refers)

to be hard evidence of dissident suicide martyrs – and the claim has been repeated by many others.[2] Sixty-five of these epitaphs were found grouped in three locations along this stretch of terrain, although their precise original locations are unknown. But the inscriptions on the tombstones are nothing other than quite normal Christian funerary epitaphs, with the name of the deceased and date of the death recorded on them. Both of these recorded facts about the deceased, including the registration of the date of death, were part of standard Christian practice for commemorating normal deaths. Nothing here betokens suicidal martyrdoms.[3] Their relevance to martyrdom has been rightly rejected.[4] There is therefore no known archaeological or epigraphical evidence pertaining either to circumcellions or to the dissident "suicides."

have such a word inscribed on them. The rise of Djebel Nif en-Nser which is nearby is located by Gsell, *Atl. arch.* f. 17, nos. 434–37.

[2] So A. Berthier, *Les vestiges du christianisme antique dans la Numidie centrale*, Algiers, Imprimerie polyglotte africaine, 1943, pp. 215 f., was the first to have believed that the stones found "at the foot" of Djebel Nif-en-Nser and Djebel Anouda were the tombstones of these precipitators: so Brisson, *Autonomisme et christianisme*, p. 321 n. 3, and text.

[3] For the notation of the day of death as normal Christian epigraphical practice, see Shaw (1996b), pp. 103–04, and the bibliography cited there. There is nothing in any of the published reports to sustain Frend's claim, *Donatist Church*, p. 176, that these stones were found "lying at the foot of a precipice" and that they therefore marked the site of suicidal deaths.

[4] Duval, *Loca sanctorum*, 2, pp. 487–88.

African sermons

I. THE MONTHLY DISTRIBUTION OF AUGUSTINE'S DATED SERMONS

The numbers in this list depend on my own collation and datings. These do not in every instance agree with the datings, for example, of Kunzelmann (1931), La Bonnardière, *Recherches de chronologie*, or Hombert, *Chronologie Augustinienne*. The results should therefore only be read as approximate, and as indicating nothing more than a general picture of the annual distribution of surviving sermons that can be dated with some reasonable certainty.

Month	Number
January	26
February	3
March	16
March/April	132 [Easter Sermons]
April	5
May	20
June	41
July	22
August	31
September	32
October	20
November	13
December	54
Total	405

2. THE DECADAL DISTRIBUTION OF AUGUSTINE'S SERMONS

The same cautions concerning chronology and dating noted for H.I above also apply to these numbers. The simple point to be made is that of those sermons that can be dated with some certainty, those preached in the decade of the 410s greatly outnumber those preached in other decades. The pattern of survival therefore reveals some selection.

Decade	Number
390–399	69
400–409	92
410–419	326
420–429	12
Total	499

3. SOME UNATTRIBUTED NON-AUGUSTINIAN SERMONS FROM AFRICA

The following does not pretend to be a complete list. It is a list of those non-Augustinian sermons from Africa, whose authors are otherwise unknown, probably dating to the fourth and fifth centuries, that I considered as part of the research for this volume. Frede, *Kirchenschriftsteller*, Isola (1990), Gryson, *Compléments*, and others, were helpful in compiling the entries.

Serm. Arm. = *Sermones Armamentarii*, ed. J.-P. Bouhot, *Opera D. Ioannis Chrysostomi*, vols. 1–5 (Basel, 1558) [see PLS 2 and 4]. Many of these sermons, traditionally attributed to the "Latin Chrysostom," are patently of African origin. Some of the sermons are derived from the orthodox "Catholic" tradition, whereas others, also found in the collection of sermons from the Escorial [see *Sermones Escurialenses* below], are manifestly from dissident sources. Many of the former sermons seem to have been collated in southern Italy from various African sources, probably in the later fifth century (J.-P. Bouhot, PLS 4: 651–52; Frede [1995], 135–36).

1. PLS 4: 656–59 (Serm. Vind. 22; Ps.-Aug. Serm. Cai. 2.51; cf. Ps.-Aug. 150)
2. De Quinta [Feria] Passionis Dominicae: PLS 2: 1124–25 (Ps.-Aug. Serm. Mai, 27)
3. De Sexta [Feria] Passionis Dominicae [I]: PLS 2: 1126–28 (Ps.-Aug. Serm. Mai, 28)
4. De Sexta Feria [Passionis Dominicae, II]: PLS 2: 1129–30 (Ps.-Aug. Serm. Mai, 29)
5. A. Olivar, *Los sermones de San Pedro Crisólogo*, Abadia de Montserrat, 1962 (*Scripta et Documenta* 12 (Ps.-Aug. Serm. Mai, 30; Petrus Chrysologus, Serm. 72B)
6. Ibid., no. 13 (Ps.-Aug. Serm. Mai, 31; Petrus Chrysologus, Serm. 72C)

7. De Latrone in Sexta Feria Passionis: PLS 2: 1130–32 (Ps.-Aug. Serm. Mai, 32)
8. De Resurrectione Domini in Pascha: PLS 2: 1135–37 (Ps.-Aug. Serm. Mai 36)
9. De Pascha [I]: PLS 2: 1137–39 (Ps. Aug. Serm. Mai, 37)
10. In Pascha [II]: PLS 2: 1139 (Ps.-Aug. Serm Cai. 2.56; Serm. Mai, 38)
11. De Resurrectione Domini [III]: PLS 2: 1249–51 (Ps.-Aug. Serm. Cai. 2.55; Serm. Mai, 152)
12. PLS 4: 665–67 (Ps.-Aug. Serm. Mai, 35) [V. Saxer, *RBén* 80 (1970), 42–50: might be the same author as Serm. Arm. 8]
13. Ps.-Leo, Serm. 8 (PL 54: 477–522, no. 8; Serm. Cai. 4)
14. PLS 4: 667–68 (Ps.-Aug. Serm. Mai, 41)
15. De Octava Paschae: PLS 2: 1141–43 (Ps.-Aug. Serm. Mai, 42)

Serm. Barré = Sermones, ed. H. Barré, *Marianum* 25 (1963), 56–93
2. De natali domini: Barré 1963: 57–58 [African?]
3. De annuntiatione dominica: Barré 1963: 60–61 (Ps.-Ambr. Serm. 167)
4. De nativitate domini: Barré 1963: 64–70; PLS 4: 1993–96 (sixth-century African?)
5. [Fragments only]: Barré 1963: 88
6. De annuntiatione domini: Barré 1963: 89–90; PLS 4: 1990

Serm. Bouhot
3. De beato Ioseph [translation of Ps.-Chrysos. PG 56: 587–90; connected to Ps.-Aug. Serm. Cai 1.45 = Serm. Cas. 1.162] text: J. Noret, ed., *Antidoron* 1, *Hommage à M. Geerard*, Brussels (1984), 48–51 (fifth-century African)

Serm. Cai. I = A. B. Caillau, B. Saint-Yves, *S. Aurelii Augustini Hipp. ep. operum supplementum* I, Paris, 1836 [PLS 2: 900–1029]
13. In Natali Domine: Africa, first half of the fifth century [PLS 2: 931–34]
19. Africa, fifth century [PLS 3: 177–79]
20. Ante Pascha, de Ieiunio: African [PLS 2: 944–46]
27. De Pascha: Africa, first half of the fifth century [PLS 2: 954–56]
28. De Pascha: Africa, end of fourth century [PLS 2: 957–58]
31. De Pascha: Africa, first half of the fifth century [PLS 2: 965–66]
32. De Pascha: Africa, first half of the fifth century [PLS 2: 966–69]
34. De Pascha, ad Neophytos: Africa, second half of the fifth century [PLS 2: 972–78]

36. De Pascha, ad Neophytos: Africa, first half of the fifth century [PLS 2: 979–82]
43. In Die Pentecostes: Africa, early, same writer as 1.44 [PLS 2: 996–97]
44. De Adventu Spiritus Sancti: Africa, early, same writer as 1.43 [PLS 2: 997–99]
46. De Zachaeo: Africa, beginning of fifth century [PLS 2: 1003–04]
64. In Natali Martyrum: Africa, citation of Old Latin biblical text [PLS 2: 1011–12]
66. Africa, same author as 67 [PLS 2: 1013–15]
67. De Ieiunio: Africa, same author as 1.20 and 1.66 [PLS 2: 1015–16]

Serm. Cai. I, Appendix
5. De Ascensione: Africa, fourth-fifth century [PLS 2: 1357–60; J. Leclercq, *RBén* 57 (1947), 121–25]
7. De Pentecoste: Africa, fifth century [PLS 2: 1024–26]
8. De Pentecoste: Africa, early [PLS 2: 1026–29]

Serm. Cai. II, 1–62 = A. B. Caillau, *S. Augustini Hipp. Ep. opera omnia multis sermonibus ineditis aucta et locupletata*, vol. 24, Paris, 1942 [PLS 2:1029–81]
Serm. Cai. II, 63–98 = A. B. Caillau, *S. Augustini Hipp. Ep. opera omnia*, vol. 24bis, Paris, 1842 [PLS 2: 1081–1123]
38. De Epiphania Domini: Africa, beginning of fifth century [PLS 2: 1048–52]
Serm. Cai. II, Appendix
57. De Ascensione: Africa, fourth-fifth century [PLS 2: 1357–60; J. Leclercq *RBén* 57 (1947), 121–25]

Serm. Canel. = *Sermones*, ed. A. Canellis, *Zénon de Vérone et 11 sermons ps. Augustiniens*, Lyon, 1988: 254–312, where the argument is made that the following sermons have African origins (see, however, the remarks by F. Dolbeau, *Rech. Aug.* 20 [1985], 15 and 53)
1. De beato Abraham: PL 39: 1743–45 (Ps.-Aug. Serm. 3)
2. De immolatione Isaac: PL 39: 1751–53 (Ps.-Aug. Serm. 7)
3. De Pharaone et parvulorum interfectione: PL 39: 1789–91 (Ps.-Aug. Serm. 23)
4. De filiis Israel: PL 39: 1797–99 (Ps.-Aug. Serm. 27)
5. De fame Samariae: PL 39: 1836–37 (Ps.-Aug. Serm. 46)
6. De sancta Iudith: PL 39: 1839–40 (Ps.-Aug. Serm. 48)
7. De eadem Iudith: PL 39: 1840–41 (Ps.-Aug. Serm. 49)
8. De beato Iob: PL 39: 1841–42 (Ps.-Aug. Serm. 50)

9. De tribus pueris in fornace: PL 39: 1855–56 (Ps.-Aug. Serm. 59)
10. De sancta Susanna: PL 39: 1857–58 (Ps.-Aug. Serm. 60)

Serm. Cas. = Bibliotheca Casinensis, Florilegium (2nd part) II, Monte Cassino, 1875
55. Africa, beginning of fifth century (Ps.-Aug. Serm. Cai. I, 46)
172. Africa, early fifth century (Ps.-Aug. Serm. Cai. II, 38)

Serm. Den.
1. Laus Cerei, Africa, fifth–sixth century [P. Verbraken, *RBén* 70 (1960) 303–06]

Serm. Eracl.
P. Verbraken, "Les deux sermons du prêtre Eraclius d'Hippone," *RBén* 71 (1961), 3–21

Serm. Esc. = *Sermones Escurialenses.* These sermons probably derive in whole from a dissident African source. New sermons that have been recognized to be part of this same collection have been commented on and edited by Leroy (1994, 1997, and 1999)
1. De Genesi et de dignitate humanae condicionis: PL 95: 1205–08
2. De Genesi: De Adam et Eva [et] De lapsu primi hominis: PL 95: 1208–10 (Ps.-Aug. Cai., 2.2)
3. De Genesi: De interdictione arboris ad Adam: PLS 4: 669–71
4. De Genesi: inimicitiam ponam inter te et mulierem: PL 95: 1210–13
5. Credidit Abraam Deo et reputatum est ei ad iustitiam: PLS 4: 671–73
6. De Iacob et Esau: PLS 4: 674–76 (Ps.-Petrus Chrysologus, Serm. Liv. 1)
7. De Ioseph, ubi a fratribus venditur: PLS 4: 677–84 (Ps.-Petrus Chrysologus, Serm. Liv. 2)
8. De Ioseph, ubi ab uxore patroni apud eum accusatur: Leroy 1999: 161–64
9. De masculis, ubi pharao praecepit nascentes masculos mori: PL 39: 1789–91 (cf. Ps.-Aug. Serm. 23)
10. De sabbato: Leroy 1999: 164–65
11. De virtutibus per legem i.e. per arcam testamenti factis et inde maiestas venerandae legis ostenditur: Leroy 1999: 166–68
12. Ubi Moyses contra Amalecitas oratione pugnabat: PLS 4: 684–87 (Ps.-Petrus Chrysologus, Serm. Liv. 3)

13. De Gedeone: Leroy 1999: 169–71

14. De Iob: Leroy 1999: 171–74

15. De confessione, super illud psalmum "confitemini Domino quoniam bonus": PLS 4: 736–37

16. Confitemini Domino quoniam bonus, quoniam in saeculum misericordia eius: PL 39: 1851–53 (Ps.-Aug. Serm. 56)

17. Confitemini Domino quoniam bonus, quoniam in saeculum misericordia eius: Leroy 1999: 175–78

18. Confitemini Domino quoniam bonus: PLS 2: 1199 (Ps.-Aug. Serm. Mai, 90.1)

18B. In Paschae: PLS 2: 1199–1201 (Ps.-Aug. Serm. Mai, 90.2–4)

19. Confitemini Domino quoniam bonus: Leroy 1999: 179–81

20. Felix qui intellegit super egenum et pauperem. In die mali liberabit eum de inimicis Deus: Leroy 1999: 182–83

20B. Dum facis, inquit Dominus, misericordiam: Leroy 1999: 183–85

21. De David, ubi Goliat immanem hostem devicit: PLS 4: 687–90

22. De Absalon, ubi David patrem prosequitur et de proelio fugiens obligato gutture arboris ramo se penditur: PLS 4: 690–93 (Ps.-Leo, Serm. Cai, 8)

23. De Helia: Vivit Dominus, si erit hiis omnibus ros et pluvia: PLS 4: 694–96

24. De Helisaeo et Syrorum insidiis et campo vel detectis: PLS 4: 696–99

25. Ubi Naaman Syrus Helisaei iussu in Iordane baptizatus a lepra curatur: PL 39: 1830–32 (Ps.-Aug. Serm. 43)

26. Ubi sub Helisaeo obsessa Samaria et famem patitur ita ut distraheretur caput asini quinquaginta siclis argenteis: PL 39: 1836–37 (Ps.-Aug. Serm. 46)

27. Diligite iustitiam qui iudicatis terram: Leroy 1999: 185–88

28. Fili accedens ad servitutem Dei, sta in iustitia et timore et praepara animam tuam ad temptationem: Leroy 1999: 188–91

29. De Esaia: cognovit bos possessorem suum: PL 65: 947–49; Leroy 1999: 192–94 (Ps.-Fulg. Serm. 76)

30. De Esaia [vel] Super illud Esaiae: si volueritis et audieritis me: PLS 4: 703–05

31. Ego sum, ego sum, qui deleo facinora tua: Leroy 1999: 194–97

32. De Ieremiae sanctificatione in utero: PLS 4: 700–02

34. De tribus pueris: Leroy 1999: 197–99

35. De Abacuch propheta: Leroy 1999: 199–201

36. Oportet semper orare et non deficere: R. Etaix, *RBén* 92 (1982), 343–45

37. In dictum Ioannis: veniet hora quando veri adoratores adorabunt: PLS 4: 705–07

38. In illud Matthaei: qui fecerit et sic docuerit: PL 39: 2243–45 (Ps.-Aug. Serm. 268)

39. In illud Matthaei: cavete a pseudoprophetis: PLS 4: 707–10

40. De Zachaeo: PLS 4: 710–13 (Leroy 1993: 215–22)

41. De arbore fici a Domino arefacta: PLS 4: 713–17

42. De eo qui incidit in latrones: PLS 4: 717–20

43. In dictum Ioannis: vos amici mei estis: PLS 4: 720–23

44. De evangelio [et] in dictum Ioannis: vos amici mei estis: PLS 4: 723–26

45. De innocentibus: PL 95: 1176–77 (Ps.-Aug. Serm. Cai. II, App. 79; Serm. Cas. 2.169b; Serm. Mai, 110; Serm. Mai, 124)

46. De martyribus: PLS 4: 726–29

47. De martyribus: PLS 4: 738–40

48. Quod oculus non vidit: Leroy 1999: 201–04

49. De principiis Christiani nominis: Leroy 1999: 204–06

50. De apostolo: propter quod rogo ne deficiatis: Leroy 1999: 207–09

51. De apostolo: nescitis quia angelos sumus iudicaturi?: Leroy 1999: 209–11

52. De apostolo id est de fide et spe et caritate: PLS 4: 729–33

53. De misericordia: Leroy 1999: 212–14 (Ps. Aug. Serm. 312; PL 39: 243–44)

54. Item de misericordia: tria sunt quae in misericordiae opere: PLS 4: 840–43

55. Item de misericordia: Leroy 1999: 215–17

56. De odio: Leroy 1999: 218–19

57. De levium peccatorum periculis quibus maiorum peccatorum pernicies possit agnosci: PLS 4: 733–35

58. De fide: Leroy 1999: 219–21

59. De pace: PL 39: 1931–33

60. De oratione: Leroy 1999: 222–25

Serm. Etaix = Sermones, ed. R. Etaix in *RBén* and AB

12. *RBén* 92 (1982), 340–42

16. *RBén* 92 (1982), 343–45

18. *AB* 100 (1982), 601–05

22. *RBén* 96 (1986), 241–46

23. *RBén* 96 (1986), 247–48

Serm. Leclercq = Sermones ed. J. Leclercq (PLS 3: 1412–25; fifth or sixth century African?)

2. De ascensione Domini: PLS 3: 1413–14
3. In Pentacosten: PLS 3: 1414–15
4. In Pentacosten: PLS 3: 1416–18
7. In natali martyrum diversorum: PLS 3: 1422–23
8. In natali martyrum diversorum: PLS 3: 1424

Serm. Vindob. = *Homiliae Vindobonenses*: a sermon book in the Österreichische Nationalbibliothek (Ms. 1616), dated to the late eighth or early ninth century (Lambot, 1958; Grégoire, 1966: 132–41, and 1980: 280–91). A fair number of the sermons seem to be of African origin.

3. De nativitate domini: PL39: 1990–91 (Ps.-Aug. Serm. 123 and Ps.-Fulg. Serm. 36; Morin, 1909: n.7)
5A. De natali domini: PLS 4: 1911–12 (sixth-century African?)
6. De natali sancti Stephani (PL 39: 2145–46 (Ps.-Aug. Serm. 215; Ps.-Fulg. Serm. 2)
10. De infantibus occisis: PL39: 2151–52 (Ps.-Aug. Serm. 219)
11. De epiphania: PLS 1: 297–300 (G. Morin, *RBén* 35 (1923), 236–41; fifth-century African?)
12. Sermo sancti Didymi de Theophania [M. Bogaert ed., *RBén* 73 (1963), 9–11]
14. De quadragesima (PLS 4: 1912–13)
19. De Fariseo et publiciano: PLS 2: 1031–33 (Ps. Aug. Serm. Cai., 2.12; Ps.-Aug. Serm. Cas. 2.114)
20. De symbolo PLS 3: 1370–76 (G. Morin, *RBén* 35 (1923), 233–35 = sixth-century African?)
20A. [Fragment only]: PLS 4: 1914
21A. Ad cenam dominicam (PLS 4: 1914)
22. De die sancto paschiae (PLS 4: 1915–16)
23. De pascha et resurrectione: PLS 4: 1916–18 (Lemarié, 1980: probably African?)
24. De pascha et resurrectione: PLS 4: 1918–20 (Aug. Serm. 375A = Denis, 4)
32. De resurrectione Domini nostri: PL 47: 1155B-1156D; Ps.-Aug. Serm. Mai, 85
36. De nativitate sancti Iohannis Baptistae: PLS 4: 1920–22

Bibliography

The periodical, serial, and collection abbreviations, other than those listed in the Abbreviations, are taken from the standard ones in *Année philologique*.

PRIMARY SOURCES

Listed below are the main editions that were used for the primary literary sources. The texts that are cited from standard series are ordinarily taken from the *Corpus Christianorum, series Latina* (CCL) or the *Sources chrétiennes* (SC) texts where these editions exist, from the *Corpus Scriptorum Ecclesiasticorum Latinorum* (CSEL) where they do not; and, finally, where all these fail, from J.-P. Migne's *Patrologia Latina* (PL). Where none of these are available, or they have been superseded, the specific alternative text that was used is noted.

CALENDARS

J. B. de Rossi and L. Duchesne, eds., *Martyrologium Hieronymianum* = *Acta Sanctorum (AASS)*, November II.1 (1894); H. Delehaye, *Commentarius perpetuus* = *AASS*, November II.2 (1931).

J. B. de Rossi and L. Duchesne, eds., *Kalendarium Carthaginiense* = *AASS*, November II.1 (1894), pp. lxix–lxxii.

COLLECTIONS OF DOCUMENTS

J.-L. Maier, ed., *Le Dossier du Donatisme, t. 1: Des origines à la mort de Constance II (303–361)*, Berlin, Akademie Verlag, 1987 [Texte und Untersuchungen zur Geschichte der altchristlichen Literatur, no. 134].

Le Dossier du Donatisme, t. 2: De Julien l'Apostat à Saint Jean Damascène (361–750), Berlin, Akademie Verlag, 1989 [Texte und Untersuchungen zur Geschichte der altchristlichen Literatur, no. 135].

This collection displays some faults of which the reader should be aware, although they are, in the opinion of the writer, not quite as severe as some of the reviewers tend to suggest. See Lancel (1988), 37–42, who is, on the whole, more favourable than the stricter Noël Duval, "Une nouvelle édition du 'Dossier du Donatisme' avec traduction française," *REAug* 35 (1989), 171–79; and see also P. Mastandrea, *Prometheus* 14 (1988), 87–95.

H. von Soden and H. von Campenhausen, eds., *Urkunden zur Entstehungs-geschichte des Donatismus*, 2nd ed., Berlin, Walter de Gruyter, 1950.

CHURCH COUNCILS

Africa

Concilia Africae, A. 345–A. 525, ed. C. Munier, CCL 149, Turnhout, Brepols, 1974.
Gesta conlationis Carthaginiensis anno 411, accedit Sancti Augustini Breviculus conlationis cum Donatistis, ed. S. Lancel, CCL 149A, Turnhout, Brepols, 1974.
Actes de la Conférence de Carthage en 411, 4 vols., ed. S. Lancel, SC 194, 195, 224, and 373, Paris, 1972–91.

Serdica

H. Hess, *The Early Development of Canon Law and the Council of Serdica*, Oxford University Press, 2002: Latin canons: pp. 212–24 [text]; Greek canons: pp. 226–40 [text].

Spain

Canons of the Council of Elvira: G. Martínez Díez and F. Rodríguez, eds., "Concilium Eliberritanum," in *Monumenta Hispaniae Sacra: La colección canónica hispana*, vol. 4: *Concilios Galos, Concilios Hispanos: primera parte*, Madrid, 1984, pp. 233–68.

ADVERSUS FULGENTIUM DONATISTAM (LIBELLUS)

Libellus adversus Fulgentium Donatistam, ed. C. Lambot, *RBén* 58 (1948), 190–222 [Maier, *Dossier*, 2: 239–85].

ANTHOLOGIA LATINA

Anthologia Latina, 1: *Carmina in codicibus scripta*, 1: *Libri Salmansiani aliorumque carmina*, ed. D. R. Shackleton Bailey, Stuttgart, Teubner, 1982.

APOCALYPSE OF PAUL

See *Visio Pauli* below

AUGUSTINE

Ad Donatistas post collationem

Contra partem Donati post collationem, ed. M. Petschenig, CSEL 53, Vienna, 1910, 97–162.

Adversus Iudaeos

Aurelii Augustini Liber ad Orosium contra Priscillianistas et Origenistas, Sermo adversus Iudaeos, Liber de haeresibus ad Quodvultdeum, ed. J. L. Bazant-Hegemark, diss. Vienna, 1969, 24–63.

Breviculus collationis

Breviculus conlationis cum Donatistis, ed. S. Lancel, CCL 149A, Turnhout, Brepols, 1974, 259–306.

Confessiones

Confessiones, ed. M. Skutella, 2nd ed., BA 13–14, Paris, 1992–98.
Sancti Augustini Confessionum libri XIII, 2nd ed., ed. M. Skutella, rev. ed., ed. L. Verheijen, CCL 27, Turnhout, Brepols, 1981.
S. Aurelii Augustini Confessionum libri XIII, ed. M. Skutella, corr. H. Jürgens and W. Schaub, Stuttgart, Teubner, 1996.

Contra Academicos

Aurelii Augustini Contra Academicos, De beata vita necnon De ordine libri, ed. W. M. Green, Utrecht and Antwerp, Spectrum, 1956 [Stromata Patristica et Mediaevalia].

Contra Cresconium

Contra Cresconium libri quattuor, ed. M. Petschenig, CSEL 52, Vienna, 1909, 325–582.

Contra epistulam Parmeniani

Contra epistulam Parmeniani libri tres, ed. M. Petschenig, CSEL 51, Vienna, 1908, 17–141.

Contra Faustum Manichaeum

Contra Faustum, ed. J. Zycha, CSEL 25.1, Vienna, 1891, 249–797.

Contra Fortunatum

Contra Fortunatum disputatio, ed. J. Zycha, CSEL 25.1, Vienna, 1891, 81–112.

Contra Gaudentium

Contra Gaudentium Donatistarum episcopum libri duo, ed. M. Petschenig, CSEL 53, Vienna, 1910, 201–274.

Contra litteras Petiliani

Contra litteras Petiliani, ed. M. Petschenig, CSEL 52, Vienna, 1909, 1–227.

De baptismo

De baptismo contra Donatistas libri septem, ed. M. Petschenig, CSEL 51, Vienna, 1908, 143–375.

De civitate Dei

De civitate Dei libri xxii, ed. B. Dombart, A. Kalb, CCL 47–48, Turnhout, Brepols, 1955.

De doctrina Christiana

De doctrina Christiana, ed. K. D. Daur, CCL 32, Turnhout, Brepols, 1962.

De haeresibus

De haeresibus ad Quodvultdeum liber unus, ed. R. Vander Plaetse and C. Beukers, CCL 46, Turnhout, Brepols, 1969, 283–345.
Aurelii Augustini Liber ad Orosium contra Priscillianistas et Origenistas, Sermo adversus Iudaeos, Liber de haeresibus ad Quodvultdeum, ed. J. L. Bazant-Hegemark, diss. Vienna, 1969.

De moribus ecclesiae Catholicae et de moribus Manichaeorum

De moribus ecclesiae Catholicae et de moribus Manichaeorum libri duo, ed. J. B. Bauer, CSEL 90, Vienna, 1992.

De opere monachorum

De opere monachorum, ed. J. Zycha, CSEL 41, Vienna, 1900, 529–96.

De patientia

De patientia, ed. J. Zycha, CSEL 41, Vienna, 1900, 663–91
Sancti Aurelii Augustini sermo de patientia, ed. F. O'Brien, Washington DC, 1970, 71–119.

De unico baptismo

De unico baptismo contra Petilianum, ed. M. Petschenig, CSEL 53, Vienna, 1910, 3–34.

Enarrationes in Psalmos

Enarrationes in Psalmos, eds. E. Dekkers and J. Fraipont, CCL 38, 39, and 40, Turnhout, Brepols, 1990.

Enarrationes in Psalmos 1–50, 1: Enarrationes in Psalmos 1–32, ed. C. Weidmann, CSEL 93.1A, Vienna, 2003.

Enarrationes in Psalmos 51–100, 1: Enarrationes in Psalmos 51–60, ed. H. Müller, CSEL 94.1, Vienna, 2003.

Enarrationes in Psalmos 101–150, 3: Enarrationes in Psalmos 119–133, ed. F. Gori, CSEL 95.3, Vienna, 2001.

Enarrationes in Psalmos 101–150, 4: Enarrationes in Psalmos 134–140, ed. F. Gori, CSEL 95.4, Vienna, 2003.

Enarrationes in Psalmos 101–150, 5: Enarrationes in Psalmos 141–150, eds. F. Gori and I. Spaccia, CSEL 95.5, Vienna, 2005.

Enchiridion

Enchiridion ad Laurentium de fide et spe et caritate, ed. E. Evans, CCL 46, Turnhout, Brepols, 1969, 49–114.

Epistulae

Epistulae, ed. A. Goldbacher, CSEL 34.1, 34.2, 44, 57, 58, Vienna, 1895, 1898, 1904, 1911, 1923.

Epistulae, I–LV, ed. K. D. Daur, CCL 35, Turnhout, Brepols, 2004.

Epistulae, LVI–C, ed. K. D. Daur, CCL 35A, Turnhout, Brepols, 2005.

Divjak Letters

Epistulae *1–*29, ed. J. Divjak, CSEL 88, Vienna, 1981.

Epistulae *1–*29, ed. J. Divjak and S. Lancel, BA 46B, Paris, 1987.

Epistula ad Catholicos

Epistula ad Catholicos de secta Donatistarum, ed. M. Petschenig, CSEL 52, Vienna, 1909, 229–322.

Gesta cum Emerito

Gesta cum Emerito Donastistarum episcopo, ed. M. Petschenig, CSEL 53, Vienna, 1910, 179–96.

In Epistulam Joannis ad Parthos tractatus

Saint Augustin: Commentaire de la première épître de s. Jean, ed. P. Agaësse, 4th ed., SC 75, Paris, 1994.

In Iohannis Evangelium tractatus

In Iohannis Evangelium tractatus CXXIV, ed. R. Willems, CCL 36, Turnhout, Brepols, 1990.

Psalmus contra partem Donati

Psalmus contra partem Donati, ed. C. Lambot, *RBén* 47 (1935), 318–28.
Traités anti-Donatistes, 1: Psalmus contra partem Donati, J. Congar intro. and notes, G. Finaert transl., BA 28, Paris, 1963, 135–191.

Regula

Regula Sancti Augustini, ed. A. Goldbacher, CSEL 57, Vienna, 1911, 356–71.
L. Verheijen, *La Règle de saint Augustin*, 2 vols., Paris, Etudes Augustiniennes, 1967.

Retractationes

Retractationes libri duo, ed. A. Mutzenbecher, CCL 57, Turnhout, Brepols, 1984.

Sermo ad Caesariensis ecclesiae plebem

Sermo ad Caesariensis ecclesiae plebem, ed. J. Petschenig, CSEL 53, Vienna, 1910, 167–78.

Sermones

Sermones, ed. J.-P. Migne, PL 38–39, 1841 and 1845; reprint: 1993.
Sermones de vetere testamento (1–50), ed. C. Lambot, CCL 41, Turnhout, Brepols, 1961.
Sermones in Matthaeum, 1, ed. P. P. Verbracken et al., CCL 41 Aa, Turnhout, Brepols, 2008.
Sermones in Epistolas Apostolicas, 1, ed. G. Partoens, CCL 41 Ba, Turnhout, Brepols, 2008.
Sancti Augustini Sermones post Maurinos reperti, ed. Dom. G. Morin, in *Miscellanea Agostiniana*, vol. 1, Rome, 1930.
C. Lambot, *Sancti Aurelii Augustini Sermones selecti duodeviginti*, Brussels, 1950 [Stromata Patristica et Mediaevalia, no. 1].
Dolbeau Sermons: F. Dolbeau, *Vingt-six sermons au peuple d'Afrique*, Paris, Institut d'Etudes Augustiniennes, 1996 [Collection d'Etudes Augustiniennes, no. 147].
Erfurt Sermons: I. Schiller, D. Weber, and C. Weidmann, "Sechs neue Augustinuspredigten: Teil 1 mit Edition dreier Sermones," *WS* 121 (2008), 227–84; "Teil 2 mit Edition dreier Sermones Zum Thema Almosen," *WS* 122 (2009), 171–213.
Sancti Aurelii Augustini De excidio urbis Romae sermo: A Critical Text and Translation with Introduction and Commentary, ed. M. V. O'Reilly, Washington DC, The Catholic University of America Press, 1955.

Sermo 163: G. Partoens, "Le sermon 163 de saint Augustin: introduction et édition," *RBén* 115 (2006), 251–85: pp. 270–85 [text].

Aurelii Augustini sermo CCCII. Testo, traduzione e commento, ed. Bruna Pieri, Bologna, 1998.

CASSIODORUS

Expositio Psalmorum, ed. M. Adriaen, CCL, 97–98, Turnhout, Brepols, 1958.

CODEX THEODOSIANUS (SEE ALSO: LEGAL TEXTS)

Theodosiani libri xvi cum Constitutionibus Sirmondianis et Leges novellae ad Theodosium pertinentes, 2nd ed., eds. T. Mommsen and P. M. Meyer, Berlin, 1905; reprint: Berlin, 1954.

Book XVI: R. Delmaire and F. Richard, eds., *Les lois religieuses des empereurs Romains de Constantin à Théodose II (312–438), 1: Code Théodosien Livre XVI*, SC 497, Paris, 2005.

COLLECTIO AVELLANA

O. Guenther, ed., *Epistolae Imperatorum Pontificum Alioruminde ab a. CCCLXVII usque DLIII datae Avellana quae dicitur collectio*, CSEL 35.1, Vienna, 1895.

CYPRIANUS

Sententiae episcoporum numero LXXXVII 'De haereticis baptizandis', ed. G. F. Diercks, CCL 3E, Turnhout, Brepols, 2004.

DE DUOBUS MONTIBUS SINA ET SION

De duobus montibus Sina et Sion, ed. G. W. Hartel, CSEL 3.3, Vienna, 1871, 104–19.

De duobus montibus Sina et Sion, ed. C. Burini, Fiesole, 1994 [Biblioteca Patristica, no. 25].

EPIPHANIUS

Epiphanius: Panarion, ed. K. Holl, GCS 25, 31 and 37, Leipzig, 1915–53; vol. 2: *Haereses XXXIV–LXIV*, 2nd ed., ed. J. Dummer, Berlin, 1980.

EUSEBIUS

Eusebius: Historia Ecclesiastica, ed. E. Schwartz, 3 vols., GCS 9, Leipzig, 1903–09.

Eusèbe de Césarée: Histoire ecclésiastique, ed. G. Bardy, SC 31, 41, 55, and 73, Paris, 1952–60.

EVODIUS

De fide contra Manichaeos, ed. Z. Zycha, CSEL 25.2, Vienna, 1892, 949–75.

De miraculis sancti Stephani protomartyris, ed. J. Hillgarth, in J.-P. Migne, ed., PL 41: 833–54.

FERRANDUS

Pseudo-Ferrando di Cartagine: Vita di San Fulgenzio, ed. A. Isola, Rome, Città Nuova, 1987.

FILASTRIUS

Filastri episcopi Brixiensis Diversarum hereseon liber, ed. F. Heylen, CCL 9, Turnhout, Brepols, 1957.

Filastrii Brixiensis Diversarum hereseon liber, ed. F. Heylen, Milan and Rome, 1991 [Scriptores circa Ambrosium, no. 2].

GENNADIUS

Liber de viris illustribus, ed. E. C. Richardson, Leipzig, 1896 [Texte und Untersuchungen, no. 14].

GESTA APUD ZENOPHILUM

Gesta apud Zenophilum, ed. C. Ziwsa, CSEL 26, Vienna, 1893, 185–97 [Maier, *Dossier*, 1, no. 29: 214–39].

HYPOMNESTICON AUGUSTINI CONTRA PELAGIONOS SIVE CAELESTIANOS HAERETICOS

The Pseudo-Augustinian Hypomnesticon against the Pelagians and Celestians, ed. J. E. Chisholm, vol. 2, Fribourg, 1980 [*Paradosis*, no. 21].

LACTANTIUS

Lactantius: De mortibus persecutorum, ed. and transl. J. L. Creed, Oxford University Press, 1984.

LEGAL TEXTS

R. Delmaire and F. Richard, eds., *Les lois religieuses des empereurs romains de Constantin à Théodose II (312–438), 1: Code Théodosien Livre XVI*, SC 497, Paris, Editions du Cerf, 2005.

J. Rougé, R. Delmaire, et al., eds., *Les lois religieuses des empereurs romains de Constantin à Théodose II (312–438), 2: Code Théodosien I-XV, Code Justinien, Constitutions Sirmondiennes*, SC 531, Paris, Editions du Cerf, 2009.

LIBER GENEALOGUS

Liber Genealogus anni CCCLXXVII–CCCCLII, in T. Mommsen, ed., *Chronica Minora saec. IV.V.VI.VII*, vol. 1, MGH AA 9, Berlin, 1892, 154–96.

LIBER GENERATIONIS

Liber Generationis: as pt. XV of "Chronographus anni CCCLIII," in T. Mommsen, ed., *Chronica Minora saec. IV.V.VI.VII*, vol. 1, MGH AA 9, Berlin, 1892, 78–140.

LUXORIUS

M. Rosenblum, *Luxorius: A Latin Poet among the Vandals*, New York and London, Columbia University Press, 1961.
Luxurius, ed. H. Happ, Stuttgart, Teubner, 1986.

NOTITIA PROVINCIARUM ET CIVITATUM AFRICAE

Notitiae provinciarum et civitatum Africae, ed. C. Halm, MGH AA 3.1, Berlin, 1879, 63–71.
"Registre des provinces et des cités d'Afrique," in *Victor de Vita: Histoire de la persécution Vandale en Afrique*, ed. S. Lancel, Paris, Budé, 2002, 252–72.

OPTATUS

Optat de Milève: Traité contre les Donatistes, t. 1: *Livres I et II*, ed. M. Labrousse, SC 412, Paris, 1995.
Optat de Milève: Traité contre les Donatistes, t. 2: *Livres III à VII*, ed. M. Labrousse, SC 413, Paris, 1996.

PASSIONES MARTYRUM

R. Knopf and G. Krüger, eds., mit einem Nachtrag von G. Ruhbach, *Ausgewählte Märtyrerakten*, 4th ed., Tübingen, J. C. B. Mohr, 1965 [Sammlung ausgewählter kirchen– und dogmengeschichtlicher Quellenschriften, N.F. 3].

PASSIO SANCTORUM DATIVI, SATURNINI PRESBYTERI ET ALIORUM

P. Franchi de' Cavalieri, "La *Passio* dei martiri Abitinensi," in *Note agiografiche*, no. 8, Rome, Tipografia Vaticana, 1935 [Studi e Testi, no. 65], 3–71: pp. 49–71 [text] = Maier, *Dossier*, 1, no. 4: 57–92 [Franchi de' Cavalieri's text, with minor revisions; and see also the revisions suggested by Dolbeau (2003)].

PASSIO SANCTI DONATI

F. Dolbeau, "La *Passio Sancti Donati* (BHL 2303b): une tentative d'édition critique," in *Memoriam sanctorum venerantes: Miscellanea in onore di Monsignor Victor Saxer*, Città del Vaticano, 1992 [Studi di Antichità Cristiana, no. 48], 251–67.

PASSIO SANCTI FELICIS

H. Delehaye, "La passion de S. Félix de Thibiuca," *AB* 39 (1921), 241–76: pp. 247–52 [text V]; pp. 252–59 [text N].

PASSIO SANCTI GALLONII

P. Chiesa, "Un testo agiografico africano ad Aquileia: gli *Acta* di Gallonio e dei martiri di *Timida Regia*," *AB* 114 (1996), 221–68: pp. 265–68 [text].

S. Lancel, "Actes de Gallonius: texte critique, traduction et notes," *REAug* 52 (2006), 243–59: pp. 24–38 [text].

PASSIO SANCTAE MARCIANAE

"De S. Marciana, virgine martyre. Caesareae in Mauretania," AASS 1 (Januarii, tomus primus), 568–70.

PASSIO SANCTI MARCULI

P. Mastandrea, "Passioni dei martiri Donatisti (BHL 4473 e 5271)," *AB* 113 (1995), 39–88: "Passio Marculi," pp. 65–75 [text].

PASSIO SANCTORUM MARIANI ET IACOBI

P. Franchi de' Cavalieri, *Passio SS. Mariani et Iacobi*, Rome, Tipografia Vaticana, 1900 [Studi e Testi, no. 3], 7–44.

PASSIO SANCTARUM MAXIMAE, DONATILLAE ET SECUNDAE

C. de Smedt, "Passiones tres martyrum Africanorum," *AB* 9 (1890), 107–34.

P. Franchi de' Cavalieri, "Della 'Passio sanctarum Maximae, Donatillae et Secundae'," in *Note agiografiche*, no. 8, Rome, Tipografia Vaticana, 1935 [Studi e Testi, no. 65], 75–97.

PASSIO SANCTORUM MAXIMIANI ET ISAAC

P. Mastandrea, "Passioni dei martiri Donatisti (BHL 4473 e 5271)," *AB* 113 (1995), 39–88: "Passio Isaac et Maximiani," pp. 76–88 [text].

PASSIO SANCTI PELLEGRINI

P. Chiesa, "Pellegrino martire in urbe Bolitana e Pellegrino di Ancona. Un'altra agiografia africana ad Aquileia?," *AB* 116 (1998), 25–56: pp. 46–55 [text].

PASSIO SANCTAE SALSAE

Passio Sanctae Salsae: testo critico, con introduzione e traduzione italiana, ed. A. M. Piredda, Sassari, Edizioni Gallizzi, 2002, pp. 66–108 [text].

PASSIO SCILLITANORUM

F. Ruggiero, "Atti dei Martiri Scillitani," in *Atti della Accademia Nazionale dei Lincei, Classe di Scienze Morali, Storiche e Filologiche: Memorie*, ser. 9, no. 1.2, Rome, 1991, 35–139.

POSSIDIUS

Indiculus

A. Wilmart, "Operum S. Augustini Elenchus a Possidio eiusdem discipulo Calamensi episcopo digestus," *Miscellanea Agostiniana*, vol. 2, Rome, Tipografia Vaticana, 1931, 149–233.

Vita Sancti Augustini

A. A. R. Bastiaensen, ed., *Vita Augustini*, in C. Mohrmann intro., *Vita di Cipriano, Vita di Ambrogio, Vita di Agostino*, 2nd ed., Milan, Arnoldo Mondadori editori, 1981, 130–240.

"PRAEDESTINATUS"

De haeresibus [?], ed. F. Oehler, in *Corpus haereseologicum*, vol. 1, Berlin, 1856, 246–59 [Book One only].

QUODVULTDEUS

Quodvultdeus: Livre des promesses et des prédictions de Dieu, ed. R. Braun, SC 101–2, Paris, 1964.
Opera Quodvultdeo tributa. Liber promissionum et praedictorum Dei, ed. R. Braun, CCL 60, Turnhout, Brepols, 1976.

SEVERUS OF MINORCA

Severus of Minorca: Letter on the Conversion of the Jews, ed. S. Bradbury, Oxford University Press, 1996, 80–124.

VICTOR VITENSIS

Victor de Vita: Histoire de la persécution Vandale en Afrique, ed. S. Lancel, Paris, Budé, 2002.

VISIO PAULI

J. Armitage Robinson, *Apocrypha Anecdota = Texts and Studies: Contributions to Biblical and Patristic Literature*, vol. 2.3, Cambridge University Press, 1893 [reprint: Nendeln, Kraus, 1967], 11–42 [=Paris manuscript: Bibl. Nat. nouv. aq. 1631].

Th. Silverstein, "Visio Sancti Pauli," K. Lake and S. Lake, eds., *Studies and Documents*, vol. 4, London, Christophers, 1935, 131–34 [St. Gall text: Cod. 317, St. Gall Bibliothek].

VITA SANCTAE MELANIAE

P. Laurence, "Vita Sanctae Melaniae Senatricis Romae," Gérontius, *La vie latine de sainte Mélanie: édition critique, traduction et commentaire*, Jerusalem, Francisan Printing Press, 2002 [Studium Biblicum Franciscanum Collectio Minor, no. 41], 152–299

Vie de sainte Mélanie. Texte grec, ed. D. Gorce, SC 90, Paris, 1962.

SECONDARY SOURCES

In the footnotes, journal and periodical articles are referred to by the year of publication, whereas short titles have been used for books and collections. Where the short title is not formed from the first word(s) of the full title, the short title is given in square brackets before the full title.

Adam, A. (1958), "Das Fortwirken des Manichäismus bei Augustinus," *ZKG* 69, 1–25.

Adam, K., *Die kirchliche Sündenvergebung nach dem heilige Augustin*, Paderborn, Schöningh, 1917.

Adams, J. N., *Bilingualism and the Latin Language*, Cambridge University Press, 2003.

Admiralty, *Algeria*, vol. 2, Naval Intelligence Division, Geographical Handbook Series, no. 505A, 1944.

Aguiar Frazão, E. R. de [*Circunceliões*], *O Donatismo e os Circunceliões na obra da santo Agostinho*, São Paulo, Universidade de São Paulo, 1976.

Aït-Larbi, M., M. S. Aït-Belkacem, M. Belaïd, M. A. Naït-Redjam, and Y. Soltani (1999), "An Anatomy of the Massacres," in Y. Bedjaoui, A. Aroua, and M. Aït-Larbi, eds., *An Inquiry into the Algerian Massacres*, Geneva, Hoggar, 13–195.

Akerström, M., *Betrayal and Betrayers: The Sociology of Treachery*, New Brunswick NJ and London, Transaction Publishers, 1991.

Albertini, E. (1938), "Un témoignage épigraphique sur l'évêque donatiste Optat de Thamugadi," *CRAI*, 100–03.

Alexander, J. S. (1973), "A Note on the Interpretation of the Parable of the Threshing Floor at the Conference of Carthage of A.D. 411," *JThS* 24, 512–19.

(1982), "Methodology in the *Capitula gestorum conlationis Carthaginiensis*," in *Studia Patristica* 17, 3–8.

(1998), "Count Taurinus and the Persecutors of Donatism," *Zeitschrift für antikes Christentum* 2, 247–67.

Altaner, B. (1951), "Augustinus und Epiphanius von Salamis: eine quellenkritische Studie," in *Mélanges Joseph de Ghellinck, 1: Antiquité*, Gembloux, J. Duculot, 265–75 = *Kleine patristische Schriften*, Berlin, Akademie Verlag, 1967, 286–96.

Alvarez, J. (1966), "St. Augustine and Antisemitism," in F. L. Cross, ed., *Studia Patristica*, 9, Berlin, Akademie Verlag, 340–49.

Amadasi Guzzo, M. G. (1990), "Stato degli studi sulle iscrizioni latino-puniche della Tripolitania," *AfrRom* 7, 101–08.

Amundsen, D. (1989), "Suicide and Early Christian Values," in B. A. Brody, ed., *Suicide and Euthanasia: Historical and Contemporary Themes*, Dordrecht, Boston, and London, Kluwer Academic Publishers, 72–153.

Anastasi, R., ed., *Psalmus contra partem Donati*, Padua, Ceram, 1957.

Ando, C. (1996), "Pagan Apologetics and Christian Intolerance in the Ages of Themistius and Augustine," *JECS* 4, 171–207.

Archambault, P. (1969), "Augustin et Camus," *RechAug* 6, 195–221.

Arendt, H., *On Violence*, San Diego and New York, Harcourt, Brace & Co., 1970.

Atkinson, J. E. (1992), "Out of Order: The Circumcellions and Codex Theodosianus 16,5,52," *Historia* 41, 488–99.

Aziza, C., *Tertullien et le judaïsme*, Paris, Les Belles Lettres, 1977.

(1985), "Quelques aspects de la polemique judéo-chrétienne dans l'Afrique romaine (IIe–VIe siècles)," in C. Iancu and J.-M. Lassère, eds., *Juifs et judaïsme en Afrique du Nord dans l'Antiquité et le Haut Moyen-Age*, Montpellier, Université Paul Valéry, 49–54.

Baldwin, B. (1961), "Peasant Revolt in Africa in the Late Roman Empire," *Nottingham Mediaeval Studies* 6, 3–11 = ch. 41 in *Roman and Byzantine Papers*, Amsterdam, J. C. Gieben, 1989, 215–23.

Ballu, A., *Les ruines de Timgad*, 2 vols., Paris, E. Leroux, 1897–1911.

Banniard, M. [*Viva voce*], "L'âge d'or augustinien," in *Viva voce. Communication écrite et communication orale du IVe au IXe siècle en Occident Latin*, Paris, Institut d'études augustiniennes, 1992, 65–104.

(1998), "Variations langagières et communication dans la prédication d'Augustin," in Madec, *Augustin prédicateur*, 73–93.

Barnard, L. (1995), "The Criminalization of Heresy in the Later Roman Empire: A Sociopolitical Device?," *The Journal of Legal History* 16, 121–46.

Barnes, T. D., *Tertullian*, Oxford, Clarendon Press, 1971 (2nd ed., 1985).

(1975), "The Beginnings of Donatism," *JThS* 26, 13–22 = ch. 8 in *Early Christianity*.

Constantine and Eusebius, Cambridge MA, Harvard University Press, 1981.

(1982), "Aspects of the Background of the City of God," *Revue de l'Université d'Ottawa* 52, 64–80 = C. Wells, ed., *L'Afrique romaine/Roman Africa* (Ottawa, 1982), 69–85 = ch. 24 in *From Eusebius to Augustine*.

The New Empire of Diocletian and Constantine, Cambridge MA, Harvard University Press, 1982.

(1983), "Late Roman Prosopography: Between Theodosius and Justinian," *Phoenix* 37, 248–70.

Early Christianity and the Roman Empire, London, Variorum, 1984.

(1985a), "Proconsuls of Africa, 337–392," *Phoenix* 39, 144–53.

(1985b), "Proconsuls of Africa: Corrigenda," *Phoenix* 39, 273–74.

(1989), "Christians and Pagans in the Reign of Constantius," in A. Dihle, ed., *L'Eglise et l'empire au IV siècle*, Vandoeuvres-Genève, Foundation Hardt, 301–37 = ch. 8 in *From Eusebius to Augustine*.

Athanasius and Constantius. Theology and Politics in the Constantinian Empire, Cambridge, MA, Harvard University Press, 1993.

From Eusebius to Augustine: Selected Papers, 1982–1993, London, Variorum, 1994.

(1995), "Statistics and the Conversion of the Roman Aristocracy," *JRS* 85, 135–47.

Barrau, P. (1987), "A propos de l'*officium* du vicaire d'Afrique," *AfrRom* 4, 79–100.

Barry, M. I., *St. Augustine, the Orator: A Study of the Rhetorical Qualities of St. Augustine's Sermones ad Populum*, Washington DC, The Catholic University of America, 1924.

Barton, C. A. (1989), "The Scandal of the Arena," *Representations* 27, 1–36.

(1994), "Savage Miracles: The Redemption of Lost Honor in Roman Society and the Sacrament of the Gladiator and the Martyr," *Representations* 45, 41–71.

Sorrows of the Ancient Romans: the Gladiator and the Monster, Princeton University Press, 1993.

Battifol, P. (1913), "Le règlement des premiers conciles africains et le règlement du sénat romain," *Bulletin d'ancienne littérature et d'archéologie chrétiennes* 3, 3–19.

(1922), "Texte de saint Augustin relatif à la destruction des statues," *BSAF*, 310.

(1923), "Le *primae sedis episcopus* en Afrique," *RSR* 3, 425–32.

Baudet, P. (1988), "L'opinion de saint Augustin sur le suicide," in P. Ranson, ed., *Saint Augustin*, Lausanne, L'Age d'Homme, pp. 125–52.

Baumgart, S., *Die Bischofsherrschaft im Gallien des 5. Jahrhunderts: eine Untersuchung zu den Gründen und Anfängen weltlicher Herrschaft der Kirche*, Munich, Editio Maris, 1995.

Bavaud, G. (1964), "Le parabole du bon grain et de l'ivraie," note 20 in *BA* 29, 608–09.

Baxter, J. H. (1924), "The Martyrs of Madaura," *JThS* 26, 21–37.

(1952), "Psalmus contra Partem Donati," *Sacris erudiri* 5, 18–26.

Bayet, A., *Le suicide et la morale*, Paris, Alcan, 1922.

Beaver, R. P. (1935), "The Donatist Circumcellions," *ChHist* 4, 123–33.

BeDuhn, J. D. (2009), "Augustine Accused: Megalius, Manichaeism, and the Inception of the Confessions," *JECS* 17, 85–124.

Augustine's Manichaean Dilemma, 1: *Conversion and Apostasy, 373–388 C.E.*, Philadelphia, University of Pennsylvania Press, 2010.

Behrends, O. (1969), "Der *assessor* zur Zeit der klassischen Rechtswissenschaft," *ZSS RAbt* 86, 192–226.

Bell, J. B. [*Generation of Violence*], *The Irish Troubles: A Generation of Violence, 1967–1992*, New York, St. Martin's Press, 1993.

Bels, J. (1975), "La mort volontaire dans l'oeuvre de saint Augustin," *RHR* 187, 147–80.

Bénabou, M., *La résistance africaine à la Romanisation*, Paris, F. Maspero, 1976.

(1978), "Tacfarinas, insurgé berbère contre la colonisation romaine," *Annales (ESC)* 33, 83–88.

Berrouard, M. F. (1985), "Un tournant dans la vie de l'Eglise d'Afrique: les deux missions d'Alypius en Italie à la lumière des lettres 10*, 15*, 16*, 22* et 23A* de saint Augustin," *REAug* 31, 46–70.

Beschaouch, A. (1976), "Sur la localisation d'Abitina, la cité des célèbres martyrs africains," *CRAI*, 255–66.

Bianco, M. G. (1980), "Abecadarium Fulgentii episcopi ecclesiae Ruspensis," *Orpheus* 1, 166–78.

Biggs, M. (2005), "Dying Without Killing: Self-Immolations: 1963–2002," ch. 5 in Gambetta, *Suicide Missions*, 173–208.

Birley, A. R. (1987), "Some Notes on the Donatist Schism," *LibStud* 18, 29–41.

(1992), "Persecutors and Martyrs in Tertullian's Africa," *BIAL* 29, 37–68.

Blok, A. (2001), "The Meaning of 'Senseless' Violence," ch. 6 in *Honour and Violence*, Cambridge, Polity, 103–14.

Blumenkranz, B., *Die Judenpredigt Augustins. Ein Beitrag zur Geschichte der jüdisch-christlichen Beziehungen in den ersten Jahrhunderten*, Basel, Helbing, & Lichtenhahn, 1946 (reprint: Paris, Institut d'études augustiniennes, 1973).

(1958), "Augustin et les Juifs; Augustin et le Judaïsme," *REAug* 1, 225–41.

Bonner, G. [*Augustine of Hippo*], *St. Augustine of Hippo: Life and Controversies*, rev. ed., Norwich, Canterbury Press, 1997.

(1964), "Augustine's Visit to Caesarea in 418," in C. W. Dugmore and C. Duggan, eds., *Studies in Church History*, London, Thomas Nelson, 104–13.

Bonnet, C., *Melqart: Cultes et mythes de l'Héraclès tyrien en Méditerrannée*, Namur, Presses Universitaires de Namur, 1988.

Bori, P. C. (1983), "The Church's Attitude towards the Jews: An Analysis of Augustine's *Adversus Iudaeos*," *Miscellanea Historiae Ecclesiasticae* 6, 301–11.

Bowersock, G., *Martyrdom and Rome*, Cambridge University Press, 1995.

Bradbury, S., *Severus of Minorca: Letter on the Conversion of the Jews*, Oxford University Press, 1996.

Brass, P. R., *Theft of an Idol: Text and Context in the Representation of Collective Violence*, Princeton University Press, 1997.

Brisson, J.-P. (1956), "Luttes religieuses et luttes sociales dans l'Afrique romaine," *La Pensée* 67, 59–67.

Autonomisme et christianisme dans l'Afrique romaine de Septime-Sévère à l'invasion vandale, Paris, E. de Boccard, 1958.

Brown, C. B., *Singing the Gospel: Lutheran Hymns and the Success of the Reformation*, Cambridge MA, Harvard University Press, 2005.

Brown, P. R. L. (1961a/1972a), "Aspects of the Christianization of the Roman Aristocracy," *JRS* 51 (1961), 1–11 = *Religion and Society*, 161–82.

(1961b/1972b), "Religious Dissent in the Later Roman Empire: The Case of North Africa," *History* 46 (1961), 83–101 = *Religion and Society*, 237–59.

(1963/1972), "Religious Coercion in the Later Roman Empire: the Case of North Africa," *History* 48 (1963), 285–305 = *Religion and Society*, 301–31.

(1964a/1972), St. Augustine's Attitude to Religious Coercion," *JRS* 54 (1964), 107–16 = *Religion and Society*, 260–78.

(1964b/1972b), "Review of Diesner, Kirche und Staat," *JThS* 15 (1964), 409–11 = *Religion and Society*, 332–34.

(1965), "Review of Tengström, Donatisten und Katholiken," *JRS* 55, 281–83 = *Religion and Society*, 335–38.

(1969/1972), "The Diffusion of Manichaeism in the Roman Empire," *JRS* 59 (1969), 92–103 = *Religion and Society*, 94–108.

Augustine of Hippo: A Biography, London, Faber and Faber, 1967 (rev. ed.: Berkeley and Los Angeles, University of California Press, 2000).

Religion and Society in the Age of Saint Augustine, London, Faber and Faber, 1972.

The Cult of the Saints: Its Rise and Function in Latin Christianity, Chicago, University of Chicago Press, 1981.

Power and Persuasion: Towards a Christian Empire, Madison WI, University of Wisconsin Press, 1992.

Poverty and Leadership in the Later Roman Empire, Hanover, NH, University Press of New England, 2001.

Brown, T. S. (1998), "Urban Violence in Early Medieval Italy: The Cases of Rome and Ravenna," in G. Halsall, ed., *Violence and Society in the Early Medieval West*, Rochester NY and Woodbridge, Boydell Press, 76–89.

Brubaker, R., *Ethnicity Without Groups*, Cambridge MA, Harvard University Press, 2004.

and F. Cooper (2000), "Beyond 'Identity'," *Theory and Society* 29, 1–47 = ch. 2 in Brubaker, *Ethnicity Without Groups*, 28–63.

and D. Laitin (1998), "Ethnic and Nationalist Violence," *Annual Review of Sociology* 24, 423–52 = ch. 4 in Brubaker, *Ethnicity Without Groups*, 88–115.

Brunt, P. A. (1971), "Violence in the Italian Countryside," append. 8 in *Italian Manpower 225 B.C.–A.D. 14*, Oxford, Clarendon Press, 551–57.

Bulst, W., *Hymni Latini antiquissimi LXXV: Psalmi III*, Heidelberg, F. H. Kerle Verlag, 1956.

Burrus, V., *The Making of a Heretic: Gender, Authority and the Priscillianist Controversy*, Berkeley, University of California Press, 1995.

Butterweck, C., *"Martyriumssucht" in der Alten Kirche? Studien zur Darstellung und Deutung frühchristlicher Martyrien*, Tübingen, Mohr Siebeck, 1995.

Büttner, T. (1956), "Die Sozial-Religiöse Bewegung der Circumcellionen (Agonisten), in Nordafrika," in *Vom Mittelalter zur Neuzeit. Festschrift Heinrich Sproemberg*, Berlin, Akademie Verlag), 388–96.

[*Circumcellionen*], "Die Circumcellionen: eine sozial-religiöse Bewegung," in Th. Büttner and E. Werner, *Circumcellionen und Adamiten. Zwei Formen mittelalterlicher Haeresie*, Berlin, Akademie Verlag, 1959, 1–72.

Bynum, C., *The Resurrection of the Body in Western Christianity, 200–1336*, New York, Columbia University Press, 1995.

Byrne, J. P. (1997), "Circumcellions," in J. P. Rodriquez, ed., *The Historical Encyclopedia of World Slavery*, vol. 1, Santa Barbara and Oxford, ABC-CLIO, 157.

Cacitti, R. *Furiosa turba: I fondamenti religiosi dell'eversione sociale, della dissidenza politica e della contestazione ecclesiale dei Circoncellioni d'Africa*, Milan, Edizioni Biblioteca francescana, 2006.

Calderone, S. (1967), "Circumcellions," *PP* 22, 94–109.

Cameron, Alan (1970), "Gildo," ch. 5 in *Claudian: Poetry and Propaganda at the Court of Honorius*, Oxford, Clarendon Press, 93–123.

Circus Factions: Blues and Greens at Rome and Byzantium, Oxford University Press, 1976.

Cameron, Averil [*Rhetoric of Empire*], *Christianity and the Rhetoric of Empire: The Development of Christian Discourse*, Berkeley, University of California Press, 1991.

(2003a), "How to Read Heresiology," *Journal of Medieval and Early Modern Studies* 33 (2003), 471–92.

(2003b), "Jews and Heretics – A Category Error?," in A. H. Becker and A. Y. Reed, eds., *The Ways that Never Parted: Jews and Christians in Late Antiquity and the Early Middle Ages*, Tübingen, Mohr Siebeck, 2003, 345–60.

(2007), "Enforcing Orthodoxy in Byzantium," in K. Cooper and J. Gregory, eds., *Discipline and Diversity*, Rochester NY and Woodbridge, Boydell Press, 1–24.

(2008), "The Violence of Orthodoxy," in Iricinschi and Zellentin, eds., *Heresy and Identity*, 102–14.

Camps, G. (1994), "Punica lingua et épigraphie libyque dans la Numidie d'Hippone," *BCTH* n.s. 23, 33–49.

Cantor, C. H. (2000), "Suicide in the Western World," ch. 1 in K. Hawton and K. van Heeringen, eds., *The International Handbook of Suicide and Attempted Suicide*, New York, Wiley, 9–28.

Carlsen, J. (1991), "Estate Management in Roman North Africa. Transformation or Continuity?," *AfrRom* 8, 625–37.

Carotenuto, E. (2002), "Six Constantinian Documents (Eus. *H.E.* 10.5–7)," *VChr* 56, 56–74.

Carrié, J.-M. (1998), "Le gouverneur romain à l'époque tardive: les directions possibles de l'enquête," *AntTard* 6, 17–30.

Castritius, H. (1986), "The Jews in North Africa at the Time of Augustine of Hippo: Their Social and Legal Position," in *The Ninth World Congress of Jewish Studies*, B.1, Jerusalem, 31–37.

(1987), "Seid weder den Juden noch den Heiden noch der Gemeinde Gottes ein Ärgernis (1. Kor. 10,32): Zur sozialen und rechtlichen Stellung der Juden im spätrömischen Nordafrika," in R. Erb and M. Schmidt, eds., *Antisemitismus und jüdische Geschichte*, Berlin, Wissenschaftlicher Autorenverlag, 47–67.

Cataudella, M. R. (1991), "Motivi di rivolta sociale in Africa fra IV e V secolo?," *AfrRom* 8, 331–43.

Cayrel, P. (1934), "Une basilique Donatiste de Numidie," *MEFR* 51, 114–42.

Cecconi, G. A. (1990), "Elemosina e propaganda. Un'analisi della Macariana persecutio nel III libro di Ottato di Milevi," *REAug* 36, 42–66.

(2000), "Donatismo e antidonatismo in Agostino alle luce dei sermoni 'Dolbeau'," *AfrRom* 13, 1819–35.

(2007), "Come finisce un rituale pagano: la caterva di Cesarea di Mauritania," in E. Lo Cascio and G. D. Merola, eds., *Forme di aggregazione nel mondo romano*, Bari, Edipuglia, 345–61.

Chadwick, H., *Priscillian of Avila: The Occult and the Charismatic in the Early Church*, Oxford, Clarendon Press, 1976.

The Role of the Bishop in Ancient Society, Berkeley, The Center for Hermeneutical Studies in Hellenistic and Modern Culture, 1980.

(1985), "Augustine on Pagans and Christians: Reflections on Religious and Social Change," in D. Beales and G. Best, eds., *History, Society and the Churches*, Cambridge University Press, 9–27.

Chang, A. T. A. and Lee, Chau-Choun (2000), "Suicide in Asia and the Far East," ch. 2 in K. Hawton and K. van Heeringen, eds., *The International Handbook of Suicide and Attempted Suicide*, New York, Wiley, 29–48.

Charles, P. (1947), "L'élément populaire dans les sermons de saint Augustin," *NRTh* 69, 619–50.

Charles-Picard, G. (1958), *Civitas Mactaritana = Karthago* 8, Paris, Editions de Boccard.

Chastagnol, A. (1958), "Les Légats du Proconsul d'Afrique au Bas-Empire," *Libyca: arch-épigr.* 6, 7–19 = *L'Italie et l'Afrique au Bas-Empire*, 67–82.

(1966), "Les consulaires de Numidie," in *Mélanges Jérôme Carcopino* (Paris, 1966), 215–28 = *L'Italie et l'Afrique au Bas-Empire*, 149–62.

L'Album municipal de Timgad, Bonn, 1978.

L'Italie et l'Afrique au Bas-Empire: Etudes administratives et prosopographiques: Scripta Varia, Lille, Presses Universitaires de Lille, 1987.

and N. Duval (1974), "Les survivances du culte impérial dans l'Afrique du Nord à l'époque vandale," in *Mélanges d'histoire ancienne offerts à William Seston*, Paris, de Boccard, 87–118.

Chiesa, P. (1996), "Un testo agiografico Africano ad Aquileia: gli Acta di Gallonio e dei martiri di Timida Regia," *AB* 114, 241–68.

(1998), "Pellegrino martire *in urbe Bolitana* e Pellegrino di Ancona: un'altra agiografia africana ad Aquileia?," *AB* 116, 25–56.

Clover, F. M. (1979–80), "Le culte des empereurs dans l'Afrique vandale," *BCTH* n.s. 15–16B, 121–28 = ch. 8 in *The Late Roman West and the Vandals*, Aldershot, Variorum, 1993.

(1987), "Carthage in the Age of Augustine," in J. H. Humphrey, ed., *Excavations at Carthage, 1976*, Ann Arbor, Kelsey Museum, 1–14.

Cockburn, J. S. (1991), "Patterns of Violence in English Society: Homicide in Kent, 1560–1985," *P&P* 130, 70–106.

Cohen, J., *Christ Killers: The Jews and the Passion from the Bible to the Big Screen*, Oxford and New York, Oxford University Press, 2007.

Coleman, K. (1990), "Fatal Charades: Roman Executions Staged as Mythological Enactments," *JRS* 80, 44–73.

(1998), "'The Contagion of the Throng': Absorbing Violence in the Roman World," *Hermathena* 164, 65–88.

Collins, E. with M. McGovern, *Killing Rage*, London, Granta Books, 1997.

Collins, R., *Violence: A Micro-Sociological Theory*, Princeton University Press, 2007.

Coltelloni-Trannoy, M., *Le Royaume de Maurétanie sous Juba II et Ptolémée*, Paris, CNRS, 1997.

Combès, G. (1948), "Le suicide des Donatistes," in *BA* 2, 635–37.

Comeau, M., *La rhétorique de saint Augustin d'après les Tractatus in Ioannem*, Paris, Boivin, 1930.

(1932), "Sur la transmission des sermons de saint Augustin," *REL* 10, 408–22.

Congar, Y. (1963a), "Le commissaire impérial Macaire," note 5 in *BA* 28, 715.

(1963b), "Le titre de martyr ne convient pas aux Donatists," note 19 in *BA* 28, 727–28.

(1963c), "Le roi maure Firmus, rebelle contre Rome et allié des Donatistes," note 21 in *BA* 28, 729–30.

(1963d), "La législation impériale sur le Donatisme jusqu'en 400," note 23 in *BA* 28, 731–33.

Connerton, P., *How Societies Remember*, Cambridge University Press, 1989.

Coogan, T. P., *The IRA: A History*, rev. ed., New York, Palgrave, 2002.

The Troubles: Ireland's Ordeal and the Search for Peace, rev. ed., New York, Palgrave, 2001.

Corcy-Debray, S., *Jérôme Carcopino, un historien à Vichy*, Paris, Harmattan, 2001.

Courcelle, P. (1936), "Une seconde campagne de fouilles à Ksar el Kelb," *MEFR* 53, 161–83.

(1958), "Propos antichrétiens rapportés par saint Augustin," *RechAug* 1, 149–86.

Recherches sur les Confessions de saint Augustin, rev. ed., Paris, de Boccard, 1969.

Courtois, C. (1950a/1975), "Saint Augustin et le problème de la survivance du punique," *RAf* 94 (1950), 259–82 = *CT* 23 (1975), 273–94.

(1950b), "Saint Augustin et les survivances puniques," *CRAI*, 305–07.

Timgad, antique Thamugadi, Algiers, Imprimerie officielle, 1951.

Les Vandales et l'Afrique, Paris, Arts and métiers graphiques, 1955 [reprint: Aalen, Scientia Verlag, 1964].

Cox, M. G. (1988), "Augustine, Jerome, Tyconius and the Lingua Punica," *Studia Orientalia* 64, 83–105.

Cracco Ruggini, L., *Il paganesimo romano tra religione e politica (384–394 d.C.): per una reinterpretazione del Carmen contra paganos*, Rome, 1979 = *Atti della Accademia nazionale dei Lincei*, ser. 8, vol. 23.1.

(1980), "Pagani, ebrei e cristiani: odio sociologico e odio teologico nel mondo antico," in *Gli Ebrei nell'alto medioevo*, 2 vols.; vol. 1 = *Settimane di studio del Centro italiano di Studi sull'alto Medioevo*, no. 26 (Spoleto), 15–117.

Crespin, R., *Ministère et sainteté. Pastorale du clergé et solution de la crise donatiste dans la vie et la doctrine de saint Augustin*, Paris, Institut d'études augustiniennes, 1965.

Crosby, K., J.-O. Rhee and J. Holland (1977), "Suicide by Fire: A Contemporary Method of Political Protest," *International Journal of Social Psychiatry* 23, 60–69.

Cross, F. L. (1949), "The Collection of African Canons in Madrid University (Noviciado) Ms. 53," *JThS* 50, 197–201.

(1961), "History and Fiction in the African Canons," *JThS* 12, 227–47.

Crouzet, D., *Les guerriers de Dieu: la violence au temps des troubles de religion*, 2 vols., Seyssel, Champ Vallon, 1990.

Crummey, R. O. (2004), "Ecclesiastical Elites and Popular Belief and Practice in Seventeenth-Century Russia," ch. 2 in J. D. Tracy and M. Ragnow, eds., *Religion and the Early Modern State: Views from China, Russia, and the West* (Cambridge University Press, 2004), 52–79.

Cutino, M., *Licentii Carmen ad Augustinum*, Catania, Università di Catania, 2000.

Darmon, J. P. (1995), "Les mosaïques de la synagogue de Hammam Lif: un réexamen du dossier," in R. Ling, ed., *Fifth International Colloquium on Ancient Mosaics*, vol. 2 (JRA Supplement, no. 2; Ann Arbor), 7–29.

Dattrino, L. (1990), "Il battesimo e l'iniziazione cristiana in Ottato di Milevi," *RAC* 66, 81–100.

Daube, D. (1971), "Suicide," in *Studi in onore di Giuseppe Grosso*, vol. 4, Turin, G. Giappichelli, 119–27.

(1972), "The Linguistics of Suicide," *Philosophy and Public Affairs* 1, 387–437.

Daux, C. (1903), *Le chant abécédaire de saint Augustin contre les Donatistes*, Arras and Paris, Sueur-Charruey.

Davies, C. and M. Neal (2000), "Durkheim's Altruistic and Fatalistic Suicide," ch. 4 in W. S. F. Pickering and G. Walford, eds., *Durkheim's Suicide: A Century of Research and Debate*, London and New York, Routledge, 36–52.

Davis, N. Z. (1973/1975), "The Rites of Violence: The Religious Riot in Sixteenth-Century France," *P&P* 59 (1973), 51–91 = ch. 6 in *Society and Culture in Early Modern France* (London, Duckworth, 1975), 152–87.

Davis, R. C., *The War of the Fists: Popular Culture and Public Violence in Late Renaissance Venice*, New York, Oxford University Press, 1994.

Dearn, A. (2004), "The Abitinian Martyrs and the Outbreak of the Donatist Schism," *JEH* 55, 1–18.

De Bruyn, T. S. (1999), "Flogging a Son: The Emergence of the Pater Flagellans in Latin Christianity," *JECS* 7, 249–90.

De Clercq, V. C., *Ossius of Cordova: A Contribution to the History of the Constantinian Period*, Washington DC, Catholic University of America Press, 1954.

Decret, F., *Aspects du Manichéisme dans l'Afrique romaine: les controverses de Fortunatus, Faustus et Felix avec saint Augustin*, Paris, Institut d'études augustiniennes, 1970.

L'Afrique manichéenne (IVe–Ve siècles): étude historique et doctrinale, 2 vols., Paris, Institut d'études augustiniennes, 1978.

(1990), "Du bon usage du mensonge et du parjure: Manichéens et Priscillianistes face à la persécution dans l'Empire chrétien (IVe–Ve siècles)," in M.-M.

Mactoux and E. Geny, eds., *Mélanges Pierre Lévêque*, 4 (Paris, Les Belles Lettres), 141–49.

(2001a), "Des manichéens en Maurétanie Césarienne au Ve siècle. L'exemple de Caesarea et Tipasa: un billet de délation," in C. Hamdoune, ed., *Ubique amici: Mélanges offerts à Jean-Marie Lassère*, Montpellier, Université Paul Valéry, 341–48.

(2001b), "Objectif premier visé par Augustin dans ses controverses orales avec les responsables Manichéens d'Hippone," in J. van Oort, O. Wermerlinger, and G. Wurst, eds., *Augustine and Manichaeism in the Latin West*, Leiden, Brill, 57–66.

and M. Fantar, *L'Afrique du Nord dans l'Antiquité: histoire et civilisation des origines au Ve siècle*, Paris, Payot, 1981.

Deferrari, R. J. (1915), "Verbatim Reports of St. Augustine's Unwritten Sermons," *TAPhA* 46, 35–45.

(1922), "St. Augustine's Method of Composing and Delivering Sermons," *AJPh* 43, 97–123, 193–219.

Delattre, A.-L. (1895), *Gamart ou la nécropole juive de Carthage*, Lyon, Imprimerie Mougin-Rusand, 1895.

Delehaye, H. (1889), "Vita Sanctae Melaniae Junioris, auctore coaevo et sanctae familiari," *AB* 8, 16–63.

(1935), "Domnus Marculus," *AB* 53, 81–88.

(1936), "Contributions récentes à l'hagiographie de Rome et d'Afrique," *AB* 54, 293–96.

Delmaire, R. (1983a), "Contribution des nouvelles lettres de saint Augustin à la prosopographie du Bas-Empire Romain (PLRE)," in *Les Lettres de saint Augustin découvertes par Johannes Divjak* (Paris, Institut d'études augustiniennes, 83–86.

and Lepelley, C. (1983b), "Du nouveau sur Carthage: le témoignage des lettres de saint Augustin découvertes par Johannes Divjak," *Opus* 2, 473–85.

Demandt, A. (1968), "Die afrikanischen Unruhen unter Valentinian I," in H.–J. Diesner, H. Barth, and H.-D. Zimmerman, eds., *Afrika und Rom in der Antike = Wissenschaftliche Beiträge der Martin-Luther-Univeristät Halle*, Halle/Saale, no. 6, 277–92.

(1972), "Die Feldzüge des älteren Theodosius," *Hermes* 100, 81–113.

Die Spätantike: römische Geschichte von Diocletian bis Justinian, 284–565 n. Chr., 2nd ed., Munich, Beck, 2007.

De Robertis, F. M., *Lavoro e lavoratori nel mondo romano*, Bari, Adiatrice editrice, 1963; reprint: New York, Arno, 1979.

De Ste. Croix, G. E. M. (1954), "Aspects of the 'Great' Persecution," *HThR* 47, 75–113 = ch. 1 in *Christian Persecution, Martyrdom, and Orthodoxy*, 35–78.

The Class Struggle in the Ancient Greek World, Ithaca NY, Cornell University Press, 1981.

Christian Persecution, Martyrdom, and Orthodoxy, M. Whitby and J. Streeter, eds., Oxford University Press, 2006.

Desanges, J. and S. Lancel (1983), "L'apport des nouvelles lettres à la géographie historique de l'Afrique antique et de l'Eglise d'Afrique," in *Les Lettres de saint Augustin découvertes par Johannes Divjak*, Paris, Institut d'études augustiniennes, 87–99.

Despois, J. and R. Raynal, *Géographie de l'Afrique du Nord-Ouest*, Paris, Payot, 1967.

De Veer, A. C. (1961), "A propos de l'authenticité du livre VII d'Optat de Milève," *REAug* 7, 389–91.

(1965), "L'exploitation du schisme maximianiste par saint Augustin dans sa lutte contre le donatisme," *RecAug* 3, 219–37.

(1966), "Une mesure de tolérance de l'empereur Honorius," in *Mélanges Venance Grumel = REByz* 24 (Paris), 189–95.

(1968a), "Candidus de Villaregia et Donatus des Macomades," note 15 in *BA* 31, 764.

(1968b), "Optat de Thamugadi," note 22 in *BA* 31, 781–83.

(1968c), "Le 'concile' de Cirta," note 29 in *BA* 31, 796–98.

(1968d), "Silvanus, évêque de Cirta," note 30 in *BA* 31, 798–99.

(1968e), "Le rôle de Lucilla dans l'origine du schisme africain," note 31 in *BA* 31, 799–802.

(1968f), "Les 'Gesta apud Zenophilum consularem'," note 32 in *BA* 31, 802–04.

(1968g), "Le diacre Nundinarius," note 33 in *BA* 31, 804–05.

(1968h), "Les violences des circoncellions d'après le témoignage de saint Augustin," note 35 in *BA* 31, 809–10.

(1968i), "L'état de la législation antidonatiste dans le 'Contra Cresconium'," note 36 in *BA* 31, 810–814.

(1968j), "Servus, évêque catholique de Thubursicum Bure," note 37 in *BA* 31, 814–15.

(1968k), "Maximianus évêque catholique de Bagaï," note 38 in *BA* 31, 815–17.

(1968l), "Le légat Sacerdos," note 44 in *BA* 31, 827.

(1968m), "Le traditio considerée par les Donatistes comme un péché d'origine," note 51 in *BA* 31, 839–42.

(1968n), "Profuturus, évêque de Cirta (Constantina)," note 56 in *BA* 31, 850–52.

(1968o), "Fortunatus, évêque de Cirta (Constantina)," note 57 in *BA* 31, 852–53.

Diefendorf, B. B., *Beneath the Cross: Catholics and Huguenots in Sixteenth-Century Paris*, New York, Oxford University Press, 1991.

Diehl, A. (1992), "La fête chrétienne," *REAug* 38, 323–35.

Diesner, H.-J. (1957), "Spätantike Widerstandsbewegungen: das Circumcellionentum," in *Aus der Byzantinistischen Arbeit der Deutschen Demokratischen Republik*, 1, Berlin, Akademie Verlag, 106–12.

(1959), "Methodisches und Sachliches zum Circumcellionentum (I)," *Wissenschaftliche Zeitschrift der Martin-Luther-Universität, Geschichts- und Sprachwissenschaft*, 8, 1009–1016 = ch. 4a in *Kirche und Staat*, 53–66.

(1960a) "Methodisches und Sachliches zum Circumcellionentum (II)," *Wissenschaftliche Zeitschrift der Martin-Luther-Universität, Geschichts- und Sprachwissenschaft*, 9, 183–90 = ch. 4b in *Kirche und Staat*, 66–77.

(1960b) "Die Circumcellionen von Hippo Regius," *Theologische Literaturzeitung* 85, 497–508 = ch. 5 in *Kirche und Staat*, 78–90.

(1962a), "Konservative Kolonen, Sklaven und Landarbeiter im Donatistenstreit," *Forschungen und Fortschritte* 36, 214–19.

(1962b), "Gildos Herrschaft und die Niederlage bei Theveste," *Klio* 40, 178–86.

(1962c), "Die Periodisierung des Circumcellionenismus," *Wissenschaftliche Zeitschrift der Martin-Luther-Universität, Geschichts- und Sprachwissenschaft*, 10, 1329–38.

(1963), "Die Laufbahn des *Comes Africae* Bonifatius und seine Beziehungen zu Augustinus," ch. 8 in *Kirche und Staat*, 100–26.

Kirche und Staat in spätrömischen Reich: Aufsätze zur Spätantike und zur Geschichte der Alten Kirche, Berlin, Evangelische Verlagsanstalt, 1964.

Der Untergang der römischen Herrschaft in Nordafrika, Weimar, Böhlau, 1964.

Dietz, S. G., *Dissertatio historica de circumcellionibus*, Leipzig, Christopher Fleischer, 1690.

Diligenskii, G. G. (1957), "Voprosi istorii narodnikh Dvizenii v Pozdnej Rimskoj," *VDI* 60.2, 85–106 [in Russian: "Problems Concerning the History of Popular Movements in Roman Africa"].

Dmitrev, A. D. (1948), "K Voprosy ob Agonistikakh i Zirkumzellionakh," VDI 25.3, 66–78 [in Russian: "On the Problem of the Agonistici and the Circumcellions"].

Dolbeau, F. (1981), "Damase, le *Carmen contra paganos* et Hériger de Lobbes," *REAug* 27, 38–43.

(1992), "La Passio Sancti Donati (BHL 2303b): une tentative d'édition critique," in *Memoriam sanctorum venerantes: Miscellanea in onore di Monsignor Victor Saxer* = Studi di Antichità Cristiana, no. 48, Città del Vaticano, Pontificio Istituto di archeologia cristiana, 251–67.

(2003a), "La Passion des Martyrs d'Abitina: remarques sur l'établissement du texte," *AB* 121, 273–96.

(2003b), "Le combat pastoral d'Augustin contre les astrologues, les devins et les guérisseurs," in P.-Y. Fux, J.-M. Roessli, and O. Wermelinger, eds., *Augustinus Afer*, 1, Fribourg, Editions Universitaires Fribourg Suisse, 167–82 = ch. 5 in *Augustin et la prédication*, 111–26.

Augustin et la prédication en Afrique: Recherches sur divers sermons authentiques, apocryphes ou anonymes, Paris, Institut d'études augustiniennes, 2005.

and R. Étaix (2003), "Le 'jour des torches' (24 juin), d'après un sermon inédit d'origine africaine," *ARC* 5, 243–59.

Dolenz, H., *Damous-el-Karita: Die österreichisch-tunesischen Ausgrabungen der Jahre 1996 und 1997 im Saalbau und der Memoria des Pilgerheiligtums Damous-el-Karita in Karthago*, Vienna, Osterreichisches Archäologisches Institut, 2001.

Dölger, F. (1932/1950), "Das Kultvergehen der Donatistin Lucilla von Karthago. Reliquienkuss vor dem Kuss der Eucharistie," *Antike und Christentum*, 3, 245–52.

Dossey, L. (2001), "Judicial Violence and the Ecclesiastical Courts in Late Antique North Africa," ch. 6 in R. W. Mathisen, ed., *Law, Society and Authority in Late Antiquity*, Oxford University Press, 2001, 98–114.

(2008), "Wife Beating and Manliness in Late Antiquity," *P&P* 199, 1–40.

Drake, H. A. (1996), "Lambs into Lions: Explaining Early Christian Intolerance," *P&P* 153, 3–36.

ed., *Violence in Late Antiquity: Perceptions and Practices*, Aldershot, Ashgate, 2006.

Drobner, H. [*Sermones ad Populum*], *Augustinus von Hippo, Sermones ad Populum: Uberlieferung und Bestand, Bibliographie, Indices*, Leiden and Boston, Brill, 2000.

Droge, A. J. and J. D. Tabor, *Noble Death: Suicide and Martyrdom among Jews and Christians in the Ancient World*, San Francisco, Harper, 1992.

Dubarle, A.-M. (1957), "La pluralité des péchés héréditaires dans la tradition augustinienne," *REAug* 3, 113–36.

Duchesne, L. [*Dossier*], "Le dossier du Donatisme," *MEFR* 10 (1890), 589–650.

Dulaey, M. (2000), "Notes augustiniennes: les donatistes et les grenouilles," *REAug* 46, 199–204.

Dunn, G. D. (2006), "Augustine, Cyril of Alexandria and the Pelagian Controversy," *AugStud* 37, 63–88.

Tertullian's Adversus Iudaeos: A Rhetorical Analysis, Washington DC, The Catholic University of America Press, 2008.

Durkheim, E., *Suicide: A Study in Sociology*, transl. J. A. Spaulding and G. Simpson, New York, Free Press, 1951.

Duval, N., *Les Eglises africaines à deux absides*, 2 vols., Paris, De Boccard, 1973.

(1995), "Les martyrs de la persécution de Dioclétien à Haïdra (Tunisie): un exemple de développement du culte des martyrs locaux entre le IVe et le VIIe siècle," in M. Lambérigts and P. van Deun, eds., *Martyrium in Multidisciplinary Perspective: Memorial Louis Reekmans*, Leuven, Uitgeverij Peeters, 99–124.

Duval, Y. (1980), "Evêques et évêchés d'Afrique, ce qu'on ignore," *REAug* 26, 228–37.

Loca sanctorum Africae. Le culte des martyrs en Afrique du IVe au VIIe siècle, 2 vols., Rome, Ecole française de Rome, 1982.

(1984), "Densité et répartition des évêchés dans les provinces africaines au temps de Cyprien," *MEFRA* 96, 493–521.

Chrétiens d'Afrique à l'aube de la paix Constantienne: les premiers échos de la grande persécution, Paris, Institut d'études augustiniennes, 2000.

Eck, W. (1971), "Das Eindringen des Christentums in den Senatorenstand bis zu Konstantin d. Gr.," *Chiron* 1, 381–406.

(1983), "Der Episkopat im spätantiken Afrika: organisatorische Entwicklung, soziale Herkunft und öffentliche Funktionen," *HZ* 236, 266–95.

Edwards, O. C., *A History of Preaching*, Nashville, Abingdon Press, 2004.

Efroymson, D. P. (1999), "Whose Jews? Augustine's Tractatus on John," in *A Multiform Heritage: Studies on Early Judaism and Christianity in Honor of Robert A. Kraft*, Atlanta, Scholars Press, 197–211.

Elm, E. [*Bild des Bischofs*], *Die Macht der Weisheit: Das Bild des Bischofs in der Vita Augustini des Possidius und anderen spätantiken und frühmittelalterlichen Bischofsviten*, Leiden, Brill, 2003.

Elmayer, A. F. (1983), "The Reinterpretation of Latino-Punic Inscriptions from Roman Tripolitania," *LibStud* 14, 86–95.

(1984), "The Reinterpretation of Latino-Punic Inscriptions from Roman Tripolitania," *LibStud* 15, 93–105.

Engelbrecht, A. (1908), "Der heilige Augustinus als Volksdichter," *Zeitschrift für die österreichischen Gymnasien* 59, 580–94.

Ennabli, L. [*Métropole chrétienne*], *Carthage. Une métropole chrétienne du IVe siècle à la fin du VIIe siècle*, Paris, CNRS, 1997.

Ermini, F. (1931), "Il Psalmus contra partem Donati," *MiAg* 2, 341–52.

Errington, R. M., *Roman Imperial Policy from Julian to Theodosius*, Chapel Hill, The University of North Carolina Press, 2006.

Eyben, E., *Restless Youth in Ancient Rome*, London, RKP, 1993.

Fedden, H., *Suicide: A Social and Historical Study*, New York, Benjamin Blom; London, Davies, 1938.

Feldman, A., *Formations of Violence: The Narrative of the Body and Political Terror in Northern Ireland*, Chicago, University of Chicago Press, 1991.

Ferron, J. (1953), "Circumcellions d'Afrique," *DHGE* 12, 837–39.

Février, P.-A. (1966a), "Toujours le Donatisme. A quand l'Afrique? (Remarques sur l'Afrique à la fin de l'Antiquité, à propos du livre de E. Tengström)," *RSLR* 2, 228–40.

(1966b), "Martyrs, polémique et politique en Afrique (IVe–Ve s.)," *Cahiers d'histoire et de civilisation du Maghreb* 1, 8–18.

(1970), "Le culte des martyres en Afrique et ses plus anciens monuments," *Corsi di cultura sull'arte ravennate e bizantina* 17, 191–215.

(1973), "L'art funéraire et les images des chefs indigènes dans la Kabylie antique," in *Actes du premier Congrès d'étude des cultures méditerranéennes d'influence arabo-berbère, Malta 1972*, Algiers, Société nationale d'édition et de diffusion, 152–69 = *La Méditerranée* 2 (1996), 771–88.

(1976), "Religion et domination dans l'Afrique romaine," *DHA* 2, 305–36 = *La Méditerranée* 2 (1996), 789–912.

(1981), "Quelques remarques sur troubles et résistances dans le Maghreb romain," *CT* 117–18, 23–40.

Approches du Maghreb romain: pouvoirs, différences et conflits, 2 vols., Aix-en-Provence, Edisud, 1989–90.

La Méditerranée de Paul-Albert Février, 2 vols., Rome and Aix-en-Province, Ecole française de Rome, 1996.

Finn, R., *Almsgiving in the Later Roman Empire: Christian Promotion and Practice, 313–450*, Oxford University Press, 2006.

Finn, T. M., *Early Christian Baptism and the Catechumenate: Italy, North Africa, and Egypt*, Collegeville, MN, The Liturgical Press, 1992.

Firpo, G. (1990), "La morte per la legge di Dio in 4 Mac. e nell'esperienza giudaico-cristiana," in M. Sordi, ed., *"Dulce et decorum est pro patria mori": La morte in combattimento nell'antichità*, Milan, 261–80.

Fischer, J. A. (1986), "Das kleine Konzil zu Cirta im Jahr 305 (?)," *AHC* 18, 281–92.

Fontaine, J. (1985), "Les origines de l'hymnologie chrétienne latine," *La Maison-Dieu* 161, 33–74.

Foucault, M., *Security, Territory, Population: Lectures at the Collège de France, 1977–78*, M. Sennelart, ed., transl. G. Burchell, Basingstoke and New York, Palgrave-Macmillan, 2007.

Foucher, L. (1961), "Découvertes archéologiques à Thysdrus en 1961," *Notes et Documents de l'Université de Tunis* 5, 30–52.

Foufopoulos, J. and N. Litinas (2005), "Crows and Ravens in the Mediterranean (the Nile Valley, Greece and Italy) as Presented in Ancient and Modern Proverbial Literature," *BASP* 42, 7–39.

Franchi de' Cavalieri, P. (1935a), "La Passio dei martiri Abitinensi," in *Note agiografiche*, fasc. 8 = *Studi e Testi*, no. 65, Città del Vaticano, 3–71.

(1935b), "Della Passio sanctarum Maximae, Donatillae et Secundae," in *Note agiografiche*, fasc. 8 = *Studi e Testi*, no. 65, Città del Vaticano, 75–97.

Frankfurt, H. G., *On Bullshit*, Princeton University Press, 2005.

Frankfurter, D. (2000), "'Things Unbefitting Christians': Violence and Christianization in Fifth-Century Panopolis," *JECS* 8, 273–95.

(2009), "Martyrology and the Prurient Gaze," *JECS* 17, 215–45.

Frazão, E. R. de Aguiar [*Os Cicunceliôes*], *O Donatismo e os Circunceliôes na obra de santo Agostinho*, São Paulo, Boletim no. 5, Departamento de História, no. 4; Curso de História Antiga, no. 1, 1976.

Frede, H. J., *Kirchenschriftsteller, Verzeichnis und Sigel: Repertorium scriptorum ecclesiasticorum latinorum saeculo nono antiquiorum*, 4th rev. ed., Freiburg, Herder Verlag, 1995.

Fredriksen, P. (1995), "*Excaecati Occulta Justitia Dei*: Augustine on Jews and Judaism," *JECS* 3, 299–324.

(2001), "Augustine and Israel: Interpretatio ad litteram, Jews and Judaism in Augustine's Theology of History," *Studia Patristica* 35, 119–35.

Augustine and the Jews: A Christian Defense of Jews and Judaism, New York, Doubleday, 2008.

Frend, W. H. C., *The Donatist Church: A Movement of Protest in Roman North Africa*, Oxford, Clarendon Press, 1952 (reprint: 1971; 2nd ed., 1985).

(1952), "The *cellae* of the African circumcellions," *JThS* 3, 87–89.

(1954), "Manichaeism in the Struggle between Saint Augustine and Petilian of Constantine," in *Augustinus Magister* 2, Paris, Institut d'études augustiniennes, 859–66 = ch. 13 in *Religion Popular and Unpopular in the Early Christian Centuries*, London, Variorum, 1976.

Martyrdom and Persecution in the Early Church: A Study of Conflict from the Maccabees to Donatus, Oxford, Blackwell, 1965.

(1969), "Circumcellions and Monks," *JThS* 20, 542–49 = ch. 19 in *Town and Country in the Early Christian Centuries*, London, Variorum, 1980.

(1970a), "A Note on Tertullian and the Jews," in F. L. Cross, ed., *Studia Patristica* 10 (Berlin), 291–96.

(1970b), "A Note on Jews and Christians in Third Century North Africa," *JThS* 21, 92–96.

(1972), "The Monks and the Survival of the East Roman Empire in the Fifth Century," *P&P* 54, 3–24 = ch. 18 in *Religion Popular and Unpopular in the Early Christian Centuries*, London, Variorum, 1976.

(1978), "Jews and Christians in Third Century Carthage," in *Paganisme, Judaïsme, Christianisme: Influence et affrontement dans le monde antique. Mélanges offerts à Marcel Simon*, Paris, de Boccard, 185–94.

(1982), "The North African Cult of Martyrs," in *Jenseitsvorstellungen in Antike und Christentum: Gedenkschrift für Alfred Stuiber = Jahrbuch für Antike und Christentum, Ergänzungsband*, no. 9, Münster, Aschendorff, 154–67 = ch. 11 in *Archaeology and History in the Study of Early Christianity*, London, Variorum, 1988.

(1983), "Fussala, Augustine's Crisis of Credibility (*Ep.* 20*)," in *Les Lettres de saint Augustin découvertes par Johannes Divjak*, Paris, Institut d'études augustiniennes, 251–65.

(1985), "The Donatist Church – Forty Years On," in C. Landman and D. P. Whitelaw, eds., *Windows on Origins: Essays on the Early Church in Honor of Jan Stoop*, Pretoria, University of South Africa Press, 70–84 = ch. 15 in *Archaeology and History in the Study of Early Christianity*, London, Variorum, 1988.

Orthodoxy, Paganism and Dissent in the Early Christian Centuries, Aldershot, Variorum, 2002.

and K. Clancy (1977), "When did the Donatist Schism Begin?," *JThS* 28, 104–09.

Frézouls, E. (1971), "Une synagogue juive attestée à Volubilis," in *Acta of the Fifth International Congress of Greek and Latin Epigraphy, Cambridge, 1967*, Oxford, Blackwell, 287–92.

Fuks, A. (1951), "Κολωνὸς μισθιὸς: Labor Exchange in Classical Athens," *Eranos* 49, 171–73 (reprinted in: *Social Conflict in Ancient Greece*, Jerusalem, Magnes Press; Leiden, Brill, 1984, 303–05).

Fux, P.-Y., J.-M. Roessli and O. Wermelinger, eds., *Augustinus Afer. Saint Augustin: africanité et universalité*, Actes du colloque international, Alger-Annaba, 1–7 avril 2001, Fribourg, Editions Universitaires Fribourg, 2003.

Gabillon, A. (1986), "Insécurité en Afrique au Ve siècle: les *mangones* et leur complices," *L'Information littéraire*, 127–28.

Gacic, P. (1957), "En Afrique romaine. Classes et luttes sociales d'après les historiens soviétiques," *Annales (ESC)* 12, 650–61.

Gaddis, M. [*Religious Violence*], *There is No Crime for Those Who Have Christ: Religious Violence in the Christian Roman Empire*, Berkeley and Los Angeles, University of California Press, 2005.

Gagé, J. (1935), "Sur deux inscriptions chrétiennes d'Hippone," *BAH* 37, 37–55.

Gaggero, G. (1991), "Aspetti politici e sociali della rivolta di Eracliano," *AfrRom* 8, 213–20.

(1994), "Le usurpazioni africane del IV–V secolo d.C. nella testimonianza degli scrittori cristiani," *AfrRom* 10, 1111–1127.

Gambetta, D., ed., [*Suicide Missions*], *Making Sense of Suicide Missions*, Oxford University Press, 2005.

Ganshoff, F. L. (1950), "Note sur l'élection des évêques dans l'empire romain au IVe et pendant la première moitié du Ve siècles," *RIDA* 4, 467–98.

Gaudemet, J., *L'Eglise dans l'empire romain, IVe–Ve siècles*, Paris, Sirey, 1958.

(1992), "Politique ecclésiastique et législation religieuse après l'édit de Théodose I de 380," in *Droit et société aux derniers siècles de l'empire romain*, Naples, Jovene, 175–96.

Gautier, E. F., *Genséric, roi de Vandales*, Paris, Payot, 1935.

Gebbia, C. (1986), "Le comunità giudaiche nell'Africa romana antica e tardo-antica," *AfrRom* 3, 101–12.

(1988), "Ancora sulle 'rivolte' di Firmo e Gildone," *AfrRom* 5, 117–29.

Geerlings, W. (1985), "Haeresis und Schisma in der Canones der nordafrikanischen Konzilien von 345 bis 525," in A. Gabriels and H. J. F. Reinhardt, eds., *Ministerium Iustitiae: Festschrift für Herbert Heinemann zur Vollendung des 60. Lebensjahres* (Essen), 161–67.

Geiger, J. (1999), "Some Latin Authors from the Greek East, 1: The Patria of Priscian," *CQ* 49, 606–12.

Gellner, E., *Muslim Society*, Cambridge University Press, 1981.

Gilliard, F. D. (1984), "Senatorial Bishops in the Fourth Century," *HThR* 77, 153–75.

Ginestet, P. [*La jeunesse*], *Les organisations de la jeunesse dans l'Occident romain*, Brussels, Collection Latomus no. 213, 1991.

Gladwell, M., *The Tipping Point: How Little Things Can Make a Big Difference*, New York–Boston, Little, Brown and Co, 2002.

Gonzales, A. (1998), "La révolte comme acte de brigandage. Tacite et la révolte de Tacfarinas," *AfrRom* 12, 937–58.

Gotoh, A. (1988), "Circumcelliones: The Ideology Behind their Activities," in Toru Yuge and Masaoki Doi, eds., *Forms of Control and Subordination in Antiquity*, Leiden, Brill, 303–11.

Gotter, U. (2008), "Rechtgläubige – Pagane – Häretiker. Tempelzerstörung in der Kirchengeschichtsschreibung und das Bild der christlichen Kaiser," in J. Hahn, S. Emmel, and U. Gotter, eds., *Destruction and Renewal*, 43–89.

Gottlieb, G. (1978), "Die Circumcellionen. Bemerkungen zum donatistischen Streit," *AHC* 10 (1978), 1–15.

Graf, F. (1998), "Kalendae Ianuariae," in F. Graf, ed., *Ansichten griechischer Rituale: Geburtstag-Symposium für Walter Burkert*, Leipzig, Teubner, 199–216.

Grasmück, E. L. *Coercitio: Staat und Kirche im Donatistenstreit*, Bonn, Ludwig Röhrscheid, 1964.

Green, W. T. (1951), "Augustine's Use of Punic," in W. J. Fischel, ed., *Semitic and Oriental Studies Presented to William Popper = University of California*

Publications in Semitic Philology, 11, Berkeley and Los Angeles, University of California Press, 179–90.

Grégoire, H. (1937), "Sainte Salsa," *Byzantion* 12, 213–24.

Griffith, S. H. (1986), "Ephraem, the Deacon of Edessa, and the Church of the Empire," in T. Halton and J. P. Williman, eds., *Diakonia: Studies in Honor of Robert T. Meyer*, Washington D.C., The Catholic University of America Press, 22–52.

Grig, L. *Making Martyrs in Late Antiquity*, London, Duckworth, 2005.

Grisé, Y. *Le suicide dans la Rome antique*, Montreal, Bellarmin; Paris, Les Belles Lettres, 1982.

Groebner, V. *Defaced: The Visual Culture of Violence in the Late Middle Ages*, trans. P. Selwyn, New York, Zone Books, 2008.

Gryson, R. (1973), "Les élections ecclésiastiques au III siècle," *RHE* 68, 354–404.
(1979), "Les élections épiscopales en Orient an IVe siècle," *RHE* 74, 301–45.
(1980), "Les élections épiscopales en Occident au IVe siècle," *RHE* 75, 257–87.
[*Compléments*], *Kirchenschriftsteller: Verzeichnis und Sigel, Aktualisierungsheft – compléments 2004*, Freiburg, Herder Verlag, 1999–2004.

Gsell, S. (1902), "Observations géographiques sur la révolte de Firmus," *RSAC* 36, 21–46 = *Etudes sur l'Afrique antique: scripta varia*, Lille, Université de Lille, 1981, 113–38.
Promenades archéologiques aux environs d'Alger (Cherchel, Tipasa, Le Tombeau de la Chrétienne), Paris, Les Belles Lettres, 1926.
(1948), "Cherchel," *DACL* 3.1, 1269–81.
Cherchel, antique Iol-Caesarea, new edition by M. Leglay and E. S. Colozier, Algiers, L'Imprimerie officielle, 1952.

Gui, I., N. Duval, and J.-P. Caillet [*Basiliques, I*], *Basiliques chrétiennes d'Afrique du Nord, I. Inventaire de l'Algérie*, Paris, Institut d'études augustiniennes, 1992.

Hahn, J., *Gewalt und religiöser Konflikt: Studien zu den Auseinandersetzungen zwischen Christen, Heiden und Juden im Osten des Römischen Reiches (von Konstantin bis Theodosius II)*, Berlin, Akademie Verlag, 2004.

Hahn, J., S. Emmel and U. Gotter, eds. [*Destruction and Renewal*], *From Temple to Church: Destruction and Renewal of Local Cultic Topography in Late Antiquity*, Leiden and Boston, Brill, 2008.

Hair, P. E. H. (1971), "Deaths from Violence in Britain: A Tentative Secular Survey," *Population Studies* 25, 5–24.

Halsall, G., ed. *Violence and Society in the Early Medieval West*, Rochester NY and Woodbridge, Boydell Press, 1998.

Hamman, A.-G. [*Monumenta*], "Monumenta vetera ad Donatistarum historiam pertinentia," *PLS* 1 (1958), 183–90, 299–302.

Hanoune, R. (1990), "Le paganisme philosophique de l'aristocratie muncipale," in *L'Afrique dans l'occident romain*, Rome, Ecole française de Rome, 63–75.

Heinzelmann, M. *Bischofsherrschaft in Gallien. Zur Kontinuität römischer Führungsschichten vom 4. bis 7. Jahrhundert. Soziale, prosopographische und bildungsgeschichtliche Aspekte*, Francia Beiheft 5, Munich, Artemis Verlag, 1976.

Hermanowicz, E. T. (2004a), "Catholic Bishops and Appeals to the Imperial Court: A Legal Study of the Calama Riots in 408," *JECS* 12, 481–521.

(2004b), "Book Six of Augustine's *De musica* and the Episcopal Embassies of 408," *AugStud* 35, 165–98.

Possidius of Calama: A Study of the North African Episcopate in the Age of Augustine, Oxford University Press, 2008.

Herrmann, L. (1950), "Claudius Antonius et la crise religieuse de 394 ap. J.-C.," in *Mélanges Henri Grégoire = AIPhO* 10, 329–42.

Hess, H. [*Council of Serdica*], *The Early Development of Canon Law and the Council of Serdica*, Oxford University Press, 2002.

Hill, T., *Ambitiosa Mors: Suicide and Self in Roman Thought and Literature*, London and New York, Routledge, 2004.

Hobsbawm, E. and G. Rudé, *Captain Swing*, Harmondsworth, Penguin; New York, Pantheon, 1968 (reprint: London, Phoenix, 2001).

Hofmann, D., *Suizid in der Spätantike: Seine Bewertung in der lateinischen Literatur*, Stuttgart, Franz Steiner Verlag, 2007.

Hombert, P.-M. [*Chronologie Augustinienne*], *Nouvelles recherches de chronologie Augustinienne*, Paris, Institut d'études augustiniennes, 2000.

Hoogterp, P. W. (1940), "Deux procès-verbaux donatistes. Quelques aspects du latin parlé en Afrique au commencement du IVe siècle," *ALMA*, 39–112.

Horowitz, D. L., *The Deadly Ethnic Riot*, Berkeley and Los Angeles, University of California Press, 2001.

Horsfall, N. (2003), "Song and Memory," ch. 1 in *The Culture of the Roman Plebs*, London, Duckworth, 11–19.

Hubaux, J. (1948), "La crise de la trois cent soixante cinquième année," *AC* 17, 343–54.

(1954a), "Saint Augustin et la crise cyclique," in *Augustinus Magister*, vol. 2, Paris, Institut d'études augustiniennes, 943–50.

(1954b), "Saint Augustin et la crise eschatologique de la fin du IVe siècle," *Académie royale de Belgique: Bulletin de la classe des lettres et des sciences morales et politiques*, 5e sér., 40, 658–72.

Hübner, S., *Der Klerus in der Gesellschaft des spätantiken Kleinasiens*, Stuttgart, Franz Steiner, 2005.

Hugoniot, C. (2002a), "Les légats du proconsul d'Afrique à la fin du IVe siècle et au début du Ve ap. J.-C. à la lumière des sermons et lettres d'Augustin," *AfrRom* 14, 2067–88.

(2002b), "Les acclamations dans la vie municipale tardive et la critique augustinienne des violences lors des spectacles africains," in H. Inglebert, ed., *Idéologies et valeurs civiques dans le monde romain: Hommage à Claude Lepelley*, Paris, Picard, 2002, 179–85.

Humfress, C. (2000), "Roman Law, Forensic Argument and the Formation of Christian Orthodoxy (III–VI Centuries)," in S. Elm, E. Rebillard, and

A. Romano, eds., *Orthodoxie, christianisme, histoire – Orthodoxy, Christianity, History*, Paris, de Boccard, 125–47.

Orthodoxy and the Courts in Late Antiquity, Oxford University Press, 2007.

(2008), "Citizens and Heretics: Late Roman Lawyers on Christian Heresy," in Iricinschi and Zellentin, eds., *Heresy and Identity*, 128–42.

Hummel, E. L. *The Concept of Martyrdom According to St. Cyprian of Carthage*, Washington DC, The Catholic University of America Press, 1946.

Inglebert, H., *Les Romans chrétiens face à l'histoire de Rome: histoire, christianisme et romanités en Occident dans l'Antiquité tardive (IIIe–Ve siècles)*, Paris, Institut d'études augustiniennes, 1996.

Interpretatio Christiana. Les mutations des savoirs (cosmographie, géographie, ethnographie, histoire) dans l'antiquité chrétienne, 30–630 après J.-C., Paris, Institut d'études augustiniennes, 2001.

Iricinschi, E. and H. M. Zellentin, eds., *Heresy and Identity in Late Antiquity*, Tübingen, Mohr Siebeck, 2008.

Isaac, B., *The Invention of Racism in Classical Antiquity*, Princeton University Press, 2004.

Isola, A., *Fulgenzio di Ruspe: Salmo contro i vandali ariani*, Turin, Società editrice internazionale, 1983.

I Cristiani dell'Africa Vandalica nei sermones del tempo (429–534), Milan, Jaca, 1990.

Jaczynowska, M., *Les associations de jeunesse romaine sous le Haut-Empire*, Wroclaw, Zaklad Narodowy Imienia Ossolinskich Wydawnictwo Polskiej Akadmeii, 1978.

Jannaccone, S., *La dottrina eresiologica di Sant'Agostino: Studio di storia letteraria e religiosa a proposito del trattato De haeresibus*, Catania, Reina, 1952.

Joannou, P. P., *La législation impériale et la christianisation de l'Empire romain (311–476)*, Rome, 1972 [Orientalia Christiana Analecta, no. 192].

Joly, R. (1955), "Saint Augustin et l'intolérance religieuse," *RBPh* 33 (1955), 263–94.

(1969), "L'intolérance de saint Augustin, doctrine ou attitude?," in J. Bibauw ed., *Hommages à Marcel Renard*, vol. 1 (Brussels, Collection Latomus, 1969), 493–500.

Jones, A. H. M. (1959/1974), "Were Ancient Heresies National or Social Movements in Disguise?," *JThS* 10 (1959), 280–98 = reprint in P. A. Brunt, ed., *The Roman Economy*, Oxford, Blackwell, 1974, 308–29.

[*LRE*], *The Later Roman Empire, 284–602: A Social, Economic, and Administrative Survey*, 3 vols., Oxford, Blackwell, 1964.

Julicher, A. (1899), "Circumcelliones," *RE* 3.2, 2570.

Kaden, E. H. (1953), "Die Edikte gegen die Manichäer von Diokletian bis Justinian," in *Festschrift Hans Lewald*, Basel, Helbing, and Lichtenhahn, 55–68.

Kantorowicz, E., *Laudes Regiae: A Study in Liturgical Acclamations and Mediaeval Ruler Worship*, Berkeley and London, University of California Press, 1946.

Kelly, C., *Ruling the Later Roman Empire*, Cambridge MA, Harvard University Press, 2004.

Kennedy, D. B., R. J. Homant, and R. T. Hupp (1998), "Suicide by Cop," *FBI Law Enforcement Bulletin* 67.8, 21–27.

Khanoussi, M. (2000), "L'armée romaine et la police des domaines impériaux en Afrique proconsulaire," *AfrRom* 13.2, 1131–38.

Khosrokhavar, F., *Suicide Bombers: Allah's New Martyrs*, transl. D. Macey, London–Ann Arbor, Pluto Press, 2005 [*Les nouveaux martyrs d'Allah*, Paris, Flammarion, 2002].

Kim, Y. (2006), "Epiphanius of Cyprus and the Geography of Heresy," ch. 20 in Drake, *Violence in Late Antiquity*, Aldershot, Variorum, 235–51.

Kirsten, E. (1954), "Chorbischof," *RAC* 2, 1105–10.

Klauser, T. (1950), "Akklamationen," *RAC* 1, 213–33.

Kleijwegt, M., *Ancient Youth: The Ambiguity of Youth and the Absence of Adolescence in Greco-Roman Society*, Amsterdam, J. C. Gieben, 1991.

Knox, R. A. (1950), "Donatist and Circumcellion," ch. 4 in *Enthusiasm: A Chapter in the History of Religion, with special reference to the XVII and XVIII centuries*, Oxford University Press, 1950 (reprint, 1961), 30–70.

Knust, J. W., *Abandoned to Lust: Sexual Slander and Ancient Christianity*, New York, Columbia University Press, 2006.

Koch, H. (1932), "Die pseudocyprianische Schrift *De centesima, sexagesima, tricesima* in ihrer Abhängigkeit von Cyprian," *ZNTW* 31, 248–72.

Kolb, F. (1977), "Der Aufstand der Provinz Africa Proconsularis im Jahre 238 n. Chr. Die wirtschaftlichen und sozialen Hintergründe," *Historia* 26, 440–78.

(1988), "L'ideologia tetrarchica e la politica religiosa di Diocleziano," in *I cristiani e l'impero nel IV secolo*, (Macerata: Università degli studi di Macerata), 17–44.

Kotila, H., *Memoria mortuorum. Commemoration of the Departed in Augustine*, Rome, Institutum Patristicum Augustinianum, 1992.

Kotula, T. (1970), "Firmus, fils de Nubel, était-il usurpateur ou roi des Maures?," *AAntHung* 18, 137–46.

(1972), "Der Aufstand des Afrikaners Gildo und seine Nachwirkungen," *Das Altertum* 33, 167–76.

(1974), "Deux pages relatives à la réaction païenne: les troubles à Sufes et à Calama," *Acta Universitatis Wratislawiensis* 205, 69–97 [in Polish, with resume in French].

(1977), "Le fond africain de la révolte d'Héraclien en 413," *AntAfr* 2, 257–76.

(1987), "Faraxen, famosissimus dux Maurorum," *AfrRom* 4, 229–34.

Kotzé, A., *Augustine's Confessions: Communicative Purpose and Audience*, Leiden and Boston, Brill, 2004.

Kriegbaum, B., *Kirche der Traditoren oder Kirche der Märtyrer? Die Vorgeschichte des Donatismus*, Innsbruck and Vienna, Tyrolia, 1986.

(2002), "Die Donatistischen Konzilien von Cebarsussa (393) und Bagai (394)," *ZKTh* 124, 267–77.

Kunderewicz, C. (1971), "La protection des monuments d'architecture antique dans le Code Théodosien," in *Studi in onore di Edoardo Volterra*, 4, Milan, Giuffrè, 137–53.

Kunzelmann, A. (1931), "Die Chronologie der Sermones des Hl. Augustinus," *Miscellanea Agostiniana*, vol. 2, Rome, Tipografia poliglotta vaticana, 417–520.

La Bonnardière, A.-M., *Recherches de chronologie augustinienne*, Paris, Institut d'études augustiniennes, 1965.

Ladage, D. (1979), "*Collegia iuvenum*. Ausbildung einer municipalen Elite?," *Chiron* 9, 319–47.

Laeuchli, S., *Power and Sexuality: The Emergence of Canon Law at the Synod of Elvira*, Philadelphia, Temple University Press, 1972.

Lambot, C. (1935), "Texte complété et amendé du *Psalmus contra partem Donati* de saint Augustin," *RBén* 47, 312–30.

(1936), "Un psaume abécédaire inédit de S. Fulgence de Ruspe contre les Vandales ariens," *RBén* 48, 221–34.

Lamirande, E. (1965a), "L'influence contagieuse des pécheurs selon les Donatistes," note 7 in *BA* 32, 696–98.

(1965b) "Effectifs des deux groupes et organisation ecclésiastique," note 10 in *BA* 32, 700–02.

(1965c), "Le crime de 'tradition' et les points de vue donatiste et catholique," note 14 in *BA* 32, 705–06.

(1965d), "Accusations lancées contre Augustin," note 17 in *BA* 32, 710–13.

(1965e), "Rapports des Donatistes avec les Circoncellions," note 20 in *BA* 32, 716–17.

(1965f), "Scelera et facinora au sujet des Circoncellions," note 21 in *BA* 32, 717–18.

(1965g), "Les enfants et les pêchés de leurs parents," note 28 in *BA* 32, 725.

(1965h), "La définition augustinenne de martyre," note 52 in *BA* 32, 747.

(1965i), "La pratique du suicide chez les Donatistes," note 53 in *BA* 32, 747–48.

Lancel, S. (1967), "Aux origines du donatisme et du mouvement des circoncellions," *CT* 15, 183–88.

Actes de la Conférence de Carthage en 411, 4 vols., Paris, Editions du Cerf, 1972–1991.

(1979), "Les débuts du Donatisme: la date du 'Protocole de Cirta' et de l'élection épiscopale de Silvanus," *REAug* 25, 217–29.

(1983), "L'affaire d'Antoninus de Fussala: pays, choses et gens de la Numidie d'Hippone saisis dans la durée d'une procédure d'enquête épiscopale," in *Les Lettres de saint Augustin découvertes par Johannes Divjak*, Paris, Institut d'études augustiniennes, 267–85.

(1984a), "Saint Augustin et la Maurétanie Césarienne: les années 418–419 à la lumière des nouvelles lettres récemment publiées," *REAug* 30, 48–59.

(1984b), "Saint Augustin et la Maurétanie Césarienne: L'affaire de l'évêque Honorius (automne 419–printemps 420) dans les nouvelles Lettres 22*, 23*, et 23*A," *REAug* 30, 251–62.

(1984c), "Etudes sur la Numidie d'Hippone au temps de saint Augustin: recherches de topographie ecclésiastique," *MEFRA* 96, 1085–1113.

(1988), "Le dossier du Donatisme," *REL* 56, 47–42.

(1989), "Le sort des évêques et des communautés donatistes après la Conférence de Carthage en 411," in C. Mayer and K. H. Chelius, eds., *Internationales Symposion über den Stand der Augustinus-Forschung*, Würzburg, Augustinus-Verlag, 149–67.

(1990), "Evêchés et cités dans les provinces africaines (IIIe–IVe siècles)," in *L'Afrique dans l'occident romain (1er siècle av. J.-C.–IVe siècle après J. C.*, Rome, Ecole française de Rome, 273–90.

(1992), "Le recrutement de l'église d'Afrique au début du Ve siècle: aspects qualitatifs et quantitatifs," in L. Holtz and J.-C. Fredouille, eds., *De Tertullien aux Mozarabes, 1: Antiquité tardive et christianisme ancien (IIIe–VIe siècles): Mélanges offerts à Jacques Fontaine*, Paris, Institut d'études augustiniennes, 325–38.

(1994), "Circoncellions," C.70 in *EncycBerb* 13, 1962–64.

(1999), "Le proconsul Anullinus et la grande persécution en Afrique en 303–04," *CRAI*, 1013–22.

Saint Augustin, Paris, Fayard, 1999 [Engl. transl. A. Nevill, *Saint Augustine*, London, SCM Press, 2002].

(2006), "Actes de Gallonius: texte critique, traduction et notes," *REAug* 52, 243–59.

and M. Bouchenaki, *Tipasa de Maurétanie*, Algiers, Sous-Direction des Beaux-Arts et Antiquités, 1971.

Lapeyre, G. G. (1931), "Saint Augustin et Carthage," *MiAg* 2, 91–148.

Lapointe, G., *La célébration des martyrs en Afrique d'après les sermons de saint Augustin*, Montreal, Communauté chrétienne, 1972.

Lassère, J.-M., *Ubique populus: Peuplement et mouvements de population dans l'Afrique romaine de la chute de Carthage à la fin de la dynastie des Sévères*, Paris, CNRS, 1977.

(1992), "Un conflit 'routier': observations sur les causes de la guerre de Tacfarinas," *AntAfr* 18, 11–25.

Le Blant, E., *Les Actes des martyrs. Supplément aux Acta sincera de dom Ruinart =* *MSAF* 30.2, Paris, 1883.

Le Bohec, Y. (1981a), "Inscriptions juives et judaïsantes de l'Afrique romaine," *AntAfr* 17, 165–207.

(1981b), "Juifs et judaïsants dans l'Afrique romaine. Remarques onomastiques," *AntAfr* 17, 209–29.

(1985), "Les sources archéologiques du judaïsme africain sous l'Empire romain," in C. Iancu and J.-M. Lassère, eds., *Juifs et judaïsme en Afrique du Nord dans l'Antiquité et le Haut Moyen-Age*, Montepellier, Université Paul Valéry, 13–47.

(1994), "Updated Report on Jews in Roman North Africa," in *Espacio, tiempo y forma*, ser. 2, no. 7, 309–23.

Lecerf, J. (1954), "Saint Augustin et les survivances puniques," in *Augustinus Magister*, vol. 1, Paris, Institut d'études augustiniennes, 31–33.

Leclercq, H. *L'Afrique chrétienne*, 2 vols., Paris, V. Lecoffre, 1904.

(1920a), "Deo gratias, Deo laudes," *DACL* 4.1 (1920), 652–59.

(1920b), "Donatisme (législation répressive du)," *DACL* 4.1 (1920), 1472–1487.

(1920c), "Donatisme: épigraphie," *DACL* 4.2 (1920), 1487–1505.

(1924), "Gamart," *DACL* 6.1 (1924), 604–10.

(1925), "Hamman-Lif," *DACL* 6.2 (1925), 2042–53.

Leclercq, J. (1947), "Prédication et rhétorique au temps de saint Augustin," *RBén* 57, 117–31.

Legewie, B. (1931), "Die körperliche Konstitution und die Krankheiten Augustin's," in *Miscellanea Agostiniana*, vol. 2, Rome, Tipografia poliglotta vaticana, 5–21.

Leglay, M. [SAM. 2], *Saturne africaine. Monuments. II: Numidie, Maurétanies*, Paris, Arts & métiers graphiques, 1966.

Lengle, J. (1937), "Tribunus (11): Tribunus et notarius," *RE* 6.22, 2453–54.

Lengrand, N. (1994), "L'inscription de Petra et la révolte de Firmus," *BCTH* 23B, 159–70.

(1995), "Le limes interne de Maurétanie Césarienne au IVe siècle et la famille de Nubel," in A. Rousselle, ed., *Frontière terrestres, frontières célestes dans l'Antiquité*, Presses Universitaires de Perpignan; Paris, de Boccard, 143–61.

Leone, A. (2006), "Clero, proprietà, cristianizzazione delle campagne nel Nord Africa tardoantico: status quaestionis," *AntTard* 14, 95–104.

Lepelley, C., *Les cités de l'Afrique romaine au Bas-empire, t. 1: La permanence d'une civilisation municipale; t. 2: Notices d'histoire municipale*, Paris, Institut d'études augustiniennes, 1979.

(1980), "Iuvenes et circoncellions: les derniers sacrifices humains de l'Afrique antique," *AntAfr* 15, 261–71 = *Aspects de l'Afrique romaine*, 161–76.

(1981), "La crise de l'Afrique romaine au début du Ve siècle, d'après les lettres nouvellement découvertes de saint Augustin," *CRAI*, 445–63.

(1983), "Témoignage et attitude de saint Augustin devant la vie et la société rurales dans l'Afrique de son temps," *Miscellanea historiae ecclesiasticae* 6.1, 73–83.

(1984–85), "Un témoignage augustinien sur les langues parlées à Hippone et à Sitifis au début du Ve siècle," *BCTH* 20–21B (1984–85 [1989]), 154–56.

(1989), "Trois documents méconnus sur l'histoire sociale et religieuse de l'Afrique romaine tardive, retrouvés parmi les spuria de Sulpice Sévère," *AntAfr* 25, 235–62 = *Aspects de l'Afrique romaine*, 243–78.

(1990), "Les sénateurs Donatistes," *BSAF*, 45–56 = *Aspects de l'Afrique romaine*, 345–56.

(1992a), "Quelques parvenus de la culture de l'Afrique romaine tardive," in L. Holtz and J.-C. Fredouille, eds., *De Tertullien aux Mozarabes, 1: Antiquité tardive et christianisme ancien (IIIe–VIe siècles): Mélanges offerts à Jacques Fontaine*, Paris, Institut d'études augustiniennes, 583–94.

(1992b), "Circumcelliones," *AugLex* 1, 930–36.

(1994), "Le musée des statues divines. La volonté de sauvegarder le patrimoine artistique païen à l'époque théodosienne," *CArch* 42, 5–13.

(1998a), "L'aristocratie lettrée païenne: une ménace aux yeux d'Augustin (à propos du sermon Dolbeau 26 – Mayence 62)," in G. Madec, ed., *Augustin prédicateur (395–411): Actes du colloque intérnational de Chantilly*, Paris, Institut d'études augustiniennes, 327–42 = *Aspects de l'Afrique romaine*, 397–413.

(1998b), "Le patronat épiscopal aux IVe et Ve siècles: continuités et ruptures avec patronat classique," in E. Rebillard and C. Sotinel, eds., *L'évêque dans la cité du IVe au Ve siècle. Image et autorité*, Rome, Ecole française de Rome, 17–33.

Aspects de l'Afrique romaine: les cités, la vie rurale, le Christianisme, Bari, Edipuglia, 2001.

(2002a), "Le lieu des valeurs communes. La cité terrain neutre entre païens et chrétiens dans l'Afrique romaine tardive," in H. Inglebert, ed., *Idéologies et valeurs civiques dans le monde romain: Hommage à Claude Lepelley*, Paris, Institut d'études augustiniennes, 271–85.

(2002b), "Quelques aspects de l'administration des provinces romaines d'Afrique avant la conquête vandale," *AntTard* 10, 61–72.

(2002c), "La diabolisation du paganisme et ses conséquences psychologiques: les angoisses du Publicola, correspondant de saint Augustin," in L. Mary and M. Sot, eds., *Impiés et païens entre Antiquité et Moyen Age*, Paris, Picard, 81–96.

Leroy, F.-J. (1994), "Vingt-deux homélies africaines nouvelles attribuables à l'un des anonymes du Chrysostome Latin (PLS 4) [Vienne O.N.B. Ms. Lat. 4147]," *RBén* 104, 123–47.

(1997), "L'homélie donatiste ignorée du Corpus Escorial (Chrysostomus Latinus, *PLS* IV, *sermon 18*)," *RBén* 107, 250–62.

(1999), "Les 22 inédits de la catéchèse donatiste de Vienne. Une édition provisoire," *RecAug* 31, 149–234.

(2004), "Compléments et retouches à la 3e édition de la Clavis Patrum Latinorum: L'homilétique africaine masquée sous le Chrysostomus Latinus, Sévérien de Céramussa et la catéchèse Donatiste de Vienne," *RHE* 99, 425–34.

Leschi, L. (1927), "Les *Iuvenes* de Saldae d'après une inscription métrique," *RAf* 68, 393–419 = *Etudes*, 349–60.

(1940), "A propos des épitaphes chrétiennes du Djebel Nif en-Nser," *RAf* 84, 30–35.

(1947), "L'album municipal de Timgad et l'*ordo salutationis* du consulaire Ulpius Mariscianus," *CRAI*, 563–70.

(1948), "L'album municipal de Timgad et l'*ordo salutationis* du consulaire Ulpius Mariscianus," *REA*, 71–100 = *Etudes*, 246–66.

Etudes d'épigraphie, d'archéologie et d'histoire africaines, Paris, Arts and métiers graphiques, 1957.

Leveau, P., *Caesarea de Maurétanie: une ville romaine et ses campagnes*, Rome, Ecole française de Rome, 1984.

Liebs, D. (1989), "Die römische Jurisprudenz in Africa," *ZRG*, 210–47.

(1992), "Die römische Jurisprudenz in Africa im 4. Jh. n. Chr.," in M. Christol, ed., *Institutions, société et vie politique dans l'Empire romain au IV siècle ap. J.-C.*, Rome, Ecole française de Rome, 201–17.

Römische Jurisprudenz in Africa. Mit Studien zu den pseudopaulinischen Sentenzen, 2nd ed., Berlin, Duncker & Humblot, 2005.

Lieu, J. and S. (1981), "'Felix conversus ex Manichaeis': A Case of Mistaken Identity," *JThS* 32, 173–76.

Lieu, S. N. C., *Manichaeism in the Later Roman Empire and Medieval China: A Historical Survey*, 2nd rev. ed., Tübingen, J. C. B. Mohr – Paul Siebeck, 1992.

Lim, R., *Public Disputation, Power, and Social Order in Late Antiquity*, Berkeley and Los Angeles, University of California Press, 1995.

(2008), "The *Nomen Manichaeorum* and Its Uses in Antiquity," in Iricinschi and Zellentin, eds., *Heresy and Identity*, 143–67.

Linder, A. (1985), "La loi romaine et les juifs d'Afrique du Nord," in C. Iancu and J.-M. Lassère, eds., *Juifs et judaïsme en Afrique du Nord dans l'Antiquité et le Haut Moyen-Age*, Montepellier, Université Paul Valéry, 57–62.

[*Imperial Legislation*], *The Jews in Roman Imperial Legislation*, Detroit, Wayne State University Press, 1987 [transl. of: *Ha-Yedim yeha-Yahadut be-huke ha-kesarut ha-Romit*, Jersualem, The Israel Academy of Sciences and Humanities, 1983].

Lindsay, M. and D. Lester, *Suicide-by-Cop: Committing Suicide by Provoking Police to Shoot You*, Amityville NY, Baywood Publishing, 2004.

Lizzi, R. (1998), "I vescovi e i potentes della terra: definizione e limite del ruolo episcopale nelle due partes imperii fra IV e V secolo d.C.," in E. Rebillard and C. Sotinel, eds., *L'évêque dans la cité du IVe au Ve siècle. Image et autorité*, Rome, Ecole française de Rome, 81–104.

Lockwood, R. (1989), "*Potens et Factiosa Femina*: Women, Martyrs and Schism in Roman North Africa," *AugStud* 20, 165–82.

Logeart, F. (1940), "Les épitaphes funéraires chrétiennes du Djebel Nif en-Nser (Commune mixte d'Aïn-Mlila)," *RAf* 84, 5–29.

Lord, V. B. (2000), "Law Enforcement – Assisted Suicide," *Criminal Justice and Behavior* 27, 201–19.

Lössl, J. (2000), "Augustine in Byzantium," *JEH* 51, 267–95.

Lottman, H. R., *The Purge*, New York, William Murrow & Co., 1986.

McClure, J. (1979), "Handbooks Against Heresy in the West, from the Late Fourth to the Late Sixth Century," *JThS* 30, 186–79.

McGinn, B., *Antichrist: Two Thousand Years of the Human Fascination with Evil*, New York, Columbia University Press, 2000.

McLynn, N. B. (1992), "Christian Controversy and Violence in the Fourth Century," *Kodai* 3, 15–44.

Ambrose of Milan: Church and Court in a Christian Capital, Berkeley, University of California Press, 1994.

(1999), "Augustine's Roman Empire," *AugStud* 30, 29–44.

MacMullen, R. (1986), "Judicial Savagery in the Roman Empire," *Chiron* 16, 147–66.

(1989), "The Preacher's Audience (A.D. 350–400)," *JThS* 40, 503–11.

Christianity and Paganism in the Fourth to Eighth Centuries, New Haven and London, Yale University Press, 1997.

Feelings in History, Ancient and Modern, Claremont, Regina Books, 2003.

Voting About God in Early Church Councils, New Haven–London, Yale University Press, 2006.

The Second Church: Popular Christianity A.D. 200–400, Atlanta, Society of Biblical Literature, 2009.

Madec, G. (1975), "*Tempora Christiana*: expressions du triomphalisme chrétien ou récrimination païenne?," in P. Meyer and W. Eckermann, eds., *Scientia Augustiniana: Studien über Augustinus, den Augustinismus, und den Augustinerorden*, Wurzburg, Augustinus-Verlag, 112–36.

(1981), "Du nouveau dans la correspondance augustinienne," *REAug* 27, 56–66.

Augustin prédicateur (395–411), Paris, Institut d'études augustiniennes, 1998.

Magalhäes de Oliveira, J. C. (2004), "Le 'pouvoir du peuple': une émeute à Hippone au début du Ve siècle connue par le sermon 302 de saint Augustin pour la fête de saint Laurent," *AntTard* 12, 309–24.

(2006), "*Ut maiores pagani non sint!*: pouvoir, iconoclasme et action populaire à Carthage au début du Ve siècle (saint Augustin, *Sermones* 24, 279 et Morin 1)," *AntTard* 14, 245–62.

Maier, J.-L., *L'épiscopat de l'Afrique romaine, vandale et byzantine*, Rome, Institut Suisse de Rome, 1973.

Mandouze, A. (1960), "Encore le donatisme. Problèmes de méthode posés par la thèse de J.-P. Brisson," *AC* 29, 61–107.

(1968), "Dialogues avec la foule," ch. 11 in *Saint Augustin: l'aventure de la raison et de la grâce*, Paris, Institut d'études augustiniennes, 592–663.

(1976), "Le donatisme représente-t-il résistance à Rome de l'Afrique tardive?," in D. M. Pippidi, ed., *Assimilation et résistance à la culture gréco-romaine dans le monde ancien: travaux du VIe congrès international d'études classiques, Madrid, 1974*, Paris, Les Belles Lettres, 357–66.

(1986), "Les donatistes entre ville et campagne," in *Histoire et archéologie de l'Afrique du Nord. Actes du IIIe colloque international (Montpellier, 1–5 avril 1985)*, Paris, Comité des travaux historiques et scientifiques, 193–216.

Markus, R. A. (1972), "Christianity and Dissent in Roman North Africa: Changing Perspectives in Recent Work," in D. Baker, ed., *Schism, Heresy and Religious Protest = Studies in Church History* 9, Cambridge University Press, 21–36.

(2000), "Tempora Christiana Revisited," ch. 12 in R. Dodaro and G. Lawless, eds., *Augustine and His Critics: Essays in Honor of Gerald Bonner*, London and New York, Routledge, 201–13.

Marschall, W., *Karthago und Rom. Die Stellung der nordafrikanischen Kirche zum apostolischen Stuhl in Rom*, Stuttgart, Anton Hiersemann, 1971.

Martroye, F. (1904), "Une tentative de révolution sociale en Afrique: donatistes et circoncellions," *Revue des questions historiques* 38/76, 353–416.

(1905), "Une tentative de révolution sociale en Afrique: Donatistes et circoncellions," *Revue des questions historiques* 39/77, 5–53.

(1910), "Saint Augustin et la compétence de la juridiction ecclésiastique au Ve siècle," *MSAF* 70 = sér. 7, vol. 10, 1–78.

(1914a), "La répression du donatisme et la politique religieuse de Constantine et de ses successeurs en Afrique," *MSAF* 73 = sér. 8, vol. 13, 23–140.

(1914b), "Circoncellions," *DACL* 3.2, 1692–1710.

(1921a), "Donatisme: législation répressive," *DACL* 4.2, 1472–87.

(1921b), "Destruction par les chrétiens des statues," *BSAF*, 151–54.

Mashkîn, N. A. (1938), "Agonistiki, ili Tsirkumtsellionyi, v Kodekse Feodosiya," *VDI*, 2: 88–92 [in Russian: "Agonistici, and the Circumcellions in the Codex Theodosianus"].

(1949), "K Voprosu o Revolyutsionnom Dvizenin Rabov i Kolonov v Rimskoy Afrike," *VDI*, 4: 51–61 [in Russian: "The Revolutionary Movement of Slaves and Coloni in Roman Africa"].

Mastandrea, P., *Massimo di Madauros (Agostino, Epistulae 16 e 17)*, Padua, Editoriale Programma, 1985.

(1991), "Per la cronologia dei Tempora Macariana," *Koinonia* 15, 19–39.

(1992), "Vocaboli unici e rari nella Passio Maximiani et Isaac," *Civ. Class. Crist.* 13, 335–42.

(1995), "Passioni di martiri Donatisti (BHL 4473 e 5271)," *AB* 113, 39–88.

Matthews, J. F., *Western Aristocracies and Imperial Court, A.D. 364–425*, Oxford, Clarendon Press, 1975.

(1976), "Mauretania in Ammianus and the *Notitia*," in R. Goodburn and P. Bartholomew, eds., *Aspects of the Notitia Dignitatum*, Oxford, 157–86 = ch. 11 in *Political Life and Culture in Late Roman Society*, London, Variorum, 1985.

(1989), "Moors and Mauretania," ch. 14.2 in *The Roman Empire of Ammianus*, London, Duckworth; and Baltimore, Johns Hopkins University Press, 467–76.

Laying Down the Law: A Study of the Theodosian Code, New Haven and London, Yale University Press, 2000.

Mattingly, D. J. and R. B. Hitchner (1995), "Roman Africa: An Archaeological Review," *JRS* 85, 165–213.

Mayer, W. (1997), "The Dynamics of Liturgical Space: Aspects of the Interaction between St. John Chrysostom and his Audiences," *Ephemerides Liturgicae* 111, 104–15.

(1998), "John Chrysostom: Extraordinary Preacher, Ordinary Audience," in M. B. Cunningham and P. Allen, eds., *Preacher and Audience: Studies in Early Christian and Byzantine Homiletics*, Leiden and Boston, 105–37.

(1999), "Female Participation in the Late Fourth Century Preacher's Audience," *Augustinianum* 39, 139–48.

(2001), "At Constantinople: How Often did John Chrysostom Preach? Addressing Assumptions about the Workload of a Bishop," *Sacris Erudiri* 40, 83–105.

Mazzarino, S. (1961), "Si può parlare di rivoluzione sociale alla fine del mondo antico?," in *Settimane di studio del Centro Italiano di Studi sull'Alto Medioevo*, Spoleto 9 (1961), 410–25 = ch. 39 in *Antico, tardantico ed era costantiniana*, 2 (Bari, Laterza, 1980, 431–45).

Mazzucco, C., *Ottato di Milevi in un secolo di studi: problemi e prospettive*, Bologna, Pàtron editore, 1993.

Melani, C. (1998), "Mascezel e Gildone: politiche tribali e governo di Roma nell'Africa romana," *AfrRom* 12, 1489–1502.

Mercati, G. (1899/1937), "Un falso donatistico nelle opere di san Cipriano," *RIL* 32 (1899), 986–97 = *Opere minori*, vol. 2, Città del Vaticano = *Studi e Testi*, 77 (1937), 268–78.

Merdinger, J., *Rome and the African Church in the Time of Augustine*, New Haven, Yale University Press, 1997.

Merkelbach, R. (1988), "Der Manichäische Codex von Tebessa," in P. Bryder, ed., *Manichaean Studies: Proceedings of the First International Conference on Manichaeism*, Lund, Plus Ultra, 229–64.

Meslin, M., *La fête des kalendes de janvier dans l'empire romain: étude d'un rituel de Nouvel An*, Brussels, Collection Latomus no. 115, 1970.

Mesnage, P. J. [*Evêchés*], *L'Afrique chrétienne: évêchés et ruines antiques d'après les manuscrits du Mgr. Toulotte et les découvertes archéologiques les plus récents*, Paris, E. Leroux, 1912.

Michels, G. B. (1992), "The Violent Old Belief: An Examination of Religious Dissent on the Karelian Frontier," *Russian History* 19, 203–29.

  At War with the Church: Religious Dissent in Seventeenth-Century Russia, Stanford, Stanford University Press, 1999.

Miles, R. (2005), "The *Anthologia Latina* and the Creation of Secular Space in Vandal Carthage," *AntTard* 13, 305–20.

Millar, F., *The Emperor in the Roman World*, London, Duckworth; Ithaca NY, Cornell University Press, 1977.

  (2004), "Repentant Heretics in Fifth-Century Lycia: Identity and Literacy," *SCI* 23, 111–30.

  A Greek Roman Empire: Power and Belief under Theodosius II, 404–450, Berkeley and Los Angeles, University of California Press, 2006.

Mitchell, S. (1999), "The Cult of Theos Hypsistos between Pagans, Jews and Christians," in P. Athanassiadi and M. Frede, eds., *Pagan Monotheism in Late Antiquity*, Oxford, Clarendon Press, 81–148.

Modéran, Y. (1989), "Gildon, les Maures et l'Afrique," *MEFRA* 101, 821–72.

  (1998), "L'Afrique et la persécution vandale," in J. M. Mayer, Ch. and L. Pietri, A. Vauchez, and M. Venard, eds., *Histoire du christianisme, III: Les Eglises d'Orient et d'Occident, 430–610*, Paris, Desclée, 247–68.

  (2003), "Une guerre de religion: les deux églises d'Afrique à l'époque vandale," *AntTard* 11, 21–44.

Mohrmann, C. (1977), "Episkopos – speculator," in *Etudes sur le latin des chrétiens, 4: Latin chrétien et latin médiéval*, Rome, Edizioni di storia e letteratura, 231–52.

Moloney, E., *A Secret History of the IRA*, New York and London, W. W. Norton, 2002.

Monceaux, P. (1902), "Païens judaïsants, essai d'interprétation d'une inscription africaine," *RA*, 208–26.

(1904/1970), "Les colonies juives dans l'Afrique romaine," *REJ* (1904), 1–28 = *CT* 18 (1970), 5–30.

(1907), "Le Dossier de Gaudentius, évêque donatiste de Thamugadi. Restitution ou fragments de ses ouvrages et des documents qui s'y rattachent," *RPh* 31, 111–33.

(1909), "L'épigraphie donatiste," *RPh* 33, 112–61.

(1913), "Les martyrs donatistes. Culte et relations," *RHR* 34, 146–92, 310–44.

[*Hist. litt. 1*], *Histoire littéraire de l'Afrique chrétienne depuis les origines jusqu'à l'invasion arabe, t. 1: Tertullien et les origines*, Paris, E. Leroux, 1901 [reprint: Brussels, Culture et civilisation, 1966].

[*Hist. litt. 2*], *Histoire littéraire de l'Afrique chrétienne depuis les origines jusqu'à l'invasion arabe, t. 2: Saint Cyprien et ses temps*, Paris, E. Leroux, 1902 [reprint: Brussels, Culture et civilisation, 1966].

[*Hist. litt. 3*], *Histoire littéraire de l'Afrique chrétienne depuis les origines jusqu'à l'invasion arabe, t. 3: Le IVe siècle, d'Arnobe à Victorin*, Paris, E. Leroux, 1905 [reprint: Brussels, Culture et civilisation, 1966].

[*Hist. litt. 4*], *Histoire littéraire de l'Afrique chrétienne depuis les origines jusqu'à l'invasion arabe, t. 4: Le Donatisme*, Paris, E. Leroux, 1912 [reprint: Brussels, Culture et civilisation, 1966].

[*Hist. litt. 5*], *Histoire littéraire de l'Afrique chrétienne depuis les origines jusqu'à l'invasion arabe, t. 5: Saint Optat et les premiers écrivains Donatistes*, Paris, E. Leroux, 1920 [reprint: Brussels, Culture et civilisation, 1966].

[*Hist. litt. 6*], *Histoire littéraire de l'Afrique chrétienne depuis les origines jusqu'à l'invasion arabe, t. 6: Littérature donatiste au temps de Saint Augustin*, Paris, E. Leroux, 1922 [reprint: Brussels, Culture et civilisation, 1966].

[*Hist. Litt. 7*], *Histoire littéraire de l'Afrique chrétienne depuis les origines jusqu'à l'invasion arabe, t. 7: Saint Augustin et le donatisme*, Paris, E. Leroux, 1923 [reprint: Brussels, Culture et civilisation, 1966].

Timgad chrétien, Paris, Imprimerie nationale, 1911.

Moorhead, J., transl., notes and intro. *Victor of Vita: History of the Vandal Persecution*, Liverpool, Liverpool University Press, 1992.

Moreau, M. (1973a), "Le dossier Marcellinus dans la correspondance de saint Augustin," *RecAug* 9, 3–181.

(1973b), "La guerre de Firmus (373–375)," *RHCM* 10, 21–36.

(1998), "Le magistrat et l'évêque: pour une lecture de la correspondence Macedonius et Augustin," *Recherches et Travaux. Université Stendhal-Grenoble* 54, 105–17.

Morgan, T., *Popular Morality in the Early Roman Empire*, Cambridge University Press, 2007.

Morgenstern, F. (1993), "Die Kaisergesetze gegen die Donatisten in Nordafrika (Mitte 4. Jh. bis 429) im Zusammenhang mit dem antidonatistischen Wirken des Augustinus von Hippo," *ZSS* 110, 103–23.

Müller, L. G., transl., intro., and comm. (1956), *The De Haeresibus of Saint Augustine*, Washington DC, The Catholic University of America Press, 1956.

Munier, C. (1979), "La tradition littéraire des dossiers africains," *Revue de droit canonique* 29, 41–52.

(1983), "La question des appels à Rome d'après la Lettre 20* d'Augustin," in *Les lettres de saint Augustin découvertes par Johannes Divjak*, Paris, Institut d'études augustiniennes, 287–99.

(1986–94), "Antoninus Fussalensis episcopus," *AugLex* 1, 378–80.

(2003), "L'influence de saint Augustin sur la législation ecclésiastique de son temps," in *Augustinus Afer: Saint Augustin: africanité et universalité*, Fribourg, Editions universitaires, 109–23.

Murray, A., *Suicide in the Middle Ages, 1: The Violent Against Themselves; 2: The Curse of Self-Murder*, Oxford and New York, Oxford University Press, 1999–2000.

Musurillo, H., *Acts of the Christian Martyrs*, Oxford, Clarendon Press, 1972.

Nathusius, D. M. von [*Cirkumcellionen*], *Zur Charakteristik der afrikanischen Cirkumcellionen des 4. und 5. Jahrhunderts in Afrika*, Greifswald, J. Abel, 1900.

Nirenberg, D., *Communities of Violence: Persecution of Minorities in the Middle Ages*, Princeton University Press, 1996.

Norton, P., *Episcopal Elections, 250–600: Hierarchy and Popular Will in Late Antiquity*, Oxford University Press, 2007.

O'Donnell, J. (1977), "Paganus," *Classical Folia* 31, 163–69.

(1979), "The Demise of Paganism," *Traditio* 35, 45–88.

Augustine: A New Biography, New York, HarperCollins, 2005.

Ohnuki-Tierney, E., *Kamikaze, Cherry Blossoms and Nationalisms: The Militarization of Aesthetics in Japanese History*, Chicago and London, The University of Chicago Press, 2002.

Olechowska, E. M. [*De Bello Gildonico*], *Claudii Claudiani De bello Gildonico*, Leiden, Brill, 1978.

Oliver, A. M. and P. F. Steinberg [*Martyrs' Square*], *The Road to Martyrs' Square: A Journey into the World of the Suicide Bomber*, Oxford and New York, Oxford University Press, 2005.

Oost, S. I. (1962), "Count Gildo and Theodosius the Great," *CPh* 57, 27–30.

(1966), "The Revolt of Heraclian," *CPh* 61, 236–42.

Opelt, I., *Die Polemik in der christlichen lateinischen Literatur von Tertullian bis Augustin*, Heidelberg, Winter, 1980.

(1983), "Augustins epistula *20 (Divjak). Ein Zeugnis für lebendiges Punisch im 5. Jh. nach Christus," *Augustinianum* 25 (1985), 121–32.

O'Reilly, M. V. (1955), *Sancti Aurelii Augustini de excidio urbis Romae sermo*, Washington DC, The Catholic University of America Press, 1955.

Overbeck, M. (1973), "Augustin und die Circumcellionen seiner Zeit," *Chiron* 3, 457–63.

Ozment, S. (1982), "Pamphlet Literature of the German Reformation," in S. Ozment, ed., *Reformation Europe: A Guide to Research*, St. Louis, MO, Center for Reformation Research, 85–105.

Pagels, E. [*Satan*], *The Origin of Satan*, New York, Random House, 1995.

Pallu de Lessert, A. C. (1901), "De la compétence respective du proconsul et du vicaire d'Afrique dans les démêlés donatistes," *MSAF*, sér. 6, 10, 17–32.

(1916), "De la compétence respective du proconsul et du vicaire d'Afrique dans les démêlés donatistes," *MSAF* 60, 23–25.

(1917), "Le conflit entre Primianus et Maximianus, Donatistes en 392," *BSAF*, 143–46.

Palme, B. (1999), "Die Officia der Statthalter in der Spätantike: Forschungsstand und Perspektiven," *AntTard* 7, 85–133.

Pandey, G. (1992), "In Defense of the Fragment: Writing About Hindu–Muslim Riots in India Today," *Representations* 37 (Winter), 27–55.

Parent, R. B. [*Victim-Precipitated Homicide*], *Aspects of Police Use of Deadly Force in North America: The Phenomenon of Victim-Precipitated Suicide*, PhD Dissertation, Simon Fraser University, 2004.

and S. Verdun-Jones (1998), "Victim-precipitated Homicide: Police Use of Deadly Force in British Columbia," *Policing* 21, 432–45.

Partoens, G. (2005), "Le sermon 163 de saint Augustin: introduction et édition," *RBén* 115 (2005), pp. 251–85.

Patlagean, E., "Les armes et la cité à Rome du VIIe siècle au IXe siècle, et le modèle européen des trois fonctions sociales," *MEFR* 86, 125–62.

(1981), "Les jeunes dans les villes byzantines: émeutiers et miliciens," in J. Le Goff and J.-C. Schmitt, eds., *Le charivari*, Paris and New York, Mouton, 122–29.

Payre, G. (1942), "Une fête de printemps au Jerid," *RT* 43, 171–77.

Perler, O. (1958), "Les voyages de saint Augustin," *RecAug* 1, 5–42.

Les voyages de saint Augustin, Paris, Institut d'études augustiniennes, 1969.

Peterson, E., *Eis Theos. Epigraphische, formgeschichtliche und religionsgeschichtliche Untersuchungen*, Göttingen, Vandenhoeck & Ruprecht, 1926.

Pettegree, A. [*Culture of Persuasion*], *Reformation and the Culture of Persuasion*, Cambridge University Press, 2005.

Phillips, D. P. (1974), "The Influence of Suggestion on Suicide: Substantive and Theoretical Implications of the Werther Effect," *American Sociological Review* 39, 340–54.

(1979), "Suicide, Motor Vehicle Fatalities, and the Mass Media: Evidence Toward a Theory of Suggestion," *American Journal of Sociology* 84, 1150–74.

Piganiol, A. (1955), "La signification de l'album municipal de Timgad," *MSAF* 3, 97–101 = *Scripta varia*, 3 (Brussels, Collection Latomus, 1973), 264–68.

(1956–67), "La religion et les mouvements sociaux dans le Maghreb antique," *Cahiers d'histoire mondiale* 3, 813–32.

Pizzani, U. (2003), "Sant'Agostino e la musica alla luce delle Confessioni," in *Le Confessioni di Agostino (402–2002): bilancio e prospettive = Studia Ephemeridis Augustinianum*, 85, Rome, Institutum Patristicum Augustinianum, 487–98.

(2007), "Agostino e il *Psalmus contra partem Donati*," in L. F. Pizzolato and R. A. Markus, eds., *Agostino e il Donatismo = Lectio Augustini XIX: Settimana Agostiniana Pavese, 2003*, Rome, Institutum Patristicum Augustinianum, 23–44.

Plass, P., *The Game of Death in Ancient Rome: Arena Sport and Political Suicide*, Madison WI, The University of Wisconsin Press, 1995.

Pleket, H. W. (1978), "De Circumcelliones: 'Primitive Rebels' in de late keizertijd in Noord-Africa," *Lampas* 11, 143–57.

Pontet, M. [*Augustin prédicateur*], *L'exégèse de saint Augustin prédicateur*, Paris, Aubier, 1946.

Poque, S., *Le langage symbolique dans la prédication d'Augustin d'Hippone. Images héroïques*, Paris, Institut d'études augustiniennes, 1984.

Potter, T. [*Iol Caesarea*], *Towns in Late Antiquity: Iol Caesarea and its Context*, Oxford, Oxbow, 1995.

———— (1996), "Recent Work in North Africa: The Cherchel Excavations," in M. Horton and T. Wiedemann, eds., *North Africa from Antiquity to Islam*, Bristol, Center for Mediterranean Studies, Occasional Papers, no. 13, 34–38.

Potter, T. and N. Benseddik (1993), *Fouilles au Forum de Cherchel, 1977–1981*, Supplement to BAA, 6, 2 vols., Algiers, Ministère de la culture.

Pourkier, A. [*Epiphane de Salamine*], *L'hérésiologie chez Epiphane de Salamine*, Paris, Beauchesne, 1992.

Prévot, F. [*Inscriptions chrétiennes*], *Recherches archéologiques franco-tunisiennes à Mactar, 5: Les inscriptions chrétiennes*, Rome, Ecole française de Rome, 1984.

Quinot, B. (1967a), "Optatus de Thamugadi," note 5 in *BA* 30, 757–60.

———— (1967b), "Les basiliques maximianistes et Primianus," note 8 in *BA* 30, 765–66.

———— (1967c), "Les accusations de manichéisme portées par Petilianus (2.18.40; 3.10.11)," note 10 in *BA* 30, 769–71.

———— (1967d), "Marculus et Donatus, martyrs donatistes," note 11 in *BA* 30, 771–73.

———— (1967e), "Les lois antidonatistes," note 18 in *BA* 30, 792–94.

———— (1967f), "Saint Augustin et le recours au bras séculier," note 21 in *BA* 30, 799–803.

Rachet, M., *Rome et les Berbères. Un problème militaire d'Auguste à Dioclétien*, Brussels, Collection Latomus, 1970.

Rapp, C., *Holy Bishops in Late Antiquity: The Nature of Christian Leadership in an Age of Transition*, Berkeley, University of California Press, 2005.

Rattenbury, J. E. [*Charles Wesley's Hymns*], *The Evangelical Doctrines of Charles Wesley's Hymns*, London, Epworth Press, 1941.

Ratzinger, J. (1958), "Beobachtungen zum Kirchenbegriff des Tyconius," *REAug* 2, 173–85.

Raynal, D. (1973), "Culte des martyrs et propaganda donatiste à Uppena," *CT* 21, 33–72.

Reitzenstein, R. (1914), "Eine frühchristliche Schrift von den dreierlei Früchten des christlichen Lebens," *ZNTW* 15, 60–90.

Rey-Coquais, J.-P. (1998), "Domini et Circumcelliones, Code Théodosien, 16,5,52: remarques de grammaire et interrogation sur le sens," *AfrRom* 12, 447–56.

Richter, M. (2009), "*Carmina autem quaecumque in laudem Dei dicuntur hymni vocantur* (Isidore of Seville, *De ecclesiasticis officiis* 1.6)," *JLA* 2, 116–30.

Rives, J. B., *Religion and Authority in Roman Carthage from Augustus to Constantine*, Oxford, Clarendon Press, 1995.

Rohozinski, J. (2002), "Ritual Violence and Societies in Maghreb: Regarding a Passage of St. Augustine's *De Doctrina Christiana*," in *Euergesias Charin: Studies Presented to Benedetto Bravo and Ewa Wipszycha*, Warsaw, Fundacaja im. Rafala Taubenschlaga, 219–23.

Romanelli, P., *Storia delle province romane dell'Africa*, Rome, L'"Erma" di Bretschneider, 1959.

Romero Pose, E. (1980), "A propósito de las actas y pasiones donatistas," *Studi storico-religiosi* 4, 59–76.

Rose, H. J. (1926–27), "St. Augustine as a Forerunner of Medieval Hymnology," *JThS* 28, 383–92.

Roueché, C. (1984), "Acclamations in the Later Roman Empire: New Evidence from Aphrodisias," *JRS* 74, 181–99.

  (1998), "The Functions of the Governor in Late Antiquity: Some Observations," *AntTard* 6, 31–36.

Rougé, J. (1983), "Escroquerie et brigandage en Afrique romaine au temps de saint Augustin," in *Les lettres de saint Augustin découvertes par J. Divjak*, Paris, Institut d'études augustiniennes, 177–88.

Rouse, R. and C. McNelis (2000), "North African Literary Activity: A Cyprian Fragment, the Stichometric Lists and a Donatist Compendium," *RHT* 30, 189–238.

Rousseau, P. (1998), "'The Preacher's Audience': A More Optimistic View," in T. W. Hillard, R. A. Kearnsley, C. E. V. Nixon, and A. M. Nobbs, eds., *Ancient History in a Modern University, 2: Early Christianity, Late Antiquity and Beyond*, Grand Rapids, W. B. Eerdmans, 391–400.

Rousselle, A. (1977), "Aspects sociaux du recrutement ecclésiastique au IVe siècle," *MEFRA* 89, 333–70.

Rubin, Z. (1995), "Mass Movements in Late Antiquity – Appearances and Realities," in Irad Malkin and Zeev W. Rubinsohn, eds., *Leaders and Masses in the Roman World: Studies in Honor of Zvi Yavetz*, Leiden, 129–87.

Ruff, J. R., *Violence in Early Modern Europe, 1500–1800*, Cambridge University Press, 2001.

Ruggiero, F. (1988), "Il problema del numero dei martiri Scilitani," *CrSt* 9, 135–52.

  (1991), "Atti dei Martiri Scilitani," *Atti della Accademia Nazionale dei Lincei, Classe di Scienze Morali, Storiche e Filologiche: Memorie*, ser. 9, no. 1.2, 35–139.

Russell, J. B., *Satan: The Early Christian Tradition*, Ithaca NY, Cornell University Press, 1981.

Sabw Kanyang, J.-A., *Episcopus et plebs: L'évêque et la communauté ecclésiale dans les conciles africains (345–525)*, Frankfurt and Bern, Peter Lang, 2000.

Salomonson, J. W., *Voluptatem spectandi non perdat sed mutet. Observations sur l'iconographie du martyre en Afrique romaine*, Amsterdam, Oxford, and New York, North-Holland, 1979.

Salzman, M. R., *On Roman Time: The Codex-Calendar of 354 and the Rhythms of Urban Life in Late Antiquity*, Berkeley and Los Angeles, University of Calfornia Press, 1990.

The Making of a Christian Aristocracy: Social and Religious Change in the Western Roman Empire, Cambridge MA, Harvard University Press, 2002.

(2006), "Rethinking Pagan–Christian Violence," ch. 22 in H. Drake, ed., *Violence in Late Antiquity*, 265–85.

Saumagne. C. (1934), "Ouvriers agricoles ou rôdeurs de celliers? Les circoncellions d'Afrique," *AHE* 6, 351–64.

Saxer, V., *Morts, martyrs, reliques en Afrique chrétienne aux premiers siècles. Les témoignages de Tertullien, Cyprien et Augustin à la lumière de l'archéologie africaine*, Paris, Editions Beauchesne, 1980.

Schäferdiek, K. (1989), "Der *Sermo de passione sanctorum Donati et Advocati* als donatistisches Selbstzeugnis," in D. Papandreou, W. A. Bienert, and K. Schäferdiek, eds., *Oecumenica et Patristica: Festschrift für Wilhelm Schneemelcher zum 75. Geburtstag*, Stuttgart, W. Kohlhammer, 175–98.

Scheid, J. (1998), "Les réjouissances des calendes de janvier d'après le sermon Dolbeau 26. Nouvelles lumières sur une fête mal connue," in G. Madec, ed., *Augustin prédicateur*, 353–65.

Schindler, A. (1980), "Die Unterscheidung von Schisma und Häresie in Gesetzgebung und Polemik gegen den Donatismus (mit einer Bemerkung zur Datierung von Augustins Schrift *Contra epistulam Parmeniani*)," in E. Dassmann and K. Suso Frank, eds., *Pietas. Festschrift für Bernhard Kötting*, Münster, Aschendorff, 228–36.

(1984), "Kritische Bemerkungen zur Quellenbewertung in der Circumcellionenforschung," *Studia Patristica* 15 (TUC, no. 128), 238–41.

Schneemelcher, W. (1962), "Epiphanius von Salamis," *RAC* 5, 910–27.

Schreckenberg, H. [*Adversus-Judaeos-Texte*], *Die christlichen Adversus-Judaeos-Texte und ihr literarisches und historisches Umfeld (1.-11. Jh.)*, Frankfurt and Bern, Peter Lang, 1982.

Schulten, P. G. G. M., *De Circumcellionen: een sociaal-religieuze Beweging in de Late Oudheid*, Scheveningen, Edauw and Johannissen, 1984.

Scribner, R. W. [*Popular Propaganda*], *For the Sake of Simple Folk: Popular Propaganda for the German Reformation*, Cambridge University Press, 1981 (reprint: 1991).

Seeck, O., "Quellen und Urkunden über die Anfänge des Donatismus," *Zeitschrift für Kirchengeschichte* 10 (1889), 505–68; 30 (1909), 181–227.

(1909), "Firmus," *RE* 12, 2283–84.

(1910), "Gildo," *RE* 13, 1360–63.

Seeland, T. (1996), "Philo and the Clubs and Associations of Alexandria," ch. 7 in J. S. Kloppenborg and S. G. Wilson, eds., *Voluntary Associations in the Graeco-Roman World*, London and New York, Routledge, 110–27.

Sémelin, J., *Purify and Destroy: The Political Uses of Massacre and Genocide*, transl. C. Schoch, New York, Columbia University Press, 2007 (translation of: *Purifier et détruire: usages politiques des massacres et génocides*, Paris, Seuil, 2005).

Sen, A., *Identity and Violence: The Illusion of Destiny*, New York, Norton, 2006.

Seston, W. (1940), "Sur l'authenticité et la date de l'édit de Dioclétien contre les Manichéens," in *Mélanges de philologie, de littérature et d'histoire anciennes offerts à Alfred Ernout*, Paris, 345–54.

Sharpe, J. A. (1985), "The History of Violence in England: Some Observations," *P&P* 108, 206–15.

Shaw, B. D. (1981), "Rural Markets in North Africa and the Political Economy of the Roman Empire," *AntAfr* 17, 37–83 = ch. 1 in *Rulers, Nomads, and Christians*.

(1982), "The Elders of Christian Africa," in P. Brind'Amour, ed., *Mélanges offerts à R. P. Etienne Gareau*, Ottawa, Editions de l'Université d'Ottawa = numéro spéc. de *Cahiers des études anciennes*, 207–26 = ch. 10 in *Rulers, Nomads, and Christians*.

(1984), "Latin Funerary Epigraphy and Family Life in the Later Roman Empire," *Historia* 33, 457–97.

(1991), "The Structure of Local Society in the Early Maghrib: The Elders," *The Maghrib Review* 16 (1991 [1994]), 18–55 = ch. 3 in *Rulers, Nomads, and Christians*.

(1992/1995), "African Christianity: Disputes, Definitions, and 'Donatists'," in M. R. Greenshields and T. A. Robinson, eds., *Orthodoxy and Heresy in Religious Movements: Discipline and Dissent* (Lewiston NY and Lampeter, E. Mellen Press, 1992), 5–34 = ch. 11 in *Rulers, Nomads, and Christians*.

(1993), "The Passion of Perpetua," *P&P* 139, 3–45 = revised reprint in R. Osborne, ed., *Studies in Ancient Greek and Roman Society*, Cambridge University Press, 286–325.

Rulers, Nomads, and Christians in Roman North Africa, London, Variorum, 1995.

(1996a) "Body/Power/Identity: Passions of the Martyrs," *JECS* 4, 269–312.

(1996b), "Seasons of Death: Aspects of Mortality in Imperial Rome," *JRS* 86, 100–38.

(1997), "Ritual Brotherhood in Roman and Post-Roman Societies," *Traditio* 52, 327–55.

(1999), "War and Violence," in G. W. Bowersock, P. Brown, and O. Grabar, eds., *Late Antiquity: A Guide to the Postclassical World*, Cambridge MA, Harvard University Press, 130–69.

(2003), "A Peculiar Island: Maghrib and Mediterranean," *Mediterranean Historical Review* 18, 93–125 = I. Malkin, ed., *Mediterranean Paradigms and Classical Antiquity*, London and New York, Routledge, 2005, 93–125.

(2004), "Who Were the Circumcellions?," ch. 11 in A. H. Merrills, ed., *Vandals, Romans and Berbers: New Perspectives on Late Antique North Africa*, London, Variorum, 227–58.

At the Edge of the Corrupting Sea, Oxford, University of Oxford, 2006 (The Twenty-Third J. L. Myres Memorial Lecture).

(2006), "Bad Boys: Circumcellions and Fictive Violence," ch. 15 in H. A. Drake, *Violence in Late Antiquity*, Aldershot, Variorum, 179–96.

(2009), "State Intervention and Holy Violence: Timgad / Paleostrovsk / Waco," *JAAR* 77, 1–42.

Bringing in the Sheaves: Economy and Metaphor in the Roman Empire, Toronto, University of Toronto Press (forthcoming).

(forthcoming), "Cult and Belief in Punic and Roman Africa," in W. Adler, ed., *The Cambridge History of Religions of the Classical World*, vol. 2, Cambridge University Press.

Sheppin, K. [*Circumcelliones*], *Selansky rukhy v rymskii, I: Circumcelliones*, Niz'h'yn, Derzh drukumi a "Nove selo," 1930 [in Ukrainian].

Simon, M. (1953), "Punique ou berbère? Note sur la situation linguistique dans l'Afrique romaine," *AIPhO* 13 = *Mélanges Isidore Lévy*, Brussels, Secrétariat des Editions de l'Institut, 1955, 613–29.

(1978), "Un document du syncrétisme religieux dans l'Afrique romaine," *CRAI*, 500–24.

Sizgorich, T., *Violence and Belief in Late Antiquity: Militant Devotion in Christianity and Islam*, Philadelphia, University of Pennsylvania Press, 2008.

Slootjes, D., *The Governor and His Subjects in the Later Roman Empire*, Leiden, Brill, 2006.

Soden, H. von and H. von Campenhausen, *Urkunden zur Entstehungsgeschichte des Donatismus*, 2nd ed., Berlin, Walter de Gruyter, 1950.

Speidel, M. P. (1993), "The *Fustis* as a Soldier's Weapon," *AntAfr* 29 (1993), 137–49.

Springer, C. P. E. (1984), "The Artistry of Augustine's *Psalmus Contra Partem Donati*," *AugStud* 16, 65–74.

(1987), "The Prosopopoeia of Church as Mother in Augustine's *Psalmus Contra Partem Donati*," *Aug Stud* 18, 52–65.

Staphylus, F., *Disputatio circa circumcelliones*, s. loc., s. edit., 1548.

Statt, D. (1995), "The Case of the Mohocks: Rake Violence in Augustan London," *Social History* 20, 179–99.

Stein, M. (2001), "Bemerkungen zum Kodex von Tebessa," in J. van Oort, O. Wermelinger, and G. Wurst, eds., *Augustine and Manichaeism in the Latin West*, Leiden and Boston, Brill, 250–71.

[*Codex Thevestinus*], *Manichaica Latina, 3.1–2: Codex Thevestinus*, Paderborn and Munich, Ferdinand Schöningh, 2004–6.

Steinwenter, A. (1934), "Der antike kirchliche Rechtsgang und seine Quellen," *ZSS* KAbt. 23, 1–116.

(1935), "Eine kirchliche Quelle des nachklassischen Zivilprozesses," in *Acta Congressus Iuridici Internationalis*, vol. 2, Rome, Institutum Pontificium Utriusque Iuris, 125–44.

Stern, H. (1981), "Les calendriers romains illustrés," *ANRW* 2.12.2, 431–75.

Stern, J., *Terror in the Name of God: Why Religious Militants Kill*, New York, HarperCollins, 2003.

Stern, K. [*Devotion and Death*], *Inscribing Devotion and Death: Archaeological Evidence for Jewish Populations of North Africa*, Leiden, Brill, 2008.

Stewart, P. (1999), "The Destruction of Statues in Late Antiquity," ch. 8 in R. Miles, ed., *Constructing Identities in Late Antiquity*, New York and London, Routledge, 159–89.

Stone, L. (1983), "Interpersonal Violence in English Society, 1300–1980," *P&P* 101, 22–33.

Straw, C. E. (1983), "Augustine as Pastoral Theologian: The Exegesis of the Parables of the Field and Threshing Floor," *AugStud* 14, 129–51.

—— (2000), "Settling Scores: Eschatology in the Church of the Martyrs," in C. Bynum and P. Freedman, eds., *Last Things: Death and the Apocalypse in the Later Middle Ages*, Philadelphia, University of Pennsylvania Press, 21–40.

Stroumsa, G. G. (1996), "From Anti-Judaism to Anti-Semitism in Early Christianity in Contra Iudaeos," in O. Limor and G. G. Stroumsa, eds, *Contra Iudaeos: Ancient and Medieval Polemics between Christians and Jews*, Tübingen, J. C. B. Mohr, 1–26.

Sullivan, T., *S. Aureli Augustini Hipponiensis Episcopi de Doctrina Christiana Liber Quartus: A Commentary*, Washington DC, The Catholic University of America, 1930.

Szidat, J. (1985), "Zum Sklavenhandel in der Spätantike (August. *Epist.* 10*)," *Historia* 34, 360–71.

Tambiah, S. J., *Leveling Crowds: Ethnonationalist Conflicts and Collective Violence in South Asia*, Berkeley, University of California Press, 1997.

Teitler, H. C., *Notarii and Exceptores: An Inquiry into Role and Significance of Shorthand Writers in the Imperial and Ecclesiastical Bureaucracy of the Roman Empire (from the Early Principate to c. 450 A.D.)*, Amsterdam, J. C. Gieben, 1985.

Tengström, E., *Die Protokollierung der Collatio Carthaginensis. Beiträge zur Kenntnis der römischen Kurzschrift nebst einem Exkurs über das Wort scheda (schedula)*, Göteborg, Elanders boktr. aktiebolag, 1962.

—— *Donatisten und Katholiken. Soziale, wirtschaftliche und politische Aspekte einer nordafrikanischen Kirchenspaltung*, Göteborg, Acta Universitatis Gothoburgensis, 1964.

Thomas, D. W. (1960), "Kelebh 'Dog': Its Origin and Some Usages of It in the Old Testament," *VT* 10, 410–27.

Thomasson, B. E., *Die Statthalter der römischen Provinzen Nordafrikas von Augustus bis Diokletian*, 2 vols., Lund, C. W. K. Gleerup, 1960.

—— *Fasti africani: senatorische und ritterliche Amtsträger in den römischen Provinzen Nordafrikas von Augustus bis Diokletian*, Stockholm, Svenska Insitutet I Rome, Paul Astroms Forlag, 1996.

Thornton, T. C. G. (1986), "The Destruction of Idola: Sinful or Meritorious?," *JThS* 37, 121–29.

Thouvenot, R. (1964), "Saint Augustin et les païens (d'après Epist. XLVI et XLVII)," in *Hommages à J. Bayet*, Brussels, Collection Latomus, 682–90.

Thümmel, W., *Zur Beurtheilung des Donatismus: Eine kirchengeschichtliche Untersuchung*, Halle/Saale, Max Niemeyer, 1893.

Tilley, M. A. (1991), "Dilatory Donatists or Procrastinating Catholics: The Trial at the Conference of Carthage," *ChHist* 60, 7–19.

(1997), "Sustaining Donatist Self-Identity: From the Church of the Martyrs to the Collecta of the Desert," *JECS* 5, 21–35.

Tilly, C. [*Collective Violence*], *The Politics of Collective Violence*, Cambridge University Press, 2003.

Why? What Happens When People Give Reasons . . . and Why, Princeton University Press, 2006.

Torhoudt, A. (1954), "Caelicolae," *RAC* 2, 817–20.

Tréhorel, E. (1939), Le psaume abécédaire de saint Augustin," *REL* 17, 309–29.

Unterseher, L. A. (2002), "The Mark of Cain and the Jews: Augustine's Theology of Jews," *Augustinian Studies* 33, 99–121.

Van Dam, R., *Leadership and Community in Late Antique Gaul*, Berkeley and Los Angeles, University of California Press, 1985.

Van der Lof, L. J. (1967), "Gaudentius de Thamugadi," *Augustiniana* 17, 5–13.

(1974), "Mani as the Danger from Persia in the Roman Empire," *Augustiniana* 24, 75–84.

Van der Meer, F., *Augustine the Bishop: The Life and Work of a Father of the Church*, transl. B. Battershaw and G. R. Lamb, London, Sheed & Ward, 1961.

Van Hooff, A. J. L., *From Autothanasia to Suicide: Self-Killing in Classical Antiquity*, London and New York, Routledge, 1990.

Van Oort, J. (2000), "Mani and Manichaeism in Augustine's *De haeresibus*. An analysis of Haer. 46.1," in R. E. Emmerick, W. Sundermann, and P. Zieme, eds., *Studia Manichaica: 4. Internationaler Kongreß zum Manichäismus, Berlin, 14–18 Juli 1997*, Berlin, Akademie Verlag, 451–63.

(2003), "Augustine and Manichaeism in Roman North Africa: Remarks on an African Debate and its Universal Consequences," in P.-Y. Fux, J.-M. Roessli, and O. Wermelinger, eds., *Augustinus Afer*, 1, Fribourg, Editions Universitaires Fribourg Suisse, 199–210.

Vannier, O. (1926), "Les circoncellions et leurs rapports avec l'église donatiste d'après le texte d'Optat," *RAfr* 67, 13–28.

Varshney, A., *Ethnic Conflict and Civil Life: Hindus and Muslims in India*, 2nd ed., New Haven, Yale University Press, 2003.

Vattioni, F. (1968), "Sant'Agostino e la civiltà punica," *Augustinianum* 8, 434–67.

Vita-Evrard, G. (1989), "La date de la Passio S. Crispinae," *AfrRom* 6 (Sassari), 308–13.

Voelter, D., *Der Ursprung des Donatismus nach den Quellen untersucht und dargestellt*, Freiburg i. B. und Tübingen, J. C. B. Mohr and Paul Siebeck, 1883.

Volterra, E. (1966), "La costituzione di Diocleziano e Massimiano contro i Manichaei," in *Persia e il mondo grecoromano* = *Accademia dei Lincei, anno*. 363, quad. 76, 27–50.

Vössing, K. (1996), "Africa nutricula causidicorum? Die römische Jurisprudenz in Africa," *AfrRom* 11, 127–54.

Schule und Bildung im Nordafrika der römischen Kaiserzeit, Brussels, Collection Latomus no. 238, 1997.

Vroom, H., *Le psaume abédécaire de saint Augustin et la poésie latine rhythmique*, Nijmegen, Dekker and van de Veft, 1933.

Warmington, B. H., *The North African Provinces from Diocletian to the Vandal Conquest*, Cambridge University Press, 1954 [reprint: Westport, CT, Greenwood Press, 1971].

Waterbury, J., *The Commander of the Faithful. The Moroccan Political Elite: A Study in Segmented Politics*, New York, Columbia University Press, 1970.

White, R. W., *Provisional Irish Republicans: An Oral and Interpretive History*, Westport, CT, Greenwood Press, 1993.

Wickham, C., *Framing the Early Middle Ages: Europe and the Mediterranean, 400–800*, Oxford and New York, Oxford University Press, 2005.

Wiedmann, C. [*Maximianistenkonzil von Cebarsussi*], *Augustinus und das Maximianistenkonzil von Cebarsussi: zur historischen und textgeschichtlichen Bedeutung von Enarratio in Psalmum 36,2,18–23*, Vienna, Verlag der Österreichischen Akademie der Wissenschaften, 1998.

Wilken, R. L., *John Chrysostom and the Jews: Rhetoric and Reality in the Late 4th Century*, Berkeley and Los Angeles, University of California Press, 1983.

Williams, A. L., *Adversus Iudaeos: A Bird's-Eye View of Christian Apologiae until the Renaissance*, Cambridge University Press, 1935.

Wilmart, A. (1912), "Un bref traité de saint Augustin contre les donatistes," *RBén* 29, 148–67.

(1931), "Operum S. Augustini Elenchus," *MiAg* 2, Rome, Tipografia poliglotta vaticana, 149–233.

Wood, N. (1985), "African Peasant Terrorism and Augustine's Political Thought," in F. Krantz, ed., *History from Below: Studies in Popular Protest and Popular Ideology in Honour of George Rudé*, Montreal, Concordia University Press, 279–99.

(1986), "Populares and Circumcelliones: The Vocabulary of 'Fallen Man' in Cicero and St. Augustine," *History of Political Thought* 7, 33–51.

Woolf, C. (2004), "A propos des voleurs d'enfants: saint Augustin, Lettre 10*," *AfrRom* 15, 1711–22.

Zangara, V. (1981), "L'inventio dei martiri Gervasio et Protasio," *Augustinianum* 21, 119–33.

Zepf, M. (1929), "Zur Chronologie der antidonatistischen Schriften Augustins," *ZNTW* 28, 16–61.

Zimmerman, M. (2006), "Violence in Late Antiquity Reconsidered," in Drake *Violence in Late Antiquity*, Aldershot, Variorum, 343–57.

Zizek, S., *Violence: Six Sideways Reflections*, New York, Picador, 2008.

Zmire, P. (1971), "Recherches sur la collégialité épiscopale dans l'Eglise d'Afrique," *RecAug* 7, 3–72.

Index

Printed in the USA
CPSIA information can be obtained
at www.ICGtesting.com
LVHW080733241123
764522LV00007B/179